READ YOUR MIND

READ YOUR MIND

Proven Habits for
Success from the World's
Greatest Mind Reader

OZ PEARLMAN

NEW RIVER BOOKS

First published in the United States of America in 2025 by Viking,
An imprint of Penguin Random House LLC
1745 Broadway, New York, NY 10019
penguinrandomhouse.com

This edition published in the United Kingdom in 2025 by New River Books
Unit 105, Leroy House, 436 Essex Road, London, N1 3QP
newriverbooks.co.uk

10 9 8 7 6 5 4 3 2 1

A CIP catalogue record for this book is available from the British Library.

ISBN: 978-1-915780-83-6

Jacket design: Pete Garceau

Printed and bound in the UK using 100% renewable electricity at
CPI Group (UK) Ltd, Croydon, CR0 4YY.

MIX
Paper | Supporting responsible forestry
FSC® C013604
www.fsc.org

This FSC© label means that materials used for the product have been responsibly sourced.

TO MY CHILDREN:
YOU'VE GIVEN ME JOY BEYOND
ALL MEASURE.

TO MY WIFE:
YOU'VE GIVEN ME EVERYTHING
AND ARE MY EVERYTHING.

CONTENTS

A Note on Terminology

In the US, "mentalist" means a performer who uses psychology, suggestion and observation to read and influence people. In the UK, it can carry different connotations. Throughout this UK edition, "mentalist" and "mentalism" are used in the US sense.

ONE

Channel Your Inner Mentalist

Picture this.

I'm a guest on a private island in the British Virgin Islands. A band plays steel drums as the clear waters of the Caribbean Sea gently lap the pristine shoreline. Chefs tend to jerk chicken sizzling on an elaborate barbecue while a team of uniformed servers weaves in and out of the crowd. The breeze smells like spices, hibiscus, and money. It's magic hour, the last golden light of day washing over us. All the beautiful people are enjoying bespoke cocktails. The other guests and I can't help stealing glances skyward; our host on Necker Island has just returned from the edge of space on his Virgin Galactic rocket.

Sir Richard Branson's people could have hired anyone to celebrate the occasion. I mean, this is a man who has Mick Jagger on speed dial, right between Paul McCartney and the King. To my surprise and delight, his team chose me. I'm working the crowd, going from group to group, building up excitement and momentum as we all wait for the guest of honor. Suddenly, his friends and family part like the Red Sea. The barefoot billionaire appears, sporting a deep tan that contrasts with his iconic white-blond hair and open linen shirt, flashing that unforgettable smile. Everything about the scene feels surreal.

A moment such as this demands nothing less than the best, and I'm ready with one of my strongest reputation-making tricks. I lock eyes with the man, the myth, the legend, and it is go time.

"Imagine someone's face, anyone at all, and see them in your mind's eye," I say. Then, using a small pair of scissors, I start slicing and dicing one of my business cards, like a child carving out a meticulous snowflake. Everyone around me whispers as they start to anticipate where this might be going.

When I ask him who he is thinking of, he casually says, "Barack." Then he adds, "Obama," in case I wasn't sure which Barack he has in mind.

I unfold the paper and hold it up against my dark gray suit, revealing the freshly cut silhouette of the former president. The audience gasps in astonishment, but Branson, who does billion-dollar deals before breakfast, isn't so outwardly effusive. Instead, he gives me a sly little smile. The best way I can describe his reaction is that it's like having the Godfather reach over and pinch you on the cheek as an understated sign of respect and affection.

Sir Richard tucks the piece of paper into his breast pocket. He looks over his shoulder to make sure no one else hears him, leans in close, and whispers, "I'll give this to him tomorrow when he arrives."

What If You Could Read Minds?

Who hasn't wished they could read someone else's mind? How much easier would everything be if we could just figure out what other people were thinking, right? I mean, you'd probably never fight with your spouse again because you'd understand that should he or she say, "It's nothing," it would *definitely* be something, and you could act preemptively.

What if reading minds gave you practical skills, enabling you to predict the right time to ask your boss for a raise, to cease self-sabotage, or to stop procrastinating and start doing? You'd be more confidently persuasive, able to influence those around you in an effortless manner. How great would that be?

Of course, mind reading would be nice to have if you found yourself in a position of weakness, because you'd have the formula to flip that power dynamic to your benefit. By knowing what's in another person's head, you could get a gatekeeper to give you what you want, whether it's an extension on an assignment or a waiver from your homeowners' association. Reading minds would make you better at understanding human nature, which makes it the ultimate cheat code in life.

What would be even *more* useful than reading other people's minds? The ability to read your own. Picture the results of tapping into your motivations and learning how to change your outcomes; of pushing past what's kept you stuck. What if you could set yourself up for success in the long term?

You can do all of this using the skills of a mentalist.

I've spent almost thirty years learning how to reverse engineer the human mind. Knowing *how* you think reveals to me *what* you think. From Tom Brady to Serena Williams, Howard Stern to Shaq, I've convinced some of the most notable people on the planet that I can access their innermost thoughts. But guess what? My entire career is built on a lie.

Ready for a bombshell?

I can't actually read minds.

What I can do is read *people* . . . and so can you! You already do it hundreds of times a day, every time you interact with another human being at home, at work, on the street, and everywhere in between, and I can help you be even better at it. Few skills will take you further in life than learning how to channel your inner mentalist. Reading people is a critical step to achieving what you want in this world. From getting ahead to getting what you want, the tactics I employ as a mentalist can be repurposed from entertainment to success in everyday life.

All of us have an internal BS detector that we developed from being around people, from getting social stimulus. What you may not realize is you were born being able to read minds. You can tell when someone's not paying attention to you. You can tell when someone's lying to you. (If you're a parent, you're *really* good at this.) You can tell when someone's interested in you or when they're faking it. We all have this sense. Well over two-thirds of communication is nonverbal[1], so it's not a matter of *what* people say but *how* they say it, and even what they leave unsaid.

Mentalism is magic of the mind. Rather than using fast hands to fool your eyes, I watch the way people move. I listen to the words they choose. I study their patterns and behaviors, often without them realizing I'm doing so. Mentalism is all about psychology, observation, memory, and communication. These small signals tell a much bigger story—and once you know what to look for, you can "read" people almost instantly. When I say to channel your inner mentalist, what I mean is this skill is instinctual. When you were a baby, long before you understood spoken language, you were able to interpret your parents' thoughts by studying their faces. The furrow of a brow, the flicker of an eyelid, the pull of the upper lip; all of it infused with meaning. The first time we smiled at our parents and they smiled back, we said to ourselves, *Oh God, when I do the thing with my mouth, that makes people pay attention to me!* And it's that first bit of dopamine that gets us going. The ability to interpret other people is innate in all of us because we're social creatures; it's why our species has survived.

The question isn't *Do you have the skills?* because the answer is *You do.* The question is *How do you take your skills to the next level?* How do you improve on your instincts and learn to trust them more?

This isn't about tricks. It's about transformation. I'm going to teach you the very techniques I've used to perform for millions of people around the world—but more important, I'm going to show you how to apply them in your own life to create real, lasting change. You don't have to be a mentalist to think like one. You just need a shift in mindset—and a few powerful tools.

So, I'll walk you through how I became a mentalist and start you on the path to honing your skills so you can learn to read people and apply the principles of mentalism to your everyday life. And, crucially, to develop the ability to look into the mirror and start to read *that* person's mind, which seems daunting, but it's not. In fact, it's easier than you think!

Like Magic

When I was thirteen, my parents took me on a cruise where I saw a magician perform for the very first time. I was captivated as I watched miracle after miracle. And then the most incredible thing happened: He picked me to join him onstage. The magician performed a classic known as "the sponge balls," where the balls appeared, disappeared, and changed in number and size in my hands. An obsession was born and, from that moment on, I spent my time stalking him because I just had to see more. (FYI, there are surprisingly few places on a ship a grown man can hide, especially from a determined kid with nothing better to do.)

When I got home, I checked out every single book on magic at the library and read them from cover to cover . . . twice. You could not find me at any point of the day without a deck of cards in hand, literally: I found waterproof cards to practice with in the shower. By the time I'd turned fourteen, it was apparent that magic was more than a passing fad for me. But I didn't need to be a mentalist to understand that my mother was tired of driving me to Wunderground, the local magic store in metro Detroit where I grew up, and paying for the tricks to satisfy my obsession. Ever pragmatic, my mom told me if I was serious about pursuing magic, I needed to get a job and start supporting my own hobby. My folks were on the cusp of divorce back then, so it's possible that my bending of spoons at the breakfast table didn't exactly ease collective stress.

Anyway, instead of taking a paper route, babysitting, or shoveling driveways, I did what seemed the most logical thing for a kid in my position—I decided to try and get a job as a strolling magician, who does close-up magic while mingling with the crowd. I imagined all the tricks I could buy and how I could take my magic to the next level. At no point did it occur to me that my idea was (a) half-baked or (b) almost certainly destined to fail, because otherwise I'd never have tried in the first place. Ignorance can be bliss. If I'd asked someone else how to land that job, they'd have told me, "First you have to do this, then you have to do that," and I would have psyched myself out of even trying.

Zia's, a family-style Italian restaurant in a strip mall a half mile from home, seemed the most logical place to give my magic gig a shot because its location was cursed. Every restaurant that opened there failed after a couple years. So I figured they could use my magical touch, pun intended.

I decided to go in one day after school with my mom, which happened to be perfect timing because at 4:00 p.m. the place was mostly empty between shifts. We sat at the bar alone, ordered some beverages and appetizers, and I started performing for my mom. This caught the bartender's eye, so I asked him if he wanted to see some magic, too—which was exactly my plan. Had I gone in during the lunch rush or at dinner, he probably would've ignored me. But because he and the rest of the staff weren't busy, he said, "Let's get a bigger crowd going." He called over several servers and, the next thing I knew, the general manager was coming by to see what was going on.

My mom, always my number one fan and a slightly pushy Israeli, gave me the eyebrow raise that indicated this was my moment. It was time to start selling. My mother and I tag-teamed, asking when their slowest night was and if they ever had entertainment. Like any good attorney, we asked our questions already knowing what answers we wanted them to give, leading them to the conclusion that I was what their restaurant was missing.

Why were they so willing to give me that shot? Maybe they were grasping for straws and thought, *We need whatever hook we can get to have this restaurant take off.* Lo and behold, I landed one night per week of strolling magic, going table to table. I was too young to drive so I walked there carrying my small bag of tricks, freshly printed business cards, and a dream.

The one thing I already understood was the concept of "Fake it till you make it." My superpower was acting like I knew what I was doing even when I didn't. I had my pitch perfected because I'd gone over it in my head a hundred times. That's why when I got in front of Zia's owners, with a proud Jewish mother behind me, I projected an aura of confidence and pulled out my best tricks. They bought it; I was *in.*

Pick Your Moment

Performing close-up magic at Zia's was probably the best education I could ever receive about learning to read people. I was able to iterate how to approach strangers and how to get a sense of what they thought of me even before I began performing. My mind would race trying to answer the questions: *What do they think of my act? How do I win their favor? How can I get them to want more?*

Through trial, error, and all kinds of rejection, I learned that my tricks were only a small part of the show as a whole. Everything counted, from my personality and my energy to the statements I'd make upon greeting them.

When I'd walk up to the table, every factor made an impression, even my smile and my body position. I learned fast that timing is everything. If people had just sat down and hadn't yet ordered, they could be flustered or get angered by my presence. They hadn't unpacked their day yet. They needed a minute with their drinks and a few calories from the bread basket to ease their tension. I used all these little bits of info when deciding the right moment to visit a table.

The sweet spot was just after they'd ordered, when the excitement of making their choices was over and there was a lull in the conversation as they anticipated their meals. Diners were the most relaxed and their guards were down. That's when I could go up to them and say, "How's everybody doing tonight?" I knew that when they saw me come over—obviously not their server or the manager—their minds would race with questions, so I would address their objections before they were even consciously aware of them. While I'd yet to study any psychology in junior high, Zia's taught me about heuristics, meaning the mental shortcuts people take to make quick decisions. My customers' default setting was assuming I shouldn't be there, so I'd immediately counter that. I'd tell them, "The owners have a treat for you tonight!" indicating that not only was I welcome, but I was a value-add and management wanted me to be there.

You've likely been in very similar situations when wanting to get something from someone and trying to find the best moment to do so. Let's say you want to ask your boss for a raise. It's important to you, so you have it on your calendar to talk to him or her first thing on Monday morning, when they're back from their annual vacation cruise. It's a big deal, so you want to get it out of the way right now. But if you do it then, even though you've worked your butt off and may well deserve that raise, you may be shooting yourself in the foot. Because your raise is not necessarily as important and immediate a concern to your boss.

Put yourself in their shoes—does your boss have a million other things on their plate? Are they normally in the best mood first thing in the morning, especially after an extended break? You know this person. You've worked with them for years. You've seen when they're at their kindest, their most receptive, their most generous, and it's rarely at 8:30 a.m. on Monday when their phone is ringing off the hook, their inbox is full, and they haven't even touched their coffee yet.

When I was working the restaurant, was I technically employed if they paid me fifty dollars under the table and sent me home with some spaghetti? I quickly learned ways to hype up a table before I'd perform. I'd ask, "Did you hear what's going on?" They'd say no, but with that one question, I shifted their hesitation to anticipation, and instead of being bothered, they were now intrigued. I'd continue, "Then you're in luck!" further piquing their curiosity. Who doesn't want to be lucky? Who doesn't want to feel in the know? Every word and phrase was designed to grab their attention and not let them go. I was setting a path in motion and that is key to tapping into the minds of others. This is Human Behavior 101: learning to anticipate the thoughts of others before they even think them.

When I'm performing, I don't use this anticipation to amaze you. I use these little sweeteners to get you to like me, to get you interested in what I'm presenting, and to win you over so the experience is all the more memorable. And you can do the same. Like in the example above, when asking for a raise: You know your boss. You know when she or he is at their best, their happiest, their most generous. Learn their patterns, make an effort to actively pay attention to their moods, and use this knowledge to strike when the time is right!

Shift Out of Autopilot

Zia's taught me the value of being an active participant, one who remains present in every moment and pays attention to every little detail. More important, I learned that I needed to make an opportunity happen, rather than wait for others to take the initiative. This is something all of us can improve in our lives and occurs only when you take charge and assume responsibility. For example, think about your day-to-day life with your spouse. How often are you truly present? And how often are you just going through the motions? We are bombarded with so much information that, with our eyes alone, we're processing one megabyte of data every second.[2] To handle the thousands of tiny decisions we make every day—from seasoning our food to picking out a tie—our brains create habits to help us process this info. These habits we develop help us to not be overwhelmed by information, yet they also make us default to autopilot. We counter this by leaning into active participation.

In lieu of going through the motions, try to view things from your spouse's perspective. Consider what might be on their mind. Are they anxious about work? Are they worried about the kids? Are they stressed about everything on their to-do list? The simple act of being able to read the room can be a relationship saver. (Again, this is tied closely to timing.)

If I performed my show on autopilot, I would mess up all the time—even though I know every formal beat of my performance by heart. I must be hyperfocused when I'm with an audience. I have to study everything they're doing, like their traits, their mannerisms, their eyes, their body language, and even their pauses. The smallest "um" uttered by a spectator at the wrong moment might seem harmless at first glance and would likely go unnoticed by the audience. But for me, even a small moment of disconnection can spell doom if not immediately addressed. That "um" may indicate that something was missed or that my participant may be mildly confused. This is a big red flag that I simply can't ignore. For example, this tells me their brain thought of one thing and then shifted to another. That one little pause could be the difference between succeeding and failing on a trick in front of thousands of people.

Failure was my teacher and my motivator in the restaurant days. When I first started working the gig, I'd walk up to a table and say, "Oh, are you ready? Let me do some magic." Then many of the diners would just laugh and go, "No thanks, kid." You're walking up to someone, ready to give them your all and they reject you? What a gut punch. (We'll delve deeper into dealing with rejection in a later chapter.) It's hard to move past that.

I could have left the rude table and thought to myself, *What a bunch of jerks.* The easiest thing is to shift the blame onto them rather than learn from this situation. Then I'd be annoyed, that tension would impact me, and I'd bring that kind of negative energy to the next group. When you're going up to fifty or more tables in a shift and three in a row treat you poorly, it can ruin your whole attitude.

My tricks weren't paying for themselves, though, so I had develop thicker skin. Instead of quitting, I tried to figure out what I could do that might yield different results, and I learned that every "no thanks" was giving me the data I needed to turn my next interaction into a "yes, please."

I discovered that instead of being mad at them, I'd be more effective in the long run if I tried to understand them. I couldn't let myself wallow in that rejection. Our brains are hardwired to register and dwell on negative events. This is called "negativity bias" and it means we feel the pain of rejection far more deeply than the balm of praise.[3]

I didn't know anything about neural processing back then. I had no idea that a negative stimulus resonated more strongly in my cerebral cortex. All I knew was that I'd feel better if I tried to put a positive spin on the situation—I'd be more focused on the task at hand instead of distracted and diminished by the recent past. So I'd say to myself, *What if their kid is sick at home? What if they had a huge fight right before they came? I feel really bad for them. They must be having a rough night. I can't wait to bring joy to the next person.*

I also started conducting after-action reviews to see where I may have veered off the rails. Maybe I'd realize that they'd been talking and I had interrupted. How would I feel if someone interrupted me? I had already started on the wrong foot when I walked up to them, and so I'd had to climb up a hill just to get their attention to win them back over. That was *my* fault, not theirs. In so many instances we tend to blame the other person instead of examining our own behavior to see what we could have done better instead—as if in a failed interaction there is only one party to blame.

When you walk up to somebody and they don't know you, what's the first thing that often happens? They get tense. You can see it. I mean, imagine you're standing at the ATM and someone approaches you—that's anxiety-provoking for sure. Your body goes into fight-or-flight. This happened to me a couple months ago. Someone was panhandling and they came up to me as I was putting in my PIN. I said, "Listen, I'm getting money out. I'm willing to help you, but give me a minute and I'll meet you outside." A better way of handling this would be if he held the door for me on my way out and then said, "If you can spare any change, that'd be amazing." He would have created a totally different feeling in me. Ultimately, I still helped him, but this is something to keep in mind if you're ever trying to solicit signatures for a petition or donations for a nonprofit. It's so important for you to consider the other person's reaction, making sure you don't interrupt or impose. In a situation where you're, say, trying to collect signatures, you're going to find the most success if you acknowledge the other person by saying something like, "I can tell you're so busy, but I have to quickly share this with you." Speak with light urgency, empathize, and validate their reactions and don't be surprised when you're able to get what you need.

Find the Right Energy

A couple of years ago I was presenting and performing at the ESPY Awards, standing arm's length from LeBron James, arguably one of the most famous people in the world. We were elbow-to-elbow backstage, and he was getting ready to go up and give a speech. We said a brief hello and exchanged pleasantries. I knew that was the absolute worst moment to say, "Hey, LeBron, can I get a selfie?" The timing was just off. Plus, I want to be seen as an equal, and coming up to him as a fan was the surest way to not get what I wanted. For him to give something of value (in this case, the selfie), I would ideally provide him with something of value first. So backstage, pre-speech, just wasn't the right moment.

However, seconds later, I met Patrick Mahomes, and he was in less of a time crunch, having just wrapped up his stage portion. I ended up talking to him and getting a good vibe. Plus, he knew who I was because earlier I'd performed for his wife, making her the star of my act; I won him over right from the start as I'm sure he typically gets most of the attention. At the end of our conversation, I said, "Patrick, it's been a real pleasure hanging out tonight, let's get a picture to remember it!" Without hesitation, he wrapped his arm around me and said, "Oh my God, get in here!" and we took the photos.

I didn't really need to ask for permission, and I could assume the close, because the timing was right and I'd locked in what matters to him most: his wife's happiness. So, when I asked for something in return, he was more likely to accommodate wholeheartedly. If I'd tried the same move with LeBron, he probably wouldn't have acquiesced because he was concentrating on what he was about to say to a huge audience, plus there was nothing in it for him. Often, getting in touch with your inner mentalist is as easy as thinking about what's going through the other person's head.

A while back, I was at an incredibly high profile event. This room was filled with the heaviest of heavy hitters in the sports world, including most of the team owners along with the commissioners of the NFL, NHL, NBA, MLB, WNBA, the World Surf League, the IOC, etc. Rarely do you get the chance to be in a room with this many powerful people at the same time. There was an über-successful attendee named Michael. One of my major objectives was to impress and win him over because he throws arguably the most exclusive party in the country each summer.

Always scheming, I planned to punch my ticket to his party that night. I was with Roger Goodell and a couple other people, and I'd already performed three close-up tricks for them while working the crowd during cocktail hour. I always aim to leave people wanting more. One of the biggest rules of success is to never overstay your welcome. If you get to a moment where you see somebody looking down at their phone or starting to check the clock, then you've missed the boat. Think about it: Let's say you're the biggest Ryan Reynolds fan in the world. You're having coffee, and Deadpool himself walks in the shop. You're not going to get distracted and check your phone. You're not going to look at what time it is. The world has ceased to exist. You could forget to pick up your kids from school at that moment because you're so focused.

Michael moseyed over right as I was finishing my very best trick. My act is structured to end on the highest note. I'd basically hit a walk-off grand slam and was leaving them on cloud nine . . . and there's no such thing as cloud ten. But then someone from the group goes, "Michael, you've got to see this!" That wasn't good. I needed to peel off and plant Michael in a group that was starting from scratch if I wanted to leave him amazed, but I had lost control of the situation. At best, I could keep going and hold the vibe at a plateau. But plateauing wasn't an option. I had to do another trick for the group, and it had to kill. Michael wasn't at the same energy level as the rest of the people in this already engaged group, though. It would be like if you walked into the end of a Bon Jovi concert and everyone else has been on this epic journey the whole night. They're screaming the lyrics to "Livin' on a Prayer" at the end of his set, but you can't match their energy because you didn't have the chance to build yours up yet. Same thing happened here. I did the trick, and it was fine, but because of the energy mismatch, it didn't produce the results I'd hoped.

I wasn't invited to perform at his party. I wanted it, but this ended up being a missed opportunity because the situation was out of my control. It's frustrating, and I've played this scenario back in my head dozens of times since. The best I can do is to learn from it. But mark my words—I haven't given up. I *will* be at that party one summer soon, because I am relentless once I set a goal.

Here's what you need to remember: In your head, replace the word *no* with *not yet.* Let's rewire your brain against what you perceive as rejection. When you're frustrated by a no, you create a self-fulfilling prophecy because you believe that your dream is not going to happen and you stop taking strides toward it. Instead of thinking of "no" as a locked door, think of it as a jammed door. A locked door is final—you can't get through. But a jammed door isn't permanently closed; it just needs a bit more effort and finesse to open. It's not a "no," it's a "not yet." If you keep at it. you'll eventually get through.

Kill with Kindness

The first rule of working in the service industry—and all industries are, fundamentally, service industries—is that the client is always right. And even if they're not right and truly unpleasant, as long as you're not in physical danger, the best approach is to kill that person with kindness. When people would snap at me during my restaurant-working days, I'd say, "Oh, I completely understand. Have a wonderful dinner and if you need something, I'm happy to send the manager right over."

When you meet negative energy with negative energy, it's just going to fan the flames.

The smartest plan is always to de-escalate a situation. A vital rule of de-escalation is that you don't charge up on someone who's running hot, who's already in a fury and wants to fight. You're far better off approaching them with a calm you may or may not feel. You want to make yourself seem smaller to calm them down. You don't match their energy, because then it turns into a competition for who can be more alpha, and that will only heat things up.

I often run into similar issues onstage. Someone in the audience wants to be combative, wants to heckle. I have learned to look at the root of what's causing them to act this way: This person wants attention. They don't want to feel like I'm putting them down, but because I'm the one in the spotlight, the power dynamic has me in a superior position. I know how to do something they don't, and it makes them feel stupid—out of place, insecure, unengaged, or not on the same wavelength as everyone else in the room. That's when I need to downshift my energy. I need to alter our power dynamic in their mind.

In situations like this, I find a way to communicate that doesn't place us in opposition, but lets them understand that we're on the same team. If you and I were on the same team, why would I ever try to steal the ball from you? If we're both trying to score together, that would be silly. I want them to know that we're on a level playing field, that I'm not some mythical messiah figure or a psychic: What I do is learnable.

What you have to understand is that my career is built on secrecy. If you get to the core of it, the truth is just that I know how to do something you don't. I build rapport with the audience, and earn their trust, by dropping little breadcrumbs of how I do it along the way. I'll create an environment where I open up to them and let them in on the secret, showing them how one of the tricks is done behind the curtain. Suddenly, they'll say, "That's so cool!" And I'll say, "Isn't it amazing?" Then I'll raise the bar and use that knowledge against them by employing a different method, and I'll use the element of surprise to my advantage, leaving the audience even more astounded. Of course, they'll want to know how I did that, too, but I'll say, "I have to keep some secrets here. I've got to try to impress you now that you're a mentalist yourself."

Letting people get a win, giving them that win, or inviting them to feel like they're in on the trick tells them you're not trying to steal the attention away from them. It's a great way to shift the energy, to de-escalate. In many instances when I walk up to a group there's often a person who wants to be the dominant alpha. They want all eyes on them, which generally stems from a feeling of insecurity. So I give them their moment. I let them call the shots within the framework of the trick I'm doing. I have them make the choices. It's no different than how I parent my children when asking them, "Do you want one carrot or two broccolis?" because it gives my kids the feeling of having control . . . and either way they eat their veggies.

It's important to make people feel like they have agency, that they have choice within the set of parameters you give them. Then, they will choose within that set of constraints, especially if you deliver that choice with a genuine smile and a kind tone. Ultimately, your hecklers can become your biggest cheerleaders. The people you think are going to be the worst in your day-to-day life can end up as your greatest allies if you get inside their heads effectively and learn what makes them tick by trying to assess their true motivation. With hecklers, what drives them is the desire to feel smart, to feel validated. They don't like when they feel lesser than, and they probably don't encounter a lot that defies logic. So they won't just let themselves lean into the wonder of it all.

People want to be seen and heard. They want to feel special. If you can win them over, it flips the script. They want attention, so give them what they want. When I work with football players, I always look for the guy who has his arms crossed, who's not smiling, because if I can win him over, everyone else will be won over as well. Here's the thing: Someone in the crowd who's negative is still engaged. If you give them a win, you can exploit that.

When I was working the private party circuit, I knew that, almost universally, people also wanted to feel like they were getting a deal. Let's say my goal was to make $500 for a show. (Thankfully my rates have gone up since then!) To get there, I'd give clients an option of three pricing packages: the bronze, the gold, or the platinum.

Human instinct is that no one wants the bronze. They want one of the better options. People will naturally gravitate toward the one in the middle, so I'd ask for $400 for the bronze, $500 for the gold, and $750 for the platinum. People don't want the basic package because there's not enough stuff in it—they easily convince themselves it's missing one or two key pieces. But the extras I'd add on to the more prestige packages are things I would have wanted to incorporate anyway, like strolling around and meeting the audience in advance because that would actually help me when I went onstage. But the client doesn't know this is something I love doing.

Even now, I run my events this way. I still want to shake hands and perform close-up mentalism. What makes mentalists unique is that there are no other entertainers—comedians, singers, athletes, keynote speakers—who work close-up for groups of two to twenty people at a time. It's such a powerful experience to be immersed in the show from only a few feet away. When potential clients see that, if they get the gold package, I'll do the close-up work, they go, "That's amazing, thank you!" When you price yourself this way, you increase your revenue by providing something extra you'd have provided as a matter of course.

What's interesting in this example is that sometimes what feels natural or easy to you has its own worth. In my case, talking to people beforehand is fun for me, so putting a price on an element of my work that I love not only increases my revenue but also helps me clearly value my own work.

Bottom line, everyone wants to feel like a VIP, and that became evident in my restaurant work. There are simple ways to create that feeling that don't cost you more than you want to invest. This is why I would walk up to people at their tables and say, "I'm here compliments of the owner, and it's your lucky night!" When you approach with that energy, right away you've established a good feeling. If, instead, I walked up and said, "Do you want to see some magic?" I'd have given people a very easy path to saying no. Human nature positions us to respond positively to hearing that it's our lucky night, especially when it's free.

Sometimes despite my best efforts, diners were rude, but I'd never give that energy back to them. Rather I'd be polite and direct, saying, "I'll see if I can come back later. Several tables have requests for me. Have a wonderful night and enjoy your meal." Then I would walk away. I wouldn't be curt; I wouldn't be emotional about their response. If I had performed one trick and they were rude, disrespectful, or apathetic, I'd think, *Okay, you're cut off. I have something special to share. Other people want it, and I'll give it to them instead.* In that moment, when they realized I was taking my talent away, many would pull a 180 and try to get me to stay. Often, if it was just one person who had been rude, the whole group would turn against them. They'd realize they'd all collectively lost something of value.

The restaurant gigs taught me the importance of aligning myself with people. One person who is an ally can open so many doors. This is basic sales. Generally, about 5 percent of your clientele absolutely love you and they become your champions. They become your promoters.

They're your hype men or hype women. Recently, my good friends had their first child and asked me if I knew anyone who could help with life insurance. I responded, "Yeah, of course! I'll put you in touch with Frank, he's my guy, he's great!" And that's what you want to be: the *go-to* guy or gal for that niche, so much so that nobody else is even considered, it's a lock.

Your fans will talk about you, whether it's business or personal. When somebody gives you a glowing over-the-top review, that is worth its weight in gold. When you get people to be your champion, you're unstoppable. So many instances in my career have come down to a handful of people who supported me. In turn, I've nurtured those relationships. I've tried to make myself valuable to them, done favors for them, gone above and beyond for them, and shown appreciation for the ways they've gone above and beyond for me, because these relationships should always be a two-way street.

Play the Long Game

Some of the biggest TV appearances I've landed I can trace back nearly twenty years to my finding the name of an event planner in the yellow pages. (For my Gen Z audience—google that move for a blast from the past.) Back then I would call event planners, saying, "I would love to swing by and give your team a very unique treat and perform a gratis show during lunch, or whenever you have downtime," knowing that they were the gatekeepers responsible for booking acts like mine. Impress a prospective client and maybe you score a show or two, but impress the right event planner and it could mean dozens of gigs down the line. This was a force multiplier and a way to work smarter rather than just harder. With a planner shilling for me, I booked my first bar mitzvah through what had been a free performance. That bar mitzvah led to another bar mitzvah, which led to a holiday party and a birthday party, and on and on. We went many levels deep into Jewish geography. Eventually this led me to the bar mitzvah of the son of a very prominent NFL correspondent on ESPN named Adam Schefter. I kept in touch with him. I made sure that I never fell off his radar, that he always received my newsletter.

Now, this is one of my best pieces of advice: Always take notes. Whenever I met someone new, I'd be sure to jot down a few lines about what was happening in their life. If someone handed me their business card, the moment I was out of their sight I wrote down the date, where I was, and everything they had said to me in the smallest font you can imagine somewhere on that card. Adam and I continued to cross paths over the next few years on the bar mitzvah circuit, and whenever I'd see him at a party, I'd always know his kids' names and what the family had been up to. We were friendly. I wrote every detail down because we had a connection and I needed him to know that what was important to him was also important to me. You don't have to be a mind reader to know that people are flattered when you recall details from previous conversations.

A lot of the time, you'll find yourself moving in the same social circles. You get hired by one person, and then someone else in their group of friends or family hires you again in a year or two. This becomes another moment to shine in front of an already receptive audience. After well over a decade of knowing each other, Adam said, "I need you to meet my boss who runs ESPN's football content."

If I had met his boss twelve years earlier, I wouldn't have been ready. But by this point, I was a seasoned pro with plenty of TV experience under my belt and was ready for this opportunity. My confidence shined; I performed the right routines and highlighted how my act could be tailored to football, could connect with their audiences. I was in the right place with the right person at the right time . . . and it only took twelve years for me to get the chance. Ultimately, your biggest goals are going to be part of a long game, and every step along the way adds up. This is the same for nearly every profession. You show me an overnight success and I'll show you the ten plus years of grinding they did to land that big break. So if your long game as, say, a Realtor is to land a million-dollar listing, every lower-dollar condo and ranch home you sell along the way builds your record and your skills.

Flip the Power Dynamic

Now, you would think that, by channeling my inner mentalist, by paying attention to my timing and killing people with kindness and tapping into human nature, I'd make all the right moves and every decision I made would be the wisest one.

That's why I need to tell you about the time I almost blew it.

I met my wife, Elisa, when I was in my mid-twenties, living my big single life in New York City. We dated for a few months; it was great, but again, I was in my midtwenties. Sometimes you have the best thing in the world in front of you and you don't even know it. You could have a winning lottery ticket and not realize it. So . . . I tried to break up with her because I was immature, too scared to commit and focused on all the wrong things. But when I told her we were done, she rejected my move and just said, "No." I was completely confused, downright flummoxed. What did she mean, "No?" Can you even do that?

In the span of just a few days, I realized how right she was. Elisa explained to me pretty much exactly what was in my head because it seems she was a far better mentalist than I was at the time. She laid out how stupid I was being, how fickle, how the problems that I raised were minor and easy to overcome. She pointed out that rather than taking the hard road of doing the slightest bit of work, I was just going to throw our relationship away. As soon as I realized what a life with her would offer, suddenly I was the one who was begging for more. With our roles flipped and Elisa suddenly in control, I pleaded with her to move in, as I'd recently bought my first apartment. She just replied, "Slow down, buddy." The shift in our dynamic reminded me of my early magician days working restaurants, when I'd walk up to a group: They didn't know if they wanted me, and they held all the cards. A minute later when I would do the first amazing trick, they'd be blown away and they'd say, "Don't stop!" Suddenly, they wanted me more than I needed them.

Learning to rely on our inner mentalist can be a challenge at first, especially when we're so likely to default to autopilot. It requires us to take a pause, really assess each situation and person, and put ourselves in their shoes. But once you're used to taking that second to get your bearings, it becomes easier and easier to figure out your timing and not rush through things, as you're far more likely to get a negative response when you come from a place of impatience. By taking a breath to de-escalate a situation, and doubling down on kindness, you make space for everyone to have a positive outcome. And when you can prove to others that you've genuinely listened to them and what they've told you is important, you're far more likely to get what you need from them.

Remember, none of this is magic; it's mentalism.

TWO

Believe It to Achieve It

The old adage says, "If you fail to plan, then plan to fail."

That couldn't be truer in my case. I never go into a performance without a series of contingency plans, in case my initial parachute fails to open. To achieve the best outcome in whatever you do, from selling software to persuading a jury of your client's innocence, it's an absolute must to not only visualize your success but also your failure. Being able to anticipate what could go wrong—and create fallbacks—goes a long way toward ensuring a positive end result, so in this chapter we'll cover how planning for every eventuality is a counterintuitive key to "reading" the minds of others.

Theory of Mind

Much of my planning revolves around the concept of "Theory of Mind," both personally and professionally. Theory of Mind refers to our ability to attribute mental states to ourselves and others, and to understand that the mental states of others may be different from our own.[1]

Picture this: It's a rainy summer day during your childhood. You can hear the heavy drops pelting the windows as the wind howls. You're stuck inside while visiting your grandmother. You and your little sister are killing time until the weather breaks, so you've decided to play hide-and-seek. You've determined that the very best hiding spot is tucked inside Granny's closet behind her dresses. However, you also know that your sister is great at finding you. Maybe she even saw your eyes dart toward your grandmother's bedroom when you decided to play. So you choose a different area because you're pretty sure she'll look in the closet first, as she's also aware that it's the best hiding place.

Taking the effort to imagine what someone else is thinking lets you step into someone else's shoes and see the world from their point of view.

And *that* is a superpower.

When I was a kid working at the restaurant, I learned to take a beat to consider the diners' inner monologues. I knew they'd wonder, *Is he any good? Because there's nothing more awkward than having someone perform badly, like a lousy singer or an out-of-tune band, and we'll have to cringe-smile. How long is this going to be? Will he leave soon?* Using Theory of Mind, I realized there were at least ten questions people were asking themselves before they even blinked their eyes when I got to their table. My challenge became to answer all ten of those questions in ten seconds or less.

Your body language and eye contact play a huge role when approaching someone else. In fact, Albert Mehrabian, a body language researcher, found that when it comes to face-to-face communication, 55 percent of communication is nonverbal, 38 percent is vocal, and only 7 percent is words, so approach and eye contact have an outsize impact on the impression you make.[2] Think of it like looking at certain animals in the eyes. When you do this, they look down. Direct eye contact can be very awkward and threatening because it feels like you're crowding them. But if you walk up to an animal at an angle, where you're really only seeing them with one eye, they get the vibe that you're one step in, one step out. It feels safer. There's a similar way to approach people that puts you in a less tense situation. So I would always walk up to the restaurant's guests in a way that was almost like I was leaving, and that's when I'd instantly address what I knew they were thinking. This was another way I'd try to set myself up for success.

Let's say you're looking for a relationship. So you sign up for a singles event, and yet when you get there, no one's mingling. Everyone is standing around, looking at their cocktails and waiting for someone else to make the first move. Clearly, it's awkward, so you could break that tension and shift the energy by calling out how uncomfortable the situation is, saying something casually to your first date, such as, "I don't know about you, but I was a bit nervous to give this a shot," all with a grin on your face. The combination of vulnerability and confidence is refreshing to others, even if you don't really feel confident and are employing a "Fake it till you make it" approach. Maybe you won't meet the person of your dreams at this event, but at the very least, you'll break the ice and make some new friends because you verbalized what they were feeling. And who knows what that could lead to?

Here's another scenario—in this one, you're a teacher. If you walk into class on the first day, how do you instantly build rapport with your students when they're on edge and they're also thinking, *Ugh, is this guy going to be dull? Is this lady going to give us a ton of homework?* There are all these expectations that are built in, so if you come in and look at the class from the students' point of view and answer the questions they might not even realize they have yet, you're going to establish that rapport far more quickly. If you immediately let them know that you're more interesting than other teachers, those kids are going to want to come to your class—they will look forward to it.

The same holds true if you're in sales. Every salesperson opens their laptop and says, "Now I'm going to work through my latest product catalog," and the potential customer's eyes are likely to glaze over, as they're so accustomed to this tactic. But if you come in and immediately address what they're thinking—especially if you guide them there by asking questions—you're going to have a more receptive audience.

The real power comes from leading with empathy. I like to present my inner monologue out loud when I perform for a big audience. When I get onstage, after the crowd has just watched a minute-and-a-half, high-octane video of supercuts of my most amazing tricks from past TV appearances, people are both intrigued and naturally skeptical. Many of them think this must be fake and like every magic show they've seen in the past, filled with sleight of hand tricks. So I'll say, "You saw my hype reel and you know what? I don't buy it. Gimme a break . . . mind reading? We all know that's impossible. Guess what, I'm the biggest skeptic in the room. If someone was up here telling me that they could read my mind, I wouldn't buy it either."

That's when I'll add, "Here's what I want you to know. I don't read minds; I read people. And each and every one of you can do the same thing, as this is a learnable skill. I just happen to have been practicing for nearly thirty years. Talk is cheap, let me prove it." Right there, I'm breaking down boundaries and promising them I'm not going to reveal what they'd prefer to keep hidden.

If I were that teacher in front of a new group of students, the first thing I would say is, "If I were you and I was sitting here thinking this class was just going to be dry lectures, I'd be bored out of my mind. So the question I have to ask myself is *How do I make this a class that you'll never forget?* One that will make you come in and you're waiting for the clock to start so we can learn about world history. I want to know from you guys how we can do that because I think this is the most fascinating topic ever, and if I do it right, you will, too."

I like putting words in people's heads. Feeding others the vocabulary I want them to use is a way of influencing them, but doing it openly, not secretly. The best speakers lead their audiences to a series of specific conclusions; keeping them engaged and entertained and unaware of the changes taking place in their minds, that is *real life mentalism.*

The first ten seconds you stand in front of someone are critical; you have to pay attention to everything the other person is giving you, from body language to facial expressions. You have to be aware of everything that might occur to someone when they look you over—how they might judge you. Their assessment of you is set in stone during those first ten seconds. I want you to ask yourself, "Have I ever been in a situation like this before?" If so, look for a pattern. What worked before? Scope out tension or resistance. It's also useful for you to be conscious of how quickly *you* judge others and understand that they're doing the same to you. What are you transmitting and what are they thinking of you? It's necessary you use that time to set the tone and take control. Verbalize what you believe they're thinking, expressing their inner voice aloud. Then, you either keep qualifying what they thought initially, such as, "I don't actually read minds," or you break down their barriers and burst the stereotypes they had of you from the start.

People always judge a book by its cover—publishers *literally* design them so you do—and that's why there's an adage telling you not to. But it's futile, because you can't avoid making a split-second decision about whether a book is for you. The beauty of mentalism is *you* get to decide what your own book cover looks like. You've got to become your own director, acquiring a real, objective perspective on yourself, which is very hard to do. We're so used to being ourselves that we can't even imagine listening through someone else's ears. We all have so much baggage that sometimes we can't see ourselves the way others do. But when you're able to step back and assess yourself, to take an unbiased, 360-degree view of how you're coming across both verbally and nonverbally, it suddenly becomes very easy for you to use that same skill to assess others.

The bottom line is that mentalists use Theory of Mind to predict and plan for what's going to happen next . . . and so do you! You probably don't realize you're already doing this. You use it every day because it helps you build relationships, solve problems, and understand the world around you by anticipating and being ready to react to what's going to happen next. It's a way of taking what people believe, what they perceive, and what they want, and then using that information to predict how they will behave.

By the way, Theory of Mind isn't just good at predicting how people will react in the future, but also helps if you're planning to try to change their reactions.[3] And it's a particularly helpful skill to hone when an unexpected event occurs . . . like when you appear on the *Today* show in front of millions of viewers watching at home and your trick goes wrong. (More on that later in this chapter.)

Game It Out

Mentalism isn't that different from cooking in a way, as both are designed to elicit primal reactions from your customers and make them feel good! Think of it like this: Chefs know the ingredients they have to work with, the sauces they can make, and have likely perfected their craft over many years of hard work, coupled with trial and error. This gives them a tremendous sense of what works . . . and what doesn't.

That foundation and knowledge allows them the option to throw this ingredient together with that ingredient and make a gourmet dish on the fly, if need be. There is a beauty to winging it and making it look easy, and that ease sometimes takes decades to achieve. I've been known to come up with my ideas for certain low-stakes TV appearances only a day, or even just a few hours, before they were set to take place. Never underestimate the power of a deadline to elicit creativity! But even on short notice, you still have to map out everything that could happen and plan effectively, not just for success but, even more important, for failure.

When it's a higher-stakes performance, you can bet that I have gamed out near infinite possibilities. I look at every step of the trick and make a contingency plan for how I'll right the ship if we veer off course. I will plan for every eventuality, storyboard each trick in my mind and on paper, and analyze the most minute details to see where I could make a mistake (or where an audience member could), and what I would or could do in each scenario. This type of stress testing is so critical and can make a massive difference in your life.

During my shows, if something goes wrong, the first thing I tell myself is to relax. I mean that on both a mental and physical level, as an audience can "smell" tension and discomfort from a mile away. Sometimes your expressions betray you, whereas with the proper practice, you can maintain a poker face even through a disaster. In fact, there have been times where I've messed up royally, but my attitude was so nonchalant and my demeanor so serene that my audience assumed my performance was going great. As Miles Davis put it, it's the *next* note that makes the note wrong.

Imperfection demonstrates that what we're doing is difficult. For example, let's say you're about to watch someone walk a tightrope strung between two skyscrapers. Nerve-racking, right? Now, if that person just flies across the rope, as effortless and sure-footed as a mountain goat, it sort of feels like something anyone could do. They made it look too easy. But if you were to watch that same person shaking on the rope, the sweat on their brow, the veins popping on their arms as they grip the wobbling balance stick, you get a visceral response right there in the pit of your stomach, your palms suddenly sweaty, because you're literally *feeling* the danger.

But it's not as dangerous as everyone thinks, because they've already gamed it out.

Visualize This

Visualization is something all top-tier athletes include as part of their training; they know the mental component is as important as the physical. Let's say the athlete is a runner: Before that starting pistol sounds, they'll have run that race in their head dozens of times, from the start all the way to breaking the tape at the finish. They'll figure out, *Here's what I'd do if my biggest competitor makes a move. Here's what I'd do if my energy flags on the last lap. Here's how I'd handle the curve in the track if it's raining. Here's how I'd proceed if my shoe rips.* And so on. They'll also envision themselves winning, again and again.

Bob Bowman, Michael Phelps's swimming coach, has had Phelps use visualization for years, and both swear by its use. Bowman says the key to visualization is starting with relaxation techniques, as relaxation helps your brain focus more on what you're trying to imagine. In fact, when Phelps was younger, Bowman gave Phelps's mother a book on progressive relaxation that she would guide him through at night, and often he'd become so relaxed after a few exercises, he'd immediately fall asleep.[4]

Whether it's Phelps picturing his pending heat, or you dreaming of winning your country club's mixed doubles tennis tournament, it's important to bring as much detail as possible to visualizing. What's the weather like at the club in your visualization? Is it bright and sunny? Or is it overcast and breezy—and how would your play differ, given those conditions? What kind of day is your opponent having? Do they play more aggressively—or less carefully—if they're tired or angry or pumped up on energy drinks? Is there a crowd gathered to watch you? Are there other matches happening close to you? How does the weight of the racket feel in your hand? How does it sound when you swoosh it through the air? Can you hear the clink of silverware coming from people dining on the club's terrace, or the rattle of ice in glasses? The more you put yourself in the scene of what you're likely to encounter, the more you'll be able to tune it all out and focus on your performance when it's the real thing.

Phelps would play out every scenario—what he wanted to happen, what he didn't want to happen, what might happen. While he went through the paces, I'm sure he could hear the din of the audience on the bleachers in the natatorium, could feel the grit under his feet on the starting block and the pinch of his goggles on his face, could taste the chlorine he'd have to expel from his mouth as he sliced through the churning water. Per Bowman, when we use vivid visualization and we've rehearsed many times, our brains can't distinguish between what is real and what's been imagined, and our bodies go into autopilot. That way, if anything goes wrong, your body is ready for it.

The more you play the mental movie in your head where you complete the task successfully, whether it's nailing your speech in front of the Rotary club, convincing your boss to give you a raise, or blowing away the *Today* show hosts, the more likely you are to succeed. That's why visualization is one of the most powerful tools you can use in your planning. Hand in hand with practice, visualization will build your confidence, help you manage pressure, maintain your focus, reduce your anxiety, and create muscle memory. I create that muscle memory by constant rehearsal, which is why my seatmate on the airplane on the way to my TED Talk likely thought I was insane, watching me pantomime with full hand motions and body language and giving my speech over forty times during that flight. While it's incredibly helpful to visualize yourself asking your boss for a raise, sometimes you need to say it out loud to yourself so you can actually hear how it's going to sound.

When I think about the value of visualization, I call to mind a classic anecdote about Neil Armstrong's moon landing. Armstrong is en route and knows he has a very limited amount of fuel, so he must execute his tasks as perfectly as possible. Due to the angle and the lunar module's position,[5] it's hard for Armstrong to identify the best landing spot. He's at the point in the journey where he's had to switch from automatic to manual control of the landing module—the computer wouldn't be able to dodge the boulder fields that scattered across the surface of the Moon. There are alarms going off throughout the capsule, which Mission Control quickly determined were harmless, but they intensified an already high-octane situation. Despite having run this—and every other scenario—over and over in their minds. Until those last few seconds, Armstrong's heart is pumping at 75 beats per minute, only slightly lower than the 110 BPM he'd experienced upon launch. While his heart rate spikes to 150 BPM in the final seconds, he still manages to put Apollo 11 on the ground perfectly, and then calmly announces, "The *Eagle* has landed."[6] (Interestingly enough, fellow astronaut Buzz Aldrin's average rate was 88 BPM, possibly because he had trained to be a fighter pilot and had shot down MiGs in combat, so he was likely better versed in visualizing everything that could go off the rails. Compare this with your own heart rate the next time you experience some nasty turbulence.)

With the Al Roker example I'll share shortly, I could not afford to panic on live national TV. But I used my time leading up to that appearance on the *Today* show to my advantage by rehearsing the entire sequence countless times assuming different outcomes, because I understood the valuc of having a contingency plan, and you should, too.

Account for Every Contingency

Around 2004, my sister surprised me with an announcement that she was going to run the New York City Marathon. Honestly, I thought the idea was ridiculous, especially as this was before celebrities decided to run marathons, before it became quite mainstream. In the past decade, everyone's started running marathons, from Kevin Hart to Karlie Kloss to Diplo. Back then, the notion of running 26.2 miles was absurd to me. But the only thing that was more absurd was knowing my older sister was going to suddenly be better than me at something, and sibling rivalry quite simply would not allow for that.

I couldn't get into the NYC race, so instead I signed up for the Philadelphia Marathon. Lo and behold, after a few months of mediocre training, I lined up at the start and went for it. Mind you, it didn't go well; I was crying (not afraid to admit it, full-on tears . . . and not of joy!) at mile 23, but I sucked it up and got it done. It wasn't pretty, it wasn't what I would describe as "fun," but I finished! And found myself suddenly hooked . . . with a desire to see if I could run the next one faster.

Over the next few years, I went from running marathons to the greater challenge of ultramarathons, which refers to any distance longer than 26.2 miles. Something I learned pretty quickly when I started to run these long-distance races is that at a certain mile marker, your mind will try to convince your body that you can't do it. Your mind will lie to your body. The worst thing in the world while you're running an ultramarathon is when your mind tricks you into giving up and starts to write your DNF (did not finish) speech.

A while back, I ran a race called the Keys 100. This is a one-hundred-mile run from Key Largo to Key West. It's really beautiful in certain spots, especially on the Seven Mile Bridge. The water all around is crystal clear and brimming with wildlife. The downside is it's hot as hell in mid-May. I've done this race twice, and each time, I've had a very rough go. The first year, I got full-blown heatstroke, which is different from heat exhaustion. Heatstroke is extremely dangerous. Your body overheats. In the span of half a mile, I went from running to walking to not being able to stand up. I was slurring my words and I couldn't tell you what day it was or even my name. Because ultramarathons are so grueling, runners typically have a race crew to help along the way. My buddies and fellow ultramarathoners, Ryan Dexter and Michael Halovatch, took time out of their busy lives to get me through this challenge. They were dumping ice under my armpits, down my back, on my crotch, and yet I had zero physical response. My body was overheating, and no matter what they did, my core temperature wouldn't seem to go down. My team attacked the problem piece by piece, never getting ahead of themselves. First things first—they had to force me to consume fluids and food. They knew they had to stabilize all my systems and try to get me back to neutral at the very least. Once I was back to talking, they saw if I was up to standing. Once I was standing, the goal was to start walking. Which I did for hours. And ready for the craziest part? I somehow got back to running and went so fast the last fifteen miles that my crew couldn't keep up with me . . . and they were in a car! I managed to finish in third place, and you bet your ass I remembered my name by that point in time.

The next year, I did the same race again, and by mile 27, I was throwing up. By mile 36, I was climbing into my stopped crew car to soak up a minute of air-conditioning. In my head, I was already rehearsing my DNF speech and preparing to tell Dexter to take me back to the hotel. You know the flowery social media posts: "It wasn't my day, but I will grow and learn from this experience, blah blah blah." But I had a contingency plan in place, by way of my crew. I knew my mind would lie to me, so I needed backup. Michael Halovatch, one of my team members who had crewed me the year before, gave me the pep talk of a lifetime over the phone. He wasn't even there with me this time, but back in New York. He said, "We're going to throw the kitchen sink at this. We're going to pull out all the stops. If you're taking ibuprofen, you're going to take more. You're taking caffeine, so we're going to double that, too. We're going to put calories in you. You've got music: Put it on, turn it up, and get your ass moving. Once you're walking, you start running. Don't give me any speeches. I'll talk to you again in five minutes."

And that was exactly what I needed. Physically, I could continue. But I needed someone to convince my mind that I wasn't done. What was so useful is that he made me stop thinking about the future and got me concentrating on the present moment, pulling every ace out of my sleeve that I'd been planning to save for later. Forget about later; all that matters is *now*. My crew member gave me exactly what was called for. I needed someone shoving me out of that car, pumping me full of everything, and bringing me back to life. The Oz Pearlman that never gives up was still in there, trapped somewhere in my mind, like a caged animal that needed to be released. When you find yourself in a situation where it would be so much easier to quit or to fail, have some tricks up your sleeve so you don't give in to what's easiest.

You might not even know what those tricks are until you're experiencing a low. Let's say you've decided to start your own business, as that's always been your dream. You don't want to work for The Man; you want to control your own destiny. Congratulations! But . . . you're not selling anything yet, and you've been at it for a while. You're not getting potential customers to call you back. You're thinking of giving up, even though you have enough of a financial cushion to tough it out.

What do you do?

At this point, you have to ask yourself, *What can I still put into this? What do I still have? Does anyone else do what I do? Is there some sort of information that I'm missing? Can I call in reinforcements?* When you get into a situation like this, set yourself up with guardrails and force yourself to utilize them, like having someone who can talk you off the ledge, buy you a beer, and tell you about the business that Bill Gates failed at before he started Microsoft. (It was called Traf-O-Data and it was a big goose egg.)

When I was in Florida running my race and it looked like the end, my buddy Ryan Dexter (aka "the Iceman") is the one who thought to call our other former crew member Michael Halovatch back in New York City. He gave the play-by-play: "He's been throwing up for nine miles. He's walking, he's a wreck. It's so early in the race." Usually in races like this, the breakdown comes 60, 70, or 80 miles in. Mine happened 27 miles into 100. The thought of walking 73 miles at a snail's pace while puking, otherwise known as a "death march," can break your spirit and overwhelm your determination. I thought to myself, *Oh my God, I'm going to have to walk the next twenty-four hours straight while feeling like this.* I would have done it but, man oh man, I didn't want to. Michael said, "We need to get you going because what you do well is run. You don't walk well, you run well. You need to get those miles in the bank. So if you can front-load those miles, you can use that to your advantage."

That's what you have to do—have plans in place that you can use to your advantage. I was in a crack-glass-in-case-of-emergency situation, and I needed someone to remind me that this was the time to crack that glass.

I was my own worst enemy in this situation. I was willing to quit instead of trying all the things my crew suggested. I was scared to take his advice because the easy way out was quitting. And in the moment, it feels good to say, "Oh, I just want to get rid of this pain and suffering and be done." But then I would have had to live with that decision for the next month, the next year, and on and on. Every time I looked in the mirror, I would know the truth, which is that I *chose* to quit. It's easy to give excuses to others, but it is very hard to lie to yourself. Quitting would have eaten me alive. I would not have dodged the pain and suffering; I would have transformed it from a short-lived experience to a long-term haunting. Knowing that your potential has not been achieved—knowing that you won't know the answer to *What if I had just done X, Y, or Z?*—will tear you apart. Do not let failure sneak up on you, but instead plan for that moment, prepare for that moment. Look failure right in the eyes and say, "Not today, I know what to do and I'm not giving up that easy."

You're not only going to succeed; you're going to improve your own brain chemistry.

The scientific effect of making plans, of having considered various backup plans, actually benefits your brain. Having something in reserve on your mental back burner will enhance your cognitive function for a couple of reasons. First, it's going to help improve your memory, because you're actively encoding that information. Planning will reinforce those neural pathways and make it easier to recall details, even under pressure; that will dovetail with improving your problem-solving skills, which will make it easier for you to decide on the fly. It's going to spark your creative thinking. In scientific terms, planning creates an interplay between our brain's prefrontal cortex and hippocampus, and that gives us the latitude to better guide our decisions and imagine our outcomes.[7] In plain English, let me break this down. The prefrontal cortex is like your brain's chief operating officer, in that it helps you with your decisions, with your goal-setting, and with thinking ahead. The hippocampus is more like the librarian who lives in your head and helps you retrieve your memories while also imagining future scenarios. When these two areas work together, you're engaging both your memory and your judgment to picture what may happen. This is key because it helps you decide what *should* happen. This interplay gives you more control over your choices and it allows you to envision different outcomes before they happen. Essentially, when these two are on the same team, they enable you to run mental simulations of the future. Imagine how useful that would that be. Plus, there's the added benefits of increasing our motivation and focus and reducing our stress when you know how it could turn out.

Planning, and including all variables, is simply a win-win.

Control the Variables

One of the best ways you can set yourself up for success is finding the means to control the variables. In a laboratory, variables are easy to control. You can isolate the experiment or the study, you can standardize the process, you can maintain a steady environment. But in life, it's not nearly so simple. Life is not a closed system. Social situations prove far more complex than a sterile lab.

The key here is figuring out what the variables are for your unique situation and how you may have a hand in guiding them. If you're a salesperson, you can't control how the potential clients react. However, you *can* schedule your pitch when you know people are most apt to pay attention or be receptive. If you've been in the business for a while, you've likely noticed patterns of when people are most alert, and you're well aware that right after lunch is the kiss of death, so you plan accordingly. If you're a teacher, your students are likely far more receptive at the top of the hour, rather than in the five minutes before class ends, so you hit them with the important concepts early. If you're wrangling your toddler, you're going to learn the hard way not to go anywhere with them right around naptime.

When I'm performing, sometimes the variable is as simple as getting a proper introduction to the audience. I never realized how important this was until I was slated to open for comedian Jim Gaffigan shortly after I was on *America's Got Talent.*

Right after *AGT,* I was hot. In showbiz, you get these moments where there's momentum and everyone's seeing you and recognizing you and it almost gives you a pass to not be as good. Stand-up comedy is my favorite form of entertainment and there is no better place in the world to see the best comics than the Comedy Cellar in New York City. The most famous comedians in the world will "drop in" unannounced, and for the first five minutes, they can just rest on their laurels. Everyone in the audience is just so blown away they are getting to see Chris Rock or Dave Chappelle from ten feet away, having paid only fifteen bucks! But if, five to ten minutes later, he's not funny, you're not going to be laughing anymore and his fame evaporates, at least in your view. With this in mind, I threw myself into improving my act because I promised myself that *AGT* was just the beginning for me, not my peak.

I was booked in early 2015 by a group of Modern Orthodox Jews that owns a very successful commercial mortgage business to perform at their client dinner later that year. This event was scheduled to take place two weeks after the finale of *AGT.* The fact that I was a fellow Jew gave me a major home field advantage. My humor was naturally going to hit better because I knew their terms, their inside jokes, I had the right "chutzpah." I knew *them.* We were just very simpatico.

It is important to note that they hired me before I'd even auditioned for *AGT*, much less made it through round after round and eventually into the finals. Their entire company watched every episode and rooted for me along the way, becoming emotionally attached as if I were their favorite sports team. And they got me for about 10 percent of the price I would have charged the day after getting third place on *AGT*. It was like buying a biotech stock whose blockbuster drug later gets approved by the FDA. They also hired superstar Jim Gaffigan, for a huge sum of money, to headline the event, and I was so excited to open for him.

The event was in Puerto Rico. It was an outdoor show by the beach, which is a kiss of death for live entertainment because there's lots of noise from the ocean and from animals, and the laughter and applause doesn't reverberate effectively with no walls to bounce off. The show is already going to be only 50 percent as strong as it could be. Then they told me to do forty-five to fifty minutes, the same as Jim. That was strange. Openers don't normally do the same amount of time as headliners. An opener should be more like the appetizer before the meal, especially because people only have so much energy to commit to entertainment on a given night.

I did forty-five minutes and I got two standing ovations. I absolutely killed it with this crowd because they got me; I was one of them. However, when I was done, they had *me* introduce Jim Gaffigan instead of an emcee. This was not the initial plan and took Jim by surprise, so he wasn't yet ready to come onstage. I read his intro and looked around, but he was nowhere to be found. About a minute or so later (but what felt like an eternity to the crowd), he made his way, flustered, to the stage. So, already, he had to contend with a bad introduction. After that, even though he's one of the biggest comedians ever, he just bombed. It was horrible, like, gut-wrenchingly bombed. It just wasn't the right crowd, and I'd inadvertently been at fault with the entrance.

And they had already been blown away by me—my show had both major moments of amazement and big laughs given our common sense of humor. (Full disclosure: My wife says that no one finds Oz Pearlman funnier than Oz Pearlman. She's right, as I just laughed out loud reading this, even though I wrote it!)

Afterward, I apologized profusely to Jim backstage about the intro because I felt terrible. I said, "You're one of the most legendary comics in the world. What went wrong?" Jim was really Zen about it, saying that bombing happens and you have to learn from a bad show and let it motivate you to do better next time. This was on a Monday night, and four nights later, he was back in New York, selling out Madison Square Garden, so I suspect he got over it. He wouldn't be where he is today without having cultivated some resilience. I learned an important show-biz lesson that night, which is: Everyone eats shit sometimes. Never forget it.

There are variables in life you can't control. There will be moments that, no matter how hard you try, you'll still fail. It's not about *if* that happens, but rather *when*: What will you do in those pivotal moments? That is what will define you. Determine what went wrong, learn from it, accept your feelings as valid, and keep moving forward. And that's exactly what I did when I didn't win *AGT.* (More on that in a later chapter.)

But failure wasn't going to be an issue on *Today*, because I was way too prepared.

The Big Reveal

When I perform on live TV, there is no safety net. There's no editing, no second take. If something goes wrong, my clock doesn't start over.

For me to extricate myself from the situation almost always involves more time. I need more time. Often, I don't have that time, as we are going to commercial or another segment, and so it's incredibly high pressure because the backup measures require me to dig myself out of a hole. And digging takes time! Now, if I'm at a live performance onstage, that's rarely a problem. It doesn't go right? It's fine because I had a plan and plenty of time to fix it. You might not even know it went wrong because it's so effortless as I swoop in with something that you didn't know I was going to do.

Live TV is more of a pick-your-own-adventure in terms of planning. On one of my *Today* show appearances, when we had about forty-five seconds left, on a whim I asked Al Roker to name any celebrity he thought could be elected the next president of the United States. When I gamed out this trick, the Theory of Mind led me to believe he'd choose Taylor Swift. I set up the trick around that specific predicted outcome. Everything I did should have led him to that choice. Unbeknownst to him, I was even wearing a Taylor Swift T-shirt under my suit for my big reveal.

Confident in Roker's answer, I said to him, "Al, who's running? Shock us."

With great confidence, Roker replied, "George Clooney," which *was* a shock, as he wasn't who I'd envisioned him picking! He had no idea that, at that moment, my blood pressure was spiking and there was the potential for millions to see me implode on national television.

And yet, in the month that I'd planned for this trick, I knew that him picking Taylor wasn't a given, although she was the most likely choice. I had visualized this scenario in my mind hundreds of times, figuring out how I could quickly get him to choose the answer I'd anticipated if he didn't pick it on the first try.

Al Roker had no idea how wrong this had just gone, and I did not allow my body language to betray my true feelings. He'd given me a catastrophically wrong answer, but he didn't know there was a *right* guess I'd anticipated. When you find yourself in a moment like this, even if the stakes aren't quite so high, the way you handle the situation determines your outcome. You keep cool, you keep calm, you shift gears. Control your emotions and take charge.

At this point on *Today*, we had maybe half a minute left of airtime. Not a lot of time to pull out the win and prompt Roker to re-guess Taylor Swift. In Taylor's own words, I was "Down Bad," and maybe even ready to cry at the gym. The clock was ticking and I had the wink of an eye to make it seem like this had been my plan all along, as the unexpected correction with seconds to spare would make the trick seem even more powerful and deliberate.

There are certain moments where you go, "Oh, he's getting it wrong but he's going to come back." But in front of millions of viewers drinking coffee in front of their televisions as they get ready for work? That's not a get-it-wrong-to-come-back moment from my perspective. I knew I couldn't lose my cool. Animals sense danger on an instinctive level. They can see it. They can smell fear. If you run from a bear, it considers you prey and it will hunt and kill you even if it doesn't want to eat you. The same thing applies when you're trying to influence people. They can sense fear, and sensing fear is almost like a smell. Your body tenses. In that moment, I had to turn into a quarterback with five seconds left on the clock. When time's running down, a good quarterback knows they have to throw a perfect pass.

I knew if I panicked, Roker would panic, and then I would not be able to impose my will on him. I wouldn't be able to get out of the situation. If you happen to watch the clip on YouTube, you'll see that I'm calm as can be.[8] Roker didn't even know that the trick wasn't on plan.

In situations like this, you must maintain your calm and composure or it actually will not work. It's sort of a catch-22; if something goes wrong, you inherently want to panic and tense up, and often that will make it even worse. In flight training programs, they do heart rate analysis on fighter pilots and astronauts. In situations of extreme tension and stress, the people who make it through are the ones who are able to maintain a low heart rate to keep their disposition, even in a situation that's life-or-death.

The stakes were high. If I failed, I would die of old age before the video clip died on social media. I can tell you about past instances when I've panicked onstage—the audience senses it and things spiral. Having visualized and having planned will help you maintain composure. It's physical. Your mental controls your physical. I've reviewed plenty of my old tapes and there are times I could see in my body if things were going wrong. I've had flop-sweat moments when suddenly my brain turns off and I go offstage and ask myself, *What just happened? I don't even remember; I was so stressed.*

I said to Roker, "Listen, the world is changing. What if it wasn't a guy who was elected? What if I was anybody else? Any women?" Instead of thinking that my setup was unsuccessful, Theory of Mind indicated that Al Roker suddenly took pause to worry that he'd inadvertently been sexist to not consider a woman.

Roker screwed up his face for a couple of seconds (that felt like an hour) and thought hard before he said, "Um . . . Taylor Swift."

I shrugged nonchalantly and repeated it slowly back, "Taylor, Swift," as if to emphasize how impossible it was that he had changed his mind, seemingly of his own volition, and with only seconds remaining before the commercial break. As he pondered, I removed my blazer and button-down to reveal my T-SWIFT FOR PREZ T-shirt. And then I asked his cohost what the word was that she'd associate with the campaign, and she spontaneously said, "Independence." Then I turned around and showed them the back of the shirt, which read #INDEPENDENCE . . . snatching victory from the jaws of defeat as Roker exclaimed, "Mind blown, again!" They were so shocked by what just took place that they bumped the next guest and kept me on for another segment. This was a near unprecedented occurrence on a show that is so tightly scheduled.

All thanks to planning for the unexpected!

(Whew!)

THREE

Make Your Fear of Rejection Magically Disappear

All too often, people shy away from accomplishing big goals because they fear rejection. What they don't realize is that by eliminating the chance of failure, there's also no chance of success. But anyone who says rejection doesn't hurt is either a liar or a masochist. It's always painful, and no one figured that out faster than me as a sensitive teenager.

Listen, I can't make the sting of rejection vanish completely, but in this chapter, I can help you shift it elsewhere. I'll show you how to separate and disassociate yourself from the skill or task at hand, to not internalize the guilt or rejection, and to prevent those bad feelings from bleeding into other aspects of your life. It's a technique I call "magic mode."

And barring that, I'll show how to let the haters fuel you, something I experienced myself after a Super Bowl trick didn't go as planned. Is it as easy as flipping a switch?

Yes, it is, and I'll show you how.

Weird Science

Rejection doesn't just hit us in our feelings. What you may not know is that social rejection causes a process in our brains that's akin to physical pain. According to the American Psychological Association, rejection can impact our emotions, our cognition, and even our physical health.[1] This stems from evolution and our biological need to be included, because being ostracized from the group and cast out of cooperative society thousands of years ago meant certain death.

Social psychologist Naomi Eisenberger of UCLA conducted a study to investigate the brain's response to rejection. Volunteers were placed into a functional magnetic resonance imaging machine, which is a type of MRI that can read brain activity, and given virtual reality goggles with which they would throw a virtual ball to other players. The subjects were told they were interacting with other volunteers, but the ball's progress was really controlled by the research team. Researchers wanted to determine what happens in the brain when we are excluded.

For those singled-out players, researchers noted that the anterior cingulate cortex, which is what responds to pain, would light up in accordance to exactly how strongly the participants felt excluded and rejected.[2] The emotional pain manifested itself into a physical response. So if you're still having flashbacks about what happened during a game of dodgeball when you were in junior high, this is why.

Rejection triggers our fight-or-flight response, meaning our heart rate increases, our blood pressure spikes, and our stress hormones are activated.[3] And that's not to mention how it hurts our self-esteem, especially if it sends us down the rabbit hole of negative self-talk and feelings of worthlessness and inadequacy.[4] Plus, being rejected can cause a drop in dopamine and that opens a whole Pandora's box of sadness, grief, and the loss of motivation.

That's a lot of baggage to lay on a kid who just wants you to pick a card before your linguini arrives, know what I'm saying?

I had no clue why being turned away made me feel bad; I just knew I wanted to *stop* feeling bad. When I was at the restaurant, my mind was constantly racing. I was always trying to find a way to be better received. In some respects, it was like I was working out a recipe; I'd see what happened if I changed an ingredient here or there and then taste-test to see what worked.

My solution then to deal with the rejection was to disassociate myself from my fear of being hurt and embarrassed. In terms of personal phobias, the fear of being embarrassed is one of the most common. It's like that Jerry Seinfeld joke where he says that more people are afraid of public speaking than they are of dying. Which means that at a funeral, more people would rather be in the coffin than giving the eulogy.

Through my trial and error, I stumbled into something that researchers describe as the ability to go from being the "actor" in the situation to being the "observer."[5] (Now I call this "slipping into magic mode" and we'll go into further detail on how to do that later in this chapter.)

What I mean by being the observer is that when I was about to perform—way back when I put on my bar mitzvah suit and walked into Zia's—I'd tell myself that I wasn't Oz Pearlman. Instead, I was Oz the Entertainer, the precursor to Oz the Mentalist. And if people rejected or didn't like Oz the Entertainer, that wasn't Oz Pearlman's problem. I turned myself into a character, meaning I separated myself and my psyche from the task at hand. I was no longer the actor; I was the observer. I made a conscious decision to not internalize how people would react to me because they weren't reacting to the *real* me.

Essentially, I would silo myself. I like to explain this with the analogy of having a bucket of fresh drinking water. If you add salt to that bucket, the whole thing is ruined; you can't drink it. But, if you were to put a divider in that bucket, you could dump salt into a little section and the rest of the water would be free and clear. I realized that if one element could ruin everything, then I had to figure out how to create silos so the salt—meaning the rejection—would only impact a small portion. That way, I wouldn't shuffle home thinking *Ugh, I'm terrible at everything*, and I wasn't derailed from my goal of scoring party gigs, which would allow me to buy more tricks. I quickly began compartmentalizing my feelings, so those negative thoughts didn't paralyze me. I'd rationalize that those patrons didn't know Oz Pearlman, and they weren't rejecting *him*; instead, they weren't into Oz the Entertainer's tricks. And that was their loss.

Ironically, while you may imagine that the pain of rejection goes away as you grow up, research shows it's just the opposite—studies show that older adults feel the sting of hurt feelings more than younger adults.[6]

So I want you to consider how disassociating could apply to the rejection you may face. Where would it be useful for you to step outside yourself and observe? If you could detach, would you feel more free to share your ideas in team meetings? Would you take the chance to talk to that attractive guy or girl you keep seeing in your apartment lobby? Would you be able to make the case to your boss for hiring an intern to help lessen everyone's workload? Could you take a bigger swing if you weren't so tied up feeling like everything was at stake?

Instead of thinking about all the ways your asks could go wrong, take a minute and envision all the ways in which they could go *right*. This is one of those "What could you try if you knew you couldn't fail" situations, so put this advice to use and prepare to amaze yourself. And if you ask and it's a no, remember, they're never rejecting you—they're rejecting one tiny piece that's separated from the rest and won't bring you down.

Failing Up

I've actually seen magicians quit performing because they couldn't deal with the rejection; they never learned to silo themselves. This is a lot like an athlete that never recovers mentally from an injury; long after they are physically healed, the fear of more pain ends their career.

This same fear can handicap you and keep you from chasing your big goals because you're not ready to risk rejection and failure.

Here's the quiet part that no one says out loud: If there's no chance of losing, there's also no chance of winning. Like in the above examples, while you may strike out, what happens when your shared ideas are implemented? When you find out the attraction to your neighbor is actually mutual? When your intern helps you shine because you're no longer bogged down with administrative work?

If you want to become stronger, whether it's mentally or physically, you must experience failure. Failure is the foundation for growth. Failing, especially multiple times, gives you the kind of resilience you just don't get from smooth sailing. Failure is the cornerstone of innovation.

Let's talk about some famous failures, like . . . one of our greatest living authors, Stephen King. King had started to write *Carrie* and became so frustrated that he ended up throwing out the entire manuscript. His wife, Tabitha, who couldn't help but be curious about his work, fished it out of the trash.[7] The manuscript was rejected 30 times before being picked up by Doubleday. It went on to sell over a million copies its first year in paperback and become a successful film.[8] Since then King has published over 60 novels, 200 short stories and won numerous awards for his contributions to literature."[9] (Imagine being the editor who told Stephen King he didn't have what it takes.)

Or how about we look at that big loser, Walt Disney? He got canned from his newspaper job because they said he "lacked imagination." (Seriously!) The Grand Ole Opry suggested that Elvis Presley return to his job driving trucks when they gave him the boot. The King of Rock and Roll! And do you clean your floors with a Dyson vacuum? Well, that's only because Sir James Dyson had the fortitude to fail 5,126 times before he created the working prototype.[10] No one sees failures in these instances; instead, they see dynamic individuals who didn't allow a bump in the road to knock them off their trajectories.

Let that be you.

Failure allows for growth. But so many have the tendency to not own up to the fact that it's easier to keep the status quo than it is to potentially suffer more along the road to greatness. Any athlete knows that if they want to get stronger, they have to break down that muscle. So it follows that, if you want to get stronger mentally, you can't protect yourself from the failure and rejection that can come from having tried.

At Zia's, one of the many things I learned (which is I why I keep bringing it up) is that landing outside gigs for my tableside magic was a numbers game. For every three tables that loved me, one would say, "Keep it moving, buddy," and for every fifty business cards I would hand out each night, maybe two would turn into a show over the next year. This required me to be patient, to plant the seeds and wait for the fruit to grow. What helped me reframe these rejections was knowing that X number of rejections would ultimately result in Y number of paying gigs. So the more rejections I collected, the quicker I could achieve my goal of working consistently as a party magician. Suddenly, rejection wasn't a failure; it was a necessary metric.

There was a popular challenge on social media called "rejection therapy," which is really just an updated term for exposure therapy. In it, people film themselves going places and asking for things, knowing full well they'll be rejected. Some of the most common challenges are asking a stranger to buy you a Slurpee at 7-Eleven or requesting a random person on the street give you a hug. The theory is that the more you accustom yourself to rejection, the better insulated you'll be. While this is not an evidence-based therapy, I have no doubt that this can help some people develop thicker skin, which in turn can help build character.

I feel lucky to have learned as a kid that getting knocked down wasn't pleasant, yet I was stronger every time I picked myself back up. It doesn't matter if you're fourteen or forty, every rejection moves you a step closer to where you want to land.

Expect the Unexpected

After *America's Got Talent*, my popularity grew exponentially, and I thought I could put worrying about rejection and failure in my rearview mirror. I assumed the road ahead would be smooth and easy from then on out . . . until the pandemic hit.

For people who held office jobs, the pivot to working from home was fairly easy. In fact, many people preferred not having to deal with commutes, dry cleaning, office politics, etc. Heck, even broadcasters were able to work from home. But when your job is to appear in a room in front of thousands of people, lockdown presented a real dilemma.

My peers began performing on and promoting themselves through social media, but I'll be honest, this scared me. Despite my best efforts,

I'm not immune to the fear of rejection, especially because social media allows for immediate responses that are easily measured. Plus there's the tendency for others to pile on when they sense sentiment has turned against the person posting. This was an entirely new medium for me. In some ways, it felt like I was starting over, though at least I was wearing better suits than my Zia's days.

Say what you will about social media; love it or hate it, the fact of the matter is it's here to stay. It seems like everyone's addicted. If you think social media doesn't impact your brain chemistry, think again. Researchers have found that the dopamine hit we get from positive interactions is similar to what's produced from using cocaine.[11] It can also diminish your ability to pay attention and to retain information, plus there's the possibility that it can negatively impact your mental health, so I'm saying all this with the caveat that it should be used responsibly. But in a time when the world was feeling so disconnected, social media was a bridge that helped us feel like we were all in it together, so I had to figure it out.

I knew that, to be successful in any endeavor, I needed to be able to scale, and social media allowed this to happen. Social media has changed our access to people, and it's the currency of our time. Think about it—you can reach out, and people can reach right back. I had no idea how mentalism would translate to a handheld screen, but I made myself try. My strategy wasn't to monetize, but to connect.

I began performing online when so many of us were still trying to figure out how to work Zoom, and I have to tell you, it felt like my early restaurant days when I was a research scientist, tweaking my experiments until they produced the desired results. At first, I was sure I was ruined and told my wife we should sell our home and move while we still could, that I'd never work again. Yes, I may be prone to catastrophizing. Yet I kept at it and within a few weeks of free shows offered to friends, family, and past clients, I came up with a successful formula of how to perform on Zoom.

Rejection is never going to go away. The possibility of failure is never off the table, no matter who you are. But the more you're willing to put yourself out there and try new things, the more success you'll experience. The ultimate failure is never getting to the starting line. When I began my career, I thought opportunities would fall into my lap, but that was never going to happen. For example, I was never going to get on television if I didn't force myself to try, so, as a bulwark against failure, I had to ask myself hard questions about what I wasn't doing.

Fortunately, during those strange pandemic times, I was able to slip into magic mode. Here's how you can do the same.

Flip the Script

I didn't have strong social skills when I was fourteen—but what kid does? If Clark Kent can rip off his shirt, throw on a cape, and become Superman, then why couldn't I do the same? In this case, my superpower was to go from Oz the nerdy, insecure teenager to Oz the Great and Powerful (as far as my audiences were concerned). Seeing people light up when I performed was a rush and I fed off it. I flipped that switch, went into magic mode, and suddenly shed the fears that otherwise held me back; I'd started on the journey to becoming Oz the Mentalist.

It's always scary to try new things. There's a possibility of failure and rejection. We worry that we're going to look stupid and feel ashamed. Neophobia is *real* and it can manifest itself in any area of your life, no matter how large or small, whether you're anxious about getting a new haircut or you're worried about making a cross-country move for that dream job. So often, our defense mechanism is to just give up instead of trying. It's easier to stay stuck, to not venture outside of that comfort zone. Keep your hair the same, stay in that dead-end job.

We've already established that visualization tricks our brain into thinking what we're seeing is real and puts our bodies into autopilot. But when you see yourself as the observer, your brain flips the script and gives you license to be a bolder version of who you are.

If you're ever going to try something new, you must be able to imagine that it's possible. For example, when I started training for my first marathon, I never allowed myself to believe that I would fail. I told myself that if I built up my endurance, if I cross-trained and fueled and hydrated properly, if I got enough rest, and if I held myself accountable to a series of small goals, there was no way I couldn't do it. I'd have built such a strong foundation that I'd be rock-solid on race day . . . and I was.

Having some healthy irrationality can be a motivating force, even though, in the back of my head, I wondered if running 26.2 miles was bananas. In marathons—and in life—the mental is just as important as the physical. You have to tell yourself you've got this, while concurrently putting in the work to make sure you've got it. Remember, *you* control that little voice inside your head. Flip that switch, and don't let it be a negative influence. Instead, become your own biggest cheerleader. Celebrate those little wins along the way, as they will add up to more than you expect over time. Repeat that positive self-talk until you believe it.

Rejection sensitive dysphoria is the name for the heightened emotional responses people can feel stemming from rejection, critique, failure, or even teasing. (This phenomenon is most common in adults with

ADHD.) One of the best ways to combat it—beyond therapy and medication if it's severe—is through focusing on the positive and your own personal strengths and abilities.

Part of magic mode is understanding the difference between rejection, critique, and feedback. Rejection is when your idea or effort doesn't work for the audience, which can be less about you and more about their individual needs. For example, you may be the best painter in the world, but if the end user wants a poem, your creation isn't going to work. Critique is more problem-focused, like when you're telling a joke and the punchline doesn't land. Feedback is solution-oriented, and it can include both strengths and weaknesses. Of course, you can certainly learn from and implement changes in each instance. The most important point is to concentrate on what is within your control. Using the Jim Gaffigan example from the last chapter: Although he couldn't control the outdoor venue's noise, he could take steps to better his outcome, such as insisting that his opener have a shorter set and getting a clear a signal before being introduced.

Magic mode is the difference between beating yourself up, and saying, "This was great, but next time will be even better," because it will help you enjoy every moment. For example, a few years ago, I ran my fastest time ever at the Philadelphia Marathon. I finished in 2:23:52, which, given my age, is likely to be the fastest time I'll ever run in my life. I was a lean, mean, running machine! Rather than savor that achievement, as I should have, I instead focused only on the negative, which was having not achieved my goal of breaking 2:20. I was hyperfixated on that number to my detriment, and that caused me to lose sight of my incredible accomplishment during that race, which I will always regret.

When I look back at that day, I realize I robbed myself of what was an epic achievement because of my mindset. I should have taken a step back, been the observer, and said to myself, *You might* never *run this fast again, don't take your fitness, your focus, your unwavering dedication and commitment for granted. Enjoy this day!*

I didn't and I regret it. Not only was I miserable, but I let my bad feelings spill over, which impacted my family and my next performance. That wasn't fair to anyone. I should have celebrated clocking the best time of my life. I should have been grateful for having the capability to run any distance at all. I should have reveled in the beauty of speeding through a historic city on a beautiful day, through crowds of supportive spectators. There was so much to love in the moment and I didn't recognize any of it: I was too fixated on four stupid minutes.

To remind myself to not let this happen again, I like to look at a picture of myself finishing the Hartford Marathon a year earlier. I was nearly two minutes slower in that race, but I didn't expect to run as fast as I did. The look on my face when I crossed that finish was one of pure bliss, unbridled joy, distilled and injected into every cell of my being. It was so striking that the next year the race organizers used it for the posters to promote the race! And what was the difference? My expectations. Letting that negative self-talk creep in and not learning my own lesson of flipping into magic mode meant that I wasn't able to shake the negative and embrace the positive.

But we're all works in progress, so remember that.

The Future Is Now

When something does go wrong, there's a technique I like to use. I tell myself that no matter how awful this feels now, it will eventually get better. The pain, the unpleasantness, the discomfort will subside and you need to visualize the sunrise just over the horizon and be patient as it comes.

Having an awareness that this pain and shame and unhappiness is temporary will help save your psyche, especially the more time passes. Will you even remember said slight or mistake three years from now? I suggest you fast-track that set of emotions, which is what I ultimately learned to do at Zia's; it's a skill I've carried with me ever since.

When I'd walk up to an unreceptive table, I'd worry about how I'd feel in the moment that they shooed me away. If they were like, "Please get out of here," that was rough. The dejection right in the moment is huge. But an hour later, a day later, the pain is virtually gone. What I suggest you do is trick yourself into speeding up that cycle. In your mind, tell yourself it's a day later instead of a minute later.

Imagine you have a remote control you can use to fast-forward your life. Right now, I want you to workshop something in your head that you're dreading and you've been putting off. Let's say you have a call with somebody that you know is going to tell you no or be mad or disappointed. You do not want to do this call. It's awful and the anticipation makes it even worse. Or let's say you're dealing with somebody that you hate, or any other situation that has you tied in knots. The mere thought of dealing with it sends waves of dread pulsing through your core, hence you keep delaying the work. Unfortunately, avoidance is only a tactic, never a solution.

I want you to catalog how you feel one minute after doing the task—just write it down. You don't even have to make the call, just record how you imagine you'll feel once you do. Then set yourself a reminder in your calendar for twenty-four hours later. How do you feel now that it's a day later? See what the difference is.

For almost everything I can think of, barring life-or-death decisions, the negative swirl of emotions subsides within twenty-four to forty-eight hours of the work being addressed. Researchers have found that, without reinforcement, memories are actively suppressed and degraded.[12] You literally will get over it. The difference is, one minute later, you probably feel an eight out of ten on a scale of terrible. But a day later, you feel maybe two out of ten, right? So let's trick our brain. Remember, the more vividly you visualize it, the more your brain accepts it to be real, and the more your body responds appropriately.

Let's repurpose the very same mentalist tricks I use in my act to get in people's heads and manipulate the way they think, but instead do it to you. In this case, speed up the clock and take what you know you'll feel one day from now and trick yourself into feeling that one second from now instead. Picture yourself hitting fast-forward on a remote control. That's how I would do it at the restaurant. So when a table would say, "Kid, get out of here," I'd trick my brain into fast-forwarding to how I'd feel a day later. Couple that with magic mode—they had an issue with Oz the Entertainer, not me—and it was easy for me to go to the next table, pass out the cards, and get the gigs.

Mission accomplished.

(Not So) Super Bowl

All of this is to say that when I finally had my chance to perform on live national TV before the Super Bowl kickoff in 2023, I was as well-insulated as I could have been for when my trick failed. The trick hinged on NFL coach Rex Ryan using a stopwatch to time Matt Hasselbeck throwing a bunch of footballs to Randy Moss, and an impossible reveal at the end that I'd predicted how long this would take. To be safe, I had the coach practice using the stopwatch with me before we went on air, even though I was worried that he'd feel patronized. I mean, showing a coach how to use a stopwatch? Why not instruct Michael Jordan on how to put that bouncy orange ball in the net? And yet somehow Rex fat-fingered the stopwatch, pressing Start and Stop simultaneously, so that the recording of the seconds—the crux of the trick—never happened.

That's right, my trick went off the rails in front of a live audience that numbered in the tens of millions. I guess if you're going to fail, fail big?

The issue was I was still sort of new to massive broadcasts like this and I didn't have proper control of the situation. My tricks have layers and can sometimes be complex, so I need total and complete buy-in from the camera operators and director, because there are certain angles and shots that they have to catch in order for it to be successful.

Afterward, I did a thorough after-action review and determined that, ultimately, it was my fault. What I wanted to accomplish was too complicated, and I was being too clever. I should have simplified the trick and made it clearer. But I was both skilled and experienced enough to not let this mistake devastate me. Honestly, I had to silo myself for the next few days after the game, because I got so much hate from people online that had placed bets based on my mentalist prediction.

So. Much.

One guy was furious. He told me, "Buddy, you owe me $1,000."

I replied, "Buddy, why are you taking financial advice from a mentalist?"

When you get that kind of pushback, the only way through is to allow the hate and the bad feelings to fuel you. What I didn't do was relive that moment over and over, berating myself with "coulda, woulda, shoulda." I had to let it go. I didn't permit one single misstep to stop me. Instead, I doubled down on my work with the NFL and have since created some of my most spectacular and iconic moments with players, like when I stunned Dak Prescott, transforming a pack of playing cards held tightly in his hands into any animal called out at random.

So now when you google *Oz the Mentalist* and *football*, you don't see the trick that went afoul, because I didn't let that one bad moment impede my progress. Instead, you'll see me correctly predicting the first thirteen picks in the 2024 NFL Draft, including Michael Penix Jr, which absolutely no one saw coming, not even the owner of the team. Or you'll see me blowing the minds of every member of the Michigan Wolverines before they won the College Football Playoff National Championship, guessing which players Coach Jim Harbaugh would think of, predicting each of their jersey numbers, which, when flipped upside down, spelled out *Go Blue*. The stadium played that moment on the jumbotron as Michigan concluded their perfect season—going undefeated and then winning the National Championship. To have my history intertwined with such a pivotal moment for my alma mater is a memory I will always cherish.

Listen, I know rejection is no picnic. But if you don't try, you're never going to achieve more. You have to face down those disappointments, and you can't let them immobilize you. While it's painful, you have the power to shift that negative energy elsewhere. Learn how to separate yourself from the fear and pain of rejection, and watch the paradigm shift that occurs in your life and your ability to start achieving your biggest goals.

FOUR

Focus on Others

In 2006, the beer brand Dos Equis created an iconic advertising campaign called *The Most Interesting Man in the World*, starring a handsome, suave, and mysterious bearded actor named Jonathan Goldsmith. He was shown doing everything from exploring Egyptian tombs to arm-wrestling in South America to surfing killer waves. After the voiceover deemed him the most interesting man in the world, he'd raise a bottle of Dos Equis and say, "I don't always drink beer, but when I do, I prefer Dos Equis." The campaign was a huge hit for the decade it ran, and it increased the brand's market share by 22 percent.[1]

Of course, that man was fictional and the product of a marketing firm. Also, the idea of being the most interesting person in the world is a huge ask.

But what if I promised you could become the most interesting person *in the room*?

If you want to be the most interesting person in the room, you don't have to be the second incarnation of Ernest Hemingway. You don't have to run with the bulls in Pamplona or survive back-to-back plane crashes. You definitely don't need to write the Great American Novel or build a boxing ring so you can spar with your guests. You never have to go fishing.

The only thing you have to do to be the most interesting person in the room is to be *the most interested* person in the room. If you want to be fascinating, be fascinated by others.

One of the fundamentals of finding your inner mentalist is to know that it's never about you. Whatever you do and wherever you go, it should always be about *them.* I'm talking about your family, your clients, your coworkers, your community, your club, your audience, etc., because when you make the interaction about them, you make them look and feel good.

In much the same way that a rising tide lifts all boats, your ability to cast your light on others to make them shine will be the secret to your success. That means connecting with everyone—and never putting your baggage on them. People want to be seen. In our heads, we're all the stars in our own movies, but to everyone else, we're just supporting characters. If you want to feel like a star, make it all about *them.*

Mentalism is a finite series of tricks. What makes a performance legendary is being a storyteller and tapping into people's emotions with genuine interest. In this chapter, I'll teach you how to make whoever is in front of you feel like the most important and interesting person in the room, and it starts with kicking away the pedestal. I will break down the steps for transforming zero-sum game situations into win-wins for everyone, and also how to apply the showbiz rule "Always leave the audience wanting more" to your everyday life.

I'll also show how to turn the mirror around so that it no longer faces you but reflects the best parts of those around you, because that adds to them wanting more. This is exactly what happened when I spent half an hour with my childhood idol, Steven Spielberg. Only it was *he* who held up that mirror to *me.*

Use your inner mentalist to try to guess how many questions I was able to ask about him.

Kick Away That Pedestal

If you want to make people look good, then you've got to level the playing field, especially when there's a power imbalance. You can't put yourself on a pedestal, and expect others to feel comfortable around you. Let's take what I've been doing with ESPN as an example. I visit a lot of NFL training camps in the preseason, and although it might look as if I'm just performing tricks—like reading Josh Allen's mind or figuring out the play fake that Joe Burrow tried to fool me with—that's not my real intent. I'm there to help build team unity. The coaches, owners, and general managers aren't just looking for a magic show, they want a morale boost. They want their team to walk out of my show feeling more connected and cohesive, which often translates into better performance on the field.

This starts with making everyone feel equal. The "pedestal effect" is a cognitive bias. What this means is, in our minds, we've created an idealized version of who someone is, especially when they're in a position of power, authority, or leadership. By default, they often make us feel "less than," even if it's not their intention. The act of taking someone off the pedestal means that we're actively trying to humanize them, because the notion of someone being on a higher level than us inherently makes us feel insecure and disempowers us.

You've got to remember that even though these men are on the same team, it doesn't always *feel* like they're on the same team, especially when the other guys are earning more, getting more attention, and simply playing more. When the second-string quarterback sees the star player laughing and being equally as amazed as he is, the invisible wall starts to come down. What I'm doing in that room removes some of that underlying tension by humanizing the superstars and coaches, making them more accessible.

Now, for some teams, this is not as much of a factor. But a few years ago, one of the teams I visited had a new coach. Everyone was on edge. It felt like I was in an army barracks during basic training. I tried to get the coach involved, to get him to relax a bit so we could have some fun at his expense. The emotional temperature in the room was significantly warmer by the time I was done. This quest to humanize others is the same exact reason I decided to freak Aaron Rodgers out so completely by making a live goldfish appear in his otherwise empty hands. (And for the record, don't blame me for the season-ending injury on the first drive of his first game with the Jets!)

A lot of times, when we elevate someone because of their position, it can bring out the worst in ourselves. I like to call this the "compare and despair" mentality. But when we're able to find a way to make it feel like we're on the same level, when we're able to make them more relatable, when we can look them in the eye instead of gazing up at them, we perceive them as less intimidating. This is why certain celebrities are wildly popular on social media, even if they're not marquee names. While it's interesting to see these icons live glamorous lives on private planes or behind the velvet rope at exclusive events, it's so much more relatable when they show themselves getting a parking ticket or spilling coffee on their pants or cheering along in sweats while they watch the Olympics. (Celebrities: They're just like us!) When you can see yourself in someone else, the gap is bridged.

When I perform at corporate events, I often provide a social context that helps promote bonding and creates an environment conducive to business. Given the power dynamics within large organizations, access to the upper echelon is a very valuable commodity, and having people at the top of the food chain know who you are as an employee is a big deal. I always make it a point to include the CEO or other senior leaders, with the goal of demystifying them. I'll either reveal something very funny about them, such as the name of their first crush in elementary school, or have them serve as my mind-reading protégé and guess something impossible to know about a colleague.

When I do this, the CEO is no longer above everyone else; they're just a woman or man like any other, who appears equally as blown away as their colleagues. This creates a bonding moment for everyone involved, and suddenly someone who'd be too afraid to even look the CEO in the eyes is their partner in crime—they're high-fiving each other in front of the crowd—and it aligns everyone to the same level. This experience serves to unite the team, creating a memorable moment that they've shared and can therefore readily reference next time they see each other.

One company I recently worked for had just gone through a big merger. Now, I've been a part of corporate America, having started my career on Wall Street. (More on that in a later chapter.) That's why I knew firsthand that mergers are inherently scary, no matter the industry. There's always uncertainty and the fear of redundancy. Everyone's on guard and they all think they're getting fired, right? So this is the perfect scenario in which to put everyone on an even footing.

I asked the event coordinator about the state of affairs, and she was a little cagey, but I insisted, "Give me the honest truth." She explained that everyone was borderline panicky and that morale was way down. I told her, "Great, good to know, I get it. And the CEO is probably in a situation where nobody wants to give them bad news, right?" She said that the company just wanted to warm up the room, to de-escalate all those bad feelings, as things truly were on an upswing and jobs were safe.

When I did the trick for the CEO, I pulled in a personal assistant, someone who'd never get face time with the CEO, and yet my trick put them on the same team. It made them equals, collaborators, coconspirators. Later, the CEO wrote to me and said, "Hey, your performance was great, but the real magic was the way you had me integrate with the team. This led to an entirely different atmosphere after the show, where people were fearlessly approaching me to laugh and joke about what just took place. The ice was broken, that glass ceiling which normally separates us shattered. I'd say that close to a hundred people, who would have been completely nervous to talk to me, walked up and said, 'Did you really guess that? How did you know their pet's name?' It was transformational and went a long way to turning things around. So thank you."

If you can find a way to put everyone on the same footing, things change for the better. It's kind of like if you get stuck in an elevator with a bunch of strangers. Five minutes in, you're all cracking jokes and full of gallows humor. You're going to get to know those people. That's the same exact mentality. The shared experience causes a shift in your brain; suddenly you can open up to others that you would've never even acknowledged otherwise.

One of the reasons I've been invited back to the *Today* show so many times isn't just because I deliver on camera (though that's important, too). The producers have told me it goes deeper than that—my repeat visits are because I bring joy to everyone on set, from the security team to craft services, makeup to wardrobe. That positive energy creates a kind of home field advantage, with the whole crew rooting for me. And here's the thing: This is something anyone can practice. When you go through life trying to make someone's day a little brighter, you'll find that people naturally want to be in your corner.

Take Note

An easy and economical way to make people look and feel good is to remember what's important to them. Doesn't cost you a penny! If you're in sales or a position where you have to influence people, and you're not doing this, you are missing a tremendous opportunity. Start to write everything down. Taking notes is so simple, and leads to such powerful results. Each note translates to a memory for that person, and there's nothing anyone likes more than being remembered. This is something I've been doing for years, as it was born out of necessity.

Much of my business involves repeat clients; if you do great work, then hopefully your clients will want you back again and again. When I head into a show, I don't want to perform the same act this audience saw the year before—in much the same way a joke doesn't hit as hard if you've already heard the punch line, the element of surprise is incredibly important to my craft. So I started writing down everything that happened at my shows to help keep track of things.

To prep for repeat performances, reviewing those notes is like studying for a midterm exam. I'd always rather be overprepared than under. I'll look up the names of the people I met and who I called onstage. I'll also have jotted down the interesting information they gave me, like their childhood dog was named Tripod because she only had three legs (that's actually true!).

When I do the next show, I'll either read their name tags, if they have them, or I'll say, "So great to see you again. Please remind me of your name." In either of those instances, I'll get the name and I'll remember where I saw that name in my notes. Let's say I was talking to John last year. And because I've looked at what I recorded last year, I'll remember that I guessed John's banking PIN.

John will often say, "That was so much fun last year!" While we're talking, I will find the right moment, usually layered with what magicians call "misdirection" (controlling where your audience members look), to check my phone and get a reminder of the info I know about John, if I don't have it memorized. When I turn back to him, I'll say, "John, I hope you've changed your PIN since last year. It's not still 2172, is it?" Even though his PIN was already revealed a year ago today, it's almost more amazing for him to perceive that I retained that info all this time.

Whether I figured out his PIN again or memorized it in the past, my knowing it still makes him feel so special. But this isn't witchcraft, it's just paying attention and taking notes. It's one tiny step that can make a huge difference. You can do this yourself in any part of your life. Let's say you meet a potential business contact at a gathering. When it's over, you jot down a note or leave yourself a voice memo about who you met and what you discussed. If and when you bump into that person again, you are ready to go, you can ask them, "Hey, how'd your kid do in the spelling bee? I know she won last year. Did she win again this year?"

People are genuinely touched when you remember something important to them. Don't underestimate how impactful these small touches can be. Even if you're not pretending to be a mentalist, you can still generate that same level of amazement by simply recalling and reflecting back information people once shared with you. Most assume that their details will have been forgotten, so when you remember, it's a moment of shock and delight. It's like getting points for free. Just remembering something about somebody, honestly, is a magic trick in many ways, and shows you care.

The first thing I do when I complete an event is log everything that happened while it's still fresh in my mind. When you do this, your notes don't have to be elaborate, just use whatever shorthand works for you. It can be as simple as, "Rhonda, blonde woman, patent attorney, friends with Louie's mom, kids go to such and such camp." This is super useful information for you to have. It's useful for connections in the future, where it's not *what* you know, it's *who* you know. For example, let's say you end up needing a patent attorney, or you want to send your kids to a tennis camp. You don't know anyone there, but suddenly that person you talked to does.

In another example, one of the ways I promote my business is by sending quarterly email blasts to past clients. Each time I do this, I receive at least 150 emails back. Most of them say things like, "Hey, congrats on the fourth kid," or "Loved your TV appearance with Tom Brady!" If I remember something about that person or have access to what we spoke about, I can write back and say, "How's Victoria doing?" or "How are your kids' costumes coming along for Halloween? Are they all still dressing up as M&M'S?" I make sure that if someone is in touch, I reach back out in a way that makes that person feel special again. And how much better is that than an auto-reply, especially when AI is making it all the easier to pretend to be personal? If I make someone else's day better, it brings mine up as well.

That little bit of effort pays dividends in the long run. What's funny is just that you're getting extra credit for the same things I do as a mentalist. And all it takes is giving people back the information that they already told you. That's the unbelievable thing. No bells, no whistles, no hidden gimmicks or difficult instructions to remember. Hell, you don't even need a good memory, simply cheat and write it down right away! People assume you've forgotten, so when you later bring it up, it makes a big impact. Of course, we remember important things about our families and friends—like birthdays—but when you're able to pull up that information about someone you don't know well, it instantly makes them feel more connected to you. That feeling builds trust and rapport, both of which are the cornerstones of strong personal and professional relationships.

My job is creating the illusion that I can read the minds of audience members, even though I go onstage and literally tell them the truth: "I don't read minds, I read people." The whole game is knowing how to reveal seemingly secret information in an entertaining fashion. And this is one of those life hacks that you can do today and start reaping the rewards from immediately.

Just imagine how useful it could be if you are just starting out in an entry level position: You're brand-new in your career, but you were savvy enough to take notes about the people at your potential new company. Maybe during your interview, the HR rep mentioned that the big boss who'd give the final approval on your hire was out of town watching his kid compete in a sport. When you later run into that executive at lunch and mention, "Hey, I saw that your son's team won the state lacrosse championship. Congratulations, you must be so proud of him!" that simple gesture sets you apart. It opens up conversation, shows attention to detail and makes you seem fascinating—because you're making it about them.

Once you start doing this, it will become almost second nature, but let me offer you this bit of advice: Exercise a little restraint. If you start rattling off details like you have a photographic memory, it might come off as a bit much. No one wants to feel like they're being stalked.

Remember, everything that might be important to others is fair game. I'm talking kids' birthdays, interesting vacations, anything that's given to you, that's been revealed, don't just let that go. Information is a commodity; it's kind of like getting a coupon that only expires if you forget it. And the longer you hold on to what you know, the more valuable it becomes.

For example, a guy texted me the other day. I performed at his son's bar mitzvah fourteen years ago, which is wild. (I was huge on the bar mitzvah circuit.) When I used to do small private parties, I'd take a photo with the kid or the guest of honor at every gig. After each of these gigs, I would send out a custom printed thank-you card within one day of their event. If I'd do the party on Saturday, they'd get the card around Tuesday or Wednesday. The parents were always so busy hosting that, most of the time, they didn't get the chance to actually see me in action firsthand, but rather just heard about me from their guests. I quickly figured out that what mattered most to them was that their son or daughter and their guests had an unforgettable experience. They had invested a lot of money into this party, and hoped their circle would remember it for the rest of their lives. So I'd always get a photo of me with their child holding a deck of cards, or in the middle of a trick, both of us smiling and engaged. This would serve as the cover of the card I'd send out. And I'd thank them, mentioning one special and specific thing about their child, like, "Wow, what a funny kid Aaron is, so well-spoken, poised, and mature for his age. What impeccable comedic timing he has!" I'd thank them for trusting me to be a part of their celebration, which is making it about them. So this guy who texted me had just come across that card. His son is twenty-seven now, but seeing it brought back a flood of memories from that special day, and he reached out to let me know.

How great is that?

Lead with Empathy

If you want to truly make others feel seen and heard, you've got to keep empathy at the heart of your interaction. Empathy goes beyond just recognizing what someone's going through; it's about tuning in and sharing that feeling with them, even if only briefly. Unlike sympathy, which is *your* reaction to someone's situation, empathy keeps the focus on *them*. Sympathy is feeling for someone, whereas empathy is feeling with someone, putting yourself in their shoes and responding from a deeper place.

Now, here's what you may not know about empathy: When you witness someone else's emotion, whether it's joy or excitement or sadness—your brain is wired to mirror that emotion. You feel it, too. How cool is that? You're predisposed to want to relate to that person; it's in your DNA, and that impulse dates back to our survival as a species. What's so powerful about this is that our empathy really enables us to feel those emotions alongside others. Empathy is the glue that binds us, that makes us feel connected.

If our current political climate feels like we're not leading with empathy . . . well, you're not mistaken. As a society, over the last four decades, we've begun to lose what they call the "empathy bone," and research has found that the average person in 2009 was 75 percent less empathetic than people were in 1979.[2] Some research shows that this stems from how much we're exposed to technology and social media, largely because social media causes us to compare and despair.[3] Even I had a couple years where my social media was a very negative influence in my life, because all I did was hyperfixate on the handful of people in my profession who I perceived were doing better than me. I had to take a step back and tell myself, *That's an insane way to go about tracking down success, because everyone in the world thinks there's someone richer, faster, better looking, stronger, more successful . . . you name it, they got it! You have to celebrate who you are and what you bring to the table.* I instead started to focus on the other side of that coin: gratitude—realizing that there are likely billions of people that would give anything to have what I have. Health, family, being my own boss, success, fulfillment, and the list goes on and on for me, but also for you! The key is hyperfocusing on the positive.

You might think that having the shared experience of social media would increase our ability to be empathetic, because we're reaching people we'd never have reached before, but you'd be wrong. Instead, witnessing the same experiences over and over again, especially in crisis, causes a phenomenon called compassion fatigue that actually numbs us to tragic incidents.[4]

Whoa.

The good news is that empathy is a skill you can cultivate. So let's bring it back! The first and best way you can cultivate empathy—especially in a world as divided as ours—is to seek out what you have in common with others, instead of your differences. I'd wager this is one of the reasons everyone loves cheering on Olympians—we all get to put aside what divides us and root for a common cause. I challenge you today to step outside your comfort zone and ask someone whom you normally wouldn't think twice about a deeper question about their life, like maybe what your Uber driver's favorite playlist is, or what the woman making your sandwich at the deli would order. See what makes them tick and give them your undivided attention while they respond without any thought to what you will say back.

If you want to be more empathetic—and you do—start with active listening. When you're just a bystander in a conversation, waiting to jump in and talk about yourself or, worse, interrupting, you're approaching the situation wrong. By actively listening, you'll make everyone feel heard and understood, especially if you're paraphrasing back what the other person has said, to demonstrate that you've been listening. Someone who's great at this is my wife. When we were interviewing at schools for my oldest son, she would take everything the administrator said, rephrase it, and repeat it. I swear, I thought she was doing a bit at first, but her way ended up being super effective, and we got our kid into the school we wanted. She showed this person that they were truly being "heard," and also demonstrated shared values that resonated most strongly with our family.

To up your empathy, actively put yourself in the other person's shoes. Sure, for example, you may be upset that your flight has been delayed again, but yelling at the gate agent is not going to change anything. Venting your frustration isn't going to clear the skies or bring in a replacement flight crew for the one that just timed out. Try to see things from that poor gate agent's perspective. He or she has probably been standing for hours. Because of storms in the area, it's been chaos for the gate agents all week. When they look up from the desk, there's just a sea of mean travelers waiting to yell at them for circumstances beyond their control. That must feel awful.

Acknowledge this to them. Make them feel seen and heard.

In fact, when you take that agent's feelings into account, understanding that you're the hundredth upset person they've dealt with in the past hour, you'll change your tone and realize it's not a me-against-you scenario, but a how-can-we-get-through-this-together situation. No one wants to be stuck at the gate, so try leaning into kindness. Smile. Make a joke. Tell them this must be a nightmare and that they're doing a great job keeping their cool. And don't be surprised when your seat is upgraded on the next flight because you're the only person who wasn't a jerk to the person assigning the seats.

To help grow your empathy, you also have to look inside yourself. How are you reacting to something external? How are you feeling? How are you expressing yourself? Is this a situation where you're expecting respect but not reciprocating? Remember, unless you're all alone in a room, your emotions don't happen in a vacuum.

Bottom line, if your feelings are going to spill out onto others, make them positive so they will lift up everyone.

Tap Into Their Emotions

I can't say this enough—mentalism offers a limited number of options. A big part of the secret sauce of what I do is having multiple methods to get the same result. I then analyze how you think I did it and reveal why your assumption isn't the correct solution, presenting an alternate method, and upping the ante yet again. It is a game of cat and mouse. Each time I do this with a greater element of surprise, and I generate greater amazement. This method is like tying the brains of the audience into pretzels, with seemingly no explanation for what they are witnessing. But what sets my performance apart, from simply being a puzzle that you cannot put together, is tapping into people's emotions by telling a story.

For example, some of my tricks include guessing a person's childhood phone number, the name of their fifth-grade best friend, or the first girl they ever kissed. I don't just say, "Think of the person who was your first kiss." There's no buildup, there's no story, the question doesn't evoke any emotion. Recognizing and tapping into emotions is critical when you want to influence others, because that emotional intimacy builds excitement and anticipation.

Instead, I go for the slow build. I help paint the picture before I guess. I want to take you back there to that sacred moment in time, because when I re-create the scene, it stirs an emotion that you can't get by just guessing a name like a carnival trick. I want you to reinhabit your nerdy fourteen-year-old self, coming home with the rest of the marching band after a regional competition. You stopped at Pizza Hut on the way, filling yourself to the brim with pepperoni and root beer. I want you to feel that awkward excitement again, the sugar and carb high you're riding, the smell of that girl's lip balm, the cacophony of your bandmates singing along to Third Eye Blind's "Semi-Charmed Life" (and it's clear why you guys were in marching band and not chorus).

I figured out how to do this because I noticed my peers were really straightforward. I realized I could differentiate myself by tying a trick to an emotion. Any good mentalist can tell you to pick a color, and then guess it. But my approach is to say, "Think back to when you were seven years old and you wanted your room to be a certain color. You drove your parents crazy about it, what was it like for you at that moment?" Creating that emotional hook is a way to package myself, to market myself differently. I learned that what truly matters is the story that person will tell about *you* in the future, and what they remember from your experience together. Some companies have figured out how to make a billion dollars just selling bottled water. What did they do? They took water, which was a cheap commodity, and they created an ultra-premium experience by packaging it in a square bottle instead of a round one, and slapped a label with a beautiful beach vista on it, which looks exotic. Now they charge you five dollars—while every other bottle of water costs two—and when you drink it, it feels like an experience because it's evocative. That's what emotion can do for you.

Mentalism is magic of the mind and there is a "trick" to everything I do, but most of what you're witnessing has taken decades to perfect. It's a skill, but nobody cares about the time I've put in. My audience cares only about the result of all that work. But what makes the trick phenomenal, what makes it memorable for the audience, is bringing everyone along as we travel back in time together. Painting that picture to create a feeling is the *real* magic, because I used that story to make it about *them.*

Early in my professional career, before I concentrated on mentalism, I was very big on learning rope tricks. There was a magician named Tabary who won the "Olympics of Magic" (yes that really exists and is held every three years in various spots around the world and is known as FISM) with a spectacular rope routine that was one of the most beautiful things I'd ever seen in my life. This ten-minute routine involved nearly a hundred moves and sleights of hand, each of which was smooth as silk and completely deceptive when deployed by the creator's hands. I spent hours every single day in front of a mirror studying where each finger should go. I was obsessed with perfecting and emulating what I saw on the video. Fast-forward to a year later, after putting my heart and soul into this routine, I finally started testing it out in front of audiences. And guess what? The rope routine just didn't connect with them the way it did with me. No matter how much I tried to get them to care, they simply did not. It was a painful lesson to learn, but the fact was that the trick was all about *me* and not *them.* Sometimes you have to kill your darlings—because the audience doesn't care about what you like. Remember this, the audience is always right. I discovered that I needed to make my performance about *them.*

(My rope tricks really were incredible, though!)

One of the tricks I performed for the New York Jets on HBO's *Hard Knocks* involved a football being thrown randomly around the room. I closed my eyes, threw it over my shoulder, and said, "Someone, catch it!" That player threw it to another player who in turn threw it to another player. Thousands upon thousands of combinations and permutations were possible for how that could have played out in a room with over eighty men, all of whom were about double or triple my size! Saying this was beyond random is overstating the obvious.

The climax of this trick involved me guessing the name of someone famous that the last player to catch the ball would think of. On the surface, this trick could be very plain and vanilla. What elevated it to another level was the story and the feeling along the way as the decision was being made, an emotional experience that was both motivated and organic. I began to paint a picture for them. I leaned into the story and truly made it about them. I said, “Imagine you catch the football and you’re in the end zone. It’s the Super Bowl. You just won the game and you’re on cloud nine. You have all this joy in your heart and your teammates are going crazy because you guys did it, you won. All that work, all that blood, sweat, and tears. You did it. Everyone’s crying and dumping that freezing cooler of Gatorade on the coach.”

And I know the player could picture that whole thing in his mind, because I guarantee he’s visualized this scenario a thousand times before.

I set the scene, “Look out at this crowd, they’re all so happy. Your family is there, your friends are there—they’re all celebrating. You notice that when you look into the stands, the front row is all celebrities. You lock eyes with a random celebrity at this moment.” Then I asked that player, “You picked that person right this second, yeah?” And he laughed, saying, “Yeah,” while deeply disturbed by where this could possibly be going. In his mind, he knew it was impossible for me to pull this off, but in his heart that, somehow, I still would.

Then I added, “There’s no way I can know who you would’ve picked, or that the guy before you would’ve caught the ball and thrown it to you, or that the guy before him would’ve caught the ball and thrown it to him. Do you agree?” The player replied, “Yeah. I had no idea.” And that’s when I said, “I’m not gonna get inside your head, no, that’s what you expect. I’m gonna get inside THAT BALL!”

I flip open a sharp pocket knife, startling several players, and plunge the blade deep into the football and saw side to side to form a large hole as it deflates. I ask him to reach in and take out what's inside, which appears to be a folded-up photo. The tension is so thick you could cut it with my knife. I look the player in the eyes and slowly ask, "Who are you thinking about?" And then he replies, "It's Kevin Hart." I point at his hands and mouth the words "open it." There it is, a gleaming headshot of Kevin Hart and the entire team unleashes a series of whoops, screams, swear words, and laughs!

Of course, when I do this, a little piece is about me, too, because my hope is that the clip will go viral. That the player will absolutely freak out, that he'll be like, "How in the . . ." and then everyone in the room will just erupt.

There are multiple methods at play when designing a trick of this sort. There are all these things that I'm anticipating along the way. A lot of times the audience is saying, "Well, you set it up with this person." No I didn't, because we threw the ball randomly around the room. Or they'll say, "Well, you stuck the picture inside the football when you were putting your hand in." No, because I made sure my hands were seen as being empty the whole time.

A lot of the time, I build these layers by using a different trick for each portion of the setup. Each portion is being done differently to make sure the audience doesn't keep up with how I'm actually pulling the whole trick off. If you saw this play out, you might actually get one of the methods. But when I change things up a second later, you'll think, *Well, that couldn't have been it*, because I've done something to exclude that method.

The point is that I'm constantly pulling from the same limited playbook. I have only so many tricks. I'm telling you: finite. And I did some version of this at every training camp. But each one felt different to the people who were witnessing it because I'd tell a different story each time and I'd home in on their feelings, making them the star of my show. Imagine how much less dramatic it would have been if I'd just said, "Think of a celebrity," and then pulled out the photo. That simple trick lacks all the buildup and it doesn't tap into that player's emotions.

Not only did I amaze them, but I evoked those feelings by making them verbalize the scene that likely plays in their head every day. I became special to these players because I made *them* feel special, and there's no reason you can't do the same when you put emotion into your stories, no card tricks required. Maybe you're in a pitch meeting and you're evoking nostalgia. (If you're a *Mad Men* fan, think of that Don Draper scene with the Hershey's bar.) Or maybe you're telling your kids why the Grand Canyon is so much cooler than Grand Cayman because it's been around since the Ice Age, and you spend all of dinnertime speculating how different your lives are from ancient humankind.

The more you pull at heartstrings—even your own—the more effective you'll be.

Leave Them Wanting More

Like nearly every kid, I was a massive Steven Spielberg fan. Who didn't grow up on *Jurassic Park*, *Jaws*, *Raiders of the Lost Ark*, and *E.T.*? He was a huge part of my childhood and his movies have stayed with me to this day.

So imagine how I felt when I got a call to perform at the ninety-ninth birthday of Steven Spielberg's dad. I was over the moon. I spent weeks thinking of everything I wanted to ask him, all the things I wanted to know. I could not believe my luck.

I kept my emotions in check and performed the show with this amazing milestone as my focus, surrounded by family and friends that adored the guest of honor. At the end of the show, Steven makes a beeline straight for me to thank me for making this day so special. And I wait for him to take a breath, to give me the pause I crave so that I can jump in organically with my one thousand questions. We did end up having a twenty-five-minute conversation . . . but I asked him precisely zero questions.

Not a single one.

I went in wanting all the highlights, like, How did you build this? and How did that work in *Close Encounters*? and How did you manage to train all those dinosaurs? But no. Not a single question. I did learn that the reason he is "Steven Spielberg" is because he's a person who is able to turn the mirror around and reflect his light back onto you. He must know that every person he crosses paths with is likely to talk about their encounter for the rest of their lives.

What's so fascinating about him is that he's naturally curious, he just has this passion for all the people around him. What's created his success is the fact that he can get completely absorbed in asking me all these questions about myself. And in my head, I'm like, *You're Steven f'ing Spielberg! Right now, I want to ask* you *things.*

His home run swing was getting me to talk about myself, getting me to open up and share about what I do. Despite having every reason to talk about his own achievements, he chose to focus on me. He held up a metaphorical mirror that made me see my worth, and feel like a star. That day I learned what a superpower that kind of attentiveness can be, and it's something every single one of us can do. Steven gave me 100 percent of his focus, 100 percent of his energy, and made me an even bigger fan of his while doing so.

When he walked away to rejoin the party, all I wanted to do was chase after him like that magician on the cruise ship. He left me wanting so much more. That was his gift, too, understanding the timing of it all. Understanding why it's important not to overstay. Had he stuck around, it might have diminished how special the interaction was for me. I got a taste, but not a whole meal, and I bet I'll spend the rest of my life savoring the bites that I had. Because he made me feel like the magician on that ship, like I was the most interesting man in the world.

You don't have to be Steven Spielberg to develop this set of skills. All you need is a genuine interest in the people around you. Be radically curious; ask questions beyond the generic small talk we all dread. Instead of "What do you do?" try "What's something most people don't know about you?" Practice active listening—don't just wait to interject but really give people your undivided attention. Notice things that make others special out loud, like, "You have great comedic timing."

Regardless of what we do in life, each of us only has a limited tool kit from which we can draw. There's only so many skills we can master, things we can accomplish, or know. What makes us truly memorable is how we make others feel.

When you help others kick away that pedestal, when you demonstrate how they're special and memorable, when you make it about them, when you cast your light on others, it all reflects back on you twice as strongly.

FIVE

Forget Tomorrow, Start Today

A few years ago, another mentalist asked me how I was able to book appearances on TV so frequently and consistently. I turned the question around and asked him, "Well, what have you tried doing?" He was taken aback, almost surprised by my question, and stammered, "Well... I haven't." I swear to you, nine times out of ten when I ask this question, I get a blank stare in return. Like it never even occurred to them to try, to be proactive, to log every producer they ever met and continue to circle back. If you meet someone while at a gig or a party that offhandedly mentions a friend who works in TV, you take their info and follow up. Never leave the ball in someone else's court when it is your future that hangs in the balance. I got the ESPN gig because I cultivated a relationship and spent over a decade keeping in touch, waiting to pounce on the opportunity when the timing was finally right.

That's the whole secret. If you want to win the lottery, you need to buy a ticket!

In this chapter, I'll cover buying that ticket—that is, what it takes to move toward any goal. I'll discuss how to end procrastination, then get through the horrible first two weeks of taking action, during which habits start to form and the dread melts away. And I'll show you how momentum always begets momentum—it's *literally* physics—by explaining how, as an adult, I went from being not very good at running to regularly winning races and setting ultramarathon world records.

Achieving goals is all about working backward from the desired outcome, whether it's personal or professional, and this starts with learning how to define and quantify them. The chapter wouldn't be complete if I didn't also give advice on how to be brutally honest with yourself and not lose sight of taking joy when you actually achieve the goals and success you've been chasing. I learned that lesson the hard way the day I ran my fastest marathon ever, a personal best of 2:23:52, but could only focus on the fact I didn't run as fast as I had hoped.

Sometimes you just have to let what wasn't perfectly on plan go and appreciate the moment.

Now, Not Later

You may not believe it, but I'm an expert-level procrastinator. This is not because I'm lazy, but because I'm most motivated and inspired by a sense of urgency. In college, I learned to procrastinate very effectively, mastering the art of cramming, pulling all-nighters to make it through. It is a bad habit to get into because you'll tell yourself that doing an hour or two of work daily seems like so much more effort than just two sleepless nights at the library immediately prior to the assignment due date or exam.

For the longest time, I believed my best work came when I was under the gun. If you told me I'd have a TV appearance in six months . . .

forget it. But if you told me I had a massive appearance in just six days, my synapses would start firing. The urgency and panic, the sense of being backed into a corner—that's when I'd lock in and come up with something incredible.

Guess what?

I'm the first to admit this approach wasn't healthy, so it's something that I've had to actively work on. I finally figured out that when I leave everything to the last minute over and over, I don't feel as good about the results and that ultimately more things are likely to go wrong.

Turns out, we're genetically predisposed to procrastination because there are two opposing forces in our brains and they are locked in battle. We all have a limbic system, which is responsible for regulating our emotions, our behavior, our motivation (that's a biggie), our autonomic nervous system, and our memory.[1] The limbic system is similar to our most hedonistic friend, the one who wants only fun, pleasure, and immediate gratification.

Our limbic system is pitted against our prefrontal cortex, which mimics our most responsible buddy. You know, the one who prints up itineraries for everyone at the bachelor party and packs a first aid kit. While our prefrontal cortex is equally as important, that bossy little voice often gets drowned out by the more dynamic and fun limbic system, especially when something is challenging or unpleasant, and this is why almost all of us procrastinate.[2]

It's not just our brain chemistry at work that causes us to put off today what we could do tomorrow. We can be paralyzed by our fear of failure, causing us to avoid trying new things and taking risks.[3] This fear can keep us safely cocooned inside our comfort zones, where we're never challenged—and we never grow, as we discussed earlier. Sometimes we procrastinate because we lack time management skills, and sometimes it's a matter of confidence.

Fortunately, whatever your issue is, it's fixable if you take a new perspective on procrastination.

The key to adopting a do-it-now mentality is to break your goal down into smaller parts and make one of them something that you absolutely do immediately. You need that spark, that initial momentum, that snowball you roll down a mountain so it grows. The resulting dopamine hit will overcome your brain's tendencies toward inertia because our brains remember incomplete tasks with far more clarity than those we've completed, and that creates stress and unease.[4] This is called the Zeigarnik effect and it means that what remains incomplete haunts our memories.[5] In our minds, an incomplete task feels like an untied shoe. If we want to move around freely, to really use our brains at their full capacity, we have to lace up that sneaker. We have to stop procrastinating.

After a lifetime of being a procrastinator, I decided to figure out how to get things done sooner rather than later (even when I don't feel tremendous, overwhelming pressure). In retraining myself, I realized I needed to change my perspective, to value getting the chore done early, rather than at the last minute, because giving myself space took a lot of unnecessary stress off me—and my wife.

We procrastinate because certain tasks seem so daunting and our brain wants the easy way out. Where do we even begin? But every marathon starts with one step, and starting small was how I shifted my perspective. For example, several years ago when I landed the gig with ESPN, I had about three weeks to plan, which is very little time to come up with somewhere between nine and twelve new tricks. (I only want to perform the latest and greatest custom content when I'm on TV.)

Not only do these concepts have many intricate machinations that take a lot of time to ideate, I also have to make sure they're going to work. While I've said that mentalism entails a limited number of tricks, the tools I have at my disposal will often mirror the common ingredients a chef might use, such as sauces and proteins. You put a dash of this and a splash of that, and the combination creates something entirely different and new. Similar to when you go to Chipotle and there are maybe twenty ingredients on the steam trays: You can combine them into hundreds of different creations with different flavor profiles. I have endless permutations when it comes to creating these tricks; plus, I have to present them in a way that feels seamless and entertaining, and I must adapt the reveals to be appropriate for the audience. I can't deliver them looking like they're still wearing training wheels. I can't come across as if I'm thinking of the lines when I say them. If I'm onstage, it's imperative that my act feels natural to everyone watching. Otherwise, it's just bad acting.

When those initial videos aired throughout the football season, I immediately got to work ideating for the following summer training camp. Had ESPN confirmed that we would be doing it again? Absolutely not, but always assume the close and be ready and overprepared when the moment you are hoping for arrives. I decided to be proactive and break the planning down into more manageable chunks. And I said to myself, *One new trick a month nets me twelve new tricks by next year.* Not only would that lower my stress level, it would also allow me to be more present with my family leading up to the events. And if I could get two tricks in a month? Even better. I'd be so ahead of the game.

By starting now, you're on your way to being more creative and a better problem solver, which in turn will benefit your overall well-being. Win-win.

Be Specific

When I mentor other mentalists, one thing they always ask is, "How do I take my career to the next level?" Now, that's a daunting question with no set answer because there's a million different ways to move forward and also my definition of *forward* might differ greatly from yours.

I'll reply with probing questions like: "What does the next level mean to *you*? Do you want to perform for more people? Are you trying to make more money?" To determine what it is that they really want, I make them hone and re-hone their answers. And then most of the time they'll figure out their bottom line, which is: "I just want a steady gig somewhere."

Now, *that's* an easy fix.

I'll say, "Great, let's look up your geographical area right now. Go to Google Maps and pull up country clubs. Look up restaurants. Let's identify places where there's a precedent for hiring a magician or mentalist. And if there isn't, we're going to invent one and we'll show them why you're such a value-add that they'd be foolish not to take you."

So often, we already know what we need to do, which is what my mentees often say when I tell them what to do. With all the information that's at our fingertips, most of the time it's just a matter of defining A and B and then drawing a line from A to B and figuring out that first step to take. The way I approach everything, whether it's coming up with a new trick or prepping for a race, is to design my plan of attack from the end and work backward. The start and the end are more important than everything else. Getting to the starting line is always the most difficult part for people. And when you get there that day, there's the dread, the fear, the trepidation. But if you can get yourself to the beginning, then you can more clearly visualize the finish and rely on your preparation to get you there. Once you begin moving your feet, it's kind of easy from there, because you're over the mental block of having started. You might still suffer, but you're past the hardest part, as starting is very often overwhelming. And remember, you can't buy achievement; you have to earn it.

I do a lot of speaking engagements and whenever I talk to sales teams, I say, "There's only one person in this room who's your top seller. I can tell you for a fact that person has had doubts creep into their mind, just like all of us do. But that person believed to their core that they would be the top salesperson for this organization. Because if you don't believe that, you will never achieve it. Some of you will believe it but not achieve it, but without that belief in your own ability, you'll never get there. The top salesperson isn't the best because of luck; They didn't stumble into it by accident. They are hypercompetitive. They're willing to battle. They say to themselves, 'Why can't it be me?'" That's how I feel when I'm at the starting line of a race. I tell myself, *I'm gonna finish this thing.* The option to give up simply does not exist in my mind. And for the people who do finish the race, they must have believed that they could do it. So you have to think that you can do it—whatever your "it" might be.

Back to my mentees—the reason I ask them those specific questions is that I'm looking for something measurable. *Next level* is too amorphous. That's like if you were to tell me you want to experience "more career progression at work," or that you want to be "happier at home." What does that mean? What are the parameters that define progression or happiness? But, if you were to say, "I want to make X dollars, get promoted to X position, buy my family a boat that costs X," I can work with that.

Often, people think of something they want from a reflex perspective, like, "I want to be successful." But if you truly look inward, you'll realize that to you, success means earning X on a weekly basis because it enables you to cover your bills without sacrificing your personal life. That's a number. We can work with a number because it's tangible. There's an end point. When you say something elusive like *happiness*, there's no hard stop, there's no finish line. It's a moving target. Having worked in finance, there's a point where making more money doesn't bring additional happiness, so it's key to drill down to what *your* definition of success is. It may have nothing to do with finances and everything to do with being able to pick your kids up from school every day and take one amazing vacation per year.

If you want a garden, it doesn't just grow—you have to plant the seeds, water them, fertilize them, till the soil, etc. You have to get your hands dirty . . . and probably sling a little manure. That's why I say, "buy the ticket." Think of it like this—how could you win the lottery without buying a ticket? One isn't going to fall magically out of the sky and land in your hands. Even if it did, it's still a lottery ticket, with only a chance of winning. One hundred percent of lottery winners took the chance. The point is, if you don't "buy the ticket," you're never going to win—100 percent of the time.

You buy the ticket by starting to make moves. (Your first move was picking up this book, so you're already on your way!) Then it's time to self-assess. Lay out the top three things that you want to see a change in, and then figure out exactly what those changes are. Then break those large changes into smaller bits.

For example, let's say your goal is to be healthier. Well, what does that mean? Let's be specific. Do you want to lower your blood pressure? Reduce your cholesterol? Build up your stamina enough that you can run a race? Or do you just want to foster the kind of endurance that lets you carry your kids on your shoulders at the Fourth of July parade because last year they couldn't see anything (and you hurt your back when you tried to lift them)? "Healthy" is amorphous. Maybe you really mean you're trying to lower your average blood sugar levels because your doctor says you're borderline diabetic, and you're terrified of having to give yourself insulin. Getting an A1C test result under 5.7 percent is measurable and specific, and you get there by upping your protein intake, eating fewer grams of sugar, and exercising regularly. When you don't break down what it is you're really seeking, you can get frustrated and fall apart because it seems too overwhelming.

Let's figure out how you can buy your ticket today.

Say you've determined your goal is to run a marathon by your fortieth birthday. Does it seem impossible? Well, if you tried to run 26.2 miles today with no conditioning and no training, it probably is. After all, the courier who ran from Marathon to Athens to share the good news that the Greeks had beaten the Persians, did drop dead at the end of his journey.

But what if you started right now by running around the block? That's it, just once around the block. You can do that, right? You may find yourself sucking wind, but you will get through it. If that's too much, start by walking, with an eye toward building up to running. And forget that it's cold out. Forget that you really need better sneakers. Forget that you don't have the right running clothes. Just get out there and do it today. Take that first step, whatever it is, like buying the URL for that business you're looking to start. The hardest part is beginning . . . yet that's also where the magic lives.

When you set a goal in motion, the neuroscience of this pursuit is called the "productive struggle." When you task yourself with something challenging, your brain starts to produce myelin as it creates a new neural pathway.[6] Myelin is a protective substance that coats your neurons to speed the path of transmission, making your nervous system quicker and more efficient.[7] (In nonscientific terms, this is totally a good thing and absolutely what you want.)

The more you challenge yourself, the more connectivity you're creating between those neurons. I know that description is sort of vague, so imagine it like this: There's three feet of snow between you and what you need in your mailbox at the end of the driveway. The first time you try to trudge through that snow, it's going to be brutal. You're going to be sweating and swearing by the time you reach your mailbox, cursing winter and your decision to live in the Midwest. But every subsequent time you head to that mailbox, you're creating a path through the snow, and it's going to be easier to get back and forth.

Metaphorically, walking through that snow, you're creating what's called "synaptic plasticity," which means that by confronting this challenge (making the trek), you're creating or strengthening new synapses (a more efficient pathway).[8] When you tamp down the snow enough, you're not even going to have to put on boots to grab the mail, because you'll have made it so much easier. You made yourself a cheat code. Your reward? Dopamine. Also known as the feel-good chemical, it's basically candy for your brain. That brain-candy reward is going to reinforce this behavior and motivate you. And who doesn't want a treat?

Define Your Goals

When I'm creating a new trick, the secret sauce is determining how to make it crescendo, each phase stronger than the last, culminating in a surprise ending with an emotional hook that truly connects with the audience. To get there, I have to analyze the trick from the audience's perspective—not only what they will see and hear, but also what they will feel and, most important, the story they will tell others afterward.

A lot of people who do what I do start with a tool, like a hammer. They'll swing that hammer around and say, "I know how to use this thing, so what can I build?" I never do that. I start with the house that's already built. Then I work backward and figure out the tools that I'll need to construct it. The final product informs every creative decision I make along the way.

Previously, I explained that my television appearances go well because I plan for every eventuality, stuff that most would never even imagine. I have thought through exactly what my plans A, B, and C are, all the way to Z. That's what is required with mentalism, because I'm reverse engineering the most complicated computer that's ever existed—the human mind. I'm thinking about what you (the audience) will do at every given moment. How can I influence what you'll do? How can I guide you through a maze so that when you ask yourself, *Am I going left, right, or forward?* you choose *left*, not realizing I've gotten you there through subtlety, persuasion, timing, and a multitude of other techniques. (That's the *real* secret sauce.) It's like a chess game where you feel like you're making your own moves, only I have already planned ten steps ahead. When you see a trick executed effectively, it's particularly mind-blowing, because everything about it feels like a free choice, *yet it's all planned by me.* Mentalism is just a magic trick with no props where I'm able to guide your thoughts.

I've spent over twenty-five years learning how to reverse engineer the human mind. And I do it to entertain people all over the world and bring joy. I want to teach you some of those same skills so that you can use them to gain an edge in your everyday life, to unlock your potential and attain the goals you thought were impossible. While I can't give you superpowers, what I can provide are tools, so that when you hit a speed bump, you know you can get through it. One of the first tools is developing an understanding of what goals you want to achieve.

The oft-used mnemonic for goals is that they should be SMART, meaning Specific, Measurable, Achievable, Relevant, and Time-bound[9] Let's say you just had your annual physical and your doctor tsk-tsks you as he reviews your chart, saying, "I want you to work on your health."

Yeah, thanks a lot, Doc, but what does that mean?

Well, that's for *you* to define.

In your head, maybe it means you should lose those fifty pounds that crept up on you these last few years. And you want to do that before your next physical in a year. So already we have a *specific* end result. We can *measure* it because fifty pounds is something tangible. You know that regardless of excuses, it can be *achieved* because you were at that weight at one point in time. Plus, you're not tasking yourself with becoming a supermodel, of whom there are only a few.

Having the sum of fifty pounds in your head is *relevant* because that number will improve your overall health, as weight loss will lower your blood pressure and your risk for heart disease and stroke, as well as positively impact your joints. (Having your knees hurt less will be an added benefit.) And it's *time-bound* because you want to do this in twelve months so you can come back and show your smug physician that you were taking his advice seriously.

To be fifty pounds lighter, let's work backward. That's only about a pound a week, or roughly a 3,500-calorie weekly deficit, equal to burning 500 calories a day more than you've taken in. What can you do to achieve that caloric deficit? Well, you can improve your diet by adding in five servings of fruit and vegetables. You can be mindful about portion control, limiting yourself to four to six ounces of protein per serving. You can decide to stop eating after 7:00 p.m. You can make sure to consume thirty grams of fiber each day. Or you can burn those 500 calories by getting a fitness tracker and figuring out how many steps gets you into that deficit. You can build muscle so your body's metabolism improves, measuring it on one of those biometric scales that are all over social media. And you can even make attaining this goal social by joining a group of friends for X number of walks a week, or X number of games of pickleball. Every one of these suggestions comes with a smaller goal, whether it's getting in a certain number of steps or tracking and maintaining your macros.

A major goal for me when I got into running was to one day run a sub-2:30 marathon, and I worked for years to achieve this by creating a series of smaller goals. What truly helped me along was folding science into my workouts, so I purchased a heart rate monitor for my training. This taught me to pace myself, because if I was going too fast and the monitor started beeping, it would alert me to the fact that I was going anaerobic. This is similar to redlining a car engine: okay for a short period, but do it too long and you'll overheat and gas out. This helped me become more efficient—and patient. The changes didn't happen overnight, but over time. With a great deal of training over the next few years, I saw my times drop from 3:21 to 2:57, then into the 2:40s and 2:30s and finally in Tallahassee I did what I thought was the impossible and nabbed a 2:29. I have since managed to run ten sub-2:30 marathons and prove to myself that it was no fluke.

The more you break down your greater goals after working backward from the end result, the easier you'll find it to move forward, especially if you're receiving feedback. Every small win feeds into the outcome. Remember, you set the importance of the goal, and it only matters how *you* define it. So let's get started already!

Make It a Habit

I said starting is the hardest part of forming a new habit, but a close second is maintaining that change and converting it into your new status quo. This can be particularly difficult if you beat yourself up when things don't go your way in those first weeks.

As my marathon times started to improve with better training, I came to realize that an even more important factor was my weight. If I could lose some pesky extra pounds, my times would get even faster. Think how much slower you'd run carrying a backpack with five bricks weighing a couple pounds each, except in this case those ten pounds might be spread out all over your body. I would implement several rules to stay healthy, while also reducing my calorie intake. These consisted of eliminating late-night snacking, setting a firm deadline to brush my teeth and be done eating by 8:00 p.m. (similar in a sense to intermittent fasting), and cutting out fried foods, sweets, and other culprits that I tended to overindulge in. After the first few days of this regimen, I would begin to fall apart. There would be an emotional induced tantrum where I'd tell myself, *This is such BS! I'm just going to pound some cake and a burrito. I don't care about any of this.* But I knew I had to be in top form to race if I wanted to be at my best and beat my previous time, so I learned to trick myself, to overcome those moments when I wanted to give up, because I can't buy achievement. I have to earn it.

Know this: Your brain will lie to you as you try to form a habit. For me, my brain will say, "Hey, I don't want to do this, I'm done." So I have to do with myself what I'd do with my three-year-old. It's Misdirection 101. I will fool myself, *Here's what I'll do. I am 100 percent going to eat that burrito and I am 100 percent going to eat that cake. But not right this minute. First, I'm going to eat a banana. Then, I'm going to drink a big glass of water and I'm going to set a ten minute timer. If I still feel this strongly about the burrito and cake when the timer goes off, then I'm eating them.* The funny thing is that as I watch those minutes and then seconds tick down, the impulsiveness and the emotional trigger, both of which are at the core of what makes me want to "break," start to melt away entirely. I am able to trick my own mind and body with simple "time misdirection"—as it is known in my business.

I started to understand the control my mind had over my body, my emotions would try to fool me into quitting a race despite still being physically capable of finishing. In the darkest parts of those extremely long runs, my mind would start shutting down and telling me, *This sucks. This is horrible. Stop. Throw your sneakers in the trash. Go back to the hotel and watch Netflix.* A lot of times, that destructive self-talk would start up because my blood sugar had dropped, and that was directly impacting my frustration tolerance. Your mood is connected to what you eat, how much you've slept, and a multitude of other factors. I found that if I could just repair that blood sugar discrepancy, my mood would lift, I could realign myself, and I'd realize my goal was more important than that quick emotional outburst. I created a mental checklist of all the systems that I thought could be causing my issues, ranging from self-doubt to exhaustion to sheer annoyance, and almost all could be readily deduced from a simple list.

This example is a direct parallel to so many things that we try, where we might commit for a day or two, and then we accidentally blow it and give up before the habit is formed. Then we beat ourselves up. Our inner monologue says, *Hey, we're not good enough to do this and it was never going to happen anyway.*

Instead, try giving yourself some space, *You know what? Today's tough. I'm putting it aside for today; tomorrow we restart the clock and we're back at it.* We live in such an all or nothing society that this kind of grace can be a challenging thing. Remember that it's okay to have a good day, a bad day, followed by three good days. It's what you do 90 percent of the time that really matters. The 10 percent isn't going to kill you.

Frequently, we get off track and we don't allow the habit to form because we're not really paying attention to our goal. How often do you stop and check in with yourself? The frequency with which you do so isn't nearly as important as the consistency over time. You have to be the chief strategy officer of your life, thinking not just about today but also next week, next month, and next year. Look at the big picture and set yourself reminders, like: Once every two weeks, you sit down for an hour and think about where you are and what you could do differently.

Most people I know—myself included—are often just treading water to get through the day. It's like we're all trying to stay afloat. We're so caught up in the day-to-day that we don't really ask big-picture questions, we're not stopping to assess ourselves. We're just plodding ahead, even when our heart's not in it, because we're wired with an autopilot we didn't thoughtfully create. We're not mindful of what we're doing or why we're doing it, so we have to create a plan to prioritize what we want to achieve, and hold ourselves accountable. So often, we think, *One day*, but what if you made "one day" today? Start right now and create the steps that will get you over that first hurdle.

You can only begin to build when you commit your mind and body to whatever it is you're seeking out. You have to make the pursuit of what you want its own habit. It's got to happen like clockwork. Once you do this, you'll start seeing positive effects. Whenever you start something new, creating change is going to be hard because you're not used to integrating the goal, so I want you to keep the "two-week rule" at the front of your mind.

What do I mean by that? Well, the hardest part of a new routine is the first two weeks. I swear. Okay? The first two weeks are everything. If I train for a marathon, I cut out crappy foods. I mean no ice cream, no eating late at night, and no alcohol. And the first two weeks are brutal because my body is rebelling and saying no, and I have emotional outbursts; that's when I have to actively trick myself with the water and the banana.

When we want something that isn't good for us—emotionally, spiritually, physically, whatever—our knee-jerk reaction is to just give into ourselves. When I'm training, it's about not scarfing down all the ice cream. My ten-minute time misdirection trick allows me to distance my mind from that emotional trigger. Often, I find that once I give it a little bit of time, I don't go for the ice cream. So I want you to figure out what *your* banana is. What do you need to do in those moments when you just want to give up? The banana works because willpower and motivation alone can't always do it for you. You need something that will help you trick your own mind long enough that you stay on track.

There's a lot of neuroscience behind what it takes to make something into a habit. For example, let's say you move a trash can under your desk from the left to right side. For the first fourteen to sixteen days, you're going to drive yourself mad by instinctively throwing your trash in the wrong direction.

Somehow, about two weeks later, something clicks. Your brain finally rewires itself and you'll notice when you get the trash in the can the first time, and you'll think, *Finally!* Be aware that it's not your fault if getting things right takes a while. There's nothing wrong with you; that's just how we're hardwired. Now that you know your limitations, you have to trick your own mind and say, *I know you're going to screw me over these first two weeks. I know it, I know going in that you're going to be my enemy. So if I can just get through this day, if something goes wrong, tomorrow is a new day, I'm going to keep going and within two weeks, the new routine will be solidified.* But the clock only starts ticking once you first move the trash can. We have to be cognizant that we're not so on autopilot that we never even move the can in the first place.

You don't have to beat yourself up forever—this kind of failure is short term. Just get through the first two weeks and you'll have created whatever habit you need to meet your goal. That's when discipline comes into play. The time it takes to create that habit is much shorter than most people expect, and yet they still give up so soon. This all goes back to having to rewire our brain with those neural pathways. As Dr. Sanam Hafeez says, "Any habit we develop is because our brain is designed to pick up on things that reward us and punish us."[10] In layman's terms from *Atomic Habits* author James Clear, "What gets rewarded is repeated. What gets punished, gets avoided."[11]

My friend David Goggins, a retired Navy SEAL and author, says that to create a habit, you've just got to clamp down on your mind. He says there's no puppy love, no simple approach, there's no motivational this or that. He went from three hundred pounds to being a chiseled ultramarathon runner by force of will alone. His approach is truly empowering, and his philosophy is that you don't stop when you're tired, you stop when you're done, although that's not a one-size-fits-all solution. You may respond better to your inner supportive friend than an inner drill sergeant; everyone is different. But the method is always the same: Define your goals and the small steps along the way to get there, and *do not give up.*

Charles Duhigg wrote a book called *The Power of Habit*, in which he discusses what he calls the "habit loop," the neurological process that causes habits to develop and take hold.[12] Habitual actions start with a "cue," which is what prompts the habit; a cue can be internal (like a feeling or a thought) or external (such as an environmental factor). The next step is the "routine," the action that happens automatically once your brain is activated by the cue. The last step is the "reward," which is the immediate sensation your brain gives you for acting on the routine.

Let's úse social media as an example. The cue could be your phone pinging, alerting you to a text from your friend. The routine is to open your phone and read the text. The reward is that good feeling you get from having heard from your friend. If you want to actively develop a habit, the most surefire way to go about it is to create that loop.

What I do know is this: The hardest part of forming a habit is the start and the following two weeks, so if tricking your brain helps, then by all means do it!

Hold Yourself Accountable

This is where the rubber meets the road. It's not enough to establish that you need to start today. It's not enough to buy the ticket and work backward from a quantifiable goal. It's not even enough to make it a habit. The final step to turning your goals into reality is to hold yourself accountable toward them. And that takes discipline.

Discipline is a tough one because nobody wants to do something that they don't like. My wife loves high-intensity interval workouts and for years tried to persuade me to try them. I finally caved the week before my bachelor party and did a session with her trainer. He had me swinging thick ropes, throwing medicine balls, doing burpees, and putting me through absolute hell. I could run one hundred miles no problem, but this was way outside my wheelhouse. When I got to my party, I was so sore that I couldn't raise my arms above my shoulders. My future wife didn't have to worry about me misbehaving because I could barely move. Come to think of it, she might be a better mentalist than me!

People assume I'm so disciplined because I run a hundred or more miles a week. But that's not it—I'm just doing something I've come to enjoy. Running provides value in my life because it gives me time to focus, a form of meditation with more cardio benefits. The difficulty is in how you trick your mind into creating and following that discipline.

In the beginning, there was a point where I didn't enjoy running. It was hard. It hurt. I was slow. The key to creating discipline is to find the things that are good for you, then convince yourself you want to do them more. With running, I found that I enjoyed it at a certain point because it allowed me to quiet my mind, even though I was slow and it was difficult and painful. For me, running helped me solve a greater problem. Ironically, I'd tried running in high school and hated it. I was bar none the slowest person on the cross-country team, hated it and gave up after one season. But when I revisited running as an adult, I was working a day job on Wall Street. While I was doing well professionally, and I had all my needs met and some material success, I couldn't stop myself from thinking, *So this is it? Global IT infrastructure? This is what I'm just gonna keep doing until I die?* I felt stuck in my life. I found myself wanting something different, something unique, something that excited me in my soul.

I found out the cure for what ailed my psyche was not just running, but racing. Even though it was painful—during my first race, I was crying for a mile or two—I kept going. There was something about it that made me feel alive in a way that a lot of other things didn't. So when you say to me, "Is it discipline?" I don't know that I'm disciplined, because I *for sure* did not want to do the awful workouts my wife did. In a perfect world, I would've said, "Hey, this bootcamp session is pure misery. So I'm going to do more of this." I've instead tried to seek out the things that will help me and that I also actually enjoy doing. Unfortunately for a lot of us, the things we enjoy are often wanting to sit and scroll while watching TV. I'm not judging that, because I do a lot of it, too. But I run much more than I would if it was all punishment, because of the benefits I get from it—both the pleasure and the physical health. I can't say if my joy is due to discipline, or if I just tricked myself into being accountable by telling myself I enjoyed it. By the way, I didn't immediately start running ultramarathons. The process involved creating a number of smaller goals, and chipping away until I felt ready to take on bigger challenges. (And yes, I absolutely wrote to my old high school coach when I won my first marathon—he was shocked!)

When you find yourself going off track from your goal, give yourself space for a day or so, but then revisit your plan and recommit to something quantifiable. Tell yourself, *I'm going to do X, Y, Z in the first month. I'm going to do this once per day, five days a week. I have no excuse not to.* Then whatever it is you've committed yourself to, whether it's sending résumés or getting to the gym or making calls to potential clients for the small business you want to create, just do it. The doing is typically where a lot of people falter because they don't hold themselves accountable for what they committed to.

If you're not at the point where you can trick yourself into accountability or force discipline on yourself, look externally. Communicate your goal to others so that they get on board. I think sometimes being a little bombastic and excited will motivate you. Make a bold claim and then put in the work to live up to it.

A lot of people confess to me they want to run a marathon. I tell them, "External accountability is an excellent motivator. Everyone's got social media now. Call your shot and make your friends hold you to it." A great way to stay on track with training for a 10K race three months from now is to post it all over your socials, even make some bets with friends, so that you're willing to do whatever it takes to maintain motivation and avoid embarrassment. Now you've got skin in the game. You've got people who are going to ask you about your training, and if you don't follow through, you're going to eat some humble pie.

You'll find that people are drawn to passion and goals, and you'll be shocked by how many support you. It's not just a good idea to involve others—there's science behind it. When you share your goals, your brain becomes like a kid in a candy store, as you'll trigger not just dopamine hits from the positive engagement, but likely also chemicals such as oxytocin (often called the "love hormone"), which are released during social interactions, and endorphins, which reduce stress and increase your feelings of well-being.[13] You'll become addicted to all that good chemistry.

Regardless of how you get there, whether it's internal or external accountability, remember that action leads to motivation (not vice versa) because it triggers a positive feedback loop. And momentum is a self-perpetuating cycle. In physics, *momentum = mass × velocity*, which means that momentum is something we control, whether we're talking about the physical act of rolling a snowball down a hill or creating a social movement.[14] To throw a little more physics at you, a body in motion will remain in motion unless acted upon by a force—so you'll keep moving unless you stop yourself. What I'm saying is, the more we put in, the more we get out.

The Final Caveat

We've covered getting past procrastination and why it's so important to start now, not later. We've shed light on how nothing will happen until you decide to buy that ticket. And once that ticket is purchased, you've got to be determined to plow through those difficult first two weeks as you form new, better habits to support you in attaining the goals you never before imagined you might achieve. Let momentum carry you as you drill down on your goals, working backward and making them SMART. And, of course, we've talked about the importance of accountability.

I'd be remiss, however, if I didn't end this chapter with a reminder to value not only your own achievements, but also the effort you put in to reach them. In this respect, enjoy the ride and not just the destination.

Don't be like me when I ran my fastest race ever at the Philadelphia Marathon. By pure chance, that was the same city I ran my first marathon in and clocked 3:21. The difference being that after the first marathon I was so thrilled at the results that I was instantly hooked on the sport that would change my life. Flash forward to the 2:23 race and I couldn't even enjoy having a new personal best time because I was so focused on getting under 2:20. Those four stupid minutes were viewed as total failure in my eyes.

Don't become so focused on where you might go that you end up stealing rewarding moments from yourself. Have gratitude for what you've been able to do.

SIX

Stack the Deck in Your Favor

Betting on yourself isn't a gamble; it's the smartest move you can make. The trick is learning to stack the deck in your favor and choosing the right moments to make your move, because timing is, indeed, everything in life. Remember, bad timing can often be a by-product of your own impatience, so I'll show you how to most effectively play the long game. For example, I didn't even make it onto *America's Got Talent* until my third try. I'll also cover the psychological impact of a growth mindset and what can happen when you effectively advocate for yourself.

Sometimes, the best way to set yourself up for the future is to pounce on an opportunity when it presents itself. I'll get into how timing led to the creation of my college side hustle. What I couldn't know then was that the savings from this little seasonal business would later give me the option to transition from Wall Street to my dream job as a performer.

Quiet Your Mind

One of the best ways to stack the deck in your favor is to learn how to quiet your mind at the right times. This is another trick used by professional and

Olympic athletes, who say the key to achieving peak performance is by turning off their inner monologue and letting muscle memory and training fully take over. When prompting themselves to swing harder or jump higher, the voice in their head goes quiet and allows them to focus 100 percent on the task at hand. Remember, the foundation of autopilot is the hundreds of times they've visualized themselves in that competition before. Two Japanese neuroscientists conducted a study in 2014 on the famous Brazilian soccer player Neymar. They compared his brain capacity to those of a whole group of second-division players. By measuring neuron signals, they found that Neymar used 90 percent less of his brain capacity than the players in the other group, the less-talented and less-experienced players.[1] Neymar was able to get himself easily into what's called a "flow state."

When competing, being in a flow state means these athletes are frequently thinking of nothing, instead of running through the aforementioned internal monologue. I realize this advice sounds contradictory to what I said earlier about shifting out of autopilot, but athletic and creative endeavors are actually instances we *want* our self-driving controls to take over.

Harvard psychologist Michael Hollander noted this difference in regard to Simone Biles withdrawing from the Tokyo Olympics when she got a case of "the twisties." He explained, "Your cortisol levels go up and your entire body is now hypervigilant to the point where you're actually making mistakes because you're hyperfocused on things. Your body is saying 'There's danger.' In a way you can think of that as you now have two tasks. One is managing the danger that's in your mind, and the other is doing your triple twist off the floor mat. And trying to do two things at once rarely, rarely works. Your focus is gone, and you stumble."[2]

How do we tap into that flow state? How do we know when to turn off our brain and when to turn it on? Researchers John Kounios and David S. Rosen, at Drexel University's Creativity Research Lab, studied jazz musicians and improvisation and they found that "it seems that creative flow can occur when two conditions are met. First, one has to gain expertise by practicing the task enough to develop, or 'bake in,' a specialized brain network for performing that task. Second, one must release conscious control so the specialized network can take over and produce ideas on autopilot, without the performer overthinking what they are doing or becoming overly self-conscious."[3]

The bottom line is, if you want to position yourself for peak performance, it's crucial to set yourself up to attain that flow state. What I want you to know is that the ingredients of preparation and visualization add up to something so much more than being ready: Putting in that time, taking no shortcuts, wires your brain to execute seamlessly when you get your big break. Being ready to access flow is key—it quiets the sections of our brains that are self-critical and allows us to be our best selves and to operate at our fullest potentials.[4]

Take the Leap

It never occurred to me that I could be a professional magician or mentalist. I certainly didn't plan for this, at least not consciously. I've met teenagers who tell me, without a moment's hesitation and with total confidence, that they plan to do this for a living. And I'll go, "How do you know that!?" I admire their determination and self-awareness.

At that age, I had no clue this profession was even an option.

When I started college, I was like one of those windup toys when it came to performing . . . once you turned the crank, I'd just go and go. From the time I was about fifteen years old, my default setting was to constantly chase the next gig. Whenever I found an opportunity, I'd take it; I never let it slip by. Let's say I met someone at a restaurant and they said to their friends, "Wouldn't this be so great at a Christmas party?" I would never, ever just reply, "Here's my card." Instead, I'd jump in with, "Amazing, I do Christmas parties all the time. What's your name and number? Someone from my team will reach out." (Spoiler alert: My "team" consisted of me, myself, and I! But saying that made people feel more secure—like I was part of a team, and therefore more legit. But never rely on someone else to get in touch if you don't have to. You need to take charge so you can own the outcome.)

My motto has always been "Do not wait for others to call you." You act, always. So even though by the end of college I was working on Wall Street with an enviable day job, on weeknights I had gigs at restaurants all across New York City, including T Bar, a steakhouse on the Upper East Side where all of Bravo's Real Housewives dined regularly, and Nino's, which served up delicious Italian fare and was a known mob hotspot. Suffice it to say I had leveled up from my Zia's days. Those restaurant performances led to parties. At those parties, I met event planners who'd book me for other events. I always took their business card and followed up early the next week saying something like, "Why don't I come by your office? Let me know a slow day. How about Tuesday at lunch?" It was a win-win, and I'd always bring something with me—pastries or donuts. Delicious treats went a long way and showed that I'd put in extra effort to make the interaction fun. These weren't just "meetings"—they were opportunities to deliver an experience to the planner's team. I loved being able to connect human to human. I always walked in knowing that they already had a roster of trusted magicians and mentalists, but knew I could prove to them that I could offer something unique to their clients.

Rather than beat around the bush, I would try to be direct and find out where I could add value and differentiate myself. I wanted to go the extra mile for them, to be memorable. I acknowledged that they surely worked with top-notch magicians already and showed respect for that, while simultaneously building the case for why I was worth a shot. It was all about getting that first gig, then proving myself and earning their trust. How could I get my foot in the door? By listening to what they said in those moments and taking action. Then once I established those relationships, momentum would build and my business would grow.

I learned that I couldn't be impatient, that I had to put in the work. For years, I was performing on the side, never really believing I would do it professionally. It always felt like a side hustle, because, in my mind, the formula was simple: you go to school, you get a job, that's how the world works. That's what my parents had taught me, that's what you see in the media and movies. That's the American Dream. In many ways, mine was the opposite of a growth mindset back then.

But two things happened that completely changed my trajectory. First, there was a magician who used to give me a lot of his overflow work. That meant gigs on nights when he was already booked, typically the most popular for private parties. Friday and Saturday nights are when most people host milestone birthdays and anniversaries, galas and similar social events. If he got calls for four different parties on a Saturday night, he'd tell his clients, "You know what? I'm not available, but I've got somebody great for you." And then he'd book someone like me, an up-and-comer. These heavy hitters acted as unofficial agents, getting us new performers new opportunities.

Getting those calls is the hard part, as is getting people to trust your recommendation over Yelp or Google. The folks who farm out their extra events either make a percentage of those gigs or they negotiate the deal and get a piece of the pie up front. This is just how it's done in the magic world.

I used to do a lot of this guy's overflow work. One day, we were hanging out—and I should point out that he was not exactly the warm and fuzzy type. He wasn't the kind of person who dished out words of encouragement or pep talks, which is why what he said next was particularly poignant. He looked at me and asked, "Why are you still working at Merrill Lynch?" I was caught off guard. "What do you mean?" I asked. Nobody had ever put it to me that directly before. His question went against everything I'd heard up to that point. Everyone else saw magic as a fun hobby, whereas working on Wall Street was viewed as the safe, respectable path.

I told him, "Well, I have a great job."

He was the kind of guy who challenged everything, so he wasn't going to concede a point. He asked me, "Do you love it?"

I had to think about that, because it had never occurred to me to consider whether or not I loved my day job before. I was just doing what I was supposed to do, and I didn't have an inkling that there were other options. I gave him an honest answer and said, "It's okay."

He continued, "Do you want to do it forever?"

That felt like a punch to the gut, imagining myself in this boring job forever. "No, not really."

He kept peppering me with very pointed questions, and every one of them demanded a yes or no answer. He wasn't trying to be nurturing or paternal, as that was not his brand.

Finally, he got to the point. "What do you need to do to perform full time?"

I totally panicked and I made up a number. No one had ever asked me anything like this before. I thought about my rent, my bills, my student loans, etc. "I've got to make $100,000 a year doing magic."

He wasn't going to let me off the hook just because I threw up such a pie-in-the-sky number. He pressed on. "How much are you making now?" And I told him. In his aggressive line of questioning, he took all these obstacles and barriers, all this baggage I had in my mind, pushed it all away and said, "Get rid of all that crap. Let's talk numbers." I saw it so clearly, for the very first time. He knew what I was making on the side, as those jobs were often funneled through him. He said, "You make this much doing magic when you do this many shows. Can you land one extra show a week for the next year? That's fifty more shows a year. And what if you charge 20 percent more? How's that math working for you?"

Everything he said made me think, *Yeah, if I wasn't at work . . .* A light bulb went off in my mind—one that should have always been on. But it took someone who was already doing magic professionally to lay it out for me and push me to think, *Holy shit, yeah, it's possible.*

That's when I blurted out, "Oh my God, I could do that."

It's so silly that I didn't realize it before, but that was an epiphany moment. I didn't quit right away, but that conversation got me thinking about an actual escape path. I needed that goal. It's like an ultramarathon; if you're going to run a hundred miles, you don't run a hundred miles all at once. I wasn't going to become the most famous mentalist in the world overnight. There are so many little steps, and they can seem absolutely overwhelming, but you've got to start by running the first mile. Most people can run one mile. I needed to just take where I was and think, *What's the next step?* For me, that was getting just one more show a week.

I had to start thinking, *Let's work a little harder and then I'm going to raise my rates this percent.* To work the system, I had to come up with realistic small goals that I could achieve, actionable bite-size things, one step, followed by another, followed by another.

Two months after this conversation, I performed for the CFO of my company at an internal event. Event planners within Merrill Lynch would hire me for shows because I had a bit of a reputation within the company, as a novelty, but also as someone who did a great job. They brought me in to perform for an intimate group of twenty top execs, bankers and their clients. I was in a beautiful office on one of the top floors of the World Financial Center, interacting with CFO James Gorman and his people. I performed one of my favorite tricks at the time, turning a stack of one-dollar bills into hundreds with the snap of my fingers and in the blink of an eye, perfect for the Wall Street crowd.

It was an amazing sleight of hand trick and the crowd was enamored. James looked at me and joked, "Oh my God, we've got to get you working here," which is what every Wall Street guy would say upon seeing that trick. I laughed and replied, "I do work here." He clearly thought I was joking as he continued to laugh. But then I paused, maintaining eye contact, and said "No, really, I do work here."

That stopped him in his tracks. He looked at me with confusion in his eyes and exclaimed, "What do you mean?" He didn't even understand what I was saying.

I confirmed, "I actually work in your global technology services department at 95 Greene Street." It was so out of character, but I broke the fourth wall, and maybe his brain a little bit, when I spouted all the corporate lingo from my group and he finally realized, *Wait, this guy actually works at Merrill Lynch.*

He looked me up and down and, in all seriousness, he said, "What the hell are you doing working here?" That was it, that was the final nail in the coffin, and I immediately asked myself, *What* am *I doing working here? This guy is the second in command at the company. If he doesn't understand why I'm here, neither do I.*

I put in my two weeks' notice less than a month later. What's so great is that everyone I worked with was genuinely happy for me; they all said some version of, "This is your calling, this is what you were meant to do."

I had inadvertently put all the pieces into place to make the seamless move into pursuing my dream. I wasn't married and I didn't have kids to send to college yet. I had plenty of savings as I built my magic business, thanks to Wolverine Spartan, which I'll explain shortly.

But what's most important is I was finally ready to go all in and bet on myself.

Learn from Every Setback

When I talk about my time on *America's Got Talent*, I refer to it as the rocket fuel that propelled my mentalism career. They say it takes ten years to become an overnight success and funny enough, it was exactly a decade after quitting my job in finance that I landed *AGT.* But by no means was this actually overnight success, especially because it took me three tries to even get on the show.

For my first audition, I had an *in.* I'd gotten a call from a producer, which is the best-case scenario because it meant I didn't have to wait for hours and hours for my turn. Think walking up to a club, skipping the line, and having the velvet rope opened for you by a smiling bouncer.

The process is pretty straightforward: You show up at an appointed time, go in and perform. In theory, this should have been way better because I didn't have to wait around with thousands of other hopefuls. The bad news was that they didn't factor in that my act is interactive, and stuck me in front of a camera with a microphone. Great setup for a singer . . . not so great for a mind reader when there's no mind available to read! I timidly explained the situation to a PA (production assistant), and let's just say this kind of troubleshooting was a few notches above his pay grade. He ran my situation up the food chain through his headset and was told to fill in as my "audience." Unfortunately, he was mildly irritated and very distracted—not exactly a recipe for success when your goal is amazement. Still, I rolled with it to show that I was adaptable. No one wants to work with a diva, right?

I tried to explain the trick I was doing and what I needed from him, but the PA kept saying things like, "Wait, sorry, what was that?" because he was half-focused on his walkie-talkie. There was no way I could pull this performance together; the cards were stacked against me.

Guess what?

It went terribly! I mean downright awful and no way to sugarcoat it. Before the audition even started, I was dead in the water. So I did the trick, and the PA was like, "Okay, cool, we done? Gotta get back to work now." There was no sense of wonder, no magic, no "Mind blown!" reaction. Immediately I realized I should have been much more of an activist for myself. I should have said, "Nope, listen, this won't work. I need somebody who's fully committed." I didn't push, I didn't advocate for myself effectively, and I allowed my audition to get steamrolled, rather than saying to myself, "Hey, this is my big shot. I'm going to do everything in my power to set myself up for success."

The mystical thing about our brains is that they are wired to help us succeed. They are on our team. Our brains have our backs. It's hardwired into our DNA to learn from our mistakes—evolution at its finest, survival of the fittest. Mistakes trigger our neurons to self-correct. In fact, the brain normally recognizes an error within one second and then continues to process after the mistake, insulating itself from making that error again.[5] My brain sent me back to the drawing board, already figuring out what I could do differently as I walked—dejected, Charlie Brown–style—out of the building. I knew the next time I got this opportunity, I'd give the producers a lot more advance notice about exactly what I needed, and I'd hold them to it.

The best advice I can offer is, if you've got your one shot, make it truly count and don't compromise when your future is on the line. Try to place all those dominoes in a row so they fall in the pattern you want. When I was setting up my audition the first time, and those producers pointed to a PA running around and said, "We have someone for you," I should have been more forceful and said, "No, I need somebody who can focus the entire time." I should have been more assertive, and more direct. I should have taken a breather, rescheduled, *something* instead of accepting a bad position. But I was so anxious to get in there and do my thing that I allowed unfavorable circumstances to crater my chances.

Please note that sometimes, even if it all goes right, the timing can still throw everything off. People will often reach out to me now, saying, "I'm trying out for the show," and I'll always lead with, "Hey, guess what? First time I didn't get on." I'm not trying to discourage them; in fact, it's just the opposite. I want to give them a dose of reality: One year you don't even make the show and the next your standing in the top three. Often, success boils down to timing, a little bit of luck, and not knowing at that moment that the producer may have already found somebody for your slot. This is why persistence and the ability to keep going is crucial, which is why we've already covered how to handle the pain of rejection. It's hard to do, separating yourself from the person being rebuffed. I didn't take the turndown personally that first time, because I know how crippling that could be. Instead, I looked at what I could have done to stack the deck more in my favor.

For the second audition, I didn't have the same *in*, probably because the first one had gone so poorly. This time I was part of the more traditional "cattle call," with thousands of people waiting long hours to get their shot. A lot of the wait took place outside, and it was a particularly bone-chilling January day in New York, with wind chills well below freezing. I stood around for almost six hours, turning into a human popsicle and then had to leave to perform a gig. I didn't realize the time commitment required and had not planned accordingly, so yet again it was not meant to be. There I was, ready to advocate for myself, and an entirely different factor stole my chance. I would not make that mistake again.

What's funny is that by that point, I was working at about 250 private parties each year. I'd developed a very thick skin from doing so many bar and bat mitzvahs in restaurants and banquet halls. In so many ways, I was already set up for success as a performer. I'd developed bulletproof strategies to win people over who were reluctant or not necessarily welcoming. Sure, the hosts wanted me there—they hired me. But the other people at the event had no idea who I was . . . and often didn't care.

If I was working at a bar mitzvah, the hosts are the parents. Teenagers, as you might well know, don't typically care about your feelings and will eviscerate you. Well, multiply that by a hundred if you're a strolling magician and they sense any weakness. Worst of all was when I'd realize that I was working my way through one segment of a social stratum across several bat or bar mitzvahs—like all the kids were in the same school, so the same group might end up seeing me three, four, or five weeks in a row, and I'd already burned through most of my repertoire. Nothing was more devastating than hearing, "Oh, I saw this last week, do something different." And some of them I couldn't shake off. They were like a rottweiler that grabs your leg, following me from group to group. My set was organized in such a way that I was repeating tricks, like a band playing their greatest hits. I wasn't set up to perform three hours of different material; there weren't songs to debut from a new album, if you know what I mean. I needed to either face the wrath and humiliation of getting called out, or pull material that wasn't my best.

When you know what's about to happen at the big reveal of the trick, then it's much, much easier to figure out, because you're watching it differently. First time around, when the rabbit comes out of the hat, your mind is blown. The second time, you're a little more wary. You'll just stare at one hand waiting for the next pivot, and you're less likely to be misdirected by that rabbit squirming around in my breast pocket, when I try to make you look away at the right moment. And when you're watching for the third time, the trick just doesn't work anymore. The secret sauce is gone. And those kids would be like, "Ha, ha, I figured out what you just did. And I'm gonna tell everybody!" (Yes, I recognize the irony of thirteen-year-olds following around the magician. I'd come full circle in life.)

The bar mitzvah circuit was not sustainable for my mental well-being. That's the reason I was more than a little anxious for the career boost I thought *AGT* could give me, especially because I was sure it would enable me to segue into more corporate gigs and away from the teen set. Again and again, I worked through every scenario of my audition, visualizing it all, to ensure this time I'd come in with the deck stacked in my favor and flow on my side, and I'd earn a spot on the show.

Answer the Door When Opportunity Knocks

I'd never have had the chance to pursue my dreams on *AGT* if it weren't for a somewhat miserable opportunity that serendipitously presented itself when I was in college. As I've mentioned, I'm from Michigan. My buddy Mark Wachsberg's parents became empty nesters when he went off to college and decided to move to a house on a lake, so we'd spend a lot of time on the water in the summer. If you know anything about lakes and cold weather, it's that every house has a boat dock that has to be installed in the spring and removed in the fall. In cold climates, the lakes freeze and you have to take the docks out or ice will destroy the structure.

If you're familiar with boat docks, then you've also encountered the guys who install and remove boat docks. Boat dock guys are not exactly known for their customer service, to put it politely. They might show up when they're scheduled and they might not; you never know. They tend to be a hard drinking, hard smoking type and leave your waterfront littered with Marlboro Reds . . . if they even show up at all. (I hate to generalize, but in our area, these were the facts.)

Dock work is a seasonal business where everybody wants their boat dock installed at the same time, so these guys were (and still are) in high demand but the work is quite miserable. When the season starts, you'll get a beautiful day in late April or early May, and everyone will want their boats out *right now* because they have spring fever.

Mark's parents got tired of waiting for the unreliable boat dock guys and said, "Guess what? You kids are about to earn your keep around here," and had us install the dock in freezing-cold water. We put on waders, which are rubberized overalls that are supposed to keep out the water. They do work . . . until the moment you step in too deep and that ice-cold water goes directly down your butt crack and fills the legs of the pants. It's the coldest, worst feeling in the world. Meanwhile, I'd be holding this heavy dock over my head while my buddy was screwing it together, and we were freezing and swearing, and his parents were just sitting on their patio with friends having drinks, all laughing at us. This was not the type of entertainment I was used to providing at my other job.

It was misery.

It was also an untapped opportunity.

Mark and I realized that installing boat docks could be very lucrative if we were also able to provide excellent customer service. We saw an opening in the market. At the time, I was attending the University of Michigan, home of the Wolverines. Mark was at Michigan State and their mascot is the Spartan. We couldn't figure out what to name our nascent company, but then we realized that 90 percent of the homes on the lake had an affiliation with one of those two schools.

My nights performing magic at restaurants taught me how critical it is to have a great icebreaker, and I thought humor would be the ticket for this type of business. We named our company Wolverine Spartan Boat Docks because it gave us a great joke right off the jump. People would look us both over and ask which one is the Wolverine (or Spartan depending on their alma mater or allegiance). One of us would answer, "'That's me, sir." And you could time your watch to them replying, "Well, I'll work with you, but I don't know about this guy," and we laughed wholeheartedly and unabashedly, as if we hadn't heard the exact same joke a hundred times before. But guess what, we just landed another deal!

We established ourselves as clean-cut college kids earning money for our future, which most people respected and wanted to support. Our company took off like wildfire because we didn't worry about failing, we didn't overthink it, and we didn't procrastinate. We hit the hardware store for two ratchets and Kinko's for flyers and business cards, the latter of which I was a pro at since age fourteen as a magician. We spent our weekends dropping off flyers in each and every lake house mailbox within a half-hour drive, while telling dirty jokes, making fun of each other, and having an overall great time.

We were so successful that we could barely handle all the business that came in. Because it was so explosive—customers hated the other providers with a passion—we ended up making tens of thousands of dollars in a short amount of time every year.

Why is this story relevant?

Because I saved all that money and it's why I had the safety net to quit my job on Wall Street less than five years later to pursue magic full time. I had no idea that I was giving myself an edge with the boat dock business; I thought I was just goofing around with my friend.

Maybe you've been waiting for your sign to stop working for The Man, but you haven't known what business to start. If you want to find what's likely a profitable enterprise, begin looking around at the pain points in your life and the lives of people around you. What is that business? Can you make money? Is there something you like to do that everybody else hates? Or maybe you hate doing something, but other people hate it too, and you hate it a little bit less? Spend five minutes on social media and you'll find something, like the Dallas woman who makes hundreds of thousands of dollars a year putting out and then cleaning up autumn pumpkin displays. Be creative and be relentless.

I will never forget the feeling of ice-cold water shooting down my back and trickling all the way down to my toes in those waders, but I'll also never forget how that frigid water led to the comfort of financial security at a time when I needed the courage to strike out on my own.

If you wait for the perfect moment to do something, odds are you're going to wait a long time. There are moments when you should act first and ask questions later. With the clarity of hindsight, you can always look back and see how the events of your life fit together like interlocking puzzle pieces. But it's harder to look at what's happening in the present and know that you have that next perfect puzzle piece in hand. There's always going to be an excuse available, like, "I don't have an idea for a business," but you can achieve greatness if you stay focused and keep pushing forward. Odds are you have your phone at hand this very moment and the full breadth of human knowledge available just a tap away. The world is at your fingertips and there are no excuses not to pursue your passion. All you do is type in "How do I do X?" and thousands of videos and articles will explain it in great detail. So, my goal here isn't to teach you how to install and remove boat docks, or how to become a mentalist for that matter.

Instead, I want to impress upon you the importance of taking those swings.

If you just keep doing the same thing over and over, it's like putting money under your mattress rather than investing it. Instead of growing in value, inflation keeps chipping away at it; the same thing applies to my profession, to any profession where you've got to challenge yourself and be willing to step outside your comfort zone to advance. It's not easy, but it's necessary if you want to take that leap—and hopefully reap big rewards. So when opportunity knocks, throw open that door—even if you're still wearing your pajamas.

There are pivotal moments in everyone's lives. Now, we've all heard about entrepreneurs like Sara Blakely betting it all on Spanx, or how Fred Smith, the founder of FedEx, went to Vegas and put all the money he had on the roulette wheel in order to make payroll. You hear about people who max out all their credit cards as they pursue their goals, and I can't deny that these are powerful stories and we eat them up. Nearly everyone wants a Susan Boyle moment—one minute she's a quiet, unassuming librarian, and the next she is discovered by the world, a superstar with the voice of an angel—but we all know that is more of a fairy tale and definitely not how things usually happen.

In real life, you have to stack the cards in your favor. For me, I had businesses since I was fourteen and I had been saving money diligently. I didn't have a fancy car or a flashy watch, like so many of my colleagues. I lived below my means and would always delay gratification. I was never ordering dessert, literally or figuratively.

That's why, when it came time to choose whether to quit my job and become a professional magician, I thought, *I'm giving myself a year to do this and I have the runway to do it.* I was lucky that timing was on my side. Wall Street was booming with a roaring bull market, and firms were hiring left and right. I told myself that the worst-case scenario was landing another corporate job in a year if this didn't pan out. Had this exact same scenario played out a few years later during the Great Recession, with widespread layoffs and uncertainty, I probably would not have gone for it. Fear would likely have held me back and made me cling to the security of my stable job.

Don't be too hard on yourself, because sometimes the timing is not right to take that leap. I saved up a bunch of money, and when I quit, I knew I could handle it for a year. Not everyone is in that position. I didn't have kids or a stack of bills to pay. Health insurance wasn't a concern because I had COBRA. Mine is not a fairy tale, but the story of all the things I'd put in place over years, so that when the moment came to make that decision, I knew where the card I needed was stacked in the deck.

Prepare for Success

I believe you're going to succeed. Still, sometimes when everything starts going your way, you can find yourself overwhelmed by free-floating anxiety. In fact, this is a common occurrence.

Psychologist Carla Marie Manly, author of *Joy from Fear*, says, "The brain's fear circuit works very quickly, and it doesn't always pause to differentiate between good anxiety and bad."[6] This is why we often feel tense and unsettled after we reach a goal or achieve an accomplishment, even though whatever happened is inarguably a good thing, whether it's a promotion or a degree or a move. Happiness can be overwhelming to some. According to Manly, for people who suffer from anxiety, the physiological change felt after something great occurs can trigger an automatic response in the body that something has gone off the rails, largely because you're not used to feeling good. It's like your system is expecting the other shoe to drop, and this feeling keeps you from enjoying your legitimate victory. There's actually a word for the irrational fear of being happy—it's called *cherophobia* and it often stems from childhood experiences where pleasure (like delighting in eating a stolen candy bar) was followed by pain (getting in trouble for stealing that candy bar).[7]

As you learn to read your own mind, better things will start happening, and that may well lead to anxiety. You can fight this phenomenon by recognizing and acknowledging it. The goal here is to force yourself out of the danger zone—to kick your autonomic nervous system out of overdrive. Clinical psychologist Alicia Clark, author of *Hack Your Anxiety*, says that one of the best tactics is to face this distress head on.[8] Acknowledge it. Allow yourself to think through all the scenarios that could happen when your dream comes true, like dealing with your snarky aunt's judgment when you're finally able to buy that lake home. Walk through how you'd handle that chatter, because the more strategies you have (such as inviting her to spend the holidays with you there), the more you'll give those unfounded worries a place to be put to rest.

Another hack when you're overwhelmed by the good (that makes you feel bad) is to intentionally try to relax yourself. Try taking deep breaths, practicing mindfulness, meditating, getting in some light exercise, or sitting under a weighted blanket.[9] One of the very best ways to de-stress is to just step outside and get yourself some fresh-air therapy. The quicker you can calm and center yourself, the better you'll feel.

If, regardless of what you try, you can't stop worrying, take that energy and use it for planning. Instead of ruminating about what happens if you get that executive level job, try to figure out how you'll tackle those new responsibilities. If you're about to live your wildest dream, create contingency plans beforehand so you can enjoy your time instead of fearing the unknown.

Remember, the world is not an either-or scenario. Something good happening to you is not going to automatically trigger something bad happening. You're not jinxing yourself by being happy.

Try to strike a balance between enjoying the present and still planning for your future. So often, we only chase short-term comfort and instant gratification because they are the path of least resistance. And I can assure you there were times when my friends went on vacations that their parents paid for and I'd say, "You know what? I can't. My parents unfortunately aren't supporting me, so I'm going to keep that $800 just in case." The sacrifices I made back then are what allowed me to now live my dream.

I'll never forget the morning after I left Wall Street, parked on the couch, still in pajamas, with a bowl of cereal in hand, watching daytime TV. I had this realization of, *Holy shit, I don't have a job and if I wanted to just veg out and watch TV all day, I could.* The weight of that thought hit me like a ton of bricks as I turned the TV off. I told myself, *I don't have a boss anymore, so I have to be the boss. This is day one, and there is no playbook for how to be successful at what I do. The phone isn't about to ring with some agent saying, "Hey kid, let me make you a star!" I need to define my goals. I need to find people that have done it and learn from them, and I need to start working. I have to make this happen because no one's going to make it happen for me.*

Which is exactly what I did.

Develop a Growth Mindset

The third time I tried out for *AGT*, I waited again for a very long time, probably six or seven hours, because I showed up to another open casting call. Here's when having some self-awareness comes in handy: I knew I was good because I was already making a living as a professional mentalist, one rowdy group of thirteen-year-olds at a time. I had a level of confidence that could only be acquired over thousands of performances for paying audiences and I understood what I had to offer.

The third time was the charm. I finally made it onto *AGT* because I incorporated what I had learned from the first audition and had the participant entirely focused on what I was doing, so I could properly showcase my talent. There was a sense of peace that came from knowing I didn't need the show to validate me, as I was doing well already. This gave me a calm demeanor and reduced any nerves that would have haunted me after my first two tries. The producers in the room absolutely loved my act and even asked me if I had any other tricks I wanted to show them after my audition set was complete. I punched my ticket to the televised shows and was ready to go! This was my chance to perform in front of Howard Stern, Heidi Klum, Howie Mandel, Mel B, and all of America. They each gave me a yes and my career would never be the same again.

Mind you I was still working the bar mitzvah circuit at this time. What's funny is, even if you're on people's living room TV every week, they don't necessarily recognize you in real life. The same week that my episode aired for judge cuts—the second round after the initial auditions—I was hired for a party in Rockville, Maryland. I was doing tricks for a small group of family members when the bar mitzvah boy's great aunt said, "Oh my God, I've got to tell you about this guy we saw on *America's Got Talent* this week." She was raving, going on and on about how great he was.

Brimming with pride, I replied, "Yeah, that's me."

She laughed at me and said, "No, it's not you."

Wait, *what*? More emphatically, I let her know, "Yes, that was definitely me. The trick you just saw? I did that trick Tuesday night on *AGT*. I assure you, it's me."

She was absolutely not having it and she went to get her husband to come back and confront me. She pointed in my face and said, "Why are you lying?"

How awkward was this?! I calmly explained, "I don't know what to tell you right now, but that was me. I'm Oz Pearlman. I'm the guy you saw. I'm Oz the Mentalist. I think I'm even wearing the same suit."

She was resolute. "No, no, this guy was hysterical," which was sort of insulting because I'd just done the same trick . . . and delivered the same joke! Then, right in front of me, she proceeded to have a full discussion with her husband about whether it was me she'd seen on television the night before! Eventually, the dad came over and confirmed that they'd booked me about eight months before I'd landed the show and that they had gotten very lucky with their timing. But that aunt could not comprehend that she'd just seen me on TV and then met me at the party.

Finally, she said, "You don't look like your picture on TV." That was it. No apology. It was the biggest inspiration yet to keep giving the show my best . . . I really had to get off the bar mitzvah circuit.

When you're looking to level up, the best practice is to adopt a growth mindset. To me, that means believing in yourself and your abilities, facing challenges, and combining hard work, learning, and dedication to create the outcome you most desire. A growth mindset is seeing a challenge and digging in with delight, confident that you'll come out better for it on the other side. It's about picking yourself back up when you fail and trying again, using the lessons you learned on the initial stumble. It's about seeking feedback and then applying it to constantly refine, hone, and improve yourself. It's about being proud of the sweat on your brow, because that exertion is propelling you closer to your goal. The best part is, with every step forward, you're making positive changes to your brain's neuroplasticity. You're clearing that smooth walkway from your front door to your mailbox.

America's Got Talent is comprised of a number of rounds. First there's the audition, then the second round, and afterward the live performances begin. With each round, more contestants got cut, narrowing the field from thousands of folks auditioning to less than one hundred who make it to TV. Every stage filtered out more people. The quarterfinals and semifinals are live, as are the finals. The pressure is intense, which I loved because I operate best when I'm backed into a corner. Reaching the finals comes with an extra performance, and that was one of my favorites. It was short—less than a minute. It felt like putting a cherry on an ice-cream sundae. That round changed the way I view TV, because up until that point, I thought that the longer the performance, the better it would be. Turns out the world was changing. This was 2015, right as social media was becoming really big (and attention spans were shrinking really small). My routine for Heidi Klum involved having her imagine an invisible deck of cards in her hand and asking her to choose any card she wanted; I even asked if she wanted to change her mind. Not only did I seemingly make a card appear in her hand out of thin air, but it was the very one she had just thought of . . . on live national TV with more than fifteen million people watching. Quick, direct, and to the point, with a palpable sense of risk and danger; I had found my sweet spot.

Going into *AGT*, I knew I didn't need to win to benefit, especially because the experience taught me so much. For example, I learned to be more creative, and that there's nothing like a deadline to get your butt in gear. Necessity is truly the mother of invention! If you have to come up with something great, and there's no timeline, you'll do it eventually, right? But if you have it forced upon you, there's no backing out or procrastinating.

The format of the show involves performing Tuesday nights live on national TV, with millions watching. Then America has twenty-four hours to vote, and the results are revealed live on TV the following night. I'd stand on the stage at Radio City Music Hall, alongside my competition, knowing full well that half of us were going home that night. With six thousand people in the audience and pin-drop-quiet atmosphere, host Nick Cannon would slowly open up the envelope, look at the results, and wait what felt like an eternity to build the tension as we each hoped to hear our name called. Then, like music to my ears, he announced, "It's Oz the Mentalist!" I'd be moving on to the next round. The timelines on the show are tight and people are chosen to perform in Week One or Week Two. I got Week Two both times. That meant as soon as I was done that night, I'd have to talk to a producer and tell them what I was planning to do the following week.

In this position, a lot of people might think, *I'm going to save my biggest and best trick for the finale*, but that's not what I did. The finale is never guaranteed, so I knew my best bet was to raise the stakes and go bigger every week, basically buying myself a fresh lottery ticket each time to stay in the game.

Ultimately, I placed third, and I was thrilled because the exposure did exactly what I'd envisioned it would do: It set me on a path to success—which meant way fewer bar mitzvahs.

I'm not much of a Vegas guy, but when it comes to gambling, I will always bet on myself. You have to play the hand that you were dealt in life and all of us have different circumstances to contend with, but stacking the deck means no more excuses. Having that positive growth mindset will help, as will self-advocating and never letting an opportunity slip through your fingers. You are in control of your destiny.

SEVEN

Don't Be Your Own Worst Enemy

Stop right now and look around. Are you at home? Are you sitting in a coffee shop? Are there other people there? Then here's something you don't know: Right now, every single man, woman, and child in your line of sight is the lead actor in their own movie in their head. They're *it*, they're the A-lister, everything in their orbit revolves around *them.* Those of us in their peripheral vision? We're just the extras with non-speaking roles, the non-player characters. We fade into their background. We may as well be wallpaper. Yet that's fine, because we're all so busy being the stars of our *own* movies.

The downside of having this main character energy is that we're also our own worst critics, harsher to ourselves than any high school bully could ever be. No online troll could poke our raw nerves and tender spots like we do when it's us trolling ourselves.

Our natural inclination is to allow our inner monologue to reinforce the negative, so in this chapter, I'll show you the important work of turning the tables on negativity, assuming the best, and treating yourself gently. We'll talk about how to quiet that inner critic for good.

I'll show how I shut down my inner critic by delving into my story of running Spartathlon, one of the hardest ultramarathons on the planet. I will walk you through my failed first attempt at this race, when my mind collapsed and gave up long before my body did. The biggest mistake of all was mentally writing my DNF (did not finish) speech and listing out all the excuses in my head for why I couldn't do it, rather than focusing on the task at hand. I soon learned the physical pain of pressing on would have faded far faster than the long-lasting inner turmoil of quitting. This was a valuable experience, as it taught me to throw everything plus the kitchen sink at problems, rather than allowing them to overtake my goals. And I'll explain how the next year, during the hottest day in race history, with the lowest finisher percentage ever, I changed my approach . . . and my outcome.

I'll also break down how to properly value yourself and your time. I'll teach you the greatest negotiation advice I've ever learned. Following my own negotiation advice led to me breaking a world record and raising six figures for Save the Children's Ukraine Relief Fund; I learned that when you do good, you're not just paying it forward for others.

Ultimately, when you learn to value yourself, you become invaluable *to* yourself, and it all starts with learning not to be your own worst enemy.

Time to Take Charge

The fastest way to silence your inner critic is to remember that just because you're the headliner in your own mind doesn't mean others perceive you that way. Not being the star of their show has nothing to do with you and everything to do with them . . . and there's nothing wrong with that. Except when we allow ourselves to stew about it. For example, when the lack of a timely response from someone else causes us to fabricate unpleasant stories, especially when we then project our unkind judgments on others and we get angry.

I'm not immune to negative self-talk. For example, recently I was waiting to hear back from a big podcast that I've been dying to be a guest on. When I didn't hear back from them immediately, my thoughts began to race about having been blown off. I let myself feel hurt and insulted, regardless of that not being anyone's intent.

Instead of just being logical, I began to beat myself up about why I hadn't made the cut and I shame-spiraled. *Where was I lacking? Was I not funny enough? Not clever enough?* Then my self-protection instinct kicked in and I started to get mad at *them*. Nothing about this was mentally healthy. I found myself complaining to my wife, who had the sense to laugh and reply, "I don't want to hear about this anymore. It's not about you, Oz. You have no idea what's happening in that producer's world. Why don't you assume the best, assume they really want you? Right now, they're probably slammed with production on other stuff and they just need a nice, friendly reminder in a week." (Yes, my wife is often more clearheaded than me.)

If you find yourself mired in negative self-talk, guess what? You're not only human, but you're an *evolved* human. This is a function of *survival*. If thousands of years ago, our ancestors hadn't allowed themselves to anticipate danger and threats, and hadn't allowed themselves the opportunity to stew, we'd have gone the way of the dinosaur.

Our prehistoric kinfolk likely sat around their caves, thinking, *You know, I don't feel fast enough to outrun that saber-toothed tiger. I guess I'll just stay in today and stare at the ceiling and eat these stupid berries instead.* They weren't depressed; they were preserving our species! And there are times your inner critic is right. If it's telling you that you're not twenty-two anymore and you don't recover like you used to in college, and refusing to be goaded into taking tequila shots out of some stranger's boot in a weird Tijuana bar means that you're lame, embrace it. Listen to that critic and be lame. Bask in your lameness when you're not crying on the toilet twelve hours later with the rest of the bachelor party. You just saved yourself a world of hurt.

The caution here is to not let your inner critic negative-self-talk you out of feeling your own worth, because that will limit your potential and can lead to anxiety, depression, and a host of other feelings.

When it comes to someone not getting back to me, my solution is normally to be proactive and to try to take the onus off them. I didn't in this situation, probably because I was too excited and the stakes felt so high. If I were coaching myself, I should have said to the producer, "I'm going to keep this date on hold for you. I'm sure you're slammed, so I'll make sure to follow up with you in a few weeks." This is effective because I'm front-loading the fact that I'm assigning them as busy. This affords them some grace and they don't have to say, "You know, I've been really swamped," especially if they've just been busy enjoying their summer break and I inadvertently make them feel guilty for the audacity of needing downtime. Then I put the job of reminding them onto myself by saying, "I'll make sure to check in with you in a couple weeks."

When I do check in, I'll say, "Hey, I promised to follow up. Let me know what's going on." Or if we're still in the planning stages, I'll tell them that I'll circle back again on X date. So I'm creating this dynamic where somebody doesn't have to make an excuse or feel as if they've been rude to me. I'm extending that extra bit of grace and runway, and people really appreciate it. Plus, assigning myself action gives me a feeling of control in the situation, which makes me less likely to turn my frustration outward and blurt out career-limiting statements to soothe my own ego.

Of course, there have been instances before where my gut tells me I need to act out, say to write a nasty email. I've learned over the last few years that it's okay to draft the email, to get it out of my system. The anger I might feel is real and I don't want to bottle it up. So I write the email. The rage channels through me and directly into my fingertips as they loudly slam each letter on the keyboard, and damn, does it feel good. I make sure to leave the address line blank, lest I accidentally hit send! And now I let that emotional brain dump sit and stew in my drafts folder, my mind free and clear. I set an alarm for the next day, and tell myself that if I still feel the same way in, say, twenty-four hours, then I'm going to send my missive. (I'm a big fan of timers and alarms to keep me on task.) And guess what happens, ninety-nine times out of a hundred? The delay has healed—or at the very least reduced—those red-hot initial feelings. I go from boiling to either simmering or lukewarm, and end up deleting the email. I've taught my kids the same move: If they're mad, they should wait a ten-count to react. You wouldn't believe how much less chaos this contributes to our household, where my wife and I are outnumbered by five kids under the age of nine.

Still, there are times I want to be petulant, like, "Hey man, I deserve more respect than this." I have to tell myself, *Stop it. Stop it right now.* The issue is that I'm just assuming that something's going wrong and it's my fault. But in reality, it's likely that whatever is happening has nothing to do with me. This is an example where creating a silo to separate myself, Oz Pearlman, from Oz the Mentalist and the associated frustration that I'm taking quite personally, is extremely beneficial. The issue is I'm one person, but if I can trick myself into two separate personalities, then I avoid anger, feelings of inadequacy, and potentially lashing out or being petty. Any of these overreactions are more likely to hurt my chances of getting what I actually want rather than help.

Try to separate a piece of yourself that can act as an agent who represents you. The best part about an agent is that during negotiations they won't take unpleasant situations as personally. Find a way to create your own good cop and bad cop in one person, so that you can extricate yourself and not feel that stress, that anxiety, those feelings that wear all of us down in our day-to-day, in both our business and our personal lives. I tell myself, *This isn't about Oz Pearlman; this is about Oz the Mentalist.* Be your own alter ego.

A good way of siloing and tricking yourself into better humor is to "Fake it till you make it." This expression is an example of "behavioral activation." According to behavioral therapist Rachel Thomasian, "Behavioral activation is a concept and intervention frequently used in cognitive behavioral therapy that utilizes behaviors to influence emotions, thoughts and mood. In other words, a therapist will often prescribe behaviors for their client to take part in, with the expectation that it will modify or ease some painful emotion they might be experiencing, such as anxiety or depression."[1]

In my case, that means if I'm feeling down because the podcast I've been obsessing over still hasn't invited me on, I let myself sit with that feeling. Rather than wallowing in self-pity, I use this no (or this "not yet") as fuel to strengthen my inner resolve and promote even greater focus on my goal.

Another important thing to consider is that sometimes you just need to take a breather. As counterintuitive as it may seem, waiting patiently can be the best course of action. The expression "a watched pot never boils" has proven true in my life so many times. So let it go, let that pot burble without you. You'll often get better results by shifting your energy to something enjoyable, like being around friends or playing a game with your kids. It helps trick your brain into a lighter, more upbeat mood. And when you're in that headspace, you're far less likely to get resentful when someone forgets that you're supposed to star in *their* movie, too.

Positive Self-Talk

No matter what the circumstance, I want you to consciously decide to be kind to yourself. Treat yourself gently. Say things to yourself that lift you up, not bring you down, because kind self-talk makes a world of difference. Maybe you think repeating positive affirmations feels silly—but they work because they rewire your brain when you say them enough.

S. J. White said in an article for the *American Journal of Health-System Pharmacy*, "The human mind seems to focus on the negative, and we tend to berate ourselves in ways we would never tolerate from a boss, spouse, or anyone else."[2]

Again, this isn't just advice I offer, it's advice I follow. I aim for an ever-running chyron of happy thoughts and positive affirmations in my head. I maintain a sense of humor about what I do as a mentalist because let's be real here, I'm not a brain surgeon or fighter pilot. My decisions and performances aren't life or death; they're purely for entertainment. I have a weird job and it's odd to me when my peers are overly solemn about the tricks we perform. Like actors, we're all effectively playing make believe. And people pay us for it! I've fed, clothed, and sheltered my family by being one or two rungs above a clown in the hierarchy of showbiz—trust me, I'm not complaining!

While it may feel temporarily indulgent to wallow in that negative self-talk, it's actually toxic and something you should avoid. When you berate and belittle yourself, you're essentially activating the "threat system" of your brain, so you feel under attack and become defensive and risk-averse.[3]

What does that mean? It means *moping doesn't help.*

You end up feeling way more stressed and this depletes you both mentally and physically. Even worse? There's a phenomenon called "emotional contagion," meaning all the negative stuff you're thinking and feeling leeches out to those around you and brings them down, too. This is exhausting for everyone!

For the longest time, before I learned to have a sense of humor about what I couldn't control, and before I really clued into the power of positive self-talk, I'd hold myself up to some of my peers and I'd give in to the compare and despair mentality. I'd watch what these guys were doing, and instead of being inspired, I'd look at myself and wonder why I wasn't at that level, too. I wasn't necessarily rooting for them to do worse, but I would feel bad about not personally doing better. Every time I looked at their success, it was a mirror revealing my own insecurities. So I'd think, *Oh man, I'm not doing enough. I'm not doing enough.* (What's ironic is that when we're on an upswing, we think nothing of others, so it's smart to remind yourself of how you felt on the downswings.)

This is another example of learning when to shift out of autopilot. My default setting was to base self-worth on how I ranked subjectively to others, and that typically sent me spiraling into a negative feedback loop. Sometimes shifting to a better state of mind is just a matter of stopping and taking stock from a different perspective. For me, I had to remind myself that I was making a living pursuing my dream and that I was doing exceptionally well. I'd certainly escaped the drudgery of global technology infrastructure, and now when I wear a suit to work, it's by choice. I have an incredible wife who loves me, five healthy, happy children who bring me tremendous joy, none of whom care what TV show I was just on or if I made as much money as a mentalist halfway around the world. I taught myself to *decide* to be happy, and if I were bound and determined to compare, to look at past versions of myself to see how far I've come. So whenever I'm tempted to start complaining or feel like crap when things aren't going exactly the way I want, I check in with myself, asking, *Are you doing better than you were a year or two ago?* That's what matters. And if I'm not doing better for some reason, *How do I try to catch up with where I think I should be? What tangible actions can I take?* In situations like this, we need to give ourselves a road map and a pep talk, not a beatdown.

How do we stop this negative-self-talk cycle? Well, there's an easy way to go about this with the clever name of Catch It, Check It, Change It, which comes from cognitive behavioral therapy.[4] This method requires you shifting out of autopilot and catching yourself in the act of thinking negative or anxious thoughts. So, let's say you're trying and failing at something, like making pad Thai from scratch. The kitchen's a mess and the dish looks terrible . . . and that's before you even taste it. And why isn't the recipe working?

Maybe you catch yourself thinking, *I was dumb to think I could do this.* In this instance, I want you to stop and examine the thought behind that feeling. Maybe it's *I'm a terrible cook*. Now, take a step back and look at the situation objectively. Ask yourself if that thought is helpful, accurate, and useful to the situation.[5] That's the Check It portion.

When you realize that thought is neither useful nor accurate, then it's time to Change It. What could you replace it with that would be accurate and useful? How about, *I make a mean lasagna that everyone loves*, or *My kids say my chocolate chip cookies are better than store-bought.* So you objectively know you're not a terrible cook. Also, pad Thai is incredibly difficult to make at home. You spend fifty dollars on ingredients you'll never use again (unless you don't give up) to make something that isn't nearly as tasty as the divine fifteen-dollar stuff from the Thai place around the corner. Don't beat yourself up; Catch It, Check It, Change It, and then hop on Grubhub or Uber Eats.

Remember, when you're trying something new or different, producing less than favorable results doesn't define you. Remind yourself of that. Because you might be killing it on other fronts. Your business might not be thriving, but business can be cyclical. You're still doing great on the home front, or your friendships are rock-solid, or you found a new hobby or something else that fulfills you. Downturns happen to everyone, but what makes the difference is how you weather those storms.

What helped me change myself and my poor attitude was, instead of comparing and despairing, I made the conscious choice to use others' success to light a fire under my own butt. When I was a little kid, I loved the movie *Rocky IV*. I thought it was so cool that Rocky kept a picture of Drago on his mirror and every day he looked at it and let that image reignite his focus. Eventually, I took that lesson to heart. Let other people fuel the fire for you, not because you want what they have, but because they inspire you to work harder. That's what I've tried to do. It's taken some growth to realize that's the case rather than just bringing myself down. I no longer view the world as a zero-sum game. Now, I let my competitors' success fuel my own ambitions. *Hey, if they can do it, so can I. What's the difference between us? Nothing. Nothing. There's nothing that's stopping me from doing what they're doing.* But real talk, my wife definitely found it a bit weird I was hanging up photos of other dudes on my bathroom mirror.

I won't sugarcoat it and say it isn't challenging to get over the hump with a new endeavor. You have to put in a great deal of work to get through said challenge. A lot of people just don't believe they can do stuff, so they half-ass their attempt in an effort to get the failure over with. By not believing in themselves from the jump, they end up self-sabotaging and reinforcing the belief that it was never going to work, so why even try? And then they feel far worse.

This is where treating ourselves kindly and offering up positive self-talk becomes so important. I'll remind you again of the snowy driveway between you and the mailbox. When you speak kindly to yourself, or when you repeat positive affirmations, you're carving a path in the snow, meaning you're stimulating those neural pathways that are a shortcut to making your brain happier and more positive. Giving yourself a positive affirmation like, "I'm a great salesperson" (or whatever affirmation you prefer), means you're actively decreasing your stress levels and you're lighting up those reward centers in your brain.[6] And that feels like a win.

This Is Sparta

I want to talk about the Spartathlon because it's one of the best examples I can share about being my own worst enemy—and what can be learned from the experience. But first, I should explain what the event entails. It is a 153-mile ultramarathon (not a typo!) with a strict 36-hour time cutoff that takes place every year in Greece. It re-creates the path, from Athens to Sparta, taken by a foot messenger in order to deliver a critical message to King Leonidas, which many believe changed the course of history. The very existence of our current civilization today can be traced back to a small band of Spartans defending a mountain pass against a massive Persian army, as depicted in the Frank Miller graphic novel *300* and the movie based on it, starring a shirtless and ripped Gerard Butler.

In 480 BCE, during the Greco-Persian Wars, the Persian armies assembled to invade Greece, which had very little time to recruit an army to repel them. In order to buy more time, a messenger name Pheidippides was sent to deliver a message to King Leonidas of Sparta. As the legend goes, he ran from Athens to Sparta in exactly thirty-six hours and instructed the Spartans to gather in a mountain pass at Thermopylae where the Persian armies couldn't attack en masse, as they would encounter a bottleneck. Three hundred Spartans defended against what they estimated were tens of thousands of Persians. Every single Spartan died, but they fought for days, which enabled the Greek army to assemble and beat back the enemy. This is considered a turning point in world history, because otherwise, civilization wouldn't be what we know it today.

The idea of the Spartathlon is to honor the memory of this one person, running this specific route in a day and a half, to deliver a message that changed the course of history as we know it. It's such an epic story. So five members of the British Royal Air Force decided to re-create the course in 1982 (the year of my birth, in an interesting twist), and the Spartathlon was born. At 153 miles, which is 246 kilometers, the race is the equivalent of almost six consecutive marathons—it's *a lot.*

There's a marble obelisk in the center of Sparta with the names of the Spartans who won medals in the Olympics, from the very first event up to modern day. And then on one side of it, for the last forty years, they've engraved the names of those who won the Spartathlon.

This is without a doubt the most iconic race I've ever participated in. When you get into town at the end, local kids ride bikes alongside you for the last few miles. Everyone in the cafés is cheering, and the cars are honking as you get closer because they all know the historical significance of this race and how hard every runner has pushed to make it this far. At the finish, there's a huge statue of King Leonidas. You bow before him and deliver a ceremonial message, receiving a hero's welcome. Race officials dressed in togas greet each finisher with a glass of water from a local river and place laurel wreaths on their head. Most runners carry a personal message—often a hope or a wish—to leave at the King's knees. (I had mine on a piece of paper, wrapped in a plastic bag.) It's an incredibly moving moment, shaped by the rich history of the race, the meaning behind the journey, and the extreme difficulty involved in finishing it.

Suffice it to say, I wanted this. I wanted this so badly . . . but apparently not badly enough.

The race proved much more mentally grueling than I could anticipate and I got in my own head. I knew I was done for when I began mentally composing what I'd tell my friends and family about why I quit. Instead of visualizing myself succeeding and focusing on how to never give up, all I could visualize was my DNF speech, and that is what did me in.

Most ultramarathoners find themselves quitting at some point. If you told me you had a gun to my kid's head, and said, "Can you keep running?" the answer is always, "Yes, of course." So you learn to look inside yourself and dig deeper. But that first year, I couldn't imagine what running 153 miles would be like. It was just unfathomable to me; I couldn't wrap my mind around it. If the race were in America, that's roughly the distance from Times Square to Albany, or Philadelphia to Washington DC.

That first year, 2011, I was running the race with my friend Michael Arnstein, and at mile 54 I was a train wreck. I'd been puking nonstop for hours, captured in all my glory in a video that has since gone viral. In a bid to uplift my spirit, he says, "We have less than a hundred miles to go!" I wanted to murder him, and on the video you hear me huffing out, "Stop talking, just stop talking right now!"

After vomiting more than eighty times, my body was in bad shape, but that's not what did me in. The issue was my mind. Rather than staying focused on the next step, the next energy gel, the here and now, I became obsessed with the daunting and overwhelming task ahead of me. There was simply *no way* I could run ninety-nine more miles feeling like this.

Therein was my fatal mistake . . . my mind was fixated on how I felt *right now and how much more I had to go.*

What I should have been telling myself is, *Things will get better, just don't stop moving.* But I had decided that I was toast and now it was just a matter of pulling the rip cord. Once I made the decision, I still had a whole lot of walking and shuffling to do before the chance would present itself to actually drop out, and by then it was the middle of the night. In the midst of this slog, I met a guy at one of the aid stations who barely spoke a lick of English. He saw my face and how I looked; he could see I wasn't going to make it. I'll never forget the way his face animated or the look in his eyes. He was like a man possessed by a demon. In halting English, he said to me, "If you cannot run, then you walk. If you cannot walk, then you crawl. Never NEVER give up!" But his pep talk came too late—I was already too checked out. I quit.

Then I sat on a bus for more than three hours, which was picking up the others who couldn't gut it out, who'd cried uncle like me. We looked at each other with varying degrees of shame in our eyes, all of us broken in one way or another. I eventually arrived at the hotel in the wee hours of night, slept in a bed, woke up, waited, and watched all the people who had been behind me finish, my heart in my mouth the entire time.

As I saw those competitors cross the finish line, I felt far more pain than I'd have felt if I'd just stuck with it. I was so mad at myself. I'm not even sure I can describe how I felt on an emotional level; I was almost crying watching people get their cold river water and leafy crowns. I was just so blown away by what they could do and I could not. (Not a single American completed the race that year, FYI.)

By Saturday of that week, I told myself, *I'm coming back*. I kept thinking about that guy I met in the night, that wild look in his eyes . . . he haunted me.

While his words didn't work in the moment, I let that man's attitude work its way into my DNA. I thought about the race every single day and I channeled him when I returned the following year. Physically, I was in approximately the same shape, but mentally, I was so much more fit. I said, *There's nothing that will keep me from finishing this time,* and I meant it.

The race the second year was two weeks after my wedding, yet I still came back. I returned again with Michael, who DNF'ed with me in 2011. (We have the YouTube documentaries to catalog the good, the bad, and the ugly from both races). If I'm being real here, I knew that first time I wasn't going to finish. If I were to have looked at myself in the mirror that day and asked, *Am I going to do this today?* Had I simply been honest with myself, the voice in my head would have said no. That voice was just overwhelming me, creating endless reasons why I could quit if I wanted to. Had I approached the race with the mindset that I was going to finish no matter what, the day would have gone so differently. You can lie to the people around you, but it is very hard to lie to yourself. I should have gone into the race with a different mindset. When quitting is not an option, everything that gets in the way is a speed bump, not a stop sign.

As I started the course in 2012, that man with his wild eyes was with me in my head for every stride. He set my cadence. On my forearms, I'd written in Sharpie, *Pain Is Temporary, Glory Is Forever* as a reminder of what these 153 miles meant to me. That became my mantra. I went into this race pumped up on positive self-talk, saying that I was going to enjoy myself and enjoy this race.

It was the hottest year on record in the history of the race, and I knew there would be no ice or outside assistance for the first fifty miles. At one hundred miles, roughly twenty hours into the race for me at 2:00 a.m., there's a 3,600-foot climb up a mountain. My brain gets loopy at night without sleep and all my ultramarathon friends make fun of me for being such a baby, but truly, I cannot function effectively with zero sleep.

I arrived at an aid station on the side of that mountain in the middle of the night. I asked someone in broken Greek to wake me in five minutes, then I proceeded to collapse onto the rocky shoulder of the dirt road. Instantly, the volunteer shook me awake. I said, "Why didn't you let me sleep?" She replied, "Five minutes, five minutes," with her palm splayed. I looked at my watch and, holy crap, she was right! It had been five minutes. I'd fallen asleep before my body hit the rocks. That was the deepest sleep of my life. But like blowing on a Nintendo game cartridge (you might be too young for this reference), the pause worked to give me the necessary reset. When my circadian rhythm kicked in during the sunrise, I shockingly felt good again.

I can't tell you how many times between 2011 and 2012 I'd visualized myself running this race, crossing the finish line, and kissing the feet of King Leonidas before drinking from the chalice of Eurotas River water. This is one of those races where the best years have maybe a 35 percent finish rate. The second year when I did it was the lowest rate in history. It was 19 percent. Only sixty-five people finished out of hundreds that year.

I was so proud to have been one of them.

I was sobbing as I ran those last few miles—it was all so emotional. But I had validated the mantra I'd etched onto my skin.

The next day, everyone who finishes is invited to a huge festival and awards dinner with around twenty thousand people packing the town squares. It's unlike any other race I've run; the history, the passion, the energy of the Greek people who embrace us like warriors. People attend from countries around the world, and the Japanese and Korean contingents all came over and bowed to us. They couldn't believe anyone had finished, given the heat. For the next two days, kids asked for my autograph as I walked through town, recovering and taking it all in.

There's no question that, before I die, I'm going to go back and run that race once again. It was both the hardest race I've ever done and the most fulfilling. When I watch Michael's 2011 and 2012 Spartathlon documentaries, I now notice that I was full of bravado in the first one, all "Let's do this!" But I knew inside that I'd likely bitten off more than I could chew.

When I decided to not finish, I fed myself lines like, "It's better to play it safe than not," and "I'm going to grow from this." But ultimately, that was all bullshit. It was me giving up before I even started. Every one of us has been guilty of this at a certain point, when we write whatever our version of a DNF speech is. When you've already thought of all the reasons you can't do it—why you should give up, why this won't work, why somebody else is better or more deserving than you—it creates an endless feedback loop of negativity. You will start to question whether your goal is even worth trying.

Instead, write the speech that you'll deliver at the finish line.

Your mindset going into a challenge shapes your results. How do you prepare for the things that might go wrong? How do you anticipate obstacles? Push through when every ounce of your being is telling you to quit? These aren't rhetorical questions and they apply far beyond the realm of ultramarathon running. You need to find the answers to them in your life and use that as fuel to achieve your goals.

I've said it before—when there's a problem, throw the kitchen sink at it. Give everything you've got. This works for anything: Let's say you're starting a new business and it's going poorly. You're not selling anything. You're not getting calls back. You're thinking of giving up. This is when you must dig deep and ask yourself, *What can I still put into this? What do I still have?* More often than not, challenging yourself can provide a fresh perspective, and maybe that's part of your solution.

Remember, whatever your Spartathlon is, if you can't run, walk. And if you can't walk, crawl. You might progress more slowly than you want, but you'll still get there.

The Price Is Right

Another way to prevent yourself from being your own worst enemy is to understand your own value. This is crucial when it comes to negotiation. When I started performing professionally early on, the biggest challenge wasn't learning the tricks. Instead, it was figuring out how I should price myself.

We know the prices of lots of things. When you go to the store, you know what the price of milk is, you know what the price of eggs is, but what in the world is the price of a magic show? This business is so niche and there are so few of us that there is no rubric for competitive pricing. This isn't like a commodity where you can go to three shops to find the best deal. I didn't know how to price myself effectively, because I didn't know the law of supply and demand.

Here's an easy hack—you keep going till people say no. When I was a kid and I walked into Zia's for the first time, I got paid fifty dollars for two hours and thought that making twenty-five dollars an hour was insanity. I mean, I was fourteen! It didn't occur to me to even wonder if I was undercharging or overcharging, because I was thrilled with what I got.

When I quit my job on Wall Street, I loved performing magic. It's a passion that became a profession. I landed my absolute dream job and it was my favorite thing to do. If you're lucky enough to work at something you love, how do you assign a value to it when you would effectively be okay doing it for free if there weren't bills to pay?

When this is the case, you have to consider opportunity cost. Think, *Hey, if I'm doing this for free for you, I can't be somewhere else doing this for money.* That's how you must value to your services. And when you have a family, the math becomes, *I'm giving you my time instead of spending it with my wife or my kids, or traveling or a vacation.* There's a finite pool of resources. I was my own worst enemy because I took every no personally. If somebody called me for a party and they turned me down directly, or tried to spare my feelings with the old "we went in another direction" excuse, it would honestly bring me down. If I got two or three no's in a week, I thought the world was ending and I'd never do another show again.

So, I would underprice myself all the time and also be very negotiable because I didn't assign myself enough value—and couldn't face those no's. At some point, you have to say to yourself, *Here's what I'm worth.* And a lot of that is confidence that builds over time. But it's very difficult early on. I was doing hundreds of shows a year for far too little money. I loved it because I liked being busy. But once I got married, I had somebody who I loved spending time with, and all those gigs now came with a cost. Parties and weekend outings that I could not attend, vacations that were impossible to book because of my performance schedule. Suddenly, I wanted some of my time back, and taking a gig became a very difficult choice, especially when I was on *America's Got Talent* and finally decided to have someone else handle my bookings.

That was a rough handoff. It felt akin to saying, "Oh, you're gonna take care of my baby," with no transition time; handing off the reins was no easy task for me after years of being a control freak. Now I have a manager who books my gigs. You have to be cognizant that it doesn't matter how much your clients love you, they will take advantage of you if you allow it. If they can get something cheaper, they will. That's the nature of the beast. That's what any of us would do. Let's say you own a market or a small mom-and-pop shop, someone walks in and says, "I want to buy that item right there." You say, "Great! It's twenty dollars." But then they say, "Eh, I'll give you fifteen." They'll want to argue that, because it's your store, you should be negotiable. But if you go to Walmart, you can't say, "I'm gonna pay you fifteen bucks." The cashier will be like, "Dude, it's Walmart. Do I need to call security?"

This is why I mentioned the concept of separating your sense of self from what you hope to accomplish. In entertainment, there are intermediaries like agents and managers, but for most people in their day-to-day lives, there is no one else representing you. The closest thing you can do is to take yourself out of the equation and become your own agent, because without that mindset shift you probably won't ask for what you actually need. But think of your agent as a cutthroat shark who believes that you are the best thing since sliced bread—and that you deserve every penny and then some. Find a way to silo yourself into Regular You and Agent You so you don't undersell your services and talents, especially because Agent You wants his or her 15 percent.

Ultimately, I'm a people pleaser. My whole job is to bring others joy and wonder. I'm there to make sure you have an incredible experience and want to generate good feelings from the moment you reach out to me until I leave the show . . . and even afterward in your memories. That's why it's imperative that I separate myself from the less enjoyable aspects of my job, parts that every profession has. You know what I mean—the awkward moments, the hard asks, the negotiations. I'm talking about when to say that things aren't right, when to say no to events, when you're not being valued properly, or when agreements aren't being honored.

If you're selling a service, you're not hired because somebody likes your smile. You're providing real value, whether for their business, pleasure, or life. You're working. So understand that you can ask for things and you can stick to your guns on certain standards. When it comes to determining a dollar amount, the only rule that matters is: You can always come down in price; you can never go up. That's not just in negotiations, it's everything in life. Whatever you want, start by asking much higher than your bottom line. Set the anchor high. Then if you negotiate down to what you really want or need, everyone feels great. You got what you wanted, they got a deal, and both of you walked away happy from this interaction.

Decide what you want, start higher, and give yourself the option to lower your price to where both people can win. Sometimes you'll be shocked by what you can get. You begin high, and some people will just say yes right away. You both feel great about what just happened. This applies to situations outside of money as well. The same rules of negotiation apply to your time, your energy, your plans, your thoughtfulness. Set yourself up to always exceed expectations and overdeliver on your promises. Let's say you're a tailor and you know you can have those pants hemmed by Wednesday. Tell your client you'll have them ready by Friday, then they're pleasantly surprised when they get that call from you on Wednesday. And they're going to tell all their friends.

When you learn to price yourself right and to leave room in the negotiations, everyone wins.

Setting the World Record

By now, you've gathered that I get a little obsessive about racing. For me it's about pushing myself as far as I can possibly go, past what I thought was my breaking point, not just physically but also mentally. Ultramarathons teach you that when you feel you have absolutely nothing left, not one drop of gas in the tank, your mind is almost always lying to you. Your mind controls your body, and in there I see a direct parallel to what I do for a living: Learning how to trick the minds of others is what I do to myself when running extreme distances. Chasing those dramatic highs and lows is intoxicating and in many ways addictive. You learn so much about who you really are when facing tremendous adversity and being able to battle through it. It's not unusual for people who have jobs that challenge their bodies to seek out hobbies that are more cerebral, and vice versa.

Running allows me to heighten my mental acuity. In fact, exercise is known to provide a litany of benefits, from aerobic fitness to improving nervous system plasticity, which helps you adapt, rewire, and learn in response to experiences, stimuli, injuries, etc.[7] My moods are more stabilized thanks to exercise. A good exercise regimen is tantamount to mental health, so if you're feeling down, go exercise. Runner's high is *real* and it will up your endorphins and lower your stress. Way to not be your own worst enemy, right?

Physical activity isn't just important for your body, but also your mind because raising your heart rate increases blood flow to the brain. You want this extra blood flow because it increases the molecules that spur the formation of new synapses, improving how sharp your mind and memory are, particularly long-term memory.[8] Now, am I suggesting you train for an ultramarathon? Ha, no. You really have to want to embrace that degree of suffering. But if you've been on the fence about starting to take walks after dinner or finally try your hand at pickleball, consider this your sign to do it. Challenge yourself, set a goal, and see it through to completion.

In early 2022, I'd spent months training for the Umstead 100 Mile Endurance Run in North Carolina. Right before I was set to travel to the race, a very successful client of mine, who happens to be a billionaire, asked me to change my plans and perform at his wife's birthday party on race day. He'd hired me a couple weeks prior and said it was so much fun that he needed me back to amaze a different set of guests. My manager declined on my behalf and explained that I had a personal obligation. I'd trained hard, sacrificed, and was super excited to run this ultramarathon. On top of that, the race was supposed to have taken place the year before, but got canceled due to COVID-19. Once it was finally rescheduled, two high school friends planned to fly in and help crew me at the race. We were all excited to get together again after many years. And my running one hundred miles provided the excuse we needed to make it happen. There are some things you can't put a price on. I did not forgo all that cake and all those burritos to change my plans at the last moment. But alas, everyone has a number.

Let me clue you in on a little secret . . . billionaires aren't fans of the word *no.* It's not even in their vocabulary. This guy was insistent that I be there, and again, I said no. But he kept asking. So I finally told my manager to quote an outrageous number that I had basically pulled out of thin air, and she said, "Whoa, I think that's going to ruin the relationship." I was absolutely fine with walking away from this gig and running my race, which is the strongest position to be in when it came to a negotiation.

Still, I persuaded my manager to throw out this ridiculous figure. (If fourteen-year-old Oz was bowled over by twenty-five dollars an hour, the sum adult Oz demanded would have *put him in the ground.*) Remember, I can read people and knew that within thirty seconds, my client would text back with a yes because he'd already heard no from us four times, which was four times too many in his book. It was all about winning.

Lo and behold, the mentalist was right and he said yes. So . . . I wasn't going to run that race in North Carolina after all. It's a weird feeling to simultaneously be furious while also trying to wrap your mind around the biggest payday you've ever gotten for taking a twenty-two-dollar Uber ride from your home.

I was in amazing shape and didn't want to waste my fitness or the long hours spent getting there. I looked for something else I could do and decided to run one hundred miles around Central Park. Totally normal and sane right? This is hallowed ground for me, the holiest of the holy: That 6.1-mile loop is my favorite place on the planet to run, and trust me, I've been to a lot of places. If I was going to do this, I decided that the run should have a purpose and be for the greater good. The world was reeling from the recent Russian invasion of Ukraine, and I saw horrific images and videos each day on TV, so I wanted to try to make a difference.

During this run, I'd raise money for children in Ukraine. I was out for a run the next morning with my training partner Tom Knight and told him about my idea, to which he replied, "Hey, last year a guy named Robbie Balenger broke the record for the most loops ever run. And it's all over the press. It was in *Men's Health*, it was in *GQ*." And then the idea became *very* interesting to me because it wasn't going to just be me competing against myself.

It's funny how ideas that are almost nonsensical can turn into something tangible. Especially if you're passionate and if there's some element of your goal that's good and selfless. I set up a page for donations and the whole thing caught fire. People heard about it and shared with others, and interest started to grow. Luckily, I'd also landed in a good news cycle, and it took off from there.

I ended up breaking the record, raising $116,000 and running 116 miles. No one's broken my record yet. Of course, when I finished, I felt I could have done a twentieth lap, which would've gotten me to 122 miles. The goal was to break the record. This is a great example of defining your goals effectively and then being relentless in your pursuit of them. I could have gotten one more loop in, but I had a small injury and I knew that if I didn't complete the whole loop, there would've been a whole lot of suffering for naught. My crew was tired and I had achieved what we set out to do, so they didn't push me to keep going. Plus it was midnight, and the next morning, I had to fly to Augusta, Georgia, to perform a show at The Masters. To do one more loop, I would have had to take a bunch more caffeine to gut it out; I likely wouldn't have fallen asleep until 6:00 a.m. and would have been a wreck the next day at my show. But I never forget the lessons of Spartathlon: Pain is temporary, glory is forever! I'm pretty good at letting things go, but there's a tiny piece of real estate in my brain that tells me I'm going to try to better that record at some point.

What's ironic is that I just wanted to do something good for humanity to balance out a healthy payday. My thinking wasn't transactional—my hope was to give back in some way while chasing a personal goal. Yet I found myself on the front cover of *The New York Times*, with a full two-page insert inside. I couldn't pay a publicist hundreds of thousands of dollars to get that kind of great press. Reuters picked up the story and it went global! This wasn't premeditated or part of some big idea. I took the initiative and went for it, the entire plan came together in ten days as I tried to turn lemons into lemonade, and all because I knew my worth.

I want you to ask yourself, *What can I accomplish when I come to terms with my own worth? What happens when I silence my inner critic and stop being my own worst enemy? How can my life change for the better when the voice in my head starts to dish out positive self-talk consistently?*

If I hadn't made changes, I'd never have learned to ask for what I'm worth. I'd never have completed the Spartathlon. And I'd certainly never have set a world record.

Never forget that a brighter, happier, more successful future awaits you, and it starts the moment you realize you deserve to be the star of your own movie.

By the way, I never slept on the goal of being on that podcast—I thought about it every day, wondering how I could get a toe in the door. I listened for years and saw where my network overlapped with past guests and close friends of the host. Then I would ensure that I found a way to amaze them and that word would slowly but surely trickle back. I played the long game, stayed patient, and never took my eyes off the prize. My persistence was dogged and my progress wasn't linear. Sometimes it would be two steps forward and one back, but I was perpetually focused and in pursuit of that goal—and I finally got on! By the time this book is in your hands, I'll have been on *The Joe Rogan Experience* and those years of planning and converting *no* to *not yet* worked! It was an amazing achievement and one that left me feeling truly fulfilled.

EIGHT

Ask for Help

We often shy away from reaching out for help when we need something because we're worried that being open and appearing vulnerable will be mistaken for weakness. This has been a particular struggle of mine because I hate the idea of being a burden. I know I'm not alone in previously having taken on more than I could handle because I wanted to be able to be self-contained . . . and doing so was often to my detriment.

One of the most powerful lessons I've learned comes from running, but it applies to all of life: If you want to be great, you have to push yourself out of your comfort zone because that's where the change happens. But what you must realize is that *you don't have to go it alone.* I'll walk you through not only how to ask for help, but also finding the right person to ask. Your best bet is seeking out someone who is currently where you want to be in five years. Even in a niche profession like mine, there are those who've done it before. I'll share the story of learning with my mentor, Bruce Kessler, who's one of the reasons I've reached the level I am at today.

The secret formula for getting a mentor's buy-in is simple: Be of value to them. Find out what you can do for them and then do it. Think like they think and make them see themselves in you. When there's a give-and-take, people are much more likely to give. When you find the right mentor, they'll ask you the questions you should be asking yourself—and that's the fast track to success. The converse here is that if you're asking for help, you should just as freely be giving it. Paying it forward is one of the best investments you can ever make, as its returns are often exponential and can be deeply impactful.

In this chapter, I'll talk about learning to let go of that need for control, to grip the steering wheel a little less tightly, or even better, to give someone else the chance to drive. Remember, you're not failing if you can't juggle every single thing—you're overwhelmed. I'll cover how to off-load what isn't mission critical.

Tear Down Your Walls

I was not good at asking for help for the longest time. I would try to shoulder as much as I could, and in many instances, took on more than I could handle, because in my head I was Superman, and as everyone knows, he has no sidekick. We think we're heroes when we try to do it all: so strong, so competent, women and men of steel. Yet when operating at the I-alone-can-fix-it level, things often end up falling apart. Right? We'll say, "Nah, I've got this handled. First, I'm gonna do this and then I'm gonna do this," despite the fact that there are only twenty-four hours in a day, forgetting that we need to sleep, shower, and eat lunch.

When we try to be a jack-of-all-trades, we inevitably become a master of none. Over the years and with a lot of trial and error, I've learned what I'm really good at and where I'm lacking. To be our most successful, we have to focus on the unique skills that set us apart and delegate the other tasks if possible. That can be a difficult realization, but recognizing this was both smart and healthy because it allowed me to reclaim my time and energy. When I finally made the decision to off-load responsibilities where I don't excel to people who are better at them than me, everything changed.

Let's be clear—asking for help can feel hard, but you have to remember that vulnerability is not a weakness. Let me say it louder for those who are trying to carry the whole world on their shoulders like Atlas: *Vulnerability isn't weakness.* Dr. Brené Brown, one of the foremost experts on vulnerability, says, "The difficult thing is that vulnerability is the first thing I look for in you and the last thing I'm willing to show you. In you, it's courage and daring. In me, it's weakness. This is where shame comes into play. Vulnerability is about showing up and being seen. It's tough to do that when we're terrified about what people might see or think. When we're fueled by the fear of what other people think or that gremlin that's constantly whispering, 'You're not good enough,' in our ear, it's tough to show up. We end up hustling for our worthiness rather than standing in it."[1]

The hard truth is that the more vulnerable and open we are, the better off we become, even though showing vulnerability can crack the door to potential rejection and pain. Still, the benefits far outweigh the costs when you look at the science behind it.

Our brains are programmed for us to be a part of the collective. We aren't meant to be lone wolves. When we're able to lower our guard and connect with others, we trigger the neurotransmitter that releases that sweet brain candy called dopamine. When dopamine is released, whatever the behaviors are that triggered it are reinforced to create a positive feedback loop.

When we allow ourselves to be vulnerable, to let others in, there's the potential to release oxytocin. Oxytocin is triggered by physical touch, acts of kindness, and positive social interactions. It's produced in the hypothalamus and it gets distributed into our bloodstream via the pituitary gland.[2] While oxytocin is most often associated with facilitating childbirth, men produce it as well. Basically, it's a love hormone, and who doesn't want a hit of the love hormone?

Also, allowing ourselves to be vulnerable can impact the anterior cingulate cortex, because when we share our feelings of pain or we empathize with someone else, we trigger this region. What I mean by that is, when we let down our guard and connect on an emotional level—whether we're expressing our own hurt feeling or someone else's—we're engaging a part of the brain that's wired for deep human connection, understanding, and even suffering. This confirms that vulnerability isn't a weakness. Instead, it's neurologically tied to empathy and shared experience.

Essentially, vulnerability lights up our neurotransmitters like a Christmas tree. The more we allow ourselves to be vulnerable, the more likely we are to build healthy relationships based on trust, mutual respect, and intimacy. You might think that being vulnerable would cause us to feel weakened and compromised, but actually, the opposite happens. Vulnerability helps us manage our emotions, makes us more resilient, and can improve our self-esteem because it leads to a more positive self-image.[3]

There are a few different strategies you can use when it comes to embracing vulnerability. Just recognizing that you're afraid to allow yourself to be vulnerable is a step in the right direction. Another strategy is to not accept your own negative thoughts as fact. We've talked at length about that snowy driveway analogy. The more you're offering yourself positive self-talk, the more you'll create that neural pathway. And you don't have to start big by sharing your every truth—you could (and maybe even should) start small by, say, asking a coworker to walk you through the new sales reporting tool because you didn't quite grasp the nuances the first time. That will build your relationship because it will create trust and good feelings between you. As always, you have to give yourself some grace when you start this process, because we're working to change long-ingrained patterns. Learning to read your own mind and tap into your greatness does take effort.

Let Go of the Wheel

I'm not saying that relinquishing control is easy, but I am saying it's necessary, so let's take some steps right now to put you on the right track. I want you to stand back and assess where you are in your life. Ask yourself, *What's bogging me down? What's keeping me from firing on every piston? What am I good at? What am I not good at? Do I even need to improve what I'm not good at? What's my highest and best use?*

The answers to these questions will help you determine what tasks and responsibilities might not need to be on your plate.

I'll give a tangible example here. Maybe you're like me and you're not good at managing your bookkeeping and calculating your taxes. First, let's recognize that this is not a personal flaw, okay? Not enjoying organizing receipts and keeping a spreadsheet is not a character defect. Poor knowledge of the tax code doesn't mean you're a bad person, in fact it likely suggests you're more fun to be around. I imagine your taxes are not something you enjoy doing or want to work on getting better at. (They certainly weren't for me.) The computations are nothing but a necessary evil . . . and a civic duty. I mean, who doesn't want roads, schools, and firefighters?

In a case like this, most likely it's time to get an accountant and say, "The money I'm spending, it gets repurposed into time. And what I'm doing with that time could yield a lot more value than sitting around for a few hours each month, bookkeeping and figuring out my deductions." I'd say this is a silly example, but it's something that every one of us has to do if we'd like to avoid jail time.

I was terrible about trying to do it all myself for a long, long time. But now I've started asking for help, even going so far as to rely on a crew (more on that shortly). I realized that time is a nonrenewable resource and becomes more finite the older we get. So I had to force myself to start spending my time more wisely and not get hung up on the things that were outside my control.

A chore that's oddly specific to what I do is creating the materials that are used in my shows. For example, I have these envelopes that have to be sealed in a specific way. In a given week, I have a bunch of things that need to be stapled or glued. My act is pretty minimalist, but there are things that I've had to make for years. I used to just sit in front of the TV for hours, doing arts and crafts until my hands started feeling arthritic, yet I felt that paying these dues were necessary for my craft. This was the very definition of labor that could be outsourced, and my stubbornness was getting in the way of enjoying my life. As my wife pointed out, I could literally train a monkey to do the same thing in twenty minutes. Let's just say the incessant hammering of the stapler while watching our favorite show wasn't exactly an aphrodisiac . . . shocker! I had to recognize that there are people on Craigslist who are very driven, ambitious, and hardworking and who want to work from home with a minimum of interaction from a boss-type. This was the perfect task to off-load . . . even though I resisted for years.

Eventually, I realized I had to hand the wheel over to them, so I did so with the caveat, "Here's what I need you to make, following these exact specifications. I'm going to reward you handsomely if you do a great job." Even though it went against every fiber of my being, I outsourced the making of those materials to others. What I never expected was that delegating this seemingly little task would be such a weight off my shoulders. I had to get past the voice in my head that kept telling me, "Wait, are they going to do as good a job as me?"

Guess what? They did. Then all of a sudden, hours in my day opened up and I realized, "Wow, that was so worth it." It's no different than fighting against, say, hiring a landscaper to cut your grass, and then finally giving in and finding yourself with an expanse of weekend.

Consider areas in your own life that you could pare down. We hire other people all the time to do jobs for us, whether it's Rick the Roofer or Pat the Plumber. While it might sound like a luxury, what if you decided to take a taxi to the office instead of driving yourself? You would buy yourself half an hour of uninterrupted time to answer your emails, and start your day ahead of the game.

An issue that gets in the way of delegating can sometimes be that we think of things too transactionally. We think, *I'm going to do this for them, which means they're going to do this for me.* We see a clear and distinct correlation, that if I take my hand off the wheel, then my expectation is that all of these other things will happen when someone else is allowed to drive. While that's often the case, it's worth noting that some of the best things that ever happen to us aren't transactional, especially when we relinquish some control. When we trust others to fill our shoes, we're afforded all sorts of new freedoms. Let's say you're organizing a large-scale event and instead of micromanaging every detail, you decide to hand off the planning to a pro. Not only can they do a fantastic job, but also they add thoughtful touches you'd never have expected or thought of. Delegating often pays off in ways you can't foresee.

Not everything has to be transactional. This is why any time somebody reaches out for an autograph, I mail them one. I don't charge; I don't need a self-addressed stamped envelope. I figure if someone is a big enough fan of me that they want a headshot or an autograph or a signed playing card, they're going to get one. You'd think I get nothing from this, but you'd be wrong. Every request galvanizes me, fills my tank, gives me a boost on the days when I might need it the most.

When I was a teenager, I would attend magic lectures, which are kind of like social hangout for magicians. Yes, there are conferences and conventions, but people really connect in their local magic shops. For me, that shop was Wunderground Magic in Royal Oak, Michigan. They hosted lectures where they brought in professional magicians. Those of us in the audience had maybe read their books or watched some of their videos; here was the chance to meet them in person and learn some behind-the-scenes material. The fun part was that afterward, people would hang out and talk shop. As a kid who was just starting out in magic, it was amazing.

Being treated like an adult by people I was a huge fan of, even though I was a teenager, meant everything to me. I've seen people nowadays who, when they meet a YouTuber, will melt into tears because of the intimacy involved, like, "Oh my God, I've been watching your videos!" To you, they might seem like a superstar, even though other people have no idea who they are. But value is all in the eye of the beholder. Having those people treat me with respect, having them say, "Come on, we're all going out," and then getting to sit down with them almost as an equal and absorb their advice was a feeling I recall fondly to this day. There was nothing really in it for them, yet they included me anyway and that just blew me away. This was a defining point for me, and it colored my whole understanding of how I should interact and connect with people in my own career. The concepts of paying it forward and having a seat at the table have stayed with me.

Here's a story that I recall far more fondly than my folks do. One night, I went out with a group of magicians after a lecture. It was 1996 so I didn't have a cell phone and ended up staying out until 2:30 a.m.

because I wasn't paying attention to the time; I was just too enamored with the company. I was fourteen years old and had never done anything like this before.

By this point, my parents had banded together, searched the neighborhood, and filed a missing person report. They were driving to every diner that was still open. When they finally found me, knee-deep in card tricks, coffee cups, and cheeseburgers, their reaction was a combination of relief that I was still alive and wanting to kill me at the same time. I was just hanging out with a bunch of magicians on a school night and never even considered going home or the time. I was sitting with magician Gregory Wilson, who may as well have been Paul McCartney to me, hanging on his every word. My parents basically had to wrestle me into the car.

Because of that experience, I've always tried to re-create it for others. We'll talk more about paying it forward later in this chapter.

Build Your Team

Becoming your best self sometimes requires recognizing that you need a team. You cannot always go it alone. When it comes to long races, crew members help get you across the finish line when you no longer believe you can do it or are an absolute physical disaster. In the ultramarathon space, *crewing* is a verb. The crew are effectively personal assistants in every regard. They're there to check on the runner's nutrition, their hydration, what they're wearing, and to be their strength when things start going wrong.

My chief crew member is Ryan Dexter, nickname "Iceman." Less *Top Gun*, more literal: He constantly dowses me in ice during hot races, ha! I like to say he is a certified badass in his own right. The man has run 150-mile races galore. We met while running 2.4-mile loops around Lake Nokomis in Minnesota for twenty-four hours straight at a race called FANS (totally normal, right?). We lost touch for about a decade or so and then reconnected. He's as selfless and loyal as it gets, and I'm honored to call him a friend. Michael Halovatch is another great friend who has been with me through thick and thin, through vomiting and you don't even wanna know what else. When I've been ready to quit, he has tough-talked me out of it more times than I care to admit. Michael Arnstein is a legendary ultramarathoner, and we go way, way back to my very first ultramarathon. And last, but certainly not least, is Dustin Emrani. An elite collegiate 800-meter runner who's now a distance athlete, he's the ultimate hype man and could get a smile and laugh out of anyone. Needless to say, it takes a village.

The thing about the ultramarathon community is there's maybe five to ten people who care about winning at any given race. Everybody else out there is on a personal mission against themselves to simply finish the race or battle the clock. Let's say you're on the road and someone's hurting and they need food, the other runners will stop without a second thought and attend to you, "How are you doing, man, take these gels. Let's get you back." They might slow down with you for the next ten miles to make sure you make it. It's such a selfless enterprise. We're all in it together, as opposed to cyclists and some triathletes (not all) who behave like scumbags. (If you know, you know. Sorry! Not sorry.)

When you're in an ultramarathon, you're battling demons. You are going to push your body in ways that somebody who's run a marathon can't even fathom. In a 100-miler or longer, you may find yourself walking for twelve hours straight while in the throes of terrible pain, GI distress, or hallucinations. It's like you're bringing a knife to a gunfight. It's a different beast. And you can always talk tough when you're sitting on the couch, but when you're out there and you're in it, it's a trial by fire where you figure out who you really are at your core when all the layers are peeled away. In this case, you cannot fake it till you make it. You can't buy the achievement; you have to *earn* it, and that is what makes it so fulfilling.

Generally speaking, in most of those races, you don't know what's going to happen. I can train for months, yet fall apart by mile 27 and not understand why. When things start to go downhill, the key is to quickly begin problem-solving. You reverse engineer the same way I do in mentalism: *Why am I not feeling well? Is this my mind tricking me? Do I have low blood sugar?* For example, when you have low blood sugar, you don't have an indicator light that blinks Low on Fuel; instead, you begin having negative thoughts.

You feel tired, you feel miserable, and you start thinking, *I have to quit.* That is the moment you need your crew. In races, as in life, having a crew makes it better, especially when you can be there for them, too. When you're part of a group you can trust, your performance improves. This is directly linked to the production of oxytocin. For example, studies have shown that when people build social ties at work, it's almost like taking a performance-enhancing drug, likely because that's what oxytocin is.[4]

Take, for example, Badwater, nicknamed "the world's toughest footrace." It is a 135-mile run from the lowest point in the Western Hemisphere to the base of Mount Whitney, the highest point in the contiguous United States. Oh wait, did I forget this is in Death Valley, the hottest place on earth . . . in the middle of July! At the start of the race, the first year I participated, it was a brisk 124 degrees Fahrenheit, or 51 degrees Celsius, with no shade anywhere in sight. One section is a seventeen-mile uphill with gusting headwinds that make you feel as if you're inside a convection oven with a hair dryer pointing at your face. My crew would dunk me in ice water every few miles, and by the next time I would see them, yup, you guessed it, I'd be bone dry. My hair would be brittle. In this setting, your crew can be the difference between life and death and are there to ensure that the goals you went in with remain the top priority, because during peak suffering you might want to give up. While the players might change up depending on who is free to lean into supporting me in a particular race, my crew is always made up of fellow nutcases who have seen and been through it all. They know all my excuses. A good crew won't let you quit if there's anything left inside of you. They do not allow you to give up on yourself unless medically necessary.

Look at your own life right now. Who do you have to cheer you on? Who's always in your corner pulling for you? Who inspires you to just keep going? These people are your crew, and if they're doing this for you, make sure you're returning the favor. Studies have shown that having a good friend literally gets into your blood: It makes changes for the better to every aspect of your health, from blood pressure to stress response to your immune system.[5] Having people you can rely on has been found to be as important a factor in your long-term health as exercise and not smoking.[6]

For running, my crew is there to remind me that I am comfort-driven and that if I want to be great, I have to break out of that zone. My crew are people I know who are going to raise me up, elevate my game. (The same should apply to your crew, whether they're in your personal or professional life.) They make it so that I can't quit, because if I did, I couldn't look them in the eye. Midrace, crewing becomes a thankless endeavor for them as I transform into a whiny prima donna. We have a running joke that at some point, usually around a hundred miles, I start getting annoyed at them. I can't even tell you why. And when I see them, I'll say, "How about some proactive crewing?" And we'll laugh because we all know they're literally about to kill me. These guys have been up since 5:00 a.m. and were organizing stuff the night before. They have no time to themselves. They're stopping every two or three miles and lathering sunblock on my legs, touching me in places they don't want to be near. They're cleaning me up, giving me food.

In addition to the crew, there are pacers who play an equally, and at times even more, important role. They run parts of the race with you. When I ran from Montauk to Manhattan in a day, I publicized what I was doing on my Instagram. And a lot of people saw that story and spontaneously decided to tag along for part of the journey. One guy was going to run with us for ten miles. He ended up running thirty-five miles that night. Wow. He was intoxicated by the experience. He kept saying, "Dude, I can't stop. It's just such a rush!" When I did the Central Park run, I only did one loop out of the nineteen alone because so many people knew about it. I even sent my plans to my client mailing list. Hundreds of people who came out had seen me on TV, and they wanted to witness the run. They brought signs and cheered. (Did it feel just like that running scene in *Rocky II*? Yes. Yes, it did.) They didn't know it, but they were absolutely my crew as well. We fed off each other's energy and it made the time absolutely fly by.

I'm always looking for opportunities to return the favor, because I get something out of it, too—it fills my cup. I like being able to help kids starting out fast-track past some of the mistakes I made, both in the world of running and mentalism. This brings me to a serendipitous meeting when I was nineteen years old with two college kids who had just started a company called Penguin Magic. They're a big part of my history. At the time, they were running the company out of their apartment at the University of Michigan, right where I happened to be going to school.

Acar Altinsel and Maxwell Murphy were hired to make a website for some Winklevoss-type investors, and once they got into it, they thought, *Why the heck are we making this for them instead of ourselves? We're the ones with the talent.* It's crucial to note here that this was in the early 2000s, when everyone still had dial-up. Broadband was just starting and streaming video was not yet a real thing. You could download music, but not video, and it took an hour. So, what these guys did was a paradigm shift.

Back then, buying magic tricks required going to a magic store and having someone demo the trick one on one. You'd point to something in a glass case and say, "That one." The magician working behind the counter would sell you the trick, then take you into a back room and teach it to you. And then you'd take the trick home with you, which was generally a gimmick or a specialty item, like a silk scarf on an invisible retractable filament, or lifelike pistachio nuts that were magnetized.

What the Penguin Magic guys did was a totally new. They started making demo videos of tricks. Their store had thousands of tricks, and they began performing the tricks on video instead of having to teach them in person in the store. This gave them so much scalability. Plus, the instructional videos were far superior to just sending you home with paper instructions. That was a huge value-add and it became a game changer.

The service altered the magic industry in the way that Uber has changed how we get rides now. By pure luck, I found out there was a magic store in Ann Arbor, which was unbelievable to me because I went to school there. What were the odds? Even better, my girlfriend's friend knew the guy who owned the shop. So I went to meet them one night after doing a restaurant gig, when I was all dressed up. I performed three tricks and they said, "Oh my God, will you do demo videos for us?" They saw potential that I didn't even know I had.

There was no money at first; I was just making their videos because

I got to learn a bunch of tricks without paying for them. I had no idea that having learned these tricks would be so important to me a few years later. (Put a pin in this because we'll get to that story in another chapter.) I was basically just giving them a hand because I loved it.

Their business grew quickly and they ended up moving to Las Vegas and getting a big warehouse in Sacramento. We made several videos together on DVD. One of the DVDs is called *Born to Perform Card Magic*, starring yours truly. This DVD is the equivalent of Britney Spears's debut album in the late nineties, as it was the highest-selling card-magic instructional DVD ever. I was twenty-one at the time this video came out in 2002 and not kidding when I say that nearly every magician on the planet between the ages of thirteen and thirty-five bought this thing. Around that time, I toured in Asia and saw a street vendor selling bootleg copies of my video, dubbed in Mandarin. My first taste of global success!

The success of these videos allowed me to travel the world. On the back of this wide recognition, I was invited to lecture in over forty countries. Magicians everywhere would say to me, "You're Oz Pearlman from Penguin Magic!" To me, that was priceless. Funny story: My wife one day invited our neighbor Karen over with her boyfriend Mike, and as I opened the door to meet them, he exclaimed "Holy f'ing s***, you're Oz Pearlman!" Turns out, he was a closeted magic nerd and had grown up with my videos. (His girlfriend, now wife, found this out at the same time as we did and had a lot of questions.)

Years and years later, a friend of mine in Israel did a trick that felt vaguely familiar. So I went to Penguin Magic's website and bought the instant download instructional video, because I wanted to understand how he did it. What happened next was like a *Black Mirror* episode, as I found that I was the one teaching the trick to myself.

What I can't get over is my own foresight. I want to say I had a master plan, but I truly just stumbled into it. If I hadn't been so willing to lend a hand in those early days, I'd probably still be working in global technology infrastructure. So if you're on the fence about lending a hand, keep in mind you never know where it might take you.

Find a Mentor

Ask yourself where you want to be five to ten years from now. The best advice I can give you is to then seek out someone who has already achieved a similar goal. For me, that person was Bruce Kessler.

After my folks got divorced, my grandma came to live with us because my mom was struggling. My escape was to perform tricks all the time so I never had to deal with all the pain. I thought maybe I could just be the dancing clown to take my mom's mind off things.

One day, my grandmother and I were at a Borders bookstore and I was playing with cards, because I was *always* playing with cards, with coins, doing moves all the time. A man in his early thirties noticed my sleight of hand and asked my grandmother about my interest in magic. Her eyes lit up knowing how excited I would be to meet a fellow magician and especially one with so much experience. He'd even been professional for a while before he went back to working a day job.

At my grandmother's behest, Bruce became my mentor and a father figure. No, it was more than that—he became my champion, my shaman. He did more than show me how to do new tricks. He taught me the value of questioning my own preconceived notions, like when he convinced me to try sushi for the first time. He helped condition me to think differently, to shift out of autopilot, and I owe him so much because of it.

Again, I met him because of dumb luck. There was no internet in

1995 and I'd have never found him if I'd gone looking on my own, especially without my grandmother's help. Bruce opened my eyes to all these new ways of thinking, and that gave me a lot more confidence. He helped me to start thinking in a more mature manner and treated me like an adult.

Basically, Bruce was the guy to give me that much needed push out of my very narrow comfort zone, saying, "I'm going to show you some new stuff. Maybe you like it. Maybe you don't.

At the time, I was very into what's called "gimmicks" in the magic world, basically props or specialty single-use items that allowed you to do one amazing trick reliably, like a modified card deck. It was like I just wanted to take a pill and get the results, instead of doing the hard work of learning. Bruce was instrumental because he made me step back and look at the bigger picture. Did I want to be a guy who bought tricks, or did I want to be a performer? He explained to me that I couldn't do a show with gimmicks alone; instead, I would have to do the legwork of reading books and learning how to do dozens of tricks with a single deck. He helped me see that I needed to build a foundation of solid skills, making mistakes along the way, rather than just going for what was quick and flashy. His lessons have stayed with me my entire life.

As important as he was to me during my formative years, eventually we lost touch when I moved away to college. But I always felt in a unique, New Agey way that when the time was right, we would reconnect because so much of who I'd become happened under his watch. His is one of the only phone numbers I have memorized to this day. Years later, I finally called him. I hadn't talked to him in more than a decade, but I'd been on *America's Got Talent* and I wanted him to know how he helped me get there. And he was just so proud of me; it was very fulfilling.

Having a mentor is important for learning to read your own mind because we often need an editor. We need someone to look at what we're doing with a critical eye toward improvement, because we're often too close to whatever the subject is.

We always consider how important mentorship is professionally, but it's rare that we delve into the neuroscience behind mentorship. Yet it's equally significant. The mentor/mentee relationship can generate far-reaching impact and results. UCLA social neuroscience professor Matthew Lieberman sums it up this way: "Being socially connected is our brain's lifelong passion."[7] Mentors fulfill so many functions that impact how we think and feel and act, from role-modeling behaviors to helping mentees develop skills and realize their aspirations.[8]

The bottom line is that effective mentoring leads directly to structural changes in the brain, with tangible improvements in productivity and goal attainment.[9]

But if you don't have a caring Israeli grandma to help you find a mentor, I'll share some strategies for seeking one in the next section.

Mentoring Is a Verb

I have five to ten people whom I mentor on a regular basis. Not daily given our busy schedules, but I have a touchpoint with them every couple of months. I think of myself almost like a Jedi sharing his knowledge of the Force, which is so nerdy and cheesy, but in some ways oddly true. I'm there at the right moment for a lot of these people, and vice versa. And more than anything else, I provide guidance, but not as some all-knowing being. Instead, I tell them what they need to hear, and what I think deep down they already know. I'm ruthlessly honest. So when somebody says to me, "I want to get on TV," I'll challenge them as to what's stopping them and to list for me all that they've done so far. I don't give them the answers; rather, I want them to figure it out on their own because then it clicks, like teaching someone how to fish rather than just buying them a fish dinner.

What's great about mentoring is that mentees reinvigorate us. We get to feel like we're helping others, and they have an effervescence that's exciting, especially when we are further in our career and it becomes easy to be a little bit jaded. Even though I'm the mentor, my mentees still call me on my crap. I might be complaining, "Ugh, I've gotta fly here, I've gotta fly there, and I have TV shoots." Meanwhile, my mentee is looking at me like, "Take it easy with your caviar problems, I would kill for a tenth of this." It gives me perspective and reminds me to have gratitude. Mentoring people helps me remain humble and grounded.

So, if you need a mentor, how do you get one?

I wish that everyone who's made it would welcome being a mentor, but that is rarely the case. Persistence is the key to recruiting one, with the caveat that there is a thin line between being persistent and annoying. A lot of those who've made it don't want to help others because they feel like success is a zero-sum game, especially if they came up without a mentor. There's an attitude of, *Why do I need to tell you what I've learned when you didn't earn it?* While that's not easy to work around, it's not impossible.

A great way to find a mentor is to make yourself of value to them. Bring something to the table. For example, a fellow performer who had been emailing me off and on for years decided he wanted to find a way to help me. He reached out saying, "I see that some of your photos on your website are out of date," because he'd taken the time (that I did not have) to sit down and analyze my social media presence, and he came up with a plan to make it all current. Not only that, he said, "Hey, let me take these things off your plate for you." It was so helpful to me that I suddenly couldn't wait to repay the favor.

It's kind of like if you buy somebody a gift: They always have to say thank you. Most people express appreciation, and that's not just manners, that's a part of the science of persuasion, according to social psychologist Robert Levine. He cites the example of charities giving you a free pen along with a request for a donation, because people are far more likely to give back if they get something. Per Levine, "Most of us are usually driven by a sense of equity and fairness. When someone does something for us, we feel obligated to do something for them in return."[10]

Getting that thank you back provides another touchpoint and chance to further the relationship. If there's a way to be of service, find it.

In every single industry, even one as niche as mentalism, there are mentors. Unlike teachers, mentors serve more as long-term advisers. You can attract mentors by asking the questions they might not even be thinking of asking themselves, and doing so will open their eyes.

As someone hoping to connect with a mentor, ask yourself, *What can I do to add value for them? What do I have to offer them that will make their life easier? How can I make an impression and create a mutually beneficial relationship?* Never be afraid to take that step, to be too scared to reach out.

If you do get an initial no, remember not to be your own worst enemy. Let it go, regroup, and try again. Turn the mirror on them. They're probably busy, they probably have a lot going on. How do you make yourself valuable to them? The truth is, it can be something as silly as inflating their ego and giving them compliments. Even better is asking if there's something you can do for them—adding value. I've had people who actually said to me, "What can I do to help you? Is there anything? Do you have emails that you need to write? Is there something menial on your website, like updating your links?" You may think this seems obvious, but I assure you that the overwhelming majority of people do not go that extra mile. Even if they think to offer that extra support, they don't execute on the intention consistently. Be the outlier, have the thick skin, and know that success is a numbers game.

Brainstorm things that you can provide, especially if they're free. If you're starting out, your time is less valuable than theirs because you're earlier in your career; you're not as busy. So offer up your time, proffer something to that person they will find valuable. The key is that once you unlock value for them, they'll often see something in you that reminds them of themselves years ago when they were still coming up.

At our core, most of us are happy to give to others. So figure out who the person who can guide you is, ask them thoughtful questions, demonstrate your interest and commitment, and find a way to get through to them. Be useful.

We're so quick to overcomplicate things in our mind to avoid doing hard things, but if you commit and follow these steps, you'll learn how to take a hand, and eventually you'll be ready to give one.

As you progress, you'll realize that to grow, you have to let go of some control, but you don't have to go it alone. Find your crew. Ultimately, the difference between success and stagnation is going to boil down to give-and-take, so be ready to give. And of course, whenever possible, pay it forward.

NINE

Turn Your Weaknesses into Your Strengths

Like most people, I struggle with areas where I feel weak or not as confident. Honestly, I'd rather just double down on my strengths and allow weaknesses to atrophy. For example, I will do almost anything to avoid a confrontation. I wish I were kidding. My aversion to conflict is a true shortcoming, to the point of being an Achilles' heel. So, in this chapter, I'll start by explaining how this limitation left me sitting, well past midnight, on the floor of a Kurdish village home, trying to get paid after a disastrous gig I'd let my mother book for me. #NeverAgain.

But having a weakness should not be considered a character flaw or personal failing. Instead, I propose we consider your weak areas jumping-off points for improvement, which starts with being able to recognize where we're not as skilled. I'll detail how to assess where we may fall short.

For the longest time, my weakness was mentalism; I thought the practice was boring. There were no "moves," no flash, and very few props. Literally nothing up my sleeve. Plus, mentalism just didn't seem *fun.* Only once I worked with a mentor did I begin to understand where mentalism could take me, especially if I added in an emotional component and made it my own. By addressing the deficiency of not having an emotional hook, I changed my professional trajectory. Finding the discipline to pursue the uncomfortable is where growth begins—I know, I've lived it.

That's why I'm Oz the Mentalist and not just Oz the Magician.

From Magic to Mentalism

I hated mentalism as a teenager. But I loved *magic* and I used to practice sleight of hand moves with cards for twelve or more hours every day. Learning to control where each card was located in the deck, focusing my entire mind on the position of a finger during a split-second move, over and over *and over* again in front of a mirror. I had an attention to detail and an unwillingness to settle for anything less than perfection that bordered on the obsessive, but that's what was required to be a top-notch performer.

Practicing magic isn't any different than a soccer player learning to bounce a ball endlessly with their feet. They know how to place the ball in the corner of their neck, how to catch it on their head. Much like the way the player can control a ball, I can control cards. This also goes for coins, ropes, and close-up tricks, which involve random household items like rubber bands, matches, glasses, pretty much any common item you can think of. There are a few people who are the best in the world with each of these items. Silly as it may sound, I could list off the greatest rubber-band magicians in the world . . . yes, that is actually a real thing. They've dedicated their lives to magic with rubber bands, which sounds insane. They could probably do fifty rubber-band tricks for you in ten minutes. And you'd be blown away seeing them disappear, shrink, rip, restore, penetrate, and change colors.

Magicians have thousands and thousands of books written about their craft, the earliest of which date back more than ten centuries. It's fascinating how in-depth magic is, how far back it goes in history. Principles of magic have been around since way before Jesus Christ, and certain tricks can be traced back thousands of years.

I found this robust history and all the sleights associated with magic fascinating. In comparison, mentalism held little appeal and was far more limited in its literature, moves, and methods. And yet, now I perform mentalism for a living. I also hated running. And now I do it for pleasure and inspiration. Your weaknesses today can easily become your strengths tomorrow, but you must allow yourself to be open to those changes.

In both instances, I had mentors and people around me who opened my eyes to new possibilities. If you're interested in something that's not yet your forte, don't be scared to ask someone who knows what you're missing.

As for my getting into mentalism, it was a practical decision. When I finally made it onto *America's Got Talent* in 2015, I did a thorough assessment of how to best plan for this opportunity. Because it was a big opportunity indeed; a lot of people would see the show. I realized the scale and that I needed to make the absolute most of it.

So often, we try to swim against the tide, when we should just let the tide wash us along. Go with the flow if it pushes you in the direction you want to go. The key is to figure out what direction that is, so you know when to let the current take you. Just after I got married, I decided that what I really wanted was to be able to spend time with my wife. I didn't want to be gone every single Friday, Saturday, and Sunday, going from party to party. I planned to have a family, and being an absentee father every weekend wouldn't work long term.

When I got my big break with *AGT,* I thought that mentalism would parlay into booking more corporate events. From a material perspective, I knew these events could be very lucrative. Leaning into mentalism would give me options in other parts of my life. I decided to represent and brand myself accordingly when on the show, in every single instance, I'd be the guy wearing a suit and tie; I'd look clean-cut. I wanted my vibe to be different and to stand out from other mentalists, many of whom lean into an edgier, rockstar look. I was not going to put on guyliner and leather jackets. I wanted to be, for lack of a better term, square. I was squeaky clean when it came to both my image and the content of my act.

The year before, on *AGT,* a magician had won. He was a white guy in his late twenties. (Shout out to Mat Franco, who is amazing!) I was a white guy in his early thirties. We weren't different enough that people wouldn't do a head-to-head comparison of us. I didn't want to be compared or confused with someone else; I wanted to be distinct and unrivaled. To me, this was the chance to carve out my unique selling proposition: Either do something different than everyone else, or do something better than everyone else. Or thread the needle and do both! Those are your options. Because there are billions of people in the world and you must find a way to stand out. Carve out a little niche that makes you incomparable, different, or the best.

At that point, I was performing about 50 percent mentalism and 50 percent magic. The magic was a crutch that I leaned on to offset the fact that mentalism carries a much higher margin for error. It is far riskier in a lot of instances and there's simply no way to know if it's going to work every time. Hence the importance of learning to create backup plans, as I covered previously.

I made the decision to transition out of physical-trick-based magic even though it was an area where I was stronger at the time, which was frightening. While mentalism would set me apart from other contestants on the show, I was about to bet my career on it. But my plan worked: Mentalism made me stand out and took me much further in the competition. The audience perceived reading minds very differently from watching a magic trick, and mentalism captured their imaginations in a different way. Leaning into what was scary and embracing what wasn't my strength is how I was able to transcend the limits I saw around me.

While I'm not psychic, I can assure you that doing the same—taking stock of your weaknesses and letting them make you uncomfortable—will spur your ascent as well. If it was easy, everyone would be doing it already.

Lost in Translation

Whether I was practicing magic or mentalism, my mom was (and continues to be) my biggest fan and cheerleader. She's been there from the very beginning, encouraging me to practice and perform. Her belief in me instilled confidence when, quite frankly, there shouldn't have been much, starting with my early days as a restaurant magician and kid's-birthday-party specialist. I'm grateful for the pushes she gave me and also owe much of my sense of humor to her. Yet as my number one fan, she sometimes wants to push me out of my comfort zone, and from time to time, acquiescing to her push is to my detriment. The promises of "Don't worry, it will be great!" aren't always necessarily true.

For a lot of us, particularly the conflict-averse, it's hard to say no to family. In fact, there's a scientific reason why it's especially difficult to say no to someone like your mother. The reason has to do with "associative learning," which is shorthand for the way the central nervous system classifies and encodes a situation as being either safe or threatening. Obeying our mothers is hardwired into our neural circuits, basically because children need their parents in order to be able to survive.[1] So it's actually *science's* fault that I found myself agreeing to my mother's idea to perform in a Kurdish village.

Here's a quick history lesson if you're unfamiliar with the Kurds, like I was. The Kurds don't have their own state, as they are an indigenous people of the Mesopotamian plain and live across parts of Turkey, Syria, Iran, Iraq, and Armenia. While the Kurds have a united culture and language, there's no standard dialect or religion.[2] Put a pin in this fact, because it becomes important in a minute. The Kurds in *this* story—my mother's Kurds—happened to live in Israel, where they have their own religion. (FYI, they've been staunch US allies in the Middle East.) They serve in the military. They're not Jewish or Muslim, and again, they have their own language. They're a nomadic people, similar to Bedouins. Even up until recently, they'd travel in packs and not stay in one place. They're very unique in that they have their own little enclaves. Think of it like an SAT comparison—the Kurds are to the Middle East like the Amish are to America. If you hear about the Kurds, it's often in reference to how they've been oppressed. The Kurdish people in this story live outside of mainstream Israel. They're not integrated with the rest of society; they have their own insular communities. A Kurdish village is probably the last place on earth where an outsider would consider going to perform mentalism. That's where the plot thickens.

One of my mom's colleagues at her job is a big fan of mine, likely because she forwards him every single one of my videos. He was convinced that my show would be a tremendous success at his village, even though he'd never organized a similar event before and his primary occupation was making decorative glass plates at a factory.

As my mom explains all this to me, numerous alarm bells start going off in my head, but she insists I don't need to worry. Upon my mother's urging, I go to this village despite my many reservations. We're trying to negotiate my getting paid to do a show, and also the ins and outs of the fact that I perform primarily mentalism, not magic. Our glass blower/artisan turned promoter promises that this is going to be a huge hit and a major moneymaker for all of us. As we talk, he's telling me, "I run big events in this community." In my head, I'm like, *Do you?* My BS detector's going off like crazy, but my mom badgers me into trusting him.

The pin I said to hold about the language? That comes into play at the event. What I didn't know from the jump is that almost no one here speaks Hebrew or English. My show requires some sort of communication; in fact, communication is the cornerstone. I'm not Charlie Chaplin and can't do a silent act. My words are my medium.

When I arrive at the venue, it turns out my mom's coworker has oversold my appearance and there are dozens of people lined up outside, because they're already at capacity inside. This guy has chained the doors against those who are trying to get in, which also *chains in* those of us who are already here. All of these Kurds are running to different windows to try to watch me, and the guys inside are trying to cover the windows because they don't want the people who didn't pay to watch. While I'm under lock and key, trying to do a show for an audience who doesn't speak my language, other people keep running to different windows and banging on doors.

Total chaos.

I end up doing a trick called a "book test." It's kind of like a pick-a-card, where the audience member picks a card and I find it. Along those lines, a book test is where you open a book, select a word, and I figure out the word in your head. There are a hundred different versions and there are a hundred different methods, as this is a famous genre within the world of mentalism. Always smart to tilt the odds in your favor and be overprepared, so I've brought along books in both Hebrew and English.

Now, my Hebrew comprehension isn't the greatest. It's been a while since my bar mitzvah. I find somebody in the audience who says they speak English. In my head I think, *They don't sound like they speak English*, but they say they do. So I give them a book. I explain what we're going to do and I have them choose a word. Tricks like this are impressive because the mentalist builds tension, teases it out, piques anticipation. The mentalist doesn't have the volunteer just say the word; that's not entertaining. The audience wants to watch the process unfold, they want to feel that suspense, the back-and-forth. The act of anticipation releases dopamine and the effect is greater for experiences than it is for material possessions.[3] What I'm saying is, for the audience, the slow reveal of the information and build up is the whole crux of the trick.

I have the person in front of me and I say, "Look at me. I'm going to guess the first letter." I continue, "Good, are you thinking of the first letter? Shhh, keep it inside your head." And they're supposed to agree and say something like, "Yes, I have the letter," as we continue our dance. Instead, the audience member blurts out the whole word. No suspense, no anticipation, no dopamine, no bueno. So I try harder to get them to understand how we're going to perform this trick together, where they *do not say the quiet part out loud.*

I try this three more times, and essentially beg them, "Please, just *think* of the first letter. Do you have the first letter? Keep it quiet inside your head. Don't tell me. Don't say it out loud. Do you understand?" And then they nod and then they *say* the letter, instead of silently keeping it to themself. I try explaining again, "No, you don't tell me. I have to guess it." After I say that, they again say the whole word out loud, which is precisely the exact opposite of how the trick is supposed to unfold, and of the instructions I'd repeated ad nauseum. There's no magic. There's no awe. There's just a Kurdish guy spouting random words from a book in front of me; it's a nightmare. If this wasn't so cringeworthy, it would have been absolutely hilarious; I am literally the butt of the joke.

As a quick aside that applies to all of us: Whatever it is we endeavor to do, sometimes our efforts will go off the rails. I wrote earlier about how Gaffigan had a bad show in Puerto Rico, even though he's one of the greatest comedians of all time. You're going to have a bad presentation, a failed sales call, a biffed opportunity; it happens to all of us. Everyone has an off day. Part of tapping into your inner mentalist means accepting failure and moving forward anyway, especially because it wasn't the Kurds' fault that they'd never seen stage mentalism before and didn't understand the nuances.

In the case of this show, the only way out was through, so I kept doing my tricks until the bitter end, taking comfort in knowing that at some point it would be over. I'd like for you to picture the worst bombing you could ever imagine. Now multiply that utter and complete detonation by fifty, and then throw on the fact that there's still people shaking chained doors to try to get in because they sold too many tickets, and also people clawing at the windows. This is the level of crash and burn where my inner voice appears and starts questioning if maybe I chose the wrong path in life altogether; even knowing consciously that external factors are mostly to blame, I still can't get over how much of a failure I am at every moment. The loop playing over and over in my head is *Oh God, please let it be over soon. Get. Me. Outta. HERE!*

This is easily one of the top three worst shows of my life. My performance gets to the point where it turns from tragedy to comedy because it's so terrible, it's just funny. (Usually *comedy* = *tragedy* + *time*, but this was so tragic that it was immediately and painfully hilarious.) I'm trapped in an absurd situation and there's nothing I can do as I'm surrounded by Kurds yelling words because they're so excited to have been visited by a semi-famous American magician.

Mercifully, the event finally ends. I want nothing more than to hightail it out of there, but alas I still need to get paid. I didn't suffer like that for nothing. The check will take a bit of the sting out of the situation.

Instead of presenting me with an envelope at the end, we have to go to the promoter's home to pick up my compensation. He lives in a house with all of his family, including cousins, grandparents, etc. There's easily thirty people under this one roof. The village isn't what I'd consider archaic, because they have satellite dishes, so it's not something rustic you might envision in the middle of the Sahara. Basically, they're exactly what I saw in the movie *Zero Dark Thirty* when SEAL Team Six killed bin Laden, which is really not the scene I want to have at the top of my mind while I'm here.

There are rugs covering the entire floor. I enter and take off my shoes, as custom would dictate, then sit on one of the rugs. They warm tea and coffee over an open fire and we all just sit there. I know that culturally, it is not appropriate to start our interactions by talking business. You have to park yourself with your host for an extended stay, drink coffee, eat—there's a rhythm. I could sense there was a courting process I was unaware of and, honestly, had no patience for. I mean, I'm a New Yorker. I'm like, "Lemme get the money. Lemme get out of here. I want to be gone. I'm flop-sweating. This is one of the worst experiences of my life. Just let me go." And my mom's there, getting nervous, yet still trusting that it would all work out. She's from a small town, where life has a slower pace, so she doesn't have my frenetic NYC energy. As we wait, everyone's talking but we don't know what they're saying. They're making us cool our heels and we're trying to be polite.

The whole scene drags on and on. As I sit cross-legged on the floor and pretend to sip my cup of tea, I'm realizing more and more that this guy has never done this before. He's not a promoter. He just works at my mom's company, heard that I could do mentalism, and he started getting big ideas. When I've been there for nearly an hour and exhausted all my compliments about the tea and the rugs, I can tell that this situation is getting tense, because things are starting to feel weird between my host and his pseudo partners in this endeavor—maybe they're his family members? I keep shooting looks to my mother, who got me into this mess. *When can we go? Do we just leave? Are they not going to pay us?* I don't want to be rude or aggressive because there's so many of them. But there's a distinct undercurrent that *something* is going on and I don't know how to proceed.

The powers that be in the compound end up negotiating me down to a third of what was supposed to be paid, and the night cost me hours and hours of my time and a good deal of my sanity. And while I adamantly swore to myself, "Never again," I do wonder if, should the circumstances ever arise again, I could be sucked in once more, because it's science's fault that I struggle to say no to my mother. Having built a career on pleasing people, I find it especially challenging to disappoint anyone, especially those to whom I'm closest.

Let's learn from my mistakes—by determining where we're weak before we end up falling into our own trap—so we can grow stronger.

Half the Battle

Let's first acknowledge that wanting to address our weaknesses is not our default setting. Like me with my conflict avoidance. Due to the fact that I hate drama, I will often give people a pass and forgive them when they've wronged me, even knowing that leaving things unaddressed only makes it more likely that the situation will repeat itself. This is the people pleaser in me; I'm like most performers and seek approval from my audiences. So many of us are guilty of the "If it's not broke, don't fix it" mindset. (Or, "If it's broken, any fix will do.") But that doesn't work for us, nor should it, largely because denial is unhealthy.

A funny example that I see all the time is on TikTok, people post videos how the guy next to them is hogging the armrest on an airplane, or manspreading into their limited leg room. But why is it that the person being crowded is much more likely to remain uncomfortable and post a shot of some stranger's kneecap on social media, rather than just politely saying, "Excuse me. Could you please give me some space?" and reclaiming their personal space?

Like me, maybe one of your weaknesses is not speaking up for yourself, which is a first cousin to conflict avoidance. This is common and there's a reason for it: Our avoidance stems from fear of rejection. Rejection hurts because it triggers the same neural pathways that are activated when we experience physical pain.[4] In a 2021 study conducted by Crucial Learning, a Utah-based performance and leadership training company, out of 1,300 people surveyed, 74 percent of them feared speaking out about social and political issues.[5] Whoa. So, if you struggle to make your opinion heard, you're in the majority. But when you suppress your emotions, it costs you. If your weakness is not speaking out, it can impair your incidental memory, which means what your brain picks up and stores without effort, as well as increase your cardiovascular activation, which is when your heart and blood vessels have to work harder to move blood through your body.[6]

If you want to, say, advocate for yourself, you have to acknowledge that an issue exists in the first place. And that holds true for whatever you consider to be your weakness. I'm actively working on this skill myself. Especially in business, I'm willing to allow people the benefit of the doubt. I always see the positive. I'm the first to say, "You know what, it's fine, I'll just do this guy a favor," and my manager will get mad at me and remind me, "He's treating you like crap; look at this example and that one. He hasn't earned the passes you keep giving."

A lot of us know where we can improve. So, congratulations—knowing is half the battle. In this case, even trying for slight growth or awareness is better than doing nothing. For example, I'm very controlling in certain elements of my business. Because my need to control things is a weakness—exerting control doesn't always benefit me and often works to my detriment—for years I did not take on a bigger team. I was not willing to let in people who would give me synergies and assistance, who would take a lot of meaningless busywork off my plate. I'm not even talking about big things. I mean emails, administrative stuff, back-office things. I kept that work all to myself for years. I didn't even farm out the manufacture of my props, even though I was earning enough. My old habits were so deeply engrained and I secretly enjoyed the monotony and the light suffering involved. It felt important to me to do the grunt work myself, as though it would keep me grounded. Ultimately, this was a great example of not reading my own mind.

But to level up the caliber of gigs and compensation I was working, I needed to free up time, and I had to recognize that my need for control was holding me back. I had to come to terms with the notion that spending money would make me more money, or that by taking a task off my plate, I'd get more hours in my day. Hell, I'd get more out of my life.

I had to learn to switch to quality in lieu of quantity for my gigs. My time is finite, so I must maximize it by charging accordingly. When I found that I was getting a yes for every booking, I realized that I was undercharging for my service. There's an inflection point when you finally ask for enough that they say no; it took a lot of trial and error to properly price myself. With quality over quantity, I've freed up more time to be in service of bigger things—like finding ways to get on television so tens of millions of people can see me and potentially book me.

Think about what your hours are worth. Not just in terms of dollars and cents, but bigger picture. What are the losses and costs to you—are they greater than if you actually did something about them? What can you do creatively if you're freed up? Personally, I thought, *What's it worth for me on a weekend to not look at my phone for four hours? And just play with my kids and swim in the pool and be fully checked out?* Not everything can be quantified, nor should it be. A lot of things have their own unique value that's even more important than money. You've only got one life to live.

Seek Out Discomfort

It's not enough just to be able to identify where you're not proficient. If you want to spur true growth, you must have the discipline to pursue what feels uncomfortable. I don't even mean addressing your flaws or your annoying traits, because everyone has those. I want you to look at bigger-picture things that make you uncomfortable, situations or instances that might keep you from living your "best life." Find those changes that might induce panic now, but long term will enable you to level up. The only way for me to grow in my profession was to get a better team around me, to let go of control; figuring out how to do that was profoundly uncomfortable.

The thing about discomfort is that if we can view it as part of our learning process—instead of regarding it as something to avoid—we experience more positive emotions, better motivation, and expanded growth, according to a study by researchers at Cornell and The University of Chicago.[7]

Let's fold my ultramarathons into this point about forcing discomfort. For example, I like to give myself rewards, especially when it comes to eating, because I run so much that I feel as though I am allowed to overindulge. But Mother Nature and metabolism can catch up with anyone and I'm guilty just as much as the next guy of letting loose, especially over the summer. So that means when I commit to the next race, I also commit to facing my weakness, and that's when I decide, *Hey, I'm on health lockdown for the next three months.* And so, I'll create my own zero tolerance policy on X, Y, Z.

Guess what? The first two weeks are abject misery. They're just torture, as I get used to this new routine that I hate and that I rebel against. But I keep going. I make myself sit with the discomfort. Part of overcoming means you have to make it through that beginning portion; that's the hardest part because you don't yet have momentum.

Then the amazing part is when I get used to my new rules and I begin to love the new spaces they're opening; I might love how I feel, or love my improved performance. The better habits become a lifestyle and soon the rewards start happening. I'm fitter. I'm running faster. I feel like a fine-tuned machine without the sugar and the grease clogging the works. And there's something to be said for being able to go to bed and quickly fall asleep because I haven't gorged myself. Without the crutch of bad habits, I find other ways to reach fulfillment, and the discipline of the new routine becomes its own driver, *even though it's not comfortable.*

I wouldn't know what to do if I landed in a new city for a gig and I couldn't go running once I'm there. Ironically, *that's* a weakness. I like to avoid certain busywork. I don't want to do boring stuff on the computer.

I don't want to write emails, so I will instead procrastinate by running twenty miles, which to the normal person sounds insane, but to me, it's an escape. In fact, I've done everything possible to avoid writing these very words you are reading right now! You hold in your hands certifiable proof that you can achieve your goals when you set your mind to them.

It sounds like an oxymoron, but to get comfortable being uncomfortable, you have to do it consistently. And that is often what burns out those who try to embrace a pursuit they don't enjoy. If you're just faking your way through something, it won't work long term. If you hate running, good luck running regularly. If you hate math, getting your accounting degree will be torture. So instead, you either have to love what you set your mind to or break through those inner limitations. I think you can do that with a lot of pursuits. You can find a way to love something that makes you uncomfortable if you can show yourself how the discomfort makes you better.

Be advised, your success will make other people feel insecure. I get this all the time with my running. I hear, "Oz, you're destroying your knees, you're doing this, you're doing that." When you take up self-improvement, when you decide you want more, when you really tap into the full power of your mind, you're going to have many haters and naysayers. There will be people around you who want to drag you down, who can't do what you're doing. Instead of saying to you, "This is amazing!" they'll give you all the reasons why you shouldn't be exceeding their expectations. You'll hear a lot of warnings from people, not because they're actually concerned, but because they're projecting their own issues and their own insecurities onto you. That's *their* self-defense mechanism that they employ because they can't handle their own feelings.

Use their negativity to spur yourself on.

Those haters, along with the people around you who might not necessarily like what you're doing, can be incredible motivation. Know that it takes a unique person to continue pushing and to change for the better, and that I believe in you. Quitting is the easiest thing in the world. Many people will casually diminish my profession saying to me, "Yeah, I had a magic set when I was a kid." And I'll think, "I did, too. So what's different between us?"

Think about this when someone challenges you on whatever your self-improvement entails as you address your weakness, whether it's training for a race, traveling across the country solo, deciding to enroll in law school at fifty, whatever. Why is it that you're somehow doing this and they're not? Why are you able to push on?

Spoiler alert: It's because you're willing to sit with discomfort.

Look at movie stars. Why are there so few of them? In part, because there's no playbook for it. Many actors carved their own path toward movie stardom, which is what I did with mentalism. If you could just go to school for four years, graduate, and say, "I have a bachelor's degree in movie star," there'd be a heck of a lot more of them. Right? So there are paths that you can carve out for yourself if you're willing to put in the work, to live with being challenged. The world has changed from previous generations and there are less surefire road maps for success. Our grandparents could graduate from high school and get a manufacturing job that allowed them to buy a home, raise a family, and send the next generation to college. With our parents, the college degree was the ticket to a limitless future. But the rules are different now and there are no more guarantees, so it's more important than ever to plot your own path.

Back to the movie star example: I believe the public admires movie stars because they understand that becoming a star is not like becoming a doctor. Mind you, a doctor is a much more important role in civilization than being a movie star . . . or, let's be honest, a mentalist. But I'll never forget when a physician called me to work a party and he found out how much I charge. He said, "That's more than I make." And I said, "It's classic Economics 101 . . . look how many doctors there are in New York City. Now, look how many magicians there are. There's a thousand of you for every one of me. Supply and demand!" He laughed; he wasn't even offended. He goes, "Oh my God, you're right. I'm getting my kid to be a magician!"

Is it easy to remain uncomfortable? Of course not. Complicating matters is the fact that the neural circuits that are responsible for self-control can buckle under stress and cause our primal impulses to go unchecked. If I have a bad day or a lousy gig while I'm training for an ultramarathon, my impulses to self-soothe kick in and I'll want to inhale a pint of Häagen-Dazs. Everybody has the same stumbling blocks: No one wants to be seen as failing, no one wants to be embarrassed, and our default setting is to get rid of things that make us uncomfortable. But the more you fight that urge, the better off you'll be.

A while back, I read a study about tennis legends. Arguably the greatest tennis player of all time is Roger Federer. He's won 80 percent of his matches. What's interesting is, in looking at the points he won in each match, you might assume that he'd also won approximately 80 percent of all the points. In the lifetime of his career, however, his percentage of points won was only 54. *That means he lost 46 percent of all points.*

To me, this is a wild data point to fully absorb because it means that you don't need to be successful *every* time. Instead, it means *you'll win if you're successful most of the time.* (It is even more pronounced in baseball, if you only succeed at the plate three times in ten, you're likely headed to the Hall of Fame.) And "successful most of the time" doesn't have to be 90 percent or 80 percent. If you're willing to keep going and going and going, your persistence at putting yourself in a situation that's uncomfortable is what's going to get you to those record wins. Federer is the perfect example of someone who has mastered his mental game and leveraged the razor-thin margins that separate the GOAT from the thousands before him that never won a single tournament.

Know that you don't have to get it right every time, so that you'll be game to try again. I mean, even the best don't come out on top every time. And they are comfortable with that fact.

Life Is a Team Sport

You can feel weak in what you're trying to accomplish when you don't have a lot of mutually beneficial relationships. You have to let people in; you're not meant to do it all on your own. Remember, almost everything in life requires some degree of teamwork, whether at work or at home, so my last piece of advice is to improve your relationships if you want to work on your weaknesses.

What I mean is, find a way to help those who help you. Create your own posse if you don't have one, where everyone assists with the heavy lifting. And be actively thoughtful, whether it's giving those who've helped you little gifts, sending thoughtful thank-you cards, or making that extra effort. Always acknowledge. When you do that, people reciprocate. I love it when I go on a podcast and the host says, "Oz, you killed it for us! Thank you. Now, what can we do for you?" I always reply, "Wow. I don't know. Let me think about it. Maybe nothing. But even just saying that helped me." Try it on for size . . . make it a mission this week to ask at least one or two people that you interact with if you can do anything for them or help them. It is so rare that someone asks that question that I guarantee there will be a light look of surprise on their face.

We often default to being self-contained because it feels safer to construct a cocoon around ourselves. So when you actively show other people who you are, it sets you apart, even though it can be scary. We live in a world where so many people feel like they're disposable and unappreciated. We're in a gig economy, where you can get anything, anywhere, anytime, very quickly at your fingertips, so what others do often doesn't feel valued. You can foster strength by taking the time to improve your relationships. Maintain networks over time, check in with people in your orbit regularly. That's been a secret to my success—regular check-ins.

Everyone's got a busy life, no one's ignoring you on purpose. Let others know you exist. Do this in a way that will add value to their life, be it via a dose of joy, a hit of dopamine, or some useful info. Anytime I write a newsletter, I want it to be something that would genuinely appeal to whoever's reading it. And I don't care if that means leaning into the lowest common denominator, like memes about cute puppies. In my newsletter to friends and clients, I'm a proud dad, a proud husband. I want to include my family here, as I leave them off my social media. What's funny is that I get more responses based on my kids and my running than I do about mentalism, probably because those areas of my life are the most genuine, and by sharing I let people know I'm a "real" person. It's like, "Hey, he's not just this guy who did these tricks at our national sales conference. He's got a real life, he's a fully formed person." What I do looks seamless and effortless, so when I allow others to witness something that I'm really putting effort in on or that I'm struggling with, it's humanizing. (Like when I had four kids with norovirus at the same time. Ugh, don't ask!)

Nothing, even in the most singular solo pursuits, happens in a vacuum. Life is a team sport and how we interact with others makes a huge difference. My career took off when I allowed myself to open up to others and to create mutually beneficial relationships, because acknowledging your community is the final piece of the puzzle.

Remember, recognizing an area where you're weak is an opportunity for growth and improvement. Even though addressing this area may be difficult and will almost certainly feel uncomfortable, you have no idea the kind of doors you will open for yourself by sitting in that discomfort. If I hadn't actively pursued things outside of my comfort zone, my life would be very different right now. I might be chained to limited ideas that kept me from being home, unable to spend the kind of time I want with my wife and children.

When you put effort into maintaining relationships and enhancing your network, there's no reason your weaknesses can't ultimately become your strongest attributes. Plus, you'll likely avoid being roped into performing for an audience that will never "get" your work. That fact alone is worth whatever the cost may be.

TEN

Make Memory Your Superpower

We've all lived this dreadful moment: You just introduced yourself to someone and vice versa when—Poof!—their name disappears out of your head like a rabbit from a top hat. That little slip is not only embarrassing, but it can also cost you personally and professionally.

The good news is that your memory can be trained just like a muscle, and even a few minutes of "working out" will yield major rewards. What's funny is that most of us, when asked, will say our memories are not that good. But in reality, it's not an issue of memory but rather of poor imprinting. You never knew the information in the first place. In most instances, the problem is related more to poor listening than to poor recall. In this chapter I will walk you through some tricks of the trade on how to train your memory. I'll teach you to turn information into an anchor in your brain so that it sticks, using the techniques and exercises I teach at corporate team-building seminars.

People assume my memory is ironclad, but that is honestly not the case. Instead, I have a variety of strategies up my sleeve. Some I already revealed in an earlier section, which includes writing everything down and taking meticulous notes. I take notes on what people tell me and what I do at every show; that way, if I see those same folks in a few months, or even a few years, I'll be able to review what I wrote and get credit for having incredible recall. While being this diligent takes a little extra effort, doing so pays dividends in the long run. What's so great about not forgetting info is that the longer you hold on to information, the more valuable it becomes.

When taking notes is not an option, there are other tools and tricks I use to anchor information; I will reveal them to you, so that you, too, will get credit for having an amazing memory. It is easier than you think!

So, let's learn how to be unforgettable.

Practice Makes Perfect

Your memory is essentially a muscle, meaning it can be coached and trained to be more effective. Consider this: Unless we're injured or ill, almost all of us have the strength to do a set of bicep curls with a one-pound weight. But successfully curling a twenty-five-pound weight for multiple reps could take some training first. And that's exactly what we're going to do with your memory; we're going to give it a solid work-out, to feel the burn. Right now, your memory might not be jacked enough to remember fifty names in a room, but remembering one name, two names, or even three names is something every single one of us can do. So let's build on that by first breaking down how memory works.

Memories are not movie flashbacks. They are not perfect recordings nor are they complete records. Information can be misremembered and falsified by oneself or others. Or by oneself *and* others, when you consider the Mandela Effect, which is when a group of people collectively misremembers an event or piece of pop culture. For example, many of us recall Tom Hanks's character Forrest Gump saying, "Life is like a box of chocolates," when what he actually said is, "Life *was* like a box of chocolates." The term *Mandela Effect* was first used by Fiona Broome when speaking with others about remembering Nelson Mandela dying in prison in the 1980s, and learning that she wasn't the only one who had that memory . . . which is strange, considering that he didn't pass until 2013.[1]

This example demonstrates that memories are extremely fragile. On top of that, it takes a lot of energy to remember something, so your brain wants to forget, filtering out whatever it doesn't consider necessary to conserve energy—and that is most things.

Memories are made every time you experience a new sensory activity, because this action forges a connection between your brain's neurons. These connections are called synapses. Synapses are already present, but they're reinforced when, say, you learn a better but more confusing way to come home from the store. The more you travel that new route, the more you remember the directions and the less confusing it becomes, until you can forget even taking it because you are thinking about something else. The good news is, your capacity to remember is practically unlimited, as your brain has eighty-six billion neurons.[2]

In the 1970s, Eric Kandel, a professor of biophysics at Columbia University, established that changes in the chemical signals between neurons are the biological basis for what makes a memory.[3] Kandel, who won a Nobel Prize for this discovery, went on to explain that the strength of a memory has to do with how often it's revisited and repeated. The more you revisit a memory, the stronger it imprints.

What's interesting is that our brains give precedence to certain memories. According to Ilker Yildirim, an assistant professor of psychology at Yale, "The mind prioritizes remembering things that it is not able to explain very well. If a scene is predictable, and not surprising, it might be ignored."[4] This goes back to my point in an earlier chapter about the complexity of slipping into autopilot, which is why you're less likely to recall an uneventful drive home from work versus when you've made the same trip in a raging snowstorm. If you're in a learning environment, note that your brain also prioritizes information you study first (called the "primacy effect") as well as what's been most recently studied (called the "recency effect").[5]

If you want to maximize your potential for preventing memory loss, understand that an active mind now will help stave off memory loss later. You've got to keep your brain busy and engaged. Researchers at Harvard University found that, in a study of participants with mild cognitive impairment, those who did crossword puzzles improved their cognition by a couple of points.[6] This is because crosswords are shown to connect short-term working memory with long-term permanent memory.[7]

While gaining a couple of points can sound paltry, this is the same amount of improvement they'd have seen from an FDA-approved memory-enhancing medication. So even a small increase is quite significant.

I also recommend practicing meditation because it's linked to increasing cortical thickness in the brain, which decreases as we age. This is important because cortical thickness is linked to intelligence, meaning a thicker cortex means stronger brain function. Cortex thickness directly impacts our cognitive abilities, like problem-solving, memory, attention, and coming up with a snappy retort on the spot, instead of hours later when it doesn't count. And another benefit is that meditation can reduce ruminative thinking—meaning when your brain gets stuck on repeat, amplifying negative thoughts again and again—which can improve the way we process our emotions.[8] So, with meditation, you can structurally alter the neuroplasticity of the brain, meaning you'll create growth in the hippocampus, which basically impacts your memory capacity.[9]

We want to make your memory your superpower, and adopting healthier habits will give you that running start.

What's in a Name?

Is there anything worse than forgetting someone's name, especially mere seconds after you just met them? How mortifying is that? Say goodbye to that feeling because I have a virtually foolproof technique to prevent this from happening to you again. Here's the kicker, though, you likely aren't forgetting their name . . . you never actually *knew* it in the first place! Memory has very little to do with it, rather this is a listening issue.

Last year, I presented at a high-profile conference, speaking alongside Netflix cofounder Reed Hastings, Katie Couric, and Paris Hilton. I gave a workshop right before the main event and had twenty-three students in my breakout session. The plan was not only to amaze them with some mentalism, but also to show them the power of their own minds and how to supercharge their memories. I would tell each of them their names and what company they worked for as a fun and fast demonstration.

Again, lest you believe I have a photographic memory or supernatural powers, I can assure you that I do not. In fact, if you ask my wife how often I forget things around the house, she will have a field day on that topic!

So, as each person walked in the room, I asked them to please remove their name badges and place them into their pockets, which right away received a quizzical expression suggesting, "What in the world is this guy about to do?" Once everyone was seated, I did a quick, secret head count, because I wanted to make sure that if extra people had come in, I could account for them. I'm so glad I knew to do this, because two extra women came in who looked an awful lot like each other, and I'd have been so embarrassed if I got it wrong. I then proceeded to go around the room and rattle off each of their names. Ever the showman, it wasn't enough to simply say their names, but I also added in the various companies they each worked for and some brand-specific jokes, too. Like, I said, "Sara, she works for Campari. Doesn't matter if I have an Aperol Spritz or a Negroni later tonight; either way, you're happy, right?" and everyone laughed.

As we got down to the last guy, I feigned panic like I couldn't recall his name, and I said, "Oh no, give me a second." Then I paused before saying, "How many of you have had this exact same feeling when you're at a party, or even at a work event, and you literally just met someone three seconds ago? And you think, *Uh-oh, what is their name? What did they just say?* Now you're sweating and your heart is pounding. You can't hear anything they're saying, because all you're focused on is, *What is their name, damn it?* Not knowing is completely consuming you. It's like you're stuck in quicksand up to your knees and sinking fast. You have this awkward interaction where you're trying to find a way to find out, because you're too embarrassed to ask them their name again. Your eyes scour the room side to side hoping and praying you find someone you know to bring over and casually say, 'Oh, do you guys know each other?' and then pray to the Lord above that they spill the beans as they introduce themselves, and a flood of relief washes over you. Heaven help you if they say, 'Yes, we know each other, great to see you again.' You're too panicked to even be mad at yourself for such an unnecessary stressor. So, how would that feel?"

Consensus? Everyone agreed they'd feel pretty bad.

Then, to the guy whose name I "forgot," I said, "I bet that doesn't feel so great for you right now, Russell, does it? But I know who you are, Russell. I would never forget you. I want you on my good side, because you work for Live Nation." He sat last, and the whole thing brought down the house, and that's how I opened up the session.

Nobody wants memory tools that will take days, weeks, or years to figure out. If you hear a name, you want to know *now* how to recall it. Like with that group, I want to teach you some tips and tricks that you can master in ten minutes and still be using *ten years* from now. Because forgetting someone's name isn't just embarrassing; it's potentially damaging. In fact, researchers at Scotland's University of Aberdeen found that forgetting someone else's name can "create a downward spiral in which forgetting undermines investment in [that] relationship."[10]

The group I'd been addressing at the conference that day were all chief marketing officers, so I wanted to use an example they could relate to. I said to them, "Everyone in the world has used shampoo, and it's a marketer's dream, because the instructions are simply three words. How can anyone get confused, much less forget those three simple words: *lather, rinse, repeat*. The repeat doesn't even matter, but Pantene needs to sell some more product so best believe they want you to repeat. Say it to yourself, *lather, rinse, repeat*, and now say it again, and again. Repetition is our friend; it imprints info on our mind. We're going to repurpose that three-word catchphrase into the following—Listen, Repeat, Reply—and you'll never again forget the name of someone you just met!"

As a quick aside, not long ago, I had the opportunity to meet and perform for Barack Obama. I've never encountered somebody in my whole life who locks in better than he does. I watched him do a meet and greet for forty-five minutes, and with every single person that he spoke to, he acted like nobody else was in the room, even though people were circling him like a frenzy of sharks. Everyone in his peripheral vision was waiting for their chance to come over, but he did not look around. He did not do that rushing thing—you know, where you're talking to somebody but they're looking over their shoulder for who's next. He didn't do that at all. If he committed thirty, forty-five, or sixty seconds to you, you had his full attention. For him, that brief exchange was just a Tuesday at 8:07 p.m. But for everyone in attendance—myself included—those forty-five seconds are most likely ones that they will remember vividly and talk about for the rest of their lives. (No, I did not use my minute to ask if he'd gotten his paper-cutout silhouette from Sir Richard Branson, if you're curious.)

When Obama meets you, he knows that the time he's giving you is valuable. When he shakes your hand, he looks you right in the eye. He focuses on you. He looks into *you*, not just into your eyes. And he's somebody who's met countless numbers of people. What I'm describing him doing is a trick that so few people know . . . it's called "listening." Most of us don't really do it.

What I want you to do, when you listen to another person, is to turn your mind off and truly *hear*. Easier said than done, as our mind rarely likes to be quiet. Instead, a hundred different thoughts could race through it, such as, *What am I about to say next? Oh my God. Who is this person? Do I know them?* But I want you to make your mind completely blank. I'm talking complete attention. We are going to *actively listen.*

When you go up to someone, tell yourself right now to do nothing but tune into them as they introduce themselves. I don't mean tune in with your ears, I mean with every part of your brain; tune out your thoughts and truly hear the words that they say. And when they say their name, repeat it back to them immediately. Always repeat it. You should say, "Ashley, oh, I love that. Do you spell it *A-S-H-L-E-Y*, the traditional spelling? Yes? Great!" We'll call this technique "Listen, Repeat, Reply." Tear a page out of my playbook and pause right now: Quiet your mind and say it out loud three times: "Listen, Repeat, Reply; Listen, Repeat, Reply; LISTEN, REPEAT, REPLY." *Listen* means you make your mind a blank. Doing so will exponentially increase your chances of remembering the name, especially if you follow up your attentive moment by repeating their name.

Here's a great visual metaphor: Let's say I gave you a stick and told you to go to the beach, to the damp sand right at the shoreline. When the water recedes from a wave, quickly write your name. If you do that one time and a wave comes by, it will probably sweep away the writing and there'd be nothing left. But if you take that stick and write your name, and then go over each letter a few more times, really pressing down with all your might, it will make a far deeper impression. Now it will take many waves to wash it away completely and leave no trace.

Brain science reveals that repetition solidifies memory because it leads to more stable representations in the cortex, meaning repetition shifts information from short-term to long-term memory.[11] The more times you can carve that person's name into your mind, the less chance there is that it will get washed away by the tide. You will retain that information, I promise you. And you don't need to retain it for life, but if you can retain it for the next minute, three minutes, five minutes, then you'll avoid embarrassment, especially if you have a profession or a social life that involves meeting new people. And don't most of us experience those situations? They might not be daily occurrences, and if they're not, you've got all the more time to practice.

We've covered *listen* and *repeat.* As for *reply*, my advice falls into three different categories. The first one is spelling the name back to the person you've just met. Simply put, make sure that you are spelling it correctly. Next, comment on the spelling. "Is that *Brian* with a *y* or an *i*?"

No matter the answer, I say, "Yes, that's the best way to spell it for sure." If their name has a very obvious spelling such as *Bob* or *Bill*, then I say, "I assume *Bill* is shortened from *William*, is that right? But you go by *Bill*?" Another way to comment on someone's name is to pay them a compliment; everyone loves to be flattered. So when you reply, use their name in a compliment, and say something like, "Brian, I love those glasses. I'm just so curious, Brian, where did you get those?" You say their name again with the glasses. Now you think, *Brian with the cool glasses.* This gives you a psychological hook, an imprint that links someone's name to how they look to you. Remember, our brains retain the thing that's different. Think about if you meet somebody with one side of their head shaved and the other side is dyed blue. When they tell you their name, you're likely to remember that person far more than attendees dressed in khakis and Patagonia vests who look like your cookie-cutter hedge fund managers. Finally, make a personal connection if there is one, or you're welcome to lie and make one up as long as you won't get caught later. Choose wisely in this case! For example, after meeting Brian, you could say, "Oh how funny, my cousin is married to a Brian!" Now is my cousin really married to a man named Brian? Absolutely not, I'm a total liar, but guess what? I also won't forget that name now.

If instead of trying to just remember someone's name, you need to remember a list of things, you can build a memory palace, a technique used in literature by the character Sherlock Holmes. To create your own memory palace, you first visualize a familiar space—it can be any place you go to or have been frequently—your childhood home, your office, or your favorite coffee shop. Then determine a course of travel through that place. In the example of your childhood home, maybe you enter through the living room, then walk through the dining room, kitchen, and family room to get to the back porch.

Once you have your place and your route mapped out, determine what it is you want to remember—say, the periodic table—and place each element along the way. If you start with hydrogen, you can picture a hydrogen-powered rocket ship on the sofa next to the front door, and then for lithium, a pack of batteries on the table. These can be found next to a salt shaker for sodium and a banana for potassium. You'll have to be creative for the more difficult elements, but maybe next you can use a mnemonic device to imagine your pretty-but-not-smart cat lazing by the fireplace. You bend down to pet that cat, associating rubidium with the motion of "rubbing the belly of a dum-dum." The more you walk through and explore your memory palace, the more that info will stick.

When I preselect people in my shows who I want to use for audience participation, I have to remember them, so I look for people wearing bright colors, big jewelry, bushy beards, etc. That way, if I'm in a crowd with hundreds or even thousands of people, and I'm onstage and I run out in the audience, I can spot them from far away.

While it can be harder to do when you're with more people, these techniques still work. Let's say you go up to a group and they introduce themselves, "That's Megan, that's Susan, that's Bill, that's Nathan, and I'm Adrian." Too many people, right? I like giving compliments when it's a smaller group, but this practice doesn't scale. If you do compliment, saying, "Megan, love the earrings. Susan, where'd you get those pants? Bill, fantastic moustache. Nathan, I dig your watch. And, yo, Adrian, I loved *Rocky*," you've tipped the balance from friendly to full-blown psycho.

If you're in a larger group, take your time as you repeat their names. Make a joke out of it. Say, "Is there going to be a quiz later? You said you're Megan. Megan, so good to meet you, and Susan. Susan, so great to meet you." Say their names back three times. People appreciate this because it shows that you took the time and the effort to commit to knowing their names, which most people don't do; that extra beat sets you apart.

As for those twenty-three marketers that day, how did I do it? Here's the inside scoop: I don't have an infallible memory. While I do work at it, it's not something I need at my level. The night before my session, at the conference registration, they gave out little yearbooks with all the attendees listed and pictured. I went through and cut out their faces. I showed everyone in class these pseudo flash cards and thought there'd be a laugh or chuckle, but suffice it to say, I may have given light kidnapper vibes. I still found it funny and promise I use my powers strictly for good!

Because I always have a plan B, while I was brushing my teeth, I made piles of the faces that were easy to recall. Some people were simple to recall because they had unique names, features, or for whatever reason, their name matched their face in my mind. Sometimes a Bob just looks like a Bob. On my first round of quizzing myself, I identified eight or nine out of the twenty-three immediately.

As I practiced and made up jokes about them, more names began to gel and I added them to the "got" file. I repeated this while flossing—gotta keep that dental hygiene y'all—then while getting dressed, and packing up my things. (Put a pin in this: Your day is full of mentally empty moments that could be filled with some purpose.) I probably did four or five passes with my flash cards. By the time I was ready to go, I had twenty-one or twenty-two of the names down 100 percent. The last two or three were more of a struggle, so I said them over and over with rapid-fire delivery.

When I arrived at the class, I tested myself as they walked in, verifying via their badges that I had the details straight. That's when I said, "Take off your name tags." In my head, it was one final pop quiz. I was like, *Oh, I know her. I know him. I know her, I know him. I know him.* So I nailed it. I got everybody right and then I taught them to do the same.

Don't worry if you still forget a name after learning this technique and aren't perfect. No one is. There have been times when I've just met somebody and I forget their name, and I'm the one here telling you how not to forget. Whenever that happens, it's because I messed up step 1. Say it with me again, do it out loud for real, I don't care if you're hunkered down in a Starbucks or in seat 24F of a plane, "Listen, Repeat, Reply." Usually, what trips me up is the *listen* portion. Often, it's when I'm about to do a trick and somebody's calling out, "Hey, come over and meet this group." I'm so busy thinking about my trick that I can't make my mind blank and receptive. It's not a faulty memory if I never knew the name in the first place. It wasn't imprinted and so it was washed away. This used to happen to me frequently at sound checks before my show, as I walked backstage and suddenly was met in the dark by a group of people all at once. I'd be going over all the technical details of my upcoming performance in my head, so I would completely screw up step 1, which is to listen. I always want to make sure that the people setting up for my show feel seen and heard, as in many ways, they are the unsung heroes putting together the entire production. Also, I'm well aware that everyone talks and word spreads, and I want to ensure that I'm easy to work with and known for being kind and polite to others. Word spreads even wider if you're the opposite! Yet sometimes I'm stressed and flustered and will completely forget someone's name because I didn't listen to it in the first place. When this happens, the very best thing is to immediately say, "Could you please remind me of your name? It's Ryan? Oh, great. I thought I heard Brian and I didn't want to get it wrong. Ryan, thank you so much for your hard work." When you show them that you wanted to clarify, it affords them an extra level of respect that you cared enough to get it right.

If you're able to wash your hair, then you're able to remember our three-word trick for names. Lather, rinse, repeat becomes Listen, Repeat, Reply. The next time you're in a social or work setting with new people, challenge yourself to remember five names. Then as you're about to leave, close your eyes and picture each person's face, and see if you can remember their name. I bet you will surprise yourself, even on the first try!

Write Everything Down

Being able to recall something about someone else creates a stronger bond and builds trust, and that connection can work to your advantage. Your secret weapon here is something everyone possesses but few do—the ability to jot it down. We went over this earlier in the book, but it is so important I feel it bears repeating and I am therefore writing it down again (pun intended!)

Taking notes was, for me, born out of necessity. I started getting repeat calls for shows. I found myself struggling, wondering, *What did I do at that show?* While I have a number of tricks, I definitely don't want to repeat them for the same audience because it takes away some of the delight of the experience for them. I want to leave crowds with a sense of wonder each time; the element of surprise plays a huge role in my act.

Writing down facts about the lives of the people you meet is the fast track to building rapport, which is so important to anyone who regularly interacts with other human beings, whether it's your child's principal or a potential romantic partner or the sales lead you've been trying to close forever. Asking something like, "Hey, how did your son do at the basketball championship? Did he win again this year?" can create so much goodwill. When people feel like you've recalled something important about them, it's huge. You don't have to train to be a mentalist to harness the sorcery of giving back information that people gave you in the past, as everyone assumes you will have forgotten it.

If you're not sure how to record relevant details, here's what I do. As soon as I'm done with my show, I write everything that happened while it's fresh. If you're in sales, build time into your schedule to log these notes as soon as you get back to your car. If you're headed to the subway, leave yourself a voice message. Just don't let too much time lapse, or you may not retain everything you should.

When you pair effort with human touch, you're unstoppable. Imagine getting brownie points for simply giving people the information that they already shared with you. And it's not cheating! My job is tricking people into thinking I can read their minds, despite my going onstage and saying, "I don't read minds, I read people." The whole game is knowing how to integrate information in a way that seems truly amazing. And this is one of those life hacks that you can begin using today. I mean, just imagine how useful it would be if you're really junior at your job. If you can remember something about the big boss when you're in the elevator, you'll be noticed, and that's a pathway to success.

Any information that's given to you, anything that's been revealed, don't just let that go. Keep it and pull it out later, because that's the kind of impression that will make you stick in *their* memories.

Anchoring Information

As I transitioned from the party circuit to working primarily in the corporate sector, it struck me that pure entertainment was no longer enough; I really wanted to provide tangible value to my clients. I realized I could be most impactful by taking the information the client wanted to convey to the audience, which has a real dollars and cents value, and making it more unforgettable. I'd say to those who hired me, "Hey, what if your clients leave your event and truly remember the three key messages or data points you are targeting? What if I could do this in such a way that the information becomes 'sticky' and remains embedded in their long-term memory because it is presented under the guise of entertainment?" Think about this for a moment: Memorizing a thirty-line poem seems an overwhelming and daunting task for most of us. Yet you can easily recall the lyrics to dozens of your favorite songs. The delivery vehicle for information determines how well it will be retained.

Turns out, authentically engaging the audience and sneaking key messages and takeaways into my presentation is a very valuable addition for my corporate clients.

Standing on the dais lecturing people tends to be less effective because only so much information can be processed, and not all of the info can ever be retained. Remember, our brains give precedence to the memories that come with higher rewards, and that isn't a lecture. According to Charan Ranganath, a professor at UC Davis's Center for Neuroscience, "Rewards help you remember things, because you want future rewards. The brain prioritizes memories that are going to be useful for future decisions."[12] So with my corporate clients, I relay the information that they want their target consumer to retain. And I do that as part of an incredibly entertaining mind-reading show. This creates a greater value proposition for their company and it's been a huge ticket to my success.

When what clients want the audience to remember is included as part of a trick, they don't really see the takeaways as part of a sales pitch or lecture anymore. When presented within the form of entertainment or humor, that core message suddenly sticks a lot better because of the way everyone pays attention. We home in on entertainment. For example, if I'm working with a charity, I will reveal a series of numbers, such as someone's birthday, the jersey number of another person's favorite football player, and maybe one final person's ATM PIN. Everyone is thoroughly blown away at this point. We then multiply those numbers together and find that the total is precisely our fundraising goal for the gala and printed on the flyer everyone has in their hands. They are absolutely floored and that's when I explain what is being done with the money and how much we appreciate the generosity of all the attendees. The audience loves it because everyone's still reeling from the trick, yet the point seamlessly sticks. The charity's patrons walk away knowing where their money is going and with a great feeling in their hearts.

There's something incredibly powerful when a speaker can shift between humor and seriousness. I once saw an exceptional presenter recount his experience summiting Mount Everest—a journey during which three people tragically died. The room grew heavy with emotion. Just as the weight settled in, he slipped in a well-timed joke, breaking the tension. That sudden shift helped guide the audience through a roller coaster of feelings and drew them in even deeper, thereby helping them to remember what's being communicated. It all comes back to our brains prioritizing things that feel different.

Even the work I do with ESPN has a purpose behind it. I'm trying to get the team to walk out of practice having shared an incredible memory; that's a huge morale boost, which is in itself an anchor. Keep in mind, even though these guys are on the same team, they aren't on the *same team.* I can assure you, there's a big difference between the player who's the star quarterback and the second-string QB and whose butt is warming that bench. The second-stringers are not wishing the starter a spectacular injury-free season, because they might see that person as standing between them and a bigger paycheck, more fame, and a better career. So I try to create team unity, and I especially try to humanize the coaches and make them more accessible. The more unified a team is, the more satisfied the players are and the more effective they'll be on the field.

If I visited the team you root for and they end up winning the big game this year?

You're welcome.

Because we've been exercising your memory in this chapter, you should be feeling the burn. Now that you're better versed in anchoring information, you'll be far more adept at remembering strangers' names, and that can foster new relationships while your new techniques for remembering information they share about themselves will help strengthen existing connections.

There's no downside to having a more powerful memory, and the more actively you listen, the stronger your memory will get. You don't have to be a mind reader; you just need to put in the effort. And if you write down the information you want to keep, it can pay dividends in the long run, creating good for you and those around you, and that is unforgettable.

The Backward Alphabet Exercise

I want to leave you with the ability to use your memory to stun your friends, so I'm going to show you how to memorize the alphabet backward, saying it in reverse as easily as you can say it forward.

If I'm teaching this at a seminar, the first thing I'll do is have someone sing the alphabet song, which is very funny, because when people are watching us, it can get nerve-racking and even the smartest person falters (or at the very least sings brutally off-key).

After I do that, I'll tell them "Now say it backward." Most people hesitate, "Ummm, *Z*, *Y* . . ." and they start to crumble. Then in rapid fire, I'll rattle off the whole alphabet in reverse lightning fast. Then I'll drop the stunner and let them know, "In ten minutes, every one of you will be able to say it that fast backward for the rest of your life."

To teach this skill, I'll create teams who break down different letters and remember them in sections. (This is less about teams and more about recalling info in digestible chunks via association.) Again, memorizing the alphabet backward is probably not something you'll use in your day-to-day life, but this is a huge confidence builder that gives you a window into how your brain works, not to mention a fun party trick. In my workshop, everyone in the room gets a poster and a thick marker. I'll tell them that we'll start by breaking this exercise down into pieces across each team. As with any goal or problem, the best way to approach it is to chop it into bite-size chunks. To make it stick, I'll add an emotional hook, something they can quickly associate with the data.

In the first group, I'll talk about how in econ courses in college, they always call the company "XYZ Corp." I'll say, "But we're disrupting the game. We just created a company that's going to change everything. You know what we should do? Let's flip things on their head. We'll call it ZYX Corp. Who's with me?"

The first group will write *ZYX* on their posterboard and we'll all say it out loud. I find that the sillier we get, the more they'll remember this. Then I'll walk over to the next table and ask, "Where did you go to school?" As attendees tell me all the places they graduated from, I'll interject, "No, you didn't. All of you went to West Virginia University, and you bleed blue and old gold. WVU! So what's our war cry? *W*, *V*, *U*!"

I'll make everyone cheer and then we'll go back to the first table, saying, "Where do we work? ZYX! Who do we cheer for? WVU, right?" After this, I'll talk about my son who is eight. I'll say, "He loves *Guinness World Records*. He likes to quiz me with his esoteric knowledge, asking things like, 'Can you guess how much the most expensive kitchen sink in the world costs?' Well, he told us that the most expensive teaspoon in the world sold for twelve million dollars, after being handed down from generation to generation." Is this true? Absolutely not. But is it outlandish enough to stick in your brain? I sure hope so. The next group will write down *TS* for that teaspoon. I'll tell them this teaspoon is made out of platinum and I have everyone imagine holding it in their hand. Together, we'll chant, "*T*, *S*, teaspoon, teaspoon."

Then I'll say the person who bought the teaspoon at auction did not want his name made public, so he called himself Robert Q. Public. Initials *RQP*. I'll tell them, "Imagine those initials engraved into this teaspoon, *TS*. His name is Robert Q. Public. *R*, *Q*, *P*." Then we'll run down the line again, starting back with *ZYX*.

To the next team, I'll start with, "You guys lucked out. It's January. It's cold. I want a day off work. And you know, the third Monday, we get to celebrate a truly legendary figure in our nation's history, Dr. Martin Luther King Jr., aka you get the day off ON MLK Jr. day. That's *O*, *N*, *M*, *L*, *K*, *J*. So you guys get the easiest string." I go down the line and have every team yell out their letters and let everyone know that we've already learned seventeen out of the twenty-six letters, and it has only been a few minutes, more than halfway there!

At this point, I'll make a heart with my hands. I'll say, "Do you know this gesture? It's a heart. Everyone in the room do this. I heart, *I*, *H*. I heart, *I*, *H*. Everybody make that gesture," and we all do it. And we'll keep doing that three or four times, and then we'll go down the line. We'll reinforce it over and over.

Next, I'll talk about how I have a new girlfriend. I'll say, "Okay, everyone write *G*, *F*, girlfriend, girlfriend." And so they write *GF*. I'll say, "You're my girlfriend. *GF.* Do you know her name? Her name is Edna, but she makes me call her Ed in public, which is very embarrassing, because that sounds weird. But she wants me to call her Ed (as in spelled E-D) not Edna. So girlfriend Edna, *G, F, E, D.*" And we lather, rinse, repeat.

Finally, I'll end with a rather silly story, "The last bit is *C, B, A*, so it's very easy, because it's the opposite of *ABC.* Like my accountant told me he's got his CBA. And I thought, *Isn't that a CPA*? And he goes, 'Nope, it's a CBA,' so he kept arguing. And I think a CBA is like a fake version of a CPA." We repeat it a few times, and then we do the whole thing.

Everybody remembers the alphabet this way. If you're willing to be silly, say this to three people that you meet throughout the course of the day. Go through it three more times at different intervals, and then go home and tell your kids, your dog, or your spouse, and then tell them again tomorrow. If you do it that many times, you will retain it for the next year. It will stick, I promise you.

I've had people come up to me years after a seminar and tell me how crazy it is that they still remember it!

Keep in mind, it's not that your memory is bad; it's simply that it's out of shape, but now you have the tools to exercise it!

ELEVEN

Disarm with Charm

I can't restate this enough: I don't read minds, I read people. And at my shows, I always seek out those audience members I feel will give the biggest, most over-the-top reactions. But in life you can't always choose who you have to deal with, be it your boss or your brother-in-law. This is why learning to disarm with charm will come in exceptionally handy!

Let's start off with how I define *charm*. To me, charm is the ability to influence people, and there are a lot of different ways to go about this. Ultimately, charm involves getting people on your team; it's finding a way to persuade them to root for you. It's about using your personality and your skills to win them over, whether it's smiling your way out of a speeding ticket with a harried traffic cop or showing empathy to the poor airline employee trying to deal with two hundred angry passengers who just deboarded a canceled flight to Dallas. What's so great about charm is it doesn't feel one-sided. When you're able to charm someone, you both leave the interaction feeling more positive. (Especially when you're the only passenger that the gate agent accommodates because you were the one of two hundred who was kind.)

Charm is like a Swiss Army Knife, useful in so many different situations. Because that presence is not only about winning a person over, but also about being able to show your appreciation. That charisma is the light that shines on all of us at the same time.

Inevitably, you'll find yourself in situations where you're forced to deal with someone who's angry or upset, whether you're negotiating with difficult coworkers, unengaged committee members, a room full of NFL players who are ready to go home after a grueling day of practice, or cranky children. I'll show you ways to use your charm to shift their energy. (I know a lot about cranky children. *A lot.*) And when you use their negative energy to your advantage, it's like a mental judo move . . . and they'll never even see it coming!

Break the Ice

I absolutely adore stand-up comedy. It is my favorite form of entertainment . . . far more than mentalism if you can believe it. Comedians are masters of charm and use it from the moment their feet touch that stage. They need the audience on the same page as them or it's going to be the longest, unfunniest fifteen minutes of everyone's lives. Humor is the tool that stand-up uses to charm the audience into going along for the ride, to tip the scales their way.

If you've never been onstage trying to break the ice with an audience, you might not realize that those seated in front of you are not immediately on your side. They're not obligated to pull for your success. It makes no difference to the audience. They can be entertained by your brilliant comedy or by the flaming dumpster fire of your failure. It's not like when your parents would come to your elementary school and applaud wildly as you played Tree No. 3 in the musical, no matter how talented (or untalented) you actually were. Odds are they still took you out for ice cream afterward.

At best, an audience is neutral and it's on the comic to win them over. Every part of the performance, from how that performer grabs the mic to the clothes they wear to the way they style their hair, is part of that charm initiative. The gestures, the actions, all of it has been planned in advance and rehearsed ad nauseam. Each choice is deliberate and orchestrated for a result, even though the performance feels totally spontaneous and natural to the audience.

Now, if we're talking about the noun itself, the dictionary definition of *charm* is the power or quality of giving delight or arousing admiration. For the verb, the definition gets at attracting or delighting as if by magic. What the dictionary doesn't say is that charm—both the noun and the verb—is the linchpin to success.

But how do you become more charming in your life? We'll break it down in this chapter because charm will power your success.

I Know What You're Thinking

In order to succeed as a mentalist, I need to ensure that audience members aren't worried or apprehensive about what's going to happen when they're involved in my performance, and potentially thinking, *Yikes, he's watching everything I do. And he knows what I'm thinking right now; I don't like anything about this scenario.* That's why the first thing I do is try to put the audience at ease, telling them that I call BS on people even being able to read minds.

Without the secret ingredient of using charm to make people feel comfortable with me, an audience could turn on me pretty quickly. I call what I'm able to do the "have a drink with you after the show" test.

I strive to leave those who see me perform wanting to say hello at the bar after the performance, because that means I connected with them. My warmth won them over. Being able to guess their ATM PIN or naming the first person they ever kissed is disconcerting and can make people feel vulnerable and unprotected. But when that information is presented with some magnetism, the equation changes and suddenly everyone's lining up to have their minds read.

We are hardwired to have an expectation of what others are going to be like. We define people by the narrative we see, for better or worse. We're often judged immediately on our appearance, regardless of whether or not this is fair. In fact, according to behavioral science professor Alexander Todorov, we can make decisions about other people's trustworthiness, competence, and likability after looking at their faces for only a fraction of a second.[1] Whoa.

But what swings them back to us (and us back to them) is charm.

For example, let's say you see a big, scary biker-type in his road-worn leathers, all muscled and tatted-up. You are likely to immediately jump to conclusions about him because our minds rapidly categorize people and situations as a way to help us respond to them.[2] This happens in the region of the brain called the amygdala, which is the part that warns us about potential threats.[3] Yet the second that guy opens his mouth to say how he's been struggling to get his daughter to eat her broccoli, it changes the way we look at him. *Wait, this isn't a scary guy at all*, we think. *He's a concerned parent—just like I am—only he happens to ride a Harley.*

When I say we're trying to charm to disarm, what I mean is disrupting people's preconceived notions, clearing them off the table. Creating a shortcut past who they think we might be to how we *want* them to see us. We all have our own preconceived notions about others, based on our pasts, upbringings, and the ways we are wired. How often have you met someone and ended up saying, "Wow, you're so different from what I thought you'd be like." It's just staggering how much we hold on to our own stereotypes. What I learned over time is that when people see me, they think, *Oh, he's a magician, he's going to do a trick*, or *Ugh, he's going to challenge me intellectually*, and that raises their guard. I have to dispel those notions quickly.

Personally, when it comes to preconceived notions about what I do, I like to immediately lay everything out in the open, telling people, "If I can read your mind, that's super off-putting, right?" I even say this during my show. I make sure to verbalize their inner monologue as soon as I anticipate their thoughts—which kind of is *real* mind reading! Then I will address their reticence to take away any residual unease and instead lean into how intriguing the methods I'm using are, and if they can start to catch how I'm doing it.

What's so monumental is that charm is a skill anyone can learn to master. And even better, you'll find that the art of mastering charm—especially when you see immediate results—is fun!

Honesty Is the Best Policy

Charm is a property that people think you have naturally, like it's part of your DNA, but that's not accurate. Charm is a tool that you can absolutely learn how to use and a skill you can build. Of course, it's true that some people are imbued with natural charisma, which isn't quite the same thing as charm. As writer Jason Vu Nguyen puts it, the difference between charm and charisma is: "Charm is 'I come to you' and charisma is 'you come to me.'"[4]

In my view, charm consists of equal parts humor, vulnerability, and honesty. Honesty truly is at the core. People can sniff out someone who's fake from a mile away. There's nothing more off-putting than insincerity, because we have an evolutionary need to establish social trust. Inauthenticity sets off our internal alarm bells and spurs psychological discomfort.[5] So when you find yourself disliking someone because you perceive that they're acting fake, there's a whole lot churning under the surface of your psyche that makes you feel that way, even if you can't put your finger on the *why*, exactly.

To me? Insincerity just grates. Insincerity makes us feel like we're being played and manipulated. I've seen many videos of magicians or people that do what I do, and when I watch them perform, I instantly say, "That's not who they really are." And I don't like it. They feel to me like a caricature of the actual person.

When I'm onstage, I'm authentically myself, but maybe dialed up an extra point or two so everyone in the back row feels included. (If I were this exuberant at home, it would be insufferable.)

What draws people in is *authenticity*. In fact, authenticity is so important, Merriam-Webster made *authentic* their word of the year in 2023.[6] Being authentic is highly valued, especially as people seek out genuineness and transparency in the digital age, as the rise of AI is causing us to question all our perceptions. Importantly, authenticity cannot be faked.

I remember once seeing an interview with Oprah where she was asked what her greatest talent was. She explained that she was especially skilled at acting in front of the camera exactly the way she'd act if she were off camera. While Oprah makes it sound so simple, that's an incredible skill to have. For so many people, when the camera goes on, they change. They feel ill at ease at the realization that they're being observed, possibly judged. By the way, freezing on camera is a real phenomenon. This happens because the camera triggers our bodies' stress responses, even though we're not in any physical danger. Just the perceived threat of having eyes on us makes our stress hormones spike in a fight-or-flight response. We feel self-conscious or we're overcome by performance anxiety. Then, that spiking cortisol impacts our cognitive function, interfering with our ability to express ourselves naturally . . . so we literally freeze up and can't find our words.

Again, the camera can be metaphorical here, meaning that anytime you're in a novel situation outside of your comfort zone, the fight-or-flight response is still real. Perhaps this happens when you're in a business setting or with new people you don't know so well. Your insecurities come to the forefront and they affect the way you behave, and suddenly you're not making the impression you'd hoped.

The good news is, employing some charm will help you turn that right around.

I feel like everybody has two different selves: There's the self we are when we're with people we love or know really well. And then there's the self we take on when we're less comfortable, when we're on guard. That first self is our most effective self, but it's not what everyone sees, because we're afraid of rejection, so we sometimes keep the best of ourselves hidden and that is a shame.

How do we fight this? Well, we have to become aware of when and how we slip away from presenting our best selves.

Now let's go back to the situation where you're by yourself in a room full of new people. The urge is to just busy yourself on your phone, right? Just avoid the unknown until it's over? But what if you used charm instead? Because charm is synonymous with honesty. If you're somewhere you don't know anyone and everyone else is in the same situation, I suggest you lean into it. Almost everyone feels awkward in a setting like this; it's human nature. So name it and claim it. Walk up to someone you don't know and say with a warm smile, "I'm a fish out of water, I don't know anyone here. Definitely nervous talking to all these strangers."

When you say that to somebody, people are disarmed and grateful that you took the risk. You're saying what they're feeling, but they're too anxious to be vulnerable and open and they're not showing their best selves, either. That creates a connection. Your honesty builds a bridge. And it will be disarming because most are so afraid to let anybody see behind the curtain, to be vulnerable. It's like we hesitate to show that we're human.

So, what are the active steps you can take to up your charm? Let's get into them.

Time to Listen

Are you ready for a staggering statistic? Eighty-five percent of all that we know, we have learned by listening.[7] So, if you want to immediately up your charm level, it's a must that you listen and be present. Per a study at the University of California, Berkeley, researchers found that when participants listened to a speaker telling a personal story, the audiences' brain activity synched up with that of the speaker.[8] What a powerful takeaway.

Listening means you're actively engaging with what the other person is saying, and you're not just going, "Uh-huh, yep, uh-huh," while you wait impatiently to say your piece. As author Jim Kwik says in an article on the science of active listening, there are five steps everyone can—and should—take when trying to improve their ability to listen.

First of all, stuff your phone in your pocket and pay attention to what's said. This is universally important, whether you're sitting in front of your child's teacher or at the conference room table with a potential client or at a trendy fusion restaurant with a date you'd like to impress. People will often tell us everything we need to know, but if we're distracted by texts or a stock-ticker push notification or the hockey game on the TV above the bar, we might miss something important.

Second, a great way to intensify the impact of your listening is to express an interest in what's being said. Not only does this kind of engagement show respect and common courtesy, but there's also science that reinforces the effectiveness of this approach. Researchers in Japan have found that "neural activation in the ventral striatum was enhanced by perceiving active listening, suggesting that this was processed as rewarding. It also activated the right anterior insula, representing positive emotional reappraisal processes."[9] In plain English? When you actively listen to someone, they get a reward of that sweet brain candy I've spoken about in previous chapters.

Kwik's next suggestion is often easier said than done, but let's do it anyway. We need to make sure we're not peppering the conversation with a lot of interruptions. Respond? Yes. Leap in and take over the convo? Absolutely not. Interruptions aren't just rude; in fact, they trigger the flight-or-fight response in the amygdala. There are times when people have interrupted me that I could clearly feel my muscles tense and my heart rate increase.

When you resist the urge to interrupt and allow the person to conclude their point, you're aiding them in activating their prefrontal cortex, leading to cognitive and emotional regulation, per Kwik. But there will be times that you have to add something for a better shared understanding, so if you do need to jump in, do so in a way that won't alienate that person. ("Wait, let me stop you right there, Bob," are words that should never come out of your mouth if you're trying to charm someone.)

Kwik recommends that you engage in the conversation, asking meaningful questions to ensure mutual understanding. This works in any situation because this kind of deft, patient manner of interjecting communicates to the speaker that they're being heard. If you say a phrase like, "Wow, I've never thought of X that way before. In your experience, how would this also apply to Y and Z?" there's not a yes and no answer there; whomever you're speaking with will absolutely want to engage more. Consider this: When you meet someone, you tend to ask the same ten questions, from "What do you do?" to "Where are you from?" Everyone has their rote answers for these questions—they don't snap us out of autopilot. But what if when you met someone, you asked, "If I met a six-year-old version of you, what would they think of you as an adult?" That takes most people by surprise and is designed to bring out some introspection. The more branches you can open in a conversation, the more you indicate interest and you can use that interest to enchant and amaze people, even if you're in a professional environment. It's also for your own benefit: When you ask questions, you engage your hippocampus, and this is key because language and memory are intimately linked.[10] Also, the more you ask about someone else, the more interesting they think *you* are. It's a win-win. So right now, I want you to think of three questions you can ask someone that will really make them stop, think, and engage.

Finally, if you want to improve your listening, one of the best ways to do that is to summarize the conversation. This is crucial because not only does it reinforce the fact that you've been interested and engaged, but it pings your prefrontal cortex and will help you retain the information.

Bottom line? Active listening is flat-out charming.

If you're ready for a master class in listening, let me tell you about how I defensively listen when it comes to my business. When I say "defensively listen," I mean that you listen not only to understand, but to prepare yourself to react in a myriad of ways. It's listening to the nth degree, both actively and strategically. One of the reasons I've experienced as much growth as I have is that I collect as much information as I possibly can. Information is power. In the early days of doing gigs, I'd take my own booking phone calls. People would call me and they'd say, "I'm having a party on such and such date." I used to field those calls anywhere because I wanted to be as accessible as possible.

I was fixated on never losing a show by missing a call, my concern being that the client or event planner would immediately call another performer who would get booked instead. Yet answering every call also put me at a disadvantage, because I'd pick up not knowing who I was talking to. I realized that if I answered the phone when I was busy, I couldn't look up info about this person, so I'd ask them where they found me. I'd drill down, querying, "Oh, was it in Roslyn? Was it Jeffrey's bar mitzvah?" If I could discern that it was Jeffrey Rose's bar mitzvah, I'd know a lot of things, including how much I charged at that event or if I offered different types of packages, or if my rates had varied over time.

Honestly, it can mean a deal slipping through your fingers if you go into something blind versus if you go into something knowing that the guy's a huge baseball fan and two of his kids play college ball, because then you can make references that are topical to him. Defensive listening is about knowing your crowd, as the more familiar you are with them, the more likely you are to be able to charm them. If you start making sports references to someone who hates sports, that material will fall on deaf ears. Defensive listening is about being a chameleon, ingratiating yourself. Building rapport with somebody because connection is a cornerstone of charm.

What I started doing was answering the phone, and after the initial pleasantries, asking, "When's the date of your event?" and then, "Listen, I'm so sorry. I'm walking into a meeting right now. I'm letting you know that I am available. I would love to be there but, respectfully, need to get back to you once I'm back in the office so our call isn't rushed. When is a good time later today or tomorrow that we can talk?"

Then I'd say, "Let me quickly text you my information-gathering form so you can fill this all out and to make your life easier." What I've done is, I've answered their phone call, I've been very responsive in the moment, I've let them know that I'm available, and I've hooked them, so that hopefully they're not calling someone else immediately after me. Also, I've used benefits-oriented language to steer them toward my booking form where they provide all of their information, including where they first saw me or who referred them. From there, I can google their names, find out who they are, where they live, where they work. Those details are useful to know going into a negotiation. Information is power and the more you know, the better positioned you are in every business.

Now that I've done my homework before the call and am better informed on how this lead originated, I'm ready with relevant info for the negotiation. So, if that caller were to come back and say, "But you gave this deal to the person who referred me," I have an immediate and honest answer as to why that is. As opposed to being defensive, I can say, "I'm so glad you mentioned that. That's absolutely true. So, the deal I had with Jared is because he hired me for three upcoming events at once and therefore received a bulk booking discount; I'd be happy to extend that same deal if you're interested" I got ahead of their objection. When you defensively listen, you're not a used car salesman. Instead, you're readily prepared with the right answers.

The bottom line is the better you listen, whether it's actively or defensively, the more charming everyone will find you because, more than anything, people want to be heard.

Charm Offensive

Being charming is another way of describing being likable. A lot of what it takes to disarm with charm is the desire to genuinely connect. Obviously, listening is a key component. But there are other areas where you can improve as well.

I've talked about how special it makes people feel when you recall their little details, whether it's about how their college kid is enjoying a semester abroad or what's happening with their plans to finally buy that vacation home in Maine. It's not enough for you to know these things—instead, you have to use them to reinforce the idea that what's going on in their life is meaningful enough for you to remember.

Let's take a question and compare a charming version that uses personal details with one that doesn't.

> Question One: "How was your summer?"
>
> Question Two: "How was the new place in Kennebunkport this summer? Congrats on that, by the way. Did you love being by the ocean? How did the kids enjoy all that boating? Did you get your fill of lobster? How great was the weather?"

Question One requires nothing but a rote answer. They could say, "Fine," and that could sum up the whole summer. But the second set of questions expresses genuine interest and will lead to a more fulfilling conversation on all sides, especially if the exchange reveals more commonalities, for example, "No, I'm allergic to lobster." "No way, me too!" Ultimately, people like to be remembered, and when you can recall the details of their life, when you can ask them questions that are meaningful, it will make you both feel good, especially when your approach is positive and upbeat.

Remember that conversation is a give-and-take, not a monologue. If you want to be charming, be interested. In *How to Win Friends and Influence People*, Dale Carnegie often referred to Publilius Syrus's quote, "We are interested in others when they are interested in us."[11] Being curious is a game changer. Asking sincere questions can be your superpower. Again, let's look at how I felt when I spent half an hour with Steven Spielberg. He was so engaged with me that he left me feeling like I was the most interesting person in the world, despite my not getting one question in about *Jaws*—not one!

Another way to up your charm is to offer sincere compliments. Again, *sincerity* is the goal here. If you hand out compliments like you're passing out Halloween candy, it will feel weird and disingenuous. But something well-timed and heartfelt will almost always hit. For example, let's say you spot and admire someone's ring. You say something like, "What a gorgeous piece of jewelry. Is that an heirloom? Is there a story behind it?" Suddenly, this person who may have never thought twice about you is creating an emotional connection with you as she relays a tale about the grandmother who sewed it into the hem of her skirt so she could smuggle it out of Poland during the war. And now you're looking at them like they're the most fascinating person in the world because it's a hell of a story, and that's how they're feeling, too. Try to walk away from that conversation without a grin on your face. Remember, when you offer up sincere compliments, you open the door to a deeper sense of connection.

If you want to take your charm to the next level, mind your manners and be respectful and polite, even if it's you who happens to be in the more powerful position. If you have the opportunity to extend a little grace, do it. Be the guy who holds the elevator for the person running down the hall. Be the woman who says, "No, after you, I insist."

While confidence is always a plus, arrogance isn't, so let's keep the bragging to a minimum. It might feel good to boast, but that good feeling is definitely one-sided, as it can trigger feelings of inferiority in the other person and, now, they're not rooting for you. (Hello, social media.) Also, bragging makes you come across as less trustworthy, according to researchers at the University of Arizona.[12] So if you're bragging to someone you hope to attract as a client, you're actually *less* likely to win the account. Sure, you can talk about your wins, but couch them in humility.

Whenever you can and when appropriate, use humor in your interactions. This is across-the-board advice, but it's especially relevant if you're dating, because the use of humor shapes the perception of creativity, intelligence, and social competence, all traits everyone wants in a partner.[13] According to Michelle Shiota of Arizona State University's Department of Psychology, "In this work, we propose that people are attracted to funny romantic partners because humor acts as a cue that leads people to perceive a potential partner as possessing other desirable traits. Of the candidate traits we examined, creative ingenuity—the ability to think and act in original and inventive ways to solve problems—emerged as the trait people most reliably inferred from humor."[14] I'm not saying you have to join an improv troupe if you're hoping to find love, but it wouldn't hurt. Humor bonds us, so no matter what you're doing, offering a funny line or a wry comeback will absolutely up your charm.

If you want to be your most charming, you have to pay attention both to the verbal and the nonverbal cues the other person is giving you. The science of positive body language is something studied in "kinesics." Kinesics encompasses so much, from gestures to shrugs to the flush of our cheeks or our intake of breath. Negative body language can be the rolling of the eyes or the stiffening of the spine.

Let me ask you this—how many times have you received a text and agonized over someone's intended meaning? (Trust me, it happens to everyone.) This is because all we have are the words—there's no body language to give us contextual clues. A recent article notes that body language accounts for between 60 and 65 percent of all communication, so it's an enormous piece of the puzzle.[15] That article's figure largely aligns with what Albert Mehrabian, UCLA professor, had to say. In the late 1960s to early 1970s, he came up with the 7-38-55 model, meaning that verbal language only constitutes 7 percent of communication, nonverbal signals being the other 93 percent, specifically breaking down nonverbal communication into 55 percent body language and 38 percent voice and tone.[16] So, yes, he established that body language is a significant component of how we get our points across.

Let's say you're in a job interview for a position you really want. You're likely to be more successful in this endeavor if you're mirroring that interviewer's body language. If they rest their hand on their chin, you do the same, because that mirroring is a nonverbal way of confirming you're on the same page as your interviewer. The more you pick up on how they present themselves in gestures and speech patterns, the more you'll subliminally convince them that you're of similar mindsets. Mirroring establishes rapport.

Your body language is something you can easily control, and doing so can be as simple as keeping your palms open rather than bunching your hands into fists, pointing your feet in the same direction as someone else, making eye contact, or leaning in when you're talking to someone. Here's a weird fact—we're attracted to being able to see people's hands. There have been studies about hands, and what researchers have found is that when you can't see someone else's hands, it impacts your degree of trust in them. If a person is concealing their hands, like having them shoved in their pockets, it can even decrease how attractive we find them.[17]

As part of my act, I pay close attention to a few things, particularly eye movements, because our eye movements indicate that we're thinking. For example, if a person looks up and to the left after being asked a question, it usually means they're accessing memories. Yet if they look up to the right, it typically means they are constructing an idea. Big difference.

For my tricks to work, I have to be 100 percent sure that the participant comprehends what I'm asking of them. In my act—and in life—it's so important to make sure you're not only heard but also understood. Your spidey senses will tell you when someone's not fully engaged, like their mouth said, "Yep," but their brain said, "Nope." So double-check because ultimately the buck stops with you.

While paying attention to these quirks and bits of movement seems like such a small gesture, it packs a major punch when it comes to increasing your charm, because these little things trace back through our evolution to when being in limbic synchrony was key to the survival of your group.[18] As it may have been awhile since you had your last bio class, limbic synchrony occurs when two people's brains start coordinating, meaning you're on the same wavelength, not just emotionally but also as your heart rates, breathing, and brain wave patterns begin to synch.

Finally, here's the greatest weapon in your arsenal. And it's a biggie that accomplishes so much, from releasing dopamine and endorphins to reducing stress hormones to improving your relationships to even boosting your immune system, because it increases the production of antibodies.

What is this sorcery, you ask?

Simple. It's a smile.

At the end of the day, charm is all about drawing people in, and if you do the above, you'll be unstoppable.

Put Yourself in Their Shoes

It's an unfortunate fact that even the best of us have bad days. It's an even more unfortunate fact that sometimes people are jerks. The good news is that the human brain is coded for compassion and empathy, so here's how to deal with someone who is not yet won over by your charms.

If somebody comes at you with negative energy, your best bet is always to kill with kindness. Shift that energy. If somebody's coming at you with a vibe that's confrontational, reply with gratitude, because that disarms people. If you want to immediately de-escalate, make the person on the other end of the conversation feel heard. Repeat what they say and empathize, "I'm so sorry you had this experience. That had to be uncomfortable and that's just not right." When you give them back empathy, you smother the fire, rather than stoke the flames.

Imagine you're the gate attendant I mentioned earlier and you're dealing with all those angry passengers. If you're a weary traveler who is desperate to get on the next flight home to your family, you're going to have the best luck winning that person over if you remain calm and speak to them respectfully. Now is not the time to make threats or invoke your million-mile club membership. Use your empathy by saying something like, "I'm so sorry you have to deal with this. This probably isn't how you hoped your day was going to go when you got up, right?" The more you can make them feel heard and understood, the faster you're going to get to your bulkhead seat. More important, by employing your charm, you're going to lighten their load, too.

Now, if I were trying to de-escalate the meltdown one of my kids was having before bed, my approach would be to first validate their feelings and to make my voice quieter. The last thing I'd want to do was be louder. Kids can lose control and it's not their fault—instead, it's often a nervous system response, so I don't want to pile on any more stress.[19] I'd probably get down on their level so they could look me in the eye, to decrease their perception of any imbalance of power. I might distract them by offering them something they like, or I'd offer them other choices, like, "Do you want to wear the red pajamas or the blue ones?"

Regardless of what kind of tyrant you're dealing with, whether it's a toddler or someone acting like a toddler, you're not going to move forward if you get caught up taking their abuse personally. Treat them with respect, with kindness, while asking them questions to clarify the root cause of an issue and showing them that you're on the same team.

This is *not* the opportunity to mirror their body language, and it's especially not the time to interrupt them, as they're already in fight-or-flight mode.

When you disarm with charm, you set yourself up for success because charm impacts everyone involved. When people root for you, they win as well. Charm is how you connect, communicate, and conjure up the best of feelings.

When there are times that your natural charms aren't enough, remember to lead with empathy and do everything in your power to de-escalate tense situations with kindness, repetition, and acknowledgment. Because at the end of the day, when you can show people that they're seen and heard, they will eventually come around. And if they don't? At least you didn't make a bad situation worse.

TWELVE

Tie It All Together with a Story

In this chapter, I'll share my greatest communication tool—being a storyteller—as I recount a couple of the tales that made me who I am today. I will kick it off with the *Ocean's Eleven*–style caper I pulled off with a group of Merrill Lynch analysts as we all channeled our inner mentalists . . . along with Prince Harry. (It's a story so shocking, even Prince Harry himself can't believe it's true!)

We jump from one of the most exhilarating nights of my life to one of the worst, which held consequences so severe they nearly derailed my entire career path, coming within a hair's breadth of preventing me from working on Wall Street. Lessons I learned on that fateful night enabled me to discover the right path moving forward, and taught me how to focus less on myself and more on the people around me. The unlikely benefit of that way of thinking made all the difference in the world. From stacking the deck in my favor and figuring out how to work my charm to planning for the unexpected, I had to pull every trick out of my mentalist tool belt to save my own skin. It's been two decades since then, and I'm only now starting to laugh about it. Let me preface the story with these three pieces of advice: Day drinking is a bad idea, orange will never be the new black, and everyone should learn a card trick as your get-out-of-jail-free card . . . literally!

As we draw to a close, let me say this—your best life is waiting for you. Your hopes, your dreams, your goals are ready to come true, and the tools and tricks I've shared will allow you to define them by reading your own mind.

The fourteen-year-old version of me performing at Zia's restaurant could not fathom all that he would achieve over the next three decades. The time is now for you to define your future.

And it all ties together with the art of storytelling.

Be a Storyteller

If you want to truly tap into your inner mentalist, there's no better way to do so than by delivering your message in story form instead of as a straightforward recitation of facts and figures or a routine PowerPoint. It doesn't matter how dynamic a speaker is, how animated, how enthusiastic or knowledgeable; what they say hits differently if that information is delivered as a story. This is scientific fact. When we were little kids, we begged our parents for a story before bed, and we've haven't outgrown this desire. That's because when a message is delivered in a narrative form, information not only pings the language-processing centers of our brain, but can also engage the sensory and motor cortices . . . and that is so powerful.

Stories help connect and inspire us by adding emotions and texture to cold hard facts and data points. Storytelling is built into our DNA and traces back thousands of years—an integral part of the human experience like creating music. It greatly enhances the audience's ability to remember and recount information, as well as sneak in lessons you might otherwise have quickly forgotten (recall the backward alphabet example we talked about . . . quick, which university did we all attend?).

Storytelling is particularly effective, because as Lani Peterson, PsyD, put it in a *Harvard Business Publishing* article:

> Scientists are discovering that chemicals like cortisol, dopamine and oxytocin are released in the brain when we're told a story. Why does that matter? If we are trying to make a point stick, cortisol assists with our formulating memories. Dopamine, which helps regulate our emotional responses, keeps us engaged. When it comes to creating deeper connections with others, oxytocin is associated with empathy, an important element in building, deepening or maintaining good relationships.[1]

Paul Zak, a renowned neuroscientist, conducted a series of experiments to determine how the use of storytelling might impact the brain. Per Zak:

> As social creatures, we depend on others for our survival and happiness. A decade ago, my lab discovered that a neurochemical called oxytocin is a key 'it's safe to approach others' signal in the brain. Oxytocin is produced when we feel trusted or shown a kindness, and it motivates cooperation with others. It does this by enhancing the sense of empathy, our ability to experience others' emotions. Empathy is important for social creatures because it allows us to understand how others are likely to react to a situation, including those with whom we work.[2]

In Zak's experiment, he divided the volunteers into two groups. One watched a video about a dying boy where the information was presented in a clinical, straightforward manner. With the other, he created a narrative arc—all the same information but told in the context of a story, including the perspective of the boy's father. Afterward, he took blood samples from all the volunteers, and those who'd seen the video that used storytelling showed an increase of oxytocin in their blood.[3]

What's particularly profound about Zak's experiment is that when he ran it a second time, he gave all the subjects money, which they were allowed to spend as they wanted. He discovered that the subjects who'd been found to have the highest levels of oxytocin and cortisol were the most likely to generously donate that money.[4] This absolutely aligns with what I do for my clients that raise money for various charities—when I relay the information they want to share using a narrative arc and an emotional hook, their fundraising is far more successful.

We tell stories not only to connect and entertain, but also to assert a degree of control over the listener or reader.[5] When we're in the middle of a remarkable story, we're holding that audience rapt—they're on the edge of their seats. Humanity has been telling stories since the inception of language because stories not only allow us to share information about what could be a threat, but also how we might maneuver past that threat. Storytelling has been a necessary part of how we've survived and evolved. And really, does anything feel better than having an audience in the palm of your hand?

So pull up a chair and gather close as I share two of my best dinner party stories, and try to spot all the concepts we've discussed in this book.

His Royal Highness

For years, magic was my way of approaching a group or a stranger. It was my secret power. Magic was how I made my fear of rejection disappear.

Instead of presenting them Clark Kent, the guy who was boring and plain and vanilla, I wanted to show them Superman. That was my cheat code to walk up to anyone and not let them know who I really was as a person. Instead, they got to know the slightly exaggerated version of me, a showman who can change a one dollar bill into a hundred dollar bill faster than a speeding bullet, who can turn the mirror back on the group and make them look good. Bringing out your inner mentalist is not so much about discovering your superpower as it is figuring out what makes you unique and special. It also helped provide me with my best dinner party story ever.

This story begins with my entry-level position at Merrill Lynch after graduating from college. I worked in the financial district right near the World Financial Center. I'd interned there the summer before and apparently performed well enough for the firm to offer me a full-time position upon graduation. Back in those days, Merrill Lynch put trainees through a ten-week analyst program. I was in the global technology sector, which is the IT division of an investment bank. Forty of us were US-based and ten were from the UK. Two of the Brits in our group were exceedingly tall, and I'm only saying this because it will be important later. (I'd say those guys were nerdy, but let me be honest, we all were.) The tall dudes were named John and Mike and we called them, respectfully, Big John and Big Mike. Yes, I know . . . very creative nicknames. One was about six-eight and one was nearly six-ten, and both of them were really lanky. Think less tough guy, more Mr. Bean.

Everyone in the program hung out together during the day as we were in a glorified version of school. Merrill Lynch would have executives speak to us throughout the morning and afternoon sessions, discussing various policies and procedures, as well as their personal journeys. Then, of course, we'd go out drinking every night. Imagine, ten weeks of being paid full salaries to have fun in New York. Those were the glory days of Wall Street.

The UK contingent lived together in long-term corporate housing, a situation that was somewhere between a hotel and a condo. (To us, it was basically a fancy dorm.) They had two rooms, and it felt almost like a fraternity. Being fresh out of college from the University of Michigan, this scenario felt happily familiar. All fifty of us partied together all the time. There was a clique of twenty who were inseparable—we just had a blast.

One night we all playing poker. In our group, a guy named Bing was an excellent communicator and connector. He was profoundly skilled at turning the mirror on other people, getting them to open up and let down their guard. Bing was an expert at walking into a room and instantly warming the group with a megawatt smile, while looking deeply into your eyes when you're speaking to him in a way that makes it feel as if nothing else exists. (Bing reminded me a lot of Barack Obama in that respect.)

This was 2003, a time when I'd say people were very familiar with British royalty as a whole however less so of the youngest heir to the throne, Prince Harry. He wasn't the household name he is now and nowhere near as recognizable. He was still quite young back then, fresh out of Eton. Apparently, there was an unwritten contract between the royals and the press at the time. The paparazzi largely left Harry alone during college, so between that and the internet still in its infancy, he was still a mystery to many Americans.

At one point, I looked across the poker table, and exclaimed to my British friend Michael Coates, "You look just like Prince Harry, bro." We all laughed because he didn't resemble him that much, save for the ginger hair. Again, how would we really know what he looked like? That's when I had a light-bulb moment.

I said, "Here's what we're going to do," and I started to lay out my plan to Michael, Bing, and the rest of our crew. Bing was a get-stuff-done kind of guy. That always impressed me about him. He was dating a girl who worked at the biggest PR firm in the city representing many notable celebs. My idea was that we go "big," creating one huge, unforgettable night by making everyone believe we were out with Prince Harry. I figured we already had a redheaded Brit and that was half the battle.

I said that Bing should have his girlfriend call a high-end nightclub and tell them we were vetting various venues for a possible visit by Prince Harry. Our plan wasn't about scoring anything free; it was about creating a splash. We all thought the idea was funny, but Michael wasn't buying it. He said, "You guys are crazy. No one's ever going to believe us." I said, "They will if we go big." I genuinely believed that if we sold people on the concept, if we played roles and committed to them, they would.

I started giving everyone tasks that night. I said, "Big John, Big Mike, you're going to be security. You guys wear black suits." Bobby was part of our group. He was British but of Pakistani descent and he looked just like Jason Statham. He was a hustler, the type of guy with an edge who may have, say, scalped concert tickets in college. He was already a master in disarming with charm.

As the idea grew in my head, I went around the poker table, assigning roles. We all had a good laugh playing out the scenario but then got back to the card game and typical witty banter. My so-called brilliant idea seemed to be forgotten. This was the second week of the ten weeks into our program. Fast-forward seven weeks later, when Bing stopped me in the hallway and said, "Dude." He could convey so much with a single word. "We're doing it."

Puzzled, I replied, "Doing what?"

Remember, I spelled out my idea one night a month and a half ago. Over the course of those weeks, I spit out *a lot* of stupid ideas. (You don't want to know.) Bing said, "We're going to do the Prince Harry thing." Having noted my confusion, he explained, "I got my girl in. She's willing to make the call."

I couldn't believe it—and I couldn't pass up the opportunity. My mind began to assemble the pieces we'd need to build a believable puzzle. How would we sell everyone else on this? Immediately, I realized that we needed to scout the right location. We decided on Underbar. This place was in the W Hotel in Union Square, which was a known celebrity hot spot. The location ticked all the boxes—centrally located, fun, a see-and-be-seen spot, very dark lighting—so it seemed like the perfect venue, largely because it felt so credible. We had Bing's girlfriend call Underbar and set up a meeting with the manager, keeping it light on details and heavy on intrigue. The first rule of show biz: Sell the sizzle, not the steak.

All of us guys picked out our suits—we wanted to look the part, as that's the only way our ploy would work—and we created dossiers on our official roles. Bobby would be the prince's official consort. We weren't sure if that was the term for it, but we barreled on. We did what research we could about our official titles and decided on our roles. I was the US affiliate liaison.

The four-person "advance team" rolled up to meet the people at the club in the afternoon. Our plan was to discuss protocol, security, what areas to cordon off, how we didn't want press interference, etc. We acted very serious because that's exactly how we figured Harry's real team would have done it. We were the living embodiment of fake it till you make it.

This story was a precursor to what I do for a living now; that night was all about mentalism, pure and simple. My job now is to fool people in a certain way, to get inside their heads. Long before I was a professional mentalist, I'd learned how people think, so when we showed up that day, I made sure that everyone committed to the fake out. I was engineering the outcome in our favor starting today. If any of us hesitated, we'd have been lost.

When you're pulling the ultimate prank, it's imperative you do everything the right way. The key is that you don't break character, no matter what. We went into the meeting and were ruthless with our questions, humorless and dour, making the W staffers feel like they weren't interviewing *us*, we were interviewing *them*. We drilled them relentlessly, asking things like, "Is this the right place? Is this not? We might have to take our business elsewhere. We need to be assured there will be no leaks. We want no paparazzi."

Ours was a basic sales technique, with the threat of the take-away, like we might gift our huge prize of a royal in attendance to a different establishment if they didn't have their act together. We got *them* to sell *us* on the Underbar. We went in there planning for every eventuality and what's so funny is it never occurred to them we'd be perpetrating this level of deception.

And why would they?

We explained to the club that we did not want word of this to get out . . . which is the best way to ensure that word will spread. It's straight-up human nature. That night, we rolled up with about fifteen of us in total. The royal escort group along with a handful of women who were in our training program, all of us dressed to the nines. We bought those little earpieces that the Secret Service wear, that loop over the ear and down the back. The cords dangled beneath our starched shirts, connected to nothing as we didn't have radios. (We barely had credit ratings!) We all wore black suits, crisp white shirts, and we were just so *bloody serious*. I mean, we were selling our association with someone in the line of succession to the British monarchy.

The plan was, any time ~~Prince Harry~~ Prince Michael walked around, I'd position myself in the front, Bobby behind, and the bodyguards left and right. We were entirely convincing as we confidently approached our velvet-roped section of the club. It was all about projecting confidence and acting like we belonged there; I was reliving that first day pitching at Zia's.

Our two bodyguards—those lanky British guys—stood in front of the rope, at attention with hands neatly folded. They were unflappable, no different than the guards you might see outside of Buckingham Palace. What worked in our favor was that the Bigs were so tall it was hard to make direct eye contact with them. Word began to spread like wildfire through that place. The bar cordoned off a corner booth for us with velvet ropes and our "security guards" stood at attention.

Now, we had to have somebody put up a credit card. You can't party like a royal without the funds to back it up. We implied that a guy in our program, Adam Prichard, was Harry's royal secretary. Adam was another IT nerd who suddenly was fast-tracked to heaven. We put down Adam's credit card and all of us twenty-three-year-olds started ordering and getting into it. We were all Merrill analysts, except for one of my college friends named Jeff who worked for BlackRock. After an hour, the gawking from the crowd was too much—everyone wanted to know who we were and what we were doing. The excitement in the air made the club feel electric, like we were on the precipice of something major. We were making the best kind of scene, so we told the management, "Here's what we're willing to do."

Because we wanted to go bigger.

We had them bring us paper napkins, saying, "We're willing to give up to one hundred autographs." The crowd went crazy and everybody on the other side of the velvet rope was chomping at the bit. Please note that Underbar was a basement bar and it was exceedingly dark; that was key. It was so poorly lit that we could have said we had anyone from Brad Pitt to Michael Jackson with us. Michael started signing autographs as we shuffled people through a hasty line and they went wild.

The other factor is that this was the pre-smartphone era. Nowadays, the jig would have been up in minutes. No one could google what Harry really looked like, plus Michael was convincingly British because he *was* British. One girl in the autograph line knew my friend Jeff because they worked at BlackRock together. She normally didn't give him the time of day, but suddenly she was begging him, "Can you get me farther in line?" Worried that she might give us up once she deduced that some nerd from U of M wouldn't be pals with the real Prince Harry, we had Jeff lean into it, suave as can be, saying, "I'll see what I can do."

The reason everything worked is that we all became mentalists that night. Every single one of us kept our shit together. No one broke character. We paid attention to how the crowd was acting and we read their expressions, giving them back exactly what we could see they wanted, and we refused to be our own worst enemies.

The whole night, Prince Michael was ordering like a fiend and he was surrounded by some of the most beautiful women in New York. He kept saying, "Adam, what do the girls need?" Michael had his arms around multiple ladies. Women who'd probably cross the street normally to avoid this dork were all over him. The best part was that at one point, he had to use the lavatory. He took the bodyguards, who knocked on bathroom doors and made everybody leave. Then they stood at attention outside while Bobby, the royal consort, went inside with him.

Imagine trying to tell a New Yorker what to do—*and having them listen!*

At a certain point, we felt like we were on the cusp of overstaying our welcome. The energy had begun to shift. The second rule of show-biz is to always leave them wanting more, so that's what we did, parting on a high note and asking for the check. Timing, as always, is everything.

Ironically, we never discussed what we'd do if our plan worked. We were the dog who finally caught the car—What were we going to do with it? We debated getting a limo and going to another location, but we were on such a high that we didn't want to blow it. We ended up not going elsewhere because our plan had been executed so flawlessly that we didn't want to risk it crashing down.

We left the poker table while we were ahead, with a story all of us would recount for the next twenty years and counting. Again, we weren't trying to get anything over on the bar financially. We paid our tab. My share was a staggering $1,800, and that was the most expensive night of my life. I mean, this was an astronomical sum, but if we wanted to play, we had to pay, and I've never regretted a single penny.

There are certain moments in your life where you feel so alive, and I can tell you some of those moments for me are the ones you'd expect, like my wedding day, when my children were born, their birthdays, and during some big races. The moment we walked out of Underbar, it felt like *The Breakfast Club* when the Brat Pack walked out and high-fived after detention. That was a moment that tied that little group of us together for life.

All of this would have been enough, except . . . the next week, *Us Weekly* published an "About Town" blurb, saying that Prince Harry was spotted at Underbar partying for his birthday.

Even the press bought our ruse!

We did it.

We gave everyone involved, from the waitstaff to the patrons to the management to my classmates, the best night ever. And we left with a tale we're all going to tell for the rest of our lives.

So that's my favorite story. But I'll share the one that could have changed everything next.

A Weekend in Jail

During the winter of my senior year of college, I drove up to Ferris State University in Big Rapids, Michigan, to hang out with my buddies Aaron and Tubo for the weekend. That college is about three hours from Ann Arbor, smack in the middle of nowhere. Big Rapids is one of those towns where there's a college and little else. In places like that, it feels like the locals somewhat can't stand the college kids, even though it's a weird symbiotic relationship because without the university there wouldn't be much of a town. In fact, the population doubles when classes are in session. This interplay manifests in an environment where the police are always eager to catch the student body breaking the rules.

When we arrived at FSU, there was two feet of snow on the ground and almost nothing to do, save for recreational consumption. Day drinking commenced in the early afternoon at a local bar, where we waited around to see if any girls showed up and played a lot of pool and darts. Little did we realize in the moment how carefree and joyous those days were, with not a real responsibility in the world . . .

Full disclosure: I am less than pleased by the choices I made that day and am thankful to have grown up a bit since. I wasn't always one to rig the game in my own favor. So, my pals and I were fairly intoxicated by 5:00 p.m. It was pitch-dark at that point and there's nothing quite so depressing as the middle of the winter in Michigan.

We had to walk back to my friend's small house on campus, just trudging through the blackness of night and all that snow, because this was before Ubers existed and there were no taxis to be found. He lived about three quarters of a mile from the bar, and we were drunk, cold, and hungry. When we spotted a warm and bright Papa Johns looming in the distance, it was like finding a lush oasis in the middle of the scorching-hot desert.

What happened next was entirely my fault, mostly because I was an idiot that day. I can't sugarcoat it; it was all me and my bad decisions. At Papa Johns, they had a bank of about twenty phones on the counter; this was before it was common to have one phone with dozens of lines. So there were these red phones that the employees were constantly answering, thanks to their brisk delivery business.

After I paid for our late-night eats, the crew and I were sitting there waiting as the pizzas baked. I noticed that one phone was broken—cracked down the middle, nonfunctional, and not plugged in. I was wearing a poofy puffer jacket so voluminous I could hide anything under it.

And the wheels inside my head started turning. A plan was hatched with not all that much thought for the consequences, just the here and the now. I said to myself, "Well naturally, I should steal that broken phone . . . and then peer-pressure my friends to also steal something." Totally logical thought, right? My plan was to use misdirection to distract the employees and sleight of hand to hide the phone under my jacket. What could possibly go wrong?

Again, since I'm giving the unvarnished truth, this wasn't the first time I'd stolen something. I used to shoplift as a teenager because I enjoyed the rush. I'd take things I would not even use. For example, I didn't smoke cigars. But at 7-Eleven, I always made it a mission to swipe a pack of Swisher Sweets and then give them to friends.

To me, stealing cigars felt like doing a trick, given the element of excitement. I liked the fact that theft required a sleight of hand, that I needed to employ misdirection. I'd wait for the right moment and palm the package, my hand shoved up my sleeve. I'd learned to be casual years before, because I would have items, such as cards and coins, hidden in my hands throughout the day as a way to practice. I'd trained my hands to palm a coin by lightly squeezing the muscles; it doesn't change how your hand looks, yet you can hold the coin in place. In fact, I could be holding three coins and you'd never know it. So when I'd shoplift cigars, in my head it was less *crime* and more *magic*.

Listen, it made sense when I was sixteen, but as I write this, I'm cringing.

Heady with the thrill of taking what wasn't mine, I turned into the ringleader because I was my own worst enemy. I commanded my friends, "You guys steal something, too." They quickly found the bathroom, which doubled as a locker room for the employees. They ran across a laundry bin and swiped three dirty Papa Johns T-shirts, shrugging them into their own puffer coats.

Remember, we paid for the pizzas; this certainly wasn't a full-blown robbery. We went back to my friend's house, where his roommate was throwing a proper house party, the entire reason we'd come. The living room was maybe three hundred square feet and it was packed with fifty people. Amazing. The drinking continued and I ended up passing out on the futon in my buddy's bedroom, likely before the prime-time shows were even over that night. Don't forget, I'd started early.

Fun fact, I was almost legally blind without my contacts or glasses at the time. I have since had LASIK and now enjoy perfect vision. In the middle of the night, I was woken up and I didn't have my contacts in and had no idea where my glasses were. I was basically blind and completely confused. Further, I wasn't even hungover because I suspect I was still lightly drunk.

Some guy I didn't know nudged me and said, "The cops are here."

Um, *what?*

I told him, "I don't live here, bro. I don't care." But he argued with me, saying, "You have to get up, they're here for you."

Again, *what?*

When we'd arrived at the party the night before, I had vague memories of putting on our Papa Johns shirts and walking around the party with the broken phone, asking, "Who wants Papa Johns?" and taking everyone's order. Because I entered college early, I was only twenty years old, so I thought our performance the night before was the height of hilarity. That is, until a virtual SWAT team came busting into the room where I was clad in a pair of tighty-whities and a Papa Johns shirt.

I was *literally* wearing the evidence.

The officer grilled me, saying, "Do you work at Papa Johns?"

I responded, "I fell asleep in the shirt," which was technically true, but the officer saw right through my ruse. I implored him to please let me put in my contacts before we did anything else. While he allowed me that small dignity, his compassion ended there. The rest of his team perp-walked me with my hands cuffed behind my back, wearing only my skimpy underwear and the stupid T-shirt that smelled of yeast. I had to wait outside half naked in minus-ten-degree weather while they collected my felon friends.

They took us to jail and put me and Aaron in one holding cell and Tubo in a separate one by himself, which had to be so scary. This was around 3:00 a.m. The detectives interviewed each of us separately. Before the interview, they put me in a prison jumpsuit. Until then, I'd been in the holding tank in my underwear, yet my friend was fully dressed. I was like, "Dude, how are you in pants?"

When I was questioned, I mustered up all the bravado a still-drunk 20-year-old could, saying, "I need to talk to a lawyer." I'd watched enough *Law & Order* and *CSI* to at least know that. I was told we were being charged with felony larceny and that sobered me right up. I was scared out of my mind, but also confused, asking, "What do you mean, a felony?" One of the men questioning me replied, "Papa Johns said you stole three T-shirts and a phone."

Even in my state, I had the presence of mind to ask, "Isn't a felony over a certain amount of money?" My superpower of a memory was pulling all up the random police procedural episodes I'd ever seen, trying to find a kernel of info that could benefit me. The officer explained that we'd stolen things the pizza place didn't sell. Had we taken $999 worth of their not-great pizza, it would still be a misdemeanor. But because we took objects that weren't for sale, what we did was considered a felony.

Shit.

Part of me needed to believe this was all scare tactics, but Big Rapids PD *did not mess around.* The following morning, they took me from the tank and placed me in gen pop at the county jail. They treated us as though we were serial killers, and not three young idiots who were trying to make people at a party laugh.

This was dead serious. I was separated from my friends, was processed and fingerprinted, and had my mug shots taken. Aaron and Tubo were taken to a separate wing, and I was on my own, the deck decidedly not stacked in my favor.

If you've never been in gen pop at a county jail, the scene doesn't quite look like the movies. Instead of cells with bars, there are doors that close with plastic windows. When I came in, the doors were open and no one was in their cells during the day, as it was minimal security.

Everything in this open bay at the county jail is self-segregated. There's a section where Black inmates are and a section where white inmates are, with a divide between them so profound there may as well have been a wall erected between them. I'm shown to the space that's my room, and the whole time my stomach is sinking—and it's not just the hangover kicking in. Instead, I am coming face-to-face with the consequences of my actions and that is not a safe space. After I put down the pillow and blanket I was given on the hard bunk, I don't really know what to do, but again, I'd watched enough *Law & Order* to know that I was considered a "fish," which is not a great thing to be.

As I took in my surroundings, I noticed that some people were watching TV, others were seated around two long tables, and again, everyone was segregated by race. For lack of another idea, I decided to lean into the one thing I did know: I decided to make my fear of rejection magically disappear. With no hesitation, I walked over to the table of Black guys playing cards, and full of confidence *I did not feel*, I said, "Hey man, how's it going? Can I see those cards?"

It felt like in a movie where the record scratches; everyone stops talking and looks at me. The guy was so shocked that the fish had walked up to him and demanded the cards that he wasn't even mad. I pressed my good fortune at not being pounded into a damp spot on the concrete floor and said, "Let me show you something with those cards."

There I was, a punk college kid reeking of privilege, bad decisions, and Jack Daniel's, demanding they give me their cards. I guess he must have wanted to see what was going to happen next, so he handed me the deck.

I performed card tricks for probably five hours straight, and what was so wild about it was that both sides of the jail came together to watch me. Black, white, it didn't matter because they were drawn together by magic.

I had won them over, one card up my sleeve at a time.

At the end of the day when I wanted to take a shower and wash the stench of fear off me, I was promised protection from all sides. Guys from both factions kept everyone out of the open shower bay so I could bathe in privacy.

Finally, around 6:00 p.m., I was allowed to call my girlfriend. I started crying because the magnitude of this screwup was really beginning to sink in. My roommate in jail was serving a year's time for his third DUI. He was fascinated that I was from Israel. When he found out I had a passport, he said, "Dude, you've got to get out of here. You make bail, you fly to Israel." I replied, "I stole a T-shirt. I'm going back to college. I'm not fleeing; I have class on Monday."

That's when I found out there was no bail and I wasn't seeing a judge until Monday or Tuesday, so I'd be there for a while.

Again, shit.

All this goes back to my point about when you set yourself up for success, you don't know what success is going to look like in the future. Sure, success now looks like Oz the Mentalist predicting the Super Bowl winner or blowing Jim Cramer's mind on CNBC. But back then, it meant that the last seven years of my life—not only practicing card tricks but performing them on video for Penguin Magic—had given me an encyclopedic knowledge of tricks in my repertoire.

Success meant I had enough tricks to make it through a weekend almost without repeating a single one. I had Travelers, two-card monte, invisible palm aces, ambitious card, assemblies, poker deals, and the list went on and on. I had an endless array of magic to perform because I'd put in the requisite ten thousand hours it took to become an expert.

It was almost as though I were set up for this scenario: seeing a magician on the cruise ship, my mentorship with Bruce Kessler and all the hours, days, months, and years spent learning and practicing magic. I performed and then performed some more. And the guards were so blown away that I later found out they were asking my buddies in a different wing if they knew how I did it. My friends found this both hilarious and a great source of relief, knowing that I was alive, given I'd been sent off by myself while they were rooming together.

Apparently over the course of that miserable weekend, I'd become a living legend in the facility—all four wings of the jail had heard about me. And to this day, I've never had a more appreciative audience. That Monday when I was finally arraigned, guards chained my friends and I together to walk into court, attached to the person in front and behind, like an old-timey chain gang. We were led through the maze of unattached buildings that make up the Mecosta County jail, courtroom, and city hall.

Fortunately, at this point, my girlfriend had helped me find an attorney and everything that I'd messed up was set to be expunged, meaning my record would carry no whiff of this incident. The lawyer employed the Holmes Youthful Trainee Act, which states that if you've never committed a violent offense or had any criminal record, you could get your misdeeds permanently removed from your record. If you perform community service, do two years of probation, and never get in trouble again, there will be no record of the arrest. It's all erased, thank God.

I didn't even have to give a Not Guilty plea, which is very lucky because if I'd had to make a plea for a larceny, it's a financial crime and I couldn't have worked on Wall Street. When I stood in front of the courtroom, the judge started reading through my file and she said, "You're the magician, right?" I was astounded. How in the world did she know? I'd never met this person, but somehow word had gotten to her too!

My bail was set at $2,000. Fortunately, I'd also set myself up for success with the Wolverine Spartan Boat Docks company, which is the only reason I had that much money in my savings account. What's funny is when my girlfriend went to pay the bail to get me out, the bondsman and the city clerk asked, "Wait, are you the magician's girlfriend?"

I was out and I was damn fortunate. I have to believe that my ability to disarm with charm was a huge factor in my freedom.

My friends and I found out later that one of the people at the party had a roommate that worked at Papa Johns and called them to tell on us. That employee in turn sent the cops to the house party and they pressed charges. I've never met that person who told on us, but for years truly detested them from afar. I must say that now with this firmly in the rearview mirror, I would thank them for giving a much-needed wakeup call to get my life on the straight and narrow.

The lesson I learned during this experience was incredibly valuable. Importantly, I learned to never steal anything again, and to be smarter. To always have a plan, and a backup plan. That lesson would not have been learned without consequences. Maybe someone could have said it to me, but without that sting, without touching that metaphorical oven and getting burned, the lesson wouldn't have stuck. Thank God it happened in a way that didn't impact my life negatively.

All things considered, I got off very lightly and I'm truly thankful for that.

But I took all those lessons, and I've carried them with me for the rest of my life in a story that I'm only now starting to tell.

Last Word

You've now taken a journey behind the curtain—not just into the world of mentalism but also the untapped power of your own mind. At some point, we've all wished we could read someone else's mind, myself included! Everything would be easier if we if we could figure out what other people are actually thinking. I'm not able to give you a superpower or magic bullet. The techniques I have shared aren't illusions or tricks; they're proven tools that you can use daily. Over time, they will become habits, ingrained in your muscle memory. Acting preemptively saves everyone a whole lot of time and effort and that's something you now have the ability to do.

When you're in a position of weakness, you have the formula to flip that power dynamic to your benefit. When you're feeling unsure, you can shelve that fear of rejection. You can get out of your own way, and you can lend—or take—a hand when needed. Your weaknesses are now your strengths and your memory is your superpower.

Now that you can deduce what's in another person's head, your ability to influence and win them over will grow tremendously. Anticipating the thoughts and actions of those around you makes you better at understanding human nature; it's the ultimate hack *and you have the key.* Because you can tap into your motivations and learn how to change your outcomes, you're going to push past what's kept you stuck, unable to move on and level up.

Remember that real transformation doesn't happen overnight. It happens in the small choices you make each day, the new habits you form, the beliefs you challenge, and the fears you face. By taking the time to learn how to read your own mind, and those of others around you, you are setting yourself up for success in the long term.

When you can read people—especially yourself—and when you can use all the tools I've shared—from planning for the unexpected to understanding how to captivate others with a story—the world becomes your oyster. This is an inherent trait that you only needed to recognize and hone. Like Dorothy in *The Wizard of Oz*, you always had the ability.

You have the skills, you have the instincts, and now, you have the techniques. So it's time to step up and take that metaphorical swing at the ball.

Pretend to look surprised when you knock it out of the park.

ACKNOWLEDGMENTS

I've read hundreds of these sections before and never realized how daunting the task is until writing my own. So many start with "it takes a village," which seems so cliché, but I have to tell you that it is actually true! There are countless people to thank, without whom I would never have taken on, much less completed, the Herculean task of writing my book. First and foremost, and without a single doubt, this book would not have been possible without my wife, Elisa Rosen, the love of my life and mother of our five children. You are a true force of nature and the foundation of our family. You were instrumental every step of the way, pushed me when I needed it, attempted to keep me focused (near impossible), and gave me the tough love required to put pen to paper no matter how much I complained. I love you and can't imagine my life without you. To my parents, for giving me life, picking a card (any card) at least a million times during my teenage years, and always believing in me, along with my twin sisters for your love. To my publishing and book team, thank you for your patience and guidance, your enthusiasm and energy, your humor and humanity, I fed off it throughout the entire process and it gave me confidence when I felt way in over my head: Laura Tisdel and the entire Viking team, as well as Jen Lancaster, Kevin Anderson, and Stephen Power. To my literary agent, Jim Levine, I love that every email you send tells me to please confirm receipt, that your eyes light up like a child's every time I read your mind, how genuine your reactions are, your sage advice no matter where in the world you might be, and your oh so casual yet oh so superb negotiation skills. To Pete Garceau, you knocked it out of the park with the cover design, incredible work! To Adam Grant, your generosity, willingness to answer my questions no matter how absurd, and your honesty meant more than you can imagine. To David Goggins, who I've been inspired by for many years and whose voice was in my head at times when I thought about quitting, but then instantly knew there was simply no way I could DNF or he would never let me hear the end of it. To Adam Skolnick, your *New York Times* article planted the initial seed that maybe I was worthy of writing a book and have a story to tell that might interest people, so thank you for inspiring me. To Adam Schefter, you've always believed in me and been my champion. Thank you for opening so many doors, being so selfless and being a great friend. To Jason Raff, *AGT* changed my life, and I will never forget all the crazy moments we shared behind the scenes, dumpster diving, your always calm demeanor, and what a surreal experience that show was. To Rmax Goodwin, your woodworking is superb, and I've heard that you're a decent mentalist, too. One day if you're lucky I will teach you the mouth coil trick.

There are so many more people that directly or indirectly have been a part of my life, career, and journey. To every person who has had me on their TV show or podcast, written a story about me, been in my audience and gasped or applauded or heckled me later, all my friends, extended family, my fans . . . thank you! To my brothers in the mentalism community, JFab, EBos, Nimrod, Kvine, Majornation, I appreciate your lending an ear and helping me brainstorm. To Bruce Kessler and Doug Anderson, you helped me catch the magic bug and it's hard to believe where it has taken me. And for the reader, I truly appreciate you and hope that these tools help you to achieve your goals and improve your life.

NOTES

CHAPTER ONE—CHANNEL YOUR INNER MENTALIST

1. Jennifer Guttman, "The Slippery Slope of Relying on Non-Verbal Communication," *Psychology Today*, November 17, 2017, psychologytoday.com/us/blog/sustainable-life-satisfaction/202111/the-slippery-slope-of-relying-on-non-verbal-communication.
2. Kristin Koch et al., "How *Much* the Eye Tells the Brain," *Current Biology* 16, no. 14 (July 2006): 1428–34, doi.org/10.1016/j.cub.2006.05.056.
3. Kendra Cherry, "What Is the Negativity Bias?" Verywell Mind, updated November 13, 2023, verywellmind.com/negative-bias-4589618.

CHAPTER TWO—BELIEVE IT TO ACHIEVE IT

1. Lindsey J. Byom and Bilge Mutlu, "Theory of Mind: Mechanisms, Methods, and New Directions," *Frontiers in Human Neuroscience* 7 (August 2013): 413, doi.org/10.3389/fnhum.2013.00413.
2. "How Much of Communication Is Nonverbal?" The University of Texas Permian Basin, accessed May 12, 2025, online.utpb.edu/about-us/articles/communication/how-much-of-communication-is-nonverbal.
3. Mark K. Ho, Rebecca Saxe, and Fiery Cushman, "Planning with Theory of Mind," *Trends in Cognitive Science* 26, no. 11 (November 2022): 959–71, doi.org/10.1016/j.tics.2022.08.003.
4. "Michael Phelps—The Journey—Ep 5—Visualization," interview with Michael Phelps

and Bob Bowman, posted August 20, 2018, by ProSwimwear, YouTube, 1 min., 57 sec., youtube.com/watch?v=p-mZhvxeK_k.

5. NASA, LSIC Excavation & Construction Focus Group, "Lunar Landing and Launch Pads," October 20, 2020, chrome-extension://efaidnbmnnnibpcajpcglclefindmkaj/https://ntrs.nasa.gov/api/citations/20205009125/downloads/Lunar%20Landing%20%26%20Launch%20Pads%20v1.pdf. See also NASA's mission overview page, nasa.gov/history/apollo-11-mission-overview.
6. Shaffer Grubb and Amina Khan, "The Apollo 11 Mission as Measured by Heartbeats," *Los Angeles Times*, July 17, 2019, latimes.com/projects/la-sci-apollo-11-mission-as-measured-by-heartbeats.
7. James Devitt, "What's Going On in Our Brains When We Plan?" New York University, June 7, 2024, nyu.edu/about/news-publications/news/2024/june/what-s-going-on-in-our-brains-when-we-plan-.html.
8. "Watch Mentalist Oz Pearlman Get Into TODAY Anchors' Heads," *Today* segment, posted March 10, 2016, by TODAY, YouTube, youtube.com/watch?v=K_K3fcfYKAY.

CHAPTER THREE—MAKE YOUR FEAR OF REJECTION MAGICALLY DISAPPEAR

1. Kirsten Weir, "The Pain of Social Rejection," *Monitor on Psychology* 43, no. 4 (April 2012): 50, apa.org/monitor/2012/04/rejection.
2. Mary Beckman, "Rejection Is Like Pain to the Brain," *Science*, October 9, 2003, science.org/content/article/rejection-pain-brain.
3. Elitsa Dermendzhiyska, "Rejection Kills," *Aeon*, April 30, 2019, aeon.co/essays/health-warning-social-rejection-doesnt-only-hurt-it-kills.
4. Guy Winch, "10 Surprising Facts About Rejection," *Psychology Today*, July 3, 2013, psychologytoday.com/us/blog/the-squeaky-wheel/201307/10-surprising-facts-about-rejection.
5. Ana Sandoiu, "Do You Fear Embarrassment? Here's How to Overcome It," *Medical News Today*, April 1, 2018, medicalnewstoday.com/articles/321378.
6. Yanhua Cheng and Daniel Grühn, "Age Differences in Reactions to Social Rejection: The Role of Cognitive Resources and Appraisals," *The Journals of Gerontology: Series B* 70, no. 6 (November 2015): 830–39, doi.org/10.1093/geronb/gbu054.
7. "Carrie Rescued from the Bin | Mark Lawson Talks to Stephen King," Interview, posted June 5, 2009, by BBC Studios, YouTube, youtube.com/watch?v=xgqj7dbLSas.
8. Lucas Reilly, "How Stephen King's Wife Saved 'Carrie' and Helped Launch His Career," *Mental Floss*, April 5, 2024, mentalfloss.com/article/53235/how-stephen-kings-wife-saved-carrie-and-launched-his-career.
9. "6 Famous Authors Who Once Faced Rejection," *WildMind* (blog), accessed May 12, 2025, wildmindcreative.com/bookmarketing/6-famous-authors-who-once-faced

-rejection; Sughen Yongo, "The Best Stephen King Books, Ranked and in Order," *Forbes*, June 9, 2025, forbes.com/sites/entertainment/article/stephen-king-books.

10. Scott Mautz, "11 Famous Failures That Will Inspire You to Success," *Inc.*, September 12, 2017, inc.com/scott-mautz/11-famous-failures-that-will-inspire-you-to-succes.html.
11. Liadan Gunter, "Neuroscience: What Social Media Does to Your Brain," *Nivati*, updated May 27, 2025, nivati.com/blog/neuroscience-what-social-media-does-to-your-brain.
12. Pam Belluck, "Memories Weaken Without Reinforcement, Study Finds," *New York Times*, March 16, 2015, nytimes.com/2015/03/17/science/memories-become-weaker-without-reinforcement-study-finds.html.

CHAPTER FOUR—FOCUS ON OTHERS

1. Kate Lunau, "King of Beer Sales, Amigo," *Maclean's*, August 13, 2009, macleans.ca/economy/business/king-of-beer-sales-amigo.
2. Harneet Kaur, "The Lost Art of Empathy," *Psychiatric Times*, February 17, 2022, psychiatrictimes.com/view/the-lost-art-of-empathy.
3. Alison Jane Martingano, "Social Media and Empathy Around the Globe," *Character & Context* (blog), *The Society for Personality and Social Psychology*, March 3, 2023, spsp.org/news/character-and-context-blog/martingano-social-media-use-lower-empathy.
4. "How Social Media Impedes Empathy," *Move This World*, January 15, 2019, movethisworld.com/mental-health-awareness/2019-1-15-how-social-media-impedes-empathy.

CHAPTER FIVE—FORGET TOMORROW, START TODAY

1. "Limbic System," Cleveland Clinic, accessed May 12, 2025, my.clevelandclinic.org/health/body/limbic-system.
2. Amy Spencer, "Want to Train Your Brain to Stop Procrastinating? Read These Tips from a Neuroscientist," *Real Simple*, last updated May 1, 2023, realsimple.com/work-life/life-strategies/time-management/procrastination.
3. Aniesa Hanson, "The Paralysis of Fear: How Fear of Failure Contributes to Unhappiness," Hanson Complete Wellness, accessed May 12, 2025, hansoncomplete.com/fear.
4. Magdalena Bak-Maier, "The Psychology Behind Task Completion: A Student's Guide," *Make Time Count* (blog), accessed May 12, 2025, maketimecount.com/how-completion-helps-students-build-confidence.
5. Mya Care Editorial Team, "The Zeigarnik Effect: Why Do Unfinished Tasks Haunt Us?" Mya Care, January 4, 2024, myacare.com/blog/the-zeigarnik-effect-why-do-unfinished-tasks-haunt-us.

6. Rishi Sriram, "The Neuroscience Behind Productive Struggle," *Edutopia*, April 13, 2020, edutopia.org/article/neuroscience-behind-productive-struggle.
7. Keiichiro Susuki, "Myelin: A Specialized Membrane for Cell Communication," *Nature Education* 3, no. 9 (2010): 59, nature.com/scitable/topicpage/myelin-a-specialized-membrane-for-cell-communication-14367205.
8. Matt Puderbaugh and Prabhu D. Emmady, "Neuroplasticity," StatPearls Publishing, January 2025, ncbi.nlm.nih.gov/books/NBK557811.
9. Duncan Haughey, "A Brief History of SMART Goals," ProjectSmart, December 13, 2014, projectsmart.co.uk/smart-goals/brief-history-of-smart-goals.php.
10. Stacey McLachlan, "The Science of Habit," Healthline, December 22, 2021, healthline.com/health/the-science-of-habit#1.
11. James Clear, "The Cardinal Rule of Behavior Change," *James Clear*, jamesclear.com/quotes/the-cardinal-rule-of-behavior-change.
12. Katie Doll, "The Habit Loop: Charles Duhigg's Theory for Continuous Actions," Shortform, July 3, 2023, shortform.com/blog/the-habit-loop-2.
13. "Oxytocin," Cleveland Clinic, accessed May 12, 2025, my.clevelandclinic.org/health/articles/22618-oxytocin.
14. Lisa Nutter and Tim Freundlich, "A Social Movement Requires Momentum," *Stanford Social Innovation Review*, March 29, 2023, ssir.org/articles/entry/a_social_movement_requires_momentum.

CHAPTER SIX—STACK THE DECK IN YOUR FAVOR

1. Michael John O'Keeffe, "Science Is Just Starting to Understand the Benefits of Athletes Putting Their Brains in 'Auto Pilot,'" *The Conversation,* June 26, 2024, theconversation.com/science-is-just-starting-to-understand-the-benefits-of-athletes-putting-their-brains-in-auto-pilot-232596.
2. Colleen Walsh, "Give Her Some Space: Psychologist's Perspective on Simone Biles at the Olympics Includes Message for Parents, Coaches," *The Harvard Gazette,* July 30, 2021, news.harvard.edu/gazette/story/2021/07/a-harvard-psychologists-perspective-on-biles-at-the-olympics.
3. John Kounios and David S. Rosen, "Brain Scans of Jazz Musicians Reveal How to Reach a Creative 'Flow State,'" *Scientific American* 331, no. 3 (October 2024): 66, scientificamerican.com/article/brain-scans-of-jazz-musicians-reveal-how-to-reach-a-creative-flow-state.
4. Nathan Cross, "Neuroscience of Peak Performance: Unlocking the Secrets of Elite Athletes and Entrepreneurs," *Medium*, September 16, 2023, medium.com/@NC_16/neuroscience-of-peak-performance-unlocking-the-secrets-of-elite-athletes-and-entrepreneurs-72ce73b026.

5. Richard Lewis, "Mindful Mistakes: How Brains Learn from Errors," *Neuroscience News*, November 9, 2023, neurosciencenews.com/errorr-learning-brain-25183.
6. Krissy Brady, "This Is Why You Get More Anxious After Something Good Happens," *HuffPost*, April 9, 2019, huffpost.com/entry/anxiety-good-things_l_5ca78fc1e4b047edf959e2fe.
7. Devrupa Rakshit, "Is This Normal? 'Every Time I Start to Feel Happy, I Get Scared Bad Things Will Happen,'" *The Swaddle*, September 7, 2020, theswaddle.com/is-this-normal-every-time-i-start-to-feel-happy-i-get-scared-bad-things-will-happen.
8. Alicia Clark, *Hack Your Anxiety* (Sourcebooks: 2018).
9. "How to Regulate Your Nervous System and Restore Calm: 12 Proven Techniques," Calm.com, accessed May 12, 2025, https://calm.com/blog/how-to-regulate-nervous-system.

CHAPTER SEVEN—DON'T BE YOUR OWN WORST ENEMY

1. Caroline Bologna, "'Fake It Till You Make It' Isn't Just a Cliché. It's Backed by Science," *HuffPost*, August 3, 2022, huffpost.com/entry/behavioral-activation-fake-it-til-you-make-it_l_62d7140ae4b0aad58d139763.
2. Lisa Lavigna, "The Dangers of Negative Thinking and How to Master Positive Self-Talk," Excelsior University, September 21, 2023, excelsior.edu/article/the-dangers-of-negative-thinking-and-how-to-master-positive-self-talk.
3. Shefali Raina, "Four Brain Science Habits to Help Neutralize Negative Self-Talk," *Forbes*, May 06, 2021, forbes.com/councils/forbescoachescouncil/2021/05/06/four-brain-science-habits-to-help-neutralize-negative-self-talk.
4. "Catch It, Check It, Change It," Headroom Wellbeing Guide, BBC, accessed May 12, 2025, downloads.bbc.co.uk/headroom/cbt/catch_it.pdf.
5. "Implementing the EASE Shift Perspective Principle: CBT Techniques," Veterans Affairs, accessed May 12, 2025, mirecc.va.gov/visn5/training/docs/Handout_Shift_Persp.pdf.
6. J. M. Dutcher et al., "Self-Affirmation Activates the Ventral Striatum: A Possible Reward-Related Mechanism for Self-Affirmation," *Psychol Science* 27, no. 4 (April 2016): 455–66, doi.org/10.1177/0956797615625989.
7. Fernando Gomez-Pinilla and Charles Hillman, "The Influence of Exercise on Cognitive Abilities," *Comprehensive Physiology* 3, no. 1 (January 2013): 403–28, pmc.ncbi.nlm.nih.gov/articles/PMC3951958.
8. Grace McGregor, "How Exercise Affects the Brain," Brigham Young University, February 8, 2021, lifesciences.byu.edu/how-exercise-affects-your-brain.

CHAPTER EIGHT—ASK FOR HELP

1. Dan Schawbel, "Brene Brown: How Vulnerability Can Make Our Lives Better," *Forbes*, April 21, 2013, forbes.com/sites/danschawbel/2013/04/21/brene-brown-how-vulnerability-can-make-our-lives-better.
2. "Oxytocin: The Love Hormone," Harvard Health Publishing, June 13, 2023, health.harvard.edu/mind-and-mood/oxytocin-the-love-hormone.
3. Jennifer Caspari, "Embracing Vulnerability," *Psychology Today*, May 7, 2023, psychologytoday.com/us/blog/living-well-when-your-body-doesnt-cooperate/202305/embracing-vulnerability.
4. Paul J. Zak, "The Neuroscience of Trust," *Harvard Business Review* (January/February 2017), hbr.org/2017/01/the-neuroscience-of-trust.
5. Alexander Heffner, "The Neuroscience of Friendship," *The American Prospect*, February 9, 2020, prospect.org/health/the-neuroscience-of-friendship.
6. Julianne Holt-Lunstad, Timothy B. Smith, and J. Bradley Layton, "Social Relationships and Mortality Risk: A Meta-analytic Review," *PLOS Medicine* 7, no. 7 (July 2010): e1000316, doi.org/10.1371/journal.pmed.1000316.
7. Lindsay Hindle, "What Does Neuroscience Have to Do with Mentorship?" International Association of Business Communicators British Columbia, April 8, 2014, iabc.bc.ca/blog/what-does-neuroscience-have-to-do-with-mentorship.
8. Angela Byars-Winston and Maria Lund Dahlberg, "The Science of Mentoring Relationships: What Is Mentorship?" chapter 2 in *The Science of Effective Mentorship in STEMM* (National Academies Press, 2019), ncbi.nlm.nih.gov/books/NBK552775.
9. "Using Neuroscience in Coaching and Mentoring for Improved Results," Vorecol, August 28, 2024, vorecol.com/blogs/blog-using-neuroscience-in-coaching-and-mentoring-for-improved-results-9248.
10. Sarah Wilson, "The Power of Persuasion," *The Guardian*, March 7, 2009, theguardian.com/lifeandstyle/2009/mar/08/power-of-persuasion.

CHAPTER NINE—TURN YOUR WEAKNESSES INTO YOUR STRENGTHS

1. Katie A. McLaughlin, et al., "Neglect as a Violation of Species-Expectant Experience: Neurodevelopmental Consequences," *Biological Psychiatry* 82, no. 7 (October 2017): 462–71, doi.org/10.1016/j.biopsych.2017.02.1096.
2. "Who Are the Kurds?" *BBC News*, October 15, 2019, bbc.com/news/world-middle-east-29702440.
3. "Anticipation: The Psychology of Waiting in Line," Association for Psychological Science, July 15, 2014, psychologicalscience.org/news/were-only-human/anticipation-the-psychology-of-waiting-in-line.html.
4. Judith E. Glaser, "Why We Don't Speak Up," *Psychology Today*, May 22, 2018, psychol

ogytoday.com/us/blog/conversational-intelligence/201805/why-we-dont-speak-up.

5. Jacob Rueda, "New Study Shows Percentage of People Fearful of Speaking Out on Their Beliefs," *ABC4 Utah News*, November 10, 2021, abc4.com/news/new-study-shows-percentage-of-people-fearful-of-speaking-out-on-their-beliefs.
6. Jane M. Richards and James J. Gross, "Composure at Any Cost? The Cognitive Consequences of Emotion Suppression," *Personality and Social Psychology Bulletin* 25, no. 8 (August 1999): 1033–44, doi.org/10.1177/01461672992511010.
7. Polly Campbell, "What We Gain by Being Uncomfortable," *Psychology Today*, June 21, 2022, psychologytoday.com/us/blog/imperfect-spirituality/202206/what-we-gain-by-being-uncomfortable.

CHAPTER TEN—MAKE MEMORY YOUR SUPERPOWER

1. Arlin Cuncic, "The Mandela Effect: How Masses of People Can Have the Same False Memory," Verywell Mind, January 3, 2024, verywellmind.com/what-is-the-mandela-effect-4589394.
2. Bradley Voytek, "Are There Really as Many Neurons in the Human Brain as Stars in the Milky Way?" *Brain Metrics* (blog), Scitable, May 20, 2013, nature.com/scitable/blog/brain-metrics/are_there_really_as_many.
3. Corinne Purtill, "The New Science of Forgetting," *Time*, April 28, 2022, time.com/6171190/new-science-of-forgetting.
4. Bill Hathaway, "What Makes a Memory? It May Be Related to How Hard Your Brain Had to Work," *YaleNews*, May 13, 2024, news.yale.edu/2024/05/13/what-makes-memory-it-may-be-related-how-hard-your-brain-had-work.
5. Kendra Cherry, "The Recency Effect in Psychology," Verywell Mind, January 16, 2024, verywellmind.com/the-recency-effect-4685058.
6. Andrew E. Budson, "Have You Done Your Crossword Puzzle Today?" Harvard Health Publishing, November 29, 2022, health.harvard.edu/blog/have-you-done-your-crossword-puzzle-today-202211292857.
7. "Why Crossword Puzzles Are Beneficial to Your Brain Health," Neuroelectrics, December 19, 2022, neuroelectrics.com/blog/why-crossword-puzzles-are-beneficial-to-your-brain-health.
8. Chuan-Chih Yang et al., "Alterations in Brain Structure and Amplitude of Low-Frequency After 8 Weeks of Mindfulness Meditation Training in Meditation-Naïve Subjects," *Scientific Reports* 9 (July 2019): 10977, doi.org/10.1038/s41598-019-47470-4.
9. "Unleashing the Mind: The Neuroscience of Meditation and Its Impact on Memory," *Neuroscience News*, June 7, 2023, neurosciencenews.com/memory-meditation-23414.
10. Rachelle Hampton, "New Study Shows How Even Innocently Forgetting Names and

Personal Details Can Harm Relationships," *Slate*, October 16, 2018, slate.com/human-interest/2018/10/forgetting-names-friendship-harm-study.html.

11. Will Houston, "How Repetition Solidifies Memory," *Neuroscience News*, May 15, 2024, neurosciencenews.com/rwpwtition-memory-26114.
12. "Brain Prioritizes High-Reward Memories," UC Davis Department of Psychology, February 12, 2016, psychology.ucdavis.edu/news/brain-prioritizes-high-reward-memories.

CHAPTER ELEVEN—DISARM WITH CHARM

1. Tiffanie Wen, "The Tricks to Make Yourself Effortlessly Charming," *BBC*, June 27, 2017, bbc.com/worklife/article/20170627-the-tricks-to-make-yourself-effortlessly-charming.
2. Marianna Pogosyan, "Prejudice in the Brain," *Psychology Today,* June 23, 2020, psychologytoday.com/us/blog/between-cultures/202006/prejudice-in-the-brain.
3. Jerry Matysik, "Implicit Bias and Law Enforcement: Reducing Blame and Understanding the Brain," Lexipol, February 15, 2017, lexipol.com/resources/blog/implicit-bias-law-enforcement-reducing-blame-understanding-brain.
4. Jason Vu Nguyen, "Charming vs Charismatic: Understanding the Difference and Figuring Out Which One You Are," Medium, June 16, 2022, medium.com/@jasonvuvu/charming-vs-charismatic-understanding-the-difference-and-figuring-out-which-one-you-are-f64cba62125d.
5. Maya Al-Khouja et al., "Self-expression Can Be Authentic or Inauthentic, with Differential Outcomes for Well-being: Development of the Authentic and Inauthentic Expression Scale (AIES)," *Journal of Research in Personality* 97 (2022): 104191, https://doi.org/10.1016.
6. Nancy Marshall, "Here's Why the Word of the Year Is 'Authentic,'" *Forbes*, January 31, 2024, forbes.com/councils/forbesagencycouncil/2024/01/31/heres-why-the-word-of-the-year-is-authentic.
7. Natalye Paquin, "(Really) Listening & (Really) Learning," Points of Light, March 3, 2021, pointsoflight.org/blog/really-listening-really-learning.
8. "The Science of Active Listening," JimKwik.com, March 2, 2023, jimkwik.com/the-science-of-active-listening.
9. Hiroaki Kawamichi et al., "Perceiving Active Listening Activates the Reward System and Improves the Impression of Relevant Experiences," *Social Neuroscience* 10, no. 1 (2015): 16–26, doi.org/10.1080/17470919.2014.954732.
10. Robert Sanders, "Brain's Hippocampus Helps Fill in the Blanks of Language," *UC Berkeley News,* September 19, 2016, news.berkeley.edu/2016/09/19/brains-hippocampus-helps-fill-in-the-blanks-of-language.
11. Dale Carnegie, "Part Two: Six Ways to Make People Like You," in *How to Win Friends and Influence People* (Simon and Schuster, 1936).

12. Kyle Mittan, "Are You Good at What You Do? Bragging About It Could Make People Trust You Less," Phys.org, July 21, 2022, phys.org/news/2022-07-good-bragging-people.html#google_vignette.
13. Brian Collisson, "Humor Is Hot: Why Being Funny Attracts Potential Partners," *Psychology Today,* September 26, 2024, psychologytoday.com/us/blog/dating-toxic-or-tender/202409/humor-is-hot-why-being-funny-attracts-potential-partners.
14. Dolores Tropiano, "Being Funny Has Its Benefits in the Dating World," *ASU News*, February 13, 2024, news.asu.edu/20240213-science-and-technology-being-funny-has-its-benefits-dating-world.
15. Kendra Cherry, "Understanding Body Language and Facial Expressions," Verywell Mind, January 30, 2025, verywellmind.com/understand-body-language-and-facial-expressions-4147228.
16. Allessio Rastrelli, "Body Language," AlessioRastrelli.it, May 3, 2020, alessiorastrelli.it/en/body-language.
17. Avelo Roy, "The Science of Being Irresistibly Charming," AveloRoy.com, April 29, 2015, aveloroy.com/2015/04/29/science-irresistibly-charming-people.
18. Alannagh Kelly, "The Psychology of Mirroring," Imagine Health, October 31, 2017, imaginehealth.ie/the-psychology-of-mirroring.
19. "How Your Child's Nervous System Impacts Emotional Regulation and Meltdowns," he's-extraordinary, March 19, 2025, hes-extraordinary.com/how-your-childs-nervous-system-impacts-emotional-regulation-and-meltdowns.

CHAPTER TWELVE—TIE IT ALL TOGETHER WITH A STORY

1. Lani Peterson, "The Science Behind the Art of Storytelling," Harvard Business Publishing, November 14, 2017, lanipeterson.com/wp-content/uploads/2021/02/The-Science-Behind-teh-Art-of-Storytelling.docx.pdf.
2. Paul J. Zak, "Why Your Brain Loves Good Storytelling," *Harvard Business Review*, October 28, 2014, hbr.org/2014/10/why-your-brain-loves-good-storytelling.
3. "Storytelling and the Brain: Understanding the Neuroscience Behind Our Love for Stories," Power of Storytelling, February 7, 2023, power-of-storytelling.com/story science.
4. Giovanni René Rodriguez, "This Is Your Brain on Storytelling: The Chemistry of Modern Communication," *Forbes*, July 21, 2017, forbes.com/sites/giovannirodriguez/2017/07/21/this-is-your-brain-on-storytelling-the-chemistry-of-modern-communication.
5. Jeremy Adam Smith, "The Science of the Story," *Greater Good Magazine*, June 8, 2016, greatergood.berkeley.edu/article/item/science_of_the_story.

INDEX

ABOUT THE AUTHOR

OZ PEARLMAN is the world's preeminent mentalist, renowned for his captivating performances and extraordinary mind-reading abilities. He first rose to national prominence as a finalist on America's Got Talent and went on to earn an Emmy Award for his acclaimed NBC special, Oz Knows. With thirty years of experience decoding how people think, feel, and act, he has turned the art of mentalism into a powerful tool for personal transformation.

Pearlman has been featured on hundreds of TV shows including Today, Monday Night Football, and HBO's Hard Knocks and has been profiled by *The New York Times*, *The Wall Street Journal*, and *Forbes*. Online, Pearlman has garnered billions of views across social media, and he is known for his unique ability to tailor his performances to any subject or audience. His elite client roster includes Fortune 500 companies, professional sports teams, and A-list celebrities.

Pearlman lives in New York City with his wife and five children. Outside of his stage and screen presence, he is an accomplished endurance athlete. He holds the world record for the most laps ever run around Central Park in a single day and is a passionate marathon and ultramarathon runner.

ozpearlman.com OzTheMentalist

THE UNOFFICIAL EVERTON TIMELINE

2014-2024: THE MOSHIRI YEARS

2ND EDITION: THE DAWN OF THE FRIEDKIN ERA

STEVE DICKINSON & LYNDON LLOYD

BRIGHTER FUTURES
PUBLISHING

Paperback ISBN: 978-1-7384977-2-0

E-Book ISBN: 978-1-7384977-1-3

Published by Brighter Futures Publishing Ltd., Queensgate House, 23 North Park Road, Harrogate, United Kingdom, HG1 5PD

BRIGHTER FUTURES PUBLISHING

Dear Reader,

When I became an author, I made the decision to set up my own independent publishing company.

It's called *Brighter Futures Publishing Ltd* - and it's the Indie publisher with a big heart.

The mission of *Brighter Futures Publishing* is: "To positively impact millions of people, through our published works, and to raise funds for cancer research charities."

Why is this important to me?

Well, my dad died of cancer. So did my grandad, my uncle and many others I have known and loved.

In fact, according to the World Cancer Research Fund, 1 in 2 people in the UK will be diagnosed with cancer in their lifetime.

It's a terrible disease. Research into cancer and its possible treatments is so important for all of us.

As an author, I choose to make zero profit from the sale of my books. My share of the proceeds remain in the publishing company.

And with my publisher's hat on, I am pleased to confirm that 75% of *Brighter Futures Publishing* profits are donated annually to Cancer

Research UK. Anything left is reinvested, for the future growth of the company.

We hope you enjoy this book, knowing your purchase is also contributing to cancer research.

Thank you for your generous support.

Steve Dickinson
Founder and CEO
Brighter Futures Publishing Ltd

Contents

Dedication

You know how it goes. You pick up a book, flip to the dedication, and find that, once again, the authors have dedicated it to someone else and not to you.

Not this time.

Because you are an Evertonian/a friend or family member of an Evertonian/know an Evertonian somewhere in your life, you will understand the pain, passion and occasional jubilation that being an Evertonian involves.

Therefore, this one's for you.

Without pain, passion and occasional jubilation, this book would never have been written.

Up the Toffees!

Steve and Lyndon

Foreword - Window Closed

During the past four decades, I have crossed paths with all but one of the club's chairmen, directors and senior executives. The exception is Farhad Moshiri. That said, the *Liverpool Echo* did publish a photograph of him holding a copy of my autobiography which was released shortly after he purchased his initial shareholding in 2016. If by chance he scanned the contents, Mr Moshiri will be aware of my prediction of a narrow four-year window of opportunity for our beloved club to catch its traditional rivals.

In the wake of the fire sale of young Wayne Rooney, the failure of the subsidized Kings Dock initiative and the despondency of too many trophy-less decades sprinkled with false dawns, his arrival provided beams of dazzling light through the aforementioned window. Surely it was our turn to benefit from a billionaire's investment, ambition, and business savvy to develop the framework for a successful, sustainable and stable future by introducing aggressive plans, modern management systems and efficient decision making processes and employing proven trailblazers to exploit the commercial opportunities available to the then twentieth most valuable brand in global football.

In anticipation of this giant leap forward, I was convinced that Everton and its success-starved followers were poised at the threshold of a new era packed with unswerving commitments, fresh ideas, clear visions and bountiful resources plus a dash or two of patience required to rejoin the English elite and lead us towards royal blue heaven. Indeed in 2016, it was an exciting time to be an Evertonian.

Agonizingly, even though Mr Moshiri kept his promise and provided funds approaching £750 million, the club behaved like an inebriated lottery winner and squandered the windfall. While there have been mitigating factors such as the coronavirus pandemic, the suspension of sponsorships with USM, Megafon and Yota due to Russia's war in Ukraine and serious injuries to Bolasie, Tosun, Mina, Gomes and Gbamin, other pains have been self-inflicted. They include a haphazard approach to recruitment of new additions - few of which lived up to expectations, and the failure to dispose swiftly and efficiently of subsequent under-performers. To compound our plight, despite Mr Moshiri's desire for stability, he and the directors have overseen the engagement of eight managers and coaching staffs as well as three directors of football – most of who struggled to make the most of the expensive resources available at Finch Farm.

Looking back, the Moshiri era was an exhausting nightmare riddled with back-to-back flirtations with relegation, enormous operating losses, the trauma of a 10-points deduction for breaching financial regulations and the inflated expectations and subsequent anger of the Goodison faithful. After failing to realize his domestic or European goals, the majority shareholder decamped leaving our beloved club in the most precarious state in its long history. Sadly, even his legacy of a state-of-the-art stadium at Bramley-Moore Dock is undermined by the future burden of massive loan payments. As a result, it remains to be seen how the new owners will navigate through the chaos in order to prosper on the banks of the River Mersey.

The Unofficial Everton Timeline has been forensically researched and expertly produced by Steve Dickinson and Lyndon Lloyd, two royal blue wordsmiths. It provides a comprehensive and balanced account of events both on and off the field between 2014-2023, and is a must-read for anyone interested in the challenges facing Everton Football Club and its future well-being.

That said, I have encouraged the publisher to include a Warning Notice for Evertonians raised in the era of Sir John Moores, The Golden Vision and The Holy Trinity, that exposure to the book's contents may cause nausea, insomnia, uncontrollable crying and alcohol dependency.

Dr David France OBE□□□
Life President, Everton FC Shareholders' Association
January 2024

SINGING THE BLUES

Well, I never felt more like singin' the blues
'Cause I never thought that I'd ever lose
Your love dear, why'd you do me this way?
Well, I never felt more like cryin' all night
'cause everythin's wrong, and nothin' ain't right
Without you, you got me singin' the blues

The moon and stars no longer shine
The dream is gone, I thought was mine
There's nothin' left for me to do
But cry-why-why-why over you (cry over you)
Well, I never felt more like runnin' away
But why should I go 'cause I couldn't stay?
Without you, you got me singin' the blues

Well, I never felt more like singin' the blues
'Cause I never thought that I'd ever lose
Your love dear, why'd you do me this way?
Well, I never felt more like cryin' all night
'Cause everythin's wrong, and nothin' ain't right
Without you, you got me singin' the blues

Oh, the moon and stars no longer shine
The dream is gone, I thought was mine
There's nothin' left for me to do
But cry-why-why-why over you (cry over you)
Well, I never felt more like runnin' away
But why should I go 'cause, I couldn't stay?
Without you, you got me singin' the blues

Composed by Melvin Endsley. Published in 1956.

Introduction

For those who know the pain, passion and occasional jubilation of supporting Everton Football Club, a knowledge of the famous club's history - as the song goes - is enough to make your heart go Woah-oh-oh.

Blues of any vintage know that studying the club's history - including its most recent past - is vital, because that's where we can find understanding, learn the lessons when things go wrong, and gain a sense of belonging and camaraderie.

In August 2010, the club unveiled the Everton Timeline at Goodison Park. Extracted from The Everton Collection and stretching around three sides of the stadium, the 123 photographic images in the timeline chart major events in the club's illustrious past.

Though updated periodically, the final image on Goodison Road celebrates the signing of Romelu Lukaku in 2014.

Did time stand still for Everton Football Club, or has it simply failed to acknowledge the struggles which occurred during one of the most eventful periods in its 146-year history?

This is the book that fills in all the gaps, on and off the field, during the tumultuous years of Farhad Moshiri's ownership, right up to and including his sale of club to The Friedkin Group.

More than a book about modern-day football, 'The Unofficial Everton Timeline:2014-2024, The Moshiri Years' documents unbridled ambition crashing into chaotic reality.

It's a comprehensive and detailed chronicle of important matches, big dreams, colossal financial investments, unproductive transfers, property deals and engineering marvels.

But most of all, it is a book about people: moneymen, conflicting egos in the boardroom, highly rewarded players and managers, and the real heroes of the story - a community of passionate Everton fans.

Formed in 1878, and one of the dozen founding members of the Football League in 1888, Everton have played more games in the top-flight than any other, scored more goals in the top-flight than any other and, through iconic centre forward, Dixie Dean, still boasts the player who scored the record number of goals in one season.

The club's Official Timeline around those three sides of Goodison Park illustrates the club's heritage: nine times English football league champions, five times FA Cup winners, one time UEFA Cup Winners Cup winner.

For well over a century, Everton were one of the great success stories of English football. Yet, it's almost thirty years since the club last won a trophy, and for each of the last three seasons, it was involved in relegation battles from the Premier League.

There is a saying that success has many fathers. The rollcall of Goodison greats falls quickly off the tongue. Players such as Dean, Lawton, Hickson, Young, Ball, Harvey, Kendall, Royle, Latchford, Southall, Ratcliffe, Reid, Sheedy, Sharp...the list goes on and on. Managers like Catterick and Kendall. Directors like Will Cuff and Sir John Moores.

They also say failure is an orphan. How did a club with the pedigree of Everton –one of the five architects of the English Premier League back in 1992 – end up facing a threat to its very existence? Who and what have been responsible for this cataclysmic decline in the club's fortunes?

Farhad Moshiri's purchase of a 49.9% stake in Everton FC was ratified by the Premier League in March 2016. After considering submissions from the club regarding the Iranian-born billionaire's proposed investment, the League noted how he had sold a 15% holding in rivals Arsenal to Alisher Usmanov, his long-time business partner, paving his way to become Everton's largest shareholder.

Soon after taking over, Moshiri articulated his vision of returning Everton to the elite of modern-day footballing giants.

He later backed up his words by increasing his shareholding to over 94% and injecting more than £750 million into the club. Yet, despite that vast cash injection, in 2024 the club found itself on a financial precipice and fighting for its Premier League existence for a third consecutive year.

In this updated second edition of our book, we've taken stock and examined what really happened after Everton's 'messiah' owner arrived on the scene, and how Dan Friedkin became the current owner and custodian of the football club.

Over the following chapters, we'll try to answer some big questions:

- What assumptions did Farhad Moshiri make before and after becoming the club'smajor shareholder?
- Why did things not work out the way he meant them to, on and off the field –not for the club and its fans, nor too for Moshiri?
- What are the lessons to be learned from the Moshiri Years, for the club, and for its supporters?
- Most importantly, in what condition is Everton FC at the dawn of the Friedkin era? And is there a brighter future ahead for the football club?

In short, we'll update the Everton Timeline. Ours is the unofficial version of events – the version guaranteed never to be included on the club's website, or on the walls of the stadium.

We hope you stay with us from start to finish. It's a truly fascinating story.

2014: Bill Kenwright and Farhad Moshiri begin talks

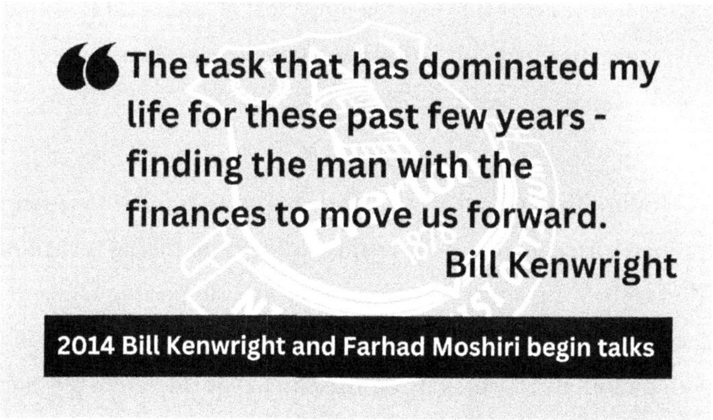

Bill Kenwright and Farhad Moshiri. Two men from very different backgrounds, whose paths would cross in 2014, and whose aims would centre around Everton Football Club.

According to Joe Strange, writing for The MailOnline in July 2016, [1]"Moshiri first met Bill Kenwright towards the end of 2014 and expressed an interest in buying a stake in the club."

Kenwright, a successful actor and theatre impresario, had been on the Board of Everton since 1989 and held the post of chairman since

2004. For years, he had made no secret of his wish to find a wealthy individual or investment group to take over at the club.

> "Once again, try as I might, I was unable to accomplish the task which has dominated my life for these past few years – finding the man, or the institution, with the finances to move us forward. Hopefully the day will come soon when I happily – even enthusiastically – hand over control of our beloved Club to a substantially wealthy individual or well funded investment group." – Bill Kenwright, Everton Annual Report & Accounts, 2011[2]

Moshiri, then 60, an Iranian-born financier, was the long-term business partner of one of the world's richest men, Alisher Usmanov. Moshiri had spent two decades advising and supporting Usmanov and, since 2007, they had each owned shares in Arsenal Football Club with ambitions to win seats on the Arsenal board before pushing through a complete takeover. For that plan to succeed, they would have to persuade majority shareholder, Stan Kroenke, to sell out to them. But Kroenke, the American magnate, had other ideas, and was determined not to sell to the Russian oligarch and his friend. It was this impasse in North London which prompted Moshiri to sell his shares to Usmanov and look for opportunities elsewhere.

Moshiri had entered the world of football as a financier with an accountancy background, rather than as a football fan, but his involvement at Arsenal had whetted his appetite for being around the

Premier League. It was a space he and Usmanov could see had good investment potential.

The investment in Arsenal by Usmanov and Moshiri, and Bill Kenwright's search for a mega-rich investor, came on the back of a major change in the preferred ownership model in the English Premier League, triggered in 2003 by the actions of another Russian oligarch, Roman Abramovich.

> "Looking back, it is hard not to regard the Abramovich takeover as the most significant single development in the Premier League era. Not in terms of what happened on the pitch, in a direct sense, but in terms of what it represented, both economically and culturally, for English football. 'We all knew,' [Sir John] Hall [formerly of Newcastle United] said. 'Doug Ellis at Aston Villa, Bill Kenwright at Everton, even the owners of Liverpool, Manchester United and Arsenal. We'd all put our money in, but the oligarch took everything to a new level. A billionaire came in at Chelsea and, overnight, there was no way we could compete financially.' – Oliver Kay, The Athletic, July 2023[3]

In 2014/15, so-called "Chelski", backed by their Russian billionaire owner had romped away with the league.

Behind them, were Abu-Dhabi owned Manchester City, followed by Arsenal, Manchester United, Tottenham Hotspur and Liverpool. The "Top-6" seemed like a cartel.

Why not a Top-7, including Everton, the team which had played more games in the top-flight than all the others?

Kenwright argued to all potential investors that his club was a sound proposition. All it needed was more investment in players and facilities, to cement its place back among the elite of Premier League clubs.

If Chelsea and Manchester City could do it, why couldn't Everton?

The potential investment upside in Everton FC was enticing, and Moshiri knew it. He had taken counsel from David Dein, a close friend of Kenwright's and former vice-chairman of Arsenal between 1983 and 2007. When Moshiri began his due diligence process in 2014, on a potential investment in Arsenal's oldest rivals, it was only natural he would turn to Dein for advice.

David Dein had joined the Arsenal board when he bought a 16.6% stake in the club for £292,000 from Peter Hill-Wood, Arsenal's chairman. Hill-Wood described Dein as "crazy" to invest his money in the club, stating that, "to all intents and purposes, it's dead money."

Dein had built up his shares until, by 1991, he owned 42% of the club. Over the next decade, debts incurred forced him to sell just short of a 30% stake to co-director Danny Fiszman for approximately £11 million. By 2007, his remaining shares were worth around £60 million.

Alongside Philip Carter of Everton, Dein had been one of the architects of the Premier League in 1992, who reshaped the structure and finances of English football.

"I felt football was really a sleeping giant and had a long way to go," Dein said. "After seeing how the Americans operated their sport, particularly American football and baseball and basketball, I felt we were light years behind. We had so much more to give as an attraction."

Greg Dyke, later the chairman of the FA, stressed the central role of Dein in the Premier League's creation, saying "David Dein was the most revolutionary bloke I've met in football. David Dein created the Premier League. It was his idea."

During his time at Arsenal, Dein had an active role in transferring players and contract negotiations, including Ian Wright from Crystal Palace for £2.5 million and Dutch international Dennis Bergkamp for £7.5 million from Internazionale. He had been behind the appointment of the little-known Arsène Wenger for the manager's job in 1996. Under Wenger, Arsenal won the Premier League three times and the FA Cup seven times, and Dein strongly backed him and his transfer plans.

Dein had also been influential in the transformation of Highbury into an all-seater stadium. Following the Hillsborough disaster, the Taylor Report required Premier League clubs to introduce all-seater stadiums. Dein was behind introducing a bond scheme, which proved unpopular with the fans, to finance the redevelopment of Highbury's North Bank and Clock End terraces into all-seater stands.

He also helped Arsenal's entry into the group of major European football clubs in 2002 and became President of the G-14 in October 2006. He was also President of Arsenal Ladies Football Club, while Arsenal vice-chairman.

The Gunners had invested heavily in the development of their new stadium, which meant the club needed new revenue to service the heavy debts they had incurred as a result. The other board members allegedly signed a contractual agreement that they would not sell their shares for a year, and they jointly expressed their intention to keep their shares in the longer term. Dein, however, was in favour of a takeover of Arsenal by an external investor, and on 18 April 2007, he left the club due to "irreconcilable differences" between himself and the rest of the board.

In August 2007, and this is where it gets really interesting, David Dein sold his 9,072 shares (14.58%) in the club for £75million to Red & White Holdings, an investment vehicle owned by Russian metal billionaire Alisher Usmanov and his business partner, Farhad Moshiri. 4

Usmanov and Moshiri appointed Dein as chairman of Red & White, which was at the time the largest shareholder in the club outside of members of the board of directors. In September 2008, he resigned as chairman of Red & White, with *The Times* suggesting it was to improve relations between Arsenal and Red & White.

But six years later, in 2014, relations between Red & White Holdings and the Arsenal board had gone from bad to worse.

With Arsenal still in a state of impasse, it was time for David Dein's close friend, Bill Kenwright, to enter the scene. Kenwright had been looking "24/7" for a 'messiah owner' to whom to sell Everton, and with it, some or all of his 26% shareholding in the club.

The relationships between Dein and Red & White, and between Dein and Kenwright, provided the green light for Kenwright and the Everton board to open discussions with Moshiri. It also opened the door to a potentially tantalising future deal with one of the world's richest men, should Alisher Usmanov ever sell his shares in Arsenal.

At the time talks began between Bill Kenwright and Farhad Moshiri, few people outside of Moshiri's circle of acquaintances knew much about him. An article published under the headline: *Iranian Moshiri Becomes Billionaire Helping Russia's Richest Man,* [5]provided some of the backstory:

"In 1989, Farhad Moshiri was an emigre in London pulling a pay check at Deloitte & Touche when he met Alisher Usmanov. Now, after a two-decade alliance with Russia's current richest man, the Iranian-born accountant is a billionaire himself.

"Moshiri who owns 5 percent of Usmanov's Metalloinvest Holding, Russia's largest miner of iron ore, and 15 percent of Arsenal Football Club, is worth at least $1.1 billion, according to data compiled by Bloomberg.

"Usmanov, 58, rewarded Moshiri, [then] 56, for years of service as an adviser and confidant in 2008, granting him a 10 percent stake in Gallagher Holdings, through which Usmanov controls Metalloinvest. 'He was consulting me for decades on different deals and exercised his option, fairly getting the stake,' Usmanov said in a telephone interview from Moscow. Usmanov and Moshiri both declined to elaborate on the terms of the option.

"Metalloinvest accounts for the bulk of Usmanov's fortune, which has swelled to more than $20 billion through timely bets on tech companies, including Facebook. Metalloinvest is worth at least $16 billion, valuing Moshiri's share at a minimum of $800 million. The company values itself at as much as $20 billion, chief executive Eduard Potapov said in February.

"For Moshiri, the road to riches started with a revolution. 'My parents fled Iran in February 1979, just before the Iranian Revolution,' Moshiri, now a British citizen, said by e-mail. 'My father was an army doctor who trained as a pathologist and later became a senior military judge. My mother came from Iran's leading publishing house, Kayhan, which is now based in London.'

"The billionaire studied accounting at the University of London and worked at Ernst & Young and Pannell Kerr Forster before joining Deloitte & Touche. He said he met Usmanov through a mutual friend, Masoud Alikhani, when Usmanov was in London as part of a 'high-level delegation' seeking ways of setting up a political-risk insurance company to encourage foreign investment in the Soviet Union.

"'I was very taken at the time by his intelligence and the speed at which he absorbed complex ideas,' Moshiri said.

"The feeling was mutual, said Usmanov, who was born in the former Soviet republic of Uzbekistan, which, like Iran, borders Afghanistan.

"'We became friends almost at once,' Usmanov said.

"'With time, Moshiri actually became my financial mentor,' Usmanov said in the telephone interview. 'I appreciate his honesty and his encyclopaedic knowledge of finance and investments, although some of my most successful investments I did contrary to his opinion.'

"Moshiri has been chairman of Metalloinvest since 2006 and represents Usmanov on the boards of some of the other companies Usmanov owns shares in, including Norilsk Nickel, Russia's largest mining company, and MegaFon, the second-largest mobile-phone operator in the country.

"Not all of Moshiri's investments involve Usmanov. He bought 9.9 percent in 2007 of Panmure Gordon, one of Britain's oldest stockbrokers, without Usmanov's help. Now he holds 4.99 percent in the company.

"Still, the partners share a love of soccer, particularly Arsenal. Their Red and White [Holdings] venture bought 15 percent of the London club in 2007 and have since increased that stake to 30 percent, worth about $238 million, based on the April 3 closing price on the London Stock Exchange.

"Moshiri is an equal partner in the investment, according *to Arsenal's* website. A 15 percent stake in the club has a market value 'I love Arsenal, that's why I'm a shareholder,' Usmanov said in an interview last year.

"Moshiri said he was attracted to Arsenal's 'position as a top London club' that had just moved into a 'purpose-built' stadium that can seat 65,000 fans.

"It's one asset they may never sell. 'We're keen to invest further to secure the future success of the club on the playing field,' Moshiri said."

Ultimately, Farhad Moshiri's time at Arsenal was frustrating. Yet, he had gained knowledge and contacts which could be put to good use. The possibility of taking control of another Premier League club was opening up before him. Was this the time to strike out on his own?

---

1. Joe Strange, The MailOnline, July 2016
2. Everton FC Annual Report & Accounts, 2011
3. Oliver Kay, The Athletic, July 2023

4. "Dein sells Arsenal stake to Russian oligarch for £75m" – The Times Online

5. Iranian Moshiri Becomes Billionaire Helping Russia's Richest Man, Moscow Times, 12 April 2012

2015: Negotiations continue between Kenwright and Moshiri

> “Farhad Moshiri was in no hurry to sign on the dotted line. 18 months of discussions ensued, throughout which Moshiri carried out his due diligence and weighed up his options.

2015 Negotiations continue between Kenwright and Moshiri

Why would anyone buy into Everton Football Club in 2015/16? And if they did, how much would it cost and what should they expect in return?

On the selling side of the negotiations was Bill Kenwright, representing himself and the other major shareholders. Kenwright, who joined the Everton board in 1989, became involved in a consortium to buy the club from the Littlewoods family in 1994 after the club avoided relegation. However, he lost out to Birkenhead-based Park Foods entrepreneur, Peter Johnson, who had owned a controlling stake in his local club, Tranmere Rovers since 1987. Johnson had agreed to inject £10 million into Everton via a rights issue, as advised by N M Rothschild from a Jersey-based family trust. When the deal was done, lifelong Liverpool fan Johnson appointed Kenwright as vice-chairman.

When the Football Association instructed Johnson to sell his interests in either Tranmere Rovers or Everton, it provided the perfect opportunity for Kenwright to realise his lifelong dream of owning Everton. He formed a new consortium that included Paul Gregg, Jimmy Mulville, Jon Woods and Willy Russell under a holding company called True Blue (Holdings) Ltd to buy Johnson's 68% controlling stake in Everton for £20 million on Christmas Eve 1999.

In an article headlined as '*Dream Script for Kenwright – Theatre impresario takes control of Everton for £20 million, as Johnson's gamble backfires,*' published in The Guardian on 26 January, 2000, Ian Ross [1]wrote:

"The theatre impresario Bill Kenwright yesterday finally assumed control of Everton. After more than 14 months of fundraising and at times acrimonious negotiation, Kenwright finally struck an irrevocable deal for the majority shareholding of the former chairman Peter Johnson.

"Kenwright met yesterday's non-negotiable deadline for completion with five hours to spare and will pay just over £20 million for Johnson's 68% stake - a deal which values one of football's oldest and most respected clubs at only £30 million.

"As Kenwright pondered how best to approach the task of transforming the fortunes of a sporting giant fallen on hard times, Johnson was left to rue a calculated gamble which backfired so spectacularly.

"The deal means that the Jersey-based businessman has not only received substantially less than he had been anticipating, but that he has also taken a loss of between £4 million-5 million on his investment when he seized control.

"Indeed, during the course of his pre-Christmas talks with Kenwright and other interested parties, Johnson was adamant that he would not do business at less than £1,200 a share, which would have valued his stake at around £29 million.

"Despite coming under pressure from the football authorities to offload his controlling interest in either Everton or the First Division club Tranmere Rovers, Johnson was content to extend his game of brinkmanship until a prospective buyer agreed to meet his price.

"However, the plan was to be undone just before Christmas when his bankers, anxious to recoup a loan he had taken out to buy Everton, insisted he accept any reasonable firm offer. Kenwright offered £857 per share, a bid which Johnson believed to be inadequate yet one which he had no option but to accept.

"With his bankers unhappy and the future of his primary business concern, the Park Food hamper group, very much on the line, Johnson gambled all believing that Kenwright would be unable to raise the funds to meet yesterday's deadline.

"As it approached, rumours began to suggest that Kenwright was struggling to pull together the strands of his consortium, meaning Johnson's gamble would have paid off. It did not. With the sort of flourish Kenwright normally reserves for his West End productions, he came up with the money to buy, at a rock-bottom price, the club he has always called his "life's passion".

"Obviously, I am very happy," he said. "It has been a long road, but I am thrilled and relieved that it is now done."

"Acquiring Peter Johnson's shares is only the first step to restoring a great club to where it belongs – to where it should be. If you are going to run a successful football club you need two qualities: you need to be realistic and you need a plan. I'm realistic and I have a plan," he added. Kenwright's consortium is made up of Paul Gregg, the head of the US entertainment company SFX, the Everton director Arthur Abercromby and John Woods, a member of the Everton Shareholders' Association.

"I do have tremendous confidence in my partners," said Kenwright, who will continue as Everton's vice-chairman. Sir Philip Carter [will be] chairman.

"To reduce a debt of about £14 million Everton will seek to sell a 9.9% stake to a media company such as NTL, Sky or Granada. There is also likely to be a new rights issue followed by discussions about the possibility of resurrecting Johnson's shelved plan to demolish Goodison Park and build a new stadium on the outskirts of the city.

"We have much hard work ahead of us but we are now on the way," said Kenwright.

The Everton manager Walter Smith can expect little benefit from the deal; he is likely to be informed that he must continue to run the team on a shoestring budget."

By the time Farhad Moshiri met Bill Kenwright in 2014, the market for Premier League teams was hotting up, and several clubs had recently changed hands. Valuations, ownership models and financing sources had been wide and varied.

Roman Abramovich had bought Chelsea for just £140 million in 2003. It had taken just 10 days for a deal to be agreed, and the meeting to iron out the heads of terms between then-chief executive Trevor Birch and Abramovich and his people had apparently lasted just 20 minutes.

The Glazer family had bought their first shares in Manchester United in 2003, escalating their shareholding until they finally had control of the club in 2005. They paid £790 million for Manchester United, but had come under heavy criticism for loading the club with over £700 million of debt.

Sheikh Mansour paid £210 million to purchase 90% of Manchester City from Thaksin Shinawatra in 2008. The Sheikh later paid extra for the remaining 10%, but it was the money he subsequently pumped into City which caused the most controversy over the years. Since their arrival in 2008, City's owners had spent more than £1.5 billion on player transfers alone.

In August 1991, the late David Moores, a member of the Littlewoods family, became chairman of Liverpool FC. Moores owned 51 percent of the club, and in 2004 expressed his willingness to consider a bid for his shares in Liverpool, Everton's rivals from across Stanley Park.

In August 2011, Andy Hunter penned an article in *The Guardian* under the headline: *Everton finances stretched to the limit, admits chairman Bill Kenwright – Kenwright tells fans' group why club is struggling. Chairman's 'desperate' search for new investors.*[2]

Hunter explained how: "Bill Kenwright has laid bare the scale of the financial problems at Everton, with a frank admission that their bankers have forced the club to reduce the overdraft and blocked additions to David Moyes's squad. In a remarkable exchange with representatives of The Blue Union, a coalition of supporters' groups alarmed at the lack of investment in Everton, the club chairman admitted that proceeds from recent player sales and Bellefield, the former training ground sold for £9 million, were taken by Barclays to reduce debts to £45 million."

The meeting turned out to be an embarrassment for Kenwright and the club, who as Hunter reported, "were now considering legal actions, amid claims The Blue Union broke an agreement not to make the conversation public. Kenwright reveals the mounting financial problems that have left Moyes without a net spend on players for three years, contradicts the evidence that Everton's chief executive, Robert Elstone, gave to a public enquiry and outlines his desperation to sell the club." They released the transcript of the three and a half hour meeting six days after the meeting which had taken place in Bill Kenwright's London offices on 12 August.

At one point, Kenwright allegedly said, "Look, we're desperate, I'm desperate."

Hunter also referred to Kenwright saying: "He is the only Premier League chairman not to take a salary or expenses from his club and reveals he has faced 'three periods of death threats' during his [then] 12 year reign as majority shareholder. He also confirmed that Keith Harris, Amanda Staveley – who was involved in the tortuous takeover process at Liverpool FC – the retail magnate Sir Philip Green, several banks and football agents, including Leon Angel, have all engaged in a fruitless search for new investment at Everton."

Andy Hunter's article ended with Kenwright's reported claim that he "was not worried about the future of Everton and that the club was looking at six sites for a possible new stadium." He denied that the billionaire Green had any involvement in the Goodison club. "He's not interested. He would say to me [adopts a mockney accent]: 'Bill, Bill, Bill, if I put facking money into Everton Football Club, you think Liverpool fans would buy from Topshop?' He's not interested. He's a total genius when it comes to money. He's like Mozart is to music. He's an adviser."

It took Bill Kenwright three more years of searching until his potential billionaire investor came along in late 2014. Yet, Farhad Moshiri was in no hurry to sign on the dotted line. 18 months of discussions ensued, throughout which Moshiri carried out his due diligence and weighed up his options.

As Alisher Usmanov's right-hand man, sitting on the board of many of his companies, Moshiri already had his work cut out. His favoured position at Usmanov's side clearly depended on him being available 24/7, 365 days a year. The case for investing in Everton may have looked attractive on paper, and both Usmanov and David Dein were supportive of the idea, but would it make sense for him personally to take on this additional project? And if he did, who would run Everton on his behalf? Who could he trust to do that?

It was time for Farhad Moshiri to prepare his business plan.

---

1. Ian Ross: 'Dream Script for Kenwright – Theatre impresario takes control of Everton for £20 million, as Johnson's gamble backfires,' The Guardian, 26 January, 2000

2. Andy Hunter ,The Guardian, 'Everton finances stretched to the limit, admits chairman Bill Kenwright – Kenwright tells fans' group why club is struggling. Chairman's 'desperate' search for new Investors', August 2011,

2016: Moshiri's Project takes shape

> "Was the Everton deal David Dein's, idea? Once lauded by Greg Dyke, later the chairman of the FA, who stressed the central role of Dein in the Premier League's creation. Dein undoubtedly had the brains, and the connections to mastermind Moshiri's acquisition of the Toffees. He was a close friend of Bill Kenwright and had been chairman of Red & White Holdings - jointly owned by Moshiri and Usmanov.

2016 Moshiri's Project takes shape

Every project begins with an idea, and either floats or sinks on a raft of assumptions. So whose big idea was it for Farhad Moshiri to 'buy and build' Everton Football Club?

Was it Alisher Usmanov's Plan B, after years of being rebuffed by Stan Kroenke and the Arsenal board? Billionaires, like Usmanov, spend their lives having big ideas, and taking massive risks. Their vast wealth is an indicator of the audacity of their ideas, the accuracy of their planning assumptions, and their ability to execute and deliver results.

As he entered his seventieth year in 2023, with an estimated net worth of $19.5 billion, Usmanov could look back on a lifetime of big ideas, many of which have delivered results in-line or ahead of his planned assumptions.

After spending six years of an eight-year sentence imprisoned in a remote Uzbek jail, on charges of which the Supreme Court of Uzbekistan later exonerated him, Usmanov steadily built up his empire through multiple mergers and acquisitions in sectors as widespread as steel, mining, publishing and mobile phones. He famously made huge returns by betting on high-tech companies. Facebook, Twitter, Groupon, Airbnb and Alibaba are among his successful investments. Even in his failed plans, such as the attempted acquisition of Arsenal FC, he walked away with a tidy profit.

Was the Everton deal David Dein's, idea? He undoubtedly had the brains, and the connections to mastermind Moshiri's acquisition of the Toffees. He was a close friend of Bill Kenwright and had been chairman of Red & White Holdings - jointly owned by Moshiri and Usmanov.

Could the idea have been the brainchild of Bill Kenwright? He had been looking for a billionaire to invest in Everton, ever since Roman Abramovich had arrived on the scene in 2003. It was an ambition he repeated in his Chairman's Statement in Everton's 2011 Annual Report and Accounts, where he wrote of his obsession with "finding the man, or the institution, with the finances to move us forward" [1]

The impasse between the Arsenal board and Red & White Holdings was clear, and through Dein, Kenwright would have known more than most. Did 'Chairman Bill' see Alisher Usmanov as his ideal 'substantially wealthy individual', and did he approach Usmanov and Moshiri with a tantalising proposition?

Or did the concept of buying Everton originate from Farhad Moshiri himself? Frustrated by years of achieving little at The Emirates, did he simply decide to sell up his shares at Arsenal, and buy out the Merseyside club to enable him to step out of Usmanov's shadow?

Through his association with Usmanov, Farhad Moshiri undoubtedly had experience in working on large, risky deals.

One of Moshiri's client accounts at Deloitte & Touche was Middlesex Holdings, a London-registered investment company in which Usmanov held shares. In 1993, Middlesex hired Moshiri, then aged 38, from Deloitte & Touche and within a few years made him an executive director. Over time, Moshiri began earning Usmanov's trust by analysing and challenging his investment ideas.

Whoever owned the original idea of 'the Everton deal': be it Usmanov, Dein, Kenwright or Moshiri; these four men came together to create an outline business plan, underpinned by a set of assumptions.

When later observing the financial mismanagement of Everton under Moshiri's ownership, it would be easy to assume there was no plan at all.

Business plans, profit-and-loss statements, balance sheets. These are the lifeblood of a person with a degree in accounting; someone with a professional career of working for major accountancy and consultancy companies for almost two decades. Moshiri had worked for Usmanov, the billionaire with a voracious appetite for acquiring businesses, for twenty-one years, employed as his principal tyre-kicker. Was there a business plan to acquire Everton FC? Of course, there was, and it was based on the club achieving success. Usmanov and Moshiri would not have touched the deal unless they believed they could bring their knowhow and capital to bear in a profitable way, and in an acceptable timeframe.

What's more, Moshiri was not walking into this deal cold. His experience as an Arsenal shareholder since 2007 had educated him in the running of an elite club within the English Premier League. From his seat next to Usmanov in the Red & White Holdings executive box at The Emirates, he had watched Arsenal play against their rivals season after season, with Everton never too far behind the Gunners:

- In 2007/08: Manchester United won the league, Arsenal finished 3rd, and Everton finished in 5th place.
- In 2008/09: Manchester United again finished top, with Arsenal 4th and Everton 5th.
- In 2009/10: Chelsea were champions, while Arsenal finished 3rd and Everton slipped down to 8th.
- In 2010/11: Manchester United were back on top, with Arsenal 4th and Everton 7th.
- In 2011/12: Manchester City were champions, Arsenal 3rd and Everton again 7th.
- In 2012/13: Manchester United were once again 1st, while Arsenal were 4th and Everton 6th.
- In 2013/14: Manchester City were champions once more, with Arsenal back in 4th place and Everton up to 5th spot.

Applying his 'encyclopaedic knowledge of finance and investments' to football, it's likely Moshiri knew more about the ownership structure and financial performance of every Premier League team than he knew about their tactics on the field, and some things must have seemed clear to him:

1. Winning the Premier League was increasingly the preserve of rich clubs. Whether that was because of the wealth of the Glazer family, Roman Abramovich, or Sheikh Mansour, the ability to fund large transfer fees and players' wages was a prerequisite to winning the ultimate domestic prize.

2. The Champions League generated a large part of Arsenal's turnover, in terms of gate receipts, commercial revenue and broadcasting income. A top 4 finish every season was therefore essential. Better still was to finish 1, 2 or 3 in the league, which led to improved seeding in the Champions League.

3. A top manager was worth his weight in gold. Alex Ferguson had proved this.

4. In Arsène Wenger, Arsenal also had a top manager. However, with the increased financial firepower of the Manchester clubs and Chelsea, the Gunners now lacked the monetary ammunition, and would likely remain as also-rans in the Premier League. Their last league title had been in 2003/04.

5. As things stood, Everton were never again going to win the league, but with comparatively meagre financial resources, they were deserving of their 'best of the rest' title.

6. Although the two clubs had once been close rivals in the Premier League, there was now a world of difference between their financial performance. For the season 2014/15 – during which Moshiri was conducting his due diligence on Everton FC, the financial comparison between the two clubs was stark.

By comparing the Arsenal Report & Accounts 2014/15[2] to Everton Report & Accounts 2014/15[3], it could be seen that the financial gulf between the two rivals was enormous.

- Arsenal's turnover of £344.5 million compared to Everton's £125.6 million.

- Arsenal's match day revenue (£100.4 million) was almost 6 times the level achieved by Everton's £17.9 million.

- Arsenal's commercial revenue of £100.3 million was 4 times that of Everton's £26.0 million.

- Arsenal's broadcasting income of £143.8 million was 76% higher than Everton's £81.7 million.

- The higher turnover enabled Arsenal to run a wage bill of £192.2 million, 2.5 times that of Everton's £77.5 million, allowing them to recruit more elite players into the squad and pay them better.

- Despite those enormous costs, Arsenal still spent a lower percentage of its turnover on wages (58.4%) than did Everton, at 61.7%.

- Arsenal made a pre-tax profit of £24.7 million, compared to Everton's loss of £4 million
- Arguably, Arsenal's greater financial muscle resulted in Arsène Wenger's side improving from a 4th place in season 2013/14 to 3rd place finish the following year, whereas Everton under Roberto Martinez dropped from 5th to 11th place.

Once discussions between Moshiri and Kenwright had opened in late 2014, and after signing a non-disclosure agreement from Everton's lawyers, Moshiri would have been privy to Everton's management accounts and other internal documents.

On the basis of their due diligence, Moshiri and his advisors drew conclusions which formed the basis of their business plan. Whilst the plan remains confidential, we can deduce some of **Moshiri's key business planning assumptions:**

- Usmanov's ongoing involvement in Arsenal prevented his direct investment in Everton, however, nothing prevented the Uzbek billionaire's companies acting as sponsors to the Merseyside club. Money, therefore, was seen as no barrier to success.
- Results in the Premier League had shown Everton progressing since Bill Kenwright and his True Blue Holdings consortium had taken over in 2000.
- Kenwright was a very experienced chairman of the football club. He had come highly recommended by David Dein, a

man well trusted by Usmanov and Moshiri.

- Kenwright, Everton's self-proclaimed *Greatest Fan,* seemed to be well-liked by most of the Everton fan base, which would be a bonus for a publicity-shy character like Moshiri.

- Fan protests against Kenwright concerning the unsuccessful Kings Dock and Destination Kirkby stadium moves had showed the strength of feeling the fan base had over the stadium issue.

- Long-standing former-chairman, Sir Philip Carter, had passed away in April, 2015. Kenwright had been close to Carter, and his death had left a void within the Everton board.

- Moshiri had no wishes to involve himself in the day-to-day running of the club, nor did he have the time. As the club's majority shareholder, there would be no need for him to join the club's Board of Directors.

- In his place, he would appoint his young associate, Sasha Ryazantsev, to the Board. Ryazantsev was already advising Moshiri about the acquisition and future strategy of the football club.

- The relationship forged with Bill Kenwright during the 18-month long negotiations had been cordial. Kenwright was the consummate salesman, with a strong network of contacts within the club, within the wider football world, and on Merseyside. Kenwright had expressed a strong desire to remain active at the club.

- Appointing Kenwright as chairman made sense to Moshiri, as long as Ryazantsev was in charge of the purse strings, and could ensure Moshiri's strategy was being implemented.

- There would be evolution rather than revolution on the Board. CEO Robert Elstone would be retained and his performance evaluated.

- No further changes to the Board, including independent non-executives, were deemed necessary by Moshiri at that stage.

- Goodison Park was clearly on its last legs. Kenwright had said, either hyperbolically or disingenuously, that the stadium may fail its safety certificates.

- Kenwright and his team had identified several alternative stadium sites. The question was which one to choose, and how much would it cost to build the stadium and facilitate the move?

- A decision on selecting the new site could apparently be made in months.

- Planning approval would be swift, given the support of Liverpool City mayor Joe Anderson.

- Interest rates were low, and expected to stay low. A 40 year 'mortgage' could be easily arranged to fund the new stadium, as others – like Tottenham Hotspur- had proven.

- If Arsenal had been able to secure a £150 million naming rights deal on their new stadium, what could Everton expect for naming rights?

- Even with a limited budget, Everton had been able to recruit quality players such as: Lukaku, Stones, Arteta and Cahill. With more investment, the squad could only get better.

- Investment in the squad and team management would lead to progression, from average 7th place to Top 6 and eventually Top 4.

- Hiring a Director of Football (DoF) was essential. Everton had never previously employed one. This was a key change to improve the club's recruitment.

- The ideal DoF for Moshiri would act in an advisory capacity, with all key hiring and firing decisions requiring sign off by Moshiri and the Chairman.

- Roberto Martinez may need to be replaced. His performance would be monitored.

- There would presumably be no shortage of top managers willing to jump on board the 'hottest project in the Premier League.'

- Communicating with the fans via popular channels, such as

Jim White on TalkSport, would make Moshiri seem like a man of the people.

- A new stadium was paramount to the success of the club. It was essential to bridge the gap between Everton and the Top 6, and could help deliver regular European football.
- The rules of Financial Fair Play, introduced by UEFA in 2009, seemed to be largely ignored by the big clubs, and would probably not be an impediment to Moshiri's project at Everton.

Later on, we'll explore how these assumptions stood the test of time, but in the countdown to the deal, they provided Farhad Moshiri with a framework. He thought he knew how to take Everton into the Top 6, he assumed he had people to run the club on his behalf, and he was confident he had the financial resources needed to achieve his goal.

All he needed now, was to bring the deal over the line.

---

1. Everton Annual Report & Accounts, 2011
2. Arsenal Report and Accounts 2014/15
3. Everton Report & Accounts 2014/15

2016: MOSHIRI BUYS THE CLUB AND SELLS THE DREAM

2016 Moshiri buys the club and sells the dream

Farhad Moshiri's signature on the contract to buy 49.9% of Everton FC in February 2016 meant Bill Kenwright's widely publicised search for a billionaire investor was finally over.

Moshiri's first communiqué – the dream he sold to the fans and other stakeholders - appeared on 12 March, 2016 in the match-day programme for Everton's FA Cup quarter-final match against Chelsea:

"I am delighted to join you here today at Goodison Park for my first match as a shareholder in Everton Football Club. I also felt it was fitting that my first message was in the matchday programme, with Everton being the first ever club to regularly produce one for home games. Indeed, it is this strong sense of tradition which appealed to me as I discussed this opportunity with Bill Kenwright to become part of the the future of the club. It is a testament to the enduring quality and consistency of the Club that Everton has remained in the top flight of English football since 1954. In more recent times this has been achieved under the stewardship of Bill, Robert Elstone and all the team behind the scenes at the Club. I am here to support them as required to ensure that the Club recaptures the glory days of the past and builds sustained success in the future. I know a lot of you want to know what my plans are. There is much to be done and things for me to learn, but I can confirm that I have committed to providing additional funds for transfers and retaining our key players to ensure that we have a strong core to build on for the future. We will also be looking at the best options in relation to our stadium. Goodison Park has served the Club extremely well but we need to make sure the Club has a suitable stage to perform on for the future. We will review the best options and how to finance, especially as it is likely to

> cost a little more than the £3,000 it apparently did in 1892. **Finally, and most importantly, Everton is about great football and winning matches.** Good luck to Roberto and the boys against Chelsea today."
> – Farhad Moshiri, 12 March 2016

Here, evidently, was a man with gravitas. A man who could spell out his understanding of the club and its history in less than 300 words. Here was a man of means, who could boldly state his vision, and his manifesto had four key elements:

- Provide additional funds for transfers,
- Retain key players,
- Look at the best options for the stadium, and how to finance it,
- Focus on great football and winning matches.

For all Evertonians, what was not to like?

***

Probably the first to break the news of Farhad Moshiri's investment in Everton, had been journalist Matt Lawton, writing in the MailOnline on 26 February, 2016[1]. He had claimed "exclusively" that a £200 million buy-out of Everton by a mystery Middle Eastern buyer could be announced in the coming days.

A report in Russia that Arsenal stakeholder Alisher Usmanov would become Everton's new owner was denied, but rumours immediately sprung up that his long-time business partner, billionaire Moshiri, was looking at purchasing the club.

For many Blues reading this news on social media, the rumours were received with scepticism. They had heard it all before.

But just three days later, the club's official website announced the news that: "Iranian-born businessman, Farhad Moshiri, has become Everton's largest shareholder."

Everton later confirmed that, pending Premier League approval, Moshiri had bought a 49.9% position that made him the club's largest stakeholder, and while it did not give him control overall, it effectively amounted to a takeover given the superior position it would afford him in the boardroom. American-based leisure tycoon Robert Earl had reportedly sold his 23% stake in Everton, while Jon Woods and Bill Kenwright reduced their own holdings from 26% and 19% respectively to usher in Moshiri as the club's biggest shareholder.

The Telegraph, along with several other media outlets including the BBC had reported that the funds had come from the sale of Moshiri's 15% interest in Arsenal to his long-time business partner, Usmanov, which was completed just one day earlier. The deal left Kenwright as chairman at Goodison, something that insiders suggested was an important factor for him personally, and which may have been one reason why an alternative investment proposal from the U.S. consortium led by John Jay Moores and Charles Noell had failed to come to fruition.

In a statement on the club website, Kenwright said of the news:

> "After an exhaustive search I believe we have found the perfect partner to take the Club forward. I have got to know Farhad well over the last 18 months and his football knowledge, financial wherewithal and True Blue spirit have convinced me that he is the right man to support Everton."

And Moshiri added:

> "I am delighted to take this opportunity to become a shareholder in Everton, with its rich heritage as one of Europe's leading football clubs. There has never been a more level playing field in the Premier League than now. Bill Kenwright has taught me what it means to be an Evertonian and I look forward with excitement to working with him to help deliver success for Everton in the future."

As Joe Strange reported in *TheMailOnline*, "After 18 months of discussions and due-diligence, a deal was struck, which included the option for Moshiri to increase his stake [at Everton] in the not too distant future."

For Everton fans, the news of the takeover and the unveiling of the mystery investor came as a welcome surprise. Suddenly everyone wanted to know about Moshiri and his connections with Usmanov, one of the world's richest men.

But it was not only the Everton fans who had taken an interest in Moshiri's background. The following year, the question of Usmanov's involvement in Moshiri's investment in Everton FC would be highlighted in a special report by the BBC programme, *Panorama*. [2]

The two-part investigation, broadcast on 5 and 6 November, 2017 focused on offshore tax havens and global finance as it pertained to some of the world's richest individuals.

By then, USM Holdings had already been announced as sponsors of Everton's Finch Farm training complex. Moshiri's directorship and part ownership of many of Usmanov's companies meant that the Uzbek-Russian's name was never too far from discussions about the Toffees' finances, but the club and the Premier League claimed there had been no conflict of interest.

Moshiri shrugged off the media's interest in his relationship with Usmanov. He said he needed to get on with the job of transforming Everton. He was a man in a hurry and would prove to be a hands-on owner, taking an active interest in the management of the first team, and the stage they played on.

---

1. Matt Lawton: MailOnline, 26 February, 2016

2. BBC Panorama: Paradise Papers: Who is in control of Everton? 6 November 2017

2016: NEW STADIUM HIGH ON MOSHIRI'S TO DO LIST

> "There is a lot of work still to be done, but this aspiration sits alongside our commitments to building a stadium as atmospheric and intense as Goodison Park
>
> \- Robert Elstone CEO

2016 New stadium high on Moshiri's to do list

In the *Annual Report and Statement of Accounts 2000 of The Everton Football Club Limited* [1]- the first report and accounts since Bill Kenwright's True Blue Holdings consortium had taken charge - the late Sir Philip Carter wrote in his chairman's statement: "The stadium debate continued throughout the year and it is likely that whilst remaining at Goodison Park is still an option, we have indicated publicly that if we are to achieve a quality stadium with a capacity of 55,000, then an alternative site must be sought. Your Board will leave no stone unturned until this matter is finally resolved and again

Everton are at the forefront of stadium design; we must ensure that our rich traditions are reflected in any new design. I reiterate that before any final decision is made, the views of our supporters will again be canvassed. Supporters can be assured that only the best will be considered, and until the appropriate time we will remain in our ancestral home, which I am sure you will agree had a much needed facelift in the summer. The 'old lady' still has pride and we love her dearly."

Plans to move the club to a new stadium had actually been afoot since 1996, ever since the 1994 conversion of Goodison Park to an all-seater stadium had reduced its capacity to just under 40,000.

Every team in the league was facing similar challenges. Some had already moved forward, leaving Everton behind.

***

First out of the blocks were Manchester United. The club carried out major redevelopment works at Old Trafford starting in the mid-1990s, including the addition of extra tiers to the North, West and East Stands, which almost returned the stadium to its former capacity of 80,000. The expansion enabled a significant rise in gate receipts; which went from £43.9 million in 1994 to £87.9 million in 1997.

***

Because of restrictions on expanding the capacity at Anfield, Liverpool announced plans to move to a proposed Stanley Park Stadium in

May 2002. They received planning permission in July 2004, and in September 2006, the City Council agreed to grant Liverpool FC a 999-year lease on the proposed site. Following the takeover of the club by George Gillett and Tom Hicks in February 2007 and a redesign of the proposed stadium, the new plans were approved by the Council in November 2007. The club said the stadium would open in August 2011 and would hold 60,000 spectators. However, Gillett and Hicks had difficulty in financing the £300 million needed for the development and construction was halted in August 2008.

In October 2012, BBC Sport reported that, rather than build a new stadium in Stanley Park, Fenway Sports Group, the new owners of Liverpool FC, planned to redevelop their current home at Anfield. As part of the redevelopment, the capacity of Anfield was to increase from 45,276 to approximately 60,000, at a cost of £150 million. It was supposedly all part of a £260 million project to improve the Anfield area.

***

Arsenal had been denied planning permission by Islington Council to expand Highbury. Feeling the same pressures to comply with new safety standards, and needing to compete with their rivals by increasing match-day revenues, the club first explored the possibility of relocating to a new stadium in 1997.

After considering various options (including purchasing Wembley Stadium), the Gunners bought an industrial and waste disposal estate in Ashburton Grove in 2000. A year later, they received the council's approval to build a stadium on the site. Manager Arsène Wenger described the project as the “biggest decision in Arsenal’s history.” Relocation began in 2002, but financial difficulties delayed the work until 2004. In the interim, Emirates Airlines was later announced as the main sponsor for the stadium and Arsenal completed the project in 2006 at a cost of £390 million, with the club’s former stadium turned into *Highbury Square*, an apartment complex.

***

Another significant stadium move took place 36 miles from Everton's Goodison Park, where The City of Manchester Stadium became the home of Manchester City. After the 2002 Commonwealth Games, the stadium was converted from a 38,000-capacity arena to a football stadium at a cost to the city council of £22 million and to Manchester City of £20 million. The club agreed to lease the stadium from the city council and moved there from Maine Road in the summer of 2003. The stadium instantly made the football club more attractive to potential investors. That culminated on 1 September 2008, when Abu Dhabi United Group Investment and Development Limited completed a takeover of Manchester City. The initial deal, worth a reported £200 million, was later dwarfed by the £1.5 billion or more the Abu Dhabi owners subsequently spent in the transfer market. In August 2015, a 7,000 seat third tier on the stadium’s South Stand brought the capacity up to 55,000 in time for the start of the 2015/16 season.

***

The opening of Arsenal's new Emirates Stadium in 2006 was perhaps the catalyst for their North London rivals, Tottenham Hotspur, to make a move with their own stadium development. Announced in 2008, but beset by revisions, disputes and delays, construction finally began in 2015. The *Tottenham Hotspur Stadium* eventually opened on 3 April 2019. With a seating capacity of 62,850, it is a multi-purpose stadium and features the world's first dividing, retractable football pitch, which reveals a synthetic turf field underneath for NFL London games, concerts and other events. The project covered the site of the now demolished White Hart Lane ground, and areas next to it, with the intention being to sell the naming rights to a sponsor. A sponsorship deal has yet to be agreed, however, and fans occasionally refer to the stadium as New White Hart Lane.

***

Spurs' delays allowed another London rival, West Ham United, to overtake them in the race to play in a new, and larger home. With an all-seated capacity of 80,000 for the 2012 Summer Olympics and Paralympics, the London Stadium served as the athletics venue and as the site of their opening and closing ceremonies. Land preparation for the stadium began in mid-2007, with the construction officially starting on 22 May 2008. Following the Olympics, they renovated the stadium for multi-purpose use. When it re-opened in July 2016, it had 66,000 seats, but its capacity for football was limited to 60,000 under the terms of the lease. The decision to make West Ham United the main tenants was controversial, with the initial tenancy process having to be rerun.

***

Farhad Moshiri's announcement when he bought Everton, of 'a new stage for the team to perform on' had come 20 years after Peter Johnson first mooted the need for a new stadium, and after several unsuccessful attempts by the club to relocate. Yet this time there was a feeling in the city that Moshiri had not only the willpower, but also the finances to make things happen.

Speaking to BBC Merseyside, then Liverpool mayor, Joe Anderson expressed his belief that the Blues would kick off in a new ground by the start of the 2019/20 season. "I'm confident the new stadium will be up and running in three years' time," the mayor said. "I think there is a real acceptance by them, and I'm pretty confident that within three years there will be a new stadium for Everton Football Club in Liverpool."

While the club released no details of the potential sites under consideration, the Liverpool Echo reported one could be in the north docks area at Trafalgar Dock, and the other at the Stonebridge Cross site off the East Lancs Road in Croxteth.

The collapse of the Kings Dock project over a decade earlier had been a source of pain for Evertonians, who had dreamt of an iconic waterfront stadium that would have put the club on the map in more than one sense.

However, much of the property on the waterfront was now in the hands of Peel Holdings, the developers of the Liverpool Waters regeneration scheme. Peel had historically been reluctant to involve a football stadium in their plans, but, were reportedly warming to the idea once Everton made their interest known in the Bramley-Moore Dock site in Liverpool's north docks area, north of the Wallasey Tunnel.

Mayor Anderson had said in August 2016 that an announcement on the club's new home could happen "in a couple of months," but the docks site depended on the Blues meeting Peel's £30 million asking price for the land.

Anderson did not comment on the specifics, but said: "Things are really positive. No option is ruled out, but everyone knows my preferred option. Everyone knows the club's preferred option. There are discussions taking place and we're at the heart of that, trying to move things on. Really, given where we were 12 months ago, we are in a much different and healthier position. The obstacle with all these things is an agreement must be reached. We did that with Anfield. We had challenges, had to buy properties and move people on. It's about negotiation and making significant concessions."

In March 2017, interviewed by Adam Leventhal from Sky Sports News, Everton's then Chief Executive, Robert Elstone, spoke of the club's ambition and hopes of finally resolving the vexing stadium issue. The broadcaster's cameras were at USM Finch Farm, covering the Blues from all angles, and speaking to many key figures. They kicked the day off with Leventhal sitting down with the CEO and club ambassador Graeme Sharp.

Elstone talked of the renewed ability of Everton to take big steps towards rejoining England's elite group of clubs now that investor Farhad Moshiri was on board.

"One thing Evertonians are is fiercely ambitious," he began. "We are content where we are. Is it where we want to be? Is it where want to end up? Absolutely not.

"Everton fans and Everton Football Club wants to push on and that burning ambition is inherent in everything we do. In our manager, in our chairman, and indeed in our new majority shareholder, Farhad Moshiri, ambition really transcends the whole football club.

Leventhal asked Elstone how the club intended to balance the 'vision' of a new stadium and the wrench of moving away from Goodison Park.

He replied, "It's the most important decision we'll make in recent times. It's a decision that will live for us for generations, so we have to get it right. It's absolutely something we need to move forward. There are lots of features and qualities about Goodison that we wish to retain and take with us around atmosphere, about proximity to pitch, around intensity, around a place where opposition clubs really don't want to come and play. If we can bottle that and take that with us, then we'll have done well.

"Financially, it's a massive decision. This is a multi-million pound investment. For Everton in a stadium that we're currently filling at 40,000 seats, it's not as if we've got a huge waiting list of any army of fans ready to move in. We have to make sure that it works for us.

"For us, it's also about future-proofing because ultimately Goodison will need us to keep investing, and it's also about a statement of intent. Both of those things are harder to put down on a business plan.

"Having said all that, we're confident now that we're moving towards a solution for the problem that has remained with us throughout this of how we're going to afford it.

"It's a big investment — where's the money going to come from to build it? There's a lot of work gone into that and we're getting close, we hope, to resolving that problem."

Regarding the projected cost of the new stadium, Mike Keegan in The MailOnline [2]quoted a figure of £350 million, that estimate also being broadly in line with the construction cost of Arsenal's Emirates Stadium, which had opened in 2006.

***

Planning for the new ground at Bramley-Moore Dock continued, following the announcement that an agreement was in place with the landowner Peel Group to purchase the dock site. In May, with the 2016/17 season drawing to a close, Robert Elstone was back in the media, when he reaffirmed the club's proposed new stadium on Liverpool's waterfront, would be "as atmospheric and intense as Goodison Park."

The outline funding proposal called for a 50,000-seat venue, but there had been speculation among supporters and the local press that the final capacity could be larger. Elstone suggested that the Everton hierarchy were confident that they could fill a significantly larger ground than Goodison Park with it's 39,414 seats.

"Whilst the Council is lending valuable support, it is important to stress that the club is paying for the stadium in full," the Chief Executive confirmed. "We will pay for our new home with a long-term lease, likely to be 40 years.

"At the end of this time, the club will take sole ownership of the stadium. These two big steps forward were critical for the project to progress.

"They give us the confidence to proceed with the next phase of our work – the work required to define, in much greater detail, what the stadium will look like and the exciting role it will play in the future aspirations of the club.

"This phase of work will require substantial investment from the club, highlighting just how committed we all are to the success of the project.

"We have reason to be confident on capacity. As evidenced this season, Everton remains as ambitious as ever and will continue to challenge for a place in the Champions League.

"And, also, right now we have 10,000 prospective Season Ticket holders waiting for the release of around 3,000 seats, so we're confident that we can fill a considerably bigger stadium.

"There is a lot of work still to be done, but this aspiration sits alongside our commitments to building a stadium as atmospheric and intense as Goodison Park."

With anticipation and momentum growing around an expensive new stadium project, the manager and his team were under ever-growing pressure to deliver more success on the field.

---

1. Annual Report and Statement of Accounts 2000 of The Everton Football Club Limited

2. Mike Keegan: Daily Mail, 2 March 2017

2016: ROBERTO MARTINEZ PRAISES NEW OWNER MOSHIRI

> ❝We're awaiting Premier League approval, but the arrival of Farhad Moshiri to Everton is something for every Evertonian to really look forward to.
>
> -Roberto Martinez

2016 Roberto Martinez praises new owner Moshiri

In 2013/14, Roberto Martinez had used his first season at the club to build on the sound defensive qualities of the squad he inherited from David Moyes. His masterstroke had been bringing in Romelu Lukaku on loan from Chelsea in September 2013. James McCarthy had also been a shrewd buy from Wigan, bringing energy and bite to the midfield; and Gareth Barry, an even more astute addition, initially also on loan. The team eventually finished a phenomenal fifth in the table.

Martinez' team had failed to kick on in 2014/15; this despite the conversion of Lukaku's loan to a permanent transfer, for a club record fee of £28 million in July 2014 – an event that proved worthy of inclusion in Everton's *Official* Timeline on Goodison Road.

A 1-0 home defeat at the hands of Spurs had confirmed a disappointing eleventh place in the table on the final day of the season. All eyes had been on Martinez at the start of the 2015/16 season, as he tried to reverse his side's downward momentum and push once again for one of the European spots.

Despite rumours that Lukaku was agitating for a move to a Champions League side, he had been regularly chipping in with crucial goals. By the turn of the year, he had already netted 18 times in all competitions. Stephen Naismith, Ross Barkley and Gerard Deulofeu were also hitting the target.

In search of additional firepower, and as cover for the prolific Lukaku, the club signed Oumar Niasse from Lokomotiv Moscow for a fee of £13.5 million at the end of the January transfer window.

January 2016 had been a winless month for Everton in the league, with away draws against Man City and Chelsea, and a demoralising home defeat to Swansea. With his team dropping out of the top half of the table, the pressure was ratcheting up on Martinez. When news of Farhad Moshiri's takeover emerged, the manager was quick off the blocks to welcome the new shareholder.

"It's really, really good news," Martinez said. "I met Mr Moshiri and the impression I got was that he is a gentleman with incredible values and someone who knows the Premier League inside out because he has been involved with another Premier League football club. He knows how difficult it is to have a vision in football and to put it into practice.

"Sometimes you get business people who don't understand it. Obviously, that is not the case here. He is someone who has been working closely with a Premier League club and he knows what it takes.

"He's someone that has been introduced to Everton and has followed the club very closely. It is fair to say, he has fallen in love with what Everton means, with the heritage and the history, and that's really exciting. Our chairman is the perfect person to introduce someone to Everton and I can speak from my own experiences.

"[He's a] new figure, someone who is going to bring a new vision and completely different push to our club. So you can imagine the excitement that we have. We're awaiting Premier League approval, but the arrival of Farhad Moshiri to Everton is something for every Evertonian to really look forward to."

Martinez expressed his belief that the change at boardroom level and the potential levels of investment that Moshiri could bring signalled a hugely positive development for the club. "What we've got is the perfect person to fit in at Everton, and you can't say that lightly. What I'm really excited about is that we're not going to lose any of the good things about the football club; it's the opposite. This is the start of a new era at Everton, without a doubt.

"We are going to show, as a football club, that we are ready to go to the next level. You can feel the excitement around the place and that's something we need to use out on the pitch. When I started, I said we have to look for the Champions League positions and we have to become a winning team. That is a very broad statement, and it's a difficult aim to achieve. Obviously, the investment and the involvement of Farhad Moshiri takes us into a different level in terms of accelerating the process.

"Clearly, it's an exciting time and every single Evertonian should know he is someone who knows our football club, someone who is a very strong addition and won't bring anything other than getting Everton to where we belong."

Behind the scenes, Martinez must have known the bar had been raised, and, if his team's performances did not improve quickly, his job would be on-the-line.

***

12 March 2016: Everton v Chelsea

Amid a raucous atmosphere at Goodison Park, and with Moshiri watching from the Directors' Box, the Toffees went toe-to-toe with the reigning Premier League champions in a tightly contested FA Cup Quarter-Final tie that featured plenty of effort and desire but precious few clear-cut openings.

Chelsea, hoping to keep their own season alive after exiting the Champions League at the hands of Paris Saint- Germain in midweek, had shaded the first half, enjoying most of the possession without really penetrating an Everton back line that was in uncompromising mood.

The first period was book-ended by a couple of Tom Cleverley shots that were comfortably gathered by Thibault Courtois, while the midfielder also dragged a shot across goal in the 25th minute, but it was a half notable more for the antics of Diego Costa.

No stranger to controversy or a bout of 'handbags' at Goodison, the Spain international was booked for catching Gareth Barry around the face in a clear act of retribution for an earlier coming together. And his teammate Kenedy was fortunate not to join him for a succession of fouls, benefitting from referee Michael Oliver's leniency.

The game picked up in terms of goalmouth incident after half-time, though. Ramiro Funes Mori rose highest to meet a Cleverley corner but could only steer his header over the bar. Costa then rounded the sprawling Joel Robles at the other but could only roll a shot across the face of the goal.

Everton had been stepping up the pressure on Chelsea's goal but had little more than set-pieces to show for it until Lukaku caught fire with 12 minutes to go, starting with a quite brilliant solo goal. The Belgian picked up a ball by Ross Barkley near the left touchline, shrugged off a foul by Cesar Azpilicueta, turned Gary Cahill inside and out before drilling a low shot inside the far post.

Three minutes later, Lukaku doubled his tally and the home side's lead with another unerring finish. Played onside by Azpilicueta, Everton's top scorer collected another pass by Barkley and drove the ball through Courtois' legs to send the bouncing Gwladys Street End into ecstasy.

Chelsea brought on Loic Remy to drag the Londoners back into the tie, but they undermined their efforts when Costa received a second yellow card for seemingly head-butting Gareth Barry with five minutes left.

Barry would follow him down the tunnel three minutes later when he too picked up a second yellow for a cynical trip on Cesc Fabregas, but Everton held on to progress to next month's semi-final at Wembley.

Could there have been a better start to the Moshiri era? It would be hard to imagine one.

Final score: Everton 2-0 Chelsea.

***

Interviewed after the Chelsea match, Farhad Moshiri said:

> "I bought into a great club. I felt it today. Let's enjoy the day and let's hope we can energise the club. I think you can never take over a club. You become part of a club and I hope to become part of the club. I bought into a new family. That's what special for me and I give them whatever I have."

The typically effusive Bill Kenwright, back at Goodison after an extended, illness-related absence, sat beaming next to Moshiri. He lauded Romelu Lukaku for two excellent goals that won the tie for Everton. He then paid tribute to his manager Roberto Martinez, who had come in for mounting criticism in recent weeks as inconsistent results in the Premier League had kept the Blues in the bottom half of the table.

> "I think we have got to acknowledge Rom's goal because it was an unbelievable goal, wasn't it?" the chairman said. "I thought his second goal was great,

> too. I thought they were all great today. I thought they were fantastic. You know what I thought today, though? What a manager. You can't hide the fact that there's been all kinds of criticism this week, [but] he's stood firm and just beaten Chelsea with some to spare."

Yet, after the euphoria of the Chelsea game had died down, the Blues recorded defeats against Arsenal and Manchester United, followed by draws against Watford, Crystal Palace and Southampton. Next up was one of the toughest matches of the season, and for Roberto Martinez, it was becoming a 'must win' game.

***

20 April 2016: Liverpool v Everton

Having suffered a 4-0 reverse in the Anfield derby during his first season in charge, Roberto Martinez' team had gained a creditable 1-1 draw in September 2014, when Phil Jagielka delivered that ninety-first minute Exocet into the Kop goal from 25 yards out, which went down in folklore as one of the greatest ever Merseyside derby goals.

In the days leading up to the 2016 all-Mersey clash on Liverpool's turf – and with an FA Cup semi-final against Manchester United due to take place just three days later at Wembley – the mantra from the under-pressure Martinez was, "We want to make our fans proud."

What ensued, however, was another 4-0 drubbing by the Reds. Instead of a proud performance, the team served-up Blues fans with utter humiliation in the worst arena possible.

Two of the goals had "Martinez regime" written all over them — acres of space afforded to the man crossing the ball, flat-footed defending and two simple headers — the first from Divock Origi and the second by Mamadou Sakho, given the freedom of Anfield in the six-yard box to nod home.

It was 'game over' by first-half stoppage time. The fight long gone out of his Everton team, Martinez stood, cross-armed and helpless on the touchline; his verbal battles now fought by his assistant, Graeme Jones.

Gareth Barry, back in the side to tie the Premier League record for games started, had to come off at half time with a groin injury that piled on the problems for the upcoming trip to Wembley. After Funes Mori received a straight red for a late stamp on Origi's ankle, Ross Barkley was also hooked; the white flag raised by the manager with dreaded thoughts turning already to the cup semi-final that could yet be his death knell, if he wasn't already out of a job before then.

If Simon Mignolet touched the ball at all in the second period, it would have come as news to Everton supporters. That the Reds weren't 4-0 up by the interval and that they didn't treble the 2-0 lead they took into the break was down to Joel Robles, who made some fine saves to deny Adam Lallana and Roberto Firmino in particular, and some poor finishing by Klopp's front line. Liverpool got it together up front on the hour mark, though, to carve the Blues wide open and present an easy chance to Daniel Sturridge to slot home. And Coutinho's accurate low drive from the edge of the box a few minutes later was well-placed beyond the Everton goalkeeper's reach to complete the rout.

Recent performances, and some damning goals for and against statistics in the last 30 minutes of matches, suggested the team weren't fit enough, didn't fight enough, weren't clinical enough, and that the mentality of the side was simply all wrong. The players seemed no longer to be playing for the manager – and when that happens, it's over.

Final score: Liverpool 4-0 Everton

***

After the match, the media found a chastened Martinez ruing a lapse in concentration at the end of the first half and a "chain of events" involving injury, illness and a red card in the horror show at Anfield.

"It was a horrible experience for everyone involved," a shell-shocked Martinez said to Darren Griffiths after the game. "You don't expect a game to change so radically. Three minutes before half time we got two actions that we don't defend properly, where we switch off and we allow a two-goal lead to be so soft in the manner that it happened."

***

23 April 2016: Everton v Manchester United (At Wembley Stadium)

In Roberto Martinez's own words, the period of the Anfield derby and the FA Cup Semi-Final against United, had promised to be a "defining week" for him and his players.

After the galling collapse at Anfield, Martinez needed a big performance, and the backs-against-the-wall, underdog spirit which had lifted Everton teams of the past against Man United, including at Wembley in 1995 and 2012. He eventually got something akin to it, whether by his own powers of motivation or, perhaps more likely, through a response from the players to the desperation pouring out of stands from 30-odd thousand Evertonians, and from the realisation their entire season was circling the drain.

The first 45 minutes produced tentative, defensive football that was lacking cohesion and organisation, and during which Everton fell behind to Marouane Fellaini's 34th-minute goal. But in the second half, the Blues suddenly discovered the intensity and drive that had been wholly lacking through a run of seven games without a win in all competitions, and they had Louis van Gaal's Red Devils on the ropes.

It yielded a penalty for the Blues, won by the otherwise disappointing Ross Barkley, who was felled in the box by Tim Fosu-Mensah. That was taken well enough by Romelu Lukaku but saved by David de Gea, a goalkeeper who had made a habit of bringing his best form into meetings with Everton over the previous couple of seasons. Then, after Phil Jagielka had denied Fellaini a second goal with an unseen handball almost on the goal-line, Everton levelled and threatened to turn the tie on its head with more pressure yet, sadly, fell short.

Instead, there was the latest in a succession of stings in the "tale" that Blues fans have had to deal with, as Martinez's defence succumbed one final time and Anthony Martial swept through the breach to plant a cruel winner beyond Joel Robles.

Little of what Martinez said in the aftermath of another crushing loss would have resonated with fed up Evertonians, but he was right that, on balance, Everton probably at least deserved to get to extra time. Their first-half display had been massively disappointing, an echo of the lifeless and unimaginative fare that had characterised a sequence of three draws and four defeats since that potentially catalytic victory over Chelsea last month.

It would have been easier to blame the loss of Seamus Coleman, the need to use Muhammed Besic as an emergency fullback, and Jagielka having to play through a hamstring injury but the second half from Martinez' side had been so much better.

The fightback, when it came, wasn't led by Martinez's self-proclaimed "style" of possession-based football; it was a last-ditch effort to raise the tempo by a group of players who were willed on by the masses of Evertonians banked in their thousands around one half of Wembley, with elimination from the cup rapidly closing in on them.

Had Lukaku prevailed from the penalty spot, things might have been so much different but, ultimately, the team had been undone by their failure to turn up for 50 minutes, their consistent failings at the back, and the leaking of yet another injury-time goal.

Final score: Everton 1-2 Man United

***

After the match, Roberto Martinez – who was insistent that his team was developing, and that he shared the Blues' ambitions – was asked if he was still the man for the job at Goodison Park. This despite another hugely disappointing season which had seen defeat over two legs to Manchester City in the League Cup earlier on, and now included a second cup exit at the semi-final stage.

"I am, yes," he replied. "I'm so attached to Everton and my ambition is exactly the same as their ambition. Over the last three years, we haven't invested any money. We've been handling assets really well. I think the squad is at a great valuation. We've got very good young players, we develop young players really well. I just share the drive that the football club has which is to getting into the Champions League, getting into positions where we can bring silverware to the football club and I'll give everything I've got to fulfil those expectations. I feel every season we are developing and showing certain things that can please our fans and bring the silverware they deserve. But clearly, at moments like this of true disappointment, it is very difficult to see through that the real good things we have developed over the last three seasons."

***

11 May 2016: Sunderland v Everton

Roberto Martinez' words after the FA Cup semi-final defeat would ring hollow in the aftermath of what proved to be his final match in charge as Everton manager. His team offered another shameful away performance, going down meekly to Sunderland who easily picked up the three points they needed to safeguard their membership of the Premier League and send Newcastle and Norwich down to the Championship.

The Blues fell behind 2-0 by the half-time interval to goals by Patrick van Aanholt and Lamine Kone. They then conceded another when Joel Robles could only parry to the feet of the Ivorian defender and he converted from close range.

Coming in the wake of the previous Saturday's abject capitulation at the King Power Stadium to newly crowned champions, Leicester, and the even more embarrassing surrender at Anfield in the Merseyside derby in the previous month, the outcome of this game came as little surprise to those Evertonians who had made the journey to the northeast.

Seven goals conceded in those two prior away fixtures soon became ten, as the Black Cats capitalised on Everton's inability to convert superior possession into chances and preyed on the Toffees' notorious weakness at set pieces.

All three goals came as the result of dead-ball situations. The first and third were incidents that Robles would want to forget, but none of the defenders covered themselves in glory and were it not for a couple of other important stops by the Spanish goalkeeper, the score might have been higher.

It had been another miserable evening for Everton. The club may have wished to delay a decision about the manager's future until after the final game against Norwich, but had he still been in charge by then, disgruntled Everton fans would have been sure to make their feelings known at what was supposed to be an upbeat occasion to see out the season.

Final score: Sunderland 3-0 Everton

2016: Roberto Martinez sacked

> “[Roberto Martinez’] record was an increasingly middling one, and did not portend a return to challenging for the European places anytime soon, were he to remain in his post. That was obviously at odds with a new era of success that fans hoped would be ushered in by the club's new billionaire owner

2016 Roberto Martinez sacked

The day after the Sunderland defeat, the club made an official announcement on Twitter and evertonfc.com that Roberto Martinez had been relieved of his duties as manager of Everton.

Bill Kenwright and the Board of Directors expressed their thanks to Martinez for his “dedication and commitment” and for conducting himself “with the utmost integrity and dignity."

The decision had come towards the end of a second-successive season in which the Toffees would finish in the bottom half of the Premier League. The defeat at the Stadium of Light had been the latest chapter in an alarming run of results stretching back to early

March 2016, in which Everton had won just twice in 12 matches in all competitions.

Humiliation at Anfield in the Merseyside derby and failure in the FA Cup semi-final had finally made up the mind of Farhad Moshiri that Martinez's time was up. While there had been rumours that the board was split on dismissing the Catalan, privately there had been a desire to see out the season and make an announcement regarding his future in the coming weeks.

The dreadful showings at Leicester City and at Sunderland, coupled with a growing clamour from supporters for his removal, forced the club to announce his departure, and head off planned protests at the final home game of the season.

While there was little doubt in the end that Martinez had to go, his departure was nonetheless tinged with regret. He had joined the Toffees in June 2013 on the heels of his FA Cup Final triumph with Wigan Athletic, but also after the Latics' relegation from the top flight. Such contrasting achievements would be reflected during his time at Goodison Park.

In his first season, he guided Everton to a fifth-place finish and their best points tally since the formation of the Premier League in 1992. It was success that not only prompted an extension to his contract, but also fostered genuine excitement among supporters that his exciting brand of football might finally deliver on the promise of the Moyes years.

The Catalan battled, however, to match the achievements of his first season at Goodison Park, with the club struggling through consecutive seasons of under-performance that ended in disappointing mid-table finishes.

In 2014-15, Martinez had become the first Everton manager to oversee exits from the domestic cups at the first hurdle, although he fared much better in the Europa League, until his side lost to Dynamo Kiev in the Round of 16 in March 2015. Many cited his decision to deploy defender Antolin Alcaraz in central defence on that miserable evening, rather than John Stones, as being indicative of the manager's defensive weaknesses that were becoming more and more damaging the further the club moved away from the solid foundations put in by his predecessor.

Martinez had steered the Blues to the last four of both the Carling Cup and FA Cup in his final season, eventually losing to the two Manchester clubs respectively, but registered another unwanted record with Everton's worst home league record in the club's history to that point, when adjusted to three points for a win.

In short, his was an increasingly middling record and one that did not portend a return to challenging for the European places anytime soon, were he to remain in his post. That was obviously at odds with a new era of success that fans hoped would be ushered in by the club's new billionaire owner.

***

Speculation soon shifted to whom the club might target to replace Martinez, with a slew of names, ranging from Frank de Boer, Manuel Pellegrini and Southampton Head Coach, Ronald Koeman.

De Boer, whose agent suggested he would love to manage a club like Everton, had just parted company with Ajax after narrowly failing to land his fifth Dutch title, while there had been tabloid claims that

Pellegrini would be interested in a job that would keep him in the Premier League and in the northwest of England following his departure from Manchester City.

The media asked Koeman on 13 May about his contract situation and his future at his pre-match press conference ahead of the weekend's final games in the Premier League.

He replied, "I am manager of Southampton. Everyone knows I have one more year of my contract," Koeman said. "What I said last week when I got [asked] the same question, is that we will sit together and analyse this season and talk about the future. That's what the news is today."

Asked outright if he would stay as Saints boss, Koeman simply stated: "Yes."

However, Moshiri would soon come calling to pitch a very attractive proposition from Everton, one the Dutchman would find very hard to turn down.

***

15 May 2016: Everton v Norwich

Three days prior to the end of of a disappointing 2015/16 season, Everton announced that Under 21s coach, David Unsworth, and former Blues manager, Joe Royle, would take temporary charge of Everton for the final match of the campaign against Norwich City, following the dismissal of Roberto Martinez as manager.

Everton also announced the postponement of their awards gala to mark the end of the season. The club followed their confirmation that the Catalan would leave his post by advising supporters that the End of Season Awards night at St George's Hall would no longer be taking place.

It was a phrase barely used in the last few weeks of his tenure at Goodison Park, but Martinez had spoken frequently of his desire to see his players "enjoying their football." It reflected his almost relentless optimism, but for all the sunniness of his disposition, it had become quite clear by the Anfield derby and beyond that Everton's players were no longer enjoying anything.

Fast forward to three days after what most Evertonians now felt was his overdue and necessary dismissal and there was much joy to be found at the Grand Old Lady — from the stands to the pitch, there were smiles and a noticeably elevated mood as the club began looking to a potentially brighter future than the stagnant one that has faced them in recent months.

As Unsworth's well-received team selection and the impressive displays by its youngest members showed, that optimism for what lay ahead was not just confined to the search for a new manager to take the helm at Everton. Four fresh graduates from the club's academy featured prominently in a handsome 3-0 victory over relegated Norwich City, lending credence to the stand-in boss's confident assertion that the next permanent manager would inherit some real gems mined from the youth system.

Matthew Pennington, starting again at right back in the absence of Seamus Coleman, would have been more familiar to Toffees fans, having featured in recent games. He would manage just 28 minutes before succumbing to the same injury as his more senior teammate and being replaced by Jonjoe Kenny — the captain of Unsworth's Under-21s side when he wasn't on loan helping Oxford United gain promotion from England's fourth tier — who made his senior bow in impressive fashion.

In midfield, the much-anticipated Kieran Dowell didn't disappoint with his hour-plus on the field and was involved in two of the Blues' goals, but it was Tom Davies who emerged as the star of the show and finishing the game as many people's man of the match. Still just 17, Davies exhibited a wonderful blend of touch, skill, steel, awareness and maturity in the middle of the park that defied his tender years, more than justifying his selection. No wonder Unsworth had made repeated mention of the need for the next manager to cherish and nurture Everton's stable of young players.

The blooding of those precocious young Blues wasn't the only refreshing thing about the Everton side that took to the field for this finale to another disappointing season. The attitude, tempo, and intensity that a team blending youth with seasoned experience brought to the contest from the first whistle was in stark contrast to the insipid, pedestrian fare that plagued them for so much of 2016.

There was also a confidence coursing through players' veins where in recent games, with perhaps the exception perhaps of 45 minutes at Wembley, there appeared to be none. That was beautifully illustrated in the 19th minute, when a lightning-quick move started by Tim Howard, making his last ever appearance, went straight down the centre of the field through James McCarthy and then Dowell, with the Irish midfielder continuing his run to meet a loose ball 25 yards from goal and bending a wonderfully crisp shot inside John Ruddy's post. Criticised by fans for his staid, one-dimensional and crab-like performances, this was evidence of the player McCarthy could be when the shackles of a flawed system were discarded.

Norwich, with their own weight lifted off their shoulders, did their best to feed off the home side's energy, and they had a couple of good moments in the first half.

Their best chance fell to Matt Jarvis a few minutes before the break, but thankfully, while he'd capitalised on space in front of him as he cut in from the left, he hammered his shot over the bar when he should have done better.

It left him to rue that miss a couple of minutes later when, at the other end, Lukaku collapsed in the Norwich box under the attentions of Robbie Brady and the referee pointed to the spot. It looked harsh on the Canaries but Baines took responsibility for the penalty as Howard declined an invitation to mark his send-off with a goal and, restored to spot-kick duties, the fullback made no mistake, slotting past Ruddy to send Everton into half-time 2-0 up.

The third goal was the one that put the game beyond Norwich's reach, but it was the one that would have Evertonians most excited by the future, given that it involved all three of the impressive-looking teenagers. Davies snapped into a tackle midway inside the Canaries' half and the ball broke to Dowell. He nudged it on to McCarthy, who fed Kenny on the overlap and his low centre benefitted from a deflection before arriving at the feet of Mirallas, who swept it into the empty net.

It was an afternoon that could only have gone better for Everton if they had piled on a couple more goals. Compared to what the day threatened to be if Martinez had still been in the dugout, it was an occasion pregnant with relief, hope for the future, and expectation at the rebuilding job ahead over the summer.

2015/16 was a season that supporters would be glad to see the back of, as the emotional toll has been a heavy one. For the second year running, Everton finished 11th in the league.

Final score: Everton 3-0 Norwich

***

Everton continued to fill the back pages as speculation over the new managerial appointment increased, and as the Blues got their search underway for Roberto Martinez's replacement, David Moyes, the man whom the Catalan had replaced at Goodison in 2013, said he would be open to returning to the club as manager. With Moyes out of work following his sacking first from Manchester United and then Real Sociedad, his name had inevitably come up in connection with the Everton post, and the former Preston boss said he would be interested seeing as there appeared to be the need for some rebuilding of the team.

"Would I consider going back? I've said if I get an exciting challenge and something that makes me feel I could get my teeth into it, then I would be really interested," he said in *The Times.*

"When we took over, we had 11 great and successful years, but we also had to rebuild the club a little bit. I just think now the change has been made, and Everton need to now go and do it again.

"If you give David Moyes an opportunity, he tends to rebuild a club, and he tends to get it going in the right direction and making sure that things are correct and I'm looking forward to getting the chance to do that again."

Rumours abounded that Bill Kenwright was supporting the return of 'The Moyesiah', but there were real hopes the club could go out and make a top-drawer managerial appointment instead. Moyes was, therefore, never going to be a popular choice. There was a tangible sense by the 2012/13 season that he had taken the club as far as he could; so there was unlikely to be broad enthusiasm for his return to Everton after a three-year absence.

In any case, this was the first opportunity for Moshiri to make his mark on the club. The fan base and the media waited to see whether he would go with Kenwright's man, or strike out in a different direction.

2016: Everton Board secure #1 Target Ronald Koeman

By mid-June 2016, the managerial speculation was at an end. Everton finally confirmed the appointment of Ronald Koeman as the club's next manager, days after reaching a £5 million compensation agreement with Southampton and completing all the remaining details over personal terms.

The Dutchman left St Mary's Stadium with a year remaining on his term there, signing a three-year contract with the Blues that would tie him to Goodison Park until 2019.

Koeman's arrival marked the completion of a process that had begun almost as soon as Martinez departed, as the 53-year-old had been touted as Farhad Moshiri's first choice to lead his new era at Goodison.

Initially, Saints CEO Ralph Kruger and director of development, Les Reed had been confident they could persuade Koeman to stay at St Mary's Stadium, at least to see out the final year of his contract. But the lure of a significantly increased salary (believed to be £6 million per year), a reported £100 million transfer war chest, and the promise of Moshiri's ambitious plans proved decisive.

"I am very excited to be Everton manager," Koeman said on his appointment. "I believe in the Club, in the team, in the fans and in our ability to achieve things in the future. Everton is a club with a great history and real ambition, and it is a proud feeling for me to be part of what we want to go and do, together with the chairman and Farhad Moshiri. I am looking forward to meeting everyone at the Club and to preparing for a big season in the Premier League."

A world-class defender in his playing days, Koeman had starred for all three of the Netherlands' big clubs: Ajax, PSV and Feyenoord. At Barcelona, he was a member of Johan Cruyff's "Dream Team" of the early 1990s, and on the international stage for his country he won the European Championships in 1988.

As manager, he had managed six teams in the Eredivisie and also had stints in Portugal and Spain before he came to England to continue the renaissance of Southampton begun by Mauricio Pochettino — despite seeing some of that club's best players sold over the past two summer windows. He led the Saints to 7th place in his first season and then 6th place in his second term, finishing just three points off the top four but securing Europa League qualification for the second year running.

Expectations of Koeman's continued success were running high at Goodison Park, and the fanbase was eager to see how Farhad Moshiri would deliver on his promises.

2016: New DoF and New Board Members Appointed

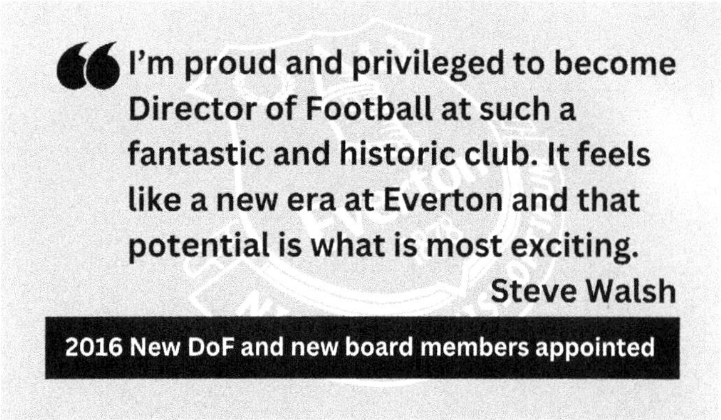

A week after Koeman's appointment, Everton announced they had also secured the services of Leicester City's highly rated head of recruitment, Steve Walsh, as the club's new Director of Football.

The 63-year-old, once described by Sir Alex Ferguson, as the most influential figure in the 2015/16 title race, filled a new position at Goodison Park and Finch Farm, one that new major shareholder Farhad Moshiri had identified as a vital part of his plans for the club.

Walsh, who once served as a European scout under Jose Mourinho and Andre Villas-Boas at Chelsea (where he helped sign Didier Drogba, Gianfranco Zola and Michael Essien) and was assistant boss to both Nigel Pearson and Claudio Ranieri at Leicester, achieved credit for uncovering the likes of Riyad Mahrez, Jamie Vardy and N'Golo Kanté, three of the main driving forces behind the Foxes' stunning 2015/16 Premier League title triumph.

Besides his 16 years at Chelsea, for whom he initially worked part time while holding down a PE-teacher role in Chorley, he had spells at Newcastle United, and Hull City. His brother Mickey, a football agent, was a Republic of Ireland international who played 29 times for Everton in the 1978/79 season, as well as also representing Blackpool, QPR and Porto.

Despite having signed a new contract with Leicester City, Walsh followed Kanté out of the King Power Stadium, as the French midfielder made a £30 million switch to Stamford Bridge.

It was reported that Koeman had recommended Walsh to Moshiri.

"I'm proud and privileged to become Director of Football at such a fantastic and historic club," Walsh said on his arrival. "It feels like a new era at Everton and that potential is what is most exciting.

"I know the club well. My roots are in the north-west and my brother, Mickey, was an Everton player in the Bob Latchford era and always proud of that fact. I also did my initial teacher training at Liverpool Hope University many years ago. I'm genuinely excited to be here at the club and very much looking forward to getting down to work."

Koeman, meanwhile, welcomed the Lancastrian to Everton by saying: "It's really good for the club to have Steve, who has shown his quality in his job at a number of clubs over many years. That's the experience and quality he will bring to us at a good time in the season. He has a great deal of knowledge about building for the long-term and the magnificent work he did at Leicester on top of the job he did at Chelsea makes us excited to have him here at Everton."

***

Alexander (Sasha) Ryazantsev had joined the Board of Directors of Everton Football Club in March 2016 following a successful career in finance and investment banking spanning over 20 years.

He graduated from the Russian Plekhanov University of Economics in 1995 with a BSc in Economics and Commercial Management, later working as an investment analyst at Global Natural Energy PLC, where future Everton major shareholder Farhad Moshiri was CEO.

After completing his Masters in Finance from the London Business School in 2002, Ryazantsev joined ABN AMRO Bank, where he led a team advising European consumer brands on their capital structures and corporate financing. He joined the corporate financing and risk solutions team at RBS in 2007, and handled bond issues and mergers and acquisitions across Europe, the Middle East and Africa.

In early 2016, Ryazantsev advised Farhad Moshiri on the acquisition of Everton, and on the future strategy of the football club.

Born into a footballing family - his father was a goalkeeper at several clubs across the former USSR in the 1960s and 1970s - and Sasha played at right-back for Dynamo Moscow boys until the age of 16 but then turned his focus towards his studies.

Darren Griffiths interviewed Ryazantsev at Finch Farm for evertontv, and he confirmed the board were delighted to have secured their top pick to succeed Roberto Martinez as Everton manager.

"[Ronald] was absolutely our number one choice from day one of the search process," he said. "It took us a while to get to him, but in the end we have absolutely no doubt we made the right decision.

"We are now one of the four north-western clubs that have brilliant managers and [there's] such a concentration [of big clubs] in the northwest that we couldn't have fallen behind. Therefore, it was very important to get someone of that stature into the club.

"Bill Kenwright ... has been the driving force for the last many years. Obviously, he is an Evertonian, and it is very important for us to keep that culture.

"We very much hope that the new manager will be the guardian of that culture as well, and that we all move forward as a big Everton family."

Moshiri had embarked on what seemed to be an ambitious process of reshaping Everton and restoring its image as one of the big players in the Premier League, with plans for squad strengthening that summer and a long-awaited resolution of the stadium issue.

Many had described his new investment in the Toffees as a 'project' but Ryazantsev felt it was bigger and more long-term than that description suggested.

"I don't know if 'project' is the right word to use," he continued. "It's probably more than that. Of course, we have the team, the performance on the pitch and, of course, we have the appointment of Ronald is the very first step we had to make in that regard.

"But we have other projects like the stadium going forward as well, and we very much want to win and be successful in whatever we do."

***

The club also announced that Deputy CEO, Denise Barrett-Baxendale MBE had become the latest member of the Board of Directors. Long considered a potential successor to Robert Elstone as the club's Chief Executive, Barrett-Baxendale had been nationally recognised for her work in heading up the award-winning charity, *Everton in the Community.*

***

In October of that year, Keith Harris, the former London banker whom Everton had enlisted to help seek investors in the club was also appointed to the Board of Directors.

Harris was previously chairman of the Football League and spent six years as Director of Wembley National Stadium until 2007 but had become noted as a broker in the sale and purchase of a number of football clubs, among them Chelsea, Crystal Palace, Swansea City, West Ham United, Aston Villa, Fulham, Manchester City, and was believed to be involved with bringing Farhad Moshiri to the table at Goodison Park, leading to his purchase of a 49.9% stake in the Toffees in February.

"I am truly delighted to be joining the club at such an exciting time," Harris said upon the announcement of his appointment. "I've known the chairman and Mr Moshiri for a long time, so I have a good understanding of their ambition. I have visited Goodison Park numerous times over the years and really enjoy the authenticity of the club and passion of the fans. The atmosphere I experienced at Goodison for the FA Cup tie against Chelsea last season reminded me just how special Everton is and I am looking forward to sharing many more experiences like that in the future."

Harris, 63, joined long-standing Chairman Bill Kenwright and deputy chairman Jon Woods on a newly expanded Everton Board of Directors which included CEO Robert Elstone, Moshiri's representative Sasha Ryazantsev and deputy CEO Denise Barrett-Baxendale.

"We've strengthened our board significantly over the last six months and I'm really pleased that we've been able to add even more experience by bringing Keith in," Kenwright said. "He has a unique set of credentials and experience, combining roles at the highest level of international business with some of the most senior positions within football in this country, and will be a great asset."

Moshiri's back-office team had taken shape. Now Evertonians were watching closely to see how the transfer funds he had promised on the footballing side would be spent.

2016: Squad changes: Money can buy you Stones

> "There is much to be done and things for me to learn, but I can confirm that I have committed to providing additional funds for transfers and retaining our key players to ensure that we have a strong core to build on for the future.
>
> - Farhad Moshiri

2016 Squad changes: Money can buy you Stones

It was clear the Everton first team squad needed strengthening in the summer of 2016 after two consecutive seasons of disappointment.

Roberto Martinez' January signing, Oumar Niasse, had looked well off the pace of the Premier League. So holding onto Romelu Lukaku was, therefore, the main priority. The Belgian's agent at the time, Mino Raiola, had hinted at some back-tracking over Lukaku's desire to leave Goodison Park, after weeks of suggestions that he would move on before the start of the upcoming 2016/17 season. The player's desire for Champions League football, coupled with his impressive goals return for the Blues, had made him an obvious target for many clubs. In remarks made to the Belgian press in the build-up to Euro 2016, Lukaku had indicated a desire to join a team that summer that represented a "project" and could offer him the chance to play in Europe's elite club competition.

However, following Koeman's appointment and a reported meeting between Blues' director Sasha Ryazantsev and Raiola, where the former outlined Moshiri's ambitions and the possibility of a much-improved deal for the player, there appeared to have been climbdown in the agent's rhetoric for his client's Everton future.

"Everton don't need the money anymore but Romelu wants to play for a club that can win trophies," Raiola told *Sportwereld* in Belgium. "Something's changed at Everton. There's a new project. If he leaves, it has to be a good deal for all parties. Romelu certainly has the qualities to play in Italy," he said. "But as the Italian landscape currently looks, there's no team that can afford him. He is too expensive for Serie A. Only a global power can pay for him – the top clubs in England, Barcelona, Real Madrid and Paris Saint-Germain."

Lukaku had talked of potential moves to Juventus or Paris Saint-Germain, two clubs that could have afforded him and offered him Champions League football. Meanwhile, a dubious report from Italy claimed Arsenal could launch a paltry £31 million bid for him, as Jamie Vardy's proposed move from Leicester to the Emirates looked to be off.

With the club now backed by Moshiri's money and with Koeman at the helm, even more players than usual were linked with Everton during the closed season. A reported fee of £30 million had been agreed with Zenit St Petersburg for Lukaku's Belgian team mate, Axel Witsel, with the expectation being that a deal could be completed after Euro2016.

Meanwhile, Everton continued to be linked with Juan Mata, more by rumour than media coverage, who may have been surplus to requirements at Manchester United.

By early August, however, with only one new signing in place, Everton's Assistant Manager, the manager's brother, Erwin Koeman, was fielding questions. He cited a combination of the delay caused by Euro2016 on the summer transfer market, the relatively late introduction of a Director of Football following Steve Walsh's switch from Leicester, the need for Koeman to fully assess the players he inherited from Roberto Martinez, and the obstacle to attracting top-class talent because of Everton's lack of European football next season as being contributory factors to the protracted wait for new faces. With the new season just around the corner and the transfer deadline four weeks away, Erwin Koeman, said his brother and the chairman were very busy, stepping up their efforts to bring in new players. Interestingly, there was no mention of Steve Walsh in terms of recruitment efforts.

The following day, the club confirmed Idrissa Gana Gueye as an Everton player, after putting pen to paper on a four-year deal.

After goalkeeper Maarten Stekelenburg's arrival the previous month, the 26-year-old midfielder became Ronald Koeman's second acquisition of the summer in a £7.1 million deal, after the club activated his release clause at Aston Villa.

Gueye had been odds-on to join the Toffees from Villa Park, when reports of their interest first emerged, and the Midlands club's new boss Roberto di Matteo admitted they had been resigned to losing him to Everton.

Meanwhile, eyebrows were raised around Goodison Park, when Roberto Martinez was named as the boss of the Belgian national team, replacing Marc Wilmots, who left the role after the European Championships. The Catalan had provided studio analysis for ESPN at the tournament and was interviewed by Anderlecht before also being linked with the vacancy at Hull City.

Back at Goodison, Everton signalled their faith in up-and-coming midfielder Tom Davies by handing the teenager a five-year contract with the club. The 18-year-old, who had only made his first-team debut in April, put pen to paper on the extended deal, which no doubt came with improved terms.

"It's great motivation knowing I'll be here for five years and that I can really push on and hopefully develop to become a really good player for the team and go on to do really well," Davies told evertontv. "Coming back from the off season and going straight back with the first team has been a good insight for me into what's required of me for the season and to be around the players, play as much as I have and train with them, it's been vital for my progression as a player.

"I just want to become a regular first. That's something I am going to work towards and hopefully, with the help of the staff and learning from other players, I can get there."

The following week, Everton sealed the signing of highly experienced Wales captain, Ashley Williams, from Swansea City in a deal that was officially undisclosed but reportedly worth £9 million.

The news of Williams signing followed confirmation of John Stones' sale to Manchester City in a deal that would eventually be worth the reported £50 million transfer fee that Everton had been holding out for that summer. Fans on social media were asking whether Farhad Moshiri was being true to his word of retaining key players, if those of John Stones' calibre were being allowed to leave the club at the first opportunity.

Interviewed later in the month, however, Stones opened up to the media about how his relationship with ex-Everton manager Roberto Martinez had deteriorated the previous season and led to his departure for Manchester City that summer, despite Ronald Koeman's arrival.

The defender, who left for what was, at the time, a club record £47.5 million fee for an outgoing player, was often played out of position or dropped for poor performances, and he said the Catalan hadn't explained why he wasn't picking him. "It was a tough period because I was doing everything right," Stones said. "I was being professional. I was carrying myself well. I wanted to do everything right, try to get in the team, how everyone should, and fight for my place.

"I felt I was doing everything I could and deserved to play and still wasn't. That's when I found it hard. It's probably a question you should have asked him at the time because he wasn't telling me.

"Roberto had his style of play and kind of changed that towards the end of his career at Everton," Stones continued. "He changed the whole style of the team and things weren't working out at that time so you could say it wasn't the best decision.

"As you know, the gaffer got sacked. It wasn't enjoyable. We weren't winning games. When we don't do that a few games on the trot, it starts to eat away at you, no matter who you are. It was a good test for me. I learned a lot about my football, about myself."

That prompted him to think about leaving Everton, three years after he arrived as an unknown teenager from Barnsley. He had put in a transfer request the preceding year when Chelsea mounted a concerted effort to sign him but, with the Gwladys Street adapting the Beatles song 'Money Can't Buy You Love' with the words 'Money Can't Buy You Stones', Martinez and the Blues' hierarchy had rejected the offer and refused to sell him so close to the 2015 transfer deadline.

A year later, he was on his way to Manchester but, having signed the veteran Williams to plug the gap in the short term, Koeman believed he had another player who could step into Stones' shoes in the form of the young defender picked up from Barnsley by Martinez in the summer of 2015.

Simon Jones in The Daily Mail[1] wrote of Ronald Koeman's faith in Mason Holgate:

> "The ink was barely dry on John Stones' Manchester City contract when the question was posed: where do Everton find the next John Stones? Ashley Williams arrived from Swansea and Lamine Kone was courted at Sunderland, but their strengths are leadership and aggression. The simple fact is Ronald Koeman believes he may have the answer right in front of him. Mason Holgate is a tall, stylish ball-playing defender that Everton signed as a teenager from Barnsley for £2million after barely 20 first team games. Sound familiar? He can play right back or centre back and has such insouciant temperament that Koeman thought nothing of asking him to mark Zlatan Ibrahimovic

> during Wayne Rooney's testimonial at Old Trafford last week. You have to understand that he is 19 years old but maybe he showed more confidence than some other players on the pitch," purred Koeman afterwards. "He's a big talent." Everton players will testify, earning Koeman's praise does not come easy and Holgate is not taking his first team graduation for granted. The manager has been great to me and not just because he put me in the team!" Holgate says. "Before I went out at United, he just said it doesn't matter whether you are 19 or 36, I'm putting you in because you are ready and you are good enough. Don't have any fear, just show what you can do. I know I have to work to impress him, I wouldn't expect anything else but it's nice to know I could get a chance this season if I keep at it. The United game was a great experience."

Koeman's efforts to improve the squad he had inherited from Martinez continued. August 15th saw Everton announce their fourth signing of the summer when Crystal Palace winger Yannick Bolasie arrived on a 5 year deal worth a reported £22.5 million that had the potential to reach as high as the club record that Everton had paid Chelsea for Romelu Lukaku, if all appearance-related add-ons were triggered.

On the same day as Bolasie signed, Farhad Moshiri said on Sky Sports there were plans to further strengthen the team before the end of the transfer window.

> "We are very pleased about today's signing," Moshiri said in the statement, "but remain anxious to further strengthen the squad. The chairman, Bill Kenwright is relentlessly pushing things forward with total support for him, for Steve Walsh and Ronald Koeman."

Two more names were added to the squad on 31 August 2016, Transfer Deadline Day, when Everton announced they had agreed a fee of £1.5 million for young Sheffield United striker Dominic Calvert-Lewin. The 19-year-old had been a target for the Blues for most of the summer. Ecuador striker, Enner Valencia also came in on loan for the season from West Ham. Proposed moves for Moussa Sissoko and Yacine Brahimi collapsed.

Valencia's impact would prove to be limited, but in Calvert-Lewin Everton had signed someone who would go on to become a hugely important player for the club and score one of the most important goals in Goodison Park's history.

Described as being physically strong with good aerial presence, Calvert-Lewin was in England's U20 squad, having made it into the Blades' senior squad in 2015 following a loan spell at Northampton Town.

The coup of acquiring him was credited to Under 23s coach, David Unsworth, who had seen his rich potential as a raw 16-year-old while coaching him at Sheffield United.

"This is an opportunity of a lifetime for him," Unsworth said once Calvert-Lewin had put pen to paper on a 5 year contract. "To go from League One to the Premier League is a massive jump, but he certainly has all the attributes to make that jump, given time, hard work and the desire I know he has."

Since Moshiri had purchased his 49.9% stake in Everton in March 2016, the club had already felt his impact and decisiveness. Through his representative on the Board, Sasha Ryazantsev and chairman Bill Kenwright, he had dismissed former boss Roberto Martinez and brought in both Ronald Koeman from Southampton and Steve Walsh from Leicester, by negotiating compensation packages with both clubs.

Off the field, the Board were still moving ahead under Moshiri's direction with plans for a new stadium, and an interim facelift for Goodison Park was also underway.

It all felt so promising, but would the team deliver?

---

1. Simon Jones: Daily Mail, 10 August 2016

2016: New season off to a bright start

> "Yes, there is a fear, definitely. When a new manager comes in, everyone has to be on their toes. There is competition for places and even the situation with the financial backing we have now adds to it all.
>
> \- Phil Jagielka

2016 New season off to a bright start

Though there had been disappointment that the club hadn't been able to hold onto defender John Stones, Evertonians were buoyant going into the 2016/17 season. Ronald Koeman had been lured away from Southampton to complete what Farhad Moshiri described as a quartet of "Hollywood managers" in the northwest, alongside Jose Mourinho, Pep Guardiola and Jurgen Klopp. Furthermore, Romelu Lukaku had opted to stay at Goodison to spearhead the Blues' attack under the new regime.

The new-found optimism following two disappointing seasons under Roberto Martinez appeared to be well-founded, as Everton began the new season with a six-match unbeaten run in all competitions.

A 1-1 home draw to Spurs was followed by four successive wins: 2-1 away at West Brom, 4-0 at home to Yeovil in the League Cup, 1-0 at home to Stoke and 3-0 away at David Moyes' new club, Sunderland. By the time Middlesbrough came to Goodison, Everton were sitting pretty, in third place in the Premier League table.

***

17 September 2016: Everton v Middlesbrough

Old habitual instincts may die hard but, with each passing game under Ronald Koeman's assured leadership, Evertonians were allowing confidence to creep back into their psyche.

1-0 down to a controversial 'Boro goal, the cavalier Blues side of early 2015/16 might well have fought back but ended up throwing the game away again; whereas the more brittle version under Roberto Martinez might have caved altogether in the face of injustice, the size of the task and the frustration pouring out of the stands.

Confidence is a powerful thing in football, though, and Koeman was restoring it in spades at Everton, to the point where they simply brushed off an awful decision by Lee Mason who overlooked Alvaro Negredo's foul on Maarten Stekelenburg and allowed Middlesbrough to take the lead after 20 minutes. Everton then turned the match on its head and had it effectively won by half-time.

Much of that was down to the combination of a vastly improved defensive setup, a visibly fitter collection of players, and their consequent work-rate that started with the front players and extended to the back, where the gladiatorial duo of Phil Jagielka and Ashley Williams refused to give 'Boro an inch.

In front of them, the imperious Idrissa Gueye, who turned in another man-of-the-match display of stunning effectiveness, again supported Gareth Barry. The Senegalese seemed to cover every blade of grass, tackled anything that moved, and again weighed in with an assist, all of which added to his burgeoning reputation as the best signing of the summer.

The game was won, however, with Everton's superior talents at the other end, once they had gathered the impetus to have a real go at Aitor Karanka's outfit. Middlesbrough had started confidently, and through their discipline and organisation, made things difficult for their hosts throughout.

It was a deep cross by George Friend that led to the opening goal. Negredo's head connected with Stekelenburg's arms rather than the ball. Everyone expected the referee to blow for the foul, but he didn't. There was disbelief and fury when he pointed to the centre circle but Everton channelled that emotion into an almost immediate response.

The second of two successive corners was swung in from the Everton left. Williams almost connected in front of the goalkeeper, and when the ball bounced through towards the back of the area, Barry had peeled away smartly to sweep it home with a nicely controlled finish.

'Boro's resistance then melted in the face of a neat move three minutes before the break, as Gueye picked out Coleman's run and the Irishman dribbled inside two defenders and drew the 'keeper, opening up both sides of the goal, to allow him to tuck the ball into the corner with aplomb.

And four minutes after that came the killer third. Bolasie engineered space for a teasing cross from the right that caught Valdés in two minds as Lukaku looked certain to get decisive contact on the ball but, whether with the aid of the merest of touches from the striker or not, it swerved into the far corner to make it 3-1 at half-time.

The second half was a bit of a non-event, save for an injury that forced Lukaku off to the benefit of debutant Enner Valencia and further evidence that the manager's decision to keep Barkley in the side was being vindicated by a purposeful display from the 22-year-old. It was he who came closest to padding the scoreline, but his powerful drive from the angle was denied by Valdés' save.

Final score: Everton 3-1 Middlesbrough

***

Asked after the game whether the combination of Koeman's more regimented management and Everton's greater financial resources had increased the pressure on the players to perform, club captain Phil Jagielka confirmed as much.

"Yes, there is a fear, definitely," Jagielka said. "When a new manager comes in, everyone has to be on their toes. There is competition for places and even the situation with the financial backing we have now adds to it all.

"Not one player is guaranteed a place in the squad, let alone the team. If the manager wants to go and buy a player in January, then the cheque book is open.

"It does put added pressure on the players, but it is a good pressure.

"That proves he has not done a bad job. At the moment, it is going well. I wouldn't say we are playing amazing, but we are getting fantastic results, and that breeds confidence."

Had Jagielka spoken prematurely? Maybe so, because Everton's encouraging start under Koeman quickly evaporated following the victory over Middlesbrough. The club's customary early exit from the EFL Cup occurred with a 2-0 home defeat at the hands of Norwich three days later. That was followed by a 1-0 away defeat at Bournemouth, two 1-1 draws against Crystal Palace and Man City, then a 2-1 away defeat at Sean Dyche's Burnley. The net result was Everton were out of a cup, and by early December they had slipped to ninth in the Premier League having won just once in 10 games.

One player who definitely wasn't enjoying life under Ronald Koeman was Oumar Niasse, whom many felt was treated harshly by Koeman.

Billed as a goal-scoring backup for Romelu Lukaku, the striker had arrived on a big-money transfer in February under Koeman's predecessor, but the new manager had decided over the summer the Senegalese should look for a new club. A move to Galatasaray had reportedly fallen through while a late loan opportunity back to Lokomotiv Moscow also failed to materialise, amid rumours Niasse's wife didn't want to return to Russia.

That left the 26-year-old in limbo, banished by Koeman to the Under-23s, without a squad number or a locker, and with just a couple of run-outs for the second-string to his name to start the season.

"It's sad, it's really sad," Niasse said in *The Guardian* at the time. "And, to be honest, I think I don't deserve this, but what I can do is just keep my head and fight to change things. I'm not going to make a drama over this. I just deal with it. I know it's just one period.

"I couldn't understand how [the manager's] decision could have been made after 45 minutes [of a pre-season friendly] but I just said: 'OK, thank you.' It's his decision. He's the manager. What can I do? I called my agent, and he said he would look into the opportunities for me. To be honest, I didn't ask Koeman to explain his reasons. I just thought, even if I asked why, I would never understand. After just 45 minutes, you cannot say to me: 'You are no good. He took my shirt number, and he told me I wasn't allowed to be in the dressing room for the first team; that I wasn't going to train with them. I had to go with the second team.

"I said: 'OK, no problem.' When you say you don't need a player, you don't have to see him. I've just kept working in training. Even if I'm training with the Under-23s, I give them the respect.

"Anything can change. Koeman just wants the best for himself and, in two months, if I can be the best for him, he will take me, because he doesn't have any problem with me and I don't have any problem with him. It's football and bigger players than me have had this problem with their coaches."

***

30 October 2016: Everton v West Ham

When West Ham arrived at the end of October, Everton were looking to arrest a run of five games without a victory in all competitions since making an unbeaten start to the new season. The Hammers were hoping to build on three successive wins in the League and EFL Cup, but they came up against a very different proposition in Koeman's outfit.

It was an Everton team featuring three changes from the one that had started against Burnley eight days previously — among them was captain Phil Jagielka who paid the price for two very poor performances with a place on the substitutes' bench — had begun the contest in less than encouraging fashion, with West Ham on the front foot for the first quarter of the match.

However, Everton headed into the break looking the more likely of the two sides to break deadlock and so it proved within five minutes of the restart. After Lukaku failed to gather a heavy infield ball from Oviedo, Reid despatched a weak defensive clearance straight to Barkley. His pass met Coleman's run on the outside where the Irishman drilled a near-post shot that Adrian could only parry and Bolasie showed remarkable speed and desire to burst past two claret shirts, swing the ball on the stretch back into the goalmouth where Lukaku had the simple task of heading into the vacant net.

West Ham began to re-assert themselves to find the equaliser but Payet's attempt to drive a free kick under the wall failed. Robles came to the rescue following an awful lapse by Ashley Williams. Substitute Andre Ayew was denied a clear goal-scoring opportunity by Oviedo's superb covering block, and when Noble attempted an impressive curling effort that looked destined to sneak inside the far post, Robles beat it away two-handed and at full stretch to keep West Ham at bay.

That paved the way for Barkley to kill the game at the end of another nicely-worked move between him and Lukaku, the former arriving in the box and meet the latter's chipped centre with a controlled left-foot finish inside the post.

It was an excellent result for the home side, earned on the back of an increasingly strong performance that was worthy of all three points in the final reckoning. Apart from Lukaku's consistent scoring record, most pleasing for Koeman was the offensive production of Barkley and Bolasie, who weighed in with assists while the former finally scored his second Premier League goal of the season.

Everton had successfully navigated an important game, keeping themselves up with the leading pack and maintaining morale as they headed into the most difficult month of the campaign so far. But would it be enough to satisfy the hierarchy?

Final score: Everton 2-0 West Ham

2017: Moshiri at AGM: 'Don't want to be a museum'

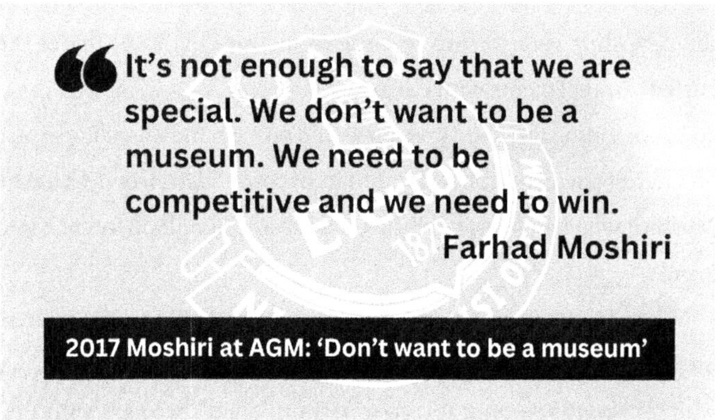

The first Annual General Meeting of Everton shareholders to take place since Farhad Moshiri had purchased his 49.9% stake in the club was held on the evening of 4 January, 2017 at Liverpool's Philharmonic Hall. Moshiri was in attendance along with his representative on the Board of Directors, Sasha Ryazantsev, and it was an occasion which offered plenty of good news, even if it did not provide a definitive update on the stadium situation.

Besides covering successful motions to reappoint Robert Elstone, Denise-Barrett-Baxendale, Ryazantsev and Keith Harris to the Board,

CEO Robert Elstone gave a review of the financial results for 2015/16, concluding the club would have made a profit but for the compensation paid out to Roberto Martinez and his staff when the Catalan departed in May.

He also announced that the club's commercial revenue would grow by £6 million that season and turnover was forecast to top £170 million for 2016/17 – a massive £50 million increase, thanks largely to the bumper new TV broadcast deals. Furthermore, the club had concluded £75 million in new commercial deals in the previous six weeks, including naming rights for Finch Farm. Elstone also expected the new shirt sponsorship revenue to increase by 300% under the current arrangements with Chang.

Elstone also said that: "Everton would save around £5 million a year on interest payments following the recent consolidation of debt under Moshiri, who had provided the club with an £80 million interest-free loan."

When it came time to take questions from the floor, the greatest interest from shareholders was in the search for a new stadium, on which Elstone was only able to report on "solid" progress with Liverpool City Council, and said the next couple of months would "be critical" to secure a location.

Everton had started an investigation into two brownfield sites within the city for suitability for a new ground, with plenty of speculation suggesting that a site at Bramley-Moore Dock on the waterfront was preferable to one at Stonebridge Cross on the outskirts of town in Croxteth.

There were enough hints from both Bill Kenwright and Liverpool Mayor Joe Anderson to confirm the waterside location was the one

Everton wanted, but the latter admitted it was a complex issue. One shareholder cautioned the Board over the prospect of moving to the outskirts of the city.

Elstone responded by saying: "Kirkby was clearly a very divisive location. In terms of Walton Hall Park, we really believed we had a viable scheme. Site location is critical. We do learn lessons. We have to find the right location. I think we can do it this time."

Kenwright backed that up by hinting that the dockside location was the one everyone wanted. "There's no real question as to where we want to be and we have alternatives, but we are working studiously towards that," he said.

The Mayor then said: "I think the elephant in the room is the waterfront site, which everyone, me included, wants but it is a complex issue. We've got plan Bs but everyone is working extremely hard to deliver on the site that you want - that we all want. On Friday, we announced £20 million for a road directly into the dock site. The reality is, there is a railway station being built there. This is the most exciting opportunity this club has had in decades."

Kenwright then discussed the arrival of Farhad Moshiri at the club, saying:

> "After meeting Farhad 18 months ago, instantly it was clear he had an astonishing love of football. I felt instantly this was a man who could get us out of the problem times we were having. This is a very special moment, I believe, in our football club."

Finally, Farhad Moshiri addressed the AGM, and in his speech said:

> "I had looked at a number of clubs. I was involved at Arsenal. Meeting Bill at his office, you couldn't be negative. His enthusiasm was infectious. The atmosphere at Goodison has far exceeded my expectations. They are really special fans. They keep buying beer for me! I don't even drink! It's not enough to say that we are special. We don't want to be a museum. We need to be competitive and we need to win. The gold standard is the Premier League (not the FA Cup). We need to do well in the league. That's where Everton's competitive edge will be measured. We don't have all the time in the world. We have a window to establish ourselves and we'll do everything we can. We need a sustainable base to be among the elite. It takes time but we're committed. That's why we're here."

2017: Koeman signs Schneiderlin in January window

> "January had started with the billing by some as the most important transfer window for Everton in many years. It ended, like the Sky-hyped Transfer Deadline Day itself, as something of a damp squib

2017 Koeman signs Schneiderlin in January window

Everton had struggled through October and November by picking up just one win in a 10-match sequence, culminating in an ugly defeat at Watford in early December. The rest of the month offered hope, however, that Ronald Koeman could right the ship again in anticipation of a stronger second half to the 2016/17 Premier League campaign.

Arsenal and Leicester City were vanquished at Goodison Park either side of a crushing loss in the Merseyside derby to Sadio Mane's injury-time goal, and when Koeman's former club Southampton were comfortably beaten 3-0 in the New Year, the Toffees sat in seventh place.

January had started with the billing by some as the most important transfer window for Everton in many years. It ended, like the Sky-hyped Transfer Deadline Day itself, as something of a damp squib. However, by then there seemed to be acceptance among supporters that, despite only bringing in two players, the club had done fairly well out of January.

Certainly, the wailing for a complete squad overhaul following the defeat at Watford in December felt like it a distant memory, as did Ronald Koeman's frustrated reaction to the FA Cup defeat to Leicester at Goodison on 7 January, where he appealed to the hierarchy to speed up the recruitment process in short order.

The acquisition of Morgan Schneiderlin from Manchester United a few days later seemed to represent the beginning of a shopping spree that would transform the squad. In the final reckoning, the Frenchman was the second and last signing of the month after Everton got cold feet over the Ishak Belfodil deal and, presumably, Koeman and Walsh's other top targets proved to be out of reach for the time being.

Of course, the dissipation of the previous urgency was due almost entirely to Everton's run of form in the Premier League since the turn of the year. Three successive wins, three clean sheets, and the impression that Koeman seemed to have finally found a reliable combination of personnel and formation lessened the perceived need for reinforcements.

Undoubtedly, new talent was needed in certain positions. That view hadn't changed, even if there was no broad consensus over which positions needed attention first. Some Evertonians had pined for a new goalkeeper, or a top-class centre-half as a long-term replacement for Phil Jagielka. Others were focused on the more attacking areas of the team where, inconceivably, there was just one reliable goal-scoring centre-forward on the books.

The collapse of Arouna Kone's move to Crystal Palace ensured that he would stay with the club until the summer, but was unlikely to be called upon at all unless something went seriously awry on the injury front.

Koeman had named Enner Valencia as the nominated backup to Romelu Lukaku, even if no one was under any illusions that he could adequately replace the club's top scorer.

It meant that Everton would muddle through another half season hoping that Lukaku stayed fit, and the manager presumably felt comfortable enough with the fact that between Valencia, Kevin Mirallas, Ross Barkley, Dominic Calvert-Lewin (when fit, perhaps by the end of the month) and even young Ademola Lookman, there were enough forward options in the side to cover for the Belgian.

The previous few games (that cup debacle against Leicester aside) may have created a false sense of security in the squad and it wouldn't take too many poor results before the voices of dissent moaned about the missed opportunity in the winter window to strengthen the side for a tilt at the top 6 or higher.

There was a nagging feeling that Everton could do better than seventh this season and that an injection of quality in January could have made the difference. With the club's powder staying largely dry until next July, however, it prepared everyone for a summer or real progress on the transfer front, one where Koeman and Walsh could take the team to the next level in terms of quality and the ability to compete for the top 4. Koeman had said he always planned for a marathon, not a sprint, and his three-year plan still appeared to be on track.

2017: City Game One of Few Highlights

> “Lord knows it hasn’t been easy being an Evertonian for much of the last three decades, but the intervening period since the Blues’ glory days of mid-1980s had been punctuated by moments, special matches and turns of events that reminded you why this football club is so deeply embedded in your heart and your soul and why you keep coming back.
>
> **2017 City game one of few highlights**

Between the turn of 2017 and mid-March, Ronald Koeman and Everton did a successful job of putting their autumn downturn behind them, stringing together a run of just two Premier League defeats in 15 matches that included nine wins.

The Blues were frustrated in that time by the form of those clubs above them and, despite the upturn in form, they were unable to lift themselves above seventh place over the remainder of the season.

Nevertheless, it was a promising spell, the best sequence of results under Koeman and it featured the high water mark of his tenure at Goodison Park – a comprehensive victory over Manchester City that inflicted the heaviest defeat in Pep Guardiola's managerial career to date.

***

15 January 2017: Everton v Man City

It hasn't been easy being an Evertonian for much of the last three decades, but the intervening period since the Blues' glory days of mid-1980s has been punctuated by moments, special matches and turns of events that reminded you why this football club is so deeply embedded in your heart and your soul and why you keep coming back.

This was one of those matches, and much more; an almost perfect afternoon, which layered on memorable moment after memorable moment, building to a crescendo as Everton inflicted on Pep Guardiola the heaviest defeat of his much-lauded managerial career. It was the Spaniard's first match at Goodison Park and, as images of him sitting slumped and shell-shocked in the dugout amid a rocking, triumphant atmosphere illustrated, it's one that would live long in his memory, too.

Had nothing of note happened for the 56 minutes after Romelu Lukaku put the Blues into the lead, the game would likely have been a special enough occasion in its own right. It had started with pre-match poignancy as the Belgian carried Bradley Lowery, the little Sunderland fan diagnosed with Neuroblastoma who was mascot for the day, onto the field, followed by a minute's applause for Graham Taylor and Jim Greenwood, both of whom had recently passed away.

Those heart-warming moments coupled with a 1-0 win, delivered by a well-worked, expertly finished goal and underscoring the incremental progress being made under Ronald Koeman, would have represented a lovely afternoon for the home fans on their own. What unfolded was as unexpected as it was thrilling.

The days leading up the game seemed focused on Morgan Schneiderlin and the hope that, following last weekend's chastening cup exit at the hands of Leicester and the manner of it, the Frenchman might make an instant impact to mark the next phase of Koeman's rebuilding process.

The expectation and, perhaps, fear was that the new signing would replace Tom Davies if they deemed him fit enough to start. In the end, while being named on the bench and coming on after 65 minutes to replace Kevin Mirallas, Schneiderlin's appearance was a footnote in the narrative of this game, as Davies took top billing on a day full of potential headlines.

The 18-year-old midfielder kept his place in the side, alongside Gareth Barry in a line-up featuring just one change from the previous weekend - that of Mirallas for Enner Valencia - but by the final whistle Davies had come of age with a personal performance to savour.

It was his anticipation of Gael Clichy's forward pass which illustrated his versatility as a central midfielder. Davies' beautifully-weighted pass to Mirallas split three opposition players down the right channel and created the first goal. The Belgian's cutback to his compatriot near the penalty spot was perfect and Lukaku side-footed confidently past the wrong-footed Claudio Bravo to make it 1-0 in the 34th minute.

If the visitors felt aggrieved going into the break a goal down, it was down to Robles, who kept his place despite Maarten Stekelenburg's return to fitness, and to Davies who ensured the Blues took a clean sheet into half time by clearing off his own goal line in first-half stoppage time.

Any attempt by City to get back into the game early in the second half was superbly halted by Everton, who doubled the lead within two minutes of the restart and then took a stranglehold on the contest as every player in royal blue seemed to grow in stature.

Mirallas, whose personal rejuvenation under Koeman's stewardship over the previous month had perhaps flown under the radar, checked his run masterfully to stay onside, receive a pass from Lukaku and made no mistake with the opportunity, rifling a low shot into the far corner to make it 2-0.

That almost nothing of note in terms of chances happened for the next half an hour was testament to how Everton stifled City's much-touted attack, but then they increased their lead with a sublime third goal 11 minutes from time, one which ended up being one of the most memorable Everton goals of the Moshiri era.

Holgate dispossessed Sterling just outside his own area. Davies picked up the loose ball and took off down the right flank. Leaving Clichy and Touré for dead with an audacious "Ronaldo chop" on the touchline, his role in the attack seemed to have ended by a collision with Stones. The teenager sensed opportunity, however, picked himself up in time to collect another precise Barkley pass and picked his moment to clip the ball over the advancing Bravo. Time seemed to slow down as it bounced goal-wards by the near post, Lukaku arriving to make sure the spin on the ball didn't carry it wide before Davies wheeled away in almost incredulous celebration in front of the Gwladys Street end.

A brilliant first ever goal for a player already rapidly blossoming into an Everton star felt like the icing on the cake, but just when you felt it couldn't get any better, the day had one last moment of magic to offer.

Koeman sent new signing Ademola Lookman on in the 89th minute to savour the atmosphere and get a few minutes under his belt as an Everton player, but within minutes he would etch his name onto that fabulous Blues performance with a moment of anticipation and a confident finish that rounded out the win in style.

In a similar fashion to Everton under Roberto Martinez, City had spent much of the first half trying to play their way out from the back, sometimes in the most risk-defying manner, so it was ironic that Stones's attempt to just knock the ball into the stands in the final minute of stoppage time ricocheted off Coleman and bounced into Lookman's path. The 19-year-old took one touch to put the ball in front of him and then buried a shot between the 'keeper's legs before he, too, made for the Street end in elation, knee-sliding towards the corner flag before being mobbed by his teammates. Robles ran the length of the field to join the party as Lukaku bear-hugged the stunned teenager, the celebrations were the last act before Clattenburg blew the final whistle as demoralised City kicked off for the final time.

More so than the win over Arsenal a month previously, where the Blues seemed to turn the game on its head through force of will, Evertonians hoped this was a transformative moment in Koeman's first season. More performances like that and Koeman's goal of a top-six finish didn't seem far-fetched.

Final score: Everton 4-0 Manchester City

***

After the free scoring win against Manchester City, Everton ground out a 1-0 win away at Palace and a 1-1 draw with Stoke at the Britannia Stadium. It was then back to Goodison for what turned out to be a remarkable game of football.

***

4 February 2017: Everton v Bournemouth

With a mad game like this one, perhaps the best place to start is to simply acknowledge a brilliant performance from Romelu Lukaku, and a personal haul that left him as the top scorer in the Premier League at the time.

Surprisingly, after waiting almost three decades for a consistent striker capable of scoring 20-plus goals in a season, there had been calls for Everton to cash in on their greatest asset. Lukaku, one of the best in the modern game still graced Goodison Park. Yet some supporters preferred to get hung up on his attitude and work-rate, when his goals return spoke simply and loudly for itself.□□□□

On his day, Lukaku was unplayable and after having precious little bearing on the proceedings at Stoke in midweek, he was in that familiar "beast" mode against the Cherries — bullish, clinical, spectacular, unstoppable. From the quick-fire build-up play involving Morgan Schneiderlin and a one-two with James McCarthy, to the curling finish that bent majestically around Artur Boruc's despairing dive, his first goal of four very different strikes on the day was a thing of pure beauty.

Goals two and four showed his opportunism and lethality; his third and, arguably, most important was a deft volley following an equally impressive disguised pass to Seamus Coleman, whose pitching-wedge centre it was that he guided past the hapless Bournemouth goalkeeper to make it 4-2.

Just for good measure, he created the second goal for McCarthy almost out of nothing, with quick feet, strength and awareness along the by-line, underscoring his peerless tally of Premier League goals in which he has been directly involved.

On any other day, Ross Barkley would probably be the one hogging the headlines. He too had had a night to forget in the Potteries on Wednesday evening, but against Bournemouth, he delivered his most complete performance of the season. Diligent in his pressing, tenacious in his tackling, purposeful, creative and incisive on the ball, and both clinical and impudent with the coup de grâce that made it 6-3 in second-half stoppage time, the 23-year-old was excellent and a close runner-up behind Lukaku for man of the match.

Everton's attacking display was breath-taking, but there were nagging frustrations with the team's overall showing, particularly on the defensive side and the way the Blues dropped off for long periods and allowed the visitors to run the game. And by the 70-minute mark, memories of the 3-3 debacle at the Vitality Stadium in November 2015 were flooding back as the visitors rallied back to 3-2.□□□□□

Haunting thoughts of the home defeats to Leicester, Stoke and West Ham last season weren't too far behind. But whereas many would bet that an Everton team under Roberto Martinez would have given up the lead this afternoon, under Koeman they were a different proposition... even if some of the defending by Ramiro Funes Mori and Ashley Williams looked like it belonged in the previous regime.

Credit to Koeman, however, for making some tactical adjustments in the final half hour to help steer the course of the game back in his team's direction. His response to the visitors drawing to within one goal was immediate. Kevin Mirallas came on in place of Lookman, whose precociously dazzling footwork and daring had been a delight at 3-0 but his comparative lack of experience on the defensive side made him surplus to requirements now that the game needed to be shut down.

But it wasn't until Mason Holgate replaced Barry with 10 minutes to go and the Blues transitioned into a back five, with the tactical shift that was missing in the last two seasons under Martinez, that the tide turned back in their favour.

Everton broke the contest open again with some wonderful attacking football. And once again, the end of the move was all down to Lukaku as he completed a brilliant hat-trick in the 83rd minute, steering home a left-foot volley before adding a fourth a minute later, while surging between two defenders and picking his spot past Boruc to bury the ball into the bottom left-hand corner.

Bournemouth's spirit was unshaken, though, and they would strike back again the final minute of the regulation 90 when Arter bundled the ball over the line to make it 5-3.

The Cherries were still going for more goals in the fourth minute of stoppage time, but in doing so, Everton picked them off one final time. Funes Mori sent Barkley away with a raking forward pass that drew Boruc well out of his box. The Blues' No.8 knocked it past him nonchalantly and, with the empty net gaping in front of him, he had time to spread his arms wide in celebration (perhaps with retribution for the winner that was taken away from him by Junior Stanislas at Dean Court 16 months ago on his mind) before slotting it home.

Koeman acknowledged after the game that he was concerned how much his team sat back at 3-0 up and invited Bournemouth back into the game. But he couldn't hide his admiration at the quality of the goals or his satisfaction at the effect his tactical tinkering had had the desired effect on the result.

That was further evidence of the progress being made under the Dutchman's stewardship. A year before, few would have bet against Bournemouth completing their comeback and sending Blues fans away muttering about defensive collapses and the team's frail mentality after throwing away a seemingly unassailable lead.

After the draw at Stoke, the three points were paramount, but the supporters gleaned plenty of confidence from the impressive way in which Everton put their foot back on the accelerator and powered their way back to a three-goal lead. Seven games unbeaten and a 100% start to 2017 at home in the Premier League showed that the Toffees under Koeman were gathering momentum at just the right time to capitalise on any slip-ups by the teams above them.

Final score: Everton 6-3 Bournemouth

***

Two days after the Blues' high-scoring win over Bournemouth, Gareth Barry lauded Romelu Lukaku's work ethic and commitment to self-improvement, but said the Belgian marksman shouldn't be in a hurry to leave Goodison Park in search of elite European football.

Lukaku had made no secret of his desire to play Champions League football, or his belief that he was now ready for it, but Barry said that Everton were once again on course to make that dream a reality with his goals capable of propelling them there.

"I don't think I have met a player who is so hungry to score goals," the veteran midfielder told evertonfc.com. "He is desperate to keep on improving. He is a great finisher already, but he won't stop there — he is working hard all the time.

"There is still room for improvement and he has got that personality and character to want to improve, so I'm sure he won't stop now. He will be desperate to keep on breaking records.

"There have been a few stories over the last couple of years about Rom wanting to play football at the highest level, and that is the Champions League.

"I'm sure he would have had conversations with the powers at the Club, and they are desperate to get there. With the signings we are making and the manager we have got at the minute, that is the road we want to go.

"Sometimes you have to be patient, but I'm confident that, if Rom sticks around, Everton can get there."

There were signs Barry's message was getting through. Just three days later, Lukaku's agent, Mino Raiola, restated his belief that his client would sign a new contract at Everton, saying talks were ongoing. Despite erroneous suggestions made in *The Express* that Lukaku had already signed a new £100,000-a-week deal with the Toffees in December, the striker had yet to reach a final agreement that would likely make him the highest-paid player in the club's history.

Raiola remained confident, however, that his client would agree new terms, although he didn't put a timescale on it.

"There are no problems right now between the player and the club, Raiola told TalkSport. "Talks are ongoing. He will sign."

***

1 April 2017: Liverpool v Everton

Prior to the 2016/17 edition of the Anfield derby, confident speeches were emanating from the Everton hierarchy.

On the playing side, Steve Walsh talked of his role at Everton and how he and Ronald Koeman were working together to assemble a team built to take the club back to the top

He was one of several club figures interviewed by Adam Leventhal during Sky Sports News' behind-the-scenes coverage from USM Finch Farm in the build-up to the game, and he explained his ethos and working relationship with Koeman.

"You're always planning and looking at good players, trying to make your team better. The fundamental question you have always got to ask is: does that player fit into what we are trying to do? If that's the case, then we try to take that forward.

"It's not just position specific - it's about trying to find out about as much as you can about that player such as his personality, has he got drive, does he want to do what we want as a football club?

"You can only do that with time. But we are certainly better than the team that started in the summer, and I think the fact we have bought people like Schneiderlin shows we have got better and will get better.

"The first thing I did [when I arrived] was I sat down with Ronald and looked at how he wanted to play. There's no point me bringing in players that don't fit with how he plays. We talked about systems and structures, and built on that.

"The most important thing is the recruitment of players for the first team, but I'm also conscious of the fact we have a good academy and good young players coming through.

"Doing that is the hallmark of a successful club. We will build on what we've got and take the club forward.

"We want to be successful. We want to get into the top four and you only do that over a period of time. Given time, we are going to get there. There's no doubt about that."

***

Would all these fine words and ambitions translate into a long-awaited win for the Blues at Anfield? Unfortunately, not that year. Another Anfield derby, passaging another season without a victory on Liverpool's patch and another painful post-mortem for Everton following a third successive defeat in the all-Mersey tussle. Blues fans had become numb to it, although the pain would never truly go.

On that occasion, the form book favoured Everton, but ultimately the league table was a better indicator of the likely destination of the points, and on an occasion that demands that star players rise above the fray, Liverpool were simply better. The Blues were badly wanting in almost all departments.

The injuries that disrupted Ronald Koeman's back line were significant, particularly that of Seamus Coleman, but it was hard to see Everton winning this game even had the Irishman been fit. Not for the first time away from home against a top-four side, the manager got his tactics wrong, and this time was let down by his main enforcer, Idrissa Gueye.

Once more the Dutchman opted for a five-man defence and, just as it was at Chelsea and Tottenham, this exposed the space in front of the defence. Pennington's inexperience, Gueye's dereliction of duty and Koeman's mystifying delay in addressing a demonstrably flawed formation were all important factors in the 3-1 defeat.

With Tom Davies, 18, in midfield and Dominic Calvert-Lewin, 20 up front, it was a very youthful Blues line-up, but it was the failure of Koeman's "big-game" players on the one hand, and the success of Jürgen Klopp's on the other, that ultimately proved to be the significant difference.

And it only took eight minutes. While Everton, and Ross Barkley in particular, succumbed unnecessarily to the increasingly out-dated imperative to indulge in the blood-and-thunder fare of the local grudge match — the Blues' No. 8 was fortunate to avoid a yellow card just six minutes in, and then a red card later in the first half — Liverpool (Emre Can aside) largely eschewed the frenetic and played the way they often do these days under Klopp: with speed and energy in attack.

Sadio Mané evaded a limp attempt at a tackle by Gueye in the centre of the park, accelerated past Davies's despairing lunge and then sucked three Everton defenders to one side of the box before screwing a shot across Joel Robles and into the far corner of the goal. The defending was atrocious really, and it threw a harsh spotlight on both Pennington and the decision to select him for such a difficult match.

Everton levelled in the 28th minute, however, with their first chance of the game. Leighton Baines's out-swinging corner was flicked on by Jagielka at the near post. Dejan Lovren couldn't react quickly enough to hack it clear and the ball fell invitingly to Pennington, who couldn't miss in front of goal.

The return to parity lasted just three minutes, though, and once again it was a failure to show Coutinho inside that would prove costly. The Reds' midfielder picked the ball up in space in central midfield and with no one closing him down until Gueye threw a lazy leg at him as he danced past, he advanced into the box, tied Pennington up in knots before curling an unstoppable shot inside Robles's left-hand post.

Liverpool's match-winners were showing up; Everton's were hugely disappointing and Barkley benefited from leniency from referee Anthony Taylor when he went over the ball and caught Lovren mid-shin, seeing his name go into the book rather than receiving his marching orders. Truth be told, apart from his failure to book James Milner for deliberate handball in the second half, the much-maligned official managed the game very well.

The expected changes from Koeman at half time never came. The manager had not been shy about replacing players or switching formations when clear they weren't working, but there was no activity from the bench until the 67th minute and by then it was too late.

There wasn't enough to suggest that keeping the five-man back line or persisting with the willing but limited Calvert-Lewin up front was going to be enough to turn the tide.

Klopp, meanwhile, made a change when Mané pulled up injured; but his replacement effectively sealed the game. Divock Origi came on in the 57th minute when Mané couldn't continue and within three minutes, he had scored.

Pennington played Holgate into trouble against the touchline. His attempted pass was picked off by Coutinho, who breezed past the lead-footed Gueye and slipped a pass to Origi behind the back-pedalling Williams. The Belgian took aim from 20 yards and smashed a shot almost down the centre of the goal.

The margin and manner of the Reds' victory were emphatic enough to render thoughts of a late push by the Blues for the top four as fanciful. Even allowing for the injuries that prompted Koeman into his ill-advised line-up, there was an unsettling gulf in ability between the two teams that sharpened the focus once more on the Dutchman's task when the summer transfer window opened.

It would also have reignited the debate over Lukaku who was, again, virtually anonymous against a top-four team and failed to register a shot in the entire 90 minutes for the third time this season, after blanks against Chelsea and Manchester United.

There was much to be said for the argument that a striker of his style can't do much without support, and without his teammates giving him the ball. Certainly, service to him was poor, just as it was in the Goodison derby in December. On the rare occasions he saw the ball, however, his touch was poor and his distribution was just as bad. Just when Everton needed him to be on razor sharp, inventive and unplayable. He was anything but.

At the end, it was a defeat that in many pundits eyes would cement Everton as only a top-seven side that season.

Final score: Liverpool 3-1 Everton

***

21 May 2017: Arsenal v Everton

The petering out of Everton's season concluded at the Emirates as 10-man Arsenal still ran out 3-1 victors against a Blues team seemingly with its mind on the summer.

The home side went ahead when Alexis Sanchez drove to the by-line, Danny Welbeck failed to connect in the centre and Hector Bellerin had the simple chance of converting from a central position to make it 1-0.

The visitors received a clear boost when Laurent Koscielny flew into Enner Valencia, scything the Ecuadorian down in full flight and referee Michael Oliver brandished a straight red card. Yet it failed to have the desired effect on Everton's performance, even after Ross Barkley replaced Tom Davies in the 26th minute, as Koeman tried to add some more guile in the final third.

Arsenal doubled their lead a minute later as Sanchez took advantage of a criminally static Blues defence, firing home Welbeck's pass across goal, after his initial shot had cannoned off Phil Jagielka.

Everton rallied briefly late in the first half and might have scored six minutes before the break, but Valencia and Barkley scuffed shots in front of goal, and Lukaku's effort was blocked near the line.

Idrissa Gueye then brought a flying save from Petr Cech with a powerful shot from distance and the Gunners' keeper had to push a header from Lukaku over his crossbar.

The second half failed to draw the requisite desire or pressure from Everton to test Arsenal, ever after Rob Holding handled in his own area and Lukaku planted a well-struck penalty to Cech's right, notching his 25th league goal of the season.

Valencia had what looked to have been the equaliser chalked off, when his impressive header from Mason Holgate's great cross was ruled-out for a push on Per Mertesaker. But it was Arsenal who got their third in stoppage time, when Ramsey took advantage of a yard of space ahead of him on the edge of the Everton box and curled an unstoppable shot around Robles to make it 3-1.

With seventh place long since guaranteed, the result had no bearing on Everton's season, but the disappointing manner in which the season meandered to a close had Evertonians eagerly awaiting the summer transfer window, when improvements to the squad were evidently needed.

Final score: Arsenal 3-1 Everton

2017: EVERTON LOSE LUKAKU, SIGN 4 NUMBER 10-S BUT NO STRIKER

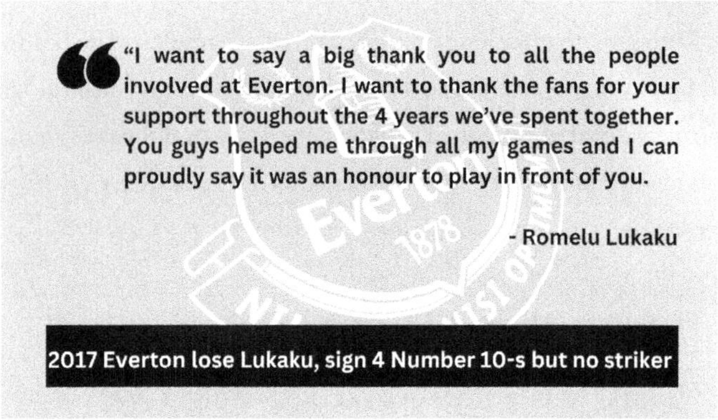

By the summer of 2017, Steve Walsh had been director of football for a year, and in that time was developing his relationship with Ronald Koeman.

The pair had been working to identify which areas of the squad needed improving after a 2016/17 season that showed progress on successive 11th-place finishes under previous boss Roberto Martinez, but which ultimately underscored a deficit in quality and depth in certain positions.

With the close season only a fortnight old and the transfer window itself not officially open for another four weeks, Walsh insisted he, his team, and Koeman had been working hard to identify the personnel they would try to sign.

"Planning never stops," Walsh said in the Liverpool Echo.

"From the day the window closes until the day it opens again, you are always looking at your possibilities. We are no different.

"We've done a lot of work behind the scenes to get the correct information about the players. I have sat down with Ronald and gone through those. Obviously, we discuss it all the time and we want to improve things, build on what we have got. That's the key message.

"My department is very well run, very organised and we make sure we get as much information about the player that we possibly can. If we like the player, I've got to try to convince Ronald that he's the player for us. It could well be that Ronald has seen the player as well, so it's a collective decision at the end of the day."

***

What followed was a series of deals that would shatter Everton's transfer record for both incoming and outgoing players. It was a clear statement of intent and ambition from Farhad Moshiri as he sought to take that next, potentially decisive step towards realising a three-year project to reach the Champions League, and it set a tone of continuing largesse in the market for the next three years.

The ramifications for the club's financial future and its ability to simply remain in the Premier League would be felt a lot further down the line, but the feeling at the time was that Everton were moving in the right direction, and that Moshiri's ambition and willingness to maintain loose purse strings would support a sustained push for qualification into Europe's elite club competition.

***

With Enner Valencia leaving at the end of his temporary loan spell, Everton were soon in the race to sign Sandro Ramirez - a striker from Malaga who had scored a remarkable 14 goals in La Liga in 2016/17 - but it would take a while to land the Spaniard in a £5.2 million deal.

It looked as though Sandro would stay with Malaga, hoping to join Atletico Madrid in January when the latter club had its transfer embargo lifted, but he eventually joined the Blues when the move was finally completed on 3 July.

***

Just four days later, Everton completed the capture of Jordan Pickford in a record deal for an English goalkeeper that would eventually be worth up to £30 million.

Having undergone a successful medical, Pickford signed a five-year contract that would make him not only Everton's most expensive player at the time, but also the most expensive British player in his position.

The Blues agreed a deal with Sunderland that saw them pay around £25 million up front for the 23-year-old, who would officially become an Everton player on 1st July when the club could register him with the Premier League.

"It's great to sign for the club," the Washington-born player said. "Last season was my first in the Premier League, so to get this opportunity with Everton now, to be able to go forward with my career and show everyone what I can do with Everton is unbelievable.

"It's a great club, a massive club and I think it's a great opportunity and the right time for me to come to Everton and show what I can do.

"This is an exciting time for the club and for me, too, with the ambition being shown. I just want to be the best I can be to help."

For manager Ronald Koeman, Pickford's signing came after a season's worth of assessment of both Joel Robles and Maarten Stekelenburg for the mantle of first-choice goalkeeper at Everton.

"I'm really pleased we've made what I'm sure will be a significant signing for Everton Football Club," Koeman said after announcing Pickford's signing. "Jordan is a very talented young professional who also has a real hunger for success, and that's important for us as we now look to make further progress in the seasons ahead.

"We've seen the quality he has through his performances in the Premier League last season and, given his young age, we're sure he will get even better."

***

Later that same day, Dutch midfielder Davy Klaassen became an Everton player after he too agreed personal terms with the club, and a £24 million move from Ajax. The 24-year-old captain of the Amsterdam side had had a stellar season with Ajax, and the Blues had led the chase for his signature before he was unveiled as Everton's second signing of the day.

"I spoke a few weeks ago with Ronald Koeman about Everton," Klaassen told evertontv. "I wanted to come here and check if this was the right club for me and since I came here, I feel so happy. It's a great club.

"The moment that I spoke with the manager directly, I got a good feeling. He's an honest guy. We talked about the club, about the way he wants to play and that gave me a positive feeling.

"It's difficult to leave Ajax, but I think this is a good step for me now and I'm really looking forward to my time here."

***

On the final day of June, Everton also completed the signing of exciting prospect Henry Onyekuru from KAS Eupen in Belgium for an officially undisclosed fee, reported to be around £6.8 million.

The Blues beat off competition from Arsenal, Paris St Germain and West Ham to land the 20-year-old who signed a five-year contract to become the club's third signing of the summer, and he was followed by another major acquisition in the form of defender Michael Keane from Burnley for £30 million.

The 24-year-old became the fifth player to be signed by the Blues during a busy transfer window, making Everton the highest spending club in the Premier League for 2017 to that point, with more than £92 million splashed out in the period since January.

Keane had been one of Ronald Koeman's and Steve Walsh's top targets, with the Everton manager breaking a self-imposed protocol by making his interest in the player public earlier in 2017 after it became common knowledge that he would leave Turf Moor over the summer.

Keane signed a five-year contract and added important competition to the back line for the upcoming season, as Everton prepared to mount a bid to make it into the Europa League group stages, as well as challenge for the Premier League's top four.

"I'm absolutely delighted to be at Everton," Keane said, "a fantastic football club with passionate fans and a great tradition, and I can't wait to come into training tomorrow to meet all the lads.

"First and foremost, the manager was a big factor in me coming to the club. He played in my position when he was a world-class player for a great Barcelona side and a great Dutch side and the style of football he likes to play will suit me, I believe.

"He's convinced me he can still improve me in certain areas of my game. I'm only 24, which, for a centre-half in the Premier League, is relatively young. I've still got a long way to go and I know this and hopefully under his guidance I'll keep improving."

***

Unfortunately, the widely expected departure of the club's star-striker finally came on 10 July, when Romelu Lukaku's club record-breaking £75 million move to Manchester United was announced, with the Belgian signing a five-year contract at Old Trafford.

Interviewed by ESPN about his switch from Goodison Park to Old Trafford and, after expressing his delight at joining the "world's biggest club" with "the best fans", Lukaku sent a farewell message to the club he had joined four years earlier, initially on loan and then permanently from Chelsea for £28 million:

"To the staff at the stadium and training ground, thank you for making me feel home from the first day I walked in. To my teammates, it was great to play with you guys. To the technical staff, thank you for helping me become a better player. Working with you guys has been a pleasure and I'll take your advice throughout the rest of my career. Thank you Everton Football Club."

***

Moving in the opposite direction was Wayne Rooney. The 31-year-old had grown up in Croxteth as a Toffee-mad kid on the Blues' books, but left the club as a teenager for Manchester United in 2004 after bursting onto the Premier League and international scene. He spent 13 years amassing a trophy cabinet full of honours and was hoping to help end Everton's trophy drought and make a concerted push for the top four under Ronald Koeman.

He put pen to paper on a two-year contract after months of speculation about his future and took the mantle of the No.10 jersey vacated by Romelu Lukaku.

"Throughout the summer I've been working out where I was going to go," Rooney said on evertonfc.com. "I spoke to my agent and said: 'Listen, you need to speak to Everton, see if it can happen.'

"He said it could, so I told him to speak to the club and get it done as quickly as possible. It's happened. I'm delighted and I'm ready to go.

"[Wearing the shirt] feels as special as it did 13 years ago and I'm just looking forward now to getting out on the pitch with it on. "[Goodison Park] has always been a special place, even when I've been on the opposing team," he continued. "You always get that feeling when you walk out of the tunnel, so to actually do it again in an Everton shirt will be a special moment for me. "I've kept it quiet for the last 13 years, but I've actually been wearing Everton pyjamas at home with my kids. I had to keep that a bit quiet!"

***

Meanwhile, his new manager was excited to have added genuine experience and savvy to the team to blend with the youthful additions he and Steve Walsh have been busy making this summer.

Rooney was the elder statesman, when compared with Jordan Pickford (23), Davy Klaassen (24), Sandro Ramirez (21), Henry Onyekuru (20) and Michael Keane (24), but he had played on the biggest stages for club and country and still kept a burning desire to push his former club back towards the top of the English game.

"Wayne has shown me that ambition that we need and that winning mentality," Koeman said. "He knows how to win titles and I'm really happy he's decided to come home.

"He loves Everton, and he was desperate to come back. He is still only 31 and I don't have any doubts about his qualities. It's fantastic he's here.

"It's all about his fitness and his desire, but he has shown me that ambition that we need. He knows how to win titles, as I said. He wants to play at the highest level that is possible for him. We have spoken several times about Everton and what we are striving to achieve."

***

Another player who could potentially play in the Number 10 role was Nikola Vlašić who completed a move from Hajduk Split to Everton at the end of August for an initial fee of around £8 million. An attacking midfielder who could operate across the forward line, Vlašić had made 87 league appearances and scored 11 goals for Hajduk since breaking into their team in 2014.

"Nikola is one of those players who can play a big part in Everton's future and in what we want to achieve as a club," Ronald Koeman said of the new acquisition.

Vlašić, meanwhile, expressed his delight at finalising the move. "When there is a manager like Ronald Koeman who wants you, there is no need to talk about it much," he said. "I wanted to come here because of the manager, because of the big players, because of the reputation of the club. It is the opportunity of a lifetime. I played a lot of games for Hajduk Split but the Premier League is something else. I am very excited about the opportunity to play for this big club. The Premier League is the best league in the world and this is one of the top clubs in England. It is such a big honour for me to be here."

***

Playing out against the backdrop of what was a busy summer of incomings and outgoings – that had seen injury-prone midfielder Darren Gibson, unfancied Tom Cleverley, Costa Rican fullback Bryan Oviedo, erratic winger Aiden McGeady, and the popular but mercurial Spaniard winger Gerard Deulofeu all leave the club along with Lukaku – was the saga of Everton's attempts to sign Gylfi Sigurdsson.

The Blues had pursued Sigurdsson for a year and seen successive offers starting at a reported £25 million rebuffed by Swansea City, including a £40 million bid in early August 2017. The Swans looked as though they were going to dig their heels in over their £50 million valuation of their star player, but they eventually negotiated a compromise package of around £40 million with a further £2.5 million dependent on appearances. It took until 15 August for the Gylfi Sigurdsson deal to finally conclude.

That deal smashed Everton's previous club record fee of £30 million paid for Jordan Pickford in June, but now, backed by Farhad Moshiri, Ronald Koeman and Steve Walsh had their top targets in place.

The open question was, after signing a goalkeeper, another centre-half, four No.10s and two untried young strikers, how would the team fill the 25-goals-a-year gap that Lukaku's departure had created?

2017: Poor Start After Massive Investment in Squad

Finishing seventh in the league in 2016/17 meant that Everton had only qualified for Qualifying Round 3 of the Europa League, and that entailed a shortened pre-season and an unusually early start to competitive action in late July.

Their opponents were MFK Ružomberok and it was hoped that the two-legged tie against the Slovakians would provide Ronald Koeman's side with the ideal ramp into the new season.

It was then that Everton's struggles under Koeman began, with the Dutch manager seemingly incapable of arresting a slide that would cost him his job in late October.

***

27 July 2017: Everton v MFK Ružomberok

Ronald Koeman fielded £60 million of new talent in his first starting line-up of the 2017/18 season, but it was the man snapped up for just £5.2 million from La Liga and a veteran fullback who made the difference in the first leg against Ružomberok.

Wayne Rooney started as expected, and there were debuts for Michael Keane, Cuco Martina and Davy Klaassen, while Jordan Pickford and Sandro Ramirez were on the bench.

Maarten Stekelenburg was in goal given Pickford's lack of pre-season preparation, while Leighton Baines captained the side.

With large sections of the Main Stand closed for renovations aimed at improving facilities for disabled supporters and Ružomberok bringing just a smattering of travelling fans, the atmosphere inside Goodison had a decidedly pre-season feel as the Blues' season got off to a pedestrian start.

Everton had their chances in the first half, but Idrissa Gueye – arguably the standout player of the first 45 minutes – as well as Rooney and Klaassen all failed to find the target, at least until the Senegalese midfielder stung the palms of Macik from distance and Dominic Calvert-Lewin saw the last effort of the half comfortably saved.

Emboldened by their hosts' torpor, the visitors controlled the early exchanges in the second half and Daniel had a half-chance, but hooked it wide before Stekelenburg had to intervene with an excellent save when he finger-tipped Maslo's header onto the crossbar.

In between, Klaassen missed with a header from Martina's cross, Mirallas's accurate drive was pushed behind by Masik, and Keane's header from a free kick deflected behind as Sandro stripped off in readiness to come on in place of Calvert-Lewin.

The Spaniard's introduction provided an immediate spark of urgency and when Everton won a corner in the 65th minute that was cleared to the feet of Baines, the captain rattled a shot goalwards that took a decisive deflection off Daniel and past Macik to hand the Toffees the lead.

With time winding down, Koeman introduced Ademola Lookman for Mirallas, but it was Ružomberok's own substitution that almost paid dividends when the ball fell to the feet of Lacny 10 yards from goal. Thankfully, he could only shoot tamely at Stekelenburg, and Goodison breathed a sigh of relief.

Final score: Everton 1-0 MFK Ružomberok

***

The return leg was played in Slovakia on 3 August in front of 4,752 fans, with Dominic Calvert-Lewin scoring the only goal, and ensuring a 2-0 aggregate win for the Toffeemen.

***

12 August 2017: Everton v Stoke

If the wisdom of Everton re-signing Wayne Rooney from Manchester United wasn't universally accepted, the 31-year-old's display over two legs in the Europa League tie with Ružomberok seemed to confirm the fears of the doubters that it wasn't so much the Prodigal Son who had returned, but the Prodigal Pensioner.

Rooney wasn't alone in performing beneath himself on the European stage — the whole team had been alarmingly disappointing against the Slovakian side — but if his contribution to the 2017/18 Premier League opener was any sign of the season to come, then Messers Koeman and Walsh (and Kenwright, too, no doubt) would be vindicated in the decision to bring the Boyhood Blue home.

Rooney grabbed the headlines by scoring the winner against Stoke, but it was the manner in which he dictated much of this contest, particularly in the second half, that was so pleasing to the Goodison faithful. Playing metronome to a side that had visibly settled once the manager had dispensed with a lopsided and, frankly, questionable formation, the Croxteth-born forward ran the show for Everton, spraying balls around at one end and chipping in with vital defensive interventions from set-pieces at the other.

His celebration following the only goal in first-half stoppage time was also a wondrous sight; the joy of scoring for Everton undiminished by 13 years away in Manchester with United.

That strike, a composed header back across Jack Butland from Dominic Calvert-Lewin's sumptuous cross at the end of the best move of the match, was also the highlight of an otherwise abysmal first period.

With Koeman determined to find a way of playing a three-man central defensive unit, Calvert-Lewin played in an advanced wingback role, one that saw Idrissa Gueye occasionally dropping off to the touchline to cover DCL's advances forward.

It was a role to which the young striker looked wholly unsuited; thankfully, he was relieved of it for the second half when Cuco Martina came on in place of Ashley Williams and Koeman reverted to a more conventional back four.

Overall, the Blues' tactics were puzzling, with a succession of floated balls to the flank aimed at Calvert-Lewin more often that not missing their target. Even the set-pieces were odd; Rooney and Sandro insisted on taking corners short, depriving the team of strikers of chances to pick up the pieces in the box.□

Stoke, looking every inch a Potters side with plenty of height sprinkled with flashes of limited end product from the likes of Bojan Krkic and Xherdan Shaqiri, offered even less threat in the first half.

The visitors had a brief flurry immediately after the restart but Everton soon established control of proceedings and Calvert-Lewin, now playing up top in a three, had two chances to double the lead but saw one shot blocked and another saved at the near post by Jack Butland.

Morgan Schneiderlin may have had another off day to go with those iffy evenings in the Europa League, and Davy Klaassen struggled to make an impact (his role in the goal where he drew defenders away to leave Rooney unmarked might get overlooked) but Gueye was excellent. And Tom Davies, the unfortunate one to drop to the bench, showed how difficult Koeman's midfield team selection will be when he came on for Klaassen after an hour to put in another accomplished display.

Despite their hugely improved second-half showing, Everton endured a somewhat nervy last 10 minutes as Hughes threw on Peter Crouch and Stoke lumped more and more balls into the home area, hoping for something to fall their way.

It was from the more cultured foot of Shaqiri that they almost grabbed a point at the death. The Swiss picked the ball up in central midfield following a corner, advanced into space and unloaded from 25 yards with a shot that was searching out the far corner. Pickford, whose only real involvement up to that point had been to display some pleasing command of his area with decisive decision-making and action, was equal to it; diving to his left to turn the ball behind his post. It was a match-winning save from the young England U21 'keeper and the first return on the massive transfer fee that had brought him to Merseyside from Sunderland.

Overall, while there was plenty to ponder from that first half, the Blues grew stronger after the break and Rooney, spurred on by his goal, employed all his experience and savvy to help control the contest after half-time.

Koeman acknowledged afterwards that the wingback idea hadn't worked as he had expected, while also admitting that his team needed to improve significantly if it was to achieve its aims this season.

He and Steve Walsh would also have to keep busy until the deadline, in finding recruits to fill the obvious gaps in the team, such as another seasoned striker who could hold the ball up and provide a physical presence up front.

Final score: Everton 1-0 Stoke

***

9 September 2017: Everton v Tottenham Hotspur

It had only been a few weeks since that Everton's expensive transfer business had been heralded by a usually ambivalent national media, and the Blues were being talked about as genuine top-four contenders.

The return of Wayne Rooney, admittedly past the peak of his powers but a world-famous name, gave the show of ambition an added layer of legitimacy and Evertonians waited for the two or three additions to the squad that would top off an excellent transfer window.

Those signings never came, of course. Romelu Lukaku, the source of football's most important currency — goals — departed for huge money but wasn't replaced. There was also no cover for 32-year-old Leighton Baines and, if there was any desire by the management to add pace and/or genuine creativity to the side, there was precious little evidence of it.

The product of this one-dimensional approach to recruitment over the summer of 2017 had resulted in Everton's uninspiring start to the new season, one which had quickly lurched from concerning into the realm of deeply demoralising.

Worse still, the team looked like a collection of individuals bereft of a plan, an identity, or any consistent attacking threat. So when the wheels came off defensively, Evertonians witnessed the humbling of their team against Tottenham Hotspur.

Seldom, if ever in the Premier League era, had a Spurs side enjoyed such an easy ride at Goodison Park, a venue that had become a veritable fortress for Koeman's side since the turn of the year. By the same token, it was hard to recall the Blues looking so lacking in desire or spirit in a home game against highly-fancied opposition other than the 3-0 reverse against Chelsea, hitherto their only defeat at Goodison in 2017.

For the first time in the league that season Koeman had abandoned the five-man defensive line he had been using, perhaps to keep one of his experienced centre halves in reserve with an eye on the upcoming trip to Italy in the Europa League, or perhaps because he had identified something in Tottenham's makeup that was better tackled with a flat back four.

Cuco Martina made his first Premier League start in an Everton jersey — many hoped, in vain, that it would be his last — while Davy Klaassen and Morgan Schneiderlin returned to the side, and Sandro Ramirez played alongside Rooney in attack.

The opening exchanges didn't offer much hint of the debacle to follow but the warning signs for the Blues would come before the match was a quarter of an hour old and the opening goal for the visitors wasn't too far behind.

A corner eventually ended up on the Tottenham right where Harry Kane tried to swing in a cross, but he ended up drifting his centre over Jordan Pickford and under the crossbar to make it 1-0 with 27 minutes gone.

Sandro saw one snapshot at the other end cannon off Toby Alderweireld's head from close range after good work by Rooney, but it was a rare opening for Everton that was swiftly followed by a second goal for the visitors.

Sucked into his six-yard box, Martina waved a leg at a cross that was flighted over everybody in the middle, which left Davies in space to force Pickford into a save but he could only push it out to Chrsitian Eriksen who converted the rebound from close range.

Dele Alli should have buried Everton in stoppage time but, completely unmarked in the middle, he mis-kicked yet another delivery from wide on Tottenham's left before Martina gifted the ball to Kane and the striker dragged his shot wide.

Kane made no mistake less than a minute into the second half, though. Laying the ball out to Davies with Martina badly exposed again, he continued his run untracked by Schneiderlin and calmly side-footed a first-time finish past Pickford to make it 3-0.

That goal ripped up whatever plan Koeman had had for the second period. Having thrown on Tom Davies and Calvert-Lewin for Klaassen and Sandro, and for the next 20 minutes, Spurs created all the chances.

Everton sputtered into a bit of life too late in the proceedings as the game ticked through the last 10 minutes after Nikola Vlasic had come on for his debut following his deadline-day move from Hajduk Split. It was a cameo that featured some neat touches and confident running that ensured he would walk off at the end as one of a tiny number of Blues players to emerge with any credit from a pitiful performance.

In the final reckoning, though, Everton had just one shot on target and failed to trouble Lloris with a shot all game... as damning a statistic as you can imagine for a team supposedly challenging today's opponents for a place in the top four.

There were supposedly mitigating circumstances: this was a team featuring several new faces, some of whom were new to the Premier

League and Everton had had a tough start to the new league season but they generally looked poor, toothless and utterly directionless.

Koeman, a man steeped in the Total Football of Holland's finest era and a Barcelona legend in his own right, was presiding over some awful yard-dog football that was marrying the worst elements of his three predecessors' reigns: the striker-less days of Walter Smith, the defensive and cowing disposition of some of David Moyes's teams, and the spineless and defensively shambolic performances in the worst days under Roberto Martinez.

Tactically, he looked to be a novice despite his lengthy CV. His team had no width, no pace, no creativity and too many like-minded players stuffed into the same line-up, not least in midfield where Sigurdsson, Klaassen, Gueye and Schneiderlin struggled to gel. The team looked lost, and it was difficult to see progress, despite an outlay of £140 million on new players.

There was plenty of time, of course but the feeling was that the manager needed to step up and figure out a way to get his side playing basic football again – or else it promised to be a very long, frustrating season.

Final score: Everton 0-3 Spurs

***

After the match, Koeman cautioned against raised expectations following the Blues' big-spending summer.

"In the second half you could see we were far away from Tottenham, but in the first half an hour we were much closer," Koeman said, following his team's second successive defeat. "I've said before, I think, along with Manchester City, Spurs are the best footballing side (in the Premier League). The difference is they have had the same group of players for a long time now.

"If you think we are trying to join them in that [top six] pack, it will be really difficult."

"I know how it works in football. If you sign some players, people stop being realistic," he said.

"Everybody is talking about Everton and the top six. But if you know the qualities, and the individual qualities of the players in the top six, it is a challenge. It is our ambition, but we need to realise it is difficult.

"We will learn from the mistakes today and we have enough games coming up to have a good reaction."

***

Throughout October, speculation concerning Koeman's position was reaching fever pitch. At the start of the month, Farhad Moshiri had once again used *Sky Sports* and *TalkSport* presenter Jim White as the conduit for a message to supporters where he gave his backing to Koeman, as the manager struggled to turn around the team's poor start to the season.

The Blues had lost 1-0 to Burnley at Goodison Park on 1 October, and left the field to boos from the home fans for the second time in three days following the 2-2 draw with Apollon Limassol in the Europa League.

Just two Premier League wins had left Everton in 16th place in the table, increasing the pressure on the manager following a significant outlay on players over the summer.

Jim White, who claimed to have a close relationship with Moshiri and who regularly passed on updates from the billionaire investor, tweeted a quote purported to be from the Monaco-based billionaire.

In the message, Moshiri said that the Burnley match was the only match so far where a defeat was unexpected, arguing that Everton had faced four of the title contenders and were tired from having to play Europa League qualifying games.

Moshiri's statement, said:

> "We're in a bad moment. But we have played the four title contenders, three away. Today was the only unexpected loss. The four Pre qualifying UEFA games and two group games on Thursdays haven't helped. There is mental and physical fatigue and seven injuries. These are early days and Koeman has my total support. We have great fans and they deserve better. We know the honest and objective expectations of our supporters and will not let them down."

On Friday, 13 October, Moshiri reportedly dropped in at USM Finch Farm.

MailOnline reported that the Iranian-born businessman was joined by chairman Bill Kenwright at the club's training facility primarily to discuss plans for the new stadium at Bramley-Moore Dock. He also spoke with Koeman, a move that was seen by some as further backing for the Dutchman, who was under pressure following a sequence of poor results that meant Everton went into an important fixture against Arsenal sitting in 16th place in the Premier League.

***

22 October 2017: Everton v Arsenal

The Arsenal match turned out to be an unmitigated disaster and it signalled the end for Ronald Koeman less than 18 months into his much-vaunted tenure. It beggared belief, really, when thinking of the vast sums Everton had spent on new players over the summer and the optimism that had been coursing through Evertonian veins just three months previously. Yet the club was once again embroiled in crisis.

Sitting in the relegation zone for the first time in 12 years and with a poorer goal difference than eventually doomed Sunderland had at the same stage of 2016/17, underscored the trouble that the Koeman regime was in.

The season before, the Arsenal fixture had marked a turning point, at least in Everton's home form in the League. It paved the way for the 4-0 demolition of Manchester City, as a cock-sure Blues side romped through Pep Guardiola's team with abandon, and six more wins at Goodison Park after that before Champions-elect Chelsea broke the sequence.

The only turning point this visit of Arsenal to L4 was likely to spark, however, was an abrupt one in Koeman's employment status... although there was no guarantee the Everton Board would be so decisive. Farhad Moshiri was seen to mouth "oh, no" as the fifth goal went in while Bill Kenwright visibly shared the pain of every Evertonian watching. It was hard to see a way back for Koeman — he looked bereft of answers.

The game exposed Everton's technical limitations and defensive frailties, while underscoring that energy and tenacity alone is not enough against sides like Arsenal when they can slice through disorganised defences like a whipsaw. The Gunners weren't at their best, but when they reached their potential, the porous Toffees couldn't live with them.

In some respects, there was a measure of sympathy to be had for Koeman here, albeit not enough to mask the mess over which he presided. He had asked for "aggression" from his players and mostly got it in the opening half hour as the forward line harried the Arsenal defence, and the likes of Idrissa Gueye were making full-blooded challenges like the one that set Wayne Rooney up for the opening goal.

Getting a boot to the ball before Hector Bellerin, the Senegalese midfielder prodded it towards Rooney and drawing on the self-belief and execution with which he announced himself to the world as a raw teenager 15 years ago almost to the day, he swept it past Petr Cech from 20 yards.

But it was over-exuberance from Gueye — in the absence of Morgan Schneiderlin, his job being to protect the back four — that got him into hot water with referee Craig Pawson 11 minutes before halftime, and which ultimately cost him his place on the pitch half an hour later when he picked up a second yellow card for one late sliding tackle too many.

Despite grabbing the relatively early goal that might have provided the foundation from which they could prey on the low morale of an Arsenal side that came into the game without an away win all season, there wasn't much more in terms of offensive production from Everton.

Jordan Pickford made himself the leading candidate for the Blues' man of the match by tipping a shot from Alexis Sanchez wide, diverting Alexandre Lacazette's shot behind to safety and making an excellent close-range save to deny the French striker after Aaron Ramsey had picked him out with an accurate centre from the Gunners' right flank. He was busy again pushing away Sanchez's free kick and then denying Aaron Ramsey from the rebound, but Arsenal's increasing pressure told. Five minutes before the break, a wrong-footed Pickford could only parry the ball into the path of Nacho Monreal and he smashed the rebound home.

Goodison was deflated, and it left plenty wondering if the Blues had it in them to re-establish a lead against a Gunners team that looked very much up for it, and was slicing through them at will.

And eight minutes into the second half, when the ball came to Sanchez, he delayed until he spotted Mesut Özil's unchecked run. One chipped cross later, the German had guided a header past Pickford to make it 2-1.

Koeman would lament after the match that Gueye's dismissal had made an already difficult task for his team impossible, but much of the fight had already gone out of them by that point. Arsenal with their tails up were just too good.

While the massed Evertonians watched angled ball after angled ball float out of play on the right touchline - the result of the manager's directive to go more direct - Wenger's men passed with speed and precision, moving through the gears with an efficiency that Blues fans could only dream of.

With 16 minutes left, Arsenal extended their lead when they carved their hosts open once more after Nikola Vlasic had uncharacteristically given it away in their half. Only the hapless Michael Keane was in the middle of defence as Ozil surged down the right flank and crossed to Lacazette, who couldn't miss from the centre of the goal.

Substitute Jack Wilshere split the defence to pick out Ramsey for the Gunners' fourth as regulation time expired but there was farce still to come in added time as Cech tried to dribble away from Oumar Niasse and the striker robbed him to knock the ball into the empty net.

Sanchez would still exert his will on the game with a final act in the final minute of stoppage time, though. Driving his way past a rank of Blue shirts, he eventually engineered space for a shot that he whipped across Pickford and into the far corner to complete the misery among those Evertonians who had remained behind to the bitter end.

But for Pickford's heroics, the result could have been much, much worse. And, even accounting for the final quarter of the contest played with 10 men, it was bad enough.

The flawed transfer strategy that saw Everton exit the transfer window with an unbalanced squad, woefully deficient in some areas and over-weight in others, was clearly a significant factor behind the slump, but the lack of consistency and clarity in Koeman's methods, team selections and tactics – and the resultant collapse in confidence among the players – were compounding the problem to a degree that was unsustainable.

There was a shortage of imagination, and what came across as a lack of passion and desire from the manager. When the buck ultimately stops at that one role, there is usually only one course of action to take. And take it, Moshiri did.

Final score: Everton 2-5 Arsenal

2017: Ronald Koeman sacked

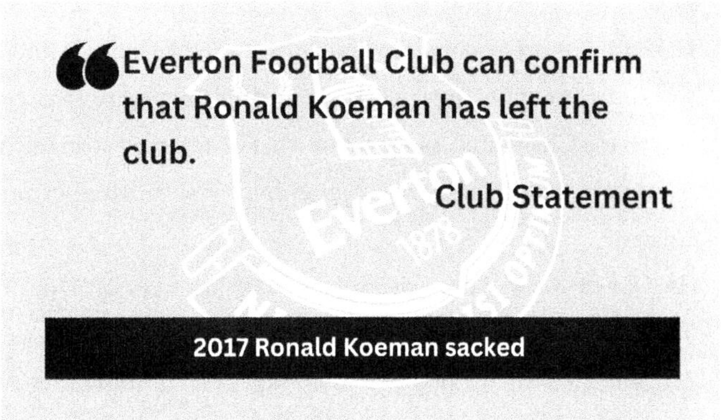

Everton sacked Ronald Koeman in the wake of that chastening 5-2 defeat by Arsenal, which had left the team sitting in the relegation zone for the first time since 2005.

A statement on the club's official website confirmed a decision from Farhad Moshiri and chairman Bill Kenwright that had become increasingly likely, despite the recent vote of confidence in the manager from the Blues' major shareholder.

Besides Everton's nose-diving form in the Premier League, the club was bottom of their Europa League group, having lost two and drawn one of their games, the worst such record for an English team in the competition to date.

Koeman had arrived at Goodison Park in June the previous year, billed as a "Hollywood" replacement for Roberto Martinez.

The Dutchman, an experienced coach who had won the title in the Netherlands three times before coming to England, had guided unfancied Southampton to seventh and then sixth place in the Premier League. Moshiri had seen him as the ideal candidate to take Everton forward.

Backed by unprecedented investment on the playing side and a club-record £6 million-a-year salary, Koeman's job was to steer the Blues into the Champions League, but what he regarded as an initial three-year project derailed in dramatic fashion with five defeats in nine league games.

The 54-year-old was insistent after the heavy loss to Arsenal that he was the right man to turn Everton's fortunes around, but a visible loss of confidence among the players and no sign of an upturn in results forced the hierarchy to act.

Koeman took training as normal at Finch Farm, but was informed shortly afterwards by CEO Robert Elstone and chairman Kenwright of the Board's decision to end his contract, including those of his backroom staff, comprising his brother and assistant Erwin, fitness coach Jan Kluitenberg, and goalkeeping coach Patrick Lodewijks. First team coach Duncan Ferguson would stay with the club.

The club statement read:

> "Everton Football Club can confirm that Ronald Koeman has left the Club. Chairman Bill Kenwright,

> the Board of Directors and Major Shareholder Farhad Moshiri would all like to express their gratitude to Ronald for the service he has given to the Club over the past 16 months and for guiding the Club to seventh place in last season's Premier League campaign."

Koeman had presided over 24 wins during his 58 games in charge, with 14 draws and 20 defeats. Though there were some misgivings among supporters about the standard of football his Everton team played, in the latter half of his first season at the club he appeared to have his team moving in the right direction.

There was, however, a feeling from club insiders that Koeman was a poor fit for the Toffees' culture, and that became a greater problem the worse results got in the weeks leading up to the dreadful display against Arsenal that triggered his dismissal.

It would also be revealed that Koeman and the club's sporting director Steve Walsh had increasingly divergent views on how to take the team forward.

Writing in *The Sportsman* on 9 November, Patrick Boyland [1]pinpointed the failed partnership between Ronald Koeman and Steve Walsh, saying that any new manager needed to learn lessons. He wrote:

> "It perfectly highlights the disconnect between Koeman and Walsh as far as the last few windows are concerned. In the case of the former, players seemingly able to deliver short-term gains were targeted in an attempt to meet a series of lofty goals over

the course of his three-year contract. As such, Morgan Schneiderlin, Davy Klaassen and Gylfi Sigurdsson were all bought on the recommendation of the Dutchman. Walsh, by contrast, largely chose to place faith in younger, hungrier players and hidden gems. In Ademola Lookman, Sandro Ramirez, Michael Keane and Jordan Pickford, the former Leicester City head of recruitment sought to buy players who would grow to form the backbone of Everton sides way into the future. The two contrasting visions have left Everton's squad lacking identity. Some players have youthful exuberance on their side and others the nous that comes with experience, but few in the ranks have both. With reliable heads thin on the ground, the Blues have been forced to place too much faith in a creaking elder statesmen and young bucks with rough edges to iron out. Whichever path is taken, Everton's director of football and new manager simply have to be on the same wavelength when it comes to recruiting players. As Koeman's demise has shown, contrasting visions cannot be reconciled. In that sense, those in power in L4 would be well advised to learn lessons from the failures of the past when appointing Koeman's successor."

***

David Unsworth, assisted by John Ebrell, was placed in charge of the first team as interim coach. With no immediate successor to Koeman lined up, the former Everton player was effectively handed an open-ended trial period to prove that he could take the job on, at least in an interim capacity, perhaps until the end of the season.

***

5 November 2017: Everton v Watford

In what was David Unsworth's fourth match in charge as caretaker boss, the Blues faced Watford at Goodison. His record in the role, up to that point, had been less than impressive. An unfortunate 2-1 defeat away at Chelsea in the League Cup was followed by 2-0 loss against Leicester in the Premier League, and a more alarming 3-0 thrashing by Olympique Lyonnais in Group E of the Europa League.

Unsworth named another changed line-up to face Watford, with Phil Jagielka, Leighton Baines and Wayne Rooney all returning to the starting XI, and with Michael Keane available again following his recovery from a leg infection, but genuine chances remained at a high premium in the first half.

The best chance of half had fallen the visitors' way when Richarlison drove forward for Watford and caught Pickford in no-man's land, but the Brazilian could only find the side-netting from the angle with the open goal gaping.

Richarlison made amends just 30 seconds into the second half, however. Everton were carved wide open again, and the forward took it wide to the left around Pickford once more and slammed it past Jonjoe Kenny on the line to make it 1-0.

By the 64th minute, Everton found themselves 2-0 down. Christian Kabasele rose highest from a corner, having lost his marker, and powered a header home.

Everton grabbed a lifeline three minutes after that, though, and sparked a dramatic and memorable comeback when Niasse toed the ball past the keeper, who had come flying out of his area. Despite being tripped as he charged through, he scored into the empty net.

Dominic Calvert-Lewin replaced Rooney, and when Leighton Baines swung in a corner, the substitute was there at the back post to head home and send Goodison into bedlam at 2-2.

As the match reached 90 minutes, it appeared the clincher had come. Holebas felled recent substitute Aaron Lennon and the Blues received the opportunity to take the lead. Baines stepped up to take the spot kick and, despite a short run-up, he placed it perfectly past the keeper to complete a stirring comeback. Yet still the game was not over.

Watford piled on increasing pressure and sunk Evertonian hearts when they too earned a penalty 10 minutes into stoppage time. Richarlison looked odds on to score his second as he neatly side-stepped Pickford in front of the goal, but the 'keeper tripped him trying to make a last-ditch tackle, and the spot kick was awarded.

Tom Cleverley stepped up with the chance to drive a stake into his former team's heart, but he screwed his penalty kick wide to spark more wild celebrations around the Old Lady; and the Blues held out for the final couple of minutes to claim a crucial victory.

This was only the second time since the relegation-defying win over Wimbledon that Everton had come back from a two-goal deficit, and it could not have come at a better time. With 10 minutes in the second half gone, the club had been staring a long battle against relegation firmly in the face. But a brilliant fightback had not only lifted Everton out of the relegation zone, it had offered hope that this collection of players had the stomach for any fight to survive in the top flight.

Final score: Everton 3-2 Watford

***

After the match, the 44-year-old Unsworth was full of praise for his players, many of them young and relatively inexperienced.

"Incredible!" Unsworth beamed in the tunnel after the game. "I'm just delighted for the club and the fans that they can go home tonight happy. I didn't expect the second half to pan out like the way it did, but to get the win, and the manner of being two goals down [makes it] very special, and it's a night that will live in the memory for a long time.

"The players have been magnificent. I've said all along that they've given me everything and they have. We've had a tough run of fixtures, but that's no excuse. When you play for this great club, you know that you've got to go away from home and give big performances and get results because our fans demand that.

"It's really important that we always go into every game and try to win. It was great to come back here tonight, to come home and get 40,000 Evertonians behind us, and that one's for them tonight."

Unsworth's prospects of succeeding Koeman permanently appeared remote before kick-off after three successive defeats, but he stressed he did not know if they would offer him the post considering the win, or if the board would look elsewhere for a new manager.

"Whatever will be, will be," Unsworth said. "I have been the proudest man in the world to take charge for thc last two weeks, and no one can take that away from me.

"I know nothing about it. I'm sure I'll speak to the chairman and owner, and I'll keep giving my best for this wonderful club."

***

Unsworth's hopes of building on his first win were tested when, a day after the Watford match, Morgan Schneiderlin came out to reports he had been "sent away" from training on the preceding Saturday, as he reaffirmed his commitment to Everton.

The French international midfielder had been omitted from David Unsworth's squad for the Premier League fixture against Watford, three days after being sent off in Lyon for two bookable offences in the Blues' 3-0 defeat in the Europa League.

Speculation had been rife that both Schneiderlin and Kevin Mirallas, also left out of the team, either walked out of training on Saturday for failing to take it seriously or were told to leave by coach Duncan Ferguson if they couldn't knuckle down.

Schneiderlin, however, rejected the reports, posting a statement to social media that read: "I have seen press stories today about me 'being sent away from training'. The stories are not true. I am fully committed to Everton and will continue to work hard for the Club and the fans in training and on the pitch."

Mirallas also addressed the situation, albeit in rather more vague terms. The Belgian posted on Instagram thanking fans for all their messages to him.

"It's a difficult situation for me," his post read. "But in life there are things much more serious than my personal situation."

Mirallas, who had signed a new three-year contract earlier in the year but then angled for a move back to Olympiacos during the transfer window, had not featured for the team since being substituted at half-time at Leicester nine days previously.

---

1. Patrick Boyland: The Sportsman, November 2017

2017: Moshiri delighted to confirm Sam as manager

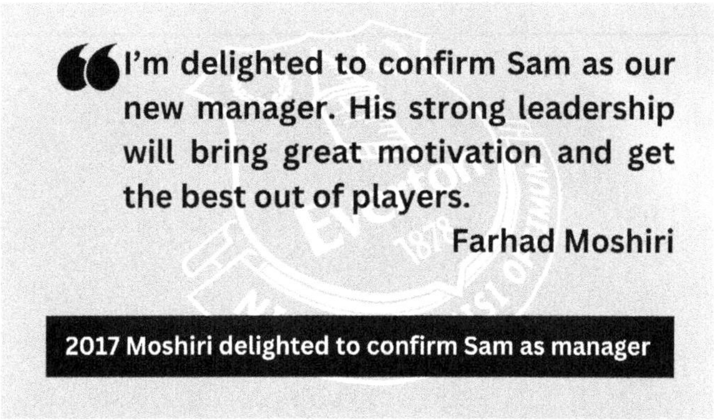

Three weeks on from the win over Watford, speculation was reaching fever pitch over who would replace Ronald Koeman. On the field, things had gone from bad to worse despite David Unsworth's best efforts. The dramatic victory over the Hornets had turned out to be a flash in the pan. A 2-2 draw away at Crystal Palace preceded a 5-1 Europa League thrashing by Atalanta at Goodison, which was followed by a heavy 4-1 away defeat at Southampton. With Everton humiliated in Europe and hovering just above the relegation zone, it looked increasingly unlikely that David Unsworth would be retained as caretaker manager for much longer.

***

29 November 2017: Everton v West Ham

The answer as to who would take the reins on a more permanent basis finally came on a bitterly cold day, when Everton were due to play a vital midweek Premier League fixture against West Ham at Goodison.

63-year-old Sam Allardyce had re-emerged as the front-runner, with a number of reliable media outlets all claiming the club had turned to the man who had built a reputation over the years for rescuing teams from relegation.

Once again, important club news was channelled through Jim White, while Everton took the unusual step of issuing a brief statement saying that Allardyce would travel to USM Finch Farm that afternoon to complete his deal.

White then passed on another message, purportedly from major shareholder Farhad Moshiri that read:

> "I really want to give [Allardyce] the support he needs. He can go as far as he wants. We need a strong leader, he gives us that."

Despite the 'official leak', stand-in manager David Unsworth took charge of the match against West Ham United, seemingly his last task in charge of first-team affairs before Allardyce would take over.

The reports claimed Allardyce had negotiated an 18-month deal on an annual salary of almost £6 million a year, and planned to bring in ex-Liverpool player Sammy Lee as his assistant. Craig Shakespeare, fired earlier this season as Leicester City's manager, would also join the backroom staff.

If Unsworth has sported the look of a harrowed man over the preceding few days, he left Goodison Park with a rueful smile, having left the post of caretaker manager with a thumping 4-0 win over the Hammers to savour.

Having lost 4-1 at Southampton just four days earlier, and seen his team fall apart in similar fashion against Atalanta the previous Thursday, the former defender knew it was only a matter of time before a permanent successor to Koeman appeared. He looked hurt in his pre-match press conference, and for stepping into the breach in hugely difficult circumstances, he fully deserved to leave his temporary post with a victory.

And how! One look at the Blues' recent form and a patched-up back four, featuring the much-maligned duo of Cuco Martina and Ashley Williams, as well as Mason Holgate, who only proved his fitness the previous night, suggested that confidence-sapped Everton might be in for a difficult evening. Instead, with controversial new hire Allardyce watching on from the Directors' Box, Wayne Rooney claimed a first hat-trick for his boyhood club in the most spectacular fashion and the home side kept its first clean sheet in the Premier League since the opening day of the season. □□□□□□

Despite the emphatic nature of the scoreline, it wasn't an entirely comfortable evening for a home crowd that was quiet and circumspect during an opening quarter of an hour. That the supporters could go home happy was also down to a vital penalty save from Jordan Pickford 13 minutes into the second half, and what was, apart from Jason Cresswell's shot that crashed off the face of the crossbar, a woeful attacking performance from West Ham on David Moyes's latest chastening return to Goodison. Rooney's world-class intervention eight minutes later, followed by atonement for Williams, merely confirmed that it was going to be the Toffees' night.

When viewed as a whole, this was not a great performance, but in the panic that had gripped the club after Sunday's defensive debacle at St Mary's Stadium, it was certainly good enough and there were some very encouraging individual performances.

With his years advancing, many observers had suggested that Rooney's best position could be in a deeper role than he occupied under Koeman and, finally, Unsworth took the much-called-for step of dispensing with two holding midfielders at home to accommodate the veteran in that more influential role.

Rooney responded by running the game from midfield, offering the industry and vision that has been sorely lacking from Morgan Schneiderlin while still chipping in with his customary striker's position for Everton's second goal after 28 minutes. His deployment as a roving "No.8" probably also left him perfectly positioned to score the third in spectacular fashion from inside his own half.

Rooney would get a deserved ovation when replaced by Beni Baningime with five minutes left on the clock, but in between Ashley

Williams scored Everton's fourth, a looping header from a corner after he had lost his marker.

And so to the impending transfer of managerial duties from the truest of Blues to the far less felicitous Allardyce, with the stabbing irony that this result confirmed what many had felt — that even hampered by injury to three more first-teamers, this Everton side was far better than performances and results had suggested this season. Indeed, several players had let Unsworth down badly since he assumed the helm six weeks earlier.

Unsworth may always regret that he wasn't able to draw better out of the team, and give the Board of Directors more time to avoid the panicked decision that had led them down the road to appointing the man sacked by England in disgrace.

It was just Sod's Law that the ink was probably still drying on Allardyce's contract as the Blues rattled in four goals, alleviated at a stroke the fear that had taken hold after their thrashing at the hands of Southampton, and removed much of the need for a relegation specialist at all. It left the Everton support having to back a manager that the vast majority didn't want, and the Board having to balance Allardyce's transfer needs in the upcoming January window with the longer-term needs of the Farhad Moshiri/Steve Walsh project, which had been on hold until the new man's hiring.

That would be an issue to wrestle with in the coming days. Rooney may have grabbed the headlines, but this had been "Rhino's" night.

Final score: Everton 4-0 West Ham

***

The day after the West Ham match, Everton 'officially' announced Sam Allardyce as their new manager, after he completed the formalities on a deal set to run until the end of 2018/19.

The arrangement represented a plain compromise between the two parties, with Allardyce agreeing to a shorter 18-month term than the three years he was reportedly after.

Everton, meanwhile, were paying him £6 million a year, a substantial increase on the £2.5 million annual salary he had been on at Crystal Palace.

Allardyce immediately called for unity and commitment from the squad following the Toffee's dreadful start to the season. "Let's try to get a healthy spirit around the club," he said. "I think that whatever's happened before we've just got to all rally around, because we are all in it together, and let's all pull in the same direction.

"We have to give the players every possibility to play to their best, really give them no excuses for not playing to their best, and get them right back up to the top level we believe they're capable of.

"Peter Reid is one of my best mates, so are Andy Gray and Paul Bracewell, whom I worked with at Sunderland. These people have always made me aware of just how special and unique a club Everton is, and I feel really enthused and energised to come in as manager."

Known as the man struggling clubs turned to steer them away from relegation, Allardyce was greeted by Everton fans with a mixture of displeasure and indifference. He was widely regarded as one-dimensional and unsophisticated. His arrival was seen by some as a sign of how far their grand old team had fallen.

Born and raised in Dudley in the West Midlands, Allardyce got his start in football as a player with Bolton Wanderers in the 1970s.

His first managerial assignment was also in the northwest with Blackpool before he moved to Notts County, the only club to that point where he had overseen relegation.

After joining Bolton, he led them to the Premier League and eventually into European competition via a sixth-place finish, but left in 2007. A stint at Newcastle followed, and he would go on to ensure the Premier League safety of Crystal Palace, West Ham, Sunderland and Blackburn Rovers before his arrival at Everton, cementing a reputation for always bringing stability and order to struggling teams headed for relegation from the top flight.

Though his achievements at Bolton remained the pinnacle of his managerial career, Allardyce's biggest appointment prior to the Everton job was that of England manager in 2017.

Hired to replace Roy Hodgson, it was an opportunity he hoped would allow him to dispel his image as a firefighter and manage at the top of the game. His spell lasted just one match, however, as the FA sacked him, following a sting by *The Telegraph* in which they recorded him apparently negotiating with an undercover reporter posing as a Far Eastern business executive looking to pay money for help in skirting FIFA's rules over third-party ownership of players.

Having rehabilitated his image somewhat at Crystal Palace, he elected to retire from the game when they parted company at the end of 2016/17. But he answered the call from Farhad Moshiri and the Everton Board in order to stabilise what had thus far been a chaotic 2017/18 season at Goodison.

***

2 December 2017: Everton v Huddersfield Town

Everton began Sam Allardyce's tenure with a second successive home win, as goals from Gylfi Sigurdsson and Dominic Calvert-Lewin were enough to see off Huddersfield Town.

Having adapted to the visitors' energetic pressing and found their own rhythm in the second half, the Blues pressed home their superiority with two goals in a match that was otherwise short on goalmouth action.

After watching Everton dismantle West Ham on Wednesday evening in David Unsworth's last game in charge, Allardyce elected to go with the same starting XI despite the availability of Oumar Niasse and Michael Keane.

That meant Calvert-Lewin played up front again, Wayne Rooney occupying the deeper-lying role in which he proved so effective against the Hammers, and Cuco Martina continuing to deputise for the injured Leighton Baines at left back.

And it was Martina who had the best chance of a physical first half, where opportunities were at a premium at both ends. The Curacao international benefited from strong hold-up play by Calvert-Lewin and hammered a right-foot shot that Jonas Lössl had to parry away with both hands.

At the other end, Laurent Depoitre came closest to breaking the Terriers' long goal drought away from home when the ball fell to him at a corner, but Jordan Pickford did enough to get a hand to it before the ball was hacked away to safety.

The second half was only a couple of minutes when Everton took the lead. Aaron Lennon's pass into the penalty area was flicked beautifully into the path of Sigurdsson by Calvert-Lewin and the Iceland international swept confidently home from a central position.

The Blues had increasingly got the measure of Huddersfield and when Idrissa Gueye won the ball in his own half and found Rooney, the veteran forward released Calvert-Lewin behind the visitors' defence with another pin-point pass. The striker bore down on Lössl's goal and profited from a slight deflection from the covering defender's lunging tackle that carried it over the 'keeper's arms into the net.

Tommy Smith had a deflected late effort saved by Pickford, but Huddersfield, who hadn't scored on their travels since the opening day, would not find a way past the Blues' back line, which kept its second clean sheet of the week.

The result lifted Everton into 10th place in the Premier League and moved them eight points clear of the bottom three.

Final score: Everton 2-0 Huddersfield

***

10 December 2017: Liverpool v Everton

Before the season started, many an Evertonian might have been eyeing this fixture as the one where the Blues would finally end their wait for a first derby victory at Anfield since 1999. Back in August, with £100 million on new players spent and the promise of more to come, 2017/18 felt like it could be the one where Everton could travel across Stanley Park as equals and with genuine prospects of winning.

15 League games and four months of the ruinous Ronald Koeman reign later and those expectations had been scaled down radically. Avoiding a Martinez-scale 4-0 humiliation was, perhaps, top of mind and if ever a performance needed to be viewed in its proper context, this was it.

In that context, the eventual reward of a point was important, because this was a horrible match to watch from the Blue perspective. The 79% of possession ceded to Liverpool was, apparently, a Premier League record at the time, which was not surprising.

Everton probably couldn't have given the ball away more if they had tried. Even Sam Allardyce, a manager given to direct, back-to-basics football, was critical afterwards of his side's inability to keep possession. And yet, the Blues escaped Anfield with a point, extended their unbeaten run to four games and took another step on the road to stability in a season that was spiralling into chaos just a fortnight ago.

That Allardyce fielded two strikers in Oumar Niasse and Dominic Calvert-Lewin, was a sign that his game plan was based on more than just defending. Unfortunately, the two spent so much time chasing wayward forward balls from Jordan Pickford that they could never get close enough to form any kind of partnership.

It meant that the ball kept coming back at Everton time after time, but two dogged banks of four bolstered by gritty performances from Mason Holgate and Jonjoe Kenny and the work rate of Idrissa Gueye meant it would take a special piece of individual play for Liverpool to get their noses in front by half time.

For all the crowing about Jurgen Klopp's attacking quartet — he had the hubris to leave two of the four, Philippe Coutinho and Roberto Firmino on the bench — they had really only threatened on one occasion prior to the 42nd minute when Mohamed Salah took matters into his own hands. He shoved Cuco Martina away from a challenge just inside the box, dribbled past Gueye and bent a shot around Pickford and inside the far post.

What should have been 2-0 and game over, came in first-half stoppage time. Sadio Mané easily side-stepped Ashley Williams as he committed himself to a sliding tackle he had no hope of winning, and raced into a four-on-one situation with just Martina and Pickford in front of him. But rather than squaring it for Salah, the Senegalese international went it alone and screwed his shot across goal and wide. Salah himself would also miss a gilt-edged chance on the other side of the break, when he headed narrowly wide with a free header from Milner's cross.

Allardyce withdrew Niasse at half time in favour or Aaron Lennon — the winger with his industry was a positive addition — and Calvert-Lewin remained on the field to provide the outlet that eventually won Everton only their second penalty at Anfield in 80 years.

In between, it was something akin to a training-ground exercise of attack-versus-defence; it was one-way traffic towards the Everton goal, but apart from an overhead kick from Mané, Pickford had nothing to do. That established the platform from which Everton could remain in the game, until it entered the final quarter of an hour, when they went in search of the equaliser.

Rooney raked a ball over the top for Calvert-Lewin, who knocked it on into the Liverpool box with his thigh with Dejan Lovren on the chase. The defender ended up shoving the striker in the back and, seeming to contact his right leg, sent him crashing to the turf and prompting referee Craig Pawson to point to the spot.

Rooney smashed the resulting penalty straight down the middle with Mignolet diving in vain to his left and it was 1-1.

While no one in Blue would have enjoyed the performance, it yielded a satisfying result, particularly given how worked up Klopp and Lovren were at the final whistle.

The point ensured a share of the spoils, avoided another painful derby defeat and kept Everton in 10th place with two games against teams below them up next. And all the while, Allardyce and his team were learning about the players they had inherited, and what they needed to do when the winter transfer window opened. It would be interesting to see how things looked by the end of January.

Final score: Liverpool 1-1 Everton

***

After the game, Sam Allardyce spoke of the positives, from what he saw as an impressive defensive display that saw Everton withstand Liverpool's dominance in possession, to grind out a point.

"It was a huge point," Allardyce said, "because we didn't create much in possession of the ball today, which was very frustrating [given] the quality of the players we have."

2018 Allardyce and Walsh sign Tosun to replace Lukaku

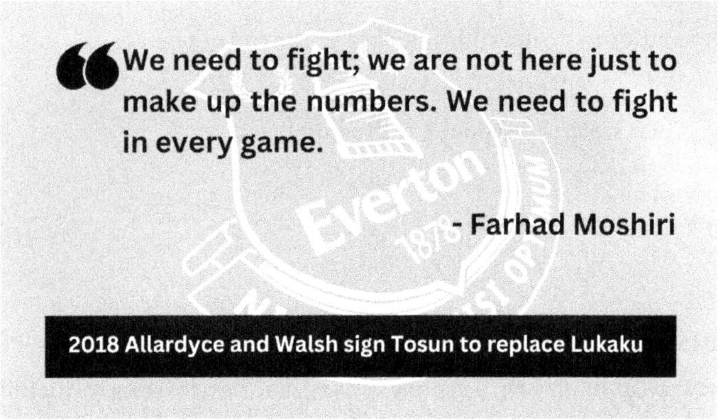

As Christmas 2017 approached, Everton announced record turnover and a post-tax profit of £30 million for the 2016/17 year. The club's turnover topped £171 million, almost £50 million more than the previous record set two seasons prior, thanks largely again to the Premier League broadcast revenue bonanza.

With such financial power seemingly at the club's disposal, the fans were optimistic about filling a Romelu Lukaku shaped gap in the first team. The Belgian had been sold to Manchester United over the summer but had not been adequately replaced.

The Turkish striker, Cenk Tosun, was rumoured to be on Everton's radar, but apparently his move to Everton hung in the balance as rival clubs looked to swoop. Everton sent Steve Walsh and a delegation to meet face-to-face with Besiktas officials to land the Turk ahead of competition from Europe.

"It's in the wind," Blues boss Sam Allardyce said of the Tosun transfer when asked if he could confirm the speculation. "There's obviously an interest because we're actively looking for a front man, but whether we are the ones to complete that deal or not, I don't know. The interest from other clubs around Europe is our biggest worry if we are to secure that transfer."

Ultimately, Everton were successful in signing Tosun in a £21 million deal. Tosun finally completed his move on 5 January.

Allardyce then turned his attention to trying to sign midfielder Steven N'Zonzi from Sevilla, a player with whom Allardyce had worked during his Blackburn Rovers days and was keen to link up with him again, but the attempt proved unsuccessful.

***

On 9 January 2018, Everton's major shareholder and de facto owner, Farhad Moshiri spoke of his confidence that the club were making significant progress on what he saw as a long road to getting the Blues back to their place among the elite of the English game.

Speaking in a rare video interview at Finch Farm, the Iranian-born billionaire shared his thoughts on the recent setbacks to his vision for Everton created by the team's unexpectedly poor start to the season and his determination to deliver a new stadium at Bramley-Moore Dock, the new cost projection for which was £500 million.

The interview on evertonfc.com was released against the backdrop of that evening's Annual General Meeting of Shareholders at the Liverpool Philharmonic Hall.

Moshiri talked about having a plan that would take several years to fully execute and one which began with investment in the playing staff and the infrastructure that supports it.

He cited the new sponsorship deal with USM at Finch Farm, the sleeve sponsorship agreement with Rovio for Angry Birds, and suggested that more arrangements along those lines were in the pipeline.

> "We have invested quite heavily in infrastructure. What you see is the visible part — buying — but there is an awful lot going on behind the scenes to make success sustainable. The commercial side is developing really well. There are a lot of other sponsorships which are coming in. On the stadium we have [also] made great progress. We have to have a [new] stadium and we will have a stadium. When the building work starts, that will be the proof of the pudding so we want to get to that stage. But until we get to that, we are in the preparation stage but we are progressing well. We have secured the land which is the most essential [part], we've picked the [site] that we think the fans would prefer. It's an iconic thing, something that Everton needs," Moshiri continued, perhaps hinting at a desire to unveil a ground superior to Anfield, "to

> have a better stadium — and that's what we have to do. I think the first part of the exercise is to make the team competitive so that the owner, the Board, the fans and the employees can be proud of the team," he said. "We need to fight; we are not here just to make up the numbers. We need to fight in every game – Farhad Moshiri, Everton AGM, 9 January 2017

***

A week after the AGM, striker Theo Walcott completed his move from Arsenal to Everton in a reported £20 million deal, becoming the Blues' second signing of that transfer window.

The 28-year-old had followed Turkish striker Cenk Tosun through the door as manager, Sam Allardyce, and director of football, Steve Walsh, looked to strengthen a forward line that had struggled to put shots on target let alone score goals in recent matches.

Everton had beaten off competition from Walcott's former club Southampton, by securing the England international's signature on a 3½-year contract and taking their spending for January past the £40 million mark. Walcott would wear the No.11 jersey vacated by Kevin Mirallas, who had joined Olympiakos on loan in the same month.

Walcott had made his name at Arsenal where he had 270 Premier League appearances, scoring 65 goals and providing 43 assists.

Despite scoring 19 goals in all competitions for the Gunners in 2016/17, Walcott had become a peripheral figure at the Emirates Stadium and hadn't started a Premier League game under Arsène Wenger for nine months.

Walcott no doubt viewed his move to Goodison Park as a fresh start where he could put himself back into the mind of England manager Gareth Southgate ahead of the upcoming World Cup in Russia, having missed the cut for Euro 2016.

"I've come to Everton because I'm very ambitious and I want the club to push to the next level," Walcott said upon signing. "I'm very excited to be starting a new chapter and felt this was the right place for me to be.

"The fact there's a new stadium going to be developing in the next few years, it's exciting times for Everton Football Club.

"I'm dead excited and I just want to do what I do best, which is playing football and expressing myself because I'm excited again. I really am.

"I do really believe that I'm going to give it my all, which is what I always have done, and this place is going to get even more out of me.

"There's something about this move which I've just felt good about."

Evertonians were keen to see whether the new strike force of Tosun and Walcott would revitalise the team's goal threat.

2018: Everton Bottom of Shots on Goal Table

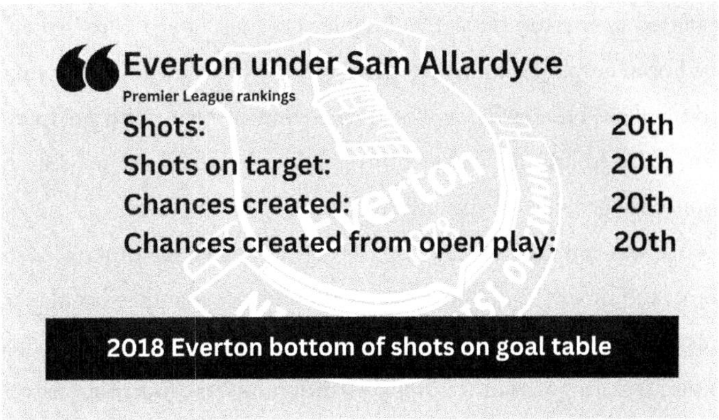

The final games of 2017 were a mixed bag for Sam Allardyce and Everton, with wins against Newcastle and Swansea, draws against Chelsea and West Brom, and an away defeat at Bournemouth.

With everything crossed for a happy New Year, the match at Goodison on New Year's day turned out to be a disappointment, with a 2-0 defeat against Man United.

Next up was an away tie at Anfield in the third round of the FA Cup, for which the expectations were low, given the Blues abysmal record at Anfield this century. That proved prescient because, for the second season running, the Toffees' FA Cup road would come to an end almost as soon as it had begun, as Everton succumbed to a 2-1 defeat.

***

13 January, 2018: Tottenham Hotspur v Everton

What happened at Wembley on this mid-January fixture was not, in theory, supposed to happen anymore after Sam Allardyce was appointed as Everton boss. The Premier League's famed "fire-fighter" had been employed to whip together a sorry bunch who had, thanks to the flawed leadership and inadequate recruitment of his predecessor, plunged into the bottom three and destroyed all the pre-season optimism generated by an unprecedented spending spree.

He was expected to shore up the defence, make the Blues hard to beat, and slowly instil in the players a confidence that they could take on anyone in the top flight and get a result. And yet, Evertonians were sat staring at another after a 4-0 drubbing – the fourth successive defeat – and with the team conceding at a rate of 2½ goals a game. Allardyce's unique selling point, defensive solidity and backs-to-the-wall defiance, has gone up in smoke since Boxing Day. It left Blues fans wondering: so what now?

Allardyce had made a decent start, going seven games unbeaten in all competitions and steering the Toffees to the comfort of ninth place in the Premier League table. However, successive defeats to Bournemouth, Manchester United and Liverpool in the FA Cup Third Round had seen Everton begin to revert to type with worsening attacking metrics that would eventually be the worst in the top flight.

This, against Spurs in their temporary home at the national stadium, was an utterly miserable performance, one only briefly lifted above the turgid and the hapless by a fleeting moment here and there early on by debutant Cenk Tosun and the brief, quickly extinguished, elation at a Wayne Rooney goal chalked off for offside.

Beyond that, there were almost no redeeming facets save the continued shot-stopping form of Jordan Pickford... that is when he wasn't left completely exposed by a flat-footed or simply non-existent back line.

Everton finished the contest having failed to register a shot on target for the third Premier League game in the previous five, and undergoing a collapse in the second half that echoed the nadirs of the Roberto Martinez and Ronald Koeman regimes.

To hear Allardyce speak afterwards of having to now make his side more boring and less adventurous afterwards beggared belief for Evertonians. The manager talked as if their maverick spirit had been punished as they poured forward in attack when, in fact, the Blues did precious little by way of getting forward beyond sending missiles forward from the boot of Jordan Pickford, aimed in the general direction of Tosun's head.

The Turk was as isolated as his predecessors in the role before he was withdrawn in the second half — proof, as if it were needed, that you can't just throw a striker into this team and expect all the problems going forward to melt away.

And for all Allardyce's renowned defensive bent, Tottenham picked their way through a system supposedly bolstered by twin defensive midfielders and around the fullbacks with ease.

The deluge began in the 26th minute as Serge Aurier took advantage of an ocean of space on Everton's left flank and drove a hard and low ball into the 6-yard box where Son Heung-min simply side-footed home from close range.

Tottenham's second was almost a mirror image of the first although this time the freedom of the flank afforded Son came from Jonjoe Kenny's inexperience as the South Korean expertly rolled him, leaving him for dead. Kane was offside when the ball was delivered to him but the defending in the middle was just as lax, with the striker easily able to steal between Jagielka and Martina.

Kane plundered a second as blue jerseys ambled about and Eric Dier then simply passed the ball into the 6-yard box again behind the static Mason Holgate and Jagielka to toe it over Pickford.

And Christian Eriksen, the like of which Everton so desperately need in attacking midfield, finished off the rout at the end of an impressive Spurs move when he swept home Dele Alli's flick.

It could have been worse. Pickford made a number of stops to deny Kane, Aurier, Kane and Son. Son also rattled the post in the second half prior to the third goal while the Blues offered nothing going the other way.

Final score: Tottenham 4-0 Everton

***

Later in January 2018, events that would have ramifications for both Everton and Sam Allardyce were playing out in Hertfordshire when Watford sacked Marco Silva as their manager on 21 January, citing

Everton's approach for the Portuguese manager the previous November, as the "catalyst for this decision".

Silva had been top choice of the Blues' hierarchy to succeed Ronald Koeman, following the Ronald Koeman's dismissal in October, but Watford had rebuffed Everton's attempts to prise him away, even after the Goodison side reportedly offered £10 million in compensation for Silva's services.

Watford fans were critical of Silva's rhetoric at the time, where he appeared reluctant to state his unreserved commitment to seeing out his contract at Vicarage Road in the midsts of reports he wanted to take the Everton job.

A statement from the Hornets said: "The Club is convinced the appointment of Silva was the right one, and had it not been for the unwarranted approach by a Premier League rival for his services, we would have continued to prosper under his leadership.

"This has been a difficult decision and one not taken lightly. The catalyst is that approach, something which the board believes has seen a significant deterioration in both focus and results to the point where the long-term future of Watford has been jeopardised."

Watford had hired Silva on the back of his impressive spell at Hull City, where he gave the doomed Yorkshire club a fighting chance of staying in the top flight with a string of home wins. He looked to be adding to his burgeoning reputation in 2017/18 and had overseen a flying start to the campaign, but after beating Newcastle 3-0 in late November, the Hornets won just once more in 11 Premier League games.

Neither Watford's faltering form nor the controversial circumstances behind Silva's form would deter Farhad Moshiri who remained determined to bring the promising young coach to Everton,

***

31 January 2018: Everton v Leicester City

The humiliation at the hands of Spurs was followed by a 1-1 home draw against West Bromwich Albion, with the Blues' saviour that day turning out to be none other than Oumar Niasse, who had survived Koeman's reign and had popped up with a 70th-minute equaliser after Jay Rodriguez had netted for the Baggies in the seventh minute.

In search of their first win of 2018, Everton faced Leicester City at Goodison at the end of January.

Allardyce made six alterations to the starting XI that started against West Brom but they appeared to have little effect on the performance in the early stages, with Everton lacking in both cohesion and direction, and overly reliant on high and direct balls aimed at Niasse up front. They managed a rare shot on target early on when new signing Theo Walcott forced Kasper Schmeichel to push a bouncing shot wide, but the tale of the first quarter of the contest was one of the home side's weakness defending set-pieces.

Everton settled, however, and when Cuco Martina pressured Ben Chilwell and the ball broke to Gylfi Sigurdsson wide on the right, the Icelandic international cut it back to meet the run of Walcott who tucked a first-time shot inside the post to make it 1-0 with 24 minutes gone.

Walcott led the way again six minutes before the interval. Michael Keane contested for Rooney's flighted ball into the box and his looping header fell invitingly for the former Arsenal forward, who volleyed it back across Schmeichel and into the far corner.

2-nil and the the Blues were flying, but their momentum did not carry through to the second half, which became a much more even affair, even if the Blues were still carrying the greater attacking threat.

Jamie Vardy scored from the spot for Leicester in the 71st minute, which led to an inevitably nervy conclusion as the home side threatened to fall to pieces under renewed pressure from the visitors. The woodwork saved them in the 77th minute, however, as substitute Kalechi Iheanacho watched a deflected effort bounce off the bar before he rapped the rebound off the post.

Everton's back line threatened to buckle again when Martina had to hack the ball out of the goalmouth to safety and Pickford flapped badly at successive crosses towards his six-yard box but escaped when Jamie Vardy curled well wide of his goal.

Everton eventually saw the game out to collect three vital points that moved them eight points clear of the relegation zone, and just three wins shy of the 40-point mark that usually guarantees safety.

Final score: Everton 2-1 Leicester

***

Just three days after that morale-boosting win over the Foxes, the Blues suffered a humiliating but all-too-familiar reverse at The Emirates

Stadium, losing 5-1 to Arsenal in what was Sam Allardyce's second defeat by four goals in North London in less than a month.

The manager was scathing of his team's inconsistency and what he described as a "pathetic" first-half display.

Aaron Ramsey scored a hat-trick and there was a goal, allowed despite a clear offside, for Gunners debutant Pierre-Emerick Aubameyang as Arsene Wenger's side racked up five goals against the Toffees for the second time that season.

Dominic Calvert-Lewin came off the bench to score a consolation goal to make it 4-1 as Everton improved after introducing Tom Davies for the hapless Michael Keane at the interval, but Arsenal's fifth underlined the paucity of the visitors' defending.

Allardyce, who vowed that the defensive capitulation he witnessed against Tottenham last month couldn't happen again, watched on from sidelines as his defence opened up again for Ramsey to complete his treble. He expressed his anger and "bitter disappointment" to evertontv after the match and suggested that the performance made it look as though he and his staff were not doing their job properly.

"The first half was a disaster," Allardyce told the cameras. "I have a lot of trouble with the players [not] taking onto the pitch what we actually asked them to do.

"That is a big worry for me. I have to say, the longer I go on, the players are showing so much inconsistency that I have to face the uphill battle of trying to get them to be more consistent and to perform at their best level, week in and week out.

"It's no good playing okay in the second half, getting the goal and trying to make the score look respectable. It's far too late. It's just a pathetic first-half performance.

"At the end of the day, I can pick as many systems as I want to pick, but if a player plays like they did today — and I'm talking about all 11 in the first half — then you've really got no chance. Tactics and systems mean absolutely nothing."

***

17 March 2018: Everton v Stoke

Performances throughout February and March resembled a yo-yo. There was a 3-1 home win against Crystal Palace, consecutive away defeats against Watford and Burnley, and a 2-0 home win against Brighton. The Blues were typically winning at home, but losing away. The away match at Stoke provided an opportunity to break that pattern.

With Gylfi Sigurdsson injured, it forced Sam Allardyce to change things in midfield where he brought Idrissa Gueye back into the side after he missed the win over Brighton through illness. The Senegalese international slotted in defensive midfield alongside Wayne Rooney, with Tom Davies given license to push forward between wingers Yannick Bolasie and Theo Walcott.

Everton struggled to get going in a dreadful first half that was not aided by periodic spells of heavy snow that settled over two-thirds of the pitch. Poor distribution from the back and a general lack of cohesion in attack meant that, not for the first time this season, they failed to register a shot on target before half time.

Stoke, who came into the match sitting in the bottom three, weren't much better, although they tested Jordan Pickford with a couple of efforts from distance, one from Peter Crouch that the 'keeper spilled before gathering at the second attempt.

Some in the Potters' ranks had declared this game as their "cup final" in their bid to beat the drop, but Charlie Adam critically undermined their cause with half an hour gone. The Scot lunged into a late tackle on Rooney midway inside the Everton half that caught the Blues' midfielder on the ankle and referee Martin Atkinson had little hesitation in brandishing a red card.

The visitors made little headway in making the numerical advantage tell, however, until there were a little over 20 minutes to go. Yannick Bolasie whipped in a cross from the right onto which Cenk Tosun got the merest of glances. Butland could only parry it to Dominic Calvert-Lewin, but Konstantinos Stafylidis stopped it on the line. Tosun was on hand to tap the loose ball home, however, scoring what should have been the decisive goal.

The Blues, however, came undone in familiar circumstances from a set-piece. Gueye pulled back his man, and when Joe Allen dropped the resulting dead-ball delivery into the space between Pickford and his back line, Maxim Choupo-Moting stole in to plunder the equaliser.

Everton wrestled the initiative back, though, with Tosun himself scoring the winner with his fourth goal in three games. This time, Theo Walcott was the provider with a cross from the right and Tosun stooped in ahead of Ryan Shawcross to power the ball into the corner.

The victory, Everton's first on their travels in three months, finally lifted Allardyce's side to the "magic" 40-point mark. Though the performance left much to be desired — even allowing for the conditions, which veered from bright sunshine to near blizzard, the manager's only concern was those three points, and the end of a run of six games without an away win in all competitions.

Final score: Stoke 1-2 Everton

***

Though Ronald Koeman had paid for his own failings as head coach of Everton's first team, the club's first Director of Football Steve Walsh had continued in his post following the Dutchman's dismissal and the appointment of Sam Allardyce.

Walsh had faced criticism, however, for the club's recruitment policy over the preceding 20 months and there was growing speculation by the spring of 2018 that he would be moved aside in favour of PSV Eindhoven's highly regarded technical director, Marcel Brands. Sky Sports were claiming from their sources that Brands, would become the Blues' latest appointment once the Dutch side were confirmed as Eredivisie champions.

Speculation concerning Allardyce's future at the club was also growing. The Dudleyite had faced routine questions about his standing at the club in the preceding weeks, amid the increasing clamour among Everton fans for him to be moved on in the summer now he had fulfilled his initial remit of keeping the Blues away from relegation danger.

He insisted he had received the clarity he sought over his future from the club's major shareholder, Farhad Moshiri, after a meeting in London but in the wake of further questions following a poor performance against Southampton in the penultimate match of the season, Allardyce admitted that he would have benefitted from public backing.

"It would have helped, yes," the 63-year-old said, "but I can't control the board, I can't control what they say.

"They are my bosses, so I can't be dictating and telling them what they should or should not do, obviously, but that has fuelled more speculation. I think results speak for themselves personally.

"You know, at the end of the day it is where it is."

Moshiri had spoken about Allardyce in glowing terms around the time of the Annual General Meeting in January, but the naturally media-shy Monaco-based businessman had said little publicly on any topic since.

The length of his initial contract suggested that Moshiri and the Everton board might have had a short-term time horizon when they hired the Premier League's renowned 'firefighter', and there had been plenty of media speculation that the Blues would move to replace Allardyce with a longer-term candidate capable of rebuilding and reshaping the team over the next few years.

Marco Silva, the man originally targeted to succeed Koeman in the autumn of 2017 before Watford refused to let him go, remained the subject of newspaper chatter, as did his compatriot Paulo Fonseca, whom Everton had also approached. Other more up-and-coming managers also cropped up in the various press stories, including the likes of Mikel Arteta and Patrick Vieira.

Former Everton players were weighing in with their opinions too.

Toffees favourite, Tim Cahill had expressed his dismay at the club's loss of identity in recent years. The Australian international became a linchpin of the team built by David Moyes, one that routinely punched above its weight in the Premier League and enjoyed forays into European competition thanks to a renowned team spirit.

Everton and Moyes battled for years on a shoestring budget while Bill Kenwright continued his stated search for a billionaire to transform the club's fortunes and to enable them to compete with the increasing riches in the old top four.

Farhad Moshiri's enormous spending had not yet propelled the club back among the top flight's elite, and the chaos that had unfolded at Goodison Park, with the sacking of Koeman and the controversial appointment of Allardyce had left Everton looking unrecognisable from Cahill's time with the Toffees.

"It's confusing. They are confused too," Cahill said on *Goals On Sunday*. "They have lost their identity as a club. There is nothing they are really building around.

"Before, there was a basis and a group of players that was built and we were adding to it and looking for the long-term plan of how to evolve as a football club.

"Now it seems like they are just making signings and the chemistry is not there, and on the pitch they are not linking well.

"It's difficult to watch because of the quality. You have to be careful what you wish for. If you want an owner with lots of money, they have that, but it doesn't always bring success overnight.

"The fans want some passion and identity. When you look back at Roberto Martinez, for example, maybe it was impatient and waiting for that style, and under David Moyes maybe they thought it was getting stale, but now you can appreciate what they have lost."

Interviewed on *Sky Sports,* former Blues forward, Kevin Campbell predicted Sam Allardyce would never gain the full support of Everton fans.

"I think Sam Allardyce has done the job he's meant to do by coming in and solidifying the club," Campbell said. "But taking it forward, I don't think the fans really take to him. I don't think they ever will and I think there's going to be a change in the summer because Everton are a year behind in their game plan.

"They really need to get somebody in there, get the plan in place and get that recruitment drive going. It might take some drastic measures to rip things up, but if that's what has to happen, that has to happen."

***

13 May 2018: West Ham v Everton

Sitting in a reasonably comfortable ninth position, after the win at Stoke, Everton lost their next home game to Manchester City, and then ground out a 0-0 against Liverpool, also at Goodison Park. Two more draws, this time at Swansea and Southampton bookended wins over Newcastle and Huddersfield which left the Blues sitting in eighth place heading into the final match of the 2017/18 at West Ham's London Stadium.

Before this match, David Moyes' reunions with the club where he spent 11 reputation-building years had been exercises in defeat. Beaten home and away as manager of Manchester United four seasons prior, the Scot had the same treatment meted out to him as manager of Sunderland in 2016/17 season and received his heaviest defeat against

Everton in November 2017 when the Blues romped to a 4-0 win under David Unsworth.

Add to that the fact that in the Premier League era, West Ham were Everton's favourite opponents; throw in a meaningless end-of-season game and you had the ingredients for an occasion where even Sam Allardyce could throw caution to the wind and go for it a bit.

The much-maligned manager did finally experiment with two strikers, although their lack of experience playing together, coupled with West Ham's first-half dominance and Everton's crippling lack of creativity meant that they weren't able to link up like a genuine strike partnership at any stage. Allardyce largely nullified any nod towards attacking adventure by deploying three centre-halves and two holding midfielders. And, if the intent was to release Leighton Baines and Seamus Coleman to conduct raids down the flanks, it didn't work.

The result was a performance that mostly made the Hammers, who began the day in 15th place, look a significantly better team than their record and recently-averted crisis suggested they were and, eventually, resulted in a defeat that may have seemed harsh when comparing chances created but which was wholly deserved on the balance of play.

Indeed, in the first period in particular, all the "joined up" football was coming from the home team, with the visitors reliant on direct balls forward and attempted penetrating passes from deep. West Ham were next to bottom when Allardyce came on board at Goodison and while he had spent the previous few months moaning that his team couldn't play with style because of the players at his disposal, Moyes simply got on with the job of getting his side playing some pretty decent football.

The Hammers were moving the ball around crisply in midfield, but after Oumar Niasse robbed Angelo Ogbonna and was denied by Adrian in the hosts' goal, Mario Lanzini capitalised on embarrassing defending by Everton to give West Ham the lead. An innocuous-looking pass from Cheikhou Kouyaté deceived Keane as it eluded the toe of Arnautovic, and Lanzini, who had started the move near the halfway line, continued his run between two blue shirts to pick up the loose ball and slot it home.

Allardyce responded at half time by withdrawing Ramiro Funes Mori, who had done nothing to suggest he has been hard done-by being excluded from the starting XI since he regained his fitness, and introducing Davy Klaassen into a midfield that now boasted four central midfielders and no width.

It resulted in more possession for Everton but precious little service to the strikers or threats to the Hammers' goal, apart from a tame effort from Klaassen from around 20 yards out, that Adrian claimed easily. Instead of taking one midfielder off and going for a more attacking formation, Allardyce stuck to type, and hooked Cenk Tosun when it came time to throw Theo Walcott on, much to the Turk's visible disgust.

Blues fans probably matched his fury; as a decision, it made no sense under the circumstances. Two minutes later, it was 2-0 from a goal largely out of nothing. Picking up a pass in a benign area outside the Everton box, Arnautovic simply rolled Keane, who was too tight and too slow to recover and smashed a shot practically through Pickford's gloves from 25 yards. The replays weren't kind to the young goalkeeper who appeared to crouch, expecting the ball to dip towards the ground before it lifted slightly at the end, and flew past him.

Niasse gave Everton hope 11 minutes later, showing some deft control and an emphatic finish to make it 2-1 from a corner, but Moyes' men restored their two-goal advantage and effectively sealed the game eight minutes later.

Lanzini was the marksman again, profiting from the yard or two's space afforded him by Seamus Coleman at the corner of the area and curling a shot towards the top right corner. Pickford went for it with his opposite hand and got fingers to it, but could only guide it onto the post and in.

It had been a disappointing end to a poor season.

Final score: West Ham 3-1 Everton

***

In fact, it had been an awful season, forgettable in almost every way except for the stain it would leave on the Blues' Premier League era.

The threat of the drop, if it existed with 24 matches left in the campaign, was largely extinguished fairly soon after Allardyce arrived. It was hard to believe there had been 12 teams worse than Everton, the paucity of quality in the top-flight rendering a finish as high as eighth flattering in the extreme.

The interim had seen a frustrating succession of dull performances, moribund football, lifeless defeats to the teams that finished above them, and a near constant yearning for 2017/18 to be over.

Now that the season was done, supporters hoped the club's hierarchy would make their key decisions – starting with the removal of the manager – that would ensure that the next season would be nothing like what had just transpired. As a fanbase, patience was being replaced by apathy, but it was not irretrievable. Another big summer was on the cards, but only if those in the corridors of power were ready to take the bull by the horns and steer it in the right direction.

2018: Sam Allardyce sacked

> "Criticised for negative tactics, a lack of attacking adventure, a chronic shortage of goals, and some heavy defeats to teams in the top six, Allardyce had failed to win over Blues fans

2018 Sam Allardyce sacked

Just 24 hours after the final fixture of the 2017/18 season against West Ham, Sam Allardyce's tenure as Everton manager was over, amid reports the club would relieve him of his duties within the next 48 hours.

The Dudleyite met with major shareholder Farhad Moshiri, when he was, as expected, told they would not keep him beyond the end of the current season.

Allardyce had guided Everton into the top half of the table and to within six points of Champions League-chasing Tottenham by mid-December, but could not sustain a consistent run of form to mount a challenge for Europe. The Toffees eventually clung on to eighth place despite losing that season finale to the Hammers.

Criticised for negative tactics, a lack of attacking adventure, a chronic shortage of goals, and some heavy defeats to teams in the top six, Allardyce had failed to win over Blues fans, and was the subject of increasingly vocal chants from the stands calling for his dismissal over the final weeks of the season. That, combined with a desire on Moshiri's part to kick start his stalled project with a fresh appointment, had led to the decision to cut ties.

Marco Silva remained the favourite to take the Everton managerial reins, although media reports suggested that his appointment would not be entirely straightforward, with the Portuguese still in a legal dispute with Watford over £750,000, he felt they owed him because of his premature dismissal from the Hertfordshire club in January.

It was also thought the Hornets Board could still pursue legal action against Everton, if they hired Silva, for what they deemed an illegal approach for him last November; that despite reports that the Blues had offered Watford upwards of £10 million to part with him.

With three managerial sackings under his belt in two seasons, the focus was once again on Farhad Moshiri. What would he do next, and would his next managerial appointment get the Blues back on track? But before that decision would be made, other senior changes were afoot.

2018: Brands in. Walsh out

> "Marcel's record of achievement has cemented his reputation across Europe and I am extremely pleased that we will be bringing his drive, energy and expertise to Everton.
>
> \- Farhad Moshiri

2018 Brands in. Walsh out

One day after Sam Allardyce departed, Everton confirmed Marcel Brands as the club's new director of football from PSV Eindhoven.

The 56-year-old Dutchman signed a three-year contract after turning down improved terms in Eindhoven in favour a fresh challenge on Merseyside.

Brands, who had formed a vital part of the team management setup at PSV that had overseen three Eredvisie titles in the previous four years, replaced Steve Walsh, who would leave the club after nearly two years rather than accept a chief scout role.

It represented a successful pursuit of the Dutchman by Farhad Moshiri, who first identified Brands as a target when he was looking to appoint Everton's first director of football two years earlier.

"At that moment I had already given my word to PSV, and I did not want to leave," Brands said of the Toffees' first approach in 2016. This time, having helped deliver another Dutch title for PSV, he felt the time was right.

"The Premier League is, of course, a great thing," Brands said on PSV's official website. "It is the biggest competition in the world in all respects. I now get the chance to do something in my own way. I am really looking forward to that."

Moshiri welcomed Brands to Everton on the club's official website, and expressed his pleasure at having landed a long-time target:

> "Marcel's record of achievement has cemented his reputation across Europe, and I am extremely pleased that we will be bringing his drive, energy and expertise to Everton. It was clear to me in our conversations that he shares in the vision we have for the club and he has much to contribute in making us better and more equipped to challenge the top teams in the Premier League."

Born in 's-Hertogenbosch in the Netherlands, Brands had an unremarkable career as a player, spending the bulk of it at RKC Waalwijk while also spending two seasons with Feyenoord.

It was as a sporting and technical director that he really made his name in Dutch football, however, first at Waalwijk and then at AZ

Alkmaar, where he worked under future Holland and Manchester United boss, Louis van Gaal.

In five years there, he helped transform the fortunes of the club as AZ won the Eredivisie in 2009, breaking the dominance of the traditional "big three" of Ajax, PSV and Feyenoord, and reaching the last eight of the Europa League.

He joined PSV as their technical director in 2010 and had developed what observers describe as an immense reputation for spotting playing talent and working the transfer market.

"It is a privilege to be joining Everton as Director of Football and I am incredibly excited to take on this challenge," Brands said on evertonfc.com. This is a great club — footballing royalty – with the best, most committed fans, and I can assure every single Evertonian that I am completely committed to driving our club forward and making the most of the opportunities that we have.

"I know what the priorities are and I'm determined that we make progress in these areas. It's also important to me that we make our progress in the right way – in the 'Everton way' – and this includes listening, consulting and collaborating on all important club matters.

"The fantastic passion of the fans for their club, the magnificent history of the club over the years and the ambition and purpose we have as people tasked with driving the blub forward all mean that we need to be competing for honours against the Premier League elite.

"It is no straightforward challenge, but this must be our motivation each and every day.

"It is only a challenge such as this which could have persuaded me to leave PSV where I am indebted to the many people whose collective effort led to some great achievements.

"Now we will look to build something really strong and lasting here at Everton."

It was also announced that Steve Walsh had stepped down as Director of Football after almost two years in the post

After first being approached by Everton two summers previously, when Walsh was eventually brought on board to become the Blues' first DoF, Brands replaced the former Leicester City scout to embark on what could become a career-defining project if he succeeds.

Incoming CEO, Professor Denise Barrett-Baxendale, said in a statement on the club's official website:

"I'm very much looking forward to working closely with Marcel, whose experience in the areas of player recruitment and development pathways for young players has forged an outstanding reputation in European football. I know that Marcel will bring an unsurpassed level of quality and prowess to his work at Everton.

"Chief among my priorities, is to structure and resource our club to enable us to fully achieve our ambitions. We will work alongside Marcel on the recruitment of a new manager, which is now our biggest focus."

"On behalf of the Board and Mr Moshiri, I'd like to express our thanks to Steve Walsh, our first ever Director of Football, who has now left the club. We all wish Steve well for his future."

***

Winding the clock forward to January 2019, Marcel Brands was appointed to Everton's Board of Directors and handed broader powers covering all aspects of the playing side at the club.

Everton's newest Board member spoke on stage at the club's Annual General Meeting at the Philharmonic Hall in Liverpool on 8 January with Master of Ceremonies Darren Griffiths, where he described how the club has exceeded his expectations so far.

"I hope to do the best things for our football club," Brands said. "To be honest, the club is more than I expected. I was working in a great club in Holland and was happy there, but I had a very good feeling about Everton from the start and that became even better when I started here. So many people have blue blood here."

Brands' promotion was one of several issues touched on during the meeting and, naturally, the executives discussed the proposed new stadium at Bramley-Moore Dock.

"Everton is transitioning through one of the most important periods in the club's history," CEO Professor Denise Barrett-Baxendale stated.

"I am aware of our long and complicated history in delivering a new stadium. We have several funding opportunities available [for the project]."

The club's recently-appointed deputy chairman, Keith Harris, talked further about what he described as a "real cracking opportunity" for Everton, saying that the goal was to build "a stadium everyone can be proud of" and "recreate the history and rich traditions" of Goodison Park.

"We are having very advanced discussions now with financial institutions which are encouraging. The money will be available. The money will be available for us to do this. Most of our raw materials will be imported.

"We cannot promise an end date because we haven't broken ground. We are hoping to put a spade in the ground next year and it would be wonderful to do it in two years, but we certainly should do it in three and it will be a wonderful stadium."

Meanwhile, Director of Finance, Sasha Ryzantsev, said that the majority shareholder, Farhad Moshiri, had committed to contribute "some equity" towards the projected £500 million cost of Bramley-Moore Dock.

Moshiri himself spoke of the stadium proposal:

> "The delivery of a new stadium, quite frankly, has nothing to do with my vision. It is a necessity. We have been given a great site which is extremely expensive. It has cost £100 million more for ground preparation, but we have to get on with it. It's a little like Mastermind — we've started, so we have to finish — and I have people I trust to execute it. I have spent £250 million to turn a museum into a competitive outfit. Throwing money at it is not the answer. You have to get it right. We always want to be top of the table. We want to be consistent, we want to do well, and we need to play a style of football which fills a 52,000 stadium."

It would not be long before details of that new stadium would begin to emerge.

2018: Dan Meis preaches to the faithful

> During the Q&A at the first of the workshops, Dan Meis was also asked what he had been told by the club concerning funding for the new stadium. Richard Kenyon, then the club's Marketing Director interjected. He said, "I can assure you that funding will be no problem."

2018 Dan Meis preaches to the faithful

In April 2018, the club, together with the new stadium's appointed architect, Dan Meis, began the next phase of supporter engagement over the proposed ground at Bramley-Moore Dock with workshops at St Luke's Church, next to Goodison Park.

With Everton having solicited feedback from fans through a survey based on 11 Key Principles that would guide the move away from Goodison, Meis was meeting with fans at the site of the Blues' current home to gather further ideas and present initial concepts.

The first images of those concepts had been surfacing on social media and they featured components that had been prominent in the minds of many Evertonians when thinking about the new development, including proximity of the stands to the pitch, a large, imposing home end and the possibility of a safe-standing section.

The conversation around capacity has also been a prominent one over the preceding weeks, ever since CEO Robert Elstone's remarks at a Liverpool business meeting in which he had intimated that the capacity at Bramley-Moore Dock would not represent a massive jump from Goodison's ~40,000.

Meis himself has also hinted that the maximum attendance at the new ground would be guided by the need for intimacy and to create an intimidating venue, and he backed that up again at St. Luke's. Meis remarked that while 99% of Evertonians wanted a 50,000-plus capacity, he was cautious of going as high as 60,000, the number favoured by most Blues.

According to the *Liverpool Echo*'s Chris Beesley, Meis said that he believed in scarcity of seats and the importance of selling out a venue. He said that the last 10,000 seats in a stadium are the most expensive and bring in the least revenue."

During the Q&A at the first of the workshops, Dan Meis was also asked by a supporter, Steve Dickinson, what he had been told by the club concerning funding for the new stadium. Richard Kenyon, then the club's Marketing Director and emcee for the workshop interjected. He said, "I can assure you that funding will be no problem."

***

Elsewhere, Liverpool Mayor Joe Anderson had revealed an alternative funding scenario for Everton's proposed stadium at Bramley-Moore Dock, whereby Liverpool City Council could build the ground and lease it back to the club.

Both Everton and LCC were discussing ways in which the club could raise the estimated £500 million cost of the stadium on the banks of the Mersey, with the leading proposal being for the City take out a £280 million loan at ultra-low interest rates that is then repaid by the club over 25 years.

Under that scheme, the ground and the club would act as security with the Council netting £7 million a year in interest payments it otherwise wouldn't receive if the Blues went entirely their own way. Everton would still need to raise the remaining £220 million privately.

Under the Mayor's alternate proposal, he told Liverpool Business News that LCC could fund the new stadium entirely if the club could not raise their share of the cost via private investment.

"There is an open door to the possibility. It is not ruled out," said Mayor Anderson.

"Everton want to own their own stadium and they are still confident they can raise the money that would allow them to do that."

Anderson explained that, "there would have to be a completely different securitisation package to go along with that," under the terms of this different arrangement and it could mean less leverage for Everton where the design, capacity, use and revenue from the Bramley-Moore Dock stadium are concerned.

The original proposal had its share of critics, with some opponents fearful of risk to city taxpayers, even though the terms of the project would put all the risk on Everton. This Plan B option would involve significantly more capital and risk on LCC's side.

Anderson gave assurances of full transparency in the process and confirmed a vote of the full council would be taken before any agreement was signed.

***

On 25 July 2018, Everton Shareholders' Association chairman John Blain had a second informal chat with Everton's major shareholder and Bill Kenwright.

As well as reaffirming his commitment to the Director of Football model at Everton and a focus on youth to bring the average age of the Blues' squad down, a key takeaway was the proposed new stadium at Bramley-Moore Dock which Moshiri still said would open in 2022. The funding model for the project was still not completed, a delay which had already contributed to the targeted date slipping by a year, and it was Blain's assessment that Moshiri envisioned the capacity of the new ground being between 52,000 and 55,000, lower than the target capacity of 60,000 favoured by most supporters (not to mention John himself), if the polls on social media were correct.

2018: Silva will be a very good manager: Brands

> “[Marco Silva’s] vision in football, the way he is thinking about football, is what we want. He wants to structure a team, and he has proved already with a few clubs with good results, so I believe strongly in him.
>
> - Marcel Brands

2018 Silva will be a very good manager: Brands

It would take until 31 May 2018 before the club announced Marco Silva as Everton’s new manager, following weeks of speculation suggesting he would become the long-term successor to Ronald Koeman.

The 40-year-old signed a three-year contract with the Blues, seven months after they first tried to lure him away from Watford and four months after the Hornets had eventually fired him for a sequence of poor results.

Silva's arrival came two-and-half weeks after the club had sacked Sam Allardyce.

"I'm really proud to be the new Everton manager," Silva told evertontv. "I'm excited and I'm really happy to take this big challenge for us as a club and for me as a manager.

"I want to express my thanks to Farhad, to the chairman, to the Board of Directors and to Marcel as well, for the confidence in my work. I know the huge history of Everton as a club and what the fans expect. I'm sure with everybody working together, I will be ready for this challenge.

"We have a lot of work to do in this next month and it is important to prepare everything in the right way. But there will be even more important work to do from the start of pre-season into the first Premier League match of next season.

"I know what our fans expect - they expect results but not only results. I want our fans to be proud when they see our team on the pitch. I want them to feel that we are committed, that we are working hard and enjoying our football because that is important as well.

"We want to build a great connection between the squad and the fans, and I'm sure that with our attitude and demands of commitment, then our style of play will see that, I believe."

The acquisition of the Portuguese was the latest in a succession of changes at boardroom and team-management level following a hugely disappointing 2017/18 season.

Marcel Brands, who had arrived as the club's new Director of Football in place of Steve Walsh on 16 May, said: "His vision in football, the way he is thinking about football, is what we want. He wants to structure a team, and he has proved already with a few clubs with good results, so I believe strongly in him. He's an open guy who wants to work together with good staff and in an environment at Finch Farm, which is conducive to building something strong."

Silva brought with him a reputation for improving every team he had managed, his last few weeks at Vicarage Road notwithstanding. After attracting attention for his exploits as a young coach on the Continent, he had gained experience of managing in the Premier League from two short stints at Hull City and Watford

Between the time he hung up his playing boots in 2011 to take up the managerial reins at Estoril Praia and his departure from Olympiakos in 2016, Marco Silva had emerged as one of the fastest-rising young managers in the European game.

Originally hired in a director of football role by Estoril, he quickly shifted to the position of manager with the small Portuguese club 10th in that country's second tier. With a run of just three defeats in the remaining 24 matches of the campaign, Estoril won the division as champions under Silva and gained promotion to the Primera Liga.

The following season, Silva steered Estoril to fifth place and qualification for the Europa League for the first time in their history and eventually left the club in 2014, having gone one better with a fourth-place finish and attracted the attention of domestic giants Sporting.

Silva spent just one season at Estádio José Alvalade where he guided the Lions to third place before being dismissed just days after landing the Taca de Portugal, their first piece of silverware in seven years, apparently because he refused to wear an official club suit in an earlier round of the competition.

He joined Olympiakos that summer to replace his compatriot Vítor Pereira where, again, he would only spend a year, but not without notching some more impressive achievements. He led the Greek club to the title by a league record 30 point margin winning 28 of their 30 league games, which included a 17-match winning streak, another record.

Silva was the surprise choice to whom Hull turned in January 2017, when they needed a miracle to escape relegation from the Premier League. The Tigers were rock bottom with just 13 points from 20 games when he arrived, far away from safety. They ended the season with 34 points, eventually falling short of what would have been an incredible escape from relegation, while also reaching the League Cup semi-final. The young Portuguese had, however, done enough to convince Watford to make him their latest manager that May after he had stepped down at the KCOM Stadium.

With a quarter of the 2017/18 campaign complete in October, Watford were sixth in the table and looking capable of finishing in the top seven and, perhaps, claiming the final European berth that Burnley eventually did.

However, the Hornets' hierarchy blamed the collapse in Watford's form in the ensuing weeks on Everton's overt approach for Silva following Koeman's sacking. Just one win in 11 matches was enough for the Hertfordshire club to dismiss him after 24 league games and lodge a formal complaint with the Premier League accusing the Blues of "tapping" their former manager up.

Mentioned in connection with recent vacancies at Southampton, Stoke City and West Ham, Silva reportedly turned down overtures from China and Continental Europe in order to become the 10th full-time Everton manager since 1992.

His staff at Finch Farm would include Duncan Ferguson, who was first promoted to first-team coaching duties under David Moyes, and Ryland Morgans, who would continue as Performance Director.

Silva named João Pedro as his assistant manager, Hugo Olivera as his goalkeeping coach, Antonis Lemonakis as his technical scout and Pedro Conceição as the fitness coach.

With a new Technical Director and a new Manager in place, expectations were high that the team would receive some much needed reinforcements during the summer transfer window.

2018: ROONEY OUT. RICHARLISON IN

> We have to look for a squad Marco can work with, and I think there always has to be a space for young players to come into the first team.
>
> -Marcel Brands

2018 Rooney out. Richarlison in

Only days after Marco Silva's appointment, Marcel Brands warned that Everton would need to trim its bloated squad of surplus players and wages before he and Marco Silva could make the targeted signings they believed would improve the team.

The Blues' new Director of Football and the new manager underwent an analysis of the playing personnel they had inherited from Ronald Koeman, Sam Allardyce and Steve Walsh, with Brands admitting that some difficult- but necessary – conversations would have to take place with certain players.

At issue was a senior squad boasting around 38 players, and some hugely inflated transfer fees and wages which were paid and offered to the preceding year's recruits in order to get them through the door.

When asked whether there would be a repeat of last summer's open chequebook, Brands was frank in his assessment, whilst also admitting that it was going to be hard to offload some players because few clubs could match their current salaries.

"No," he said in *The Guardian*. "First, we need to offload players to raise money [for transfers], and also salary-wise. But it's not only a money thing. Of course, money is important but also, for a coach, it is not workable to start with 38 players in your squad.

"We have to look for a squad Marco can work with and I think there always has to be space for young players to come to the first team.

"That has to be, let's say, 25-30 players. Now there are 38 and a lot are not young anymore. They are players who have arrived.

"We have to be honest when we take the decision with these players. Do they have prospects here at Everton? Some of the conversations will not be nice, but I think Marco must start with a squad that everyone is eager to play for and has prospects to play."

Wayne Rooney was predicted to be first out the door, as his slow-moving negotiations over a switch to DC United were nearing conclusion. According to other reports, Morgan Schneiderlin and Davy Klaassen were two more players signed by Ronald Koeman on wages north of £100,000 a week who could have followed him.

Schneiderlin seemed keen on finding a new club, with speculation linking him with a return to France. Sandro Ramirez, who had arrived for just over £5 million but was also on a big salary, had stressed he had no desire to play for Everton again after securing a loan move to Sevilla in January.

Klaassen, meanwhile, had publicly stated his desire to stay at Goodison Park to fight for his place but was reportedly being eyed by Besiktas, initially on loan. According to *The Mirror,* Yannick Bolasie was the subject of interest from at least one Premier League club.

"If you make a new signing," Brands continued, "with the salaries in England and the player is not successful, then what do you do? In most countries, players cannot make the wages they get in the Premier League, so a lot of players who don't play here cannot play anywhere, because the salaries are not comparable.

"Hopefully, I will succeed in offloading the right players. They are good players, so I hope there will be interest for a few of our players."

***

The first manifestation of the changes Brands had intimated was Wayne Rooney's move to DC United, with confirmation he would officially sign for the Major League Soccer club coming on 10th July 2018.

According to the Washington Post, the 32-year-old had agreed a 2½-year contract, with an option for a third year, and a $13 million (£10 million) compensation deal that would seal his departure from Everton for the second time in his career.

Rooney, who left Goodison Park as an 18-year-old star-in-the-making in 2004 before returning in the summer of 2017 on a 2-year deal, was keen to see out the final year of his current terms with the Blues, but was informed that he was not part of the club's plans.

Everton would ease their wage bill to the tune of £8m for the coming season with Rooney's transfer.

Rooney could not play for DC United until after the MLS transfer window opened, which meant that the first match for which he would be eligible was his new team's home game on 14th July, which also marked the opening of Audi Field.

When asked about his feelings on leaving Everton for a second time, Rooney said, "It's football. Everton is the team I grew up supporting and I was grateful for the chance to go back there last summer. But in football you never know what's round the corner. I've made the decision to come here and I'm sure there are a lot of questions on why I left Everton and the people who want to know can ask Everton Football Club and let them answer it. But I've made the decision to come here and, as I keep saying, I'm excited and I'm just looking forward now to the first game."

***

On American Independence Day, Everton's new management team reportedly travelled to London to discuss transfer strategy with Bill Kenwright.

According to the *Liverpool Echo*, Marcel Brands and Marco Silva made the trip to the Capital for a first summit with the club's chairman, showing the duo were preparing to make their first signings.

To that point, three first-team players had left what Brands had admitted was an overly large squad — Wayne Rooney and Ramiro

Funes Mori were both sold, while Joel Robles was released after his contract expired. They would be followed by Davy Klaassen whose hugely unsuccessful stint in England came to an end when he joined Werder Bremen for half the fee Everton had paid for him 12 months earlier. Yet, while there had been plenty of links to potential targets, Blues fans were still awaiting the first acquisition of the summer.

Silva and Brands had hoped to start the new season with a group of just 25 players, having trimmed the wage bill from the previous year, and they set about making targeted additions aimed at bringing down the average age of the squad and ensuring that the bulk of Everton's incoming signings would have a resale value should they need to be moved on before their contracts expired.

***

The marquee acquisition of that summer would be Richarlison who arrived in July on a five-year contract, in a deal worth a reported £40 million. It was a big price tag around his neck but he was a player with enormous potential.

The move represented a reunion with new Toffees' boss, Marco Silva, who had signed Richarlison from Fluminese for a little over £11 million the year before, persuading him to join the Hornets rather than Dutch giants Ajax.

The then 20-year-old had starred for his country at the U20 World Cup, and showed his star quality with five goals in his first 12 games for Watford as they ascended to the top six early in 2017/18.

He had begun his career in his native Brazil with América Mineiro from Belo Horizonte, where he scored nine times in 24 games in

2015/16. Fluminese bought him for the following season, and he struck another nine goals in 42 appearances before Watford came calling.

"I want to have a lot of success with Everton," he told evertonfc.com after they announced his arrival. "I think it is going to be important for me here to be with Marco Silva again. I will learn more because I am still learning as a player and I aim to develop and grow here.

"Everton have put their faith in me and I intend to honour this shirt and demonstrate on the pitch why I came here.

"I want my dreams to become a reality here at one of the biggest clubs in England."

***

The signing of Richarlison was followed by that of Lucas Digne, whose move from Barcelona to Everton was announced on 1 August, when he signed a five-year deal with the club. A fee, reported to be worth around £18 million, was negotiated with the Spanish club, and the 25-year-old used the time to mull over a decision between regular football at Everton and the prospect of playing second string at the Nou Camp.

Digne ultimately opted for the fresh challenge on offer in England where he would provide long overdue competition for Leighton Baines, before eventually replacing the Goodison favourite at left back.

***

The rest of Everton's transfer business, of what proved to be a busy summer, culminated on Transfer Deadline Day of 9th August 2018 when four more key additions were made to Silva's squad.

With all incoming deals needing to be done by 5pm that day, time was running out to plug the few holes in the team that still needed to be addressed.

The Blues started the proceedings by unveiling Bernard, their third major signing of the summer, who was acquired as a free agent from Shaktar Donetsk.

There was high confidence that Yerry Mina would complete a £28 million switch from Barcelona and despite late reported interest from Manchester United and Lyon, Everton won the race for his signature.

He was joined by Andre Gomes, another Barcelona player deemed surplus to requirements at the Nou Camp, who was signed on a season-long loan. That just left a late scramble to land Kurt Zouma from Chelsea, also on loan. A deal sheet for the central defender was submitted to the Premier League just before the deadline which gave Everton's staff two hours to complete the deal, which they did successfully to conclude the summer's business.

2018: RICHARLISON BRACE GETS THE NEW CAMPAIGN UNDERWAY

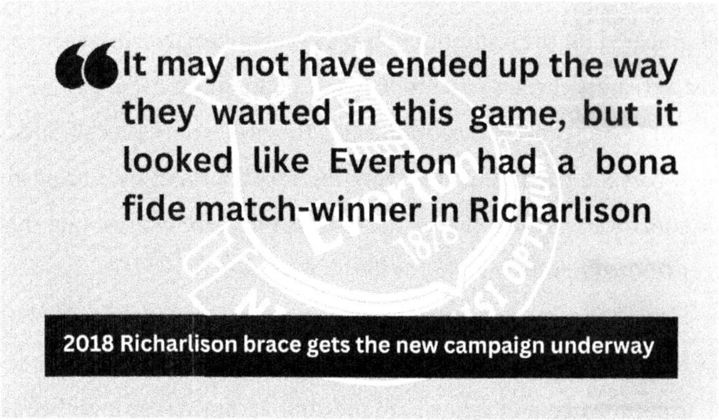

Several watchwords had characterised the following of Everton since the surprising 2013/14 season under Roberto Martinez and one of them was *frustration*. It was the overriding feeling again as the Toffees kicked off their first campaign under Marco Silva against Wolves at Molineux.

***

11 August 2018: Wolves v Everton

The Blues were 10 minutes from a first opening-day win away from home in 17 years and, had they been able to hold on to the lead handed back to them by a moment of brilliance by new signing Richarlison, it would have felt like a huge victory in several ways.

After all, it was only a few short months ago that largely the same XI was labouring under Sam Allardyce's limited stewardship, struggling to register shots on target, let alone win games with any regularity. It was only a week since a similar starting XI had looked worryingly ill-prepared for the resumption of the Premier League when they had lost a friendly curtain-raiser to Valencia at Goodison Park.

But having proven categorically that they were ready after all, Silva's men had the rug pulled out from underneath them by a moment of controversy at the end of the first half against Wolves, one that contributed significantly to the loss of two points.

Having largely quelled the enthusiasm and momentum that Wolves carried into their first game back in the top flight, amid pyrotechnics that illuminated and echoed around this famous old ground before kick-off, Everton were riding into the half-time interval on the back of a 1-0 lead at the time thanks to Richarlison's first goal for the club since his big-money move from Watford.

The 21-year-old debutant had been in the right place at the right time after 16 minutes when Michael Keane challenged for a corner from the Blues' left, the ball dropped to his feet and he had the simple task of firing home from close range to open the scoring and silence the buoyant home crowd.

Joao Moutinho's rising half-volley midway through the first period was as close as Nuno Espirito Santo's men had come to troubling Jordan Pickford, while Everton had looked composed and good value for their lead.

But then a momentary lapse of concentration... a square pass from Keane squirmed away from Phil Jagielka and towards Diogo Jota arriving on his blind side. Desperately trying to atone for his slip, Jagielka slid through the ball, diverting it forward before catching his opponent's foot and sending him sprawling. "Over the ball" it was not, but his stretch meant that he led with his studs and it was one of those incidents where the tackled player's reaction can have a huge bearing on the referee's course of action. No surprise, then, that as the Wolves player writhed in pain on the turf, referee Craig Pawson went straight to his pocket to pull out the red card.

Wolves added insult to the injury, with an equaliser; one which owed plenty to Ruben Neves surreptitiously moving the ball forward — unseen or unchecked by the officials — five yards into the ideal spot for a curling free kick over the wall. The Portuguese's shot was spot-on; Jordan Pickford's fateful step to his right to peer through his wall less so, meaning he got his fingertips to the ball but couldn't keep it out.

Credit to Everton after half-time, because they could have folded, and under any of Silva's immediate predecessors, they might have done. Kudos also to the manager himself, whose faith in Richarlison was demonstrated by the decision to keep him on the field, although he had picked up a yellow card in the 14th minute.

The Brazilian rewarded that faith midway through the second half. Collecting Tosun's lay-off near the touchline, Richarlison took a few steps into the Wolves box before whipping a bending low shot around the goalkeeper's despairing dive and inside the far corner. It was a strike where the element of surprise in its early despatch was as important as the crispness and accuracy of the finish and it felt like a massive goal for the 10 men in Blue.

They couldn't keep the lead, though. Holgate and the much improved Michael Keane repelled cross after cross at the back, but the numerical disadvantage meant that stopping those deliveries from the wide areas was much more difficult.

With ten minutes remaining, Neves capitalised on the space wide on the left to check back and curl a wicked cross over Keane's jump to Jimenez, who buried his header at the back post to make it 2-2.

It denied Silva a memorable victory in his first game in charge at Everton, but there was plenty to admire about his team and much that gave hope for a strong season ahead if the performance showed what was to come.

Importantly, there was a spirit and fight in the face of adversity that had been absent for so much of the previous season, which hinted at both a unity of purpose in the ranks and the effects that true competition for places can bring.

It may not have ended up that way in this game, but it looked like Everton had a bona fide match-winner in Richarlison. Even better, all four of Silva's deadline-day signings, among them Bernard and Andre Gomes, had yet to make their first appearances. It felt like exciting things were just getting started.

Final score: Wolves 2-2 Everton

***

After the game, Silva was fulsome in his praise of his players' work ethic and commitment.

"I saw a fantastic attitude, fantastic spirit in our squad and good organisation even with 10 players," he said afterwards. "I believe we were better with our organisation, even with the 10.

[After we scored] we didn't give them any chances and [it was] one really harsh decision from the referee. Of course, not only was there a red card but they score a goal as well, so it made a big impact on the match.

"Because we were having a good game, but one decision can impact the match. We felt it was not the right decision and where there are moments where something [like this] happens, we are to work together to help each other, which is what we did in the second half."

***

29 August 2018: Everton v Rotherham

A week after the promising performance at Wolves, the Blues opened their account at Goodison with a 2-1 win against Southampton. Seven days later, they led 2-0 at Bournemouth, before being pegged back to 2-2 by Eddie Howe's side. Twice in away fixtures Everton had led, twice they had had a player sent off in controversial circumstances — this time it was Richarlison given his marching orders for a barely perceptible motion towards Adam Smith's forehead — and twice they had come away with only a point.

Marco Silva's first cup match in charge was against Rotherham United. A crowd of 31,972, the highest attendance for a League Cup second round tie at Goodison Park for 50 years, turned up at Goodison and watched Everton ease into the draw for the Carabao Cup third round after what was a comfortable win over the Championship side.

Everton started in nervy fashion at the back but scored just shy of the half-hour mark to settle the nerves. Sandro Ramirez took on his man and fired the ball across the box. Gylfi Sigurdsson stuck out a leg and diverted it past the 'keeper to make it 1-0.

Rotherham came very close to equalising almost immediately, but the ball ricocheted off Kurt Zouma and bounced wide of Maarten Stekelenburg's goal. It wasn't until an hour had elapsed that the Blues doubled their advantage when Digne swung a cross to the back post where Calvert-Lewin nodded home.

Niasse should have made it three not long afterwards, but he headed Sandro's cross over from six yards out and though Rotherham rallied late in the game and went disturbingly close to making the game interesting, Calvert-Lewin cut back on his right foot and curled a beauty over Price and inside the far post to restore Everton's two-goal advantage.

Final score: Everton 3-1 Rotherham

***

21 October 2018: Everton v Crystal Palace

Progress in the cup at Rotherham's expense was followed by a 1-1 draw against newly-promoted Huddersfield Town draw at Goodison. Then came a home defeat to West Ham, and the customary away loss at Arsenal, resulting in a slide down the table to twelfth position.

The positive vibes felt in August suddenly seemed like a distant memory. A 3-0 home win against Fulham restored some confidence, but could the Blues find some consistency?

Next up was Southampton, in Round 4 of the League Cup at Goodison. The match finished 1-1, a tie decided on penalties. Everton went out after Richarlison skied his spot kick over the bar, and Theo Walcott's effort was saved.

Four days later, Everton were on the road again, recording their first away success under Silva with a 2-1 win at Leicester.

After the international break, it was back to Goodison for another Premier League match. This time, Everton and Silva engineered victory when it appeared a typically obstinate Crystal Palace side would shut them out.

Recent years had seen frustrating encounters against Palace, starting with a crushing 3-2 defeat in Roberto Martinez's first season, that effectively ended the Blues' Champions League hopes. It was the same scoreline the following campaign despite Romelu Lukaku getting the home side off to an early lead, and the following two seasons featured annoying 1-1 draws. A 3-1 win over the Eagles at Goodison Park in 2017/18 had bucked the recent trend.

Another point looked to be on the cards in this match as well until all three of Silva's substitutes weighed in to win it with a thrilling conclusion. Fortune favoured the brave because on an afternoon when little had worked for Bernard, when Theo Walcott had been ineffective, and when Richarlison had often been guilty of over-elaboration or a stubborn refusal to give up the ball, it needed something different to pick the lock to the visitors' defence.

Pleasingly, Ademola Lookman supplied a deft cross for Dominic Calvert-Lewin to steer a header past Wayne Hennessey and Cenk Tosun, forced back to the bench for the last two games, rapped home the killer second goal, all within the space of less than two of the dying minutes.

Blues fans were also toasting Jordan Pickford for that third successive Premier League win. The England international pulled off a brilliant stretching save in the first half to deny Cheikhou Kouyaté, as Everton almost buckled from another set-piece, and then made a superb stop with his trailing foot to prevent Luka Milivojevic from putting Palace ahead from the spot with an hour gone.

The penalty save proved to be the turning point of what was a scrappy and testy affair, punctured incessantly by referee Anthony Taylor's whistle. It was also the moment that ignited a Goodison crowd that was becoming anxiously Everton weren't going to find a way through.

After all, besides Palace's reputation as playing the spoiler at Goodison and the recent stumbles against Huddersfield and West Ham, Everton had a miserable record in Sunday televised matches, and there was the rather curious statistic that the last time they had won one without Tom Davies playing was December 2016... and the 20-year-old midfielder was not in the starting XI for this match.

That was because the manager had handed André Gomes his long-awaited home debut, ten long weeks after he signed on a season-long loan from Barcelona. Finally deemed fit after picking up a hamstring injury on the Spanish club's pre-season tour in America, the Portuguese international had lined up alongside Idrissa Gueye in a partnership that immediately looked like it would be the way forward for Silva that season, if both could stay fit and healthy.

Gomes's Premier League baptism was a hugely encouraging one, as were the performances of Michael Keane, Kurt Zouma and Lucas Digne at the back, as they restricted Palace to few real chances of note from open play.

Three league wins in succession and a move back into the top ten had Silva's side well placed as they prepared for their next game, a trip to Old Trafford. It would be difficult matches like those that would show just how far Everton could conceivably go that season so early in the new manager's tenure. The future looked bright and the future looked blue.

Final score: Everton 2-0 Crystal Palace

***

Afterwards, Silva credited his team for their patience as they eventually prevailed over a typically stubborn Palace.

"Tough game, tough game, like we expected," Silva said. "Like I told my players, always when Crystal Palace come here to play, it's always a tough game for us.

"[To make Goodison a difficult place for teams to play] is what we want. The Premier League is really hard. Opposition teams respect our team, they come here to wait, to keep good defensive organisation and we have to find the solution to play faster in some moments.

"But we are creating and today our team had the patience and moments to not lose our balance too easily. Our fans, they were fantastic because they didn't lose patience as well; they kept supporting our team the whole time and in the end everybody is happy because we played together, us and our fans."

2018: Ryazantsev: 'We learn from others'

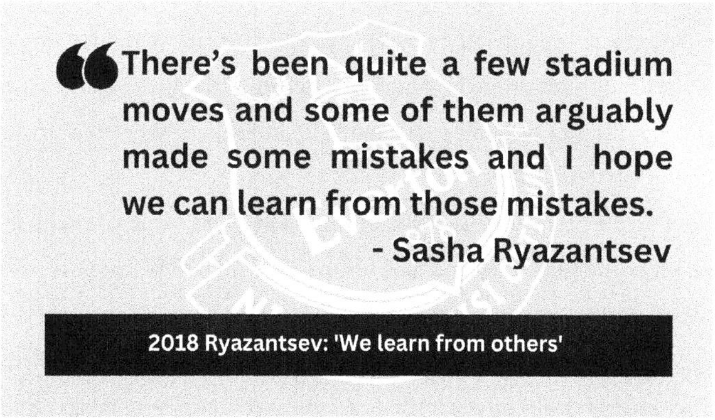

While Everton were beginning life under a new manager in the Autumn of 2018, off the pitch planning for the new stadium at Bramley-Moore Dock was continuing apace. In October, the Toffees' Director of Finance said the club would use the experiences of rival clubs as learning opportunities.

Speaking at the Leaders Sports Business Summit at Chelsea's Stamford Bridge, Sasha Ryazantsev said that while the decision to leave the Blues' current home at Goodison Park was a hard one, avoiding some mistakes made during the planning and construction of other stadiums would make their transition to the banks of the Mersey that much smoother.

Ryazantsev, who joined the club with Farhad Moshiri in 2016, as the owner's presence in the Boardroom, didn't mention any specific examples in the quotes attributed to him, but the delays and cost over-runs of Tottenham Hotspur's new stadium served as the most obvious instance.

West Ham's move to the London Stadium, meanwhile, had been fraught with complaints over policing and a lack of atmosphere in the wide expanses of a former athletics venue.

Ryazantsev said that if Everton could get their move right, it could be the catalyst for propelling the club back into the elite of the English game, while also providing enormous financial benefits to the city of Liverpool.

"There's been quite a few stadium moves and some of them arguably made some mistakes and I hope we can learn from those mistakes," Ryazantsev said.

"Sometimes it's good to be a trailblazer, but when you're not first, you can learn from others' mistakes. It is a very long-term project and it will take several years before we move.

"We see it as an opportunity to close the gap on the top six and the stadium itself will create a huge amount of new life.

"It will breathe new life into the team, create new jobs in the area and be worth one billion pounds of economic value to the city."

The proposed new ground at Bramley-Moore Dock still had a target completion date of 2022 but the financing of the project had yet to be finalised, leaving the planning application, final capacity and design up in the air.

It was a message Ryazantsev repeated in June 2019, two weeks after the opening of the Tottenham Hotspur stadium. He said that Everton's proposed move to Bramley-Moore Dock was vital to the club's future. He also commented that Spurs had shown how it was possible to remain competitive while still funding such a large-scale project.

Speaking to fcbusiness magazine, Ryzantsev explained that the new ground would give Everton a leg up in terms of commercial performance, with increased matchday revenue and wider sponsorship possibilities. He reiterated that the club's hierarchy envisaged that the build would take three years from the time the planning application was approved and the first spade plunged into the ground at the historic north docks site.

"We see the new stadium as an opportunity to further move the club towards the Premier League elite again," Ryazantsev said. "We will have more capacity and more concourse space, enabling us to offer a better fan experience.

"We also hope to attract better partnership deals and earn more broadcasting revenue with an iconic setting for our stadium on the Liverpool waterfront.

"And the one thing that we very much hope to bring from Goodison is the atmosphere of our amazing fans.

"I think every year in the Premier League is a challenge for all of us, whether it is a new stadium, competing for the title, European places or if you're in a relegation battle. It is a very challenging league.

"I would almost rephrase it: would it be challenging for us not to move to a new stadium over the next decade? I think that it would be a much bigger challenge.

"If you look at the obvious example of a similar project recently," Ryazentsev continued, referencing the Tottenham Hotspur Stadium, "that team has managed to build a new stadium and compete on the pitch.

"We hope we can learn from that in terms of managing the construction process while also performing on the pitch and increasing our commercial growth."

Ryzantsev was asked where Everton were regarding plans for the new stadium and when the club envisage breaking ground.

"We have made steady progress so far," he replied. "We are on track to submit a full planning application for a new stadium before the end of the year.

"In terms of funding, we are in a good place; we have options available to us in both the private and public sector and will carry out due diligence on the best deal for the club.

"I am as keen as every Evertonian to break ground, but we have been clear that this can only happen once we get planning permission and once we do, we estimate it could be a three-year build."

He concluded with the message that the club continued to plan for the team kicking off at Bramley-Moore Dock for the first time in 2023, but everything depended on the planning application and securing the required funding.

2018: Blue Crimbo at Moshiri's Liver Building

2018 Blue Crimbo at Moshiri's Royal Liver Building

The prospect of a gleaming new stadium on the banks of the River Mersey allowed Evertonians to dream of reclaiming a significant share of the local limelight from neighbours Liverpool, and the club's *de facto owner*, Farhad Moshiri, took a step towards that in 2017 when he led a consortium to buy the iconic Liver Building on the city's waterfront.

Together with Luxembourg-based Corestate Capital and a group of international investors, Moshiri bought the grade 1 listed building for £48 million, with the British-Iranian businessman understood to own 49.9%.

With a view of the club's future home a mile and a half to the north at Bramley-Moore Dock, Moshiri moved Everton's operational headquarters to the Liver Building, and the world-famous Liver Birds atop the two towers were lit up in Everton blue for Christmas in 2018, triggering a spectacular firework display above the River Mersey.

They floodlit the iconic statues in blue to launch the Football Club's *Blue Crimbo* campaign and it would remain a fixture of the city's skyline throughout December.

Everton chairman Bill Kenwright and X Factor finalist Anthony Russell pulled the lever that covered the top of the Liver Building in the Club's colours, with hundreds of fireworks immediately shooting skywards to mark the occasion.

First-team stars Yerry Mina and Michael Keane, Director of Football Marcel Brands and former WBC cruiserweight boxing champion Tony Bellew were also on stage, along with Ambassadors Ian Snodin and Graham Stuart, joining 350 invited supporters and guests in attending the high-profile waterfront event.

"We've got a wonderful community programme and we've established Blue Crimbo over the last seven years, but tonight was something for everyone, a feeling of Liverpool, the best place in the world," said Kenwright.

"It's the start of Christmas and, of course, we all want Anthony to do well for us this weekend.

"He's a real Blue, a typical Scouser. He's up against two extraordinary vocal talents but it's called the X Factor and he's got it."

Everton Chief Executive, Denise Barrett-Baxendale said: “It’s been fantastic. Despite the wind and rain, Evertonians have collected outside to come and see the start of our Blue Crimbo campaign.”

It wasn't the last time that the two mythical Liver Birds would be lit up in Everton blue – the club would take the opportunity to do so ahead of Merseyside derby matches in future years – and it was a visible sign that the city's first club was beginning to take back some of its former prominence.

2019: Results show Silva's Blues can't defend set pieces

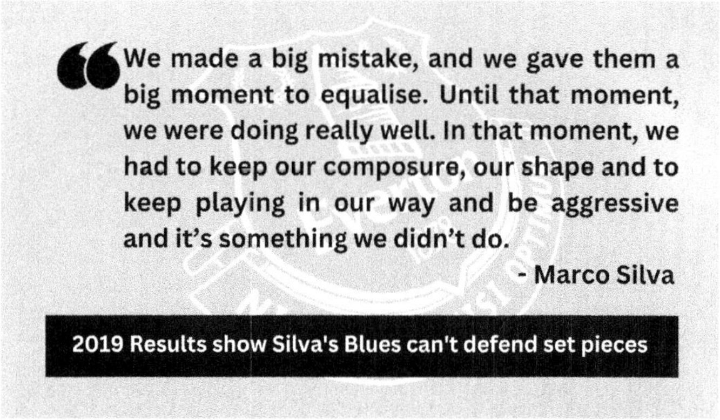

Back on the field, Marco Silva's largely positive start, which had seen his team lose just three of their opening 13 matches in the Premier League between the opening day and late November, had given way to a more difficult patch that would see them slip from sixth place to mid-table.

There had been defeats in away games at Manchester United, Liverpool and Manchester City. However, 'Fortress Goodison' had seen wins against Brighton and Cardiff City, followed by draws against

Newcastle United and Watford. Another stern test would be in store for the Blues when Spurs were the visitors two days before Christmas.

***

23 December 2018: Everton v Tottenham Hotspur

If Everton had shown what they were capable of in their five previous meetings with the top five that season, this latest meeting with Spurs was supposed to be the moment they finally fulfilled that promise, on home turf against a "big six" team.

The attacking adventure they had shown at the Emirates in September, ultimately let down only by poor finishing and the fine form of Petr Cech, defensively robust displays at Stamford Bridge and Anfield in November where chances to score went begging, not to mention some promising spells against Manchester United at Old Trafford in October... it all hinted at what the new Everton, the positive, attack-minded Marco Silva Everton, could produce.

With the backing of the Goodison Park faithful and fuelled by the determination to make up for recent disappointments, the Blues hoped they could finally put together a complete performance. Instead, a veritable nightmare before Christmas unfolded at a stunned Goodison as Spurs meted out a thrashing of unforeseen proportions.

It left in tatters for the time being, any notion that Silva's nascent Everton revolution could keep the top five within reach and capitalise on any continued upheaval at Manchester United. His Everton team was miles away from touching that elite clutch of clubs, and there could have been no doubt about the scale of the task required to bridge that gap.

This was an agonising result, on a weekend where supposedly inferior teams like Crystal Palace and Leicester achieved what Everton couldn't do in recent weeks — namely win away against a top-5 team. It was now 23 games since a Toffees side had recorded a win over England's six richest clubs, and if they played like they did that day against Spurs, it would be a good deal longer before they got another.

Once again, this was a game littered with poor performances up and down the Everton ranks, with only Lucas Digne, Gylfi Sigurdsson and, perhaps, Dominic Calvert-Lewin emerging with any credit. Sigurdsson helped create one goal with Calvert-Lewin, and he scored with a brilliant solo effort of his own. While the young striker, DCL, was hugely unfortunate to have a headed goal disallowed. That, coupled with the episode of Keystone Cops at the other end shortly afterwards, proved pivotal in the contest.

Where the rest were concerned, it was hard to know where to begin. Jordan Pickford added another howler to further tarnish the glowing reputation he took from the World Cup in Russia; Richarlison was anonymous save for two off-target headers; Theo Walcott converted the opening goal with aplomb, but did nothing else for 90 minutes; Tom Davies, André Gomes (before he went off injured) and Morgan Schneiderlin (after he had come on for the Portuguese) cut gallingly vulnerable figures without the injured Idrissa Gueye when they didn't have the ball; and, with a black hole of a midfield in front of them, the rest of the back four simply caved as Spurs romped through them, seemingly at will.

The players' collective display, as bad as anything the Goodison faithful had endured the previous season under three different managers, only told half the story, though. The other component of this collapse was naïve tactics by their manager and a stunning inability or refusal to make any alterations to address a midfield being badly overrun.

Trying to play Spurs at their own game with an attacking bent, a dangerously high defensive line, and an inconsistent high press, they invited one of the most dangerous teams in the country to pick them off with balls over the top or into the channels or simply parted the waters to allow the visitors to stream through.

Harry Kane helped himself to yet another brace. The hugely impressive Hueng-Min Son bagged two of his own and there were crisp first-time strikes from Dele Alli and Christian Eriksen to underline the talent assembled at Tottenham in recent years. They stood as the example that Everton had to follow, but it felt like an awfully long road on days like these.

Final score: Everton 2-6 Spurs

***

Silva admitted that his team had made critical mistakes against Spurs and the humiliating result left Evertonians in familiar doldrums going into Christmas, with the Blues sitting outside the top half of the table with no wins in five games.

"Of course we have to feel really bad," Silva told Sky Sports afterwards. "For sure, we wanted to do something different than the score we achieved.

"We started really well. Of course, we scored first and scored the second goal as well — it's a key moment in the game, in my opinion, when we scored the second goal but the referee saw something there and didn't give the goal to us.

"Afterwards we made a big mistake, and we gave them a big moment to equalise. Until that moment, we were doing really well. In that moment, we had to keep our composure, our shape and to keep playing in our way and be aggressive and it's something we didn't do.

"At this level, when you make mistakes against a team like Tottenham, they can create problems and we lost many, many things after that moment."

***

26 December 2018: Burnley v Everton

Everton responded to the mauling by Tottenham by putting five past Burnley and recording their biggest away win since 1985.

Yerry Mina scored his first Premier League goal to set Marco Silva's men on their way inside two minutes, Lucas Digne added two fine strikes in either half, while Gylfi Sigurdsson scored from the spot, and Richarlison came off the bench to put the icing on the cake in stoppage time.

The four-goal margin might not have shown the general pattern of play — Everton only shaded possession and there were long spells where they were content to sit back a little and see what Burnley could come up with — but you can't argue with a 5-1 victory.

The win moved Everton back into the top eight but, of course, one impressive score-line in isolation would mean very little if it wasn't followed up with a string of positive results over the upcoming seven games before the next meeting with a top-six side.

Win at Brighton in the following game, and follow it up with a victory over Leicester on New Year's Day and Silva could legitimately feel that his side had recovered somewhat from the Spurs debacle, to embark on a long road to Wembley in the FA Cup and remount a challenge for that sixth place that Manchester United currently occupy.

Final score: Burnley 1-5 Everton

***

Afterwards, Silva praised his players for the manner in which they bounced back from the humiliation by Tottenham and thanked the fans for their support.

"We learn every time, not just when we have a bad result," Silva explained. "We had a really tough result in the last game and even today we won the match clear, but we learned as well, for sure. It's part of our process as a team.

"My first words are for our fans and for our players. The fans welcomed our players before the match [which was] fantastic after a really tough result.

"And our players deserved this win and the three points. It was a good win for us. We got three important points for us and now is the time to rest and prepare for the [next match].

"Our last game wasn't a normal one from us, but we are here to fight, to compete, and to show the ambition we have as a club."

***

5 January 2019: Everton v Lincoln City

The Burnley result turned out to be the only win recorded by the Blues in December 2018, and there remained a lack of fluidity and confidence about Everton that suggested it would continue to be a difficult road. The manager searched for the answers to the poor run of form that began with the Merseyside derby in early December, with its last-minute punch in the gut. That had been followed by disappointing home draws against Newcastle and Watford, defeats against Manchester City, Tottenham and Brighton, and a 1-0 home reverse against Leicester City on New Year's Day.

For a team struggling through that run of poor form midway through the season, a home tie against a side in the fourth tier of the English football was precisely what you would want. Any game against a lower league side is a potential banana skin but a healthy home win to calm the nerves was surely on the cards.

That it didn't turn out that way underlined the shortage of confidence and composure that had suddenly afflicted Marco Silva's team. The Toffees won, but the manner in which a fast start gave way to a disconcertingly disjointed display – during which Lincoln more than held their own for long periods – would not have dispelled the doubts that had crept in during recent weeks.

Ademola Lookman found the net via the unexpected route of his head 11 minutes in, as Everton's early pressure and slicker passing told. Spreading the ball across the pitch, the Blues eventually worked the ball wide the over-lapping Baines who curled a cross to the back post where, unmarked, Lookman looped a header over the goalkeeper and over the goal line where the covering defender couldn't keep it out.

Two minutes later it was 2-0 and Everton were flying. Another nicely worked move saw Gylfi Sigurdsson find Dominic Calvert-Lewin in the area. He played Bernard in behind the last man and the Brazilian lifted the ball expertly over Josh Vickers.

After that, the impetus suddenly and inexplicably left the Blues' game, and Lincoln started coming forward. John Akinde had been giving Kurt Zouma plenty of problems early on, not least when the Frenchman gave the ball away in the middle of the park and was then "skinned" by the burly striker as he tried to ward him off. But it was Mina's cheap foul that handed the Imps a free-kick opportunity from which they scored.

The dead ball picked Jason Shackell out free in the six-yard box and while Jordan Pickford repelled his point-blank header, the rebound fell straight to Michael Bostwick, who converted from close range.

For the next half hour of the match, Everton struggled to rediscover their rhythm, even after Silva had attempted at half time to address the lack of control in the middle by replacing the disappointing Davies with Gomes. This was a match that Sigurdsson, Idrissa Gueye and Bernard, all of whom had played in World Cups, should have been absolutely bossing from start to finish, and for the likes of Davies, Calvert-Lewin and Tosun, it was a chance to really shine.

Of the younger players drafted into the side, Lookman was the only one who made a strong case in patches for a regular first-choice berth, and only Baines lived up to his billing as a former international and Premier League star.

Still, in the cup, the final score is always paramount and, in that respect, what mattered was the Blues being in the hat for the next round. While this wasn't the dominant performance Evertonians would have hoped for, both Silva and Marcel Brands would have added more information and context to their plans for further strengthening the squad during the January transfer window or over the summer.

Final score: Everton 2-1 Lincoln

***

13 January 2019: Everton v Bournemouth

Ever since the Roberto Martinez fairy-tale turned sour, somewhere between the Europa League defeat in Kiev in March 2015 and the consecutive home defeats to Leicester and Stoke the following Christmas, Goodison Park's atmosphere had periodically been a topic of debate among Evertonians.

Where the library-like milieu that away fans liked to mock was concerned, there was often a push-pull between those who felt it was incumbent on the crowd to generate the atmosphere from the off and those who put the onus on the team to excite the fans. Then, of course, there was the altogether more concerning toxicity that was prevalent on occasions under Martinez and Ronald Koeman. That was brought into sharper focus by midfielder Nikola Vlasic when he spoke of Everton's players being paralysed by fear.

There might not have been outright fear to this point among the Blues' ranks by January 2019, but the psychology had been off kilter since the derby defeat at Anfield in early December, and concerns over Everton's home form since. While there may have been a consensus that Marco Silva was going to need time and a good deal of patience to rectify the problems sown during the two regimes that preceded him and the interim Sam Allardyce tenure, it was fairly obvious that supporters were disappointed with how yet another season was coming off the rails.

Under those circumstances, it probably wasn't surprising that there was an air of uneasiness about the place when what was an important game against Bournemouth kicked off. With no home wins since late November and on a run of just one Premier League win in eight since then, the importance of three points wasn't lost on anybody.

By the time the hour mark approached, however, roused by an additional common enemy — the villain of the piece wearing black — and an improving, more robust and committed display by the players, Goodison was a good deal more animated; and, half an hour later, the Evertonian collective was celebrating a victory. An ugly victory that masked some continuing issues, but a victory which fans hoped would inject some confidence into the Blues' veins.

Silva had routinely asked for more aggression from his team, and he got plenty of it even if, spurred on by seething injustice at one of the most inept refereeing displays seen at Goodison in quite a while, André Gomes threatened to cross the line on more than a few occasions.

Having been harshly yellow-carded when he reacted to the latest in a litany of bafflingly poor decisions by Anthony Taylor, the Portuguese dangerously toed a tightrope in the closing stages and was fortunate not to see red.

Ultimately, though, Taylor's horrendous refereeing provided the focal point that roused the Goodison faithful from that uncomfortable silence that had enveloped most of the ground as Everton laboured through a fairly torrid first half hour. Where Bournemouth, a side on a run of 10 defeats from 13 coming into the game and five losses on the bounce away from the Vitality Stadium, were zipping the ball around comfortably the Toffees struggled to string three passes together in the face of the visitors' pressing.

All the openings in the first quarter of an hour were created by Eddie Howe's team, the best of them falling to David Brooks when played into a one-on-one situation with Pickford, but he struck his shot off the post, with Goodison erupting in boos at referee Taylor for failing to bring the play back for an obvious foul on Kurt Zouma.

It was the first of many baffling and infuriating decisions by the official who ratcheted up Evertonian ire when he awarded Adam Smith a free kick for falling into Gomes on the edge of the box. Pickford was equal to it, pushing Junior Stanislas's free kick behind.

Everton, who had been passed off their own patch for 30 minutes, gradually came to life and by the hour mark had taken the lead with a goal fashioned by Lucas Digne. The Frenchman drove to the by-line and, going away from goal, he expertly hooked a cross to the edge of the six-yard box where Zouma powered home his first Everton goal.

Bournemouth were unbowed, though, and an often bad-tempered affair remained nervily close until stoppage time and when one last boot downfield from Jordan Pickford was collected by Lookman who he held up long enough for substitute Dominic Calvert-Lewin to arrive about 16 yards out and stroke the winger's pass into the net with a wonderfully composed finish.

It was a reminder of what the young striker could do. Calvert-Lewin had struggled to show the consistency required of a first-choice starter but it was clear he could produce clinical moments like that one and chip in with important goals.

What remained to be seen was what effect this result would have on Everton's performances from then on, and whether it was a fillip that could get them back to playing the way they were pre-Anfield. The lack of passing options, an over-reliance on getting the ball wide for crosses into the box, and the misunderstandings that are often clear between the midfield and the two central forward players, all continued to be concerns and challenges for Silva to resolve.

Final score: Everton 2-0 Bournemouth

***

26 January 2019: Millwall v Everton

Everton's army of away supporters never disappoint. They turn up in their thousands for every game, and deal with whatever life throws at them. On a visit to London for an FA Cup Fourth Round tie against Millwall, it was bricks, bottles and blades, as sections of the home supporters ambushed the Blues' fans on their way to the New Den.

One Evertonian, Jay Burns, was slashed in the face, and received life-changing injuries.

As Jonathan Humphries, Crime Reporter for the *Liverpool Echo*, wrote: "Jay Burns made the trip to East London on Saturday but never made it to Millwall's ground, The [New] Den, after being caught up in a mass brawl in Hawkstone Road, Southwark, at around 4.45pm. Mr Burns, 29, told the *ECHO* the group of Everton fans he was travelling with were 'not looking for trouble' and were being escorted by police when they were attacked by another group. Mobile phone footage shows a man in a flat cap appear to make a slashing motion towards Mr Burns, who then staggers backwards clutching his face.

"He was rushed to hospital where he required over 25 stitches to a wound stretching from beside his right eye down to his chin. He told the *ECHO*: 'I just don't understand why people carry knives to a football match.'

"The fight ahead of the game was not the only incident of violence on the day. Coaches carrying Everton fans were pelted with bricks and bottles near The Den, smashing windows."

On the pitch, Everton were turfed out of the FA Cup by the Championship side, amid fury at an obvious handball goal and familiar frustrations over the team's inability to defend set-pieces.

Marco Silva's side twice led in a tie played in sodden conditions at and occasionally torrential rain, but squandered their advantage on both occasions, before one more silly foul handed the Londoners the chance to win the tie from a free kick.

Silva and Everton were livid that Jake Cooper's controversial goal, which levelled the contest at 2-2, was allowed the stand — despite this being a televised match, the Football Association had elected not to employ Video Assistant Referee technology — but it couldn't mask the Blues' attacking shortcomings, nor their galling weakness at defending high balls into the box.

An unsurprisingly poor game didn't see its first shot on target until the 43rd minute when Richarlison gave Everton the lead. André Gomes' pass found Richarlison with space to shoot from outside the area and his slightly deflected shot squirmed under goalkeeper Jordan Archer with two minutes left of the regulation 45 in the first half.

Millwall were level less than two minutes later, though, when Everton failed to deal with a free kick. Cooper nodded forward for Lee Gregory and the striker looped a header over Jordan Pickford and into the net.

Everton were better in parts in the second half but had only a scuffed Sigurdsson shot to show for their efforts before Cenk Tosun replaced Dominic Calvert-Lewin with 25 minutes to go. The Turk had been on the field for seven minutes before he notched his third goal of the season. Sigurdsson played him in between two defenders and Tosun tucked his shot inside the far post to make it 2-1.

A sloppy free-kick conceded by Lucas Digne set the home side up for an immediate reply, however. Everton's defence were beaten easily in the air again and though Pickford saved the first shot well, the rebound hit Cooper on the arm and bounced over the line. Referee Michael Oliver consulted his assistant to confirm the decision, and the goal stood despite Everton's vociferous protests.

The Blues were heading for a replay until another ill-advised transgression in a dangerous area by Digne led to a stoppage-time winner.

Once again, Millwall prevailed as they swung the ball in. There were more blue home jerseys than visiting white shirts in the six-yard box going for the second ball, and Murray Wallace pounced to consign Everton's Wembley hopes to the bin for another year.

Silva would point to the injustice of the second goal, but the problems in all areas of the pitch that showed no signs of abating were what lay behind a performance that yielded just three shots on target and precious little of the control that is expected of a Premier League side playing against lower-division opposition.

The painful defeat effectively ended Everton's season in late January, and increased the scrutiny of the manager and several of the Blues' expensive but under-performing players.

Final score: Millwall 3-2 Everton

***

7 April 2019: Everton v Arsenal

Following their FA Cup exit, Everton's form under Marco Silva could be best described as inconsistent .

A 1-0 away win against Huddersfield was followed by three consecutive defeats: against Wolves, Manchester City and Watford. Respite came through a 3-0 away win against Cardiff and a hard-fought 0-0 draw against Liverpool at Goodison Park. Another defeat, this time 3-2 away to Newcastle, preceded two consecutive 2-0 wins, against Chelsea and West Ham that lifted the Toffees back into the top half of the table.

With another home game against a "Top 6" side in the offing, the key question was once again, could Everton attain some of the consistency that had eluded them all season?

Prior to the visit of Arsenal in early April 2019, it had also been over two years since an Everton side earned three successive clean sheets. But thanks to a solitary Phil Jagielka goal and a laudably resilient performance against a team looking to leapfrog their neighbours, Tottenham, into third place, Everton saw off the third London team in a row without Jordan Pickford's goal being breached.

Pickford's wild punch dropped straight to Aaron Ramsey early in the second half and might have been punished on a different day but, thankfully, the Welshman volleyed over. Then apart from a couple of tame efforts on his goal, Pickford's role mostly centred around his distribution from the back which was, pleasingly, hugely improved.

Instead, the focus was, rightly, on a Blues display under-pinned by determined and impressive defending, phenomenal work-rate throughout the side and the hit-and-miss nature of Everton's counter-attacking which, if they could get right, would make them a seriously dangerous team.

The Blues had taken just 10 minutes to make the breakthrough via the somewhat unlikely source of Phil Jagielka, a player who wasn't even supposed to be on the pitch. Silva had named an unchanged XI but, with Michael Keane unable to shake off the effects of a virus, the club skipper stepped into the team and was on hand to tuck home what would prove to be the winning goal.

There was a note of controversy in the game's assessment afterwards, with some observers of television replays suggesting that Lucas Digne had stepped over the touchline in delivering one of his tomahawk throw-ins but it was rightly deemed legal by the officials as Jagielka flicked it on and then profited from a fortunate ricochet when Dominic Calvert-Lewin's header fell to him in front of goal and he couldn't miss.

From then on, it was a question of Everton suffocating the visitors with tireless closing down, remaining on the front foot for most of the first half, but just lacking the killer instinct to extend their lead, as their overall performance warranted.

As the game opened up later in the second half, a slew of opportunities were created for Everton that they just couldn't convert into further goals. Bernard, Gylfi Sigurdsson, Richarlison and Dominic Calvert-Lewin all spurned decent chances.

Meanwhile, at the other end, Arsenal attempted to find an equaliser as full time approached, but Everton saw the game out with a flurry of late substitutions.

This could and should have been an even more handsome victory, but Silva's men had found turning those quick transitions and interceptions into goals a challenge all season. Everton racked up 23 shots over the 90 minutes but only six on target and while good goalkeeping by Bernd Leno was partially responsible for the home side only scoring once, poor ball control and decision-making also prevented this from being a hiding for an Arsenal team that hadn't travelled well all season.

Having at times looked so bereft of answers this season, Silva finally looked as though he was finding his feet again at Goodison Park, with some real signs of progress. As galling as the defeat at Newcastle had been, that second-half collapse at St James' Park (and, perhaps, 45 shaky minutes before half-time against Chelsea) stood as an aberration in a six-match sequence that had yielded four wins, a goalless draw in the Merseyside derby, and progress back up the table. The Blues were back to within a point of seventh place and looked to have established a platform on which Silva and Marcel Brands could build in the summer.

Final score: Everton 1-0 Arsenal

***

13 April 2019 Fulham v Everton

Everton could really be beyond parody at times. An "Everton, that" phenomenon had become a running joke on social media for years, a product of the relentless mediocrity and fallibility that had plagued the club for the past three decades, and it was made for days like this one.

Given that Fulham came into this game with their relegation back to the Championship confirmed, without so much as a point from their previous nine Premier League matches and with just one clean sheet to their name all season, Evertonians might have asked themselves if there was there anything more nailed on than what played out at Craven Cottage.

Credit went to Scott Parker and his team. Relieved of the pressure of a battle to avoid to the drop, Fulham were energetic, physical and became increasingly confident once it became apparent that the visitors were having a day to forget.

After a first half in which they had given the Blues a couple of scares, Marco Silva needed to deliver a similar half-time team talk to the one that spurred the second-half display against Chelsea a few weeks earlier, and which had ignited what looked like a strong charge to finish in seventh place.

Instead, the home side came out from the half time interval and immediately scored. Everton then descended into the irredeemably awful display that fans had hoped had been consigned to the history of a frustrating 2018/19 season.

For the hosts, it was all about Ryan Babel and Aleksander Mitrovic, with the Serbian striker rattling the crossbar and forcing a point-blank reaction save from Pickford, while the Dutchman set up Tom Cairney to score within 30 seconds of the start of the second half.

He then galloped away into oceans of space behind Everton's leaden-footed back line to dink the ball over Pickford and make it 2-0 with 21 minutes to go.

There was ample time for Everton to summon some kind of reaction, but against the second-worst team in the Premier League their response was pitifully bad, with players seemingly unable to even control a routine pass and even three changes from Silva failed to improve the fare. From an attacking perspective, there was almost nothing of note to report from the Toffees' 100-odd minutes of "action" – against a defence that had already been breached 76 times to that point in the season, Everton managed just one shot on target.

The depressingly familiar tendency for Blues teams to descend into maddening disarray lived on, regardless of the occupant of the technical area. Eradicating it would be one of Silva's big challenges.

Final score: Fulham 2-0 Everton

***

"It was a disappointing result," Silva admitted afterwards. "We didn't perform the way we want or the way we expect.

"We knew before the match and we spoke in the dressing room before how difficult it is to play here always. For us, it's not important that they were just relegated — they always put big pressure on the player with the ball.

"It wasn't a good game for us at all — I think they were more aggressive than us and faster than us."

***

21 April 2019: Everton v Manchester United

Atonement for the debacle at Craven Cottage came the following weekend as Everton powered their way to an impressive 4-0 drubbing of Manchester United. It was arguably Everton's best result for two years and it was the kind of performance that hinted at what could be under Marco Silva, with another transfer window under his belt and the chance to build on a 2018/19 season that would finish in very positive fashion.□

Not since they had hammered Manchester City by the same scoreline in January 2017 had an Everton team looked so strong against "big six" opposition and they set the tone early by pegging United back for long periods before taking the lead in the 13th minute.

Lucas Digne's long throw-in was knocked on by Dominic Calvert-Lewin and Richarlison swivelled onto it to slam the opening goal into the roof of David de Gea's net.

Marcus Rashford went close on what would be a rare attack for United when he fired over after collecting a ball over the top of the home defence, but Everton broke away nine minutes later and Sigurdsson drilled an excellent shot into the bottom corner from 30 yards.

With Michael Keane back in central defence alongside Kurt Zouma and Morgan Schneiderlin slotting into midfield seamlessly in place of the suspended André Gomes, Silva's side were in dominant mood, hustling United out of their stride and forcing errors.

Silva withdrew Richarlison with a rib problem a few minutes into the second half, but his substitution in favour of Walcott didn't halt the momentum established by Everton, who extended their advantage in the 56th minute.

Sigurdsson's attempted shot deflected behind, and when De Gea punched the resulting corner clear, it fell to Digne, who rapped it back past the Spaniard with a crisp first-time effort from 25 yards out.

De Gea was stranded again in the 63rd minute when the Icelandic star sent Walcott away and the substitute finished with aplomb, guiding the ball into the far corner.

Final score: Everton 4-0 Manchester United

***

The fine victory against Manchester United, secured in brilliant Easter sunshine at Goodison, moved Everton back into 7th place on goal difference; but, after a goalless draw at Crystal Palace, a comfortable 2-0 win over Burnley, and an entertaining 2-2 draw at Tottenham – where they almost pulled off a win to end the campaign on a high – Silva's men had to be content with finishing in 8th.

Despite being pegged back late on in North London, the season had ended in hugely encouraging fashion. It meant that Everton fans could consign some really poor form over the winter months to the history books and hope there would be an injection of more genuine quality over the summer.

Question marks remained over the futures of loanees Kurt Zouma and Andre Gomes, but there was clear evidence of a structure, a plan and a process about Silva's work at Goodison that pointed the way to a more stable and competitive future for Everton.

Unfortunately for the Portuguese and the Blues, it turned out to be anything but.

2019: Bramley-Moore Dock Stadium Visuals Revealed

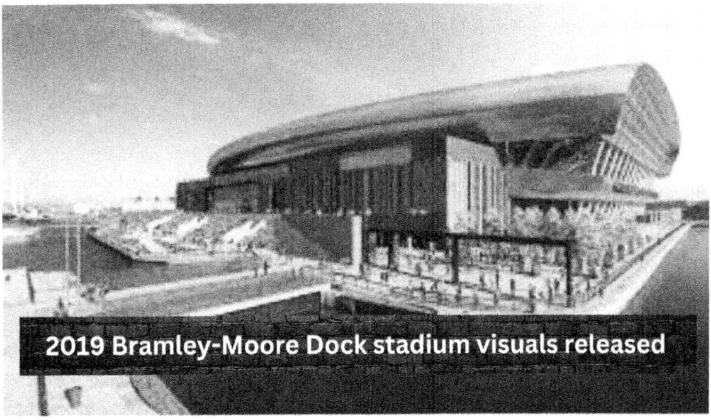

Everton's quandary over Goodison Park, its ageing infrastructure and the need to either redevelop the "Grand Old Lady" or move to a new, purpose-built, modern stadium had been rumbling on since the days of Peter Johnson in the late 1990s.

The dream of a waterfront home had died with the collapse of the Kings Dock proposal in 2004; and what many Evertonians felt was a potentially disastrous move to neighbouring Knowsley was avoided when the Destination Kirkby project was killed off by local opposition; whilst a plan to develop a ground on Walton Hall Park in 2012 had never really got off the ground.

Farhad Moshiri's arrival as major shareholder and chief benefactor in 2016 had finally allowed the club to get a new stadium project moving forward, and on 25 July 2019 Everton unveiled the first visuals of their proposed new stadium at Bramley-Moore Dock, at a special presentation on the eve of the second phase of its public consultation into the scheme.

Architect Dan Meis was in attendance at a special event for supporters that coincided with the release of artist's impressions and a brilliant CGI fly-through of the new ground.

Around 1,000 invited supporters at the Titanic Hotel, along with the Chief Executive Denise Barrett-Baxendale and chairman Bill Kenwright, gave Dan Meis a standing ovation. The structure would feature a floating roof above a brick facade, designed to embrace the unique waterfront location in Liverpool's north docks.

It was said that the design of the stadium celebrated the club's history, and the architect's aim was to try to replicate the best characteristics of Goodison Park while improving on it, with modern facilities to meet the expectations of Evertonians.

The brickwork on the exterior would pay homage to the famous Archibald Leitch latticework at Goodison Park – and supporter experience would be at the forefront of shaping the fan plaza.

Additionally, the club planned on investing more than £55 million to preserve, restore and celebrate the heritage assets at Bramley-Moore Dock. The site had been inaccessible for many years and had sat behind locked gates, while the Everton scheme aimed to bring the dock into productive use and open up the area for the public to appreciate its heritage.

Working with local and national heritage bodies, Everton had committed to saving and restoring the Grade II listed hydraulic tower. It was anticipated that they would use the tower all year round.

The water channel would also be maintained, to keep the integrity of inter-connecting docks. Other historic features, such as cobbles, capstones and tramlines, would be kept, as would the dock walls under the stadium.

In embracing its future, the club had also planned how to care for its past. Goodison Park has been a cultural icon of the city for almost 130 years and a Legacy Project was initiated that planned on delivering health and wellbeing facilities, education amenities, business start-up facilities, community retail, a youth zone, homes – including sheltered housing for the elderly – and a permanent tribute to Goodison Park through green space, using the area of the famous pitch's centre circle.

The future still looked promising, and Farhad Moshiri's vision for Everton had never looked brighter. However, just one day later, the Club announced that Jon Woods and Deputy Chairman Keith Harris were leaving the Board of Directors, saying the changes had come about following a period of "review and strategic planning".

Dr Harris had been charged with leading Everton's plans to relocate to a new stadium Bramley-Moore Dock. It was also announced that CEO Denise Barrett-Baxendale would oversee the work of Stadium Development Director Colin Chong, and take responsibility for the new stadium project — including the delivery of a community-led legacy at Goodison Park — with Sasha Ryazantsev responsible for finalising the funding for the schemes.

2019: Changes to Silva's squad, on and off the field

> The seeds of significant financial woes were sown when north of £140 million was splashed out on five players, none of whom would end up making the kind of impact their transfer fees and wages required.

2019 Changes to Silva's squad, on and off the field

The close season is often a time of change in football and the summer of 2019 was no different at Everton, where within three weeks of the final game of the season, surprise news arrived on 1 June, when the club confirmed that Assistant Manager Joao Pedro Sousa had left the club to take up a managerial role in his native Portugal.

Marco Silva's Number 2 had accepted a two-year contract to coach at newly promoted Famalicao.

Sousa had worked with Silva at each of his five most recent clubs, including Everton, and the pair were also teammates at Trofense during the late 1990s. His departure was unwelcome news for the young Everton manager.

***

Three weeks after that, Everton confirmed the first of their summer signings aimed at further strengthening Silva's squad to support a push towards the top six in 2019/20. In all, six players would come in before the unusually early transfer deadline on 8 August (for one season the Premier League tried closing the summer window before the start of the season) but, with central-defensive stalwart Phil Jagielka leaving on a free transfer after 12 years with the Toffees, it was the signing the club didn't make that, arguably, came back to haunt them.

Furthermore, the seeds of significant financial woes were sown when north of £140 million was splashed out on five players, none of whom would end up making the kind of impact their transfer fees and wages required.

Following the arrival on goalkeeper Jonas Lössl on a free transfer, André Gomes was acquired for £22 million in a deal struck with Barcelona. The Portuguese midfielder signed a five-year contract and made permanent his switch from the Nou Camp after a successful season on loan at Goodison Park in 2018/19.

"I know the Club made a massive effort to sign me and I'm very happy and thankful to them," Gomes told evertonfc.com at the time. "I said during the year that I felt part of a family and that is the most important thing to me.

"Last year was a really good experience for me. I just wanted to feel part of something special and I found it here. It was good for me in that moment and right now, after signing for Everton, it's even better.

"I always got massive support since day one. I'm really happy to have this badge on me right now.

"I want to give all the fans my best because I think they deserve the best. I have to thank Marco and Marcel, too, because they made a really massive effort for me to be here."

Following his impressive form for Valencia and on the international stage for Portugal, where he was in the team that won the 2016 European Championships, Gomes had joined Barcelona in a big-money deal in 2016 that was worth €35 million up front and included another €20 million in appearance-related add-ons.

He made just 29 starts in all competitions for the Liga giants, being used more as a substitute than a first-team regular as his much-vaunted move turned sour. Linked strongly with a move to Tottenham in the summer of 2017, Gomes would end up staying at Barcelona. He had been open about the psychological toll his poor form was taking, and he welcomed the chance to join Everton on loan a year later.

A hamstring injury, suffered during Barcelona's pre-season trip to the United States, prevented him from making his Blues debut until October. Thereafter, he quickly established himself as a vital member of Marco Silva's team and formed a strong partnership with Idrissa Gueye in central midfield.

***

On 15 July, Everton completed the signing of 29-year-old Fabian Delph from Manchester City in a deal initially worth £8.5 million pounds, by agreeing a three-year contract that would keep him at Goodison Park until 2022.

“I’m hungry,” he said after the deal was announced. "I don’t like losing. I see myself as a winner. I’m at an age now where I am probably one of the most experienced players, so hopefully I can help my teammates here to do better.

“I’m really happy to be here. I’m going to give absolutely everything — nothing less than 100 per cent.

“Every time I have played against Everton, whether it was home or away, straight away the first thing that comes to mind when you see the fans is passion, Everton fans seem to know football, seem to understand it, it seems to be in their blood and they really back the team.”

Having initially come to prominence at Leeds United. Delph had been linked with a move to Everton ten years earlier after he had helped the Yorkshire club gain a promotion from League One. He eventually signed for Aston Villa and became a full England international during the latter stages of his time there.

Despite verbally committing his future to Villa in the summer of 2015, Manchester City tempted Delph away with an £8 million move as they sought to bolster their squad. He made 89 appearances in all competitions for them, scoring five times.

Originally deployed in his natural central midfield role, he had played more recently as a left-back, to cover for Benjamin Mendy who sustained a long-term injury.

Delph had battled injuries of his own, however, in recent years but, with him being available for a cut-price fee a year before his contract expired at the Etihad Stadium, Marcel Brands and Marco Silva imagined the value in adding his versatility to their midfield options.

***

Early in August, Everton tied up the £23 million transfer of Jean-Philippe Gbamin from FSV Mainz 05. He also penned a five-year contract to become the fourth new face of the summer and was followed a few days later by the 19-year-old Italian striker, Moise Kean.

Both players fitted the profile that Brands and Silva were now principally targeting – young, exciting and with potential sell-on value down the road if they were successful at Goodison.

Ademola Lookman, a £10 million acquisition made by Steve Walsh in January 2017, had fitted the same bill but had struggled to settle on Merseyside, and was sold to RB Leipzig for a fee rising to £22.5 million in between the arrivals of Delph and Gbamin.

Gbamin, 23, had broken into the Lens first-team in 2013 after spells with Aire-sur-la-Lys and U.S. Saint-Quentin Blessy's youth setups.

Mainz had brought him to the Bundesliga in 2016 as a promising France U21 international, but he switched his international allegiance to Ivory Coast, the country of his birth, shortly afterwards, for whom he had won 11 caps to date.

Gbamin was intended to be the replacement for Idrissa Gueye, who had just joined Paris Saint-Germain, but he could supposedly also operate at centre-half if needed. He would wear the No. 25 jersey.

"It's a big moment with a lot of emotion and now it's on me to prove on the pitch why they bought me," Gbamin said.

"I'm excited because Everton is a great club here in England with a big history and ambition, so I didn't think for more than a moment — I wanted to come here."

***

Moise Kean, meanwhile, was drafted in from Juventus in a deal that was officially undisclosed but said to be worth £25.1 million.

The Blues won the race for the highly rated teenager, fending off reported interest from the likes of Arsenal and Manchester United, and he signed a five-year contract after completing a successful medical.

The Serie A club would have first option on Kean should Everton decide to sell him in the future but there was no buy-back clause in the deal, negotiated to be paid in three instalments, that would rise to £27.5 million if appearance-related add-one were triggered.

"I am very proud and honoured to wear the Everton shirt. I will give my best to this team," Kean said on evertontv.

"I was convinced to sign because Everton is a club looking to the future and so am I.

"I know about the size of the club. It has big ambition and I will work very hard to help us fulfil what we want to achieve.

"I am used to winning and I want to bring this winning attitude to the team. I hope I will be very good on the field and bring the fans joy."

After the signing, Marco Silva, said: "A striker was one of our priority signings this summer.

"Moise is strong, fast, with many good qualities as a striker and he is just 19 years old. He has talent, and he is ready to work, ready to improve our squad and gives us different solutions."

***

As July was drawing to a close, Marco Silva had publically stated that Everton needed to sign five more players before deadline day if the club were, in his words, to do "better than last season".

Gbamin and Kean filled two of those spots but the manager also reportedly wanted a centre-back to replace the departed Jagielka, a winger, and a new right-back and admitting that a shortage of options in that position had forced him to "risk" playing Seamus Coleman in two pre-season friendly games in Germany that summer.

Asked if he thought it possible for Everton to complete their business in less than two weeks, the manager said: "It should be if you really want to be competitive and to do better than last season. Because, at the end of the day, it is what we want to do: do better than last season."

***

This transfer deadline day was Thursday 8 August. As usual, there was lots of last-minute activity and speculation in the media with Everton known to be targeting a wide player and a centre-half as the window entered its final 24 hours.

The French full-back, Djibril Sidibé, became the sixth Everton signing of the summer when he arrived on loan from AS Monaco for the season, but the Blues had been unable to persuade Chelsea to part with Kurt Zouma who had excelled during his loan spell with the club the previous season.

With the benefit of hindsight, it was clear that Brands and Silva had put too many of their eggs in a Zouma-shaped basket, and were left with few options to bolster their defence as time ran out.

An approach to sign defender Chris Smalling was reportedly knocked back on deadline day by Manchester United but, otherwise, the speculation was dominated by the search for a winger, one that became more urgent after Everton were foiled in their attempts to sign Wilfred Saha from Crystal Palace.

Farhad Moshiri had made no secret of his admiration of the Ivory Coast attacker and the Blues were believed to have offered as much as £52 million for him. Palace, who would have to pass on 25% of any fee on to Manchester United, would not lower their asking price, said to be around £70 million, even after the player handed in a transfer request. With 90 minutes to go before the deadline, word came through from Selhurst Park that Zaha was not leaving the club under any circumstances.

That left Moshiri and Everton to scramble in the waning minutes of the window to try and agree a deal with Arsenal for Alex Iwobi. In between, Steven Bergwijn of PSV Eindhoven had been floated as a potential alternative but it was Iwobi who re-emerged as an option with just 15 minutes to go before the 5pm cut-off.

It would later emerge that Iwobi was on a boat in Dubai when the call came through from Marco Silva sounding him out over a potential move to Goodison Park, but he and his potential new club faced a race against time to get the paperwork filed on time.

"We told them it was an emergency, like we needed to spin the boat [around] and get back quick, because we were in the middle of nowhere," Iwobi would later recount. "I have to give props to the driver because I don't know how he sped back to get us back in time to try and sign the documents."

In the end, Everton were able to submit a deal sheet to the Premier League almost within seconds of the deadline and successfully completed the transfer for an initial fee of £28 million rising to £35 million depending on appearances.

On balance, Iwobi's move to Merseyside was not the success all concerned hoped it would be. The winger would struggle for consistency for his first couple of years as a Toffee, and it would take another Londoner, Frank Lampard, to draw the best out of him just when Everton needed it most in order to stay in the Premier League. Eventually Iwobi would return to London, after a move to Fulham late in the 2023 summer transfer window.

2019: Blues keep faith in Marco Silva

> "We'll improve. I don't have doubts. If you ask me about the performance today, it was not our best. We could do better and we will be better for sure in the future. I don't have doubts that we will play with more quality.
>
> \- Marco Silva

2019 Blues keep faith in Marco Silva

The way in which Everton finished the 2018/19 season, with just two defeats in 11 games and with impressive home victories against Chelsea and Manchester United that helped secure an eighth-place finish, had engendered real optimism for Marco Silva's second season in charge.

Though there was concern over the failure to sign a centre-half to cover the loss of Phil Jagielka and loanee Kurt Zouma, there as cautious excitement about the new signings the club had been able to make during the close season.

***

17 August 2019: Everton v Watford

The first home game of 2019/20 was against Silva's former club, Watford. After the disappointment of the opening day's 0-0 stalemate at Crystal Palace the previous week, this felt like one of those games Everton needed to win if they were to improve on last season's 8th place finish.

Seeing Goodison Park in full voice with 38,000 blue-and-white flags waving as the blaring siren gave way to Z-Cars, and Everton then taking an early lead, it felt as though a more convincing result was in store than ultimately proved to be the case. But a win was a win; three points are three points.

It could easily have ended in an irritating draw, and the Blues had contrived to throw away two points or more on so many occasions in recent years that it would have come as little surprise if they had. Certainly, when there didn't seem to be much of a central midfield, with André Gomes looking like he was playing with the benefit of pain-killing jabs and Jean-Pierre Gbamin fading after an impressive start, or when Watford launched their aerial bombardment in the last quarter of the game, you couldn't help but sense a dreaded equaliser in the offing.

But this was an Everton team that, stretching back into last season, had now kept 10 clean sheets in its last 13 Premier League matches and hadn't conceded a goal at home since the beginning of February. Despite the departure of Zouma, Michael Keane had simply picked up where the Chelsea man had left off the previous season, and Yerry Mina was quickly converting the doubters with two towering displays to start 2019/20. And in Jordan Pickford, Silva had inherited a player capable of preserving winning positions with his bravery, presence of mind and sheer shot-stopping ability... even if that sometimes meant keeping the ball out with his face!

If a solid defensive foundation appeared to be in place the fluidity and potency of the attack looked like it would take more time. Richarlison and Gylfi Sigurdsson, in particular, had yet to pair their industry off the ball with effectiveness on it. Dominic Calvert-Lewin, full of running and work-rate himself, still didn't look like the best fit for Silva's current system; the 22-year-old didn't have a shot during his 72 minutes on the field whereas his replacement, Moise Kean, quickly showed that he might already fit the profile, and could have scored twice, which really would have put the seal on the afternoon.

Thankfully, while chances were at a premium, Bernard proved to be the difference on the day. The little Brazilian had taken his time to adjust to life in England but against Watford, he showed signs of his growing confidence.

The match was just 10 minutes old when Lucas Digne swept a sublime ball down the left channel for Bernard to chase. The No. 20 cut inside, showing all the signs of looking to play in a teammate, but instead fired an early, low shot inside the near post and past Ben Foster before the goalkeeper could react.

So far, so good for Silva's men, who were looking a great deal more inventive than they had been at Selhurst Park the previous weekend. As the only player among the new signings to be making his home debut, Jean-Philippe Gbamin was in the spotlight. He was given plenty of the ball and showed in consistent flashes over the first half hour that he could be both a physical but also enterprising presence in the midfield's heart.

Watford posed a regular threat from set-pieces and they came close to cancelling out Bernard's goal midway through the first half when Craig Dawson's header come back off the post, and the second period didn't start in encouraging fashion for the home side, either.

Former Goodison favourite, Gerard Deulofeu, accelerated between Digne and Richarlison and knocked the ball into the path of Troy Deeney by the penalty spot, but Pickford was off his line quickly and took the shot squarely in the face to preserve the clean sheet.

Everton still remained the more dangerous of the two sides in attack, especially following Kean's introduction with 18 minutes left, and the tide turned back in their favour. With the Hornets chasing the contest late on, Bernard sent Kean clear but the young Italian blazed a shot high and wide from around the edge of the box and screwed an even better chance an inch the wrong side of the upright in stoppage time.

Had it gone in, it might have taken the roof off Goodison, but there was plenty from the teenager to suggest that he would prove to be a very exciting addition to the team. Deceptively powerful, he showed superb strength against some large defenders and proved he could turn on the jets as well when presented with space in front of him.

In the end, the one goal was enough. That kind of resilience could only stand Everton in good stead while the new boys bedded in. Four points, two clean sheets, and with none of the summer acquisitions yet fully embedded in the team, it represented a pretty good start to the new season.

Final score: Everton 1-0 Watford

***

Afterwards, Marco Silva said he was sure that Everton would play better but he was pleased his side had seen out an important victory.

"It was not our best performance, for sure," he said. "We played really well [for] the first 30 minutes, but even when we weren't doing so well in the game, the fans were always behind the team and supporting the players.

"I think we deserved the three points. Of course, it's always a tough game in the Premier League but we created more chances to score.

"We'll improve. I don't have doubts that we will play with more quality."

***

On 27 August Everton confirmed that their new midfielder, Jean-Philippe Gbamin had damaged a quadricep tendon in training and was expected to be out for at least eight weeks.

The club's statement indicated that they would be consulting experts in Europe for possible advice on how best to rehabilitate the injury. Sadly for Gbamin and the club, this would turn out to be the first in a series of major injuries for the player.

***

1 September 2019: Everton v Wolverhampton Wanderers

The second away game of the season had seen Everton give a debut to new signing, Alex Iwobi, who came on as a second-half substitute. Frustratingly, the Blues squandered many chances, eventually going down 2-0 to a spirited Aston Villa side.

The midweek Carabao Cup game away at Lincoln had been far more positive. Goals from Lucas Digne, Gylfi Sigurdsson, Iwobi and Richarlison were enough to secure a place in the 4th round, in a 4-2 win.

Back on home turf, where they were on a five-match winning streak going back to the end of the previous season, for Sunday afternoon kick off against Wolves, they entertained the Goodison crowd to a high-scoring match against Nuno Espirito Santo's side.

Had this match ended 2-2, as it looked like it might with 15 minutes to go, Evertonians would have gone into the international break feeling somewhat deflated.

Five points from a possible 12 would have felt like a poor return from the relatively comfortable opening set of fixtures to the new season, but seven points and 6th place heading into the first enforced two-week hiatus of the campaign had a much rosier look to it.

Everton were still reeling to a degree from the debacle at Villa Park nine days prior and Silva needed both a reaction and a strong performance from some key individuals. And in Gylfi Sigurdsson, Andre Gomes and Richarlison, in particular, he would have seen three players who responded in pleasingly strong fashion, while also getting some telling contributions from another trio making their full Premier League debuts.

Alex Iwobi scored with his second header in the space of four days. Moise Kean played a vital role in the opening goal and Fabian Delph helped coordinate things in the middle with the energy and combativeness that was so sorely lacking in the matches against Crystal Palace and Villa. If he could stay fit, the £8 million acquisition from Manchester City looked as though he could prove to be the steal of the summer.

Not that it was all plain sailing, of course. Wolves twice pegged Everton back with goals that were poorly defended. Sometimes the Blues' central midfield was a little too porous and in the first half especially, the visitors were getting behind the fullbacks with worrying ease. But, having twice lost the lead, this was a test of character and resolve that Silva's boys passed, even in the face of some typically one-sided refereeing from Anthony Taylor.

The biggest headlines deservedly belonged to Richarlison, a player who was perhaps fortunate to keep his place in the team after the opening three matches of the season. Silva had enough faith in the young Brazilian and was rewarded as he got the hosts off and running inside five minutes of kick-off.

Conor Coady miscued a back-pass to Rui Patricio, the keeper's attempted clearance struck Kean and fell invitingly into the path of Richarlison who fired a shot that bounced off the ground and looped up into the goal.

It was a lead that would last just four minutes, though. Lucas Digne failed to deal with a high ball down Wolves' right flank and Adama Traoré took it off him and burst to the byline, out-stripping the Frenchman for pace again as he powered inside before fizzing it low across the face of Jordan Pickford's goal. Seamus Coleman could only block its path and Romain Saïss prodded home the loose ball to level the match.

Everton were back in front just three minutes later. Richarlison hooked an excellent pass down the line for Sigurdsson and he whipped an equally impressive ball into the middle where Iwobi was on hand to steer a header past the goalkeeper.

In contrast to the previous home game against Watford, this was an open, entertaining and often breathless encounter between two attacking sides. Everton came out of the half-time break still willing to push to extend their lead but, having dealt with the threat from the visitors fairly well, they succumbed meekly in the 75th minute when Willy Boly flicked a throw-in to the back post and Raúl Jiménez stole in untracked by Digne to head in the second equaliser of the game.

That could have been another of those pivotal, confidence-draining moments, but Everton would be back in front for good when Digne and Richarlison underlined the precious value of quality when they combined beautifully with 10 minutes left.

The Frenchman appeared to be going nowhere, closer to the corner flag than the penalty area but he cracked a superb cross in from the byline that Richarlison met with a towering leap over Boly that he guided past the keeper's fingertips and inside the far post.

3-2! Goodison was bouncing at three well-earned points that lifted Everton above three of last season's top six heading into the international break. More than that, in contrast to this same fixture in 2018/19 where the Toffees were played off their own park, it showed just how good Silva's team could be when they had their best players firing on all cylinders.

Final score: Everton 3-2 Wolves

***

21 September 2019: Everton v Sheffield United

How the pendulum swings! No sooner had Marco Silva and Everton sent a signal that the blue touch paper might have been lit on their fledgling season with the hugely encouraging victory against Wolves, than they followed it up with the huge disappointment of a 3-1 away defeat at Bournemouth.

In his latest pre-match press conference, the manager had spent his time with the print media fending off the notion that his team were in an early-season crisis. Yet, come the final whistle at Goodison Park following an utterly dreadful performance against Sheffield United, the Portuguese's dishevelled hair and flustered countenance betrayed a man who could be under no illusions about the mess he and his team were now making of the new campaign.

After finishing 2018/19 so promisingly, Everton were arguably better placed than most to start the new season strongly and help set the early pace in the Premier League. A favourable start against two newly promoted clubs and three that had "bottom half" written all over them should have provided the ideal platform to do so. The proverbial door to the top six was open; instead, there was now mounting evidence that the Blues had probably already scuppered their hopes of finishing among those coveted positions come May.

As it turned out, it wasn't too early for such doom-laden prognostications following an utterly dire display. Sheffield United won 2-0 with just two shots all game and only one on target (Yerry Mina inadvertently scored a first-half own goal) with a performance that their manager, Chris Wilder, described as their worst with the ball so far this season.

Everton had 70% of the possession but — stop us if you've heard this before — did almost nothing with it, forcing just three meaningful saves from Dean Henderson, none of which were taxing of the Blades' goalkeeper.

The most worrying aspects of the whole match, however, were the set-piece defending, the galling lack of character and attacking punch in the Blues' side, particularly in the second half, and the desperate moves made by Silva to salvage something from the game.

Eyebrows were raised when Alex Iwobi, arguably one of the most effective Everton players in recent games, was dropped to the bench to accommodate Bernard, while the manager persisted with two holding midfielders against a limited attack. Moise Kean's return to the starting XI was less surprising, given Silva's desire to bed him in at home, but by the end of 90 minutes the hosts had a five-man forward line, just three defenders and not much of a midfield to speak of, after Morgan Schneiderlin and Seamus Coleman were withdrawn in the second half.

As the Toffees chased the game in the final quarter of an hour, it was not surprising that John Lundstram was able to capitalise on the space. He slipped Lys Mousset in, to double the lead and kill the match with a clinical finish past Jordan Pickford. That Everton failed to muster a chance worthy of the name in the ensuing 11 minutes plus five of stoppage time told you everything you needed to know about a team going nowhere.

Final score: Everton 0-2 Sheffield United

***

Speaking after the defeat, veteran midfielder Fabian Delph said that Everton's players needed to shoulder their share of the blame for the dire reverse against Sheffield United.

"The manager always ends up coming under a lot of pressure, but us players need to have a good look in the mirror and look at each other," admitted Delph.

"I hate losing. I have three little girls and cannot let them win anything. I'm a nightmare.

"But you get your frustration out. You speak about the game individually to people and collectively. Now we focus on Sheffield Wednesday [in the League Cup].

"We weren't good enough. We planned well all week, and it didn't click. It is a big club with a lot of history and we expect more from ourselves.

"The fans always turn up and they have made their feelings clear."

***

3 November 2019: Everton v Tottenham Hotspur

Following that alarming loss, Everton steered themselves into the League Cup Quarter Finals with wins over Sheffield Wednesday at Hillsborough and Watford at Goodison Park, but had slid worryingly down the Premier League table in the interim with defeats to Burnley,

Manchester City and Brighton – although the loss the Seagulls on the south coast was an especially cruel one. The Toffees had largely been spared, to that point, of any controversy by the recently-introduced system of Video Assistant Referees. But, having played well against Brighton and come from behind to lead 2-1 in the second half, their efforts were derailed by an astounding recommendation by VAR Lee Mason. He proposed the on-field referee award the hosts a penalty, when Michael Keane inadvertently stood on the foot of Aaron Connolly. Neal Maupay converted the resulting spot-kick to level the game at 2-2, Everton never recovered and a miserable afternoon on their part was complete when Lucas Digne put through his own net in stoppage time.

By the time Tottenham came to Goodison Park in early November, it was feeling like a 'must-win' match. But not only were the Toffees denied all three points, they would lose a first-choice midfielder in André Gomes to an horrific ankle injury as well.

Two teams struggling for form and sitting in the bottom half of the table before kick-off played out a first half depressingly bereft of quality, made worse by typically horrendous officiating from referee Martin Atkinson.

Richarlison had Everton's brightest moments before half-time when he spun on Digne's low cross in the 32nd minute but fired straight at Gazzaniga in the Spurs goal and later rolled Davinson Sanchez before lashing over.

The second period had begun in the same vein until the match came to life with an hour gone. First, Richarlison finished a smart move by latching onto Digne's cut-back but was foiled by a good save by the Tottenham keeper.

Then, a costly mistake by Alex Iwobi in his own half allowed Spurs to take the lead. The former Gunner passed straight to Son Hueng-Min, who released Dele Alli to turn inside his marker and drill a shot past Pickford to make it 1-0.

Everton tried to push in response, almost prompting Ben Davies to turn the ball into his own net. A lengthy VAR check looked like it might hand the home side a spot kick after Alli handled the ball in his own box, but, controversially, no penalty was awarded.

The contest then turned from frustrating and fractious to sombre in the 78th minute. Son, aggrieved not to have been awarded a free-kick in Everton's half, chased Gomes down as the Portuguese advanced down the hosts' left flank and impetuously lunged in from behind.

Gomes collided heavily with Aurier and was left prone in unmistakable distress near the touchline, with the horrified reaction of supporters in the Family Enclosure nearby leaving the television audience in no doubt that the midfielder had suffered a terrible injury.

Under advice from the VAR official, Anthony Taylor changed Son's initial yellow card to a red and the Spurs forward, wracked by tears at the extent of Gomes's condition, walked down the tunnel. Meanwhile, Silva prepared a double change that saw Gylfi Sigurdsson and Dominic Calvert-Lewin come on, with Tom Davies the other player to make way.

Calvert-Lewin came close to equalising when he headed an excellent Sigurdsson cross over, but it was Tosun who finally made the breakthrough with 97 minutes on the clock to ensure that the spoils were shared.

The result kept Everton in 17th place, one above the relegation zone, and still searching for the consistency expected of an expensively assembled side.

Final score: Everton 1-1 Spurs

***

Afterwards, Cenk Tosun described how he had tried to comfort Gomes whom, it would transpire, had sustained a dislocation fracture to his ankle following Son's reckless tackle. Insult would be added to that injury a couple of days later when the South Korean's red card was downgraded to a yellow.

"Everybody is so sad inside," Tosun said. "Some players, they nearly cried.

"[André] was in shock. His eyes were open so big. He was crying, shouting, and screaming. I just tried to hold him and speak to him; I tried to tell him to stay calm. We couldn't understand him. He was the one who had got the injury.

"It will be a tough time for Andre, but sometimes in football, these injuries happen.

"I just hope and pray he comes back stronger after his surgery. We will give him the motivation he needs. My goal is for him, the point is for him. If we had a few minutes more, we would have won it for him."

The circumstances of the horror injury to Gomes, one that looked at the time as though it might cost him a year of his career at least, were just a part of a match that was officiated badly by Atkinson and ruined by yet more VAR controversy. Taylor was called upon in Stockley Park to review three potential penalty incidents, all three of which were deemed not to be fouls, even though there was clear contact on Richarlison by Aurier for one and an even more obvious handball by Dele Alli in another.

The Dele incident, subsequently explained by the Premier League as not being a penalty because Yerry Mina's presence supposedly caused Alli to handle the ball, took three minutes of review by VAR before a decision came back to Atkinson, further undermining the credibility and usefulness of a tool that had failed Everton on two successive weekends.

"It is really tough for us to talk about what has happened on the pitch," said Marco Silva, who accepted a dubious penalty decision by VAR that went against Michael Keane in Brighton the previous weekend. "What I want to tell you, all of us love football and we play for our fans and I am 100 percent sure they didn't like what they saw this afternoon."

On Gomes, Silva said he was waiting to learn of the extent of the injury but photographs of the aftermath of Son's tackle left no doubt that he had suffered an awful injury.

"He's gone to hospital. Our medical staff are in control. This is a bad moment for us and our team — this was [about] more than a football game. We will give all support to André and his family."

As it turned out, Gomes would make a stunningly rapid recovery and, remarkably, he was back playing again just 112 days later.

***

23 November 2019: Everton v Norwich

Everton had followed up the draw against Tottenham with an away win at Southampton. Yet, at the halfway stage of a home match against newly-promoted Norwich City in late November, Evertonians were feeling as though they were stuck in a familiar pattern: just biding their time for Theo Walcott to be substituted around the 70-minute mark; for Alex Iwobi to come on like a fortnight previously to make some telling contribution that made a mockery of his selection among the substitutes; for Gylfi Sigurdsson to finally be deployed in the No.10 role; or for Marco Silva to throw on Dominic Calvert-Lewin either in place of, or in addition to Cenk Tosun.

Mostly, though, it felt like the Everton fraternity was simply marking time until Silva's time was up, and the Board put a merciful end to what was looking increasingly like a failed tenure. After the Norwich game, there was a sense that timescale had compressed dramatically.

Many Blues expected Silva to pick up three points against a Canaries side who came into the match rock bottom, then to eke out a few points from a daunting December programme, and limp his way to May where, maybe, the Everton hierarchy would make a bold decision to replace him with someone more experienced and more qualified.

Yet, there was an urgency about the managerial situation at Goodison, with the team in danger of spiralling out of control in a manner evoking the death throes of he Ronald Koeman and Roberto Martinez reigns. Indeed, there was a very "last days of Martinez" feel to this match, after Norwich took a second-half lead and the dread set in that, not only would Everton not recover but, just like Sheffield United did in September, the Canaries would complete the job with a late second.

That they did, and it triggered a chorus of loud boos and a rapid emptying of the stands, as disgusted fans poured out into the streets around Goodison amid a crushing sense of collective déjà vu, while many of those who remained to the bitter end made no secret of their feelings.

That Everton always provided accommodating opposition for any team or player struggling through a poor run is the stuff of gallows humour and social media meme, but after two wins and a draw since the frustrating events at Brighton last month, there can't have been many Blues who foresaw what unfolded today.

Norwich had arrived on Merseyside without an away win, with just a single goal on their travels since they regained promotion, and a stench of the doomed about them. But they matched Everton in a dull first half and by full-time, they had run rings around a desperately poor Toffees outfit, carved them open to score their first in the 55th minute, added a somewhat fortunate but predictable second in stoppage time and were just a Teemu Pukki goal from putting the cherry on top of the "Everton, That" cake.

It was that bad – so disorganised, passionless, lethargic and lacking in leadership – that even if they had rescued a point, it wouldn't have been enough to dampen the growing sense that Silva's week-to-week case for remaining in the post needed to come to a definitive end.

Final score: Everton 0-2 Norwich

***

4 December 2019: Liverpool v Everton

This fixture had become so painful as the years stretched on after Everton's last win on Liverpool's soil in 1999 that by the time Roberto Martinez had overseen two 4-0 defeats at Anfield, many Evertonians had developed a self-protective numbness to the derby. A certain level of defeatism and realism in the run-up to the game helped Blues fans cope with the agony of defeat and no one really gave Everton a chance when they crossed the Park in early December 2019 with manager Marco Silva under mounting pressure.

Whether this latest drubbing at the hands of the old enemy was as bad as feared or simply just depressingly predictable probably depended on who you asked, but at the base level, it felt as though Silva had failed the Blue faithful.

The injuries to his three preferred central midfielders continued to provide somewhat mitigating circumstances but where Silva arguably erred was in persisting with Gylfi Sigurdsson in midfield alongside Tom Davies, rather than restoring Morgan Schneiderlin, a player more used to playing in a withdrawn role in front of the back four, to the team.

Just as he had against Leicester on the preceding Sunday, a match that also ended in defeat for Everton, Davies struggled with the demands of covering more than just his usual duties alongside the Icelander, who was anonymous for long stretches even by the holographic standards he had set that season. It made for a vacuous midfield compounding a high defensive line that Liverpool ruthlessly exploited.

Given the reds' form and reputation, and the calamity that had recently befallen Everton in the final half hour at the King Power Stadium, at the very least one might have expected a compact and concentrated performance during the first half; one designed to nullify the Liverpool attack. Instead, the Blues were cavalier in the early going and, just as they had been by the Foxes the previous Sunday, were undone with depressing ease by fast transitions and then balls over the top that were so simple in their conception, it was a wonder how Silva's defence was still being caught out by them.

Sadio Mané should have completed a hat-trick, but far from learning from the error, Silva persisted with the high line, and was probably fortunate to escape Anfield without an even bigger deficit. Klopp's side quickly showed that all they had to do was catch Everton on the counter-attack, or ruthlessly exploit a ponderous and shambolic back line with long balls behind the defence to tear up the Portuguese's game plan.

They took all of six minutes to get the humiliation underway. Mané and his precision pass caught Michael Keane flat-footed and Jordan Pickford in no-man's-land off his line, allowing Divock Origi to take it past him and roll the ball into the empty net.

Ten minutes later, it was 2-0. Mané carried the ball to the edge of the Toffees' box and waited for Xherdan Shaqiri's run across him before slipping it into the path of the Swiss who cut it past the stranded Pickford. Cue remonstrations between Mason Holgate and Sidibé and earnest conversations between Keane and Davies.

To their credit, Everton didn't immediately fold, and they were back in the contest within just four minutes. A short corner routine almost broke down, with a poor ball by Sidibé, but the ball broke to Davies, he slid it to Alex Iwobi who drove the ball into the box where it came off the sliding Dejan Lovren and Keane knocked it over Adrian to make it 2-1.

Four minutes after that, Iwobi sent Calvert-Lewin away with a beautiful slide-rule pass but the striker was barged over by Virgil van Dijk just as he was pulling the trigger. If there was a VAR check, Everton would never have got a decision off Martin Atkinson, so play continued.

Unfortunately, what could on another day have been a turning point in the contest in favour of Everton's, prefaced a third goal for Liverpool. Once again, it was galling in its simplicity. Lovren looked up and sent a missile over the top behind Keane and Holgate, which Origi controlled and then steered high into Pickford's net.

That prompted an early change from Silva, who hooked Sidibé, who had been dreadful, and threw on Bernard; moved Holgate to fullback; and pushed Richarlison further forward alongside Calvert-Lewin.

But when an Everton corner was cleared, a rampant Liverpool sped away to score their fourth. Mané turned inside Iwobi in his own half and sent Alexander-Arnold away into a two-on-one situation. The young right back waited for the Senegalese to arrive before teeing him up for a tidy side-foot finish inside Pickford's right-hand post.

If there had been a beacon of light for Everton on an otherwise bleak and harrowing evening, it was that their two Brazilian lads never not lost their heart or desire. They combined to great effect in first-half stoppage time to send the visitors into the dressing room with some hope. Played down the left by Lucas Digne, Bernard despatched a left-footed cross towards the penalty spot and, throwing himself at it between the two centre-backs, Richarlison sent the ball flying past the goalkeeper into the net, off his shoulder.

It wasn't until the last 10 minutes that what had been a typically fractious derby opened up again. Despite a one-on-one chance for Kean against Adrián, it was the Reds who added insult to injury with a fifth goal in the 90th minute. Firmino twisted and turned Holgate near the by-line, cut it back to Gini Wijnaldum who sent an early shot through three Blue jerseys and inside the far post.

With his hands dug into his pockets, Silva had spent much of the second half with an expressionless demeanour, perhaps knowing that his team was struggling its way to another defeat. It had been men against boys for much of the match and it resulted in another psychologically damaging defeat.

Final score: Liverpool 5-2 Everton

***

Silva would rightly point to injuries to key players, cite awful officiating and injustice by VAR and bemoan some pretty rotten luck, but the scale and nature of this defeat unfortunately underscored that in a very Martinez way, Silva was struggling to prove that he could learn from his mistakes.

Amid reports that the Board of Directors would imminently discuss the manager's future by conference call, the axe was expected to fall swiftly. Whom they would bring in to replace him would be just as important as the decision to put Silva out of his misery. And those decisions would say a lot about the state of play in the boardroom, and just how much sway Marcel Brands now had.

2019: Silva sacked after 5-2 mauling at Anfield

> Everton's players were reportedly asked to stay behind after training to be addressed by the owner, and at 7.00 pm the first report emerged via the BBC claiming that Silva had been sacked and would not be in charge against Chelsea on that weekend

2019: Silva sacked after 5-2 mauling at Anfield

The morning after the debacle at Anfield, and amid fevered media speculation that Marco Silva would receive his marching orders, Everton's owner Farhad Moshiri was photographed leaving Runcorn train station before travelling to the club's training complex at Finch Farm. He was joined by Sasha Ryazantsev, his representative on the Board, and chairman Bill Kenwright for what bore all the hallmarks of the executioner coming to end Silva's time as manager.

Just a week earlier, following an interview by Director of Football, Marcel Brands, in which the Dutchman had stressed the club was going to stay united behind the manager, it appeared as though the Portuguese would be given more time to turn things around. But the nature of the derby defeat, in which Everton conceded four first-half goals for only the second time in the Premier League era, combined with the supporters' reaction, might have forced Moshiri's hand.

In truth, Silva had been clinging onto his role for weeks, lurching from damaging defeats to brief periods of apparent stability. However, successive defeats to Norwich City, Leicester and Liverpool proved to be the final straws for the club hierarchy who felt compelled to act.

Everton and their manager had left the field at Goodison to boos at the end of the 2-0 reverse to the Canaries, the third time this season that Silva's side had lost to a newly-promoted side without registering a goal. And, despite a promising showing against the Foxes, a weakened reds team had humiliated them in the Merseyside derby.

Those results had left the club sitting in the relegation zone, having lost nine of their opening 15 games of the Premier League campaign; a miserable return from what was, until that week, a relatively comfortable run of fixtures. Silva left the club with an overall win percentage of 36%, lower than Ronald Koeman's 40%, below Roberto Martinez's 38%, and a shade under the 37% managed by Sam Allardyce.

On a strange day at Finch Farm, Everton's players were also reportedly asked to stay behind after training to be addressed by the owner. By 7.00 pm the first report had emerged via the BBC, claiming that Silva had been sacked and would not be in charge against Chelsea on that weekend.

Indeed, sacked Silva was; 18 months into his three-year contract. First-team coach Duncan Ferguson was appointed in a caretaker capacity to take charge of the clash with the Londoners at Goodison

Park, while a club statement confirmed that Everton would look to appoint a new permanent manager as a quickly as possible.

Billed as potentially the next Jose Mourinho, Silva had been an ambitious hire by Moshiri who had pivoted from the experience and more staid style of Koeman and Allardyce to what he hoped would be a more dynamic style under a young, innovative coach.

But in Silva, many Evertonians had found echoes of Martinez's reign as boss, with an undercurrent of stubbornness against changing formations and defensive vulnerabilities that frequently cost his side points. In the wake of the miserable game at Anfield, few were left in doubt that Moshiri had needed to act.

2019: Big Dunc's Blues beat Chelsea

> Anyone who was at Goodison Park when Duncan Ferguson took charge of his first match as stand-in manager would have been in no doubt of the level of anxiety coursing through the crowd, given the outpouring of emotion and relief that greeted what happened that day.
>
> **2019 Big Dunc's Blues beat Chelsea**

In the years following his departure from Goodison Park, Marco Silva would lead Fulham back to the Premier League and rebuild his reputation as one of the most promising young managers in the game by achieving a top-half finish in the Cottagers' first season back in the top flight. As Everton lurched from one managerial crisis to the next, it would prompt much discussion about the culture at the club and the root causes behind so many failing coaches.

Even back then, there was a feeling that Evertonians might look back on the start of December 2019 and wonder – as they did two years previously when the club lifted itself clear from relegation danger during the transition from David Unsworth to Sam Allardyce – what all the panic was about.

But after the humiliation of the Merseyside derby, Everton sitting in the relegation zone for the second time in the space of two years, and with a daunting set of fixtures looming in the run-up to Christmas and into the New Year, there was still an understandable sense of foreboding among supporters.

Indeed, anyone who was at Goodison Park when Duncan Ferguson took charge of his first match as stand-in manager would have been in no doubt of the level of anxiety coursing through the crowd, given the outpouring of emotion and relief that greeted what happened that day.

7 December 2019: Everton v Chelsea

Duncan Ferguson had taken his first press conference as interim boss at Finch Farm the day before, where he expressed the pride he would feel standing in the dugout as manager of the team he represented with such passion as a player during two stints in the 1990s and early 2000s.

"It'll be an incredibly proud moment for me," Ferguson said. "Everybody knows how I feel about the club and I'll be emotional, nervous, excited and obviously looking for a positive result."

The 47-year-old admitted that he wasn't entertaining thoughts of taking on the managerial role at Goodison Park on a full-time basis, expressing that he didn't feel ready, and he repeatedly stressed during his presser that the focus was all about the match against Chelsea.

The Everton hierarchy had tasked Ferguson with rousing the players following Silva's dismissal and a damaging defeat in the Merseyside derby, and he admitted that while the team was going through a difficult time, sending a positive message would be really important.

"It's not nice for a manager to lose his job," the Scot said. "We all felt for him, everybody at the club supported him as best we could and it's unfortunate that he's lost his job but results determine that, don't they?

"[The reaction from the players has been] mixed as you can imagine .... but we've got to try and pick them up now. That's the great thing about football — there's always another game."

Away from the cameras and behind closed doors with the press journalists, Ferguson betrayed a little more emotion and explained that his message to the players would be one around the need to acknowledge the gravity of the situation facing the club and to give everything for the badge.

When asked whether Everton falling into the bottom three had hurt the players as much as it did him, Ferguson said, "Is that possible?" Well, we all hope it is, don't we? That is the kind of message we gave the players. We have to bleed for this club. We have to bleed on that pitch.

"I am looking forward to the team talk. Rallying the troops, no? There is not a lot you can do in this situation, a short period of time. You keep the message simple.

"There will be a rallying cry to get blood and thunder, but we also have to be sensible because we know how good Chelsea are. They can hurt you on the counterattack, so we need a good defensive balance and then take it from there.

"I believe in this squad. I believe they can turn it around and I believe that is what we will do. I have my ideas. I know what I am going to go with. My message is clear."

Everton badly needed a result against Chelsea; one point would have done in the circumstances but three would have been priceless. And cometh the hour, cometh the Talisman – wearing Howard Kendall's watch, it would later be revealed – to inspire from a hitherto listless and directionless team a performance of high intensity, desire and determination that was matched by a raucous and then rapturous Goodison Park.

The team sheet, featuring the much-maligned Gylfi Sigurdsson, Morgan Schneiderlin, Theo Walcott, and Dominic Calvert-Lewin - a player who hadn't scored since October – was not greeted with much enthusiasm. Yet the trust instilled in them by Ferguson was returned tenfold.

In a pleasing and long-overdue break from Silva's reliance on a lone — and all-too-often isolated — striker, Ferguson deployed Richarlison up front with Calvert-Lewin and the difference in terms of the latter's game was significant. Both players were involved in the opening goal, a well-worked move that Richarlison started by collecting a pass from his strike partner and laying it off wide to Sidibé, who still had plenty of work to do before whipping in a perfect cross for Richarlison to meet in the middle with another unstoppable header. A goal straight from the playbook of Big Dunc, the player.

With fresh instructions from Ferguson at the break, Everton emerged from half-time with the same sense of purpose that had served them so well in the first period, and they doubled their lead just four minutes after the restart. Kurt Zouma, back at Goodison for the first time since his loan spell with the Toffees ended in May, could only slice a loose ball into the air.

Calvert-Lewin jostled with Andreas Christensen as it dropped, got a fortunate bounce off Zouma that took it beyond the defender and had time to weigh up his shot before steering it beyond Kepa to make it 2-0. Ferguson, who had leapt down the touchline in unbridled joy for the first goal, went galloping out of his technical area again, this time scooping up a ball boy, as he celebrated what felt like a massively important second goal.

Chelsea were back in it within three minutes, though, thanks to an accomplished finish by Mateo Kovacic. Frank Lampard's side attacked down their left flank and when Digne could only sweep a cross as far as Kovacic, the Croatian guided a controlled first-time shot past the unsighted Pickford and inside the post to make it 2-1.

Sensing that his team might need bolstering in midfield, Ferguson withdrew Richarlison with 20 minutes to go and introduced Tom Davies, a decision that did not sit particularly well with the Brazilian.

Christensen had too much space to advance into in the 79th minute and he pinged one narrowly off target from distance. A minute later, Holgate, another particularly impressive performer on the day, blocked Mount's volley and Pickford tipped Azpilicueta's shot over from the rebound as Chelsea continued to press for an equaliser, but it was to be Calvert-Lewin's day.

Kepa's pass out from his area missed Zouma and was intercepted by the alert Walcott, who tucked a beautiful pass between two Chelsea players and into Calvert-Lewin's path. He back-heeled it to Davies who couldn't quite dig it out from under his feet, Kanté blocked the loose ball and it ricocheted nicely for Calvert-Lewin to stretch out a boot, knock it through the legs of both Azpilicueta and the keeper and into the empty net. Lady Luck, who had utterly abandoned Silva, smiled on the Blues.

It was not clear how long Ferguson would remain in charge at Goodison. If he was to be given the responsibility of overseeing the next few games or even asked to stay on in the role until the end of the season, it was hoped that future results would not tarnish what was a magical day for him and a match that will live long in the collective Evertonian memory. The way he spoke after the game, you got the feeling he would have loved to take this match and result back home with him, put it on the mantlepiece if he could, and just be happy with that for the time being.

More than a few supporters questioned the wisdom of appointing Ferguson, a first-team coach about whose abilities fans knew very little, to the job of taking up the reins from Silva with the team in such dire need of a pick-me-up. But he answered the call in typical "Duncan" fashion — with a passion and hunger that left no player on that team in doubt of what it means to represent Everton Football Club. The reaction that he and a bear-pit crowd inspired in the players could not have been understated.

His influence spurred the Blues to a massive victory that smashed through the wall of worry that had surrounded the club and its supporters as they viewed a pre-Christmas schedule with dread. A trip to rejuvenated Manchester United next would test the team to the limits, but there was no question that a performance of this ilk would have struggling Arsenal quivering in their boots back at Goodison in a fortnight's time, and there was renewed hope for the looming League Cup Quarter-Final tie against Leicester as well.

Final score: Everton 3-1 Chelsea

***

After the final whistle, Duncan Ferguson was revelling in what he described as an "incredible experience" at a bouncing Goodison Park but he insisted that he wasn't thinking about becoming permanent boss.

"It was incredible today!" Ferguson beamed to *BT Sport*. "Honestly, I've felt nothing like it in my life. It was unbelievable. What an atmosphere.

"I know we had to defend a lot and probably sit back and keep in a good shape and pick a time to break. I think we did that well. We kept our shape well and, as you can see, it was a 4-4-2 screening their two holders. I thought we did that well, and we pressed the ball well when it went wide.

"I thought all the players were absolutely fantastic."

Asked if he was looking beyond the events of the day, towards the next few matches or even contemplating putting himself forward for the role permanently, the 47-year-old quipped: "I'm just looking to get home for a lie down, I think!

"No, I'm not looking too far ahead at all, to be honest with you. I was just looking at this game and that is it. We're just savouring the moment. It's three fantastic points for us, that's the main thing.

"I think they (the hierarchy) saw how enthusiastic I was on the touchline, but it's one game, it's one result."

In his post-match press conference, he joked with the media, "I don't think I could go through it again, to be honest with you!

"Listen, it was just one game at a time for me. I was asked to come in and I'd never turn down Everton Football Club, but I'm also realistic. It was a game. I'm made up and delighted for the fans. Three points is massive for us."

***

A week after the Chelsea triumph, Ferguson held onto the managerial reins for a tough away fixture at Old Trafford, and his side came away with a deserved 1-1 draw before entertaining Leicester City in the last eight of the Carabao Cup. Everton bravely rallied back from being 2-0 down to the Foxes after just half and hour, with Tom Davies pulling one back before Leighton Baines smashed home a stunning strike in stoppage time to force a penalty shootout. Unfortunately though, Baines was one of two Blues players to see spot-kicks saved and the visitors went through.

Meanwhile, talk of who would become the club's next permanent manager was rumbling on in the background. The broad consensus was that Ferguson was too raw and inexperienced for the role and Vitor Pereira, a name that would surface again much further down the line, quickly ruled himself out of the running by committing his future to SIPG Shanghai.

For a while it seemed as though the most likely successor to Marco Silva was none other than David Moyes who was unemployed at the time, having been overlooked for a permanent role at West Ham in favour of Manuel Pellegrini. The Scot would later describe how close he came to coming back on board as the Toffees' manager that month – all the pieces were being put in place for that after Moyes' interview in Germany with "the people who run Everton." Then, at the last minute, Farhad Moshiri saw an opportunity to land an unexpectedly big fish.

The day before the League Cup Quarter-Final against Leicester, Everton had moved to dampen what seemed to be bizarre speculation that coaching legend Carlo Ancelotti had committed to become the club's next manager.

The Italian, one of the most decorated head coaches in European footballing history, had just been sacked as manager of Napoli and was on the market, but the Blues released a statement asserting that, despite reports the Italian had agreed a deal to succeed Marco Silva, no firm contract offer had been made to Ancelotti.

Everton's statement read: "In the 11 days since Marco Silva left the club, the Everton Board have been working to recruit a new manager - and has held meetings with a number of candidates. We can confirm that thus far no contract offer has been made, and no candidate has chosen to withdraw from the process."

Everton playing coy might have been because Ancelotti still had to return to Naples to complete the details of his severance from the Serie A club, but media reports, both on the Continent and in Britain continued to suggest that he was set to become the next incumbent of the Goodison Park hot seat.

Sky Sports News and their sources in Italy claimed that Ancelotti, having been persuaded to join by Moshiri in a telephone conversation, had already travelled to England and agreed a deal in principle with

Everton. Incredibly, within days the Italian would be in the Directors Box at Goodison next to his new bosses.

2019: Carlo Ancelotti is Blues' surprise Christmas present

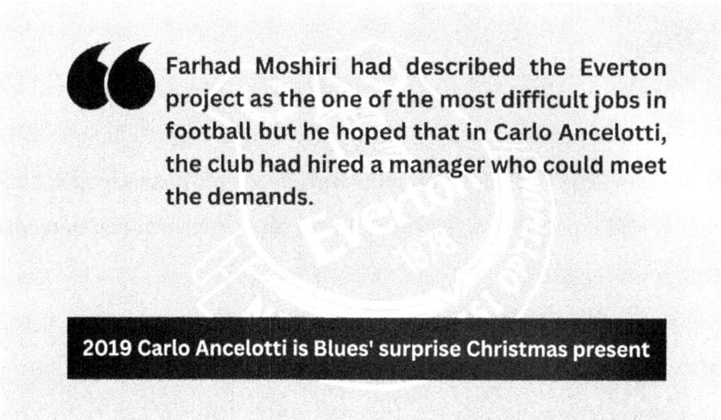

Just hours before they were due to face Arsenal at Goodison, just four days before Christmas, Everton confirmed what had become one of football's worst-kept secrets: Carlo Ancelotti was the club's new manager, succeeding Marco Silva following his dismissal from the role on 6th December and the Italian's departure from Napoli.

Ancelotti signed a four-and-a-half-year contract and became the third permanent appointee under Farhad Moshiri's reign at Goodison Park, following the high-profile capture of Ronald Koeman in 2016 and the protracted pursuit of Silva that led to the Portuguese being hired in May 2018. Previously, they had installed controversial coach Sam Allardyce on an interim basis after sacking Koeman only 18 months into the job, having achieved Moshiri's goal of avoiding relegation in 2017/18.

Ancelotti, meanwhile, had had his contract ended by Napoli, despite leading them to the second place in the Italian top flight the previous season, and securing their passage to the knockout phase of the Champions League just before he was fired. It had ended a difficult relationship with the Serie A club's chairman, Aurelio De Laurentiis, one that had made a parting of the ways at Stadio San Paolo seem inevitable.

The then 60-year-old coach – who had infamously been fired by Chelsea in a corridor at Goodison following a league game against Everton in 2011 – had begun talks with Everton's hierarchy five days earlier, and reports emerged that evening that Ancelotti had agreed a deal in principle .

Negotiations had continued, amid rumours Everton were prepared to make Ancelotti one of the highest-paid coaches in Europe. There were also reports he was seeking assurances from Moshiri and his board that there was scope for investment to upgrade the team.

He would officially take charge on Boxing Day when the Toffees faced Burnley at home, which left the reins in Duncan Ferguson's hands for the Premier League clash with Arsenal. It meant Ancelotti would watch on from the stands, near to the Gunners' own newly-appointed head coach, Mikel Arteta.

It had also been agreed that Ferguson would stay on at the club as one of the new man's assistants, alongside Ancelotti's son, Davide.

Ancelotti was one of the most successful managers in the game and his appointment represented an impressive acquisition for Everton and another statement of intent by Moshiri. The Everton gig was the Reggiolo-born coach's 10th managerial role, having helmed some of the biggest names in European football, including Juventus, AC Milan, Paris Saint-Germain, Real Madrid and Bayern Munich.

He had won 15 major trophies in his 24-year career, was one of a select few to have already won the Champions League three times, and had won league titles in four different countries.

The day's match against the club from North London almost seemed like a sideshow, and the dull goalless draw that played out seemed to reinforce that notion.

Final score: Everton 0-0 Arsenal

***

Farhad Moshiri had described the Everton project as the one of the most difficult jobs in football but he hoped that in Carlo Ancelotti, the club had hired a manager who could meet the demands.

The Blues' majority shareholder was speaking with Jim White of *TalkSport* at Goodison Park after the draw with Arsenal and he spoke of his gratitude to Duncan Ferguson for restoring the passion to Everton's game while also explaining how he felt Marco Silva struggled to cope with the pressure brought on by the supporters' expectations.

With the appointment of Ronald Koeman in 2016, Moshiri felt he was hiring a man capable of fitting into the "Hollywood" of managers that he felt the northwest of England had become, with Jurgen Klopp in place across the park, together with Pep Guardiola and Jose Mourinho in Manchester.

While Ancelotti certainly fitted that bill more than Koeman, the Iranian-born billionaire distanced himself from that description in his chat with White:

> "We've had managers from Wigan, Southampton and Watford and they've all had their impact, but we've invested heavily in a group of players. They're all internationals, so we think they could benefit from someone of this pedigree. It has nothing to do with 'Hollywood' really. You know, we've rediscovered Everton in the past two weeks. I've had my most enjoyable time with Duncan and we're really grateful to him. This is the club and I think we just need to keep this; that is the most valuable aspect of Everton, not Hollywood. This passion, celebrations of fans and the manager together. Carlo is a real football man and we hope with Duncan next to him we keep the passion, and we build on it.
>
> Everton is a very difficult job in football because you're two home losses from being disowned by fans. It's very hard and what we've noticed for younger managers is that it's difficult to cope. Because you have the bad runs, but I think the fans don't give you any

time and the strength of Goodison is the passion of the fans and once you lose that it's very difficult. I think Silva was a very talented coach and when the gods of football aren't kind to you, what can you do? You know, we lost six points through VAR, he loses 70% of his midfield but I think a good general is a lucky one, that's the thing. I think this is one of the most difficult clubs. We don't have the financial base but the fans' expectations are huge so I think this mismatch somehow needs to be resolved. So we've put a lot of money in to give the club a platform to match the fans' expectation and sometimes it's just too much for a young manager so we hope that an experienced manager can cope and deal with it better."

***

26 December 2019: Everton v Burnley

If Marco Silva was reclining somewhere watching this game with his slippers on he might have been nodding ruefully in the second half, as Everton struggled to break down a Burnley side who had brought their most defensive of game plans to Goodison Park for Carlo Ancelotti's first game in charge.

As the contest ticked towards the 80-minute mark, the visitors had failed to register a shot on target but the hosts, who had enjoyed almost 70% of the possession overall, had still failed to break the deadlock. As for so much of the Portuguese's tenure, Everton were dominating the ball but struggling to find the inspiration and penetration in the final third and it was all very reminiscent of the previous regime.

There was, however, a fluidity to the Blues' system, one which alternated between 3-4-3 with Djibril Sidibe in a more advanced right-midfield role and Seamus Coleman tucking into the back line, and a more conventional 4-4-2. Besides an assurance about their possession of the ball overall, there was also greater positional dynamism in Everton's midfield which allowed Bernard, in particular, to drift into the middle and Richarlison to drop back into the hole, creating the space and opportunities for the Blues to break Burnley's lines in quick transition in a manner that wasn't always the case under Silva.

With a bit more decisiveness and composure in advanced areas, it might have yielded an earlier goal, but there were embryonic signs of the flexibility and ideas that Ancelotti could bring to the team. As it was, just when it looked as though the Italian was realising first-hand the shortcomings of the side he had inherited, everything came together with 10 minutes to go.

Sidibé received the ball on the right flank and the Frenchman delivered another of his telling crosses that Dominic Calvert-Lewin met with a gloriously old-school diving header that bounced in off the far post to hand Ancelotti his first three points as the Toffees' boss.

Though the lead was a narrow one, Everton never really looked to be in any danger of giving up the points in the closing stages and they comfortably held out for the win that lifted them into 13th place and within three points of their next opponents, Newcastle, who were sitting in 10th place. Ancelotti described it as the perfect first game and while it was short on genuine thrills and entertainment, few

Blues would argue given the wider context of the season and the key absentees in the squad, particularly in midfield.

Final score: Everton 1-0 Burnley

***

28 December 2019: Newcastle United v Everton

Within six days of Carlo Ancelotti taking his first training session as Everton's new manager, he already had six points on the board and, depending on what happened with other teams, the Blues could have had the comfort of starting 2020 in the top half of the Premier League table.

That felt like an awfully far cry from how Evertonians were feeling on the 5th of December following a third successive defeat, and humiliation in the Merseyside derby that had left the club sitting in the relegation zone with three more of the "big six" still to play in successive games.

Duncan Ferguson, of course, had played his part, rousing a squad depleted of personnel and morale to a win and a draw before Farhad Moshiri landed one of the biggest fish possible as Marco Silva's successor.

It was very early days but the contrasts between the vastly experienced Italian and a comparative managerial novice were already clear, not least in terms of tactical shifts and game management, both of which elements lay at the heart of a 2-1 victory at St James's Park.

It was hard not to draw the distinctions between this result and the corresponding fixture on this ground last season. On both occasions,

Everton were winning 2-1, with 25 minutes to go but where, in March, Silva's side collapsed in the final 10 minutes and lost a match they had been leading 2-0, this time Ancelotti's charges held on in disciplined and increasingly assured fashion to secure the points.

Aside from the first couple of exchanges, Everton dominated the first 25 minutes, hogging almost 70% of the ball, and a spell of pressure that began in the 10th minute eventually told.

Gylfi Sigurdsson's direct free-kick cannoned back to him off the defensive wall, his shot on the rebound deflected off a defender and fell to Dominic Calvert-Lewin in front of goal, and he picked his spot beyond Dubravka to give the Toffees the lead.

It was a mostly professional away performance, particularly after Calvert-Lewin had slid the ball home to put Everton back in front after Fabian Schär had cancelled out his first-half opener.

With a win that had given Everton 11 points from a possible 15 since Silva's departure, things were certainly looking up for the Blues as they looked ahead to 2020. And after 22 shots on goal to add to the 21 they registered against Burnley, there was no shortage of attacking endeavour in the team now.

Ancelotti rightly pointed out afterwards that his team could and needed to play better football. It disappointed him with the way they ceded the initiative back to Newcastle in the first half, but he was justifiably pleased with his return of maximum points so far.

The trip to Manchester City on New Year's Day and an FA Cup date at Anfield would pose altogether more difficult challenges, but Evertonians would travel to both games with a good deal more confidence that their side could produce something away from home.

There was a long way to go with some key parts of the side that the new boss would eventually want to improve, but the way things were going, there was hope it would be a happy New Year after all.

Final score: Newcastle United 1-2 Everton

***

In January, 2020, for anyone wondering how Everton could fund further investment in Carlo Ancelotti's squad and simultaneously finance a new stadium, news that billionaire businessman, Alisher Usmanov, was pondering greater involvement at Everton was timely.

Usmanov's name had already come up in reports suggesting he had personally spoken with Ancelotti to assure him of financial backing for improving the squad, and he admitted that he was considering increasing his investment in Everton, including the possibility of buying naming rights in the club's new stadium.

By this point, the Uzbek-born tycoon had sold his 30% stake in the Gunners after the London club's owner, Stan Kroenke, confirmed he had no interest in letting him onto the Board of Directors at the Emirates.

Usmanov said in an interview with the *Financial Times* in December 2019 that he would think seriously about increasing his exposure at Everton beyond the current sponsorship deals with USM Holdings and Megafon if Moshiri wants him on board:

> "Yes. With great pleasure, if he asks. I am thinking about my investment in this club. I cannot reject Arsenal. I will not leave them as a fan. But if I join Everton, then I will wear an Everton shirt, because I am a professional. They are going to build a new stadium. Why not the USM Arena? It is not obligatory for me to participate myself. I could just sponsor them."

***

5 January 2020: Liverpool v Everton

Carlo Ancelotti had only been in his post for 12 days when he took his new side across Stanley Park for an FA Cup Third Round tie against Liverpool, and it seemed that not even the venerated Italian was immune to the malady that so often afflicts Everton teams at Anfield.

Gutless. Spineless. Witless. Hapless. It was a case of choose your adjective on a harrowing night. Everton's long-suffering fans had witnessed some pathetic performances at Anfield in recent years, but this one, against a Liverpool team featuring nine changes and stuffed with inexperienced kids, took the proverbial biscuit.

Everton turned in a second-half display so bereft of fight, quality, spirit and urgency that it left fans wishing they could throw half the players out the club immediately. Sadly, as the imminent financial accounts would show, the club was counting the significant cost of almost four years of horrendously expensive and just plain poor recruitment that would no doubt require Ancelotti to use all four-and-a-half years of his contract to fix.

The second 45 minutes was indescribably bad from a group of players who, it was felt, couldn't provide much worse than some of the dross they had already served up that season. Whether through fatigue, or a simple sense of the futility that had embodied this fixture for Everton for two decades, they appeared to just give up.

For so much of this increasingly dejecting match, the team full of youngsters was the one playing with all the composure while the one with four players 30 or older and packed with internationals was struggling just to do the basics. And it was a reliance on the basic, later abandoned, that had served them so well in the first half hour of the game when they had gone close to taking the lead.

A low drive from around the penalty spot from Dominic Calvert-Lewin was perhaps too accurate, in that he put it down the middle and Adrian saved with his feet. Mason Holgate latched onto a whipped free-kick from Gylfi Sigurdsson, but he planted a free header straight at the goalkeeper. And when Theo Walcott cut the ball back from the by-line for Richarlison, he too was denied by the goalkeeper's foot.

With Liverpool failing to trouble Pickford, it felt as though it was only a matter of time before Ancelotti's men made the breakthrough but the tide started turning in the second half and Everton gradually disappeared from the contest. Pickford pushed out a bouncing, speculative effort from Divock Origi before Curtis Jones produced the moment of magic that the match had been sorely missing, particularly from those in blue jerseys.

The 18-year-old collected Origi's pass after good hold-up play by the Belgian and he sized up a shot from the edge of the area that he curled over Pickford's despairing fingertips and in off the underside of the bar.

The effect on Everton, with all the experience in its ranks playing in front 8,000 expectant supporters, was utterly demoralising, because Ancelotti's men appeared to lose all belief and any remaining ability to string together a series of passes.

Ultimately, Everton's failure to put a single effort on target in the final hour of the match was a damning indictment of the performance, and of the players who plumbed new depths of awfulness.

Just four games into his new job, Ancelotti would have had his eyes opened to the problems that existed in this squad, and the amount of work that would be required to turn it around. So early in his reign, this one wasn't on the manager; this was squarely on a group of players who had largely escaped the worst of the criticism and allowed Marco Silva to carry the can, but now had nowhere left to hide.

Final score: Liverpool 1-0 Everton

***

1 February 2020: Watford v Everton

Although Carlo Ancelotti had begun 2020 with successive away defeats, to Manchester City in the Premier League and Liverpool in the FA Cup, he stabilised Everton's form over the following month with three wins and two draws that lifted the Blues into the top half of the table for the first time since the previous September.

Two of those points had slipped away in almost comical fashion at Goodison against Newcastle in late January when Everton, leading 2-0 going into stoppage time, somehow contrived to draw 2-2 as the Magpies netted two quick goals in the 94th and 95th minutes.

However, they would make amends three days later with a thrilling victory at Watford with their own last-gasp goal.

It was rare that Theo Walcott completed 90 minutes in an Everton shirt by that stage. Indeed, before this match, he hadn't managed it since the final day of the previous season at Tottenham — also the last time he had scored — and had it not been for Fabian Delph's dismissal in the 72nd minute of this game at Vicarage Road, it's possible he would have been hooked again well before the end.

Such are the quirks of fate that meant that Walcott, a rival to Delph for the worst performer in blue on the day, remained on while Dominic Calvert-Lewin was sacrificed. That enabled the introduction of Michael Keane to shore up the back, and Walcott was there in the final minute of regulation time to score a dramatic winner that capped an equally stunning Everton comeback from 2-0 down.

If Carlo Ancelotti's men needed to get the final minute of that recent Newcastle 2-2 draw out of their system, this certainly did the trick and they exorcised a few other demons, not least Marco Silva's failure to engineer victory from a losing position during his stewardship of the team. The last time an Everton side had come back from being down prior to this had been in December 2017, and the last time they'd overcome a 2-0 deficit away from home was under Roberto Martinez when they beat West Bromwich Albion in 2015.

This Everton team also didn't tend to score from corners and yet, thanks to Yerry Mina goals that came around like buses, they bagged two and then stymied Watford enough when they were a man down to allow for the counter-attack that led to Walcott becoming the unlikely hero of what was ultimately an unforgettable afternoon.

Gerard Deulofeu created the opener for Watford by bringing the ball out of the air deftly laying it to Adam Masina who had driven forward, completely untracked by Walcott. He fired a shot into the ground, past Pickford's left glove and inside the far post to score. Of course, his first ever goal for the Hornets.

A dreadful error from Delph led to the hosts' second when he gifted the ball straight to Troy Deeney outside his own penalty area and the striker paused before playing Roberto Pereyra in to drive a shot past Pickford three minutes before half-time.

Just as they had done at West Ham a fortnight previously, however, Everton pressed in the dying phases of the first half and were rewarded when Yerry Mina met a flighted corner from Lucas Digne, the ball dropped to Holgate who couldn't force it past the man on the line, but it finally broke nicely back to Mina who prodded home.

That would end up being more than just a fillip to take into the dressing room because two minutes later, Everton would score from their second corner after Pereyra had blocked Digne's attempted cross. Sigurdsson took the honours this time from the opposite side and he swung his delivery over everyone except Mina who easily stepped in front of Craig Cathcart to plant a downward header into the unoccupied side of Foster's goal to make it 2-2.

Suddenly the whole complexion of the game had changed and with fresh instructions from Ancelotti ringing in their ears, the Blues emerged for the second half with much more intensity and tempo about their game. However, despite the overall improvement from Ancelotti's men, chances were few.

The prospect of victory appeared to evaporate in the 71st minute, however, with the latest of Delph's bone-headed lapses in judgement. The midfielder had Etienne Capoue safely up against the touchline and going nowhere, but elected to tackle him and ended up chopping him down to concede the free kick. As stupid as the supposedly experienced midfielder's challenge was, it was a ridiculously soft decision by referee Craig Pawson to book him but, in making the challenge, Delph had given the officials a decision to make, one heavily influenced by Capoue's theatrics and the urging of Watford's players and the crowd, and it ended with Everton finishing the game with 10 men.

Ancelotti sacrificed Calvert-Lewin for Keane, moving the excellent Holgate into midfield alongside Schneiderlin and the move proved inspired, giving Everton the defensive solidity to hold Watford at bay before they pinched all three points at the death.

Masina couldn't bring Holgate's defensive header from Mariappa's long throw under his spell, and Kean nipped it off his toe into the path of Richarlison who raced off down the left while his strike partner and Walcott sped forward with to his right. The Brazilian delayed until he got within 10 yards of the box before slipping it in to Moise Kean who, depending on your point of view, either missed his kick or helped it on to Walcott arriving at the back stick in time to steer home a composed finish.

The release of emotion, perhaps pent up from that frustrating conclusion to Everton's last game, was palpable as all the players and substitutes mobbed Walcott near the corner flag in front of the delirious away fans.

Indeed, this was the perfect, albeit slightly mad, antidote to the utter emptiness with which Toffees fans greeted the final whistle against Newcastle. Whereas that draw with the Magpies had seen Everton throw away two points at the end of arguably their best performance of the season, this time they first looked to have retrieved a point from a seemingly lost situation, and then they grabbed all three just when it looked as though a draw would have to be enough, even after being reduced to 10 men.

It meant that they would finish the weekend in at least 10th, and, at most, just four points off fifth place with a series of fixtures against last season's top six to come that presented real opportunities for further upward progress. If this was the Ancelotti effect, long may it continue!

Final score: Watford 2-3 Everton

2020: COVID-19 GRIPS FOOTBALL

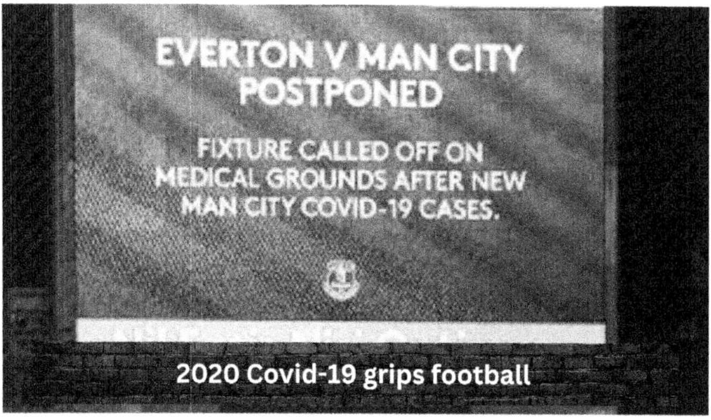

2020 Covid-19 grips football

On 11 January, 2020, the Chinese National Health Commission notified The World Health Organisation that they had identified a new type of rapidly-spreading coronavirus, SARS-CoV2. The world was about to be turned upside down.

By 31 January, Italy had flagged that its first infections had occurred, in two tourists from China. Spain reported its first cases the next day. The U.K. saw its third case confirmed on 6 February, with the patient having visited Singapore.

Throughout February and early March, the number of cases of this mysterious new virus reported around the world increased exponentially. Deaths followed cases. Dramatic scenes of Emergency Departments at full stretch filled our TV screens hourly.

The UK government was relatively slow to implement restrictions on large gatherings. Sporting and cultural events, including football, continued into March. Everton drew 1-1 with Manchester United on 1 March in front of a packed Goodison Park, followed by an away game at Chelsea on 8 March.

The Cheltenham Festival took place from 10th to 12th March, attended by 150,000 people. Meanwhile, Liverpool hosted Atletico Madrid on 11 March, with thousands of Spaniards flying into the city for the Champions League match.

Despite the spread of the coronavirus, and the fact that the rest of Europe's major leagues had either been suspended or scheduled to go ahead behind closed doors, the Premier League released a statement saying that the full programme of matches would go ahead on the weekend of 15 March.

The situation quickly changed, however, when Arsenal manager Mikel Arteta and Chelsea players Callum Hudson-Odoi both tested positive for the virus and both squads went into "lockdown", prompting an emergency meeting of the Premier League and EFL. The Premier League then issued a statement, initially suspending English football until 4th April, which read:

"Despite the challenges, it is the Premier League's aim to reschedule the displaced fixtures, including those played by Academy sides, when it is safe to do so. In this fast-moving environment, further updates will be provided when appropriate."

Premier League Chief Executive, Richard Masters added: "Above all, we wish Mikel Arteta and Callum Hudson-Odoi speedy recoveries, and everyone else affected by COVID-19. In this unprecedented situation, we are working closely with our clubs, Government, The FA and EFL, and can reassure everyone the health and welfare of players, staff and supporters are our priority."

The suspension of all Premier League, EFL and top-level women's football in England meant the friendlies against Italy and Denmark, scheduled for 27 March and 31 March respectively, were also shelved.

In addition, Everton closed Goodison Park, Finch Farm and their headquarters at the Royal Liver Building once an un-named player went into self-isolation after exhibiting symptoms suggestive of coronavirus or influenza. In statement, the club said:

"Everton Football Club can confirm that one member of the Everton first-team squad reported a high temperature last night and is now undertaking a period of self-isolation for seven days. In line with Government guidelines no other players are self-isolating at this stage but the Club's USM training facility has been closed as a precaution and staff, including players, have been advised to stay away from all Club sites until further notice."

***

By 24 March, there was a mounting acceptance among Premier League players they would have to play to empty stadiums if any attempt to conclude the 2019/20 season by June 30th was to be successful.

That was the date by which UEFA had said that Europe's domestic leagues needed to have played their remaining fixtures but, with the COVID-19 crisis still unfolding, there were fears that the new 30 April timeline set by the Football Association for the resumption of matches would come too soon.

Certainly, with Prime Minister Boris Johnson having only just moved the country into a "suppression" phase of the virus contagion, by mandating that citizens stay home except to conduct essential errands and business, and experts predicting that the U.K. could be as hard hit by the coronavirus as Italy and Spain, there appeared to be little chance that fans would assemble under one roof again only five weeks later.

While *The Mirror's* back page screamed, "No Fans, No Way!" amid claims the players would revolt if asked to play behind closed doors, a report by David Ornstein for *The Athletic* following conversations with PFA deputy chief executive, Bobby Barnes, suggested the players were taking a realistic view towards the need to finish the current season and were increasingly aware that they wouldn't be playing in front of people.

Barnes admitted that, at the outset, there was significant opposition to the idea of empty stadiums, but the financial realities of the situation would ultimately hold sway.

"I've been speaking to players — including two or three very high-profile Premier League players more or less on a daily basis — and the conversations I had with them at the outset were based around not wanting to play behind closed doors, if at all possible," Barnes explained.

"I said to them, 'Look, none of us, in an ideal world, want to play in front of empty stadiums. Football is about fans. But the reality is that, for the vast majority of the players, particularly at the highest level, television money funds their income and there are contracts that have to be adhered to. In order for us (the PFA) to be able to protect those players in terms of securing their salaries... if that's the only offer we have on the table to complete the season, then that is what it will be'.

"The players get it. They understand the alternative. Quite frankly, if we're going to get the season finished in a timely fashion so that we can even consider starting next season, we've got to be open to all options.

"If it means playing behind closed doors has to happen in order that contracts are protected, fixtures fulfilled and commercial deals honoured, then I think we've all got to come together and accept we've all got to sacrifice to try and find a solution for the industry as a whole."

Britain, together with most of the developed world, was soon in full lockdown, and Carlo Ancelotti said that he believed football, like so much of the world, would emerge changed from the Coronavirus crisis when things eventually returned to some sense of normality.

The Premier League entered its third week of forced shutdown as the COVID-19 pandemic continued to sweep across Europe, with the United Kingdom still on a depressingly upward curve in terms of positive cases and deaths from the virus. Meanwhile, the timeframe for when football could return kept getting moved further out.

Speaking in an interview with *Corriere dello Sport,* Ancelotti insisted he wasn't concerned with when matches could resume, but he admitted that, financially, the game will necessarily 'downsize', amid the predicted economic fallout of a severe global recession.

"I'm certain we're all going to have to get downsized, starting with football," the Italian said. "Today's priority is health to limit the contagion. Everything else is secondary.

"When you start again when you finish, the dates, the promises, the hopes... believe me, I don't care in this moment and [that is] the last of my thoughts.

"The initial idea was to restart in May, but it's out of the question that we can do it. I hear talk of salary cuts, suspension of payments. They seem to me to be untimely solutions.

"Soon the economy will change, and at all levels, television rights will be worth less. Players and coaches will earn less, tickets will cost less because people will have less money. Let's prepare for a general decline."

In the media, there was soon talk of players needing to defer salaries and agree potential wage cuts, as football of all levels grappled with the effects of lost income and the unknown duration of the shutdown.

***

By the end of April, a plan was starting to come together. English clubs were discussing plans that could see the 2019/20 season restart on 13 June, albeit behind closed doors as the nation remained in the coronavirus's grip.

By that time, the Premier League had already been shut down for over six weeks. The COVID-19 pandemic which, according to Government figures, had already claimed the lives of over 20,000 Britons, made the prospect of playing top-level football matches unthinkable.

With the threat of millions of pounds of default payments due, because of lost broadcast revenue, the top-flight clubs committed to finishing the campaign rather than voiding it entirely. Yet there was still little scope for holding matches, even without fans in attendance given the testing requirements of players and the estimated two to three hundred people needed on site at each game.

UEFA were pressuring each of its member leagues to furnish them with plans by 23rd May, for either completing or cancelling the current season.

According to *The Mirror*, the Premier League had scheduled the middle of June as a date on which matches might resume, with the season running into August if necessary to clear the backlog of 90-odd fixtures.

English Clubs met again to discuss "Project Restart" in further detail. In the meantime, France effectively called an end to the season, after their government ruled out any matches, even behind closed doors, being held until September.

It was 10 June before they finally made the decision to allow the derby game to be played at Goodison Park on 21 June behind closed doors, with a 7.00 pm kick off.

That followed weeks of speculation, by Liverpool City Council's ground safety advisory group, after most local entities (the police, the mayor, the clubs) had expressed their support for the game going ahead at Goodison Park.

The Goodison derby had been on a list of fixtures which the United Kingdom's football policing lead, Deputy Chief Constable Mark Roberts of South Yorkshire Police, said local forces had requested to be played at a neutral venue.

However, Merseyside Police appeared to contradict DCC Roberts by saying they were happy to police matches in Liverpool. Then, at a meeting of the council's Safety Advisory Group, they gave Everton

remained uncomfortably short of quality in attacking midfield, something that would hopefully be addressed in the summer.

Final score: Everton 0-0 Liverpool

***

27 July 2020: Everton v Bournemouth (Behind Closed Doors)

Between the derby game on 21 June and the final game of the season, Everton had languished in mid-table. There were wins against Norwich, Leicester and Sheffield United, draws against Southampton and Villa, as well as defeats against Spurs and Wolves. The players had adjusted to playing in eerily quiet stadiums and on an accelerated schedule that crammed nine games into a little over a month, and the season would be concluded by 27 July. With the final game being a home match against Bournemouth, there was an opportunity for Carlo's men to sign off in style.

At an empty Goodison Park, another weak and uninspiring performance and a fifteenth Premier League defeat of the campaign condemned Everton to their lowest league finish since 2004. Hardly a fitting occasion for one of the finest players of the modern era to bow out and yet a result entirely in keeping with this wretched season.

Leighton Baines came on as a 70th-minute substitute, made one last goal-denying tackle and then called time on his magnificent career after the game. He would leave the Blues having never won a trophy, but departed with the adoration of Evertonians everywhere.

Baines would not be a part of what came next at Everton (at least not in a playing capacity), but in some ways he might have felt like he was better off out of it; because unless Carlo Ancelotti could effect more than just the "evolution" he promised, there was more frustration to come with this collection of players.

In the final reckoning of this match, one that condemned Bournemouth to relegation despite them recording the league double over Everton for the first time in their history, the only positives came from a trio of youngsters: Jarrad Branthwaite, deputising again for Mason Holgate, again exhibited poise and cool beyond his tender years; Anthony Gordon came off the bench to inject the urgency that had been lacking up to that point; and Moise Kean showed some lovely touches and distribution while also notching his second goal in Royal Blue with a simple tap-in late in the first half.

In his post-match interview, Ancelotti explained he had told the players who would remain that summer, that they would need to show more motivation next season. If finances were to be as tight as many expected, the Italian would not be in a position to replace almost all of his midfield, sign a new goalkeeper and fill the other roles that badly need attention. But if he and Marcel Brands were able to add some genuine quality in key areas, it would help. Whether it would be enough to build a bridge to the top six in 2020/21 remained to be seen, and much would depend on Ancelotti's own managerial talents.

"I want a better team," he told the press. "We want a better team. We will have a better team. I want to see more fight."

Once again, Everton would go into a vitally important transfer window, with long-term irrelevance beckoning if they couldn't get it right.

Final score: Everton 1-3 Bournemouth

2020: Allan, Rodriguez and Doucouré sign for Don Carlo

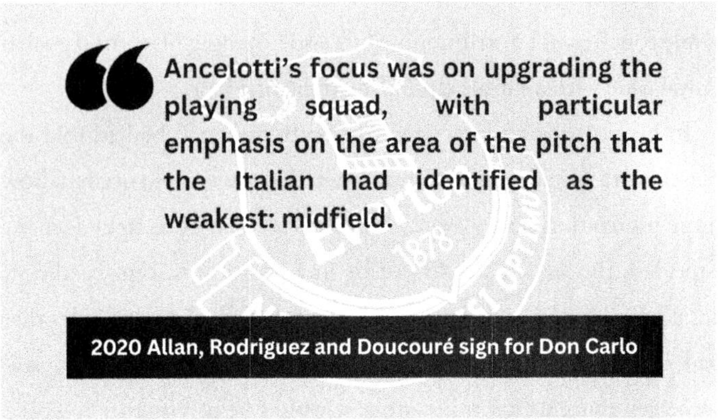

The delayed finish to 2019/20 meant that the calendar for the following season had to be pushed out accordingly. The new Premier League campaign would kick off on 13 September and the transfer window, which usually closed on or around 1 September, was shifted so that the new deadline would fall on 5 October.

At Everton, where Carlo Ancelotti was preparing for his first full season in charge, all the focus was on upgrading the playing squad, with particular emphasis on the area of the pitch that the Italian had identified as the weakest: midfield.

The veteran, Fabian Delph, had made just 13 league starts as he battled with a succession of soft-tissue injuries, while Jean-Philippe Gbamin, the highly-anticipated addition from Mainz a year earlier had had his first season in England wrecked by a thigh tendon tear, and then by a ruptured Achilles. In their absence, that limp conclusion to the campaign underscored the galling lack of drive, guile, imagination and presence in Everton's midfield.

Ancelotti had seen enough and it probably didn't take much persuading on his part to prompt Marcel Brands into making a sizeable change in his recruitment policy, by advocating the need to sign some players capable of making a genuine and immediate impact, even if it meant acquiring talent at the upper end of the age range.

The result was the arrival of three significant signings in the space of three hectic days, a week before the new season was due to kick off.

***

Brazilian midfielder Allan Marques, one of Ancelotti's most dependable players during his time at Napoli, came in for £21 million. The price was half of what Paris Saint-Germain had offered Napoli for the 29-year-old in 2019 before that proposed deal collapsed. Since then, it had been Allan's desire to link back up with his former boss, Carlo Ancelotti, and he got his wish when he signed a three-year contract and joined compatriots, Richarlison and Bernard on Merseyside. He would wear the number 6 jersey.

"It is a real pleasure to sign for Everton. I am immensely happy to be here," he told evertontv. "It is a club with a rich history in the Premier

League, has real ambition, and then there is Professor Ancelotti. He has done everything possible to bring me here.

"It is the size of the Club and the name of the coach, which means you don't think twice about coming to Everton."

Allan promised to add strength to that part of the team and more of a box-to-box presence than anyone currently at the club. While not a prolific goal scorer — he had scored 16 times in 212 appearances in all competitions for Napoli — he could get forward, reportedly had a good turn of pace, and offered both strength and technique on the ball.

***

Just two days later, Everton confirmed the signing of James, the Colombian star from Real Madrid in a deal that, it was eventually revealed, cost the club almost nothing by way of an up-front fee. In what was a potential coup for the club, the 29-year-old linked back up with Carlo Ancelotti, the man who made him the fourth-most expensive player in world football in 2014 when he signed him for Real from Monaco for £63 million and then brought him to Bayern Munich on loan for two seasons starting in 2017.

Indeed, Ancelotti helped to persuade James to join him at Goodison Park, vouching for him personally and making several phone calls to him to describe the project he is working on with the Toffees.

Rodriguez signed a two-year contract, with the club, keeping the option of a third.

"I am really, really happy to be at this great club, a club with so much history, and here with a manager who knows me really well," he told evertonfc.com. “I’m looking forward to achieving great things here — and winning things, which is what everyone’s aim is. I’ve come here to improve, to get better. I’ve also come here to help the team to win, to play good football — entertaining football.

“I’m convinced, with Carlo and his technical staff, we can achieve big things, and one of the big reasons [I signed] was the presence of Carlo Ancelotti. I have enjoyed some great times with him previously at two different clubs. That was a massive reason to come here.

“I’m a winner... a real winner. I like to win things and I’m convinced we can have a great season. I know we have a very talented squad, full of top players, and, I think, with the additions we’re making during this transfer window, it’s going to make us even stronger.”

***

The next day, Abdoulaye Doucouré left relegated Watford to join the Toffees for an initial £20 million, although a further £5 million in appearance-related add-ons would eventually bring the transfer closer to £25 million.

It was believed that Brands had long had his eye on the Frenchman and, based on Doucouré's comments following his unveiling as an Everton player, the feeling had been mutual.

“I have been waiting a long time to come here and now it has happened so I am very happy,” Doucouré told evertonfc.com. “I had some interest from other clubs, but from the beginning, when Everton showed an interest in me, I told my agent to focus on Everton.

“It was the only club I wanted to join. Everton has a big history in English football and it is a good club for me to have a step up in my career. I am very happy now to be an Everton player and very excited for the future."

"I can bring my energy - I am a powerful player, I can run a lot, all the game. I can add goals as well. I will try my best to score goals and help the team.

***

Almost overnight, Everton's midfield had been completely overhauled, with indisputable power, tenacity, physical presence, flair and a bona fide playmaker added to the ranks. A disjointed mid-section that had ambled its way through the final weeks of 2019/20 with the lackadaisical Gylfi Sigurdsson, the faltering Tom Davies, the ill-fitting Alex Iwobi, the half-fit André Gomes and the timid Bernard, now had plenty of options and much-needed competition for places.

With a total outlay of over £60 million that summer, once young defender Ben Godfrey had been added to the ranks in a £20 million move from Norwich City, Director of Football, Marcel Brands, was under pressure to recoup transfer funds before the transfer deadline.

However, while the club were reportedly willing to listen to offers for a few first-team regulars and fringe players, they only managed to collect £1.8 million for Morgan Schneiderlin who left for Nice, and Fraser Hornby who joined Stade de Reims for the same fee. Otherwise, those players who left did so on free transfers, with Sandro Ramirez, Oumar Niasse, Cuco Martina and Luke Garbutt departing alongside goalkeeper Maarten Steklenburg and academy graduate Kieran Dowell.

As such, it had been an expensive close season. When the expenditure on incoming transfers was added to the estimated £12 million a year being paid to Ancelotti and the club-record salary for James – that was variously reported to have been between £150,000 and £250,000 a week - it represented a big gamble by Farhad Moshiri.

In many ways, it was the last roll of the dice for the Everton owner; a sizeable bet placed on the managerial abilities of Ancelotti and his ability to fashion a winning side from the players he had inherited and those who had arrived in the summer.

For a few heady weeks early in the season and again after Boxing Day 2020, it looked like the gamble might pay off. Evertonians might have been restricted to following their team from their own homes but they were imbued with a rare sense of optimism as Ancelotti's new-look side began the campaign in electric form.

***

As ever, things were also moving off the pitch as Farhad Moshiri and the Board of Directors sought to push forward on the issue of Everton's new stadium. In late August, the club had announced they would submit a revised planning application in September, which would include architectural and design changes to the proposed structure at Bramley-Moore Dock.

The club's original planning documents had been submitted to Liverpool City Council in December 2019, with a decision expected sometime in 2020. Although the application had been made just before the outbreak of the COVID-19 pandemic, Everton insisted their plans, which were very much in line with the Government's "build,

2020: Ancelotti's Blues off to a flyer. Second by Christmas

2013 — the last time Everton had won away at a "big six" team; 2012 — the last time Everton had beaten Tottenham; 2008 — the last time Everton had won on Tottenham's home turf. All three unwanted statistics tumbled on the opening day of the 2020/21 season, and while there was a discussion to be had around the extent to which the absence of fans reduces home advantage, it would take nothing away from the Toffees' performance, the magnitude of the result, or the transformation the team had undergone since the same fixture just seven games previously.

***

13 September 2020: Tottenham Hotspur v Everton (Behind Closed Doors)

This was night and day from that miserable display in early July when a pretty awful Spurs edged an utterly dreadful Everton thanks to a Michael Keane own goal. A defeat that effectively ended any notion of the Toffees sneaking into a European qualification place had been attributed on fan website, ToffeeWeb, to "a black hole of a midfield, one devoid of guile, imagination and drive, where the first instinct was to go backwards because of an inability to play through an opposition press." In the first game of the new season, they found victory through a completely revamped mid-section, with three new signings making stellar debuts in royal blue.

From front to back, this was an Everton that looked hungry, determined but also finally confident in its own ability thanks to the new boys, and they dominated the early exchanges. Mourinho admitted in his pre-match press conference that on the back of their transfer business, he now considered the Blues genuine rivals for the top six but even he might have been surprised by the way Ancelotti's men set about controlling the ball, at least until Spurs finally got to grips with them to a degree as the first half wore on.

Everton should have been a goal up after a quarter of an hour, but Richarlison ignored Dominic Calvert-Lewin – free in the centre waiting for a tap in - went for glory and sliced an off-balance effort well off target.

Spurs then broke at speed in a two-on-two situation where Dele Alli could have slipped Kane in for a clear chance on goal but also went for it himself, and Pickford reacted brilliantly to push his shot over the crossbar. Later, Matt Doherty, played a one-two with Kane, latching onto the latter's scooped ball over the top and aiming a shot for the far corner of the goal but Pickford was equal to it, making an impressive save with his foot to divert the ball away to safety.

For Everton, Allan was efficiently going about his business closing down spaces, winning the ball, and handing it off with the minimum of fuss and Abdoulaye Doucouré was covering ground, claiming second balls, driving forward with purpose but was also alert enough to put in an excellent stretching tackle to stop Lucas Moura from racing away for the hosts.

James Rodriguez, meanwhile, was oozing class with every silky touch and pin-point accurate cross-field pass and he would create more chances in a game than any Everton player had for two years.

The goal, when it came, though, was not from the cultured boot of Rodriguez or the mercurial Richarlison but emphatically from the head of a man about whom questions had been raised at the tail end of last season when he failed to score at all during the nine games of "Project Restart". When Richarlison was fouled wide on the left and Digne whipped the ball behind the defence, it was Calvert-Lewin who rose powerfully and purposefully in the image of his Finch Farm mentor, Duncan Ferguson, and despatched an unstoppable header high into Lloris's goal. It was a thumping finish worthy of any Everton No.9 and a well-deserved winning goal.

Ancellotti had promised that his Everton team would be more competitive in his first full season in charge and his players delivered on that pledge in spades. Combative, resilient but also confident and composed, they bossed this match and were more than deserving of the points, despite Jose Mourinho's churlishness.

This was just one match at the start of a long season and Evertonians were more than accustomed to disappointment, heartbreak and false dawns but this felt different — the effect of a top-class manager stamping his will and class on a team with targeted acquisitions and a touch of magic. If this was to be the platform from which this side got better as the new players settled in and attained full match fitness, then these could be the beginnings of exciting times at Everton... if so, the Blues hadn't half earned them!

Final score: Spurs 0-1 Everton

***

Afterwards, Ancelotti expressed his satisfaction with Everton's impressive win, saying that the players did exactly what was expected of them.

"Unbelievable," Ancelotti said. "The game was good. The game was what I expected from the team. I know it was not easy, but I thought the new [players] brought energy, brought quality and the others supported really well.

"So the performance was brilliant. We had some difficulties in the beginning, but we were comfortable on the pitch."

Asked if it surprised him at how quickly his new signings had bedded in, Ancelotti smiled, "Players that are able to play football don't need a lot of time to adapt. James knows very well what he has to do, and Allan and Doucouré are the same.

"I told them to show their quality and I think they did. I think we have a good combination in midfield — we have quality in Gomes and James, we have Allan [who does really well] in possession, and we have Doucouré who can work box-to-box.

"Last season, we had a lot of players with quality on the ball, but in football sometimes you have to play without the ball."

***

19 September 2020: Everton v West Bromwich Albion (Behind Closed Doors)

2020 might have felt like an interminable year, but it hadn't been all that long ago that Everton, under Sam Allardyce, ranked rock bottom in the Premier League for attacking prowess: 20th for shots taken, 20th for shots on target, 20th for chances created, and 20th for chances created from open play.

While there was always the feeling that Farhad Moshiri would choose to get his over-arching dream back on track by binning one of the most unpalatable managerial appointments in the club's history at the end of 2017/18, nothing was guaranteed. It was that uncertainty which had made for sobering times for Evertonians.

Fast forward two-and-a-half years and the outlook at Goodison Park had been transformed. In between, Marco Silva's tenure did come to an unsuccessful end, but he was at least responsible for buying Richarlison. Now, thanks to Carlo Ancelotti and three astute signings over the summer, Everton were an entirely different proposition from an attacking perspective.

It was hard to overstate the importance that a primarily defensive acquisition such as Allan had been to the side, but it was James Rodriguez, a player who promised to be a goldmine of assists for the Blues, who predictably grabbed the headlines.

In his first two games as an Everton player, the Colombian magician had created more "big chances" than André Gomes, Tom Davies, Fabian Delph and Morgan Schneiderlin had created in all of the previous season combined. He weighed in with an assist on his first Premier League appearance at Goodison Park against West Brom, scored what Evertonians hoped would be the first of many goals in royal blue when he put the Toffees ahead on the stroke of half-time, and underscored the size of the coup Ancelotti and Marcel Brands effected when they brought him from Real Madrid.

And it was Dominic Calvert-Lewin who stood to benefit most from the transformation in midfield. The 22-year-old ensured that the lion's share of the limelight was his this time by grabbing his first hat-trick, to bury a spirited Baggies outfit as Everton ran out 5-2 winners and temporarily topped the Premier League table for the first time in three years.

Although the Baggies levelled the game at 2-2 early in the second half through an admittedly brilliant Matheus Pereira free-kick when they were playing with only 10 men following Kieran Gibbs's dismissal in first-half stoppage time, Everton's irresistible attacking options eventually prevailed.

Richarlison's header from a 54th minute free-kick by Lucas Digne was pushed away by the keeper but Michael Keane was on hand to tuck away the rebound.

Eight minutes after that, Everton scored arguably the pick of their five goals on the day when James knocked a perfect ball over the top to Richarlison who prodded in on past the keeper and Calvert-Lewin slid in to toe it over the line and make it 4-2.

Calvert-Lewin wrapped up his hat-trick when he met a Rodriguez corner with the back of his head and sent it flying in past the stranded Sam Johnstone.

Including the 3-0 midweek win against Salford in the Carabao Cup, it was now three wins out of three in all competitions and a brief stint at the top of the Premier League to mark a terrific start to the new season for Ancelotti and Everton.

Things would get better, too – at least until a controversial Goodison derby temporarily derailed Everton's excellent start.

Final score: Everton 5-2 West Bromwich Albion

***

30 September 2020: Everton v West Ham United (Behind Closed Doors)

After a 5-2 win against Fleetwood in the cup, and a fine 2-1 away win at Crystal Palace in the league, Everton booked their place in the last eight of the Carabao Cup for the second year running as Dominic Calvert-Lewin grabbed his second hat-trick of the nascent season to propel the Toffees to another handsome win over the Hammers.

Ancelotti had named another strong line-up, keeping his in-form strike force intact, but this time adding James Rodriguez for his cup debut and Allan in midfield alongside Gylfi Sigurdsson and Fabian Delph. Niels Nkounkou and Jonjoe Kenny continued as the full-backs with Lucas Digne putting in another impressive display at centre-half partnering Michael Keane.

Keane had impressed over the first few games for his defensive work but it was his peach of a ball over the top that set Calvert-Lewin up for his first goal of the evening. The striker pulled the defender's pass over the top out of the air with jaw-dropping control and then stroked the ball past Darren Randolph to make it 1-0 with 11 minutes gone.

Everton had barely had time to set themselves for the second half before West Ham were level. Attacking straight from kick-off, the Hammers worked the ball forward, and it ended up at the feet of Robert Snodgrass in too much space and he whipped a shot past Pickford from 20-yards.

The home side's response was emphatic, however, and they restored their lead when Richarlison again terrorised the visitors' back line by running at them and then across the edge of the box, where he unleashed a shot that deflected off Declan Rice and flew past the keeper.

Then, following a short corner, substitute Alex Iwobi curled a shot off the right-hand post and Calvert-Lewin was in the right place at the right time to tuck home the rebound.

And the shoo-in for an England call-up completed his hat-trick six minutes after that. Rodriguez was involved again as Sigurdsson slipped 'DCL' in behind the defence with just Randolph to beat, which he did with calm aplomb and a tidy left-foot finish. It was Calvert-Lewin's eighth goal of the season already and it capped another strong performance from Ancelotti's men.

The newfound confidence in the side was again in evidence. Where Everton teams of recent years might have crumbled after giving up the lead, then losing key members to injury and, perhaps, struggled to a draw and had to survive the lottery of penalties, Ancelotti's 2020/21 edition simply carry on undeterred and score again themselves.

After a strong showing over their first three rounds in the cup, Everton had a break until the third week of December when the quarter-finals were scheduled to take place. At least five of the other seven sides left in the competition were from the Premier League, four of them from the so-called 'big six', but injuries permitting, the way they were currently playing, the Toffees would fear few sides.

Final score: Everton 4-1 West Ham

***

Once again, Ancelotti was really pleased with what was his team's sixth straight win in all competitions to start the season.

"[It] was a very good performance. We did well and [we have] good momentum, we have focus, we have motivation and we keep going and winning, which is really important.

"We have to pay attention because [other] games can be more difficult [and] we don't have a lot of time to recover and prepare for the game against Brighton, but I hope we can [produce] a repeat performance."

That fixture against the Seagulls at Goodison Park just four days later ended up posing little problem for Ancelotti's men. For the fourth time in seven games, they scored at least four goals, with James Rodriguez grabbing a brace in a 4-2 win that put Everton in dreamland – top of the Premier League heading into the first international break.

Despite not being able to witness any of their team's early-season successes in person, Evertonians were in ebullient mood heading into the Goodison derby. As the catchy 1980s song 'Spirit of the Blues' was used in more and more memes on Twitter and Instagram, a groundswell movement eventually propelled the song to Number 1 on the UK iTunes charts as more and more fans bought digital versions of the track.

The phenomenon carried over into the following day, with 'Z Cars' climbing to the No.2 spot followed by the 1985 FA Cup song 'Here We Go' at No.3. The recently-released film 'Howard's Way' about the glorious 1980s side also ascended to No.1 on the iTunes Movies charts. 'Spirit of the Blues' would become the club's unofficial anthem over the next years, and the soundtrack to two desperate struggles against relegation.

***

Just six days before hosting Liverpool at Goodison, news emerged that Everton's neighbours from across the park, together with Manchester United, were driving a radical overhaul of the Premier League power structure. A one-off, £250 million rescue package and hugely increased ongoing funding for English Football League clubs, in exchange for a reduced Premier League and consolidated voting power among England's biggest clubs, were among a raft of proposals in a 'Revitalisation' document that was revealed by *The Telegraph* and given public backing by EFL chairman, Rick Parry.

Amid the onset of the COVID-19 pandemic, which was triggering a financial crisis in football, particularly in the lower reaches of the English professional football pyramid, Manchester United and Liverpool were working with Parry on what they dubbed *Project Big Picture*, one that had the potential to reshape the finances of the game.

Under their proposals, the Premier League, the most lucrative sports league in the world, would see a reduction to 18 teams, with automatic promotion from the Championship for two clubs each season and the next three best-placed teams playing off with the 16th-placed Premier League club to determine which gets a place in the top flight.

The League Cup and Community Shield would be scrapped, allowing for greater participation of England's top clubs in an expanded UEFA Champions League. It was also proposed that the distribution of broadcast revenue be altered, with one portion based on performance in the league on a rolling three-year basis.

The existing system of parachute payments to clubs dropping out of the top division would stop, with 25% of the Premier League's TV income distributed among clubs across the second to fourth tiers instead.

In exchange for these measures designed to safeguard the future of the domestic game, the Premier League's nine longest-serving clubs — the so-called 'big six' of Arsenal, Chelsea, Liverpool, Manchester City, United and Tottenham, plus Everton, West Ham and Southampton — would get greater voting power, with a majority of six required for certain decisions, including, for example, the power to approve or veto takeover bids for clubs.

The Premier League itself came out against the proposals, saying that while it supported, "a wide-ranging discussion on the future of the game, including its competition structures, calendar and overall financing ... in the Premier League's view, several individual proposals in the plan published today could have a damaging impact on the whole game and they were disappointed to see that Rick Parry, Chair of the EFL, had given his on-the-record support."

Parry told *The Telegraph*: "What do we do? Leave it exactly as it is and allow the smaller clubs to wither? Or do we do something about it? And you can't do something about it without something changing."

Three days later, *Project Big Picture* was slapped down by a majority of the top flight's other clubs and unanimously declared a non-starter during a meeting of the 20 Premier League clubs. Instead, the League resolved to undertake a wide-ranging 'strategic review' that would seek to implement the key measures, particularly those relating to a greater share of the money to the EFL.

According to *The Guardian*, Everton CEO, Denise Barrett-Baxendale, demanded an apology from Liverpool and United, which was denied by the clubs' representatives, Tom Werner and Ed Woodward.

***

17 October 2020: Everton v Liverpool (Behind Closed Doors)

If the directors of Everton and Liverpool had been allowed to mix at an appropriate social distance before and after the derby match, it was possible the atmosphere in the Goodison boardroom would have been a little frosty.

On the field, it was clear you could take the fans out of the derby but you seemingly could not take the 'derby' out of this historic local rivalry, with this edition seeing four goals, an almost obligatory red card — 88 minutes after Jordan Pickford could have received his marching orders — and a last-gasp intervention from VAR's hair's-breadth rulers. In a fixture that so often failed to deliver the greatest exhibition of football from both sides, there were plenty of talking points and drama to chew over.

Everton came into the game with a 100% record and greater optimism of ending their miserable record in this fixture than they had done for many years, but they didn't do themselves justice. For long periods, there was just too much of the 'old Everton', the one that struggled to beat the opposition press, relied too heavily on Pickford's boot to launch 'attacks' and lacked the crisp, clinical passing of the like that Liverpool used to race into a very early lead.

With players possessing the ball-moving qualities of James Rodriguez, Allan and André Gomes — and certainly given the start they'd made to the new season — Evertonians were expecting more from their team, especially in the first half where they struggled to contain a reds side operating near their peak.

When Everton were fleetingly sublime, unsurprisingly it was James who was at the heart of it, but the Colombian had a mixed performance himself (which, when you consider he was still probably the best player in Blue on the day, was quite something), while Richarlison, like Yerry Mina displaying the effects of trans-Atlantic travel on the Thursday, was peripheral until he took centre stage late on.

But if the feeling was that Adrián was a weak link in the reds' side and that the loss of Virgil van Dijk being forced off with an injury within the first 10 minutes gave the Blues another big advantage, the hosts didn't end up taking full advantage. Apart from having to pick the ball out of the net and denying Dominic Calvert-Lewin prior to the first equaliser, the Spanish keeper wasn't sufficiently worked by Everton.

Instead, the home side finished the match with 10 men after Richarlison's deserved dismissal. They also played a Get Out of Jail Free card in stoppage time when Pickford, who had kept his side in it with an impressive display, almost threw a point away. Jordan Henderson's goal – another potential heart-breaker for Blues supporters – was, however, ruled out for marginal offside.

If there were fears that Everton would take the brunt of Liverpool's response to the 7-2 battering they had taken at Villa Park before the international break, they were realised right at the start of this contest. Jürgen Klopp's side came flying out of the traps and were ahead inside three minutes.

A rapier-like move through the hosts' midfield ended with the ball being played out to Andrew Robertson wide on the left and he centred hard and low for Sadio Mané to slam the ball high into the goal with a first-time finish.

Sensing blood, the Reds came forward again in the fifth minute and when Virgil van Dijk threatened to meet a ball to the back post, a knee-high tackle by Pickford cleaned him out. With the whistle having already gone for offside and Pickford's 'tackle' deemed serious foul play and not violent conduct, there was no scope for VAR to review the incident and either award a penalty or send the goalkeeper off.

It was a massive let-off for Pickford, and Everton then gradually settled and equalised with 18 minutes on the clock. Calvert-Lewin collected a ball down the right-hand channel and stung Adrian's palms with a powerful drive from the angle. James took responsibility for the resulting corner and deposited it into the six-yard box, where Keane connected with a strong header through the keeper's gloves.

That should have been the cue for the Blues to slow things down a bit and play their game a bit more, but the passes just weren't hitting their mark and, all too often, the midfield was bypassed by Pickford's long kicks forward.

Then, with half an hour gone, Everton lost an important player of their own when Seamus Coleman suffered a recurrence of the hamstring problem that had prematurely ended his game against Brighton last time out. Ben Godfrey replaced him, and acquitted himself very well on what was a baptism-by-fire debut.

Thiago Alcântara fired narrowly wide, Mané sliced a shot off target, and Calvert-Lewin's side-foot touch slid past Adrian's post as the two sides traded blows late in the first half but it was all square at the half-time interval.

The second period started in similar fashion to the first, with the visitors driving forward and seeing efforts from Fabinho and Henderson fly over the crossbar but Everton found some rhythm of their own and James was at it again with another quite brilliant cross. Richarlison dived to meet but his header came back off the post before the Colombian star had an effort of his own diverted away from goal by the keeper.

It was Liverpool who took the lead again in the 72nd minute, though. Mina cut out a cross from the right but only presented it on a platter for Salah, who took an instinctive snap-shot that spun beyond Pickford's dive and inside the far post.

And 2-1 almost became 3-1 five minutes later. Joel Matip lost his marker in the box at a corner and headed towards the top corner, but Pickford pawed it out the air superbly to deny the defender before parrying a stinging Salah shot over the bar.

Everton hit back again, however, nine minutes later as James and Digne combined to serve up the second equaliser for Calvert-Lewin. Rodriguez, who had ghosted over to the left flank, fed the Frenchman down the line and his deep cross hung up perfectly for Calvert-Lewin to meet it with one of his amazing leaps and then steer his header back across the keeper.

"Now win it," was the collective refrain from Evertonians watching on screens across the world over but Richarlison effectively killed the Blues' hopes of taking all the points with a dreadful and needless challenge on Alcântara in the centre-circle.

The incident almost proved to be even more costly because Liverpool tried to press home their numerical advantage in the last few minutes, and looked to have claimed victory with yet another sickening stoppage-time winner. They played Mané in down their left and he cut the ball back into the centre for Henderson, whose side-footed effort looked routine enough for Pickford to palm away. Instead, the ball spun off his glove and over the line, but Liverpool's celebrations were cut dead by Video Assistant Referee, David Coote, who adjudged that Mane's shoulder had been beyond the last defender.

It was a huge slice of fortune for Everton, but then the Blues had been due some derby luck after years of dodgy refereeing decisions and last-gasp winners. Reds fans would have felt aggrieved at VAR and moaned for months that Pickford should have received his marching orders after just five minutes; but after years of refereeing injustice in Merseyside derbies — Dirk Kuyt's flying kick on Phil Neville; Steven Gerrard's two-footed lunge on Gary Naismith; Joleon Lescott getting assaulted with no repercussions; Luis Suarez's histrionics in getting Jack Rodwell sent off; and even cynical a kick out at Allan by Robertson that went unpunished in this game — Evertonians wouldn't be losing any sleep.

Despite being well below the best of what they had shown to that point in 2020/21 season and never seeming to get out of second gear, Everton had grabbed a draw against what Klopp described as his side's best away performance of his tenure. The spirit of a side that knew the meaning of how to come twice from behind was admirable and hugely encouraging.

That was definitely something to build on for Ancelotti, but it was a relief that the next tortuous derby wasn't until February, when the Blues would slay two hoodoos at once.

Final score: Everton 2-2 Liverpool

***

By December 2020, ten months into the pandemic, the decision was taken to allow a limited number of spectators, sufficiently spaced out for their protection, to attend Premier League matches in certain cities designated as Tier 2 or better in terms of COVID-19 restrictions.

That meant that for three matches that month, 2,000 Everton fans were drawn by lottery for the home games against Chelsea, Arsenal and Manchester United. It would be another five months before more supporters were allowed back into top-flight stadiums, and even then they were capped according to coronavirus protocols.

Since the fractious Merseyside derby in mid-October, the Toffees' form had suffered due to James Rodriguez struggling with an unspecified groin injury, as a result of being pole-axed by reds defender Virgil van Dijk, and Richarlison's three-match ban following his sending off for fouling Thiago Alcântara. Having won all seven of their opening fixtures in all competitions, Everton registered a victory in just one of the next seven and had fallen to ninth place following a dismal 1-0 home reverse to Leeds United and a 1-1 draw at Burnley.

By the time Arsenal came to town, back-to-back wins over Chelsea and Leicester had vaulted Ancelotti's side back up to fifth; and by the time the final whistle had blown on their last match of the calendar year, against Sheffield United at Bramall Lane, Everton were in second place and primed for a tilt at finally qualifying for the Champions League.

***

19 December 2020: Everton v Arsenal (2000 spectators)

A year into their respective managerial tenures, Carlo Ancelotti and Mikel Arteta found themselves in very different positions. Everton, heading into Christmas, were sitting in the top three, while Arsenal languished towards the bottom of the Premier League table. The visitors' early approach showed their lack of confidence, as the two teams sized each other up in cagey fashion for a quarter of an hour before the first real moment of excitement presented itself from the unlikely boot of Michael Keane.

The centre-half strode forward as space opened up ahead of him and unleashed a swerving missile of a shot that bent agonisingly within a whisker of the post from thirty-plus yards out.

Seven minutes later, Alex Iwobi, playing against his old club, capitalised on more space afforded him by Arsenal to whip the ball in from the right where Calvert-Lewin got a glance on it with his head and it flew in off Rob Holding for what would go down as a 22nd minute own goal.

Arsenal responded and received a route back into the contest when Tom Davies clumsily felled Ainsley Maitland-Niles as he tried to collect a loose ball. It provided referee Andre Marriner with an easy decision to award a penalty. Nicolas Pépé assumed responsibility for the spot-kick and calmly slotted it past Jordan Pickford to make it 1-1.

With Allan out injured, the manager had asked Davies to step into the breach, and whilst he had a decent enough first 45 minutes, he was emblematic of a lack of creativity from the Blues that largely characterised their performance. It was a display crying out for the invention of someone like James Rodriguez and, in the second half, someone like Bernard; but in the Colombian's absence, the onus fell in Alex Iwobi and Richarlison, both of whom popped up now and then with decent contributions without ever really stamping their authority on the game.

Importantly, in the absence of any consistent imagination or attacking ideas, Everton fell back on the industry of Calvert-Lewin and their threat at set-pieces to reclaim the lead. The striker's overall work-rate deserved a goal, and he almost got it on the stroke of half-time when he tested Bernd Leno with an excellent left-footed strike from the edge of the box that was heading for the top corner until the keeper finger-tipped it behind.

From the resulting corner, Gylfi Sigurdsson delivered the ball to the near post to meet Mina's run and the big Colombian defender steered a header impressively on goal and past Leno at his near post for his second goal of the campaign.

Old habits seemed to die hard for Everton in the second half and it made those dogged and professional games, where Everton got themselves ahead and then dug in to protect what they held, nerve-wracking to watch. Evertonians of any vintage remember all too well how often their side would try to sit back against opposition teams down the years and inevitably concede to toss away points; but they were now having to get used to the pragmatism and game-management of Ancelotti, a man not averse to finishing a match with seven defenders on the pitch in the interests of seeing out a match.

The second 45 minutes against Arsenal were not a comfortable watch but by the end, the Gunners were banging their heads against the same brick wall that had confronted Chelsea and Leicester in the preceding week. It said much for how far the Gunners have fallen despite their impressive cup form that Everton almost completely ceded the midfield battle in the second half and only fleetingly looked like being punished for it.

Arsenal came close to wiping out their hosts' lead for a second time early in the second half when David Luiz hit the crossbar and it needed a save from the returning Jordan Pickford in the closing stages to ensure that Ancelotti would toast a third successive victory. Hardly a performance to set the pulse racing but the win was paramount and the fact that it was secured without the team playing especially well in an attacking sense – not to mention without three of its best and most creative players – boded well. With just two shots on target, Everton were a model of efficiency as they climbed into second place in the Premier League.

Final score: Everton 2-1 Arsenal

***

Following what was a third successive win for the Toffees, Phil McNulty, Chief football writer at the *BBC*, wrote of a result that:

"Capped a superb week for Ancelotti and Everton after wins against Chelsea and now Arsenal at Goodison Park, flanking a midweek victory at Leicester City.

"And as Ancelotti took the acclaim of the 2,000 fans inside Goodison Park, especially those on the Gwladys Street, the 61-year-old's status was confirmed.

"If Ancelotti had plotted out a week to mark his first year, three months of which were without action as football went into lockdown because of the Covid-19 pandemic, then this would have been his perfect script.

"Everton were left in 15th place after that draw with Arsenal last December, Ancelotti sitting a few seats away from Arteta in the directors' box on that freezing lunchtime.

"And how glad Moshiri and Everton must be that the cards fell neatly into place in those decisive days when both they and Arsenal were seeking a new manager, the Gunners having sacked Unai Emery.

"Ironically, Arteta had supporters of his own inside Everton's boardroom and his appointment may well have been warmly welcomed by supporters, while Arsenal were linked with Ancelotti because of his global stature and his previous success in the capital with Chelsea, where he won the Premier League and FA Cup double.

"Arsenal went with the rookie with roots at Emirates Stadium while Everton pushed for Ancelotti - both clubs satisfied with the outcome.

"Ancelotti, typically, refuses to get carried away. He has seen it all and knows rough times may still be around the corner as he contemplates Wednesday's EFL Cup quarter-final against Manchester United at Goodison Park.

'We did very well in our last few games - brilliant performances and fantastic results,' he said. 'We showed more consistency. This season we started well, then we had a difficult moment, but right now I'm really pleased. The position in the table is really good. But as I said last week, it is not the end of the season. We have to keep fighting but this was a top, top performance.'

"One year on, Everton and owner Moshiri have every right to be elated at the acquisition of a man regarded as managerial royalty."

***

At the club's AGM on 14 January 2021, a major topic was the planning application review for the club's proposed new stadium at Bramley-Moore Dock, which had been delayed by the pandemic; but Professor Barrett-Baxendale expressed her confidence that the impact would not be unduly detrimental to the timeline which called for the first spade to go into the ground that year.

"Liverpool City Council's public consultation period closed in October and the club is confident of securing a successful planning determination very soon, with the potential to commence construction on-site shortly thereafter," she told shareholders.

"While the Club awaits the determination of a planning application, we continue to pursue a range of funding opportunities, including senior debt, alternative sources of equity and subordinated debt.

"Phase two due diligence is currently being conducted to support the funding process, including direct research with supporters to help shape what match days will look like at the new stadium."

***

10 February 2021: Everton v Tottenham Hotspur (Behind Closed Doors)

Perhaps occupying the dizzy heights of number two position in the league had caused a collective team nosebleed. Certainly results after the Arsenal game had been mixed. A home defeat against Manchester United in the Carabao quarter final, was followed by the Boxing Day away win in Sheffield, and by a New Year's Day home defeat against West Ham. The next seven games included 4 wins, 2 draws and another home defeat, this time to Newcastle.

The next match at Goodison saw Everton drag themselves into the last eight of the FA Cup, with a gutsy, if defensively suspect, display and a dramatic extra-time winner in a back-and-forth, goal-laden thriller against Spurs made famous by Carlo Ancelotti's gloriously nonchalant reaction to his side scoring to go 5-4 up.

It was Spurs who had came out of the traps with more purpose and within three minutes of the kick-off, Everton's zonal marking system had utterly failed with Davinson Sanchez rising unchallenged to nod home a corner from the Tottenham left.

Hugo Lloris tipped a Dominic Calvert-Lewin effort onto the post as the home side found their attacking belief and after Yerry Mina headed a corner wide 10 minutes before the half-time break, Everton sparked a burst of three goals in seven minutes when Dominic Calvert-Lewin hammered in his 18th of the season and 50th for the Toffees, via Lloris's gloves.

Two minutes later, Digne's headed lay-off from Sanchez's awkward header was heel-flicked neatly to Richarlison by Calvert-Lewin and the Brazilian, finally looking like his usual self, took a touch to his right before drilling through a defender's legs and into the bottom corner from 20 yards to make it 2-1.

Five minutes after that, when Pierre-Emile Højbjerg accidentally clipped Calvert-Lewin's heels as the striker went to collect a pass inside from the left flank. Referee David Coote had no hesitation in pointing to the spot and, after a check by Video Assistant Referee, Chris Kavanagh, Sigurdsson stepped up to roll home the resulting penalty.

That should have seen the Toffees into the interval with a two-goal cushion, but an awful lapse in concentration from Mina allowed the ball to slip by him in the box and Eric Lamela was on hand to clip it past stand-in keeper Robin Olsen deep into injury time.

Everton's slender 3-2 lead felt more precarious when, just nine minutes into the second half, Calvert-Lewin had to be withdrawn with a recurrence of his recent hamstring problem and Richarlison moved into a central attacking role.

Indeed, it was an advantage that would last only a couple of minutes longer and once again it was schoolboy defending at a corner from the same side as before that was the Toffees' undoing. Sigurdsson kept his attentions on Sanchez and not the ball, which meant it was the Colombian who tracked it and, holding off the Everton man, stuck out as a leg to stab it home and level things up at 3-3.

If the pendulum had swung toward Spurs, Richarlison would ensure that the hosts landed the next blow. Sigurdsson played him in nicely between the lines and the Brazil international powered past his man before lashing a superb left-footed shot across the keeper and in off the far post from a tight angle.

With 82 minutes gone, however, Everton's defence was breached again, following yet another corner. Olsen's glancing fist on the ball ended up with Lamela again, his shot headed off the line by Abdoulaye Doucouré, but when Son Hueng-min collected the loose ball on the far side and bent a cross to the back post, substitute Harry Kane was there, unmarked, to head in from close range.

Once more, with their deeper bench and their tails up at having made it 4-4 to force extra-time, Spurs might have felt the momentum was with them, but it was Everton who grabbed the deciding goal that finally broke Spurs's resilience – and it was one worthy of settling any tie. Bernard played a ball inside to Sigurdsson. He controlled it and then chipped deftly over the defence for the little Brazilian to track and then half-volley sweetly past Lloris with his left foot.

On the sidelines, cameras caught Ancelotti nonchalantly sipping his tea in his technical area as the Blues' bench celebrated behind him.

Perhaps he couldn't feel confident that the ninth goal of the contest would be the last; or maybe it was emblematic of his generally calm demeanour. Either way, he had steered Everton into the last eight.

Final score: Everton 5-4 Spurs

***

In other news, two days after that mad-cap Spurs game, Ancelotti's Crosby home was burgled by masked thieves who were disturbed by his daughter, but not before they had taken off with a safe.

A report in the *Liverpool Echo* partially substantiated a rumour that had began on WhatsApp and quickly spread to social media that the intruders had held the Everton manager up at knife-point. However, Ancelotti, who had regularly expressed how much he enjoyed living in the area, was not at home.

Merseyside Police said: "two men wearing balaclavas and black waterproof clothing perpetrated the crime." They reportedly gained entry to the property and removed the safe. When they noticed Ancelotti's daughter, they fled the scene.

The Police later said the safe, which had been forced open, was found dumped in a car park off Runnells Lane, near Masefield Road, in Thornton.

It was later rumoured the harrowing incident played an important role in the Ancelotti family's decision to prematurely leave Merseyside.

2021: Liverpool 0-2 Everton

> "This time it was different, and it was over. It was finally bloody over. 21 years and five months since Everton last won at Anfield, the most depressing sequence of results in the club's 143-year history ended as Carlo Ancelotti's team beat Liverpool 2-0.
>
> **2021: Liverpool 0-2 Everton**

When Kevin Campbell scored a fourth-minute winner in the Merseyside derby in September 1999, little did he know that it would be more than two decades before Everton would win again at Anfield. The Toffees' record since the turn of the 21st Century, on the ground they had called home until the 1892 split that led to Liverpool FC's formation, had been depressingly torrid. The more years that passed since their last victory on the Reds' turf, the more anguished the fixture became.

20 February 2021: Liverpool v Everton (Behind closed doors)

The psychology behind the fixture appeared to trump the law of averages, but in February 2021, 22 years of pain finally came to an end as Carlo Ancelotti oversaw a precious victory on the other side of Stanley Park.

For far too long, Campbell been the last man to score an Everton winner at Anfield. That accolade now went to the warrior-like Richarlison, the player who fired home unerringly in the third minute to send Everton on their way to a cathartic, misery-ending victory. Gylfi Sigurdsson's late second merely ensured that the points in a Derby would go the Blue side of Merseyside for the first time in over a decade.

To outsiders, the spontaneous outpouring of emotion at the final whistle, the jubilant hugs, clenched-fist bellows and boisterousness in the changing room may seem curiously excessive, but they were a visceral illustration of how much this meant to Everton's players and staff, and not just a local like Tom Davies or the long-haulers like Seamus Coleman and Duncan Ferguson. Newcomers like Ben Godfrey, James Rodriguez and even Ancelotti himself had also grasped the importance to the club and its supporters of banishing this rotten hoodoo.

In the end, it didn't take a fantastic attacking performance, but as expected against the defending champions, it required a resolute defensive stand and some heroics from Jordan Pickford.

That last part was gloriously poetic. Everton's goalkeeper has been the subject of some shameful media scrutiny and criticism over what happened in the Goodison derby last October; hysteria that continued right up to kick off this evening. But he responded with a man-of-the-match display, playing behind a defensive unit that could probably all have laid claim to that accolade, such was their individual and collective effort.

Mason Holgate had had an inconsistent season but was immense, as were Michael Keane, Godfrey, Coleman and Lucas Digne, who left everything out on the pitch in terms of effort and desire. This was a towering display by Everton's rear-guard that began at the front, but which was founded on discipline and shape throughout the team against a notoriously dangerous Liverpool attack.

It needed to be, because the Blues often made it more difficult for themselves than need be with some poor ball retention and it was no surprise that in the final reckoning they had just 28% of the possession. It didn't matter, because they were more than good enough at the back.

The tragedy, of course, was that no fans were there at Anfield to see it. Two decades of Blues had gone across Stanley Park and suffered either valiant draws or painful defeat, but the hope now was that with the hex gone, Evertonians would savour victory at Anfield in person some day soon. Until then, Blues just had to drink the feeling in.

Final score: Liverpool 0-2 Everton

***

On 25 February, Carlo Ancelotti told *The BBC* he hoped he could extend his time at Everton beyond the terms of his existing contract, saying he would like to still be there when the club moved into its new stadium in the autumn of 2024.

The Italian had signed a 4½-year contract when he became Everton manager in December 2019, which meant his existing deal would expire at the end of what looked at that stage like it would be the Toffees' last season at Goodison Park.

Everton's proposed new ground on the banks of Mersey was being reviewed by the Secretary of State following a unanimous vote by Liverpool City Council to approve the extensive planning application for the project. If all went well, the Blues hoped to kick off the 2024/25 season in their new home.

Ancelotti had spoken before of his desire to stay longer than his original contract and he reiterated that, saying: "I would like to stay as long as possible.

"I would like to be there when the new stadium will be opened. It will be a good achievement for me, of course.

"I think to finish the contract in 2024 you did a good job and when you did a good job, the contract will not be stopped in 2024, it will continue."

Meanwhile, speaking of more immediate concerns at his press conference regarding Everton's ambitions this season, Ancelotti said:

"For us, it will be really important to play in Europe next season and it means a step forward for the players, a step forward for the club. In my opinion, we don't have to look at the table. We have to play game by game and see where we are at the end of the season. We have to work hard, because it will not be easy, because a lot of teams are involved there, but I think we can compete until the end.

"The result [against Liverpool] was really good, and the performance was also. We [have] showed we can compete in some games and now I think we have to look forward because we have a home game and our run in the last period was not good. If we want to fight for European positions, we have to improve our form at Goodison."

2021: BMD PLANNING PERMISSION RECEIVED

On 23 February 2021, just three days after the success at Anfield, there was more good news for the Blues. Everton's planning application for its new 52,888-seat stadium at Bramley-Moore Dock was approved unanimously by Liverpool City Council, taking the club a major step closer to realising its plans to move from Goodison Park. Following a recommendation from the Council's Planning Officer last week, the local authority convened a special Planning Committee Meeting composed of 11 councillors to approve the proposals,

which were originally submitted in December 2019 before being updated in September 2020.

The Blues' CEO, Denise Barrett-Baxendale, and Stadium Development Director, Colin Chong, were both in attendance to outline the club's case for the project, which they expected could bring £1.3 billion worth of revenue to the area and create 15,000 jobs. Colin Chong had been steering the project since the departure of Keith Harris from the Board of Directors in July 2019.

The club's vision for the redevelopment of Goodison Park in Walton also got the green light.

Barrett-Baxendale said in an email to supporters: "The planning consent from the City Council means that our application will now be referred to the government — a standard procedure for an application of such scale. The government will have an initial 21 days to review the plans and make its decision.

"Once that process has concluded - and provided it is a positive outcome - we can press ahead with the plans we have developed over the last few years.

"I am sure you are aware of how important a new stadium will be for us - providing the state-of-the-art facilities befitting of an ambitious Premier League club — as well as the important role it can play in boosting our local economy at a time when it's never been more needed.

"The project, which will be one the most significant infrastructure projects our city has seen in many years and one of the largest single-site developments in the country at this time, will provide a £1.3 billion boost to the local economy and deliver more than 15,000 jobs."

"If we achieve the final planning approval, we have all worked so hard for, then we will be in a position to complete our funding arrangements and confirm our schedule for the build process at Bramley-Moore Dock."

Chairman Bill Kenwright said: "Whilst today is just one more step in our long journey, it is a very important one. Farhad [Moshiri] and I would like to thank Denise and Colin and their dedicated team for the extraordinary hard work and commitment that has got us to today.

"We are also enormously grateful to the many organisations and tens of thousands of individuals across the city region who have given us their feedback, ideas and support along the way. It's been a good week for Everton and Evertonians."

The project still faced objections from UNESCO, however, who insisted that the stadium "would have a completely unacceptable major adverse impact on the authenticity, integrity and outstanding universal value" of what is part of a designated World Heritage site. They were urging Secretary of State for Housing, Communities and Local Government, Robert Jenrick, to call the project in for full scrutiny, which would delay any final decision from Westminster, but it never came to that.

***

The good news regarding the stadium was followed by the announcement that Farhad Moshiri had taken up a massive new share issue.

New shares worth £200 million were issued to him in exchange for new cash injections and the conversion of old loans into equity.

Everton received £50 million of new money from the majority shareholder, which came on the back of an injection of £50 million in November.

Moshiri's input of £100 million in cash came in combination with the conversion of existing loans into share equity, thought to be around £100 million.

In total, 100,000 new shares in Everton FC were created, 66,667 of which were issued to Moshiri at that time, which increased Moshiri's ownership stake in the club to 93,698 shares, representing 92.16% of the 101,667 shares issued to that point. Bill Kenwright's shareholding remained at 1,750 but it reduced his stake to 1.72%.

***

A month later, on 26 March, Everton's plans to develop a new stadium at Bramley-Moore Dock were finally given the green light after the club's planning application received government approval.

The Secretary of State for Housing, Communities and Local Government, Robert Jenrick, had asked for more time than the statutory 21-day review period to assess the plans but he and his department agreed with the LCC that the Bramley-Moore Dock project would provide a boon to the city of Liverpool and the Merseyside area.

The club's first step, ahead of starting construction that summer, would be to purchase the site from Peel Holdings for £22 million and confirm Laing O'Rourke as the preferred contractor to move ahead with a final construction schedule.

The exact details of how the estimated £500 million development would be funded were yet to be finalised, but Everton owner, Farhad

Moshiri, had already committed to sourcing private investment and sponsorship in preference to a public funding model involving the Council that was initially floated.

***

By the middle of June 2021, Everton had begun preliminary inspection work at Bramley-Moore Dock in anticipation of construction work on the new stadium beginning later in the year, with the first project being the filling in of the dock itself.

The *Liverpool Echo* reported that specialist firm Boskalis Maritime would send a boat out onto the Mersey to carry out various checks on the dock and its hidden contents.

Their team would conduct a survey of the bottom of the dock and check for any potential hazards like unexploded devices from the Second World War – they would find around a dozen – while also assessing the condition of the dock wall ahead of the infilling operation.

The *Echo* report also suggested that other work would include a survey of microbiological organisms present in the water and the recovery of panels and materials installed to better understand the local climate, with construction work set to start in late summer or the autumn.

2021: Everton join fight against European Super League

Whereas the final two decades of the old English Football League Division One had produced nine different champions, the 20 years after the formation of the Premier League in 1992 saw just five teams win the title. It was an illustration of the increasing dominance of the domestic game's major honours by a small group of elite and monied clubs, and it extended to that same group's grip on England's four Champions League qualification places.

That situation ensured that the millions of pounds of broadcast and participation revenue, which naturally grew the longer teams remained in Europe's elite club tournament, was consistently going into the coffers of these same clubs, widening the gap between England's 'haves' and 'have nots' and reducing competition within the Premier League.

It also had the effect of heightening the jeopardy for clubs that failed to qualify for the Champions League in a given season – their spending, wage bills and commercial arrangements were all predicted on dining at Continental football's top table. With the quartet of clubs once dubbed the "Sky Four" (due to the satellite broadcaster's focus on England's most powerful clubs, Arsenal, Chelsea, Liverpool and Manchester United) having extended to the so-called 'Big Six' with the addition of Manchester City and Tottenham in the 2010s, it meant two of these teams would miss out on qualifying each season.

When Leicester City upset the apple cart in 2016 and romped to their first title as 5000-1 outsiders, three of the six finished outside of the Champions League places, a precedent that many observers believe was part of the impetus behind the spectacular hubris of the notion of a breakaway European Super League of 12 clubs from Europe's 'Big Five' Leagues.

England's Big Six, along with AC Milan, Atletico Madrid, Barcelona, Inter Milan, Juventus and Real Madrid suddenly announced on 18 April 2021 that they would be the founding members of a new competition that would directly challenge UEFA's Champions League.

Three more clubs were expected to join the competition for its inaugural season, which ESL signatories said was "intended to commence as soon as practicable", possibly as early as 2022/23. They proposed offering five further places each year to qualifying teams, in an effort to blunt FIFA's objections to 'closed shop' leagues.

The concept, a cynical attempt to further consolidate more earning power in the hands of a dozen or so of the Continent's most powerful clubs was met with swift condemnation and a revolt by supporters horrified at the implications for England's domestic leagues, the oldest in world football.

Within hours, the Premier League had issued a statement saying the six member clubs would face expulsion if they elected to take part in the Super League, in what a spokesperson described as "a proposal that attacks the principles of open competition and sporting merit which are at the heart of the domestic and European football pyramid."

A joint statement by the Football Association, UEFA and the Premier League said that they were "united in our efforts to stop this cynical project" which was "founded on the self-interest of a few clubs, at a time when society needs solidarity more than ever. This persistent self-interest of a few has been going on for too long — enough is enough."

UEFA and FIFA, football's global governing body, warned that they would ban any player who took part in such an unsanctioned league from appearing in the World Cup and European Championships.

The European Club Association, the body which represented 246 leading clubs in Europe, joined in the near-universal denunciation of the plan and reiterated its commitment to revamping the Champions League instead.

Reportedly led by the American owners of Liverpool and Manchester United and chaired by Real Madrid president Florentino

Pérez, the ESL was to be backed by JP Morgan bank. They would supposedly put up £3.5 billion to launch the league and pay each of its member clubs €350 million just for participating.

Former Manchester United defender Gary Neville voiced his disgust at the breakaway and called on the respective leagues to come down hard on the rebel 12.

"It's pure greed; they're imposters," Neville said. "The owners of Manchester United, Liverpool, Chelsea and Manchester City, they are nothing to do with football in this country.

"Manchester United, Arsenal, Tottenham aren't even in the Champions League. And they want a God-given right to be in there? They're an absolute joke.

"The time has come now to have independent regulators to stop these clubs from having the power base. Enough is enough."

***

Everton's owner, Farhad Moshiri, branded the ESL proposal as "preposterous arrogance" and on 20 April joined the call from the Premier League's other 14 clubs for disciplinary measures to be taken against the rebel six.

Meanwhile, in a statement from the Everton Board of Directors and an email to supporters from CEO Denise Barrett-Baxendale, the club outlined its commitment to the football pyramid and principles of open competition and sporting merit.

The messages from Everton came as reports suggested that at least two of the English six were wavering in their commitment to the controversial new venture.

The Guardian claimed that "a well-placed executive at another club approached to join the breakaway league" said that Chelsea and Manchester City, the last two clubs to commit to the Super League on Saturday, already had second thoughts following the fierce backlash to the plan, particularly in England.

The Telegraph, however, said that according to their sources, legally the ESL clubs now could not reverse course without being sued for billions of pounds because of the "binding agreements" they signed.

The following day, opposition to the Super League continued, with FIFA president, Gianni Infantino finally breaking his silence by saying that, "there is no doubt whatsoever of FIFA's disapproval of this," but while he warned that, "concretely, ... you cannot be half in or half out of [European football]," he stopped short of threatening action against the rebel clubs.

U.K. Prime Minister, Boris Johnson, meanwhile, offered "unwavering support" to the football authorities in their fight against the Super League and, in a statement from 10 Downing Street, said it, "was clear that no action is off the table, and the government is exploring every possibility, including legislative options, to ensure these proposals are stopped."

Moshiri, who sold his stake in Arsenal before his business partner Alisher Usmanov did the same after failing to gain entry to the North London club's board under their owner, Stan Kroenke, spoke to *TalkSport* where he voiced his disgust at the betrayal of the Premier League:

> "Every facet of this is against the very idea of British football. Football clubs are community assets, they

> belong to fans and their communities. This just takes much of their romance away. It just makes it a money game — it's not football any more. This is six clubs attacking the very heart of the Premier League, and I think they should be disciplined."

The statement from Goodison Park, meanwhile, urged their rival clubs to withdraw the proposals for the breakaway league that "[disenfranchised] supporters across the game — including their own — by putting the very structure that underpins the game we love under threat. Moshiri continued:

> "The backlash is understandable and deserved — and has to be listened to. This preposterous arrogance is not wanted anywhere in football outside of the clubs that have drafted this plan. On behalf of everyone associated with Everton, we respectfully ask that the proposals are immediately withdrawn and that the private meetings and subversive practises that have brought our beautiful game to possibly its lowest ever position in terms of trust end now. Finally we would ask the owners, chairmen, and Board members of the six clubs to remember the privileged position they hold — not only as custodians of their clubs but also custodians of the game. The responsibility they carry should be taken seriously. We urge them all to consider what they wish their legacy to be."

Later that day the 'rump' of 14 Premier League clubs convened in a meeting led by the League's chairman Richard Masters and issued their statement afterwards that said: "The 14 clubs at the meeting unanimously and vigorously rejected the plans for the competition. The Premier League is considering all actions available to prevent it from progressing, as well as holding those shareholders involved to account under its rules."

In a separate memo sent to the 14 clubs, Masters reportedly wrote: "This venture cannot be launched without English clubs and we call upon any club contemplating associating themselves or joining this venture to walk away immediately before irreparable damage is done."

By that same evening, the controversial breakaway Super League all but collapsed, as Manchester City formally withdrew from the ESL, followed by Chelsea, Arsenal, Liverpool, Manchester United and Tottenham.

As fans clogged the road at the players' entrance at Stamford Bridge ahead of Chelsea's Premier League match against Brighton, the London club had seemingly become the first to lose its nerve.

The *BBC* were first to report that Chelsea were preparing the paperwork to withdraw, but City were the first to provide official confirmation later in the evening. Sources at Chelsea suggested that extricating themselves from the binding contract they signed was complicated, but it was little surprise that the two clubs believed to have been the last two of the 'Dirty Dozen' to sign up were the first to bail.

Shortly before 11pm U.K. time, the two north London clubs, and both United and Liverpool, confirmed their intention to walk away from the Super League, with only Arsenal offering an apology in their statement to supporters.

The Super League company itself refused to give in, announcing that the launch would be delayed and reshaped.

A statement read: "Despite the announced departure of the English clubs, forced to take such decisions due to the pressure put on them, we are convinced our proposal is fully aligned with European law and regulations, as was demonstrated today by a court decision to protect the Super League from third party actions. Given the current circumstances, we shall reconsider the most appropriate steps to reshape the project, always having in mind our goals of offering fans the best experience possible while enhancing solidarity payments for the entire football community."

The dominoes would fall in Europe as well, however, and when the dust settled, just three clubs – Real Madrid, whose president Florentino Perez had been the primary driver behind the original proposal, Juventus and Barcelona – were still clinging to the ESL idea.

Few in the game were under any illusions that the "hydra" of a European Super League had been killed off forever, but the furore did help usher in a new format for the Champions League that would take effect in 2024/25 and which was designed to not only increase the money earned from participating by increasing the number of games, but also gave richer clubs a greater chance of qualifying each year.

To its critics, it would simply be a watered-down Super League, while the cynics surmised that the Continent's most powerful interests would always get their way somehow.

2021: Everton: European hopefuls to mid-table obscurity

> “It was sobering, pretty humiliating and, perhaps most alarmingly, not all that surprising; the final ignominious chapter in a season that promised so much but ended on perhaps as flat a note as it could for a team that sat in second place in the Premier League on Boxing Day.
>
> **2021 Everton: European hopefuls to mid-table obscurity**

Back on the field, Everton had slipped steadily down the league table and further away from European qualification; and at the heart of it was their dreadful home form. While the absence of crowds had no doubt helped the Toffees rack up a record-equalling 11 victories away from home, their results at Goodison Park consistently undermined their bid to finish in the top four.

While not helped by injuries at times to key personnel like Allan and Abdoulaye Doucouré, or the fact that James Rodriguez had become an increasingly unreliable presence in the side as he battled a niggling calf problem, it was still a conundrum that Carlo Ancelotti couldn't solve despite all his experience and coaching ability.

Relegation bound Fulham came to L4 and won, followed by Burnley who stunned Everton 2-1, before Aston Villa and then doomed Sheffield United also left Goodison with all three points before the end of the season.

***

19 May 2021: Everton v Wolves (6,068 spectators)

With hopes of Champions League football long gone, the best the Blues could hope for was a spot in the new Europa Conference League. Their opponents for the final home game of the season were Wolves.

This was not a good performance, but it was enough to earn the Toffees their first home win since the start of March, and it was fitting that Richarlison bagged the winner.

Evertonians had mused that few players feed off the energy of a crowd more than the mercurial Brazilian, and the way he rose to the occasion of supporters being let into Goodison for the first time since December seemed to bear that out. Quiet in the first half, Richarlison scored a terrific headed goal just two minutes into the second and, by the end, he was looking very much like the player Blues fans had come to love since he joined from Watford three years earlier.

Given how tentative and typically ponderous Everton had been in their build-up play, it was perhaps not surprising that the winner came from a set-piece. The fans in attendance had been desperate to see James Rodriguez in the flesh but were left wanting when the

Colombian withdrew from the squad due to "fatigue". The team lacked creativity without him.

But in his absence, Gylfi Sigurdsson provided the energy in the press even if he wasn't as productive when Everton had the ball, and it was his corner that served up the winner. The Icelander's out-swinger was placed perfectly for Richarlison to leap highest and guide his header into the far corner.

Sigurdsson went close to sealing it either side of a penalty claim for handball by Wolves against Doucouré, first with an attempted curler that hit the stanchion on the right side of goal, and then with another effort searching out the same corner that took a nick off a defender on its way behind.

But after months of misery on their home soil, Everton had ended their campaign of fixtures at Goodison Park on a high and with a victory that meant they could still qualify for the Europa Conference League if they bettered Tottenham's result on the final Sunday of the season.

The failings at home against the likes of Leeds, West Ham, Burnley, Fulham, Newcastle and Sheffield United – where just a point in each would have meant Champions League qualification would still be possible heading into the final day – would forever hang over this strange pandemic-affected season, but Ancelotti would have learned plenty about these players and what he needed to push for in 2021/22.

Final score: Everton 1-0 Wolves

***

Ancelotti had shown that he and Marcel Brands were aligned over what Everton would have to do in the transfer market over the summer in order to improve the squad, and he laughed off the notion that the club might be sanctioned over financial fair play rules, in view of the failed Super League.

Just like the previous year, the Italian appeared committed to making impactful signings in the close season but there has always been assumption that Everton would need to offload fringe players first in order to remain within UEFA's Financial Fair Play regulations and the Premier League's own profit and sustainability rules.

Fans expected outgoings when the current season ended, with Moise Kean topping the list of players who could be sold but Ancelotti, somewhat naively as things turned out, said the club would not need to wait for sales to come to fruition.

"The Premier League has to solve different problems than the financial fair play of Everton [because of] the fact that six teams wanted to go in [to] the Super League," he told print journalists following his pre-match press conference in front of the broadcast media yesterday afternoon.

"First of all, they have to take care of this and then, maybe, they can have a look at Everton. But we are going to look at ourselves.

"If they looked at us, with the problem they had with the top six that wanted to join the Super League, that would be funny. Of course, we will take care of our financial aspect, but we can buy without selling players this summer for sure."

"We're all agreed on the plan. We have to improve the squad and there is no doubt we are totally focused on this," Ancelotti continued.

"We are totally agreed, from the manager, the club and the technical director, Marcel Brands."

***

23 May 2021: Manchester City v Everton (10,000 spectators)

In what Blues fans hoped wasn't a portent of what was coming the following season, Everton wore their 2021/22 black away kit at the Etihad Stadium for their final attempt to secure European football for the 2021/22 season. But it was less The Black Watch and more the death watch as they extinguished the last breaths from European-qualification hopes that had been on life support for a few weeks and had effectively died a week previously with a horrible home defeat to Sheffield United.

Manchester City, true to their exacting manager's footballing philosophy, were merciless. Pep Guardiola eschewed any notion that his mind and those of his players was on the looming Champions League Final against Chelsea. He named an almost full-strength line-up, watched them tear the Blues apart, and still had plenty of time to bring on the departing Sergio Agüero for his triumphant swan song. Just as they were for Arsenal's title party in 1998 and Leicester's in 2016, Everton were obliging guests who laid down the welcome mat and got trampled amid the revelry.

It was sobering, pretty humiliating and, perhaps most alarmingly, not all that surprising; the final ignominious chapter in a season that promised so much but ended on perhaps as flat a note as it could for a team that sat in second place in the Premier League on Boxing Day.

So much seemed possible heading into the New Year, not least because Carlo Ancelotti was fashioning his side into one of the most effective away from home. Increasingly, the formula was a simple one centred around discipline, hard work and the deployment of the low block, in the expectation that the Toffees could pinch a goal on the break or from a set-piece and then dig in for the points.

Aided by the lack of home supporters, it worked an impressive number of times; which is why it was curious that the Italian chose a game away at the newly crowned Champions, who had fans in the stands for the first time since February last year, to abandon the tactics that had served him so well to this point.

By his own admission Everton tried to play further up the pitch and take the game to City and while it was laudable in their pressing need to win to have any chance of making the Europa Conference League, in retrospect it was puzzlingly naïve.

The visitors had some bright moments in the early exchanges but the floodgates opened in the 11th minute when Kevin De Bruyne's run into an ocean of space in front of Everton's defence went untracked and he had the time to pick his spot with a typically excellent finish inside the far post.

Three minutes later, Michael Keane tried to dribble through a clutch of City players near the halfway line and the hosts pounced, with De Bruyne picking out Jesus who easily turned Mason Holgate and fired home to make it 2-0.

A potential route back into the game for the Toffees arrived ten minutes before the break, though, in a moment of controversy where Everton felt that Ruben Dias should have seen red for denying Richarlison a goal-scoring opportunity.

The Brazilian raced onto a through-ball and was caught by the Portuguese defender's slide-tackle and then clattered by Ederson, with referee Michael Oliver electing to only yellow-card Dias.

Gylfi Sigurdsson stepped up to take the penalty but placed his shot at the ideal height for the goalkeeper and Ederson pushed it away, while Richarlison's shot from the rebound was charged down by a recovering defender.

Phil Foden made it 3-0 eight minutes after half-time with another impressive finish after Abdoulaye Doucouré's loose pass was cut out on in the centre-circle and City attacked quickly.

Ancelotti sent on Alex Iwobi for Doucouré and then Bernard for Sigurdsson, but neither player made much impact. Instead, it became the Agüero send-off party as Tom Davies became the latest player to be dispossessed cheaply in his own half and Agüero navigated his way around Holgate before guiding the ball into the far corner with the outside of his boot with 20 minutes left.

Six minutes after that, Everton's misery was complete. Fernandinho crossed from the right for Agüero, who had positioned himself inside the 10 yards of space between Godfrey and Keane and the Argentine steered a header beyond Pickford's reach to make it five.

In the final reckoning, even had Everton pulled off the improbable against a City side that existed in another universe to its own, it wouldn't have mattered, anyway. Displaying a good deal more spirit and enterprise than has been in evidence from the Toffees in recent weeks, Tottenham Hotspur came back from 2-1 down to beat Champions League hopefuls Leicester 4-2 at the King Power stadium, securing a spot in the inaugural Europa Conference League.

For Everton, the wait to play Continental football again would have to wait at least another year, but of more immediate concern was the way what seemed, as recently as March a hugely promising season had unravelled so dramatically, with Ancelotti seemingly powerless to do anything about it.

Final score: Manchester City 5-0 Everton

***

Richard Jolly, writing in *FourFourTwo*, on May 26, asked the question on the lips of so many of the club's fans:

Everton: How did things go so wrong this season for the Toffees?

His answer made sombre reading: "Carlo Ancelotti's Everton went from European hopefuls to mid table obscurity in a pitiful 2021. [The Man City result] was the heaviest defeat of Carlo Ancelotti's coaching career and, indeed, the heaviest suffered by any manager with three European Cups in his trophy cabinet.

"The juxtaposition between Ancelotti's past and his present has rarely felt as clear as during Manchester City 5 Everton 0. This time, the silverware being celebrated on the pitch was not anything Ancelotti won. His side had the carrot of European football - but were thrashed by a team with nothing to play for and recorded his lowest league finish of any full season in charge anywhere.

"The sight of Everton in 10th underlines the way this season was a missed opportunity and not merely because it is logical to assume that Liverpool and Chelsea will be stronger next season and thus the bar for a top-four finish will be set higher.

"Everton got historic wins away at Arsenal, Tottenham and Liverpool, triumphed at Leicester and West Ham for good measure and finished two places lower than they did under Sam Allardyce in 2018 and Marco Silva in 2019. Their four major signings – James Rodriguez, Allan, Abdoulaye Doucouré and Ben Godfrey – all succeeded to some extent, but the season concluded with the tone-deaf Colombian tweeting pictures of himself on a plane bound for the Copa America when Everton's destiny was still to be determined. 'Tiredness' was an inadequate reason for missing important games.

"It was a campaign when, even when Everton got some things right, others went horribly wrong.

"Everton ended the campaign without a regular system or a style of play. Ancelotti switched shape intelligently at times, adapting to the rotating cast on the treatment table, but it also betrayed Everton's inability to find a settled 11. It felt damning that, in the end, they were better when they had less of the ball and when less was expected of them.

"Everton were prisoners of their past, Ancelotti encumbered by previous poor signings like Alex Iwobi and Bernard, lumbered with an imbalanced squad that contained too many midfielders and yet, because of their injuries, too few at times; but they were also architects of their own failure. Too many games felt a failure of mentality, leading Ancelotti to use the word "unacceptable" after the Sheffield United game. Seamus Coleman was often more scathing; the captain may be in decline but his own attitude was invariably beyond reproach.

"His frustration stemmed in part from the awareness he will not have many more chances to accomplish something seismic. Everton will not have many better ones. Ancelotti was brought in to elevate them to the next level, not to see them finish below a promoted club, plus their former manager, David Moyes. He showed a sure touch in 2020. Yet Everton's demoralising 2021 meant even an eminently amenable man seemed irritated. One of the season's achievers ended up among its underachievers".

***

For Evertonians, who would spend the coming days wondering whether the summer would bring some positive signs, what happened next was a real shocker.

2021: Ancelotti Leaves Everton in the Lurch

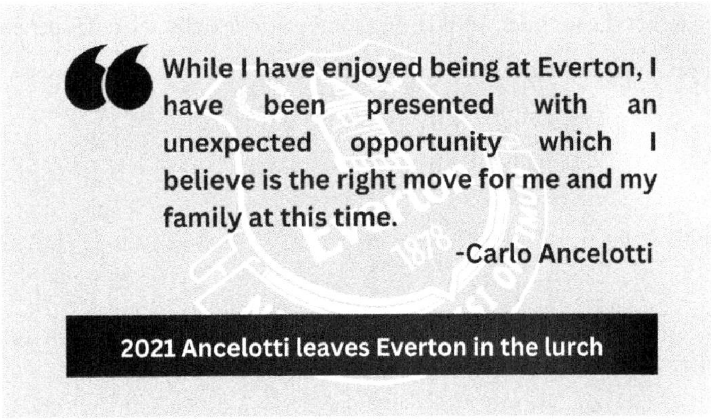

Gone! Less than 18 months after he joined Everton as a surprise managerial appointment to succeed Marco Silva, Carlo Ancelotti abruptly left Goodison Park to return to Real Madrid, the club that sacked him six years previously.

Only weeks earlier, the Italian had been talking in terms of extending his contract to enable him to see the club into their new stadium, so the Blue half of Merseyside was stunned by reports that broke in the late afternoon on 31 May, that the Italian was being lined up to replace Zinedine Zidane at the Bernabeu. Events moved quickly, to where Ancelotti was confirmed as Real manager that evening.

It left Everton having to put their summer transfer plans on hold and scramble to draw up a shortlist of candidates to replace Ancelotti, with the likes of Eddie Howe, David Moyes and Nuno Espirito Santo among the early names being linked.

Zidane's decision to step down at Madrid had been on the cards as the 2020/21 season drew to a close and it sparked rumours that Ancelotti might be among the candidates to replace him; suggestions the Italian had laughed off during his final pre-match press conference of the season ahead of the Manchester City match.

The lure of Madrid proved too much for the 61-year-old, however, and after firm contact was made with his representatives, Ancelotti came to a final agreement that saw him sign a three-year contract at Real, which was reportedly worth less than half per year than he was earning at Everton.

One wondered what impact the burglary of Ancelotti's home in Crosby had had on the willingness of his family to stay longer on Merseyside. Certainly, they were unlikely to come across the same problems when living within a luxurious, gated-community, in the salubrious part of Madrid that would become their new home.

"While I have enjoyed being at Everton, I have been presented with an unexpected opportunity which I believe is the right move for me and my family at this time," Ancelotti said once the club confirmed he had left for Madrid.

"I would like to thank the Board of Directors, the players, and the Evertonians for the tremendous support they have all given me during my time at the club.

"I have complete respect for everyone associated with Everton and hope they can achieve the exciting opportunities they have in front of them."

***

Meanwhile, Everton's board of directors held an emergency meeting to discuss the club's next steps.

Just 24 hours after the news of Carlo Ancelotti's departure had rocked the club, the Blues were reportedly set to open talks with former Wolves boss Nuno Espirito Santo after installing him alongside David Moyes as a preferred candidate to replace the departed Italian.

The Portuguese had left Wolves last month after four years in charge and had been in discussions with Crystal Palace about succeeding Roy Hodgson at Selhurst Park.

Sky Sports claimed Nuno would be the first candidate to be interviewed by the Everton hierarchy.

David Moyes, who was still expected to accept a contract offer from West Ham, had come close to being re-appointed as the Toffees' boss 18 months ago but had been pipped to the post by Ancelotti. Former Leipzig boss and onetime candidate to replace Moyes in 2013, Ralf Rangnick, was also thought to be in the frame.

In the interim, Josh King, who had been curiously under-used by Ancelotti, was one of five confirmed departures on 4 June, together with Muhammed Besic, Yannick Bolasie and Theo Walcott, all of whom were released from the first-team squad.

But incoming transfers had to be put on the back burner while the search for Everton's new head coach dragged on to the end of the month. The appointment when it finally came, was as controversial, divisive and destructive as any in the club's history.

2021: Moshiri: Benitez is a proven winner

> “Rafa has managed clubs with big expectations and won some of the biggest trophies in the game. He’s a proven winner. We are confident that his winning mentality will bring success to us at Everton.
>
> - Farhad Moshiri

2021 Moshiri: Benitez is a proven winner

On 30 June 2021, after days of speculation, Everton finally announced former Liverpool manager Rafael Benitez as Carlo Ancelotti’s successor, a little over four weeks after the Italian had abruptly left the club in the lurch to return to Real Madrid.

Benitez arrived at Everton’s Finch Farm training ground ahead of the official confirmation that a deal with the club had been finalised, despite a vociferous outcry from a significant section of the fanbase who continued to react with shock and horror at how he could be the new Everton boss.

Because of his long association with the reds and comments he once made about the Blues after a Merseyside derby in 2007, Benitez's arrival was highly contentious for a section of the Everton fanbase. Banners protesting the Board of Directors' decision appeared outside Goodison, and someone left a reprehensible one near his Caldy home, with a threatening message warning him not to sign on with the Toffees.

Everton's majority shareholder, Farhad Moshiri, pushed through the appointment despite the protests, stating that Benitez was the best candidate to bring success to the Blue half of Merseyside – or, at the very least, to keep the club on an even keel.

In a curious twist of fate, Benitez had become Ancelotti's immediate successor for the second time in his career — the Spaniard replaced the Italian at the Bernabeu in 2015. He also became Moshiri's fifth managerial appointment in as many years, starting with Ronald Koeman's much-vaunted appointment in June 2016.

He signed a three-year contract with Everton and became the first man in the modern era to have managed both Merseyside clubs, having coached Liverpool between 2004 and 2010. He brought fitness coach and long-time associate Paco De Miguel with him to the club, while Duncan Ferguson, Leighton Baines and goalkeeping coach Alan Kelly remained in their existing roles.

"I am delighted to be joining Everton," Benitez said. "Throughout this process, I have been greatly impressed by the ambition shown by the senior representatives at the Club and their desire to bring success to this historic club.

"I believe this is a club that is going places. I'm determined to play a big part in helping this great club achieve its ambitions."

In a statement lacking his usual effusiveness, Bill Kenwright, said: "Rafa Benitez is joining Everton Football Club at an exciting time. On behalf of the Board of Directors, I wish him well in achieving success for our football club - success our supporters long for and deserve."

Moshiri's rationale for hiring Benitez was likely based on his previous success as a manager – as well as his affinity to Merseyside, where he still lived with his family – although by the time he arrived at Goodison Park it had been eight years since his last trophy.

Following an unremarkable, injury-affected playing career between 1978 and 1986 Benitez moved into management in 1993 with Real Madrid's B team. Spells at Valladolid, Osasuna, Extremadura and Tenerife followed before he joined Valencia, where he emerged as a noteworthy coach by twice winning La Liga while also guiding Los Murciélagos to a UEFA Cup triumph in 2004.

Those achievements caught the attention of Liverpool who hired him to replace Gérard Houllier, and in his time across Stanley Park he won the FA Cup and reached two Champions League finals, beating Ancelotti's AC Milan in Istanbul in the first in 2005.

The reds regarded the 2009/10 season as a campaign of decline and Benitez left Liverpool in the summer, when he joined Inter Milan to replace Jose Mourinho. While he won the Supercoppa Italiana and the FIFA World Club Cup, they dismissed him just six months into the job as the reigning Serie A Champions slumped to 6th place under his stewardship.

Two years later, he became interim manager at Chelsea, where he ignored supporter discontent at his appointment to guide the Londoners to a Europa League triumph 6 months later.

Benitez returned to Italy to take the reins at Napoli where he won the Coppa Italia. Then came a brief tenure at Real Madrid, where he managed James Rodriguez. That was followed by three years at Newcastle United. Brought in late in the 2015/16 season, he could not keep the Magpies in the Premier League, but he remained with the club and secured an immediate return to the top flight.

His final season on Tyneside was a middling one, dominated by reports of a testy relationship with owner Mike Ashley and disagreements over transfer policy. Though he was loved by Newcastle's fans, his contract was allowed to expire in 2019, and he took up the invitation to try his hand in China with Dalian Professional, an assignment that was curtailed by the COVID-19 pandemic and Benitez's desire to return to his family on Merseyside.

***

On the Everton FC website, the club published an interview with the owner under the headline: FARHAD MOSHIRI: WHY WE WANTED RAFA.

In it, the club's owner explained that Benitez had "stood out as the best candidate," fulfilling the remit of, "a manager with experience of managing at the highest level, who has a strong track record of delivering success, who can work within our structure and who fully buys into our vision for the future.

"We want to be playing in European competitions and challenging for silverware at home and abroad - so it was vitally important we have a manager who has been there and understands what it takes to achieve that level of success.

"Rafa has managed clubs with big expectations and won some of the biggest trophies in the game. He's a proven winner. We are confident that his winning mentality will bring success to us at Everton.

"I know that the last few weeks have not been an easy time for our supporters, so I'd like to thank them for their patience throughout this process. Hopefully now we can come together and be confident about our plans on and off the field. There are some exciting times ahead and I hope the supporters know that they have my full commitment in terms of delivering our ambitions."

***

Another shock announcement came on 20 July, when Everton confirmed they had suspended a first-team player pending an investigation by police.

A brief statement by the club said that they would continue to support the authorities with their inquiries and would not be making any further statement.

The bulletin from the club came in the wake of a report by the *Daily Mail* that a Premier League club had suspended a 31-year-old player because of inquiries by police.

The player in question, who wasn't ever named in the British press for legal reasons, would eventually have his contract terminated and never again played for the Toffees.

***

Later that day, desperate for some good news, Everton announced the acquisition of Andros Townsend on a free transfer from Crystal Palace, the first signing of Rafael Benitez's tenure as the Blues' manager. The 30-year-old winger agreed a two-year contract that would run through the end of June 2023, bringing to an end a five-year spell at Selhurst Park while renewing his association with Benitez who managed him briefly at Newcastle United in 2016.

Townsend explained that reuniting with his old boss and the prospect of playing for a "massive and ambitious" club like Everton meant he could not turn down the chance to sign when it came up.

"I think everyone knows what Everton is. It's a massive football club, it's very ambitious, a club which has been trying to get back to where it belongs into Europe and beyond," Townsend told evertontv. "I'll be doing all I can to help the Club do that.

"Everton is a massive football club and has big ambitions next season. As the old cliché goes, it was a no-brainer.

"Rafa is very experienced. He does a lot of work on the tactical side on the training pitch. He leaves no stone unturned. But more importantly, he's a great man, a great man-manager, and he's always talking to you. I'm sure he will be very successful here."

***

Then, hot on the heels of signing Andros Townsend, Everton confirmed the signing of Asmir Begovic as goalkeeping cover for Jordan Pickford over the coming season for an undisclosed fee and on a 12-month contract from Championship side Bournemouth.

***

Just two days later, Everton completed another signing with the confirmation of the capture of winger Demarai Gray from Bayer Leverkusen.

The Blues activated a clause in the former Leicester City player's contract and landed him in a deal with around £1.7 million. Gray signed a three-year contract that would keep him at Everton until 2024, but there was an option for the club to extend it by a further year.

"I'm delighted to be back in the Premier League at such a big club and I'm excited to play with the team and get to work," Gray told evertontv. "Speaking to the manager and Marcel Brands, I had a really good feel for the Club and I feel this is a place where I can continue to develop.

"The manager, with his ambition and what he has won in the past, is important and we'll look to push forward and compete with the top clubs. I think a club of this magnitude has all the potential to be right up there.

"I want to push on, be a pivotal player in the squad, and help the team score goals and assist goals," Gray continued.

"I'm a speedy, tricky winger. I enjoy running with the ball. I like to play anywhere along the front three and I feel like I can be dangerous in all areas."

***

Having been linked with many strikers, and in need to sign more firepower, Everton completed their fifth signing of the window on transfer deadline day with the acquisition from Dalian Professional of Salomon Rondon, who linked back up with former boss, Rafael Benitez. The oft-mooted transfer happened ahead of the 11pm transfer deadline, after the Venezuelan striker ended his contract in China.

Remarkably, the 31-year-old, who signed a two-year contract with the option of a third, was the only addition to the Blues' squad on a day that looked as though it was going to be hectic, but ended up being a damp squib.

***

Though there was disquiet among large sections of the Everton fanbase, concerning the appointment of Benitez, the club continued to make progress on the stadium project and it was soon confirmed that the start date for construction work at Bramley-Moore Dock would be Monday, 26 July, 2021. Main contractors Laing O'Rourke would immediately begin the first phase of the project to build the club's new 52,888-seater stadium.

That was the day the club took possession of the site from Peel Holdings and the enabling works to prepare the dock site in readiness for the build could begin.

Work would include the repair and preservation of the Grade II listed dock wall, stabilisation of the old hydraulic tower, the development of welfare facilities for Laing O'Rourke construction staff, the preparation for demolition of existing non-listed structures, and raking of the dock floor. Pipework would also be installed, needed for infilling of the dock.

Bill Kenwright, said: “We are thrilled to be able to confirm that construction work will commence on our new stadium later this month. This will be a momentous day in the history of the Club and is testament to the ambition and financial commitment of Farhad and the determination and talent of Denise and her executive team at the Club.

“Like every Evertonian, Goodison Park has been a massive part of my life but in moving forward we could not have found a more fitting nor more glorious site for our new stadium — one which will both honour our history and celebrate our magnificent future.”

Meanwhile, Everton’s Chief Executive, Denise Barrett-Baxendale, commented: “This moment will rank as one of the most important in the Club’s history as it symbolises a new era for Evertonians, an era which will see our supporters, their children and their children’s children supporting their team in one of the finest stadiums in world football.

“This project presents such an exciting future for our club and is a clear demonstration of our owner’s commitment and ambition."

***

On the eve of another new season, and with the team under the control of yet another new manager, Evertonians finally hoping to see James Rodriguez in the flesh at Goodison Park were disappointed to hear the Colombian was not in the squad.

Like Moise Kean, James had been training away from the rest of the first-team squad in what they presumed to be a precaution. However, Rafael Benitez said some of his players were quarantining in line with COVID-19 protocols, with Rodriguez among them.

Rodriguez had been using the video community Twitch to interact with his fans over the previous couple of weeks and had given little sign his future belonged at Everton.

Against a backdrop of media talk that Rafael Benitez had apparently told him he didn't suit the Spaniard's plans for the team, James claimed that he simply wanted to play where he was wanted.

He cast doubt on his participation in the season-opener against Southampton when he said on his channel: "There is a game on Saturday... but I don't know. I don't think I'll play. Everything can happen until the end of the month. Soccer always changes fast," he concluded.

If he was successful, it seemed like Evertonians would never get the chance to see Rodriguez play for their team in person. Certainly, supporters wouldn't see him play against Southampton.

Benitez said in his pre-match press conference that he had spoken with James and that the club would do its best to find the right solution for him.

"I have had my conversation with him and he knows my idea," Benitez said. "Now, he is not available, so not an issue for tomorrow. We will discuss with every single player with their agents to find the best solution."

Kean, meanwhile, had reportedly made it known that he wanted to leave the club before the transfer deadline, and had removed all photographs from his time at Everton from his Instagram feed.

A permanent move to Paris Saint-Germain, where he had spent the preceding season on loan, did not look to be on the cards after the French giants refused any other arrangement than another temporary spell, having just signed Lionel Messi from Barcelona.

***

14 August 2021: Everton v Southampton

Meanwhile, Benitez began his reign with a rousing season-opening victory over Saints, as Everton welcomed a practically full house back to Goodison Park for the first time in almost 18 months.

Buoyed by a positive reception for Benitez from the fans, Everton made a positive start but were undermined by a horrendous error by Michael Keane midway through the first half. The defender, playing alongside Mason Holgate with Yerry Mina on the bench because of his lack of pre-season activity following a delayed return from the Copa America, was caught dallying on the ball inside his own half and was robbed by Che Adams. Adams prodded it forward to release Adam Armstrong, who made no mistake, lifting the ball past Jordan Pickford and into the top corner of the goal.

Benitez's half-time talk and a tactical shift that swapped the positions of the two centre-backs and switched Demarai Gray to the left with Richarlison moving into the centre did the trick, however, in spurring his charges into more purposeful action. Gray won a 47th-minute corner that was only cleared as far as Townsend. He nodded a looping header back towards the six-yard box where Richarlison stole in behind the static Mohammed Salisu and stabbed it into the roof of the net.

That ignited the home crowd, but it would take another half an hour for the next goal to arrive as Southampton responded in what was an even encounter until 15 minutes from the end. Despite a couple of nervy moments claiming aerial balls from a flurry of Saints corners, Pickford didn't have a save of note make after denying Armstrong in the first half.

Instead, it was Alex McCarthy who was picking the ball out of the back of the net following a wonderful strike by Doucouré. Operating much closer to the opposition box than was the case in the latter stages of Carlo Ancelotti's tenure, the Frenchman was involved in the build-up to the goal when he fed the ball out to Seamus Coleman on the right flank.

The Irishman's scooped pass found recent substitute Alex Iwobi, who headed it back to Doucouré just inside the area. He took one touch to turn his marker and then unleashed a fabulous effort into the top corner to make it 2-1.

That became 3-1 in the closing stages and Iwobi was involved again. Picking up the ball on the right from Richarlison, he then threaded a perfectly weighted pass between two defenders and the Brazilian whipped a peach of an early cross to the six-yard box where Calvert-Lewin stooped to force a diving header into the net, to set the seal on a superb afternoon for Everton.

It was a performance wholly at odds with the team's struggles at home under Benitez's predecessor and a victory earned by playing to the Blues' strengths as a side. The previous season's games in an empty home stadium were too often a story of capitulation and attacking ineptitude, but against Southampton, the character and response from the team was exactly what was required.

They owed much to Richarlison, who was excellent in the second half and a driving force in attack, but both new signings played important roles and the new boss got his tactics right on the day.

True football was back with the return of a ground full of supporters who enjoyed a stirring victory that would, for the time being, banish the cloud of pessimism with which many fans approached the 2021/22 season.

Final score: Everton 3-1 Southampton

***

The positive start to the season under Benitez continued with a creditable 2-2 draw at Leeds, followed by a 2-1 away win at Huddersfield Town in the Carabao Cup, and another impressive 2-0 win away at Brighton.

Unfortunately, the win on the south coast in which Dominic Calvert-Lewin had notched his third goal in four games to start 2021/22 would be his last until January 2022, by which time Benitez was on the brink of losing his job at Everton.

The striker, who had been so impressive during Ancelotti's only full season and become the long-awaited replacement for Romelu Lukaku by default, suffered a serious quadricep tear that would not only sideline him for a significant portion of the season but would trigger a series of soft-tissue complaints for months afterwards.

***

13 September 2021: Everton v Burnley

Everton returned home after their win over the Seagulls for some Monday night football where they came from behind for a second successive home game to sweep Burnley away at Goodison Park, which was bouncing by the end of what had threatened to be a frustrating evening under the lights.

The Blues had toiled through a disappointing first half, playing with a five man defensive formation under Rafael Benitez for the first time, and fell behind early in the second half to a Ben Mee header, a goal that evoked painful memories of a string of home defeats under Carlo Ancelotti last season.

Rather than wallow in impending defeat, however, Everton responded in almost immediate and irrepressible fashion, scoring three goals in six mesmerising minutes – the pick of them coming like a rocket off the boot of Andros Townsend – and coming close to adding a fourth soon afterwards, but Abdoulaye Doucouré's effort was ruled out for offside.

The equaliser arrived within seven minutes of Mee's opener, just as Benitez was preparing his first change in order to alter the course of the contest. A short-corner between Lucas Digne and Demarai Gray ended with the latter firing disappointingly into a defender but the Blues kept the ball, worked it to Townsend on the opposite flank and he whipped a perfect cross onto the head of Keane who just had to guide it past the stranded Pope to make it 1-1 on the hour mark.

Five minutes later, the game was turned on its head in the same manner Everton had flipped it on Southampton a month ago on the opening day. Andros Townsend cut back inside off the flank with a couple of touches and then unloaded a quite magnificent left-foot shot from 30 yards out that crashed into the top corner, leaving Nick Pope with no chance.

Just over a minute later it was 3-1, as Burnley's attack following the restart broke down in Everton's area. Townsend knocked the loose ball to Doucouré, who spotted Gray's run through space in the centre-circle and released him with a perfect pass that allowed him to bear down on keeper and bury it past him in front of the ecstatic Park End.

The hosts threatened to turn it into a rout and there was a late cameo for another new signing, Salomon Rondon, but Everton were content otherwise by that stage to see out their second 3-1 home win of the campaign and move joint-top on points in the Premier League table.

Final score: Everton 3-1 Burnley

***

21 September 2021: QPR v Everton

If Rafael Benitez had made a surprisingly impressive start to life as Everton boss, leading the Toffees to a fourth-place berth by mid-September, the wheels would come off in spectacular fashion, starting with a 3-0 defeat at Aston Villa and then the club's almost customarily premature exit from the Carabao Cup.

Indeed, an Evertonian of any pedigree knows there was nothing shocking about the result in a third round tie at Queens Park Rangers which once again saw the club out of the League Cup before autumn had officially begun.

Everton have never won the competition, and it's highly unlikely they ever will; not just because the Carabao Cup is under threat from the burgeoning international calendar and calls for the fixture list in England to be pared down, but also because the perennial down-playing of the tournament by playing weakened sides means that successive Everton managers are always playing with fire.

Benitez was the latest to get burned.

The rationale for making wholesale changes to the team for cup fixtures is well-established, of course. It's an opportunity to rest your stars and give some game time and a chance to impress for fringe or younger players against the calibre of opposition that Everton should beat regardless of which mix of the first-team squad is out there.

Benitez's impulse to rest some key players was justifiably strong. He was already without Dominic Calvert-Lewin, Richarlison and Seamus Coleman (although none of them had played in the previous round at Huddersfield) and could ill-afford to lose any more ahead of Premier League matches against Norwich and Manchester United.

The bigger inquest really surrounded the paucity of Everton's squad and the disastrous recruitment decisions that had left the squad so shallow in terms of quality. Nevertheless, whenever you make wholesale changes, you leave yourself wide open to the danger of being picked off by a lower-division side and on this occasion it came at the hands of Queens Park Rangers and the lottery of a penalty shoot-out.

Still, given that six of the 11 that started at Loftus Road had been in the line-up at Huddersfield in the previous round, where his charges still squeaked through despite going down to 10 men in the second half, the Spaniard might have expected better than the dreadful fare Everton served up for much of this contest.

He was let down badly, particularly by the centre-half pairing of Ben Godfrey and Mason Holgate who struggled to cope with veteran striker Charlie Austin before improving in the second half, and a limp midfield duo of André Gomes and Tom Davies that contributed to QPR enjoying, at one stage, 70% of the ball... against a Premier League team!

If Benitez was relying on a repeat of the Huddersfield tie, the early knockings might have comforted him but it only took 18 minutes for Everton to fall behind. The porous nature of Everton's below-strength midfield and right flank, where Jonjoe Kenny offered little resistance, underscored QPR's first meaningful attack. Chris Willock twice made a mug of Davies before finding Ilias Chair, who knocked it to Sam McCullum. When Asmir Begovic could only palm his cross straight to Austin, the striker simply nodded into the empty net to make it 1-0.

Digne had the Toffees level within 12 minutes, though, when QPR's offside trap was sprung by a delicious ball over the top by Townsend, that picked out the run of the Frenchman who calmly side-footed it home first time.

Parity lasted just four minutes, however, as Everton's soft centre showed again. This time it was Chair who swung the ball in from the Rs' left and Austin capitalised on the yard's worth of space afforded by Godfrey by rising above him and glancing a header inside the far post.

With their manager's half-time team talk no doubt ringing in their ears, Everton got the early goal they needed once the second period resumed. Gomes scuffed a corner to the near post, Holgate knocked it across into the mix in front of goal, where Townsend converted from close range to make it 2-2.

That should have provided the platform from which Everton won the game, but they lacked the requisite cutting edge or drive in midfield.

Benitez hooked Gomes and introduced both Abdoulaye Doucouré and Demarai Gray but there was never enough cohesiveness or penetration about the team to enable either to fashion or score a winner... although the Frenchman probably should have had a penalty in the 74th minute when he appeared to be tripped in the box.

Once it had gone to penalties, Everton's League Cup curse took over, manifesting itself in the worst spot-kick of the shoot-out from Davies who invited Dieng to save it at full-stretch and set Dunne up to be the hero with QPR's eighth successful kick.

Once again, the aftermath to an early League Cup exit was dominated by recriminations over the manager fielding a much-changed side. Gary Lineker had quipped before the previous round that, "the Carabao Cup is where a bunch of teams enter a competition and Manchester City win it at the end," and there was more than element of truth about the futility of this tournament where teams like Everton were concerned.

By the same token, though, progression through each round narrowed your odds, and for a club like Everton – trophy-less for what would be 27 years by the time the finals of the domestic cups came around the following spring – could they not put their best foot forward in every round and do everything possible to win a piece of silverware? The 3,000 fans who packed the away end on a Tuesday night in London deserved much, much better.

Final score: QPR 2-2 Everton (Pens 8-7)

***

More bad news was to follow. James Rodriguez finally left Everton in a permanent transfer to Al Rayyan of the Qatar Stars League for a fee that was officially undisclosed, but reported to be around £7.2 million.

It ended James's one-year association with the Toffees that began in a hail of publicity and some scintillating early performances, but which ultimately became a constant source of frustration as the player battled injury during the 2020/21 season, with many also questioning his commitment to the Everton cause.

The departure from Goodison Park of his mentor Carlo Ancelotti in June seemed to signal that Rodriguez's time with the Blues would also be cut short; but there was a point when the summer transfer deadline passed in England and he could not find another club, where it looked as though he could yet stay.

The suggestions in the media were that with Benitez unable to see a role for him in the team, Everton kept pushing James to find an exit to a country where the window was still open, so they could get some or all of his reported £200,000-a-week salary off the books.

Indeed, though Benitez had tried claiming that, "It's always up to the player; in the end he has the final decision," the manager had hinted earlier in the month of September that the former Galactico's exit was required as Everton worked towards remaining within the Premier League's Profit & Sustainability limits.

"We are talking about a special situation for this club," the Spaniard said after the Carabao Cup defeat to QPR, "[With] the financial fair play rules, we have to manage everything in the best way we can."

As he parted ways with Everton having never experienced the magic of Goodison at its most passionate, the Columbian wrote on Instagram:

"I ... want to thank Everton fans. A pity not to have played in Goodison Park with you. It would have been very nice. I always tried to give my best, and I always wanted to win. That is my mentality. I wish you all the best."

***

23 October 2021: Everton v Watford

Everton moved on from the cup defeat to QPR to register a 2-0 home win against Norwich, and began October with a 1-1 draw with Manchester United at Old Trafford. Those results put them in good spirits for the visit of West Ham to Goodison on 17 October, but an Angelo Ogbonna goal for the Hammers in the 74th minute decided the match and sent the restless crowd home frustrated. The defeat saw the Blues slip to 8th in the league.

The following Saturday, there was an opportunity to atone, when Watford were the visitors to Goodison. What unfolded was quite the opposite and it was an early harbinger of poor performances and results to come under Rafael Benitez as a former player, perhaps with a point to prove, ran riot.

In the expectation of a busy summer of transfer business, few had questioned the decision by Everton to let Josh King go at the end of 2020/21. The Norwegian international had shown flashes of promise off the bench in his few months with the club after arriving from Bournemouth in January, but Carlo Ancelotti has largely overlooked him and he failed to make a single start under the Italian. If he wasn't going to play, better to release him and sign someone more to the manager's liking.

Ancelotti left Goodison Park at the start of June, of course, and following an alarmingly austere summer, Everton effectively ended up trading King for Salomon Rondon, a player whose limitations were already obvious, and who once again proved to be utterly ineffective up front for the Blues. King scored a hat-trick as Everton fell apart in the final quarter of an hour.

Benitez's team were utterly shambolic, particularly in the closing stages as Watford players poured through their midfield and defence on the way to a four-goal assault in the space of 13 minutes. It was an absolute horror show, evocative of some of the worst collapses in a recent club history littered with embarrassing and gutless capitulations.

Michael Keane and the 2021/22, post-COVID version of Ben Godfrey made for an awkward and susceptible-looking pairing at the best of times, but against Watford, with both players turning in often shocking performances, it looked like a doomed partnership.

Yerry Mina had been a big miss against West Ham the previous weekend, and he proved to be again, side-lined as he was by a hamstring complaint. With Abdoulaye Doucouré and Dominic Calvert-Lewin also missing, Everton proved that without those important components of their metaphorical spine, they had no real spine at all.

In Doucouré's absence, Tom Davies looked to have stepped admirably into the breach by grabbing an early goal. Anthony Gordon fed Demarai Gray and when he crossed low into the six-yard box, where Davies arrived to slide home from close range to score his first goal in over two years, in only the third minute.

The Toffees' good work was undone, however, by another failure to deal with a set-piece. A free-kick, whipped in from the right near the corner flag, came off Ben Godfrey's head and dropped to King, who was free to prod it into the gaping net.

Disconcertingly, the goal visibly drained much of the Blues' early belief and it would be a while before they rediscovered some of their mojo. What should have been the turning point of the contest came just past the hour mark when Richarlison, absent for the past few games with a knee injury, came off the bench to score within three minutes of his introduction. The Brazilian ghosted into space to connect with Keane's clipped ball into the box and launched himself to guide a header past Ben Foster and send Goodison into rapture.

With 16 minutes left, Keane could have killed the contest but crucially planted his header off a free-kick the wrong side of the post. Just four minutes later, Watford were level again. Sloppy play by Davies forced Keane to put the ball behind and the resulting delivery found Juraj Kucka, who bulleted a header past Pickford.

King's second goal turned the game on its head at 3-2, and any chance of Benitez's charges getting something from the contest evaporated three minutes from the end of the regulation 90. Godfrey failed to clear his lines as three Everton defenders got in each other's way and the ball was poked through to King who side-stepped Keane and slotted past the keeper to make it 4-2.

And Everton's misery was complete in added time, as Emmanuel Dennis took advantage of an AWOL defence to stroke home Watford's fifth in front of rapidly emptying seats.

So, just as in the previous year, Everton had seen a flying start to the season massively undercut by injuries to key players and the poor recruitment that had left the squad so thin. All of that capped with questionable decisions from a manager whose "honeymoon" was well and truly over. What began as a campaign infused with optimism that the wily, experienced Spanish campaigner could navigate a squad – lacking in depth, but blessed by sufficient quality when everyone was fit – to an improved final placing on those achieved in recent seasons, was supplanted by fears that the Blues' chief focus should be on getting to 40 points as soon as possible.

Back-to-back defeats at what is supposed to be Fortress Goodison ratcheted up the pressure on Benitez to find the solutions to his team's inability to defend set-pieces, and to plug a large, Doucouré-sized hole in midfield with the winter transfer window still over two months away.

Final score: Everton 2-5 Watford

***

Since overcoming Norwich in late September, Everton's form had slumped, with the team registering two draws and six defeats in the ensuing eight games and falling from 5th to 14th place in the Premier League in the process.

They had undoubtedly struggled in the absence of players like Richarlison, Abdoulaye Doucouré, André Gomes, Dominic Calvert-Lewin and Yerry Mina, but all but two of those team members were now back fit so the excuses were starting to run out.

The latest of those disconcerting defeats had been a humiliating 4-1 home defeat against the manager's former club, Liverpool. For those stalwart Evertonians, watching on glumly at a rapidly emptying Goodison, while 3,000 away fans sang merrily about Rafael Benitez, it felt like the final straw.

Farhad Moshiri had been pushing back against speculation that Benitez could be sacked, though, by expressing his belief that the Spaniard would turn things around at Everton in the coming weeks.

The Toffees' owner and the Board of Directors came under fierce criticism from the club's fans after the derby mauling and there had also been calls for Benitez to be fired after a miserable run of just two points from the last 24 available.

In a text exchange with *TalkSport* host Jim White, however, that the Scot read out on air, Moshiri blamed injuries for Everton's abysmal form:

> "Football is about crisis one day and glory the following day. Rafa is a good manager and underperformance is largely due to the injuries. Next two weeks, we will get to a full squad and, in the meantime, results will improve. Rafa needs time to have his mark on the squad. He will be supported to add depth to the squad. Managers need time."

***

Supporters, however, were growing ever more frustrated and concerned. A collection of fan groups on social media called for Evertonians to leave their seats in the 27th minute of the televised clash with Arsenal on 6 December.

Dubbed "27 Minutes For 27 Years", the initiative signalled to the club's hierarchy the frustration Evertonians felt at the club's lack of progress, and the team's shocking run of results in recent weeks. Form the fans put down to poor player recruitment.

Since the release of initial hashtag and social media announcement, the campaign leaders published the full rationale for their initiative and the goals they hoped to achieve.

They said: "The #27minutesfor27years was to be a campaign highlighting Everton's longest peacetime trophy drought, 27 years in May 2022 since club captain Dave Watson lifted the FA Cup at Wembley. Why 27 minutes for 27 years? It was designed to bring attention to the majority shareholder Farhad Moshiri who despite investing approximately £685 million since February 2016 (£450 million into the club, £100 million into the Bramley-Moore stadium and £135 million approx. in buying existing shares) had not seen an improvement in the club's fortunes with multiple managerial appointments, a weakened and less competitive first team squad and declining performances on the pitch."

In a message to supporters, the group expanded on their aims, and there was a call to action for all attending the next match at Goodison Park:

> "**The Campaign:** Monday 6th December, Everton vs Arsenal, Goodison Park. At the 27th minute fans supporting this campaign to leave their seats as a visual representation of the need for change at Everton. The

campaign respects individual decisions to leave their seats for 5 minutes, until half time or for the remainder of the match. The campaign is a bringing together of supporter groups, fan organisations and individual supporters. Its sole purpose is to engage Farhad Moshiri and promote changes in the running and management of the club. Something that can only be addressed by the major shareholder. The individuals supporting the campaign continue their support of the football club and are fully committed to supporting the players on the pitch to better performances and results.

The campaign welcomes and acknowledges his financial commitment to the club. However, the campaign draws attention to the governance and management of the club during these last 6 years. The campaign recognises that without investment and fresh recruitment in the board and executive teams the prospects of a change in fortune in the club remains slight. The campaign recognises that the fans' emotional investment and financial commitment to the club are totally aligned with Farhad Moshiri's investment. We seek the same outcome, a better return for both our investment. We call on Farhad Moshiri as major shareholder to make the management changes necessary to see an improvement in performance. We call on

> Farhad Moshiri to communicate in future through official club channels. We call on Farhad Moshiri to engage, meet and discuss fan concerns with the fans. The campaign will seek the widest possible support across the fanbase and is committed to maintaining the campaign until such a time as Farhad Moshiri engages and agrees to the changes necessary to resolve the club's decline." – #27MinutesFor27Years Campaign

***

6 December 2021: Everton v Arsenal

Arsenal, who had travelled to Merseyside in good form and had designs on moving back into the top five, began the game well and played the more impressive passing football without really threatening Jordan Pickford's goal.

Halfway through the first half, it was Everton on the attack. Gray flashed a dangerous ball across the face of Arsenal's goal, just as the clock was about to tick into the 27th minute marker when the #27MinutesFor 27Years campaign had called for fans to leave their seats. With most eyes still focussed on action on the pitch, a smattering of disillusioned Blues left their seats and walked out. Watching on from the Directors Box, Bill Kenwright and Denise Barrett-Baxendale would have been relieved that the spectacle was not more dramatic.

The game came alive, just before the interval when Richarlison was fouled outside the box. From Townsend's free kick, Richarlison thought he had put the Blues ahead with a typically excellent header. Sadly, the VAR adjudged him to have been fractionally ahead of the last man as he leaned forward to make his run to meet the ball.

Two minutes later, and well into injury time, Everton were undone at the back. Kieran Tierney got beyond Seamus Coleman to centre for the untracked Martin Ødegaard and he side-footed home from close range.

Everton were undaunted, however. They had the ball in the net for a second time shortly before an hour's play had elapsed. Allan passed to Doucouré, who picked out Richarlison to drill it past Ramsdale and wheel away in vindication. But, once again, VAR returned an even more agonising hairline verdict.

With Goodison burning with a sense of being hard done-by, Benitez brought André Gomes off the bench and Everton dug deep to turn the match on its head in thrilling fashion.

In the 79th-minute, Gomes' shot rebounded off a defender to Gray just outside the box. He attempted a delicious curling shot with his instep that cannoned back off the face of the crossbar to the waiting Richarlison, who looped it deftly over the stranded goalkeeper to finally get his goal.

Then, as the game moved into stoppage time, Gray took centre stage by firing home an Exocet missile from 25 yards to complete a stirring comeback.

The hard-fought win was Everton's first since late September and arrested a slide of six defeats in seven games to lift the club up to 12th place in the table, ahead of back-to-back away games in the capital against Crystal Palace and Chelsea. Was there still a chance that Benitez' team could turn things around?

Final score: Everton 2-1 Arsenal

2021: Everton Director Ismailov Steps Down

> "Ismailov's initial brief was Commercial Director of the Woman's team but within four months of his arrival, on 2 November 2021, he suddenly stepped down from his duties, officially for personal and health reasons.

2021 Everton Director Ismailov Steps Down

If there was a regular criticism of Farhad Moshiri's reign at Everton, it was that the Board of Directors under the British-Iranian businessman hadn't been augmented either in size or capability under his leadership. So it was a surprise when the club announced the departure of Sasha Ryazantsev in August 2021, and indicated it was part of a reorganisation of the Board which also saw Grant Ingles appointed as Chief Finance Officer.

Ryazantsev had joined the Everton Board as the Owner's Representative in 2016. He then became the Club's first Chief Finance and

Commercial Officer in 2018, and was also appointed as Managing Director of Everton Women in 2020. He had seemingly performed well, at least in public, and his sudden departure fuelled speculation that some heavyweight external talent was incoming.

Instead, the vacuum was filled by 25-year-old Sarvar Ismailov, the nephew of Alisher Usmanov. Ismailov was made a Director of the Club Board and Moshiri's Executive Representative. He had initially joined Everton in 2019 as Global Commercial Consultant, before becoming Everton Women's first Sporting and Commercial Director and a member of the Everton Women Strategic Leadership Team in 2020. It was confirmed that Ismailov would retain his role at Everton Women and will also remain on the Club's Stadium Board – a post he took up in 2019. It was hoped he would bring some fresh ideas to the boardroom. But more significantly, it also hinted, perhaps, at greater involvement from Usmanov himself.

Within four months of his Board appointment, on 2 November 2021, he suddenly stepped down from his duties, officially for personal and health reasons.

Three weeks later, Ismailov was charged by Westminster Magistrates' Court with GBH for an incident that occurred in London on 11 June 2021. Together with his brother Sanjar, Ismailov, he was accused of causing grievous bodily harm to Edmond Krasniqi at a flat in Hyde Park Gate.

According to *BBC News,* Sanjar Ismailov was further charged with causing actual bodily harm to model Astrid Fajcsi.

It was the kind of publicity all concerned could have done without.

A month later, Daniel Sandford of *BBC News* reported that: "The case against former Everton director Sarvar Ismailov has been dismissed due to a 'lack of evidence'. Following a three-week adjournment, Westminster Magistrates' Court heard the case had been discontinued. No further details were given in court by the Crown Prosecution Service. But a spokesman later said: "We have a duty to keep all cases under review and on further consideration we decided this case no longer met our legal test. It has therefore been discontinued and we have written to the complainant explaining our decision."

In July 2022, Joe Thomas in the *Liverpool Echo* reported that: "Former Everton director Sarvar Ismailov has been sanctioned by the British Government. Ismailov, a nephew of already-sanctioned Russian oligarch Alisher Usmanov, was today named among a list of new figures to be hit with action. The sanctions follow the Russian invasion of Ukraine. In a statement, the Foreign, Commonwealth and Development Office said: 'Also sanctioned today are Sarvar and Sanjar Ismailov, nephews of major Russian oligarch Alisher Usmanov who has close ties to the Kremlin. Both Sarvar and Sanjar have significant interests in the UK, it is believed that they own homes in Highgate and Hampstead Heath.' Both men had their assets frozen. Their father, Gulbakhor Ismailova, was sanctioned in April 2022.

***

In other news, the panel commissioned with performing a fan-led review of Football Governance published its findings and recommendations on 25 November 2021.

The Fan Led Review of Football Governance had resulted from three crisis points: the collapse of Bury FC, the COVID-19 pandemic, and the attempt to set up a European Super League (ESL) in April 2021.

The panel was chaired by Tracey Crouch, Conservative MP and former Minister of Sport, and included Everton CEO and recently-named 'Business Woman of the Year for 2020,' Denise Barrett-Baxendale.

Their report included some far-reaching recommendations, which sought to wrest overall control of English football from the Premier League and its six dominant members. Their 10-point plan said:

1. To ensure the long-term sustainability of football, the Government should create a new independent regulator for English football (IREF)

2. To ensure financial sustainability of the professional game, IREF should oversee financial regulation in football.

3. New owners' and directors' tests for clubs should be established by IREF replacing the three existing tests and ensuring that only good custodians and qualified directors can run these vital assets.

4. Football needs a new approach to corporate governance to support a long-term sustainable future of the game.

5. Football needs to improve equality, diversity and inclusion in clubs with committed EDI Action Plans regularly assessed by IREF.

6. As a uniquely important stakeholder, supporters should be properly consulted by their clubs in taking key decisions by means of a Shadow Board.

7. Football clubs are a vital part of their local communities, in recognition of this there should be additional protection for key items of club heritage.

8. Fair distributions are vital to the long term health of football. The Premier League should guarantee its support to the pyramid and make additional, proportionate contributions to further support football.

9. Women's football should be treated with parity and given its own dedicated review.

10. As an urgent matter, the welfare of players exiting the game needs to be better protected — particularly at a young age.

Subsequently, it became known that the Premier League was ardently opposed to the appointment of an independent regulator for English football. It would remain to be seen whether Denise Barrett-Baxendale's participation in the panel and Everton's very "anti-ESL" stance would have negative consequences for the club.

2021: Moshiri backs Benitez. Brands resigns. Digne sold

> "On Friday, following a personal conversation with the chairman and my fellow Board members, we agreed that I would step down from my post as Director of Football and as a member of the Everton Football Club Board.
>
> \- Marcel Brands

2021 Moshri backs Benitez. Brands resigns. Digne sold

The evening of 1 December 2021 had been one of anger and frustration at Goodison Park. Everton had just been trounced 4-1 by Liverpool, suffered the ignominy of reds' fans taunting them with chants hailing Rafael Benitez, and supporters were demanding action. Boos and chants of "Sack the Board" rang out at the final whistle and Marcel Brands was accosted by one irate supporter as he left the Directors Box who admonished the Sporting Director for the poor quality of the playing squad.

In what was interpreted by some as Brands suggesting there was plenty of blame to go around, he responded by saying, "It's not just the players, is it?"

Within two days, the 27 Minutes for 27 Years campaign had called on fans to stage a walk-out protest during the Arsenal game on 6 December, as a means of highlighting the urgent need for change at Boardroom level.

Two days later, the club announced that Brands' 3½-year stint as Everton's Director of Football was over after he agreed to leave the club by mutual consent because of a clash of visions for the future of the club.

Shortly before midnight on 5 December, Everton finally confirmed media reports that started earlier in the day with *The Mirror* claiming that the Dutchman, who had only signed a new three-year contract in early 2021, had agreed to leave the club with immediate effect.

The Blues' hierarchy had come under mounting pressure for the club's declining fortunes. Though many of the problems that led to Everton being unable to spend more than a paltry £1.7 million over the summer in the transfer market pre-dated Brands' arrival, he was seen as part of the issue.

However, given the opaque nature of the club's structure and general lack of communication on the division of responsibility, it was never clear how much power Brands ever had for player recruitment and the hiring of managers.

In a statement, Brands explained his departure:

> "On Friday, following a personal conversation with the chairman and my fellow Board members, we

> agreed that I would step down from my post as Director of Football and as a member of the Everton Football Club Board. This decision has taken some time and some consideration and was one of the most difficult I have faced in my career. The Board and I agreed that there is a clear difference in the vision and direction for this beautiful club and, with that in mind, the decision was taken. I want to thank everyone in the club who I have worked closely with over the last three and a half years. There are a lot of talented people at Everton with huge passion and commitment to move the club forward, both on and off the pitch. I want to wish all of the squad every success, and I am convinced that there is enough quality to improve the current situation quickly. It has been an honour for me to work at this fantastic club and I wish everyone associated with Everton the very best for the future."

Though reports suggested that Rafael Benitez would take on full responsibility for player recruitment, Everton's own statement pledged a "strategic review" of operations on the playing side:

> "A strategic review of the football structure will now take place, which will inform the best model for the Club to proceed with in the long-term. In the meantime, the Owner and Board of Directors will continue to provide our manager, Rafa Benitez, with their full support."

It was also rumoured that Chief Executive Officer, Denise Barrett-Baxendale had been "seeking alternative employment" for some time, and might have been the next board member to move on. It turned out that she would remain in her post for another 18 months, by which time things would become a good deal worse.

2022: Benitez Sacked After Defeat at Norwich

> "Everton's depressing loss at Norwich did, indeed, prove to be the last straw for Farhad Moshiri and Rafael Benitez's ill-advised reign as the Blues' manager was terminated following a dreadful run of results of just one win in 13 Premier League matches.

2022 Benitez sacked after defeat at Norwich

It would have been nice to say that an Everton defeat to a Norwich City side that had comfortably been among the worst in the top flight all season - who came into this match on a six-match losing streak, and who hadn't scored a Premier League goal for seven weeks - was unthinkable but it really wasn't.

15 January 2022: Norwich City v Everton

Indeed, any Blue would have been well aware that there was no better team to face than this version of Everton when you've not won for ages and can't score for, well, toffee. And Rafael Benitez's side were all too obliging, handing the Canaries their first league win since Dean Smith's first match in charge in mid-November.

Benitez had proven incapable of producing results at Everton since the last time they met Norwich in September and beat them in comfortable, if rather unconvincing, fashion at Goodison Park. Since then the Spaniard had overseen just one victory in the Premier League, one inspired and secured by the individual brilliance of Demarai Gray and Richarlison as they turned the match against Arsenal on its head a month earlier.

Rather than act as a springboard, that adrenaline-fuelled, crowd-backed triumph over Mikel Arteta's vastly improved Gunners proved to be an aberration in what had become a miserable sequence of nine defeats in 12 games under Benitez; games blighted by mystifying team selections and formations, even allowing for absences from injury and positive COVID-19 tests.

This match was no exception and by the time it had ended, few could have been left with any doubt that Benitez's time as Everton's boss was over. Certainly, Farhad Moshiri would finally be compelled to act with the Toffees in a tailspin and sinking towards the relegation zone.

Benitez did at least dispense with his bizarre five-man defence, overly staffed by full-backs, and opted for what looked, on paper, to be 4-4-2 at Carrow Road. It ended up with Salomon Rondon operating almost as an awkward and baffling number 10 behind Dominic Calvert-Lewin.

Calvert-Lewin himself had been a welcome returnee to the team after sitting out the narrow win at Hull City in the FA Cup the previous weekend, but there were long stretches of this contest where it was easy to forget he was playing, such was Everton's impotence as an attacking force.

Indeed, apart from some early probing forays by Demarai Gray and the occasional threat posed by Anthony Gordon, Everton didn't really pose much danger to Norwich's goal until Richarlison came on as a second-half substitute to score a spectacular goal that, sadly would be forgotten, given the result.

Credit went to Norwich for a spirited performance where they capitalised on Everton's mistakes and defended doggedly to prevent the Toffees from salvaging a draw in the closing stages, but the story was all about Benitez and his team's incomprehensibly bad form.

The deadlock was broken in the 16th minute, when Josh Sargent's cross came in from the Canaries' right and Michael Keane stuck out a leg that diverted the ball past Pickford to give the hosts the lead.

They were two goals to the good almost immediately. Everton were trying to attack at one end when Seamus Coleman sold Anthony Gordon short with an attempted pass that was intercepted by Brandon Williams who strode forward and calmly threaded the ball to Idah to fire past Pickford.□

When Benitez finally made moves to change his approach with his two substitutions, it took Richarlison just six minutes to make his mark. A corner from the Blues' right was cleared, but Everton kept the ball and when Tim Krul failed to get purchase on a punch from Mykolenko's deep cross, it sat up invitingly for Richarlison to overhead-kick it cleanly into the top corner from near the penalty spot.

What should have been the catalyst for an all-out assault on the Norwich goal failed to spark much more attacking penetration from the Toffees, however, as Norwich defended in numbers and dealt with the slow-tempo play in front of them.

As ever, Benitez deflected all the criticism for this latest defeat onto the shoulders of the players, blaming them for making mistakes while commending them somewhat for a more purposeful second-half display. It was true that he couldn't really legislate for Keane's clumsy own goal or the sloppy distribution that led to Norwich's second and his players had more than enough time to claw things back to at least earn a point.

Yet they looked utterly lost under a manager who seemed clueless how to get the best out of them, or set them up to win matches in the Premier League. The feeling was that Benitez's time at Everton had been up for a while. That Farhad Moshiri had waited so long to end the farce merely sacrificed precious points and prolonged the fans' frustration.

Many of the club's irate travelling fans aimed chants of "you're getting sacked in the morning" and a now-familiar banner imploring the former Liverpool boss to "Get out of our club" was unfurled in the away section before and during the game. Within 48 hours, they would get their wish.

Final score: Norwich 2-1 Everton

***

16 January 2022: Benitez Sacked

Everton's depressing loss at Norwich did, indeed, prove to be the last straw for Farhad Moshiri and Rafael Benitez's ill-advised reign as the Blues' manager was terminated following a dreadful run of results of just one win in 13 Premier League matches.

The decision to part ways with the Spaniard was, apparently, made at an emergency board meeting, and they made an official announcement after an agreement on compensation was reached by both parties.

The writing had arguably been on the wall for Benitez since that chastening evening of the Goodison derby at the start of December and the 1-0 defeat at Brentford that had preceded it, and where the travelling Everton supporters had first made their displeasure with the Spaniard known.

However, the early-warning signs had emerged in September after Calvert-Lewin sustained his serious injury that side-lined him for four months, when Benitez' gamble of playing a weakened side at QPR failed, and when his side collapsed in that horrible 5-2 home defeat to Watford.

Between a come-from-behind win over Burnley in mid-September and the calamitous loss to Norwich, Benitez presided over just two League victories. He had been pointing for weeks to a debilitating injury list — the squad was certainly down to the bare bones because of injured players and positive coronavirus tests — but he could not escape criticism for poor tactics, player selection and game-management, not to mention his team's frustrating passivity, particularly in the first-half of matches.

In a form table encompassing matches since week eight of the season, Everton were sitting rock bottom, and looked to be heading for a desperate fight for survival given the team's inability to pick-up points under his watch. There was an argument for his dismissal after the embarrassment of the Goodison derby but whether Moshiri simply wanted to give him as much time as possible or was trying to avoid sacking another manager, he let the situation drift until mid-January.

By then, it felt as though Benitez had lost the confidence of the players and any lingering support from the fans, particularly after he had frozen out key first-team player, Lucas Digne. The impasse had eventually forced the French left-back out of the club altogether. Digne signed for Aston Villa in early January 2022, further weakening the Toffees' squad and strengthening the feeling that Moshiri had afforded Benitez and his ego too much power.

***

The board's list of candidates to replace Benitez reportedly included Wayne Rooney, who had been impressing as Derby County boss, Niko Kovac, Rudi Garcia and Roma manager Jose Mourinho, although the Portuguese reportedly took himself out of the running, as did Brighton head coach Graham Potter. Vitor Pereira, never too far away when there was a managerial vacancy at Goodison, was also said to be in the mix. Meanwhile former Derby and Chelsea head coach, Frank Lampard, indicated he would prefer to assume his next post in the summer and with the benefit of a pre-season to prepare.

Suddenly Roberto Martinez emerged as the 'clear frontrunner' and the wheels appeared to be turning quickly on that front, until the Belgian FA, who wanted Martinez to lead their team at the World Cup in Qatar later in the year, blocked his departure.

In the interim, Duncan Ferguson, an outside bet for the full-time role himself, retook the reins. He had led Everton to a thrilling 3-1 win over Chelsea in front of a raucous Goodison crowd in December 2019 following the departure of Marco Silva. There was no doubt he would relish the opportunity to manage the team again when Aston Villa came to town.

***

22 January 2022: Everton v Aston Villa

Evertonians had no doubt envisaged this match going differently. An expectant Goodison Park crowd was ready to back Duncan Ferguson and the players to the hilt for 90 raucous minutes. Meanwhile, by posting some long-overdue communication with supporters from Farhad Moshiri via email ahead of the match, the Everton hierarchy no doubt felt that they had blunted one of the 27 Years Campaign's chief gripes ahead of a more unified atmosphere around the club.

By the end of the clash with Aston Villa, their most feared outcome had occurred, and the post-match protests by supporters aiming their ire at the owner and the Board of Directors felt as justified and as urgent as ever. Not that any immediate change off the pitch could address the very real near-term threat of relegation. The Blues had found themselves in a mess created by many years of mis-management; but those in charge's next act — the appointment of a successor to Rafael Benitez — would have a huge bearing on whether this famous old club remained in the Premier League after that season.

You had to feel for Ferguson at the final whistle. There wasn't a soul who doubted how badly he would have wanted to lift the gloom around Goodison a little by guiding Everton to a badly needed win. That "lightning in a bottle" first match as caretaker boss against

Chelsea a little over two years prior was always going to be hard to replicate, but the Scot clearly felt that a repeat of the passion and the high-octane, more direct football that delivered that famous win would be enough on this occasion.

Unfortunately, Ferguson came up against a Villa team that was reaping the benefits of having made their own managerial change early in the season, and of savvy recruitment in a squad that balanced silk with steel. Everton had plenty of the hard stuff themselves, but little of it was constructive and when the intensity of their spirited start inevitably abated, they didn't have sufficient guile to fashion a vital goal.

It was supremely ironic that one of Benitez's most controversial acts (sanctioned, of course, by the club) – namely the sale of Lucas Digne to Villa just days before he they fired him – should come back to haunt the Blues. It was Digne who provided the assist for the game's only goal by Emiliano Buendia from a corner in first-half stoppage time.

Employing a less refined, more direct approach than the visitors, Everton had hoped to make the most of Dominic Calvert-Lewin's aerial prowess and Richarlison's own physical attributes but the pair got little change from Tyrone Mings and Ezri Konsa, particularly in a first half where the Toffees failed to register a shot on target.

It took the introduction of Anthony Gordon, a surprise omission from the starting XI, for Everton to carve out their first genuine goal-scoring opportunity of the contest after just a couple of minutes on the field. Gordon whipped a ball in from the right that Richarlison could only steer high and wide of goal. Three minutes later Ben Godfrey sent a brave header goal-wards, but Tyrone Mings headed off the line.

That was as close as Everton would come to scoring, and with this latest defeat they were now very much in the thick of a battle to avoid relegation – a notion that was unthinkable just a year before, when they had Carlo Ancelotti at the helm and were sitting in fifth place.

The belief that this team was too good to go down wasn't misplaced. It had been stripped of its most creative elements over the previous few months, but there was still talent there if they could harness it under the right system and remain as motivated as they were against a highly-organised Villa side.

Things would probably hinge on the Blues' best players remaining fit, however and the club hopefully making a move to bolster central midfield before the transfer deadline. More than anything, the hierarchy needed to make one of the most important decisions they've ever had to make in terms of a new manager. This was a team crying out for a fresh approach from new eyes, but it would be an appointment that the club could not afford to get wrong.

These were harrowing times to be a Blue, and a hugely important month in the football club's history lay ahead.

Final score: Everton 0-1 Villa

***

After the match, Duncan Ferguson couldn't hide his sadness at not being able to deliver three desperately needed points on his return to the touchline as caretaker boss this afternoon against Aston Villa.

The result, coupled with wins for teams below them that weekend, left Everton hovering precariously above the relegation zone with just one League win in 14 games.

"I think I got a reaction from the players," Ferguson said afterwards. "The first half we were not quite on it. The second half, they had a good go at it and they gave me everything. I could not fault their effort.

"I am on the floor. I am gutted. I was kicking every ball. I am sick for the fans. I was desperate to get the win. I feel for them because I am one of them. It's a bad moment for me."

A couple of hundred Evertonians remained behind in the stands after the final whistle to protest the failings of the Board of Directors and owner Farhad Moshiri. Before kick off, a plane trailing a banner calling for Bill Kenwright to stand down had flown over the stadium and was captured by television cameras.

The interviewer asked Ferguson for his thoughts on the protests.

"The fans, for me, can protest and they can say what they want," he said, "because it's their club at the end of the day, and they have the right to support in any way, shape or form they want. I know how sick they are, believe me. I'm gutted as much as them."

***

As had been the case when Ronald Koeman was sacked, and again when Carlo Ancelotti left, there did not appear to have been a coherent succession plan at place at Everton when Benitez was terminated. 10 days after the Spaniard's dismissal, there was still no clear candidate to replace him; although a shortlist appeared to have three names on it.

One of them, Vitor Pereira took the unusual step on 26 January of pitching his credentials for the Everton job with a live phone call with *Sky Sports*, as the club's search for a new manager verged on farce.

Interviewed by Bill Kenwright nine years previously as a potential successor to David Moyes, the Portuguese's name resurfaced on most occasions that the Goodison hot seat became available.

A journeyman manager since leaving Porto in 2013, Pereira was a controversial candidate with supporters because of his chequered record that includes that short stint with 1860 who were relegated from 2. Bundesliga under his stewardship. He also had a couple of unspectacular stints with Fenerbahçe, won titles in Greece and China, but had no extensive experience or demonstrable success in any of Europe's top five leagues.

Nonetheless, he emerged as the favoured candidate to succeed Rafael Benitez with reports in the media that Everton might announce him as the new Blues boss before the end of that week.

However, amid a backlash from supporters that included graffiti on a wall at Goodison Park against Pereira's appointment and in favour of Frank Lampard, the *Daily Mail*'s website claimed that the 53-year-old was considering withdrawing from the running.

In his conversation with *Sky*, Pereira said he felt his interviews with Everton officials had gone well, and he had laid out what he felt he could bring to the role. He also defended his performance at 1860 Munich five years earlier and implored supporters to look at his overall record.

"I've had more than one interview with different people," he explained. "I think they were enthusiastic about what I proposed to them — an intense, pressing game with possession. We need to give confidence again to these players, to approach the fantastic supporters again.

"I think the first decision from the manager in the club is to bring again the organisation, the way to press and the intensive game I saw a few years ago. To me, to watch at Goodison, to show other teams. Goodison is a fortress, and it's difficult to play.

"They have other candidates. I understand this is the time for decisions. They have told me to wait for the decision and to be calm. They are grateful for interviews and that was all.

"In my opinion, some of the critics are not for me because they do not know me very well. They do not know my work or me personally. I have worked in a lot of countries and at different levels. I've got several titles. I understand the feeling of the supporters because in the last few years they didn't get results.

"Of course, this is the first time in my career that I see this kind of things," he continued, regarding the graffiti at Goodison. "Never in my career have I seen these comments. My CV speaks for itself. I think these [criticisms] are not directly [aimed at] me. It's something to do with [the environment]. I don't take this as a personal attack.

"This passion is the power of the club. The spirit of the supporters can change the game. The passion in football can be on a positive side or a negative side. What a manager should do is bring the positive side.

"If you look at the top managers in the world, we have titles in different countries. Teaching young players. I started my career with 8 years in Porto. In Munich, it was a very difficult money situation. They were relegated because of the money, the money to pay the players. You must look at the titles I've won. You must look at the positives.

"I have built my career with passion, organisation, competence. This is what I can offer to the club. I give 100% of me, football for me is 24 hours. This is my life, my passion. All of my career I have worked under pressure. The pressure is to be at the best level.

"I still want the job, of course. Now it's a club decision. I will move forward with my life. If they want me, they must call me."

***

Another protest against the Everton board by disgruntled fans took place that evening, next to the Dixie Dean statue at the gates of Goodison Park.

Hundreds of fans assembled outside the ground after a tweet was sent out alerting supporters of the proposed action.

Chants of "sack the board!" were accompanied by ironic banners reading "No Status No Optimism" and "School of Silence."

The criticism came against the backdrop of mounting frustration with Everton's owner, Farhad Moshiri, and the Board of Directors for what the fans perceived to be their shambolic stewardship of the club which had left the Blues hovering above the relegation zone and searching for yet another new manager.

Though not organised by the 27 Years Campaign, the group lent their support to the protest and planned to be in attendance. It followed similar protests in the stands after the defeat to Aston Villa, and a display of banners outside Everton's headquarters at the Royal Liver Building.

2022: Moshiri increases Blues shareholding to 94.1%

> The Club has announced today the conversion of a £100 million loan to the club into equity which is a clear demonstration of my commitment and greatly strengthens the balance sheet. I am a private man and I do not speak publicly very often. But I promise you that my determination to deliver for Everton will not waver.
>
> -Farhad Moshiri

2022 Moshiri increases Blues shareholding to 94.1%

In a personal letter sent to all Official Everton Members and season-ticket holders on 21 January, 2022, Farhad Moshiri announced he had further increased his ownership commitment to the club by converting an additional £100 million in loans to equity in Everton shares. The move increased his majority shareholding in the club to 94.1%.

In the lengthy letter, one that represented rare direct communication with supporters from the Monaco-based billionaire, Moshiri recognised the poor run of recent results that had led to the sacking of

Rafael Benitez and put himself firmly behind Duncan Ferguson, while also referring to the strategic review underway into the footballing side of the club and the search for a new manager. Moshiri's letter also trumpeted the creation of a Fan Advisory Board which was underway in concert with Everton Stakeholder Steering Group (ESSG) and which, with the separate news that the Board intended to amend the Articles of Association so that the commitment to an Annual General Meeting of shareholders was removed, looked as though it would become the prime method of engaging supporters over the long term.

Moshiri's communiqué read in part:

> "I understand the frustration felt by everybody who loves Everton because of our inconsistent form in recent seasons, despite significant investment in the playing squad, The money that has been spent since 2016, not just on the playing squad but also on key projects including our new stadium, demonstrates my commitment to Everton. I write to you to assure you that my commitment remains strong and focused. The Club has announced today the conversion of a £100 million loan to the club into equity which is a clear demonstration of my commitment and greatly strengthens the balance sheet. I am a private man and I do not speak publicly very often. But I promise you that my determination to deliver for Everton will not waver. The strategic football review that is cur-

> rently ongoing will ensure we have the best model in place moving forward. I am working closely with the Chairman and the Board as part of that strategic review - and I can assure you the recruitment process for a new manager is aligned to that. It is vital we appoint a manager that fits the structure we are putting in place and so, whilst we are keen to make an appointment as quickly as possible, we will work together to ensure it is the right candidate to deliver the success we all crave." – Extracted from Farhad Moshiri's Open Letter, 21 January 2022

Meanwhile, chairman Bill Kenwright rejected the core message of protest groups like the 27 Years Campaign and The Originals that the Board was the problem at Everton.

A group of fans had remained behind in the Gwladys Street and Park End stands after the 1-0 defeat to Aston Villa to demand changes at boardroom level at the club.

The frustrated Blues supporters blamed the club's owner, Farhad Moshiri and the members of the Board that included Kenwright and CEO Denise Barrett-Baxendale for the situation that had left Everton facing severe spending restrictions because of the Premier League's profit and sustainability rules, searching for yet another manager, and hovering above the relegation zone following the Rafael Benitez's disastrous tenure.

In mobile phone video shared in a tweet that was later deleted, Kenwright was barracked by fans in Goodison Road after the Villa match with calls of "let go if you love the club" as he made his way to his car. The chairman stopped to confront some of his critics and hear their pleas.

Kenwright agreed that the team's form this season had been "horrible" but when challenged that fans have had to endure 27 years of misery without a trophy, he retorted:

> "It hasn't been 27 years, has it? We've had some good times."

To another fan, he argued that changing the Board "is not the answer."

***

On 28 January 2022, the long-standing requirement that Everton Football Club Company Ltd shall call an Annual General Meeting of shareholders was cut from the Articles of Association provided to Companies House.

For many years, the AGM had been the means by which small shareholders (numbering around 200 people) could express their opinions and concerns about how the club was being run.

But things came to a head with a raucous AGM in 2007 when Bill Kenwright found himself strongly challenged over issues with the previous failed stadium venture known as Destination Kirkby. Kenwright took the unilateral action to suspend AGMs for the next 7 years, denying the small shareholders any voice.

Resolute action by the Everton Shareholders Association forced an Emergency General Meeting in 2013, at which AGMs were reinstated, and had been operating normally until the COVID-19 pandemic, with the AGM in January 2021 being held virtually.

Because of continuing COVID restrictions, the club canvassed shareholders that November for future AGMs to be held virtually if necessary. Several vocal shareholders who saw it as a further limitation to the expression of shareholder opinions met this with resistance.

While publication of Everton's Report and Accounts for 2020/21 was delayed and the expected timing of an AGM for 2021 came and went, the club took an executive decision on AGMs, sending a written resolution to Companies House dated 24 January 2022, rescinding Item 10.1 of the Articles of Association, which read:

10.1: Once in every calendar year, the company shall call a general meeting

However, the rest of Section 10, dealing with Notices of General Meetings, remained in place, suggesting that meetings could be called in the future. They subsequently filed the revised Articles of Association at Companies House.

Instead of AGMs, the club said it was working with selected fan groups already associated with the club — through the Everton Stakeholder Steering Group (ESSG) — to put in place a Fan Advisory Board by the end of the season, as well as instigating some supporter representation at board meetings.

2022: Moshiri Praises New Manager, Frank Lampard

> "Frank is an impressive young man on and off the pitch. I will provide the system to support him. The process is vital to ensure all components of Everton fully support the manager. Fans are the most important part of that. You can buy any player; you can't buy the 12th man.
>
> \- Farhad Moshiri

2022 Moshiri praises new manager, Frank Lampard

Vitor Pereira's bizarre on-air telephone call with *Sky Sports*, where he had publicly stated his case to become the next Everton manager, had caught many at the club off-guard. That, in combination with supporter sentiment appearing to coalesce around Frank Lampard, may well have taken Pereira out of the running for the position.

Five days later, and more than two weeks after Rafael Benitez had been fired, Everton officially unveiled Lampard as their new head coach, after he had signed the final paperwork on a 2½-year contract.

The then 43-year-old became the sixth managerial appointment since Farhad Moshiri had come on board as the club's major shareholder in 2016.

The makeup of Lampard's backroom had also taken shape, with Joe Edwards handed the role of Assistant Manager, Paul Clement First Team Coach and Chris Jones coming on board at Finch Farm as Head of Performance.

Though rumoured he might step away, Duncan Ferguson remained on the coaching staff, as did goalkeeping coach Alan Kelly. Lampard also offered a coaching position to his former Chelsea teammate Ashley Cole.

"It is a huge honour for me to represent and manage a club the size and tradition of Everton Football Club," a beaming Lampard said at his unveiling as the new boss. "I'm very hungry to get started. After speaking to the owner, chairman and the Board, I very much felt their passion and ambition. I hope they felt my ambition and how hard I want to work to bring it together.

"You can feel the passion Everton fans have for their club. That will be hugely important. As a team — the competitive level that the Premier League brings and the position we are in the table — we certainly need that. It's a two-way thing. I think Everton is a unique club in that you can really understand what the fans want to see. The first thing they want is fight and desire, and that must always be our baseline.

"My first message to the players will be that we have to do this together. We'll try to do our job and I know the fans will be there backing us."

A playing legend at Chelsea where he had a glittering career and established himself as one of the best midfielders of his generation, Lampard had cut his coaching teeth at Derby County whom he led to the final of the EFL Championship play-offs, just falling short of promotion to the Premier League in his first season in charge when the Rams were beaten by Aston Villa.

It was enough, however, to persuade his old club Chelsea to hire him in the summer of 2019 where, in his first season there, he guided the West Londoners to fourth place in the league and into the FA Cup final where they lost to Arsenal.

Despite huge investment in players in the summer of 2020, his second season at Stamford Bridge proved to be more challenging, and with Chelsea sitting outside the Champions League places he was sacked by the notoriously trigger-happy Roman Abramovich and replaced by Thomas Tuchel the following January.

Lampard had been out of work for just over a year when he joined Everton but, according to those close to him, had been keen to get back into management, and had used the time off to reflect on his two previous roles while expanding his coaching knowledge.

He assumed responsibility for a Toffees team that had won just one Premier League match in 14 games and had plummeted from the European qualification places in September to sit just four points above the relegation zone with 18 games left.

The club had moved in the background to address the most pressing issue Lampard would face, namely significant problems in central midfield where Abdoulaye Doucouré, Tom Davies and Fabian Delph were all side-lined for at least a month, by agreeing a loan deal with Manchester United for Dutch midfielder Donny van de Beek who would be the first signing under the new manager. Just before the transfer deadline, the Blues also added fallen Tottenham star Dele Alli to the squad in a complicated deal.

Two young full backs who arrived at the club prior to Lampard's appointment were Nathan Patterson from Glasgow Rangers, in a deal that could ultimately be worth £16 million, and a replacement for the outgoing Lucas Digne by the name of Vitalii Mykelenko, who joined from Dynamo Kiev for a fee reportedly worth £18 million.

Lampard would take charge of training for the first time on Monday 1 February 2022, with the FA Cup Fourth Round tie against Brentford his first assignment at the weekend, before a crucial trip to Newcastle in the Premier League.

Moshiri appeared rarely at USM Finch Farm, but he arrived along with Bill Kenwright to welcome the new boss. The Everton owner called on Everton's fans to give new manager Frank Lampard "that Goodison feeling" and suggested that bringing in a man that supporters could unite behind might be the most important move the club would make this month.

Among the 27 Years Campaign's biggest gripes had been a lack of footballing expertise in key areas of Everton's hierarchy, particularly after Marcel Brands had left both the club and its Board the preceding month. However, striking legend Graeme Sharp had been promoted to the boardroom earlier in January, and there were rumours that Tim Cahill would be appointed to head up a new technical department at Finch Farm, after Moshiri confirmed the Australian was very much involved in the negotiations to bring Lampard in as manager.

"We ensured a lot of expertise went into it," Moshiri asserted. "We had Graeme Sharp, with his vast football experience on our board. Tim Cahill was advising me personally and attending all the interviews. He did very diligent, serious work.

"Our chairman is very important. We are keeping the chairman as long as we can. He manfully fulfils his functions, and I really appreciate what the chairman does."

***

5 February 2022: Everton v Brentford

In contrast to Rafael Benitez's aloof and somewhat dispassionate demeanour, Frank Lampard brought welcome enthusiasm and warmth to Finch Farm and his energy was welcomed by supporters based on the fragments of video of training sessions that were disseminated by the club over its social media channels in the first few days of his tenure.

Telling his players to "enjoy the ball", Lampard offered the promise of a young and hungry manager who could not only transform the mood of a dispirited camp in the short term but might also lay the foundations for a more progressive and successful style of football than had been in evidence under his predecessor.

That feeling was bolstered by his first match in charge as his reign began with a flurry of goals and a first win as the Blues swept Brentford aside to progress to the fifth round of the FA Cup.

The new manager oversaw what would be Everton's biggest win of the season as Yerry Mina, Richarlison, Mason Holgate and Andros Townsend all found the net, rendering Ivan Toney's second-half penalty meaningless.

Lined up in a 3-4-3 formation and exhibiting a more settled passing style and more confidence with the ball at their feet overall, Lampard's side made all the early running in this all-Premier League tie and Mina made the breakthrough from a 30th-minute corner. Demarai Gray swung a dead ball in from the left and Mina won the match-up with his marker to power home a header from six yards out.

The second half was less than three minutes old when Everton doubled their lead. Allan picked the ball up in midfield, chipped it deftly into the path of Richarlison and the Brazilian forward took advantage of the goalkeeper's decision to rush to the edge of his box by knocking it calmly into the open net from 18 yards out.

Brentford responded when Christian Nørgaard picked Ivan Toney out with an excellent defence-splitting pass. The striker smartly left his foot in as Pickford slid across to close him down and referee Michael Oliver pointed to the spot.

Toney sent Pickford the wrong way with his penalty and halved the visitors' deficit, but it would take Everton just eight minutes to restore their two-goal cushion. Gordon's cut-back found Gray, but his shot deflected behind and from the consequent corner, the Blues scored their third.

Once again it was Gray the taker, and when Bech Sorensen got a head to the ball under pressure from Mina, he could only knock it into the path of Holgate, who nodded inside the far post to make it 3-1.

Two late substitutes helped Everton put the gloss on Lampard's day with the Toffees' fourth in stoppage time. Alex Iwobi touched Cenk

Tosun's clever ball inside on to Andros Townsend in the box and the winger had time to pick his spot and whip a shot past the keeper.

It was a perfect start for the new boss, the biggest margin of victory in a first match in charge for an Everton manager since WJ Sawyer, 104 years earlier, and safe passage to the next round.□

Final score: Everton 4-1 Brentford

***

Afterwards, Frank Lampard thanked Everton's fans for the terrific reception they had given him, not only for his first match in charge, but all week since his appointment as the club's new boss.

The media asked Lampard afterwards for his thoughts, both on how the team performed and what pleased him most after just a few days' training under the new regime.

"It was the things that we'd talked about in the week and worked on," he said. "I know the players have been through a tough time results-wise, and that knocks confidence.

"So, when you ask certain things of them, like being brave on the ball, and trying to play through the lines like they did for the second goal, that makes me really happy.

"I certainly won't be getting carried away with one win in the FA Cup. We've got big games coming again, particularly in the League as we know, so it's important that the players keep level-headed about it. But there's so many things from today that we can take as positives and take them forward."

Lampard's arrival had given an enormous lift to a fanbase that had felt hugely let down by the hierarchy's decision to appoint Benitez, and four months of dire football under the Spaniard once his initially good start had fallen away.

Goodison gave Lampard a rousing welcome and also applauded the new signings, Donny van de Beek and Dele Alli onto the pitch at half-time, for which the manager expressed his gratitude.

"I can't thank the fans enough for the support I've had before this," he said. "Today was something very special and something I'll never forget.

"Coming to this club last week in difficult times... they've given me messages, the feeling in the city for the last week since we've been here and then the reaction they showed [in the ground] today... that means a lot to me so I thank them for that.

"But what means even more is when they support the team. When we are trying to play, there'll be moments after today when we're trying to do things and sometimes passes may go astray or people are trying to do some different things on the ball...

"But that's the way I want us to go and so we need their support and we absolutely got it today."

***

12 February, 2022: Everton v Leeds

Everton's post-1980s history may have been mostly barren, but Goodison Park has witnessed some truly memorable occasions in that time — the quarter-final victory over Newcastle on the way to the 1995 FA Cup triumph, the vital win over Manchester United under

David Moyes to press the Blues' Champions League qualification hopes 10 years later, impressive home triumphs over United and Arsenal during Roberto Martinez's first season in charge, and the 4-0 thumping of Manchester City under Ronald Koeman, for examples.

In terms of sheer visceral emotion and roof-raising atmosphere, however, many have come in the face of adversity; when Everton's players have needed the unbridled, raucous passion of their fans and the famous Goodison 'bear pit' to help drag them over the line. The 4-4 draw against Liverpool in the FA Cup in 1991 required that the Toffees come back from a goal down four times; Duncan Ferguson's first goal in that famous derby came at a very low ebb for the club, as did his first win as a caretaker manager 25 years later; another famous night under the lights against Fiorentina began with the team 2-0 down from the first leg in Italy; and the two skin-of-our-teeth scrapes against relegation in 1994 and 1998 took place with the Goodison roar behind them. It's proof positive that when the chips are down, Evertonians rally around their side and they would prove it over and over in 2022 and 2023.

Though there were still 17 games to play and 51 points still on offer coming into this fixture against Leeds, there was a feeling that Everton could enter a death spiral of shattered confidence and a horrible losing habit if they were beaten in this game. Their fantastic fans brought their flags, their banners and their voices, and the players responded in spades to ease the immediate threat of relegation battle with a magnificent victory.

There were smatterings of desperation, exasperation and trepidation and helpings of determination, inspiration and motivation all channelled into a super-charged, high-octane performance played out against a deafening Goodison Park atmosphere. This was the Arsenal home game of two months prior cranked up to 11; individual brilliance from that evening augmented by a front-to-back display of unity, cohesion and maximum effort. This was irrepressible front-foot dynamism, high-press intensity and final-third productivity. This was Everton.

Having endured the end of a short-lived honeymoon at St James's Park on the previous Tuesday, when the Toffees had gone down to a 3-1 defeat, Frank Lampard needed a big performance form this new team.

His selection – which left Dele Alli on the bench, dropped Alex Iwobi into the starting XI for only his eighth League start of the season and his first since mid-December, and deployed Jonjoe Kenny as an emergency left-back – was bold but paid off handsomely as the players, in the manager's own words, "delivered".

There were stories of redemption written through this pulsating victory. Iwobi was terrific throughout, tracking back and harrying Leeds players out of their stride in the press, giving and going with teammates and putting in his best performance yet in a Blue jersey.

Kenny, a player on whom the club had given up – his continued presence at Everton only because of a lack of willing suitors - was stellar, operating out of position on the left side of defence. Raphinha, a man looking for this fourth goal in as many games against Everton, was rendered so peripheral that he had to be substituted at half time. The Cruyff turn Kenny executed down by the Leeds penalty area was just further proof that the hometown boy wasn't phased by the weight of the occasion or his unfamiliar role.

In the centre of a defence stripped of arguably its two best members, two players who have had their critics this season rose to the occasion. Michael Keane turned in a rock solid defensive display and stepped into Yerry Mina's set-piece scoring role at the other end. Mason Holgate, at fault for Newcastle's equaliser the previous Tuesday, was composed and assured.

Donny van de Beek, meanwhile, was imperious in the double-pivot alongside Allan, turning in a full-debut display that made his treatment at Manchester United over the past 18 months seem utterly mystifying. Coming deep to collect the ball, an integral part of the press and provider of a "pre-assist" for Everton's opening goal, the Dutchman made an instant impression.

Then there was Seamus Coleman, the long-serving captain who appeared to be at a loss somewhat at the club's latest bout of chaos, and whom many questioned could handle a third game in the space of a week. The Irishman rolled back the years with a swashbuckling display that was epitomised by some committed defensive work at the back and a tenacious 10th-minute diving header on a memorable afternoon.

It was a fine move, too. Coleman began a neat passing exchange that saw Anthony Gordon touch a lovely ball inside two defenders for Van de Beek and when Dominic Calvert-Lewin couldn't quite divert the Dutchman's low cross home under pressure from a defender, the ball sat up invitingly for the skipper to crash it home with a lunging header ahead of Mateusz Klich on the goal line. The importance of the goal, what it meant to him and the catharsis of the moment etched onto his face as he wheeled away towards the Main Stand in clenched-fist celebration.

Everton doubled their lead when Richarlison's determination won them a corner on the right and some clear work on the training ground paid dividends. Gordon swung the set-piece in beautifully as a conga line of blue shirts prepared for its delivery and Keane battled his way to meet it with an unstoppable header.

Unable to maintain the furious pace of the first 45 minutes, the Toffees, understandably, sat off a little in the second half and focused on containing their opponents, which they did with aplomb for long stretches. They restricted the Yorkshiremen to one wayward Dan James effort and a rising Rodrigo shot that would never trouble Pickford's goal and then wrapped up the scoring when Allan laid the ball off to Richarlison. The latter Brazilian danced along the 18-yard line and fired a low shot that crept inside the far post via Gordon's heel, with the goal ultimately awarded to the young winger who had, again, been superb throughout.

With relief having already poured off the stands following the killer third goal, the final whistle was met with jubilation and full-throated renditions of "Grand Old Team" and "Spirit of the Blues" as the players and their new manager milked the applause of a top-class display and massively important victory.

Lampard reiterated afterwards that he was just getting started and the Blues weren't out of the woods yet. But if ever they needed to prove that they were too good to go down, today was the day. Indeed, with a more inspiring figure in charge, together with a team of forward-thinking coaches and more results like this, Everton could start looking forward to a brighter future rather than nervously over their shoulders. And they could do it having reclaimed a lot of their identity as a club.

Final score: Everton 3-0 Leeds.

Man of the Match: The 12th Man

2022: Russian invasion of Ukraine changes everything

> “Following a statement that 26 individuals with close ties to Vladimir Putin and the Kremlin would be subject to measures, Usmanov’s assets in the EU were frozen, and he was barred from travelling through any member state.
>
> **2022 Russian invasion of Ukraine changes everything**

In comparison with the terrible acts of warfare Russia has inflicted on the Ukrainian people, beginning with the invasion of its neighbour on 24 February, everything else pales into insignificance. However, that was also the day everything changed in Farhad Moshiri’s grand plan for Everton.

Just four days later, Alisher Usmanov, the Uzbek-born tycoon who co-owned two of Everton’s biggest sponsors, found himself on the list of Russian oligarchs being sanctioned by the European Union. The United Kingdom and United States would soon follow, as the international community levied an unprecedented series of economic and trade sanctions against Russia.

Following a statement that 26 individuals with close ties to Vladimir Putin and the Kremlin would be subject to measures, "In respect of actions undermining or threatening the territorial integrity, sovereignty and independence of Ukraine", Usmanov's assets in the EU were frozen, and he was barred from travelling through any member state.

Usmanov, a Russian citizen who at one time was Britain's richest resident with an estimated £20 billion fortune, was named specifically as a "pro-Kremlin oligarch with particularly close ties to ... Putin. [He] was referred to as one of Vladimir Putin's favourite oligarchs ... [who] actively supported materially or financially Russian decision-makers responsible for the annexation of Crimea and the destabilisation of Ukraine" and "actively supported the Russian government's policies of destabilisation of Ukraine".

Usmanov offered a response in writing in which he said:

> "On 28 February 2022, I became the target of restrictive measures imposed by the European Union. I believe that such decision is unfair, and the reasons employed to justify the sanctions are a set of false and defamatory allegations damaging my honor (sic), dignity and business reputation. I will use all legal means to protect my honour and reputation. I hereby suspend the exercise of my duties as the President of the International Fencing Federation, effective immediately until justice is restored."

According to *The Athletic* at the time, Moshiri, who had always insisted that his investment in Everton was entirely independent of Usmanov, declined to comment on the situation. However, almost immediately, Everton suspended their sponsorship arrangements with three of their key sponsors. Not long afterwards, the club announced that Farhad Moshiri was severing his links with USM Holdings, the Russia-based conglomerate he helped found with Usmanov.

This was a hugely significant move for Everton and it would have lasting and profound implications for Moshiri and the football club he owned.

USM Holdings – the conglomerate that Everton owner Farhad Moshiri chaired and of which Usmanov owned a 49% stake – sponsored the club's Finch Farm training complex and had purchased a £30 million first option on the naming rights for the new stadium at Bramley-Moore Dock. Its subsidiary MegaFon was a key matchday sponsor at Goodison Park and, along with Yota, sponsored Everton Women.

A statement from Everton read:

> "Everyone at Everton remains shocked and saddened by the appalling events unfolding in Ukraine. This tragic situation must end as soon as possible, and any further loss of life must be avoided. The players, coaching staff and everyone working at Everton is providing full support to our player Vitalii Mykolenko and his family and will continue to do so. The Club can confirm that it has suspended with immediate effect all commercial sponsorship arrange-

> ments with the Russian companies USM, Megafon and Yota."

All signage relating to MegaFon was removed from Goodison Park overnight and Everton Women played their next fixture against Aston Villa with blank jerseys after the same company's logo was dropped from their kit.

2022: Kevin Thelwell appointed as new Director of Football

> **Following a rigorous search and recruitment process, Kevin was the standout candidate to become our new Director of Football. He brings quality, experience and an outstanding track record for developing young players.**
>
> **-Bill Kenwright**

2022 Kevin Thelwell appointed as new Director of Football

On 25 February 2022, the day after the dreadful news concerning Russia's invasion of Ukraine, but prior to the termination of the club's most important and lucrative sponsorship deals, Everton announced the appointment of Kevin Thelwell as the club's new Director of Football. It was almost three months since Marcel Brands had left the role following a disagreement over the strategic direction of the football club.

For 12 years, Thelwell had held the same position at Wolves having been promoted from Head of Football Development and Recruitment after originally joining the Midlands club from Derby County in 2008 as academy manager.

In 2020, he made a switch to the United States where he assumed the role of Head of Sport at New York Red Bulls. Former Blues favourite, Tim Cahill, may well have played a role in facilitating Thelwell's move to Everton.

As a player, Thelwell represented Northwich Victoria, Winsford United and Congleton Town in a semi-professional capacity after coming through the ranks at Crewe Alexandra and serving an apprenticeship at Shrewsbury Town.

Thelwell had earned his FA/UEFA and FAW/UEFA Advanced Licences and the UEFA Pro Licence, before completing a B.Sc (Hons) degree in Sport Science at Warwick University and fulfilling the role of Director of Coach Education for all of Welsh football. He was arguably more qualified on the football and coaching side than the other candidate who was heavily linked with the Everton job, Steve Hitchen, formerly of Tottenham Hotspur.

According to a statement on evertonfc.com, Thelwell would report directly to the Board of Directors, "acting as the strategic lead for recruitment and all the club's football departments, including First Team, Academy, coaching, sport science, medical services and analysis."

Upon taking the role at Finch Farm, Thelwell said: "I'm so pleased to be joining Everton and to have the opportunity to play a part in the club's ambitious journey. I'm greatly looking forward to working with Frank and the players, and to helping the owner and board achieve their long-term footballing objectives.

"The Owner, the chairman and the CEO all presented compelling reasons for me to join this great club and I am really excited to have the opportunity to work with them all and to move Everton forward. I can't get wait to get started."

Bill Kenwright said of the man credited with identifying and bringing in the likes of Diogo Jota, Ruben Neves, Adama Traore and Leander Dendoncker to Wolves: "Following a rigorous search and recruitment process, Kevin was the standout candidate to become our new Director of Football. He brings quality, experience and an outstanding track record for developing young players."

***

On 12 April, six weeks after Kevin Thelwell's arrival, the club announced that David Unsworth would leave his position as Everton's Academy Director and Under-23s manager, to pursue his ambition of becoming a first-team head coach elsewhere.

Unsworth was originally appointed as Everton's assistant Under-21 manager in 2013 following roles in the Championship, including as assistant manager at Preston North End and Sheffield United.

He progressed into his last role of Academy Director and Under-23 manager and enjoyed success, winning the Premier League 2 title in 2016/17 and 2018/19 the Premier League 2 and Premier League Cup double in 2018/19.

He had also twice taken caretaker charge of Everton's first team — first, at the end of the 2015/16 season and then for 8 games in 2017.

In terms of player development, Unsworth had overseen progression to the first team of several young players, including then regular first-team players Tom Davies, Anthony Gordon, Jonjoe Kenny, Mason Holgate and Dominic Calvert-Lewin.

Unsworth described how hard it would be to leave the club he has represented as a player and coach for 30 years:

"This has been one of the hardest decisions I have had to make in my career," he said. "Everyone knows what Everton means to me.

"However, to give me the best chance of achieving my aspirations and becoming a first team manager, I believe now is the right time for me to move on."

Bill Kenwright said of Unsworth's impending departure: "Since coming back to Everton, Unsie has shown everyone what he is — a great coach, a great Evertonian, and a winner.

"While we're sad to see someone with his talent and love for the club moving on, we completely understand and respect his decision."

It was also announced that former player John Ebbrell would take charge of the Under 23s until the end of the season, as changes initiated by Thelwell at Finch Farm began to roll out.

2022: Everton reveal massive losses for 2020/21

On Tuesday afternoon, 29 March 2022, Everton published their accounts for the financial year ending June 2021, showing losses of £120.9 million on turnover of £193.1 million, the highest losses in the club's history.

Coming on the heels of a record loss of £139.8 million in 2020 and a further £111.8 million in 2019, these amounted to £395.4 million over four seasons, an eye-opening illustration of the financial lengths to which Farhad Moshiri had chased the dream of seeing the Toffees playing in the Champions League. The club would later explain the mitigating circumstances behind these losses, such as COVID and the early-stage costs of building its new stadium at Bramley-Moore Dock.

Indeed, the losses were said to include at least £170 million attributed to the impact on the club of the COVID-19 pandemic, with £103 million of that figure coming in the 2020/21 financial year.

Salaries had risen from £164.8 million to £182.6 million, pushing the club's wages-to-turnover ratio up from an already-high 89% in 2019/20 to a staggering 95% in 2020/21.

Only a financial injection in the form of two share issues by Moshiri — of £100 million in 2020/21, and a further issue of £97 million in January 2022 — had stabilised the club's finances, with Everton reporting current net debt of £58 million.

With top-flight clubs in England restricted to losses of £105 million over a three-year period, on paper than put Everton significantly outside the bound of the Premier League's 'Profitability and Sustainability' rules.

However, having maintained a constant dialogue with the Premier League since the summer of 2021 – discussions that included oversight and sign-off by the league of incoming transfers – the club were insistent that the latest accounts complied with the financial fair play regulations. It believed its accounts were fully compliant, due to allowable deductions for unforeseen losses attributed to the pandemic, continued investment in the new stadium at Bramley-Moore Dock, Everton's women's team, and the club's official charity, Everton in the Community.

Commenting on the accounts, Evertonian and finance expert Paul the Esk wrote:

“The club is caught in a perfect storm of underperformance on and off the pitch whilst funding capital projects, having too big a cost base, and having little idea as to how to grow its commercial income. From a financial perspective, the club is entirely dependent on Moshiri’s willingness and ability to keep funding extraordinary losses.

"From a regulatory perspective, i.e., profitability and sustainability, the club is suggesting that, such is the level of COVID-related contributions to losses (£170 million in two years) that the club remains compliant with the Premier League rules. The club has confirmed, as reported here that discussions have been ongoing for a considerable period with the Premier League. The warning signs for the club are there for everyone to see. We have an individual who is prepared to fund these losses, but equally the same individual must be held responsible for allowing the existing board and management teams to perform in such an unsatisfactory manner.

"We are a shadow of the club Moshiri inherited despite his financial backing. He has to address this through bringing in a competent board to run the club without his involvement. A continuation of a deteriorating performance can only result in non-compliant losses and probable relegation despite the progress at Bramley-Moore Dock. This set of accounts can bring no comfort to any Evertonian and should bring no satisfaction to Moshiri."

2022: Everton beat Palace to secure Premier League status

> The celebrations went on long after the final whistle, only this time the Goodison pitch was a high-decibel mass of jubilant Evertonians; a chorus of relief and joy following an evening of high drama and true Blue spirit.

2022 Everton beat Palace to secure Premier League status

Against a backdrop of all the off-the-pitch developments surrounding Alisher Usmanov, the loss of Everton's key sponsorship deals and the club reporting record losses, team manager Frank Lampard and the players were fighting a battle to preserve the Blues' top-flight status.

The consequences of Everton falling out of the Premier League were potentially disastrous. This was a fact no one seemed to understand better than the club's beleaguered but indefatigable fanbase, who were doing something unique in the history of football over the final few, emotion-fraught weeks of the season.

If the atmosphere at Goodison Park during the emphatic win over Leeds in February had set a new bar for the kind of support and energy that could be transmitted from the stands of the Old Lady to the pitch, the Toffees' fans would find new levels as the weeks went on and victories remained depressingly hard to come by.

Following the Leeds match, Everton had lost four straight games in the Premier League, against Southampton, Manchester City, Tottenham and Wolves, and had struggled to overcome non-League Boreham Wood in the FA Cup Fifth Round. They sat 17th in the table when Newcastle United, resurgent under Eddie Howe and new ownership from Saudi Arabia, came to town.

***

17 March 2022: Everton v Newcastle United

Defeat for the Blues at home to Wolves the previous week seemed to have sapped the morale from the supporters but, perhaps grasping the gravity of a situation that meant even a draw would have done little for the club's parlous position, Evertonians shed their nerves at kick-off and dragged the players through 90-odd minutes of fire, brimstone and controversy. There was even the bizarre interruption of an anti-oil protester, cable-tying his neck to one of the posts early in the second half, to what ended up as one of the most important results and most memorable games in the club's history.

The crowd seemed to live every throw-in, every tackle, every refereeing decision, practically every kick of what was, in truth, an ugly game of football played against the backdrop of gnawing anxiety leading up the game so tangible you could have cut it with a knife. Even as the odds stacked up against the Blues — the loss of Donny van de Beek and Jordan Pickford to illness before-hand, being deprived of kicking towards the Gwladys Street in the second half, and then the infuriating circumstances behind Allan's red card — the fans maintained the volume.

And then... sweet, blessed relief as Alex Iwobi pivoted from being a ceaseless bundle of industry chasing black and white shirts around the park, to the scorer of what was, in truth, a lovely goal and one worthy of settling any game.

In a purely footballing sense, Everton offered desperately little. Newcastle, with the benefit of having had Howe in the job longer than Lampard and with some savvy recruitment having beefed up what was a woeful side prior to January, were more composed and penetrative over the 90 minutes. Yet they came up against the bristling intensity of a Blues team that responded to the urgency of the moment through sheer commitment.

The Magpies didn't shrink from the ferocity of the atmosphere in the way that Leeds seemed to; indeed they gave as good as they got in what was a very physical contest that straddled the line between legal and not. So it was fitting that referee Craig Pawson, having cultivated a permissive stance over the course of the game, only booked Allan for his cynical and late tackle on Allan Saint-Maximin with nine minutes left of the regulation 90.

His decision, however, at the prompting of Video Assistant Referee Stuart Attwell sitting a couple of hundred miles away in Stockley Park, to upgrade that yellow card to red was shocking, and it simply ratcheted up the fury in the crowd, while simultaneously under-cutting what little chance Everton seemed to have of getting the victory they so badly needed.

Newcastle had been denied the chance to make their numerical superiority count by dogged Everton defending by all nine remaining outfield players, and by goalkeeper Asmir Begovic who denied Willock with another good save at his near post.

Then, after future Magpie Anthony Gordon was denied a penalty when barged over in the box, enter Iwobi, the unlikely hero of the hour, a player whose only previous league goals in a Blue jersey had come at Wolves in each of the last two seasons and who was, perhaps, only in the starting XI because of Van de Beek's absence.

Seamus Coleman, who was back to his tenacious best in this game, won a full-blooded challenge against Saint-Maximin, bouncing off the French winger in the centre-circle and moving the ball quickly forward to Iwobi.

The Nigerian glided inside Dan Burn, left him for dead and found Dominic Calvert-Lewin on the edge of the box. He composed himself when it looked like his first touch might have got away from him before turning and laying a lovely reverse pass into Iwobi's path who slotted across the keeper and into the far corner to send Goodison wild.

On the sidelines, Everton's management team erupted, with Lampard admitting afterwards that he might have broken a bone in his hand in the process while the Goodison crowd, which had fought every moment along with the players all night, turned into a mass of limbs.

In the final reckoning of a rollercoaster season, this would prove to have been a vital victory.

Final score: Everton 1-0 Newcastle

***

The win over Newcastle may not have had a transformative effect on Everton's results but it did demonstrate once again to the Toffees' supporters the power of Goodison and the huge role that Evertonians could play in hauling their club away from the trapdoor to the Championship. Frank Lampard's side faced three away games over the ensuing 3 weeks and lost them all, bombing out of the FA Cup at the Quarter-Final stage with a miserable 4-0 defeat at Crystal Palace, one that that had the manager questioning whether his players "had the bollocks" for the fight, and going down to defeats at West Ham and relegation rivals Burnley.

The loss at Turf Moor had been particularly demoralising given that Everton had come back from conceding an early goal to lead 2-1 at half-time, only to then lose 3-2 to an 85th-minute Maxwel Cornet goal. The result closed the gap between the two clubs to a single point in the table with nine games to go. By the end of April 2022, after beating doomed Watford at Vicarage Road by two late goals, Burnley were sitting level on points with Leeds and five above the Toffees who were in the relegation zone.

With third-place Chelsea next up at Goodison, the situation was starting to feel desperate. But Evertonians refused to be bowed and, spurred on by an initiative from supporters groups, they crammed the streets around the stadium before kick-off and filled the air blue with smoke canisters to give the team coach a rousing welcome.

That energy flowed into the stands and fired up the team ahead of a match that, like the one against Newcastle, produced indelible moments, images and a single goalscoring hero. This time it was Richarlison who scored the game's only goal a minute into the second half and celebrated by raising a billowing blue "flare" aloft as he celebrated a vital goal that lifted Everton to within two points of safety with five matches of the season left.

Sent on their way by a unique coach send-off by fans at Finch Farm, a first away win since way back in August 2021 was secured at Leicester City thanks to a stunning volley by Vitalii Mykolenko, the Ukrainian full-back who had been signed to replace Lucas Digne in January, and a winner from centre-half Mason Holgate. All Everton needed to do to virtually guarantee their survival was to beat Watford, a team that was on a club-record 11-match losing run, in their next match; if not, Brentford at home offered another chance to put the issue of relegation to bed.

Unfortunately, a lethargic contest at Vicarage Road ended 0-0 and after a devastating 3-2 home defeat against the Bees four days later, Everton were likely entering the Last Chance Saloon in their last fixture of the season at Goodison against Crystal Palace. Because looming on the final day was a trip to Arsenal and no one of a Blue persuasion wanted to travel there needing anything by way of points.

It called for one last push of passion and energy, blue smoke and thunderous renditions from the Everton catalogue of chants; a collective summoning once more of emotion and devotion; and the use of the power of Goodison Park and all its history to drag this club out of the mire and preserve its Premier League life.

***

19 May 2022: Everton v Crystal Palace

For a third successive home game, fans lined the streets outside Goodison Park to usher the team coach towards the players' entrance and turn the air blue. It was the most vociferous welcome yet for Frank Lampard's team, and the hope was that it would be enough to propel Everton to the three points that had eluded them at Watford and against Brentford in the preceding nine days.

By 8:30pm, the Grand Old Lady was a murmuring shell as Evertonians contemplated a relegation battle going right to the wire at The Emirates four days later, with all the uncertainty and danger that would entail. Everton were 2-0 down at half-time to Crystal Palace following a fairly dreadful first 45 minutes, with many of those lessons from a chastening season seemingly unheeded, as a two-man midfield featuring the struggling André Gomes had been overrun by Patrick Vieira's confident charges, and the Toffees' infamous vulnerabilities at set-pieces were exploited by Jean-Philippe Mateta.

To add insult to injury, another one of those dangerous tackles that were supposed to have been outlawed by the Premier League failed to yield a red card for Jordan Ayew, and the forward would pop up just two minutes after his ugly challenge on Anthony Gordon to bundle in a goal that was horribly reminiscent of Gary Ablett's almost comical own goal against Wimbledon 28 years ago.

But, just like that "That Game" in 1994, the Toffees – more Goodison Gang than Crazy Gang – refused to lie down. Over 45 minutes that are now irrevocably woven into Goodison folklore, amid an atmosphere that somehow surpassed those that had stunned neutral observers in the preceding weeks, they dug down deep and pulled off a thrilling comeback victory. Win number 1,878 in England's top flight... as if written in the stars.

On this occasion, thanks largely to the transformative introduction at half-time of Dele Alli and a decisive switch, from 3-5-2 to 4-3-3, it was enterprising and smooth. Mostly, it was scrappy and ugly; direct, uncompromising, and uncultured football tailored to the desperation of the stakes. Yet it was spirited, visceral and, by the end, pure Everton, as a classic diving headed goal scored by a No.9 in front of the Gwladys Street secured a quite remarkable 85th-minute winner.

This was a night that Dele, a largely forgotten January addition who had remained an enigma after leaving Tottenham, and Calvert-Lewin, a player who had struggled to recapture anything close to his 2020/21 form, joined the ranks of the redeemed.

This was vintage Calvert-Lewin: all committed running, prodigious leaps, flick-ons and chest lay-offs before the decisive lunge to meet Demarai Gray's curling free-kick and bury a header past Jack Butland to spark pandemonium in a stadium that was rocking to its foundations.

Behind him for 90-plus minutes was a cast of tireless heroes, most prominent among them Richarlison and Michael Keane who had scored the goals to bring Everton back from the dead to 2-2, Alex Iwobi who never stopped from start to finish, and veteran captain

Seamus Coleman who atoned for a first-half error to roll back the years to play a vital role in a game for the ages in L4.

And on the sidelines, Lampard got to reprise those fist-pumping, bulging-vein celebrations that marked his arrival at Everton, but this time knowing that he had completed the first part of the massive job he undertook back in January.

Everton had started in the frenetic and adrenaline-charged fashion that had characterised their performances recently under Frank Lampard but in the 21st minute it was 1-0 to Patrick Vieira's side who went ahead. And it came in all-too familiar circumstances for Everton's supporters. André Gomes fouled Jeffrey Schlupp on Palace's left flank and when Eberechi Eze swung the resulting free-kick into the box, Mateta easily got in front of his marker to plant a header past Jordan Pickford from a central position in front of goal.

10 minutes before the break, Ayew doubled Palace's lead amid calamitous defending from Everton. Pickford only parried Mateta's cross away from the goal out to Wilfried Zaha. The 'keeper then got a hand to the Ivorian's bouncing first-time shot. Tragically, the ball span onto Ayew's head. It was he who bundled it over the line, as Mykolenko desperately tried to keep it from going in.

Gomes had once again struggled in a midfield that was being overrun by Vieira's men, prompting Lampard to send Dele out to warm up during the half-time break. The former Spurs man had made sporadic appearances until then, but his impact in the second half was seismic and it was the foul on him that led to Everton pulling a goal back in the 54th minute.

Mykolenko swung in a deep free-kick. Mason Holgate headed it back into the danger area, where Keane took a touch before guiding a lovely left-foot finish into the far corner of Butland's goal.

Demarai Gray replaced the willing but flagging Anthony Gordon to re-inject some pace and verve to the Toffees' attack, Palace briefly rallied, requiring another match-winning contribution from Pickford who batted Mateta's shot behind with a raised glove, and then Everton regained their footing. With 15 minutes of an increasingly bruising contest to go, they were level.

Coleman turned inside his man and clipped the ball to the back post, Dele's cross-shot was knocked back to Richarlison, and the Brazilian dug it out from under his feet before scooping it past Butland with the help of a slight deflection off a Palace leg.

And then, with five minutes of the regulation 90 to go, Everton completed their amazing recovery after Zaha dragged Coleman down, setting up a free kick for Gray to line up on the Blues' right flank.

The winger arced the ball behind the Palace defence and Calvert-Lewin threw himself at it, powering a wonderful diving header home. Goodison erupted and a small, ill-advised invasion of the pitch by ecstatic fans ensured stoppage would stretch beyond seven agonising minutes.

Everton hung on, though, as the home faithful cheered every throw-in and free-kick earned before referee Anthony Taylor blew his whistle and charged towards the tunnel as the stands emptied onto the pitch in unbridled joy at survival achieved.

As they did after the wins over Chelsea and Leicester, the celebrations went on long after the final whistle, only this time the Goodison pitch was a high-decibel mass of jubilant Evertonians; a chorus of relief and joy following an evening of high drama and true Blue spirit.

Police and stewards formed an arc around the dugouts within which the players stayed after fans had mobbed them, some held aloft on the shoulders of supporters. Arm-in-arm, they chanted along with the crowd from the Goodison hymn book and eventually Lampard made his way through bowels of the Main Stand to emerge triumphantly in front of the Directors' Box to bask in adulation.

In his post-match interview, the manager once again struck all the right notes, acknowledging that while Everton hadn't won anything, the supporters' celebrations were an out-pouring of emotion from a fanbase that has gone through a horrible year, looked square in the face of relegation from the top flight for the first time in 68 years, and emerged with their proud membership of the elite intact. And they'd done it all together.

Final score: Everton 3-2 Crystal Palace

***

After the match, Richarlison said Everton's incredible comeback against Crystal Palace, that ensured Premier League survival and ended a turbulent campaign, was one of the highlights of his career.

"The invasion of the crowd was something I had never witnessed in my career," he told *Globo Esporte*. They were all very distressed, worried about the situation, and in the end, it was a relief for everyone to win and escape relegation. It was all very exciting.

"It was one of the most special games of my career. A moment I will never forget. We went through a very difficult situation during the season. There was nothing calm during the year and what remains is the learning of all of us, because a team like Everton can no longer be in a situation like this."

No doubt feeling the effects from the jubilation that had followed the dramatic events of win over Palace, Everton travelled to the Emirates for their final fixture of 2021/22 and were soundly thrashed 5-1. Those Evertonians who had made the trip were in celebratory mood, however, and treated it as a day out and a way to decompress from a frustrating, stressful and emotional season that they hoped would not be repeated for a very long time. Years of costly mistakes and the lack of a clear-eyed strategy and vision for the playing side of the club had nearly cost Everton their place among the elite.

Not all the players who came across with Frank Lampard to the away section, to thank the fans for their unprecedented levels of support, would be around for the reconstruction of the squad that needed to be undertaken. Changes would be demanded at higher levels of the organisation as well.

The Blues had found collective strength in adversity; but would the warnings from 2021/22 be heeded?

2022: Moshiri apologises in letter to supporters

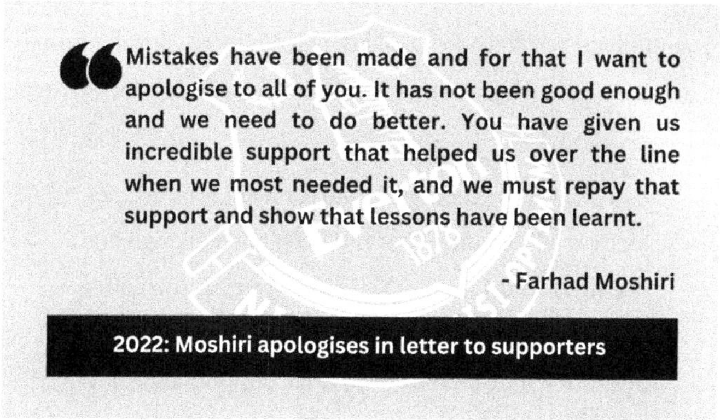

Still under fire from supporters angered by Everton's close call with relegation, Farhad Moshiri, wrote to supporters on 8 June to apologise for the mis-steps that had culminated in a traumatic struggle to stay in the top-flight in 2021/22, and to pledge that the club would do better.

The Iranian-born businessman had been in *de facto* and now *de jure* control at Goodison Park since 2016 and had ploughed historic levels of funds into the club, chiefly on the recruitment of players, many of whom failed to make the grade or improve the team's fortunes.

The massive expenditure, combined with compensation payments to sacked managers and the big hit to revenues that came from the COVID-19 pandemic, had left Everton with historic losses and hamstrung by the Premier League's profitability and sustainability rules.

A mis-matched squad of players proved incapable of dealing with injuries to key players and struggled badly under the management of controversial hire Rafael Benitez, which left the club in danger of being demoted from the top flight by the time the Spaniard was sacked in January. His successor, Frank Lampard, eventually steered the club to safety, thanks in huge part to unprecedented backing from Everton's fans, which had enabled the hierarchy to consider mistakes made and to plan for a more sustainable approach. Moshiri wrote:

> "Mistakes have been made and for that I want to apologise to all of you. It has not been good enough and we need to do better. You have given us incredible support that helped us over the line when we most needed it, and we must repay that support and show that lessons have been learnt. I am committed to securing the future success of the Club by delivering a fully funded stadium that will underpin our status as a leading Club. Of course, the stadium alone will not help us achieve our objectives and we are committed to not making the same mistakes again including how we have not always spent significant amounts of money wisely. During the 2021/22 season, the Board led a strategic review of our operations which included looking at working practices, our recruitment

> process and the whole structure of our footballing operation in order to clearly identify the causes of our under-delivery on the pitch. Many of the learnings have already been implemented."

Moshiri cited the appointments of Frank Lampard and Kevin Thelwell as examples of the new way forward, and he concluded his letter by mentioning the tremendous response from club officials and the fans to Russia's invasion of Ukraine, and the support shown to Vitalii Mykolenko, as well as a planned friendly against Dynamo Kyiv to raise funds for the war-torn country, before signing off with a note of thanks to Evertonians for their unwavering support:

> "Thank you for everything you did to support your Club so brilliantly during such a challenging season. You did not deserve the frustration and fear that the season brought. Your incredible support is never taken for granted and together we move forward."

***

The consequences of the mistakes to which Moshiri admitted, both potential and real, would continue to be felt going forward.

Earlier in May 2022, it was revealed that Leeds United and Burnley had written a joint letter to the Premier League accusing Everton of breaching 'Profitability and Sustainability' rules and asking for an independent commission to investigate Everton's financial situation within six weeks of their correspondence.

The two clubs, embroiled in a battle to avoid the last relegation slot, threatened to start legal proceedings and bring about a claim for substantial damages against Everton and the Premier League, after the Blues reported combined losses of £370 million over the preceding three years. According to the Premier League's P&S rules, a club could lose a maximum of £105 million over a three-year period. Should there be a breach, a club could face sanctions – including possible points deductions for serious breaches.

Everton had responded by saying: "We have worked so closely with the Premier League to make sure we are compliant, and we are comfortable we have complied with the rules. External auditors have told us what we can and cannot claim against the pandemic. If they want to take legal action, then they can do so by all means."

***

Later in the summer, one of the heroes of the preceding season left the club as Everton urgently moved to offset the operational losses incurred in the 2021/22 financial year with the £50 million sale of Richarlison to Tottenham.

Richarlison had, inevitably, become the subject of transfer speculation linking him with a move away from Goodison, and a recent change of agents sparked suggestions he was preparing to leave after four years with the Toffees. Everton's failure to challenge for European football in 2021/22 would prompt him to seek a club that could offer him a better opportunity to in the Champions League. From the club's perspective, his value would significantly reduce their financial deficits and may yet avoid them falling foul of Premier League rules. It was the trade-off for losing a key player and a gamble that Richarlison's goals and general contribution would not be missed too much during the forthcoming season.

2022: Kenyon consortium fail in Blues takeover bid

> *The Telegraph* on 14 June suggested that Peter Kenyon's group had been granted exclusivity as talks continued over a potential buyout, and Kenyon was likely to take a role in the club's running if the takeover is successful.
>
> **2022 Kenyon consortium fail in Blues takeover bid**

Six years after he had first bought into the club, and with his project at arguably its lowest ebb in that time, media speculation began that Farhad Moshiri would listen to reasonable offers to either buy out his 94% stake-holding in Everton entirely or just a portion of the club.

Moshiri's estimated net worth had reached as high as £2.9 billion at one stage but had taken a hit following Russia's invasion of Ukraine, the resulting personal sanctions against his business partner Alisher Usmanov, and the general impact of the war on USM Holdings.

June, 2022 saw the first concrete reports indicating he was ready to sell up, with *The Telegraph* claiming that Peter Kenyon, the former CEO of Manchester United and Chelsea, was reportedly spearheading a consortium intent on taking over Everton. The consortium, which included the chief executive of Minneapolis-based Talon Real Estate, Maciek Kaminski, and American entrepreneur John Thornton was being advised by investment specialist Michael Klein, along with the U.S. law firm Weil, Gotshal and Manges.

According to the report, the group were already in talks with the Blues' majority shareholder and that the discussions, which initially centred around financing the stadium at Bramley-Moore Dock, had developed into a proposal to buy the entire club outright. While still said to be in the preliminary stages, *The Telegraph* suggested that heads of terms – the first step towards a sale agreement – were already in place, signalling the intent by both parties to progress.

It was said Moshiri valued Everton at over £500 million, a figure that included the club's debts, but *SportsMail* said that Kenyon's consortium was only offering £400 million at that stage.

Furthermore, Kenyon and his partners were apparently seeking assurances that Everton would not be subject to any action from the Premier League, either through a heavy fine or points deduction in relation to breaches of Profit and Sustainability rules. The club had consistently maintained they remained compliant and had comfortable headroom regarding the League's financial regulations.

In his recent letter to supporters, Moshiri had reiterated his pledge to deliver a fully funded stadium, with the rest of the estimated £500 million construction costs also expected to be funded privately. These costs would also have to be factored in by any buyer and would likely affect the price of any buy-out offer, which would, as a result, be the biggest stumbling block to any takeover deal.

Further updates from *The Telegraph* on 14 June suggested that Kenyon's group had been granted exclusivity as talks continue over a potential buyout, and that while Kenyon was likely to take a role in the club's running if the takeover is successful, it was Kaminski who was "providing the greatest financial weight behind the bid".

***

By the end of the month, however, the deal was dead in the water. The U.S.-backed consortium did not have its period of exclusivity extended beyond 30 June, and its bid to take the club did not proceed any further, with *The Athletic* reporting that Moshiri had walked away from the talks with the American investors having lost faith in their ability to fund the buyout and cover the cost of the new Everton stadium.

According to *The Times* and *The Liverpool Echo*, it was understood Moshiri would now be "moving on from discussions with Peter Kenyon's group." Meanwhile, Moshiri reportedly maintained his commitment to delivering the club's new ground at Bramley-Moore Dock, but would still entertain advances from investors who would help fund the stadium.

He also apparently intended to focus on strengthening Frank Lampard's' playing squad over the summer of 2022, following the sale of Richarlison to Spurs.

According to *The Athletic*, however, the Kaminski camp remained keen on extending their period of exclusivity to undertake full due diligence of Everton's accounts.

Liverpool Echo journalist Dave Powell passed on the Kaminski family's' stance via Twitter, saying:

"I'm told by [the] Kaminski group that their position hasn't changed and that 'paperwork was exchanged overnight' with regards to exclusivity extension. [The] group say the situation hasn't' changed despite reports to the contrary and that they remain 'the only show in town.'

If the deal was dead as suggested, the news came just days after reports suggesting that Kaminski had visited Merseyside, and that Maciek and his son planned to be installed as directors on Everton's Board while Kenyon was eyeing the role of Executive Chairman in place of Bill Kenwright. All the while, however, there was reported interest from other parties, perhaps from the Middle East and the Far East, although no concrete details were revealed.

2022: Striker-less Everton in Dreadful Start to New Season

> "We need to make sure [we're not back in a relegation fight come March] for those supporters who are travelling down every single [game] to watch us play in Bournemouth or Newcastle or wherever it may be. We've got a lot of learning to do and we've got to do it quickly.
>
> \- Conor Coady

2022 Striker-less Everton in dreadful start to new season

By the summer of 2022, few Evertonians were under any illusions as to the difficult conditions under which their club was operating. That Richarlison's transfer to Tottenham had gone through on the final day of Everton's 2021/22 financial year was indication enough that the Blues had needed to sell to satisfy Premier League Profit and Sustainability rules. Given those constraints, whether, and to what degree, the club would be able to replace the talismanic Brazilian was a different question.

It was a situation compounded by Dominic Calvert-Lewin's ongoing injury problems which were very much in line with the adapted cliché: sometimes it feels like if it weren't for bad luck, Everton would have no luck at all. The club, under Farhad Moshiri's stewardship, had rightly been criticised for poor recruitment decisions and profligacy in the transfer market, but it was also cursed by a succession of serious injuries that had robbed the Blues of key — or potentially key — players for long periods.

James McCarthy's and Seamus Coleman's double leg breaks, Yannick Bolasie's torn ACL and meniscus, André Gomes's sickening ankle fracture dislocation, Jean-Philippe Gbamin's thigh and Achilles woes, successive knee injuries to Cenk Tosun (not a key asset, of course, but a saleable one) and, more recently, Dominic Calvert-Lewin's quad tear, all of these formed the bulk of a sorry list of serious injuries to have befallen Everton players over the past few years.

***

6 August 2022: Everton v Chelsea

The season opener against Chelsea was a chance to see whether Everton's fortunes were about to improve. Alas, it was not the case.

Yerry Mina had been available for less than half of the games for which he was eligible since arriving from Barcelona in 2018, due a frequency of his injuries that had become almost tragically comical over the past 12 months. A £27 million signing and arguably Everton's best centre-half, through no fault of the club's, he played in just 11 of 38 Premier League games in 2021/22. And, after "crocking" himself again in the season opener against Chelsea, he would make just seven more starts.

Then there was Ben Godfrey, who had battled COVID and a torn hamstring, worked his way back to full fitness and was rewarded with a starting role for this game, only to break his leg inside ten minutes. The footballing gods were evidently amusing themselves at Everton's expense.

At least in Godfrey's position, Frank Lampard had replacements on whom to call, and against Chelsea he drafted in Mason Holgate, who continued the run of good form he had had since the new manager took charge at the end of January.

Up front, of course, Lampard was pitifully short on options: with Richarlison sold to Spurs in June, Calvert-Lewin missing, and Ellis Simms out on loan, he didn't even have Salomon Rondon as an alternative. That left him trying to fashion a forward line geared for pace on the counter-attack against a superior opposition and, rather than deploy Dele Alli as a false nine, he plumped for Demarai Gray and Anthony Gordon as the two most advanced forwards, with Dwight McNeil making his debut in support.

Predictably enough, the Toffees struggled in attack without a genuine focal point and, with neither Gray nor Gordon renowned for their consistency of end product in the final third, they carved out few clear-cut scoring opportunities. And as if to remind Goodison of the large DCL-shaped hole in attack, some tempting deliveries into the box would go begging; particularly in the first half. You felt that, had the No 9 been there, Everton might have scored and won this fixture for a fifth successive season.

Ultimately, though, the contest was settled by one moment of clumsiness by the otherwise impressive Abdoulaye Doucouré, and a controversial penalty award.

Everton had been doing a decent job of keeping the visitors at bay and restricting them to half chances and dead-ball opportunities but their good work and that of Doucouré was undone deep into the time added on for Godfrey's injury. Raheem Sterling jinked into the box and was clumsily barged over by the Mali international, leading Craig Pawson to point to the spot.

Though Mina and Pickford did their best to put him off, Jorginho made no mistake with the penalty, sending the keeper the wrong way.

Doucouré had a shot from around ten yards out saved well by Edouard Mendy in the Chelsea goal early in the second half but, on the whole, the Blues struggled to create chances.

Thomas Tuchel's men, meanwhile, had resorted to delaying tactics and time-wasting. They barely threatened Pickford's goal until seven minutes from the end of the regulation 90 when Vitalii Mykolenko made a goal-saving intervention to prevent Sterling from putting the game to bed off Marc Cucurella's cross.

It was easy to dwell on the disappointment of a rare opening-day defeat — that was Everton's first loss in their first game of a new season for 11 years — and to miss the elements of this performance that were genuine cause for optimism.

The Blues' passing was crisper and more accurate than was the case the season before, and they played their way through the lines with a confidence and efficiency that was almost entirely absent by the time they sacked Rafael Benitez in January.

James Tarkowski had slotted right in and cut an assured, leader-like figure at the back; Nathan Patterson made a hugely promising Premier League bow, displaying some exciting attacking instincts while betraying some rawness against the trickery of Sterling; the defence faced a dizzying succession of corners but held firm where last season they would surely have conceded; and Alex Iwobi continued his unforeseen but massively welcome rebirth as a midfield play-maker under the new boss.

At first blush, and contrary to some neutral observers' dire prognostications, the 2022/23 edition of Everton didn't look doomed to another battle against relegation; however, the rest of August and what lay beyond would provide far more worrying signs.

Final score: Everton 0-1 Chelsea

***

After the match, it was revealed that Godfrey had fractured his tibia and would face months on the side-lines.

The Blues suffered a double blow in the game, with Godfrey's central-defensive partner Mina sustaining yet another injury, this time to his ankle, that would side-line him for a period of months.

***

With young defensive prospect Jarrard Branthwaite out on loan, it left Lampard with only three fit senior centre-halves. Two days later came the news that Frank Lampard and Kevin Thelwell had secured much-needed central-defensive cover with the acquisition of Conor Coady from Wolves on an initial loan deal, with an option to buy the following summer.

"I'll give absolutely everything, every day, for this football club," Coady told evertontv in his first interview:

"I feel privileged and lucky to be given this opportunity. We want to be sure we're going out and making supporters happy and improving the club at the same time.

"I'm someone who was desperate to come here, to play for this club. I know how big it is and I know the passion people have for Everton. It's an important day and a proud day for me to get it over the line.

"As soon as I heard the interest from the manager but also the Football Club itself, I really wanted to be part of it straight away. I'm over the moon to join.

"I've grown up around the city," the St Helens-born, former Liverpool youth player continued. "I know the Football Club, how big this club is and what it means to the fans."

Coady brought with him a wealth of Premier League experience, reliability and, like James Tarkowski who had been drafted in on a free transfer earlier in the summer, leadership qualities from having been captain at his previous club.

While Idrissa Gueye's slow-motion return to Goodison Park from Paris Saint-Germain continued, amid reports that the Senegal international was undergoing a two-part medical in France and was awaiting international clearance to travel to Merseyside, Everton landed their biggest signing of the 2022 close season in the form of Amadou Onana from Lille.

Having beaten off competition from David Moyes's West Ham, the Blues negotiated a £33 million deal involving a low up-front payment in return for additional appearance-related add-ons and a sell-on clause benefitting the French club.

Tall, rangy and still only 21, Onana was a recently-capped full Belgian international and widely regarded as one of the finest central prospects in Europe. As such, it was something of a coup for Everton, and Lampard was delighted to bring him on board.

Transfer deadline day saw Gueye's protracted return finalised for around £2 million and highly-rated young midfielder James Garner arrive for an initial fee of £9 million. Yet it was the lack of effective cover for Dominic Calvert-Lewin at centre-forward that remained a vexing issue for supporters.

Thelwell and his recruitment team had tried for weeks to strike a deal with Southampton for Che Adams but were put off by a lofty asking price, reported to be as high as £20 million. An approach to take Guinean international forward Serhou Guirassy on loan failed when Rennes insisted on a permanent cash deal instead and nothing came of rumoured interest in the likes of Samuel Chukwueze of Villarreal, Joao Pedro of Watford or Ben Brereton Diaz of Blackburn Rovers.

However, Everton almost pulled off one of the signings of the summer when they came to the brink of capturing Mohammed Kudus from Ajax Amsterdam. In what was, perhaps, one of those sliding doors moments in terms of Lampard's future at the club, a proposed loan deal for the exciting Ghana international looked to have all but been arranged when the Dutch club pulled the plug.

In parallel to their talks with the Toffees, Ajax were also negotiating the blockbuster sale of winger Antony to Manchester United for around £85 million and once that was agreed, they insisted they had no interest in losing both of their star attacking midfielders in the same transfer window.

Kudus temporarily went on strike and refused to train in an effort to force through a move to Goodison Park, but the matter was resolved at Ajax a few days later and Evertonians had to watch him turn heads at the World Cup in Qatar three months later, and wonder at what might have been.

In the end, the only forward who arrived at Everton was Neal Maupay from Brighton & Hove Albion in a deal worth a reported £12 million. Prolific at Brentford in the season they won promotion to the Premier League, Maupay had been less successful with the Seagulls where he was averaging a goal every four games, a far cry from what Everton needed.

Nevertheless, the Frenchman was, at least, a nominal striker who, it was felt, might be able to bring some of the qualities that Richarlison offered in terms of work-rate and generally being a pest in opposition penalty areas.

Nottingham Forest, who were in the midst of a record overhaul of their squad in preparation for their return to the Premier League after two decades in the second tier, had apparently agreed a reported £15 million fee with Brighton for Maupay. But once Everton's interest became known and Lampard spoke with the player personally to convince him to join his project at Goodison Park, the 26-year-old's mind appeared to be made up.

"Everton is a great club with unbelievable fans and I am so, so happy to be here," Maupay said. "It feels amazing.

"It was an easy choice for me when I started to talk with the club. I knew straight away I wanted to play for Everton and help the club to succeed."

Frank Lampard expressed his satisfaction at having added a much-needed attacking option to his squad, while he awaited Calvert-Lewin's return to fitness from his knee injury.

"We're delighted to bring Neal to Everton, a player of proven quality in the Premier League. We wanted to strengthen our attacking options and Neal provides a goal-scoring threat, as well as bags of energy and a fighting spirit that are vital to what we're building."

Much to the fans' chagrin, Everton had already played four Premier League matches without a recognised striker, with Lampard forced to mend and make do with Anthony Gordon and Demarai Gray as forwards. Infuriatingly, because of the late August Bank Holiday and a bizarre ruling that required player registrations to have been completed one full working day before the next match, it would be one more game before Maupay could come in.

The new signing was forced to watch from the side-lines as Everton took the lead at Leeds, but the Blues couldn't hold on to claim their first victory of the new season and had to settle for a draw.

***

18 September 2022: Everton v West Ham

No one had really wanted to put too much emphasis on one match, but with an international break coming up and an always tricky away game at Southampton looming on the other side of it, Everton really needed to beat the Hammers and earn their first win of 2022/23.

With defeats against Chelsea and Villa, and draws against Forest, Brentford, Leeds and Liverpool, three points were urgently needed. Another draw wouldn't have been catastrophic, of course, but to have completed a fifth of the season without picking up a victory would have been an unsettling return for the Blues in view of the previous season's close call with relegation.

As it was, they battled their way to a 1-0 victory, reversing the scoreline from the corresponding fixture the previous season, on the back of Neal Maupay's first goal for the club.

Everton didn't get much change from referee Michael Oliver but their luck held once more – an opposition player struck the post for the seventh time in four games but the ball again stayed out – and though there were a couple of other scares late on, they largely held the visitors at arm's length, with the defensive quartet of Nathan Patterson, Vitalii Mykolenko, James Tarkowski and, newly installed as deputy captain, Conor Coady excelling when it mattered in the closing stages.

Idrissa Gueye came into the starting XI for his first start since returning from Paris Saint-Germain and formed part of a midfield three that helped cancel out the visitors, but this wasn't a performance that would live long in the memory. Everton managed just two shots on target in the 90 minutes, both coming early in the second half and their forward play was often let down by the final ball. Indeed, neither side managed an effort on target until the stroke of half time, when Asmir Begovic comfortably caught a header from Kurt Zouma.

West Ham had the first chance of the second period when Pablo Fornals got to the byline and centred for Bowen, but he swept a first-time effort narrowly over. Soon afterwards, the lively Demarai Gray was involved in the game's only goal.

He knocked a neat pass inside to Alex Iwobi who then picked Maupay out on the edge of the penalty area. Having gathered the ball with a tidy first touch, the Frenchman fired a crisp shot wide of Fabianski and inside the near post to hand Everton the lead. He didn't know it then, but it was the only goal he would score for Everton all season.

The Londoners came very close to grabbing a point when Gueye lost the ball and Said Benrahma advanced towards goal before curling an effort around Begovic. The Bosnian keeper watched it bounce off the inside of his right-hand post and fly across goal before being cleared.

Begovic pushed Maxwel Cornet's shot behind and had to tip a sliced Jarrod Bowen cross over in stoppage time as the Toffees held out to claim three points that lifted them away from the bottom three.

As Lampard remarked afterwards, "there's a good feeling about the place."

The Blues still hadn't scored more than once in a game so far that season, and it looked as though goals would continue to be scarce, at least until Calvert-Lewin came back into the side. But the graft, the solidity and the character was there to suggest that the club could start looking upwards rather than over their shoulders.

Final score: Everton 1-0 West Ham

***

Three weeks before the 2022/23 edition of Everton v Crystal Palace, the club received a £300,000 fine for the two incursions onto the pitch by their supporters during the club's emotional win over the Eagles in May. Fans came onto the field in the 85th minute when Dominic Calvert-Lewin scored the dramatic winner at the Gwladys Street End, the goal that secured Everton's place in the Premier League, and then again in celebration after the final whistle.

Though there had been no physical altercations between supporters and opposition players, the Football Association cited 'threatening and violent behaviour from fans' as justification for the unprecedented financial penalty - a reference, perhaps, to the goading of Patrick Vieira that prompted the Palace manager to kick out at one individual fan.

Merseyside Police spoke to both Vieira and the supporter and, along with the FA, took no action over the incident. But, to show a strong hand in trying to crack down on pitch invasions, the game's governing body acted retroactively with a steep fine, after a hearing chaired by David Philipps KC – a lawyer who would later be selected to chair the Premier League's Independent Commission over Everton's alleged breaches of Profitability and Sustainability Rules.

The incidents at Goodison Park in May had been just one instance of fans pouring into the pitch after a game — similar incidents occurred at Nottingham Forest, with one supporter charged for assault for a head-butt on Sheffield United's Billy Sharpe, and at Manchester City, where home fans confronted opposition goalkeeper Robin Olsen.

***

22 October 2022: Everton v Crystal Palace

With November approaching, Everton had only managed three goals in their five matches at Goodison Park, but against Crystal Palace they doubled their home goals tally for the season in some style, putting three past their opponents for the second time that year.

There were many pleasing aspects to this performance: Dominic Calvert-Lewin was fit, firing and back among the goals; Anthony Gordon was demonstrating the marauding and tenacious form he had shown in the second half of the previous season; Seamus Coleman kept Wilfried Zaha in his back pocket; and Alex Iwobi was absolutely revelling again in his roving midfield role, weighing in with two assists – the second a delicious back-heel to present Dwight McNeil with the Blues' third goal.

After a seven-game unbeaten run had taken them to the brink of the top half at the start of the month, three successive losses, to Manchester United, Tottenham and Newcastle, had the potential to send the Blues into a bit of a tailspin. Coming into this game, the bottom three was looking ominously close again.

Lampard needed a big performance, back in front of a highly charged home crowd, and he got it with a high-intensity start that yielded an opening goal that was all down to Calvert-Lewin's physicality.

The 25-year-old dispossessed Luka Milivojević ten yards outside the Palace box. When Iwobi threaded the ball back to him, Calvert-Lewin took a neat touch past Marc Guéhi, then had the strength to hold the defender off before drilling a shot across the goalkeeper, Vicente Guaita, who couldn't prevent it from finding the far corner.

Palace were being kept very much at arm's length in the first half but Vieira's men came out of the half-time interval the more purposeful of the two sides. Everton re-asserted their dominance not long after the hour mark with a superbly-worked goal. It started with a goal kick in their own half, involved some confident passing out from the back and a lovely pass from Iwobi through the lines to Gray, whose pass to Amadou Onana found Mykolenko arriving in acres of space on the overlap.

Guaita got a hand to the Ukrainian's low shot but could only palm it into the path of Gordon, who had the simple task of knocking the ball into the empty net. The referee's assistant had raised his flag for offside, but a check by VAR resulted in what was clearly the correct decision — a second goal for Everton.

Dwight McNeil entered the fray in a 72nd-minute change and he took the invitation to drive at the Palace defence. He slipped a pass into the box for Iwobi, who deftly back-heeled it back into the winger's path and McNeil tucked it home to make it 3-0.

It was a lovely goal that underlined how good the side could be when it had its tails up and was in full flow. It wouldn't happen very often that season – all too often the Blues had been tentative and bereft of attacking invention – but what was the most complete performance under Lampard since the win over Leeds in February, had the potential to serve as a benchmark for future home matches, as the manager looked to take his side to the next level.

Final score: Everton 3-0 Palace

***

12 November 2022: Bournemouth v Everton

For a club that had become synonymous with false dawns, the handsome win over Palace and the slick nature of it proved to be yet another flash in the pan. No one knew it at the time, but it would be almost 12 months before Everton would once again score more than a single goal in a match at Goodison Park.

A dull but creditable goalless draw at Fulham had followed a week later, but when struggling Leicester came to Merseyside and left having collected three easy points with a 2-0 win, the alarm bells started ringing for the Blues' long-suffering supporters.

Worse was to follow with two trips to Bournemouth in the space of four days, one in the Carabao Cup and one in the Premier League, after which doubts started to solidify about Lampard's ability to steer the club clear of relegation for a second season.

The performance from a much-changed side in the cup-tie, against an equally under-strength Cherries side, had been abysmal. Yet there was hope that, when those first-choice players that were fit to play were reinstated for the second fixture between the two clubs at the Vitality Stadium, things would be a lot different.

They weren't. Far from making amends, the Blues left the south coast having been comprehensively beaten again by a Bournemouth team that hadn't won a league game in five attempts coming into the weekend, and who wouldn't taste victory again for another eight matches. Another chastening defeat meant the Blues were hovering above the relegation zone going into the six-week break for the 2022 World Cup.

A horrible mistake by Jordan Pickford gifted the Cherries the opener in the 18th minute. Dominic Solanke's cross was inexplicably batted into trouble by the England goalkeeper and Marcus Tavernier gratefully seized on the loose ball to knock it into the empty net.

11 minutes after that it was 2-0 as the Toffees failed to deal with a corner but then stopped to appeal for referee Craig Pawson to halt play for a clear head injury to Tarkowski. The official allowed play to continue, Pickford parried Phillip Billing's shot away, but when Tavernier put the ball back into the six-yard box, Kieffer Moore was there to power a header in from close range.

Everton didn't manage their first shot on target until the 40th minute, a fairly tame shot from Alex Iwobi that was comfortably gathered; while Maupay's appeals for a penalty in first-half stoppage time fell on deaf ears where Pawson was concerned.

The Toffees produced arguably their most dangerous moment of the contest shortly after half-time, when Amadou Onana laid the ball back to Idrissa Gueye who blazed over rather than work Travers in the Bournemouth goal.

But any hope that the visitors had of clawing their way back went out the window with 20 minutes left. Lewis Cook swung a free-kick into the Blues' box and with no one tracking the runner, they left Jaidon Anthony unimpeded to head powerfully past Pickford to make it 3-0.

The defeat left Everton going into the break for the World Cup sitting just two points off the bottom three. The manager's inability to find any consistency from his players, and the erosion of the defensive solidity that had been one of Everton's strengths earlier in the season, were the larger concerns looming over the team.

Final score: Bournemouth 3-0 Everton

***

Afterwards, Conor Coady was scathing in his assessment of how Everton had collectively performed at the Vitality Stadium, saying that it was "shocking."

"[I]t's nowhere near good enough from our point of view," the Wolves loanee said. "I don't want to speak about it, to be honest — the referee's done his job today and, whatever… Listen, we speak about referees after every game and I'm certainly not going to do that when we've put out a performance like that against Bournemouth.

"So, no, I'm not going to speak about the second goal. I'll speak about the performance and it was nowhere near good enough. It was nothing that represents an Everton team, that represents Everton Football Club, that represents our supporters; so one hard look in the mirror for everyone of us that plays for this football club."

Asked what the desperately poor team display was down to, Coady replied flatly: "Personal pride; standards; we have to set standards every day in training. It's not just about today; it can't be anything to do with the manager, his staff; it's nothing to do with that.

"It's up to us as players to have standards, to have personal pride in what we do every single day and we don't have that at the minute. So we have to make sure we have that because things like [today] are going to happen. So we need to look at ourselves long and hard... because it was shocking and nowhere near good enough.

"We've got to look at it because we've got a second half of the season where we have to be better, no matter what. We can't go into the second half of the season like that without a long talk in the dressing room in terms of what's going on and what needs to be done.

"[Bournemouth] wanted it more than us. [We're] massively short of where we need to be because this is Everton ... and we're not representing that as a team or as a club for the supporters.

"We need to make sure [we're not back in a relegation fight come March] for those supporters who are travelling down every single [game] to watch us play in Bournemouth or Newcastle or wherever it may be. We've got a lot of learning to do and we've got to do it quickly."

Referring to the uncomfortable scenes after the final whistle where those players who went over to the away supporters were booed by the Everton fans, Coady said:

"Today, for me, will take a lot of time to get over, if I'm being honest, because that feeling out there on the pitch at the end was absolutely horrendous. We need the supporters behind us, but how can we expect them to be when we're [playing like] that?"

2022: 27 Campaign writes to Moshiri demanding change

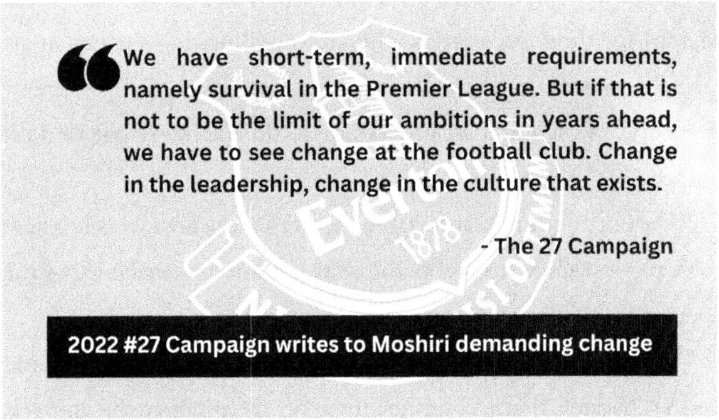

As the World Cup reached its Quarter Finals stage in Qatar, the 27 Campaign group released a second open letter to Farhad Moshiri, in which they outlined finances, ownership, leadership and direction as the main concerns that "directly relate to [Everton's] performance on the pitch" and which they wanted to see urgently addressed.

As part of that, the 27 Campaign (so-called because 2022 marked 27 years since the Blues had last won a trophy) was agitating for a change in the leadership of Everton – the group had highlighted a boardroom shake-up as one desired development they wanted to see happen – as well as a change in culture at the club.

The full letter read:

> Dear Mr Moshiri,
>
> **Change required:** Since our open letter in July 2022, we respected your request to all Evertonians to "judge you at the end of the (summer) window". We gave you the benefit of the doubt. We have continued to provide the manager, Frank Lampard, his team and the players, the very highest levels of support particularly on match days, home and away. A year ago, the 27 Campaign was formed to highlight the time since our last trophy win. Our actions, alongside other fan groups, then and since are driven by concerns as to the financing, ownership, leadership and direction of our great club. We believe that issues surrounding finances, ownership, leadership and direction directly relate to our performance on the pitch. Regrettably, given the absence of communications and any degree of change in the running of the club, we have in an open letter format, to ask you the following questions:

Finances: Other than the minimum statutory requirements, the club provides no information on its finances. On the back of constructing a new stadium, having extensive, continued losses, and profitability & sustainability issues, it is reasonable for shareholders and fans to expect regular updates on our finances. Our finances directly relate to our ability to compete. **Ownership:** Since the summer, messaging from the club has been confused. Is the club for sale? Are you seeking new investors to fund our working capital requirements? Other Premier League clubs seeking new investment or owners have appointed investment banks to handle their requirements. They have been clear with their communications. What is your intention, what are you doing, and when will you communicate it clearly? **Leadership:** In the near seven years since you acquired your initial shareholding, you have persisted in retaining the current Chairman and Chief Executive Officer. There is nothing in the club's governance, commercial, financial and indeed footballing performance, that suggests they warrant continued employment. As a result of huge losses and the squandering of resources, our competitive position declines on an annual basis in all respects. How can you justify their performance? **Direction:** What are your ambitions (if any) for the club?

The building of a new stadium, in isolation, will not cure the ills that have befallen Everton in recent years. So much more is required for us to be a competitive Premier League and ultimately European competitor once more. We have short-term, immediate requirements, namely survival in the Premier League. But if that is not to be the limit of our ambitions in years ahead, we have to see change at the football club. Change in the leadership, change in the culture that exists. You, as the majority shareholder, are the only person who can bring about that change. Surely you, with the financial commitment you have made, must recognise that change is necessary? With respect, we ask you to directly answer the questions put to you. Tell us what changes are to be made to change the direction the club is heading.

Yours Sincerely, The 27 Campaign.

***

26 December 2022: Everton v Wolverhampton Wanderers

Everton returned to competitive action, looking to set a very different tone to the one with which they went into the break for the World Cup in mid-November. They emerged from Boxing Day with a fourth successive defeat in all competitions, as the bottom club Wolves won this tense 'six-pointer' in stoppage time.

Julen Lopetegui picked up his first win as the Black Country club's new manager in his first game at the helm thanks to substitute Rayan Ait-Nui's last-gasp goal, while the Blues' boss, Frank Lampard, hustled down the tunnel with Goodison Park's frustrated boos in his ears at full-time.

Everton had their chances to put this game to bed long before a poor Wolves outfit caught them cold on the break in the final minute of time added on, but wastefulness plagued their attack, which was creating and scoring precious few goals.

Yerry Mina, playing instead of the ineligible Conor Coady, had settled the nerves of a shaky start by heading in what was Everton's first goal that came directly from a corner all season after just six minutes, glancing his header across Jose Sa and into the far corner of the goal.

However, Wolves hit back 15 minutes later with a corner routine of their own, as the ball was pinged to Joao Moutinho on the edge of the box. Rather than have a crack at goal, the Portuguese lofted a clever ball over a static defence where Daniel Podence arrived completely unmarked to guide it past Pickford and make it 1-1.

Everton's best chance of the rest of the contest arrived 11 minutes before the break when Idrissa Gueye made a fine interception and immediately threaded the ball through to Anthony Gordon in the box, where the young winger took one touch and tried to tuck it past Sa, but the Portuguese pushed his shot away one-handed.

Then, in the 42nd minute, a loose touch from Nathan Collins gifted possession to Maupay, but the striker fired another great chance straight at the keeper.

The onslaught for which the Goodison faithful were baying in the closing stages never came, with Lampard's charges continually recycling the ball in injury time rather than trying to play the percentages with a target man spearheading the attack.

There was a cruel irony, however, that as soon as they shed their inhibitions with one final attack and lost the ball on the edge of the opposition area, a sucker punch hit them hard. Wolves tore away on the counter-attack with numbers, Adama Traore centred and Rayan Ait-Nouri took a touch to set himself in front of goal before lashing it home.

It was a harsh and dispiriting end to a game that had been billed as must-win for an Everton side who would be in the bottom three when they travelled to the home of the champions, Manchester City on New Year's Eve.

The result also heaped more pressure on Lampard to solve his side's timidity and profligacy, and on Kevin Thelwell to bring in attacking reinforcements as a matter of dire urgency when the transfer window opened.

Final score: Everton 0-1 Wolves

***

That had been Everton's 4th defeat in eight home matches so far in 2022/23, a worrying trend for a team that had relied so heavily on results at Goodison Park to stay up the previous season. The grave concern for supporters who were looking for signs of progress having been made during the hiatus for the World Cup, were reflected by the frustrated reaction from the crowd at the end, a fact not lost on Lampard.

"I think the lads had all the right intentions, so for that I'd love the crowd to stick with them," the manager said afterwards.

"We saw what a positive it (Goodison Park) can be last year, so let's not come away from that.

"I'm in the dressing room with them, and I know they want to do the right thing. I'm not asking the players to play 100 passes in our own final third, but to be a bit braver on the ball. Good players want to play so I'd like that to get some backing as the reality is we haven't got Dominic (Calvert-Lewin) for the direct option. We have to take it on the chin. We are trying to improve off the back of where we last year and it will be baby steps."

***

3 January 2023: Everton v Brighton

If a surprise draw to close out 2022 at the home of the Champions Manchester City had ignited some optimism among the Toffees faithful, the first match of the New Year would plunge Evertonians to greater depths of concern.

A home clash with Brighton & Hove Albion under the lights at a sodden Goodison Park, turned into a footballing disaster, as the Seagulls humiliated Everton, first by carving them open in the first half to take the lead, and then by extending their advantage with three quick goals in the second half, each as concerning as the last.

There had been a contingent of supporters who felt that Lampard should have been sacked after the twin embarrassments in

Bournemouth before the World Cup, and their number grew following the dreadful display against Brighton. To make things worse, the Blues once again dropped into the relegation zone on the back of the result.

It was no surprise, then, given the rising tide of discontent that Everton's fans turned on the club's owner and board of Directors as they witnessed the astonishing collapse in the second half. The crowd loudly booed Lampard and his team at half-time and again at the final whistle, with chants of "sack the board" ringing out once again inside the Grand Old Lady.

Final score: Everton 1-4 Brighton

***

While reports in the immediate aftermath of the match claimed that no assurances had been given to Lampard about the safety of his position, within a couple of days it emerged that the club were planning to stick with him for the time being.

The Telegraph suggested that there was "a growing belief he was fighting a losing battle to keep his job" and, given that Everton hadn't won a game since confidently despatching Crystal Palace on 22 October and were now in the bottom three, the next three fixtures would be pivotal for both Lampard and, perhaps, the club's ability to avoid the drop this season.

Following talks with Director of Football, Kevin Thelwell, at Finch Farm and the club's Chief Executive Officer, Denise Barrett-Baxendale, it was decided that Lampard would take charge of the FA Cup tie against Manchester United at Old Trafford. The hope was that with a positive result against Manchester United, or at least, a promising performance, the manager might be able to imbue confidence among the board in his ability to take Everton forward.

Meanwhile, several Everton supporters groups, including fan websites like ToffeeWeb and the newly renamed NSNOW group, put their name to an open letter to the Blues' majority shareholder, Farhad Moshiri, calling on him to change the club's leadership.

The move came after a similar missive from NSNOW (then known as the 27 Years Campaign) appealing to Moshiri for greater communication around the governance of Everton FC and, in particular, the ongoing funding model for the club's new stadium.

That letter received no response from Moshiri's office, but the Brighton result had given the owners' critics greater impulse for action to be taken at the top of the club.

The latest letter from the supporters groups read:

> "To Farhad Moshiri
>
> The time to save our club from its continued decline is now. For too long, despite your investment, we have seen diminishing returns that now threaten our existence as a Premier League club. We the undersigned fan and social media groups call on you to make sweeping changes at Chair, Board and Executive levels. Bring in competent, experienced professionals

who can reverse our decline and make us competitive once more. The narrow window of opportunity you spoke of is all but closed. Act now, while we still have a chance. Change the culture of the club, change the Chair, Board & Executive. NSNO - our standard not just our motto."

2023: Insecure Board stays away from Goodison

> "Following a thorough risk assessment, and in response to tangible threats received by the Club and intelligence we have gathered, the Club's board members have been told they must not attend today's fixture.
>
> \- Unnamed Security & Safety Advisor

2023 Insecure Board stays away from Goodison

Farhad Moshiri's response to the latest plea from the NSNOW campaign came two days before the latest 'must win' game to be played at Goodison Park – this one against Southampton, the newest incumbents of 20th place in the Premier League – and yet again he used the controversial medium of Jim White and *TalkSport* as the conduit to communicate his message to supporters.

A year before, he had informed White that he would no longer be calling him on air following pushback from fans who could not understand why he refused to use the club's official media channels to communicate with them. Now he was choosing, at perhaps his lowest point since coming on board as a major investor in 2016, to break that self-imposed exile.

On the phone call to the radio host, Moshiri defended his efforts as owner, gave Lampard the dreaded vote of confidence and, surprisingly, suggested that the sacking of previous managers like Roberto Martinez, Ronald Koeman, Sam Allardyce, Marco Silva and Rafael Benitez had all been driven by fan sentiment.

Asked if he thought Evertonians still had faith in him, Moshiri said "he hoped so," before reiterating his support for manager Frank Lampard and the need for continuity in the head coach role:

> "I put my money where my mouth is and that is the most an owner can do and I have done that. Some of the decisions we have taken is together with the fans, right? All the managers who have left have been driven by the fans, not me initially. I think you have got to stay with the manager to get the systems going, the players he brought in. I have a lot of faith in Frank that he will get it right."

On the likelihood of upcoming protests that weekend at the game against Southampton – demonstrations of discontent that were likely to have been intensified by Moshiri's decision to speak to *TalkSport* again – he agreed that:

> "Protest is a democratic right of everyone ... I think the feeling is well-known if you are communicating. But I would say the biggest thing is to support the team. So we need to give it and they will give it back to us."

One of the biggest bones of contention among many fans, and in particular the NSNOW movement, was the perceived lack of expertise in the boardroom. But the owner was unequivocal in his support of Bill Kenwright, Denise Barrett-Baxendale, and newer members like Grant Ingles and non-executive director, Graeme Sharp:

> "They have been there a long time. Some are new appointments but they are longstanding, they are dedicated, they are local and it is so important to keep the club in Liverpool and its roots in Liverpool. Those are the roots and the roots of the club. They love the club and they have been attending games under every condition, and it is just building a £760 million stadium that will be one of the best in the country [that] is an enormous challenge for a club. I think [the fans] need to acknowledge that [the directors] are going through a transformation and they are working extremely hard, and I have added to the board every now and again with support and we will do it again. You can't just make rash decisions. We have two big games, Saturday, and on the 21st (against West Ham), and that is the only focus."

Then, just three hours before Everton were due to kick-off against Southampton, the news broke that, in an unprecedented move, Everton's directors had been instructed by the club's security team not to attend the critical fixture at Goodison Park.

It came on the back of developments in the fans protest movement earlier that week, coordinated by NSNOW, who called for a peaceful sit-in at Goodison after the game against the Saints to show their concerns over the state of the club.

The order to the Board was apparently because of "malicious and unacceptably threatening correspondence" that had been received, along with "increasing incidents of anti-social behaviour – including targeted physical aggression - at recent home matches."

An unnamed Security & Safety Advisor said: "Following a thorough risk assessment, and in response to tangible threats received by the Club and intelligence we have gathered, the Club's board members have been told they must not attend today's fixture."

A spokesperson for the club added:

> "This is an unprecedented decision for Everton Football Club – never before has our entire Board of Directors been ordered not to attend a match on safety grounds. It is a profoundly sad day for Everton and Evertonians."

Merseyside Police later issued a statement saying no incidents or offences had been reported by the club.

***

14 January 2023: Everton v Southampton

Meanwhile, on the pitch against fellow strugglers, Southampton, the mess the Blues had become under Farhad Moshiri's ownership was laid bare once more, with Frank Lampard powerless to prevent his charges from slumping to what was their seventh defeat in eight games, despite taking the lead through the imperious Amadou Onana.

The Belgian, so impressive in defeat at Manchester United in the FA Cup eight days earlier, was brilliant again, and rewarded with a goal from a towering first-half header that should have been the platform from which Everton won the game. However, yet more calamitous defending saw the lead evaporate and the Toffees descend into crisis on and off the pitch.

Southampton, who came into the fixture on a two-game winning streak in the cups, one of them an impressive League Cup quarter-final victory over Manchester City, went close to capitalising on yawning gaps in Everton's back line, first when Mohamed Elyounoussi's shot looped towards the far post and dropped wide and then when Mohammed Salisu's header was parried by Jordan Pickford on the line.

Everton broke the deadlock, though, with seven minutes left in the half. Some neat footwork from Demarai Gray ended with his attempted cross being blocked behind. From the winger's corner, Onana fought his way through the crowd to meet the in-swinger, and planted a downward header home off Bazunu's glove.

It was his first goal for the club and a potential mood changer. If only Everton could have hung on, but they tossed the lead away with less than a minute gone of the second half.

A simple Adams flick-on past James Tarkowski found Ward-Prowse in plenty of space to draw a sliding block attempt from Ben Godfrey and then stroke the ball past the helpless Pickford to make it 1-1.

Everton briefly rallied, with a marauding run by Ben Godfrey allowing him to set Calvert-Lewin up just outside the box, but his shot took a vital deflection off a defender's out-stretched leg and smacked off the underside of the crossbar and away from goal.

Lampard tried to change the course of the game by throwing on Anthony Gordon for Seamus Coleman, but instead of making the difference at the Gwladys Street End he played an important role in Southampton's winner with a clumsy and needless foul on Che Adams that gave the visitors a free-kick in prime James Ward-Prowse territory.

With Pickford and his wall all at sea, the Saints Talisman simply picked his spot and drove the ball into the left-hand side of the goal as the goalkeeper stood rooted to the spot.

For the third time since Christmas, the players left the Goodison Park pitch with the frustration, ire and boos of the fans in their ears, before the demonstrations of disaffection with an absent board took centre-stage behind the Gwladys Street goal.

Everton urgently needed an injection of goals in the transfer market and a change of ideas in the dugout. Off the pitch, it was hard to see the wholesale shift in culture and leadership that was required coming in time to stave off relegation to the second tier for the first time in 72 years.

Final score: Everton 1-2 Southampton

***

Writing in *The Guardian* that evening, Jonathan Liew rather eloquently summarised the situation, with the sadness of an outsider all too aware of how far the giant that is Everton had fallen:

"I've been particularly enjoying the protest banners. Everton is a furious club right now, its fans and its ownership in open warfare, a mixture of rage and desperation and powerlessness. And yet for some reason all this anger seems to express itself in perfect, playful rhyming couplets. 'Everton were magic, Kenwright is tragic.' 'A football giant owned by a clown, all you'll achieve is taking us down.' 'A chairman who won't let go, an under-qualified CEO.'

"Only Everton fans, you feel, can capture an existential cry for help with the levity of a child's nursery rhyme. I don't propose to analyse the metre and scansion of the Everton banners in too much detail, but on some level I wonder whether the jauntiness of the medium is a subconscious counterpoint to the opacity and obfuscation of the Everton board, with their woolly "Official Statements", their anonymous briefings to favoured journalists, the intentionally imprecise messaging. You put out your press releases. We bring poetry. The natural instinct amongst many rival fans, and even some voices in the media, has been to poke fun at Everton's plight, chide their sense of legacy entitlement, deride their supporter base as delusional, demented, perhaps even dangerous. And as with any mass protest movement – and not to equate the aims of Just Stop Oil or Black Lives Matter with, say, the underwhelming signing of Neal Maupay in the summer – the focus invariably shifts towards the methods of protest rather than the substance of the protest itself.

"After the 2-1 defeat to Southampton on Saturday – a game the board did not attend citing vague and unspecified safety concerns – a small group of fans surrounded the cars of Anthony Gordon and Yerry Mina as they tried to leave Goodison Park. A little unsavoury, but essentially harmless. Perhaps so Mina, who grew up amid the barras bravas of Colombian football and has presumably seen much worse, looked so calm as he stepped out of his car to talk to fans and listen to their concerns. "Show us a bit of heart," one fan urges him. "All we want is passion. Show us a bit of passion. Start speaking up, lad, show them you're the man." There was a touching and curiously human quality to the whole exchange, one that really strikes at the heart of what Everton fans are really angry about. Because at its heart, this is not a protest about net spends or sporting directors or even league form. It's about hope and connection, the forlorn and obsolescent idea that a football club can still be an expression of its people, that those who run and administer it can still want the same things they do. What do Everton fans want? And can modern football even provide it? "The fans expect the best," reads another banner. Nil satis nisi optimum, the club motto from which one of the main protest groups takes its name, means "nothing but the best is good enough".

"You see the problem here. Everton had for a time one of Europe's best young strikers in Romelu Lukaku. Manchester United bought him for £75m. They had one of the world's finest managers in Carlo Ancelotti. Real Madrid took him. Gordon had half a good season before Chelsea started making eyes at him. What do we think happens to Amadou Onana if he starts tearing up the Premier League? Or Ben

Godfrey? Or Nathan Patterson? And these were the good decisions. But outside the game's VIP circle nothing good can ever last. For fans of smaller clubs, perhaps you make your peace with this fact sooner rather than later. But those one level removed from the elite, your West Hams and Aston Villas and Hamburgs and Sampdorias, are essentially trapped in a doom cycle from which there are only really two escapes: relegation or an autocratic benefactor. This isn't entitlement. It is simply the howl of a club and fanbase that, whether they make the right choices or the wrong choices, will simply never be allowed to grow. One of the interesting elements of this protest is how young the banner-wavers and slogan-shouters are. They're mostly young men in their 20s and 30s, some even younger. These guys aren't high on nostalgia. They're not pining for the days of Sharp and Sheedy. But they are slowly realising, perhaps for the first time, that the dream that was sold to them no longer exists, at least not for them. The game they were bequeathed by their parents, a thing of romance and aspiration, has been sold off and converted into crypto.

"There will be no trophies. There will be no famous Champions League nights at Bramley-Moore Dock. You will not get to see the world's finest players in an Everton shirt. You do not even get the giddy underdog rise through the divisions like fans of Brighton or Brentford or Wigan. Your owner is a billionaire who will never speak to you or attend a game, and if he wants to run the ship aground there is not a damn thing you can do about it. No matter how loudly you sing, no matter how many blue smoke canisters you let off, the limit of your ambition will always be top seven and occasionally signing someone promising from Burnley. Or, to put it in terms with which Everton fans will perhaps be more familiar:

"THREE DECADES OF FINANCIAL STRATIFICATION, HAVE MADE IT HARDER TO FIND GRATIFICATION. A REVIVAL OF EVERTON'S SUCCESS ON THE PITCH, WILL FOREVER BE THWARTED BY THE SUPER-RICH."

***

21 January 2023: West Ham v Everton

By the third weekend in January 2023, the situation at Everton appeared bleak. Following the loss at home to Southampton - the club's 10th game without a win – the Toffees sat joint bottom of the Premier League with the Saints and West Ham, the much vaunted search for a striker having turned up empty with just 10 days left of the transfer window. Frank Lampard was the proverbial 'dead man walking.'

As if to underline the gravity of the situation and the vulnerability of the manager's position, the Board of Directors, absent from Goodison the previous weekend because of security concerns, were all in attendance at the London Stadium for another 'six-pointer', this time against the Hammers. Not only that, but so too was Farhad Moshiri, who hadn't watched an Everton game in the flesh since October 2021.

That, surely, was Lampard's last chance to turn a tide threatening to wash away the Toffees' proud 69-year unbroken membership of the top flight in a league where, theoretically, any team could beat another on its day... any team, it seemed, except this Everton one.

Unfortunately, against the Hammers, with his 'executioners' watching on, Lampard's men turned in the display of a side crippled by a lack of self-belief, overseen by a manager who looked incapable of instilling any confidence in them or changing a game to rescue a losing situation.

Frustratingly, if Everton had started the game with the relative tempo they showed in the second period, they might have preyed on the tangible nervousness among the West Ham faithful in the opening stages. Both teams appeared frightened by their own shadows, but the visitors were at least looking fairly comfortable on the ball.

But that dominance of possession lacked any urgency, with Amadou Onana, so effective and purposeful the previous week against Southampton, disappointingly hesitant to drive forward.

Everton might have had a penalty when Angelo Ogbonna appeared to handle a cross from Gray with a quarter of an hour gone, but neither the referee nor Video Assistant Referee, Andre Marriner, felt it was worthy of being penalised as an infringement.

However, the Hammers got the encouragement they needed to come out of their shells as the half progressed and the opening goal came 11 minutes before the interval. The ball was chipped back into the Everton box following a West Ham corner, Yerry Mina and Conor Coady got in each other's way and Jarrod Bowen was on hand and fractionally onside to knock Kurt Zouma's flick on past the keeper from close range.

1-0 became 2-0 three minutes before half-time when an attempted pass by Iwobi was cut out, the Hammers countered and Michail Antonio skipped past James Tarkowski's ill-advised lunge on the touchline. The burly striker centred past Coady and Bowen arrived to thump it home and claim his second goal of the afternoon.

Iwobi went very close to giving the visitors hope just before the interval, but his low drive took a decisive deflection off Declan Rice skidded wide off the outside of the post and Gueye's shot from 25 yards was tipped behind by Lukas Fabianski early in the second period.

Meanwhile, Pickford did superbly to turn Emerson's shot onto the crossbar in the 65th minute, and Nayef Aguerd headed over from the subsequent corner. Then Rice was inches away from making it 3-0 following a run down the left flank and a shot that just missed the far post.

Aston Villa's win at Southampton kept Everton from dropping to rock bottom in the division but without a win since October, no sign of one coming under the incumbent manager, and Lampard having now overseen the worst points return from the first 20 games of a season in Everton's history, his continued employment at the club seemed inconceivable.

Everton was a club gripped by apathy at the top, and agony and frustration among a helpless fanbase. But with things still so compressed at the bottom of the table, it was still not an irretrievable situation if the board acted decisively. A new managerial appointment would need time ahead of the visit of Arsenal, as well as help on the player recruitment side over the next 10 days.

The inevitable question was, 'who could do a better job than Lampard?' Sadly, with a run of results that now represented the worst record after 20 matches in the club's entire history, it became more a case of could anyone do any worse?

This Everton team looked bereft of everything apart from in goal — poorly coached with no confidence, no belief, no cohesion and no direction... except down.

Final score: West Ham 2-0 Everton

***

Afterwards, Farhad Moshiri and Bill Kenwright tried to beat a hasty retreat to their waiting cars outside the London Stadium but were intercepted by Gary Cotterill of *Sky Sports* who asked both men if Frank Lampard's time was finally up.

Neither could give the reporter a definitive answer but, perhaps suggesting that there would be better ways of delivering such news, the visibly harrowed chairman said: “It’s been a bad run of results for us all but, no, I would never say such a thing to you.” He added, it was “a bad time” for Everton and that “We just need to start winning games.”

Moshiri offered little more, except to say:

> “I can’t comment [on the question of whether Lampard would now be sacked]. It’s not my decision.”

The owner's response was taken by many as an indication that this would be a joint decision made by the Board, in concert with Director of Football, Kevin Thelwell, rather than a unilateral one made by Moshiri himself.

Less than two days later, 53 weeks after Rafael Benitez had been terminated, the axe fell again.

2023: LAMPARD SACKED. MOSHIRI PROMISES FANS A NEW STRIKER

> “Lampard’s departure marked a sad end to a managerial tenure that held so much promise in its early days, and which reached its peak on an emotional night at Goodison in May 2022 when the Toffees secured their Premier League survival with the stunning come-from-behind win over Crystal Palace.

2023 Lampard sacked. Moshiri promises fans a new striker

Two days after the West Ham defeat, and in a decision made unanimously by Farhad Moshiri and the club's Board of Directors, Everton dismissed Frank Lampard from his position as head coach, less than a year into the role following a string of defeats and the club sitting in the relegation zone.

The 44-year-old had overseen just three Premier League wins all season, the worst 20-game sequence of results to start a season in the club’s history, and failed to progress past the third round of either domestic cup competition.

Lampard's departure marked a sad end to a managerial tenure that held so much promise in its early days, and which reached its peak on an emotional night at Goodison in May 2022 when the Toffees secured their Premier League survival with the stunning come-from-behind win over Crystal Palace.

Fans had commended the former Derby County and Chelsea manager for the way he had tapped into the passion of the Everton faithful, and there had been high hopes that he could continue to develop not only his management skills but also the Blues' squad over the course of what was to be his first full season in charge.

However, having lost his best player, when Richarlison was sold to Tottenham Hotspur, Lampard was dealt another cruel blow just three days before the start of the 2022/23 campaign when Dominic Calvert-Lewin, a big miss for much of the previous season, suffered another serious injury and wasn't really able to recover full fitness for the entire season.

The failure on the club's part not to sign a reliable goal scorer of Calvert-Lewin's ilk, acquiring instead Neal Maupay from Brighton, further hampered the manager's attempts to build a winning side, even as it appeared he was making progress when Palace returned to Goodison Park in October and were swept aside with an impressive display that yielded a 3-0 win for Everton.

That was the last time Everton won under his stewardship and over the ensuing three months the club dropped from 12th place to 19th, with games running out to mount another great escape and avoid what would be a catastrophic drop into the Championship.

Everton would embark on the search for their eighth managerial appointment in ten years, and in the end, it came down to a choice between two wildly different candidates.

***

It would be a week until Everton unveiled the seventh managerial appointment of Farhad Moshiri's reign. In the meanwhile, a transfer window that, in the context of the desperate need for a reliable goal scorer, many fans had regarded as being potentially the most important in the club's history, was entering its final week without the Blues having signed anyone.

With the anticipated arrival of Arnaut Danjuma, on loan from Villarreal until the end of the season, it looked as though Kevin Thelwell had landed a player capable of providing much-needed attacking threat to a team that had scored just 15 times in 20 games.

However, having agreed personal terms, undergone a medical and completed most of the media duties associated with the unveiling of a new signing, a delay in the arrival of the paperwork from the Spanish club's end gave the Dutchman enough time to rethink his decision. In a stunning, last-minute U-turn, he opted instead to sign for Tottenham Hotspur.

***

On the same day, Everton released a video interview with Farhad Moshiri conducted by Jazz Bal, chair of the Fan Advisory Board, to address some of the key questions posed to that body by supporters. The discussion produced two headlines – first, that the owner promised in no uncertain terms that the club would sign a striker before the transfer deadline on 31 January; and second, his insistence that the club was not for sale but that he had been talking to top investors to bridge the funding gap on the stadium.

"I can't do it myself," Moshiri said. He added, "I want to bring top sports investors into Everton [to provide] more talent, and we are close to having a deal done. It's not selling the club at all, it's just bringing more expertise in terms of global sponsorship and commercial development."

Given that the interview had been recorded a week earlier, it was likely that Moshiri's confidence in making a striker signing was based on the positive discussions with the representatives of Danjuma and that player's willingness to sign.

The winger's *volte face* before heading for North London sparked a scramble in the transfer market to land either a centre-forward or a goal scoring, attacking wide player before the window closed. It proved fruitless. To the utter dismay of their supporters, Everton failed to bring in a single new face that January, leaving whoever was to take over from Frank Lampard worryingly short on firepower.

2023: Sean Dyche wins the two horse race

> "I know about Everton's passionate fanbase and how precious this club is to them. We're ready to work and ready to give them what they want. That starts with sweat on the shirt, effort and getting back to some of the basic principles of what Everton Football Club has stood for over a long time.
>
> \- Sean Dyche

2023 Sean Dyche wins the two horse race

Although the bookmakers and sports writers had reeled off a number of potential candidates to fill the void left by Frank Lampard's sacking, it quickly became apparent that the club had narrowed the search down to just two options with vastly differing styles – Argentine maverick, Marcelo Bielsa, and former Burnley boss, Sean Dyche.

On 26 January, it was reported Marcelo Bielsa had jetted in to England to hold talks with Everton, with the Board hoping to make an appointment by the end of the week.

Bielsa had been dismissed by Leeds almost a year previously after four years in charge at Elland Road, where he had become a folk hero for engineering the Yorkshire club's return to the Premier League following a 16-year absence.

Early newspaper reports suggested the Argentinian was 'warming' to the prospect of taking on the Everton project. For his part, Dyche who had been out of work for a similar period, was said to be enthusiastic about the opportunity, even if it was on a short-term basis, just to keep Everton in the top flight.

It was widely believed Bielsa was the first choice of majority shareholder, Farhad Moshiri, but the former Leeds manager was famous for preferring to take new jobs in the summer, so that he could get the benefit of a full pre-season to bed in his methods and playing style.

According to reports, he proposed to Everton that he and his eight-person support staff take charge of the Under-21s for the rest of the season and then he would become first-team head coach at the end of the season.

That plan was unworkable, leaving Moshiri and the Board of Directors to turn to Dyche as the alternative, a safe pair of hands hopefully to guide the team to safety over the remaining 18 games of the season.

With Bielsa turning down the opportunity to take the first team reins with immediate effect, Everton finally confirmed Dyche as Lampard's replacement on 27 January 2023.

The 51-year-old signed a two-and-a-half-year deal and brought former Everton youth player Ian Woan in as his Assistant Manager, ex-England international Steve Stone as First-Team Coach, and Mark Howard to provide additional sports science expertise.

Dyche had been out of work since leaving Turf Moor, after a decade in charge of the Clarets. During his time at Burnley, he led them to European qualification in 2017/18, but was dismissed in April 2022 by new owners with the club heading for the Championship.

Burnley, under Dyche's long-term replacement, Vincent Kompany, were the runaway leaders of the second tier and on course to return to the top flight, whereas Everton's new boss was charged with making sure the Blues didn't pass them on the way down.

Dyche took over with the Blues on a run of just one win in 14 games and sitting joint-bottom of the Premier League. He faced a baptism of fire with clashes against leaders Arsenal and local rivals, Liverpool, in his first two matches.

"It's an honour to become Everton manager. My staff and I are ready and eager to help get this great club back on track," Dyche said on joining the club.

"I know about Everton's passionate fanbase and how precious this club is to them. We're ready to work and ready to give them what they want. That starts with sweat on the shirt, effort and getting back to some of the basic principles of what Everton Football Club has stood for over a long time.

"We want to bring back a good feeling. We need the fans, we need unity and we need everyone aligned. That starts with us as staff and players.

"Our aim is to put out a team that works, that fights and wears the badge with pride. The connection with the fans can then grow very quickly because they're so passionate."

***

If Sean Dyche had been promised any reinforcements to the squad, come transfer deadline day on 31 January, he must have privately felt as aghast as the fans when the club finished the day empty-handed.

Many Everton fans had billed it as potentially the most important transfer window in the club's history, but the club finished January weaker than before. Despite selling Anthony Gordon, Everton failed to make a single signing, while the teams struggling with them in the lower reaches of the Premier League table all strengthened their squads.

Somewhat gallingly, fellow strugglers Southampton ended up beating Everton to Stade Rennais winger Kamaldeen Sulemana, with the player ultimately plumping for St Mary's over Goodison Park after both clubs had bids of around £22 million accepted.

Links of varying veracity for the like of Genk striker Paul Onuachu, who also went to Southampton, Udinese striker Beto, Fenerbahçe's Michy Batshuayi and Manchester United's Anthony Elanga all came to nothing, on what was a damp squib of a transfer deadline day.

When the transfer deadline passed, the Blues were the only club in the top flight not to sign at least one player since the turn of the year, a staggering failing that left new manager Sean Dyche desperately short of creativity in the wide areas and goal scoring threat up front.

Only Wolves had scored fewer goals than Everton to that point in the season, but Dyche would have to engineer them from places that his predecessor Frank Lampard could not, and he would have to do it without the club's joint-top scorer, Anthony Gordon, who, like Richarlison before him, was sold without being replaced.

***

4 February 2023: Everton v Arsenal

The winds of change blew through Goodison Park again — not in the Boardroom, of course; but on that score, protest was in the air. Yet, so too was defiance and a refusal by almost 40,000 Evertonians to let their club sink without a fight. Sean Dyche took his place in Everton's dugout (or, more accurately, the touchline where, in contrast to his more passive predecessor, he was a constantly animated and vocal presence) for the first time. There he oversaw one of those electrifying home wins over a superior foe, amid an atmosphere that vanquishes visiting teams regardless of their talent and standing.

Likely needing at least seven more wins to stay up, this was one of the most difficult of Everton's remaining assignments in 2022/23. Arsenal, unbeaten in the Premier League since September under Mikel Arteta, were an excellent side. Yet there were precious few moments during the 90 minutes where they could exhibit their quality. They had just three shots on target and only one of them, a powerful drive from substitute Leandro Trossard 12 minutes from time, really tested Jordan Pickford.

Another effort from Bukayo Saka in the first half, might well have gone in on another day, but this time, the positioning of Conor Coady, rejuvenated and inspired along with the rest of the Blues' team in a highly organised 4-5-1 formation, was exemplary and he cleared his England squad-mate's volley off the line.

Eddie Nketiah and Martin Ødegaard wasted the other couple of decent chances that fell Arsenal's way, but the best opportunities came at the other end and had Everton won by two or three goals, Arteta probably couldn't have had many complaints. They might have done had Abdoulaye Doucouré and Dominic Calvert-Lewin not spurned excellent headed chances in the latter stages of the first half, but James Tarkowski's first goal for the Toffees, fittingly enough scored under the coach who really made him as a player, was all that was needed.

This was a day reminiscent of the first game Duncan Ferguson oversaw in December 2019 against Chelsea — a high-octane, determined and feisty display that leveraged the power and tenacity in the squad together with that legendary 12th man in the stands. On a day which saw thousands of Blues march from the Royal Oak, up Spellow Lane and around the Grand Old Lady before kick-off-time, fears that the demonstrations against the club's hierarchy would detract from support for the team proved unfounded, as the fans raised the roof once more to roar home three points.

The decisive goal came right on the hour mark. Everton won a corner on their right,

McNeil swung it in and Tarkowski muscled his way past Martin Ødergaard to meet it and guide a header back across goal past Ramsdale before wheeling away in celebration of his first goal for the Toffees.

Arsenal had howls for a penalty waved away not long afterwards and Leandro Trossard stung Pickford's palms with that strong shot that was beaten away and cleared before the Belgian missed the target with a curling attempt a few minutes later.

The Gunners were increasingly desperate by the end and were finding their hosts hard to break down. They would have just one more chance to salvage a point in stoppage time, but Oleksandr Zinchenko blasted it over the bar. And then, mercifully, it was over after six minutes of injury time, the referee's whistle triggering relief and celebration in the stands.

This wasn't quintessential Dyche-ball, as his reputation had, perhaps unfairly, painted him at Burnley. Yes, the Blues went direct when they needed and the deciding goal came off a set-piece but the new boss had clearly set out to put legs in midfield and marry the technical ability and speed over the ground that existed in the team with its physicality and aerial ability.

When combined with a disciplined shape and an effective mid-block without the ball, it's a formula that would stand him in very good stead.

Dyche was right, however, when he stressed in his post-match comments that this result is just a start. Wolves's win over Liverpool and West Ham's strong performance at Newcastle illustrated how difficult the fight was going to be at the bottom over the rest of the season.

It was going to take eight more performances of high effort and concentration at Goodison and some vastly improved results away from home if survival was to be achieved, but this win over the worthy League leaders definitely pointed the way.

Final score: Everton 1-0 Arsenal

***

18 February 2023: Everton v Leeds United

After the disappointment of a 2-0 away defeat in the Merseyside derby in a Monday night game at Anfield on 13 February, Sean Dyche registered his second successive home win as Everton manager, and the Blues lifted themselves out of the bottom three thanks to Seamus Coleman's stunning second-half strike against Leeds at Goodison Park.

Everton were the better side on the day but frequently let themselves down in final third, although Illan Meslier had to be at his best to deny James Tarkowski a first-half opener from a corner, Max Wöber headed out from under his own bar from Conor Coady, Weston McKennie cleared a Neal Maupay header off the line, and Abdoulaye Doucouré made a mess of a gilt-edged chance to put the game to bed at the end.

Leeds failed to test Jordan Pickford in the Blues' goal despite being gifted several chances to put the hosts' back line under pressure in the latter stages of the game.

Everton, by contrast, made most of the early running, with Amadou Onana and Idrissa Gueye missing the target, Vitalii Mykolenko seeing appeals for a penalty waved away and James Tarkowski testing the keeper Meslier with a header from a corner.

Then, in the second half, Neal Maupay failed to work the goalkeeper with a shot on the turn eight and Mykolenko had another effort comfortably saved before Coleman broke the deadlock in stunning fashion.

Iwobi chipped the ball over the last defender down the right flank to find the skipper's run and with no blue shirts gambling in the centre, Coleman appeared to chance his luck by going for goal from an almost impossible position, the ball arrowing behind the keeper and inside the far post to light up what had been a nervy Goodison Park.

An increasingly desperate Leeds side pegged Everton back after that but the Yorkshiremen weren't able to muster a decent goal scoring chance while Everton really should have killed the game in the 88th minute.

Ellis Simms, on for Maupay, did superbly to loft the ball over the top for Abdoulaye Doucouré to gallop towards the Leeds box but rather than gamble with a left-foot shot, he tried to bring it back into his right and it ended up getting caught under his feet before it was hacked clear.

Though there were wins for all three teams that had begun the day in the bottom three of the Premier League for the first time in eight years, this win vaulted the Toffees out of the relegation zone and into 16th place.

Final score: Everton 1-0 Leeds

***

After the match, Seamus Coleman said he probably wouldn't be able to replicate too often the brilliant finish that had settled the game, but he acknowledged how important it was.

"I knew that there was no one in the box and I presumed the keeper would anticipate that maybe a cross would come in and he would maybe go half a yard and I just tried to hit the target.

"Listen, I could do that 20 more times, 30 more times and I wouldn't hit it as sweet, so, thankfully, for me and the team, it went in."

"[The game] was very high stakes," the Irishman admitted. "You try and play it down as best you can before the game and see it as just 90 minutes of trying to be better than the opposition but in the back of your mind you're aware of how big the game would've been if Leeds had've won; they pull away a little bit.

"You could feel that in the stadium, but the fans were right behind us in every tackle, every ball we had to chase into a corner — they were so loud so they played a massive part in this."

Asked how difficult it is to keep your nerve when there is so much riding on the outcome of the game, Coleman said:

"It's tough; there's no getting away from it but you have to do the right things. You know, we've been stung a few times here at Goodison, where it's been 0-0 and we're trying to push for the first goal and we get stung on the counter-attack.

"So we're starting to learn a little bit from that and the manager's done a lot of work with us on that as well. So to get the goal and hold out was important, but there's no getting away from it — there were plenty of nervy moments."

***

11 March 2023: Everton v Brentford

Sean Dyche could not work his magic in the next home game against Aston Villa, where the Blues suffered a disappointing 2-0 defeat which dumped them back in the relegation places. That was followed by a 4-0 thrashing away at Arsenal, and a 2-2 draw away at Nottingham Forest, results which still left Everton 18th in the league a third of the way into March.

Every game was becoming a 'must win' and the tension around Goodison before the match when Brentford came to town was palpable.

The Bees had not lost in 12 Premier League matches coming into the weekend and had their eyes on an unlikely European qualification place but, though they showed why they have been such difficult opposition in what became an increasingly panicked second half from the Toffees' perspective, Dyche's men held firm.

Everton had set themselves on their way to what was a vital victory when Dwight McNeil put them ahead with just 35 seconds on the clock and they could have been out of sight by half time had David Raya not made two smart saves and Video Assistant Referee, David Coote, not scandalously overturned a Demarai Gray goal that would have made it 2-0 at the break.

It was the perfect start for Dyche's men, however, as they broke up a Brentford attack from kick-off and launched the ball forward quickly, with Alex Iwobi slipping it inside to Abdoulaye Doucouré, who moved it on to McNeil, approaching the opposition box.

The winger, reborn under his former manager at Burnley, exhibited close control before firing a crisp shot across Raya and into the far corner. It was a lovely finish,

Michael Keane headed a fine a chance wide, Amadou Onana spurned a gilt-edged opportunity, side-footing disappointingly wide from Iwobi's fizzed cross from the byline and Demarai Gray aimed a shot inside Raya's near post, but the goalie did well to divert it wide with an out-stretched leg. From the ensuing corner, Iwobi must have thought he had scored from just a couple of yards out, but Raya was there again to save with his foot and Onana mis-kicked the rebound wide.

Meanwhile, Bryan Mbeumo forced a first save from Pickford in the 24th minute that the England keeper initially spilled, but then gathered at the second attempt; while Ivan Toney was inches away from equalising with a header from a cross from the Bees' right a minute later.

The second goal that the Blues were so keen to get looked to have arrived three minutes before half-time when Keane headed a free-kick it into the area. Ethan Pinnock hooked the ball off the line but only into Gray's chest and it ricocheted into the net. The referee, Simon Hooper, allowed the goal to stand, but after taking a long look at an inconclusive replay, Coote on VAR overruled Simon Hooper's decision on the field and ruled it out.

If Dyche had hoped his men could keep the initiative and try to pad their lead in the second half, he would be disappointed. Brentford, spurred on by the much-lauded Thomas Frank, seized control of the contest almost from the restart.

However, the Toffees kept them at bay, with Coleman making a vital block from point-blank range to deny Rico Henry, McNeil rescuing Pickford after he had made a mess of coming for a resulting corner by whacking the ball off his goal line, and Raya coming forward for a corner in stoppage time, only to plant a header well off target.

The win, combined with defeats for Nottingham Forest and Leicester and Leeds United's home draw with Brighton lifted Everton out of the bottom three and into 15th place for the time being, and offered hope once more that they had enough to win their battle to avoid relegation for a second season running.

Final score: Everton 1-0 Brentford

2023: The Cult of Bill

> “[Kenwright] owns only 1.3 per cent of the club these days. Everton is - theoretically at least - under the control of the British-Iranian businessman Farhad Moshiri whose company Blue Heaven Holdings owns 94.1 per cent. But Kenwright remains front and central, for better and for worse.
>
> - Ian Ladyman, Daily Mail

2023 The Cult of Bill

With Everton Football Club on its knees following one close call with relegation in 2021/22, with another one looming in 2022/23, and forced into extreme austerity as the largesse and mis-steps of the Moshiri years started to bite, supporters had started to demand both accountability and change – in the Boardroom at first, but increasingly at the ownership level as well.

In line with the feeling in general that the club needed an injection of fresh ideas and genuine corporate, commercial and footballing expertise, the clamour for long-serving Chairman Bill Kenwright to either stand down or be moved aside by Moshiri was growing beyond a disaffected and vocal few in the fanbase.

Writing in the *Daily Mail* at the end of January, with Kenwright and the rest of the Directors in self-imposed exile from home matches and in the period of uncertainty between the sacking of Frank Lampard and the appointment of Sean Dyche, Ian Ladyman pulled few punches in describing what one insider at another club labelled the 'Cult of Bill':

> "He owns only 1.3 per cent of the club these days. Everton is – theoretically at least – under the control of the British-Iranian businessman Farhad Moshiri whose company Blue Heaven Holdings owns 94.1 per cent. But Kenwright remains front and central, for better and for worse. Given the stress and the heartache, why is he still putting himself through it for the sake of what is essentially someone else's football club? 'I asked him this at a game not long ago,' one senior executive at another big club tells *Sportsmail*. 'Usually, he just laughs and ducks it. But this time I pressed him and he just said it was impossible for him not to still care.'

> "[S]even years after the sale and with the club once-again managerless following the sacking of Frank Lampard, Kenwright, according to those who

> know him, continues to believe that Everton would simply sink on Moshiri's solo watch.' Bill has a belief perhaps bordering on arrogance that he can still save the club from itself', said one long-term ally. 'Farhad likes big gestures. He can be impetuous. Bill thinks he needs to be there to temper them and gets frustrated that fans can't see this. Some think Bill feels guilty, that he feels he sold to the wrong person. I haven't heard him say that. He does have an insane love for the club but also for the limelight, even when that focus is bad. He loves the glory of being in the middle of a grand old football club, even one as broken and divided as this one. It's like a drug to him but it's one he needs to kick for his own sake. '

> "'It's very much the Cult of Bill,' one Premier League chief executive tells *Sportsmail*. 'And it's the same when they come to us to be fair. But in a nice way. At many Premier League clubs it's hard to recognise anyone in the boardroom but it's not like that at Everton. It's like the old days and there is something to be said for that.'"

The insight in Ladyman's article came from the quotes from figures within the game and those close to the Chairman himself, and they exposed the confusing internal structure that existed at Everton thanks to the competing forces of Kenwright's acolytes and Moshiri's faction, which routinely affected everything from player recruitment and transfer negotiations to selecting the club's next manager.

Ladyman's piece also revealed Moshiri's inability or reluctance to hire his own people in place to run the club, as well as Kenwright's fear that if he didn't remain actively involved, the whole thing would fall apart. As things turned out, they almost did, despite his best efforts.

***

Around the same time, in January 2023, another figure seen as controversial by some elements within the fanbase took the opportunity to publicly deny having an out-sized influence on Farhad Moshiri when it came to player recruitment and even managerial candidates.

Using the same platform deployed by the Everton owner to defend himself, infamous player agent and facilitator Kia Joorabchian said on a call with Simon Jordan and Jim White on *TalkSport*, that his relationship with the Blues formed only a small part of what he and his operation did.

Rumoured to have been behind the push to sign Alex Iwobi from Arsenal at the eleventh hour on transfer deadline day and other less successful moves like the loan of Anwar El Ghazi from Aston Villa in the winter transfer window of 2022, Joorabchian's name had become synonymous with the meddling in transfers and controversial managerial appointments at Everton because of his close relationship with fellow Iranian, Moshiri.

The unease among supporters surrounding his influence over Moshiri had peaked in January 2022 when he recommended his client

Vitor Pereira for the vacant head coach role following the sacking of Rafael Benitez, but under a more collegiate decision-making process, Frank Lampard was chosen.

Joorabchian confirmed to Jordan and White that he had put Pereira's name forward for the Everton job but suggested that CEO Denise Barrett-Baxendale had been influential in pushing for Lampard instead.

He admitted that Anwar El Ghazi had been his doing but also claimed to have suggested players like Bruno Guimaraes and Militao to the club before they were expensive targets and Everton passed on them.

Whatever the truth of the matter, Joorabchian largely melted out of the picture from that point on, and stood to have any influence reduced to almost nothing were Moshiri to be successful in selling Everton.

2023: Blues' accounts reveal 'Going Concern' bombshell

2023 Blues' Accounts reveal 'Going Concern' bombshell

Everton's financial position vis-à-vis Profitability and Sustainability rules had been a concern of the Premier League's since the end of the 2020/21 season, a time when clubs in England's top flight were beginning to recover from the effects of COVID-19 and to assess the impact the pandemic had had on their operations and bottom line.

To that end, the Blues had been required to maintain ongoing dialogue with the League regarding the club's finances, and all of their transfer business was subject to oversight, starting with the summer

2021 transfer window. From then on, Everton had operated on an austere sell-to-buy basis while also working hard to structure incoming transfer deals with small up-front payments and the fees spread over the lifetime of the players' contracts wherever possible.

The enforced pivot away from what had been a period of significant outlay on player transfers and salaries in the first five years since Farhad Moshiri had arrived on the scene at Everton had the effect of significantly trimming Everton's losses in the annual accounts for the 2021/22 financial year which were finally released on 31 March, 2023.

The report showed revenue of £181 million and losses totalling £44.7 million, a £76 million improvement on the previous year, but the club's cumulative three-year losses were in excess of £305 million and net debt had increased to £141.7 million.

The biggest outlay had been on construction costs at the new Everton Stadium at Bramley-Moore Dock, which topped £200 million, and £10.5 million was attributed in the accounts to compensation to former manager Rafael Benitez and his staff following his dismissal in January 2022.

However, player acquisitions like those of Nathan Patterson from Rangers and Vitalii Mykolenko from Dynamo Kiev in January 2022 were offset by the sale of Lucas Digne to Aston Villa that month and Richarlison to Tottenham Hotspur in June, while high-earning players like Bernard and James Rodriguez were also moved on.

The club attributed £90 million in crystallised losses and further unspecified 'uncrystallised' losses (for example, unrealised revenue from player trading that was affected by the pandemic lockdown) to the COVID-19 pandemic, the latter of which had been a major point of contention from rival clubs.

The statements from the club in the accounts revealed, however, the extent to which Everton FC still relied on Moshiri's willingness to cover its losses and they contained the bombshell revelation that the club's very survival might be at risk in the event of relegation from the Premier League, should the owner not cover the shortfall.

"Despite the substantial financial impact of several unexpected and unprecedented factors in recent seasons, the club remains in a secure financial position thanks to the continued support and commitment of our majority shareholder," a statement in the accounts read.

It was clear the club had become entirely dependent on Farhad Moshiri's own finances. The key question was, with Alisher Usmanov now barred from sponsoring the club, for how much longer would Farhad Moshiri continue to pump cash into his failed project?

Such was the uncertainty, the auditors insisted the Everton Board include this alarming statement in their annual report and accounts:

> "**GOING CONCERN:** As outlined in detail in the notes to the financial statements, the Directors recognise that there is uncertainty attached to the timing and quantum of the anticipated revenue levels, cost savings and the future funding required by the Group over the forecast period in a relegation scenario. Efforts are currently underway to secure funding as referenced in the Directors' report. If the assumptions in the relegation scenario were not achieved, then the Group would have to seek further funding from its majority shareholder. They have provided a letter of support confirming ongoing financial support will

> be provided to the Group but this letter does not represent a legally binding commitment. Collectively, the above conditions indicate the existence of a material uncertainty that may cast significant doubt about the group's ability to continue as a going concern." - Everton Football Club Report and Accounts 2021/22

In other words, if Everton was going down into the Championship, it may also lead to the club being plunged into administration. As time would tell, Farhad Moshiri's written commitment to provide the club with ongoing financial support would prove to be worthless.

2023: EVERTON REFERRED BY PREMIER LEAGUE TO 'INDEPENDENT COMMISSION'

When Everton's annual accounts for 2020/21 were published in 2022, showing further losses of £120 million, it had prompted Leeds United and Burnley to write a joint letter to the Premier League requesting that an independent commission be established to investigate Everton's finances, and threatening legal action should the Blues be found to have breached Profitability and Sustainability Rules.

Everton had responded with a statement insisting they were in compliance with the PSR rules, a claim that was bolstered by the revelation that at two separate Premier League shareholders' meetings, first in March 2022 and then again that summer, it was stated that the club had no case to answer.

"We have worked so closely with the Premier League to make sure we are compliant. We are comfortable we have complied with the rules," the correspondence from the Royal Liver Building read. "External auditors have told us what we can and cannot claim against the pandemic. If they want to take legal action then they can do so by all means."

So, it was to Everton's shock in late March 2023 when it emerged that the Premier League had referred the club to an independent panel after all, charging them with breaching PSR rules during the 2021/22 season. Meanwhile, some executives at other top-flight clubs were uneasy at the apparent U-turn by the governing body which some felt might have been was politically motivated — Premier League CEO Richard Masters was set to go before a Parliamentary hearing on sports governance where the Government would push for an independent regulator to oversee English football — while others were asking why, if the Toffees had broken the rules, had the matter not been dealt with in the summer of 2022?

"The Everton charge is very surprising," one Premier League executive told *The Mail On Sunday* at the time. "We sat in front of the Premier League around March last year and they categorically told us there was no case to answer.

"Then, in the summer, we were told Everton could sign players as they were working together with the League to stay the right side of the line, and their COVID losses made them compliant.

"The Premier League made these points in open meetings and also held private meetings with individual clubs who had expressed concerns."

With the Premier League's charge having no precedent and the exact nature of the infraction undisclosed, the football world was left to speculate about all aspects of the commission. Initially, there were no details of when the hearing would take place — preliminary estimates ranged from six months to a year and a half — who would make up the panel, or how long they would take to reach a decision, while potential penalties ranged from a fine or more official transfer embargo to a points penalty or even expulsion. The fact that the League had charged Manchester City with no fewer than 115 counts relating to their own commercial dealings, and the reporting thereof, simply added another dimension to the potential ramifications of the commission's ruling.

As the season reached it's final month, external criticism of the Everton owner and board was piling in from all directions and pressure was mounting from those clubs embroiled with them in the battle to avoid relegation for the situation to be resolved before the end of the season.

Some contested newspaper reports claimed that Leeds United, Leicester City, Nottingham Forest, Southampton and Burnley all believed they were entitled to compensation from Everton should the club be found guilty, and that they were preparing to sue the club for damages if Everton stayed up.

At the very least, the clubs concerned asked that the Premier League ensure the work of the independent commission be completed before the end of the 2022/23 season so that any sanctions could apply to the ongoing relegation battle, particularly where a points deduction was concerned.

However, the League had to inform them that they were powerless to bring forward the verdict of the commission as they had no say in how swiftly the review process would be completed.

As it turned out, the panel wouldn't meet until October that year and Everton would go into the 2023/24 season with the threat of an unknown punishment still hanging over their heads.

2023: Chairman Bill's letter

> “Putting your chairman on a bed sheet in a distasteful way is something that, although it hurts, I have to get used to but...Grant and Sharpy?!?! On banners?!?!
>
> - Bill Kenwright
>
> **2023 Chairman Bill's letter**

When Bill Kenwright's decade-long search for a billionaire benefactor to bankroll Everton's return to the elite of English football came to a seemingly successful conclusion with the arrival of Farhad Moshiri in February 2016, there was a school of thought that it might provide a watershed moment where the theatre impresario could begin to step aside after 12 years as chairman.

Though he had only been a major shareholder at the time, with a 49.9% stake, Moshiri's stated aim back in 2016 was to eventually increase his investment in the club. That would then provide him the opportunity to overhaul the club's leadership with fresh faces, new ideas and commercial acumen.

The British-Iranian businessman opted, instead, for continuity and a heavy emphasis on local influence, with Kenwright remaining in his post to offer his experience of running a Premier League club, even as his shareholding eventually dwindled to less than 2%. Moshiri, meanwhile, would resist taking a place in the boardroom himself until June 2023, almost two years after his representative on the Board, Sasha Ryazantsev had left the club.

Over time, however, as the progress promised by the new regime stalled, both on and off the pitch, confusion over just who was making the big decisions became a source of frustration for a growing contingent among the fanbase.

The agitation for change in the boardroom that had begun in earnest in December 2021, when it became clear that Rafael Benitez's tenure as manager was destined for failure, and it would build over the following 18 months as the Blues struggled to avoid relegation to the Championship. Fans began by imploring Moshiri to make personnel changes to the Board of Directors that could inject fresh blood and demonstrable expertise in business, commerce and top-level football into the club. By the turn of 2023, however, as Everton's situation in the Premier League became more perilous and a second successive fight for survival ensued under another failed head-coaching appointment in Frank Lampard, the clamour was now for a wholesale clear-out of the hierarchy.

That meant calls for removal of all the existing directors, including CEO Denise Barrett-Baxendale, Finance Director Grant Ingles, Non-Executive Director and playing legend Graeme Sharp, and

Chairman Kenwright himself, who had become a lightning rod for criticism from the most vocal opponents to the status quo at Everton.

Either a meddlesome and reactionary presence, a necessary check on Moshiri's more destructive impulses, or something in between, depending on which fans you asked, "Blue Bill" was seen by many as someone who would robustly defend his record without taking personal responsibility for the club's failings.

By January 2023. of course, Kenwright had been self-exiled from the Directors Box, with the members of the Board opting not attend home games, and he used the forum of the club's 2021/22 accounts to express his "pain" at not being able to attend Goodison Park.

In his Chairman's Statement at the front of the annual reports and accounts, he wrote:

"I may have been castigated by some fans for sharing my opinion, but I have enjoyed many [good?] times at Everton, and even though we have sadly been trophyless under my Chairmanship, it is with no fear of further criticism when I say two league games from last season's 38 will stay with me forever.

"Do I have to say more than that night against Crystal Palace? While the afternoon I stood alone in the stand at Leicester City after a monumental away, when listening to our outstanding travelling supporters, sing passionately and enthusiastically — for a full 20 minutes after the game had ended!! — was inspiring, humbling and genuinely moving.

"Memories of occasions like these have made the recent instruction given to myself and my fellow board members not to attend Goodison Park all the more painful that has hurt deeply.

"Looking forward, we know we have challenges to overcome. The absolute priority is, of course, to secure our Premier League status for a 70th consecutive season and we can all play a part in helping to secure that.

"As we proved in the run-in to last season, a unified football club is a stronger football club."

***

That unity would continue to prove elusive, however, and in April, the supporters movement going by the social media tag #AllTogetherNow, penned on open letter in which they reiterated their call and that of the 27 Campaign (now known as NSNOW) for the removal of the club's Board of Directors.

In their announcement, #AllTogetherNow said that the protests, staged before each home game since the turn of 2023, calling for wholesale change in the Boardroom, would cease if Moshiri confirmed that changes would occur in the running of the club.

Somewhat controversially, the movement's letter made mention of Kenwright's well-documented ill-health over the preceding few years as being a potential impediment to his running of the club, and this was addressed directly by the chairman in his own public response in which he defended the calibre of the Board's individual members.

In a highly personal letter, posted on the club's official website, Kenwright stressed that running the club in the competitive environment of the Premier League was difficult, as was securing the funding for Everton's new stadium at Bramley-Moore Dock.

He also dismissed the notion the club would be better off without the current board in place, when he wrote:

"Dear #Alltogethernow,

"I have read your letter to the Club. Firstly, can I thank you for your care and concern regarding my health. You may well know that in April 2015, I was advised I had a chronic illness that would probably be with me for the duration. This is, pretty inevitably, only the start of a journey where the issues usually increase. And they have. What you may also know is that most people find a spirit that will not give in and hopefully not be beaten. Sometimes it's not easy but there are many worse off than me.

"If I may, I will take this opportunity to address a couple of points from the rest of your letter. The Chairman does not run the football club. We have a Chief Executive Officer who does that, as is true with most clubs. In the eyes of most of the football world, Denise is amongst the best of the best. The truth is she has to be to deal with what every other Premier League club copes with in a hugely competitive environment in addition to the problems that the world has thrown at us over the last three years and, closer to home, in the last year or so. You may think it is not a massive challenge to relentlessly push forward the new stadium currently taking shape on the waterfront. I promise you it is! Financiers amongst your group will tell you why.

"You write that 'The rumours tell you from 'well placed and trustworthy sources' that investment is imminent.' Right now, that could be half right, a quarter right...etc. But that has been the situation for some time now. Again, those of you that know about raising hundreds of millions in investment will tell you it's a relentless journey where hopes are built and squashed in a heartbeat. But it's a quest that we undertake relentlessly and we will succeed. We are succeeding. Farhad and myself are on it hourly ... along with the Board and its advisors.

"For what you believe to be the best interests of the Club you are committed to the removal of this Board. As you've shown. For me, the horror of seeing Grant Ingles, our Chief Financial Officer, and Graeme Sharp being attacked is more than difficult to comprehend. Putting your chairman on a bed sheet in a distasteful way is something that, although it hurts, I have to get used to but...Grant and Sharpy?!?! On banners?!?! The short window you refer to will, you infer, be helped by the removal of your Board. Have you ever pondered whether your manager and players would agree with that? Whether Frank would have rubbed his hands with glee last year at the thought, rather than rushing to the Directors' Box to acknowledge where his biggest support had come from? And what about other clubs around us? Are they thinking 'the Everton Board has gone... it's going to be easier for us now!!!?' I'm confident of the answer to each of those questions. Finally, there is one indisputable fact. Your Board cares. It's not nice going through what we have gone through but it hasn't stopped the work rate, the desire to grow and improve and the loyalty to this Club and to Evertonians.

"I've often said that I would never deny the right of protest to any football fan, especially Evertonians. I know, inevitably, your day will of course come. Just as I knew that I would find you a billionaire when the loud and long protests claimed I wasn't even looking. In the meantime, I thank you again for worrying about my health problems. In truth, a week off would be great...but I can't see it happening...as it hasn't for many years. I wish you what I have wished every Evertonian since I joined the Blue Family nearly seven decades ago…a happy weekend…the season end we all hope for…and a return to better days thereafter."

Chairman Bill

***

It took just two days for the #AllTogetherNow Campaign to deliver a return salvo in what was becoming a public war of words with Kenwright, reiterating their calls for the Everton chairman to stand down.

Both the tone and the timing of the chairman's letter, coming as it did on the eve of an important match against Crystal Palace, were criticised by sections of the fanbase and in their follow-up, #AllTogetherNow cited Kenwright's response as further evidence of his unsuitability to the role he fulfilled at the club.

They pointed to Everton's desperate fight for survival in the Premier League as an indictment of the Board's failings and, describing his position as "untenable", they suggested he would never be able to restore the fans' faith in his ability to lead the club.

At that point, Everton sat in the bottom three of the Premier League with six games to go in the season, in danger of losing their top-flight status for the first time in 72 years. And, if that were to happen, the club's directors had confirmed just three weeks earlier that if the club was relegated, there was "material uncertainty about [its] ability to continue as a going concern."

Besides the Campaign's response to Kenwright, they took the decision to call off the scheduled protest before the potentially massive home game with Newcastle United on 27 April, and instead asked supporters to "stand shoulder to shoulder" to welcome the team outside Goodison Park.

#AllTogetherNow's second release followed statements issued on social media by both the Everton Fan Advisory Board and the Everton Fans' Forum expressing their disappointment with Kenwright's decision to release his letter at a time of distress and concern among supporters. It read:

Dear 'Chairman Bill',

"Every Evertonian is gobsmacked to read your reply to the All Together Now Movement. As Chairman of the Board, you are the apparent leader of OUR club. Under your control and leadership, our great club has endured its longest ever spell without a trophy and has been in more relegation battles than cup finals. You have thrown our CEO under the bus, something which will no doubt cause more upheaval in the boardroom of the worst-run club in the league.

"We now find ourselves in yet another relegation battle, our club's finances are shot, and we are under investigation by an Independent Panel of the Premier League. OUR club is in crisis. Yet, your first statement in months is to complain about bedsheets. We are afraid that all your letter has done is confirmed the size of the gulf between you, the board, and Everton's fans. The players alongside Evertonians kept our club up last season. You trying to claim credit for our survival last year is an insult to the Evertonians who greeted coaches and sung our hearts out. Frankly, your letter reads as delusional.

"Your letter adds weight to the fact that you cannot and will not ever win back the confidence of Everton fans, nor are you ever welcome back to Goodison Park. Your position is untenable, the timing of your self-centred response was scandalous. As a movement and Evertonians we care about the future of our club and are putting all of our effort into backing the team on Thursday as opposed to protesting, this is all despite your tone deaf media release on the eve of the huge Palace game.

"Out of respect for our club, go now and allow us to unite for the relegation fight your mismanagement has left us in."

#AllTogetherNow

***

Kenwright's controversial open letter to the #AllTogetherNow fan group elicited a further statement from the Everton Fan Advisory Board calling a vote of no confidence in the chairman.

The FAB – comprised of four elected representatives, including shareholder and then chair Jazz Bal, and fans drawn from supporters' groups, including the Everton Fans' Forum, Everton Supporters Club Committee and the Everton Heritage Society – was assembled to act as a liaison between Everton's ownership and Board on the one hand, and the fans on the other.

In the weeks preceding the war of words with Kenwright and supporters' groups, the Advisory Board had presented Everton's Board of Directors with several concerns raised by supporters at the running of the club, and the FAB itself had voiced their own reservations about a lack of timely or adequate communication from the hierarchy, particularly around player recruitment, the ongoing search for investment, the funding models for the new Everton Stadium, and owner Farhad

Moshiri's own medium- to long-term plans as they pertained to his position as majority shareholder.

In their statement, the FAB remarked on what was "a second successive relegation battle threatening our Premier League status", the alleged breach of financial rules, and their own calls for "proactive leadership, communication and engagement" from the club hierarchy, when the relationship between large parts of the fanbase and the Board had become fractured, and for some, irreparable.

***

Over the years as a journalist covering Everton for the *Liverpool Echo* and more recently the *Daily Mail*, Dominic King had defended the Everton hierarchy and Bill Kenwright from criticism, but as the club fought for its Premier League life, the evidence of "years of bad decisions" has finally opened King's eyes to what he saw as the biggest problems afflicting the club. He claimed, "The board have ripped the soul out of Everton and everything it stood for has gone."

In his article following Everton's demoralising second-half collapse against Newcastle in late April that left the club in 19th place in the Premier League, King blamed "a constant cycle of bad decisions from the board" that have been compounded by "a raft of performances that have been an affront – there is only so much misery people can take."

Even the *BBC* were commenting on the civil war between fans and board ripping Toffees apart. It was a rift symbolised by the fact that in March, the Everton Timeline panel dedicated to Kenwright's successful takeover of Everton in 1999 had been ripped off the wall of Goodison Park and thrown into a canal.

"To add to the toxicity and uncertainty around the Merseyside club, a civil war has erupted between the Everton board and disgruntled supporters, who feel chairman Bill Kenwright is not up to the job and owner Farhad Moshiri has squandered much of the £750 million he has invested," wrote Shamoon Hafez for *BBC Sport*.

There were few Evertonians who would have disagreed with that pithy summary.

2023: Dyche steers Blues to Premier League Survival

> I said to the players, 'We shouldn't be here. Enjoy this today and you've earned it, but at the end of the day it has got to change.' It's a horrible day for all concerned. There is no joy in it for me other than getting the job done.
>
> -Sean Dyche

2023 Dyche steers Blues to Premier League Survival

Everton's gritty win over Brentford on 1 March had been their third 1-0 home victory since Sean Dyche had taken charge and, like the slender triumphs over Arsenal and Leeds, seemed to have established a template by which the Toffees could save themselves from relegation to the Championship. They sat in 15th that day, albeit just one point above the bottom three, but they failed to win again for the next two months.

An impressive equaliser from Ellis Simms had salvaged a draw against Chelsea at Stamford Bridge; likewise a spectacular,

90th-minute Michael Keane goal against Tottenham at Goodison Park a fortnight after that, but those relative highs were followed by fairly dismal defeats to Manchester United at Old Trafford and to Fulham and Newcastle at home.

The 4-1 drubbing at the hands of Newcastle had been a particularly crushing blow. Everton had dropped back into the drop zone following a goalless draw at Crystal Palace five days earlier and, with home games running out, the visit of Eddie Howe's Champions League-chasing Magpies was seen as vital to Everton's survival hopes.

It was decided by the various activist groups that the pre-match protests against the owner and Board would be suspended for the week and another raucous, blue-hued coach welcome was planned to greet the players in the streets outside the ground. In short, Evertonians had planned to expend every ounce of effort in supporting the team with another of those famous "bear pit" atmospheres inside the Grand Old Lady, but what they got in return was a hefty loss.

It meant that Dyche's team had to eke enough points out of their final five matches of the season – four if they discounted the visit of Champions-elect Manchester City – to lift themselves back out of the bottom three before the end of the campaign.

***

1 May 2023: Leicester City v Everton

Clashes didn't come much more important than the one between Leicester and Everton on 1 May at the King Power Stadium, a veritable 'six pointer' between the teams sitting in 18th and 19th place respectively before kick-off. Victory for either club would have taken them a step towards guaranteed safety; as it was, each had to be content with just a point.

Everton left the East Midlands much the happier of the two having avoided another damaging defeat thanks to the heroics of Jordan Pickford and a redemptive second-half strike from Alex Iwobi.

With Dominic Calvert-Lewin making a third straight start to add a much-needed extra dimension to the Blues' attack, Everton were easily the more dangerous of the two teams for the first quarter of the contest.

And their early superiority was rewarded with a quarter of an hour gone when the ball was flighted towards Calvert-Lewin just inside the box, and he went down under a clear shove from Timothy Castagne that left referee Michael Oliver in no doubt about the award of a penalty.

Calvert-Lewin stepped up himself to take it and swept a perfectly struck effort high down the middle of Daniel Iversen's goal. There was a chance to make it 2-0 almost immediately when Iwobi played the striker in, but Calvert-Lewin's shot was blocked behind. Michael Keane could only nod the resulting corner wide at the back post.

The Toffees' lead lasted just seven minutes, though. Dwight McNeil gave away a cheap free-kick inside his own half and when James Maddison's set-piece wasn't dealt with, Wout Faes headed the ball back across goal. Keane failed to track Caglar Soyuncu and the Turkish defender swivelled it in off Pickford's hand to level the match at 1-1.

Iwobi, having received a let-off when dispossessed in midfield and Maddison's curling effort failed to test Pickford, was not so fortunate shortly afterwards. The Nigerian's ill-advised cross-field pass across the centre-circle was intercepted by Youri Tielemans, Maddison quickly threaded the ball through Everton's defence and the 36-year-old Jamie Vardy easily out-stripped Keane for pace, rounding the keeper and slamming it home to turn the match on its head.

To their credit, Everton responded, and when McNeil surged forward and cut the ball across to Calvert-Lewin almost on the goal-line, the striker somehow prodded the ball to the only part of the gaping goal where the keeper was, and Iversen kept it out.

Leicester counter-attacked immediately, when Vardy twisted Keane into knots before drawing Pickford and chipping a shot over him, but the ball bounced off the crossbar and over.

That wasn't to be the end of the first-half drama , though as Coleman, who had been having a very good game to that point, went down in a heap clutching in his knee after being pole-axed by Boubakary Soumare. He was eventually carried off – the skipper still geeing his teammates up from the stretcher – and replaced by Nathan Patterson.

Then, in the ensuing injury time, Iwobi lost the ball again in an advanced area, Leicester poured forward once more, and when Harvey Barnes's cross struck Keane's out-stretched arm, referee Oliver pointed to the spot again, this time in the home side's favour.

Pickford elected not to pick a corner, though, and stood tall in his goal to beat away Maddison's penalty as he tried to drive it down the middle, keeping it at 2-1 heading into the second half where the contest became more and more akin to a winner-takes-all cup tie.

Everton came out of the changing room the more purposeful of the two sides and almost got their reward again when Calvert-Lewin's effort was kept out by Iversen's out-stretched foot at the near post.

Two minutes later, however, it was 2-2. McNeil's cross came off the head of Faes and dropped invitingly to Iwobi arriving on the other side of the box and he steered a beautifully cushioned half-volley past the keeper.

That sparked a sustained period of Leicester pressure and James Tarkowski had to clear Vardy's goal bound header off his line. But as the game moved into the final quarter of an hour, it was Everton who looked the more likely to grab a winner and Doucouré went very close to stealing the points three minutes from the end. The Mali international found himself with time on the edge of the area to line up a left-footed shot that he despatched in search of the bottom corner, but Iversen had sight enough of the ball to dive to his right and palm the ball behind.

So, not the result that Everton needed with just four matches remaining – two of them against the daunting opposition of Brighton and Manchester City – and with the club still sitting in the bottom three of the Premier League.

Individual errors and amateur defending continued to be huge issues that Dyche seemed incapable of addressing but the manager was buoyed by the spirit shown by his team, the attacking threat they posed with Calvert-Lewin leading the line, and that they had scored twice away from home for the third time under his stewardship.

Salvation was still possible, but matters were out of the Blues' hands. They needed help in matches involving their relegation rivals until Everton could try to help themselves at the Amex Community Stadium the following Monday against Brighton and Hove Albion.

Final score: Leicester 2-2 Everton

***

After the match at the King Power Stadium, the club confirmed that Seamus Coleman had suffered a serious, season-ending injury.

"It's really unfortunate," manager Sean Dyche said. "We're waiting on news. "It could be serious, a knee injury. I thought he was terrific. The medics have had a look at it and it doesn't look great. We'll hope for the very best for him."

***

8 May 2023: Brighton v Everton

One of the surprise packages of the season, Brighton & Hove Albion had become somewhat of a feared opponent during the 2022/23 season. They had lost Graham Potter – the architect of their emergence as an established Premier League presence and their impressive possession-based style of play – to Chelsea earlier in the season but, far from lose their way in his absence, they had arguably become even better under his successor, Roberto de Zerbi.

By the time Everton travelled to the south coast in early May for a game billed on social media as the match between 'a well run club' vs 'a poorly run club,', the Seagulls were in eighth place, just four points shy of fifth. The general consensus was that the Toffees would do well to get anything from the game, particularly in view of what had happened in the reverse fixture at Goodison Park at the turn of the year.

Indeed, the bookies had given Brighton 7/19 for the win; Everton, with only two away wins in the last 34 games, were 8/1 for the victory. In the end, fans on both sides could hardly believe their eyes, as the visitors defied the odds.

By the final whistle, the jubilant hordes in the rammed away end easily outnumbered the rapidly diminishing home crowd, most of whom had seen enough by halftime to believe it would not be their day.

Everton had blown much-vaunted Brighton away on their own ground, registered their biggest win in 4½ years and lifted themselves out of the relegation zone with a counter-attacking masterclass at the Amex Stadium. In the context of their battle for survival, it was up there with the most important results of the season.

For Everton, the result was also a remarkable reverse of the match between the two teams at Goodison Park the preceding January when Brighton tore them apart on the way to a 4-1 win that drove another nail into the coffin of Frank Lampard's tenure as the Toffees' boss. It was also their best result on their travels since beating Sean Dyche's Burnley by the same scoreline under Marco Silva in December 2018.

With Dyche finally caving and dropping Michael Keane back to the bench, Yerry Mina returned to the team for a rare start at centre-half alongside James Tarkowski while Nathan Patterson came in at right-back for the injured Seamus Coleman and James Garner kept his place in central midfield.

And Everton got off to the perfect start with a goal after just 33 seconds. Patterson made an important block to intercept Kaoru Mitoma's attempt to knock it past him, Dominic Calvert-Lewin executed a perfect pirouette to take Alex Iwobi's pass around his marker and after driving into the box, the striker crossed perfectly for Doucouré to knock it in assuredly at the back post.

In the 26th minute it was 2-0. Dwight McNeil raced away down the left flank, spotted Doucouré free on the other side of the penalty area and found him with a perfect cross, which the Mali international volleyed home brilliantly.

Remarkably, it was 3-0 six minutes after that, and the goal came from another superbly executed breakaway. Iwobi's ball into the box was a little too far ahead of Doucouré, but he kept it alive and found McNeil, who took it to the byline and attempted to drive it across the face of goal. The cross caught Steele's out-stretched leg, though, and bounced in.

McNeil squandered yet another promising counter when he just failed to find Calvert-Lewin as the pair raced away in a two-on-two and Garner must have thought he had registered his first Premier League goal when he side-footed wide of the keeper from close range, but Lewis Dunk got in a crucial block that ensured Brighton's deficit was only three at the halfway stage.

Roberto de Zerbi responded by making four changes at the interval, throwing on exciting young striker Evan Ferguson and the tricky Julio Enciso and for the first 15 minutes of the second half it was one-way traffic towards Jordan Pickford's goal.

The England keeper stood tall, however, saving bravely at his near post inside the first minute of the restart, parrying Enciso's fierce drive up and behind to safety and then brilliantly turning a Ferguson header onto the post with a one-handed save at full stretch.□Ferguson grazed the crossbar with a shot via Pickford's fingertips and, from the ensuing corner, then Alexis Mac Allister thumped a header off the face of the bar as Everton just about kept their clean sheet intact.

Dunk dropped a header wide of the far post shortly afterwards and Pickford made another top-drawer save to palm Mac Allister's header away before Everton defied all expectations by scoring a fourth.

Iwobi surged down the left flank this time and drew one defender to him that opened up the space for McNeil to steal into and. When the Nigerian found him with a perfectly-weighted pass, the former Burnley man faked to shoot, turned inside the last man and keeper and walked the ball into net before wheeling away in delight.

Brighton reduced their arrears to three again almost immediately when Mitoma slid in to meet a deep cross from the right. Although he could only steer the ball onto the post, it bounced off Mac Allister and then into the empty net to make it 4-1 with 11 minutes to go.

The Amex Stadium began to empty at 4-0, and those who remained did not get to witness a miraculous recovery. Indeed, it was Everton and McNeil who put the icing on the cake in stoppage time.

Once more it was a counter-attack, this time sparked by sub Amadou Onana's ball from inside his own half that released McNeil who used Iwobi in the middle as a decoy before leathering it inside the near post and into the top corner of Steele's goal.

A quite stunning result, against a very good side who could still have mathematically moved as high as fifth if they won their games in hand, lifted Everton out of the bottom three, taking full advantage of Leicester's 5-3 defeat at Fulham and Leeds United's loss at Manchester City that weekend.

Everton's next clash, with the new League leaders Manchester City at Goodison Park, promised to be a Herculean task of even bigger proportions but Dyche's men had given themselves a great chance of preserving the club's top-flight status providing they could reproduce this kind of form in their final three fixtures.

Final score: Brighton 1-5 Everton

***

20 May 2023: Wolverhampton Wanderers v Everton

Everton's comedown from that miraculous display in Brighton was swift and predictable as champions-elect Manchester City and Ilkay Gündogan, in particular, underlined the chasm in class between the two clubs with another world-class performance and a comprehensive 3-0 victory at Goodison Park.

Knowing that the Blues' final two games against Wolves and Bournemouth offered far greater opportunity for picking up valuable points, Sean Dyche, no doubt, was keeping the bigger picture in mind.

Watching from the sidelines as the match at Molineux ticked into the ninth minute of injury time with his side 1-0 down, the Everton boss must have felt his side had left far too much to chance for the final day clash with the Cherries. Indeed, were the Blues to lose to Wolves, a Leicester victory at Newcastle two days later would vault the Foxes into 17th place and wrest control of their destiny from Dyche and company's hands.

What followed, delivered by folk hero Yerry Mina as the clock reached 98:52, was another stunning moment in Everton's fourth great escape of the Premier League era.

With Calvert-Lewin passed fit despite feeling tightness in his groin during the defeat to City, Sean Dyche and his men were no doubt confident that, despite having to start Dwight McNeil at left back in place of the injured Vitalii Mykolenko, they could carry on from their magnificent performance at Brighton, and pick up three precious points against a Wolves side that had already secured their Premier League future.

And they started well, with Calvert-Lewin firing into the side-netting and then despatching Alex Iwobi's dangerous centre narrowly over the crossbar. However, the injury crisis at full back was about to get worse as Nathan Patterson was involved in a collision of legs that would force him off with an injury with less than half an hour gone.□

Everton remained the dominant side and their best chance of the first period should have fallen to Calvert-Lewin, but Mina got in ahead of him to meet McNeil's corner and the defender couldn't keep his header down.

The visitors' momentum and good work to that point was undone shortly afterwards, when Doucouré's weak pass was intercepted deep in Wolves territory and the hosts broke away through Adama Traoré. Jordan Pickford saved his shot but could only palm it into the path of the untracked Hwang Hee-chan who turned the loose ball home.

As if the afternoon couldn't get much worse, Calvert-Lewin's afternoon also came to a premature end on the stroke of half-time when he went to ground grasping his thigh before putting his head in hands. It was yet another recurrence of his troublesome hamstring injury and it would be mid-September before he saw action again.

With Calvert-Lewin and Patterson missing and Demarai Gray and Michael Keane on in their place, Everton struggled for coherence and balance in the second half. There had a few bright moments but after Pablo Sarabia passed up a great chance to kill the contest when he curled his shot, the Blues' attempts to grab something from the contest became increasingly desperate and ineffective.

By this point, Keane had been pushed forward into an emergency striker's role after Dyche had introduced Mason Holgate in place of Amadou Onana, and the visitors then launched the ball forward hoping for something to break their way.

Wolves almost put the game to bed two minutes into the nine added on by referee David Coote for stoppages, when Matheus Nunes raced clear on the breakaway, but Pickford denied him with an out-stretched foot that diverted the Portuguese's shot wide.

Then, just when it looked as though Everton's huffing, puffing and ineffective long-ball football was to be in vain, Gray flighted a long ball to the back post. Tarkowski beat Bentley's gloves to the ball to head it downwards where Keane knocked it square and Mina converted from close range to send the distraught visiting fans into delirium on their side of the stadium.

In the battle to avoid relegation, the Toffees had really needed a victory but the draw salvaged with almost the last kick of the game would prove to be one more crucial result overseen by Dyche during those final few weeks of the campaign.

Final score: Wolves 1-1 Everton

***

28 May 2023: Everton v AFC Bournemouth

The point secured against Wolves ended up proving vital, as did the 88th-minute save by Newcastle United's Nick Pope on Monday 22 May that denied Timothy Castagne a dramatic winner for Leicester City at St James's Park. It meant that, going into the final day of the

2022/23, Everton needed to win to once again secure their Premier League status and preserve 69 years of unbroken top-flight football at Goodison Park. Anything else and the Toffees would be at the mercy of the results in the matches between Leeds and Tottenham at Elland Road and, more pertinently, Leicester and West Ham at the King Power Stadium.

The visitors to the Grand Old Lady were Bournemouth who had already twice beaten Everton in convincing fashion at the Vitality Stadium back in November, so there would be nothing routine about the fixture.

With Dominic Calvert-Lewin and Vitalii Mykolenko ruled out, Sean Dyche had to cobble together a team capable of beating the Cherries, who had already achieved safety but had not travelled to Merseyside to simply make up the numbers.

The manager turned to a starting back three for the first time since taking over from Frank Lampard, deploying Dwight McNeil and the excellent James Garner as wing-backs, with Demarai Gray charged with leading the line.

It was Everton who began the game on the front foot, but it took them a quarter of an hour to threaten the visitors' goal when Gray drilled a shot that faded away from the target. Idrissa Gueye was then played in superbly by Amadou Onana, but Mark Travers tipped his rising effort over the crossbar, and the goalkeeper had to be alert a few minutes later to push away another strong effort from the Senegalese international.

An error by Tarkowski almost condemned the Blues to a half-time deficit but Yerry Mina got back to get a crucial touch on Dominic Solanke's shot to divert it behind while, back down the other end,

Garner's curling effort was heading for the top corner, but Travers batted it behind.

At the halfway stage, Everton were heading out of the Premier League, with Leicester - who had a superior goal difference - beating West Ham, but the Blues had another 45 minutes to save themselves from relegation and potential financial Armageddon.

That breakthrough should have come just six minutes after the restart, but Gray failed with a gilt-edged chance from close range. The ball was nodded on to him in the six-yard box and he just had to get a decisive touch but, perhaps fearing contact from an approaching defender, he miscued his header and Travers pushed it off the line before it was prodded behind to safety.

Six minutes after that, though, Abdoulaye Doucouré imprinted his name indelibly on Goodison folklore with a stunning 20-yard strike. Gueye's floated ball was initially cleared by a Bournemouth defender and when it fell to Doucouré, he smashed it home with such velocity that Travers barely moved.

The Old Lady erupted as one in elation. There were incredible scenes of joy in the stadium before the hosts dug in to try to both defend the lead and extend it if they could.

Gary O'Neil's introduction of Kieffer Moore threatened to add unwanted drama to the occasion. The Welsh international's added height caused havoc. It was his knock-down that fell to Solanke in the box, but Pickford made a decisive intervention, apparently dislocating a finger in the process, while Mina finished the job by clearing his lines.

With Gray wasting one great opportunity when he slipped trying to test the keeper from the angle, the industrious Alex Iwobi seeing a shot deflect inches wide of the far post and Tarkowski heading over following a corner, a second goal to settle the nerves never came.

Instead, Goodison held its collective breath at the other end as substitute Matias Viña lined up a crisp volley that Pickford beat away to safety.

Anguished Evertonians bayed for the final whistle as a couple of late free kicks gave the visitors chances to heave the ball into the box, but Everton's back line held before referee Stuart Attwell finally blew for full-time. For that season at least, Everton were safe, and the relief was palpable.

Final score: Everton 1-0 Bournemouth

***

With his post-match comments, Dyche struck a purposeful and less restrained chord, saying that the necessary work to change things significantly at Everton was already underway.

The 51-year-old had completed his initial remit of keeping the Blues in the top flight by steering them to safety, despite the loss of key players and having an imbalanced squad. He quickly dispensed with his well-worn rhetoric around shifting the mentality in the dressing room to talk of making Everton think and operate like a big club again.

His message carried a tacit challenge to the hierarchy to assist in that transformation, but it was also grounded by what would be possible in the short term, with Dyche insisting there was a lot of work ahead and there would be no quick fixes.

Dyche told the media, "I said to the players, 'we shouldn't be here. Enjoy this today and you've earned it, but at the end of the day it has got to change.' It's a horrible day for all concerned. There is no joy in it for me other than getting the job done.

"There is no point in sitting on it and saying, 'Look how great we are,' because it is not like that. There is loads to change here and a lot of work to be done, but it was a big step to secure it.

"The work on next season started the day I got in here. Don't think I thought this was an easy fix, because it is not. Far from it. There is a massive amount of work to be done. The thing I've learnt about Everton is the fans have been amazing. They want the club to be in the top end of the market, but the club is not at the top end of the market.

"It's a big club, big history, but we are not performing like a big club. We have to find a way of changing that. This is two seasons now. There is a massive amount of change to build to a new dawn, a new future, a bigger future.

"I think the Evertonians, as remarkable as they have been, have to remember that. This is a bigger project than just, 'Oh well, it's all right now.' I don't have magic dust, I can only make things happen I think are believable. It is definitely a reason to be happy, but we have to demand more internally. The fans know the truth. They know this wasn't a walk in the park.

"You have to build a belief in a new culture. If you ask five die-hard Evertonians what the club stood for, they would probably give me five different answers. The club has to realign. There was a time when it was 'earthy, hard-working. Give a lot to the shirt. Pride'. I'm not sure they are as obvious now.

"That's the base I want to build but I want to play good, attractive, winning football but it has to start with something. There have been signs this team will work, fight and give everything. Don't think Pep's [Guardiola's Manchester City] side just play beautiful football. They work, they defend, play hard, as well as being ultra-top footballers.

"There's a chance [I'll have to sell players]. I'll find out about that. There's been peripheral talks based on ifs, buts and maybes. I'd be very surprised if they say there is going to be another war chest. There is a beautiful stadium down the road and someone has to pay for that.

"But that will come over the coming weeks when we find out the truth of what we have got. We had to get this sorted out. We've got it over the line."

2023: THE SEARCH CONTINUES FOR NEW INVESTORS

> **According to reports, MSP Sports Capital had secured exclusivity in their negotiations with Farhad Moshiri as a precursor to an investment deal that could provide Everton with much-needed funds and lead to change at boardroom level.**

2023 The search continues for new investors

As Everton fought for their Premier League lives throughout the spring of 2023, confusion continued to surround the future ownership of the club. Press speculation over much of the season had suggested that Farhad Moshiri was prepared to listen to offers for his majority stake, but the Iranian-born businessman had been steadfast in insisting that the club was not for sale.

Media reports in March had put that down to Moshiri's concerns that selling Everton could cause his relationship with Alisher Usmanov – who was already sanctioned by the United Kingdom and

European Union following Russia's invasion of Ukraine in 2022 – to be scrutinised by the U.K. Government.

Indeed, Government sources had told the *The Daily Mail* that they were keeping a watchful eye on any sale of Everton. Perhaps there was still a suspicion – first aroused by the leak of the so-called Paradise Papers in 2017 - that Moshiri's original shareholding in Arsenal had been a gift from Usmanov. It was the proceeds from the sale of his Arsenal shares which Moshiri had used to buy into Everton in 2016.

Any involvement from Usmanov in the running of Everton was always denied strongly, both by the club and Moshiri's camp, but it remained a constant source of conjecture in the media, not least when it was claimed that as many as five prospective candidates for the Everton manager's had reported having held direct conversations with Usmanov during their interview processes.

Everton had cut their commercial ties with Usmanov's business entities in the spring of 2022 following Vladimir Putin's attack on Ukraine, which meant the loss of key sponsorships from USM Holdings and subsidiary Megafon, but there remained a possibility that Moshiri might yet be drawn into the sanctions equation. This concern grew when Usmanov and USM were reported to have been targeted with further sanctions by the U.K. government amid scrutiny of individuals and companies whom it accused of acting as "financial fixers" for Russian oligarchs like Usmanov and Roman Abramovich.

Britain's Foreign Office said in a statement, that they were aiming the new measures at those helping the two prominent businessmen (Usmanov and Abramovich) to avoid the full cost of financial sanctions which, by implication, could have included his long-time business partner – and the "M" in USM – Moshiri.

Indeed, *The Guardian*'s Simon Goodley reported that the Treasury's "sanctions police" were investigating Moshiri's finances, considering his long-time association with Usmanov which made him a "person of interest" to the Office of Financial Sanctions Implementation (OFSI).

That reportedly prompted the Everton owner to hire an expert sanctions lawyer at Peters & Peters, 'one of the U.K.'s largest law firms', but in an echo of the situation at Chelsea where Roman Abramovich had been forced to sell his club while receiving none of the proceeds, Goodley raised the possibility that an offer of investment or buy-out of Everton "would result in Moshiri losing control of the club without being paid a penny" if he, too, was subject to punitive measures by the Government. Or if it was proved conclusively that Usmanov's money directly funded his shares in the club.

USM Holdings bristled at the moves by Whitehall, saying in a statement:

"We consider the U.K. sanctions adopted against USM Holdings and its shareholders to be unjust and unfounded. Alisher Usmanov has not been engaged in business activity for a long period of time," the statement added.

Moshiri rejected the allegation in the same way he had strenuously denied claims it was Usmanov who effectively owned and controlled Everton, and that the oligarch had been in attendance during interviews for managerial candidates like Rafael Benitez and Frank Lampard.

***

In the meantime, Moshiri and the club continued negotiations with prospective investors in Everton from the United States. Talks with Florida-based private equity firm 777 Partners over a full takeover had reportedly stalled in March, and MSP Sports Capital took their place at the negotiating table with an offer of investment up to £150 million in return for a minority stake, perhaps in the form of preferential, convertible shares.

MSP, headed by former sport agent Jeff Moorad and businessman Jahm Najafi, secured exclusivity in their talks with Moshiri as a precursor to a proposed investment deal that was intended to provide Everton with much-needed funds, largely for the remaining construction costs on the stadium at Bramley-Moore Dock, and would also lead to change at boardroom level.

The New York-based investment firm, who already had stakes in Bundesliga side Augsburg, Spanish club AD Alcorcon, Estoril in Portugal and Belgian outfit Beveren, as well McClaren's Formula One team and the X Games, had been in discussions with Moshiri on and off for months and, by May 2023, all the indications were that an agreement was imminent.

However, a deal that would see MSP Sports Capital take an initial stake in Everton never materialised. Weeks passed and the 2023/24 season dawned without any sign of badly-needed funds to cover the next tranche due to stadium contractors, Laing O'Rourke. Then, on 23 August it was reported that MSP had withdrawn from talks with Moshiri.

No official reason was ever given but the claim was made by Matt Slater, Senior Football Reporter at *The Athletic*, that one of the stumbling blocks to the proposed deal had come in the form of opposition from Rights and Media Funding Limited, the offshore lender with whom the Blues had an estimated £200 million in outstanding loans and who had 'negative pledge clauses' which prevented Everton from pledging any assets if doing so would jeopardise R&MF's security.

According to Slater's report, that made MSP's proposal unworkable, with R&MF not convinced that the New York company would be injecting enough capital in return for its planned equity position of 25% unless they paid off tens of millions of pounds of what the club owed them first.

Nevertheless, MSP did agree to furnish the club with a £100 million loan for the Everton Stadium. In the meantime, the door was left open for 777 Partners who would soon reach a non-binding agreement with Moshiri regarding an outright takeover of his 94% stake in the Blues.

2023: Three step down from Everton Board

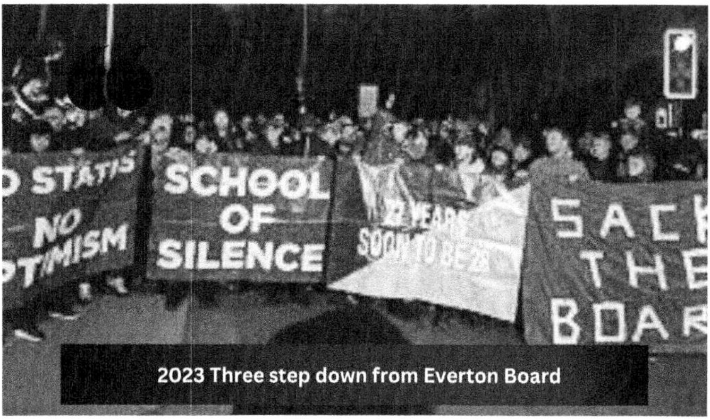

2023 Three step down from Everton Board

The winds of change in Everton's Boardroom finally arrived in June 2023 with the announcement that Chief Executive Denise Barrett-Baxendale, Finance Director Grant Ingles and Non-Executive Director Graeme Sharp had all stepped down from their respective roles with immediate effect.

The fate of chairman Bill Kenwright was expected to be announced shortly thereafter but it would take another 11 days before his position was clarified and, ultimately, it was Farhad Moshiri's preference that the 77-year-old theatre impresario remain in his post.

"We have all been fully committed during our time here and are disappointed to have made the decision to leave Everton," a statement from Barrett-Baxendale, Sharp and Ingles said.

"We have worked tirelessly alongside our chairman in what has been a challenging period to deliver some of the most significant projects in Everton's history – projects that will safeguard and sustain the commercial future of the club for generations to come.

"We are proud of the commercial growth projects progressed during our time on the board, including the construction of the club's new waterfront stadium. This construction project — the largest currently on site in the U.K. — is progressing at pace.

"It has been an honour and a privilege to serve as directors. We would like to thank everyone who has supported us during our time here. We wish the club we have loved to serve every success in the future."

***

On 15 June, Andy Hunter from *The Guardian* reported Everton fans had vowed to intensify protests against the club's hierarchy unless they removed Bill Kenwright as chairman. He wrote:

"Given the clear need for improvements in a squad that has only just survived two relegation battles in succession, and this latest example of Everton's dysfunction, the supporters group #AllTogetherNow has urged Moshiri to take decisive action.

"The group, which represents several Everton fan organisations, stated: 'We call for the immediate removal of the chairman of this football club – who has been the most unsuccessful chairman in our history. For the football club to move forward, and fans to unite, this without doubt has to happen. The protests will not cease and will only further intensify if you [Moshiri] allow 'Chairman Bill' to stumble on, continuing to fail in his position, despite clear evidence for a need for change. We ask you to respond without delay to this loyal fanbase, do not cause any further unnecessary hold up to a deadline that the football club's leadership team set out.'

"Kenwright described the outgoing directors as 'a great board' when their departures were announced on Monday. While work is advancing on an impressive new stadium at Bramley Moore dock, Moshiri is yet to secure the funding needed to complete the project. Everton face other financial problems, including the threat of legal action from Leicester, Leeds, Southampton and Burnley should they be found to have breached Premier League financial rules. Their former manager Carlo Ancelotti is also suing the club in London's high court. The #AllTogetherNow statement added: 'That 'great board' have left us in a perilous financial position with constant poor decision-making, leaving the club in a dire situation with an FFP court case hanging over our heads. They have brought us zero trophies and two back-to-back relegation battles. Not forgetting in recent times throwing the club's biggest asset, its fans, under a bus with no remorse or apology.' "

2023: Moshiri joins Kenwright on Everton board

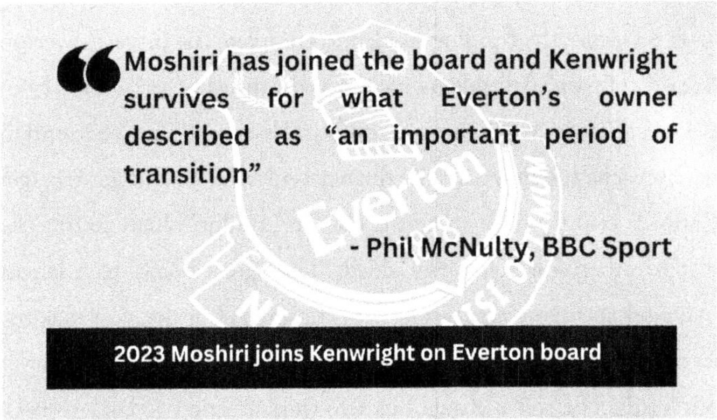

On 23 June, the position of Bill Kenwright and the make-up of Everton's interim Board of Directors were clarified when the club released of a statement in which it was announced that Colin Chong had been appointed as interim Chief Executive Officer and director.

Chong had served as the Chief Stadium Development Officer, focused on the delivery of Everton Stadium, as well as "the operational management of the club's business headquarters at the Royal Liver Building."

James Maryniak was promoted from Director of Finance to interim Chief Finance Officer, while two Non-Executive Directors were added to the Board in the form of the majority shareholder himself, Farhad Moshiri, and John Spellman, a Chartered Accountant, businessman and lifelong Blues fan.

Kenwright would remain as chairman, with Moshiri saying: "I wanted Bill to remain as our chairman during this important period of transition for the Club and I am delighted that he has accepted my request to do so. Bill's knowledge and vast experience will be crucial for us as we look to reset, deliver on external investment and position Everton for a successful future.

"In John, we have an experienced finance professional who has held Chief Executive and senior finance roles for international firms and I welcome him to the Club.

"In Colin and James, we have two experienced senior club professionals who have agreed to take on enhanced roles on an interim basis, and who we know can and will deliver immediately."

***

In an article for *BBC Sport*, Chief football writer Phil McNulty wrote of his scepticism that the news at boardroom level was unlikely to quell the mood of rebellion among fans:

"The early expectation after chief executive Denise Barrett-Baxendale, finance officer Grant Ingles and non-executive director and former player Graeme Sharp left the board was that long-serving Kenwright would follow.

"They formed a boardroom quartet whose relationship with the fanbase was so broken they have decided not to attend home games since January, citing safety reasons, amid growing protests among supporters, with Kenwright and owner Farhad Moshiri primary targets.

"Instead, Moshiri has joined the board and Kenwright survives for what Everton's owner described as 'an important period of transition' as incoming investment is expected from New York-based MSP Sports Capital to secure more funding for the club's new stadium at Bramley Moore Dock.

"It may well be that this is a boardroom holding operation until the MSP deal is finalised as it is expected they will understandably demand a strong boardroom presence in return for their investment, but the continued presence of Kenwright is in danger of overshadowing the wider context.

"Everton supporters' groups had already vowed to intensify protests if Kenwright stayed on and there is no doubt Moshiri has risked the further wrath of large numbers of fans by placing his faith in the 77-year-old, even if it may only be for a short period.

"Kenwright and Moshiri have taken heavy criticism for Everton's current parlous plight after two seasons of near relegation and being referred to an independent commission by the Premier League for alleged breaches of financial fair play rules.

"If Everton's statement was intended to calm the mood among discontented fans, early indications suggest it has had the opposite effect."

2023: Interim CEO updates fans on stadium progress

> The aim has always been to deliver on a promise to build something that all Evertonians can be proud of. When you finally walk through the entrances in that boundary wall, I'm sure you will agree it will be that, and much, much more.
>
> -Colin Chong

2023 Interim CEO updates fans on stadium progress

Colin Chong would serve in his dual role as Interim Chief Executive Officer and Chief Stadium Development Officer at Everton, and within days of his addition to the Board he would provide an update on progress made on Everton Stadium which had, by this stage, taken full shape at Bramley-Moore Dock.

He took the opportunity to address supporters in his capacity as acting CEO and address mischievous tabloid reports suggesting that the stadium was behind schedule:

"There was a time, not long ago, when peering over the boundary wall, or looking through the gates, was necessary to check on the progress of our future home on the banks of the River Mersey.

"Now, Everton Stadium towers into the north Liverpool skyline, and we've all enjoyed watching this magnificent super-structure emerge from the former dock.

"The scale of progress in the past 12 months has been staggering, and that is testament to the planning, commitment, professionalism and ingenuity of our trusted construction partners, Laing O'Rourke and their partnership with the hard-working staff here at Everton.

"A year ago, the site was receiving the delivery of steel work and we were seeing the skeleton of each of our stands come to life. Since then, we have seen milestones that have included the arrival and departure of tower cranes, terracing lifted into place, brick panels delivered and installed, a complex series of roof truss lifts completed and the ramping up of internal works, which has included making the building watertight and the start of the mechanical, engineering and plumbing fit-out.

"Within one year, the site is literally unrecognisable.

"Supporters have understandably shown a great interest in the project, from concept to consultation, and for that, I warmly thank you.

"It's also fair to say the one question I'm asked more than any other is 'when will the stadium be ready and finished'?

"Contrary to some ill-informed media reports, there is no delay, and the project remains firmly on track and on-schedule.

"A precise moving-in date for our new stadium has never been publicly set by the Club. We have repeatedly stated that the schedule of the development will see the keys for our new home handed to us from Laing O'Rourke during the 2024/25 season.

"This means we won't be starting the 2024 season at Everton Stadium – but, to reiterate, the Club has never publicly confirmed an intention to begin the 2024/25 season at our new home. If the project remains on schedule, it raises the question as to whether the Club moves in mid-season or alternatively, do we wait and give the Grand Old Lady a fitting send-off before commencing competitive league games for the senior men's team at the start of the 2025/26 season?

"Whatever decision is reached, it won't be based on sentiment; it will be reached in consultation with fans, while also considering the impacts it will have across our football club in terms of our football operation, our commercial partners and third-party contracts, our staff, seasonal workflows and the impact, of course, on supporters.

"Moving mid-season may offer some commercial benefits, but also presents a series of challenges and hurdles that could negatively impact other aspects of the Club – and other commercial considerations.

"What I can say categorically is that, today, the project is several weeks ahead of schedule, with another winter to come.

"The aim has always been to deliver on a promise to build something that all Evertonians can be proud of. When you finally walk through the entrances in that boundary wall, I'm sure you will agree it will be that, and much, much more."

***

While there was no indication how long Chong would remain as interim CEO – the assumption was that he would remain at the helm until there was clarity over investment into the club or an outright takeover was agreed – he assumed the role having overseen the one shining light of Farhad Moshiri's reign as majority shareholder.

Everton Stadium had been rising out of the north Liverpool docks precisely according to architect Dan Meis' vision and its successful completion promised to be one of the most important developments in the club's history. Financially, it offered stability, if not salvation – given the mountain of debt with which the Blues had been saddled – but that stability was also dependent on Everton's continuing membership of the Premier League, a status that would come under renewed threat during the 2023/24 season.

2023: Another Fine Mess You Got Me Into

> "Bill has a belief perhaps bordering on arrogance that he can still save the club from itself', said one long-term ally. Farhad likes big gestures. He can be impetuous. Bill thinks he needs to be there to temper them and gets frustrated that fans can't see this. Some think Bill feels guilty, that he feels he sold to the wrong person.
>
> \- Ian Ladyman, Daily Mail

2023 Another fine mess you got me into

On 12 March 2016, Moshiri wrote in the matchday programme: "Most importantly, Everton is about great football and winning matches."

His intent was clear, but the results under his ownership have been far from impressive.

In the 276 league games played since Moshiri bought his stake in the club until the start of the 2023/24 season, the team achieved only a 34.4% win rate, with a goal difference of minus 101. It was a desperately poor return from such a significant outlay in transfer fees, players' wages and the cost of managers, directors and support staff.

Everton's Cup runs had been no better. After the League Cup Semi Final defeat against Manchester City and the FA Cup Semi Final defeat against Manchester United in Roberto Martinez' last season, the Blues had exited both the League Cup and FA Cup in the early rounds on five occasions. They had not progressed beyond the Quarter Final stage in either competition since 2016. The club's only foray into Europe ended with elimination at the group stage of the Europa League in 2017.

The absence of a footballing identity and strategy had been alarming since the early days of Moshiri's tenure, and it was somewhat ironic that the closer the Iranian-born businessman got to the exit door at Everton, the more coherent the overall vision on the playing side had looked – as forced as it has been by circumstance, austerity and a need to get back to basics.

A club that in seven years, had burned through eight managers and coaching teams, two interim managers, plus three Directors of Football, looked lost at sea. The result had been a plethora of coaching ideologies, haphazard recruitment of players and managers, multiple power-bases in and around the club – each using favoured agents, advisors and media to promote their vested interests.

In the years of Harry Catterick, Everton was known as 'The School of Science'; in the mid-eighties, Howard Kendall's side was acclaimed by Brian Clough as the "best young side in Europe," after winning the League Title and the European Cup Winners Cup in 1985. Joe Royle's 'Dogs of War' won the FA Cup in 1995. David Moyes' teams were tough, pragmatic and productive, enabling the club to hold the 'best of the rest' title for years. But what moniker could be applied to Everton during the Moshiri era? 'The Magnificent 7th' in 2016/17 was Moshiri's high-water mark.

Even the golden half-season under Carlo Ancelotti in 2021 - when the club was second in the league on Boxing Day – turned out to be a prelude to a slide into mid-table obscurity, in which Ancelotti seemed to lose interest and eventually left the club in the lurch at the end of that season. Hindsight is a wonderful thing, but Ancelotti leaving for a more prestigious club was always going to be on the cards, wasn't it?

In Moshiri's opening communiqué, he also wrote, "I have committed to providing additional funds for transfers and retaining our key players to ensure we have a strong core to build on in the future." Yet, his pledge to keep key players turned out to be hollow. Within his first two years, the club had sold John Stones, Romelu Lukaku and Gerard Deulofeu.

Yet he did offer an open chequebook to Ronald Koeman, as he explained on *TalkSport* in November 2016:

> "**We have no restrictions to spend**. The manager is totally committed and ruthless; if a player is not up to it he uses another player and eventually he buys one. There are no sentimental issues there. The manager will strengthen the team in the areas he feels necessary. Koeman is Koeman: he does what he wants and I support him. I think the job of an owner and chairman is simply to hire and fire the manager; the rest is down to him. He has the personality, aura and ability and

> we trust him. In Everton's culture the manager is the most important individual."

Moshiri's actions would once again prove to be at variance with his rhetoric. Indeed, he supported Koeman for a further twelve months, until he sacked him.

Furthermore, despite Moshiri's claim that: "the job of an owner and chairman is simply to hire and fire the manager, the rest is down to him." it became increasingly clear that was not how he and his chairman behaved.

The Dutchman was followed into the Everton manager's hot seat by as varied a group as you could wish to meet: each one hired and fired by Moshiri and Kenwright. The cost of early termination of Martinez and his six successors, plus their support teams exceeded £50 million.

Of course Everton was not the only club in the Premier League to hire and fire managers. Yet the lack of a clear footballing strategy and the absence of a consistent identity at the club, led to a chaotic merry-go-round that burned money whilst only yielding that 34.4% win rate.

In the results business of football it's impossible not to draw comparisons, and in the football-mad city of Liverpool the benchmark club sits just half-a-mile away, across Stanley Park.

Since signing for Liverpool on 5 October 2015 – just five months before Farhad Moshiri's arrival at Everton – Jürgen Klopp had faced Everton 17 times by the start of the 2023/24 season. He had won ten of those matches, drawn six and lost one. He had faced eight different Everton managers. The anticipation of who would come next presumably keeps him on his toes.

2023: Following the money

Back in March 2016, Farhad Moshiri also made a commitment to provide funding for the team, as well as for a new stadium. It was a hugely ambitious statement, but he was apparently a man with a plan and access to significant assets.

Remember, he graduated with a degree in accountancy from the University of London and worked at Ernst & Young and Pannell Kerr Forster before joining Deloitte & Touche. He then spent twenty years tracking the business plans and performance of Alisher Usmanov's companies.

Before he bought into Everton, Moshiri produced a business plan complete with spreadsheets and financial projections, all based on his key assumptions. His plan was verified by 18 months of due diligence and detailed discussions with Bill Kenwright. Even if Kenwright purported not to know what 'other operating costs' were, the qualified accountant who would become Everton's owner most certainly knew.

***

What Moshiri's spreadsheets did not tell him was by early 2023 he would have already pumped £750 million into the club through his own companies, he would still need to find another £350 million to complete the stadium, and even more to fund his loss-making club's working capital and squad-investment needs.

The cash requirements of the football club had spiralled far beyond the projections made in his business plan. The mismanagement of the club, by Moshiri and his board, had turned Everton from a tightly-run but undercapitalised unit in 2015, into an organisation that was still haemorrhaging cash in 2023.

In making his public assertion in January 2023 that the stadium project would top out at £760 million, Moshiri was confirming the cost was perhaps three times his original estimate. And, because of planning delays, COVID-19 and other factors, the projected cash-flow benefits of playing at Bramley Moore Dock in front of a crowd of over 52,000 had been pushed into 2025.

Once Moshiri's principal benefactor and intended naming rights sponsor for the new stadium, Alisher Usmanov, had been taken out of the game thanks to the events in Ukraine, Moshiri was financially standing all alone.

***

It was clear since the days when Moshiri and Usmanov owned 30% of Arsenal FC that the two men and their finances were closely linked. Moshiri sold his shares in Arsenal to his friend, Usmanov, in order to fund his initial stake in Everton. What's more, Usmanov's companies became Everton's principal sponsors between March 2016 and February 2022.

What is less clear, is how Moshiri funded his ongoing investment in the club after he arrived.

According to Simon Goodley, writing in *The Guardian* on 26 September 2023:

"The Everton Football Club owner, Farhad Moshiri, received more than £400 million from Alisher Usmanov companies in the run-up to the Russian billionaire being placed under sanctions, documents suggest, raising fresh questions about the financial ties between the two men.

"Records seen by *The Guardian* appear to show that Moshiri borrowed £145m from a company wholly owned by the Russian-Uzbek tycoon from about 2020. The papers also set out how, between 2018 and 2022, Moshiri sold about £270 million of shares in a company whose largest shareholder was Usmanov. Moshiri did not pay for those shares, public accounts imply, which accounting experts suggested could mean the share sales were a gift.

"After being presented with the information laid out in the internal documents, a spokesperson for Usmanov declined to discuss precise details of the funding but said: "Mr Moshiri and his companies are indeed indebted to Mr Usmanov and entities affiliated with him. We hope that the debt will be repaid after Mr Moshiri closes the sale of the Everton club, which is now being actively announced in the press."

Putin's decision to invade Ukraine shocked the world, even after months of Russian forces posturing on their neighbour's border. Then, in the aftermath of 24 February 2022, Usmanov, was sanctioned by the British and EU governments. Sponsorship funding from Everton's principal sponsor literally dried up overnight. What's more, Moshiri was suddenly and unexpectedly required to resign from the chairmanship of the $20 billion Metalloinvest Management Company Limited - the Moscow headquartered company owned 60% by Usmanov and 10% by Moshiri. With much of Moshiri's personal wealth tied up in the company, his Russian bank accounts were apparently frozen as part of the sanctions.

To his credit, Moshiri did not shirk his responsibilities to provide funds to the football club through his own companies – he said he would, and he did that at tremendous cost. That ongoing support throughout 2022 enabled the stadium build to continue, and the club to function semi-normally, albeit under a 'special measures' regime from the Premier League.

To date, he has paid out £300 million to Everton for new shares, and £490 million in shareholder loans. (Source: Everton FC Annual Report & Accounts; and TheEsk.org)

However, as Moshiri's funds dried up in 2023, the club was forced to extend its credit facilities with anyone who would lend it money. By September, the club's borrowings included:

- A £200 million rolling credit facility provided by Rights and Media Funding – funding provided by offshore entities at annual interest rates of around 12%. That facility being secured against all the assets of the football club, including future TV revenues, bank accounts and properties (excluding the new stadium).
- £140 million of debt provided by MSP Sports Capital (including Andy Bell and George Downing as limited partners) – secured against the shares of the Everton Stadium Development Holding Company.
- A COVID related loan of approximately £25 million with Santander.

Unsurprisingly, by the beginning of the 2023/24 season, with Moshiri's magic money tree looking sadly bare and every asset owned by the club currently mortgaged to the hilt, Everton's financial position was more precarious than ever.

***

In 1849, Charles Dickens wrote about the relationship between money and happiness: "Annual income twenty pounds, annual expenditure nineteen pounds, nineteen and sixpence, result happiness. Annual income twenty pounds, annual expenditure twenty pounds and sixpence, result misery."

If only Moshiri and the Everton board members he appointed had adhered to that principle from day-1 of his ownership, rather than follow a fatally-flawed 'money is no barrier to success' model.

A look back over Moshiri's years of ownership highlights a progressively worsening situation:

In Moshiri's first full year in charge (2016/17) the club achieved a turnover of £171 million[1], a massive £50 million increase on the previous year thanks largely to the bumper new TV broadcast deals. Operating costs also increased significantly to £184 million, resulting in an operating loss of (£12 million). Nevertheless, after the sale of John Stones and with a profit on player trading of £52 million, there was a **pre-tax profit of £31 million.**

The following year (2017/18), turnover increased to £189 million. Yet operating costs shot up to £287 million, bringing about an operating loss of (£98 million). It took the sale of Romelu Lukaku to push the profit on player trading to £88 million, ensuring **the pre-tax loss for the year was only (£13 million).**

2018/19 was the first year the club's finances spiralled out of control. Turnover dropped slightly to £188 million, while operating costs increased still further to £315 million. This resulted in an operating loss of (£127 million). With the club's previous top two playing assets already plying their trade at the other end of the

East Lancs Road, profit on player trading was only £20.5 million. **The pre-tax loss rose to (£112 million).**

A similar picture emerged in 2019/20. Once again, turnover fell slightly to £186 million, whereas operating costs were £361 million, and the operating loss a resulting massive (£175 million). Profit from player trading was £41 million, and **the pre-tax loss came in at (£140 million).**

In 2020/21, turnover rose slightly to £193 million, and operating costs fell slightly to £319 million, meaning there was another huge operating loss of (£126 million). After a modest £13.2 million profit on player trading, the **pre-tax loss for the year came in at (£121 million).**

The latest club results to be released are for the year 2021/22. Turnover fell back to £181 million. Operating costs were still high at £284 million, bringing about an operating loss of (£103 million). The sale of Richarlison to Spurs brought about a £67.7 million profit on player trading, and **resulted in a pre-tax loss of (£44.7 million)**.

It was at that point that the club directors were obliged by the auditors to issue a blunt notice about the club's continuation as a going concern, in the event of relegation. The auditors signed off the accounts only having received a (non-legally-binding) commitment from Farhad Moshiri to continue to fund the club.

***

In summary, in the first six years of Farhad Moshiri's reign, he and his Board oversaw a period where costs exceeded turnover by more than £640 million. The club's operating losses were reduced by making a £282 million profit on player trading in that period, meaning the pre-tax loss was 'only' £400 million.

Moshiri and the club would argue that the losses in 2017/18, 2018/19 and 2019/20 included around £50 million of exceptional stadium-related costs. All stadium costs incurred after planning permission was granted in 2021 have been capitalised and are included on the club's balance sheet.

The Board claimed significant COVID-19 related losses were also incurred. Besides obvious losses, such as gate receipts for all the games played behind closed doors, the club included losses relating to player trading during the depressed transfer market.

Moshiri may also point to delays in the Bramley-Moore Dock project – partly due to COVID and partly due to the need to submit a revised planning application; the consequences of which mean that the expected £50 million per annum of additional stadium-related revenue will only materialise several years later than his original assumptions.

Approximately £50 million of the club's operating costs resulted from compensation in the hiring and firing of managers and their coaching staff during the chaotic managerial merry-go-round that has characterised the Moshiri era.

Interest costs sapped a further £40 million from the club. And now, with external debt spiralling, at a time when interest rates for borrowers have quadrupled, the interest bill will only grow in the short-to-medium term.

Half of Moshiri's investment has gone to fund the operating losses in the football club.

***

In Farhad Moshiri's business plan, he expected revenue growth to play a major part in the turnaround of the club's fortunes. Billionaires are not averse to investing money to enable a promising project to get off the ground. The successful projects achieve good returns. The failed projects either get culled or sold on, hopefully before the losses become too serious. This is what billionaires do.

Farhad Moshiri and Alisher Usmanov had each owned a 15% stake in Arsenal since 2007. We don't know what turnover forecast Moshiri had pencilled in for Everton, but his experience at Arsenal must have been on his mind. The Gunners had moved to their new stadium in 2006 and attracted crowds of 60,000 who paid to watch Premier League football, Champions League matches, and plenty of domestic cup games. Their new stadium attracted Emirates Airlines as its naming-rights sponsor, and its extensive corporate hospitality facilities proved highly profitable.

With a turnover of £344 million in 2014/15, Arsenal could afford to spend £192 million on wages (well under the sustainable limit of 70%) and still make a profit of over £24 million. Was that the aspiration Farhad Moshiri had for Everton? If so, the Blues had a lot of ground to make up. In that same year of 2014/15, Everton's turnover was only £126 million. With wages of £78 million, the club was left with a loss before tax of £4 million. [2]

Billionaires, like Moshiri and Usmanov, are not typically known for their patience. After ten games in charge, Roberto Martinez became the first casualty of the new Moshiri era – although it cost £11.3 million to get rid of him.

Ronald Koeman replaced Martinez, and a new position of Director of Football had been filled by former Leicester City Head Scout, Steve Walsh. It was their job to ensure Everton upped their game and became more competitive, in order to give the Top 4 a run for their money in the race for Champions League places every season. In the meantime, Moshiri and his board nominee, Sasha Ryazantsev, moved ahead with the urgent task of building a new stadium, while simultaneously attempting to grow the club's revenue streams.

***

Revenue Streams:

Broadcasting Revenues: Everton's first growth spurt was expected to come from a hike in broadcasting revenues, which in 2015/16 - the season of Farhad Moshiri's takeover at Everton - stood at £81.7 million. In 2016/17, broadcasting revenue rose to £130.5 million on the back of the new TV deal.

Did Moshiri and the Everton board believe the TV rights would provide an ever-increasing income stream? Whatever their assumption, by 2021/22, Everton actually saw its broadcasting income fall back to £115 million. Failure on the pitch, including the lack of success in the domestic cups, meant the club relied solely on income from league matches. The profitable drama and income from hoped-for European football was replaced by the nail-biting reality of relegation battles. [3]

***

Gate Receipts: In 2014/15, with Farhad Moshiri eyeing up the acquisition of Everton FC, whilst still an Arsenal shareholder, he saw Everton's matchday income of £17.9 million totally eclipsed by Arsenal's £100.4 million. No wonder Moshiri prioritised the new stadium project in his first address to the Everton faithful.

Yet, it is still likely to be season 2025/26 before the Blues first run out to Z-Cars at Bramley Moore Dock. In the meantime, Goodison Park is full every week. With no European games, and few domestic cup matches, gate receipts have remained static at around £16 million. [4]

***

Sponsorship/Merchandising: Another area where Everton had previously lagged way behind the likes of Arsenal was in sponsorship and merchandising. Alisher Usmanov was unable to invest in equity at Everton while he remained an Arsenal shareholder, but providing sponsorship was another matter. By 2021/22 Everton's Sponsorship/Merchandising income had risen to £35 million, largely thanks to the club's deals with Usmanov's companies, USM and MegaFon.

But in February 2022, in the wake of Vladimir Putin's invasion of Ukraine, the club announced that Farhad Moshiri had immediately severed his links with Metalloinvest, the Russia-based conglomerate he helped found with Usmanov. That move came only days after the Blues announced they were suspending their sponsorship deals with USM Holdings and two Usmanov-owned telecoms subsidiaries, MegaFon and Yota. The club removed signage relating to MegaFon from Goodison Park overnight and Everton Women played their match against Aston Villa with blank jerseys after the same company's logo was dropped from their kit. The financial impact of these cancelled sponsorship deals (estimated at £20 million per annum) will become known when the club publishes its 2022/23 accounts. It remains to be seen whether Everton have been able to fill this significant gap by finding other major sponsorship and merchandising deals. An even bigger blow to the club, was the loss of the USM naming rights deal on the Bramley-Moore stadium, worth an estimated £200 million.

***

Operating Costs:

Without sight of Farhad Moshiri's business plan for the Everton FC acquisition, we will never know how quickly he expected his new club to achieve Arsenal-like annual revenue figures of circa £300-£350 million. However, he wasted little time in allowing the club's operating costs to emulate those of their illustrious North-London rivals. And when the turnover growth failed to materialise, he did little to cut costs; thereby creating a £642 million operating loss in the first 6 years of his ownership.

It's time to take a deeper dive into the main drivers behind the 'operating costs explosion' under Farhad Moshiri.

***

Wages:

The biggest cost to any football club is the wage bill for the players and staff.

Under the regimes of various managers and Directors of Football, Everton's Wages/Turnover ratio ramped up from 61% in 2016/17 to an unsustainable 95% in 2020/21. [5]

Not only were many players signed on high wages, but long-term contracts were handed out to average performers at the tail-end of their careers.

For many of the players recruited by Moshiri and his appointees, their deal with Everton marked the high-wage point of their career. If they failed to perform at Everton, no other club would pay them what they earned. It was virtually impossible to loan them out, unless Everton picked up most of their wage bill. Sales of these players proved virtually impossible, so most stayed on the Goodison Park payroll until their contract expired.

Consider the following roll-call:

Bolasie: £22.5 million fee. 5 year contract.£19.5 million wages

Schneiderlin: £20 million fee. 4 year contract. £20.8 million wages

Williams: £9 million fee. 3 year contract. £10.8 million wages

Sigurdsson: £44.5 million fee. 5year contract. £26 million wages

Rooney: No fee. 2 year contract. £16.8 million wages

Sandro: £5.2 million fee. 4 year contract. £13.5 million wages

Tosun: £21 million fee. 5 year contract. £15.6 million wages

Walcott: £20 million fee. 3.5 year contract. £18.2 million wages

Mina: £28.5 million fee. 5 year contract. £31.2 million wages

Bernard: No fee. 4 year contract. £25 million wages

Gomes: £28 million fee. 5 year contract. £29 million wages

Gbamin: £23 million fee. 5 year contract. £19.5 million wages

Delph: £8 million fee. 3 year contract. £12.6 million wages

Dele Alli: No fee. 3 year contract. £15.6 million wages

Maupay: £13 million fee. 3 year contract. £7.8 million wages

It's a sobering thought that over £500 million of Moshiri's cash went to pay the transfer fees and wages of these fifteen players, some of whom rarely played for the club, all of whom failed to justify their huge wages, and none of whom provided the club with a decent sell-on fee. (Source: Spotrac.com and ToffeeWeb.com)

***

Other wage costs:

Player costs are the main cost driver, but headcount was allowed to balloon across the entire organisation. Prior to Farhad Moshiri's arrival, the club employed 274 people. By June 2022, the number had swollen to 491, with all departments seeing a significant growth in headcount and costs.

Players, training, management: 98 (2014/15); 169 (2021/22)
Youth Academy: 38 (2014/15); 66 (2021/22)
Marketing & Media: 32 (2014/15); 78 (2021/22)
Management & Admin: 71 (2014/15); 116 (2021/22)
Security/pitch/safety: 35 (2014/15); 62 (2021/22)
Total: 274 (2014/15); 491 (2021/22)
Total wage costs : £77.5 million (2014/15); £162 million (2021/22)[6]

Except for Colin Chong and his team supervising the work of Laing O'Rourke at Bramley-Moore Dock, and the growth of the Women's Football team, it's hard to imagine why the club which finished 16th in the league in 2021/22 should require a significantly more complex and costly organisation than the one which had finished 11th in the league six years earlier.

***

Financing the Stadium:

When Farhad Moshiri announced in March 2016 that he would look into the best options for the stadium and how to finance it, there was no mention of how much he had budgeted for this in his business plan. However, he knew it had cost Arsenal £390 million to build their 60,000 capacity stadium on an industrial and waste disposal site in Ashburton Grove in 2004. Emirates Airline bought the naming rights for the stadium, in a 15-year deal estimated at £100 million that also included a 7-year shirt sponsorship, starting in the 2006/07 season. Emirates and Arsenal agreed a new deal worth £150 million in November 2012, and shirt-sponsorship was extended by five years while they extended naming rights to 2028.

Another reference point could have been the City of Manchester Stadium, which was built at a cost of £110 million as the home for the 2002 Commonwealth Games. It had a capacity of 35,000, part of which was temporary seating. Soon after the event, the athletics track and pitch were removed, and the ground lowered to create space for additional tiers of seating in a football-specific configuration. The temporary stand behind one goal was dismantled and replaced by another permanent construction, identical to the one at the other end. This all cost an extra £30 million and enabled Manchester City to move there from their historical ground – Maine Road – after signing a 250-year lease. In 2011, the club was given a naming rights deal with Etihad Airlines for £150 million. It was a record deal for British football. Further investment will take the capacity of the Etihad Stadium to 60,000.

Everton had their own reference point in Kirkby, where they proposed to build a 50,000-seat stadium. It was estimated to cost £150 million and be the centrepiece of a huge retail development in a scheme driven by supermarket giant, Tesco. The Destination Kirkby project had a divisive effect as soon as it was announced and when Bill Kenwright opened the decision to a vote of 36,662 Everton fans. The outcome in August 2007 was 15,230 in favour, with 10,468 against and a further 10,901 abstaining. As Andy Hunter wrote in *The Guardian* on 25 November 2009: "The vote followed claims from Everton's then chief executive, Keith Wyness, that Kirkby represented 'the deal of the century' for a club that currently cannot afford a new stadium without an enabling project. It was also voted on before details of the new stadium were revealed and which, when published, prompted the leader of Liverpool City Council, Warren Bradley, to describe it as 'A glorified cow shed built in a small town outside Liverpool.' The project was finally ditched, when government Communities Secretary, John Denham, rejected the club's proposals."

Three Premier League clubs, three stadium projects, in a cost range from £150-£390 million, two of which had attracted sizeable naming rights deals to help them defray the capital costs. Was that the ballpark that Farhad Moshiri was thinking of when he prepared his business plan?

If so, the decision to develop the new Everton stadium on the banks of the Mersey as part of the Peel Holdings' Liverpool Waters scheme, then a World Heritage Organisation site, quickly blew those ideas out of the water. In committing to Bramley-Moore dock, the club had to pay around £30 million to Peel Holdings for the site, paid tens of millions to drain and infill the dock, and committed to spend "more than £55 million to preserve, restore and celebrate the heritage assets at Bramley-Moore Dock.

In selecting that city-centre, waterfront location and the magnificent design from Dan Meis, Moshiri aimed high. No glorified cow shed for him; instead, he committed to build Everton their Nil Satis Nisi Optimum stadium, one that would come to be nicknamed Liverpool's "fourth grace" and be selected as a host venue for the 2028 European Championships.

Club officials had long suggested the project would cost £505 million and Denise Barrett-Baxendale, then chief executive, was credited with negotiating a fixed price with contractors, Laing O'Rourke. But in an interview on TalkSport with Jim White in January 2023 and a meeting with the Everton Fan Advisory Board, Farhad Moshiri revealed that the completed stadium development project would cost around £760 million.

Though external funding had always been part of the original plans for paying for the Everton Stadium, none was secured until the summer of 2023 – and even then it was in the form of loans rather than investment. Up to that point, Farhad Moshiri had found himself in the painful predicament of everything coming out of his bank account. **Current estimates are that Moshiri has already paid out £400 million, for everything from the site cost, design and planning to the renovation of the heritage assets and construction costs to date.**

That left around £360 million to find over the final 18 months of the construction timeline.

Combined with funding the loss-making club to the tune of around £500 million since 2016, it's easy to see where over £800 million of Moshiri's money had gone.

No wonder he was desperately searching for additional funding.

His plan, ever since signing an exclusivity deal with MSP Sports Capital in May 2023, seemed to be based on the acceptance of their offer to inject over £100 million into the stadium funding pot and £50 million into the club, in return for granting MSP two places on the Everton board.

He hoped the MSP funding could not only trigger construction finance from major investment banks, but would also enable him to restructure the Everton board and bring in fresh ideas on how to take the club forward.

As had proved to be the case all too often, events did not work out the way Farhad Moshiri expected them to.

As the Toffees began their 121st season in the top-flight, on and off the field, the situation was about to become even more precarious.

---

1. Everton FC Annual Report & Accounts -2016/17
2. Arsenal Report & Accounts 2014/15; Everton Report & Accounts 2014/15
3. Everton Report & Accounts
4. Everton Report & Accounts
5. Everton FC Annual Report & Accounts

6. Everton FC Annual Report & Accounts

2023: MOSHIRI'S EVERTON WALKING THE TIGHTROPE

While Sean Dyche had successfully steered Everton to Premier League safety by almost the slimmest of margins thanks to that final-day win over Bournemouth in May, the club had remained under a cloud of uncertainty heading into the 2023/24 season.

The situation was summarised in gloomy fashion by Phil McNulty in his pre-season Premier League prediction column for *BBC Sport*:

"Where to start with a club who have narrowly escaped relegation for the last two seasons, and have yet to show any evidence they have learned the lessons? Everton have lacked quality back up for injury-plagued striker Dominic Calvert-Lewin for 12 months and they have yet to bring in anyone who looks ready to fill that role, with Leicester City's Patson Daka the latest to be linked.

"The scale of Everton's financial mismanagement over recent years means they are scraping around in the bargain basement. The squad is currently smaller than the one that escaped the drop on the final day of last term, although the addition of 38-year-old Ashley Young on a free transfer may be a very smart move.

"Everton's expected reset at board level has yet to materialise, along with the long-touted investment from American group MSP Sports Capital. Three boardroom members left in June but deeply divisive chairman Bill Kenwright remains in post, which continues to be a source of discontent among fans. The 77-year-old has not even felt able to attend a game at Goodison Park since January, citing security concerns.

"Manager Sean Dyche's organisational skills may just keep Everton up, although there is also the concern about a hearing in October after the club was referred to an independent commission for an alleged breach of the Premier League's Financial Fair Play rules. Everton strongly deny any wrongdoing but the prospect of a points deduction lingers if they are found guilty, which will obviously impact this particular prediction. Prediction: Everton to finish in 16th place."

Three games into the new season, Everton had managed to underperform McNulty's predictions. With a record of 3 games played, 3 losses, no goals scored, 6 goals conceded, zero points, the club sat bottom of the Premier League – the worst start in its history.

The bad news was not confined to the football results. On 23 August, Matt Slater of *The Athletic* reported:

"Everton's hopes of improving their financial situation have received a huge hit after MSP Sports Capital withdrew from talks about taking a minority stake in the club. The New York-based investment group signed an exclusivity deal with the Premier League side in May and the plan was to invest up to £150 million ($190 million) in convertible debt that would become a stake of approximately 25 per cent in the 145-year-old club.

"In a complicated deal, £100 million of that investment was meant for Everton Stadium Development Company, the subsidiary club owner Farhad Moshiri set up in 2017 to oversee the construction of Everton's new ground at Bramley-Moore Dock, with the rest going to the club. But that exclusivity period is now over and the deal is dead, with the stumbling block being opposition from one of Everton's existing offshore lenders, Rights and Media Funding Limited."

For many Evertonians, the news that a relatively unknown lender, Rights and Media Funding could block the new investment deal came as a shock. It raised many questions, including who was behind Rights and Media?

It was a question that had been partly answered at Everton's AGM in November 2015, just three months before Farhad Moshiri took over at Everton. In an article written by Ed Aarons in *The Guardian* in December 2016, he recalled how:

"The CEO, Robert Elstone castigated shareholders who asked questions about [Philip] Green's potential involvement before revealing that the club's net debt had increased from £28.1 million in 2013/14 to £31.3 million in 2014/15, despite announcing record turnover and a bumper TV deal. 'We have three sources of lending,' he said. 'We have a long-term loan with the Prudential that expires in 2026, an overdraft with Barclays that is not enough to manage the day-to-day cash flow of the football club and, to address that, we borrow from JG Funding (a private company) against the TV money. It is all fully disclosed in our accounts, is approved by the Premier League and paid back at the end of the year.' "

Less than six months after the latest loan with JG Funding was taken out, Moshiri paid his £87.5m for a 49.9% share in Everton, valuing the club at £175 million. The publication of Everton's 2015/16 accounts revealed the Iranian businessman had also provided an interest-free loan of £80 million 'with no agreed repayment date.' That funding was used post year-end to reduce the club's long-term debt by repaying the entire other loans balance of £54.8 million at 31 May 2016.

Despite that, Everton's accounts showed that another loan was taken out on 26 August 2016. This time, it was registered to a company called Rights and Media Funding Limited, which had changed its name from JG Funding at the end of 2015.

This practice of 'payday' lending, whereby clubs borrow at higher-than-market interest rates from offshore entities, was not a new practice, nor was it unique to Everton. The security offered against the loan was typically the club's TV rights money. The loan is normally repaid annually and renewed as necessary. As Aarons explained in the same article in *The Guardian*:

"By the start of the 2011/12 season, Everton had debts of more than £40 million and faced the prospect of having to sell some of their better players to balance the books. With banks unwilling to lend in the wake of the financial crash, Kenwright turned to Vibrac [Corporation] to arrange a deal worth £14 million a year, although they were to take out loans worth more than £80 million in loans over the next four years. Fulham also borrowed £16 million, while Reading took out an £11.7 million loan for which they were later fined £30,000 for contravening Football League rules."

A recent search on the Companies House website revealed that Rights and Media Holdings is a U.K. company based in Altrincham. It has no employees and two directors, David McKnight and Jonathan McMorrow. In its accounts, for the year to 30 June 2021, it had assets of £190,934,023. The lenders of these assets were named in the charge documents as:

- M H Finance Limited, a company incorporated and registered in Bermuda.
- Galloway (Cyprus) Ltd, a company incorporated and registered in Cyprus.
- Carroch (Bahamas) Ltd, a company incorporated and registered in Nassau.

But who is behind these companies?

In *Football's Secret Trade,* published by Bloomberg in 2017, Alex Duff and Tariq Panja revealed that the British tax exile and racehorse owner, Michael Tabor – who made his fortune selling the 114-shop

Arthur Price betting chain to Coral in 1995, and subsequently split his time between homes in Monte Carlo and Barbados – "Employed David McKnight, a soft-spoken Mancunian in his late 50s... Tabor also called in Graham Shear, a partner at law firm Berwin Leighton Paisner, who could put together a contract in as little as 24 hours."

According to Duff and Panja, Tabor used McKnight and Shear to organise loans to Athletico Madrid, Deportivo La Coruña and Getafe. Tabor also "took over some of the business of Investec in English football, advancing money due to Everton, Southampton, Fulham and Reading before the start of each season, in return for promissory notes from the Premier League....The arrangements in the UK were through another company domiciled in the British Virgin Islands, called Vibrac Corporation."

Michael Tabor's name is nowhere to be seen on the loan agreements between Everton Football Club Company Limited and Rights and Media Funding Limited, but the agreements are signed for Rights and Media by David McKnight. The documents are copied to Bryan Cave Leighton Paisner LLP, for the attention of Graham Shear.

Seven years after Farhad Moshiri took over at Everton, the club is more indebted to Rights and Media Funding than ever. According to Everton's 2021/22 accounts the club's borrowings, aside from shareholder loans, amounted to £174.1 million. Included in that figure was a £150 million, 5-year facility with Rights and Media Funding, which appeared to be fully utilised. The club is likely to be paying 10-12% interest on that loan.

In the charge document signed by Everton directors, for the loan taken out from Rights and Media Funding on 22 August 2016, there is a negative pledge attached to the loan. That means the terms of the loan agreement prohibit or restrict the company (Everton) from creating a further security that will rank equally with or ahead of the charge.

In layman's terms, you can't mortgage your house twice, at least not without the consent of your first lender.

This is standard practice in such matters, and MSP Sports Capital must have known about the club's loans from Rights and Media Funding. Why it took so long for this to become the deal-breaker (if indeed it was), remains an open question.

So at the start of the 2023/24 season, Everton remained in financial limbo. Farhad Moshiri continued the search for his own messiah investor –someone who would help him keep the club afloat, and enable him to fulfil the dream of a new stadium for the Blues to play in. In the meantime, the owner, the club and its fans continued their tortuous tightrope walk; knowing that a slip into the Championship could prove fatal.

2023: From Moshiri's frying pan into the 777 fire?

> “I believe they [777] are the best partners to take our great Club forward...As a result of this agreement, we have an experienced and well-connected investor in football clubs who will help maximise the commercial opportunities, and we have secured the complete financing for our new stadium.
>
> – Farhad Moshiri, 15 September 2023

2023 From Moshiri's frying pan into the 777 fire

By the turn of 2023, Farhad Moshiri’s search for external investors in Everton had become reminiscent of Bill Kenwright’s increasingly desperate efforts to find his own billionaire more than a decade before, but Moshiri's discussions with USA-based investment firms MSP Sports Capital and 777 Partners hinted at progress on that front as the year wore on.

The narrative had initially been around Moshiri trying to find a co-funder for the stadium. Yet the fallout of Russia’s war against Ukraine, the resulting sanctions against Alisher Usmanov, and Everton's worsening predicament on the pitch, moved Moshiri's discussions towards the outright sale of the football club and its half-finished stadium.

Less than six months after providing a (non-legally-binding) letter to the auditors confirming his ongoing financial support for Everton Football Club, news broke on 15 September, that Moshiri had signed an agreement with 777 Partners to acquire his full 94.1% stake in the club. The precise nature of the deal remained opaque, with the exact terms of the agreement undisclosed, but *The Telegraph* reported that it could eventually total £500 million with the Miami-based private equity firm agreeing to making staged payments over a period of years that would depend very much on whether the club remained in the Premier League.

In an open letter to Evertonians, Moshiri said:

> "The nature of ownership and financing of top football clubs has changed immeasurably since I first invested in Everton over seven years ago. The days of an owner/benefactor are seemingly out of reach for most, and the biggest clubs are now typically owned by well-resourced PE [Private Equity] firms, specialist sports investors or state-backed companies and funds. I have been open about the need to bring in new investment and complete the financing for our iconic new stadium at Bramley-Moore Dock, on the banks of the Mersey, which I have predominantly financed to date.

> "I have spoken to a number of parties and considered some strong potential opportunities. However, **it is through my lengthy discussions with 777 that I believe they are the best partners to take our great Club forward, with all the benefits of their multi-club investment model. As a result of this agreement, we have an experienced and well-connected investor in football clubs who will help maximise the commercial opportunities, and we have secured the complete financing for our new stadium, which will be the critical element in the future success of Everton."**

Completion of the transaction was expected to occur by the end of the year but the 777 bid was subject to regulatory approval, including from the Premier League, the Football Association, and the Financial Conduct Authority (FCA). As a slew of newspaper and investigative pieces published over the ensuing weeks illustrated, this promised to be no mere formality.

Despite Moshiri's claims that 777 were "the best partners to take our great Club forward," serious doubts were being expressed over the American firm's ability to follow through on their purchase of the club in the first place, with numerous observers questioning whether they had the funds necessary to complete the deal, even on a phased basis.

Beyond that, reports of missed or delayed payments in parts of their existing sporting portfolio – one that includes Sevilla, Standard

Liege, Genoa, Hertha Berlin and Vasco da Gama in football and the British Basketball League – placed a question mark over 777's ability to complete Everton Stadium, cover any debt that must be repaid in the event of a successful takeover, fund day-to-day operations, and invest in the playing squad.

As if all of that weren't enough, concerns were being raised as high up as the UK Government over 777 Partners' suitability for buying into the Premier League based on their ongoing involvement in several court cases in the United States. 777 and sister company Sutton Park had been accused of fraud, offering illegal loans and failing to pay bills totalling hundreds of thousands of dollars, all potentially disqualifying events under the Premier League's beefed up owners' and directors' test.

That was the "postage stamp" version. The seedier and unsavoury accounts of how co-founders Josh Wander and Steve Pasko had built 777 Partners in the first place could form the outline for a Hollywood film. Originally under the banner of Sutton Park, the pair had found their niche in the lucrative business of "structured settlements" – the practice of offering highly discounted cash settlements, often to victims of accidents who have been awarded annuities in compensation for their injuries – and they had grown the firm into arguably the biggest player in its sphere in the US.

Starting with Wander's arrest for drug trafficking and possession as a student at the University of Florida (for which he was later sentenced to 15 years' probation for possession of drug paraphernalia after pleading no contest to the charges), through the lawsuits filed by two American women accusing 777 subsidiaries of predatory lending practices and allegations of racketeering activities, including 'kidnapping, bribery, extortion and dealing in a controlled substance,' all the way to claims of fraud and breach of contract in relation to their budget airline business, legal problems have never been too far away from Everton's prospective buyers.

Where the experience, the financial resources and the management skills to take forward a club the size of Everton were concerned, there was little evidence that 777 would have the wherewithal to pull it off.

At the time of their takeover bid, the firm had barely two years of experience in owning and controlling football clubs and their success rate in that time had been decidedly mixed. As Paul Brown and Philippe Auclair wrote in the first of a number of exposés of 777 for *Josimar*, a Norwegian investigative publication, in July 2023, "Multiple club-owner 777 ... has a patchy record in honouring its financial commitments.

"[I]n less than two years, 777, a private company which insists it does not invest other people's money but only the wealth of its owners, has become a multiple club owner only surpassed by a handful of operators such as Abu Dhabi's controlling entity City Football Group in terms of the depth and breadth of their investments in club football.

"777 now owns in full or in part seven football clubs in seven different countries on three continents, for an outlay which Josimar estimates could run up to 900 million dollars in total, debt burden not included, a colossal sum for a company which is nowhere near as cash-rich as other US equity funds which have recently set their eyes on, in particular, European clubs."

Though 777 Partners' moral and ethical compass appeared to be at odds with a great British footballing institution that prides itself on its standing and work in the community, it was their ability to successfully fund and run Everton FC that was of greatest concern to its supporters. In that respect, the sight of fans of Standard Liege and Hertha Berlin displaying banners of protest aimed at their club's Floridian owners, reports from Brazil that FIFA had threatened Vasco da Gama with a transfer ban for non-payment of transfer fees (777 came up with the payments at the eleventh hour) and further delayed tranches related to their investment in British basketball all cast doubt over a company that claims to have the funding necessary to acquire and develop a major Premier League club.

No one could say for sure, as the end of 2023 approached and the club awaited the conclusion of the vetting by the Premier League and FCA of the bid from Florida, whether a takeover by 777 Partners would be a good thing or a bad thing for Everton FC. Though 777 had a chequered history of meeting their obligations in a timely manner, they had a habit of finding the money in the end and there were signs in 2023 that their stewardship of Genoa, in particular, had brought stability and firmer fiscal foundations than had previously existed.

Indeed, 777 at least appear to be going about things in the right way in terms of structuring a portfolio of clubs across three continents in fairly short order. Don Dransfield, formerly the Chief Strategy Officer at City Football Group, was appointed Chief Executive Officer of a dedicated 777 Football Group division in May 2022. He met with Everton supporter representatives as well as finance expert Paul The Esk and joined Wander and Pasko in the Directors Box at Goodison Park for the home game against Luton Town in September 2023.

Additionally — and equally as encouraging from the point of view of structure and intent — Johannes Spors, previously director of football at Vitesse Arnhem, now General Manager at Genoa, and someone who was seriously considered for a senior role by Tottenham, was appointed Sporting Director for the 777 Football Group, reporting to Dransfield.

777's intent, as Wander told French newspaper *L'Equipe*, is to invest in a club's long-term success rather than to try and turn a quick profit.

"What is important in our eyes is not to build a club which generates profit just for the sake of profit," he said. "We want clubs that are capable of living and developing over a number of decades."

Those goals were echoed by Spors in an interview with *The Telegraph* in December 2023 in which he described Everton in terms of being "the missing link" in the firm's stable of clubs.

"We want the clubs to be the best versions of themselves," the German explained. "We have the challenge that every club that joined the group was having, in recent history, a development going in the wrong direction. We have to turn around all the clubs' development and all of them are now in a better situation.

"So we made the teams younger, we made every team cheaper in terms of the wage bill, but we increased the value of the squad."

Everton's financial hole is considerably deeper than any of the teams 777 Partners have acquired to date; nevertheless, against the backdrop of a drumbeat of negative headlines around the company – at the time this book went to print, reports emerged that the US Department of Justice had launched an investigation in 777's financial dealings – Messers Wander and Pasko were making good on their intent to invest in Everton. By the end of 2023 they had furnished the club with loans in excess of £100 million, to cover working capital and the ongoing cost of building the new stadium at Bramley-Moore Dock.

Would that form the starting point for a takeover that would end the Moshiri Era or would the mysterious money-men from Miami become the latest in a lengthening line of Everton's creditors?

2023: The End of an Era

> "There can be no mistaking that Bill loved Everton Football Club. He admired the hard work, dedication and effort of every member of staff across the club and Everton in the Community but most of all he recognised and empathised with the passion, loyalty and support all the Everton teams have had from Evertonians be that at home, away or abroad.
>
> - Farhad Moshiri

2023 The end of an era as Bill Kenwright dies

Ever since he and his True Blue Holdings Consortium had launched their successful bid to buy the club from Peter Johnson in 1999, the figure of Bill Kenwright had loomed large over Everton. It would be another five years before he assumed the mantle of chairman but, in everything from the firing of Walter Smith and the appointment of his successor David Moyes in 2002, to the formulation of the Blues' first proposed waterfront stadium at the Kings Dock two years later, there was no question who was shaping the club's future.

Even after Farhad Moshiri came on board in 2016 and eventually increased his holdings to 94.1%, reducing Kenwright's stake to a 1.3% in the process, the renowned theatre impresario remained entwined in many key aspects of running the club, especially when the Board of Directors – and he in particular – had become a lightning rod for criticism and frustration from supporters.

This was true even as he battled ill-health in his 70s but, in the summer of 2023, Kenwright was admitted to intensive care for a period of weeks due to complications following surgery to remove a cancerous tumour from his liver. He returned home to begin his recovery but apparently suffered a heart attack shortly thereafter. He passed away on 23 October at the age of 78 surrounded by his loved ones, bringing to a close a defined era in the club's history.

"The club has lost a chairman, a leader, a friend, and an inspiration," a statement from Everton read.

The club's majority shareholder, Farhad Moshiri, sent his own message via evertonfc.com in which he expressed his sadness at the passing of his "great friend".

"There can be no mistaking that Bill loved Everton Football Club," Moshiri wrote. "He spoke with an infectious enthusiasm about every aspect of Everton, from the legends of yesteryear to his unconditional support for everyone that wears the Blue shirt and represents the club. He admired the hard work, dedication and effort of every member of staff across the club and Everton in the Community but most of all he recognised and empathised with the passion, loyalty and support all the Everton teams have had from Evertonians be that at home, away or abroad. He was a special soul, a man successful in so many different walks of life. We will miss him but never forget him."

A life-long Everton fan and one-time small-part actor on *Coronation Street*, Kenwright built his career as a nationally renowned producer of plays. He was first elected to the Everton Board of Directors on 23 October 1989, and, after leading the successful takeover a decade later, he decided to take the title Vice-Chairman and installed former supremo, Sir Philip Carter, as Chairman before eventually taking the helm himself in 2004 when Carter became Life President until his passing in 2015.

Though the first decade of Kenwright's tenure as chairman would see much-needed stability on the pitch under David Moyes, the club's financial footing was gradually eroded as the Board battled to keep the team competitive on the increasingly un-level playing field of the Premier League.

He had always maintained that he was the ordinary fan from the Boys Pen who had 'done good' and realised the dream of owning his beloved Blues; merely the custodian waiting for someone with deeper pockets and much bigger resources to eventually step in and buy him out. It took him longer than he initially envisaged but he eventually found someone fitting that bill in the form of Farhad Moshiri.

Likely even by his own admission, the next seven years didn't pan out the way Kenwright had envisaged. His dream of a new home for the Toffees on the banks of the Mersey was well on the way to being realised but his death came at a time of deep uncertainty at Everton, both on and off the pitch, with the club struggling financially and facing the prospect of a third successive battle to avoid relegation.

His role in the decline in Everton's fortunes during the Moshiri Era may have been debatable, but in the minds of many supporters he had, unfortunately, come to be seen as complicit in the majority shareholder's failings. Though he had been retained as chairman while the rest of the board stepped down in the summer of 2023, it was expected that in the event of any takeover, Kenwright's time as chairman would have come to an end anyway.

He would not get to see that next chapter in the history of his beloved Blues, nor take a seat at Bramley-Moore Dock but Bill Kenwright had left an indelible mark on the club. A memorial service was held for him on 18 December at the Anglican Cathedral in Liverpool.

2023: Everton stunned by Independent Commission's verdict

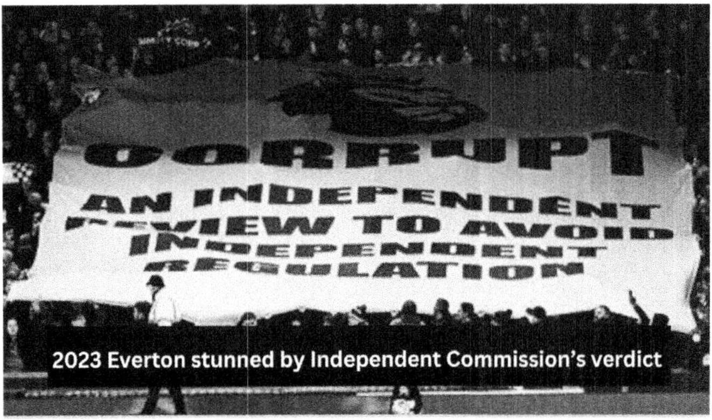

2023 Everton stunned by Independent Commission's verdict

The decision in March 2023 by the Premier League to refer Everton to an independent commission after charging the club with breaching its Profitability and Sustainability Rules (PSR) during the 2021/22 season had hung in the background while the Blues first battled to avoid relegation for a second successive season and then set about trying to improve their playing squad. All the while, they were still operating under strict austerity measures that had, by that point, been in place for two years.

The club's attempts to not only remain compliant with the League's spending rules, but also take demonstrable strides towards improving their standing vis-à-vis PSR, required Director of Football Kevin Thelwell to work the loan market and structure deals for incoming players in such a way that required the bare minimum in up-front payments.

38-year-old Ashley Young was drafted in on a free transfer following his departure from Aston Villa. While Arnaut Danjuma, the player who had infamously snubbed a move to Goodison Park at the 11th hour in the January transfer window, was secured on loan at the second attempt. Another season-long loan arrangement was concluded for Leeds United winger Jack Harrison, and Youssef Chermiti, a promising teenage striker was signed from Sporting Clube de Portugal in a deal that could eventually total £12 million.

The initial outlay for the youngster was thought to be a quarter of that, and when another January target in the form of another Portuguese striker Beto was secured shortly before the summer deadline for £26 million, Thelwell and the club were able to structure the deal in such a way that no payments were due until the next financial year.

Meanwhile, the outgoings continued. Yerry Mina's £6 million-plus annual salary was jettisoned from the wage bill when his contract expired, and almost £50 million was raised with the sale of seven players from the first and Under-21 teams, with Alex Iwobi the most prominent when he left for Fulham in a £22 million deal. When added to the departures of the likes of Anthony Gordon and Moise Kean earlier in 2023 it meant that Everton had realised close to £120 million in outgoing transfers for the calendar year while spending almost nothing by comparison on the five new faces they were able to welcome to the club.

It may have been an imperative given the parlous state of the club's finances, a situation that would require further loans from external lenders to prop up day-to-day operations as the year wore on, but it also represented significant risk. Sean Dyche had been left with a more balanced playing squad that finally had striking alternatives to Dominic Calvert-Lewin, whose 2021/22 and 2022/23 campaigns had been wrecked by injury, but there was precious little depth. Any significant injury crisis could have seriously undermined what was expected to be another long fight for top-flight survival.

All of those moves to slash the losses racked up in the preceding years came too late for the purposes of the Commission that finally heard the Premier League's case against Everton and their PSR breach in October. A three-person panel made up of David Phillips KC, Alan Greenwood and Nick Igoe was appointed by the Premier League to hear the case. With no precedent or established framework for sanctions in place, the Commission's powers of censure were essentially limitless.

While outright expulsion from the Premier League was deemed unlikely in the extreme, speculation among observers varied from Everton being handed a fine or temporary transfer embargo on the less punitive end of the scale to a points deduction on the other. In what was a hugely controversial development, however, newspaper reports surfaced on 25 October that the League were pushing for a points deduction of as much as 12 points and it would later emerge that they had advanced a formula by which the Commission might calculate an appropriate sanction: 6 points for the initial breach and then 1 point for every £5 million Everton had gone over the £105 million threshold.

So it was that on 17 November, it was announced, to the astonishment of Everton FC, its fans and much of the domestic football that the Commission had recommended the club be deducted 10 points with immediate effect, plunging the Blues back into the relegation zone. Worse, it was also revealed that in a decision reached by Mr Phillips in May earlier in the year, the door was opened for the likes of Burnley, Leeds United and Leicester City to launch their reported £300 million joint lawsuit against Everton for lost revenue due to relegation in the two preceding seasons which, they would argue, would not have occurred had Everton not broken spending rules.

In the Commission's report, it was detailed that Everton had admitted to breaching PSR but only by £9.7 million, an assertion the Premier League countered with their own calculation that the club had gone over the limit by £19.5 million. Mitigating factors put forward by the club's counsel relating to the outbreak of the war in Ukraine that led to the suspension of key sponsorship deals with USM Holdings; the club's firing of Player X following his arrest in December 2021; interest paid on costs related to the construction of Everton Stadium; further losses and complications caused by the COVID-19 pandemic, including the inability to raise funds with the sale of Player Y; and the Premier League's 4% Transfer Levy on transfer fees were all dismissed as considerations.

Instead, the League put forward a number of Aggravating Factors that they felt were appropriate in determining the extent of Everton's culpability, including "overspend despite repeated warnings", "misleading the Premier League about stadium interest" and "misleading the Premier League about the intention to sell Player Y". The Commission decided to eliminate the last factor from consideration and agreed with Everton's assertion that an improving trend towards PSR compliance went "some limited way to diminish [the club's] culpability", but they ultimately sided with the League on the other factors, agreed that Everton had, to an extent, acted in bad faith. The Commission ruled that only a sporting sanction not a financial penalty would be appropriate for 'a serious breach', given owner Farhad Moshiri's personal wealth.

On the day the 10-point penalty was announced, Everton issued a statement saying they were "shocked and disappointed by the ruling of the Premier League's Commission. The Club believes that the Commission has imposed a wholly disproportionate and unjust sporting sanction." An appeal of the decision was lodged 14 days later, with a new independent panel to be appointed to assess its validity in the coming months.

In the meantime, an Everton team that, under Dyche, had started putting a run of form together and was climbing the Premier League table was thrust into another battle for survival. The struggle on the part of the three newly-promoted clubs – Burnley, Sheffield United and Luton Town – offered hope that the Blues could overcome the significant handicap of losing 10 points and stay up. Even if they managed it, however, the club's parlous financial state and the uncertainty over 777 Partners' takeover bid continued to pose further existential threats to one of Britain's oldest and most venerated institutions.

2024: We Shall Not Be Moved

With Farhad Moshiri's signature on an exclusive agreement with 777 Partners to acquire his full stake in the club, the Iranian-British businessman's active ownership of Everton effectively came to an end on 15 September, 2023 – but the deal could only be completed if the Florida-based investment firm passed the Premier League's owners and directors test. Originally expected to take around 12 weeks and be wrapped up Christmas, that vetting and approval process would bleed well into 2024, with the prospect that the sale might not come to fruition at all growing ever stronger.

With the Blues already indebted to 777 to the tune of a reported £142 million – that on top of the other liabilities that had piled up under the Monaco-based billionaire's reign – it wasn't clear what would happen should the takeover collapse, and where that would leave the club.

In the meantime, the peril in which Everton had been placed by the Moshiri years deepened with the announcement by the Premier League on the 15 January 2024 that the Blues had been referred to *another* independent commission for a *second* alleged breach of Profitability and Sustainability Rules for the three-year period ending 30 June 2023.

Under new guidelines from the League aimed at expediting any penalties for contravening spending rules, member clubs had been required to submit their preliminary accounts and PSR calculations by the end of December 2023. Still in the process of preparing for their appeal against the first charge and sanction, Everton had been forced to submit accounts in line with the decision from the first independent accounts and declare themselves in breach of PSR.

If found guilty, of course, that carried the threat of a further points deduction, to be imposed before the end of the 2023/24 season, and the very real prospect that Everton could be relegated from the top flight – with all the existential crises that would trigger.

Everton responded to the second charge with a pointed statement highlighting the fact that 75% of the financial period in question overlapped seasons for which the club had already been penalised, a sanction for which they were currently appealing:

"The Premier League does not have guidelines which prevent a club being sanctioned for alleged breaches in financial periods which have already been subject to punishment, unlike other governing bodies, including the EFL. As a result – and because of the Premier League's new commitment to deal with such matters "in-season" – the club is in a position where it has had no option but to submit a PSR calculation which remains subject to change, pending the outcome of the appeal.

"The club must now defend another Premier League complaint which includes the very same financial periods for which it has already been sanctioned, before that appeal has even been heard. The Club takes the view that this results from a clear deficiency in the Premier League's rules."

The situation meant that outcome of that appeal, expected to heard in February 2024, was of critical importance to the club's future and to Moshiri's legacy as Everton's owner.

Moshiri's track record in accountancy and consulting, together with his skills and experience in mergers and acquisitions, had once taken him to the chairmanship of Metalloinvest, Alisher Usmanov's $16 billion conglomerate, and the reward from the oligarch of a 10% shareholding in the company.

Yet Everton's appalling performance on and off the field over his almost eight years at the helm, the club's referral to two independent commissions, coupled with the deep concerns around Moshiri's choice of buyer in 777 Partners all raise serious questions about his governance and judgement.

□

As we've seen repeatedly in The Unofficial Everton Timeline, since taking control in 2016, Moshiri's miscalculations had caused considerable damage to the football club and to his own reputation.

After nine years as an Arsenal shareholder, he must have felt as though he knew what it took to run a successful football club. Arsenal may have been an entirely different kettle of fish to Everton –on the field, Arsène Wenger provided the leadership and regular Champions League football, and the Gunners had completed construction of the Emirates Stadium before Moshiri and Usmanov showed up – but, as the intervening years have shown, the Boardroom leadership of Arsenal has been far more suited to steering an elite Premier League football club.

Given his other responsibilities as chairman of Metalloinvest, Moshiri surely never intended to be involved in the day-to-day running of Everton. Nor should he have been. His job was to appoint serious, heavyweight, experienced professionals to the Everton Board. Instead, he allowed Bill Kenwright to convince him that some continuation of the old regime was the answer. When it came time to appoint a new chief executive, a new finance director and a non-executive director, he allowed Bill Kenwright to fill those posts with his devotees rather than bring in industry-leading expertise to establish a forward-looking, innovative Boardroom. And when it came to the big decisions on the playing side, Moshiri never seemed able to resist the temptation to meddle, or to take the advice of self-interested 'advisors' from outside the club.

Indeed, while Sheikh Mansour hired top professionals to run Manchester City, leaving them to recruit Pep Guardiola, provide him with the funds to recruit the players he needed, and lay the foundations for City to win 14 major trophies since 2017, Moshiri, in that same period, interfered in areas he had no expertise in and has experienced nothing but failure. He personally hand-picked a succession of managers and coaches, most of them with little in common in terms of their approach and style, while Directors of Football also proved ineffective within Moshiri's structure, where he and Kenwright remained in charge of player recruitment.

Moshiri clearly had good intentions when he arrived at Everton and he did have an aggressive plan for the first few years following his takeover aimed at vaulting the Toffees into the promised land of the Premier League's top four and the Champions League.

He once told an AGM of shareholders that while he was at the club, money would never be in short supply, no doubt because he had mistakenly banked on the continuing financial support from his friend and business partner, Alisher Usmanov, and his companies. And Moshiri described to the independent commission in October 2023 his strategy of significant outlay on upgrading the playing squad in his first three or four seasons as major shareholder.

As Evertonian and finance expert, Paul Quinn, commented in November 2021:

"The casual abandon with which cash was spent in the early days of the Moshiri reign, combined with extremely poor recruitment decisions on and off the pitch, have created a significant cost and liability that Moshiri could not have foreseen when he arrived in February 2016."

It shouldn't be overlooked that Moshiri's efforts at building a successful team were hampered by some terrible luck, in terms of serious injuries to the likes of Yannick Bolasie, Jean-Philippe Gbamin, Andre Gomes and Yerry Mina. Such setbacks robbed the Toffees of their services for long periods and prevented them from ever having a significant impact on the team's fortunes. But while his ambitions were grandiose, Moshiri's plans lacked any contingency for the eventuality that either European football's gravy train proved elusive, the supply of funds from USM Holdings was cut off – or both! Putin's invasion of Ukraine was never in the plan, and the consequences of the UK government's immediate sanctions on Usmanov deprived the club of its main sponsors overnight. It also dashed any hopes Moshiri had of completing a £200 million naming rights deal for the new ground at Bramley-Moore Dock.

Beyond the shorter term speculation on a 'Hollywood' manager and big-money signings, with the goal of Champions League qualification within three or four years and all the riches that would entail to fund future growth, Everton Stadium was seen as the main solution to the club's problems.

The planning, design and execution of the new stadium stood in stark contrast to the shambles that Moshiri's reign became on the pitch and if the good ship Everton was able to ride out the stormy waters currently threatening to pull her under, the reclusive and somewhat enigmatic British-Iranian would have solved one problem that had vexed successive owners for generations.

Yet as the stadium continued to rise out of Liverpool's north docks, the existential threat that Moshiri referred to in his videoed meeting with Jazz Bal of the Fan Advisory Board in January 2023 hung heavier than ever over the club.

With the club's interim directors in the process of appealing against the ten-point deduction imposed by the Premier League's Independent Commission, the threat of further sanction posed by a second panel, and with Captain Moshiri about to abandon ship, off the field the club's future remained far from certain.

***

On the field, however, things were looking up as 2023 drew to a close. Even though the Premier League had handed Everton the largest sporting sanction in English top-flight history, plunging it into another battle against relegation, it had taken the Blues just two weeks to win the same amount of points back and haul themselves out of the bottom three, as Sean Dyche and his side shrugged off the setback against Manchester United on 26 November by winning four straight matches.

Indeed, it was fitting that Chelsea – the free-spending Londoners – were the opponents at Goodison Park on 10 December. Fitting because the respective experience of the two clubs over the majority of the Premier League era, and their standing in the game with regard to treatment by the media and the powers-that-be, had been so very different.

In hoarding players and farming them out on loan to places like sibling club Vitesse Arnhem, spending close to £1 billion on incoming transfers in just a couple of years, and by signing those players on seven and eight-year contracts, not to mention selling club-owned hotels to sister-companies, Chelsea had bent the rules to breaking point.

They were under the brief threat of having their day in front of an independent commission for their own PSR breaches, but few could miss the irony – not to mention the mockery of the notion of financial fair play – in Mauricio Pochettino's response to his team's latest defeat at Goodison Park being a call to spend yet more money on transfers in the upcoming January transfer window.

Everton, by contrast, would almost certainly have to sell one of their crown jewels in the forthcoming summer transfer window to cover costs and spiralling debt, especially if 777 Partners either proved incapable of completing their proposed takeover or were deemed unworthy of owning the club by the regulatory bodies concerned. In the interim, however, survival as a top-flight outfit remained top of mind and fortunately, under Dyche at that time, Everton had in spades what money can seldom purchase: spirit, mentality and belief.

It may have been tempting for neutral observers to put the Blues' four wins prior to Christmas2023 down to the galvanising effect of the Premier League's potentially devastating posts sanction, but Dyche's team were already atoning for a poor start with a run of four wins in eight games before the unfair and disproportionate loss of those 10 points.

They would need to draw on all of those aforementioned qualities over the remainder of the season, even after the punishment recommended by the first independent commission was reduced to six points following a partially successful appeal in February 2024.

The team's winning streak, however, had came to an end with a painful exit from the Carabao Cup in a penalty shootout against Fulham and three successive League defeats that left the club hovering above the bottom three to close out the year. The manager and his players would be challenged by injuries and suspensions as they struggled through a 13-match winless run that broke an unwanted Premier League record that had stood since the infamous days of Mike Walker in the mid-1990s.

Meanwhile, the second independent commission into Everton's PSR breaches returned a verdict in April that the club should be docked a further two points, making the Blues the first club in history to be sanctioned twice in the same season and reducing the cushion between themselves and the bottom three to just two points.

Everton would push on, however, displaying the kind of character, defiance and fight for the badge that Dyche had so admirably harnessed in his first year in charge at Goodison, even after an alarming 6-0 defeat at Chelsea had temporarily sapped belief.

The harrowing night at Stamford Bridge was the kind of performance and result that had the potential to send the Blues into a tailspin with just six games left in the season. Sean Dyche and his players travelled back to Merseyside sitting just two points above the relegation zone but in the knowledge that they had the unusual advantage of three successive home games with which they could vault themselves clear of danger.

Which is exactly what they did. Everton followed that humiliation at the hands of Chelsea with three wins in the space of six transformative days in front of their home fans — a fine 2-0 win over relegation rivals, Nottingham Forest, and a 1-0 triumph over Brentford bookended a pulsating night under the Grand Old Lady's lights in the Merseyside derby.

Against the backdrop of a pulsating atmosphere, Jarrad Branthwaite pounced in the 27thminute to put the Blues ahead and while Jordan Pickford's heroics at one end protected the precious advantage against Liverpool, Dominic Calvert-Lewin headed home the killer second goal at the other 13 minutes into the second half.

Luis Diaz came the closest to opening the door for the reds in Jürgen Klopp's last Merseyside derby when he fired off the upright with 20 minutes to go but it always felt as though Everton were in control on a memorable occasion, where Sean Dyche's men became the first Toffees team to beat Liverpool at home since 2010.

Dyche had called for a typical derby display and, having set the team up perfectly, he got one in spades as Everton came out with high-octane intensity.

With greater composure from Abdoulaye Doucouré, the Toffees might have grabbed the lead as early as the third minute but the Frenchman side-footed disappointingly wide while, at the other end, a terrific, two goal-saving interventions by Ben Godfrey kept things level before the home side grabbed a 27th-minute lead.

A Dwight McNeil free-kick was only partially cleared and James Tarkowski hooked the ball back into the box where Jack Harrison cushioned it square to Godfrey. His shot pinged off Andrew Robertson and then Curtis Jones before Alexis MacAllister miscued horribly to Branthwaite who squeezed a shot under the goalkeeper and in off the post, with Calvert-Lewin sliding in to make sure as the ball squirmed over the line.

Goodison erupted but the goal sparked a sustained spell of Liverpool pressure. Darwin Nuñez seemed odds-on to score but Jordan Pickford made himself big and blocked his shot and England's No.1 was there again in the 44th minute when the Uruguayan striker nodded the ball into the path of Diaz, and Pickford quickly adjusted his feet to stop the goal-bound effort in superb fashion.

He was called into action one final time in a frenetic close to the opening half when he beat away Robertson's low cross and Everton went into the break a goal up and worthy leaders.

Far from the anticipated onslaught from Klopp's men after half-time, it was Everton who had the chances in the first quarter of a hour after the restart which led to them doubling their advantage before the hour mark.

Having stung Alisson's palms with a thunderous drive from outside the box that forced a corner from the Blues' right, McNeil swung a trademark delivery to the back post where Trent Alexander-Arnold completely lost Calvert-Lewin and the striker rose unchallenged to power a downward header into the goal to send the home fans into delirium.

It was a scene very much evocative of Joe Royle's first game in charge almost 30 years previously, when Duncan Ferguson had leapt with similar prowess to score his first goal for the club. That time it sparked Everton's remarkable drive to safety and FA Cup glory; on this occasion the famous win effectively secured the Toffees' top-flight status for another year while driving an emphatic nail into the coffin of Liverpool's League title hopes in Klopp's final season as the Reds' manager.

Final score: Everton 2 - 0 Liverpool

Dyche's team ultimately finished the 2023/24 season in 15th place, 14 points clear of Luton in 18th and with a final tally that would have matched that of much-lauded Brighton & Hove Albion if the eight points they were deducted were removed from the equation.

That baseline of determination and togetherness, on the pitch and in the stands, that had been a feature of much of the campaign, had continued to be a vital ingredient in a season that finished far more positively than it might have done. **Or, to put it in fewer but all-encompassing words: We shall not be moved.**

2024: Dodging the Bullet

If Sean Dyche's Everton side had needed a jolt to inspire that remarkable six-day spell in April 2024 when they won three straight home games, including a first victory in the Goodison derby for fourteen years, the 6-0 humbling by Chelsea on the 15th of that month had provided just that.

That date also had the potential to be seismic in terms of the club's ownership saga, as midnight on the 15th of April represented the deadline by which 777 Partners had to have provided the funds to pay off the £158 million loaned to Everton by MSP Sports Capital the previous summer. Failure to do so would hand MSP the opportunity to take a 51% controlling interest in the club, were they to activate a clause in their agreement with Farhad Moshiri.

No doubt over-awed by the amount of debt Everton had accrued as they pressed on with the construction of the new stadium at Bramley-Moore Dock, the New York private investment outfit ultimately declined to take up the offer. Still in financial limbo, Moshiri extended 777's deadline until the end of May, by which time they would have to prove to the Premier League that they could also fund an escrow account with £60 million to cover the club's ongoing working capital requirements.

If it all felt rather pointless, given that at no point had Josh Wander or Steve Pasko, 777's founding partners, ever seemed close to meeting either condition in order to pass the League's Owners and Directors Test, the end of the charade eventually arrived when the revised date of the 31st of May came and went without incident.

777 Partners' doomed bid to buy Everton had officially come to end but the firm itself was already beginning to unravel in spectacular fashion as the extent to which they had over-reached became apparent. The Miami-based firm's collapse had its origins in the decision by US agency, A M Best, to downgrade the credit rating of 777Re, a reinsurance subsidiary of the parent company based in Bermuda.

That prompted Advantage Capital Insurance Group (A-CAP),another, larger player in the insurance arena — and, as it turned out, the major backer behind 777's attempt to build a global stable of sport teams — to begin to pull back from Wander and Pasko's organisation.

The real catalysts to 777's implosion, however, came in April, first with the collapse of their Australian budget airline, Bonza, which was forced into administration at the end of the month. A fortnight later, the firm's assets in Belgium were seized by authorities at the request of the chairman and former owner of Standard Liège, Bruno Vernanzi who alleged that 777 still owed a sizeable instalment of funds for the purchase of that club two years previously.

At the same time, a Brazilian judge ordered that another 777-owned club, Vasco da Gama, be taken out of their control and handed back to the *Sociedade Anônima do Futebol* (SAF), while Wander, Pasko and three others were removed from Vasco's board of directors.

A day later, 777 Partners' two managing partners resigned their positions at the firm following the filing of a massive civil lawsuit against them in a New York district court by London-based Leadenhall Capital Partners, who alleged that they had fraudulently borrowed against £350 million in assets that "it didn't own, didn't exist or were already promised to someone else." There were also allegations of forged documents, faked records and the assertion by Leadenhall that 777 had been operating "a giant shell game, at best, and an outright Ponzi scheme, at worst".

Everton and their fans might ordinarily have watched the soap opera that played out over the remainder of 2024 with a sense of detachment and even perverse amusement, but 777's crisis had ongoing implications for the club and remained an obstacle to fresh takeover moves from other interested parties over the summer.

Indeed, the Blues were named in Leadenhall's complaint which said that, "Everton is the latest shiny object of Wander's fraudulent scheme, solvency aside. Despite the fact that 777 Partners and many of the operating businesses and professional football teams that Wander owns are deep in debt, behind on their obligations, and on thin ice with regulators, Wander's strategy has been continued expansion — using debt to acquire new assets that he can then use as collateral for more debt, which he then fails to timely pay off, in a seemingly never-ending cycle of 'robbing Peter to pay Paul'."

Wrapped up in Leadenhall's case against Wander and Pasko —and, by this point, A-CAP, who had assumed control of 777's assets — was the £200 million the Floridian company had loaned to Everton while their proposed buyout of the club had been pending. Those funds, crucial to the on going construction of Everton Stadium, formed a large portion of the $600 million Leadenhall were seeking to recover and the judge in the case granted an injunction stating that they could not be repaid to A-CAP without the agreement of the London firm. Not surprisingly, the messiness of the situation, not to mention the air of impropriety that hung over it, would provide an impediment to any other takeover proposal that Moshiri might hope to entertain while the legal wrangling continued.

Despite the ongoing uncertainty, for Everton's supporters, many of whom had seen the investigative work by the likes of *Josimar* vindicated as the digital magazine's revelations concerning 777 Partners were corroborated and confirmed by the Miami firm's spectacular fall, there was the overwhelming sense that the club had unequivocally dodged a bullet.

If 777's origin story had painted its founders as ill-suited owners for a club like Everton, the evidence that reinforced that notion kept piling up as the months wore on, with their takeover seemingly no closer to coming to fruition before everything came to a head in the spring of2024.

Yet, no sooner had Wander and Pasko exited "stage left" than the story of Moshiri's seemingly endless search for new owners of the club gathered fresh momentum. In truth, the game had been up for a few weeks and even before the expiration of 777's revised deadline to meet the Premier League's demands, the Monaco-based businessman had been holding talks with a number of would-be buyers.

Initially, despite demurring when the chance to take a majority stake in the Blues presented itself in April, MSP Sports Capital, together with their Evertonian partners Andy Bell and George Downing, appeared to be the most likely takeover candidates. Together, with their loans still outstanding, they remained significant creditors of the club and, as the2023/24 season was drawing to a close, talk persisted that Bell and Downing were working to attract additional investors with whom they might form a viable consortium, possibly with the backing of the family office of US billionaire, Michael Dell.

Media speculation suggested that A-CAP, substantial creditors themselves, might entertain a bid but, with their hands effectively tied by their own financial crisis and that of 777 Partners, that seemed fanciful at best.

Meanwhile, five new players entered the arena, with Vatche Manoukian stepping forward at the head of a group of investors that purportedly included Middle Eastern royalty and the Australian Myer family, who, together, were prepared to submit an all-equity bid in the region of £400 million.

Their interest was rivalled, at the prompting of former Everton director, Keith Harris, by the hitherto unknown Vici Private Finance, who were prepared to match Manoukian's bid, and American billionaire John Textor who had expressed his interest in the Blues even while he was trying to offload his 45% stake in rival club, Crystal Palace.

However, there was one outfit that emerged in June as the clear favourites when they agreed a period of exclusivity with Moshiri's Blue Heaven Holdings. Like 777, they already had significant interests in global club football but, pleasingly for Everton's weary fans, they were a stable, successful American firm with an owner whose personal wealth dwarfed that of the Anglo-Iranian. It looked as though the seemingly never-ending search for a buyer had come to an end and the Moshiri Years would soon be over.

2024: The Dawn of the Friedkin Era

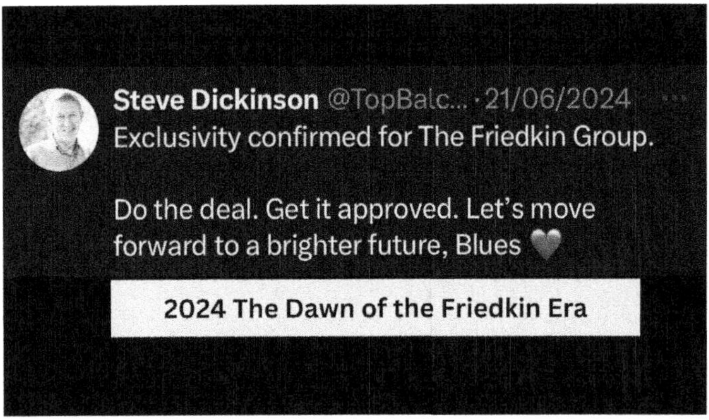

On the 15 June 2024, news broke that The Friedkin Group, a Texas-based firm helmed by billionaire Dan Friedkin, had agreed a deal in principle with Farhad Moshiri to purchase his 94.1% stake in Everton Football Club. The group received a period of exclusivity to conduct their due diligence and, hopefully, pave the way for Everton's controversial owner of eight years to sell up and move on.

The question on everyone's lips, of course, was who were The Friedkin Group, and would they be suitable owners for the Merseyside club?

Born in California, Dan Friedkin, now 59, was only 35 when he took charge of Gulf States Toyota, the company founded by his father in 1969 that became the largest private Toyota distributor in the United States. Over time, he broadened TFG's business interests, moving into sports, film production, luxury resorts and conservation in Africa. A trained pilot and collector of vintage aircraft, Friedkin gained notoriety as the stunt pilot for the scene at the end of *Dunkirk* where Tom Hardy's character lands his Spitfire on the beach following an aerial dogfight.

With an estimated personal fortune of around $9billion, Dan Friedkin is also the president and owner of Italian Serie A club, AS Roma, and French fourth-tier outfit, AS Cannes. As such, for Evertonians weary of years of under-performance on the pitch and 18 months of uncertainty over the future ownership of their club, Friedkin and his firm represented a legitimate and attractive prospective owner of the Toffees,

TFG had bought their controlling interest in AS Roma in 2020, when they paid $591million for the shares of James Pallotta. They inherited Paolo Fonseca as manager (a man linked with the vacant head coaching role at Everton on more than one occasion) but, despite having led the *Giallorossi* to a respectable fifth and seventh place finishes and the last four of the Europa League, the Friedkins elected to let him go in May 2021, and hired his Portuguese compatriot, the colourfully controversial Jose Mourinho.

Typical for the managerial career of "The Special One", Mourinho's tenure lasted less than three seasons before he was sacked, but he had ended an 11-year trophy drought for Roma by steering them to glory in the inaugural Europa Conference League in his first year at the club, and then the final of the Europa League the season after, only to lose to Sevilla. For his failure to qualify for the Holy Grail of the Champions League, he was relieved of his duties in January 2024.

Evertonians liked what they heard about the ambitious, wealthy businessman with strong ties to Toyota and other major commercial partners. Significantly, he had showed he knew how to turn around an ailing football giant, already investing more than £1 billion into AS Roma. According to reports, he had also told his friends that Everton "was a brilliant football club in need of polishing up."

However, no sooner had the Everton fanbase become comfortable with the prospect of the Friedkins acquiring their club, than on 19 July, a joint statement from Everton FC and The Friedkin Group announced that talks between the two parties had collapsed. The deal was off!

The announcement said,

"Following a period of exclusivity, discussions between Blue Heaven Holdings and The Friedkin Group over a potential sale of a majority stake in Everton have ended, and The Friedkin Group will not be progressing with a purchase of the Club. Both Blue Heaven Holdings and The Friedkin Group entered discussions in good faith to explore whether a sale could be agreed. Those discussions have concluded. The parties agree it is in both their interests for Everton to explore alternative options. The Friedkin Group will remain a lender to the Club and is proud to have played a key role in enabling the new stadium to be built, which will help ensure a bright future for both Everton and the City of Liverpool."

As the official statement intimated, TFG agreed to inject around £200 million of loans into Everton, enabling the club to pay off the existing debts to MSP Sports Capital and their partners. The TFG loan being secured against the new stadium and Moshiri's shares in the club.

The stumbling block for TFG had been the £200 million loan Everton had previously received from 777 Partners, one that was still tied up with the ongoing legal case between Leadenhall Capital Partners and777/A-Cap in New York, where the district court adjudicating the case had granted the London firm a legal injunction over the latter's assets until the matter was settled. Friedkin and his lawyers, it seemed, had concerns over the legal morass and shied away.

It was a devastating blow for the football club. The optimism and hope that had grown in late June and early July vanished, plunging Everton's employees, playing staff and supporters back into uncertainty.

And, if a savvy businessman like Dan Friedkin had been deterred by the 777 loan, who else would come in to buy the club? Would Everton once again be the target of unscrupulous, bargain-hunting financiers, whose only interest was to buy the club cheaply, sell off the stadium and try to make a quick buck?

Moshiri had once said, "it is through my lengthy discussions with 777 that I believe they are the best partners to take our great club forward." What lengths would he go to next, to rid himself of his loss-making football investment?

Not only was the long-term future of the club once again in doubt, but short-term questions over cash flow, working capital financing and the ability to complete and fit-out the new stadium were all hotly debated in the press and social media. Speculation was rife throughout the summer transfer window that Manchester United was attempting to seize upon Everton's financial weakness by offering low-ball offers for Jarrad Branthwaite, with rumours also circulating around the future of Jordan Pickford and Dominic Calvert -Lewin. One major outgoing transfer occurred on 22 July, when Amadou Onana was sold to Aston Villa in a deal reported to be worth £50 million, to ease concerns over further PSR breaches.

The end of Friedkin's interest provided an opportunity for John Textor, another pretender to the Everton throne, who expressed his interest in buying Moshiri out. The Missouri-born entrepreneur spoke glowingly of the Toffees and what it would mean to him, personally, to own a club with such a rich history. In an interview with Sky Sports in the summer of 2024, he even speculated on the calibre of players and manager he would bring to Everton were he the owner.

There had been hints there might be substance to his designs on the Blues in some of Everton's transfer dealings during the summer window, with both Jake O'Brien and Orel Mangala arriving from Textor-owned Olympique Lyonnais in France. In retrospect, however, Textor's shareholding in Crystal Palace meant he was never close to completing a deal with Moshiri.

Just as well, because Textor would have his hands full in France. With Lyon failing to bring in enough revenue from player sales before the August 2024 transfer deadline, that club was provisionally relegated from Ligue 1 in November for violating spending rules.

Meanwhile, Dan Friedkin and his son, Ryan, were busy dealing with their first real challenge as Roma's owners, when they faced a backlash from the club's hardcore "ultras" for the sacking of club legend, Daniele di Rossi, as manager just a few games into the 2024/25 campaign.

If events off the field looked bleak for Everton, the team's performances at the start of the 2024/25 season did little to lift the gloom. By 21 September, Everton had suffered four defeats and picked up only two points from their first six league games. This despite the fresh blood that had been injected into the squad, with the addition of the talented forward, Iliman Ndiaye, winger Jesper Lindstrøm, midfielders Orel Mangala and Tim Iroegbunam, defender Jake O'Brien, and loanee striker, Armando Broja.

They say it's darkest just before the dawn, and the first light of a possible new day for Everton was spotted by Financial Journalist, David Hellier on 23 September when he reported that Friedkin was back in the game, reporting on Twitter/X: "Dan Friedkin agrees to buy Blue Heaven's stake in Everton FC." The deal would, of course, be subject to regulatory approval from the Premier League, the Football Association and the Financial Conduct Authority but, given TFG's ownership of Roma, the consensus was that would be a mere formality.

It appeared, behind the scenes, Dan Friedkin had negotiated a better deal with Farhad Moshiri, and Friedkin's lawyers had put in place a settlement of the 777 loans which satisfied Kenneth King at A-Cap, enabling TFG to proceed with less risk than had seemed likely back in July. That settlement still needed to satisfy the terms of the New York Court injunction, which appeared not to be a major impediment.

Furthermore, TFG had come to an agreement with long-standing lenders, Rights and Media Funding, to pay back their £225 million loan, which was costing the club £30 million a year in interest.

Subsequently, while the regulatory approvals process meandered on through the autumn, TFG provided further loans to enable Everton FC to complete the fit-out work at the new stadium, in readiness for its official opening in August 2025.

A project initially estimated by the club to cost around £350 million and be completed by 2022, the new stage on which Everton FC would play had morphed into an £800 million project on the banks of the royal blue Mersey, financed by a combination of equity from Farhad Moshiri and high interest, short-term debt. That outcome was far away from the assumptions made in Moshiri's original business plan, and at times it appeared the financial gamble of building the new stadium could bring the entire club down; particularly when Moshiri failed to secure long-term, low-interest funding for it, and when Alisher Usmanov's financial support was severed. But the near-completed stadium has clearly been a significant hook with which to attract TFG and other potential investors.

A naming rights deal, and other commercial opportunities that the stadium will attract, should provide much needed future revenues for the club. That much, at least, *was* always part of Moshiri's plan.

The responsibility for realising the rich promise of the new ground – with its 52,888-seat capacity (an increase of 33% compared with Goodison Park), steep stands, and a roof enclosure built to keep the crowd noise in – and the rebuilding of a once great institution, now falls to The Friedkin Group.

If ever an organisation needed restructuring, it is Everton. With Dan Friedkin's extensive business experience, honed by the trials and tribulations of his AS Roma experiences, he finds himself with a rare opportunity to oversee an almost complete reset of the club. From selecting key personnel for the Boardroom, deciding who sits in the

Director of Football seat, and who manages the team, to shaping the very core of the culture at Everton FC itself.

He and his team would be wise to engage with the Fan Advisory Board — not simply pay lip-service to the FAB, but to engage meaningfully and regularly with them so that they can disseminate the message widely to all Evertonians and seek feedback.

Friedkin's success in the coming years will be largely determined by the quality of his recruitment decisions, and his ability to set out a clear vision and framework from Day 1. His appointments of chairman, CEO, finance director and independent non-executives will tell us a great deal about his leadership style and aspirations.

Prior to Moshiri's involvement, Everton FC under Kenwright was struggling financially, but was holding its own in the top-half of the topflight. The decline of the club, which, in reality, had set in during the onset of the Premier League, sped up during the Moshiri years. His previous experience as a 15% shareholder in Arsenal FC and his access to the vast wealth of his business partner, Alisher Usmanov (at least until the untimely Russian invasion of Ukraine) caused Moshiri to believe he knew how to return Everton FC to the elite of English and European football. But in the words of Warren Buffett, "Risk comes from *not* knowing what you're doing."

This book has highlighted that Moshiri fell into the trap of believing he knew what he was doing, whereas most of the evidence we have presented proves he did not.

Moshiri retained Bill Kenwright as chairman, and Kenwright appointed his devotees to key positions; comfortable relationships, with everyone protecting their own interests and ensuring no-one in a position of power would point out the emperor had no clothes. Rival power bases in London and Liverpool, each vied for control of key decisions. Throw in the influence from the sidelines of Alisher Usmanov, players' agents and corporate advisers, and it is little wonder reporting lines and responsibilities blurred, and the organisation became chaotic and dysfunctional.

Moshiri meddled in footballing matters in which he had no expertise and showed time after time his ineptitude with recruitment to the club's board, its football management and its playing staff. He blamed the fans for voicing strong opinions about failing managers when the responsibility for recruiting better ones in the first place and creating a framework capable of delivering success was his. As we have explored, his ambitions were grand and his intentions noble and while his complicated legacy includes a gleaming edifice on Liverpool's famous waterfront, his footballing project — it's results on the field that determine the health of a football club after all — was doomed to failure.

Massive change is required at Everton FC, both on and off the field. Dan Friedkin must note what Farhad Moshiri did during his eight years in charge and largely take the opposite path.

Knowing the club's history is vital, because that's where we can find understanding, and learn the lessons when things go wrong. Taking a leaf out of the Everton playbook of 1892, when they last moved to a new stadium, could also prove valuable.

That year, having won their first League Championship Everton left their old stadium at Anfield over a rental dispute and moved across Stanley Park to Goodison Park. Prior to the split, boardroom rivals had quarrelled, politics were prevalent, and the fanbase unhappy and divided.

The move to Goodison and the clarity of vision of the remaining Everton directors in 1892 enabled the club to move forward and establish itself with even greater purpose in the fledgling Football League. In often raucous public meetings, the Members of Everton Football Club debated and voted on key issues, including board membership. The fanbase of today is just as opinionated as their predecessors, and rightly so.

132 years later, could the move to Bramley-Moore Dock and the change of ownership provide the Friedkin Group with the ideal opportunity to reunite Everton Football Club with its passionate fanbase?

***

The long-awaited news and the end of the Moshiri years was finally announced at 10.00am on 19 December, with an official club statement that said:

> "Everton Football Club has been acquired by Roundhouse Capital Holdings Limited (Roundhouse), an entity within The Friedkin Group (TFG). The transaction was finalised following an agreement between Farhad Moshiri's Blue Heaven Holdings (BHH) and Roundhouse for the sale of BHH's majority stake in the Club.
>
> The deal received the necessary regulatory approvals from the Premier League, Women's Professional

Leagues Limited, the Football Association, and the Financial Conduct Authority.

Marc Watts, incoming Executive Chairman of Everton Football Club, expressed his enthusiasm:

"Today marks a momentous and proud occasion for The Friedkin Group as we become custodians of this iconic football club. We are committed to leading Everton into an exciting new era both on and off the pitch. Providing immediate financial stability to the Club has been a key priority, and we are delighted to have achieved this. While restoring Everton to its rightful place in the Premier League table will take time, today is the first step in that journey."

Farhad Moshiri, the outgoing majority shareholder, stated: "I truly believe that the transaction with The Friedkin Group is the best outcome for the Club and its future success. There has been a huge team effort in getting to this stage and I would like to personally thank my Board colleagues John Spellman and Colin Chong and all the senior management team including Katie, James, Richard and of course Kevin and

Sean for their huge commitment to the Club. Despite a challenging geopolitical backdrop, a significant amount has been achieved over the last couple of years including the delivery of a new sporting department, the stabilisation of our finances and the delivery of our iconic new stadium. I now hand over to new owners confident in the outlook for the Club and that our incredible fans will see the success on the pitch that they so thoroughly deserve."

Dan Friedkin, Chairman and CEO of TFG is proposed to be Chairman of the Board. He has appointed Marc Watts to serve as Executive Chairman, who will be responsible in this role for the management of the club. Ana Dunkel, TFG's Chief Financial Officer and Colin Chong, the Club's interim CEO will also serve on the Board. Additional appointments will be made in the coming weeks.

TFG's vision for Everton Football Club focuses on building a sustainable and successful future. Key priorities include:

- Strengthening the men's first-team squad through thoughtful and strategic investment.

- Cultivating home-grown superstars through Everton's Academy.
- Fostering a distinct on pitch and commercial strategy for the women's team.
- Respecting the Club's traditions and keeping Everton at the heart of the community.
- Maximising the potential of the new stadium through long-term commercial partnerships and events that benefit the city of Liverpool.
- Enhancing Everton's reputation as a unique and historical name in world football.

In view of recent changes to the Premier League's shareholder loan regulations, Everton took proactive steps prior to the transaction's completion. These included increasing the Club's share capital to convert outstanding debt owed to BHH into equity, thereby facilitating additional equity investment from Roundhouse.

With this acquisition, TFG is committed to delivering a strong and sustainable future for Everton Football

Club, restoring its competitive stature and maintaining its deep connection with fans and the community.

Nil satis nisi optimum."

In a letter to supporters, Dan Friedkin said,

"Dear Evertonians,

Following the completion of the takeover of Everton Football Club, I want to express my gratitude for your continued support and introduce the incoming Executive Chairman of Everton, Marc Watts.

I take immense pride in welcoming one of England's most historic football clubs to our global family, The Friedkin Group. Everton represents a proud legacy, and we are honoured to become custodians of this great institution.

The Friedkin Group is a diverse family of companies with a global footprint spanning industries such

> as sports, automotive, entertainment, hospitality, and adventure. Across all our endeavours, we strive to deliver extraordinary experiences that ignite people's passions. We are thrilled to bring this ethos to Everton and the Liverpool City Region.
>
> Whilst we are new to the Club, we fully understand the vital role Everton plays in local culture, history, and the lives of Evertonians here and around the world. We are deeply committed to honouring this legacy while contributing positively to the community, economy, and people of this remarkable city."

Newly appointed Executive Chairman, Marc Watts added,

> "We are proud to be the new custodians of your club. Together, we will usher Everton into a new era, one that is marked by ambition and professionalism. As stewards of Everton, we look forward to showing our commitment to the club through actions, not words."

The change in ownership has come at a challenging time for the club, but challenging has been the name of the game for Everton for over thirty years. With the Blues standing in 16th position in the Premier League on the day the Friedkin Group acquired the club, having amassed only 15 points from 15 games, all eyes will be on

Dan Friedkin and his newly appointed board and executive team as they aim to steer the club away from yet another relegation battle in Everton's last season at Goodison Park, and prepare for next season in the new stadium on the banks of the Royal Blue Mersey.

Everyone who knows the pain, passion and occasional jubilation of supporting Everton Football Club, will wish Dan Friedkin and his team every success. That passionate community of Everton fans deserve a brighter future and will be cheering him and the team on, as collectively the club and its supporters write the next momentous chapter on the Everton Timeline.

Up the Toffees!

The Continuing Story...

That's the end of this edition of *The Unofficial Everton Timeline.* Thank you for following the long and complex story of what has been one of the most fascinating and traumatic decades in the history of Everton Football Club.

Why is this edition so long? It's simple. There's a lot to tell, and rarely a day goes by when the club is out of the news. The second half of this season could be even more tumultuous than the first half. Imagine that!

We'll be back with more *Unofficial Everton Timeline* insights: telling the story of Everton Football Club, on and off the pitch, and giving perspectives that will never be shown on the club website, nor mounted on the walls of Goodison Park or Bramley-Moore Dock.

Until then, Up the Toffees!

Steve and Lyndon

ACKNOWLEDGEMENTS

Huge thanks go to Lord Grantchester, Keith Wyness, Tony Tighe, David France plus his wife Elizabeth, and the other wonderful people associated with The Everton Collection, who developed The Everton Timeline which adorns Goodison Park.

Owned by The Everton Collection Charitable Trust, the collection is housed at the Liverpool Record Office where it is conserved in purpose-built facilities meeting the highest standards for long-term preservation and under the care of professional archivists. With support from the Heritage Lottery Fund, the Trust acquired The David France Collection – treasures lauded by experts at Christies and Sotheby's as the world's greatest club collection of football memorabilia – in late 2007 for a fraction of its market value. In addition, Dr France and his wife donated the priceless 29 official minute books, which document all board meetings between 1886 – 1964, to the Trust and detail the decisions made at 5,000 meetings recorded in over 10,000 handwritten pages signed by the likes of John Houlding, George Mahon, Will Cuff and John Moores.

The archive also contains over 6,000 football programmes, around 90% of all programmes involving Everton in league games, cup competitions, friendlies and reserve-team fixtures since 1885, including all home editions from the inaugural League season. Other highlights include season tickets from the club's days at Stanley Park, Priory Road and Anfield, gold medals for every major competition won by Everton including an example of the first-ever League Championship medal in 1890, the earliest team photograph taken shortly after the club changed its name from St. Domingo in 1881, players' contracts dating back to 1890, the tender documents for construction of the grandstand at Anfield in 1884 and much more.

The club's own modest archive was added to The David France Collection to form The Everton Collection. In total, it contains 20,000-plus items which chronicle the week-by-week story of life as well as football on Merseyside.

Further information can be found at www.evertoncollection.org.uk

In addition, the authors would like to express their appreciation to David France (Life President, Everton FC Shareholders' Association) for his contribution to the book. In turn, he would like to extol the unyielding dedication and tireless hard work of Colin Chong (interim CEO), Richard Kenyon (Chief Commercial and Communications Officer) and their staffs at the Royal Liver Building, Finch Farm and Goodison Park following the departures of the club's chief executive, chief finance and strategy officer and non-executive director in June 2023, and the death of chairman Bill Kenwright in October 2023.

It would be impossible for the authors to write a book about Everton and its amazing supporters without also acknowledging the tireless and essential work of all those involved in the 'Everton In The Community' charity https://www.evertoninthecommunity.org/, as well as Speedo Mick and all the incredible fundraising work he does for mental health charities through the speedomickfoundation.org

On a personal note, Steve would like to thank his family and close friends for helping him deal with his Everton addiction.

Lyndon would like to thank his wife, Natalie, and two daughters, Elyssa and Anna, for putting up with his passion for Everton FC, the many hours of devotion that goes into covering the club for almost three decades and all the wild emotional highs and lows that go with it!

About the Authors

Steve Dickinson

Steve was born in Liverpool, England in 1957. At the age of three, his grandad 'introduced him to the Blues.' The rest, as they say for a lifelong Evertonian, is history. His first memories of watching the Blues on TV was their 3-2 win against Sheffield Wednesday in the 1966 FA Cup Final. His first live match at Goodison Park was a 2-0 win against West Ham, during the league-winning season of 1969/70. Life for the Toffees was sweet back then.

Between then and now, he graduated with an engineering degree from the University of Liverpool and spent a forty-year career in the world of construction and manufacturing: running projects and businesses, restructuring companies in the UK and overseas, and travelling the globe.

He is now an author, publisher and Everton season ticket holder.

Steve can be found at SteveDickinsonBooks.com and on Twitter/X @TopBalconyMan

***

Lyndon Lloyd

Born in Johannesburg, South Africa, Lyndon was chosen to be an Evertonian comparatively late in life when he moved to England at the age of 12. Though he graduated from the University of Wales, Swansea with a Masters in History, he pursued a career in graphic and web design that took him to California during the Dotcom boom at the turn of the Century.

In parallel, he built Evertonia.com, an independent website covering the Toffees, that was merged with ToffeeWeb in 2001. The resulting behemoth is the biggest and longest-running website devoted to Everton, and one of the oldest football sites still in existence.

Lyndon can be found at ToffeeWeb.com, on Twitter/X @EFCLyndon, and on the weekly ToffeeWeb Podcast.

Did you enjoy this book?

Thank you for reading *The Unofficial Everton Timeline: 2014-2024 The Moshiri Years.*

2nd Edition: The Dawn of the Friedkin Era

Your feedback helps us provide the best quality books and helps readers like you discover great books. It would mean the world to us if you took two minutes to share your thoughts about this book as a review. You can leave a review online, wherever you obtained the book, and/or send us an email with your honest feedback.

Best wishes and Up the Toffees!

Steve@SteveDickinsonBooks.com

Lyndon@ToffeeWeb.com

Printed in Great Britain
by Amazon

61472929R00408

Re ey

Else Jerusalem
für Herrn Georg Bachrich zum
Angedenken u

Red House Alley

Else Jerusalem

Introduction by Sophie Haydock
Afterword by Stephanie G. Ortega

RECOVERED BOOKS
BOILER HOUSE PRESS

Contents

Introduction

by Sophie Haydock

"To You! You girls dancing, laughing, brides, mothers at play. This book belongs to You."

Else Jerusalem is starkly clear in the epigraph to her one and only novel. This book is for women—the ones who are joyfully in "the apex of Your lives." Don't take it all for granted, she instructs: the lashings of privilege that our society bestows upon you, whether as a wife or mother or caught in courtship. She guides her potential readers to "direct Your gaze into darkness." Hear the voices, she demands, of the women who have not been so fortunate, whose names must not be forgotten: Milada and Rosie, Bina and Anna, Olympia, Putzi and Fanny. The young women of the Red House, down on their luck. Don't turn away.

As the novel's protagonist Milada says in an impassioned speech to an erudite client: "It's always the same story. The will of every person is destroyed here. Nothing is predictable. Nothing is secure. We are subject to every misfortune. We're thrown into danger with no hope of being saved. Illness, getting old, debt—it's an endless cycle of crises for us. We can never break out of the cycle. Every move to security comes at the cost of the inevitable descent into ruin."

The Red House is a brothel in Vienna—the city itself is never mentioned—as it would have been experienced in the late nineteenth century. The Habsburg dynasty has reigned for centuries; the Austro-Hungarian Empire is strong—politically and economically. By 1900, it boasts forty-six million inhabitants. Vienna is the epicentre of radical thought, art, music, decadence, and glamour, but the glittering façade hides an uglier truth—one of stark inequality. The age of consent is just fourteen. Women in Austria won't receive the vote until 1918 (and prostitutes will be excluded for a further five years). Among the big questions of the day, debated by men in coffee shops across the capital, is whether women have a soul.

Else Jerusalem was thirty-two years old and mother of two children when she published *Der heilige Skarabäus* (*The Sacred Scarab*) in 1909. She was experiencing an apex of her own. The novel received critical acclaim and best-seller status—it went through twenty-two printings in its first two years and was translated into many languages. But what motivated this young woman to turn her attention to the underbelly of the Empire's most glittering city?

Else Kotányi was born into a respectable Jewish middle-class family in Vienna in 1876—her father was a wine merchant—and she received a university education, which was rare for women of the day. She studied literature and philosophy at the University of Vienna, one of the first women to attend, although she was denied a formal degree because of her gender.

Why not, people might have asked at the time, write about masked balls, theaters and horse-drawn carriages, rather than a "disreputable" little alley and its denizens? Jerusalem didn't turn her attention to "fallen souls" gratuitously or sensationally or with sales in mind. Even at her most cynical, she could hardly have guessed that the public would clamour for a book of this content. She wrote over six hundred pages on this topic to shine a light into society's hidden corners, much as other realist and socially minded authors did, including Émile Zola. Ultimately, she was unafraid, undeterred by the criticism that comes with being a provocative woman.

As an influential feminist intellectual, Jerusalem always gravitated towards taboo topics: controversial sensitivities that were deliberately brushed under the carpet: female sexuality, sex education for young women (and education in general), gender relations, and prostitution, radically shown through the lens of the women living it. In 1906, she was granted permission, as one of only two women, to attend the trial of a Jewish brothel madam who would later be convicted of embezzlement and fraud. It's a testament to Jerusalem's energy and insight that, as a result of what she learned during that infamous trial, she chose to turn her gaze, with sharpest vision, to the prostitutes who were overlooked, ignored, seen as disposable.

Jerusalem knew, just as her heroine Milada expresses, that women are condemned by their own limitations, those imposed by a patriarchal society. "However we got here, we do not have to be destroyed here, Madame! If people go to work in a factory, they do not have to wait until they lose a limb in a machine. Between what we have to do and what we want to do is a door. We only have to open it. We stay put if we believe the door is closed. I believe it's open. I don't believe a door can keep me here. Or anybody in the house for that matter."

Later in the novel, the question of money and desire and sex is pulled into a perfectly knotted problem for Milada when she falls in love with one of the young men who frequents the Red House. The irony can't be lost on readers that Milada gives Gustav a gold coin to commemorate their relationship. That coin, an inversion of the flow of money between client and prostitute, directs us to the crux of this novel: will Milada, a woman who grew up in the Red House and who was plunged into prostitution at the age of fifteen, who has been forced to accept money for sex—not much of which directly benefits her—be willing to accept a very substantial amount as a negotiation for terminating her love affair?

"We offer you 20,000 kroner, paid to you in cash, the moment you hand me a farewell letter to Gus," goes the bribe from Gustav's father. This is a fortune with which Milada could build a new life—a life in which she can realise the dreams that "consume and sustain" her—ones she'd have had better access to if her own father, a landed estate owner, had not discarded her mother, Katerine, who was, as a result, forced into a life of prostitution that culminated in her banishment and early death.

Milada, I hope you'll agree, is a heroic figure in a literary tradition of pitiful fallen women. She carves a fate for herself, without forgetting those with whom she stands shoulder to shoulder. All she asks from you, the reader, is that you see her and the women of the Red House for who they truly are—without the rouge and stockings, without objectification and titillation.

"What do you men know of us, you men who come to us in the evening? You are drawn to the light of the salon, where we wait tarted up with rouge and baubles to service you with the warmth of our bodies, but do you know us? What do you know of these women who relieve you of your earthly sorrows with our frivolity.... Who among you has the courage to ask one of us with shuttered souls, 'How do you look in the light of day? Please show yourself.'"

It's an incredible privilege to read this unabridged English-language version of *Der heilige Skarabäus*, translated as *Red House Alley* by Stephanie Ortega. An abridged version was first published in English in 1932. So, more than a hundred years after the book's first publication, we're among the first English language readers to receive Jerusalem's words, her thoughts, her manifesto, in full. It's also significant to see such a ground-breaking novel brought back from obscurity by Boiler House Press as part of their Recovered Books Series—it so deserves our attention and shouldn't be lost.

Now it's up to you to see if this novel has an ending that's happy or sad. Will the strength of these women prevail? We're invested in the struggle of Milada and want to see her triumph. Sadly, Jerusalem died in Argentina in 1943, aged sixty-six, "alone and somewhat forgotten," as her daughter later put it. There had been much grief in her life, but her story mustn't be seen as tragic. By reading *Red House Alley*, I believe that Jerusalem likely shared Milada's outlook, which may be ours, too: "I do want to live—to live and live and live. I want to see what's in the future. I'm eager to see it.... And at the end I'm going to say, 'The journey was beautiful.'"

Red House Alley

by Else Jerusalem

Translated by Stephanie G. Ortega

To You!
You girls dancing, laughing brides, mothers at play,
This book belongs to You.
From the apex of Your lives may You hear down to the nadir.
From the light of Your lives direct Your gaze into darkness.
May You feel where You have long judged.
Stop to think where You have too long passed by.
And let Your empathy greet with grace these You have offered up for Your
Good fortune.

Chapter 1
Black Katerine

> *If I were a wife at home and had what I need,*
> *I would be true to my man and happy, cuddle and kiss him.*
> *This is what, among some coarse songs, a wench sang*
> *To me in Venice, and never have I heard a more devout prayer.*
> *—Goethe*

There, just behind the glittering street, a center of social concourse in the big city, on its wide sidewalks of clean asphalt where, daily, hundreds of elegant gentlemen and adorned ladies, people out for a leisurely stroll, smile at each other and greet one another, suddenly and without warning—in an almost too abrupt change—right there the realm of darkness begins. When you turn the corner at the Louvre de Luxe, a high building in a sleek, modern style, and go a few steps along the elegant, simple side of its façade, and make a second sharp turn, you are standing at the entrance to a cul-de-sac whose upper end is closed by a high garden wall. When twilight falls and the dull, pleasant gray of the evening sifts over the roofs of the big city, our small side street sinks immediately into miserable night. The little houses shrink together, the arches of the gates become lost in shadow, and, while the main street is putting on its glistening evening attire, here in the alley only one red lantern is burning. It envelops its immediate surroundings in a ring of blood. Hands that know their business put smoldering oil lamps in some of the small, low windows.

The small, pale flames, blown by wind from cracks and holes, jump about and lure and beg. They are the silent signposts.

The main street grows quiet, then even quieter, shops close, and the elegant people on their leisurely stroll have returned home. One after another the sputtering lanterns start to glow, and gray draperies cautiously cover up the finery and the sheen and the luxury. Behind them life awakens and opens, hungrily, its sleep-filled eyes. Windows open, rusty door hinges creak, the air is filled with questions, chatter, laughter. There are clouds of musky perfume, the fragrance of violets; silk rustles, and silver wheels clatter, as figures in bright clothing, readying their petticoats, emerge from nameless, dark alleys.

There they are!

Painted lips upon which a gay tune blossoms. Swaying hips deformed by tightly laced corsets! Gleaming eyes that struggle with the light. And their easy laughter entombed in a grimace. This is how the train of women moves onto the nice main street. The market of love is open!

The stalls of good fortune are made ready, and the peddlers call out to their clients. They do not have long to wait. The men come from their mothers or from their brides, from wine or from serious books, from the dance floor or from church—all one and the same—they find their way here, join in the dance. Now the evening rustles her black skirts. Greetings, giggles, and hasty calling begin. Numbers are thrown out between whispers and curses. An uncomfortable agreement is struck between sighs of desire, and the prostitute's obstinate insistence wins out over the unrestrained lust of the one pleading. The men, collars turned up, follow as the women lead. They hurry back into the nameless alley, and the red blood of the lantern drips only a short moment, haltingly, over the strangers' faces.

Then darkness covers what it had paired up in her realm.

During the day, this little corner of the world lies still in a web. The curtains are all drawn closed, the gates bolted, and the sound of children or neighbors talking is seldom heard. Children in this quarter do not grow up happily at play. Vice and its company live here outside the law, as do crime and its hidden acceptance; everything has an agreeable hiding place, and it is kept tucked away without scruple from respectable society. The thief and his fence, con artists, hustlers, and the "easy clients," as the police say, are to be found together in both of the smoke-filled cafés at street level, one of which is run by the infamous Mama Zimmermann. This is where young men with pockets full of money hang out, let the girls caress them, admire them, and then start talking and become expansive. They plunk jewelry on the table while making a fuss—until someone lays a brazen hand on their shoulder and causes them to reel and tumble.

Girls walking the streets flood the small, damp, poorly built houses because the place is lucrative, very popular, and sure to have ready clients.

Except for some raids, which happen from time to time and which the women who run the places and housekeepers expect, there are not really any disturbances. There are no mean-spirited disruptions or any trouble. Sometimes a certain fellow will be picked up or someone with stolen goods will be apprehended, but in general the police do not bother the "nice girls" all that much. Routine supervision by the police is never really rough; what goes on here is tolerated. And in suspicious cases, it is the housekeepers who take care of the girls they protect.

"The poor kid is as clean as can be, Your Honor, Your Grace—well, sure, a bit of trouble with some guys—but such a sweet lamb, Your Honor! The answers Your Grace wants are easy to find. We only have to ask her."

Disreputable and tiny as the little alley looks, in the district it counts as good luck. It is a kind of security, a place to hide out.

The rooms and the beds are never empty. There is always a new bunch of "fresh young guys." The housekeepers do replace the ladies. Theirs are the hands that stay flush with money from the women who make it.

Above the thick, high wall of the Soldiers' Hospital that crosses the alley at the other end, old, tangled acorn trees rustle, and the wind blows leaves, dirt, and twigs across the unkempt sidewalks of broken concrete. All kinds of trash lie around, broken dishes, rags blown about, kitchen garbage, newspapers. Little streams of water carelessly pitched out of doors and windows make large puddles that get in the way of the women who curse, hitch up their skirts and hop over them. They run around, one by one, with their hair disheveled and in ragged clothes, carrying baskets and mugs out of the houses. They make their way around the watchman on patrol and disappear again into one of the bars.

Wherever you look, everything is messy, seedy, worn out. Only one single well-maintained, multi-story building with reflective windows across the front rises above the small, low buildings in the area. Here, too, the red lantern shines, the eye of the street, and, in thick, black letters on its brightly colored glass, it bears the name Red House. Its builder had named it that because of the odd, blood-colored roof that covers it all over. Red House is the pride and centerpiece of the nameless alley. The elite among its inhabitants is a select group of the prettiest and most successful young ladies. The house was not so much a special designation as it was the assurance of better and regular income. Here you were well taken care of if you worked and did not drink. The gentlemen—noblemen, too, even cavaliers—were glad to visit Red House since there was something there that always inspired trust among men of inaugurated circles in those who rented rooms there. Yes, as far as that goes, everything would be fine and good if it were not for Madame Lorinser. She rented the rooms only with maintenance and the day's clean laundry. Madame Lorinser was the porter, actually the manager of the house and the single person of authority. There was no appealing anything she had made up her mind about. Red House was the property of a retired old major, and he did not take any part in its administration. He let the old hag run things as she wanted to and was happy enough when she paid the monthly rent, and in this regard she was just as reliable and punctual as she was in demanding daily payment from her ladies, which included the considerable sum of twenty gulden. Twenty gulden per day! Sometimes the tenants could make that much, even more. But even the most beautiful and hard-working had bad days. What then? Lorinser was not in the habit of giving credit. Those who could not pay landed in the street. Oh, she was not afraid of finding new renters, Old Lady Porter was not.

Fine and elegant, that is how Red House looked. The windows were clean and had no cracks or holes. There were short white curtains and here and there live, potted flowers, which gave the house a friendly appearance, even when they were dusty and in need of attention. Yes, now there was a woman who was dutiful and punctual. She did her job like a workhorse, that Lorinser.

If her renters could only get hold of all that money! There were also shoes, clothes to buy, the cost of laundry, and just about everybody had a few "dependents," parents, brothers or sisters, who came by the little alley a few times every week, asking for money.

The women handed it over.

After all that, what was left for love?

The food in Red House was rather good and plentiful, but there was no wine or liquor, and these stimulants were a necessary part of their life. Old Lady Lorinser sold cognac and wine and was not happy when people bought it elsewhere. That ate up the money as fast as a cow eats grass. Good God, when you counted the money you made, it did not always cover expenses, and Lorinser grabbed her debtors like the devil grabs fallen souls.

So there was a lot of packing and clearing out, moving in and running away, swearing and flattering going on in Red House. It livened up the environs and aroused the residents' sharpest interest. Lorinser, for her part, did not like the "stable ladies." They took liberties and found friends and protectors; they screamed bloody murder over every alleged injustice. They started rumors and put up a fuss, but, in the end, they still came up short of money.

No, no way, did she give credit. It was better, in her book, to have fresh, young replacements. That filled her pockets. New renters were open and easy-going and did not sniff exploitation right away. They did not see her power games behind every arbitrary and urgent demand. Old Lorinser had a habit of standing around train stations or sneaking around alleyways and attaching herself to pretty girls new to the city. Sometimes it worked out for her, sometimes it did not. Either way it turned into a kind of business for her. The neighborhood was, because of its location near the city center, good and productive, and those in Red House—well, they were as good as aristocrats. Yes, those who were fresh and new really had a fine time. And Madame Lorinser, on account of them, did, too. The police were well acquainted with her. Those who knew her asked her advice, knew what her signals meant and supported her, so that in the execution of her duties she had nothing to fear, no unpleasantness or surprises.

In the junk store on street level with Red House, a sputtering petroleum lamp burned during the day. That is where ice-gray Mother Lorinser sat among cartons and shelves, crammed so full of stuff from top to bottom that there was just one small space free in the middle. There were clothes, linens, boots, hats, soap and brushes, beauty preparations and perfume, fat novels in out-of-date bindings, lurid pictures and incense holders, mirrors, spittoons, petticoats that shimmered like silk, things for daily use and other things that had rotted there for years, things nobody could use. Most of the stuff was pawned. But some items had actually belonged to former tenants. Lorinser had greedily grabbed these things when she could not squeeze any more money out of the tenants. A scrawny little canary bird peeped in a homemade cage. It had been the darling of its former owner. It had been requisitioned from her together with her few pieces of clothing after a short stay in Red House, and the little animal had some nasty words to say to the porter in passing when it was not fed right. He had given up singing and did not have a mate. He did not want to sing.

Only one pair of eyes in the overpopulated Red House saw the tragedy of this small creature. These eyes, large, gray, and attentive, belonged to a little girl not more than six years old.

On spring days, when the bird was hung outside the store on the wall of the house, the little girl, dressed in bright clothes that were far too big, stood and watched him flee from perch to perch.

Very quietly her little brown finger poked in between the bars. "Sing, sing!" she begged from outside. But the bird hid himself above his food cup and made a weak little peep.

"You're scared, aren't you?" thought the little girl. "Mama knows, and she always sings. She's not afraid of her." Mention of the porter had gotten the girl a rough shove before, first from that Lorinser, who absolutely hated the "worthless little Bohemian," and then from her mother Black Katerine. Her mother gave the child a good wallop, as laughter formed on her full, red lips. When she was done giving the child a whack, she broke into laughter, leaned way out the window, and let her laughter break on the ears of Lorinser, drooling below. Then Katerine turned to her friend Janka who was busying herself quietly in the kitchen.

"Go on, say what you want. That kid is a little toad, she jumps and spits."

"She's like you," Janka answered with a sigh.

"Then she's like that by rights," Black Katerine answered mockingly and stretched out, slim and comely. "She needs to watch out, the little bitch, and learn to spit on everybody—like me."

Janka cast a pleading look toward Katerine. But a threatening glance from Katerine stopped Janka short. She shook herself like a cat and went in her room.

When Janka was in her "pious mood," Katerine knew it was better to leave her alone.

Black Katerine was the only one in the house who had any kind of free autonomy alongside the regime of Lorinser. She lived in a separate section of the house with her friend Janka and the child Milada. It had a kitchen, main room, and pantry. She paid the rent quarterly and directly to the property owner, with whom, it was widely rumored, she had once had a sweet relationship. The porter just had to put up with this painful breach of her control. She was powerless against this one woman and her open laughter. Katerine was one gorgeous, lissome woman. She looked very Slavic, with bright cat-like eyes and a broad, sweet and sensuously curved mouth, whose charm dominated the rest of her face. She lived alone and withdrawn, did not make friends, and never took part in others' celebrations or arguments. People called her proud; but she was not. She was apathetic and tired, and nothing more caught her interest. Not even jewelry or silk clothing. She was beautiful and sought after and was paid handsomely, but money slipped right through her fingers.

When Janka asked, "What are you doing with it?" then she answered, "I think I lose it. I put it in my pocket, but—my word, look!—it has a hole in it."

And she laughed aloud, an unholy laugh that came out of her mouth harshly, like the ring of a bell. "But what does it hurt? We have food and drink, my love, and a warm place to sleep, what more do you want?"

She lay about in bed, weary and uninterested, until evening fell. Katerine watched her friend with angry eyes as she scrubbed and cooked for her, at times talking to herself, without waiting for an answer, without asking for one. "Oh, Jan, I'd like to stay here in bed and not do another thing. Not eat, not drink, just die of tiredness. I don't want to lift another finger to live this stupid life. It doesn't matter if people like us are dead or alive. That's just how things are. Aren't you alive because you have to be? There, you see, at the hour of death, when you don't want to live any more, at the hour you're going to die, it's all over, done."

Janka peeled potatoes and dropped them with a plop in the boiling water. The smell of fine coffee filled the kitchen.

The fresh cool air of autumn blew in from the next room where the luxurious bedding of Katerine was airing.

"Stop working, Janka. Just look, your little hands are all red and rough from working. Sweetie, bring some wine so we can laugh a while."

She drank a whole glass, jumped out of bed, and stood in front of the mirror. "My laugh, you know, it's like this," she put her hands far behind her back, bent backwards a little, and laughed.

"How about that? The men downstairs go crazy for my laugh. But I can be different. Just look, Jan! I can be like this." Slowly her face changed, the corners of her mouth curled, an expression of greed and delight filled her eyes, and she laughed to herself softly. With great restraint she emitted a laughter with a crimson hue, a scream of delight and cruelty. "Do you like that? I mean you, Sir?" She gestured toward the other room. "You like that. I can tell by your eyes. They're getting red and hot, like fire's leaping out of them. You're getting hot now. But I'm not! I'm only putting on an act. You fools! I practice in front of the mirror. The face in the mirror, it's always my best friend." She nodded to her reflection. "Isn't that right, what all you show me? I can be a proud lady, a lady at court! Now I'm a fine, rich lady who sits at the window on winter evenings, spinning. Or I could be a holy little nun! Just look, Jan, am I the pious Sister Cecilia?" In a flash Katerine had made a nun's hood out of a handkerchief. She rolled her eyes upward, and with the blue ribbons of her nightgown she wound a wreath around her finger. "And now??"

Janka laughed, "You're a real comedienne."

Katerine made a serious face, "That's how I entertain myself. If I didn't, I'd curl up and die of boredom. Sometimes I pretend I am this person or that person. There's just one thing I don't imagine, being cold, stiff, dead." She put her head on her shoulder, closed her eyes and squinted at herself in the mirror. "Poor Katerine, what will you have to say then? But the dead don't talk, and the real Katerine died a long time ago."

Janka set Katerine's coffee down for her, and she drank it down greedily. The steam of the hot liquid rolled out of her mouth.

Then she went back to bed and pulled the covers up over herself, freezing from cold.

"Hey, Jan! That little student was here yesterday, the little blond guy, the one who used to come in the afternoon, you know, and drink coffee. That's a funny young guy, but he's gone now. We used to go all kinds of places, and he didn't want anybody to follow me. Oh, what a goldmine!" She laughed out loud, "So now we know why we ain't got money. And you, you don't go out anymore!" she threw out with an accusatory tone and pulled a choice apple out from under the covers.

She took a hearty bite and continued, "When that student was here, I used to imagine I was his mother. I took his hand and warned him about that Katerine. I was sweet to him, just like a mother." Janka stirred up the flames in the stove without turning her head and mumbled, "But you've got your own kid!"

"Just leave me alone about that. The kid's my own real flesh and blood, I'm not happy about that. What I'd like to have is something different, a dumb little blond thing, someone who needs somebody. That little toad doesn't need anybody, she's a know-it-all. She can take care of herself out on the street."

"Jesus and Mary, a sin!" Janka moaned.

"What? I'm right here. Is that toad any better than her own mother? No, she's not! She belongs right here. She'll end up on the street. Stay out of this, Jan, don't talk! It's my business, enough! Lord Jesus, if I didn't have the kid, I swear, last year I would've taken off with that Jew from Berlin. I swear, I would've gone. I'm sick of putting on an act when those guys come, those asses. It would've been sweet to laze around my whole life long." She spat out the apple core, turned around on her back, and looked at the ceiling. "You're young and healthy. You've got a bit of fire left in you. The bastards, those bastards, drain me, day after day, drop by drop. They've taken the little bit of youth and fire I had left. Sometimes I don't go out looking for them, but they come right on over, the pigs. I get angry when I hear them knocking. You know how it is. Some guy shows up and gets his bit of fun. And I have to shut up and hold on. He can roll his eyes, the fucking fish, when I'd like to give him a swift kick. Sometimes you have to, sometimes you want to cry a river, but you keep it to yourself. Oh, Jan, at times a stupid little student does a body good."

"Where's the little one? She left her bread. It's time for her to have some lunch."

"I don't like to go round and round with that old bitch downstairs. The kid needs to stay away from her," Katerine said stubbornly.

"You don't ever listen to one single thing I say," Janka said with a sigh and opened the door to the hall, "Milada! Milada!"

Janka went back inside. Around her furrowed mouth there was a twitch, as if she wanted to cry.

She was small and worn and very often kept her head down on her sunken chest. Her stature had something oddly unformed and not mature about it, as if a hard kick had checked her growth. She might have had a lung ailment, but she rarely coughed and never complained. The skin on her face was covered with makeup and powder, but there were areas of bare white skin on her forehead, neck, and temples where lots of large freckles were visible. They covered her forearms and hands, too.

Katerine looked out from behind her pillows, ill at ease.

"Why are you always worried about that little brat? She'll be alright. If she needs something, she can steal it."

Janka's voice sputtered and broke, "She's just a child. What are we doing to her soul? Honestly, it is a mortal sin, Katerine. It really is!"

Katerine blew up. She hissed, and flames shot out of her eyes. She had been expecting something like this for days now. She knew it was coming ever since that letter arrived. Janka had thrown a towel over it, but she had seen it, that letter. Stupid hiding game! They had no right coming to her with that, not a one of them.

"Keep it to yourself. She's my kid. And always will be, even if I die on a pile of shit. I'm the one who decides. No, no, that's not how we play this game, you and me."

"What set you off?"

"Shut up, Jan! You act like a lamb of God! I don't have to answer to you. I could've left last year with that Jew if I didn't have the kid. If I'd gone, you'd have packed up and taken her home—fast as one, two, three. Then you'd have put her on her little Daddy's lap! Yes, you would've."

She jumped out of bed and shook her red-brown hair. "And here I am her mother. No, no, no, I'm not playing along with you and your backwoods yokels. You think you are so smart, but I'm smarter. We're workers here, and we're poor, but what we have we hang onto. We're tough." She stomped off.

"You don't have to talk so mean and be so crazy, Katerine, you know?"

"You don't have to act so holier than Thou, you bitch. I can see in your eyes what you want to do. No, she's staying here, and she can walk the streets just like me. Do you care about me? Wasn't I a kid just like her, wasn't I? No, I'll say it again, and that's that. I'm going to wake up one more time and have a good laugh at the end of the day."

She drew her legs up on the edge of the bed and propped her head on her knees. An expression of hate and scorn twisted her face. "Just wait till he hears his only child, his flesh and blood, is walking the streets for three or four gulden. He'd love to bring the kid to his house in a coach with four horses and velvet pillows because his rich wife can't give him one. Janka, if you say anything to him, if you betray me..." She jumped up and lifted her arm, then let it fall slowly. She nodded to her beautiful reflection in the mirror and said softly, "But I know, sweetie, you'll never do that to your poor Katerine." She went to the kitchen window and hollered down to the courtyard, "Milada! Mi-la-da!"

"She's down there playing with the cats."

Katerine smoothed her hair quickly with a comb and brush and started to sing with a resounding voice:

Kde domov muj?
Kde vlast je ma?
Kde voda huci po lucinach[1]

Suddenly she stopped, turned around. She was calm and in a pleasant mood.

"Janka, sweetie, stop cooking and cleaning! Your poor, pretty hands! Go get the laundry woman. Tonight we're going to have some money, I'm tellin' you. Today Katerine will be good and

---

1 A song of Czech resistance: *Where is my home? / Where is my homeland? / Where water roars across the meadows.*

smart. Just you wait and see! And by the way, why don't you get yourself all dressed up like you used to? It's been two weeks since you've gone out, my angel. No wonder you're so miserable."

She ran her elegant fingers over her friend and flattered her until Janka lifted up her head and looked at Katrine with her washed-out eyes.

At that moment the little girl pushed her way in the door. Katerine told her, "Come on, quick! Let's make your aunt beautiful. She needs to laugh. Tell her to laugh."

"If you don't laugh, Auntie, you won't pick anybody up," Milada said seriously. Katinka, as Janka called her, gave her friend a little nudge and laughed a hearty laugh.

"There we go, nobody'll think she's a goodly little country girl. Sweetie, your hair's a mess. Lanolin, powder! We need tonic and some toilet water. Go get some, be quick!"

She was in a good mood and sat Janka down on a big chair. With a flourish Katerine tied back her own thick, curly hair and started putting cream and pink powder on Janka's face and hands. She waved her hands, chatted and told little jokes, throwing in affectionate words in Czech. She splashed violet water on the back of Janka's neck, her ears and hair, tamed her frizzy hair into waves around her forehead, and finally put a black velvet ribbon with sparkles around her neck. Then she stepped back to admire her work and clapped her hands.

"Just see how your aunt looks now, why don't you?"

"Beautiful!" Milada said and nodded, deftly putting up the bottles and boxes.

"Now, go get the red dress for your aunt."

"No, no!" Janka protested, looking in the mirror. "Not an outfit like that in the middle of the day."

But Milada had already hauled out the dress. It was a conspicuous, bright-red dress with ruffles and fluttering ribbons, and, despite her protests, Janka put it on. Milada helped, knew what to do, pulled it back and used her little hands to smooth the flounces and bows. Then she took her place beside her mother and admired Janka.

"Tonight you'll get a baron, Jan," Katerine said approvingly. "But you really have to walk where there's light."

Milada tugged at her dress. "And if you get a lot of money, then you'll be sure to buy me the bird from Lorinser, Auntie," she whispered. "She'll sell him cheap. He hasn't been eating."

Janka strutted over to the mirror and admired herself. But really, how she looked! You wouldn't recognize her. She was fit to kill out on the street.

With her knees apart, Janka sat down stiffly and carefully. With her handkerchief across her breast to protect her dress, she drank her coffee. "There are potatoes and some butter in the cupboard for you," she said to Milada.

"Later," the child answered secretly and skipped out of the room into the kitchen, this time carrying more things. Milada brought fresh laundry scented with violets, pins made of shell, hair combs and pearls. She propped herself against the armoire, opened it, and pulled out rustling skirts, hung carelessly. "The yellow one?" she called out.

"The white one!" Katerine ordered.

"Even if it's already dirty?"

"It's still all right."

Katerine took off her nightrobe and stood there in only her nightdress. Her arms and the back of her neck shimmered the color of ivory. She shook out her short, thick curls and pinned her hair on top of her head in a wide crown. She changed her underwear and pulled a skirt with a train made of very thin, white fabric over her hips. She drew the red silk laces of her dress closed and wrapped herself up in a black knit cloak that half covered her head and hid her slim figure completely. Because of this cloak the alley's visitors had nicknamed her the Woman in Black. With a flash of her eyes she said, "Come on, Jan!"

Milada gave her mother a disapproving look. She did not like to see Katerine dressed so shabbily when she had nice silk clothes in the closet.

"Make a fire in the stove!" Katerine called back behind herself. "Eat something!" Janka said. Then the two women made their way down the steep stairs.

For a moment, the child listened. Then Katerine's fluttering voice rose up the stairs again, and the child nodded earnestly as if she had not quite grasped what she knew. Right away she started picking up furiously. There were clothes thrown everywhere, laundry, combs and ribbons. She put it all away. Then she jumped up on a chair and piled up the dishes. The dirty bowls and glasses clanked in the sink. She dragged the rumpled bedding off the bed and stuffed it into the cupboard. Then she replaced it with clean silk pillows with the scent of violets from Katerine's showpiece bed. She had just enough time to run her little brown fingers over the smooth, cool material. With unbelievable skill and systematic carefulness, going from one corner to the other, she cleaned the mess all up. Like a busy little hobgoblin she raked up the coals and, stepping carefully, carried some to the iron stove in the next room. She put red apples under the pillow on Katerine's bed and put out a bottle of wine. Janka did not need anything. She was not as special as her mother. Finally she surveyed her work with satisfaction.

She did not have to check. She had not forgotten a thing. The red glow of the lamp, which she had turned down, filled both the rooms with a mystical darkness. How beautiful it was there! But now she had to hurry. Katerine was coming back, and she needed the light as it was. She put a few warm potatoes in her pocket along with some wax candles and matches and slipped out. Red House would have to be home for you to find your way around at night. You had to wend your way over a wooden balcony, up steep stairs, and through long halls and corridors, the whole time on a worn and damp path, to reach the basement-like arch of the entrance hall. That is where the girls stood together in bright clothing with floating feather boas and white veils as they exchanged comments. They were loud and unaffected. Some went into bars; others stayed out on the street; most spread out around the city.

"Standin' around in bars costs a ton of money, and then you're still taking a risk," one young thing said with an attitude while she poked a thin walking stick into the toe of her patent-leather shoe. "'Cause the waiters are mean and they're crooks. You have to give 'em some cash first. But then they'll get you a trick, even more 'an that."

"To hell with that!" another spat out.

"Shut up now. Here comes the Hungarian slut."

"She'll do it for a gulden."

"A gulden! That's a good one!" the Hungarian replied with a laugh.

"Anything goin' on?" the young woman with the patent-leather shoes asked a couple of others who had been walking the alley.

"It's all right, but there's a horrible guy out there tonight."

"That's how they all are here. Back in Budapest..."

"God, my stomach's growling I'm so hungry, and it's awful cold out here!"

"Want a piece of candy?" the Hungarian offered.

"Sure, give me some."

"One gulden, that's what it'll cost," the Hungarian said. Her face was red as a brick, and she had a pointy nose. She said with a grin, "There you go."

"Hungarian trash!"

"Who you callin' trash?"

"I'm callin' you trash! That's right. Anyone wants that much for a stinkin' piece of candy is a..."

"Move over, some guys are coming!"

"Oh, God, don't tell me it's that Italian from the police, the Commissioner."

Janka stepped aside. "He doesn't bother anybody," she told them. The girls dispersed.

They slipped out of all the doorways and corners and, humming aloud, hurried past the official into the bright light of the bustling main street. As they did, he looked them over with disapproval.

"Auntie!" said Milada seriously and pushed her way over to Janka who clomped on toward her under the weight of the rustling dress, "Didn't you get a couple of gulden? Was it like last time when the girls were mean to you?" Janka waved her away sadly, "I know, I know," she said. She was upset and pushed her way on into the apartment.

Enveloped in her black shawl, slim and elegant as a fir tree, with eyes that had a strange glow and pierced the darkness around her as if with flames, Katerine stood beneath a sky strewn with stars. She let people pass her by without noticing them, uncaring. The girls shot her spiteful glances, or, feigning an accident, they shoved her rudely with an elbow. Some hurled mean curses, but they missed their mark and fell like a stone. She never turned around to look. She took deep breaths, drawing in the cold night air. She wanted to fill her lungs after having smelled perfume, kitchen odors, and the warmth of bed. She walked with lightly swaying hips past houses. She was in no hurry. She did not hum, and the wide hem of her white skirt dragged on the ground, sweeping up debris. The others moved around the corner and tried to lure their clients. She stayed in the alley. The visitors came to her.

Only on rare occasions did Katerine go downtown. If there was no money in the house and Janka was complaining she needed to buy something, she dressed up like a lady in rustling finery. She walked slowly up and down the busy main street in the middle of the day in a feather hat with a veil. If she turned into her alley, she could lure a companion of her choice with an inviting laugh. She charged as much as they needed at home, sometimes ten gulden, but as much as a hundred or more. People rarely haggled with her. That was during the day.

But in the evening men came all on their own. She took some with her down the alley in a rush, like baggage carriers, never looking around to see them. She did not even move her covered arms to give them a signal. She opened the door to the house, whistled softly, and Milada flitted to her with a candle and lit the way for her as she stepped in front of the visitor, stiff and silent. But every so often there was someone Katerine walked around with, laughing and joking. She told him stories or listened to him attentively until she began chattering away hotly. She cuddled up to him sweetly like a wife, and then she followed his soft promptings willingly. At those times a little song would blossom on her lips that mixed oddly with the sound of the rusty house door and the creaking of the wooden stairs. Then Milada would run behind her mother, and, without realizing it, the little child would share in her mother's excitement.

"She really likes that guy," the child was happy to think, and she hummed along with her mother. On those occasions she went out to the street to find Janka. She knew she was not allowed upstairs. Katerine did not want that. Milada was proud her mother was so desirable. Dutifully she counted up the visits on her fingers and was happy when she did not have enough fingers for all of them.

There was a wild, reckless strength, a victorious taking and holding-on about this woman. Katerine had a seductive charm that the child attached to her felt, too.

Katerine was the type of person who is, an any situation, naturally superior. She was in control. Others were quietly resigned to her mood of the minute. They attended her, hoping to bloom in the sunshine of her good moments. In her good moments they forgot the wrongs and slights of her many dark hours. If she was fond of someone, he stuck fast and came back again and again.

This prostitute knew how to awaken and keep alive the illusion of an intimate partner and unusually good-hearted woman, even though the man was paying for this affection and for the hugs that were empty. Men did not forget her, and often it was only an impetuous movement—a questioning word or her abrupt laughter in the middle of the night—that fueled a man's fantasy. The curve of her body was enough to refresh and enliven men's fantasies.

There were brief, pleasant episodes when she lured and kept this or that man in her apartment for days on end. She served him and busied herself with him. She was sweet and compliant like a new wife. At those times she insistently locked her door to other visitors, put up with Jan's yapping, would rather sell her silk clothes if she needed money, and belonged unwaveringly to this one man alone.

One time it was a young student; another time, an artist who had mistakenly walked into the alley, looking for a model, and had been taken by the beauty of Katerine's body; at other times, it was some old comedian or idler who had become trapped, willingly, by her talent for femininity. She found these people interesting and asked them eagerly about their families and lives, offered them advice, made plans for the future, put to right difficult relationships with her quick words, eased their discomforts and passions with flattery, smoothed everything over, and then let them go with her warm glances and sweet kisses, just like an enchanted goddess of love.

Many a man returned and suggested he would set her up in respectable, new circumstances. Yes, he promised to marry her, if she wanted that, but she always rejected these offers with great decisiveness.

It was the awareness of her very deep degradation that gave her the strength to jettison her sweetest and most intimate qualities. She had been abused and mistreated.

"You see, Jan, what I want to happen does happen." How often had Janka heard just these words out of the lips of her friend when they were young! She nodded faithfully. Every now and again these words still fell from Katerine's painted lips like tatters of some long-lost purple fabric; they emerged later from lips she had carefully defined with a brush. And still Janka nodded faithfully.

When Katerine was asleep or out shopping in the neighborhood, the two, Janka and the child, sat close together on the stack of wood by the stove and spoke about her in whispers. How good the new dress looked with her face and what they might cook her for lunch to make her really happy! And they spoke about all the money they had found in the drawer that morning. The fine gentleman with the top hat had left it there with his address. Milada had found the note crumpled on the floor, smoothed it out and put it up carefully in a box with foil and tinsel.

"It is quite possible she can use it," the child said, old before her years.

"So what's going on there with the tall councilor that they have so much to talk about?" Janka remarked pensively and with concern.

"They're just having a good time!" said Milada. "There's nothing really interesting about him. Mrs. Marek says he hardly pays."

Janka shook her head. When she was worried about something, two deep furrows settled on her brow, and she closed her eyes halfway.

"I think he wants to take her away from here," Janka said slowly with a heavy voice. Milada's eyes flashed, "But she won't do that, right? She won't. Mommy won't leave this place, not for somebody like that!"

"Wouldn't you like to go with her yourself?"

"Me? No. I'm gonna stay right here all my life, just like Mommy."

"Oh, my love, the world is so beautiful, so bright and good. There are places where you don't see all these houses, and there's nothing but sky and fields and meadows—and then just forest. Oh, Jesus!" A sob arose from her soul.

"But, Auntie, we have flowers, and we'll get that little birdie Hans, too. Just you wait until he starts singing," Milada announced, reproaching Janka. "Honest, he'll sing for me!" She clapped her hands, then caught herself and looked toward the next room. Milada crouched down and was quiet. "And later, when the fuchsia blooms, Auntie, you'll see how beautiful it is right here!" She whispered to reassure her because Janka was staring at the floor downcast.

The Councilor Raffel was generally known as the Italian Councilor because his lady love—though he rarely took her out—was from Tuscany. Raffel was one of the most eager visitors to the alley.

He hung around one girl at a time, went out with her, and brought her fine fruits or greens. He supervised her clothing and changed her hair. He gave her a sense of "style" and offered her good advice. But he always backed right off when a serious client showed up for her. When he was grooming someone, he had dozens of special ways of talking. Sometimes he was serious like a pastor, or else he was silly like a clown. The girls laughed about him, but they also found him annoying since he was shabby. Except for the fruit he got free as Commissioner for the Markets, he never had anything to offer. He never dropped any money, not even for the little blandishments the girls showed him in sentimental moments. He did not repay them with the smallest tip.

For a time he visited Katerine who, up to this point, had intimidated him with her proud and arrogant behavior. Katerine was the first one to figure out that behind his "foolishness" was a need to act out. He needed relief from the narrow confines of propriety. She also saw his moods and erratic behavior paralleled her own. She was thankful for anything different or new that came her way in her own narrow sphere, and she responded to his oddities with understanding and warmth.

Every evening she went around with him and laughed when he called her "m'lady" or "madame" or put on airs, kissing her fingers when he arrived or left. "Why not?" he said coolly. But there was a difference in the tone of his behavior with her and with the "nice girls" of his social circle. Nice girls, he said, did not know how to keep their distance and became uppity and self-conscious about their sexuality when they were alone in the proximity of maleness. He had found his experiments in playfulness were without prospects among bourgeois women. Furthermore, he said, it was difficult to stir up the woman in proper ladies. Raffel was interested in a pure woman. “If you please, not in the sense of ‘untouched’ or anything like that.” What he was after was, rather, essential sexuality freed of appearances and egoism. If they are single, their sexual functions are for the task of getting married and nothing else. There is not a hint of uncontrolled excitation. And then there are the married women! Dear God! Those were dolls, monkeys for show. As a man you were useful to them as a provider or decoration, at best for stud service. There were some women who had desire. But they only wanted their little lust satisfied. They were not interested in the desire of the other. He had no use for that. He required someone who understood him, understood him completely, not as any lover or some nice model client, by no means. He wanted someone who was interested in him and only him, Hugo Raffel, Commissioner for Markets, with his knock knees and Adam’s apple, naked as he was, and ready for love in his very own way. No, he did not sleep with anybody who did not suit him or anybody who did not want him, just him. Oh, yes, he had all the time in the world. He could always wait, just not too long. Katerine detected a real sincerity behind these words. She liked that.

“You know, m’lady, the nice girls from our circles do not want to know about a natural, easy, and, of course, unmethodical relationship. But if they do, then under conditions that make a relationship with a man of my qualities impossible. And if these nice girls do have easy sex, then ten minutes later they don’t want to be reminded that they did. And you can never let on that you know that they knew what was going on; that’s not sufficiently ‘sensitive.’ And you always have to beg up front and afterwards play penitent and remorseful. Lord God, how complicated this whole business is. It's enough to make you impotent!"

He removed his hat and wiped his sweaty brow with his handkerchief.

"Up to the very last minute, even past that, you have to pick your way along a narrow bridge. Then, of course, you lose your balance and at best come tumbling down. Where is there, I ask, any room, realistically, for personal instincts? What happens to free expression? People can't inspect each other, feel at home with somebody, and, so to speak, get to know each other physically. Because the sexual instincts, exactly like the social habits of two people, have to come together in such a way that they work toward an agreement that is mutually beneficial. Take me for example," he said as he took hold of a button on his overcoat. "I'm one of those guys who can read a newspaper in the act. I have no use for illusion. I am *perdu*, lost when someone wants a lot of game-playing from me. There are guys who need a gentle sadness. You can't disrupt them with a loud word or a laugh. They are done after some stupid little joke. Then there are others who beg and wheedle to the last second and swear the whole time they never ever would have gotten this woman if it hadn't been for their extreme efforts. Ridiculous fantasies! They're trying to fix nature! Like children they water down some sweet drink so that it will last longer. I am one of those very guys who is fine reading the news in bed. I don't ask for a prelude, any heavily charged expectation. I require no preparation for days in advance. Madame, don't rob me of anything real, and I can do it all."

For effect he stretched out his arms. The girls sifting past turned around and laughed at him. He grimaced with disgust.

"Your colleagues, Madame, are conventional idiots. They have taken their techniques from 'respectable girls.' That's all it is. But that's as far as it goes. If a guy like me goes for one of them, then they don't ignite, exactly like wet gunpowder."

"You don't have to promise them anything. You don't have to make a fuss or anything like that," Katerine replied slowly and thoughtfully. "A girl can just expect a little something, don't you think?"

"But of course," he said in a hurry and happily, "I do see that I am understood. Take this girl Rosa I saw last week for instance. Atrocious!"

She narrowed her large, gray eyes. "You practice acting in front of a mirror," she offered frankly with disdain.

"Atrocious! She's wild and eager and pants and gushes and explodes with excitement. We talk intimately, bitch and moan, and call each other names! May the devil come and haul me off. That woman is a crime against nature. It's true, I can't bear it. It makes me into a little old woman. By all that's holy, I swear, that unmans me. It makes me a nervous wreck, goes to the core and makes me vulnerable. I see dirt and filth. I see every little wrinkle. I am sensitive. Slut, don't impose on me, girl! Pay no attention to me! Eat your food right out of the wrapper! Wipe your nose. Go get me the newspaper, it has to be around here somewhere. Don't take away my illusion of regular life. Deceive me with a marital, philistine, groggy indifference in bed. Don't be too pure, Phryne. Don't wear perfume! Blabber, gossip, and be crude! And don't ask if we need light. When I go out to eat, I don't ask the waiter for gastronomic gestures he tried out in front of a mirror. I like chewing each bite slowly, thoroughly. I have some bread after each bite. I read a chapter after the act. That's just the way I am."

He kept interrupting himself when Katerine turned around or someone got her attention. Then he let go of her arm, lit a cigar, and patiently waited till she returned and listened to him with her head down as she walked beside him.

She very much liked talking with him. When he was not around, she wore an expression of disappointment and was irritable and sharp with people. She was angry when the girls laughed about him. "Stupid idiots!" she said with scorn. Men teased her.

"Well, Lady in Black, looks like he's your guy, huh?" She defended herself, saying, "Not at all, I'm way too young for him. He needs someone old and tired."

And he could be more than just funny! She felt a strange burning desire leapt out of his words, and something of that desire got in her blood. She did not resist that. Things were really sweet with him around.

He could wait he had said.

And he could also wait with a bit of heated passion. She liked that, too.

Sometimes she walked on by him like a stranger, stiffly, but her eyes followed him restlessly and with excitement as his lone figure with his coat flapping in the wind strode through the alley.

If another woman cozied up to him, she came between them like a hurricane, hurling insults, so that he exclaimed, "Goodness!"

That often led to some rough arguments, yes, to physical fights, which amused people in the neighborhood, just not Janka. Janka watched the man with jealous hate because she was afraid Katerine's reputation would suffer from her "need" for this man. It did not take long for the spoiled woman to feel an unusual, breathtaking desire for the big blowhard who threw looks of disapproval at her when she cuddled up to him and let her white breast show through the black cloak pulled tight against herself. Her usual "Come on!" did not cross her lips. And, yes, as her blood ran hotter and went to her head and her desire teased her, she became all the more cool and mocking and laughed about the men who stuck to her like burrs.

One evening he explained to Katerine that he would be glad to have sex with her after he had finished smoking his cigar. She blanched with anticipation, and her heart began to pound. She murmured something, then walked around with him not saying anything. She motioned the other girls away with a shake of her head.

"There's still time," he said once when one of her clients came up to her. "This cigar will last a while," and he flicked the ashes of his cigar between his thin, red fingers.

"But I don't want to!" she flew off the handle, stomped her foot and kept standing there.

"Ah-ah-so," he drew out the words unruffled and looked her up and down.

She bit her lower lip and was defiant, but she said nothing as if foiled.

Suddenly she was overcome with the fear he might turn down the next street, simply leave without a word, with no explanation—and never come back. He might never want to have anything more to do with her because he saw that she was crazy about him. That did not sit well with him! That man was so crazy he could honestly leave. It was possible he did not care one whit about her, about anybody. He could honestly drop her. Yes, he could do that pretty easily, the cheapskate. The one guy she wanted—one of thousands—was not going to brush her off. Holy hell, no! She swallowed hard before she could speak in her normal voice.

"I'm sick and tired of the whole world. I don't want anything, nothing at all."

"Why is that?"

"Jesus! People like me have our worries," she sighed. "You can believe me. We laugh and play around the whole sweet day, but when we start to think about things, well, we see what's what! People like us always end up hurting the worst. And then we just have a drink."

"Can I offer you a glass of wine?" he asked gallantly. "Wait a minute, you poor dog, I'll get you wine."

He pulled some money out of his pocket and began turning over small coins. Very laboriously he counted his change.

"Don't do that!" she said eagerly and took a piece of silver out of her bag. "Here's enough for a bottle of wine."

"You're right," he replied and slipped the coin into his pants pocket.

She did not know what to do. She stood in front of him almost embarrassed, playing with his long, red fingers. He held the cigar sideways in his mouth and chewed on the end. She felt a sharp pang of fear in his presence. And the sharper the pangs, the more tempting was her desire. It confounded her otherwise sharp senses.

She had trouble breathing. And with an abrupt, small movement she let her other arm drop. Her cloak fell, and her throat and breasts shimmered in the darkness like sparkling silk.

"Little tart," he said and stretched out his hands. She took his fingers and ran them across her breasts.

"So, do you like me?" she whispered imploringly.

"Wait, I'll get some wine," he replied with a husky voice. She nodded, shivering at his touch.

"I'll wait upstairs," she whispered. "The child will lead you. Just whistle and say, 'To Katerine.'" And she left. She threw out a few quick words to Milada, shoved Janka out without giving her an explanation, turned down the lamp, and threw herself on the bed with her arms up over her head. The large decorative pillows sent out the smell of violets as they fell to the floor.

But, no, that was just a man!

The sensation of her own, personal femininity was now, after a long pause, again awake, and it mixed hotly and sweetly with her inflamed fantasy. She, Katerine, wanted just this once...

Not because he suited her or because he paid good money, or because she was drunk on wine—not at all. Only because she wanted to taste a bit of good luck. She wanted to kiss and be kissed. She longed for a man she had feelings for. She wanted to feel close to someone and not keep her distance. She wanted to know a man without that ugly feeling: he is a client.

She wanted a man of her own, someone after her own taste, and he...

No more acting, good luck for once. Ooh, she let herself be swept away. She stretched out across her silken bed feeling good. It rustled and shook beneath her and made her dizzy with soft scents.

Then she heard light, careful footsteps in the stairwell. That was the little girl. She was walking ahead. There were unsure and heavy steps alongside the light, fleeting ones. He tripped in front of the door, laughed, and the door opened. Cold air rushed in. It seemed to Katerine he took forever looking for a coin. He smiled, and chucked Milada on the chin. "There, you little thief!" He felt his way into the room, and a soft hand reached out for him.

In the middle of the night Janka slipped downstairs to look for the little girl. Her eyes were filled with anger and swollen from lack of sleep. She found Milada asleep in a doorway, blue from cold.

"Come on!" she said and took Milada upstairs.

"No, we can't go upstairs," Milada stammered, surprised. "We can't go near Mommy today, right, Auntie? Mommy is..." Janka let out a sigh. Then she took the thin, sleepy little creature in her arms, pressed her close to herself in a moment of tenderness and whispered.

"May God forgive us all the sins against you, poor soul!"

During the days that followed Katerine did not philosophize. She went about the small apartment chatting and singing. She peeled large red apples, even helped Janka with daily chores, and told the most impossible tales in detail about her newest love story. She rummaged around in the laundry and clothes, put together a pile by her bed, and said, "Today I'd like to go out for a real afternoon stroll, just like a lady in her finery. Here are your orders: Cook, make something wonderful. And I'll go out flaming and beautiful on the streets shopping. And then I'll come home and tell good, goooood, stories. Ooh, it seems so stupid and lazy to do nothing the live-long day but talk a blue streak." She stretched out her arms. "I want to do something busy today, Jan, something downright busy so I only have to think about doing busy things. And when I've caught my breath a bit, I'll have to think about my good luck and right away again about getting on with things. I want to be a teacher. If only things had gone the way my grandmother wanted them to! She always lamented, 'It's enough to make a body crazy, dear God! My Katinka got on the wrong path.'" Katerine kept prattling in a good mood, chewed the apple and spat out the core. She started putting on her clothes slowly, tried on a frilly nightgown, threw it aside, and put a serious, black, tailored dress on her lovely, slim body.

"Jan, I could also sit at the window sewing fine fabric with beautiful silk thread and golden pearls. That would suit me. Good heavens, I'm going to go buy myself something like that. You know, Jan, I would have fit perfectly in a cloister. At the end of the day I'll give up this business here and feed myself by doing pious work." She laughed and stretched.

"Sinful talk!" Janka muttered and plucked the leaves of a head of lettuce.

"And how wonderful it is," said Katerine, "to turn over in bed, and the guy doesn't plop on the floor! It's so wonderful to have a man who lies next to your body. You don't want to take money from someone like that, Jan, even if—God help me—it's pure gold."

Janka did not answer.

An unusual look of grief and sorrow lay on her yellow, dry face. She moved her lips silently, as if she were praying. Katerine looked at her uncomfortably. What was her problem this time? Everything was fine. They had enough money. She could not bear her judgment. When Janka pulled a face, it bothered her even if she was in an especially good mood.

"Want an apple? He says rabid eating drives away evil thoughts. That might help you, sweetheart!" Her bare teeth crunched into the apple.

"Cook something nice! I want to look forward to something all day long till the evening, Jan. That's when my man will come again. So what's wrong with you? What's going on? Talk to me!"

Katerine narrowed her eyes. Her upper lip drew up a little, revealing the coral red of her gums. Her forehead was slightly rumpled.

"You a little angry? Well, are you? You can talk or not, suit yourself. Are you being a bitch?"

A particular nervous uneasiness vibrated in all these questions.

"Do you always have to spoil my good times, sweetie?"

"I am somebody, too, and can't sit by and watch this anymore," Janka growled out her complaint.

"What?" Katerine sat up straight, and her sweet, thick upper lip was pressed hard against her teeth. Her cheek bones showed sharp through her skin, while her jaws were clenched.

"You, her own mother, who has a God-given conscience, you laugh along with him when he calls the child a thief or a bastard. Such a little child, and he calls her things like that, and you laugh with him.

"Little Milada stands downstairs on the look-out for men and says, 'There's somebody with Mother already.' That," Janka raised the spoon she was cooking with, "Goes against God's wish." Her red hands fell on top of her head, "That's like murdering the child, that's what it is."

There was a pause while Janka listened as her heart rose in her throat.

The other woman spoke slowly with a voice that was weak. Her gaze fluttered to the windows, covered with fog. She was like a bird that had become exhausted.

"It would have been all right if the kid had died."

"Give her up! Why don't you give her up?" Janka whimpered softly.

"No! No! I'm not going to let you people take her away from me. Not a one of you knows Katerine at all! Do you understand me? What would I have then? Would I get some more little letters from the precious wife of the squire, offering to take Milada for herself and her husband Lord Andreas? This time I smell the Church in all this. I'd rather die a miserable wreck than let them get their fingers on her. Did Mrs. Squire write you again, hm? Tell me! Where do you go when you sneak out?" She grabbed Janka by the arm. "You are all one nest of rats. To hell with all of you!" Katerine was done and spat.

Janka looked her in the eye. "What is it that you want? I won't stay around for that. I'm tired of this whole life. What am I to you? You treat me like I'm your... I want to go home. There's always a place for me there—always."

"You're pretty sorry about leaving, aren't you?" Katerine sneered savagely. "You're sorry you left your lovely home and your special Uncle Andreas, lord of the estate. Back home you can play the fine, groveling servant to his stupid wife, the high and mighty lady."

Janka threw her a mean look. She stirred up the coals, and the fire licked her face with its weak flames.

"Don't worry about me. You don't have to say any more about me, Katerine," she said reproachingly. "But your little child, look at her. If she stays here, her soul is lost, here and in heaven. She might already be lost, Katerine, while we're looking the other way and don't lift a finger. It's just like watching a bird die and not giving it a drop of water or a bit of bread when you know it'll die today or tomorrow. You laugh about that creature of God, how it suffers and flaps its wings. Go ahead and scream—scream! But it's true all the same. The sin is terrible. It will come back to haunt us all. Katerine, stop this, and bundle her up! Katerine, give her to a cloister! Promise her to Holy Mother Anne, and save your little child. Take her to the school at the cloister where she can learn to work and pray, where she might want to spend her life.

Sure as there is a God in heaven, I would never betray you, never say a word to her father. You can trust me, I wouldn't tell Andreas anything about his daughter, not on my deathbed. My poor soul has no peace, I confess it."

She knelt down on the floor and sobbed, her face pressed in her hands.

Katerine's heart had become hardened to anything that suffers and perishes. But Janka there tore her up! A harsh, raw word was stuck in her throat.

They had both grown up together in the cloister, Janka, a daughter of the wealthy Matschak family, and Katerine, the child of a weaver. Katerine's eyelids burned over her staring eyes. They glowed with treachery. Her buried soul now listened to the primal cry in her memory. Katerine sank down intuitively beside Janka who was kneeling on the floor. Tears streamed down the pale, haggard, hollowed-out cheeks, and they fell on Janka's hands, which Katerine tried in vain to pry apart.

"Janka, my love, please stop. Laugh, my dear! Don't look away, look at me! You know your Katerine has nobody, nobody on Earth like you. Nothing in this world means as much to me as your dear face. We'll do what you want. Yes, the child has to go to the cloister school. To the good sisters, all right? Maybe she'll want to stay there and pray us all into heaven. No, not you, just me, me. You are as blameless as an angel of God, you are."

And she rocked Janka's head on her breast with sweet words. And her old magic, the power of this proud soul, broke through and soothed the pain and suffering of her friend. Katerine even promised to drop the man, never to let him come to her again if it mattered to Janka.

"And you know, my sweetie," she whispered in Janka's ear, "We won't let in any man at all, and we'll crawl into bed together, just like we used to in the cloister school. Remember? You stood on the cold floor, shaking, afraid of a ghost. We wrote notes about it, don't you remember?" And she nudged her and laughed and beamed at her with her gray eyes so long that Janka warmed and started chatting,

When Milada showed up to see about lunch, it had not been cooked and was sitting on the cold burner. Then all three of them laughed together, and Milada ran to get them sausage and pickles, chocolate, wine, and apples—lots of apples—and raisins and sugar. When they had eaten, Janka pulled a blue silk ribbon out of her shoe and started to braid the child's unruly hair.

"Wow, are you really doing my hair up nice, Auntie?" Milada asked curiously.

"We're going to the cloister school now where nice children have their hair in braids and learn and pray."

"But I don't want to be with the nice children!"

"Oh, my! Why don't you want to? They have pictures and books and beautiful needlework. What all they have there!"

"Can little Peter and little Hans come, too?"

"What's that? Those stupid little urchins go to school?" Janka answered Milada.

Janka looked with satisfaction at the two stiff, thick braids that fell in a curve at the nape of the child's neck.

"Maybe you'd like to be a pious nun! If you behave nicely and pray, you can even stay in the lovely cloister."

Milada shook her head firmly, "I don't want to. I just want to stay here in Red House forever."

Katerine looked at her friend with amusement. "Go on with your holy pilgrimage!" she said with a yawn and stretched out across her bed, "I'll take a little nap."

At the cloister a lay nun listened patiently to Janka's story. At the end she shook her head thoughtfully, and, while promising much, did not so much as look at the poor, needy little thing who looked around with extremely serious eyes and rubbed her nose from time to time. The nun then said she would go to the mother superior who was booked up with appointments that day. But for a matter like this there was not much hope. Well, Janka offered, she could by all means wait. And because Janka looked at her so imploringly, the nun added kindly that, while they wanted to help everyone, the school was already more than full with children of married parents. And with that, she left.

Janka did not stop fussing nervously over Milada and muttered as she fussed, "It's beautiful here, you know. It's really all festive just like in church. Look," she pointed to the schoolyard where there were children in blue smocks who came up to the window with curiosity. "Say a prayer! Pray you can play with them, dear child."

"I don't want to. I want to stay with you," Milada answered without being defiant but with determination.

In the meantime the lay nun had returned in the company of a nun, a fat elderly woman with a pleasant, slow disposition who carried a heavy ring of keys.

Janka shoved Milada in front of her and tried to start talking, but the nun motioned her away and said, she knew all about it. No, the poor urchin could not attend the cloister school. That would not be good for the other children. Besides she was only six years old. That was much too young.

The lay nun signaled she wanted to speak, and the nun nodded in agreement. "Of course it would work if... Oh, you poor urchin!" she interrupted herself and put her hand under Milada's chin in a gesture of goodliness.

She then explained in a fussy manner to the attentive Janka that on Oberhoff Street—"What is the address again, Regina?" Regina looked it up and wrote it down for Janka. On Oberhoff there was an elementary school with the first three grades for needy children. It was run by the Church, of course. Every year one of the girls from the third grade was selected for a cloister. There she would have, if she was nice and pious and a good little girl, a chance to be taken care of in either this or another religious institution.

Janka hesitated. She had, with thankfulness in her eyes, pleaded for more, perhaps a recommendation. No, no, that was not necessary. The Oberhoff school would certainly accept the child. Janka need only tell dear Mrs. Coelestine she had been sent by Holy Anne Cloister.

"Allow me to kiss your hand!" Janka hurried to offer while bending over the hand of the good sister.

"That's not necessary, it's fine."

Milada did not want to kiss her. She made her way to the door and pulled Janka by the skirt. "You're scared of the dark woman, right?" Milada left and waved the sister a friendly goodbye.

On Oberhoff Street there was a long, low building painted white. It had bars at the windows and a narrow entrance with a white cross.

They accepted Milada then and there. Janka had to beg and promise, threaten and wheedle, and hide outside the classroom before she was able to leave the disruptive child, averse to obedience, in the strange environment.

"Aunt Coelestine" was a woman with some experience. She took the little, sobbing creature to a big room filled from floor to ceiling with books, globes, and stuffed animals. There was even a live monkey on a perch. Turtles crawled around slowly and heavily over a pile of moss, and white mice with long tails and red eyes scattered into hiding as they entered.

Mrs. Coelestine moved the planets, let the moons revolve, coaxed the monkey off its perch, held out a mouse for Milada's cupped hand, took out a book with colorful tables, opened it and said, "Listen, you will be able to read all of this. You'll understand everything. You'll know exactly what's in the sky and what's below you in the earth you stand on. But you have to agree to stay here and mind me. Would you like that?"

The child looked around as if under a magical spell. She opened her gray eyes very wide and perhaps ardently for the first time in her life. Milada shot hungry, glowing, curious glances around the room. A new expression appeared on her little thin, brown face. Suddenly she looked fresh and childlike. She pressed the book close to herself and nodded, nodded full of greedy expectation.

"Are we going to start right away?" she asked the woman who greeted her reaction with a smile.

"First tell me your name and where you live!"

"Milada Rezek, and I'm from Red House."

"And you will learn to love me, won't you?"

Milada shook her head earnestly, "Oh, no, I only love Mother, my Aunt, little Peter and little Hans."

"All right, that's just fine," Mrs. Coelestine advanced pleasantly. She led the child back to the classroom where she was happy to stay. And at this moment, a new life began for Milada.

She no longer stayed on the street or in the courtyards, climbing over the walls in between; no longer did she float from door to door or carry messages, run errands to the pawnshop or to some other place; and she no longer looked with worried eyes at every man who walked down the street. Her young soul was shaken awake and taken over by the desire to learn. She wanted to leap with extreme swiftness over the barriers between herself and complete immersion in the mystery of books and ideas.

For hours on end she looked for the letters she knew in bits of newspapers, small pamphlets booksellers stuck in the doors, and in fat, old and yellowed calendars. She put them together into syllables, and she pestered Janka until she taught her how to put together words and make words into sentences.

Stoked by a tough determination she grasped it all unusually quickly. Her little classmates had hardly learned the basics, and Milada was already sitting in the stairwells with whole books she had begged from Lorinser's junk store. She ran her fingers along the lines, deciphering the swirl of dark print on the page; she read with intensity and great urgency. And of course she hung on Janka's apron strings the whole time. "Auntie, what is 'recompense'?" "Auntie, what is 'a sinful l-l-love'?" Right away Janka explained these puzzling words as well as she could. Even Katerine noticed the child's fervor and had to laugh when she found her lost deep in the pages of an open book. Learning to read was the first real experience of Milada's childhood, and even in much later years it remained the pivotal event for ordering her memories.

"That happened before I could read."

Business at Red House and everything that went with it gradually lost its appeal for her. She lived in a new world.

Tired from the mental exertion—as well as from the long walk to and from school—she required peace and quiet in the evening. She often fell asleep in the kitchen by the stove, a piece of half-eaten bread in her hand. When that happened Janka picked her up and spirited her away since there were visitors who objected to a sleeping child.

And when "Madame Teacher" sent a note, suggesting a "separate sleeping arrangement" for the child at night, Janka made up a space for Milada's bedding in a small, unused room in the attic where only rats had lived, a very unusual type of rat with black and white spots. They sniffed around the strange, quiet new arrival with curiosity. Milada tried to catch them and to play with them. She warmed them up at night under her covers, put out rolls for them to eat, and called them out of their hiding holes with a whistle. She showed them books and tables, showed off with what she had learned, and taught them, trying hard to copy her teacher. She told them about the Lord Jesus and His Disciples. The wonders of the Savior sounded believable in these four solitary walls where a little girl preached and the tame rats listened spellbound, pushing each other out of their way.

Once Janka overheard her teaching. She folded her hands in prayer and crossed herself three times, as if before a visitation.

Katerine listened to the child's praying with indifference, but Janka's piqued interest annoyed her. It made her secretly, painfully jealous.

"You're pleased about the toad! She's just like you used to be, and you like that. Bookish and spiritual."

The good mood that had blossomed in Katerine soon wilted. After just one week the good time with Raffel was over. He had told her off one day coldly, saying his way of conducting himself was only a system. He had his own style of weaseling a bit of intimate woman, for little or no money, out of what was on offer. His system got him a bite of confection that he, a poor connoisseur, could otherwise not have tasted. He tried it out with all the ladies, and most usually his experiment worked out for him, or so he said. That was sobering news for Katerine, of course. He used to read his poetry aloud to her all afternoon long. He expected enthusiasm for these "red lyrics," as he called them, and became nasty when she was distracted or yawned.

So they parted soon thereafter, and he attached himself to another girl, and Katerine resumed her work as before.

Cold, closed, and not of a sensual nature, as are all headstrong people, Katerine was not suited to this business. Baubles, glitter, expensive jewelry or costume jewelry, these pitiful comforts her coworkers spent their money on, did not attract her at all; they offered her no pleasure. She was tired of it all, and, though she was proud of her beautiful body, she was not interested in wearing jewels or dressing up. The fantasy she had filled her proud and willful soul with and had soothed herself with was now flagging.

Very slowly the misery and hopelessness of the years to come dawned on her, years that would eagerly and inexorably slink up on her like hungry wolves on the prowl.

She placed her hands in front of her eyes and refused to heed the future. She tried to live for the day as she had before. But she was no longer able to ignore the inevitable.

Increasingly more often this struck her: In two years you will still be sitting here, waiting to pick up men, laugh, and make love as they want to. But in five years men will not be interested in going out with you. They will come closer, look at your face and jeer. You will have to beg, Katerine, cajole them, and talk in the wind like other women do.

Then in ten years you will be old and arthritic, have wrinkles and dyed hair, and live on the edge of town. You will sit on men's laps, toast to their health, if they are friendly, and make the rounds from bar to bar for a trick.

She burrowed down in these thoughts, wallowing in the pain. She saw herself a wreck, cruising the alleys, brash like the Hungarian woman or like the flower girl who lived at Mother Zimmermann's.

In secret she examined her body and face to see if she could already see wrinkles, gray hair, or the horrible blue puffiness from rotten cosmetics and poor circulation that never goes away or becomes smooth again. She ran her hand over her firm, young flesh, looking for signs of decline and decay.

Thoughts of death arose in her mind again and again.

Death did not frighten her, only living till she died. She feared the slow, terrifying years of waiting that would destroy her body with its iron claws, ongoing and inexorably. Before death came she would have to live out the years. To live the rest of her life she would have to watch as death approached. And so she brooded.

When will it come? She simply had too much life still in her. Sometimes she could be crazy when she was playing or laughing. At those times she drank and danced, got dressed up, and enjoyed people. And that, all of that, would fall away, one thing after another spent—gone. Fun, drinking wine, looking in the mirror, wearing silks, the excitement of men and of her vengeance would go. Before losing that she could not die. Start, Katerine, start, there was a warning inside her. Let it all go, be done with it! It will happen regardless!

She put her hands to her temples and tried to chip off thoughts of death and misery that clung like frost. She made new friends, spent days or weeks with them, talked about God and joy, tried the usual experiments to improve oneself, and skillfully made a theater of contrite conversion.

These tactics distracted her for a short while, and the attentions of men did her good. A student brought her books and the literature of the Berlin Magdalene Home. She wrote them an inquiry, but in a momentary, savage and desperate mood she threw away her resolve and went to the bars the prostitutes who knew better avoided. She brought home money and various jobs. Once she made an appearance—just this one time—in a club for men who worked in the stock market. On stage she was overcome with muscle cramps and fell flat on the floor. This unpleasant event angered the management, and the club could well have brought charges against her for inebriation at work if an influential man who had been in the audience had not come forward on Katerine's behalf. He advised the club not to prosecute, and they let the incident drop.

And so she tried anew living life as she had. But an unrest that led again and again to excesses and wild scenes took hold of her in cycles and never again let go. The single cause of her violent internal distress was this: she had lost faith in the possibility and lethal power of revenge.

For miles and miles around his flourishing estate the one man she wanted to destroy, Andreas Matschak, sat ensconced, safe and secure. He laughed the resounding laugh of people who have no worries and are powerful, and Katerine's long and deadly fall did not disturb the sun-filled air he breathed. She had prepared herself calculatedly, cold and sure of victory. The idea of his demise had taken hold of her as if with talons. Go down and take what you can with you. That is the only way to destroy him, this proud gentryman, lord of the estate. His peasants called him The Prince. He had subjected his niece, his child, and his lover to shame and destruction. His pride and his fortune would have to bleed to death for what he had done.

She knew the steely anger that shot like lightning out of his blue eyes. Under the shade of night, when no one was looking, he reached out to Janka and his child. But by day his brow was lit with pride and satisfaction, and his servants greeted him submissively as he passed. But still! She had had some victory over him in his moments of fear. He once sent a messenger, a priest, to demand his child. "His child," the young servant of God had said as he rolled his eyes from hell below up to heaven.

His messenger was so formal that he rang the doorbell. She had to laugh. He offered her money, the ass! He offered a lot of money and a cottage somewhere in Bohemia for Janka with a little garden and some acreage. The pastor smacked his lips with delight at the luxury of this offer. "No," was her answer, and once again, "No. The child is mine and that's that!" Without insult or argument she showed the men the door. Janka had begged with her eyes like an injured cat. "No," she said once more, and that stuck. Ha! Had that gotten to him? Had it? She listened to people back in her childhood home. She watched Janka's moods. She combed the letters that came and went. Did he really see his good blood in this child? Did he truly? Well then! She sacrificed the pure little soul. His betrayal of his own child should result in a thousand scenes of horror, just as his betrayal of her had destroyed her life.

Just you wait, you fine lord, until they bring you your blond niece Janka on a funeral carriage! Just wait, fine Prince, until men from the back alley and vagabonds bring you the tramp, utterly destroyed. Then you will reach for your revolver, the one you carry. "Pull the trigger, asshole!" and her eyes glowed. "Finish what's left of you!"

Katerine used to spend hours imagining in detail the scenes she wanted to witness. She lay there, her head buried in the pillows, and was seized with delight when an especially wild scene came to mind.

And she always enjoyed how hot and eager her fury was and how it burned her victims, victims she had chosen for revenge, like flames.

But gradually and completely without her noticing it, the last of her energy sank into the spongy ground she lived on.

The battle of her life, which daily threw her onto the street so she could laugh, love, and earn a living, the battle that led to enervation she tried to deaden with her deceptive fantasy, had to, necessarily, mercilessly, use up the last, most carefully kept remainder of her strong being. Each and every chance to do something effective was more and more elusive. Her hate and vengeance became ever more meaningless. The past sank into shadowy fog. The frame that held together those scenes and objects that rose and fell in her thoughts—thoughts with no coherence or lasting effect—that frame was shattered. Her thoughts became a swirl of ugly, dark spots that duped her blind soul.

When Milada turned eleven and was ready to advance to the next-to-last section of the third grade, things began to happen in the alley. Renovations and remodeling threatened the residents of Red House with an unhappy fate. Big events followed upon small, insignificant incidents. The alley was paved and plastered, sidewalks were put in, and a municipal streetlight was erected, which, new and victorious, outshone the feeble light of Red House that had for so long fought valiantly against the surrounding darkness. And at long last! The nameless street was formally baptized with a black lacquered sign with white lettering. From now on the street bore the official name Red House Alley. Thus far everything seemed fine and in good order, and, in general, people were happy about the improvements, at least those who had cause to be. Lorinser blew out the smoking petroleum lamp in her junk store as soon as the streetlamp was up. Her visibility was established vis-à-vis her junk store. A street with an official name and sign seemed the legal recognition of her authority. The less pleasant aspects of her business were obviously downplayed. All bureaucrats of the city and the health administrators had, seemingly, come together to effect these changes. They flooded the forgotten corner with regulations, admonitions, leaflets and warnings. Workmen showed up with picks and shovels. They tore up the dirt, pounded it flat, and spread out gravel. They inspected sewers and water pipes for damage and repaired them. Inspectors snooped around, overseeing this and that, pushing their way into entry halls, basements and attics. It seemed there was no end to their invasion. Property owners and maintenance members hewed to strict rules: access pipes and wastewater pipes had to be kept clean; it was forbidden to pitch dirty water and refuse out the window; and, daily, the tall, slatted garbage wagon rattled around the corner off the main street down the Alley.

At first begrudgingly, and then with laughter, the ragged women got used to giving the grinning and wise-cracking garbage collectors their baskets and crates filled with trash. Lorinser, who had a finer nose than the other women, immediately began to gripe and complain loudly about the transformation of the area.

All those strangers poking around Red House Alley did not suit her. She sensed a force behind all this activity that went well above the authority of her own power, a force she could certainly have no personal access to. Once she was rudely stopped because she had dumped out a carton of refuse by the wall of the hospital, and ever since then she let anybody who would listen know that these newfangled "rules and little measures" had been put in place just to make the lives of poor people more rotten and miserable than they already had been. Moreover—and she put her hands on her hips—she was going to see to it that this business of "slicking things up" in the alley was going to stop. "We could use less of that. The place would be better off without it!" "That's for sure!" people around her chimed in cautiously. Lorinser had to realize, much to her dismay, that the human power of authority always had its limits.

The man who called himself "your patrol officer" shrugged his shoulders considerately and said the clean-up was a matter of city authority and did not concern the police. All right, but things got even worse! The renovation project now involved the property owners, the renters, and subletters. They were all shocked to be called before the police. They had to show papers from their place of origin, shop licenses, police ledgers, and medical certificates; in a word, a thorough set of official documents.

Almost everyone who operated a business in the alley was fined for violations by a judge of the court. "May you land in hell! Who authorized you to charge for sex? Zimmermann, Elisabeth, have you registered your renters? Are you paying taxes on your income?"

"Your Honor, Your Grace, I beg you," the accused little woman whimpered.

"Enough from you. Order in the court! I'll teach you to keep six individuals captive in one place! You are disgraceful."

Then the little woman launched into a wild outpour of explanations. No, no, these women did not disappear without paying their taxes. They had paid their taxes just as the law required. But why did they have to pay anyway? She had always paid that way where they were before. One girl left, another arrived, and the housekeepers had done their best to make them pay. His Honor would have to see she had made some effort to comply with that, she muttered.

But the proprietors had nothing to say when a certain paragraph of the law was read aloud to them and explained in clear language.

Keeping a large number of individuals in one building was not permitted. In accordance with the law most of the girls were removed from the houses in the alley. "Where will we go? Where?" the girls complained. The officials shrugged.

They could only repeat, "First get papers from your place of origin, then go back to the police and register again!" The police told them to do as the law prescribed. There was no other course of action.

The girls were given a stay of twenty-four hours to take care of this, which was to be time enough. But when the time had elapsed, the complaining and begging began anew. Most of the girls owed money to the housekeepers and had to leave their possessions as collateral.

Oh, dear God! The best thing to do was jump in the river naked and drown!

What could they do about it? The temporary residents were properly plucked like birds, rousted, squawking, out of their warm nests and thrown out into the cold, hostile light.

Some of the girls yielded to force. Three patrolmen came and helped them move out.

These men evicted them peacefully, without unnecessary force, knowing they were vested with the heavy weight of legal authority.

Yet there were a few individual scenes that got ugly, when people gathered and cursed all the way down the alley to the main street.

In Red House Alley there was one patrol left behind to make sure the wares in Lorinser's junk shop were cleared out. Half-grown boys stood around and snatched items, while merchants, a few gray, haggard Jews, protested the looting vigorously. Old Lorinser looked on dully as the junk she had greedily piled up was stuffed in sacks and hauled off forever.

"No permit on file for operating a junk shop," is what the police had said. The commissioner slammed his fist on the table so hard and looked around the room with such fury that Lorinser jumped up on the bench for the poor.

She had to be locked up and fined in court.

"All-merciful God!" Lorinser exclaimed and looked up at the windows, where women were lined up eagerly, gleefully watching her in her misery.

"Grimy business is what it is!" said one policeman to another, yet loud enough for Lorinser to hear, and she turned around to him filled with venom and ready to strike.

"A crime and a shame the way they treat us poor folks! We're just regular folks," one observer said.

"You're wrong there!" a policeman interrupted her gently, "We need law and order. That ugly mess in the alley has gone on long enough. What's the government here for anyways? It's not like there was a public riot here. We're only doing our job!"

Red House, too, came in for some scrutiny.

But not as thorough as in the other houses because the landlady Lorinser was, at least in this instance, careful to heed the advice of her friends. She only took in girls whose papers were in impeccable order. Nonetheless the Hungarian, Helene Marsner, and the two very young Ressel sisters were directed to leave because of incomplete or, in one case, suspicious papers. The Hungarian had a crying fit, lay in the middle of the alley, and was conveyed farther down the street by a police wagon.

Katerine and Janka had always had their legal papers in good order, and they stayed put. Above and beyond an official permit, Katerine could show, almost as a dutiful mission, the correct, weekly certification from the physician for the police, documentation almost unthinkable, given the miserable conditions in the alley.

The administrative official gave her a good-natured thump on the chest. "That's the way it ought to be!" he said.

Peace set in after that.

The empty nests filled very quickly with new wares, young,

cheerful girls, fully documented with papers and passbooks. The housekeepers had no concerns and were happy to find them rooms since the newcomers paid something like an excise tax should they have to "relinquish the rooms of their apartments to the next renter."

In short, the look of the alley, apart from the street sign, the city streetlight, and the closing of the junk store, had not changed at all—almost not at all. There was no change except in prices. Due to the cost of maintenance the "poor housekeepers" bore, prices were now a good forty percent higher. That was the result, as they told the ladies, of the "city's damned fines and taxes."

These housekeepers were careful to add as appeasement, "But now there is no more dirty competition. Those rich girls have no business here for their own enjoyment. All that is gone. The girls here in the alley are all decent girls on their own."

The way was paved for the last and best surprise, which came completely unexpectedly. It felt like a bomb had hit. Red House was sold and turned into an elegant, fashionable brothel with grandiose style. Its new owner was a Madame Goldscheider.

It threw the whole alley into turmoil; everybody had something to say. Unrest and commotion prevailed throughout the house. Good God, a brothel in Red House Alley! Well, all right, the independent girls could pack up and leave. It was the end of an individual doing business. Something like this ruined those on their own. You were in luck if you had a place at all.

Lorinser came up with the most fabulous stories. The new gracious madam of the house had called for her services and had informed her in detail about what would happen, but she could not divulge anything. No, not one single thing. Everything would be revealed in good time. She did, however, have one message right away for everybody. "Sale of the house curtailed rental agreements," she told the girls, who protested and were upset. In eight days everybody needs to be out. No ifs, ands, or buts.

They had to pick up and move again, roam around once again. And here is where Lorinser cleaned up. They had paid the porter well above and beyond the rent just to stay put in Red House. Oh, woe! Where could a person find a place in the middle of the month? Places in town were all rented out. There was not a free room anywhere. Fine and fancy as they were, they now had to make do with two-bit rentals on the outskirts of town. They had to go around in hunger and misery. They shuddered.

There was no more laughter or idle talk in the house. The girls slunk around, were gloomy and complained. In the evenings they lamented their fate to the clients.

Katerine wore a furrow on her white brow. Having to roam the streets, to roam about, now when she was almost done living, to hell with that.

"Where can I go? I don't want any strange, new place. I don't want to settle in again. I am sick of fixing up a new place up to make it work." Janka sat on the ledge of the stove and broke wood into pieces. That was her favorite thing to do. She made thin little kindling, and Milada, who squatted on the floor, laid them out in nice small piles, while the dying embers in the stove bathed them both in a friendly red glow.

"Right, where can we go?" Janka said with a sigh, "Everybody would really like to stay in the alley. People are paying Zimmermann fifteen gulden a day just for a room. Making your own money for yourself is not an option in the alley anymore."

"Here in this little alley," Katerine echoed Janka's words, scathing and full of wrath. After a while she said abruptly, "People are supposed to pull themselves together and make a new start in times like these. But that can't happen for people like us. Nothing new will come about for us. Wherever you go, you drag your same old misery with you. When you're stripped naked and you've got nothing, you go." She stretched her arms up in the air as if she wanted to fly upwards. "It doesn't matter anymore. Sing the same little song, move on, keep going and keep laughing … Not for me. I'm done."

She spat. "For all I care, stick me in Mother Frietschen's place, six to a room."

"Why don't we go to a snow-white house with a weathervane and a great big garden full of rosemary and marigolds, Auntie? I mean now. It would be the best thing for us," said Milada in the pause of silence.

Katerine curled her upper lip, showing her coral-red gums, an expression typical for her.

"Ah-huh, so that's what you'd like to do," she said calmly. Janka looked her way with guilt in her eyes.

Now I want to jump up, take hold of something and throw it on the floor, smash it to pieces, Katerine thought. She waited to see if she would do it. Or scream and yell in anger. Why not do that, she thought and kept sitting numb. Janka sat curled up in guilt and fear. And the child felt the discomfort. She crouched down just like a bird without a nest outside in foul weather. Janka and Milada were afraid for Katerine.

Oh, Jesus! Fools! stuck in Katerine's throat. She asked herself, Don't you see your Katerine has given up the fight? She's scared, too. Scared. She is afraid and doesn't even know what she's afraid of. Maybe she's afraid of what you both think and are plotting in secret and afraid of the things you say in whispers when you think she is asleep.

She turned to face the wall and, burying her head in the pillows, sank into a dull, go-nowhere dream state that stirred through things past and present, as if she were in a light, sympathetic delirium. Janka, you're right. We should go home. Yes, let's go. Wasn't it beautiful at home? The Matschak estate rose up in her mind like a vision. She saw the white, lonesome grounds up above the fields, with the gates to the yard flung wide open both day and night. Oh, she knew it well, this country manor.

She had loved it with a wild, senseless and inexplicable passion.

She ran around it with Janka for hours on end, wondering at it, dividing it up and thinking of plans.

Imagining had been a game she played, and it made her dizzy like strong wine.

To be the lady of the estate! Here, where the very ground smiled and smelled of wealth!

Her pride rose up in her and caught her unawares. It would have to come to pass. She was the most beautiful, the best. Here she fit right in.

And that is how the Prince won her over. When? In a few summer nights. How? Playfully, laughing, and lordly all at once. With a handful of sweet words he wooed her, a girl no man had gotten.

"Girls in the cloister are not allowed to kiss."

"Ahh, then I will teach you, girl."

These were days in late summer. They were warm hours lost in dreams and desire, this hide-and-seek of their glances, hands, and lips in the cool, hidden halls of the great house.

She had never really loved the prince of the manor, that fat, heavy man. Truly she had not.

But she was proud of him. He was the lord of the estate and the richest man in the region.

When she began to feel the child under her heart, she embraced her body, giddy with good fortune. Now he had to, had to ...

Lord Matschak would not bring a bastard into the world. Katerine went about in distress. She could not return to the cloister. Was he not preparing for a wedding? ...

Little Janka embroiders. She is embroidering a bridal gown for her. Coral-red is the color of the adornment of a Matschak bride. She tries it on, an ancient, beautiful robe. It is the color of blood, she thinks, and she lays it around her white neck. And all of a sudden the beads come unstrung and scatter everywhere like drops of coagulated blood. Damn! Then something terrifying happens. She cannot recall what, but it lies in wait behind her thoughts, and she is afraid of looking at it. "That's how it always goes when I try to remember," she murmurs a lament and tosses around in her bed. The leaden hours of the afternoon emerge.

"Your precious dresses and things are all over the place!" Lorinser throws open the door and flies into the room.

Confused and with her eyes half closed, Katerine sits up in bed.

The coarse voice pierces the sweetest half-light of her thoughts.

"There's a filthy washtub out there in the yard and crappy pieces of clothing. Get that garbage out of here. I can't stand it anymore! And from now on there won't be an extra piece of meat for lunch for you Bohunks."

Janka quickly grabbed a laundry basket and ran out to collect the wash, while Milada opened the kitchen window and said, "She's just the kind to tear our laundry down."

"What's going on?" Katerine asked in a hushed whisper, a way of speaking new to her.

Milada explained hurriedly, "It's all because we have our laundry out in the yard. All of a sudden it annoys her. And she's angry about the washtub, too. Wait here. I'll go help Auntie."

She left the window open and ran out into the hall. A cold gust of air wet from rain rushed in and sobered Katerine right up. "Calm down!" she hollered out and jumped out of bed.

She put her fists to her temples, and her gaze ran slowly, deliberately, as if looking for something, along the broken courtyard wall up to the ceiling brown from smoke, which was covered with fly specks and spider webs. With rising terror, as if she were seeing all this for the first time, she opened her eyes wide and took on the wild expression of someone being tortured.

Only moments ago she had seen a world in bloom, trees, shimmering meadows, and a house in the background, blue with the light of the moon.

Her temper erupted. It was nearly vicious. She looked at

the large, black pots, greasy and smoke-covered, and then at the dirty water in the sink; then, at the muddy shoes. Holy God, could somebody not keep things clean! She was going to take the furniture and leave.

Underneath the battered kitchen cabinet were cardboard shims. It fell apart when you opened it. Up and move with this old piece of junk? The stink of cheap soap and old coffee grounds—to hell with it all! The place looked like a dump. It was after noon and nobody had thought to clean up.

In deep shadow she glimpsed the vision from her dream briefly as it floated away. There was the brightness of the sun. There were whitewashed rooms, oak furniture, and lots of shiny tin utensils that reflected the sun; there was a momentary flash of yellow linen with colorful embroidery at the windows...

Everything in that realm was well cared-for and solid. Where did it all go? Away, it was all whisked away, as if someone had wiped it out. Yet something of it lingered and was true.

Clear-sighted she looked at each thing around her and saw the stains, the dirt and the filth. And whatever she touched became etched in her mind. A rude scream and the sound of a fight interrupted her thoughts. Then the door opened, and with great effort Janka dragged a basket of wet laundry into the room. Milada entered after her with a sack of colored wash in one hand and a bundle of black rope in the other. Katerine stared at them blankly.

"Look, I got away with a bunch of clothesline!" said Milada triumphantly.

"And you can hang it right back up, my love. It's a shame about the laundry we did," Janka sighed and shook out some pieces of clothing that were covered with dirt from the yard. They started hanging up the clothesline, running it back and forth across windows and doorjambs. The laundry sagged so low in the room that even little Milada had to stoop to get around. They paid no attention to Katerine. She was sitting quietly on her bed, chewing her fingers and throwing quick, angry glances all around.

"This is making my fingers stiff."

"Pin the line up with a nail," Milada suggested as she jumped like a cat from her chair to the floor.

All of a sudden and without warning Katerine exploded. Milada stared at her, eyes wide open, while Janka tried to fend off the rampage by raising her arms.

"Rotten, lousy shit!" she opened fire, breathing heavily. "Get rid of it, I'm telling you. Don't hang that sopping crap over my head, I'm telling you. I want peace and quiet. To hell with all this crap here. Damn it, damn it all to hell! Just take a look at this shit!" She pulled down the weak, old line with both hands, and the laundry flew in all directions.

"We'll drown in this filth and rot. Can people live like this, I ask you? In the middle of the day the place is all full of laundry and crap. I swear to God I'll throw it all away if you don't get it out of my way. Stupid bitches!"

She screamed even louder, screeched once again, and pounded with her fists against the kitchen cupboard. The shim fell out, and it crashed down. Everything inside tumbled out all over the floor with a clatter and a clang. Katerine stood in place, breathing heavily.

With terror in her eyes she withdrew to her room. The whole furor had blown over. She was not thinking anything. She was calm. She looked around. She almost laughed. She observed how the fury subsided. She was sick of this whole business. Crazy! Of course everything was filthy rotten. But did that mean get rid of it all? The crap is sweet, keeps you warm.

All the laundry looked like it had died. A pair of red flannel pants lay stretched out in front of her like a man who was satisfied. She let out a hefty, loud laugh.

"One person can't do it all alone," Janka started to say with a whimper. "I just can't do this."

"Don't talk nonsense, Jan. From now on the washerwoman is going to do the laundry. And do go get me some wine to drink."

She stood in place and shot a quick look around to test things. Then she said defiantly, in a flip tone, "Oh, well, once in a while you need some peace and quiet." And she went to her room.

None of it mattered. She was fairly calm after that blow-up. All was well and good. She sat down in the one and only armchair, which was by her bed, and stuck her feet into the yellow fur of the rug at the side of her bed.

She did not want to think about the bad things all the time, no, she did not. How long had she been like this? Her mind was filled with death and falling apart—all this fear! She had become afraid of anything new. It was fine the old building had been sold together with the life she had. Luxurious, fun and light-hearted, that's how life would be in a brothel like this. Why make yourself miserable about it? Be nice to the madam and flatter her a little. Stay on and let yourself be taken care of, like a real lady. Now things would be very lovely for her. A bottle of wine was shoved through the crack in the door. She lit into it. Such a good idea! Get away from here? Nothing doing, for the time being stay put. Laugh and be happy so that that new Jewish madam will see her in a good light. But first, have some wine. She sat down and started drinking. Janka, sorry I can't help. I'm doing fine for the moment right here in Red House.

Jesus, pious Janka should go back home. But of course. It's best she go back home. Andreas would like to have her back. He was her uncle after all. But eventually, some time or other, he would have to curl up and die.

She poured more wine in her violet-perfumed glass and drank it down. If they were gone, she would have the place to herself. She was an idiot to be so attached to both of them. She was not going to heaven like this. The situation had to change. Janka should take the little one and place her on an altar. What did she care?

Sure, let it be. Hate? Did she still hate him?

She wailed aloud as she had back then when she left the manor in the dark of morning, hopeless.

If he had made her his wife, had made her lady of the house, by God, she would have been a proud woman, as was fit and proper for the household. She knew that. She was still able to feel that beneath the rubble of her soul. The proud gentlewoman of the house, that is what she would have been. She would have invited guests over and attended to them, and she would have filled the wardrobe and pantry with luxury goods. Yes, and managed the peasants with her glances. That would have suited her. But most of all she would have cared for the child! If the girl had been born heir of the Matschak estate, if her father had recognized her openly under the sun, then how she would have loved that child! She would have rightfully had the best of everything.

But her regrets were not for the child. She only regretted her own ruined pride as a mother. What did she care about that poor urchin? She was a bastard child. A sin for a sin, that was fitting. Did the girl need love? She would learn to get drunk, that was all. Get on with it!

A sacrifice for her sacrifice! Her pride and the child were slaughtered at the altar together. By him! The child's own dear father did that! Broad and crude, with his hands on his hips, he had laughed at her in scorn.

"What's that!? Do you maybe want to be a married woman here? Katerine, don't think so highly of yourself! If you like the foreman of the farm, then I suggest you marry him. He makes eyes at you."

Then she grabbed his chest and hit him with all her might. She punched him in the face. And what did he do? He liked it and laughed. "You little cat!" he said and took it like a wall. Then she let him go and, despairing, went inside.

In the early morning light she went to see Janka and told her everything. And the poor little thing knelt on the floor and kept stroking her hands. Katerine moaned and swore, "My love, come with me! If I leave alone, I'll throw myself into the lake. Don't abandon me and the child! My love, if we go together, he will come get all three of us, for you alone."

And the miserable young thing kissed the fingers of blond Janka, which were frozen in fear of death.

They fled the house in secret before the break of day, left the village. Exhausted and with no idea what they were doing, they arrived without a penny in the big, strange city. The first thing Katerine did was write to the man and tell him she wanted to come right back with Janka, if, as was proper, he was willing to marry her. Janka, too, who longed to return, wanted him to marry her. She was not asking for his charity but for justice. He surely knew who she was. She did not chose to mention their love.

"Our joy this summer is not dead. Andreas, it is very much alive and has a beating heart under mine. It moves me toward you. Man, come to your senses and do what is right. We can be happy."

Right away she got an angry answer, more for Janka than for her. He would not take orders from a wayward girl. Janka was to come home right away and by herself. Then he would see to it that her tramping around with a strange slut would be forgiven. He was willing, as a decent man, to recognize the child and take care of it. That was it, end of discussion.

The girls sat on a bench in a garden in the light rain, pressed against each other and freezing. Janka's blond face with her childlike flat features was hidden as if lost in Katerine's shoulder. Katerine sat there upright and numb. With blank eyes she stared into the falling darkness.

So that was the kind of man he was! He had chosen her to use her. The lord sat in his warm house, and mother and child could go to hell.

"But I have her." At that moment it dawned on her, and a momentary flash rose over the blond head at her side. "Come on, Jan, come on!" she whispered with a rasp. To get warm they sat down in a small coffee shop at street level. There a strange woman chatted them up. She acted friendly and comforting and asked clever questions. She flattered them and praised them and got to hear their story from Katerine's lips, which were moved by disdain and anger. Oh, he will change his mind, she said. Such a lovely young woman, and then her good young friend along with her. Yes, certainly, he would change his mind. She just had to wait and to hang on to her defiance. The woman talked about this and that, told funny little stories, and spoke of mysterious things, lots of money and clothes of silk. She paid the tab and finally, with compassion, took the girls along with her.

After another eight days the gentleman and lord of the Matschak estate was so eaten up by rage and fury he took a carriage to the city to settle the score with his lover and to pick up his disobedient niece.

But it was already too late. They had been conscripted as registered prostitutes and lived in a house of disrepute. This was a moment of intense and sweet revenge. And had he killed her at that moment, she would have seen him like nobody in this world had seen him, that proud man of the estate. He would have been destroyed, blanched down to his fat neck, the neck of an ox, as if he been bled out, with his fat, yellow flesh looking horrifying, like dead meat.

"The devil, the devil!" he said between clenched teeth, and that was all.

And with his foot he shoved Janka. He spat on her as she lay whimpering and left.

"The devil!" Yes, at that moment she felt something like the thrill of desire, the ecstasy of evil.

And she threw herself down on the ground next to Janka, pulled her hands from her face and laughed. She laughed so loud the housekeeper rushed in and asked her to keep quiet.

This laughter had finally blotted out her memory of his laughter, which was embedded in her ears.

You cannot trifle with the devil and his deeds, isn't that right, big farmer? And then, at that moment, Janka wanted to go back home. And why not? Be quiet, Jan! Don't cry! He will forgive you. As time goes by his anger will surely soften. Somewhere in a quiet little corner you will have a house. He has carpenters enough, the lord does, to build a house for you. They would see it as an honor to do that. Whatever happens, you are always a daughter of the Matschak family. The priest blesses you for a good sum and implores our dear God to grant you heavenly joy.

Your family always receives blessings just like that.

Janka was truly no longer of any use here. All she could do was snivel and blubber. She did not go out soliciting. That business calls for fresh human flesh.

Katerine raised her bottle and drank. What did she care about anybody else? She cared about herself. Dying, what stupidity! Who can say what she might expect in a brothel? Maybe she will find a baron, and in her imagination she flopped about on the cushions of a carriage.

Now she entertained thoughts that made her feel good and comforted her.

The feeling she might have done something wrong earlier became fuzzy, and the wine made her soft-hearted. She got up out of bed.

She opened the door and left her room humming. My heavens, the two of them were down on their knees and scrubbing. Dear God, how hard they were working! All the pots were outside, and the water flowed. They were so intent on their work, they did not stop to look up at her.

"Janka," she whispered.

She had let go of her need to ridicule her friend. She did not lift her drunken eyes from the figure on the floor. The woman of twenty-eight was hunkered down like an old woman. There she was, the daughter of the Matschak family, the blond woman beneath her. Wasn't that Janka? Why, oh why, was she down on the floor scrubbing? And the child along with her? Were they doing grubby chores together for her? So who was she anyway that they were working for her?

These ideas were all new to her. For the first time they resounded in her soul.

What suddenly came alive in her was not regret. It was fear of herself, as is visible in great geniuses or in infamous criminals when they close their eyes and shudder at the power of their own being. Without saying a word she walked across the kitchen and stepped out into the hall. A veil of blood flickered in front of her burning eyes. She leaned against the wall. She was dizzy.

Now with each new day came important new things. Lorinser was called several times to gracious Madame Goldscheider and always returned excited and with a sackful of reliable messages.

There was a certain Mademoiselle Olympia, a lively person they called *vif*, dark and beautifully attired. Purportedly, Olympia had confided all kinds of things to Lorinser. Then there was Madame Goldscheider herself. Oh, said Lorinser, Goldscheider did not say much. Madame Goldscheider simply came and left. With but a single word of parting she had taken her leave. She was reportedly a fine lady, wore only silk clothing at home and large pieces of green jewelry; yes, that was a true lady.

A large wine tavern on prominent Ring Street had belonged to Goldscheider for a good while, and for the time being she had rented it to the "Italian woman," Sucher's mistress. Sucher, who was called The Spy, had made it possible for Goldscheider to run Red House as a licensed brothel. He did this to thank Goldscheider for renting to his girlfriend. It would be exactly like those in Paris: fine, sparing no expense in anything. The girls nodded, resigned, at

Lorinser's report. Yes, if Sucher was behind it all, then everything was in order, and there was nothing more anyone could do about it. But the biggest piece of news Lorinser, the great lady's messenger, had to share was this: Lady Goldscheider was going to come herself to look the girls over, and, maybe, she would keep a few of the prettiest and youngest for her new business.

Lorinser was sure, in telling her story, to make herself out the big person, and she let it be known a lot depended on her good reports to the lady and on her protection. A sense of expectation, mixed with hope and fear, filled the residents of Red House.

Like young girls before a ball, they got together and in lively chatter spoke of their hopes and expectations. Many of them had heard of some such undertakings or had even known about them firsthand, and they added their words of doubt and concern.

"No, not me. I'm not interested," said tall, thin Rosa decisively and shook her head of disheveled blond hair. "I know what I am talking about. I saw the same thing in Dresden with Aschermann. You don't have to worry, that's true, but you don't get paid either. And if you get sick, what does the madam do? Throw you out on the street. Right away. If you do business yourself, you can get by, but in a brothel, you're done for."

"Go on, there were 'opportunities,' you had 'opportunities,'" said Lorinser. She had picked up this word from Mademoiselle Olympia and threw it around. There would not be men off the street, that is what she said. Only well-dressed men, only men with money were allowed. They got a fine meal and then could choose to go on upstairs.

Little Fritzie, a very small personage with coarse hair and a scar above those red doll lips, knew the story of one woman, a Polish Jew, who had found a count in a brothel—and had actually married him. Altogether in a house like this your clients were gentlemen. That was of course much better than guys off the streets who haggled over every penny. There were even men who argued, left in the dark and did not pay. And there were the constant nasty scenes with the housekeeper. You always had to hold your purse open, play it sweet, and watch out with those bitches. Otherwise you could have bad luck. And then what? Try putting in a complaint to the police! Jesus God, you were sure to lose working on your own. But a lady like this new one, she made sure a girl got paid.

"Sure, a lady like that!" a woman named Hatschek said scornfully. "She can make her own demands that'll make your hair stand on end. I know what I'm saying."

Every day over the next few days the women made an effort to get ready for the arrival of the new owner of the property. A strained excitement filled the whole house. Lorinser cleaned up the dirt that had collected for years in the stairwells and halls. The girls made themselves up and did their hair in the mornings. They dressed with greater care and ran lightning-fast to the windows when the doorbell rang. Only Katerine became all of a sudden cool, untroubled, and indifferent.

She snapped her fingers. Ridiculous! She was not going to let the pitiful little life there scare her very much. It could be here or anywhere. She claimed she had looked around, and there were plenty of other places somebody like her could go. She was happy to stay here, but if that Jewish woman did not want her,—bah! She cleverly avoided Janka's questions and her outbursts of fear. Janka was plagued by bad dreams and terrible anxiety, but Katerine did not get caught up in this. "Drink something when fear makes you sick, girl!" was the only advice she gave her.

On a rainy Sunday, quite early in the afternoon, Madame Goldscheider showed up, just when nobody was expecting her. People did not even know who had let her in or how she had gotten in the building; all of a sudden, she was standing inside and looking around. She measured the height of the ceiling, tried the windows and doors; she ran her fingers over the wet outside walls and lifted the loose floor tiles with the tip of her silk umbrella. The girls, who were for the most part drowsy, disheveled, and in their old underwear, all came running down together and stared at the slim lady with wavy, red hair and an elegantly curved Jewish nose, above which she wore a golden monocle, through which she surveyed the place.

Lorinser shoved her way in front of the others and melted in bows and devotion. Madame Goldscheider waved her away, opened her jacket, and sat down on an easy chair. She had the girls march in front of her.

One after another they had to show their papers. She read through them carefully, taking her time, now and again asked questions, simply, in a harmless tone. She nodded when things looked in good order, but, when the materials looked suspect, she looked out past the woman in question and smiled. It was only a glance and a smile, but that was enough. The girls who had gotten this kind of treatment blushed. Gradually the room became full. Lorinser was on the spot and constantly made every effort to attract the attention of Madame Goldscheider. Some of the young women had put themselves together hurriedly. Their hair hung down loosely. They had applied some rouge and draped themselves with a piece of silk. But Goldscheider was not fooled. Only those who were truly young and looked good found acceptance in her eyes. The bright light of day, however, made even the young ones look old and drab. More than two thirds were rejected.

"Well, I cannot use you," she said to Olinka Brecher. She smiled friendlily to pretty Gisi with the lovely blue eyes. Gisi turned red and clapped her hands like a child.

She wanted to keep Rosa Hatschek, too. But Rosa said curtly, "No way I'm going to a brothel!" "As you like," the madam responded calmly.

Janka had put on a red collar and stood there in her bare feet freezing. "You are old," said Madame Goldscheider, turning her away with a golden pencil. She then turned to Katerine who looked straight at her with bright, unshaken eyes. "Well, and me?" she said jeering. Goldscheider lifted her eyes, and, with the look of someone who knows her business, she assessed the young woman. Yes, she could use her. She was the sort she had in mind. "That one stays here!" she stated with an inviting wave of the hand. She was the fifth and the last. All the rest would have to leave.

"You have eight days," she spoke, turning to the porter who was crouched down like a cat, "to get everything cleared out. You have some time for the fees. You," she addressed those she had selected, "I will put you up somewhere else. Be agreeable and things will go all right for you. Each of you will receive a fine wardrobe, the garments and dresses you will need. In my establishment you can earn good money and live well. I do not treat people unfairly."

She stood up. Katerine's eyes sparkled. She took a step forward. Hatschek said defiantly, "We're not dogs here. You're throwing us out in the middle of the month." "We've got a rental contract here," another woman spoke up in support of Hatschek. "Sale of the house curtails rental agreements. You have heard that," Goldscheider announced. Lorinser nodded vigorously, "I did, your Ladyship, tell them right away, but one of these poor women would like to say something."

"So now you think everything's just taken care of for us, right?" said the woman indignantly. Goldscheider buttoned up her jacket. "You five go see Dr. Lamberg for me this week for a health examination. See to it that each of you brings me the signed certificate from him for the police. That will be all!"

Katerine stepped up in front of her, "There's something else I have to bring up." As she spoke, Goldscheider kept fastening her headdress and shook her copper-colored hair. "There is a child who lives with me." Katerine's eyes met those of Janka who looked expectant. "And the woman over there comes with me, too," she said quietly after a pause.

"The woman will have to find some place else to stay. But how old is the child?"

"Eleven, twelve years old. She is quiet. She doesn't bother anybody. She knows how to make herself useful. Isn't that true?" Katerine looked around. The other women listened but did not respond. Only Janka nodded. She even stepped forward and spoke loudly and decisively.

"She's a capable child. She already knows how to do tasks and work hard."

Katerine stared at her. Janka! What was she doing?

"The police do not take kindly to school-aged children in the house," Goldscheider said considering.

"In the fall," Janka chimed in again, "She will be done with school. Then she can work here as a maid."

"Well, fine, you can keep her with you for the time being," Goldscheider decided. And quickly, while preparing to leave, she said, looking at Lorinser, "Of course, Madame, your position is, as of the Fifteenth, terminated." And with that she was gone without having said goodbye.

Lorinser was rooted to the floor. "Lousy red-haired bitch!" she hollered and stamped her foot. After this visit life in the house was tumultuous. Neighbors came over out of curiosity to ask what the result of the visit was. People cursed, gave praises, quarreled, and rejoiced. Lorinser encountered a general gleefulness at her misfortune. People felt sorry for the ones who were turned away, but the girls who were going did not feel rejected and asserted it would not have worked out for them there anyway.

There was a loud hubbub and commotion, and Gisi's voice pierced the noise like a blaring trumpet, "What a promise! Dresses, garments with monograms, even silk clothes! And it won't cost anything, not one little penny."

"That's what you think!" added Backwoods Victorine who was brimming with envy and wished them ill. "You'll see, you bumpkins, what it will really cost!"

"Her, take care of me in a brothel? Not on my life! If she

gave me a hundred gulden, I wouldn't do it," Rosa Hatschek was proud to say. "Independent women, that's what I'm for. We have to take care of ourselves. In a brothel, you're trapped, like a bird in a cage. If you want to go out, you can't. Even if you want to go to church, you can't."

Katerine stood off to the side, completely confused by all that was going on. It had all happened so fast. Had she had good luck, or not? She did not understand one bit of it. And Janka? Where had she gone? No, her Janka could not get along with these girls in a brothel. Suddenly she wanted to belong. She approached the other women with curiosity.

"There you have it. Folks are going to fly right out the door now that things are this tough," said Little Fritzie. Fritzie had been in a good mood, too, but was now sad and defiant.

"That's just how it goes. It shouldn't scare you," Katerine joined in, "Let's not be afraid at this point, right?"

"No, absolutely not," Little Fritzie agreed approvingly. "Cheers, enjoy! Be good. I'm leaving."

"Do tell, you hustling Jew," Olinka yelled with venom after Little Fritzie who was walking out the door.

"Fritzie will have to adapt to the change," Hatschek remarked philosophically and followed her out. "This business is only about making money."

"You're in good shape, and you get to keep the little girl with you," Gisi turned to Katerine. Usually she was not venomous. But now the few Goldscheider had selected had to stick together against the others. When she was addressed, Katerine rose up out of her reflective mood.

"The little girl, sure. I can't just toss her on some pile of manure," she said coarsely and left. She had to get a grip! What was going on here now? What had Janka been thinking? Did Janka and her family not want the child anymore? Had the child become too infected with filth for them? Now when they could have her if they wanted? She waited for days for some word from her friend Janka. But there was none. Then she made no further effort. Why not?

During this time Janka sat on the pile of wood in front of the stove, as was her wont. Tears streamed down her cheeks as she held Milada between her knees and spoke to her hurriedly. She comforted the child with a torrent of words and held her small hands in her own work-hardened hands. The child listened carefully and only nodded earnestly to show she understood, “Yes, Auntie, I know.”

“You have to take care of her now,” Janka admonished little Milada urgently. “And when she flares up at you, when she acts stupid and crazy, my dear...” she stared off in the distance and pushed her hair off her forehead. “Remember she is good, she is good. Don’t pay attention to what she says when she’s angry. Take good care of her, and stick by her because she doesn’t know how to do regular housework. She doesn’t like sweets. But do go buy her wine and apples every day. She has to have her apples. Little old white-haired me, I’ll be fine for years to come. And, my love...”

“Get out of my way!” said Katerine brusquely to Milada when she arrived in the kitchen where they were. She put her hands on her hips, looked at the two of them, and laughed with derision.

“What are you whispering about? We’re going to pack up and get out of here. All together, just like we arrived. We’ll stay together and get out. End of topic.” Startled, Janka looked upward to heaven. Then she held out her hands.

“No, no, Katerine, you stay here. You belong in a house like this. You’re still the most beautiful one here, and who knows what might...”

“Don’t talk crazy talk!” Katerine said darkly and crossed her arms. “I spit on the Jew and on her brothel. We’re all leaving together. I mean it.”

“Don’t talk like that! Don’t bring bad luck on yourself, Katerine. You can live here like a lady and not worry and have money.

Somebody like you will do fine in a place like this. Don't throw away your lucky chance, Katerine!"

"And you?" she replied derisively. "You're going to die in misery without me, right?" Her gaze became penetrating. "Are you thinking you'll go back to the cloister?"

Janka shook her head. She spoke with her eyes, the worried, true-blue eyes of a dog. A light shone in her eyes. She did not need words.

"Well, now, I thought you would. A Matschak can't be loyal."

"Katerine, I have been loyal to you. As long as it helped you, I stood by you. You are starting a new life now, and I have no place here. You know that yourself, Katerine. I have not counted the years, and don't you count them either. What Uncle Andreas owes you, I can't begin to pay. I haven't counted all these years. It's only a small bit of money that has mounted up this whole time, Katerine. Who can say how much the Matschak family still owes you." Janka glowed red and shook.

Katerine grew limp. Softly pleading, she said, "And the child? Do you want her to be destroyed in this house? You know very well what will become of her here."

Janka replied, "I have thought about it and thought about it. Am I doing the right thing? And I did think she has to get away, for the sake of Jesus, she has to get out. I have wanted to tear her away with all my strength. But the years have made me weak." She smoothed her hair with her fingers. "Her way of being is tougher. She doesn't let go, doesn't give up. It's your way of being, Katerine. You belong together for better or worse. Don't push her away. Listen to me, hold your child tight."

Katerine, who had stood partially turned away, made an abrupt movement with her hand. Janka held this hand tight and said as if making a vow:

"No, don't push her away, I tell you. Pay close attention to her. She's your child. She wants to be with you. You, when I look at her, when I see how she is, I tell you, Katerine, pay attention! You will need her when things get tough!"

Chapter 2
In Goldscheider's Salon

Agency sets you free: That is the true lesson of freedom.
—Nietzsche

In September of the same year, the old Red House was opened anew and immediately had lots of customers. After a few weeks, Madame Goldscheider saw that the undertaking would be successful and that its existence was secure. Old friends and curiosity seekers came around; the regulars brought guests, who also helped business. Soon, people were aware the goods and quality of this business could be called first-class.

The prices were also high enough to keep a certain type of customer from coming, and the new rates resulted in a pleasant, social cohesion. Customers were not coerced; they were never pressured to pay a surprising amount. What struck guests as most agreeable was that neither Madame Goldscheider nor the ladies looked askance at a customer if he only had an ale or a glass of wine, paid, and left. To be sure, that was a rare occurrence since the ladies were young, pretty, and very well dressed.

Truth be told they were almost well-bred. They had nothing of the seedy look of ruination about them, so people said, nor were they idiotic or brash women on an adventure. People even ascribed a singularity to the salon. People in town spoke about it with praise or condemnation, but, whether they praised or condemned it, all had to agree spending an evening there was "interesting." Enough said. The opening of the residence was something of a premiere. People took note, and that is, in such instances, a guarantee of success. Goldscheider had at first gone forward with this undertaking not without external pressure—or rather with her own reservations.

In the course of her ever-more-extensive engagement with the business, which secured her a steady but not large income, she felt impelled to put in a reputable wine cellar with the option of service by the ladies to bring in otherwise uncollectible funds. Since Goldscheider was not familiar with the operation of such an establishment, she was happy to leave the management to the former head waitress of her wine cellar on Ring Street, a crafty woman of Italian heritage, Carlotta. This woman, moreover, happened to enjoy the privilege of being the lover of the man about town and friend to nobody, Teobald Sucher. The feared police agent supported Carlotta most effectively in the management of her business. Business in the wine cellar flourished, made good money, and after barely one year the ambitious Italian woman had had enough of serving and bookkeeping. She pressured Sucher to get her a rental agreement from the property owner. Most likely Carlotta's suggestion did make sense to him. The advantage of running her own business was something he could not dismiss, but he also knew Goldscheider was as savvy as his girlfriend. He was afraid Goldscheider would give the proposal a decisive no. It also was not in their favor that Goldscheider herself or even more so her factotum, the former high-school assistant principal and current private tutor Horner, liked to come by the wine cellar in the evenings.

Goldscheider and Horner watched the goings-on and joined in conversation with the guests or the waitresses. Horner offered advice. He tried various wines and rejected some. He also seemed to push Goldscheider to play a bigger role in the operation of the business. He was especially interested in the compensation given the three waitresses who, from time to time, disappeared from the floor on the watch of the Italian woman. Officially, according to police ordinance, they were not permitted to have anything to do with customers in the wine cellar. Of course these girls had gotten into a hugely dependent relationship with the Italian and had to do the grubbiest chores in the house in the mornings. They were also under the Italian woman's surveillance when they went out. She took every bit of money from them, yes, and, not uncommonly, even subjected them to physical searches for any stolen tips. Those were three thin, unhappy creatures, all over the hill, not exactly old but played out and worn down with constant worry. They put on a pained smile, just as they applied rouge to their cheeks, and they were unabashedly lavish with their caresses and flirtations. They let the men do what they wanted, and they put up with all of it because they knew the shelter under this roof was just the prelude to worse misery, which they strove to ward off by any means possible. When Horner made the clear insinuation he saw these "wenches" were regularly disappearing and wondered aloud how their work was paid and how it was recorded in the books of the business, Carlotta remarked curtly and with annoyance,

"Tips, and only tips! I tell you I don't make any money from this."

Horner shook his head and tried to snoop in the "written ledger." But Carlotta became rude and said she would have to complain to Teobald Sucher.

After Carlotta had spun out a scenario for a franchise to Sucher, he presented Horner a brilliantly thought-out offer to convey to

Goldscheider. One evening he sat down next to Horner, "privately" had a bottle of wine brought to the table, and laid out his plan. Sucher stipulated a ten-year contract with the right to purchase and offered in exchange twelve percent of the capital interest, should Carlotta sell, and—he gently stroked his shiny, black beard, after the fashion of the Emperor's—"At no cost there would be, reciprocally, the concession of running a brothel, according to the most propitious terms of business."

"Doctor Horner, I am not exaggerating when I say there is money right there on the street."

Horner sat as if hewn of stone and stared at the dregs in the bottom of his glass. Sucher refilled his glass and continued suavely. It was evident the good lady would be interested in such a business. And, naturally, it would be a business on a more extensive basis and not just a little operation on the side, like this one, where there was no money to be made. The good doctor would certainly share his opinion. Horner grumbled something that Sucher cunningly countered with, "Certainly, of course." He would like to emphasize, very importantly, the most fortunate location of the property for the brothel at a node of public traffic with ready public access. Currently it was a quiet, accessible niche, a well-known, centrally located house of prostitution. It had recently come to his attention that the place would be up for sale. Up to this moment it was in the best of hands. It would only take a simple voucher from him about a future business, nothing more, to secure a loan from the bank for the house. All in all, a very fair deal.

"The initial outlay would be nothing in comparison to the position, the acclaim, and the investment potential! Gold, dear Sir, is lying there in the dirt unrealized. With respect, each cobblestone of the alley is worth a fortune."

"We should really make a deal to rent the wine cellar, shouldn't we, most honorable Sir? We could make an agreement on the basis of your illustrious name, couldn't we?"

"Doctor Horner, you are making me embarrassed, of course I mean on the basis of the name of the esteemed lady. I am simply a bureaucrat." He inclined himself as if with a pain in his chest. "I can only suggest, Doctor Horner, and express my opinion. And that is this: we write a contract for what is available. At the moment, the business there is disorderly—in that alley, I mean. There are women all over the place without a license. But it doesn't matter. I can put a few police officers on the job. We can make sure the property is in order, clean up, make it sanitary, empty out the buildings, and put in sewers, everything in accordance with regulations. We would determine the conditions of a new establishment and control the influx of people. We would raise the rates—set the rates—you understand me.

"Yes, dear gentleman. Hey, hey, we could light a little fire under the girls there. I can take care of that, Doctor Horner! If a girl doesn't pass regulations, we throw her out on the street, and then we'll put in a regular establishment, isn't that right?"

"She is an idealist," Horner murmured and tipped his glass.

"Another bottle!" Sucher called out and nodded to Carlotta. He slid closer to Horner. "You see, Doctor Horner, I could keep the whole business for myself, but our bosses don't like us to be engaged in too much outside work. You have to recognize people do have their own small ambitions and weaknesses. Here is an example: between noon and midnight waitresses in a bar can take some time off on the side. But a brothel in this district, a brothel like I am talking about, is something else." He knocked on his chest, "It's the undertaking of a lifetime. I guarantee, with solid management, it would bring a pure profit of one hundred twenty percent. There'd be twelve to fifteen small rooms, well appointed, and a few people working in the kitchen. There would be coffee, a food bar, a wine bar in the cellar, an elegant salon with music, and a room for playing poker off to the side, say, twenty chips per person. Doctor Horner, with this kind of traffic, just do the math! Terrific, isn't it?"

Horner raised his fat, pale, unhealthy face. "What...? Where is this coming from?" his voice was sloshing in wine.

Sucher was stopped short. He picked up on a hidden message. That Horner was a slippery fish.

"Well, sure, sometimes things can get a little unpleasant. But we're talking about an establishment that's entirely different. This would be nothing but an elegant, warm salon, yes, a sweet, warm little place to go for the evening. And there would be girls of your choice, man oh man, Doctor Horner! There would be girls according to your liking."

"Tell me something, my kind host. Is this whole idea spinning around in your smart little mind alone? Your mind is filled with infamous ideas, most honorable Sir."

"Doctor Horner!" Sucher made an endearing gesture toward his heart, "I will not appeal to my position."

"It would only work against you!" Horner added a poisonous rejoinder.

"I understand. Let's speak frankly. We are talking about Red House." He paused for effect, looked meaningfully at Horner whose face betrayed nothing, and took a package of papers from his briefcase. He threw them out across the table: plans, calculations, and legal papers. He sorted them out quickly with his short, fat fingers, spreading them out over the table.

"You need to look at these, Professor Horner!"

"Go away, get yourself out of here!" Horner growled.

"See how carefully I have already looked into this. There are the petition, cost estimates, and construction plans. You are familiar with Goldammer, aren't you? The architectural firm? And here you have the new building. Look it all over at your convenience. I only have to think of the name, Red House, right, Doctor Horner? What a great business venture that is, don't you think?"

Horner put on his glasses and studied the materials.

"You can't discount it," he said.

"Excuse me? It's a plan. Old friends would think it couldn't be more sound. Red House offers the city, so to speak, a new dimension in business. It would be giving something old new life, so to speak, new blood, hey, hey?"

Horner stuffed the papers in his pocket.

"Madame Goldscheider will be hard to convince. She has her own business, a very good business, much too good, unfortunately."

Shaking his head, he immersed himself in the bottle of wine that had arrived at the table. Sucher stood up and left the man to his considerations. Yet before Horner had reached for his hat to leave the place, Sucher whispered in his ear in passing, "About the three-and-a-half percent, Doctor Horner. I'm a bureaucrat and not a businessman. I could split with you, fifty-fifty."

Goldscheider listened to her friend attentively with twinkling, short-sighted eyes.

"Horner," she then said, "What you are proposing, don't be offended, doesn't suit me at all. No, it's not at all for me. I'm not embarking on an adventure like that."

"Just as I thought. You have been ruined, utterly destroyed. That's what that damned Jewish learning, those stupid ethics from your precious David have done to you." He tromped back and forth in the room. His eyebrows were raised in a threatening gesture.

"As a young woman, Elise, you wouldn't have turned down an offer like this one. Back then you were unspoiled, which was good."

"Horner, do not misunderstand. I am simply not clever enough for that. I'm a simple businesswoman, and of course I'm open to expanding my business where possible. And when it comes to conscience! Bah, I'm not that concerned. But what we are talking about here is, first of all, experience. I don't have that experience. Man, how I have lived since I was eighteen years old!...and how I am now."

"Virtue, my precious, is a well-known liability in the course of business. It has to be overcome."

"Too late, Horner. I am not going to learn anything more of that sort. My God, if I had misgivings, it would be because of my child." She spoke the name softly with pursed lips, "Alma Luzie."

"I have to say if you're dealing in old clothing or young flesh, your sweet daughter with the long braids in Dresden doesn't have to know. I don't understand much about Mammon and how people make money, but the profit the gentleman drew up, that impresses me."

She looked over the papers, made some notes for herself, and shook her head again and again, discouraged.

"It is quite a business," she said as she exhaled. "I will give you that. But how would I learn the business, the practical ins and outs, the strategies? Good grief, something like this you'd have to learn from the ground up. Imagine!"

"Elise, you're being too serious. You need to be playful and have some grace of spirit. You're a person who's careful, thorough, and completely down to earth. I've told you that plenty often, and now you are showing me how true it is. Good heavens, just think of the concept! You would be the person in charge of the pleasure of love. Your job is to put the right woman with the right man, and you'd make a profit in the process. Let the idea carry you forward. The natural sequence of things, the details, will come to you. Smart entrepreneurs find their own solutions to the most difficult matters. It's all a game, I'm telling you, a game." He snapped his fingers, "Elise, why don't you take a business trip and look into the profession? Why didn't I think of that before! Go see how other people run their business. Take a page from their book if you have to."

She remained hesitant and undecided but, nonetheless, visibly excited and captivated. She talked about capital, about the necessary licenses, and the precipitous purchase. She was especially concerned about the healthy sum of money construction would chew up.

"Now I see," he said sarcastically, "dear little David Goldscheider's widow, with all her business acumen, was mired in an old-school attitude. With God's help you can fleece an upper-class gentleman and use the money to help the poor." He dropped the topic. But he played up Sucher to her. The good gentleman did not make his appeal with nice words but with solid calculations. He had made an unconditional guarantee of a one-hundred percent profit on the initial outlay. And that was only at the onset. With time it would have to be more, Madame, it would have to! He himself knew of such houses that made a profit of one-hundred-fifty or two-hundred percent. And he took paper and pencil and showed her all the math. The small businesswoman became greedy and hotly interested. The columns of figures danced on the paper.

But she still claimed truly not to understand one iota. She complained in distress, once again, she had led such a limited life.

Sucher completely dismissed these misgivings. "Laughable," he asserted. "There is no course of education or instructional program for this, you simply use your basic instincts. Old women from the backwoods, hags from the villages, have come to town and set themselves up as successful madams."

"Grab the reins, gracious lady, just like you're taking control of horses that are spooked! Pull hard on the bit! Dig in your spurs! Then the dumb animals will run." After all, had it not been Sucher behind the whole suggestion, Sucher? Horner only had to throw the idea out to her, and she would grasp it. That's how easily things would go. His job was to present the plan to her and then bring in Sucher! Hey, hey, they'll get along fine, like bugs in a rug.

And at the end, when she was halfway won over, he brought up the topic of the trip to learn about the business. Once again, he thought to himself, it looks like Doctor Horner is right. A trip was an eminently brilliant idea. Doctor Horner is after all a friend as well as an insightful, excellent person! He could offer the best recommendations in nearby towns in the monarchy, Budweis,

Olmuetz, Znaim, and Aussig. There was good business there. Successful people. Then she could turn her sights to the other side of the border, Dresden, Hamburg. Those Germans do smart business. If she was able to sniff out their sources, it would be really advantageous to connect with them and with agents in other countries who generally avoid doing business with narrow-minded Austrians. There we have it! He stretched out his hand for her to shake on it. And she, although she had not relinquished all her misgivings, shook his hand and decided to go with the deal.

Horner was triumphant. "Did the idea finally grab you?" he addressed her in a pompous apostrophe. "Do you not see how limited you have been?" She was impatient and put her hands over her ears.

"Horner, don't make me crazy with your speeches. Your speculations and everything else that goes with them are obscure to me. All I know is I have a lot to do. Liquidation. Get the money together since you all think I have it on hand. Me, the one who has no sense of style or color, no taste at all, I'm supposed to decorate fourteen rooms. And take care of getting linens and clothing for a bunch of young women. It's all so foreign and new to me. Well, to pick it up I'm going to have to do some traveling. And in Dresden I'm going to give my darling child one thousand kisses." She narrowed her near-sighted eyes and said, "Now that I stop to think about it, I've been running this whole stupid business all along just to have a few extra days with my daughter."

Horner hated Goldscheider when she waxed sentimental. He made a grimace and turned away. After she had taken care of the necessary tasks, she took off on her travels. And while she was away, just as Sucher had said, an iron broom swept Red House Alley clean.

Goldscheider visited the famed officers' brothels in Austrian cities with garrisons. She saw the big and small houses in the underworld and tried to gain as much insight as possible into the management and workings of those operations. Armed with letters from Sucher and other authorities from his department, the energetic, beautifully attired, and universally charming Madame Goldscheider was received without the usual mistrust in the trade of curiosity seekers. The managers were in no small measure flattered that someone from the metropolis came to visit and was interested in their industry and how they outfit their buildings. In fact, this woman wanted to learn. And they were not sparing in giving her their advice and sharing principles. Goldscheider kept her eyes open, and she was possessed of a sound, sharp mind. With piercing insight she identified what was salient and necessary. And before she had finished her round of travels, she had arrived at the decisive conclusion that an operation run like a bourgeois household had the best prospect for profit. She immediately dismissed anything that smacked of bar milieu, of seedy music halls or street traffic, which did attract some visitors. And, she learned that a constant turn-over of guests caused an up-and-down in the profits. She saw the most widely diverse combination of business strategies in Hamburg where she visited the internationally renowned sailors' hotels and houses of prostitution. Here she had the impression of chaotic, senseless barbarity, which flourished at the expense of the proprietors. They admitted to her, with a sigh, this kind of sketchy, unrestrained behavior, which was routine night after night in their establishments, was only dangerous and never profitable. But they were unable to do anything about it. Business was based on word of mouth, and that had to remain as it was.

Often the owners themselves lured the sailors into their place of business, gave them booze, and got them all riled up. But outside that very same city, Hamburg, in the district of fine villas where the Alster River flowed, in the immediate vicinity of simple yet elegant houses of merchants and shipowners, Georgette de Villiers kept her villa. She was a charming old woman with an elegant, discreetly powdered face. Goldscheider had been referred to her by an agent in Lübeck.

Goldscheider, who in the meantime had acquired some experience and become rather thick skinned, was taken aback at the style and tone that prevailed in "Salon Georgette." Madame de Villiers said with a motherly little laugh visitors were received only three times a week since socializing in the evenings was so demanding and her little girls did love their precious sleep more than anything.

The first half hour of her visit Goldscheider had to keep fighting the insurmountable, miserable feeling she had gone mad. She reassured herself with all her might and main that she was where she was; otherwise, she would have surely lost her composure. These were lovely, well-bred, young women, clad in white or pink, with gowns most discreetly cut at the throat. They received the guests with bright chatter and pleasantries, very often in broken French, which Georgette corrected without tiring. "My auntie" straightened a bow or put a wayward curl in place, and no one took notice when, in the course of the evening, several of the girls disappeared and there were four rather than seven who kept the party going. More than three, Goldscheider took note, never left the room at the same time. In between their intervals away, they served tea and English cakes. "The cakes got a little burned," a girl admitted to Georgette, who waved a threatening finger at her while laughing.

Money did not change hands. There were no tabs. Refreshments seemed to be offered at no charge, gratis, just as in elegant society. From time to time there was the command, "*Pahlez français, mes dames!*" One or another played jolly operettas on the piano, and they sang in pairs or three together. And, often, the guests even joined in. When one of the girls, a very beautiful girl from Berlin, preferred not to sing, Villiers spoke to her kindly and concluded with a grand gesture, "But, my dear child, our friends aren't critical. They are here to enjoy."

After that the shy girl sang a sweet Romantic tune with a simple, pastoral melody: "Mama always said look nice, don't go out such a mess." When she was done, Georgette began clapping with enthusiasm and said with beaming eyes to one of the gentlemen, who bowed slightly, "Now, Consulate Wychers, we regret we must let that sweet girl go for her education. Paris should be thankful to us, don't you agree?" And in this very house something else happened that drove Goldscheider, the observant nonparticipant, to distraction.

Madame de Villiers arose all of a sudden, walked over to one of the gentlemen, and, as she put a diamond cufflink in his hand, announced in the most free and easy way in the world, "Lord von Palestra, our silly Suzanne relieved you of this attractive item, probably to tease you. But before you notice it is gone, *voila*!" Palestra turned dark red, grabbed the cufflink and stashed it away. He had given it as a gift to Suzanne, a darling woman from the Alsace, who liked it and had fingered it coyly. But Georgette found this behavior "shocking" and returned it to him. When, a few days later, the young Alsatian wore it prominently as a brooch, not another word was said.

And you can make money in a place like this?? Goldscheider must have asked herself a thousand times. She could not believe her eyes. The salon was very popular in certain circles. It was frequented exclusively by elegant, handsome, well-built men with upper-class names who exhibited the most polished manners and had the most exquisite presence. Georgette wore jewelry, genuine jewels, and clothes of rare distinction. She had her lovely villa and her carriage, and the whole of her passion, as she admitted herself, was to let the horses run. As Goldscheider was preparing to leave, Villiers, flattered by the impression her system seemed to have made on the stranger, started disgorging her wisdom. "Is it inevitable," she said, "that only an ugly business can be made out of the sweet necessity *de la belle usance*, of the enjoyment of love? I would never for any amount in the world pair up my girls with crude men who are unsavory. It would burden my soul, Madame, for me, in my inattention, to do these innocent girls—innocent because they are born for the pleasure of men—any harm. Rather they should attain higher positions as a result of my help. You see, Madame, my philosophy is this: all life is a great marketplace. One either buys or sells; there is nothing more. *Voyons!* What is sold in the market is available because merchants are smart. They make availability their vocation or an artisanal business. Love is the same, Madame. Let us not delude ourselves further. Love is a hunger within the individual, and, like hunger, it must be satisfied. Wouldn't you say? Butchers, bakers, and candlestick makers feel they are of value; they see their work as a necessity. Yet a woman who gives happiness, who creates the most precious moments of forgetfulness and joy—the most wonderful, best, and lasting wares ever—sinks into shame. Is there anything more natural than a young person giving herself over to youth? And people look down on these women! I don't see why people nowadays vent their spleen over this."

"Nowadays, Madame?" Goldscheider intervened, risking her head.

"For two thousand years, since the beginning of Christendom, this attitude has been around. What will this span of time mean in the history of the world? Two thousand years is but a momentary flash for the Lord. But I want to be clear about this to you. We entrepreneurs, I mean we capitalists, are the ones who will bear the responsibility for this: We rob these girls of their humanity and make them into slaves who have neither will nor pleasure in living. People are only happy when they have free will."

Elise Goldscheider said, spiritedly, that de Villiers's views were certainly original, in fact worth admiring. But at best they could only be implemented in an international and wealthy city like Hamburg, where a monarchy did not prevail and then under the precondition of a goodly—you will excuse me—patronage with powerful capital. In small places or in other modern big cities, hunger would dictate the law.

The madam interrupted her with a little laugh of disdain that was not to be misunderstood, and then she spoke effervescently, "Oh, Madame, *tranchons le mot!* I'm familiar with that fashionable view of things. *Excusez, Madame, je suis une femme bien âgée et je me suis vue quelque fois en face d'affaires differentes.* This is simply the view of the avant-garde speaking from their own perspective. Please do not mistake me for a missionary, *pleine d'altruisme. J'ai mis mon bien a couvert.* I act on my own interests. But not, Madame, as you do, no, not like that. What was it people said a hundred years ago? Workers and peasants have no need of an education, of thinking for themselves. That is dangerous. They only need God, catechism, and *le roman obscène*. And today? And one hundred years from now, where will we be then? We hold onto old ideas hard and fast. The pleasure girl, since we require such a person and see her as an indispensable surrogate in society, should live in clean, not just tolerable, rather in decent circumstances. She doesn't have to be some idiot with a sweet tooth, a lazy liar, or someone who is deathly ill. In small towns and big cities, in high-price establishments or in cheap bars, everywhere she should have the same access to the law, to medical treatment, and to social justice."

Madame de Villiers stood up and finished her speech with these words, "My ladies would be shocked if some uncouth person would say he despises them for their lifestyle. You saw them, Madame. Are they not lovely, smart, and enchanting, these children? They believe they are loved and desired because of their attributes, because they are so young and pretty. Their lovely appearance, their laughter, and the charm of their most intensive femininity is what Nature gave the courtesans. And I, Madame, I, too, give them dignity."

On their return trip the agent from Lübeck told her wonderful things about Georgette, as she was known in short in certain circles. It was said she earned a huge amount of money and had a lot more than she needed to retire.

But she did love the business and did not wish to give it up. It was just amazing how she supported the girls while protecting them. She was known to demand women who were racial types, and it was very difficult to supply Georgette with wares. She probably sent back twenty women before one met her expectations. She cultivated—this is how the agent expressed himself—the aristocratic type of the *grande mondaine*. Purportedly people in town knew that Georgette, for instance, firmly closed the doors of her house to men with a bad reputation, whether they were rich and elegant or not. There was a famous piece of gossip that a patrician's son and multi-millionaire had to bring a doctor's note as well as the entrance ticket, which cost a thousand, in order to be received by Georgette.

The depiction of the Hamburg idyll had an inordinately large effect on Horner, to whom Goldscheider reported about all she had seen. Something like Georgette's met his wildest dreams! There was really, truly, such a thing in modern Europe! Luckily he could not afford to go because he would have gladly stayed to throw himself at Georgette's feet. He uttered her name only with expressions of the highest esteem. He said,

"This woman alone grasps what is needful in this era of philistine dissipation and degradation. She aims to elevate the most refined wisdom about the female body. The soul of a Greek dwells in your French woman, let me make this clear to you." He slammed his fist on the table. "Emulate her! Educate a young woman, someone fresh," he continued, rubbing his hands, "someone in the middle of the fray, active and ambitious about business. Find a woman with a talent for leadership, a genius of organization, and with the appeal of the Love Goddess. Then those who make the law and male pride itself will have to pack up and leave! And all those who uphold the law for their sense of their own importance, let them be gone! Oh, yes, Elise, the two of us will hold the whip over the monstrous vanity of the powerful in a society that is going under. Elise, I'm telling you, find me this young woman! Then I will instruct her about the conditions of the new order. Further, we are going to instate the morality of the prostitute as law. Oh, you commoners, you who make brooms and pots, wait and see! You who find sin in others will be punished! The wisdom of the religion you exalt will finally be actualized." He strutted back and forth around the room in a state of excitation. "Excellent, Madame! Your little hands are holding a dangerous explosive, and for that I want to kiss your little hands." He smacked his thick lips in the air.

"Horner, drop the stupidity!" Goldscheider gave him a dry warning, "In my house never!"

"Do you want to stop me from coming up with ideas?" he replied sharply.

"Do whatever you'd like! But remember Georgette and her circle are not an option here. We don't have Palestras and Bingens and Johnstones who can cover a bill of a thousand German marks for a visit to the brothel. The agent from Lübeck is right when he says Georgette is running a finishing school for courtesans. It's like going to dine in the finest culinary academy. I can't replicate that! You'll have to pursue your ideals in Red House," she said in conclusion to keep him from getting upset. She still needed him.

The opening took place in early fall. The new house was finished, true to its name, with red roof tiles. It had a bank of eight windows across the front and a porch, above which hung a sparkly little flag to catch the sun, though it did not. There was a brass bell on the yellow and blue lacquered front door, which made a sharp rattling that filled the house. The ladies arrived in three cabs. There was a carpet that led across the hall and up the first step. In the lobby were ivy trellises, and a marble child held a lamp up high. Everything was so clean and light and pure you would think you were at the theater. The ladies from the former Red House gave each other significant looks. You could really tell what kind of place you were in. The new porter, Mrs. Polifka, a strong, plump person, came from her apartment and gave everyone a friendly greeting.

"The bitch of my nightmares is gone," Little Fritzie mumbled, completely captivated and tapped Katerine.

Goldscheider's trusted Madame Olympia, a lady tightly corseted with dark features and a forehead full of burned curls, greeted everyone very eagerly. She conducted them into the salon, which was decorated with Bordeaux-red velvet furniture and white lace curtains. It looked extremely cozy and elegant. There were marble tables with vases and figurines, charming bunches of flowers and peacock feathers. Everything had been positioned about the room to look fine and elegant. The height of glamour was the carved golden mirror that stood as tall as a man between the windows. Katerine clapped her hands.

"Jesus, they really did it all," she said. In this short time the expression on her face had already changed. She also had, in the ensuing time, learned to style her hair and to use makeup—a lot of makeup—to erase wrinkles and furrows. But the cosmetic brush had only made her face banal; her features, which were moved only by hearty laughter to please herself, had, in the transformation, lost much of their once-riveting originality.

The women who had formerly rented rooms in Red House could not stop looking around in astonishment.

The others, who were only there to observe, were blasé, or tried to be, and shrugged their shoulders. They would not have minded participating in something like this. Even Mademoiselle Olympia piped up to say she found everything indeed quite cute. But, for someone like herself, who claimed to have been to Paris, there was not really anything that remarkable left to see. Goldscheider took the girls to her office and put a sheet of paper filled with print in front of each of them for their signature. They all signed without hesitation. Most of them had no idea whatsoever what they were signing. Some said they thought it was a contract "that they could not leave." But for the time being that did not enter their minds. One slim, blond Austrian, who had been a maid in a hotel in Switzerland and brought with her the allure of a princess, did have an idea about the contract. She explained there were "a whole bunch of numbers;" it was a bill or something like that. It was likely a big bill. Well, what did it matter? You got lovely garments and dresses. If it turned out that this was a bill, there was plenty of money for everybody, or so they consoled one another.

What most impressed the girls who had been in a brothel was the tone the madam used right from the start. Goldscheider's announcement had a rare inspirational effect on their downcast mood: "Behave yourselves, everyone can succeed. Don't be messy with your possessions. And don't sneak around and get yourself drunk on booze! Here in my establishment you have opportunities. Each and every one of you can still have a fine, respectable life if you're smart." At that moment she was able to push down a feeling that kept surfacing: desire and ambition were absolutely fruitless. It was an awareness of the prostitutes' frailty. Their morals and their ruin were at stake. But what the girls heard in these words and ideas was this: "You're all still young and attractive. You'll be able to do well!"

They were afraid of the madam, but at the same time they respected her.

"She's a hard nut to crack, but she knows what she's talking about! And she's not just saying hand over the money and then some more. She's not leading the guests on and playing them, that's true. The woman is tough, but she's the same with everybody." And they also said there were a lot worse places to be. Just think of all the dresses you got! Yet just about everybody had something bad to say about them. It was not that they were out of style or shabby. Quite the opposite, everything was silk and attractive. But they were like the traditional, local "housemaids' costumes," as Bibi put it, like outfits from provincial towns like

Aussig and Teplitz. Over at the Excelsior House the girls were only allowed to wear a lace tunic with a silk "baby" top over that and nothing else. Nothing like that was worn here, not even late in the evenings. One girl or another had tried coming into the salon half-dressed, but Goldscheider sent her back right away. In such matters she had no sense of humor.

In all things and at all times, the madam ran a tight ship. Breakfast was served at eleven in the morning. Everybody got a decent-sized pot of coffee and a piece of cake that tasted "delicious, like mother made it." Naturally she saw to it that the girls ate well. They were not allowed, as were girls elsewhere, to have frivolous foods or candy. "Things like that may fill you up, but they don't give you strength." "That's right," said the girls and ate their dumplings right up.

Goldscheider applied her highly professional punctuality and pedantry to the rhythm of this business. She was insistent the girls be in a good mood when they "worked." When they gossiped or hatched up mean tricks, as was customary in such places, their hopes the madam would take their side were dashed. Goldscheider was unshakeable in her sense of justice. She did not play favorites, nor did she always find fault with the same people. Anybody who was disruptive or ineducable and did not care to adapt to the clear rules of the house had to leave. Goldscheider was in regular communication with brothels in the provinces. She was especially fond of a lively and active business. She encouraged the girls to be cheerful by calling out to them and speaking with them individually. She was also unobtrusive and pleasant when giving the girls guidance about keeping the guests happy.

"People have to have a good time here, do you understand? They have enough to worry about everywhere else. The gentlemen should say, 'Those girls are extra-special sweet.'"

Fueled by Goldscheider and buoyed up by her even-handed, positive treatment, which was neither harsh nor despotic, the ladies tapped the wellspring of merriment that bubbles up from youth and folly. Goldscheider was not unhappy to take the girls in hand one by one and to instruct them almost individually.

"Look here," she said to Helene Nippich, a pretty but dimwitted Jew who belabored every utterance with a whiny complaint and ruined a good laugh with her sighs and piteous laments, "your endless stories are dumb, and nobody believes a word of them. They laugh along to be polite. Tell the truth when somebody asks you a direct question, and if you don't want to answer, make a joke. But don't go around bemoaning the opportunities you lost."

"Does anybody want to dance?" Madame once asked. "Me, me!" there was a chorus from all sides. Irma, a smart Hungarian, did not say much. She just hiked up her skirt and danced a real, traditional csardas so lively that the tiles of the floor shook and the fancy vases rocked. Goldscheider had her practice a few dances with the music director James Stoll who played in the salon every evening. She performed these beautifully to the great satisfaction of the guests. People loved her, and for several weeks she was a star.

The other girls tried it, too, but since they were clumsy at it, the dance did not catch on. Bibi, who was clearly very popular, knew how to do a little art presentation that the French waiter at the Excelsior had shown her repeatedly until she got it. She placed eight thin wine glasses of various sizes filled to various levels in a row and tapped them with an ivory chopstick to make the sweetest melodies. Her best number was the "Marseillaise." When she played it, her eyes glowed with ferocity while she kept the beat forcefully with her right foot. She twirled the chopstick in the air, exactly as she had seen Monsieur Charles do it.

After her performance this or that person came forward bashfully with her little talent show. The performances set off a new and real competitive edge among the girls. A healthy, youthful eagerness made their eyes glow—almost made them happy—and livened up the conversation. What they offered was not much, but they truly did forget why they were performing, to what end. And that is what Goldscheider with her mind of profit wanted, and she watched and laughed.

One evening Katerine stood next to the piano player, told him something and, inclining her head in a posture of yearning, began singing melancholic Bohemian love songs. The young ladies were deeply moved. At first the gentlemen were taken aback, then they exclaimed for joy. Instead of singing in her former light, pleasant voice, Katerine was emboldened by the sudden hush in the audience and began to belt out the songs; she let rip. She drew out the sentimental notes of longing as she looked upward to the ceiling. Afterwards she was unusually proud of what she thought was her triumph, and she talked with Olympia about it. Her singing was, she said, more beautiful and wonderful than a bit of clinking around with wine glasses.

Katerine was over thirty, and her characteristic riveting style was, little by little, eroding in the new milieu. She was already showing signs of the whore who is scraping for some advantage in life, a person using cheap games to stave off the years of most appalling misery. When Janka left, she lost the connection between her soul and her past; it loosened, then was torn away. She was free. She no longer had a past. Her dreams fell to ashes. Her vengeance had died out. Her life was made up solely of the noise of the night and the tips she brought in—had to bring in. She wanted to be the most beautiful and most desirable and used ordinary enticements and seductive artifices. Quite unlike her earlier self, she had attached herself to Olympia, to whom she was sweet and admiring. Olympia, who was aware Katerine was not a productive commodity, outfitted her with a story that was romantic. Olympia outfitted all the girls with a story. She wove her tales with oohs and aahs. But Katerine's story was, as people could tell at a hundred paces, the usual stuff of fairy tales. In this tale there was a wicked stepmother, a horrible old seducer, and a wonderful, handsome aristocratic student Katerine was very proud of. She preferred him above all others, praised him, and believed in him so firmly that she adamantly defended his thoroughly impeccable honor against slander.

Katerine was a person who had never known peace or taken pleasure in small things. She had needed inebriation to quell her escalating anxiety. But now she enjoyed the warmth of company and exchanging tales of woe. She became trustworthy and opinionated. She listened to others and shared with them. Her bad temper seemed to have cooled. Her lovely, slim body still attracted and gratified men, and Katerine had regular, loyal clients, just as she had had soliciting on the street.

At Olympia's suggestion she dyed her wild auburn hair flax-blond and called herself Carmen.

She also wore a crocheted stole about her neck and bangles that looked like coins. She made up a secretive heritage about Gypsies who stole children. The two, Carmen and Olympia, loved to play solitaire, read tea leaves morning, noon, and night, and read trashy novels that came in installments with the weekly tabloid, which they cut out carefully and assembled.

She treated recurring heavy bouts of asthma and palpitations with homeopathic remedies, and since they did not help, she started to drink, in secret naturally. She had Milada smuggle wine to her room in rather considerable quantities.

And the wine drove the tiredness from her limbs. She called the eerie numbness that tended to flood her legs and lower body "poor circulation." Milada spent her days with the porter and slept in a room in the attic whose small window pushed open out onto the roof. Her old friends the white and black rats once again found their way to her room. She carried out all kinds of tasks in the house and was sent on errands in town. She also accompanied Goldscheider on her walks when she had to carry something or pick things up. She had to pin her hair up and wear long, shapeless skirts, and often she had to wear a large, knit shawl to hide her child's body.

When Katerine first arrived at the new house, Milada was standing at the door, full of expectation. She was waiting there for word of her mother. She had been separated from her mother for months and had lived with strangers. They were sullen people who did not look after her more than a stray dog. The child had become withdrawn. While her mother was away, Milada had surrounded her image in memory with a halo of the sweetest tenderness. Her mother's warmth and laughter sustained her lonely heart. As she stood leaning against the wall, waiting for word of Katerine, an innocent longing moved her little brown face with excitement. And there was Mother on the arm of a lady, wearing a silk dress with a feather hat and gloves. She looked around while laughing and almost did not see Milada. Katerine was intent on moving toward the door. But Little Fritzie held her back and said, "Look, the little girl is here." Katerine looked back slowly and raised her eyebrows. After a moment she said, "Jesus, she has gotten big." Then she deftly gathered up her rustling skirts and shoved her way up to Olympia at the entrance. There was not another single word.

The child lowered her head even more. When the chatter and laughter began, she trundled out into the dark well of the courtyard.

With the coin the good Mrs. Coelestine from school had given her as a going-away gift the child had bought apples and put one under her mother's pillow. She had also made sure Katerine was given a nice room, although the porter had told her, "Here everybody gets the same treatment." Milada answered her as an older, superior person, "Oh, gosh, Mrs. Polifka, you'll see how Mother is." And the porter, who liked the helpful child, let Milada put the most colorful pillows and vases in her mother's room. Once the child had seen her mother, she had her first and most terrible disappointments. Her mother no longer counted with the other ladies in the same way. Mother was good to them and laughed with them, and she even chatted with Little Fritzie and Olinka. Since her return she shared wine with people she had not noticed before and crawled in bed with them. Every time Milada came over to see her mother several people were sitting in her room and talking, and Katerine listened to their talk, burying her hands in her light-blond bouffant hair. The women all kept their wine glass hidden under their skirts, but Mother drank right out of the bottle and buried it under the pillows. She was now afraid of the madam. Oh, no, how she had changed!

The child observed and was sick at heart. The great, deep-rooted pride she had in Katerine gradually, without notice, fell to bits. She was unaware why she had become disappointed in her mother. People still found her mother beautiful, and men came around. But she was no longer Katerine in Black from Red House who threw her head back in resounding, defiant laughter. The child understood in her heart Katerine had come down from the heights where she alone had been. And she had dissolved the distance between herself and others. She no longer passed others by with a song or an arrogant shrug of her shoulders when they called out to her from their jealous bickering. Katerine said gently and wearily, "For pity's sake, you women, can't you just get along? I am tired of this." Or she took the wine glass from Gisi, her rival, the person she often quarrelled with. Then she shouted angrily, "Don't you drink my wine, bitch, if you're going to tangle with me!" If the argument got more intense, she unleashed a flood of coarse swear words and insults, which were returned in kind.

Weeks and months went by in Red House in unvarying monotony. Business flourished and expanded. The girls were in good spirits and busy. And Katerine passed by Milada without noticing her as she scrubbed the steps and picked up the rooms. Katerine acted as if they were strangers with no connection in life. She did not ignore her out of hate or bitterness; she was empty of feeling. She pushed away everything that came into her icy, blank orb.

Her soul was hobbled and did not keep up, and her proud will seemed to lie beyond reach in some far-off future.

She was completely unaffected when Milada stood in front of her door and slipped in when she found the room empty. She stood in a corner, quite still, or picked up all around. She waited till the woman who sat in front of the mirror or lay in bed noticed her presence and turned to her. Katerine's reaction was always the same. She either gave Milada errands to run or said hastily, "I don't need anything." Then the child left. In her apron she took along half-rotten apples from the cabinets or off the floor. She no longer liked Katerine. When Katerine had asthma or palpitations and curled up in bed gasping with blue lips, she sent Milada away with angry gestures and curses. She wanted no one. She wanted to be alone and did not need anyone to care for her or tell the madam on her. She was not ill, she said. The little spell would soon pass, and she would be up right away. She bolted the door and admitted no one when she felt weak. Milada had to shove a bottle of wine into her room and then leave, just as she had done in earlier times. Otherwise, Katerine would call her names. By herself she could at least wheeze and moan as she liked, and there was nobody in her face to delight in her misery.

Katerine did not see how Milada longed to stay close and be her caregiver. "Yes, she's like a hawk," she once told Olympia, "She'd be happy to sell me for a penny, I'm telling you."

Milada's fantasy of her mother died long and hard. The old Red House, Janka, and the Katerine of Milada's early years, her mother with her sweet laughter and teasing and with her fond wishes and fantastic ideas—even with her flashes of anger—sank into oblivion. And a dull, swollen wreck of a woman surfaced, someone who went by Carmen and sifted about from room to room reeking of wine. The madam spat insults at her, and she defended her warm little corner of the house like a scrappy cat.

The half-grown child was left to her own devices. She lived

alone in the room of rats. She had lost her feeling of belonging with this woman. The iciness that flowed from Katerine's heart drove her ever deeper into a solitude with only rare moments of relief. Her abjection was oh-so unchildlike.

And yet! The seeds of love are strong and indestructible. "Mother" remained a warm and friendly word for her. Its sound was mixed in her thoughts with a vision of a small, thin woman who drew the covers over her and comforted her as she slept, a woman with hard, red hands.

Her whole life long, as she was falling asleep and the warmth of the bedding comforted her exhausted limbs, she had an indescribably lovely feeling she did not have during the day. The sensation was these mother hands gently patting her.

One evening Katerine had an attack in the salon. Her breathing was distressed, her heart beat wildly, and a terrifying leaden feeling overtook her belly and legs. She looked for the door with glassy eyes and fell to her knees in front of her chair. People ran to her immediately and carried her to her room, where the next morning Goldscheider appeared and watched over her. She told her it would be better for her to be in a small town in a less stressful job as a woman in a cafeteria or as a cashier in a pub. She would be happy to find something like that for her. Katerine looked at her, and her pale lips quivered with horror. She asked whether she had not been doing the work there? Was she not as good as anybody else that Goldscheider would treat her so badly?

The madam asked in return why she was so attached here, and said she had certainly been in this place long enough. She asked whether she was reluctant to leave because of her little girl.

Oh, her? No, it had to do with the fact she had gotten used to things here. It was familiar. But really and truly! There was nothing wrong with her. She had been a person who was healthy and hardy her whole life long! She put her hands on her hips and hummed.

"Of course," said Goldscheider calmly, "nobody can stay here forever. In this business the main thing is variety and change. But you know that."

"But why me?" Katerine muttered, and she sensed the worst defeat was at hand.

"For my part, it doesn't really matter. But the guests demand change, here as anywhere. You will be happy somewhere else, too. In a new setting you're sure to have money." And with that, Goldscheider left the room.

A few days later Doctor Lemberg came to the house and gave Katerine a thorough examination. She stood there, legs astraddle, and laughed. He was also in a good mood, slapped her on the back, and said she would probably outlive him and a couple of young cats. She kissed both his hands and felt as if she had eluded danger. Nonetheless he confirmed to Goldscheider an advanced, long-standing case of kidney disease with its attendant heart damage. He advised the madam to get that evil out of the house posthaste. "This woman is eating and drinking you out of house and home, and on top of that you have the ugly mess. Get this damage out of here!"

Goldscheider, who certainly had bigger items on the agenda, took the news well. Katerine's appeal had, naturally, also suffered over the course of time.

In accord with protocol in the house on a certain day Goldscheider informed the ladies who had been selected to leave they were to pack their bags and prepare for their travel that evening. Little Fritzie had gone to the town of Pilsen; two others, to Troppau. And Katerine's destination was Braunau.

Goldscheider made a point of telling Katerine that she had made an effort to find her a good position. It was in a fashionable, modern American-style bar, only for civilians, and tips were good. Then a man in a cap and jackboots nodded to her. He had been waiting for Katerine in the office. She listened while looking at the floor. Her face was swollen, and beneath the red makeup her ashen, sallow skin was visible. Her body, which had lost its slender and attractive voluptuousness, was now enfolded in white flab.

Goldscheider adjusted her gold monocle.

"Furthermore, I will keep your little girl here. I'll relieve you of that concern. The doctor says you need rest. And don't you drink!"

Katerine made a tired gesture with her hand. While the porter brought in large, black-lacquered suitcases, Olympia ran around laughing and triumphant. She then sat down next to Katerine who was throwing clothes and laundry in one pile. "Stop: perfume and the hairdressing set stay here. They belong to us."

A sunken expression of hopelessness set in around Katerine's mouth. She no longer hid her misery. She moaned at times and sat down.

"Braunau, Braunau, wherever that may be! It's got to be a good nest. I'd surely be glad if they got me a job there. But they just won't let me go." That is what Olympia said full of fake satisfaction, and she flung one foot over the other. Gisi stuck her red face in the door. She was half asleep and surprised. "Jesus, Katerine, is it true you're leaving? What news!" She came closer and looked at Katerine and spoke to her softly and kindly. "You're going to be sitting at a beautiful counter with artificial flowers and pouring champagne. Oh, girl, that's something nice!" "But not in Braunau," Olympia said maliciously.

Katerine hardly heard what they were saying. She slammed the lid of the suitcase closed and sat on it like a horse, put a bottle to her mouth and yelled, "Take us to the knacker!" But her laughter became a hateful, leaden smirk, and both the others left feeling moved to tears.

She then slept till the hour of her departure. It was almost ten in the evening when the porter woke her up. The sounds of music and voices were already coming from the salon. Wrapped in a shawl she shielded herself from the guests who were arriving and got herself a hat box and an umbrella from the office. Outside it was raining in sheets. There was not a soul there for her to say goodbye to. The only thing that surrounded her were fourteen years of memories. They were like hungry, gloomy, screeching birds of prey.

She did not look around; she spoke not a word. The porter called out, "So where's your little girl now?" She hollered "Milada!" toward the kitchen and rushed off to the courtyard.

When she returned with Milada, the handle of the carriage was closing, and it set off.

"Clean as a whistle," the porter thought, shaking her head. She gave Milada a miserable shove of annoyance and shut the door.

Katerine's fate played out awfully fast. In Braunau she was loaned out to a "private circle" by a speculator Markus Schleicher, owner of a variety and singing show and bar. He saw right away that this person was not the great acquisition his esteemed guests had been promised. In this private circle she had to serve, three times per week, the most disgusting and lowly debauched types.

Schleicher consoled her jokingly, "You can take care of yourself, my child!" And he cleared out a small hole for her in the unheated building at the back. She had to buy her own food with the tips she got now and again. "And you won't need any clothing," the businessman informed her. Katerine was indifferent and apathetic, as people wanted her to be. She spent almost all her time in bed wrapped like a piece of sausage in patched, coarse wool blankets. An ill-tempered woman paid by the hour got her the most basic necessities. She only pulled herself up off the mattress when hunger drove her to earn some money. She went over to the door or lay about the window to look enticing. She was not allowed to solicit on the street. Her health declined more rapidly than her mental state. She was no longer able to tolerate the rotten fare the woman brought her. She breathed heavily and vomited. She numbed her weak, malnourished being with large quantities of alcohol. Wine had become too expensive for her; it came down to hard liquor.

After a while people in the "private circle" started complaining.

"This person isn't much," they said. "She's like a sponge, always soaking up the liquor."

"She should clear out," said one unhappy customer. "She offers nothing, just stands and stares. You could expect a little something, right?"

Schleicher was angry and betook himself to the "hole," tore the half-conscious woman out of bed with a crude "stupid, lazy bitch!" and threatened her with a "damn good whack" in the face. He ordered her to watch out and do a better job. If she did not, he would have to see to it, he said threateningly, "Not one more lousy drop of booze will go down your gullet. You've got a nice life. Some people have to haul coal when they're off work." He swore at her and slammed the door.

Katerine came to the conclusion she would not drink all morning long on those three days a week she went to "work." Just before she had to be on the floor, she allowed herself a moderate amount so that she could, for a while, feel a bit fresher and livelier. Then she could follow, if struggling, the lousy goings-on around her. But the unholy rotten luck of those marked by doom followed her once again. One day she drank more than was useful. While posing naked, holding a burning candle, she fell into the middle of a circle of men. They pulled back. And a stinking liquid poured out of her mouth onto a white fur carpet, which was the extravagant showpiece.

Schleicher carried through on his promise. He gave her a few hard slaps in the face, packed a small bundle of clothes and laundry for her, gave her a ticket and a coin for the road, and delivered her in a late-night hour back to the city she had come from three months ago. To cover his "losses" he kept most of the clothing she had brought with her from Goldscheider's.

It was late autumn and the worst and least productive season for work. And there she was, just one more miserable, shapeless woman painted the red of roof tiles there on the streets on the outskirts of town, approaching men and begging with needy eyes and curses.

The tragedy of this misery is always the same. Exactly as Katerine in her prime had imagined her future in hours of terror, that is how in fact it was. Her physical weakness kept her from making tireless pilgrimages from bar to bar until someone picked her up. This type of prostitution was paid in food and drink, and the few measly coins a person got panhandling went to the woman who runs the pub. She snatched the money right up.

The disgusting old witch in the suburbs that Katerine had become soon came to curse the "nag" that fate had dealt her. Yet she was still aware that Katerine with her large, black-rimmed eyes and wild, red hair looked good, pretty good, when she put herself together. "You're not worth your own salt," she said to herself deprecatingly.

So Katerine put herself in a dubiously white bed that smelled of cheap soap and powdered bleach, put a fan in her hand, sprinkled this broken woman she had become with perfume and brought this nag visitors. There were soldiers, manual laborers, half-grown boys, and men who had been out drinking. She lured each of them with veiled promises and with unsavory hints of a fine lady who happened to be interested in a man just like him. This lady did not charge, of course, but she asked a small tip, naturally.

Night after night for many nights Katerine lay there with rattling breath, forcefully keeping her eyes open, and waited.

A stinking lamp burned on the ledge of the stove, and the glow of the iron stove cast rays that exposed her sallow complexion. The self who offered love arose and gave the man who entered a drunken laugh. She was more and more deferential as it became increasingly more difficult for the former Katerine to prepare the other self, prone on the bed. It became almost impossible to pull this woman together for customers. One evening even the old

Katerine's wildest rantings and ravings failed to rouse her other self. She thumped and whacked and swore. Finally she enticed her with liquor. She poured it with force between her clenched teeth. But nothing helped, she did not move. Only vague sounds came from this other woman's lips.

Then the former Katerine got scared. She keened and wailed and alarmed the neighbors. She swore to anyone who would listen that she had taken care of this other Kate like her own child. She whined to the policeman observing the dubious situation who vainly asked for papers. At last she fell to her knees with fear and also with relief as the door closed behind the men who carried the bier out the door with heavy, resounding steps. Katerine landed on Louise Street in the charity hospital. They pressed her with questions but could not determine her identity. And when the treating physician called the case hopeless, they left her in peace. Barely conscious, she asked for a drink. But when the woman orderly brought fruit juice or milk, she groaned her objection.

After a number of days the staff brought in a girl who recognized her. She had been at Goldscheider's salon a short time with Katerine.

"She's got a little girl in Red House," she told them. "She's young, a maid there at Goldscheider's. I can tell you for sure this woman's name is Carmen." With a light shudder the still youthful creature turned away from the swollen body, the blue lips, and the chest filled with frantic, rattling breath.

Goldscheider was informed, and the next day the porter Polifka appeared with Milada. The girl was pale and looked around with confusion.

"There are people here from Red House!" the orderly cried out. Katerine panted. She opened her eyes slowly. "Come here, she's awake now," explained the orderly and waved them over.

"It's us. We're here. Yes, look, here we are," Polifka said and pushed Milada forward. Katerine opened her mouth. "Jan?" she whispered her question.

Milada spread her fingers across the blanket and looked at the cadaverous face. "Mother? No, it's only Miss Carmen," she thought fleetingly. "How horrible she looks, horrible!"

"Say something to her!" the porter admonished. Milada's thoughts swirled in her mind. Red House. Janka. Mother. The person there, Mother? The improbable thought that was her mother occurred again and again until it overwhelmed the horror. Her throat closed from fear and fright. Mother died there, Katerine in Black. The hospital room, the beds of iron, the gasping body there, Mother died.

She whispered, "Mother."

Completely silently, hidden, moved by a longing and repulsed by horror, she stretched out her brown hand, rough from working, and reached for her mother's curled fingers. The coldness of ice rose in her young blood. Behind her the porter was whispering animatedly with the orderly. Polifka put something in her hand, and the orderly nodded. Then the orderly pushed the child away and bent over the bed.

"She is not awake now. Pray for her when her breathing stops. It will be in a short while." She supported herself on the edge of the bed. "There, there," she said too loudly. "Watch her now, there, there. You're just dying, that's all. You'll be happy to see the guests from Red House. What, you're opening your eyes?! There you go! You want a drink of schnaps? Is that what you're saying? She's alert."

Katerine opened her eyes and looked around.

"There are people here from Red House!" the orderly yelled. She put her arm under Katerine's pillow and raised her up.

"Janka!" the ill woman whispered again.

"It's crazy, she keeps saying her name." To Katerine the orderly said, "For God's sake, please sign for the girl to stay there in Red House! Listen to me, sign!" She put a piece of paper in front of her and put a pen in her hand. "Someone should have gotten here earlier," she mumbled and looked around fearfully.

Katerine's eyes showed she understood.

"Jan," she choked, "it's not...not...very bad."

The orderly placed the pen in her hand and closed her fist around it.

"Sign!" she pressed her. "Do it for Janka," the orderly urged her.

Katerine refused. She pushed away the paper and the arm of the orderly who was holding her firmly.

"Come over here!" the orderly called out to Polifka. "Show her the little girl!"

The porter came near. "Miss Carmen!" she shouted. "It's me, Polifka, yes, me. Polifka, that's right. The girl should stay with us, the little girl!"

"The girl," Katerine whispered. Then she said it again, "the girl!" A little smile brightened her face, and she willingly allowed her fingers to be moved to sign.

"Now you've got it, you're doing it," the orderly encouraged her. "When the doctor comes, I'll have it done."

Katerine lay motionless. Her typical way of holding her mouth, almost a smile, was there in her agony.

The orderly stood in the corridor and chatted with another orderly. It was midnight. The seven other patients in the ward were asleep in their beds, and Katerine was in the grip of death. Sweat stood on her forehead, and her tongue moved heavily in light, senseless talk. Doors opened and closed. A physician came, looked over at Katerine, and told the orderly who was busily scurrying about, "Give her milk!" Disregarding his orders, she went out into the corridor and continued her conversation. As it was approaching one in the morning, a male porter arrived and said, "Dr. Rössler would like to know if there's a free bed in Ward 25. He called to ask me to bring a gurney upstairs."

"Well, he will know when I tell him. It's occupied. That's where we are."

"But Rössler told me there would be a bed free."

"I am here, and he is downstairs. But he thinks he knows better."

The orderly decided to go check for herself and found Katerine growing cold. Her mouth and eyes were wide open from the struggle with death. She looked like a ghost, but her body lay still in very deep peace.

Amid arguments and opposing words they wrapped the body in a sheet and carried it downstairs for Dr. Rössler to perform the post-mortem examination. He ordered them to get the bed ready for the next patient who had arrived.

In the meantime, at Goldscheider's there was fun and merriment. One more season had passed wonderfully well. There was a host of fresh, elegant young girls with high temperaments who joked amicably and a bevy of interested, generous gentlemen who laughed along with them. There were expensive wines in the cellar, and in the salon there was a beautiful piano that sounded like silver bells, which the music professor handled masterfully. In a friendly mood and with plentiful tips he played an extra portion of "Classics," as he proudly announced. True enough, in these very rooms one could listen to Franz Abt's "A Maiden's Prayer" or Wagner's "Isolde's Love Death." For what it is worth, this was something of value.

Twice a week the doctor came to the house and examined the girls. Those who were ill were banished without ado. But if the good doctor made faces and said a case was harmless and the usual precautions were sufficient, Goldscheider stood by her rights and had her taken to the hospital. If girls returned after recovering, they were sent to other houses, usually to the one in the province with which the madam had a lively exchange. The madam never let a girl stay around in the house after she had been assigned to A2, as the hospital's division for prostitutes was called.

Of course Goldscheider could rarely use a girl for trade who had been returned to her. Here Theobald Sucher performed his duty, and so did Carlotta. Carlotta had transformed herself into the most subservient of servants and always had advice to offer in matters. Both she and Sucher had an enormous circle of acquaintances among owners of cheap music halls, wineries, cabarets, and among owners of police-approved and underground brothels. They did extensive business in trading out fading creatures, driven to ruin by prostitution. Carlotta collected them from Goldscheider's and, in exchange, provided young wares. She generally entrapped girls at petty-bourgeois dance halls and from inns. She went to these places with a small, grotesquely ugly seamstress, Moosmann, who was useful for just about everything. Goldscheider had brought Moosmann along with her from her former businesses. Of course, in most instances, Goldscheider could not put the girls they had enticed and enlisted directly into living quarters at the brothel.

There were some who were employed, admittedly for poor pay, in the most varied day-time jobs. They worked as governesses, receptionists, models, a certain type of chic salesgirl, and cashiers. Some were young, naïve girls who did needlework. They were engaged at Goldscheider's a few hours in the evening and had to split the money they got with her. Carlotta suggested married women, too, the notorious wives of men who traveled or of agents. But Goldscheider rejected her suggestion out of hand. The part-time girls were usually single. They paid regular, unreduced prices for what they consumed in the salon and left with a tolerable sum. They were not in the salon on a regular basis. Goldscheider had them on call for certain occasions so that she was never short-handed. The cautious woman on call knocked at Sucher's door, and the agreeable bureaucrat provided her with dozens of passbooks to have on hand, should the police request them.

Goldscheider had established one last reliable source for acquiring girls. This source was secure: public maternity clinics and hospitals. She took in these schoolgirls, effectively raised them, and exploited them. She maintained friendly, well-paid connections to the porters and women orderlies at these centers for assurances they would inform her when someone suitable for her business arrived.

These injured children were from deplorable circumstances and now a disgrace in society. They saw their life as a burden. They were desperate for hope and eager to believe the depictions and promises of a care-free life. The women orderlies at the maternity clinics let sweet promises flow like honey from their lips. They spoke of how wonderful everything there would be and how exceptionally fine and dandy pleasure-filled days there would pass. Once the way was paved, Goldscheider appeared and resolutely banished any doubts the girls had. She promised to place the baby with a foster mother in the countryside. Foster mothers, she promised, were always looking to take on children. It was obvious most of these mothers were glad at heart to be rid of the pressing burden of a baby. For all of them motherhood meant the dreadful awakening from a foolish dream of pleasurable sensuality. In those iron beds with course, grey-linen sheets lay women who tutored by the hour, housemaids, and those who did needlework, alongside daughters of the middle class who had been disinherited. There were also very immature children of the working class, fourteen to sixteen years old. They lay abed ashen and emaciated, glad to have a roof over their heads in their suffering.

Milada had to accompany the good madam on these and similar business trips. She sat with the driver of the coach and kept watch over the meager baggage of the new acquisition. From inside the carriage Milada heard screaming and crying at first, but Goldscheider calmed the girls with a friendly tone so that by the time they arrived at Carlotta's or Red House, the eyes of the "fresh" girl were glowing with expectation. Goldscheider's gravitas in acquiring girls between respectability and downfall gave her salon its special quality. The new acquisitions gave Red House a certain nuance that sparked the interest of the smart set.

Hers was an establishment for love in which the common type of whore was almost completely absent.

Dangerously systematic and predatory, Goldscheider gained entrance to the ranks of the bourgeoisie and made inroads wherever she was able to find a crack or fault in that milieu. And truth be told she was able to find plenty.

Since the proprietor of Red House was not able to accommodate all the young flesh that came her way by these means in either her or Carlotta's business, she came upon the idea of trafficking. And like anything this brilliant woman put her mind to, this business, too, was a smashing success.

Under her leadership an extensive trade in girls was established, and interested parties across Europe knew about it right away. It was in high demand. This undertaking became the main source of her wealth, which was fast accruing. Simultaneously she ran Red House in its original, fine style, the maintenance of which, it goes without saying, cost her dearly.

She took a certain hidden pleasure in the fact that aristocrats, foreigners, globetrotters, and writers often frequented her salon. Universally they found it a unique attraction of its kind. Quite a few of them engaged Goldscheider in conversation, and they talked on a wide range of topics. They followed the accomplishments of this practical woman with interest. She was forever occupied with an array of ideas and ambitious plans. She was thinking of expanding, perhaps putting in a few intimate rooms with newspapers and billiards, like in a club or a modern cabaret. But she was so very busy with all her interests that she did not have time to do it all.

Even though she did not remodel Red House as fully as she intended, the residents found it sufficiently satisfactory. There were no arguments and no complaints. Money was there, and they had it for a while. They enjoyed their young lives. True enough, as long as they were young and happy, healthy and productive,

Goldscheider surrounded her ladies with ease and every comfort. One of Goldscheider's greatest and most useful bits of wisdom was never to use the full extent of her power against someone she had at a disadvantage. She was in league with the greatest social injustice, the one that hovers darkly on the wing over the depths of human existence. Allied with that she had her triumph.

In the course of time at Red House under Goldscheider's administration, Milada, the little housemaid, shot up tall. Her slender, agile body may have been put to better use had she not hidden herself in the most pathetic and raggedy clothes that Moosmann tailored for her from the clothes others had thrown out. She wore her heavy, brown hair in braids—a far cry from Katerine's distinctively coiffed red hair. Milada pinned her braids behind her head in a lump. With open eyes she watched. Her lively, glowing eyes revealed an unusual awareness and keen assessment of people and situations. They resembled light fog pierced by the sun. The girl ran upstairs and down, slipped in and out of rooms, cleaned, fetched, and listened to gossip. She was abused as the listening ear for secrets, gossip, petty and mean-spirited intrigues—all of which gained them less than it would have in any other part of society. She lived as a small, unobtrusive grub among bright-colored, fluttering butterflies. Nobody, it seemed, was aware of her. Nobody was concerned about her.

She served in the salon deftly and quickly. Milada took care of the needs of the guests and seemed to understand their every wish and their individual tastes. She did the ladies' hair, dressed them, made the coffee, and kept tabs on the silver and porcelain. She knew all things at all times in each and every corner of the house. She garnished sandwiches with a flair that made them appealing. Everything she did she did naturally. Why, then, was Milada there? One person alone understood how indispensable she was. That was the madam. Elise Goldscheider hardly spoke to her, did not acknowledge her. But in the swirl of people and their loud chatter, she did not miss a thing Milada did. Goldscheider took note. The importance of this experience would resound throughout Milada's future.

While she tidied up the ladies' rooms, she listened to their chatter with astonishment.

"I don't even want to think what'll happen to me. Things can only get worse," one of them said. Another replied, "Well, whatever happens is bound to happen. We will all leave here sometime. When I leave, I just want to go out happy." Milada could not imagine. Why did they talk like that? These were people who had the good fortune of being at Goldscheider's! The words of the madam to the new arrivals sounded very different: "People don't have to leave here penniless and without hope. Be smart and save your money! That's how you'll get ahead."

How many times had Milada heard that! And how often had she herself observed this to be true. Goldscheider's words of practical wisdom became the foundation for this young soul and lifted her out of total nihilism.

This observation from Goldscheider also gave her security: "Anybody who comes to Red House is worth something. If you leave and take money, the world is yours." Milada took this message personally as we all take certain messages that inform our souls and give us strength. Milada was proud of this house and its reputation and renown. Her pride was the same as the pride middle-class people have about their families. These feelings of worth from early childhood found our complex emotional structure.

Milada had a strong, richly endowed soul to take sustenance from such a poor and limited diet. Milada was proud that Red House, the place she was born and where she lived, was famous. In no other establishment in town were there such lovely, sweet girls or such impeccable service as here, and people knew that. She had heard generous praise from guests and agents repeatedly.

As one gentleman said to another, “It’s worth it to come here for the madam alone.”

Yes, Goldscheider! Her name had a positive ring in the area. Quite often guests or agents from other countries came, bought girls, and took them along. What you find at Goldscheider’s is *chic*, they said. “It’s *chic* and good fortune,” said Olympia with a sigh as they walked out the door. But what did all that fame and fortune mean? Most of the girls had to move on to houses like the Excelsior or La belle Francaise. Or they went to Zimmermann’s. They indulged in all kinds of idiocy with their money. They threw it away without a thought. They drank, they smoked, bought lottery tickets, and spent large sums on piles of expensive clothes they did not take care of. And the seamstress Moosmann flattered them and encouraged them to waste their money. Their tabs grew bigger and bigger; and their way out of debt, narrower. Milada’s mother had always drunk and bought treats. Katerine never held onto money. But not Milada! She did not want to sink into penury like that, absolutely not. She did not want to fail. She sought to be reliable, competent, and productive, someone everybody in Red House, even Madame Goldscheider, could be proud of.

Milada took stock. Quite a few of the girls left Red House and went on to something better in life, like Anka Balling. The young Count Laurin had taken her along with him. He had her take ballet lessons, and now she was dancing around under lots of lights in a silver dress. There was even a piece in the paper about her. If Anka did that, what was not possible! Admittedly Anka was beautiful, and Milada was not.

Day and night the small, gray housemaid thought about her future and kept her thoughts to herself. All her time was taken up with work. She loved work. Her lonely thoughts carried her from one task to the next. She was not the sort to sit idle. Milada was always completely engaged in whatever she was doing. That was her way. It made her feel good to clean up messes, roll up her sleeves at the sight of disorder, and make sure everything was clean and in its place! She simply could not understand how ladies lay about in bed and watched the flies buzz around. To be sure they were up at night working while she was fast asleep. "It does make them tired," she thought. "When I'm in the salon, I'll be like that, too."

She knew it would come to that. Goldscheider had promised her that when her mother died, and Goldscheider always carried through on her promises. Milada's flights of fancy were quite unlike those of most young people. The arc of Milada's dreams and her image of her future were bound to a strict, excruciatingly serious reality. Her fantasies were spun of earnestness and concern. They came from the facts of the life she knew directly. This child learned from harsh experience. She had witnessed people dying in a miserable morass. She had seen tired bodies and souls broken. Out of these real memories she constructed for herself a way upward into the future.

She had no idea about the scorn of the masses that hung over her young being and threatened to destroy her just as she planned to spread her wings. Completely unaware of this danger, Katerine's daughter slid through childhood. She carefully saved each penny and kept her pennies in a box. She was happy when she heard them rattling against each other and fingered the silver coins in the heap of copper with pleasure. She did not want to be ruined, no, no! She did not want to end up ill and in misery at Zimmermann's or the Excelsior. That is why Milada loved money. It would help her. This smart child of the street deliberately confronted mounting barriers. She tried to understand them and take them on. Her lips were narrowed in thought as she went about her work. She prepared herself against approaching threats. Yet danger from afar awaited her. She was armed.

"Mrs. Polifka," Milada asked one Sunday afternoon as they sat in the kitchen that had been scrubbed clean, at a moment when the world was asleep and peaceful, "Mrs. Polifka, what would you do if you had to leave?"

The porter replied, "Me? Leave here? Go away? Did you hear something?"

"No, I didn't," Milada assured her. "Not a word, nothing. It's because things will always change, won't they?"

"I'd be very unhappy to go! My old man is a mechanic at Eger train station. I could be a porter there. After this." She sighed, "I've worked in new places plenty often enough."

"Well, and after that?"

Polifka looked at the girl long and hard.

"And when both of you don't have work anymore," Milada went on, "where will you spend your golden years?" The fourteen-year-old made a serious face as she used Mademoiselle Olympia's favorite words.

Polifka answered, "We'll go to the old folks' home, my old man and me. But probably not the one for poor folks. Folks like us can go to a place you pay for. When the time comes and if you stay a good girl, you can come visit me in the garden there."

Milada stared off. "A garden," she repeated unsure. "Are you sure there is a garden there?"

"Pretty sure, yes. For example my husband's aunt is there, and she has a good life. She's got a small garden outside of her window. Folks who pay have it better. His aunt is a housemother. Everybody treats her nice. And she gets paid a bit of money to boot. I'd sure like to be a housemother."

She put her hands on her lap and looked off contentedly into the future.

"Mrs. Polifka, can anybody go there?"

"I think so!" Polifka became defensive. "You need some money, that's why they call it the old folks' home for people who pay. And you need to be reliable. Those are the two things you need. On top of that you have to be decent." She gestured to the floor above. "For the likes of those useless women, there's the poor folks' home." She held her tongue. Milada was silent, too. All of a sudden, she had found a way out of the alley. She allowed her thoughts to play in a garden, a large, expansive garden with chestnut trees and benches, just like the garden of the Soldiers' Hospital you could see from the window in the corridor. That would be a while! Over there, people were very old and tired and had no more wishes. They were not concerned about being prettier or more charming or more elegant than everybody else. The windows in an old folks' home, she imagined, ought to look just like the windows of the women's rooms in the Soldiers' Hospital. They had thin white curtains, and inside where the sunlight shone there was the bed. That was the "blessed end."

Mademoiselle Olympia could not come up with anything better when she spoke about the end. The child weighed and weighed out this thought. Could she arrive at this destination? Polifka had said you have to be reliable. That she was. Money! She let go a sigh. You always needed that. It was part of "staying on top," in the beginning and at the blessed end. Money was important for everything! She had to tend to that while she was young and smart and had opportunities.

But decent? Was she decent? What did that mean? She took the word one syllable at a time to try to make sense of it, but she could not. So, with a sigh, she gave up trying.

Before she went to bed that day, she embraced Polifka and looked at her with her large, gray eyes.

"Polifka? Can we go some day to see your aunt? I'd really like to see what it's like at an old folks' home. Can we?"

And without waiting for her answer, with a lively spark in her eyes and on her cheeks and forehead, she left in a hurry.

"Yes, we can go look in on the old woman," Polifka muttered and sank into pleasant thoughts.

At the time there were ten lovely ladies in Red House. They were very comfortable there under Madame Goldschelder's regime. Above and beyond their abundant tips they received a small percentage of the money for having guests. Goldscheider kept careful track of these amounts in her books, and she never ever held back a penny when someone departed. You had to admit there was never any dirty dealing in Red House. Goldscheider never added in the cost of transportation. She also did not charge for theater or circus tickets, should a person choose to go. Goldscheider picked up the tab for that herself. Little benefits like these certainly spoke for her.

Angela, a very lovely seventeen-year-old Italian, had been at Zimmermann's for two days and ran away. She left all her cash behind. She told horror stories about this obscure little business. You paid for breakfast, for maid service in the morning, for a bath, for the hairdresser, and for a manicure. A toiletry set with soap, powder, cosmetics, and perfume cost twenty, and on and on. You were surely better off living on your own than at Zimmermann's.

"Yes," another woman sighed, "in the city that might be so, but where will you ever find a room to rent? And once you have a room, then you have to go out and pick up customers. Then you have to pay the landlady, the municipal inspector, the police, and the neighbors, and on and on. You're up to your eyebrows in expenses. And after fourteen days they can still throw you out."

Lulu Wollner, a slender girl with dark hair and the dreamy eyes of a madonna, agreed with a laugh. She had to go looking for a place ten times in one month. She bounced from one house to the next just because some Protestant preacher had made it his business to follow her. He ratted on her to the police and hunted her down. The preacher told the police his "little girls were on their way home from school every day and had to see that woman." Yes, these things do happen. "The last word is when you can't even go sit in a café. Take my friend Poldi for instance. She does quite well for herself in Berlin. She works in a bar and had a boyfriend. He had her charged 30,000 marks for being around his kid."

Angela raised her hand as if to ward off evil. In her broken German she said, "I have bad things there, me, too. Work in bar!! All that, all things bad. Police damn. Police no let go."

All of them agreed. The police rode on their backs like Satan and spat in their soup. If a girl was owed money and the man was putting up a fuss on the street, the police snarled at the girl. And if she stood up for her rights, then the cop took her by the arm, shoved her back into her house, and made sure the porter kept her inside. If there was an argument with the housekeeper, the housekeeper was always right—whatever the situation. The housekeepers knew the undercover police, paid them off with the little money they made by ugly means from their renters, and that was how it went.

Working on your own was definitely not worth it. You were forever looking for a new place to stay, had to get registered with the police, and then you had to go upstairs to service "some old man." You could not stand the way a man with the police looked at you and asked you questions. You ended up having to bring him gifts, usually things customers had given you, like rings, bracelets, or blouses. Then the customers saw you gave away their gifts, and they cursed at you. Somehow you had to please them all. You were lucky to have a nice, good-looking guy all your own. You wanted someone who was not looking around and choosey. It was good luck to find somebody to take you home and keep you warm. That was real luck!

Lulu told the girls about a young officer she had a stint with last year in the town of Bruck.

"I used to wait for him in a small house at the window across from an open field. Man, was that sweet! Such a darling guy!"

Angela threw up her arms. "An officer!? They all lousy! I no do with officer. No for much money." She spread out her ten fingers. "No for so much gold."

Angela had come from Trieste. When she was fourteen her parents set her up with a wine dealer in the big city. She tried various things there but was soon fired. She had been a nanny, a model, and the girl who encouraged guests to drink liquor in coffee houses at night. Then she took up with officers and had some bad experiences. Finally she got a job in an infamous theater where she sang in her little birdie voice and made bawdy gestures. In this theater, together with a couple of men, she coerced inexperienced men to gamble after the show. Sucher and her "old man" picked her up and, despite her protests of innocence, kept her in jail for fourteen days.

When she got out of jail, Carlotta generously found her a job. The crafty Italian, ever on the look-out for profit, had upgraded her place of business in recent years. The pub was expanded, and a number of elegant private booths had been added. A quartet played for guests in the common room. A buffet was put in where the bar had been. At the buffet there were the most seductive little pastries on display. Three elegant ladies in black silk dresses served these pastries, while four other ladies, provocatively done up in party dresses, serviced the men in the private booths, where the only beverage was champagne.

Angela was neither smart nor temperamental. She was very pleasing primarily because she had kept a certain, unstudied way of casting down her eyes and a soft, feminine way of withdrawing when she was unhappy with things.

She had one strong point, but it rubbed Carlotta the wrong way. She was immovable—either with bribes of money or threats of hunger—when it came to going with officers. She simply up and disappeared if pressured to service them. She hid in a corner and cried. Angela was filled with such fear that the Italian had to look away, whether out of sympathy or anger.

A fine young bourgeois man, moved by good qualities, started to take an active interest in the lovely, helpless Angela. Since he was also a valued regular guest in the establishment, he was allowed to take her out of the house after having had a generous number of rounds of champagne. Carlotta allowed this because she knew Angela would have to come back to her in the not-too-distant future. After an excursion of fourteen days in Berlin, the young man brought her back at her fervent request. Angela wept copiously and refused to return to Carlotta. So Goldscheider picked her up.

At Goldscheider's she enjoyed the peace, the quiet, and the laziness and folly of the ladies, but at times she had to shudder, remembering certain events in her life. "Don't go near an officer," remained her motto after her bad experiences: "Me no do with no officer, sure not, no."

"Money is like liquor in their hands," Goldscheider said to Horner. "The girls are incorrigible when they have money. When they've got it, they have a feeling of power, and that's like a rush for them."

"You and your smart owl! I kind of like the idea of Goldscheider as Minerva. You, too, are partially responsible here for their squandrous spending."

"Well, they can't use it anyway. I don't want to make them feel like dogs because when people feel like dogs, they show their teeth. And then some young gentlemen with their mania for saving people will surely do some stupid things to spite me."

"Your practical love of humanity never fails to impress me. You are the only person I know who feels and thinks."

"Horner, I'll let you in on something. When I think about how I might spend the rest of my life, I mean after being in business, I could do something worthwhile. But after me, things here might go to hell."

He had a lascivious grin on his lips. "My dear Elise, what do you imagine you will manage to do in all your grandeur when this is done?" he asked slyly.

She looked at him with amusement. "Since you don't tolerate liquor anymore, your mean spirit is in good form and slips right from your thoughts to your tongue. You were almost sweeter to be around when you were drunk."

"I know," he said snidely. "You are a Jewess. And you are sentimental. You love to see other people's hearts break, hear sorrowful nightingales sing, and read cheap romances where innocence triumphs in the end and vice curls up and dies. You love all those things you don't see in life. Would you perhaps like to be a Catholic?"

She saw through his insults to the emotional discomfort that engulfed him when he was around a person with a strong will.

"Thank God I distinguish between my good business and my poor person," she said with a laugh, "because I do want to enjoy myself."

"I might have guessed," he scolded her enraged. "I never should have had anything to do with you in the first place. I should have just left you stuck where you were, stuck in your old ways. You still can't let go at all! Your Jewishness holds you back. You need to learn a thing or two about ancient Greece, but trying to teach you would be a waste. Judaism always wins out, and your dear departed David is always right! Clearly all you know of Fichte and Spinoza came to you predigested. Your mind is caught in a loop."

She fiddled a while with some papers, gave some instructions to Olympia who had come in, looked at some light-blue material Moormann had laid out for nightgowns, indicated with her finger a model in a fashion magazine, and then returned to Horner. He sat sunken with glassy eyes, staring straight ahead.

"Say you're grateful, Horner, for what I am about to tell you. I have at long, long last come to see the truth of your words. You've always called me an egoist, but I never ever believed you. I thought your judgment was unfair to me. At the time I worked like a dog and made sacrifices for others, for my precious mother, for my brothers and sister, for my father, and for all the lazy asses in our house. Then I got married and kept doing the same old sacrificial things. At first I slaved away diligently for my nasty mother-in-law, working like an idiot in her business. I ran the errands in town, took care of the baby, did it all until David got sick. Taking care of David was no easy job, Horner. He was looking at dying, and I had to keep going. I did not rest for one moment. At the time I saw myself as terribly good. I thought I was selfless. But you saw who I was. You looked deeper. You called me a sentimental egoist. Today I see that's true. I almost killed myself caring for them, for all of them—yet all for myself. I was absolutely thorough in working for their well-being. The craziest part about it was I didn't care one iota about them, their interests or their pain. I did not care what any of them thought, not one of them, not even my own mother. They were all aliens to me. I worked my fingers to the bone, but I only ever really cared about myself and about my daughter. I live for Alma Luzie! I can't help all of you. What I do in my life is for her." With that she stood up.

"Don't make faces, Horner. You would have given up on me if I hadn't been an egoist. Helping this one, helping that one: what does that mean to me? I am here for myself, and I keep on going—even when things get dirty."

"My dear Elise, you're in a dirty business because of me. Getting out..." He laughed a poisonous laugh.

"Don't you worry, Horner. I will pull myself up out of this mess on my own. People have done that before me. Isn't that right?"

"*Apage*, may the devil be gone, you Jew!" he pronounced coldly and made the ecclesiastic gesture of exorcism that was supposed to banish her.

"Maybe it helps you be rid of Jews! The likes of us do not bargain with some heavenly reward. It's very possible this is a Jewish trait. But our race has taken the hit far too often. No wonder, Horner! We deal in money! We love ourselves and our families and nothing else in this world."

The means by which this clever woman had arrived at the pinnacle of her life were unusual and gnarled.

She spent her childhood in wretched poverty. This scrawny, neglected Jewish child evolved into a voluptuous, sentimental young woman, full of longing for the love of a man and erotic tenderness. She lived in a two-room apartment in a basement with her father Jonas Chaim Koch, six siblings, and just as many shift bed-renters. The care of her mother, who had a lung ailment, and of the younger children, as well as minding the business fell on her young shoulders alone. Sixteen-year-old Elise found it a random stroke of good fortune that David Goldscheider, a student of the Talmud and temple scribe, came into her life. He used gentle words and showed a friendly interest in her, although she had lived a life of unrelieved misery. To her he seemed a better, higher cut of human than any of the men around her; better than her father and much better than the renters—all from Galicia. They lay about, unwashed and dressed shabbily, all day long on sacks of straw or wooden crates. They sat and chewed onions on salted bread. These men intoned their prayers in loud, singing voices and asked each other snappy questions in their dialect. They descended on these questions like hungry ravens, diving for a piece of meat in their midst. Not a one of these strong, young men worked. When money in the household was tight, then one or another of them would get up, half asleep and feeling put upon, and crawl up the steps of the cellar. Then he would shake himself like a bird rustling his feathers and look around for some kind of job. But most days these men preferred to hang out together and wait for *nissim* (that is: miracles). To the members of the Koch Family, David Goldscheider looked like a learned man. He had a reputation in Talmudic circles and was an honored guest. He was small and homely. His complexion was sallow, and he had a small, blond beard, which rose in a thin line to his side curls. David was certainly not the type that Elise especially liked. She was slender and had red hair. Her thoughts sooner turned to the elegant, tall men who worked in the trenches. She saw these men when she was on her way in town. One of them would have suited her. But a poor Jewish girl had to take what was available. And David was the first man who brought a whiff of love into her musty life.

The young creature who had to grow up so quickly showed him sympathy; also, desire and encouragement. She was happy and had a strange, tingly satisfaction when she saw him blush while she leaned against him. She took hold of his cold fingers that crawled timidly around her thin blouse and put them tantalizingly in her hands. Then he stumbled over his words and only came out with a sigh. What struck her about him more than about any of the men in her vicinity was that he came from a nice family and had a regular job.

His mother Judith Goldscheider was known all over the neighborhood. She had a small resale shop, which she ran with steely diligence and tough determination. She had turned it into a reliable store with clothes to rent or buy. She was a tough, robust woman, all wrapped up in Orthodox prejudices. She kept the people in her house in line, and she doted on her one son. She fretted over him. She set store by the fact he was too fine, too delicate, and too educated to work in her shop. His uselessness was both the source of her pride and the cause of her suffering.

"He'll marry and have a wife," she said with a sigh to the people she knew. "Then he will be hers, and she'll have a business. She'll have God's blessings."

Although the old woman loved her son beyond all telling, she would never have tolerated any lazy slacking-off. When, after a three-year period of study at the Merene Row Wolfe Schlomo Ashkenazi School in Bratislava, he returned exhausted and weak, straight away she found him a position as scribe. His modest income, from Sundays, clanked in the pockets of his long black robes and deeply impressed the Koch Family. They felt honored in no small way that such a "pleasing" man was in their midst. And the hazel eyes of all the Kochs looked upward with humility whenever they ran across Judith Goldscheider, who did not have much use for these friends of her son. Once Elise was in her shop to get some used clothes for the children, and she looked around in amazement at this new, fine, quiet world free of sighs and sorrows. There were no sick people groaning, children screaming, nor any biting stench of onions. How lovely it was there! She saw heavy oak furniture, chairs covered in brown velvet, silver candelabra—"heavy, not expensive!"—but, most of all, she saw the mysterious chest for the Torah. It was adorned with golden cloth and contained silver for the Holy Days and David's costly books.

The old woman with her strange, motionless eyes, looked intently at Elise for a moment, then said, "A house full of healthy people, and not a one moves a muscle to work. The couple of coins you earned for clothing is more of a gift than a piece of gold. Pay attention to what I am telling you: *Gebentsht*, blessed are the hands that do everything on their own. Here, take this wine along for your mother—*nebbish*, if you don't mind."

What David's mother had said did not sit with Elise. She picked up a hateful, even malicious undertone to her words. But the powerful, advantageous way the old woman spoke to her resonated with something similar in her own being. When Elise returned home, everything looked even darker, uglier, and less bearable. Her mother moaned and held baby Jainkef to her breast. But the child squirmed around, angry, and pushed away her empty breast. The fourteen-year-old flower of a girl cooked gruel and put it in a bowl for her little brothers who stuck their dirty fingers in the sticky, sweet treat. Nearby the men hunkered around and shot the breeze, chewed on their onions, and told each other stories or sang songs in Hebrew with low voices.

Father Koch was at the train station, looking for renters. And he found a cheap place, like his own, for those he did not take on—this is how resourceful he was. The Russian and Polish emigrants were especially thankful for his help and gave him small tips. Those tips were his earnings. He was extremely attentive when he was on the job. The eyes of the small, agile man with a dark beard, shot through with silver, sparkled. He listened to the stories of each man, heard about these men's hopes and prospects, took in pieces of advice, registered meaningful gestures, and handed out addresses. He counted the names of the good donors and hoped he might receive a small gift. And, at the end of the day, he invited these strangers to his house for a *plausch*, a chat. His mouth and his legs kept going without stop. But he could not bring himself to put them in the service of a regular job. He was not able to do the simplest of tasks his innumerable well-wishers and doners gave him because of his keen sense of Talmudic devotion. He rested on the Sabbath and observed prayer times and dietary laws. Since he exerted a strong influence about observance on his renters and friends and enticed them to inactivity free of need, a whole mob of strong men lived there from donations and gifts. Sometimes charities sent these men to Jonas Chaim in his basement.

At the time David started to warm up to the Koch Family the darkness of their need dawned on them—dimly. In his company Elise suddenly landed in the realm of a fine, romantic and imaginatively gifted being. His mind was filled with ideas and problems that to this point had been as distant to her as stars in the heavens. David was unencumbered and in harmony with the world. He had no big ambition and did not agonize over impossible wishes. What he needed was there for him in abundance. And that is why he was good.

When Elise complained to him and described the direness of their poverty, David asked, untroubled, "How is that possible? How can this be? How do people live like this?" Or he quickly pulled a book out of his pocket and started to read aloud to her. He read from a novel in which free, brave people performed heroic deeds.

Or he read Elise sweet poems about a shining moon and snuggling violets, or he read her passages from the mystical philosophy of an Oriental man who embraced adversity with arms of love. Then she blushed and her face changed. It became softer, more childlike. And when the breath of her mouth came closer and brushed the coarse blond hair of his beard, she could feel his body tremble, and his thin hand reached for hers. In these moments, she took pleasure in her own power. She did not stifle the feeling of desire that arose, and she was happy to forget her misery.

But things at home became more desperate and serious. Quite often there was no milk in the house for the children or for her failing mother. They chewed bread. They pawned the feather beds, and the silver-plated clock Chaim inherited through the line of fathers in the family went, too.

David was not able to help. His mother had spoken clearly. And the way things looked, she was right.

"Money that's scrounged falls into pockets with holes," she said.

David said, "Elise, couldn't your father just get into some line of work? Some things would work out better if he did." After he spoke, to ease the directness of his words, he said, "Listen, here's some sausage Mother sent you." And he timidly put a package on the lap of the girl who was lost in her worries.

And at long last the stifled willpower of the pensive, miserable girl erupted. She pushed the book David was thumbing through aside and said, "Don't read, David. Today we need to talk. David, you tell your mother we don't need charity anymore, not from her, not from anybody. Things will have to change at our house, otherwise..." She took a deep breath, "Something terrible will happen."

Indeed, a change did take place.

With a start the girl rousted the bevy of men up out of their dull inertia. She became their guide and their boss. She issued commands. She assigned tasks. She pressed them into action with brutal force. She made one last appeal to Chaim's supporters.

She plied them with requests and entreaties. And those who had stopped helping because they were exhausted and saw no returns gave it one more try and did contribute. She did not ask for money or used clothes. She asked for work from the men and work from her older siblings. All of the earlier attempts to find jobs were pursued anew, and the jobs that were offered were accepted.

A stove for roasting chestnuts that had sat rusting in a corner was put to use. This stove was entrusted to the oldest boy. Others took over getting food for breakfast for the employees by working in a kosher warehouse. Another renter went from house to house, hawking "Holiday calendars" and memory books that had been gathering dust in a crate. The care of those who were ill and the meager family business went to the second oldest, the darling. And Elise scurried from house to house and from shop to shop, scouting out piecework.

"Kind Sir, our people do all kinds of work. We distribute fliers, deliver packages, gather information, write out addresses—whatever you have. Please do think of us. We need the work." She turned down money, "No, Sir, please give us work!" And then she repeated the address and her intent, and people began to take note and had sympathy for the red-haired Jewish girl with a firm set about her mouth. She kept after the men and stamped her feet, ran around them like a cat if they slacked off. She made their life of sitting around the house miserable. She ruined their enjoyment of idleness with her acrid words. When, however, they returned in the evening and plunked the money they had earned on the table, she beamed. She invited them to sit down, gave them something to eat, laughed with them, and asked them about their day. And she took charge of the money. She closed her fist around the coins.

"She's making me *meshugge*, driving me nuts," old Chaim bellowed at least one hundred times a day. She had gotten him a post running figures for currencies from client to client at the stock market. The activity did suit his restless temperament since he hated keeping still. But it took up his time. And the trains kept coming, from Kiev, Warsaw, and from Ternopil. They brought Jew after Jew while he was there running figures to clients. Elise kept him on task with sweet words and even sweeter foods.

"When people see you working, they start working. They always follow you, you see that." And then she seasoned the onion sauce and the bread for supper that went on the table.

"How good the bread tastes when you've been working!" She encouraged the young men to work with similar tactics. "You can treat yourself with a bit of meat, white fish in oil, or challah for the Sabbath. And you can get yourselves a nice pack of cards to play games." As things went better and better, she bought one or another a sporty cap he had long wished for, a little pipe, or a green silk bag for his tefillin. She teased wishes and desires out of their dispositions, which had been emptied of hope. She gave them the needful human pleasure in small things they could attain.

But a small bit of leftover change always landed in her slender hands, which were not rough from hard work. Worries about tomorrow were done away with. And in no time at all the bitter misery of the apartment in the basement was shot through with rays of comfort that each of the residents had earned a part of. Their existence was still not dignified. Mother still had no medical attention, and the wretched little children still had no sunlight on the floor. But at least they had enough bread and got sweetened milk, and a satisfaction from eating filled out their haggard faces almost as if they were lit with good fortune. Indeed, it looked as if Elise's attitude had changed in all respects.

Instead of passively receiving David's stories or listening to his reading, she pressed him to teach her German, mathematics, and bookkeeping. Much as he regretted doing this, he had to acquiesce to her wishes. "David, it will really help me. Once I am working in the shop, it'll be too late to learn," she said with importance. And so many an evening, when the others were sitting around visiting and munching, Elise and David sat on a crate covered with white paper and studied. Her mother's anguished, shallow sighs were audible in the next room.

Elise was not one of those students who are sharp and eager, who whip through material, looking to move on. She applied herself to learning a limited amount, but in detail. She was uncommonly thorough, and what she grasped she made use of from then on.

"I have to get this and this and that," she said and divided up the lessons into daily bundles, just as she had parcelled out tasks for others. "I do have to learn some letter writing, and I really need to learn to work with figures, to get that down."

A quiet, unspoken agreement arose between the two of them, although David had not committed to anything.

Often when he wanted to break off the lessons because of his nerves and agitation, Elise kept him going. "David, let's practice some more of these math problems, then I can do all the problems like this by myself. Then on Sunday we can go to the theater. And I invite you," she added proudly.

It is true, Elise had gained a lot of power over him, and he was so strongly attached to this creature that his mother, who had tried to get him to be independent, finally and with reservations, started to relinquish control. David asked for nothing, and he demanded nothing. But he was not eating and slept poorly. He awoke covered in sweat and had headaches.

Old Doctor Robitschek shook his head. "Madame Judith, get advice from a matchmaker!" he said seriously.

"Dear Doctor," she cried, "a child, such a child, and then to lose him like this."

"Is his girlfriend really so awful? As I know David..."

The old woman shrugged. "Does he say anything, tell his mother anything? All I know is these people are shirks and avoid work. Oh, Doctor, people live by working and eating bread. How can one of those people fit in our family?" As a mother, she knew she had to seek out good advice. After a stormy conversation with her son, during which she swore amid tears she would never ever give in, Judith put on her silk dress and her sable stole, old as the hills, and brought Elise from her apartment in the basement to her house. She jealously studied Elise's pale, angular face, red hair, and thin, tense mouth with her penetrating, swollen eyes. And she was astonished.

Afterwards she spoke with her friend Esther Schwarzer who was blind. "Esther, if you could see, you wouldn't have chosen this girl for David, not for ten thousand gulden. But I bit the bullet and said yes."

"You did the right thing, my child," the blind woman said. The old woman felt obliged to add a condition after agreeing to the match. The Koch Family had to go back to Galicia.

And since all those concerned stated they were happy to agree, Chaim and his family were packed off to their homeland, supplied with money and decisive words of farewell. This was before the marriage ceremony.

Then the two of them had a wedding.

The intern and the maid at Judith's shop were relieved of their jobs, and the newly married woman worked in their place.

Judith very quickly recognized the attributes of her daughter-in-law and put her talents to maximal good use. And Elise adapted. This did not mean she had reached a standstill in her evolution or that her budding independence was interrupted. Rather her soul felt filled from the bottom up with the air of natural well-being. She had things that belonged to her, possessions she first regarded with awe before she allowed herself to use them. She had underwear and clean, nice tunics with lace and her name embroidered on them. And she had a dress for the store, one for wearing in town, and another of black silk for the Sabbath.

Together with David, who beamed with joy, she took over the alcove in the apartment, and Judith slept in the next room.

Judith slept on a narrow, hard, upholstered velvet sofa. However much her son begged her and however much Elise encouraged her, the old woman remained stiff-necked in her resolve to stay on the couch. She told David simply, "Don't you know why you got married? Where do you think your mother should sleep?"

Slowly, very slowly, what had been unthinkable to Elise came to be, and she came to accept the new order of things. Yet she always retained a respect for her mother-in-law and felt gratitude toward her; she felt gratitude toward her hard, yellow hands that had accomplished it all. Elise worked and slaved unshrinkingly and cared for Judith after she had a severe infection of the peritoneum and edema. She held up under the malice from this mother who was never satisfied or at peace.

"She's poisoning me, my son. She wants to get rid of me, believe me. I'm not making this up. Nobody should touch that red woman," she whispered to David, while Elise calmly mixed her medicine and her husband, with tears in his eyes, lifted up his mother and smiled.

"I pulled her up out of the *dreck*, out of the mud. I got her her first real dress," the ill woman complained to her guests. And when guests tried to remind her of her daughter-in-law's industry and dutifulness, she waved their words away with her swollen hands. "I want to tell you something. She does work, it's true. But who is she doing this for? For me? How does her work help me? Is she taking care of my future or her own? What I needed on Earth I got with my own hands. I managed everything, right up to preparing my death shroud. Ever since she's been in this house—just ask her yourself—she's taken me aside and said, '*Nebbish*, just let me do it.' And him? What is a loving son? Haven't I seen with my very own eyes what kind of wife she is to him? And what kind of a man is he? God is just. You can believe me, she'll never carry a child."

Soon after their wedding Elise felt well and was optimistic. But carrying a crate of clothes from the warehouse to the shop was more than she could do. She was sorely aggrieved, cried in private, and complained. To distract her, David hit upon the idea of giving her lessons as he had in the past. But accounting did not interest her anymore, and she could not put her head to learning algebra. She said, when he asked, that she would like to learn German and a bit of natural history.

And although the old woman, as expected, was put out by these *narishkeiten*, her idiocies, David asserted himself and found Elise a tutor who came twice a week. Her new tutor was an old customer in Goldscheider's shop. The old woman called him dismissively, "a blasphemer and a master shuffler." He had a doctorate in philosophy and was a retired assistant principal of a preparatory school, Arnold Egidy Horner. With the absolute intellectual superiority of a dissipated being he met with the red-haired and, as he calculated, inevitably dissatisfied Jewish woman.

He put on airs, loved to say, "we Aryans," wore common clothes, and with trepidation gave the scrappy watchdog Judith a wide berth. He also slunk around her space. He said she had the nasty habit of assessing, right through the heaviest trouser fabric, money, and other unimportant things.

He said of Elise, "It's strange. She's not gifted. She doesn't learn quickly. But when she grasps something, then it expands in her mind, evolves of its own, and reaches out in all directions. Out of one idea, one concept, she comes up with hundreds of her own. Difficult entrance, solid flooring." He poked David in the side and grinned lasciviously. David did not understand him and smiled out of politeness.

The twice-weekly lesson they had originally agreed upon soon became a lesson a day. Tutor and student spoke in lowered voice in the apartment's alcove, and David defended this arrangement when the old woman wanted to intervene. When Judith was feeble and bed-ridden, she was forced to look on during the newlyweds' dreaded "comic theater." Elise made a greater effort than did David to avoid provoking the old woman's dissatisfaction and bad temper. She buried her books away from Judith's searching gaze. She never spoke about her lessons. Horner had to take off his shoes when he came in the house, and they spoke in whispers until the old woman's rattling breath told them she was asleep.

"That woman has the mind of a slaveholder," Horner swore. He was always full of words of rebellion, but a rebellion others would have to mount.

Elise looked at him coldly with her gray eyes.

"It's all hers," Elise said. "She owns everything. And she should have everything just as she wants till the end." Then David looked up from his book and thanked her with a gentle smile.

Elise's mouth had, since birth, corners that were twisted down in an expression of irony. She had never been aware of this feature or the way people understood it. It misled Horner for a good while. He imagined he could persuade her to participate in his alcoholic debauchery and much else. He stated he wanted to liberate her from thinking of finances and discretion. He saw in her the perfect comrade to share in his vices. Together, he imagined, they would display the colors of the providential Superior Individual of the coming age, quasi after Nietzsche. He told himself that would be their common goal. She struggled to follow his disjointed philosophizing, which inevitably was a departure from the topic. His rambling usually wore her out.

Elise remained adamant on certain points. Horner did not register her resistance at first. He let himself get carried away with the notion he had found the right young woman. And he let his fantasies, born of abnormal impulses, run wild. Much later he came to understand that Elise's sober, no-nonsense temperament never did accompany him on his strange flights of fancy. But when he fully understood she did not share his interest, the realization did not bother him. Her slim, milky-white body, which in the first years of their acquaintance had excited and distressed him, had lost its appeal for him.

This same year, as Judith Goldscheider was preparing to die, Elise gave birth to a girl who was given the name Miriam after the old woman. The new child also received an expensive pearl necklace with the understanding that only she would wear it—but not until the day she married in a Jewish ceremony under a traditional canopy. The old woman held the child in her shaking arms. And when looking at the little one with a sculpted face and red hair, she pronounced in her selfish, old-woman way, "Just like David." She loved the child. Elise had to smile. She called the girl Alma Luzie and did not put up with people calling her anything else once her mother-in-law died.

The little girl was surrounded with luxuries her mother never would have deemed fitting for herself. The baby had a room painted blue with white furniture, and she had a Christian maid. Elise did not want her to hear the grim Hebrew prayers or bedtime stories.

David, the weakling without will, looked on while these things happened. He became more seriously ill and tired, and he had relinquished the position of scribe. He sat bent over his books, day in and day out, and wrote letters she did not have time to write herself. Everything was going well. The business flourished under Elise's hand. David was almost completely happy. Only this disturbed him and sometimes even terrified his devout, gentle soul: his child was a stranger to him. Was it his child? Sometimes he tiptoed into the child's room where a Christian woman in a white apron was sitting, attending the little girl.

"Papa," said the child and extended her hand to him politely. When David called her, the syllables of this strange, elegant name were difficult for him to get out, "Alma Luzie." He was almost afraid of this child.

"What will happen," he worried at times, "if my child is ashamed of her father?" He was as he was, wore long black robes and sidelocks. Is that good? Is it a blessing? He never mentioned a word of these doubts to Elise, although these worries pained him like nothing else on Earth.

Elise ran with her hair flying and face glowing out of the warehouse, out of the shop, the places where she spent her time, into the child's room. She lifted the baby on high, shouted with joy, and ran back to work beaming with delight. How she rejoiced in the sweetness of Alma Luzie! She was charmed by her round, pink, flower-like little body. She surrounded her daughter with the brightness and happiness she had never known.

Fate protected David from future conflicts.

As Alma Luzie was paddling around in the nursery, a case of influenza cut him down. He never got back up.

His illness lasted months. Elise cared for him devotedly and conscientiously. She did not let anyone else care for him, although Dr. Robitschek strongly recommended a caregiver.

The child was not allowed into the sickroom. Her mother was afraid of contagion. He agreed with that.

In the afternoon of a spring day he passed. Just that morning he had said his prayers as he always did. Elise came in her apron, smelling of almond soap, rice flour and chamomile.

She said in an uplifting tone, "We washed Alma's hair with chamomile so it won't be as red as mine."

David sighed, "What all you plan for this child! Make sure you don't raise a Christian goy."

She narrowed her eyes. "David, David!" she said with a laugh, mocking a warning.

"Do what you like," he murmured. "It is, thank God, only a girl."

She straightened his covers, put the buzzer in his hand, and went back to the store. Yes, and at eleven she ran upstairs to check in on him since the electric buzzer kept ringing loudly. It was still ringing when she stood at his bed where she found him soaked with sweat in a fetal position. The buzzer rang on in his stiff hand and drove her half-mad. A hemorrhage of the lungs had ended his life.

Six months later Alma Luzie became Protestant, and Goldscheider kept with a difficult decision. She placed her six-year-old daughter in a well-known boarding school in Dresden. The luxury of an English education almost eclipsed her financial resources. But after she experienced the ambience of Goethe Street, she firmly resolved Alma would spend her childhood at this school. She should never again have to enter the resale clothing store, brown from age and dirt, where her mother-in-law had slaved away, selling. Alma should never become a girl of the ghetto, contained within those very narrow social limits. She should not be dragged from one *beshoy* meeting arranged by a Hasidic matchmaker to another until the moment she is married when, in the best case, she is set up by her husband in some bourgeois misery. To avoid this possibility, Alma's mother knew she had only one thing left: work and more work.

Nobody knew her in Dresden, no one had heard anything about her or her work. There she was only Alma Lucie's "little mother." Twice a year she went to visit and always returned delighted by the appearance and bearing of her one and only. Oh, what a slender, elegant little creature she was! This child had the romantic thoughtfulness of her father and the radiance of her mother's gray eyes.

True enough, this child was well suited to the quiet, prestigious setting of Goethe Street. She lived in a house full of paintings, statues, and people who were fine, gracious, and laughed—people like Alma.

Red House under Goldscheider's hand was much better than it would have been in a sequence of years in its former state.

And when Elise finally gave up this business, it was worth a fortune. She had succeeded! The shimmer of its future state, which no one could have imagined, became a ray of sun that slowly sank on the horizon. Horner was caustic in his criticism about her future.

But he was mistaken in his criticism. Goldscheider knew she was in complete control of her life and felt strong enough to climb up from its former depths to relish her life completely. Theater, music! She had a new life.

These images arose in her thoughts quite often in the midst of the noise and rush of wine that filled the salon with laughter and merriment. And her cold, watchful eyes became misty as they encircled the heads of her happy young ladies with a wreath of joy. All the while she kept her secret, kept it hidden from everyone, and zealously kept it from Horner who had witnessed her past. The cynical mind of her old friend dare not penetrate her secret future, however he tried to intrude, sniff around, and dig. She had to be sovereign and relieved of everything.

Through her untiring work, all the while suppressing herself, a bridge was thrown up between her pure child and this world. She alone had the right to cross this bridge—she alone, the mother.

Chapter 3
The Philosopher

If you do not want to miss out on life,
Live it as if
You could lose everything
By living as you now are.
—Goethe

Milada knocked at the door of Miss Dubbe Martel. She was sitting in front of a mirror, vigorously rubbing off her makeup with a washcloth. "Oh, it's you, Milada!" she said, turning her head from side to side to see who it was. "Come right on in. Tell me, did I get all the rouge off?"

"You can put some more on later if you need to," Milada told her, knowing what she was talking about.

Dubbe was amused and laughed. "Well, if you think so. I'll try again later without makeup. Pale but pretty, right? The Spaniards call that '*morbidezza*,' the look of the dead." She looked in the mirror at her sweet, narrow, oval-shaped face, surrounded by ash-blond hair. "Tears wash away the glow of the eyes," Dubbe muttered and nodded to her reflection. "It doesn't really matter."

She sighed and put her arms around Milada's neck, opened her blue eyes wide, and whispered, "I'll take the next caller, Milada, I will." Then she got up, ran out the door and down the stairs. Milada watched her and shook her head. Without thinking what an unusual person Dubbe was, she took stock of her room, which was a mess this morning. It evinced an active business. The beautiful, yellow-silk dress with its many frills the seamstress Moosmann had spent two days on lay on the floor just where Dubbe had taken it off, and the heels of her shoes were still hung in its folds.

"How sloppy!" Milada pressed her lips together and picked it up, shook it out and laid the pleats flat, then draped it across the ottoman. And then, yes, she had to put up all the clothes and underwear the laundress Miss Martha had so carefully folded and stacked. "It looks like somebody had to leave in a rush," Milada thought. There were cigarette butts, the ashes of cigars, wine bottles and glasses everywhere. Please no, not in the bedroom! Dubbe is a bit dotty. Everybody in the house knows that. But what an unholy mess to pick up on just a normal day. What if the madam saw this! The sun shone in the window at an angle and fell on the dirty water in the basin of the sink cabinet where it was splashed about, sparkling like drops of silver. "Well, get to work!" thought Milada and rolled up her sleeves. She was in the middle of cleaning when the door was pushed open abruptly. Dubbe flew in, pale as a sheet with distress. Her eyes were open unnaturally wide. She was trembling all over. She swept past Milada, charged around the room and stammered, "What ever will I do? Everything is gone! My life is over! God help me! Why won't she let me go? I'll go crazy here. She doesn't understand this place is making me ca-razy!"

"But, Miss Martel, you've got it good here," the fifteen-year-old Milada said, broom in hand, as she came over to comfort her. She knew these outbreaks of despair and how quickly they blew over. But this looked more dire.

Dubbe looked at her but did not register. She took a deep breath, grabbed Milada by the arm and held on, "You, dear child of God, you know how she trapped me. She's a vulture. It's that woman and her helpers! They did this to me, and I went along. And now she says I chose this, didn't I?"

"Miss Martel, please don't take this all to heart. Lots of things happen, but they pass. And in the end, you have to admit, this is the best place. Everybody says so."

"Everybody?! What do they know? They should try this out. Not me! I don't belong here. I came here from another world. I want to go back." She choked out the words, swallowed hard, and threw a large gold coin on the floor.

"She says I owe four hundred. For what I ask you? That monster destroys souls. She tells me I owe four hundred and that she saved me. Saved me from what? To do what? I would be happy to pay. Here is a payment of one hundred of the four she says I owe. There's this guy, and he promised me he'd give me the money." She sifted around the room, distracted. "But it's already too late. Even for that, it's too late."

"Madame Goldscheider," said Milada, thinking things over, "does not make arrangements to pay."

"She needs to let me go. Then I can pay her. He gave me that coin last night as a gift. He's from England, and he trusts me. He could see I was telling the truth. We spoke English. And he said he would be waiting for me at the consulate at eleven thirty. But it's too late now. She won't let me go. She wants to kill me."

Someone in the next room pounded on the wall for quiet.

"They want to sleep," Milada warned as she put the bedding on the window ledge to air and straightened the flounces of Dubbe's gown that were in disarray.

"I'll get revenge. I'll destroy her, just like she did me. I'm going to write to the Councilor to the Emperor—today. I was a tutor in his house for three years. I was like one of his own children." She grabbed Milada's arm again. "I'm a decent, respectable girl, you know. I can't take it here."

"This is really the most respectable and best brothel in the whole city," Milada replied.

Dubbe looked at her for a moment. Then she broke out in shrill, hysterical laughter.

"That's really good. You're a gem. That's the most insane thing I've ever heard. Maybe you mean what you say, you and all the others. You should be in my shoes. I come from some place else. I am a teacher, an English teacher. I have a teaching degree. You can look into it. I have the credentials. I've taught aristocrats, Montholon, Lucie. I shouldn't say their names out loud within these walls. They called me dear lady. I used to take care of sweet children. I've lost everything." She sat at the vanity and wept tears of rage.

"But just look, Miss Martel," Milada spoke to the wall as she brushed the clothing, "with only one out of four hundred gulden and your pleas, you won't convince Madame Goldscheider. That won't be enough. If you're really set on leaving, just start saving your money. You have the most elegant foreign visitors. They pay above and beyond. Save up the four hundred! And when you've got three hundred together and make an appeal to her, then Goldscheider might let you go. If you're nice to her."

All of a sudden Dubbe turned around. In the mirror she had seen the face of someone listening. Goldscheider had walked in unobtrusively. She leaned against the door and looked around, laughing lightly to herself. Not seeing her, Milada continued, "Just don't go to her when you're angry. You're better off going to her when you're calm. I'm sure of that."

"There, you've got your dirty money!" Dubbe shrieked, made furious by the madam's appearance. "Take the money for the balance." She pushed the coin on the floor with her foot toward Goldscheider. "People like me have connections, thank God. I'll get some of them to help." She put her hands on her hips and looked right through Goldscheider.

Milada broke off in fear.

The madam waved to her. "Go downstairs, girl, and see Moosmann. She'll give you a green-silk dress." She bent down to pick up the coin. "This is yours. I'll keep it for you for the time being. And you, my sweet child, pull yourself together. You're leaving in two hours. I demand respect here. It's a shame that you with your education and teaching didn't do better for yourself. You know I made sure your baby was taken care of, made sure you were spared from your awful debts. And I groomed you, too. And now you are putting up such a fuss. No, my child. Wash up, comb your hair. I'm giving you the green-silk dress as a going-away gift. Make yourself as sweet as you can. In two hours my agent will be here for you."

With surprise in her eyes, Dubbe stared at her. "Going away?" she stammered. "I'm going away now?"

"Yes, what else can I do? You might have worked out for me. You know that. But Red House is not the place for you to act out."

And with that, Goldscheider left. Dubbe ran after her. But Moosmann caught her in the hall, looked at her with sympathy, and pushed her back into her room. She was carrying a package carefully under her arm. "Shhh, don't cry, don't worry. It'll be all right."

Moosmann opened the package. "Let's make lovely Dubbe more wonderful, and the young barons will be sure to make eyes at her. There you go!"

Milada helped, and they presented Dubbe with a green-taffeta dress covered in jet beads. It made her neck and arms shimmer, and sunbeams did a lively dance across the fabric.

"It's like a million candles, a million!" Moosmann cried out and hopped around with delight. "It's so luxurious! That dress looks like a flood of light. Miss Dubbe has a large bust and long arms, just like Madame Goldscheider had told me."

Dubbe looked around in despair. She spoke out, filled with fear, "I have to go. She doesn't want me here."

"But where will you go?" said Moosmann. "She's letting the most beautiful person go?! That can't be true. Go downstairs, Miss, and show her how beautiful you are. Then she won't get rid of you. Like candles in a church, how magnificent!"

Milada did up Dubbe's hair, wiped away her tears with violet water, while cheering her up and smiling. Dubbe let her do this, humiliated, broken, and hopeless as she was. She regarded herself in the glamorous dress in the mirror.

"If she will only keep me on!" she said with agitation and hurried off down the steps.

"Now that's one poor idiot," Moosmann said nastily. Then she pulled out her measuring tape to see how tall Milada was.

"Jesus, you're measuring me?" Milada said with embarrassment and pulled away.

"Do you think you could walk around in the salon in this old sack of a dress?" the seamstress asked.

"In the salon...?" Milada echoed her words.

"Well, where else would you wear it?" the old woman muttered as she rolled up her measuring tape.

"She's keeping me, she's keeping me!" Dubbe hollered jubilantly over the railing of the stairs. "She took a big, long look at me, and I said, 'I'd be really happy to stay here, dear lady.' And she said, 'I'll agree to that.'"

"There, you see! She wouldn't throw you out, not a person like you," Moosmann said in a flattering tone.

Milada clutched her broom and stared anxiously out the window down to the street. What!? Was she supposed to work in the salon already? How could it happen so soon? Did the porter Mrs. Polifka know about this? Would they put a dress on her and just push her into the salon? To dance, sing, and entertain the gentlemen? Maybe she would have a green-silk dress. And they would put some rouge on her. Then maybe it would work, it might work better. She looked across the room at herself in the mirror. No, she was not pretty like Gisi or the Jewish girl Laura, or even Dubbe. When she laughed, her whole face moved. She had dimples in her chin and cheeks. But even then she looked serious. Maybe that would be all right. She tried on a coquettish laugh in the mirror while Dubbe stood in front of her. She did not like how she looked. Her dark face, her thin lips, and her eyes, however she turned them, did not look cheerful. With a sigh, she gave up trying. She would not be doing Goldscheider any favors. Well, if she was not right for the salon, she could be put to good use working. She could always rely on work. Suddenly she blushed. She blushed all over. She did not want to think like this. Quickly she grabbed her broom and left.

Dubbe applied her rouge and traced out her thin, high eyebrows with a brush. "Four hundred, and then on top of that the green-silk dress, that makes five-hundred eighty. I can get that. She'll get her money. What, you don't believe me? The way I look and the way I talk? I make men weep. Guys will see that if they have any sense. Guys like those," she said, indicating the men in the lobby. "There are dozens of guys like that. A girl as interesting as I am will never end up here. 'End up here,' that is the way to put it. I'm like the daughter of a king here among the discredited."

She let down her hair and smoothed the ash-blond strands over her ears. "Does that look good on me? It makes me look a little old, doesn't it? That looks a bit better." She tried putting her hair in various styles and flirted with her reflection. "And now I should go out for a walk. Milada, go downstairs and ask the old lady if we can go out for a stroll."

She dressed hurriedly and sang off key as she did. In her shrill, little voice she sang in English: "My heart is in the Highlands / My heart is not here."

Mrs. Polifka, as it turned out, knew nothing about Milada's new role. The day went by as usual. Milada served in the salon until midnight when she was relieved by the other maid. Then, sleepy and tired of working, Milada sat down in the kitchen where Polifka was making coffee. The coffee smelled good, and she closed her eyes and let the images of the day filter up in her thoughts. The memory of that morning smarted in her awareness like an open wound. The madam must have heard what she said to Dubbe. Goldscheider had picked up the gold coin and kept it. Such a lot of money, a hundred!

And then Moosmann had measured her for a dress. Did all this come together? How might these events come together? Milada racked her brain over suspicions and interpretations. There was a lot in life she simply did not grasp, and she had learned not to spend too much time agonizing. "It will all resolve itself," she told herself. When the doorbell rang, she ran out to open the gate, let the maid know, and returned to the kitchen where she sat by the stove and warmed her feet.

The music of the piano in the salon as well the sound of chatter and laughter wafted over to her in the kitchen. It was especially loud when the door of the salon opened and the girls accompanied their guests to their room.

Polifka poured the boiling water over the coffee, and a gray cloud rose up.

The maid shouted in the kitchen door, "Your coffee doesn't have any grounds in it today."

"Then I'll have to put a spoonful of ashes in next time," Polifka grumbled. She was proud of her cooking.

Milada polished up a bunch of glasses and arranged them in a row. Suddenly she turned to Polifka and asked, "What is a decent girl?"

The porter was holding a strainer in her hand and answered loudly, "Girl, what ideas you have running around in your head! It's enough to make a body crazy."

"But I want to know," Milada said hesitantly as she put her hand to her forehead in a gesture that showed she had thought a lot about it without coming up with an answer. "Are there decent girls here in the house, or don't they, decent girls I mean, come to a brothel?"

"Don't bother me with all the questions you dream up!"

Milada came up behind Polifka and put both her hands on the porter's shoulders. The girl had such an intense look of wanting to know in her eyes that Polifka, who was usually stern, was moved. Without realizing her voice was hushed, she said hastily out of sympathy, "Well, a decent girl doesn't like it if she has to do it with a man on Sundays. Now off to bed with you, and go to sleep!"

Polifka was distressed and rattled around in the kitchen with pots and pans.

"She belongs under the protection of the Church," she thought in shame. "Such a little bit of a thing!"

Milada took a deep breath, "Oh, I was only asking."

Polifka's bad temper erupted, "Now get to bed, you silly little trollop! I don't want to hear another thing out of you." She pushed the child out of the kitchen and swore a good while so loudly people could hear her. She cursed God's rule here on Earth.

A few days later Goldscheider left her office and ran across Milada on the floor, scrubbing the tiles. She looked at Milada's small, brown face, which was turned up to her.

"This kind of work isn't right for you," she said, standing over her. "We have a maid here for this."

"Today she's doing laundry, so I thought I'd do this."

"You're like your mother," Goldscheider said directly. "Just be smarter than she was. How old are you now?"

Milada muttered, "Sixteen," so that Goldscheider would hear what she wanted to hear.

"The same age as Alma Luzie," went through Goldscheider's mind, and a glimmer of warmth shot into her cold, gray eyes.

"Porter!" she called out. The porter appeared right away. "This girl will not be doing any heavy cleaning from now on. Just look at her hands! And where is it this girl sleeps?"

"In the small room in the attic, m'lady. In the corner with the rats."

"Do we have a room available? How about the small room off to the side near Serafine? Is that free?"

The porter answered, "In the evening we do use it."

Goldscheider said in a pinched voice, "Well, that's in the evening."

Goldscheider's gaze returned to Milada's face. Truly, she did have Katerine's eyes. They did not waver.

Goldscheider understood there was useful material here. She nodded and left.

"Well, Missy, my congratulations. You're in luck," the porter said in ill humor, making a mock curtsy.

Milada leaned against the staircase, silent, and stared off into the distance. It felt as if she had suddenly awakened in the night and all her dreams had evaporated. A host of new images arose and danced before her inner eye. There was a room with a closet and a door that locked, and there were candles, as many as she could use, books and newspapers, and strangers, always new strangers; free time and no more work. Gold coins. And underneath these visions there was something huge. There were things she could not articulate, and she sensed a terrible force, violence.

Milada felt the presence of the world breaking in upon her. It was another world, the world of others. These ideas balled together in her thoughts like a hard knot. She let out a deep sigh, lifted her head, and looked around in confusion. In front of her lay the dusty entry hall. It rose abruptly from the damp, shiny pieces of tile she had just scrubbed clean.

She dunked her trembling fingers into the pail, picked out the rag, and continued scrubbing without taking notice of the porter, who watched her, shaking her head.

"She'll never make a good prostitute," thought this primitive creature.

What kind of God is it who imbues a child with the tools to survive deep disturbances of the soul, to reach out to someone at hand and do what is necessary?

When Milada awoke in the new room, she found a light-red corset, a thin, white blouse with red cuffs, and matching hair ribbons.

Mrs. Moosmann was there and helped her with her hair and putting on the new clothes. Amid cries of admiration, the seamstress braided her thick, brown hair and fastened the braids on top of her head.

"There you have it, there you go. Now the eager robins will come to feast. They'll take a good look at you. And the madam will be amazed when she sees you!"

Milada went downstairs to the office, her heart pounding. Goldscheider looked at her fleetingly and said "Wait!" and kept writing.

For ten minutes Milada waited and used the time to look at herself in the mirror. The clothes fit her slim figure like a glove. She was tall. The fine, natural curls that surrounded her temples framed her sharp face with its calm, gray eyes, in which there was no trace of youthful longing. She had the eyes of a person edging her way over dangerous terrain, taking each step forward with caution.

For ten minutes she waited. She studied Goldscheider's face, which she had not seen before at close range. In the bun of her reddish hair there were streaks of silver. Milada noticed imperfections in her complexion, lots of freckles around her nose and on her cheeks. She had an unusual, sweet line buried in the corners of her mouth when she wrote. Goldscheider had on earrings with turquoise and large balls of gold. She wrote with great care and moved her lips as she wrote, and as she wrote, she tapped the small finger of her left hand on the desk. Suddenly she shook her feathers.

"Come over here!" she said, looking the girl over. She nodded.

"I will put you in the salon. You are the child of Katerine, and she was useful here. The clothing you'll get I give you at no cost. When I leave the business, you owe nothing to anyone. Your debt here is only to me. Do you understand what I'm telling you? You owe only me.

"Yes, m'lady."

"You worked here as a maid for four years. Your clothing and supplies are payment for your work. The point here is this: when I'm gone, you don't owe anybody one single thing. You are free to go wherever you want. So now sign." Goldscheider pushed the sheet of paper over to Milada.

Milada picked it up and started reading it over. Surprised but not saying a word, Goldscheider watched her. Then the young girl nodded and wrote her name at the bottom awkwardly with her stiff fingers. The madam folded up the paper slowly.

"Conduct yourself well, and things will go well for you. The fact you grew up here and know this life gives you an advantage over girls who come here from elsewhere. You have seen enough and gotten experience. Make use of that! You don't have to be ruined, to drown in the muck. If you leave here with some money, then the world is open to you."

Madame Goldscheider became quiet. She had said more that she had wanted to. She had spoken directly from her soul, and that surprised her. She had thought about herself and about quiet, pure Dresden where her daughter lived on Goethe Street and looked forward to seeing her mother.

All that melted together in an inexplicable, new feeling of responsibility and eroded her tough exterior of haughtiness.

"I think I will do all right, m'lady," Milada replied and kissed the hand the madam offered her.

"Stay upstairs in your room and wait. This afternoon Sucher will take you to the winery. There you'll learn how to act with guests. You can keep what you get in tips. Do you understand? You simply say you earned it. And in six weeks you'll return here. Adieu."

Now Milada was one of the ladies. She had her own room in the apartment of the Italian Carlotta. She was allowed to receive guests there.

In the evening, she was busy in the private booths, and her primary duty was to see that much champagne flowed. Milada pocketed a percentage of this, even though Carlotta generally kept the girls' tips when she tallied things up.

The six weeks she was supposed to spend in the winery became six months because she had a stroke of luck. Her luck might have been even better if a certain incident had not come to pass.

After Milada had been the plaything of an aristocrat for several weeks straight—for which, upon leaving, he had given her an account with five hundred crowns—she was given to a man in the upper echelons of the military. After that she went to the arms of a banker from Berlin. He was satisfied with her and promised her he would keep her for the whole of his stay in the city. Milada got the clothes she wanted, flowers, candies, small tokens of appreciation, an emerald brooch, and the promise of a diamond rivière necklace if she was well-behaved till the end of his stay. He stayed, by the way, camped in Milada's room during his free time, ate what the Italian woman served there, bought and drank the most expensive wines, and secured for himself a respectable lodging with his girlfriend.

"You're not pretty, and you are not a little wench either. I like you because you aren't those things. My old Heda back home, I thank you for this time. With you, Milada, my piggy, I can recover from my decent marriage."

He showed her a picture of his wife in Berlin, a fat, blond, aggressive person who appealed to Milada quite a lot. Later, when she looked at herself in the mirror, she was taken aback. The carmine-red makeup did not go with her brown face, and whenever she could, she wiped it off in private. She admitted to herself that here, too, the girls were more cheerful and lively than she could ever be.

The girls at the winery boasted that, at the end of the day, the whole business—whatever they did there—was "nothing at all" to them. They said they were only performing like actors. Fritzi's lively banter or Paula's sparkling eyes around officers, or the blush that burned on Paula's cheeks when these men teased her—all of that—was only theater, comic theater! The first time Milada experienced this herself was in the establishment of the Italian woman. Milada watched and understood, and, for the first time, her soul hardened. Immediately she came to see the barriers between social classes, and she put the societal sphere of her origin in perspective. She had a keen sense of the gradations of social disadvantage; she perceived the small and the fine nuances of what was permissible and tolerated. And she assessed her own value by the standards of the world. The heady smell of this world initially drew her in. She was consumed like a twig curled by fire.

Very precisely, while at first gingerly, her sharp vision cut through the insensible mass of humanity around her; it parsed light and shadow. With the sureness of a sleepwalker, she climbed up and down the rungs of the social ladder. She moved in an artificial light not cast by the sun. She crept into the depths of the abyss and witnessed the last twitches of life. Intellectual acuity comes as a result of grasping relationships. Here in the establishment of the Italian Milada acquired this acuity. She saw the difference between herself and the young, plucky waitresses in black silk; she saw the relation between those girls serving at the buffet who got their ears boxed when they piped up and the girls who unabashedly begged guests for sandwiches and liquor.

Most acutely she noted the gap between the waitresses in black-silk dresses and the ladies from outside who, each and every evening, arrived and went to the private booths. Those were stylish women who wore heavy jewelry. They spent their time in the company of upper-class men, smiled a smile of understanding to Carlotta, and greeted the early morning with champagne.

They laughed and joked with everybody, but only the man they belonged to was allowed to make love to them.

These ladies were in secure hands, and only rarely did they change lovers. Here at Carlotta's there was, after a manner of speaking, the money-market of love. Here the terms of the leisure set were registered, scrutinized, and maintained. When people who lived by these "terms" were in the private booths, the waitresses were not allowed to serve their tables. Milada was not allowed to either. The waitresses were not even allowed to talk to the gentlemen, to ask for a cigarette or a sip of wine.

"They ain't no prettier than us," Paula commented out of envy. "And they don't talk no better either. They got it pretty crappy though."

Milada was not content with explanations like these. The difference between people of her ilk and these special ladies, who used their elegant lovers' names after their nickname, had to be understood at a deeper and more fundamental level. Milada's small, unhappy friend Paula was not interested in looking deeper. What was that difference really about? Milada could not put a name to that either. She did not brood over it. Her nimble brain at first simply took in the information with curiosity. She also took note of how very disdainfully the girls of dubious elegance were treated when they slipped into the place with shaded eyes, both brash and embarrassed, and looked around for an empty table. Carlotta shooed these lowly creatures out and tolerated them only when they came in the company of a man.

Jargon for these girls was "bar skirts." And some, in defiance, hoisted up their skirts triumphantly to reveal a shimmering silk petticoat.

They were not particular and did not play games. They hungrily ate up everything they were served. They were humble, almost submissive, to the waitresses and grateful to the men who paid them.

Then there were the "dark ladies" who sometimes came to Carlotta's. When they arrived the guest room got quiet. These women wore veils and subdued clothing. They came in pairs or in groups of three with their gentlemen. The gentlemen, too, were somber. They looked around in the room and ordered wine by the glass. Carlotta said these were the "decent women."

She said she had no use for them. The atmosphere of frivolity went by the boards in their presence. Carlotta did, however, act friendly to them, but, behind their back in the tap room, she made faces and bad-mouthed them. "They should stay at home and wash diapers and not show up here like they were at the theater."

Milada liked these dark ladies a lot. They stuck together and whispered. Milada noticed these "reputable" people were always very serious. Almost sad. They took sips of wine but did not laugh or tell jokes. Sometimes Carlotta went over to their table to liven things up and chatted about the weather and rising prices at the market. Then a gentleman would call out to this or that waitress, offer her something to drink, and talk light-heartedly. But no merriment ensued. Even Paula, who was usually in a good mood and swished around in fun with her skirts when someone was querulous, became glum when these reputable ladies were present and left whenever she could.

Paula left in annoyance and mimicked one of the men, "'When do you turn in in the evening?'" She continued, "'So where should we go for a stroll? Are your parents living?' Such tiresome stick-in-the-muds! Who needs them anyways?"

Once, while Milada was serving, she saw a lady point to her and say, "Oh my God, look how young that poor thing is!"

Milada thought, "So what of it? I am lucky to be young and fresh."

Later a man called her to his table, pinched her cheeks, and told her he was glad to see she did not wear makeup like the other girls.

"Would you perhaps like some wine, Madame?" one of the dark ladies said to Milada. At first she did not understand the lady was speaking to her. No one had ever addressed her as an adult. A strange feeling stopped her in her tracks. The woman's voice had sounded so gentle, even timorous. Why was that? Then the man with her gulped down his wine and boomed, "Aw, come on. These little sluts guzzle their share. Isn't that right, kid?"

Paula called out across the room, "We like to turn around and spit it out. In general, we like to spit." The ladies looked at each other. Milada heard someone in the next room call her name and quickly ran out.

"She looks pretty stupid," one lady said with a sigh once Milada had left. Afterwards Paula laughed scornfully. From that moment on Milada was intimidated and always looked around the room carefully before entering.

Her first encounter with morality in society did not go favorably.

In the hours of the afternoon, the girls were allowed to go for a walk. Usually they went to the Prater, the central city park, and then they stopped at Meier's for a coffee. They watched the carriages roll up and riders stop by on their horses. Automobiles sped past. When Paula saw someone she knew, she became quite excited and clapped her hands for all to see.

Here, for the first time, Milada witnessed the concourse of daily life among the urban upper class. She sat there numbed, watching all the people laugh as they greeted one another, nodded recognition, and sat down together to pass the time with idle talk.

She stirred her coffee mechanically and listened absent-mindedly to Paula's loud comments. Yet all the while her head was exploding with all kinds of questions for which she had no answer. All these people! Who are they? How do they live? And what do they have to laugh about all the time? The women did not have to wear makeup or wear low-cut dresses. They did not wave to men or sashay for their attention. These ladies sat quietly, and the gentlemen bowed and approached them slowly and carefully. "The gentlemen seem to tiptoe," Milada said in amazement to Paula, who hung on her arm.

Once two very slender, blond, young women arrested Milada's attention as they got out of their carriage. They looked like sisters. Both wore white lace dresses and were covered in jewelry. A swarm of men on horseback greeted them deferentially. As the sisters looked for a place to sit in the café, people inclined their heads and spoke in hushed voices.

"Look at them!" Milada said discomforted and watched as they went by.

"Those women have nothing else to do but deceive their husbands. That's how they get those diamonds and lace dresses," Paula replied disdainfully.

"You're really the smart one!" Fritzi called out. Fritzi was lovely and the star of the winery. She was a wonderfully beautiful blonde with fine, regular features. On walks in the park she was most interested in the little children. She smiled at them, shook their tiny hands when she passed, and tried to get them to talk with her.

She had a six-year-old girl at her mother's house back home. She idolized this child, and every child she saw reminded her of her longing for "Susie Mousie." "My, what a sweet little outfit! Just look at it! I'll have to sew one for my Susie. Look at how it's made: six pleats for the skirt and three on the sleeves. But for Susie it should be blue as the sky."

And then, at this very moment, something happened that had been bound to happen all along. The event at hand illuminated the darkness of Milada's observations and questioning; the light was sharp and intense. The three of them, Milada, Paula, and Fritzi, arrived at Meier's Café and could not find a table in the garden. It was completely full. They sat down next to an old married couple who signaled with a welcoming nod for them to sit with them. The woman had a friendly, sallow little face. She wore a black lace hat and smiled pleasantly at the pretty faces of the three. Paula looked around to see who might be there and said, "There ain't no soldier here," sighed without pretense, and began to flirt with a group of men who rode bicycles. After a bit, the old couple put their heads together in a private exchange. With painstaking awareness, Milada studied the old woman's air of unease as she looked the three women at her table up and down.

"Hey, Fritzi, she's talking about us," Milada said as she tugged at the arm of her neighbor who was reading the comics. Fritzi looked the old couple over with her light-blue eyes. "Well, just let them." She was used to situations like this.

"What does she think about us?" Milada brooded to herself. "She thinks we are prostitutes, that's what. She thinks, 'Oh, how disgusting. I want to leave.'" Milada tried to read the inscrutable face of the old woman.

At that very moment a boyish, young officer passed by the table. Paula turned as if electrified and called out to him. He looked disconcerted and kept walking. "Oh, my God! He could have been my sweetie."

The old man pushed back his chair and called out, "Check, please!" The old woman had already left Meier's Café.

Milada's eyes were wide open. They jumped and flashed as she reviewed what had just taken place.

"Such a stupid old lady!" said Paula.

"You can keep your mouth shut!" Milada returned in anger. "We don't need to attract attention, all right?"

Fritzi, who was normally easy-going, took Paula's side. "We didn't have to sit here with people who have such sensitive noses." Fritzi was unhappy with Milada and kept flipping around in her magazine.

"The old bastard! Just 'cause I didn't play footsy with him," Paula hollered loudly, almost as if she was trying to be heard at the neighboring tables. Light laughter from the other tables grew louder. People shrugged their shoulders and turned away. And then something exceptional happened: while Fritzi was reading and Paula was turned around looking at the passers-by, Milada absorbed the disgust all around her. People shot both open and stolen glances at their table. For the first time in her life, Milada cast down her eyes knowingly. She saw the gaping chasm that divided her sphere from that of the world at large.

The looks people gave them were curious, cold, and gruesome. Milada sat motionless as she registered the disdain. It felt like her due.

She heard someone say, "Those girls should see us and think about what they're doing. The young one is one of them, too. Disgusting!"

That was the truth. All three of them were prostitutes. Milada lifted her head. She had grown up at Goldscheider's! She should go back where she came from. The gentlemen at the café probably knew exactly what a brothel was. And the ladies probably did not. They had every right to laugh derisively. One woman there swiveled around to gawk. What they whispered to one another was irrelevant. The fact of the matter remained. She was young and fresh, and in the evenings she was available to men. When these people did go to Carlotta's place, they sat quiet as cows and did not grumble. They all wore gray faces. Milada relied on her usual way of coping. She thought of how to get out of the situation; she thought of fleeing. She could not simply keep sitting there, but she did not know how to extricate herself either. A heavy, unbearable feeling of isolation overwhelmed her. She used these people's stares, their barely audible words, and their unmistakable gestures—as well as the thoughts whirring in her mind—to build a wall, brick by brick. This wall closed off "other people." They could live on the other side with their pride and their disdain. They could keep their good fortune and pain, their furnishings and rules. The wall separating them was absolute.

Many years later, whenever Milada made an effort to explain just what her relation to the world of "other people" was, a host of disparaging faces swirled in her mind. They were the faces, filled with derision, of that hour at Meier's Café. All those faces were staring at her. It seemed they held some magical power over her. They stifled her. She always felt exactly as she had felt that one decisive day.

At this very moment at Meier's an awareness of her own reason for living began to take shape. It became bedrock, and it stayed with her, unaltered, throughout her life; it was in place through all her tribulations.

Half a year later the banker from Berlin left the city, and Milada returned from Carlotta's establishment to Red House.

One rainy evening in January, unannounced, Goldscheider went to see Milada in the salon. She took Milada by the hand and conducted her to Horner who was sitting in his usual place by the stove. "There you go, man. Now you've got someone to keep you from falling asleep on me. She's young. She's Katerine's daughter. You surely remember Katerine! We were both younger then, and this girl was only knee-high."

He lifted his fat, unhealthy, pale face. "Katerine, ha! Yes, I remember. That was a wildcat. And her? She's young, really young." He shoved the rest of his cigar into the left corner of his mouth. "Hey, girl, do you like the food here? It's rich, isn't it?" He made a face. "Do you use liquor to digest the food here? You should have some, just wait!" He pulled her over to himself and wrapped his arm around her hips.

Milada could not help feeling repugnance at the touch of his soft, flabby fingers.

"Stay, just stay put," he mumbled. "I'll give you some good, strong liquor. It'll offset the fatty food here and purge your stomach of indulgence. It cleanses excrement." He mumbled this in her ear.

From time to time he put a glass of lemonade to his mouth and sipped on it constantly.

Even though the girls openly ridiculed Horner and even though Horner was himself monotonous, Milada stayed at his side. She heard something new she had not imagined in what he had to say. She found what he said in bits and pieces exciting.

Increasingly Milada felt physically drained when she was around Horner, Yet, at the same time, her soul was filled with a delightful sweetness she had never dreamt of in her numbness. "Let people laugh, dance, act crazy, but you must remain calm and upright. Just watch them. Do you think they can wrest free of the weight of their existence? Ridiculous, girl! Nobody lives life as if it were final. We all carry within ourselves a bit of the continuation of some alien matter that struggles for permanence. Life is only about this matter and not about momentary, idiotic consciousness. You can start out an empress and end up a prostitute. But it's the prostitute who in her dreams helps her bit of this matter to triumph. Having a goal in sight is everything. But who ever reached a goal? Who ever arrived at his goal, completely conscious and the absolute master over this matter? Who realizes this? Goethe? Jesus, hmm? Immortality is all we wish for. It is the rhythm of the dance we dance. What opens us to living falls away because it is not essential. It will return. You existed before, and you have to return. Oh, Greek Phryne, oh, courtesan! Can this little bit of filth of your existence harm you in this eternal consciousness? Do what you want, laugh, dance, sing, despair, but do not believe this life is what is meaningful about you. Do you know what is important? What is important is this: coming to an end in good time. Live lavishly, be wasteful, transfer out, and do not burden the matter with too much egoism."

From time to time, Milada had to get up obediently when either Goldscheider or Olympia waved to her. She disappeared to the salon for a while to serve guests and wait on them, but then she returned automatically to Horner. She racked her brain to make sense of his dark, puzzling words. They clattered like heavy stones against a gigantic wall.

"You appear out of millennia, you return in millennia, and you live here a second as an idiotic consciousness. You are part of an idea blown by indeterminable circumstances onto a pile of manure.

"Bear your fate as if it is a matter of course, and you will come forth again. Put down roots in the Earth's realm from which you come. Draw strength and vital fluids from the Earth, and you will reach your innermost goal.

"Take dung beetles for example, scarabs. They're not disgusting creatures. They know how to live. They have *savoir vivre*! These bugs are simply happy their luster is golden. It doesn't matter to them people think they stink.

"Have you ever seen a real dung beetle, the Scarabaeus coprophagous or sacer, to use its scientific name? No, you've never seen one," Horner repeated Milada's answer. "You're a careful, slow learner. Well, this beetle is small. It's adorable and shimmers green and gold. It's extraordinarily beautiful and precious. It's a pleasure to behold. But if you hold it in your hand, it squirts a dark-brown fluid from its posterior hole, and a vile stench assails your curious nose. The dung pile instantiates a concept.

"The dung beetle says, 'I am here because you people made this dung heap. You piled up this fowl stuff, the filthy excrement and urine. Ha, ha, and I flourish in it. I grow large and get fat. If every corner of your world was clean, dear folks, then creatures like me wouldn't be here in their glory. I wear pants of green silk.'"

Horner grabbed Milada under her skirt. He continued, "The beetle says, 'I wear little, golden shoes and golden, sparkly baubles around my neck and on my bosom. You people need your dung heaps. And how odious those heaps would be without me.' Just see how these creatures swell up.

"Lift yourself up, Milada, above this momentary evanescence, and you can help the idea of a you triumph. Millions of incarnations struggle and then fade away into irrelevance and redundance. They pass like excrement through the gut of existence. Dung, dung, that's what we all are. We live by our instincts."

He looked contemplatively down at his empty glass. Then he brandished the glass.

"Bring fine sugar, two lemons halved without seeds, and water. I will teach you how to make lemonade. Then you'll have another skill in life. I could like you."

She took the tray obediently and left.

Olympia called out, "Jesus, Horner, you make me want to retire." She had become a businesswoman and strutted around proudly carrying a wad of keys and a money bag.

"That is what we old people do," he replied gruffly.

Olympia looked at him angrily and passed by him quickly.

To make himself comfortable, he stretched out his legs. "Ha, ha, life always offers small, sweet humorous moments..."

He had, metaphorically, turned the dung beetle Olympia over on her back, and she struggled in anger to right itself. And the other noxious bug? The young one? She used all her strength to crawl around him in loving servitude and kept her antennae in the air. Of course a little tickling did Horner good. His friend Elise knew that and took care of him every so often and sent him girls. Then the girls listened to him. One listened because she believed he would pay her something; another, because she believed he would pull her up out of the muck by the scruff of her neck. They all had their reasons for listening to him. But, after they had shown him generosity and it had brought them nothing, they made fun of him. Ridicule did not faze him! He was in his own hog heaven, that was all. Did he really want to find the sacred scarab beneath the scramble and commotion of living? He kept on laughing to himself, especially at stupidity. He was no longer on a quest. He was much happier about the sour, stupid face the novice wore when he took her off his lap and left without "reaching into his pants pocket," a behavior he had become known for. People regularly swore at him. Curses restored his soul. Nothing bothered him. Nothing lay on his soul. He did not act defeated as people "normally" do. He took insults in stride and walked away laughing.

Milada withdrew after some while, and he brewed his own lemonade, complaining about the inconvenience. "You have to mix this up for me every day," he said.

He made accusations against her. "It's because of you that I've made an enemy of Olympia. I won't climb that mountain ever again. Do you know what I'm saying?"

She nodded.

"You seem to be a girl without any feelings. What's your name again? Milada. Sounds good, sounds right. How old are you anyway? Sixteen."

Horner's manner of talking to people was quite odd. He looked at people from the side, bent his right ear to them, which was stuffed with cotton, and spoke in a whisper. All the while he ran his glassy eyes over their person. Milada directed her gray eyes straight at him and did not let him gaze at her with his sick eyes.

"You'd like to get out!" he rasped while swallowing lemonade. "Then go! It's not worth staying here. Go and be gone, never to return again. Leave!"

Milada shook her head emphatically. "That won't work," she said. "I owe the madam hundreds."

"Very good, ha, excellent!" Horner snorted. His spittle sprayed across her face. "You fool! You are free. Don't you know? Completely free. Nobody has any strings on you. The door there is open. The steps are clear. The city out there is quiet. Only bums are out on the main street, walking around the gutters. Go, I'm telling you, go! Ride the current. No one will miss you. No one will try to find you. What do you mean to them?" He pointed in the direction of Goldscheider. "You're just bad debt, nothing more. There's the door. I tell you go!"

Milada was so deeply affected by his forceful suggestion that she arose and went to the door. But she felt him watching her, pulling her back. He turned, full of curiosity to see what she would do, For the first time, he took her seriously.

"Strange," he mumbled, almost shocked. "Strange, everybody else laughed. But that one there, she left."

And that is how a friendship was cemented. The mind cannot fathom how strange and bizarre this friendship was.

Horner had gone off the rails of bourgeois life. A resistance to law and order and middle-class norms, likely the result of physical irregularities, dominated him. He hated the idiotic ladder of success, just as he hated, in his words, "the stupid translation of natural talents and work into honors, offices, titles, and positions in a hierarchy."

"I've been destroyed," he told Milada, and his piercing gaze bored into her face. "And how did this happen? It happened because a vain lieutenant pilloried me for my personal aversion to jumping on a horse and swinging a sword. He called me an intractable coward. He branded me a clown to my schoolmates and the world. And it happened again because of the lousy honor of the director of a preparatory school. He punished me for certain unmentionable pleasures and the physical enjoyment I had become accustomed to. He claimed they were disgusting, filthy acts fit for the tabloids. I stumbled and fell because of this guy, tripped over him like a stone, and landed in the muck. And that's where I've stayed."

After Horner had lost the few advantages and status he had attained through his university studies, he took up the company of the dispossessed, the enslaved, and disenfranchised. Here he had a place. He had done this in part because it suited his interests but also to retaliate against the destructive authority of the dominant society. They had let him feel their power by relegating him to the realm of the dispossessed, enslaved, and disenfranchised. And, to be sure, he did have a role to play among them.

He belonged to that group of talented but unanchored individuals who find peace and moral security only in the lax atmosphere of the demimonde. Horner resided here since society relinquishes its expectations at this border. A person arrives here and is rid of all cultural shame, prejudice, and all discretion. Here one finds shelter for the human impulse to lawlessness. One can live by his animal instincts for gratification.

Horner had never felt comfortable in society, and he did not feel comfortable now among prostitutes and their clients. But this corner of society offered him pleasure in his gruesome game of destruction. Everything in this game drives inexorably toward obliteration.

He called the brothel the "residence of instincts." Here anything that lifted its head or triumphed bore in itself a priori the seeds of decay. This milieu aligned with his odium.

Horner knew these types, the ups and downs of their fate, their shocks and convulsions, the creeping exhaustion, and the numbing of their psychic functioning. He understood how their pathos toward themselves is extinguished and their primal love of self is quashed.

He knew first-hand the gruesome disgust that people shunned by society have for themselves; he knew for himself how, in the end, outcasts are defeated. Horner understood how outcasts curse, till the bitter end, the deterioration of their bodies as their bodies contend with their inborn soul.

The people of the moral world had long tried to convince the creatures they shunned of the baseness and vileness of their profession. And Horner saw that righteous, goodly people had, through their laudable efforts, succeeded in inculcating self-loathing and defeat in their outcasts. People of the moral world had even convinced their victims it was their societal duty to find themselves disgusting. Yes, victims were duty-bound to be wrecked.

What had he not seen here? There were girls with great will and a thirst for living; also, girls with high intelligence and high spirit who fought like flies against the sticky poison that held them fast. Then there were the girls who lost their girlish innocence in the morass. And all of them, the good and the bad, the strong and the weak, were ruined—necessarily had to be ruined.

Everything that lives had to perish and decay.

Oh, Life, how he hated it. All the while he pursued it greedily. He never had enough.

This great life triumphed and replenished itself perpetually; it was universally victorious. Nothing denigrated or tainted it. It stood sublimely above hate and love. This imperial force endured, hidden away, blow after blow and defeat after defeat. The most sacred flame at the ancient altar once burned with ferocity, but the last remnant of humanity was snuffed out of its priestesses. Other people's morality threw ashes and sand on the flame. Eternal, infertile wasteland! The Sahara of morals! Oh, prostitution!

"Try to show me conformity to law, harmony, a mathematical rule, or a finer reincarnation! I tell you, Miss, there are only chaos, deceptive puzzles, and regression. I deny, deny—thrice deny—there is any progress or any education that lifts us up. The prostitute is the symbol of Nature. And what we call life is nothing other than the unrestrained use of the whore's randy, juice-emanating, unthinking, vain body. She lies down to fornicate at every opportunity. You all have your philosophy. It's an impenetrable bramble. All exegesis is just chopping around in the brambly growth as if it were art. People hang around like apes in the jungle, cracking empty nuts."

That was Horner. The odd thing about this man was that, despite his undeniable dissipation and loss of cultivation, he had, alongside his sponge-like weakness of will, a tough, curious energy that shone forth in all its fullness.

He was like the fat, unmoving carnivorous plants in whose slime the insects that flew to it suffocate motionless. And just like a carnivorous plant, Horner had one active interest: attracting people to himself expressly to impregnate their minds. As a very young person he hankered after vulnerable people and glommed onto them tenaciously. His tenacity was unsavory. And after a while his mounting bitterness and disappointment caused him to lash out against those he had singled out.

His whole life long he had expressed his will in a wild surge of ideas. But he needed someone else to actualize what seethed in his selfish mind. He wanted to externalize his ideas and reveal them to an avaricious world. He wanted to show people what a powerful mind they had discarded. He wanted them to know they were missing out on a genius.

He was looking for someone to embody his will. He sought a person who could carry out an "act." Oh, how much unsatisfied desire for triumph and how much creative spirit he invested in his search! He longed to watch his protege participate in the actions of this world.

Horner called his fixation the "damnable thrust of the immaterial" in his blood. It kept him from having any peace; it disallowed him any traction in this world. It tore at him and bellowed. It drove his ego, and his fat, flabby body, which had long ago become slave to his instincts, followed without resistance.

Perhaps what drove him was simply the age-old human longing for possessions and security or for something intransient. Maybe he wanted a material marker of his fear of dying. He was terrified of disappearing from this earth without a trace. And because he had no children to give him the illusion of immortality, he sought this illusion in an unusual and complicated way.

In his search this cynic and anarchist, who was happy to denigrate anyone or anything, wallowed in the suffering people's massive scorn caused him. His perverse suffering was excruciating since he imagined himself invulnerable. Each disparaging word and every dismissive gesture pained him. People's opinion of him broke him like the beggar who had no moral or physical capital to fight back. That is why Horner constantly looked fixedly at the world around him with a pained gaze that was filled with derisive superiority and distrust. He was on the look-out for mockery and insult and preemptively slandered those in his sphere before they could call him a weakling behind his back.

In Goldscheider's salon he was wrathful and lay in wait like a hunter in a blind. He delighted in tracking the progressive decay of society. The salon held all types: women with paid positions, women laborers, girls from the middle class, and women of some means. Women of all varieties left the bastion of the bourgeoise and found their way to the lawless land of the salon by the back door. And the gentlemen who were squires, knights, and cavaliers flowed in streams out of their barracks into these women's bedrooms and spread their poisonous bacteria among the purest of flowers. Horner called them the cupids of the devil, ha ha!

He visited Goldscheider's salon and Carlotta's establishment alternately. He even went to Zimmermann's place to sniff around. He also went to the infamous Salon Agular, a hidden circle where girls of the middle class mingled with aristocrats and high-placed ladies met up with coachmen. But he always returned to Elise where he felt most at home. He felt he was in the home of an old friend. Here he could see whole cloth the threads of individual lives. One prostitute was intelligent; another had only her five senses. Some snagged whoever was available; they sucked the cavaliers dry and, without caring, let them fall flat on the floor. Goldscheider spun her web with artifice and plucked from it only the golden, only the best little flies. She did this with a creative flair for extravagant waste. She let the rest go. She did not murder her victims; she anesthetized them and granted them movement and latitude. Her tactic allowed this most strange collection of types to work to good effect. At other establishments these women's entrapment descended into an empty theater of marionettes.

Horner said to Goldscheider, "I connect the concept of roundness, the state of being closed off, bounded on all sides and free-floating, with complete purposefulness. This state is perfection. The concept of roundness is completion. Its ideal form is a sphere. I have rarely seen perfectly round things, but your business is one. You impress me with that. At the onset I did not think you were up to this work. But I now admit my opinion of this business was informed by an outdated understanding of theater. Once you decided to take on this business, you founded a new societal institution, based on the Greek temples' cultivated and revered hetaerae. In your hands they have become proletarian courtesans." He added, lurking around, "You built a gallows for the society. And you treat your girls like the workers on this project. Well done! Impart to them an awareness of their role as 'commodities.' Inform them it is socially needful. Your next step is conserving this institution. You preserve what you have built by securing its financial underpinnings: organization, a bevy of consumers, fixed prices, and alliances. And presto you are a woman who is a leader among us. You will dictate the rules of the game. Ha, Madame Elise, what do you think of a role like this? Seize it while you can. There is something heroic about this role that even your girls understand. We men have lost our strength. We have played our roles; we are on our way out. We men are poorly armed and depleted. We are moldering thinkers. But you women have brains that are fully rested. The future belongs to you!"

In happy moments, when he sat in the salon and watched people with eyes that looked glazed-over and unseeing, his old euphoria about ideas returned to him. Then he selected one of the girls, preferably one who was "fresh." He was looking for a creature who was new to him and full of mystery. He put her on his lap and started talking. "A modern class of ancient, venerable hetaerae can blossom on top of human manure. It will have to be organized well, spiritualized, and aware of its immense social power." He shouted for joy, "That would be a slap in the face to the laughable, arrogant society that draws up laws for itself when it is hit in the gut. This society is excrement, and it will flow into the sewer! You girls will give the bucket of crappy morals a swift kick! Oh you girls, you girls, who surrender your body, your youth, your aspirations to the pleasure of strangers, you must demand a hundred times more recognition! You deserve as much justice and honor as the pale maidens behind the barbed-wire fence of false rules. Men will have to die the miserable death of Adam for having made these rules. Men have been the instruments of Nature! Insipid domestic animals! But you little children, you despise what they have done. You are here for yourselves. You will be profligate royalty!"

Goldscheider's recent disinterest in his fantasies and sarcasm deflated him much more than he let on. When he visited her in her private office to vent about one thing or another, she nodded distractedly or made irrelevant, joking remarks. She openly showed her skepticism, and she dismissed his schemes and suggestions for improving her business. Her stance told him she made her own decisions. Her interests and aims did not include him or his views. Her avoidance posed a danger to the requirements of his ego. Goldscheider hid herself and her intentions behind an agreeable, unruffled formality. She kept her impatience and annoyance to herself and persisted in keeping her distance. The longer she maintained her silence, the more ill at ease and agitated he became. Fueled by gall, he began to make insinuations and wheedled her. He provoked small altercations and quarrels that inevitably ended in loud, unloving scenes. He accused her of betraying their friendship, playing deceptive games, and swindling. These accusations spewed quite often from his rancorous, nasty mouth.

Truth be known, he did see through Goldscheider. She had deported herself impeccably as the madam of Red House. She had taken the path shown to her without looking ahead or behind herself. She had acted mechanically out of necessity. She had spent almost nine years ceaselessly following her ambition with no nourishment for her soul save for the letters Alma Luzie sent on vacation and her brief, annual trip to Dresden. This had netted her a generous amount of capital. Then, one day when she was struck down with exhaustion and tender longing, she asked herself: What good does all this money do me? What does piling up wealth matter, if I am dragging myself around through this mire for the years of good health I have left? I have to limit my undertakings. I cannot magically make Alma Luzie a rich princess. What I can lay at her feet is the humanity I have left. If I stay at Red House, then my lovely little daughter with sun-lit eyes will not have a mother. She will have the madam of a brothel.

A long, unaccustomed shudder rattled her person. She had, up to this point, not thought through these ideas; she had not turned her attention to these considerations. Her sense of self, which had been shuffled over with a thousand concerns, erupted with powerful force and brought her to these realizations. A genuine, absolute disgust suddenly gripped her. She was disgusted by this business and its dealings. And there she was at the core of it all. Again and again she tortured herself with the question: What is all this for? What is the point? She was prone to forget that originally it had been all about the money, and it now lay in the bank.

Open rebellion came to the fore. Her interest in books and beautiful language returned. She appreciated old tales of honorable deeds and sweet circumstances. It felt as if the gentle spirit of her dear, departed husband David surrounded her and gave her strength for her plans.

She felt close once again to the past and, without realizing what she was doing, hummed Hebrew melodies to herself. And she smiled remembering the faces of the vagabonds her father brought home and the stories they told each other on Saturday evenings. She let the business wind down and cashed in her bonds and market shares. She called in outstanding loans and turned her assets into money. She entered no new deals, took her name off of operations where she could, and gave people in the business credible excuses for discontinuing contact. She talked with Sucher, with whom she had always done business, about selling the brothel.

It was the end of winter. And Sucher advised her to wait till the summer to close out favorably since eager buyers in the provinces always contacted him at the beginning of a new season. In the winter they would have to look for buyers and make proposals; they would be at a disadvantage. So Elise decided to wait. During this time Horner became uncomfortable. He started snooping around in her affairs, very much to her dissatisfaction. She did not, as a result of something she had let drop, want to have this man in her future. Horner made her careful, incremental disengagement more difficult. She understood how closely attached to her he had become. He never admitted to himself that his plans and expectations were lost on her. She had taken the path he had once pointed her down for her benefit. This man, who was inclined to deceptions and compromises, had salved his wounded ego with this fact. Goldscheider now took stock of the current situation and felt both superior to him and emotionally responsible to him. After all he was the one she had to thank for much in life that had been positive. It seemed she was beholden to him and had to find this man a credible, new illusion to replace the old, disintegrating one.

On a rainy autumn evening Goldscheider sat Milada down on Horner's lap. She was prepared. She had a plan; she was not making a snap decision. Later, in the course of the evening, when Milada was off on an errand, Goldscheider went to Horner and said directly and forcefully, "Hey, Horner, pay attention. You need to take that girl seriously. She's someone special. When I presented her with her contract and asked her to sign, Milada studied it." Horner was snide and mean in response to her announcement. He growled something and slumped deeper into his chair. He accorded her the formality of listening. He sensed her announcement had something to do, somehow, with Elise's Jewishness. This was the glorious manifestation of the Testament! Essentially he had nothing to hope for other than a finale. He acquiesced there to accepting Milada as his scion. The two, Goldscheider and Horner, were guided by their selfish interests. They put their chips on the gambling table. What they could not see at that moment will be revealed in the course of the game.

What they wagered was not a playing chip that clinked and sparkled. It was hard, genuine metal—not counterfeit. It was the best human material that had ever run through Horner's manipulative fingers. Now this material was going to take on its own shape. It would receive the proper stamp and be credited what it was due.

In Milada Horner had his last pupil. Educating her meant putting down roots.

For as long as she could remember Milada had been exposed to tiresome, arcane concepts that had no echo at all in her world; there was no reflection there. These elusive concepts had never troubled or confused her with some shadowy form. On leaving Carlotta's establishment, however, she was sobered by the chilling reality of her profession.

All the desires, hopes, and expectations she had invented for herself began to fall away. They dried up. Milada told herself that in this life of ours nothing is worth striving for. We are taking steps, one at a time, backwards. We become ugly, old, or ill. These are the three mortal enemies of the prostitute, and they await us inexorably on the horizon.

As she saw things after her term in the winery the only options were Red House Alley and the Luisa Hospital where her mother had died. People who are better off end up in the poor house.

What seems uplifting—momentary moods of elation, betterment in standing or money—does not last; these are transient. They are only a detour on the way.

At the very beginning she had placed some hope in the guests. Some gentlemen were lovely to the girls. They became friendly. But, although she was popular in the salon, she could not count them as friends. They often asked her how she had gotten to Red House. She said simply she had grown up there since her mother had been there. The gentlemen did not find anything special in that and asked nothing further. Other girls were clever and told more of a story. The men listened to them. Camille, for example, came from Geneva, and Gisi had even spent time in the Orient with a Turk. These were stories.

Finally Milada had stopped wanting anything more or different than pleasing the madam or her clients for the moment. This worked for her because she was young, peaceable, and she liked order.

Only one thing oppressed her: She had no real work. Since she was not used to being idle, she suffered for having nothing to do. So one morning she went down to the salon and began picking up before the housemaid arrived. The maid looked at her in surprise. "Anna, don't get upset. I took care of some things myself before you got here. If you don't tell on me, I can help you every day, upstairs and down. I like doing this. It makes me feel good."

And that is how it went. When she was cleaning and in a good mood, she could reflect. At those times she let herself forget heavy thoughts. When she did think those same old heavy thoughts, then she saw the gray outlines of Luisa Hospital. She saw the long corridors with the gossiping orderlies and the serious, bespectacled doctors. "That's how it will have to end," she said to herself with a sigh. Red House wore you out and took away your will!

She felt blank until a rough shake woke her up. She was in the ambit of Horner's fog. "The hopeful fool" propped her up with his new material. He transported her in one swoop from her spiritual desert to the shining pinnacle of the tower of his worldview.

"Can you imagine, little girl, that you are holding onto a point high on a tower and clawing your way up higher and higher till you have the whole of the world at your feet? The alleys and streets with their people look like squiggles and little dots to you. Gobs and gobs of tiny insects are crawling around down there. They're running around, helter-skelter. They drool, slither, and dance about, but after a while they all merge onto one wide street. It's dark down there and gloomy because all the people are crowded together. They are all scurrying, mindlessly, into a great abyss that swallows them up. Hey, girlie, up there on the highest peak of the roof, do you want to say something? Do you have an opinion about which one went the right or the wrong way? Do you see the ones who went right on down the hole with dignity? Way up on your pinnacle do you see a straight or crooked path? Are there evil and good paths? Your buddy who drinks himself into a stupor and you the Queen of Spain with a rose for honor, you and me, we don't care which direction they take. It's all about the energy of the eternal matter. Some difference may be visible from on high. But on the ground there is no difference; it's all the same."

Milada shielded her eyes from the blinding light that fell on her. It hurt her. She became aware of the narrowness of her soul. She had the perception this light was greater and more significant than she was. It wanted to pierce her.

Milada asked, "Do we prostitutes have to be ruined, do we?"

He answered her with the keenness of a grammar-school teacher, "Imagine you are in a jungle in Africa. You're plagued with hunger and thirst. Overhead, within reach, are fat, sweet fruits, golden dates and bananas. No creature would have any qualms about grabbing them. You wouldn't either. The forest primeval has no rules. You can even throw things and spit. Spit! Now, my daughter, tomorrow go to the Prater, the Royal People's Park, and pick a little yellow rose. Pick the one you like. Snicker-snack! The policeman will catch you. Do you follow me? That's what you get for taking a little yellow rose, which may have lost its petals by tomorrow. But in the jungle you can fill your belly with wonderful fruit. Don't you know? Connect the dots. Where do rules apply? Listen up, why aren't you allowed to pick a rose in Prater?"

"Because it's forbidden, and the policeman keeps watch," Milada answered thoughtfully.

"There you go! You're clever. The high and mighty society proclaims, 'The person who picks a flower has committed theft.' That's what they call a legal paragraph. And they put a man in a uniform there to see to it the paragraph is enforced. Fine and good! So you are stopped short by the policeman. You don't want to end up in the pen. You're tough and agile. All you really need is your two legs to run, right?

But then he whistles, and another cop comes and a lot of people, too. "And there you have it," he said very pleased with himself as he leaned back in his chair. Light shone in his eyes. "Now you see the situation for what it is. And one more person shows up and then another, and then one more. The law is enforced on all sides, and you, the thief, the little girl with the little rose as yellow as the devil's sulphur, the bad girl with good taste, you are standing there all by yourself. Everything depends on the law; everything hangs by a cord society has strung across the landscape. And the person who does not depend on the law trips and falls and is trapped. And the person who screams is muzzled. That's how it is. You have your two hands, but the man holding you down has fifty. For your two feet he has one hundred. It is the masses that make it so, the power of minions on the street. Being on your own in that space can only mean being in league with evil. The force of gravity applies to the space where the cord is strung."

In educating Milada, one last time, his innermost secretive plans flew on high.

"You are the creature," he rejoiced, "that can realize my plans. Your birth and your development make you the bearer of an extraordinary idea.

"You are the child of a prostitute, a child of revenge. You were nursed with hate and raised with scorn. Thus you are the material expression of the animalistic egotism of the strong. Hey, a bitch full of revenge dropped you in a nest of prostitutes. She abandoned you. It's magnificent! Your mother was a seeress with talent, I tell you. She had a higher vision. Men were thrown, danced or slithered to the bitch. And the small child lay in the filth, even before it could move its little legs. This little Jew bastard might have fallen in anyone's nest. Just you broom-makers and pea-pickers wait! This cuckoo's egg is going to surprise the hell out of you."

Systematically, old teacher that he was, Horner employed logic to teach her. With neither too much haste nor eagerness he proceeded to sort out the chaos of Milada's memories. He ordered her experiences and unformed thoughts. Her intellect was turned over like soil ready for new seed. Horner corrected her primary education. He had a well-thought-out and far-ranging plan. He instructed her in the natural world, geography, and history; he gave her lessons on art and beauty. Horner thoroughly purged her thoughts of prejudice and fantasies and of superstition and fatalistic rules, which greedily suck weak souls out of this conception of life.

His primary principle in teaching was never exhaust a topic. He set no firm boundaries.

He told her, "Everything that a person can think, express, or create is an image of Nature that has been filtered through the human mind. Most people see things mediated by and confused with the dregs of their physicality. Intelligent people see things most clearly and immediately. We owe them a debt of gratitude for the most complete understanding of Nature and for the most useful truths. Every truth is spiritualized Nature."

This phase of Horner's life could be called the best and richest. He appeared markedly more collected. During his tenure as principal at a private boys' preparatory school his concentration had diminished daily. But, while teaching Milada, he was attentive for hours. He was communicative and engaged. His wit lost its acerbic edge. His whole being was recharged, and he became sociable.

Madame Goldscheider watched and smiled.

He had said to her once, "You women with your bourgeois pasts, with your sentimental memories and relationships to this world are captives. You are valueless. Your primary asset is your womb; in other arenas you are sterile. Milada, by contrast, has nothing to lose. She is not attached. She's not a mother and not a daughter; nor is she a person with any status. The horror of being disgraced does not hang over her.

"I tell you, the person who can put down roots in the desert sand has to bear peculiar fruits!" quoth Horner.

"Milada might bear bombs," Goldscheider replied.

"No, she'll bear the hard, bitter nuts of my knowledge," he told her, rubbing his hands in delight.

The most valuable and important lesson he imparted to Milada was this: her individuality was hers and hers alone. Up until then she had seen herself as the product of her environment. She was Goldscheider's useful tool; she carried out the madam's orders. She felt delivered up to a fate she accepted without complaint or resistance. She had become, in the truest sense of the word, selfless.

She stayed loyal to her sense of pride in Red House and its growing renown in the city. This pride alone gave her a sense of dignity.

She was dutiful in her performance at Red House. She had never violated any of the eight rules of the house, which were copied out and hung in a frame on the wall of every room.

She had a deep need to honor and to serve. In the most limiting of circumstances people erect an altar and place on it a god they create in their own image.

Horner took away her primitive belief in the importance and value of the place she lived, and he gave her in return a fundamental belief in the freedom and invulnerability of her own ego.

She listened to him, meditatively. She watched him.

"I tell you: you can go right out that door. Milada Rezek, you are free. The name Milada may well mean humility. But your essence, what is ineffable and eternal in your bodily being, that is free. Bodies are numbered and trapped; they can disappear, never to come again. Yet the essence within is free. Hadn't you ever thought of something like that?"

"No, never," she answered excitedly in a lowered voice.

Horner continued, "The I and the you, those two do not go together well. Please understand me correctly! The you eats, drinks, sleeps, and kisses when the madam says to. And the I thinks, has desire, and negotiates when it has to. I am addressing the you. But your I gives me an answer. Never be misled by the mistaken belief anyone or any rule has any rights or any power over the I. Chains can tear the you apart. But they cannot touch the force that forges our inner thoughts. What transpires within you is most significant. External events are nothing. Each step you take forward and every gesture of your hand stirs through external circumstances. Is this world," Horner indicated the space around himself, "the contents of your being? Do you start out life or end it with this? Will you die and have been nothing other than a prostitute? What foolishness!"

He grabbed her forehead.

"That is the center. What happens in there, what you consider and what you decide, that remains for centuries. This body of yours is only your subordinate servant. Train it, and you have fulfilled your duty. Live as a prostitute or as empress, it does not matter. You need a change? Good! You want to change out the theater sets? Just wait!"

He put a fat finger on his nose as he thought.

"Do you know the flat meadows outside of this imperial city? Have you looked up under the skirts of this city? There's the smell of dirt, isn't there? Fields of green and yellow stretch out before you, and there are rows of trees laden with flowers in the spring. Behind them are the hills round about. Farther back they get darker, more defiant, stronger. The high forest reaches upwards behind the hills and bounds the sky. In these mountains and forests, in the valleys and basins, there are people living their lives. The boys and girls are young and strong like you. They live in isolation with the animals. On summer days you hear nothing but the humming of the bees, cow bells, and the calls from pasture to pasture. When strangers come, these boys and girls go hide; they're shy of people. They don't want to know about your world or your friends. Your rules don't apply there. Your evil doesn't exist. You can pick a bushel of flowers, inhale their scent, and throw them away. You can gather aprons full of berries from the forest, and you can let the ice-cold water of the stream flow over your tongue. You can play chase with the animals, chew stalks of grass, and look off toward the sun. Get up and go there. And find yourself some work! Lots of women are looking to hire a strong girl like you. You do know the door downstairs is open. What are you waiting for, huh?"

She held her slender, brown hand with long, narrow fingers to her forehead.

"I can't imagine what it's like," she said, complaining about the pressure.

"No matter. The world is large and varied. It was only a setting from the theater. Now onto something different! In the evening you might go out into the alley with a shawl and a dark dress instead of going to the salon. For the sake of my story now you aren't wearing any makeup," he said sternly. "You have to leave the little alley. You step out calmly into the harsh light. You are already making accommodations. Life is about adapting."

He stretched out his hand. "Hey, are you with me? You are standing in the heart of our dear city."

"Yes," said Milada as if hypnotized.

"Now go swiftly down the side streets. You study the notes on the doors of the houses. This one doesn't suit you; that one doesn't either. But here's one: 'Room cheap, with food, for respectable young lady.' Great! Go take a look! You share the room with a pasty-looking milliner girl. That's fine, too! The landlady is the widow of a bureaucrat. She wears a lace cap and horn-rimmed glasses; her lips are mobile. She has flowers in the window boxes and old photographs on the table. This woman listens to you and hears you are an orphan. She swallows her tears and makes you a sandwich. Your pasty roommate is immediately on friendly terms with you. She tells you about her cousin who travels and cannot be reached. All that is fine. Then you go out to find a job. Work, I can tell you, is always available in our fair city. There are seamstresses, nannies, women who embroider, knitters, women who mend clothes, and so on. What you want is only day work. You're firm about that. You want to spend evenings sitting together with the pasty milliner while the bureaucrat's widow tells tales of joy. If things go nicely, she'll brew some tea. Does that appeal to you? Then go get a situation like that! You can always find a little corner like that. You just need to go after it."

Horner continued while a twisted smile played on his lips. His expression had something of deep sorrow about it.

"At this point your life can go any number of directions . You're waiting for something. You do know something will happen. You and the milliner girl are both longing for something that unsettles your landlady.

"Ha! Do you know springtime in the Royal People's Garden? No, you don't know it. Trees and shrubs are in bloom and send out aromas. It all seems to sing. A warm whisper floats about in the breeze. It calls to each young girl. To you, too. Your eyes are wide open and look wistful, just like the eyes of the pasty girl. You are looking for something. The wind tears at your hat. The wild wind of spring blows your hair in your face. You hold onto your hat with both hands, and your skirts dance crazily. That is spring in the People's Garden."

He took a moment and stared straight ahead.

Then he continued, "Each and every morning you think to yourself, 'Today is the day. Certainly it must be the day.' A young man speaks to you. He's well-bred and honorable. He smells of nice soap and violet pomade. But that is irrelevant. I'm going somewhere else with this."

Horner cleared his throat, and his smile became a grimace.

"And now love has appeared in your life, but not as you have known it before. For God's sake, girlie, you have to forget all your encounters up till now. For God's sake, don't be too pure, that's always suspicious. Hey, first you look each other over. Then you speak sweetly and purr. Sometimes you squeal with delight; other times, you cry. Then you girls slowly come to understand what is marvelous." He placed his finger tips together and spread out his hands.

"You marry him, naturally. You have children, learn to cook, and wash diapers. That's another scenario! Does it appeal to you?"

Milada answered, "First of all, I don't really believe you when you say I am all that free. The police can run me down and bring me back here if Goldscheider wants. I can't sew either. I don't knit or anything like that."

She put her hand on her young body. "I can't even have a baby. Having children is good, just like you say. But it's not something I wish for."

"It doesn't matter. Satan was only putting some wonderful things in life on display for you," Horner said affirmatively. "Anything can be attained. Anything you can imagine is possible.

"Enjoy yourself, play with ideas. Roll the dice! But do take note. Any one life or another is not better or more important than any other; none is more worthy of aspiring to than another. Everywhere you look, you find people on a quest. They long for something and rush around, moving forward into the abyss. That's what's amusing. Whether you take yourself seriously, making strides with confidence, or whether you stoop down or hunker in the dirt, in the end—one by one—all the puppets tumble down the hole.

"You have to investigate each and every option. You can play any role at all. Try on all the scenarios. You hold all of these within yourself simultaneously. In you is everything that was, is, or ever will be.

"There is no moment of rest. There are no hard and fast boundaries. Everything is fluid and in flux, just as the Greek philosopher said. Goldscheider puts this principle into practice. She never smuggles women who work, upright shop girls, nannies and other angels over the borders of this county."

And, thus, this most difficult experiment of Horner's went well. Milada's imprisoned soul gradually tore itself out of the soil it had been anchored in. Her thoughts, which had been bound to the next, immediate situation, were cast afar into unbounded realms, and they returned laden with wonderful, new seeds. The unnatural narrowness of her imagination gave way to a spirited, delightful ascent. And she soon felt the pulse of the universe, standing right there where she was. She understood, "Nothing is ever completely cut off, lost, or dead. Everything belongs together. All things change."

The girls of the salon, these brightly attired, rouged girls she lived with, and those who walked up and down Red House Alley in the shade of the night, the proud ladies who strolled past her with disdain, and the happy girls who walked safely arm in arm with their mothers—all of them—belonged together. They constituted one concentrated mass in the world of phenomena. Neither rules nor selfish decrees could efface their original and eternal unity.

The end of the season brought the lovely young lady Camille good fortune. A Russian engineer, who arrived in the merry company of the salon by coincidence, had fallen head over heels for the pretty, blond girl. After having generously paid off her debts, he took her along on his travels.

Camille had been the attraction of the house, yet Goldscheider let her leave without much resistance. She took leave in a very strange way. She looked like a happy, young woman when she left Red House. She wore a decorative dress for travel, smiled, waved, and kissed her intimate friends sweetly.

Dubbe, as might have been expected, took the occasion of Camille's departure to make a theater of her own distress. She hung on Camille's neck so tightly, as she sobbed and wailed, that poor, dear Camille was shocked and turned bright red. She began to choke.

Vassil Milevitch, the engineer—who looked like a Jew or a Gypsy—gave Dubbe a swift kick to the stomach. She laughed and jumped back like a cat. Afterwards she stayed in her room and bawled her eyes out. Milada, whom Lefty Anna called The Nun, brewed chamomile tea for her. It might help her get an engineer.

"Oh, well," Olympia sighed. "Traveling is wonderful. You have fine hotels, silk clothes, and the whole time you have just the one man."

People were curious to know who Camille's replacement would be since there had never been fewer than eight young women in the house. The part-timers had never made up the difference.

"Maybe Goldscheider will get Fritzi from Carlotta," one person ventured.

The porter Olympia shook her head knowingly. She was the only person who was in any way informed about the madam's dealings.

"Last year Fritzi had Doctor Iserstein tell us she isn't leaving Carlotta's. Her trip to Berlin was only a vacation," Olympia explained. So people kept on waiting to see who the replacement would be. Such matters always provoked interest, but people were particularly eager to know since this post had been for the house favorite, the so-called Champagne Lady.

The girls were happy enough when two days later a large, rawboned girl with cheeks as red as roof tiles and straight blond hair moved into Camille's former room. It was outfitted with polka-dotted batiste curtains and yellow furniture. It was a more rustic style than the madam, a woman of sophistication, usually chose for her house. There was something quite crude and provincial about the new arrival.

The newcomer shook people's hand and told them her name was Bina Michal and she was glad to meet them.

The girls made a fuss. Laura pulled a poppy-seed cake and some sausage out of a hastily wrapped package. This brightened their mood even more.

But then the newcomer turned around resolutely and told the convivial woman Laura, a Jew, she could not offer her hand in greeting. She explained she was just "like that." Bina made the excuse her hand was not working right. Anybody could look and see it was impaired. She held her arms stiffly at her side.

Rosa with the pockmarks knew this type of provocation well. She turned around indignantly, took a deep breath, and said these country attitudes were not acceptable in the city. She did not know where the newcomer had learned this behavior, but she found it vulgar. Rosa left the room solemnly, and the rest followed her.

Unruffled and with a defiant look on her fresh face, the new member of the house installed herself.

Goldscheider had not let the attitude of this recent acquisition affect her. One morning, as she was sitting in her office, the porter had brought in a country girl in clean clothes. This girl with the pleasant, bold confidence of a farm woman gave Goldscheider her card. All that was on the card was her complete address, written in crude, broken script. The girl was young and strong. The madam saw she looked useful and beyond this seemed to know the score.

Michal spoke very little when she arrived but showed a lively interest in what was going on around her. She was eager to work. In her eagerness she stood up and smiled at the many guests when they entered the salon, much to their amusement. She gave up this practice when Goldscheider, who in former times never would have accepted Bina in her salon, informed her it was out of place. We can say Bina was overly friendly, but she did her work well.

Milada thought, "She'd be a good fit for Zimmermann's business." But Goldscheider's refined clientele got along all right with this bit of raw Nature.

Milada, it turned out, was the only person Bina had any connection with. "Rezek is a name we know back home. They're people from the border. Are you from the German-speaking part of Bohemia?"

Milada answered she did not really know. It was possible though. Her mother was from that area. She did remember her mother often sang Bohemian songs.

After a while Bina entrusted Milada with her money. This was the best proof of trust this limited, rough soul could offer.

Bina's most rancorous enemies remained Laura, the Jewish woman with the hair of Titian, her pride and glory, and Anna, who was nicknamed Lefty because her left arm was partially paralysed and hung forward. Laura and Lefty were quite harmless compared to Annie Meitner, who came from the Czech city Olomouc. Annie was proud to say that by the time she was eleven she was not good for anything but prostitution.

"You should have seen my breasts. They stuck out like bombs."

Laura and Lefty took every opportunity to tease the newcomer Bina. They made fun of her way of walking and her posture, but mostly they made fun of the way she spoke. Bina had the habit of ending every story or any argument with the words, "I have Cyrill."

Nobody could figure out who this Cyrill was. Any attempt to find out met with Bina's scorn. She shook her head, smiled, and said nothing.

Right from the start Bina brought order to the disorder of life in the brothel. She made sure duties were distributed evenly. She showed up in the salon every day at noon with remarkable punctuality, well rested, dressed and coiffed. She always had a piece of heavy, gray homespun linen she was embroidering in jarring bright-blue. She embellished aprons, blankets, and curtains—all in unbelievably short order. After lunch she napped, and when she awoke she banged around in closets and cupboards, washing, polishing, scrubbing, and sewing her clothes. Bina put her possessions in good order every single day. At seven o'clock, filled with energy and a thirst for activity, she appeared in the salon. She went along with all the mean jokes and never once put on a bad face. People palmed off the most unpleasant and burdensome guests on her. She took them on, even later in the evening, without complaining. She understood serving these guests was part of the job.

"The ladies here have it pretty easy," she said to Milada when they were alone. It must be said that she had come to understand only the most lovely and beautiful came to Red House. She also understood the advantage of being in Red House was she did not have to work like a dog, as did laundresses and scullery maids who did heavy cleaning. She let it be known she was no longer willing to do that kind of work. The light and relatively well-paid way of earning money made her giddy, yet she was always prepared for some random stroke of bad luck. She watched her every step closely. Bina was able, quickly and unobtrusively, to slot into the group of young ladies who had an air of urbanity about themselves as well as charm and sophistication. Goldscheider knew just how to bring out these qualities in the girls and how to showcase them.

There were two of them who were inseparable, Fanny Schwabe and Putzi Bleier. The first was really named Fanchon, French for whimsical. She had been around the block a few times before arriving at Red House. Goldscheider had taken on this thin, wispy proletarian child with the consumptive face and blue eyes, hungry for living, at the behest of a very influential supporter who had taken pity on her. Fanny had a childlike, unselfconscious joy about her. She had the sweet, dalliant playfulness of a waif. Her manner could captivate a tired, old man who was used up by life. She could seduce him into expressing secretive sentiments. Goldscheider's supporter had had great plans for Fanny! He had bought her a villa and placed Fanny, who was deathly ill, in the sunshine out in the country. He surrounded her with the best fare. But she slipped away from him. She was not interested. What she wanted was to live fully, to laugh and have friends. Fanny needed a scintillating, busy, exciting environment of song and dance and idle illusions. She had a musical rhythm and a breath of beauty about her thin, pale limbs, and she was looking for the most dramatic, quickest descent into death. She danced and twirled and got others to join in her rush. And she sat in place for hours on end with her knees pulled up and recited prayers, letting her rosary slip through her small, white hands, paralysed by the fear of death.

She was the child of a mason, and she readily told the story—too readily—that her five siblings back home were his real children. Before her mother had married the mason, she had had a relationship with an architect, a lively man of good humor, who built churches.

"I think," Fanny said, "he was rather spiritual. Mother always said there was something blessed about him."

Lefty Anna said, "Then he had to have been a circumcised Jew."

"Well, if all he had was little Fanny, maybe so. I am so very happy to be alive," she said openly.

She could talk an unbelievable lot, and nobody listened to her so attentively and eagerly as Putzi, a very beautiful but limited and sexual being. Putzi had no imagination, and her sole interest was plain sexual desire. She was the daughter of a well-regarded merchant in the city. Many men had already used Putzi in hidden corners by the time she was fourteen. When she became interested in money and her appearance but did not know how to sell her body, she fell into the hands of a procuress. This woman could not take her away from her family, so Putzi met with her secretly. The procuress walked the streets of the metropolis and addressed gentlemen out on a walk with these words: “Lovely, young girl, are you interested?” For a few days the business went smoothly, but then the police got wind of it. Both Putzi and the procuress were stopped and arrested. At the ensuing trial, the girl told her father, who was in tears, short and to the point: she was sorry to inform him, but she could not get along without a man. She asked her father to be so good and let her do this. She promised to change her name and never return home.

Putzi was lazy and not a fast thinker. She listened to the animated, fanciful Fanchon while nestled in the pillows with half-closed eyes that sparkled. Fanchon decked out stories of her experiences with bright colors. She had learned a lot from her time as a model. She knew how to relate stories about the fun, exciting life of painters, their imagination and conversations. When she was telling her stories, she always jumped up, ran to the mirror, tried on scarves and veils, and put flowers in her hair to show the girls how the painters had depicted her. She posed with her thin, blue-white body in coquettish and stylized positions. She lay down like a slumbering nymph with an artificial palm representing the forest, using a jug of water as a spring. Her time as a model had obviously been the happiest and richest of her life. There were other “noble moments” that followed. Yet she had never lived so comfortably as among the young artists in whose ateliers she had long been the most special girl. They had been good and jolly and generous when they had some money. They never cursed, did not ask for anything objectionable, and they were grateful for any small service. “Fanchon is the one who is stable,” is what Happy had said about her. His real name was Temple, and what a golden guy he was! If he had something, everybody had enough. He shared sausage, beer, cheese and cigarettes they rolled themselves. He had a honky-tonk piano, a funny child's instrument, and Happy played waltzes and songs, and some pieces of opera, too. His playing was so beautiful and moving that people would listen for hours. What a guy Happy was! She had loved him! Heavens above, he was very dear. But he had a deformed foot. Happy had almost become a doctor and not an artist at all.

"Can you all imagine how he was? There was always humor and dancing when he was around. But he could also play tragic roles that made you so scared you cried." Then she strutted around again. "They sketched and painted my hands, my feet, my back, all of me, and then showed it to their teacher." Happy had once draped a gray veil over her body. It was white and black around her head, and on top was a wreath of dark-red roses. She had to pose with her eyes closed and her arms outstretched as if she were indicating a path. All the artists painted her in that posture. One of them put his painting in a beautiful silver frame and sent it to an exhibition. "Twilight" it was called, and it cost five hundred gulden.

"You are cheaper now," Lefty Anna said philosophically.

Afterwards at a café she had a seat high on the bar wearing that gray veil.

"You had red flannel underpants on underneath, right?" said Putzi.

Fanchon did not get angry. Undisturbed she kept on with her story. Inevitably the good time soon came to an end. They could not paint Fanny alone. The professor had once thrown a brush in anger and said to the students, "You always paint this one girl. You can't do that!" Then Happy brought in another model for them.

"That model was a big, fat women with red hair. She acted proud and said, 'Only my head, please, nothing more.' How odd! These were artists! This was where the finest of ladies said 'thank you very much' and paid to pose. So Happy suggested she undress, just as an experiment, behind the screen and stick her head out because the head of a naked woman has very different coloration. So she did that, and Happy quickly pulled the screen away, and there she was. Then it was clear why she had pretended to be prudish. She was old. Happy asked her to go home and send her daughter to model. I tell you that woman was fuming!"

Fanny took special delight in telling the story of her departure from the circle of painters. Bina Michal sat by quietly and contentedly, enjoying the stories as great entertainment she got free. She could not comprehend how someone was so moved by an event in the past. How animated everything about small Fanchon was! She was completely alive, just as she had been when the Bohemian artists loved her and painted her.

"And that's just how it was. Happy told me, 'You can't become a maid. But that's all right. Read books! What else can you do with your health? Be sure to drink a lot of milk.' That's what he said. That's how it went. They brought me pictures, and the sculptors brought presents. I got a red ashtray. But some dumb bitch kept my things. She was my first encounter with a nasty landlady. So, fine. That evening we all went to the Alhambra. I picked up the tab—for that bitch, too. And she told me then and there that was the last time she would have anything to do with me. What an ass! We had coffee, wine, and cake, and nice tidbits to eat. I was glad to offer that. Then the men walked me home. At eleven that evening someone came to visit. It was Happy's uncle, a guy from the countryside who was in town to buy livestock. Happy was a good guy, wasn't he? He sent his uncle to see me right away. But he had cooked something up, of course."

"Did that uncle have a bum leg, too?" Putzi asked and had a good, loud laugh.

"A bad leg runs in families," Anna said.

"I don't know anything about that," Fanchon picked up her story, eager to continue.

"Happy had told this uncle he was taking him to a virgin. It would cost a hundred gulden. Fifty, up front. Happy would give that to the mother of the virgin and the other fifty..."

"Of course it was a virgin," Lefty Anna said laughing.

"And the other fifty the uncle could give the girl. He could pay the girl himself. Well, then Happy told him all kinds of wonderful things about this girl, what she was like, and so on, until this uncle was crazy for her."

"For you," Anna corrected her.

"Yes, slow poke! I...at the time...and then afterwards... A virgin would have gone to pieces. Well, I don't remember. My heavens," Fanny assured people. "I should have known better than to lie down. I tell you all, it was a spectacle. He started cursing. And Happy was outside the window with a group of guys, and they chanted, 'Blue, blue, the thimble's blue. It fits the uncle like a hat. Now the virgin has to dance, rutting with a dolt like that.'

"I tell you it was dreadful! At first I thought the old guy couldn't handle it and had gone mad. He cried out, 'I want a virgin. Where's the virgin?'

"My landlady, what a fat mouth that woman had! First she dumped a pot of water on his head and said, 'There's an avalanche for you. Your virgin isn't far away.' All right, so then a policeman showed up. Happy's uncle grabbed the policeman's head and screamed that the girl wasn't a virgin and, if he didn't believe it, he should see for himself, please.

"And I said, 'Please stop this.' And the uncle screamed, 'I was cheated out of fifty gulden, fifty gulden.' And my old landlady said, 'Fifty gulden for a virgin?! What a stupid yokel! For fifty gulden you can't get an old sow let alone a virgin pig.'

"Afterwards this uncle had to pay ten gulden, and he split quick as lightening."

Everybody loved the story, and Fanny's audience was in a good mood.

"So why didn't Happy marry you then?" Bina asked her practical question.

"Well, he went on to study medicine," Fanny defended herself with gaiety.

"Yeah, and then there was the problem with his game leg," Putzi giggled.

"But," said Bina emphatically, "if he was your fiancé, he should have married you. A fiancé marries his girl."

"Like Cyrill," Lefty Anna said with compassion.

"You nasty bitch!" Bina responded.

"Go to hell," said Lefty.

"The nastiest people are the ones who start things."

"Maybe in hell it's nicer," Anna said slyly to cool her out, as she poked her.

At that moment Olympia slowly opened the door, looked at everybody in the room, and made an announcement. The tone she used was portentous—she was good at that. "Here you all are telling your stupid little stories when there is big news. Our madam is going to sell the house."

Crash, slam! That really hit hard. All the girls jumped up and barraged Olympia with questions.

Only Bina sat there without making a sound. Milada was leaned against the door with her eyes wide open and just listened.

"I've known for some time something was up. The madam had let on there was something afoot. But I thought 'don't go spreading rumors.' Then yesterday while we were sorting clothing," Olympia turned to Milada who nodded, "Madame Goldscheider said Sucher had come to see her. He had said as he left, 'You're a true pal. You're smart and know how to do business.' She replied, 'Nice to hear. But it is a shame for the business.'"

"Oh, all of us will suffer! A man will run the business. There will certainly be beatings," Putzi asserted almost with an undertone of contentment.

Gisi Geyger chewed on her beautifully manicured nails.

"I'm packing. Ferdi will surely come get me, and..."

Olympia waved her hands emphatically in protest and said, "Since the house is being sold, everything will be sold with it. There will be a complete inventory."

"If I don't like things, I'll go back to a respectable job. I have credentials, and the Baroness in St. Pölten, not far away, will be glad to have her Rosie back."

People were emotionally wrought and made plans. Everybody felt wishes, unrest, and agitation rise within herself. Only Bina and Putzi were not disturbed. Putzi said, "Look at Amshel's brother, the one who limps. He beat us, too, my God!"

There was a boundless, turbulent distress! Olympia, as she usually did in times of stress, started prattling about Paris. She lost herself in a monologue about her best memories.

Milada closed the door. She, too, felt a storm brewing within. Sold! We're being sold off! Early childhood memories surfaced in her. She saw her mother with her red curls in her cotton dress roaming around the room, singing. At the same time a deeper, more primary fear gripped her, a fear that lay beneath the women's noisy chatter.

Janka made a pale appearance in her thoughts as a pale woman. A vision of Janka floated out of the mist of the past. Where were Mother and Janka now, right now? It was her turn this time. But she was free, free—free. But not as Horner had meant. Not just free in her own thinking rather actually free. Goldscheider's words returned to her, "When I leave this business, you owe nothing to anyone. Your debt here is only to me." Milada closed her eyes and felt dizzy like a person approaching the edge of an abyss. Where should she go now? The world is so large. Where was she going? Should she shake off this world and find herself a soft, warm, new nest? She stayed in her room and locked the door. She pressed her forehead to the windowpane.

A while ago she had shaken Dubbe assertively when Dubbe had clung to her in despair. Did she imagine things were any different for her than they had been for Dubbe? Ultimately Dubbe had to—absolutely had to—leave, didn't she? She should take her child and go back to Germany! This Dubbe! She was completely foolish during the day. She was always hissing and screaming and forever repeating her story, which nobody cared about anymore. In the evening she became very loud in her madness, in her abandon and wild behavior. She was so unrestrained that Goldscheider often had to intervene. Milada used to think Dubbe should just go away. Now Milada wanted to calm herself down and think about her own future. Horner called that "organization."

She did have some money, maybe four hundred, and a very nice wardrobe. She would be fine for a while with that until she found something else. She could find some kind of work that was good and secure. She was in good health, like a lot of the girls. She was afraid for Fanchon though. Milada knew she was coughing up blood, and Olympia had reported Fanny, without her makeup, looked chalk-white. Goldscheider had only kept her on because she had made a promise to an old supporter of hers. Milada had heard this supporter even sent money for Goldscheider to keep Fanny on. If there had been a new girl, Fanny would have to go, that was certain. And she was such an adorable person, that Fanchon. She was as dear as a child and just as helpless. There will be plenty of noise over her fate.

But how did all that concern her? She would be far away, maybe even in Paris!

Regardless how hard she tried to imagine herself in another situation, she kept coming back resolutely. The look of shock on the faces of the girls returned again and again and disrupted any image of the future she tried to put together. Milada was not making choices or ordering her thoughts. That was the way she thought when she feared something new. Whatever came would bring danger. Clinging to the present works. The girls were afraid and lived in fear. There was no inkling of courage or faith among them. She wished for the security of an unshakeable faith in herself.

She heard Horner's words, "Nothing will happen to you. You are invulnerable." Who could give them a curative dose of that message now? She rambled around in her room without direction. Horner's message was all well and good. But, at base, were these not just words made up of letters, like the words "trapped," "desperate," or "cowardly"? Was she in actuality any better off here in this body with its heart trapped inside? Hunkering down was the only possible future. It was easy for Goldscheider to say, "The world is large." Horner might preach, "Be free in your thoughts!" But the chains and shackles were more real to her that the messages from Goldscheider and Horner. She had the courage to open the door. But could she comfortably look people in the eye and ask for a friendly word? Was she in any position to ask for kindness? Could she lie about her life and everything at Red House? Never! Something erupted in her. It was not hatred of this world, and it was not aversion to it.

She had a strange inkling. She felt compassion. She felt sympathy for those gripped by fear. What were these feelings? She had the feeling of being together with others. It was intimate and inviolable. She was connected with those who would stay on, if she did leave. She was tied to all girls whose lives are entwined in the lap of the night. She was one with the girls who dance out of the depths into the harsh light of sin only to fall back when it is extinguished.

Milada recognized guilt was not what had bound her all along to Red House. What bound her was her own indestructible will. Her own compassion enfolded all the girls who needed protection. She did not have words to frame this elusive, dreamlike feeling. It was forcefully present. Milada also knew the feeling would last and snap her back, wherever she might land. It converged with everything she had known. It was in tension with her will to be an individual; it clashed with her personality. This awareness of connectedness triumphed over Horner's beatified "I."

The power of her emotions was so intense that when Horner opened the door, she blurted out, "Horner, Goldscheider is selling the place, and I am going out into the world. I want to go to Paris. I want to live there—finally!"

He put his dirty, fat finger on his nose.

"Paris is good. Beautiful. Who brought that to your attention?"

"It was Olympia," she answered lost in thought. After being so shaken by emotion she was exhausted and silent. "Why? Do you have anything against my leaving?"

"Yes, well, is Olympia your oracle now? In earlier times I knew her well. She had been a proud woman. Her first lover was a university student. Their relationship had all the signs of becoming a good bourgeois engagement. There were lyrical rendezvous in hotels and jejune passions, things like that. And then an artist from the circus swept her away. She left with him for Paris on a trip into the sunset toward heaven. That was cause for jubilation. There she found a generous lover, the company of men in the German Artists' Club. After she had become acquainted with Paris, she developed, naturally, a taste for the exotic. She took up with a juggler from Japan and worked with him. She juggled her way around the whole of the Botanical Garden until she acquired a wild interest in higher-order aristocrats. Naturally, there was a pretender to the throne among them. That was the apex of her gaming career. Now let's come back down to Earth. Olympia is not one to climb on bare walls. A true swindler from the circle of the aristocrats entertained her some good long while. He bought her genuine diamonds and a charming little castle, which originally had been Spanish. As things go, at this castle she received a German prince, from whose good offices it took her half a year in the charity hospital to recover. She had the typical convalescence: she returned to morality. She became a nanny in Beauvais and, after two months, got a kick in the pants from her employer as well as travel money to return to Germany. Here she climbed to the top of the social ladder, from which she fell and landed at Goldscheider's.

Now let's add things up! From her glorious trek all around, this is what she had accumulated: an enormous lot of middling portraits, fifty colorful balls of celluloid, two loose diamonds, syphilis, and a photo of the family of a gracious gentleman. Why did she need Paris? How did it help her to take her beauty, youth, and strength across the border? You can do anything she did in Paris right here, can't you?"

Milada thought, "Why am I telling him what I think? He will only make fun of me." Aloud she asked, "So what do you suggest I do? Stay here?"

"Take a look around yourself," Horner said. "Learn to look! Learn to recognize what's going on! Learn to take something spiritual from the facts, and then digest it! Gather all this together!"

"Yes, Horner, but wouldn't you say I already recognize what's going on here?"

"So you think you recognize things," he continued. "Ha, you don't recognize a thing! You do not make distinctions. You only smell filth! You can touch a dead body with your fingers, but that's all. Learn to distinguish the cause from the effect. Make a distinction between the fundamental and eternal on the one hand and the temporal and transitory on the other. Begin to amass information. What is typical of you and people like you? What is repetitious in the myriad ways of playing the game? You'll easily recognize the special things in life; they stand out like red veins on a white ground. Learn to relate what is daily and what is common! Learn to love what you pass by perhaps in arrogance. Put yourself out there, and squeeze humanity from lead-gray masks! Show me the enigma of humanity before you tell me you are proud to have the answer!"

"I think I understand," she began enchanted. "I see what you are saying. Ideas and plans are fine. But I am too full of myself." Her words came from her mouth excitedly, "But I'm not as good as you think. I chew myself up."

"Don't break your teeth chewing, my little one! The person who believes he has to crawl into the sun to understand its essence is making a mistake. Unfortunately we can't be rid of our guts. If we could, the art of knowing oneself would be further along. Watch at a remove. Invest yourself in external things. Use your intellect to go on a trip rather than to drill down on yourself. Looking to yourself brings no benefit. Don't count your little cache of money like a petty merchant; exchange it, lend it, buy and sell. And then when you're back home, take account. What you've gained is you! Every action is the measure of our I. No amount of craftiness, however crafty it may be, no philosophy, however dark it may be, can offer you more enlightenment about yourself than the very tiniest bit of instantiation of your own will. Get out there and perform acts, and you will know yourself. Hey, you girl, did I find you and guide you to higher things for you to amuse some empty-headed Frenchman?"

Horner turned his probing eyes to her face. "You've got to stick it out here. You can conquer the world from here. Drink up and drink only from the cup you have poured for yourself. You don't need anything else. You are rich enough as you are. You have learned to think. You've got courage and defiance, uniqueness, and soul. You are rich. And now you're talking about taking all that out into a world that is suffocating in excess? You want to throw it away on those people? Waste it on their good fortune? Look around yourself, and create order! Make enlightened people of the proletariat of prostitutes! Organize them. Teach them to fight! That's what I raised you to do. Girl, your education is good for negotiating, lashing out around yourself, stabbing and punching, and for being so smart it is ridiculous. Do you know the story of Don Quixote? You have to read it. Quixote is a true hero. You have to believe in him your whole life long. All the other heroes are shit heads because they have had everything laid out for them in black and white, telling them what they stand to gain by fighting and what the prize is.

"I'm going to tell you a secret. Come closer! Prostitutes laugh like little girls. Queens roll around in filthy beds. Poor mothers cry. Human flesh depends on small words without sounds. There are burdensome speeches whose meaning is empty, like the tolling of bells in the air. Recognition ennobles. Make your world noble! Exhaust your being by giving! You should pray at the altar where you have made sacrifices. It is an old wise saying! I tell you this: you will love the lepers, the down-trodden, the wounded and wretched. And perhaps, just perhaps, this love of yours will be a torch that burns up altars. You will not lose yourself in this great self-sacrifice. Listen well! As wild and tumultuous as the sea of human love you traverse may be, its culmination is only a small ripple in the mud; its name is egoism."

It was a gray morning. Milada left the salon all done up. She had her makeup on and her hair coiffed. The distress that had gripped the whole house today still quivered within her. She, too, was at a crossroads. Goldscheider had sold the house and told some of the regular guests about it. She had gone to Milada late in the evening and said to her laughingly, "Well, now, pull yourself together."

The madam had had quite a loud fight with Horner. For the first time Milada could remember he did not show up in the salon. There were lots of guests there. Fanchon, Gisi, and Dubbe were acting impossibly foolish. There was something about their noise that was unhealthy, shaky, even sick. Dubbe led her gentleman, a small, blond count, out of the salon by the arm. He gave her his wallet. Bina lay flat on the floor and complained loudly.

Wild scenes of the evening danced in Milada's head. And behind those scenes there remained a sharp awareness that pierced each fading dream. The muck shuffled over her dreams. There was nothing she could do about it. Others will come, young ones in full bloom. And they, too, dance and float, weighted down with the same suffering, with the same burden. Myriads come and go. Some are young, eager, and happy; others, pale, and ragged. They look tortured to death. They raise their hands, crying "Help us, please you, help! At least give us your soul."

Milada sat at the window and leaned her head against the wall. She was already feeling the need to sleep. But there was someone standing in front of her, waiting for something from her. Milada felt like screaming, "I can't!" Cold fingers shook her bare shoulders. "Milada, it's me." It was Dubbe in her nightgown and barefoot. She was bare faced and looked destroyed. She appeared like a ghost.

"Thank God you're awake. I have to talk to you," said Dubbe. "There's a sweet boy in my room asleep. He's staying all night, the sweetie, thank God! Our life of misery is over. Did you hear? The madam is selling the house! Oh, I'm nobody now."

Dubbe fell on Milada's bed and moved over to the edge.

"Go to bed now, Martha," Milada said.

The shadows from the candle played over Dubbe like ghosts. She stuck her beautiful arms out of her nightgown. "I still look really good, don't I? Two years, my God, that's not so awful. I'm a teacher. I've got credentials, Living here was only..." She turned all the way around, let her arms fall, and continued, "an idiotic interlude. Now I'm going back to my world."

"Martha, going back is not always that easy." Milada stood up, moistened her face, and spoke, "How do you think you will live? How do you think you will find students out there?"

"The whole world out there can use me. There are newspapers, institutes, and the embassy. I used to tutor at the house of the ambassador. I speak really English. I'm not afraid of looking for work."

"Martha, have you talked to Goldscheider yet?"

"Her?!" Lightening shot out of her blue eyes. "She's the one who picked me up, like a dogcatcher picks up a stray dog. Do you know why she has kept me here and not ever sent me to Carlotta's? It's because she's afraid I'll tell on her and the others who've helped her. She tore me out of bed after the birth of my child. She tore the baby from my breast. The first thing I want to do is get my child back."

"Do you have an address?" Milada asked, tired and played out, having heard this story a million times over. But Dubbe's eyes were filled with fear and begged for an answer.

"Goldscheider has it. She took care of placing my baby some place in the country with strangers. She placed my baby with a woman who raises children. Now I'm going to get my baby back. No, Milada, I'm not afraid for myself. For Christ's sake, two years here don't mean the end. I'm not lost. I will give lessons, live like I had lived, and have my child with me. It's true, Milada, two years like this are nothing. I knew a girl who was bedridden for four years with tuberculosis of the bone. And when she was well, she married a lovely young man. What do you have to say to that!"

Milada made a gesture of helplessness. Others in the house had called Dubbe crazy when she went on about her fantasy of getting her child. Someone had said the baby died right after birth. Milada held Dubbe's arm. "You need to talk with Madame Goldscheider. Do you hear me? You can't go to the new owner of the house. You're only an amount of money to the new owner, nothing more."

"You're right," she replied with the voice of a child. "Goldscheider's got to let me go, I mean it. She's done way too much to get away with." Dubbe leapt up and threw her arms around Milada's neck. "Oh, Milada, you're so good to me. I'll talk to her calmly. I've got a hundred things to do. What do you think I should do first? Rent a room or go get my baby? My child shouldn't spend one more minute with somebody else." She looked for an answer in Milada's face. Innumerable hours of fear lay submerged in Dubbe's eyes.

"Ask yourself," Milada whispered, "what if I never find the child again? Martha, sweetheart, come see me tomorrow morning, and we can talk it through. And we'll send the porter Polifka to the home for foundlings. She can give us real information. But for now, go to bed and sleep."

"Sleep?! Me, now? Never, you dear nun. I think I'm never going to sleep again."

"Dubbe, Dubbe!" Milada took hold of her hands. "How are you going to talk with Goldscheider tomorrow if you haven't slept? You need your rest, now go to sleep!"

"There's somebody in my bed," Dubbe said in a strange, singing tone. "But that doesn't matter. I can't sleep feeling like I do. I'm really tired, but I'm not going to sleep."

Milada let go of Dubbe's hands and stroked her gently.

"Oh, Milada, you little nun, your hands are warm, and I am freezing. I'll go to sleep and then see my baby. My baby's crying, calling for me. Don't you believe me? My baby calls me every night."

Downstairs the clock chimed loudly. After a short while, someone knocked heavily on Milada's door. "Miss Milada, is Dubbe there with you?" the maid called through the door. "Look what she has done! She left a count all alone in her room. If the madam gets wind of that!"

Dubbe jumped up. "Jesus, and here I am without any makeup on, and it's already light. Milada, go look and see if the sweet young man has left." She stood in front of the vanity mirror, put on rouge, painted up her lips and traced out her eyebrows. The wrinkles that showed her tiredness disappeared, and her eyes gleamed. She splashed cologne over her hair until it was dripping. She gathered up the lace of her skirts coquettishly and—slam bang!—she was out the door.

"What had that been about? Was Dubbe serious? Was she playing a game or putting on a mask? Was this foolishness or despair? Probably some of each," Milada thought defeated. Then she undressed, lay down, and slept deeply till noon the next day.

When she awoke, she heard the latest news of the house. Sucher had been there that morning with another gentleman and had a long, important conversation with Goldscheider. Olympia reported that all three were very pleased when they left the office. The porter brought clean wine glasses, and what they drank was not bad stuff, Fanchon assured people. She knew her wine.

Then Dubbe went to see Goldscheider. After the two men had left, she and Goldscheider went in the office, although the porter had tried to prevent Dubbe from entering. At first only Dubbe's voice was audible; she was loud, emotional, and she gushed. Then Goldscheider spoke. After that Dubbe, the poor distraught thing, thrashed about and screamed. When the porter heard an armchair crash, she went in. Dubbe was on the floor. Goldscheider only called out, "She needs to be flogged with a whip."

An hour ago the madam was said to have departed in a carriage, wearing a silk dress and decked out with green baubles. Bina related all this to Milada calmly and peacefully as she sat embroidering a runner, at moments holding up her crude handiwork for approval.

Several of the girls sat around in Fanchon's room whose walls were covered with placards and nudie pictures. They were talking excitedly about the events. "We just don't know what's coming next. The madam wasn't the worst of them," Rosa said with a sigh. Rosa had been quite happy there.

"She's a real bitch," Mitzi stamped her foot. She had just arrived a few days ago from the hospital. "Who wants to stick by her!"

"Let other people here have their own opinion," Laura piped up nastily. "Did you ever have someone like Big Amshel beat you? There could be somebody like that here next."

"What, me get a beating and have red marks? That bastard!"

"First I want my gold ring back, the one you stole from me."

Mitzi fired back with disdain, "If somebody turned you upside down and shook you as hard as Amshel, he wouldn't get a gold ring out of you, you suspicious flea bag. At most your false teeth would fall out."

Lefty Anna laughed loudly, "Mitzi, you can really dish it out."

Fanchon yelled over the argument with her high voice, "Be quiet, you can't even hear yourself think."

Then the maid stormed in the room with excitement, "Ladies, ladies, get yourselves dressed right away! The new lady is downstairs. She's down there on the street talking with our madam." The maid hurried off. She opened all the doors and announced the news in all the rooms of the house. Everybody ran to the windows. Only Dubbe did not go to see. She lay on the bed with her eyes closed and wailed.

Goldscheider had been standing on the other side of the street for quite some minutes with a lady of medium size dressed in gray. She lowered her noticeably small head nervously under the gazes that fell on her. A small, gray feather boa about her neck heightened the impression she gave of a bird. The ends of her veil blew in the wind.

"Her name is Lora for flower," Anna giggled. Nobody laughed. The fever of expectation was too high.

Goldscheider touched the arm of the stranger as they spoke, making an inviting gesture with her hand. The woman in gray ran her hand over the top of her head to smooth her hair; it was a motion of obvious self-consciousness. Then she took hold of her skirt and walked across the street with Goldscheider. The doorbell rang. A shudder ran through the house, and the girls dispersed without speaking.

Yes, indeed, it was true! Red House had been sold and was now in the possession of the well born lady Josefine Aglaia von Miller. She was an aging, thin, meritorious lady who had cared for a man of the cloth for almost twenty-five years. That had been in the heart of the wealthy state of Styria. Oh, what a marvelously rich diocese! There were fields, meadows, cattle, and gardens full of fruits and vegetables. Everything was there in rich abundance! The lady dabbed at her eyes at the mention of Styria.

A few days after Pentecost the transfer of Red House was definitively concluded. Goldscheider was sitting in her office by early morning. People came and left. Delivery people and agents, even some of the guests who had become close to the house dropped by briefly to take their leave of Madame Goldscheider. People knew she was leaving the city for good. She said dismissively she was leaving for "some place in Germany." The ladies of the house came down to say their goodbyes. They all had a request, one last wish, or some pressing concern to raise. They hoped she would smooth over old arguments or, out of a sense of decency, offer some final word. They sought her advice. Goldscheider explained everything of that nature was to be addressed to the new madam and that nothing further could be changed about the situation. People had to live with this.

Olympia was the only one who had a travel destination. The new owner refused to take on a manager or anyone to oversee the house. She asserted she had had plenty of experience managing things. She said she was fine on her own. She knew what she was doing.

"That one especially looks used up," the new madam said of Olympia. "I don't need her." And so Olympia, this veteran of love, had to leave. This time she was bound for Galicia in the North of the Empire to a large military canteen. She pulled a long face, and Sucher comforted her with these words, "The job there is only selling milk. The men have services."

Toward noon Goldscheider had finished up her business and was only waiting for her successor to arrive. Goldscheider laughed to herself at the thought of the word "successor." The thin person with pale, greedy hands was timorous. She lived with the constant fear someone from the remote village where she had been twenty-five years in the pastor's service might wander into Red House!

This was von Miller's ultimate aim in picking up the reins Goldscheider laid down: "I want to be buried next to the venerable pastor."

Goldscheider recalled her first meeting with the old woman and Sucher. When he named the amount her investment would earn her in profit, her soft, brown eyes had glowed with greed and delight.

"Yes, but the risk, the risk," von Miller kept saying. "Couldn't I lose money? There are sickness and death."

"But it's not like you have livestock, dear lady," Sucher said. "If somebody falls ill, she returns to the job at no cost to you. If she doesn't work out, you can send her away. You have a first-class business with the perpetual option of exchange. You have contacts: you have Fischer in the town Budejovice, Mr. Kohlmann in Teplice, Meher in Bruenn, and so on, don't you?"

Goldscheider nodded.

"And then you've got Jonathan in Chernowitz. Which of the girls did you get from Jonathan, Madame Goldscheider? Those girls put plenty of change in your purse, they did." Sucher snapped his fingers.

"That's right. There was Rosamunde," Goldscheider lied on the spur.

Sucher picked right up, "That little Rose! She was quite a live wire. She must have sold three hundred worth of champagne every evening. How much would you say you made in a day from having Rosamunde here, Madame Goldscheider?"

"One-hundred fifty," she responded.

"So, I'm telling you, you can only realize a profit," Sucher leaned back. "And that was just on the sale of champagne. How much do you think you realized from food sales? And from the girls? What do you charge for just one cup of coffee?"

"One fifty," Goldscheider answered.

"And what is the cost to you for a cup of coffee?" Sucher continued.

"Fifteen cents."

"Well, there you have it!" Sucher said while leaning back and waving his hands about.

Goldscheider reviewed these endless, boring meetings with von Miller. She sat through all the debates and discussions until the old woman finally took the bait like a hungry fish.

As far as Goldscheider was concerned, Red House could flourish or not. She was done with the business. She was resolute in her decision not to have a formal leave-taking and to leave in secret once Miller arrived on the spot.

She wanted no goodbyes, flowers; no speeches or to-do. It was icy. And how would a public exit like that have gone for a woman like her? People might have cursed her or dumped waste on her head. She just wanted to put Red House behind her as quickly as possible. The perpetually cool and collected madam was quite nervous and filled with ugly thoughts. She removed her key from its ring, chucked the ring in the desk drawer, put the key in an envelope, sealed it, and wrote on the envelope "For Madame von Miller."

Yes, then there was leaving Horner! They had been yoked together. She laughed mischievously, thinking how Horner had recently distinguished himself! He had heaped venom and gall on her and had barraged her with a thousand petty acts of meanness. He had made undignified, unnecessary scenes, completely without rhyme or reason. And what had his meanness availed him?

Horner was now attached to the girl. He boasted about her. Maybe she was really valuable. Goldscheider stood back and considered. She found it truly astonishing that from the moment of her arrival in Red House up to the moment of her departure this girl had always been there, right before her eyes. Goldscheider had watched the development of this child with a certain curiosity.

The very first decision she had made as the new madam concerned this child. All these many long years, Goldscheider had felt there was something known about Milada. She was aware, every time their paths crossed; she felt a connection to this girl. Milada was part of the place. Goldscheider felt good about having her around. So why not then leave her last orders in Milada's hands?

Milada entered.

"I trust you will say nothing. I'm going to leave here in an hour. A carriage will be here later for me. Send it to Hotel Royal. And keep crazy Dubbe in check until I'm gone."

She looked contemplatively down at her nails, which she was polishing with a cloth.

"I want to tell you before I'm gone not to let Horner muddle your thinking. Living is a practical matter and not as complicated and high-flown as he sees it. Take direct paths! All his considerations and brooding are only weakness. I advise you to keep watch to see about..." Goldscheider pointed toward the office desk, "taking over from the new madam. She will need guidance, the dumb cluck. If you're smart... Well, here she is right now, the new madam."

Goldscheider nodded to Miller as she entered and quickly threw Milada a quick, knowing, and earnest look.

"Good, Madame von Miller, that you have arrived punctually. Everything is in order. There are the books, the cash box, and here are the keys. And here is your competent young lady! This is Milada. She understands the business from top to bottom."

Miller raised her monocle and nodded awkwardly. "Yes, fine, but do tell me who is raising such a ruckus here in the house?"

"That's how things are here," said Goldscheider nonplussed. "There is noise here at times." Milada took a step toward the door.

"I can't let you in there, m'lady. Jesus, Mary!" said the maid. A heavy body pressed against the door, then it was thrown open, and Dubbe flew in the room. She was dressed to go out for a stroll with a jacket and umbrella, however, without a hat.

Dubbe addressed the madam, "Madame Goldscheider, you're not leaving yet. Oh, no, you're not making such a shabby exit. Get away from me!" she screamed as Milada approached her, and she threatened, "I've got a knife."

Goldscheider halted Dubbe's furor with her ice-cold gaze and said, "Here is the new madam. If you want something, speak to her. I have nothing more to do with any of you here."

Dubbe shook her fist. "No, I have a score to settle with you and nobody else. I don't need the new madam. She doesn't know me. But you do, you brought me here." She made a fist and pushed her away. "You dragged me here. Tell me what you have to say, Madame! Do I stay here or not? Am I going to stay?"

Goldscheider got up. "You owe this new madam, Madame von Miller, one hundred gulden. I doubt she'll let you go because of that. Beyond that people here also love you."

Miller stared at both of them uncomprehendingly.

Miller stammered, "What's going on? I don't understand."

Dubbe blasted, "Slave driver! Executioner! I'm going to run away from this place, from you and that new woman. I'm going to jump out the window. That's what I'll do. I've had enough of lining your pockets. Stop, you can't go yet. Don't take another step. Today I won't collapse. I am standing here. Today I'm asking you where my child is. Do you hear me? I don't want money. I want the address."

"Madame von Miller," said Goldscheider, feigning resolve, "Dr. Kahane represents me. I am prepared to dismiss two thirds of this woman's debt. Let her go."

"Oh, God, don't try to dissuade me, you old cheat! I want the name and the address. My baby was so tiny when you tore him away from me."

At that point Dubbe's theater was too much for Goldscheider.

She only wanted to leave, drop everything, and escape. But looking at Dubbe who was ready to assault her, she was held back.

"You've come a bit too late with your show of emotion," she said, making an effort to put an superior sharpness to her tone. "Go to the maternity ward. They'll know."

"I went. I went there three different times. Milada will tell you, she knows. Tell this cheat if they know anything there. I'll make sure you are tried, you lying bitch, if I don't get my baby back."

Goldscheider kept her composure.

She turned to the people standing around, to the porter, Milada, and Madame von Miller whose eyes were popping out of her head, as she strained to breathe. There were also people pressed against the door. "You girls, and you, Madame, I tell you all, when I found this person she was in debt up to her ears. She didn't own the shirt on her back. Her landlady had kept her suitcase. She was in debt to the hospital and was going to be thrown out on the street. Isn't that so?" Raising her voice, Goldscheider went on, "It was out of compassion I took her on. Her child was a burden to her, a further misfortune in her misery. I took care of that child." She yelled in her agitation. "I took care of it like any foundling. The mother begged me to take her to the brothel. She didn't know who the father was. Maybe the child died right away, maybe it was a week later. Did she ever ask about the child then? Did she make any effort at the time to find out what happened to the child? It's been almost three years. Now that this woman is well fed, strong, and outfitted with clothes, now she wants the child."

"Jesus, Mary and Joseph!" Dubbe exclaimed and rocked back. All of a sudden she stopped screaming. There was no more defiance or furor in her; she was broken. She looked at the truth.

Dubbe mumbled, "She doesn't know anything about my baby. She let it go out into the world like a thing, a tiny baby! She tore that child naked from my breast. It can't be true. All you feel is anger at me. For God's sake, you have no mercy! It's crazy, isn't it? A child can't just disappear. That was a Christian child, and the birth was registered in the records."

Dubbe approached the desk. "You have a lot of paperwork here. All the drawers are full of paper. Somewhere there's got to be an address. "Please listen," she said with her hands folded to plea, "if I was foolish then, I..." She turned around. "I can't sleep. You can laugh at me, but it is true. I long for that child. I hear my baby calling me day and night."

The porter, a robust woman and herself the mother of four children, went to stand next to Dubbe.

"M'lady, we'll go to the police. We'll find the child. It must be possible to look through the records. The records will show when the baby was born, what name it was given."

Dubbe turned to her and, shaking, put her hands on Polifka's shoulders.

"I don't know anything. I don't know how my baby looked. I didn't even get to see my baby's little face. I go cold thinking about that. The orderly and Goldscheider did everything. They said they sent money every month, that they would send it for six years. In six years I would be out of debt, that's what they told me. I was half starved in the hospital. I was weak with pain and from roaming around. They hit me and said, 'Hand over the child.' And I did. A complete stranger took my little baby. How I suffered. I was hungry and cold, and people beat me. It was over, and I didn't even see his little face."

"She is insane," Goldscheider muttered and picked up her purse and umbrella.

"She belongs in an insane asylum," Goldscheider said to von Miller who stood mouth agape.

"Yes, but don't you want to..." Miller began horrified.

"Lock the door behind me," Goldscheider hissed to the porter. She passed by all the people with their astonished faces and turned her back to them.

The sound of the door slamming shut brought Dubbe back to her senses.

"Don't let her go!" Dubbe screamed as she fought her way free.

But Milada's strong arms held her tight.

"Calm down, Martha, be calm. Come along with me. Everything will be all right. Just be good and calm down." And speaking to her softly, Milada led the pale women out of the room as she looked around in confusion.

"She's a bitch," the porter murmured and spat. Then she went out to the street. But there was no trace of the old madam. She had left without her hat.

Madame von Miller stood in the office in shock. Her eyes showed she was completely unable to grasp what had happened. Her small head sank on her round breast with the velvet shawl of an old mother.

The new madam fiddled with the nail file Goldscheider had left. Then she threw it away from herself, horrified, as if she had been holding a viper.

"I really got myself into a fine mess," she blubbered. "This is a fine howdy-do. The beginning is an omen, I have to say."

Chapter 4
Miller's Salon

A monument to the shame of our times
—Schiller

The new madam who took over the direction of Red House was not made of the same stern, weather-tight stuff as her predecessor. She brought none of the most important attributes for getting things done to the job.

At the parsonage in the little town of G. she had indeed held an excellent position as caretaker. She had been a pious, eager servant of the church and of her priest. This venerable gentleman had, in recognition of her service, often called her the "most precious being" when, in the evenings, he sat at the round table with the notables in town.

"Oh, yes," they responded to him, "Madame Josephine manages things well and is thrifty." But many of the notables thought to themselves, "God protect us from the devil." If there had been a vicar assisting the priest, he would not have been able to take working with Miss Fini, as she was called. When Fini hired day laborers for the heavy work of the harvest, they complained about the way they were treated and about the food. Two retired farm workers, eighty-year-old Katie and little old Ursula, who was one hundred, opened and closed their toothless chops and turned their little old eyeballs toward heaven when recalling their work with Fini. Well, more accurately, cranky Kate did since Ursula, as Kate said, "has gotten quite childlike."

Fini's cooking was pretty meager in view of the fat stipend the church gave the priest. She scrimped on every pat of butter, inventoried every hen, and cursed the chicken that built a nest next door. She kept track of the necessary payments and donations; she negotiated for and haggled over every bit of change that went for the expenses of church services, weddings, and baptisms; she finagled about the amount of fabric in a shroud for the dead; also, she oversaw the venerable priest's cadence at the funeral service and the number of times he shook hands with the pallbearers. The pastor had swollen up with the volume of potatoes and peas she served him. Miss Fini was also opposed to eating meat. She held it made people angry and un-Christian.

Josephine made exceptions for his little niece who was taken care of at the parsonage. This slender, moony young lady bore an uncanny resemblance to Aunt Fini, especially in her pious, soft brown eyes and in her thin yet comely lips. In the older Fini these lips were clenched and repressed any gentleness, while in the younger niece these lips revealed much secretive longing and a cleverness about acting on her desire. The niece's pale, spongy complexion and characterless pug nose resembled those of the priest, her "godfather." This man doted on the child "as is usual" from the time she was very young.

The aging woman Fini was the scourge of the village. Every unmarried prostitute who left her child at the church was received with accusations and a loud scolding.

"The holy water is wasted on this child," she was wont to say.

Miss Fini washed, cooked, sewed, and spun. In short she performed the tasks of keeping house all by herself. If someone complimented her work, she replied softly and humbly, "When the good priest takes in two strangers, it is fitting he receive help in this way."

There was plenty of money coming in. The two bank books showed a generous number of deposits. One was inscribed with the name of the pastor; the other, with the name of the "niece." The bank books did not account for the promissory notes and bonds hidden in the desk.

The young lady of the parsonage spent most of the winter in the palace of Baron Waldek in Vienna. He had an extensive manor and was a patron of the church in G. Miss Petronella, the estate manager for this baron, was a devoted friend of Miss Fini.

When the niece was twenty-one, something happened that quickly unsettled the idyll of the parsonage.

Following a stormy conversation with her aunt—the details of which remain forever hidden from the world—this niece packed her bags on a September morning and took the omnibus of the hotel to the train station. No one escorted her to the station. Aunt Fini recovered after some time and spread around this story: The young niece had great good fortune in Paris. The baron had assumed the costs of her education. The niece did, however, look older now and had become more bitter and less sociable than she had been.

Two years later the very blessed priest died and left Miss Fini, "the most precious soul," both bank books as well as the movable goods and property.

After Fini had, while heaving a sigh, given her successor the duties of the house and yard, the pantry and the cellar, she retired to a small house on a mountainside. She lived there in absolute seclusion, surrounded by lumber farms and cow pastures. It was called Sunny Heights.

While she was spending her days like Katie and little old Ursula, doing nothing, she was struck with fear about the rest of her life. She was running out of money. Would she have to enter the lay world after living in the security of the parsonage? Would she once again be thrown into public concourse? What should she do? She did not have enough to keep living at Sunny Heights. Should she play the market and invest like her father the cavalry officer had done? Her father had lost his shirt speculating. Where should she start?

She could not stay on in this isolated situation.

Fini knew that women who had fallen on hard times and gone to Paris had ended up on the rocks.

Her thoughts probed dark corners of her past in search of someone who might help, and finally she hit upon the man her drunkard father had trusted. This man had gotten everything of value in the Miller estate: the horses, all the jewelry and paintings. He was the agent and money lender J. Kessler. He assured the people he knew in business he was not—as they might suspect—a Jew. It was Kessler who had suggested Josephine for the position of manager at the parsonage twenty-five years ago when she was in dire need. He had secured that post for her.

One fine day Miller sat down and wrote to Joachim Kessler. She described her current circumstances and asked for his friendly advice. He answered by return post. His reply came on fancy, new professional stationery. The letterhead stated he dealt in realty, purchases, sales, and exchanges. He also made inquiries, transacted currency exchanges, advised about dubious investments, and much more of the sort.

Kessler wrote Josephine he would be pleased to offer his humble assistance in finding her a good investment; he would do his best to put her nice little bit of capital to good use with a secure contract.

Spring arrived and Miller and Kessler exchanged several letters with no real content. Then a telegram arrived to Josephine in little G. and disrupted the tranquility of the mountain. "Luxurious existence. A very rare opportunity. Your presence needed immediately. Come right away." She packed at breakneck speed. Her little house on Sunny Heights was rented to a neighboring farmer, and on a frosty morning in March Madame von Miller stood with her nose red from excitement in the great, bright lobby that opened upon the private office of Mr. Kessler. He was still the active man with the convivial demeanor of the expansive agent. The only thing different about him was that he had acquired a gut, upon which lay a heavy gold chain. There was another pronounced change in Kessler. He said, "Although I am a Jew, people in the best circles know and use my name. And I'm proud of that since I've never denied my religion as so many people nowadays do."

Kessler did not talk much about his suggestion to Josephine. He presented her with Goldscheider's account book, and his fat thumbs ran up and down the columns of figures like an accomplished agent. At first Madame von Miller was shocked, then horrified, and then confused. And in her confusion she experienced a rush of breathtaking greed like someone in front of a roulette wheel for the first time who hears how probable a great win is.

"In the name of God," Miller finally said and quickly signed the bill of sale. She signed, although she understood nothing of the loan Goldscheider offered, the obligation to pay interest, or the fact that the house, the business, and the income were now hers. The reason the purchase price was relatively small did not dawn on her. Kessler gave her his word of honor that she had just concluded a very sweet deal. He called it the best transaction he had brokered in his career of forty years.

Miller was possessed of a wealth of passivity. She knew how to wait people out, to hold on, and all the time persist in implementing her own plan. She used pleas, wheedling, threats, and, if none of those worked, tears, curses, and melodramatic scenes. She understood perfectly how to break someone's will with persistent, gentle, treacly, niggling resistance. But she had no trace of diligent, aim-oriented activity or of the forthright confidence and composure that comes of superiority, the kind of composure Goldscheider had brought to bear in making her business a great success. Most fatefully Miller lacked what Goldscheider had possessed in large measure: an understanding for the needs, interests, and wishes of these fallen souls. Goldscheider had had an immediate and close connection with each of the individuals in the house.

As long as Miller was in the house, the girls felt she was an outsider. They did not understand her. They did, however, understand she had a deep need to control, but it only aroused their resistance, willfulness, and at best their laughter. No one ever took her seriously. When Goldscheider was in the house, there was a feeling of cooperation. The girls knew what her gestures meant and understood her orders. They even knew her severity and rash decisions made sense and had a purpose. The saying was, "She's a bitch, but she knows what she's doing."

From the moment Miller arrived on the scene, there were two camps: the new madam and everybody else. The girls were unhappy, exploited slaves who worked against rather than for the interests of the madam. Her stinginess in the smallest detail, her greed, her insecurity and pandering deference in exchanges with the guests, and Miller's rude way of dealing with the girls oppressed them and made them, in the flick of a wrist, her adversaries. The girls ridiculed and derided her flashes of anger in the salon when something happened that Miller found "inappropriate." These occurrences were, however, quite normal within the context of the milieu. What people found most oppressive about Miller was her intrusive curiosity and her mistrust of everyone and everything.

Miller saw enemies and adversity all around. She tried to recruit spies and set people against each other.

Her system of espionage did not work for her. When she believed her unctuous flattery had won a girl over, that girl told the other girls what the madam suspected or imagined. And so there were daily grievances. People were in a bad mood, complained, and wore distraught, disgruntled faces.

The purely economic side of the undertaking was, of course, absolutely alien to her. She had some greedy instinct there was an enormous amount of money to be made here and quickly, but she had no notion where to begin. Where did the money come from? She never risked spending money up front to double her return. Rather she haggled over every nickel with every merchant and vendor as if she were doing personal, daily shopping at the market. And the people who were used to Goldscheider's unforgettable generosity soon started giving Miller poorer goods at higher prices. Miller was happy when she believed she had pinched a penny here or there, and she shouted for joy, "Just you wait and see! You thought you'd get the better of old Miller."

Goldscheider had employed publicity agents, and she always left a tip or a token of appreciation after visiting some place, like the hospital or the maternity ward. She left something for her connections in the police department and with the porters of small hotels in out-of-the-way places and flophouses. She was, thus, assured inexhaustible resources for girls for prostitution. She used these channels to speculate. They were the source of her best and most lucrative deals. Miller, by contrast, resisted any connections of the sort kicking and screaming. She called prospective informants in hospitals, at the police station, and in hotels robbers and thieves. She thought they wanted to cheat her out of her hard-earned money. She dismissed their inquiries, announcements, or offers out of hand. She claimed she needed nothing; she already had plenty. She was not interested in an exchange or any changes. Wherever possible she cut back on connections and advertisements.

She charged the girls the former high prices for cheaper clothes and lower-grade undergarments. When she tried to charge them for their regular allotment of candles, soap, perfumes, and other essentials, there was a unanimous outcry, and so Miller had to back off. But she limited the delivery of these nice items and made a point of showing disapproval when she dispensed them. Even the portions of food and volume of drinks sold in the salon were reduced while the prices were increased.

The girls got the regular customers riled up about this or that new practice of Miller's. Not uncommonly a guest would refuse to pay the amount of the tab and demanded he pay what Goldscheider had charged.

Measures like these did not help morale or engender a feeling of frivolity, which depend on an atmosphere of cooperation rather than on the actual degree of comfort. Keeping an atmosphere of frivolity in play is the secret of this business.

People who had been regulars said, "Red House has changed. It's gotten tired. It's not interesting anymore. The girls are constantly complaining. That new madam is an unpleasant character."

Or else people commented, "Before, when Goldscheider was there, the place was alive! It's dead now. It's really come down a notch." Comments like that went on and on.

Miller's bookkeeping was not organized as Goldscheider's had been. She contented herself with keeping excruciatingly close tabs on daily accounts receivable and payable. So when the first quarter of the year was up, Miller discovered the amount she made did not nearly approach what Goldscheider had made.

"I knew it!" she erupted. "I'm no good at this business. I'm much too good for this. I've been a fool."

Then Miller called in Mrs. Polifika, the porter, and blamed her for the poor results of the business. She was so bitter in her accusation that the porter, who was otherwise not an irascible person, decided finally to accept an offer of employment from a competing business.

"It's no wonder the customers shudder on the porch steps at the sight of your face. You're supposed to be the porter. It's no wonder. They see you, then they complain a bit and take their business on over to Madame Zimmermann, right?"

Polifka made her exit with only a shrug of her shoulders. She said nothing to Miller in response. Throughout the house there was an enormous uproar. Miller swore, cursed, and snapped at people. No one would have guessed a woman accustomed to working with aristocrats and people of the cloth knew language like that. She tore around the rooms of the house like a madwoman with her face contorted in evil. She threw back the shutters and ripped open trunks, rummaged through people's suitcases and tossed bedding all around, looking for what had been "stolen" from her "personally." Miller threatened to have everybody thrown in jail on criminal charges of theft. She accused anyone and everyone she ran across of contriving her misfortune. She had lost her mind. She believed she had been dumped in insurmountable circumstances with no chance of salvation. These circumstances were beyond what her poor strength and intelligence could handle. As is the case with people with a weak constitution, it did not occur to her to consider her own behaviors and make any change.

What really aggravated Miller in her contracted little thought-world was the knowledge that she was in the middle of an opportunity to make a huge lot of money. She told herself she needed nothing more than her two eyes to spot money all around and both her claws to snatch it up. The money was there, it was right there! Goldscheider had gotten rich off it. But, fatefully, she was not as sly or slippery or as unscrupulous as Goldscheider. She, Miller, was cautious and had a conscience.

She regretted her own goodliness and gullibility. She cursed Kessler who had convinced her to go into this business and Goldscheider who had sold it to her. She even resented the good priest whose death had driven her to take this on. And, yes, those girls!

They did this to her. She balled her fists against the open revolt they were waging. She made an oath and had a plan.

Gisi had always come downstairs any time she wanted to in any state. She went so far as to appear in a high-cut black slip. From that moment on Miller had not even let her downstairs. Miller was, after all, the woman who fed Gisi's stupid face bread, meat, and cake at her own expense. Gisi was on the take. Mitzi was another one, but at least Mitzi listened up when they fought. Mitzi did have a brain. But when it came to controlling Dubbe, Miller was unstrung. She flew off the handle with rage. Dubbe had been in bed almost three months, nursing a case of poor nerves as if she were a fine lady. "She needs milk," the doctor had said, "and plenty of rest." Miller found the doctor impossible. He said, "The hospital does not take patients like this." And wouldn't you know! When the doctor made a surprise visit, there was Dubbe in the salon, making a spectacle of herself.

"So what do you think, Madame Miller?" the doctor joked. "Should I send her to the spa and you foot the bill?"

It had to be a plot. They were conspiring against her! Then that piece of trash Dubbe stayed in bed and did not move for another fourteen days. "Let her wait and see!" thought Miller. "I intend to wipe the floor with her."

Miller went upstairs and stood listening at Dubbe's door. As she might have suspected, there were a couple of people in there. She put her ear to the door. Were they talking about her and making plans? Of course! Was that Milada?

Miller had a strange relationship with Milada. She both respected and disliked her. At first she had allowed Horner to visit her because she thought he was a paying client. Then she tolerated him because he was completely invulnerable to her passive-aggressive slurs and mean carping. He kept visiting Milada the same as ever, but he had cut back considerably on his visits to the salon. The salon under her regime had simply lost its appeal to him.

While she was listening at Dubbe's door, a girl passed by and cleared her throat loudly. Before Miller could get away, Milada opened the door and said, "Oh, it's you, M'lady." "Yes, it's me," said Miller. "And what's going on here? Is Dubbe still in bed? Get her up! I'm getting rid of her."

She pulled back the light-red curtains, so that the light of day fell on Dubbe's sunken face. As Miller kept on talking, Dubbe's face contorted into a derisive grin. She put a compress that smelled heavily of menthol to her forehead and temples.

"Enough! I am not going to put up with this any longer. I've been in touch with Sucher. She's going away. Do you understand me?" The madam stood imposingly over Dubbe. She sat up, looked the woman over, and taunted her, "Am I going with a hot-air balloon or with the green truck for garbage? I really don't give a damn. I'm actually quite happy. Nothing else can happen to me."

"I'll have you carted off to jail if you don't go willingly. You've got to get out of my house. I can't stand having you around anymore."

"So, you probably want me to get dressed, right? You'd like me to paint myself up and just keep laughing. Isn't that what you want?" With great effort, Dubbe put her hand on the side of her head to hold it up. "I'm not doing that for you—or for anybody ever again," she wailed and fell back on the pillow. She turned to face the wall and paid no further attention to Miller, while Miller pitched her voice higher and called down the judgement of God on this accursed creature. At that moment Miller was struck by such a profound feeling of complete powerlessness over all matters in her life she could only sob. Her sobbing swallowed up her words. She sounded like a small, thwarted child, throwing a tantrum.

Milada stood at the head of the bed. Her gray eyes became increasingly more stern. She looked at Miller with mounting disdain.

"Send her to a hospital," Milada said after a pause.

"To a hospital?!" Miller echoed her words. "A hospital won't take her off my hands. She's healthy. Doctor Lamberg said so. She is healthy. She's healthier than I am," Miller croaked out. "She's just lying around drinking booze." She went over to the bed.

With composure Milada raised her arm and spoke, "Don't you touch her!" She went on, "Our Madame Goldscheider surely would not have left someone this weak to stay in her room, especially if Doctor Lamberg had said she was ill. Lamberg wouldn't expect anybody in this condition to work. And he wouldn't charge his standard two gulden for his visit either."

"Two gulden?!" Miller groaned and wrung her hands.

"We pay that ourselves," Milada said. "Goldscheider would have paid Lamberg's fee to smooth things over. He does what you, Madame, want. Furthermore, Goldscheider kept on the good side of the porter at the Luise Street Hospital. And she wouldn't have forgotten the official in the city office. She could send anybody to the hospital, even without Doctor Lamberg's orders. He wouldn't mind. Dubbe here should have gone to the hospital three months ago. She has more than just a bad case of nerves. For a while now she has been having seizures when she has a visitor. People know about that. Something like that is illness. If Dubbe goes to the hospital, then give Gisi the big room. Gisi would love to have it. She'd be in a better mood right away."

Milada's confidence and authority caused Miller, in her driveling, nervous distress, to cling to Milada's every word like a fly to fly paper.

Miller was no longer thinking of herself. She was attentive and said, "Well, sure. All that's fine. Let's say I do these things, will the business work out for me? I don't know what to do about Gisi! She tore up the lace curtains in her room. And now she's slammed herself away. Is she really on my side? I don't mind if she gets her way. But I won't put up with her mean treatment. Take Mitzi for instance. She's always up to something. And you and I are forever on the outs. I can't take that."

"Dear Lord, there are dozens of girls like Mitzi. She's not a real problem."

Milada took Dubbe's cold compress and freshened it.

"You're better off not confronting Gisi with the torn bits of curtain. That will only make things worse for the business."

"I don't think so. Tearing up curtains in anger costs me money."

"But if she gets angry, it will only cost more money," Milada answered promptly. "When Gisi's visitor Schöller came to the salon to see her, he regularly dropped five hundred on champagne. And more than half of that is pure profit. Last night he didn't even buy our cigarettes. He brought his own, that's how unhappy he was."

After a while Milada pulled the covers up over Dubbe and said quietly to herself, "I know this business like the back of my hand." As unintentional as Milada's remark was, it hit its mark. Miller's expression softened, her color returned, and she assumed a gentle demeanor.

"She's asleep now. I'm going to go." Milada opened the door, let Miller leave first, and she looked down the length of the hall. Or so it seemed. What she was really looking to see was the play of emotions on Miller's face. Miller tried to conceal her feelings, but they were visible. She was miserable. She reached out her hand to Milada as if to hold her back. At long last she uttered these carefully chosen, formal words through her tight lips, "Madame, Madame Rezek!"

'Yes?"

"You've been here a long time?"

"Twenty-one years, as long as I've been alive." Milada then looked right at the madam. Her gaze was challenging and showed she felt superior.

"Then I can learn!" Beneath her green-plaid wool blouse her feelings and wishes were pulling her apart. Miller's red face with its blinking eyes could not hide her inner conflict. Her sense of mistrust was stronger than her feeling of helplessness. Her mouth hung open, and it closed with a sigh. She turned her back to Milada without saying another word. As she walked down the hall toward Gisi's room, she let out a troubled sigh.

"Oh, God, oh God! Twenty-one years in this business. It's true."

The years of a quiet, peaceful life in the house of the parsonage floated like evil spirits before her inner eye. "I ought to have learned something about decency," she thought as she opened the door to Gisi's room, which fortunately was not locked. The girl lay across her bed in a black-silk dress, smoking a cigar from Havana. Next to her was a bottle of cognac, which she covered with her blanket when Miller entered. A man called Bert had smuggled it into the house. Gisi had just been considering Bert's offer to spend the summer in Munich and work as a model for some painters. Should she or not? He had told her about the advantages of taking this excursion, but she was not ready to move and live with all the new commotion. She was relatively comfortable here and knew going to Munich would mean having to install herself in a new place and go on walks as an advertisement for the men. She had done that with the Jewish traveling salesman who had taken her along from city to city with his display of books. Bert would give her presents, clothes, and jewelry, but when he was done with her, she would be standing all alone on the streets, in "blissful solitude."

She was just mulling over the pros and cons of Bert's offer when Miller walked in. "Well, there goes the evening," Gisi thought. "My peace and quiet is over once that woman starts bitching."

Miller minced around the room, examined the lace curtains in shreds, pretended to laugh and consider the damage with a "hmm." But she could not bring herself to put the contentious matter to rest.

"So, she's drinking cognac someone brought in," she thought to herself in anger. "And the lady is smoking cigars. She'll probably fight if I charge several gulden. I'll only ask for half," she concluded.

Gisi kept right on puffing away unapologetically, although she, too, wanted to be done with the issue of the curtains since she was increasingly less interested in leaving the nice spot she had for a future in the artists' quarter of Munich.

Gisi got up yawning, spat on the glowing cigar and tossed it in the wash basin. Then she sat down on the edge of the bed and started putting on a pair of black, lacquered, high-button shoes. She held her feet up so that wherever Miller looked, she saw the whole of a solid, white leg bobbing in the air. That embarrassed Miller quite a bit.

"I'm going to have to have new curtains made," she was able to get out the words and immediately felt miserable she had not approached the topic well.

She got this prompt reply, "I would have paid the full cost of the curtains right away. But Bert wouldn't let me. He was dead against it." The shoe buttoner flew through the air to the basin with the cigar, and Gisi stood up on her beautifully shod feet. Her attitude could not be mistaken. Miller went cold. She sensed shit was going to fly. Miller had a paralyzing awareness she could do nothing to stop it. She knew she could stop nothing in the house. She was aware she could not avoid the fate that awaited her and that it was coming nearer day by day. Miller lifted two fingers of her right hand and yelled out in great agitation, "The hand of God smites those who are corrupt and those who are vain. Woe to all of you!"

With that unconscious act Miller accomplished much more than she had ever achieved through her niggardly calculations and her underhanded little tricks. Gisi was speechless. If the madam had given her a good slap in the face, she would have understood. But what Gisi had just witnessed had never happened before. Once Miller was out the door, a feeling of gratification filled her from head to toe. She lay back down on the bed and thought a good long while about the strange occurrence.

As Gisi pondered she came upon the decision to decline Bert's offer once and for all. Here at Red House amazing things were happening. Miller had ceded control.

The next afternoon Madame Miller sent Milada a request via the porter. She asked Milada to dress immediately to take care of what she, the madam, had begun yesterday.

Miller and Milada walked side by side to the hospital. They did not say a word along the way. Miller looked askance at Milada with mistrust and curiosity. But Milada's serious, brown face showed no emotion. The porter at the hospital knew Milada well. Miller felt incensed at the way he stuck the two gulden Milada pressed in his hand right in his pocket like he expected it.

He said, as far as he knew, the transport was going to leave right away. They are "already informed upstairs, M'lady."

Milada and Miller went upstairs.

"Money, please," Milada said. With a sigh the madam reached into her green-velvet coin purse. Milada shook her head.

"Not enough!" she said. "An official doesn't take less than five gulden." Since Miller still hesitated and looked around nervously, Milada added, "That's how much Madame Goldscheider used to give." That did the trick.

Then she paid the fee for the transport stretcher together with another tip. And after Miller had paid all these people with a sigh, there was nothing in the way of Dubbe's stay in the hospital.

"Who's going to pay me for all this?" Miller carped as she stepped out onto the street. "I bet this money is completely wasted, isn't it? Who can I go to to get my money back? Who's going to pay!"

"The new girl," Milada answered laconically.

Miller looked at her without comprehending.

"Well, you the madam are going to have to look for a replacement. You will have to find someone agreeable who comes cheap."

"That Sucher is mean," Miller admitted.

"Sucher would also be much too expensive," Milada gave a curt reply.

Miller paused. Milada strode quickly on her way, and Miller tripped along behind her. Miller was in a bad frame of mind.

Time and time again Miller stretched out her arm, then drew it back. She came up with a hundred plans. She made a hundred stabs at speaking, but she always broke off.

When they finally arrived at the entrance to the main street, Miller took Milada's arm and said in a whining voice, "Let's go to that place where we can get someone agreeable, really agreeable, I mean, some place we can find a girl that won't cost anything. Can we?"

"It will cost something," said Milada. "But it will be cheap."

Then she turned around and went back the way she had come, while Miller paddled along behind, filled with rage and self-loathing.

"That's where it is, right there," Milada said, pointing with her umbrella to a quay.

"It's probably some dealer who works with procurers. I've had my fill of those people," Miller picked up the conversation.

"What are you thinking!" Milada said disapprovingly. "They wouldn't give us the time of day."

Milada's word "us" shocked Miller. Nonetheless she kept on bravely, "These hotel porters aren't that reliable."

"We are not going to see a hotel porter," Milada dismissed her remark.

For a brief moment Miller entertained the misguided notion she would take control and drop the plan. She wanted to curtail things, which seemed to be getting more uncomfortable. She was after all the madam. But she was helpless and had no idea what to do.

"The best thing to do is ignore her. Don't say another word. Act like I have a servant with me. I'll give her a tip when we're done. I'll say, 'Here, this is for the trip, thanks.'" Miller was filled with a sense of satisfaction as she accompanied slender Milada who was walking at quite a clip. When they arrived at the banks of the quay, Milada stopped, unsure. She first looked up and down the long row of elegant houses that lined the bank. It was a new district of the city. She shook her head.

"So! Now she doesn't know where to go," Miller was venomous and jumped in front of Milada. "Well, this isn't good. We've taken a wrong turn. I should have brought Goldscheider's list of addresses with me."

"If you think, Madame, you're going to find an address for this place," Milada pointed to a dark corner where a few forgotten houses clung to one another between construction sites and mounds of coal, "then I suggest you go there tomorrow by yourself."

"Of all the gall!" Miller's pent-up anger gushed out her mouth. "How dare you! Who do you think you are?"

"Let me tell you, Madame," Milada touched Miller's arm, which she had pulled back. "I'll tell you why I hesitate. I don't feel good about taking you there. Up there," Milada paused and then continued, while she drew figures in the sand with her umbrella, "it's not safe for outsiders. There are wonderful goods up there. And when Rough Eddie, that's what they call him, is in a good mood, you can get half of them for nothing. But every time you go, you're taking a risk. Once Zimmermann got a horrible beating up there. But Eddie's known me for a long time. I don't think he'll bother me, even if we have bad luck and he's not plastered. That's when he's very nasty and I can't get anything done."

"All right, but who do you think you are bringing me to a guy like that? Things are getting out of hand. I can handle a regular dealer, no problem, but I don't need a killer. You're not going to get me," Miller said, pointing to the little houses, "to go into that den of thieves."

"Madame," Milada whispered, almost shocked and walking a few steps ahead of Miller, "don't yell like that. That man over there is watching us."

A policeman walked passed them, looking serious and imposing. His sharp eye did look them over.

Miller blinked. "That's, that's..." Miller blubbered, "How can you, how can I, I...?"

"In this business you've got to know these corners," Milada said with authority. "Other people only tell you what everybody knows. They're talking about exchanges. But Eddie delivers new wares, special goods! He has girls people will be talking about in a week. Once, when business was slow, but not as bad as it is now, Goldscheider got a girl here who..."

Miller interrupted impatiently, "If you leave me here by myself, I'll sink into the pavement. I can't just stand around for God's sake. What am I supposed to do on my own?"

Milada's tone had changed appreciably. She now used a voice with the strength and confidence of someone teaching an apprentice. "Look over there at that new neighborhood with the elegant houses. Do you see it? Go walk around that area, go walking back and forth. Pretend you are looking for an apartment. Wait there till I'm back. Over there you'll be safe."

Then Milada crossed the street quickly, without waiting for Miller to agree. She walked into the shadow of the lost houses.

When half an hour was up, Milada returned with a spring in her step, pleased. She waved to Miller, who was walking quite a way off. Her wave showed an intimacy Miller would not have accepted an hour ago. But in those thirty minutes of walking along the quay in the presence of pimps cruising and a policeman on patrol, she was now ready to submit to Milada's strong personality. Milada meant protection and safety.

"Well?" Miller asked peevishly. "It took you long enough."

"I took care of things," Milada replied. "Come on."

Miller's brown eyes glowed like suns with greed and delight. The light smell of alcohol and musk floated around Milada.

"I had to drink with them," she told her. "It was a real stroke of luck Rough Eddie was drunk. Just look at my dress, it's full of the stuff! We toasted each other back and forth pretty heavily."

She laughed and brushed the spots on her dress. "So, Madame, just imagine. We're going to have a girl for one week, starting on the first of the month. She is a married woman. Her husband is going to be hanged soon."

"What?! Jesus, Mary, and Joseph," Miller said and stopped dead in her tracks.

"Yes, her husband snuffed out a lawyer. She's done time, too, but she was released. Everybody in town knows her story. Eddie's wife picked her up right after she got out of the clink. She took her to her private residence, of course. Eddie's wife is an elegant person, you should know. She wears diamonds and always wears silk. She's regal. She was upstairs just now, and I put everything together with her. She gets five hundred gulden for making the deal. And Eddie, she promised, wasn't going to get a penny of it. And all this happened because she'd just had a big fight with Eddie."

"Five hundred gulden! For God's sakes, that's a huge lot of money. What will she do for all that money?"

"Madame, if you don't want to pay, I will with my money. And I'll take the earnings from it, too."

"What crazy talk! You have money? You should pay your own debts. Such stupid talk!"

Miller pulled herself together to look respectable, and for the rest of the way back, neither of them spoke at all. They were icy.

Soon thereafter Dubbe left Red House. She was remarkably calm and did not resist. She did not make a scene, rather complied with orders.

Supported on the arms of two hospital orderlies, she slid down the front steps. "I'm coming back, I'm coming back," she said, downplaying people's farewells. As she was stepping out onto the street, she suddenly became very weak. She stood stock still and seemed to be remembering something. She looked for Milada who was paying the cab driver. Milada was struck by something unusually tragic and pitiable in Martha Dubbe's face. But before she could go to her, the men lifted her in the cab, and the door closed.

Without waiting for Miller's orders, the porter and Milada emptied out Dubbe's old room. They cleaned, washed the floorboards, and polished the furniture. They put fresh, rose-red curtains at the window and decorated them with ribbons. Then they brought in vases and flower pots, put out lovely, satin linens from storage, placed items like perfume, atomizers, crystal bottles for toiletries, and small ivory boxes, which Goldscheider had in large supply, all about the room. At noon they brought Miller to see.

"This will be for the new girl Birkner. Pretty nice, don't you think?" said Milada.

"I want this to go to Gisi," Miller said defiantly.

"But Gisi is her old sweet self. We don't have to do anything else to perk her up, don't you think? What a good mood they were in yesterday at Eddy's, weren't they? We got a good deal, right?"

Miller did not deign to answer.

Milada ran her hand over the rose-red silk bed cover.

She said in an off-hand way, "It would be better to serve afternoon coffee again, like we did with Goldscheider here. Those old practices are the best. Coffee really picks people up. We're going to make little sandwiches today. We'll sell them for twenty-five cents, but they'll cost us five. You have to spend money to make money."

"Give her an inch, she takes a mile," Miller said derisively, but she did not countermand Milada. She only turned and went out the door.

Milada went to the kitchen to talk with the cook.

"Mrs. Riedl, go to the cellar and get cold cuts and caviar. I will be making sandwiches. And, listen, if Miller comes sniffing around, tell her Goldscheider used to serve sandwiches with sardines, but Milada is saving money by serving them with chopped boiled eggs, all right?"

"Jesus, Madame," said the successor of resolute Polifka, an inveterate worrier. "Just look at you and how you can make this business fun!"

Milada said, "Soon enough I won't be involved anymore, Mrs. Riedl. I'll tell you," Milada whispered secretively after a pause, "I'm going to get an inheritance from my father's family. He had a big estate. And now he's gone so the family is dividing his holdings. Keep it to yourself, Mrs. Riedl. I'm going to be independent."

Riedl clapped her hands. "That's great news! I always did have a feeling you'd take over. And now it's really going to happen."

When Horner showed up, Milada was going through the letters Dubbe had left between the mattress and springs of her brass bed.

"Madame Secretary," he said, "at your service."

She tossed the letters down and laughed in answer.

"Horner, I've got Miller by the horns. She twists and turns, but she can't get away. I'm circulating rumors, very funny stuff. And if I do carry through on my plans, they fit very well with how things run here. The story of my inheritance has gotten around. Everybody's coming to ask me about it. They think that book by Marx you sent me yesterday was a bundle of legal documents. Everything is going to work out exactly as I planned."

Milada flung her arms up, and her slender young body was energized.

"I think I'll be able to…" Milada broke off.

And Horner finished her sentence sarcastically, "Knock the old brothel madam off her throne and crown yourself Queen of Red House."

She picked up his banter, "Yes, and I'll dash around after your ideas like butterflies."

"Well, all right, but you're not that far along yet," he said with satisfaction. "So tell me quickly, what kind of role have you made up for yourself? What will your new title be? Will you be Regent of the Lumpenproletariat or Grand Inspector of the Raggedy? Which of the seventy-six devils of vanity has gotten into you? Just you wait and see, you'll give birth to outright bastards! This is going to yield bad seed! Unconsecrated union! But I really don't care! I'll just sit by and watch you have at it."

He put his glasses on and snooped around in the papers. "So are you going to cart off the remnants of Dubbe?"

"Right, this is all there is of her meager possessions. There's a certificate of birth from her town, examination certificates, other credentials, letters, and poems. I found all these stuffed under her mattress. Poor creature! She was so attached to her credentials."

"A lot was lost when she departed?

Milada shrugged. "Well, she had a lot of misery coming. These things are just numbers that Miller sits and broods over."

"So what did she die of?"

"She's not dead at all."

"Nonsense! Do listen to me, please," he barked at her. "If somebody wants to die here, she is already dead in the world outside."

"I'll grant you that," said Milada and placed her hand on the bundle of papers. "Dubbe came from a good family. She was an English teacher and tutored a university student at his house. She was young then and beautiful."

"Stop right there! You've laid out inevitable destiny: love, honor, innocence, anguish, despair, abandonment and helplessness. Done and over," Horner interrupted her.

"Horner, what you call destiny is not inevitable; it is not a given of Nature," Milada said. "As far as I can tell all your great books fail to explain why women are reduced to this destiny. It is unnatural. Women are physically designed to bear children. Why do men disdain women with healthy, mature bodies who carry out their venerable role? Why does the vengeance of the law fall on them? It makes no sense! Explain it to me."

"Your question," he said with a sneer, "honors the man you asked enormously. I will take your question to a policeman and place his explanation at your feet."

"Sorry, Horner, this time you're not getting around me. I want a clear answer. Are the laws truly only there for people who are secure and fortunate? And anyone who is disadvantaged is not served by the law? Nobody's ever thought this system should fall apart?"

"You have to give it a kick, that's what the Honorable Codex states," said Horner with grim irony. "But keep your sympathies to yourself, and don't bother me. A mother with her child is not helpless. She is not lost. Mothers do not need your pity. They have their vengeance. They have their revenge. Look here! Children with no father have an immense power. Is it for better or for worse? Who can say?"

Horner made his fists into a ball. "We hold power. If people were smart, they would be more afraid of fatherless children than they have been. People shouldn't let these children grow up with such uncontrolled, independent freedom, children like you and me. If they were smart, they'd keep us within their sweet little laws. They should have legislation requiring us to wear muzzles. Look at how things are in this world! Take the list of criminals! Look at who the victors are. It's the prostitutes! They are the children without fathers. The government is the loser I'm telling you. Take your stupid average capitalist, a woman like Miller. She's fearful each day about her profit. The future will slip through her fingers." Horner lifted his index finger. "Only in the treadmill of marriage can a person produce a valuable, pious, meek and useful citizen of the state. Some gratuitous impregnation is not allowable. The children that are imitations of the official trademark "Human Being" are persecuted. They are punished as unfair competition on the market. What more is there to say, Homunculus?"

"Punished," she repeated with her forehead in wrinkles. "That's right. In an instant Dubbe lost the life she had. The people of the embassy threw her out. The man who got her pregnant went off on a trip. His father almost beat her to death in his rage. His mother went around, wringing her hands and telling everybody what Dubbe had done to her boy. Only the housemaid helped Dubbe by bringing her food. When she was about to have the baby, she was thrown out in the cold with no doctor. Horner, for one whole day and a night she went from hospital to hospital, from one home for unwed mothers to another, but there was no room for her. As an unmarried woman, she was told, she should have come three months earlier to work. She stood in the street and writhed in fear and pain. A woman orderly came out to her and made her promise that if they took her in, she would go to a brothel when the birth was over. Then the woman took her in and told people Dubbe was her cousin. Finally she was given a bed."

"So now you see how careful people are," he added.

"They took all her clothes off," Milada said with a clear image of the events in mind. Her voice revealed she was seeing everything that she was talking about. "'It was like a blow,' Dubbe said, when she tried to keep her dress. The supervising orderly yelled at her, 'Lie down, you idiot! We don't have separate laundry here for each person.' Then the doctor arrived and asked, 'Is she married or not?' The orderly answered, 'Unmarried.' The doctor whistled and said, 'Take her dress off.'

"Listen, Horner, after that what Martha Dubbe went through was even worse. When she was at her most desperate here in Red House, she never forgot the time they took her in at this hospital. She told the story over and over. And she talked about the child, how they treated her baby." Milada stopped for a moment. "Here's what happened then. They put the new baby on a small pallet on the floor. Martha was so weak she could not get out of bed to see the child. She couldn't even ask someone to lift the baby up for her to see. She was afraid to ask. She was ashamed to tell someone to bring her the baby. Her shame was that she was not married. All night the child whimpered. She was afraid for the baby and could only say, 'drink.' The orderly poured water in her mouth, but she meant the baby needed milk. Her milk had come in, and she wanted to nurse the baby. But she was afraid to say that.

"Do you know what Martha wrote in her diary, Horner? Every three months there was a terrible fight here. She saved her money diligently. But finally she spent it on silks and champagne. It's always the same story. The will of every person is destroyed here. Nothing is predictable. Nothing is secure. We are subject to every misfortune. We are thrown into danger with no hope of being saved. Illness, getting old, debt—it's an endless cycle of crises for us. We can never break out of the cycle. Every move to security comes at the cost of the inevitable descent into ruin."

Horner looked at her. His eyes were filled with wrath. "Yet there are people who hauled themselves up out of the muck by the scruff of the neck. That's what people say."

Milada continued with her position. "That's why we are resigned to what happens to us. Horner, it's evident when someone owns something in life, whatever it is, that the person has hopes and dreams. That person is able to negotiate for himself. He takes himself seriously and lives with security; he can make things happen. We can't do that. We destroy ourselves first."

"And that's why one day down the line you all will be forgiven your idiocies, my fine little lady! What's your relation to heaven, most esteemed lady?"

"That's not an issue, Horner! Hell never threatened any fine lady. And no maid could ever afford the promise of eternal bliss. Material security makes a person strong. Living in the clouds doesn't help for very long. I've never felt as strongly as I do now that material security fuels our talents. The person with no security goes to ruin. I tell you, Horner, I'm going to live intentionally.

Whatever happens to me, I will never let things roll over me and take away my will. I do not want to go to ruin like all the rest."

Horner rubbed his hands, giggling. "That's karma, little girl, difficult karma! What are we going to do about that?"

"I'll grab it by the horns and turn it around. And so be it! If what I'm daring to do now ends up being my demise, then I will accept that. But then it will be the fate I chose and not a trap someone set for me."

Horner jumped up. He was quaking, and his face was contorted. Spit was running out of the corners of his mouth. "Triumph, my girl!" he blurted out. "So I haven't sat around the dung heap, waiting, for nothing. It stinks. The sacred scarab has arrived!" He took two steps back and bowed forward, doffing his greasy hat to the floor in a gesture of humility.

One afternoon at a rather unusual hour Horner went to Red House. He found Milada in the office, talking eagerly about plans with the seamstress Moosmann. Moosmann was, all of a sudden, once again in favor here.

"Today we placed an advertisement in the paper," Milada said. "It's for Birkner, the new girl, you know. Three newspapers won't run the ad, but eight of them will post a notice tomorrow. In three days things are going to be lively here. That's it for today! We're going to need you to make new dresses. I want all of them the same. And Birkner will be wearing white."

Upstairs in Milada's room Horner shifted his weight from one foot to the other in distress. "I don't understand. You talk too much; you think too much. You've become very important recently. Hey, you have unbelievable success to your credit now, don't you? I'd just like to know whether you're so sure where you're going to have your body interred."

"For heaven's sake!" Milada said. "I haven't ever thought about it."

"Because you are an idiot. How can you ever achieve anything in life? How can a goal that's near or very near be important to you, if you haven't even planned your final destination? How can you go on an adventure or engage in speculation? How can you fling yourself into a sea of a thousand possibilities unless you're sure your body, which you're risking in the game, has a final resting place?

"You have looked into the mystery of the cemetery, of the crypts of the lofty ancestors and the luxurious coffin. You see these as what follows the heroic acts of individuals here on Earth. But that's all you've done! You are caught in the midst of the game. It gives you life, energy, and courage for the moment. You have your fantasies and a taste of the world's good fortune. But first you have to put a solid peg in the soil of this Earth! If you haven't done this, your dreams cannot take flight. You will lack true ambition. Your decisions are folly; they have no spine. I had hoped for the best for you, but now I can't bear to see where you're headed. I'm tired."

Milada looked at him. His face was more lined, puffy, and unsettled than ever. His bushy eyebrows were closely knit together. They partially occluded his greatly contracted pupils. She recognized these symptoms.

"Horner, you're drinking again," was all she said.

Without looking at her, he rummaged around in his pockets and, from an inside pocket, he produced a large envelope. "There you have it," he said hastily. "Take it. It's free and can't be taxed. The corpse will be absolutely lovely."

Milada looked at him speechless.

"You should know that I have often thought, with intense feeling, of your dead body. I like it, love it. You won't attract anybody anymore. Nobody will desire you, and no one will pay for your fond attention. Just don't think that I have invested any ambition or feelings in offering you this. Ridiculous!" He snapped his fingers.

He went on, "I take a pagan pleasure in wielding and brandishing the only weapon, sharpened daily, that is lethal to life.

The last fantasy I allow myself is imagining everything that lives and breathes after it is gone.

"I tell you, girl, only the intimacy of this house creates the fine and true atmosphere that relieves me of the desire to live. Being here dissipates the energy of the will, bit by bit. I bask in it, every day anew, and emerge a victor. Just look at me! Don't I look like somebody who triumphs in the end?"

He sat up straight. His eyeballs rolled around in his head, and the tips of his mustache shivered.

"Have you ever considered," he suddenly began to speak softly, "the fact that everything will be over for you all of a sudden? With one fell swoop, you're done! For the time being you can see the gray wall, can count the cracks in the ceiling, and listen to the noise of the traffic. You can speak. You can talk about supper and say you prefer radishes, nice red ones, and then—ha! All of a sudden, it's over.

"Think about what comes after that. Think about it clearly and in detail. But don't think about progress, about the biology of it. Don't think of evolution or the theory of reincarnation!" he shouted. "Forget about history, culture, or some nonsensical drivel about eternal life. Nobody actually knows about that. Consider this: you won't think or feel anything. Thinking and feeling will be miles away from you. You won't think about dinner, the nice warm dinner you won't digest if you up and die after you've had cake and coffee in the afternoon."

He pulled Milada toward himself by the arm, talked right past her, and his raspy voice sank to a whisper. "Think about the next hour, and think about the little minutes that are vile, crawling ants that bear an action, an accomplishment, or an event out of life. Think about the pleasure of watching someone lighting streetlights, one after another, how they glow red and appealing in the November fog, and consider you won't see them anymore once they have lowered you in the leaden light of the afternoon down into the earth. That's what's terrifying, what our living body can't fathom. That's what our gray brain matter resists and denies. Our brain is big enough to survey the future of culture in the coming millennium. But it shrivels up to nothing when it comes to comprehending the hour after it's ceased to be. Throw yourself into the chasm of this hour. You will emerge again for me, I tell you, immune, with an impenetrable hide around your tender little soul."

Milada had put her hands up to frame her face and listened to him intently.

His voice was a rasping whisper that was hard to hear.

"How does it go? You're lying in your room. Flies and other crawling things are on your forehead. The gray of the morning has become light, and sunlight plays about your nose. Now the milkmaid arrives, and then the baker's apprentice is at the door. All this happens at the hour you used to lie around in your warm bed, hungry. Someone in the kitchen feigns a complaint, 'You can forget the two rolls with seeds for the gentleman.' That's who you are. 'He died.'

"There are people in your room, throwing around useless stuff, an ironing board or wet laundry. They're doing things you wouldn't put up with in life. With no inhibition they take paper and pen off your desk. They talk loudly and gossip. And you're just lying there while flies shit on your face. What?! Then you feel a bony hand at the back of your neck. What are the millennia that were promised against this one dawn that no longer breaks for you? What are all the stars in the sky that twinkle in the face of streetlights you can no longer see shining, when you've croaked in the afternoon? This is where the wondrous power of the fear of death is lodged. This wonderous power has made us beggars, idiots, and saints because no one has the courage to subject this image to light, to take away its power, or to scatter the phantoms. We apes would rather tumble into the most eternal eternity with one cowardly leap, we'd rather do that than...I'm telling you, girl, imagining this moment takes some doing, some courage! When these thoughts first occurred to me, I shook and groaned like a little boy. I was a boy at the time and called out for Father Brains and Mother Wisdom to comfort me. But they did not come. That's when I came upon these ideas, in my search, in my numbness. Do you understand me?"

Horner slammed his fist on the table and cried out, "Lust helps! It's a distraction, a vile deception! There's nothing else like it! There's nothing as singular or lasting as bodily lust. Take note of this, you prostitute, and exploit it as you will. Physical lust is the only thing we've invented that quashes our thoughts of death. Only in those moments when we are in the throes of lust do we have anything to wage against death. Our mortal and spiritual life is, momentarily, free of decay. Everything is laughter. Gravity is suspended. The little boy sits there and quivers with desire. He is both creator and creative power. There is new life coming to light. Worlds recognize each other. But ultimately the little boy was alone, all alone. The little boy was only playing. Ha-ha!" He laughed a raucous laugh. "He had, for a moment, hoodwinked the great Mr. Death!" Horner looked disgusting. His face was pinched; his mouth, slack, and he drooled. His spongy body quivered with excitement after his speech. Milada moved away.

"But now," he began anew, "I am fine where I am. I see the Old Gentleman rather near, Mr. Death. I rub elbows with him. I know his elaborate stage tricks. Bottom line: I have no attachments. I love nothing. I don't get used to anything that I'm not used to watching with the eye of a survivor. You, all of you," Horner indicated a large circle around himself, "are as good as dead for me. My nerves no longer squeal in pain. There are no more surprises. How comfortable life is for me now. It's broken in like an old shoe." He rubbed his hands, slowly got back to his topic, and turned to face his audience, Milada.

"So there you have it, Milada Rezek," Horner bowed deferentially. "In recognition of your honorable and loveable dead body, for which the Easter bells will soon toll," he bowed once again, "I have, most humbly, taken the liberty of offering you a small token of recognition." Milada took the envelope from him and, filled with curiosity, opened it.

"Well, sure, it's second class, but it's just fine," he said with pride. "It was surprisingly inexpensive, when you think about what all you get with it. You get a black shroud, four candles, thick ones, too! I chose them myself. And a wreath of pearls for the top. In case there's nothing else, it will look very nice. Since it's for you, I'm assuming there probably will be another wreath.

"Take a look! It includes a coffin, the usual medium size. That should be right. People generally reckon fifteen centimeters more. Bodies do stretch out a bit."

Milada turned around. "Horner, I think this is really insane of you," she said, and a shudder flew through her.

"I think that's really impertinent of you. Now you can lie down and die anytime, anywhere you want. Doesn't that mean anything to you? Don't you have a feeling of peace and a tremendous sense of security? Is what goes on around you nothing more than shit? What's left to worry about, to fear? Your life now seems to be just about ideal. I won't have to worry about anything else for you."

"Horner, tell me, do you think you're going to live to see me die?"

He blew up. "You stupid idiot! All doors are open for you. Now you can finally live fully! Until you have overcome the anticipation of Mr. Death so completely that you can say goodbye to him, wherever you encounter him, you won't be free. Then and only then will your power upon life be available to you. Now you can take on anything. Do what you want! Get rid of the madam, make your way into the decent life, become a tailor, or a tightrope walker above the market square! You can buy yourself three new dresses and be independen—any of that! You hold the reins now. Pull hard."

He pushed the closed envelope over toward Milada.

"Put the honorable funeral away in a safe place. Be done with it!" said Horner.

Without answering the overwrought man, she took the envelope and put it in a drawer. He lit a cigar from Virginia.

"Does the grave have a number?" is all she asked.

"But of course! Everything is according to protocol. The grave has a section number, group and row number. You can look and see," he replied, pleased with himself. "You'll be in a nice spot! There aren't many neighbors around. It's in a new section. The air there is very clean. Third class looked a bit too shabby to me. It was common, up against a wall, and cramped. People are packed in there like sardines. Third class is probably for minor bureaucrats. That's how it's laid out."

The cigar hung from the corner of his mouth. His face was a mass of tired, listless wrinkles.

Milada was familiar with the abrupt onset of exhaustion in Horner. Consuming alcohol or heavy physical exertion brought it on. Exhaustion frequently befell him in the middle of a conversation. It made him impervious to what was going on around him.

"Yes, well, let it be. Believe me," he stuttered, "it's all foolish, all foolishness."

Milada was standing by the window with her back erect. She had the feeling narrow little Red House Alley stretched away to green fields. Beneath the pale skies overhead she saw a straight row of small, dark hills rise up. One of them was her grave. Quiet, dark earth awaited her. This grave was the first thing she owned. It was the first thing she had for her security. A strange feeling came over her. She felt youthful and marvelous; she was fit for any battle. Why had this happened? A new feeling of power welled up inside her. Her stern face looked young, and she looked good.

"Think whatever you want to, Horner! I do want to live—to

live and live and live. I want to see what's in the future. I'm eager to see it. And at the end..." Milada turned to him and finished her thought, "Horner, there's one thing I am sure of. At the end I'm going to say, 'The journey was beautiful.'"

Miller sat in her office and read the *Reporter for German-Speaking Catholics*. It was an extraordinary thing for her to do!

She sat there with a cap of black lace on her graying hair and with her pale face momentarily relieved of its usual thousand sullen wrinkles. This was on the morning of Palm Sunday! Miller had just come from mass. She counted the money from last night with fingers still smelling of the incense she had lit in church. She put the money in the till with a look of great satisfaction. She had taken quite a profit these last few days!

This new girl Birkner! It was unbelievable how much business she brought in! She was not very special. She had a plain, chubby face with watery blue eyes, and her hair was done in a ponytail. She wore a white dress with red shoes and had a red ribbon around her neck. But she did tell great stories! She talked about how her husband had murdered the lawyer. At first Miller could not take the horror, but then she got used to it. Every evening Birkner told the same story. Miller hardly paid attention anymore. Yes, Birkner had had an affair with the lawyer, or so she said. Her husband Robby had not known about it. He had always wanted her to live well, have nice clothes and fine foods. But he only made fifty-three gulden as an accountant! Her old man had been so parsimonious.

When this woman arrived there was an uproar in Red House! The men ran around after her like crazy. There were always new men, and they lined up. The commotion went on half the night until the porter had to lock the door because the house was full. The men who came were, of course, cavaliers; they were true gentlemen! If someone did not want to pay fifty gulden for Birkner, he visited another girl. God knows, a devil had gotten into them.

Miller made the sign of the cross quickly. They were boisterous in their fervor. One after another the men ran after the girls from room to room. They pursued them up the stairs and down the corridors, hooting and hollering.

They went through all the champagne in the house, even though Milada had bought a large supply. The men paid prices that had seemed impossibly high to Miller. They drank it all up.

At eight in the morning Milada Rezek went off for a new supply of foods for sandwiches, goose liver, fine pastries, and caviar. The frenzy had been going on for five days. Praise God! This Lent season had been going very well! The madam could only be grateful for this.

Miller immersed herself in the *Reporter* once again. She read an article, "Catholic Charity for Abandoned Children." Then she picked up the mail the porter had put on her desk. There was a lot of mail coming in. Miller read the whole article with great care, praised the good author generously from her heart, and leaned back in her chair, sighing with comfort. Milada was also picking up the mail these days. Milada was the one who had brought all this about. And she, Miller, was there to reap the rewards. There were inquiries, announcements, and offers. She, Madame Miller, was now giving orders to move on these. Her life had become less troubled, even effortless. Having Rezek do all this was a great idea of hers. Of course Miller could not show Milada she knew. But Milada was aware. Miller believed she had put together a fail-safe plan. First she would delegate everything, watch what Milada did closely, oversee her closely, take note of everything and retain it, and then...hmm, leave. She would take it all with her. Milada might think she is making herself indispensable. Miller would let her think she is becoming more important than the madam. It was appropriate to have someone looking over the books. If things kept going as they were, she was fairly certain she could execute her plan in another six months. She certainly did not want to die here.

In reality Miller had completely subordinated herself to Milada's rule. And in so doing, she had entirely lost sight of running the business. Milada dealt with the agents, with the delivery people, with the girls in the house, and with the guests. She oversaw the kitchen, the tailors, and accounting. It was Miller's belief she kept the till all for herself. Nobody was allowed to touch the hard cash. Miller was convinced the money coming in was what made her head of the whole business.

Milada was too smart to let it appear she ran the ship. She always spoke about the madam as the mover and shaker, but not one transaction occurred without Milada's authorization and oversight. She made sure Miller had the impression she had seen to everything and orchestrated it all. The magical incantation Milada used to win over Miller when they were at odds was and remained, "just as it was under Goldscheider." These words pushed back against the stinginess, meanness, and blind resistance that, at times, overwhelmed Miller. This charm worked when Miller became high-handed and headstrong like a child who had been spanked.

If there was pressure from agents or the girls, Miller knew how to stall people with excuses and canned phrases until she had gotten Milada's opinion. At those times she said, "Rezek, Rezek, I'm busy at the moment. Take care of the gentleman I spoke with yesterday."

After a while people caught on to the maneuver and took their business directly to Milada. Milada addressed their concerns more quickly and easily than did Miller, who was always blabbering out of insecurity. For the first time since she had assumed the business Miller had a feeling of well-being and peace of mind. This was the comfort she had waited for.

In the kitchen everything ran smoothly. The new cook Riedl managed things, and the girls had no complaints or arguments. Milada had told her, "The madam talks too much with the girls.

You shouldn't do that. It interferes with their respect for you. Tell them what they need to know, and that's all."

And the cook hewed to this advice. Milada's relation to the other girls had also changed considerably. This came about slowly and without notice as time went on. In part the story she had circulated about an inheritance, and which she kept alive with sparse comments, had given her new standing. And Milada used this adeptly and cleverly whenever she needed to. By implication she suggested Miller was not doing especially well with the loans and perpetual tactics for saving money and that she, Milada, was happy and delighted to step up and help Miller out financially where she could. She put out the message people should cooperate and stick by her, so that finances did not go amok. From the get-go these strategies had secured her the power base she was putting in place. Everybody knew Milada had not needed to attach herself to Goldscheider. Her good pedigree, together with the history of Black Katerine, preceded her and was credit enough. People also knew that the former madam had been smart to keep Milada at her side.

Under Milada's direction the girls had at first grumbled and had their occasional disagreements and suspicions. Especially Mitzi did what she could to undermine Milada's status with the other girls. But those who thought about it soon saw that there was not a hint of favoritism or arrogance in Milada's behavior. They accepted the fact that Milada was in charge. Her expanded activities did not strike people as excessive. They could readily see that it was to their benefit to deal with the madam through Milada. They understood a brief, reliable bargain with Milada was not nearly as upsetting as a long-winded battle with Miller, which, in the end, brought nothing.

Very possibly one girl or another had said to Milada, "Leave! You're a complete idiot! You're letting yourself be used by the madam, and you won't get any credit." Gisi, who, like all the girls, got along with Milada, told her she should open her own business, maybe a very nice winery. Gisi suggested her friend Bert would support her. "If you stay at Red House," said Gisi, "you'll have nothing to show for all your efforts."

Milada replied, "Listen, I grew up here. I really care about Red House. I can't bear seeing her let it go down the drain. That's why I'm staying right here."

Milada's companions understood her uncomplicated position, and they respected it, each as she could.

Outsiders or girls who came along later were free to leave without second thoughts if that is what they cared to. A girl could leave when she fell ill or when she believed working at Red House was not for her. But Milada stuck fast. She was the child of Red House Alley.

There was a knock at Miller's door. It was Milada's knock, quick and sure. Without waiting for the words "come in," she walked into the office. She had a hat and jacket on, and her face was red from the harsh wind of spring.

"It was a great inconvenience," Miller announced in a bad mood, "for me to put together all the things we need for Sunday. Nobody delivers on Sunday. That cost a lot of money in tips."

Milada presented Miller with the bills, and Miller looked them over with concern. While standing at the desk in coat and hat, Milada opened the mail. She read aloud, "'Madame: Luncheon set for six. To Birkner, from the Jockey Club. To be served from noon till two.' That event will make us a lot of money." She kept reading and laughed.

"Some people are complete idiots. They send us inquiries from the provinces. They think we rent Birkner out. Those inquiries go to Eddie. And here are more bills. This one's from the shoemaker. It's a contra-account. We only enter it in the books. This one is an offer from Ascher in Saint Pölten. You can look at it if you'd like to. Ascher writes he has a widow there. Dear God, I'm tired." Milada sat down.

While she was fluffing her hair with her fingers after taking off her hat, Milada initiated their decisive conversation. Miller sat there like a block of stone. Milada had a disruptive, subterranean awareness she should be disinterested about what she planned. She told herself she was watching the fall of a distant fate at some remove. Miller, for her part, felt so confident about Milada's behavior that she was caught fully off guard by their exchange. Miller was thrown off and made unconsidered decisions. Only later did she understand how fateful her reaction had been.

Milada began, "I have to talk with you about me."

"All right. What's going on?" Miller peeped in a high-pitched voice. She was clueless, while Milada answered her with a calming coolness.

"Oh, not much. I want to leave."

For a brief moment Madame Miller saw images of green mountains and a quiet forest. She recalled a young, red mouth that had said these same words. But she dismissed these images and shouted, disarmed, "Whatever has gotten into you all of a sudden? Well, it would be better if you did go." Miller clung to her rights, "You're on the record. You're in the books. It would be fine by me. Anybody could come and say at any time, 'I'd like to inform you I'm leaving!' And how am I supposed to respond?"

"I don't know how you do things with other people. It's different with me though. I'm not in your account books because I didn't owe Goldscheider one penny. In the last few months, I've accrued some debt for shoes and clothes. I'd like to know how much I owe you for those."

"What you owe me?! Mother of God!" Miller laughed hysterically. "Fifty-three thousand gulden that I paid in cash, minus what Kessler pocketed. And all those bills I paid. What you owe?! All the money the most honorable priest left me for twenty-five years of loyal service. Mother of Christ! If he could only see me in my despair. He always warned me, 'Josephine,' he said, 'you might do stupid things, but you are never mean, never.' He was right. Time and time again, he was right. Now I have done something very stupid."

Miller rolled her eyes upward as if she were lodging a plea.

"You see, Madame, I have to think of my future. I have no one who'll take care of me if I'm in need. I have to look ahead and make something of myself."

"Make something of yourself? Why are you telling me that? You've already made something of yourself."

"So what am I then, Madame?" Milada took pleasure in making the madam squirm. She had forced her into a corner before delivering the final blow.

"What, what does that matter to me?" Miller stuttered. "That, that is..." Then her tone of voice changed. She began talking quickly. Her words tumbled out.

"Rezek, are you maybe thinking of leaving me? You, of all people? Haven't I kept you here like, like...even though people resent me for the way I treat you? You're going to stay right here with me, Rezek. Right here."

Milada shook her head. "You just want to keep me as long as it suits you. What would you do with me if I fell ill?"

Miller replied, "You, ill? Why all of a sudden are you talking about falling ill?"

"Because one after another we all become ill with this work. And we die early."

Miller screamed, truly terrified, "Mother of Christ! What am I supposed to do? What kind of business is this anyways that it goes to pot little by little?"

"The business will not die. We die, we girls," Milada answered her with scorn. "The business always needs young girls. Bringing in new blood is what this business is about."

Miller's head sank. That was, of course, an ongoing struggle here. It never ceased. She had not gotten used to the turnover. It seemed the minute the problems with a new girl were resolved, then there were difficulties with other girls that needed attention. Things like this were more than she could handle.

"Yes, you have to think quickly and find new personnel," Milada said. "Keeping the same personnel is not an option. And since that's how it is here, I thought I should move on. While I'm still young and strong, I need to make plans to take care of myself."

Since Miller did not answer, Milada continued, "I'm so well known I won't find anything here. But I'm also tired of this business. I want to try something else. I've got some money."

There was a silence during which Miller's eyes were astonishingly wide open.

"I understand accounting. Either I get a job in that field, or I go to the theater, like Gisi did. If I lived someplace else, I could also get married."

Miller sat unable to speak and stared off into the distance. This was the way this business operated. It had been presented to her as a wonderful investment that would run on its own without a hitch. Just perfect! One person gets married, another one dies, and another goes off to dance on stage. Everybody does what she wants, but what about Madame Miller?

And there she was left to pay and pay, talk with agents, advertise, slink around, and lie in wait. She had to pay off spies so that the police did not nab her. If that happened, they would take the prize she had worked so hard for right out of her hands. What if all the girls she had gotten hold of acted like Milada? What would she do then?

Miller pulled herself together and hollered out with empty emotion, "Why did you come here in the first place? Nobody lured you here. You came here all on your own."

"To begin with, my mother left me to Goldscheider," Milada

said. "But," and she spoke with the conviction she was speaking for everybody in the house, "however we got here, we do not have to be destroyed here, Madame! If people go to work in a factory, they don't have to wait until they lose a limb in a machine. Between what we have to do and what we want to do there is a door. We only have to open it. We stay put if we believe the door is closed. I believe it's open. I don't believe a door can keep me here. Or anybody in the house for that matter."

The floor fell out from under Miller.

Without compassion Miller went on, "I won't mention the religious organizations you only have to write to if you want to leave." Miller whimpered to herself that these organizations worked against her. A religious organization foiled her work! Then suddenly an idea came to her.

She addressed her, "Milada, as sure as there is a God above, I am talking with you now very honestly. If you stay here a few years, maybe only two, and I've gotten as much money as I plan to have, then I'll give you the business. So help me God." She was delighted. "I've been promised a place in a nunnery. To hold my place will cost a lot more money. It's with the Congregation of the Sisters of the Cross of Jesus in Styria. When I've paid that, you'll have Red House from me. You'll have it cheap. Or maybe it won't cost you anything at all."

She buried her head in her hands. She had just surrendered everything she had on Earth. She could not bear to hear anything Milada would say.

"Madame Miller," Milada said, "you probably mean well. But your offer is not certain enough for me. Who can say how things will be here in the house in a few years? Let's make a firm, regular plan.

"I'm not interested in making you uncomfortable, Madame, and I do care about this business. I would like to count on your offer, especially since you are so sincere. I am upstanding and reliable, thrifty, and I work hard. I know this business. And you, Madame, can't get along without this business. Taking on some stranger to manage the business would cost you a lot more. If you're willing to keep me as manager with one fifth of the profits and with no obligations in the salon, then I would be happy to stay."

"One fifth of the profits?" Miller asked horrified.

Milada expected an onslaught and stood arrayed for battle.

"Of the profits?" Miller repeated.

"That's right, Madame. My work is worth that." Milada was firm, "And when you do leave, I have first right of purchase since, as you know, I do have money. The business can revive. It'll be as good as it was." She leaned against the desk with composure. "So what do you say, Madame? Is it a deal? You go for it, and you'll see Rezek get down to work."

"One fifth," Miller repeated the third time. But this time, considering the offer, she said it as a promise. She felt almost victorious. When Milada held out her strong, brown hand to Miller, she took hold of it, almost as a reflex. She held it for a moment.

"Sure, all right, I agree. My main concern is being rid of this. Soon! I swear by the name of God you'll get your one fifth! Rezek, now we are bound to each other body and soul. You understand?"

"And we'll put it all in writing, Madame," Milada replied happily and waved her hand. Now the bargain is made! Let's first make our job easier. Laura will have to go. And Anna Meitner, too. This evening we'll make a bowl of punch. It doesn't cost much, and people like it. That will be at midnight. Five and a half kreuzer a glass. I'm counting on selling forty portions. Then we'll have to have a couple of girls on loan from Spizzari for the next few evenings. We don't have enough girls in the house. And..." Milada was interrupted by the doorbell. "Ah, the food stuffs have arrived."

Milada opened the door and spoke to Miller, "It would be

a good idea if you let people know I'm staying on. They knew I wanted to leave." And Miller acknowledged her with a nod and disappeared into the kitchen.

On Maundy Thursday before Easter Bina Michal asked for one day off. She wanted to go home to see her parents and siblings, and Cyrill, too, who was "going to have furlough from the military." She can certainly take off, Milada said, and Miller agreed.

"I'd like to ask something else," Bina said and took a gold coin out of her purse. She held it between two fingers in the air.

"Do you want to send it home? You can take it yourself."

Michal shook her head. "No, I want to get something nice for Cyrill! I don't like shopping in town, and I don't trust the other girls to get something for me. When I go home for Easter, I'll give Cyrill something really nice. This should be enough money, don't you think?"

"Sure, that's enough. What would you like me to get? A walking stick, a wallet, or a cigar case? Can you tell me, is Cyrill a relative of yours?"

"On, no!" Bina stood up proudly. "He's my betrothed."

In response to Milada's look of surprise, Bina said in confidence, "He's been in the military for a year now. Since he's the only son and his father is gone, he'll be out soon. I'm not sure how to say it in German. In the fall he'll be free, that's what he says. And then! Well, I've been saving my money all this time. He's going to be surprised, don't you think?"

Milada replied, "I know you've really saved your money. So do you two want to get married then?"

"Hmm, I'm not sure. His mother has taken over the household. There's a cow in the barn. In one year I've sent them over eight hundred gulden. And I'm going to take some more money with me on my trip. I don't want to put it in the bank or buy bonds. I'll tell you something about his mother. She's very strong."

"I see, all right. But tell me, Bina, does his mother...I mean, does Cyrill know what you do here?"

"Probably, I think so. After Cyrill joined the military and left for Hungary two years ago his mother told my mother, 'Send your daughter to the city.' My mother is the second wife of my father. She's my stepmother. Cyrill's mother told my mother her daughter should make a little money for the house and the livestock."

"What? Your mother sent you to Goldscheider's?"

Bina shook her head. "I got the address from the fish monger who comes to our village on Sunday. Cyrill's mother is like a mother to me. She had worked in the city as a cook when she was a girl. She told me this is the nicest house, that I should come here. When I sent her the last bunch of money, she wrote that Cyrill is looking forward to the wedding. She wrote he's been stationed in the forests of Hungary this whole time and can't come see me. In all her letters she writes that he had told her, 'Send greetings to my dear bride.'"

Milada said contemplatively, "Then things will all turn out for you. I'll buy a walking stick for you to give him. But I want you to listen to me. Be more careful with your money! You shouldn't give it away unless you get something in writing—not even to Cyrill's mother. You never know what will happen."

"Dear Jesus, I went to school with Cyrill. When my mother died," Bina made the sign of the cross, "no one was as kind to me, no one took care of me like Cyrill and his mother. I love them more than anybody in the world."

Once she had broken her silence and finally spoken about her life, she was light-hearted and wanted to talk. "My father's strong, too, but I don't trust him now that he has a new wife. Whatever she wants, he does. And she doesn't like me because everybody in the village knows I was always the best at the dances and in lots of things, and her two daughters weren't."

"Do you two want to get engaged finally at Easter?"

"Oh, no! People in my village don't do that. They just get married, and then everything's all right."

Milada shook her head. She promised herself to a young man in the village and then goes to work in a brothel just like she had entered domestic service, a job a girl can leave at any time intact and in good spirits. She lives a decent, righteous life here. One could even say she is happy to perform the tasks of her job. She finds her work commendable and believes she will return home with this experience. Bina brings structure and order and all kinds of domestic virtues to the chaos of living as a prostitute. And now she is waiting for a husband, a house and home, work in the fields with flowers, and a bit of good fortune in her town. She expects children, too. Naturally she cannot imagine a life without rocking the cradle and children running around. Incomprehensible and yet true. Life has spoken. Countless men have paid her in the meantime for affection and physical warmth. This has weakened and destroyed her strength and health measurably. These men have done this without remorse just as they pillage and lay waste in war. She grants them this. It does not impinge on her soul, which keeps alive the dream of good fortune for women.

"If they were honest with her!" Milada said aloud, unusually moved. Milada did not trust them. This Cyrill does not even write to her! Oh, well, the hide of a farmer is thick, and, in the end, money speaks louder to them than their old-fashioned notions about virginity.

Little Fanchon lay in bed. Nothing was wrong with her, she said it was nothing at all. It was some little thing; just an infection under her arm. She did not show it to anybody, and she was adamant her friends not tell Miller. Or even Milada. But it did keep her from coming down to the salon in the evening, though she truly wanted to. She did want to participate.

"Every spring my skin breaks out. It has happened to me

from the time I was a little girl. The doctor always said, 'April is bad for you.' But when I get through it, I'm fine for another year."

Bina Michal had returned from her vacation beaming. She now sat patiently at the bedside of Little Fanchon and listened to the stories she embroidered with her imagination. Fanchon loved to tell these stories and tried her best to make them sound believable. She was happy to listen to the tale of the huge triumph Bina had celebrated at home in her village. Cyrill was not there. He was just too far away in Hungary to make it. "Father was very happy. He spent a lot of time with me. He had to touch my silk dress and hat and my little purse with perfume in it. Too bad, Cyrill's mother had to be at the annual fair in Dobran. But she did write a lovely letter and enclosed a pressed flower, a forget-me-not from Cyrill.

"And my stepmother and her daughters were furious when they saw me," Bina said victoriously. "I'll tell you what kind of person she is. She cried out I would get slapped in the face if I walked around town all done up with my hat and fancy shoes. But father stood fast and said, 'Don't you dare talk that way to her. She's a lady. Go give your two ugly daughters a good slap in the face.'"

In the meantime two new girls had arrived at Red House. Without a word and without any ado Mitzi, who was moody and sassy, and Anna, who was fat and slow, had to leave. They left as simply as girls had left when Goldscheider was in charge. Who arrived to replace them remains to be told.

At first there was Ilonka Arrigazzi. She was assuredly the rising star in the firmament of Red House. She immediately took up the position due her. She brought her own fabulous toiletries with her. She was versed in the behaviors of a woman of the world and had a photograph, signed personally by a fat, European potentate.

Ilonka had, in fact, been a maid at the spa in Marienbad. She left that position after an altercation with the administration at the spa and went to an aunt who took in girls. Fat Auntie Breslauer initiated Ilonka with two other nieces into the world of international baths. At the end of the season she was invited to come to the capital via Aussig. Ilonka's mother in Tirol was delighted that her daughter with the Hungarian name—all she had to remind her of her father—was able to advance so well in the cold, hard world, the *freddo mondo*. This mother wrote her daughter daily that she prayed to the Sweet Madonna that life would be better to Ilonka than it had been to her, Giusta Arrigazzi.

There was less to-do about the arrival of the other girl. Karla Neuern was a fashionable blonde. The only problem with her was her pale face. It made her look like she was terrified. Her eyes were suspiciously red and she could not bear direct sunlight. Miller had seen reliable medical certificates for Karla, but she was experienced and had her doubts. "Don't worry," Milada said. "Neuberger, the agent in Prague, has always been reliable."

It turned out that the inflammation in Karla's eyes was a completely harmless condition. The new girl had to overcome shyness in her new environment since she was, as Neuberger had written, "a very decent girl who, till then, had worked only in a winery." She did not talk about her personal circumstances except to say she was on her own in the world and that was fine by her.

The whole time the bell at Red House kept ringing, and Fanchon could no longer stand lying in bed. She looked out into the hall with curiosity and sat on the window ledge to "feel the warm sun" since her legs were cold and painful, a situation she defiantly hid.

"Miss Ilonka, go to the salon, please!" Miller said sharply.

"Look how people compete for her!" Fanchon said with sadness.

"Miss Bina, to the salon, please!"

"Good Lord, how much traffic is going on down there," Fanchon called out in shock and watched as it went on.

"It's Saturday!" Bina remarked with a philosophical disinterest as she put down her needlework.

Fanchon put on her red-satin evening gown in her excitement. "Listen! There's the piano! Already?" Yes, business was booming. The hustle and bustle around Birkner had burned the salon into the people's memory for a reason.

People greeted Milada warmly as the manager. "She's from the School of Goldscheider," people said as a compliment. She received the guests in the salon in a high-cut, black, silk dress with a white lace apron. Her sharp, watchful eyes oversaw the whole of the salon. She had a renowned sensibility for all types of visitors.

With pleasant questions and without being overly solicitous, she served the regular guests. She never allowed the girls to approach a visitor or show him any personal attention until he had expressed his wishes to Milada.

"All of you are pretty, young girls," Milada told them. "You're healthy and full of fun. Why would you throw yourselves at the men and then at some point get turned down? You can afford to be choosy. Don't worry, they'll come to you. When it comes down to it, if you aren't interested, you don't have to see anybody. Or, if you're not interested in someone in particular, you don't have to see him. Just stay upstairs in your room!"

Milada's latitude allowed the girls to feel they were treated fairly; there was virtually no insubordination. The worst thing Milada did was insist a girl leave the salon and stay upstairs. She did not burden the girls with long-winded, useless conversation. Rather she made all the girls available to customers. Milada never acted rashly in the interest of the business. She was never a brutal or offensive madam.

There was no noise or any nasty fighting; there were no accusations or reproaches that could damage the reputation of the salon or reveal the reality of the lives of prostitutes to guests. Lovers were disappointed to know such things.

Milada had learned from Horner to keep customers unapprised.

On evenings in the spring the salon was full till the late-night hours. The ladies appeared from their rooms, looked around, then took their leave only to rush into the hall with interest when the doorbell rang.

Arrigazzi sat at a table decked out in a cherry-red velvet dress. She was radiant and happy about the attention she got for her femininity.

She was entertaining an elegant-looking man with a slightly graying goatee who listened with interest as attentively as if he were sitting in the boudoir of a great lady. Champagne was at hand, but both disdained to drink it.

In a corner by the window of the salon, half-hidden by plants, Gisi let a well-known traveler offer her sympathies about Bert's sudden departure. He was portly and kept reaching into his pants pocket and jingling his change. But the fat man was not for Gisi, and she kept turning her beautifully coiffed head to the door to see if another girl could take this unpleasant guest off her hands. Fanchon had hardly appeared in the door when Gisi popped up and conducted her to the table with the fat man. Gisi pronounced, "This is our Little Fanny." And then she was gone.

At another table there were two young men deeply engrossed in their conversation. They sat over black coffee and smoked cigarettes. Gisi stood at their table and ran her hand flirtatiously over the high forehead of the older of the two who had a head full of dark curls. "Oh, do stay this evening," she said sweetly.

"Sorry, Mitzi," he answered. "We're going to have to disappoint you."

"I'm Gisi," she announced, irked, and threw her head back.

The men laughed. "And what's so special about you personally, Gisi? What do you do that makes you different?" the man with the dark hair asked.

"I'm loyal," replied Gisi, insistently.

"That won't help you much," the other man with the glasses

piped up.

"If I love someone, he doesn't need to pay. But you, Sir," Gisi sized up the man who had spoken, "you're not one of those."

He narrowed his eyes behind his thick glasses. "And why then not?" he asked.

"You're too much of a smart aleck for me," she said and left.

"Bravo, girl! What about the name Sibyl then?"

"Isn't that just like a woman! It seems the sweetness was only meant for me," the dark man laughed out loud and followed Gisi. At the door he ran into a friend of his, the physician Gustav Brenner.

Gustav took him by the shoulder, turned him around and said in jest, "Sorry, the room's full, Seidner!"

Seidner with the dark hair had this rejoinder, "Our philosopher here looks into the salon like he's going enter a lecture hall. He thinks he's a live wire and tempting. It's physics and math, isn't that right, Gus?"

Seidner sat down foiled and shrugged, "You've got to take advantage of a situation when it presents itself," he said dryly.

"We playboys have disgraced ourselves, Gus old pal. The sensation Birkner left some time ago. And so what have we fine fellows concluded about this place? I for my part find the coffee's passable and that girl over there isn't bad. And our companion the nearsighted philosopher is electrifying."

Gisi was at the door again. Her blond hair was in a ponytail, and she had on a light-blue princess gown. She approached the table coquettishly. "Well, Seidner, glad to make your acquaintance."

"My pleasure, but I will have to request an early departure this evening. I have to get back to my little pad," Seidner responded to Gisi.

"I beg your understanding. It's our privilege as men," said Seidner to his friends at the table and jumped up next to Gisi. Her laughter rang out.

The bespectacled philosophy student was Joe. Joe turned to

Gustav and said, "As I know Seidner, it looks like it will be you and me, Gus, at the table here."

Milada then took away their empty cups and asked the newcomer, "Sir, would you like a coffee, too?"

"I'll take a beer if you have one, please," said Gustav.

Milada nodded and said, "A bottle of Pilsner then."

Joe asked Gus, "Did you see her eyes?"

"Everything about her is beautiful," Gustav gushed while looking over at Ilonka Arrigazzi.

"No, I mean the waitress at the table, the dark one," said Joe.

"Her? She's old."

"Yes, but she has great eyes. Those are the eyes of a carved sphynx dreaming off under Egyptian skies."

Milada asked, "Would you like anything else?"

Then Gustav looked up at Milada, who had served him a glass of beer with a conventional smile.

"The way she uses her eyes does not appeal to me," said Gustav, and he was soon drawn again to the charms of Ilonka, the new girl from Tirol, who sat back in her chair to be more seductive.

In the meantime the salon had become full of guests and girls. The man playing piano hammered out a march, and a fat, immobile violinist accompanied him with a masterful stroke.

Joe remarked, "He's an accomplished violinist at the conservatory. I know him."

"And so why is he here?" Gustav asked.

"He earns more here than by performing at the literary salon of Baroness So-and-So," Joe answered.

Fanchon had taken the fat traveler Gisi had palmed off on her off to her room, but she returned very soon thereafter and joined the company of some elegantly attired young men, barely past boyhood. They had come in with a loud lot of noise and taken up seats at a table where they occupied some girls with their demands.

Joe was annoyed with them and commented, "Those are the

ruffians of the salon. I want to move out of their way. I don't like being around them."

Gus drank his beer and decided to look on quietly. He wore a purposeful look of disdain, which made him visible as a newcomer to the environment of the salon. Joe, by contrast, swore and cursed audibly, making sarcastic comments about the place. He let go a tirade of angry words about the boys at the next table who were guzzling their beer and treating the girls badly. They were here for the girls.

One of them in particular was very crude. He was a thin, pale little guy whose eyes were glazed over from alcohol. The corners of his mouth twitched. When he ordered more, he plunked his money down on the table. He yelled and flailed about and behaved himself like a unruly child. He put his head on Putzi's bosom, and she pulled away from him.

He hollered out, "Let me put my boots there. They're dirty. What's the matter, aren't they nice, my shiny boots?" He put his feet up on the table and displayed the boots on his little feet.

Lefty Anna spread out her arms and asked ironically, "Maybe put them here?"

"Hell, yeah! Put my dirty boots on your breasts? Girlie, I'll pay for that, come here!"

Anna said, "On my dress? You're not that interesting." She smoothed out the yellow silk of her dress.

Bina then lifted the legs of the pale boy straight up in the air and placed them on a napkin she had spread on the table.

"I don't like you doing that," he cried. "You're awful. Why did you put my good boots on a napkin? I don't like you at all, you Bohunk. My shoes are getting dizzy up there."

Gisi had returned to the table of the students Gustav and Joe. She had a flower in her blond hair, which now hung down loose.

Joe asked her in a rage, "Is there an axe in the house? He looked over at the group at the next table.

Gisi asked him, leaning over him, "So why didn't you come along? Oh, you have a girlfriend, don't you?" She pointed to a ring on Joe's finger, which had a heart-shaped red stone.

"Maybe it's from my dear, departed grandmother. She had no taste. But listen, I'm getting very angry here just sitting watching that guy. Couldn't you throw something caustic on him? If you do, I'll write a poem about your pretty eyes."

Gisi replied, "The madam's good at taking care of guys like that. She's all right with that guy Menzel there, the idiot with the boots."

"The girl at that table is the madam?" Joe asked, indicating Bina.

"Heavens, no! I mean the older woman. She's Milada."

"So that's her name, good. I like it when a name fits someone. If I look at her eyes and hear the sound of her name, I have to think of a throne, but a throne that's gradually sliding into the mud. Gustav, pal..."

Gustav, against his better judgment, had to laugh as he watched the scene in front of him. It escalated and got nastier. "That guy's a real ass, but he is funny."

Menzel had gotten hold of a crown out of tin foil and placed it on his head. The musicians played a cakewalk to get people to dance. Fanchon lifted up the hem of her skirt and swayed rhythmically to the music. She had not put on her makeup carefully. There were prominent red blotches on her forehead and cheeks. When she laughed her face looked stark and grotesque.

"Take a look at your face, Salome," Menzel declaimed, indicating Fanchon. "My shiny boots can be your mirror." As he spoke he put one foot, then the other, back up on the table.

Joe was at his limit. "Scum! He's repulsive," he hissed.

Menzel kept on, "Dance, do a dance for your daddy. I'll pay for everything, I'm Herod. I'm your father. We have a relationship."

Joe yelled, "He's drunk as a skunk."

"Ah, get out of here! You have to be Saint John," Menzel roared at Joe.

The guys with Menzel found this funny and laughed heartily. One said, "Menzel, you're hysterical today!" Menzel laid his head on Putzi's breasts and swung his feet up and put them on Fanchon's shoulders.

"I have to leave," said Joe. "I'd like to pay now."

"Goodbye then, John! We'll chop your head off later," Menzel yelled.

Gustav was still watching pretty Ilonka Arrigazzi. He said, "Oh, look, she's leaving, too." Ilonka fled the scene with her gentleman.

Miller's shrill voice pierced the air, "Fanchon, get out!" Milada had told Miller about the ruckus. "Fanchon!" she yelled.

Fanchon ordered Menzel, "Let me go. I tell you, let me go!" To Miller she wailed, "He won't let me go!"

Fanchon tore his foot off her shoulder. But Menzel kept putting his foot back on Fanchon, each time more deliberately and more forcibly.

Suddenly a loud voice rose above the noise in the salon. "Listen up here! This has gotten out of hand." It was Gustav.

"I'm going to hit that guy," Joe cried out as he went over to Menzel.

Menzel stood on both his feet, plastered, not knowing what was going on.

"So what's your problem?" he drawled in his drunkenness as he looked at Fanchon who had wrested herself free.

The people who had gathered around dispersed in short order.

"Joe, get over here and help me out!" Gustav Brenner's voice rang out crisp and clear in the room, which had grown silent.

Fanchon had collapsed, and Milada was bent over her. She lifted Fanchon's head. She had turned white as a sheet. Her mouth was twisted in pain.

Young Doctor Brenner put his head with his straight, blond

hair down to listen to Fanchon's faint breath.

"Is she ill?" he asked, looking up.

"God, no," said Miller. "The idiot is just drunk."

Milada asked people, "Do any of you know anything?"

One of the girls answered reluctantly, "She's been walking around with an abscess for a week now. And with the way Mr. Menzel was trampling her, it must have ruptured."

"So!" Gustav's blue eyes smoldered. "Take hold of her, Madame!" he said to Milada. "I'm a physician," he added. He supported her head while Milada raised her feet. Joe stood back. He wrung his hands so hard that the bones cracked audibly. Joe was whipped up like a warrior preparing for battle.

"What do you know! What can I say for myself? I hurt somebody with my nice, shiny boots," said Menzel, laughing like a fool and looking down at the floor. When he looked up again, he saw Joe squared off before him with his arms folded across his chest. A few moments ago, Joe had been ready to punch him or hold him in lock grip with his face on the floor. Menzel had it coming.

"But he's just a kid, a kid who got drunk," Joe thought disgusted. His eyebrows were knit and formed a continuous line. His sight was fixed on Menzel like a snake's on a bird flapping around. "That's right," he began with an eerily friendly tone, "Your boots, Sir, are nice—nice and shiny." Joe paused. Menzel was trying to focus, but he was too drunk to see.

"Your boots are disgusting," Joe blasted out. "They're filthy. They're for clomping in dung." He then took a deep breath and kicked Menzel's elegant footwear twice, very hard, with the heel of his solid hiking shoes. Menzel tumbled backwards, bleating like a lamb. "Would any of you gentlemen care for the same?" Joe asked Menzel's companions. "My name is Joseph Wallner. You can find me in the university caféteria any day from noon till two. I sit to the right of the window."

Joe went outside while little Menzel sat on the floor,

half-conscious and furious. He removed his light boots so they would not hurt his swollen, throbbing feet.

In the meantime Fanchon had revived. Gus had put vinegar on a cloth to her nose. She looked around terrified and answered Gus's questions with, "Nothing, nothing, nothing's wrong with me."

It was obvious she was afraid and ready to break into tears. Milada spoke to her, "Please, Fanny, it's all right. The doctor's trying to help. He only wants to help you. Doctor Lamberg would send you to the hospital, and that would be worse."

Milada then turned to Gustav, "She's afraid she'll lose her place here if she's seriously ill. Please be thoughtful and don't let people know about her health." Fanchon then lifted her arm and showed Gustav the sore. He found an abscess under her left arm. It was the size of a nut, fiery red and half open, dirty, and irritated by the lace of her dress. Her whole arm was swollen and painful down to the wrist.

Gustav cleaned the wound and lanced it to drain. The whole time he repeated she was a "brave girl" since she neither winced nor cried. "It hurts a lot less now," she said softly. The doctor asked Milada to bring a disinfectant, gauze, and tape. She could not find gauze, so she tore up thin handkerchiefs. He nodded his approval.

The strong smell of the disinfectant and iodine in the gauze quickly spread down the corridor. Milada assisted Gustav without speaking. She had followed his instructions ably and quickly, and she showed no sign of disgust or weakness. She kept Fanchon supported with her arm raised while Gustav drained the wound. When the procedure was over, Milada stood at the foot of Fanchon's bed and joked with her. Fanchon looked relieved. Her face relaxed after the application of the bandage. Milada cheered her up. All of a sudden Fanchon became aware she was naked. She tried to cover herself with a silk blanket.

It was a very strange reaction and even more strange in this setting. Young Gustav's face showed he was perplexed at her modesty, and he looked at Milada, unsure. The depth of her gray eyes drown her anxious questions, "What do you think? Are you laughing at us? At Fanchon? About the whole occurrence?" He blushed deep red without knowing why. He forcefully averted his gaze from Milada's eyes. Her eyes had captivated him, and he took large steps over to the wash basin.

Exactly as he had learned from his professor in the clinic, he gave Fanchon instructions for further care as he washed and dried his hands.

"You should move your arm as little as possible, and you need rest. Do you understand, Madame? You need bed rest for one or two days. It should heal completely, and then the problem will be gone. If you don't take care of the wound, it can drag on." To Milada he said, "She's not to eat spicy foods. And rest is important." Gustav was so filled with the seriousness of his job that he completely forgot where he was. As he was handing Milada the washcloth, he wanted to commend her for her help, and so he said, "You, Madame, are a very good..." He had wanted to say "assistant" but broke off since he was met by a light in her eyes that expressed gratitude. Her eyes also expressed her intelligence and hope. Immediately Gustav realized it was inappropriate to call her his assistant, and he fell silent with embarrassment.

"So I can't go downstairs to the salon?" Fanny asked shyly out of concern.

Milada lowered her head and said with marked formality, "Would the good doctor care to return to the salon? We are grateful for your good offices."

Suddenly he took stock of how obviously ludicrous the situation was. He was there in a public house of prostitution, and he had offered his medical skills, given medical advice, and instructed a patient to rest. Such foolishness! Gus had never been one to feel superior, and he had never had a sense of formality. He looked over at Fanny and felt shy. She was in bed, looking irritable and sullen. And he looked at Milada's waitress apron with the pockets for coins. Then he mumbled a few words and made his way modestly to the door. Unhappy with himself and, all of a sudden, oppressed with God knows what, he looked for his coat and hat. Milada brought him both. She was hardly aware how excited she had become, yet her cheeks glowed red, and her hands shook. Her hands tightened as she handed him his coat.

It annoyed him to think how Joe and Seidner would have a good laugh over his little show of Good Samaritanism.

Once he had found a little boy on the street freezing and homeless and taken him back to his place. The next morning he discovered the boy had left with his watch and wallet.

Gustav hated being taken advantage of, and he hated anything that might impinge on his personal pride. For this reason he said gruffly to Milada, "Madame, take her to your own doctor! Her condition is complicated and requires proper medical treatment."

Milada asked, "You won't return, Sir?" The plea she kept from articulating moved him.

"I won't call Doctor Lambert in on this case," he avoided the question she did not voice.

"That's not a concern. He wouldn't come for something like this. There's so much else to treat here. Perhaps you will consider coming again," Milada said.

Hat in hand he left Fanny's room, walked down the corridor, took the stairs to the entry hall and stepped onto the street. Beset with thoughts about the experience, he shook his head and was contemplative and inward, an attitude not at all usual for him. He went his way. And he arrived at the coffeehouse he usually frequented, but he hesitated before entering. A genuine reluctance overcame him at the thought of the company of his friends, especially Joe. Joe would ply him with all kinds of questions. He joked about everything. Gustav had no patience for this. He did not see the events of the day as significant, but he did not want to be teased about them either. He was clearly not comfortable with Joe's teasing. Gustav stuck his hands in the pockets of his overcoat. He knew how to shut them down if they did start to tease him. But if he did that, they would take it wrong. They would twist his reluctance and dig around.

Gustav also considered telling them what happened just as it was. But he would not mention the bit about Fanny covering herself, Milada's eyes, or his blushing. There were some things that did not concern them. Unthinkable! There was no way he could explain this to anybody, not even Joe, his best friend, a person he held in high regard. He could not explain why the whole event had affected him so deeply. When he entered the coffeehouse, he found his friends engaged in some philosophical debate. Joe sat there carefully regarding his shoes. While turning his feet back and forth, he greeted Gus fleetingly. Gus was untypically serious. Gus sighed and thought, "Joe hasn't talked about this event with David. Ergo, he, too, takes it to be of real consequence." This thought solidified his deep emotional reaction.

As Gus and Joe were walking home, without provocation Gus suddenly told his friend the details of the day's events. Joe nodded and puffed on his Cuban cigar, then said, "It's a good idea to keep all women at arm's length. Ones like that especially. That's my advice."

Gustav could feel his face turning red. It was the second time today he had blushed and both times about the same event. Nonsense! "Why would you tell me that?"

"Well, it just occurred to me. The whole state of affairs brought an old event to mind. To tell the truth, I've been through some things myself." Joe was very sparing with information about his past. Since Gus knew Joe never said much, he understood Joe had had an experience of the same sort.

"Had you known one of the girls there before?" Gus asked,

eager to know.

"Someone there? Heaven forbid! But once I did have something sweet like this happen to me. It was long, long ago! So, if you'd like to hear about it, I'll tell you," Joe tossed the rest of his cigar. "At the time I was younger than you are. I was quite the man about town and an honorable gentleman. And one fine day I took a girl away from a nasty fellow. This happened in a coffeehouse. He gave her ten gulden. And for this money she was supposed to...ahh, damn," he interrupted himself. "The upshot was I fell for this girl. I was crazy about her. It's hard to imagine now, but at the time I thought this girl—of all the people in the world—had been made for me. I felt I could never ever leave her. I was out of my mind and dead serious about her. It was like nothing I had ever felt in my life. I was good-natured, sweet, industrious, ambitious—anything you can say along those lines." Joe lit a cigarette and continued, "Dear God, it cost me a lot of money to extricate her from her rotten situation. Once she was free, I was thankful to God. She wept to see her new room. We did not live together because—don't take this wrong—I wanted to marry her. I also imagined she would heal, that the damage to her as a woman would heal, if she was on her own. I believed she must be disgusted by life and by men. I believed in my wisdom of the time that if I did not touch her, I would take her to be my wife.

"The end of the story is this." Joe threw away half of the cigarette he had been smoking. "She took up with the baker's son." He choked or coughed. "I heard this from the postman who was angry she had sent him away. When I confronted her, she didn't deny it. She said she couldn't stand not having sex. And since I wasn't interested, so she said, she took the little snotnose to bed."

The two young men were silent. Joe said, "You don't have to try to say anything, Gus. There's really nothing more to say about it. Some things that happen just aren't very nice. They're pointless, like my life will be, most likely. It was one of those circumstances you feel miserable thinking about and end up asking yourself whether it wasn't some kind of bad joke."

"That was awfully mean of her," Gus erupted, angry for his friend.

"Awful? Mean? That's what I told myself, too, when it first happened. And that feeling stuck with me for months. Going through something so awful and mean was new for me in my naiveté. It helped ease the horrible pain. I was a nervous wreck and had no energy. After a while colleagues and Philistines, beer-drinking buddies, told me anecdotes from their own lives. (I should mention parenthetically they were always heroes in their stories and had done bolder things.) Hearing them talk helped me put the thought out of my mine, and finally I was over it. My old sense of morality changed. I heard myself whisper this question in my ear: 'Tell me, old friend, what made you think you had the right to take this creature out of her context, to cut her off so completely from the world she'd known, and to covet her? Why did you want her to live according to your values? Your little fantasy has made a fool of you. You might impart some of your traits to a small child, but you can't give another individual a new soul. It was a misplaced feeling of being a big man, my friend, to use brutal force to put a woman in a corner and think you could give her your desire and the torturous longing of your moralistic abstinence.' I arrived at this view of my experience, and it has stayed with me. As you see, I don't take your side here. The whole event came back to me today when I saw what happened to you. That's it. Good night. Here we are at your door."

"Come on in, Joe. Let's have a drink and talk about it. It'll do you good."

"For God's sake, man, don't treat me like a little girl with a broken heart. But your offer sounds good. Let's have a toast to the day and fill our bellies with the wine of the Romans! I long for longing. 'Longing' is a great word, repeat it, Gus." Joe stood in the entry hall and stretched out his arms. "Oh, Ancient Goddess, we need you this evening in the monastery to bless our conversation. You are the temptress with supple hips, most sumptuously round. My heathen soul would rise up for joy if, behind this column you would..." Joe dreamed off, looking out in the dark at the courtyard behind the Brenners' house. He continued, "If you would appear to us and in your inimitable, elemental way would declaim, 'Don't bring me wine. I want a blood sacrifice.'"

Gustav laughed. He was captivated and dreamy, and Joe's strange outbreak of emotion encouraged him to enjoy immersing himself even more deeply in his own emotional state. Only at moments in his dreaming was he aware of these things: prostitution, the eyes of a prostitute, and the business of a brothel. As soon as he was struck by the awareness of the actuality of the situation, a wave of passion arose in his young heart and banished the uncomfortable truth.

Joe stopped for a moment at the head of the stairs and asked, "How are things between you and your father?"

Gus shrugged. While they were climbing the stairs, he answered, "He's always trying to spy on me, same as ever. He doesn't even recognize me when I say hello. He's a traditional gentleman, though, from head to toe, when I ask for money. It's boring to think about. Nothing ever changes."

In the afternoon of the following day Gustav Brenner was once again at the door of Red House and rang the bell. He could hardly believe he was doing this. He wore an expression of dutifulness, reserve, and decisiveness. He was completely sober. After he had articulated his intention early that morning, he had to laugh at his crush of the day before; his laughter did hold a personal feeling of pleasure. How abundant his sense of warmth was still! Last night had been a long night filled with happiness.

Early that morning Gus had watched Joe snoring on the couch, still dressed in his street clothes, with the knot of his tie at the back of his neck and his collar rumpled and sweaty from drinking. "Well," thought Gustav, "even now, however he may try to act, my good friend is still quite the Bohemian. He's a bit *deraciné*, out of his element." To this day Gus used French, the language he and his mother had used when he was a child to exclude his father. Gus could not rouse Joe at all. He only coughed and turned over.

Last night had been very nice. Drinking wine had lulled the two friends into a good mood. But, dear God, Joe could have still taken his clothes off and put them on a chair.

He picked Joe's silver watch up off the floor. It was three in the morning, the hour made him wince. He was almost indignant. He bathed, shaved, threw on his clean clothes and went out to the coffeehouse. All the while his friend snored on—it was not pleasant—and slept in, later and later.

At this point Gustav had not thought about Red House. Perhaps a snippet of his memory surfaced, but in his usual pedantic style, he put it out of mind for some later time. When he got to the tram that runs in the morning, he recalled yesterday's events in vivid detail. He ordered the events chronologically, just as he would as a critical observer. He reviewed things devoid of emotion. There was the time in the salon, the waitress with the gray eyes and her apron with the ominous pocket for money, and the health crisis of the girl and administering first aid. All of it was most likely quite banal. Fanchon was apparently cold, that must be why she tried to cover herself. And the other girl with some kind of limited medical education did not want to call the regular physician, Doctor Lamberg. She must have wanted to avoid paying the fee for a call. She seemed to be a very practical person.

He spent the morning in the clinic as usual, had lunch with Joe in the caféteria, but declined the afternoon visit to their regular coffeehouse. He said he had a pressing professional duty, and that is when, half an hour later, he rang the bell at Red House.

The porter greeted him, and the maid rushed around, said a friendly hello, and asked if he was interested in a particular girl.

He answered brusquely he had come to look in on the girl he had treated yesterday. The maid looked pensive and said, "Just a moment, please." She then went to knock on the door of Miller's office. Gus was indecisive and annoyed with himself for putting himself in the same ridiculous role he had been in yesterday. Miller opened the door of her office and came out, wearing her pious smile. She had heard that the blond physician Gustav Brenner was the son of the filthy rich industrialist in the iron business. And she was enough of a businesswoman to encourage his visit.

"Oh, Doctor, Sir, we are immensely thankful you dropped by. It is so very kind of you!" Then she pressed a buzzer and said, as she withdrew, "Madame Milada will have the honor of receiving you."

He went to the stairwell and met Milada at the landing.

"Oh, how very lovely," she said with a sigh.

"And how has the patient been?" he asked.

"She suffered and complained all night long," said Milada as she helped him with his overcoat. "And now she has a fever."

"Did Doctor Lambert come?" he asked. He was moved and uncomfortable.

"No," said Milada. "He wouldn't come for something like that. I took her temperature."

"You did? Well." He was taken aback and did not know what to say. He was amazed how remarkable her face looked to him at that moment. He was so taken with her large, gray eyes, he was hardly able to walk down the hall.

"Where is she?" he asked impatiently.

Milada walked in front of him and opened the door to Fanchon's room. He armed himself with the authority of a chief surgeon and began to copy the expression, demeanor, and generic good humor of this medical position. Fanny was in bed, pale and uncomfortable. Her thick, blond hair fell over the blanket and hung down loose.

There was a girl next to Fanchon, sitting, doing needlework. She was large and sturdy with assertive eyes. She got up immediately. "Stay here," Fanny said to her in a whiny voice.

"I'll be back in a while," Bina answered.

"But what he's going to do will hurt," Fanny said.

Bina stroked her hand but then pulled her own hand away. "It will be all right. He's a good person," and with that Bina made a provincial curtsey.

Bina's gesture of deference fueled his attitude. "So how are you doing, Madame?" he asked Fanchon kindly.

"I'm not as well as you are, Sir."

He laughed and asked, "So what do you know about me?" He raised her arm. "Well, you have abscesses forming all around, but that's not so serious. We'll nip them in the bud. She doesn't have any fever now, Madame Professor."

"Because she's had only milk to drink," Milada answered.

He took off the bandage, palpitated the wound, cleaned it and applied a new bandage. He did all this with professional confidence, and he worked so quickly that Fanny did not have a chance to make a fuss.

"You know quite a lot," he said amused. "That makes us doctors almost unnecessary."

"Hardly," Milada said warmly. And her gaze met his as he looked at her dartingly and unsure.

"I'm in pain," Fanny began, finding the two of them were not paying enough attention to her. "How am I supposed to lie down when it hurts here and there and all over? And it itches a lot, too."

"We'll use powder to absorb the fluid," Gustav said to calm her. And once he was again comforting and attentive, she was quiet. "You will have to swab the infected areas with salicylic acid. Do you know how to do that?"

"Yes. You make a small puncture."

All right, thought Gustav. She was an orderly in a clinic and learned some techniques. But in any event, she is smart. And he felt relieved of a heavy burden to think she had some training.

"Can I write a prescription for her?" Gustav asked.

"You'll have to make it out for me," Milada answered.

"But you are coming back, aren't you?" Fanny begged him. "And what should I eat? She isn't feeding me at all."

"Soups would be good, also milk and white meat. She shouldn't have spicy foods. And no alcohol."

"I don't like alcohol anyway," said Fanny.

"But, Fanny, what about the cognac you always want me to get you?" asked Milada.

"Is cognac really alcohol?" Fanny wanted to know.

Gustav went out into the hall, and Milada followed him with her face contorted. And then things brightened up. Milada put her hands on her thighs, bent forward and started to laugh. Gustav crossed his arms, leaned against the wall, and, like a boy, found her laughter infectious.

"Please, oh please," Fanny called out from her room, irritated.

Milada tapped his sleeve, pulled him down the hall, and said, "I'll take care of her."

"It won't be difficult to manage," he replied, and both of them went to the next room.

There was a table set up as a desk between the windows. Here there was no hint of the intense, undefinable smell that permeated Fanny's room. That smell had been rather oppressive to him. Here the window was open, and the day's raw, foggy air blew in. It was a simple, unremarkable room. If it had had the requisite toiletries, books and some pipes strewn about, it could almost look like a student's quarters. The room was carefully ordered. Milada opened the letter case and gave him a pen and paper. Then she quickly cleared away the papers on the desk, and Gus sat down. Everything here looked to him to be in regular use.

He wrote, "Three times daily wash and powder the affected area. The abscesses can be covered with a bandage. They will, however, reappear, but they are harmless." Gustav spoke to Milada, who was behind him, and noticed a row of books on the dresser. The titles on the spine, printed in gold, unsettled him much more than the ominous, mysterious toiletries in Fanchon's room. There was Marx's *Capital*, Max Stirner's *The Ego and Its Own*, Schopenhauer's essays *Parerga and Paralipomena*, and Ludwig Buechner's *Force and Matter*; there were titles by August Bebel, Charles Fournier, and more. Gustav was dazed. He was almost pained at the flood of thoughts that rolled over him. What kind of woman is this, and how did she get here? Was this a novel way of entrapping men? He got up brusquely. Milada's expression was serious, comprehending, and straightforward. It grabbed him.

She had partially opened her mouth but did not speak. She lowered her head so that the thick braids of her chestnut hair were visible.

He tried to come up with something to say that would be appropriate to the situation, something that would conclude his visit.

She raised her head and said slowly and calmly, while weighing her words, "How good you are!"

"You mean a good fellow, a bit like a simpleton," he was able to stammer out the words. Immediately he was annoyed with himself for speaking with her with such intimacy.

"Where did you work as a medical assistant?" he asked right after that.

"I never did."

"Did you spend time talking with medical students?"

"I've never been out of this alley. I was born here. I don't know much else of the world."

"How can that be?" he asked disconcerted, and he looked over the books.

"For some years I've had a friend, a wonderful teacher who

was happy to take me on as his pupil." She ran her hand across her forehead and spoke the following words very quickly, "I was at a very low point in life. I had given up on myself when Horner, my teacher, arrived. Do you know the school director Horner?"

Without listening to her question he blurted out, "How can you stand it here with your good mind? How can anybody who has learned so much stay on in this milieu?"

"They need me," Milada said softly.

"Are you part owner here?"

"No!"

"Do you have," he coughed, "any duties here in the house?"

"Not anymore."

A violent rage overwhelmed him. "That's disgraceful," he muttered under his breath. "No, it is one thousand times worse." His protective instinct was to look for the door.

"Will you come by tomorrow, Sir?" Milada asked without moving from the spot. His blue eyes clouded. In his nervousness he tugged on his properly trimmed English moustache. "Well, I am the one who got himself into this foolishness," he said clumsily.

Milada's face showed she was eager to know. He could not leave like this. He felt obliged out of courtesy to look at her once more before he left.

"Is it all right if Fanny gets up?" she asked quickly, not knowing what to say. She had asked him to return. He strutted about and looked at her with disdain, "You are a businesswoman and have a lot to do," he said.

"Do you have something against this business?" she returned.

"I despise making money from these creatures."

"Do you know that a lot of these creatures, Fanny included, were completely weakened by lack of basic food before they came to this profession? Do you realize they would have died without this business? At least they are safe here from the most terrible fate."

"And will they not, Fanny included," he echoed her words,

"be destroyed in this house? Don't you think so?"

"You are right," she acknowledged very seriously. "They will be destroyed here, too."

"I think that helping here is a tragic job."

"Are you making the business responsible for this misery?" she asked, shaking her head in discouragement. "This industry is only the economic response. It exists only because there is a demand for it far and wide. That demand is found on every street."

"Life requires sacrifice. We are talking here about the ethical responsibility of each individual," he said importantly as he put on his overcoat.

"It is a shame, but hunger and despair are usually stronger than ethics," she replied softly.

"Hunger and despair! It's the same old tune for every situation. Why don't the people who eat well throw off these chains?" He gestured with his hand, "All these young people, and you, Madame?"

"It's some people's fate to live in chains."

"If they want to cash in," he forced a laugh and went down the stairs.

A strange mood beset him all day. He was conflicted and unsettled. Later, when evening fell and he was preparing to go to bed, everything that had moved him during the daylight hours circled around this mysterious and breathtaking core: expectation. It enveloped all considerations and all decisions and dissolved them in foolhardy dreaming. His last waking thought as he drifted off was, "Tomorrow I'll see her again, tomorrow."

The upshot of their conversation was that the young physician went to Red House daily. Fanchon's wounds healed without difficulty, and he oversaw her treatment until the girl returned to the salon. To be sure, she had to rest every day after supper for the visit of the Doctor, as he had come to be called. She complained and whined a little, but she let herself be weighed and put up with the diet he prescribed. She was somewhat recalcitrant and a bit comforted. She was also rather at odds with Doctor Brenner. The off-putting feeling the setting had originally given him dissipated as he became acquainted with the daily life of the residents. He also dropped his need for irony and superiority, which he had used like armour to protect himself from insecurity and embarrassment. He became confident and comfortable. His loveable nature came to light.

As a child Gustav withdrew to avoid the moodiness of the women around him and other inimical influences. When he was a student, his older colleagues dominated him, especially Joe with his superior sophistication and Seidner with his Jewish dialectics. He was the spoiled child of his mother, and he readily subordinated himself to his friends. He was helpless against their influence.

And yet he did have the instinct to defend himself. He did have selfish impulses. They were only waiting for an opportunity to emerge and to take over.

Red House provided him with ample opportunity to exercise authority. Over the course of the eight semesters of his university studies, the girls there allowed Gustav to diagnose and treat their illnesses of all sorts.

He was conservative in prescribing medications and used powders and salves that an educated layperson would know and could get hold of. You could not belie the fact that the authority and respect he had in the house—from Miller right on down to the porter—helped his confidence immensely. He had an inflated feeling of his own importance. His importance was most likely linked to his interest in being of service where needed. He told himself his role in Red House had become necessary and significant. He was pleased to think that he, son of a patrician, was engaged as a physician to help the dispossessed and disenfranchised.

He asked himself: if Christian missionaries travel to the

interior of Africa and subject themselves to certain danger with uncertain outcome to reshape a few primitive souls into Christians, why then should people like himself from the bourgeoisie not enter the sphere of desolation and abandonment that is prostitution? Thus, daily, he went down the path of self-interest with a heightened consciousness. The path was paved for him. He did not tell his friends what he was doing. He did not subject what he took to be his heroic choice of paths to their judgement. He was not up to Joe's long, drawn-out "I told you so!" or David Seidner's satirical attacks.

Hardly did he arrive at Red House but what everybody who was awake rushed to see him. They gathered around him with questions and their wishes. They asked to be consoled. The girls wanted advice, medication, or a new diet; mostly, they wanted him to tell Miller they should have wine, at least once a day. Gustav's visits broke up a long day of this and that.

Without realizing it, he came to be on a personal basis with the girls. He told them stories about the clinic and about life as a student, and he told them about trips he had taken. He knew all the news of the district where Red House and the hospitals were. He recited the news in a way that was entertaining. The girls listened attentively and retold his stories in every detail, even the oldest, as matters of great interest. His stories were unceasingly new and exciting. They were thankful to him for this.

Gustav was a breath of fresh air in the house. It was astonishing to see how mischief, wit, and levity all came together and rescued the souls of these repressed, imprisoned women. It was also astonishing to see the girls had not become cynical or needy. They played funny tricks on each other and made the most childlike jokes. They laughed themselves silly when they were able to pull the Doctor into their games. Their feeling of ebullience had been awakened.

If Gustav had known these words from Goethe, he could have

applied them hundreds of times: "A girl's earliest inclinations gradually make up her character."

It did not occur to him to link the youthful playfulness that welled up and flooded the house with his presence. Yet it was Gus and only Gus, the loveable, young man with radiant blue eyes and solid, warm hands—hands that readily took hold when necessary—who had wrought this miracle of spring. He was, by nature, sensitive and considerate, just as his high-strung, hysterical mother had been. And, like her, he deeply loved beauty, lightness, elegance, and everything that reached and delighted his senses. He was not indulgent and did not enjoy rude gratification or the ecstasy of physical desire.

While he had admired beautiful Arrigazzi, she did not bedazzle him when she lay naked and perfume-scented in her bed, complaining of arthritis. He massaged the shoulder in pain and then covered her gently. "Joints are susceptible to drafts," he said. The constitutional purity and lack of pretention of this man healed their dignity as women, which had routinely been dragged through the mud. He restored their innocence.

He chatted with Gisi in perfect French, the language he had spoken as a child with his mother. Their conversations were lighthearted.

Karla, who was generally icy, thawed out, and her eyes glowed with emotion when Gus remarked at the beauty of the mountains of her homeland. Fanchon kept asking him if he did not know her friend Happy. When he said he did not, she could not believe it. She suggested Gus go to the magistrate's office where he worked and say hello from her. There, said Fanny, Gus would certainly meet a great guy!

There was someone who pushed Gus to put aside the initial brusque attitude of arrogance he used it to shield himself from these "creatures," who, in his bourgeois judgement, were doomed to ignominious ruin. This someone was the strange, intellectual woman who managed Red House, the woman he still could not sort out, Milada Rezek. With her eyes of a sphynx that dreams of unfathomable secrets under Egyptian night skies she remained inscrutable to him.

Milada's cold, introverted intelligence, which precluded any coquetry, attracted him with a power he could not resist. At the same time he was constantly repelled by her unwavering assuredness about her social sphere. She set and maintained clear boundaries, and this brought out his class prejudices. Despite his discomfort, step by step, he drew closer to her. She piqued his curiosity and enlisted his sympathies. When she told him about the circumstances of each person, she showed how what was touching was also disturbing. She pushed him to recognize the social mechanisms that were not apparent. She caused him to see the tragedy in vice these mechanisms hid. Finally she allowed him the vain pleasure of thinking he was the trailblazer and pioneer in the wilderness of these people's fate.

"She's dreadfully interesting. She captivates me," he told himself. "She's interesting somewhat like Emile Zola's characters Germaine and Nana are supposed to be. I'm sure Joe would be enthusiastic about her."

This was his justification for his undeniable need to look into the depth of Milada's eyes once a day. "She is not attractive to me. I almost forget she is a woman and only a nuisance to me," he repeated to himself daily to reassure himself and keep himself safe. He repeated this as a person living in pain coats his medicine with sweet sugar.

It never occurred to any of the girls to ask him to visit the salon in the evening or to ask him to start up a physical relation with them. At no time in his exchanges with even the most vain or lascivious of them was there ever an improper intimacy. No one ever made intrusive advances.

Milada once told Gustav straight up she would be

uncomfortable if he met up with Horner. She had not mentioned the Doctor's visits to Horner. She had justified her relation to Gustav with the fabrication he was not interested in her. She also thought Horner would misunderstand anything she said about the effect Gustav had in the house. But, oh! how Milada had, during the phase of his visits, toyed with "He loves me, he loves me not." Those days were bathed, her whole life long, in a shimmering, rosy light. Vacillation was at odds with her usual, clear-cut way of thinking.

When she spoke to Gustav about meeting Horner, he asked, "Uncomfortable? I think it's probably true. But he's the one who'd be uncomfortable. He is extremely put off by anything with any muscle. What? You didn't know that, Madame? Everybody in town knows that. Just mention Joe Wallner to him in passing."

Milada laughed in response, "I'll be sure to keep it to myself." She was inwardly happy about her secret.

Horner had become increasingly restless. He had fallen into a sullen funk. He could not bear anything new or unexpected. Milada found the wonderful things she saw, thought, and expected, so precious that she kept them safe within. She was loathe to share in mangled, distanced words what was on her mind with the prying old man.

Then a storm broke out in the idyll. One of the girls who had, for some good while, been unwell and taken a lot of medication suddenly fell seriously ill.

That was Putzi Bleier. She was overcome by a high fever. It persisted despite the compresses Gus prescribed and in the face of her feigned cheerfulness and Miller's ill temper. For several weeks Miller had been sick and tired of this "doctoring business" in the house. On day four of Putzi's fever Gus spoke up, "She's generally weak and has poor circulation. She's not getting good nutrition. I cannot find any particular disease. Give her lots of milk. If her fever abates, then give her roasted meat and red wine.

Under no circumstances should she get out of bed!" That is what he told Madame Miller right to her face. She looked at him in an attitude of friendliness.

But as soon as Doctor Brenner was out of the house, Miller stormed into Putzi's room in a paroxysm of rage. She swore at her, calling her an ass, a whore, and a malingerer. If she wanted to play the invalid, she should get herself to the hospital. And, moreover, she was fed up with this doctoring. If that doctor came to the house again, she would personally throw him out on the street. If someone had a real illness, then she would call Doctor Lamberg and pay his regular fee. As she saw it, that Gustav Brenner was actually bringing diseases into the house. He was just using the girls in the house like lab rats. No thank you! She was going to call Lamberg then and there. She left saying they would see!

Putzi cried and complained. Then she got up out of bed and went down to the salon. She wanted to show the madam there was nothing wrong with her. Why would she call Lamberg?

Naturally Milada sent her back to bed, all the while bearing up under accusations and insults from Putzi. There was Putzi cursing Milada while appealing to her. Milada shrugged.

The following day Doctor Lamberg was brought in. He diagnosed Putzi with typhus. He cursed because no one had called him earlier and ordered her to be taken to the hospital without delay. He demanded her room and her possessions be disinfected.

"Well, now, ain't this pretty! We know where that disease came from," Miller said full of bitterness. Milada had to go directly to admissions at the hospital and had no time to look in on little Fanny, who was acting out of control. Miller had asked Doctor Lamberg to see her, too. Lamberg said he remembered Fanny from the time Goldscheider had been there. Back then he had found her to be in questionable health. So he believed it would be wise, while he was there, to check out "the dangerous little girl." He tickled her on the chin, and then said she had to leave the house immediately.

"She's got tuberculosis and shouldn't be entertaining nice guests."

Lamberg was hardly out the door when Miller let loose. She told Fanny she ought to kiss the hand of that dear Mr. Gustav for having kept her in the house this long. Fanny sat there in her nightgown, completely out of her mind. One with typhus, another with tuberculosis. Gustav was supposed to be a physician. But what kind of a doctor was he? He came right from the morgue to Red House and puddled around. It had been to her disadvantage he had not diagnosed her with tuberculosis. But she could accept the detriment to her health as long as she and the other girls were protected from being thrown out.

Fanny only registered one thing. She had to leave right away. She had felt she was at home in Red House. Everybody was nice to her. Here she was Little Fanchon.

She propped her head up in her hand. She was aware enough to know she could not show Miller how the news had hit her. "Am I really that ill?" she asked from behind her fingers like a child.

"Yes, really!" Miller replied. "Lamberg said he's never seen a case as bad as that. It's like someone had tromped around on her."

"Eventually I'm going to die," Fanchon said all of a sudden and let her hands fall. Her face was that of a petrified, emaciated child. Her eyes were full of fear. Miller turned nasty, "Sure, just die!" She added, "Go ahead and die. Such stupid talk. Dubbe didn't die. She's in Hungary and is carrying on over there. And I didn't get a thing for setting that up either," she finished with venom.

Since Fanny had no response, Miller was afraid. She simply shrugged and left the room. She listened outside the door. But there was nothing to hear. There was only silence.

"I can't take care of everybody and keep the upper hand. That girl was talking about dying, but next week she'll be up and swishing around in her silk clothes."

When Milada returned from the hospital, she was greeted with the news Fanny had to leave. Zimmermann, who ran a low-end brothel in the district, had told her a few times that if they wanted to let go of a couple of girls in the summer, she could use them. Fanny would be one of those. Putzi would eventually be the other.

When Milada asked Miller whether Fanny was aware she had to leave, Miller answered with embarrassment, "Well, yes, Lamberg told her."

Milada went upstairs to Fanny's room but found the door locked. The other girls told her Fanchon had been telling everyone who went to see her, "I'm going to die. I'm going to die. It's over for me, poor Fanny."

"She's in there praying," Bina Michal reported. She had looked through the keyhole.

"Boy, am I glad I never let that Brenner touch me," Arrigazzi said arrogantly. "He would have infected me, too."

"Who's been talking such nonsense?" Milada asked each of them.

"You can say it's nonsense about that good-for-nothing. I'm fine with that. But just look what happened!" Arrigazzi screamed and stepped forward. "I'm telling you your filthy little student brought these diseases in the house."

What was going on? Who had started this? Milada wanted to start with Arrigazzi who had trotted off all high and mighty in her bespangled petticoat. But Milada caught herself. Where had Gustav been with his helpful hands? The idea hit her so fast and hard she could not collect herself. She could not conceal her distress. She found it better not to listen.

Milada turned around and went down to the office. Gisi followed her, dear, blond Gisi, the girl she felt closest to. Gisi whispered, "Mila, I'm so scared! Why did he do that to us?"

Milada found this painful and asked Gisi, "You believe this, too? Why do you let yourself get pulled into this?"

"Yes, Mila, you should take this seriously. When my mom was in the hospital in Krakow, they gave her some kind of shot, and after that she had red blotches and blisters, just like Putzi has now. It's the truth!"

Milada stood stock still. "Everything's going to hell in a handbasket. You've all gone mad. Why do you blame the Doctor, Gustav, for bringing these diseases into the house? Who came up with this idea anyway?"

"Just think. He's only a student and still learning, and he thinks we don't matter. We're only prostitutes."

Milada replied, "No, he doesn't think that. You know him yourself. You know he's good and wants to help."

Gisi defended herself, "He only wanted to help out after a while. At first he thought he'd just give it a try."

Milada was pale from distress and sat down at the desk. That's what he gets for his efforts! That's what comes of his help. This good person came to this place of sorrow and tried to do his work, and this is how they reward him. These prostitutes! These people are unthinking and blind. They nestled together like a flock of birds, stared at the light and carped at it. Gustav had given Putzi an injection for the pain that plagued her. And now they were virtually making him out to be a murderer. He would have to laugh! He would not take it too much to heart. He was too strong and confident and too evolved. She raised her eyes and had the sense she could see him smile. His image was warm, calming, and composed.

She thought, "We want to do what is necessary, isn't that right?"

"We?" Suddenly her illusions fell apart. Whatever had she been thinking? What had misled her? What had drawn her to him? What was going on with her? "Gus is a stranger, a complete stranger, after all. He has no idea what you want or how presumptuous and foolhardy you see his goodness to be. For all you care he can leave and never return.

"Does all effort and each and every endeavor come down to satisfying our paltry egos? Had Horner been right to say so?" But all of Milada's thoughts were forced; they felt false. She was filled with a resistance. She had a certain angry disgust for whatever it was she did not dare think. Yet it was where her thoughts took her: "We! Both of us!" She had to deal with the fact this notion had real power over her. The recognition caused her to become more and more agitated. She had envisioned him, this man, at her side in everything she wanted or planned, in all of her dreams, near or far away. She was powerless and surrendered.

In her fantasy she told him, "We've got to do something for Fanny. We've got to help this sick little girl. She's a lost soul who's paralyzed with terror and dread. Gustav, Zimmermann can't get hold of her, just so Miller can collect her seventy-five percent. We need to prevent that!" In her mind she told him Fanchon's story. "She was the child of laborers who, at thirteen, gave herself to a construction boss on the work site for a bit of meat, something she had never eaten. It was 'a few sausages with sauce.' Her mother listened to her lively tale about the good meal her oldest child had gotten and said with envy, 'Yes, well. That's as good as what I once got.'"

The bell at the entrance to the house rang. Milada looked at the time. It was time for him to arrive. Gus was there. She ran to the front door, opened it, almost without saying hello, and dragged him into the office. As she stood there, she realized she was still in her coat and hat, just as she had arrived back from the hospital.

"Just imagine, Doctor," she said without an introduction, "Putzi has typhus and is already in the hospital."

"Oh, so it did happen," he said while nodding.

"She was delirious all night long, and Lamberg came early this morning. They took her right to the hospital."

"But of course she had to go to the hospital. Are people disinfecting her room?"

"Yes, they're doing that now. But Fanchon is also ill. Doctor Brenner, just think, poor Fanny has to go, too. She has tuberculosis. That's what Lamberg says. And Miller wants her gone."

"So that's how things are," he said, affected by the Milada's discomfort in presenting the situation. "Lamberg has known her a long time, since Goldscheider was here," he was quick to explain.

Gustav was perplexed and twisted the end of his moustache.

"I'd really like to be able to help her," she said softly. She was ashamed to have lost her composure. "They told her about her condition, that it's fatal."

"Who told her that?" Gus interrupted.

"Lamberg and Miller."

"That was cruel of them," he said with resentment. The openness of his reaction was a relief for both of them. "How dare they treat her like that! And this was from a physician?! It's unbelievable behavior."

"Fanny's upstairs in her room now, crying and praying. I don't know what to do."

"Clearly she has tuberculosis. The diagnosis is correct. But to tell her that, to say that to such a young person, is just cruel," he said, pacing back and forth around the room. "So what's going to happen to her now?"

Milada said, "Look across the street. You can see where that window with the curtain is. That's where Zimmermann lives. She takes girls. She either takes them on or sells them. Things aren't that bad at her place, but the poor girls are really captives. They don't get any fresh air all year round, except once a month. But Zimmermann is connected with very terrible people. Young girls with a health problem like Fanny disappear never to be seen again. I want to make sure Fanny doesn't land there."

Gus continued pacing.

"So they told her right to her face! That's mean of them. The poor girl! Does she owe a lot of money here?" Gus asked.

"The books show she's square with Miller, you should know."

Milada was interrupted while speaking. Miller carefully pushed her way into the office. With a small nod of greeting she addressed

Gustav, "It's you, the little student!" Gus did not greet her in return.

"Madame Milada," Miller pronounced with respect, "Madame Zimmermann wants a copy of the invoice for Fanny."

At that Gustav planted himself firmly in front of Miller. He was decisive and enraged as he started out, "Fanchon is going to the hospital, you do understand. She's not going to the madam across the street."

"At whose expense, I ask you?" Miller said sharply. "This is a financial matter, you must know. I do not consider keeping her here in the house."

Miller looked at him through narrowed eyes like a cat sizing up an enemy. Should she attack or carefully lull him into submission?

"The girl will be sent home from the hospital to her family. She must have family. They'll take care of her until she's healthy again."

"She doesn't have family," Milada offered.

Miller said, "She owes me a large amount of money. I can't lose that much on one person. She is still useful. Isn't she, Madame Milada? If you need to know about her, Doctor Brenner, there's information for you."

Gustav moved his hand across his temples just as he had seen his training physician do in very serious cases.

He thought to himself with some pleasure Joe would accuse him of being arrogant. Gustav accepted this. He knew feeling superior helped him deal with the situation at hand. At this point he took control. He had seen through Miller and knew she was weak and incompetent, and so he announced forcefully, "We will come up with someone to cover your financial loss."

Milada looked over at Gustav with large, compassionate eyes. Drawn to her, he turned to face her. He spoke to her quietly, "Don't worry. I'll take care of this." Miller was disquieted and in doubt, "Certainly, Doctor, but I need concrete information. I need to know what you will offer. Fanny is very sought after here. Zimmermann knows how attractive she is. Milada will know what it takes to cover my costs. It's five hundred gulden." Miller continued since she could see Gustav was surprised at the amount, "I'm not young anymore. I'm not in good health. I'm ill, too. Milada can confirm this. I am not well."

Milada did not move from the spot and said, "The madame has anxiety." Miller then yammered, "I'm ill, very ill." Miller had an inkling of a trap and had a dark feeling that Goldscheider would not have tolerated Doctor Brenner's visits. She would have thrown him right out if he had gotten mixed up in her business. But she had no way of doing that. She had neither the courage nor the strength of mind.

"I need to go to a care facility, not the... I need to be taken care of, not the... I'm losing all my money and my peace of mind. My nerves are in a terrible state. Who's looking out for me?"

"Then you should take tepid baths every morning and use warm compresses," Gustav gave her quick instructions.

Miller put her hands in front of herself in defense. "No, absolutely not! Don't touch me!" she screeched in a nasty tone as she backed out the door.

Milada could not suppress her laughter as she thought how the madam stuck her long nose in warm, soapy water every morning.

Gustav spoke up, "This business is truly horrific. It's made her thoroughly hysterical."

Milada said politely, "She's not useful here."

"So what are we going to do? Are we going to find the girl some place to go? What do you think, Milada?"

That was the first time Gustav had called her by her given name. She had been so tightly bottled up that hearing him say her name brought tears to her eyes.

Gustav continued, "Doesn't Fanny have an aunt or somebody in the country? With a year of breathing air in the forest, drinking milk, and resting, she could recover. At least she would live longer."

"She's barely seventeen," Milada said under her breath and felt lost.

"Dear God, just seventeen! There's no protection for these children. They just end up on the streets. That's dreadful!"

He thought Joe was not right to say he was motivated by elitism and that he had the "ethos of the leisure class." What dawned on Gustav was the realization the society he belonged to had placed an outrageous, gruesome responsibility on weak children already burdened with hardship.

Milada was decisive. She walked over to him and addressed him formally. "Mr. Brenner, the issue here is not money. If it were money, I would pay myself. I'm not poor. What's at issue here is privilege. Wherever I go, a madam, people dismiss me with disgust. We have our own hospitals, physicians, and police. We live on our own economy. And that's all we can ask for. Whatever I try to do—if that's trying to gain Fanny a few miserable years—I need the establishment and the law on my side. I need privilege. What I need is the world you live in."

He stared at her. "What an strange girl you are! Once you told me a person's fate plays out unopposed. Why do you have to live here? Please, tell me!"

He took hold of her arm. His touch pervaded her body. She stood stock still.

"Don't you care for anything except for this misery, Milada?" he asked. His voice was harsh.

For the first time in her life the touch of a man shook her. It was a strange, unknown feeling. It ran through her senses like a drug. And all her energy and all the strength she had ever mustered were stirred through. She felt like straw. The feeling took over so completely she lost her grip on reality. This street, Red House, Fanchon, and her own wishes, lay far—unreachably far—away.

There was only this man holding her arm. All of life had hold of her arm.

"I belong in this misery," she said with great effort, as if suffocating.

"All right, I will help you," he said in a raw voice and stepped back. "Fanny won't go to Zimmermann. She will be saved, as far as possible, of course. My father helped found a clinic for tuberculosis patients. There are beds available. They'll take Fanny there. Are you happy with that?"

She exhaled a deep breath. But her gray eyes looked past him, shy and unsure. She looked out past Red House.

"Fanchon has to want to go to this clinic. She is finicky and so frightened."

"I think she trusts me. I'll take care of talking with her. You take care of making Miller agreeable. He laughed out loud, but it was no longer the laughter of a simple, carefree boy. "First slay the dragon, then rescue the fair damsel. Saint George and my sword!" The joke was inappropriate and did not go over well. He could see it fell flat. In a sober mood he opened the door for Milada.

Fanny sat propped up in her bed and was busy arranging the thick, golden curls on her forehead and at her temples. Her eyes were a bit swollen and red from crying, but her mouth had taken on a fantastic expression of laughter. She wore the mouth of a doll. It was an expression she liked to put on when she was in a good mood.

When Fanny saw Gus and Milada enter, she let her arms fall. She looked both shy and serious.

"Well, Fanny, how are you?" Gustav said as he pulled up a chair.

"Our regular doctor wasn't at all happy with my condition," Fanny answered uncomfortably.

"Well, let's see now," Gus began with the tone of the head physician in a ward who pronounces important information as if nobody and nothing in this world existed except the physician and his pronouncement.

"You do understand that your lungs have been acting up."

She interrupted him to say, "Zimmermann told me people like me live to be eighty."

Milada entered the conversation, "Zimmermann came to see you?"

"She sure did! And she told me..."

Gustav retorted, "That Zimmermann is a nosey old witch. She ought to keep her opinions to herself. But she is right. If you take sound care of your health, you can live to a ripe old age. Madame Milada and I want to make sure you leave here and go to a place where good people will take care of you."

"Take me away from here?" Fanny said numbly as she sat up in bed.

"You'll get better resting in the country under the supervision of a doctor."

"Jesus, Mary, and Joseph," Fanny blurted out. "Did you talk bad about me to people?" She threw off the blanket that was covering her. "Shame on you, shame on you, if you talked bad about me to Zimmermann. What kind of a person are you anyway?"

She balled her hands into fists and broke out crying like a small child. Milada tried to get involved, but Gus moved her out of the way. He spoke sternly.

"Don't be foolish, Fanny! If you stay here, you will become worse. We're trying to help you. If you'd like, you can let your parents know how you are. They can take you home and then..."

"I won't do that, you quack! Take me back home?! I don't want that, and I won't go. Do you hear me? First you botch up my health, and then you want to make sure I die so that nobody will know what you did. You don't know anything about me. I'm going to the police. They want me to stay here in Red House. I have my official city registration!"

She jumped up out of bed, put both feet on the floor, and tore the nightgown off her shoulder. Her eyes shone full of meanness. Tears ran down her pale, emaciated cheeks.

Gustav lost his composure and stood like a block in the middle of the room. He looked at her as if dazed while the small Fury hurled curses at him.

Milada had foreseen Fanny's reaction and took her by the arm. "Shut up," she said forcefully. You should be thrashed till you understand, you silly goose. Get back into bed now. You need to get well by going to the country."

"Get well?" Fanny, out of her mind, ridiculed Milada. "By eating cow shit and grass? And thank him for saving me! He won't get rid of me like he did Putzi. I'm real tough."

"Those awful people!" Milada said in disgust as she gave the bed a push.

"You just wait and see. I'll tell the police about your quack medicine. Lamberg told me that. And he's a real doctor. You're only a student."

"Hush now!" Milada hollered in anger and raised her hand. And Fanny crawled back into bed like a beaten little dog.

"Are you standing up for your sweet boyfriend?" Fanny called out from under the covers.

The door of the room opened and closed. Milada did not look up. She knew he had left. She did not want to see him. No. Suddenly her legs began to shake so hard she had to hold onto the table. He could not be too far away. He was on the stoop at the front door.

She should have run after him. Said a couple of words. Made some explanation. About Zimmermann. But, as if in a dream, she could not move. He left. And she could not run after him. She froze. It felt as if the air had been shaken. It passed. She left without looking at Fanchon.

She walked through the corridor as if sleepwalking and looked in the office. His hat and coat were gone. He had left his student walking stick in the corner.

He had left the house like a refugee on the run.

Esteemed Doctor Brenner!

I have agonized all week before composing this letter.

Every time the bell rings at a certain hour, I have thought he has returned. But one week has passed, and I know you will not return. Now I am…

Is it possible that you are angry with that terrified, distressed child who is hanging on so tenaciously to the miserable life she has known? Are you angry with a child who clings to what she has rather than any one of a thousand favorable options alien to her? These options only terrify her.

Please consider that if your promises meant health and well-being, she would still be afraid to exchange them for the certainty of daily work and income. Nobody has lost more courage and trust in the future than those of us at Red House.

These last couple of weeks I have asked myself whether your experience here has tainted your sense of joy in doing good.

Doctor, please take this example to heart. I tried to play a melody on Gisi's zither. I could almost tease out some notes, but my thumb hurt when I plucked the strings. The pain was severe and persistent. I had to stop. Right after playing a blister formed on the tender area. Gisi, who plays the zither, told me, "You have to keep at it to develop calluses. You'll never make beautiful music unless you have calluses. You have to push on despite sore fingers." I said to myself, "Look what this wooden box asks of you."

How much more difficult it is to pull a beautiful song out of a human soul! Don't we have to develop a thick skin to protect our delicate, bruised compassion? You will have to pardon me for sounding as if I am lecturing you. I see in reading over my words it may sound like that, but it is not my intent. To tell the truth, I myself have need of this lesson more immediately than ever before. I have lost my courage. Everything escapes me. Fanny does, too. I am incapable of taking hold of the situation. I have lost my grip.

Horner is pedantic. He is a master of theory. When I hold out my hand to him and say, "Lead me to something real, to some fact," he fails miserably.

Our Fanchon will go to Zimmermann. The only thing I have been able to get her to do is promise me not to leave the alley without informing me. Whatever life she has left will be destroyed there. It may be that I come to you for help for her. I do not allow myself to think there is nothing left between you and us.

I bid you farewell,
Milada Rezek

When she sent off the letter, Milada's anxiety evaporated into hundreds of timid hopes.

Three days later—almost too soon for her to expect a reply and before her secret fever had abated—his reply arrived in the mail.

A little letter in brown parchment lay in the entry hall among advertisements, photos of nudes, and the bills.

She pulled it out of the pile, held it a moment, then opened it. She saw gold lines and small, fine letters written clearly. She felt the letter released a certain perfume. He wrote:

M'Lady, here I am. I am not upset. Your letter has the same effect you have. It is earnest, intelligent, and somewhat mysterious. Please accept my thanks for writing. I am not angry at the little rage monster. Let us hope God soon puts an end to her foolishness. Otherwise it will be too late. I would like you to know that my offer to transfer her to the Humanitas Clinic still stands. She may go there at any time.

Madame Milada, I hold your incomprehensible reasons for your own enigmatic martyrdom in high regard. I hope you will not hold it against me that I am not interested in hardening myself. I do not care to engage in such thankless affairs again. This letter shows I harbor no prejudice, does it not?

I have been in Berlin and expect to spend the upcoming summer semester there. Before I leave, there is Pentecost. For me this time is about birds singing, the green of the meadows, the aroma of the forest, and a hundred other things of beauty. When I return, let us talk. Shall I visit you, or would you care to visit me?

In expectation of your reply,
Gus Brenner

Milada put away the letter and opened the accounting book. Mechanically she entered figures, calculated, and wrote. Her great expectation had blown over and left her with an emptiness almost like physical pain. She asked herself, "But what great act did I expect from him? What did I expect? The most elemental comprehension? Did I think he would bridge every chasm to reach out his hand to me and help me? To offer all of us help? How ridiculous! Pentecost is something special he has every year. It is a time of joy he looks forward to. He went to Berlin. He plans a future. When she put herself in his place, those things did seem natural. When she stopped to think about it, of course they seemed natural. Gustav's visits were weighty, meaningful experiences for her. His absence brought about a conflict within her that almost devastated her. But for Gustav? For him all those visits dissolved into meaningless moments. They were lost without a trace in his life of wealth and privilege. The miscalculation was her mistake, and the notion of a couple did not comport with the actual nature of things. And that was that. He had a certain goodness and interest in helping. But the direction of the tide pulled him away from her and her milieu off into another world. It was a world his powers belonged to. This world would destroy her. Whatever had misled her to believe he had entered her world with its interests? Why did she think he would be drawn to the path that had brought them to each other? All his goodness and his lively confidence came from the freedom of the outside world. For a brief while it had illuminated the rooms she inhabited. While she and Horner laid imaginative plans and looked to concepts and constructions, Gustav looked for established systems. He made decisions out of hand. For him there was a clear yes or no. His mind was not cluttered with barriers; he dispensed with them.

Again Milada opened his letter and looked again at the clean, unaffected handwriting. "Shall I visit you, or would you care to visit me?" It looked like there was a bridge laid from her to him. Dare she cross it? She read on, probing, "I hope you will not hold it against me that I am not interested in hardening myself. I do not care to engage in such thankless affairs." He was clearly standing on the other bank. He was firm and unwavering. He was shored up by his own will. "I am not interested." She imagined him before her, saying these words.

Horner was having a bad time. Gustav's visits and various details about what he had done in the house had gotten back to him via Miller. He detected an interest in the "young dandy" behind Milada's hard-necked silence. He attacked Gustav with mean-spirited accusations, poisonous barbs, and pompous reproaches.

"I hear you're spending time in earthly delights! Horrible credentials! Bogus credentials! I am no risk to you. Did he arrive fresh from the battlefield?"

"I don't know what you've heard, Horner. But it certainly wasn't the truth."

He made a dismissive gesture with his hand. "It's your business! I granted you the right to keep your own council a long time ago. It's laughable to expect great things, the grand tour from any one person! I'll just look on while you swim with the flow. Miserable woman! This is all that remains for your sex."

"Horner, you've always preached to me 'Don't be afraid. Do what you want. Do what's unprecedented. Don't let go. Enjoy what you can in life.'"

"But I also said don't go for what you can't handle. Don't waste your time on superficial things. Don't eat fine fruits and specialty foods. You need honest nutrition. Don't get involved in luxurious undertakings. They are the most egregious betrayal of your personal happiness. That, dear lady, is what I've always told you. But, my mistake! You are in love, and you must be happy. I must tell you, Madame, being enamored is only a secondary phenomenon. There is no life in this emotion. The primary evil lies deeper. How? Why? Are you turning away? Is your happiness standing on feet of clay? But, of course, I'm forgetting here. You are in love. People limit themselves to what they have. You are wise to have given up sounding to the depth of things."

A deep resistance to this type of conversation swelled up within Milada. What was it all about? What was the point? What does it matter? She was tortured by Horner's blather.

He pointed his filthy forefinger at her.

"Do go on!" she said softly, unmoved. She looked at his malicious eyes.

He slammed his fist on the table. "What? Isn't this coming from your poor, hungry womanhood? You throw yourself blindly and without resistance at the first, best dandy who comes your way. You attach yourself to some green youth whose mouth is full of honey and sweetness. He can only roll his eyes toward heaven and waggle his dick."

His vulgarity made her indignant. She grew a whiter shade of pale. With composure she told him, "What you're saying is slander."

"Oh, sure," he blubbered. "Madame feels herself to be honored, we could say sainted and free of sin, isn't that right? Now you attract this wonderful, new person and you cast aside your own ethos like dirty clothes. You break with what was and will be, hey? She's counting on this boy like a good bourgeois woman just because his male privilege tickles the ruined shreds of her girlhood. You disgust me, I spit on you! Don't you see it? The whole, sorry humor of the whole affair is he tucks away his wallet and doesn't fork over any cash."

Darkly, in an attitude of hatred and with her lips tight, she stood in front of this drooling man.

"You have trespassed against any rights you used to have, Horner," Milada said, breathing with difficulty. After a pause she added, "You're welcome to think whatever you want to. You don't even know him. What's worse and hard for me to imagine is this: You don't understand who I am despite the fact you know me. You talk rubbish. It doesn't hit home with him or me."

He was taken aback. Milada's steely, simple words were neither pointed nor digging. They hit him like heavy, dull blows.

"So, I don't know him, just fine! All right, I don't," he spoke with a contorted face. "Four years he sat at his school desk right in front of me. And I had the pleasure of looking at his milquetoast face. So I don't know him. His autobiography in French began, 'Mon pére *est le troisieme plus riche de la ville.*' I had to laugh at him when he was in knee pants. He represented the parasitic aristocracy. At the time I called him the Sponge, your beloved. Just so you know. I can show you my teacher's ledger." He pounded on his chest. "Yes, you'll see after his surname I wrote 'Sponge.'"

She was done answering Horner. He looked at her out of the sides of his eyes. He knew he had made a mistake and retreated slowly. "Is it your fault? Is one responsible for the secondary phenomenon of emotion? I showed you primary evil because you were interested. I'm telling you it is an ongoing battle with our physical bodies. Other people's bodies are a constant burden to us. We are plagued by invisible enemies. What kind of man should you have?" He was proud of himself. "A true prince would have been a shame for your womanhood. Such an exemplar of humanity! When I look at you, girl, I have to feel bad for you!"

His voice was squeaky. Milada's silence and her severe, dismissive posture were oppressive to him. He turned around, begging, pathetic, and deceitful.

"Do you think I'm worried about you? You'll find your own way out of this mess. That's what I think. You will. And you won't be the worse for having taken a tumble. You are invulnerable. Well, now, why are you so silent? Milada?"

He tugged on her sleeve. "Be so kind and hold your tongue, why don't you! I am a peace-loving person. What does any of this matter to me? I'm not interested in any more drama. Spare me. You won't see me around here anymore," he screeched. "What do I care? You and your friend can both go to hell. For all I care you two can lead a happy life. Happy, did you hear me? I won't stand in your way. My health won't bear it. I wish you happiness, Milada. I hope you have nine children."

"Spare me!" Milada said and turned away. She moved heavily and mechanically toward the door.

Horner held her by the hem of her skirt and scolded her. "Milada," he hissed, his face twisted in fear, "Don't be so theatrical! Don't go around talking bad about me. I am unwell. Getting upset like this can kill me. Say whatever you want to. Go ask for his advice. Take off! You'll hear nothing from me, do you understand? If you ever find me here again, you can spit in my face. Do you understand? Spit in my face! Spit in my..."

Milada stood her ground and looked directly at the pained expression on his face.

She thought to herself, "And this is the man I held onto? I thought he could help me?" She ran her hand across her brow.

"Yes, I'm ready to go now. But first give me your word of honor you won't tell anybody. I'm an old, old man who talks too much.

Farewell then." He grabbed his hat, adjusted it on his head, and made his way to the door. She let the hand she had raised fall to her side. It hung down stiff.

She thought, "I had no idea. I took him for a man of courage who practiced what he preached. I thought he was someone who would die for his ideals. It was all a pack of lies! It was only a fantasy. Am I making no progress toward the truth? Nothing is as I had understood it. Time and time again I was wrong."

And Gustav's words came to mind, "We kids used to scare him with ladybugs. He'd run around the classroom. It seems he plays the big man here in Red House. He's still the same, a coward."

So schoolboys had seen through him, but she had not. For her he had been the person who saved her. She rested her head on the windowpane. Was everything he had ever told her nothing? Was she left to retreat to the empty, useless despair of her childhood without any will? She felt the icy circle of her earlier isolation. It enclosed her life firmly, ever more firmly.

The Holy Days of Pentecost arrived full of springtime and joy. It was time to celebrate! On Saturday an envelope with a picture postcard of the mountains came in the mail. There were two signatures on it, Gus and Joe. Gus had written a few cursory, ringing words, "It's wonderful being here." Milada studied the colored photo with snow-topped mountains, the small houses strewn in the valley among the cliffs, and the tumbling, white waterfalls. But her imagination was limp and unwilling.

It was not really like that!

At noon Bina flew into Milada's room, flushed and excited.

"Milada," she called. "Will you let me go home? Just for one day? I'm happy to have you take that day from my earnings. Just look at this. I got a message Cyrill has off for the holidays and is coming home."

"Cyrill wrote to you?"

"No. Toni Stadler wrote. She's an old friend. Toni wrote, just look! There's going to be a big festival and a dance, and Cyrill's coming to visit. Milada, I have to go home. I'll pay whatever you want if you let me go."

"Me? I won't say no." Milada took the letter and read it. Was it the right thing to do to spoil Bina's naïve joy with her mistrust? "Bina, why didn't your family write you?" was all Milada said.

"I think they didn't believe the madam would let me go since I was there at Easter. They didn't want me to be sad. But if I come home and surprise them, there'll be quite a stir!"

"I'll tell the madam. Do you want to go tomorrow?"

"I'll be back by evening. Please tell the madam my mother's ill. I'm going for her sake, that's what I'd like you to say."

Without waiting for Miller to agree, Bina was packed and ready to leave. After a rather difficult battle with Miller, Milada told Bina Miller had agreed to the day off. Bina had packed a small handbag with a red-satin housedress. She also packed a considerable pile of embroidered pieces she had amassed.

There was a lot of noise and racket the night before the holidays, as is always the case. A new person arrived, too. It was the widow from Saint Pölten Ascher had offered Miller a while back. She was small, blond, and voluptuous. Her eyes were light and friendly as was her laughter. She enjoyed chatting and at times laughed so loudly she could be heard above everything else. This irritated Miller, and she signaled her discontent. She was unhappy when business degenerated into conversation and the reason and purpose of an exchange was lost in frivolous talk. The widow had brought this chatty behavior with her from nice society.

It so happened a Mr. Albrecht from St. Pölten was also in the salon. The widow was supposed to serve him and then disappear. Albrecht delivered shoes to Red House. He was someone Goldscheider had trusted. His trade with Miller was only delivering shoes. He explained Miller had no understanding of "other merchandise." He was an unpleasant customer. He never paid and never left a tip. He also wanted everything to be written up punctually and deducted from what he was owed. Miller did not like him. She wanted him to be served quickly and then shown the door. He did not fit in the milieu with his rough, red hands, his clumsy bearing, and his unkempt red hair. Miller found his tedious narratives and awkward jokes insufferable. The widow did not like him either. She tried to get rid of him but in vain. He came to the city from Saint Pölten twice a week. So twice a week the bungling shoemaker was in the house, sweetly wooing the widow. He told her he was glad to be rid of "bo-or-ring Ka-Kar-la."

"When the bo-oot-ts are too s-mall, Miller gi-give-s them ba-ack. Wh-at am I su-po-sed to do?" he laughed crudely.

The widow was usually well appointed. Her past life as a bourgeois woman, which she spoke of like a star, made her quite the item.

The salon emptied out as the morning sun began to glow in the east and the rays began to disperse.

Spring arrived with Pentecost. It was a fresh morning. People wrapped up in their overcoats left Red House and went busily about their day. The lights at the window went out one by one.

Bina left at 5:30 a.m. She wore a large feather hat that obscured her face. She offered Milada her hand in parting. It was cold and quivered.

She whispered half to herself, "How I am looking forward!"

"Please do get back on time for me," Milada said as she stood at the door. "You know it's important."

"I know," said Bina and rushed off.

Milada was tired and played out. She had put up with Miller's complaining and cursing. She had taken care of the girls and kept them in line since early that morning.

As soon as guests left, Miller ran into the rooms and demanded the money she was due. She spied on the girls to see if the men had left them too large a tip. Miller was forever snooping and poking around behind people's backs. She also wanted to make sure Milada had not kept money for herself.

While Milada was helping the porter put the messy salon back in some kind of order, once again a scene with Horner transpired in all its unpleasant, filthy details. Milada was more clearly aware than ever before she wanted nothing further to do with him.

What the man had to offer, she had gotten. He was finished. The only fire left in him was hatred and loathing. He was ruled by fear. Looking back she could understand his poverty. He hated everyone who was stronger or richer than he was. Milada had no inkling what would follow later that day!

She opened the windows in the salon. The light of the morning shone in and pierced the thick, gray smoke in the room.

"Don't let Horner befuddle you. Go your own way! Happiness is the most basic of feelings." That is what Goldscheider had to say. At the time Milada had believed she had a mission and a future, and she had trusted Horner as a teacher. One after another, the bubbles had burst. Truth shone out like the sun, which eclipses the small light of the stars.

She gave the porter the morning off. She could still hear the heavy footfall of the guests coming downstairs. Doors opened and closed. Finally all was quiet.

"Everyone's asleep," she thought. "They were very tired and fell right asleep. I'm alone in the house." And just as this idea occurred to her, she saw it portended more than she had first understood. Sleep! Yes, everyone was sleeping. They were having dreams rich in images. Their dreams of life deep in their sleep were richly colorful. The shutters of their souls were closed; the door to reality, locked. Playful fingers had closed their eyelids. "Darkness is good. Sleep and dreaming are a blessing. Don't wake them, don't call them. Let us poor creatures feel happy in our dreams."

Milada chose rather to look at the light. She knew the sun.

Hot fire filled her eyes and pierced her through. Dust and all that was the enemy of light rose up before her and flew apart into thousands of atoms.

As a wise woman she watched the characters from her milieu as actors in a theater. She knew what happened in the performance would catch them up. She was familiar with the brutality and the greed of the entrepreneurs and their games. They laid their traps skillfully, lay in wait for their victims, and led them to their demise. She also knew the system that exploited these characters. She knew it flourished without societal restraint. She was well aware of the position the prostitute's work forced her into. This position was outside the law in countries that were cultured. In this position women are subjected to unchecked violence. They are robbed of any and all possessions; they are further robbed of their health and freedom.

Milada knew the type of business Zimmermann ran kept girls captive like prisoners. They were allowed only the most basic clothing so they could not go out in public to escape. Even the legal revisions the police put in place made the whole alley into what everyone knew was an orgy. Here men took up with a pretty girl while the officers of the law fell asleep in the middle of the free-for-all, naked, holding a bottle of cognac. Milada knew about discarding girls who were not appealing or broken; they disappeared into the night. Milada saw how innocent girls were entrapped and their virginity was systematically exploited. All this she knew too well. She was tired and disgusted from seeing it again and again. She had become inured; she was deadened. She could no longer cry. She had no illusions about this business. No laughter dispelled the pain; no words healed the wounds. No thought could deliver one. No one scaled the pyramids up out of this evil.

She walked over to the window and tried to look directly at the sun without wincing. Milada held a dialog with him. "Evil holds me in its iron grip," she said. "I can't move. The circle that encloses me is so narrow I can't breathe. I do want to help, make things better.

"And live here and help the way I used to, by working hard and taking charge. Slowly I am climbing my way out, but over dead bodies. I don't want to do it. I don't want to go on." Those were her angry thoughts. They ran in circles.

"What would you do, if you were truly burned out, empty and desolate? If you were a black hole? What if you had no light and no fire about loving the world you live in and the people you know? What if you had no fire to keep them warm? But you want to go on. You have to. You would still have longing in your deadened heart. It would make you cry."

A wave of warm air blew into the cool morning. It brushed her face tenderly and stroked her hands, which were balled in fists on the windowsill. The warmth opened her hands and made her raise her palms. In this quietude, there was a voice, "Fool, there would be nothing left to love. The sun would burn itself out and take the world with it. I wouldn't be able to love. The eternal call of life is still love. Love—love. With love we become the power of love. We carry the sun within. It can't be destroyed. The person who knows love has words of warmth and hands that do good. This person has helpers. You have them, too."

Slowly she moved away from the window.

"And I have this power?"

She put aside words, images, or ideas that might bring her back to normal consciousness and make her feel unmoored. She put aside those words, images, and ideas that had earlier blinded and foiled her and asked: did she have the power to change reality? Could she shape it? This idea was huge and filled her with a wonderful shudder. Put her hands to the task, work, and create anew! Feeling lucky and eager like a small child, she began to review her memories. She took the measure of things and fortified herself with details from many episodes in her life.

A wealth of events came together felicitously and lifted a heavy weight from her soul. It was true: here and there this or that had actually happened. There were times she had known power and helped. She recalled that in taking on a challenge, she had not felt doubt or despair. Dubbe came to mind, Fanny, and Camilla, and lots of other people she did not know. She had offered restless souls a moment of respite. She lifted them up skillfully out of their internal abyss. She had never let despair win out even when it looked inevitable. She had pointed those with sight to those who were blind; she had shown those who eat well people who were hungry; and she had reminded the living of death. A spark of courage always stuck fast. The sun within us shines on as long as we evolve.

But what does all this come down to?

The feeling of sheer good luck that had pervaded Milada died out. Shadows slipped in. What does lifting others up have to do with the individual? What is Gisi's good faith or the careless, joyous laugh of Fanchon in comparison to the enormity of terrifying misery? Thousands of people suffer hardship and adversity. Who will speak up? Who throws a bridge over the morass with no shore? "Don't any of you out there know? Your silence condemns us all, all of us." Milada lifted her arm against the waking city. The first dreamlike smile of life in the city appeared. She addressed people on the streets:

"What do you women know of our lives, you women who gather your skirts when you walk past us and look us over with curious disdain?

"And what do you men know of us, you men who come to us in the evening? You are drawn to the light of the salon where we wait tarted up with rouge and baubles to service you with the warmth of our bodies, but do you know us? What do you know about us women who relieve you of your earthly sorrows with our frivolity? Once we have satisfied you, you slam the door behind you, unfeeling. What do you care about the tragedy of our aging, our losses, the curse of our illnesses, or our depersonalized souls? Do you know how the present shatters to bits for us, the past becomes a shudder, and the future holds only a grave? Who among you has the courage to ask one of us with shuttered souls, 'How do you look in the light of day? Please show yourself.'"

Milada took a deep breath. A strong will needs to surface. It must be joyous. This will is sure to win out and to blossom. It will arrive like the spring, blow the leaves of fall away, and inspire everything to thrive. This has to come. There must be a man who stands up and says, "Come all of you, come follow me!"

She sat at the open window, leaned back, and pulled the red curtain over her cold arms. The sunlight intensified, danced and shimmered. What was that? She opened her eyes wide.

Had not someone been here? Was there not a person talking to her?

Who had uttered the words "Come follow me"?

Gustav? It could not have been Gus.

In her daydream she had recalled her grade school for the poor and the man who had hung on the gray wall, all bloody and horrible. He held a heart in his hands, and a flame shot out of the heart.

"Be quiet, be quiet!" Madame Coelestine had admonished. She spoke of the Savior. She told the story of Jesus of Nazareth on the Cross.

Gustav was not like that. He was beautiful and happy. Gus was alive.

She smiled softly and fell sound asleep.

When she awoke the sun was streaming into every corner of the room. The light was filled with dust particles and was numbing. The maid was dusting and sweeping. She said to Milada, "It's Pentecost, don't you know, Madame Milada?"

It was Sunday and Pentecost, and the house was quiet! Miller had given in to Milada's urging and bought tickets for the balcony at the circus. The girls were full of expectation. They crammed themselves into two carriages and rode off. People were surprised the "Old Witch" had arranged this.

Putzi put her nose in the air and said at the last place she worked they sent the girls to evening performances and not to something as shabby as the circus. Circuses were for children and, at most, a few students, and all the tickets Miller bought were half price. But none of that kept her from dressing to the hilt with a feather hat so large everybody was envious. Gisi made the observation, "She's probably ashamed to be out with us. She looks like an actress on stage."

Milada stayed at the house with Karla. The widow and little Rosie had decided to stay back so that the house had a skeleton crew. It was not completely empty, as Miller had feared it might be.

Rosie plunked around on the piano. The widow munched bonbons from under her colossal bouffant. Karla was asleep in her room. She had fallen asleep with a prayer book on her chest. On her lovely, damp cheeks there were trails of tears that made furrows in her makeup.

Milada sat in her room. She tolerated Rosie's tedious playing and let her thoughts roam. She thought of blond Camille and wondered if she was still sending money every month to the monastery for women in Geneva.

Milada thought of Bina who was probably home with her family, sitting next to Cyrill at the head of the table, happy as can be and proud. Then her thoughts drifted to luxuriously beautiful Arrigazzi, who had been taken to Abbazzia on the Austrian Riviera for a few days. Fanchon's narrow face came to mind as it had looked earlier among red-checked pillows in the clinic. Her eyes had been filled with fear. They shimmered a strange gold. Fanny was very ill and unable to move. But the orderly had said, "This little idiot will get back up."

Milada had brought her fruit and chocolate, but Fanny, untypically, hardly looked at them. Her face was swollen from crying. She whispered, "I'm a bad person, a bad person."

"Do you think you've been bad to me?"

"I'm bad," Fanny spoke between clenched teeth. That was the only audible thing that came out of her, as the bright sun of this early Pentecost morning fell on her pale fingers.

At the time Milada had thought, "It seems the whole world and all its people are happy today and feel joyous, but here she lies, weeping the most bitter tears.

"It seems the world is filled with people who are fortunate and healthy and not with people lying in bed in a clinic without hope and feeling abandoned." Milada had told Fanny, "I am with you." Then Milada banished these ghosts.

And in her daydreaming an image of Gustav suddenly appeared to her with surprising intensity. Milada was completely swept away with this vision. She listened for his voice. She felt his eyes look deeply into hers. The smell of his person next to her was so strong it startled her.

"I want to tell you I'm here with my hat in one hand and a bottle of wine in the other at the top of the highest mountain, greeting Nature."

That was the whole of this man. He was young and on the move. He had laughing eyes. That man was also the other world, the embodiment of everything that wants to live, to take hold of fortune and enjoyment.

A shadow fell suddenly over Milada's view of the alley in full sun in front of her. On the other side of the street she saw Horner, swinging his gnarled walking stick in the air. She nodded and went to open the door. He raised his eyebrows in surprise, but since her relatively good mood remained unruffled by his arrival, he only mumbled a few words. He entered.

"These damned holidays," he swore. "Nothing disrupts one's peace and quiet like a holiday. If it weren't for holidays, a body could almost believe he was dead. Then a holiday arrives and rattles me awake. And the maid comes at eight in the morning instead of at six. You can't find clean clothes. What you do get is church bells ringing and the guy next door singing some tune, 'Live well, you quiet house.' I say to hell with all of it. All I smell is burned butter. And do what I will, I still have some glow in these old, red eyes. I see everything as it is. The dirty spots on my coat and my run-down shoes embarrass me. Then there's the fine filth of years on my hat." He looked with melancholy at his hat and rotated it. "At every turn I run into this world, the people, the facts and what's important. In other words, I have the feeling I'm alive. There's this attitude of celebration that comes of sweet Christianity. It puts me in mind of a little braid, bound and pomaded with bits of bright-blue tinsel, on some small, snot-nosed girl. I feel like a louse in her hair, sickened by the smell and aggravated." He used his walking stick to hit the floor.

"Yes, well, Horner, living is the practice of great art."

"Living here isn't great art," he said. "That's why I always come back. The atmosphere of everyday life is stalled out here." He made himself comfortable and lit a cigar. That felt right to him. He wanted to forget.

She was ridiculous. And that Gustav was only some little boy. But he, Horner, had made her who she was. He had made her the person standing right there, living as she did.

"I will tell you something, little girl. Pay attention. When you are miserable and your will is weak, the internal power of your being lifts you up high. The eternal matter within you pursues its own goal. Your part is in the details. Life is self-perpetuating and has the rhythm of a clock pendulum. Look at its birth as the onset of movement. It requires no effort from you. You are listening to the best advice I have from slogging around on Earth. I offer this to you as a gift." He sounded sentimental and affected, as he always did when he was pontificating and had his own agenda.

"I'll tell you what else. Human life is like a bottle of fine wine that has spilled out into a puddle. Who recognizes the qualities of this aristocratic beverage in this gummy slop? It's become a blob of filth. It's decomposed into thousands of atoms. The flavor is gone, and its aroma has flown to the four winds. Its vitality is wasted, yes it is." He yawned and wiped his mouth with the back of his hand.

"What are our ideas, emotions, and the actions of our will? What are our great deeds except colored bubbles that float over the sewer of our existence. With the slightest pressure they rupture like fleas. They disappear beyond the periphery of our vision. They have no use or any direction. Furthermore, we don't see them at all. That's what is special about them. We know nothing about them. Therein lies the irony and falsity of all personal happiness."

After having served him his lemonade, Milada returned to her place at the window. She listened to him halfway and wove his words into her own train of thought.

"His philosophizing, Fanchon's bitter tears, the monotone of sounds from the salon, the rustle of Arrigazzi's silk flounces—how bizarre they seem. Yet in their essence they all come together. They all add up to the same feeling and emanate the same sweet enervation. Each of these elements on its own would seem different, but for the moment they are all awash."

Horner kept talking, hoping to draw her in. He wanted to enchant her as he had before. His speech became more halting and strained as the silent figure at the window grew darker with the shadows of late morning.

She was transported by sunny moments, high mountains, Gustav, and laughing women. She tightened her fists. These things, too, were all of a piece. The afternoon at Meier's Café came to mind. She remembered looking at the faces of the women, one by one. One of these women belonged to him. There had to be one of them to whom he wrote long letters about his travels. He must be eagerly sharing his experiences of beauty in letters with one of these nice women. In the dusk, when night drapes objects and feelings with its silver veil, he must hold the hand of one of these women. An expression of anguish escaped her lips.

She shook her head. Be gone, be gone...

Horner held forth. Rosie's piano playing wound its way through his words like a sluggish snake through a mass of roots and undergrowth. Time was hypnotized. The afternoon was an eternity. Weren't the girls back from the circus yet? She pressed her lips together.

Horner pointed his index fingers at her. "You are going to die an agonizing death. That's because you are tough. I mean it."

Milada's voice floated over to him from the window. "You are wrong. I will have an easy death because I want to die. I will be tired."

She came over toward him and supported herself on the table.

"I believe everybody has her own strength that she puts to use through work. Everybody makes a necessary contribution."

"Get to the point, why don't you? Don't chew around on ideas like a goat munching grass!" Horner hollered out. He did not like listening to her.

"Listen. If there's difficult work to do, people set themselves to the task without thinking of the obstacles. They fix their sights on the goal. Strength buoys us up. I often kept on like this when I had to deal with Goldscheider and worked in the salon. That was at a time when I longed for freedom and before I spoke with Miller about quitting. After that I was constantly surveying what was ahead. I weighed every move forward and each advantage I sought against the strength I had left. I spent my energy. If I were up against that situation today, I would not be able to do what I did. It would cause me anguish. I wouldn't want to put forth the effort. It does not seem that wonderful to me now. I don't see the value. Some people are stuck here; others, there. Each person gets as far as she can while her strength holds out. I am sure of this: the less strength we have, the easier our death. A person who is used up does not resist death. People who have truly loved living and freely spent their energy, those whose souls are exhausted from suffering, refuse to go on. They long for peace. We die like the golden leaf of autumn frees itself from the tree. There is no regret, and there is no awareness of surrendering something precious."

Horner interrupted and without a moment's pause continued in a flat monotone.

"But energy that has not been used up and tapped out ferments and tumbles around in an old body. It demands to be put to use and recycled. It wants to avenge the sloth of its master. It plagues him from one desire to the next, from goal to goal; it chases him through all districts of hell and down all the streets of craving. At length it traps him in the labyrinth of longing and martyrs him there.

"In the end it disintegrates into the fear of death. It falls apart with the blind, abysmal fear of dying and, among the faithful, with the fear of judgement. It ends with a fear that sits in live veins like lead. What about that?"

He jumped up from his seat. "You're right, brat! You little rascal! You've said your piece very well. Slam, bam! Did you swat the little fly that was buzzing around your sweet face, did you?" Horner's eyeballs rolled around in his head. His lips quivered with an excitement unusual for him. His spit sprayed across her. "Bravo! You have thought this through brilliantly, slut! A philosopher could not have done better—and she did it with style. And God knows, what she said here is true enough! Now use your wits to twist a noose and hang old Horner by the neck. He's the site of rotting energy." He ripped off his vest and tore at the gray tricot of his shirt. He beat his brow, "And here is where she exposed his fantasies. She threw garbage and stinking muck on my body and fouled up my life. She made me erupt in toxic boils. Scenes of hell, death, and the Devil, and these nightmares! Would I were tired, girl. I wish to God I were tired, too."

He pitched forward. "Come over here. I want to tell you something. My soul is horny. It's horny, shameless, naked, and disgusting like a fat old whore who itches with lust. I deceive anybody I can. I prey on the poorest of the poor and people with nothing. I buy their souls and make them my slaves. So did you notice? I bought and paid for you, too. You came cheap. I got a good deal. I paid off your debts to Goldscheider. She was glad about that.

"You say you surveyed what lay ahead, is that right? Did you look to see what was behind you?" At this point he began to whisper. His tone was almost intimate. It held a gruesomeness. "You see I am not certain about this. I'd rather have nightmares and dread. I won't stand still. I intend to keep watch."

He lowered his head so that all she could see was the gray hair of his head and the dark-gray fat rings on the back of his neck. His disgust of himself was transferred to Milada.

All of a sudden he jumped up high. "The old man is hanged! Is he drooling still? Is his tongue hanging out of his mouth? He's not moving. You haven't done anything new to this old head. I'm familiar with this, too. I've experienced execution before, old wretch that I am. I'm a sweet piece of candy." He assumed the posture of a body hanging from a noose.

"Horner!" she yelled in horror.

"No, it's not me. After an execution, you know, people don't go on. But after an orgy people recover, the old assholes. When the body is played out the soul has to keep going. Pretty funny, isn't it? A bit of onanism doesn't affect the mind." With that he rapped on the table wildly for more lemonade. He raised his glass.

Without wiping the pained expression of disdain from his face he made his way to the door, taking steps backwards.

Let him leave. Let him go. She wanted to hear and see nothing more of him. She could not bear it. "He's like a dead body. He is a corpse," she surprised herself with her own words. "I have to get away from this man. I need to save myself. He's killing me."

Without thinking she made her way to the salon, sat down next to Rosie, and was glad to inhale the smell of life her blond hair emanated. She ate sweets the widow offered, went to see Karla and told her to make herself up beautifully. Nice guests were on their way. Milada went to the kitchen and tasted the meal for the evening. She dished herself a plate full, then pushed it aside. Her mind kept turning on this one thought: "There's a dead man upstairs in my room."

She went to wait with the porter in the entry hall, watching out for the carriage that would bring the girls back to the house. That's when she spotted Horner. He had come downstairs and left by the back door. She pressed herself against the wall and took hold of the porter's apron. She said something or other.

Horner stood in front of her. He laughed and said sardonically, "Well, it's appropriate for us to take leave of each other. We despise each other."

He went to the gate while she extended her hand as a reflexive motion of parting. She knew it was useless to speak. She had no words.

The sound of the latch of the gate closing reached her ear. She exhaled. An odium about life filled her heart. She sensed she had been freed from the embrace of a corpse.

Thus Horner left the house of the unfortunate and retreated to his world. Surreptitiously he took along with himself Milada's inheritance: compassion.

In this moment Milada was set free.

Gratitude blessed her. It surged, seemingly, from the cosmos and flowed back again into the cosmos. It was restorative. For a second her profane body was blessed.

Chapter 5
Experiences

A conscience that is independent is sunshine in your age of propriety.
—Goethe

On the second day of Easter holiday, early in the morning, completely unexpectedly, Bina arrived back at Red House. Nobody saw her come in. Nobody remembered having opened the door for her.

When Milada walked past her door, she heard a faint sound. She opened the door and found Bina, sitting atop her black suitcase, fully clothed, as she had been when she left the morning before. But the state of her clothing tipped Milada off something was awry. The bodice of her dress was buttoned askew. The lace inset hung backwards over her collar. Her black feather hat was fastened loosely; it was slipping off her head and pulled her braids down to the nape of her neck.

"Bina, what's going on?" When Bina looked up slowly and dully, Milada understood: something miserable had happened.

"What happened to you? Get up, please! I beg you, get up, Bina!"

A twitch contorted her transfixed, pale face. It was the first movement as she began to stir. It was as if she was waking from a deep, heavy sleep.

A dreadful outburst was unleashed.

She threw herself down across the floor and began to scream and cry. The floorboards rattled as she knocked her head against them violently.

In no time her room was full. The girls in their nightgowns gathered around in confusion, asking Bina as she thrashed about, "What's wrong?" "Didn't you go home?" "We should call the doctor. She's got some kind of poisoning." "Jesus, Mary, and Joseph."

Milada tried in vain to get her to stand up. The girls supported her. Putzi resolutely poured a pitcher of water on Bina, while Lefty Anna, wearing an odd grimace, doused her with cologne. But Bina, rigid and stiff as a board, clung to the floor. In the middle of her screaming she blurted out words no one understood. She shoved away the arms of the girls who wanted to help. She tried to slap Milada's hand when she held her head to keep her from hurting herself.

"Nothing helps," Anna said, dropping the bottle of cologne with resignation. "It will take a man to hold her down. We'll have to let her thrash it out."

The porter pushed her way forward through to Bina and spoke to her, "Madame, you aren't telling us what's wrong. You should be ashamed of yourself for raising Cain like this in the house. Just look over there at the window. People have come to see what's going on. Pretty soon the police will be here. It's going to be as bad here as over at Zimmermann's place."

What the porter said seemed to have an effect. Bina lay motionless. Milada was then able to lift her up. "What is it, Bina? What happened to you?" the girls all chimed in. "For God's sake, please tell us what's going on."

"I don't really know. I... I'm..." Bina stood there dazed and stared at everybody. Her face was sunken; her eyes, swollen and red. "I sat in a field all night long," she said quietly to Milada.

Milada asked, "Were you at home after all? Didn't you go home, Bina?"

"I should've known," Bina gasped heavily, tired. "I should have known about everything—everything." Then she looked around at each person standing there. She did this mechanically, looking from one to another until she stopped at Milada's face. Bina's immense pain sank in Milada's kind, gray eyes.

"I'll be calm now," she whispered to Milada and nodded. And then she resumed her spot on her wooden suitcase, putting her arms on her knees and her head on her arms. She stayed like that, no longer moving at all.

The people in the room were shocked and uncomprehending. They just looked at one another.

"She's drunk," asserted Anna.

"*Meshugge*, crazy," Putzi said.

Only Milada understood it was something grave. "Go back to bed," she told them.

Without trying to rouse Bina again, Milada took her wet hat off her head and draped a blanket around her cold shoulders. Then she shooed everybody out of the room.

An hour later Bina was stretched out in her bed fast asleep. Her usual healthy, happy face now looked raw and depleted. Her fingers were spread in front of herself as if she were fending off some force. Her breath was a restless rattle. She looked as if she had been running and running without stop.

"Poor devil," said Gisi who had been standing at the head of Bina's bed. She asked Milada, "So what do you think?"

Gisi looked lovely in a green housedress of light fabric. With a comforting, motherly movement she straightened Bina's pillow.

"Some grave insult," Milada answered briefly.

"From him?"

"From him, yes."

"It's always some bastard when one of us goes on the rocks," Gisi said in anger. "After this, save your heart for somebody decent." She kicked Bina's hat across the floor and her gentle face hardened.

"Do you think she's sleeping?"

"I don't know."

"Doesn't he want her anymore?"

"Does that surprise you, Gisi?"

"It does and it doesn't," Gisi said despondently. Then she sighed and left.

Toward noon some of the girls told Milada that Bina Michal had bolted her door. People could hear her milling around inside. But when Milada went to see her, she readily opened the door. Bina had put away her things and made the bed. She had dressed and made herself up. She had, in fact, Milada noted, put herself together for the evening. It moved Milada to see this. Her face was emaciated. It revealed the blow she had been dealt. Her red eyelids stood in stark contrast to her powdered complexion.

"Can you tell me, Bina? What happened to you last night?"

"Oh, last night? I went crazy from sitting out in a field."

"Didn't you go home?"

Bina turned to Milada and looked at her meaningfully. She held her sobs in check and pronounced with a constricted voice, "It's over." Then she walked over to Milada with her usual, lumbering gait and took Milada by the hand.

"You knew everything about me the whole time. Why didn't you shake me and ask, 'Idiot, what are you thinking? You're bad, a fallen woman. You're nothing for a good man. You're a whore, trash.' Why didn't you shake the truth into me?"

"Who told you those things?"

"Who?! Everybody, everybody. The pastor of our church, Father, my stepmother, even Bozenka. And, and..." Bina swallowed hard, "Cyrill! Milada, sure as I am standing here, it's true. It's true, isn't it, Milada?" Bina did not wait for an answer, she continued.

"It's gone. It's gone—all of it. The money, the little house, the cow, and the man. Everything. Just look how terribly they treated me! They threw me out of my own house and home like a Gypsy. And then they said a prayer and spat to rid themselves of evil!

"So there I was standing like some poor dog in the rain. What did they want from me? They hit me and cursed at me. Then they slammed the door on me. They made me get out. So now you know the whole story."

"Oh, Bina, that can't be everything. Tell me the whole story. Tell me everything that happened," said Milada as she stroked her cold hand.

Milada got the following story from the jumbled narrative Bina told in a flood of angry tears: Bina had imagined her surprise arrival would please her family. But she caught them off guard and embarrassed them. She found the house decked out for a celebration and the table set for the holidays. But there were no guests around. When Bina asked where everybody was, she got short, dismissive answers. So she confronted her father and asked what was going on.

He said distractedly, "Mother knows something about you." Then he hurried off. Cyrill was not to be found, so Bina went to his mother. But her door was bolted closed. The maid told her everybody had gone to church over in Bohemia. Back at her family's house things were in an uproar. Her stepmother gave her nasty looks and sneered at her. Her stepmother screamed at her younger stepsister Bozenka for taking Bina's hat. Bina was so distraught by her behavior she did not dare ask for an explanation. Her stepmother and stepsisters put their heads together and whispered. Then the servant called out from the window, "He's waiting outside in the courtyard." Bina's stepmother was startled to see Bina was there and had heard this. The woman launched into a tirade against her. As she was raging Bina began to put things together. She asked, "Who's waiting in the courtyard?"

"You can guess. Go on over. He'll tell you himself."

So, Bina went over to the courtyard, but nobody was there. Then she heard a dog whining because he recognized her. She went toward the sound and saw a man at the dogs' cage, holding the dog's mouth closed. It was Cyrill in uniform.

Bina was struck dumb. She simply stared at him. As Bina told the story, she extended her hand to greet him, but he pushed it away, saying he knew she had become a whore in the city. He said he was ashamed for her to the whole family. He told her his mother would take his head off if he had anything to do with her. He had not put a hand on the dirty money she sent. The good pastor, Cyrill said, had eventually taken the money. He admonished her to leave right away and get back to her life as a whore where she could wear silk clothes and necklaces of gold.

When Bina started to speak up for herself, she noticed there was a crowd standing around. Her father and mother were among them, and they were swearing at her. Bozenka joined in with the others. Bina threw her arms around Cyrill's neck and looked up at him, laughing hysterically. She understood it all. Cyrill fumbled with his sword and yelled out he would love to run her through. Andulka told him, "Cyrill, put your sword up. It will only work against you." Bina ran over to her mother and announced, "This was all your doing. You did this."

"Yes, yes I did. You're upset he'd rather have a decent girl."

Bina asked her father, "Where's my money?"

Her mother yelled out, "Money? We don't need money from a whore, a miserable whore. Go ask the Holy Reverend what happened to your money!"

The pastor was standing right there. He was a tall, dark man from Bohemia Bina did not know. He said he had come upon an idea how to purify the money. He would have an altar made to the Holy Mother Magdalene.

Bina concluded her story, "While the pastor was talking, I looked over at Andulka. She was laughing, and Cyrill was laughing with her and twisting his mustache." Bina stood up to tell what happened. "I ran over to her and threw her down on the ground and pounded her with my fists. I choked her with all my might. What happened then," Bina shook her head, "was nothing. It was over. Everybody had gone inside. Except the pastor. He stood there like a block of wood, praying for my soul. Somebody brought my suitcase out to the courtyard. My hat flew out the kitchen window. Cyrill cried out, 'Trash Bohunk!' And it was all over and done.

"I can't tell you how I got to the train station. That night I rode back and sat outdoors in a field. I don't know if I was asleep or awake. All I know is I wanted to die." Bina leaned her head against the wall and nodded to herself. Milada stood up abruptly.

"No, Bina! We're not going to let it go like that. Give me the receipts from the post office for the money transfers you made. I'm going to take them right away to Doctor Morgenstern. He will help."

Bina looked at Milada through her swollen eyes, uncomprehending.

"We're going to take this to a lawyer. These people willl have to think about the scandal a legal case will bring down on them. It's clear to me what they were doing."

Bina made a gesture of futility. "Can you, can any lawyer, make Cyrill love me again?"

Gisi was in the doorway, listening. Putzi stood there, too, and watched with her large, blue eyes.

"What the hell! They knew damn well where you were. They took you for your money. They're thieves. And that soldier is a shit."

"No, that's not true," said Bina decisively. "When we were kids, back then, he did love me." A brooding demeanor washed over her, "The folks back home are right to do what they did. I really am a bad person. There's no place for me back there."

Slowly, ever so slowly, an awareness of social priorities began to dawn on this simple creature. It registered on her face and worked on her soul. She suffered visibly to make sense of this gruesome, new recognition.

"I always thought—I thought from the very beginning—that there has to be something sinful about having all this money and such a good life where everything's so nice. And each and every month when I went to the post office to send money, I thought to myself, 'You got this money without doing any real work. But then nothing bad's ever happened to me. Things will be fine. It's possible to live well and not have bad things happen to me.' But now I know better. When I was little and poor, Papa loved me. Bozenka did, too. And so did Cyrill. Everybody there at home did. But now that I wear gold jewelry, they run me out of town. Punishment did come my way."

Putzi commented, "People in your village get ruffled pretty easy."

And Gisi put in, "You can find a lot nicer guy than that lousy Cyrill."

Milada said, anger shooting out her eyes, "He owes you that money."

"And you didn't give him a good smack in the face?" Lefty Anna wanted to know. "A pox on that stuck-up ass! He's the Bohunk, snarfing up all your money like that!"

She did not have a chance to finish because the doorbell rang downstairs. All the girls poured into the hall.

"Bina, listen to me," Milada said in haste. "Keep your head up and keep going. I'll help you any way I can. Let those idiots do what they want. You think about the future." She did not have the heart to unpack all the lies any further. This poor creature had had enough for the time being. Milada wrapped up the conversation with something of a plea, "Bina, you've been all right here, haven't you? You've been pretty happy, haven't you?"

Bina nodded agreement. "Yes, I've been happy. But that was because I was thinking about home. I was always thinking about

Cyrill and about the little house with a garden we'd have. I kept in mind how nice life would be."

She arose. The brooding expression she wore on her lips became more intense. The deliberateness of her speech revealed her suffering, how broken she was.

"There's something good and beautiful about earning money from hard work, you know? It is real work. And there's real pleasure in it, too. You know? And there's something sinful in money that comes quick and easy. It doesn't make people happy." After a pause she added with the certitude of someone who has arrived at a sure conclusion, "They were right after all. A good man can't marry someone like me. It would be a waste and a shame."

"A good man does not behave like he did."

Bina held Milada's arm and spoke. "Cyrill is a good man. He did not want money from me. That was my stepmother. She sent me here." Her eyes glowed with hatred. "I had to run away, had to leave my father's house. The devil has taken my soul."

"They have to give you your money back," Milada repeated, although she did understand that money was not at stake for Bina. Milada clung adamantly to her position. Her angry demand expressed her bitterness, but it had no effect on Bina's view of the facts.

Something balled up inside Milada when Bina said, "I was a stupid young thing when I came to the city. Mother had given me an address, and the policemen laughed at me when I asked how to get here. My only thought was things will work out. If someone had told me, 'Girl, don't do that, stay away! Hard work is better for you,' things would have turned out all right." Bina shrugged her shoulders.

"But nobody tried to stop me." Both Bina and Milada sat in silence. The clock struck the hour. Both of them listened up.

Someone downstairs hollered out, "Miss Bina!" The sound of footsteps drew near. Obeying her reflex mechanically, she opened the door and stepped out. Milada followed her. She saw Bina's full, heavy figure slowly approach a man. She watched as Bina extended her hand in greeting. She heard Bina return his greeting. The pair passed her in the corridor. Bina kept her eyes level and straight ahead. The man held her arm tightly and emitted a crude laugh. And then they disappeared behind the door to her room.

The summer began with intermittent storms and showers. In the midst of bad weather Milada made her way to the Luise Hospital. Several days prior she had gotten a letter from Fanny, telling her she was going to leave the hospital. She wrote she would rather jump in the river than return to Zimmermann's. Zimmermann had taken all Fanny's clothes to make sure she would return. Milada knew this tactic from the housekeepers, so she packed up a bundle of clothes and underwear to take Fanny to help her out of her most immediate need.

Milada took along Little Rosie, a tall blond girl with a sweet face. The widow from St. Poelten had recently brought Rosie along with her to Red House. Rosie carried the large box of clothes for Fanny and used her free left hand to keep her hat from blowing off in the strong wind.

"It's good I'm wearing short knickers," she said as she looked down at the puddles of water.

Rosie came from a nice family. An officer in the military had seduced her when she was sixteen. This liaison had consequences. Her family threw her out brutally, and the officer made arrangements for her to stay with a midwife in St. Poelten. But things did not go well. A scandal broke out. The officer was found out and dressed down, and the arrangement with the midwife fell through. Rosie's parents turned her out permanently, and she fell ill. Once she was nursed back to health in the hospital, the widow took her in under the pretense that she would find Rosie employment in the city. After placing her in various jobs, the widow took her to Miller in Red House. But Rosie was only on loan at Red House since the widow had to be seen around in St. Poelten with Rosie every so often.

Milada followed a dark instinct and took Rosie along with her to the Luise Hospital. She was used to feeling no sympathy or having any pangs of conscience about exposing girls to harsh reality. In fact, she thought it would do Rosie good to see where the life of ease inevitably landed one. Milada hoped seeing the hospital would be a tacit warning to her. Possibly her sweet, child-like illusions would be disrupted. On their way to see Fanchon Rosie prattled away without stopping. She talked about dancing lessons, her girlfriends, and about her first ball gown, which she had gotten for graduation from high school. She talked about the glass display case her mother had for fragile toys, where she kept a little doll that could walk.

"Mama is so odd. She kept toys locked away in that case. There was no playing with the things in there, and we cried." By contrast she rarely spoke of her own tragic fate. People had to prod her to talk about that. She referred to the officer who seduced her as "the young gentleman" and to the aristocrat who later owned her as "the old gentleman."

Milada was curious to know what impressions the life and goings-on in Red House had made on the seventeen-year-old. But Rosie did not talk about that. "Gisi is the prettiest. She has such a lovely way with the gentlemen. But Putzi flits around like an idiot." She was afraid of Madame Miller. It was her dream to have just one man, maybe two men, all to herself. She also wanted to be rid of the widow in St. Poelten who always wanted money. And that was all Rosie had to say for herself.

"Fine," said Milada. "But what would your parents have to say about your life now?" Rosie dropped her jaw. Her response was to repeat that her mama did not have to be like that, always too strict. She put a doll in the glass cabinet, and if somebody took it out, they got a good spanking. Just think of that! Mama acted like a doll was not a toy! This was the temper of Rosie's conversation until they arrived at the hospital.

Fanny came up to them in a gray hospital gown. She was very pale and emaciated but, she said, "healthy as a horse,"

She was in a great mood, outright happy—quite unlike Milada had expected her to be from her letter. She thanked Milada for the clothes and put them up. Then she showed them, secretively and laughing, a dark-brown velvet dress with a décolleté. It was used and a bit worn. Fanny was proud to tout it as her own. Then she began complaining about the woman orderly in the hospital and about Zimmermann. Both of them had stolen from Fanny. But she did not care a whit about them, so she said. She was lucky. She was oh-so lucky! There was a whole story to tell about the dress. Olympia, who had been in business with Goldscheider when Goldscheider had Red House, was now a patient in the hospital. Fanny had gotten the dress from her. Fanny called it "quite a deal, absolutely wonderful and completely on the up and up."

"Olympia?!" Milada had to remark.

"Yes, Olympia. She's in bad shape. She's in a room in the back, can you see? Only two people are ever in there at a time. Did you know she hates me? She really hates me, and I hate her. She worked in a winery in Prater, the public park. Downstairs there is a pub and every evening they have music. Olympia played the harp, and I had to sing. We all got white dresses with white ribbons. The name of the place is Puszta's Tavern. Pretty nice, huh?"

"Olympia is that ill?"

Fanny made a sad face. "Yes, she is. She doesn't have long. That's what the doctor said. If you're in that section of the hospital, you're not going to make it. That's why she gave me the brown dress. She won't take a walk in the park ever again."

Milada got permission from the woman orderly to visit Olympia, and the orderly took her over to the section where she was.

There lay lovely Olympia in her bed, a ghost with ashen-gray, sunken features. Her hands shook, and her voice was shockingly weak and without inflection. It took a while for Olympia to recognize there was a strange, dusky presence with a shadowy face, bending over her. She looked around with great effort, then focused. Dear God, she had come from far away.

"Ollie, how are you?"

"Here, here," the ill woman clutched at her neck. "The air in Prater Park is too humid, too humid."

"You'll get better," Milada whispered, moved.

Olympia's former fashionable curls hung down, gray, from her forehead to her cheeks, wet with perspiration.

"It's in tune," Olympia whispered. "In a bit I will..." She made a motion as if playing the harp. "And Fanny will sing. Do you think she'll be as good as you?"

Milada bent down toward her.

Olympia spoke, "He didn't say much, only a little, but... but..." She shrugged her shoulders in frustration at her failing voice and wrote on a board near her bed: "Fanny very very ill. Dr. say not long."

She whispered with great effort, "He told her."

Milada asked, "Is he good to you?"

Olympia put down the board and shrugged. Then she gave a quick nod and closed her eyes. Milada took her hand.

"Ill!" Olympia whispered, and there was a chasm of suffering in this one word. A tear slipped from her eye and soaked into the coarse material of her gown.

Milada tried to be light-hearted, "You should go to Paris. It'll be better for you there."

Olympia shook her head, yet there was a faint smile on her lips.

"Say hello to everybody for me," she said under her breath. "It's been wonderful."

What images might be dancing in her brain empty of blood! Perhaps Goldscheider's salon, the black-silk dress of the barmaid, the apron for money, and music! Or maybe even moments as far back as Paris, laughing and living, ravishing parties, a spin in the park on a sunny day, dances where beautiful naked flesh was in its glory, and passionate love in her heart!

It's been wonderful! The flesh joyously making its peace with fate. All tension let go. Peace!

"Don't talk!" the orderly said harshly. "Oh well, she had to go. The doctor did say so."

Milada bent over the patient momentarily and kissed her on the forehead, then pressed a gold coin into the hand of the woman hovering in the wings.

"We are the ones who have it hard," she excused herself quickly.

When Milada returned to Fanny's ward, she heard her eagerly describing the wonders that had befallen her. The white and green ribbon she used to wear in her hair played a prominent role, as did the rosette of ribbons. And then there were the Hungarian cavaliers who came. "We called them magnates. They came in golden carriages with green feather crests." And Rosie opened her blue eyes wide in wonder. "After the show the gentlemen invited the artistes to have champagne and oysters and whatever the most expensive item on the menu was. And on Sunday real Gypsies came, dark men with eyes like coals. They were guys you could truly fall in love with." And as she was talking she glanced at herself coquettishly in the darkened mirror above the wash basin and spat into her handkerchief. Fine, light-red streaks remained around her mouth.

Fanny finished up with a promise to Rosie she would keep her in mind if a job came up at Puszta's. She said, "If he's open to it, I'll tell him about you. But personally, I would rather pose for artists. Like this, 'Longing,' or like this, 'Twilight.' 'Twilight' I do with veils. Eventually I would like to do theater."

"Having a talent like that must be wonderful," Rosie sighed, completely enraptured.

"Well, people like us don't get jobs like that very often," Fanny consoled Rosie. Fanny was delighted that she had made such an impression on Rosie. Fanny then accompanied Milada and Rosie down the hall, still chatting away and asking them questions. She greeted everybody along the way.

"Listen, Mila, there was a doctor here the day before yesterday, your doctor, Gustav. He was in our ward of the hospital. I said hello to him, and he told me I wasn't well. Do you still like him?"

A coughing fit stopped her from talking. The fragile girl swayed back and forth, unable to catch her breath. Her airways were blocked with blood from her lungs.

"You'd better get on home, man, the weather's terrible!" the orderly said as she passed them, carrying a load of cotton. "You better watch out that the skipper doesn't see you," she said to Fanny. Fanny quickly stuck her bloody handkerchief in her pocket. She nodded to Milada and Rosie to say goodbye and ran back to her room, accompanied by the warnings of the orderly. "Fanny's using up all the reserve she has," the orderly remarked to Milada and shook her head with exasperation.

"Did you see the blood?" Rosie asked with a shudder.

"People die as they live," Milada thought to herself.

"It's true, isn't it?" Rosie asked, "She hasn't got long to live." She held her hat with both hands because a storm was gathering around them. Rosie did not wait for Milada's answer. She was lost in her own thoughts.

Rosie continued, "Just when she was having such good luck! It's a shame, isn't it?"

Milada did not answer. Memories were swirling around in her soul like birds of the night flying toward a light.

Gus is here. Gus was up there in the hospital. Fanny saw him. So, did he not go to Berlin after all? She had thought that might be the case. But now she knew he was here, right here in town, where she could see him. Tomorrow, or the day after? She was sober and felt fearful and hapless. Gus might return. He would be in charge, the guest. If he asked, she would have to oblige him and take him to the room of the most beautiful girl.

The poor thing cried out in pain, "No! I can leave the house at any time, I can leave Red House Alley, leave it all. I can forget all of it. I can."

She stopped for a moment to collect herself. Rosie begged to go into a confectioner's shop, and Milada nodded consent. The shop was empty. Rosie enjoyed eating pineapple and smiled with pleasure at the waitress, who in return eyed Rosie with suspicion.

"I have to get over this," Milada thought. "I have to do something quick—quick—before I get back to Red House and maybe find Gus sitting there. He might be with Gisi or with Thea. Nobody should know about my feelings. I don't want that. I don't."

As her thoughts ran away with her she was simultaneously aware that, realistically, it was almost impossible to run into him. She had thought too much about sharing her most intimate life with him. She was not over her feelings for him. The touch of his hand, his smile, his gaze, his desire, and his attractiveness fetched her. But, she told herself, that is not what Gustav Brenner is, not what that stranger is, the actual man. What she did possess was a rich private thought world. The morning of Pentecost with its eternal promises rose up in her mind enticingly. Make her dreams come true—could she do that? How many times before had she told Horner, "I can do what I want. I'm sure I can. I know for sure my wishes will come true."

And now? Had she lost her power? Her faith? Now, when acting on her will would mean gratification for her?

"You don't want your pineapple? If you don't eat it, it'll be wasted. You can't eat it later," Rosie spoke softly while Milada sat quietly. Milada rose and went to pay while Rosie quickly ate up the plate of fruit and cream Milada had shoved over to her.

On the way back to Red House Milada held a conversation

with Rosie. They kept returning to one topic until they got back, illness and the hospital. When they walked down the carpet-covered hallway, the notion Gustav would be there hit Milada with such force that, truly, she had to clutch the banister of the stairs. She entered the salon with her face radiantly aglow. She looked so wonderful that two new guests, sitting over coffee, stared at her with curiosity and astonishment.

The thought of his presence burned in her so hotly that she went straightaway into the salon and flew through it. Gisi was sitting there with her friends and nodded to Milada.

At another table Bina was sitting by herself in a new, blue-satin dress, trimmed with lace. She had a bottle of Rhine wine on the table and toasted the men at the next table as they laughed.

When Milada wanted to go to her own room, she was still under the spell of this inexplicable fixation Gus would be there. Miller stopped her. "What, Madame, do you think of Bina? Just look at her now! She brought in fifty gulden in wine tabs from one customer alone. Right here in the middle of the afternoon! My stars!"

"Why is Bina doing this?" Milada asked.

"Well, while you were out," said Miller in a wily tone, "I went up to her room and laid that satin dress out for her. That was all. Five minutes later I looked through the keyhole, and she had the dress on and was spewing like mad, making faces, and waving her fist in the air. But now she's in a good mood. She fleeced one customer for all he had. I have various tactics to roust people to work."

Milada went back into the salon with Miller.

She knew the idea Gus would be there had been an illusion. She no longer expected to see him. The evening took over. Guests came and left. They had to see if Zimmerman had anybody available. They called in girls on the reserve list. Sweet Rosie went from arm to arm. And with the demands of the work that evening Milada forgot the hope of surprise and expectation that had held her captive earlier that afternoon. Her attention was taken up by one further event in the salon that day.

She spotted Bina. Her face was red from wind. She was standing in the middle of a circle of people who were laughing. Milada heard her excited, loud voice and registered the anger in her movements and clenched fists. The girls squealed loudly, and the men listened eagerly. It was rare to see such intimacy among them. Bina held forth, saying that people in villages could sure pull some mean tricks. And, said Bina, as you might expect, there was always a man of the cloth at the bottom of their high jinks. Milada made her way over to Bina to hear.

"And so I grabbed the bitch by the neck, like this... 'Get out of here, your low life!' And then I said, 'Go to hell.' And that was that!"

Bina tried to make an interesting tale of her own despair. She was so drunk on wine and whipped up with her own furor that her eyes were filled with blood. There, in front of these guffawing men, was Bina, the careful, wary, reserved Bina! By God, she had snapped.

"Keep your voice down. Control yourself!" Milada said as she took Bina by the arm.

"Down with Cyrill!" Bina slammed her fist on the table. "I hope he goes to hell," she shrieked in her rage.

"Bravo! You're right," the men egged her on. "Don't take that from him."

Milada only shrugged.

Miller pulled Milada aside, "So what do you think of that, m'lady? We've sold another twelve bottles of Rhine wine. My stars!"

This was how Milada's incessant work that evening went: up the stairs, down the stairs and through the poorly lit corridors, stop to listen at the door of each room, and demand money from the girls while they complained; calm them down, then run downstairs once more, fly through the salon and deposit the money from the girls with Miller; keep people in line, explain, contest something or shrug, and keep suspicions under wraps. As she was doing all this, she was also taking notes about new orders, serving in the kitchen, making sandwiches, taking care of regular customers, and bidding them farewell.

Button someone up, do up someone else's hair, put things away, keep tabs on the waitresses, make sure the girls whisk away the traces of lovemaking, and deal with the constant fear that unnerves all salon proprietors and business women, the fear that keeps them in a certain twitchy, nervous state: untimely inspections might bring certain unseemly situations or proceedings to light and stir up a scandal, the ramifications of which may well be incalculable.

At two in the morning things got out of hand.

Milada was not in the salon when Miller ran upstairs in distress and called for her manager in despair. By the time Milada had come downstairs the whole scene was in full swing.

Bina was standing half naked in the middle of the salon, holding up a chair and screaming. She was out of her mind. The men had cleared out of her way in haste and fear.

The worst part of the scene was that Miller, wringing her hands and in distress, had fallen apart in front of an official. The gentleman had shown her his credentials and was making a probing inquiry.

He wanted to know how much truth there was in what the girl had to say. Was Bina officially registered for her work with the City? He inquired whether the books for the business were in order. Had this girl been forcibly detained? He asked since it was clear to him she was not here by her own free will. He wanted to know whether this business was licensed for both liquor and prostitution.

He asked all manner of uncomfortable questions.

Quaking and bewildered, Miller was like a criminal who had been caught in the act of a heinous crime and had to answer to a grand inquisitor.

"I knew it," she thought. "It's going to fall apart on me. It has happened, it's happened. The police, the court, the newspapers, jail—good night." Miller's fears were swirling in her mind when Milada arrived. She assessed the situation right away.

In one swift, clever move she spirited Anna, who had been borrowed from Zimmermann, and Rosie with her into the coal bin. She whisked the widow from St. Pölten, who was posing as kitchen help, into the capacious larder in the cellar. Then, while Bina ranted away with a voice raspy from wine, the chair she had lifted came crashing down on wine bottles and glasses. Milada rushed in to rescue Miller who had waved to her like someone on the verge of death. Milada addressed the official in a tone that evinced confidence as well as deference and explained the situation with Bina to him.

She offered to show, on the spot, the licenses and credentials of the girls. She produced the impeccable documents of not only Bina but also the others. They had the stamp of approval of the Commissioner. She showed the results of the last inspection of Red House and said they had the word of Mr. Theobald Sucher all papers were in order. He had, she stated, supported the terms of this salon from its inception.

Of course, Milada offered, the good madam was prepared to close the business immediately until such a time as a thorough examination of the premises had been satisfactorily concluded.

He replied he would, for the time being, dispense with an inspection. Her statements were sufficient. His concern came, he assured her, from the drunken creature who deserved to be given a citation. However, in order to show due diligence, in the course of the next few days... As he spoke, he slipped into his coat, which someone held ready for him to put on.

Milada exchanged glances with Miller and left it to her, once she had regained her composure, to offer the final formalities to the departing gentleman. With the help of the porter Milada threw a tapestry over Bina's head and dragged her out of the room.

Bina sat on the floor with her eyes rolling wildly around in her head. She was staring around the room. "Get yourself into bed!" Milada yelled at her and barricaded her in her room.

Not until the next morning was there peace in the house.

As Milada was getting ready to retire to her room, Gisi ran toward her in her nightgown. "Mila, that guy David Seidner was here last night. But his friend Joe, the tall guy, wasn't with him. Seidner says Joe's not interested in seeing girls anymore. Not a one, he said. And his other friend Doctor Gus sends his regards. He said you should go visit him!" Gisi added, "Aren't you happy?" She looked at Milada.

"Oh, don't be silly. What do I care about him?" Milada said calmly, quietly.

"Sorry," said Gisi softly and a little annoyed. "I thought you'd be excited to know."

Gisi came closer to Milada and said, "Just look here!" In her hands she held a huge golden apple with red veins. "Seidner gave it to me. Joe is a philosopher. Too bad he wasn't there. I could be sweet on Joe. If only..." Gisi shook her head, then threw her arms around Milada's neck and kissed her heavily on the mouth.

"The apple's for you," she whispered, tearful, and disappeared. Milada pressed the smooth, cool piece of fruit to her cheek and smiled. If there are strange messages, then a good one had come to her today.

Two days later, after supper, Bina went to see Milada in her room.

Milada was sitting, writing, and she did not look up. Her head was down. She did not move.

"Do you want something?" Milada asked as she looked up fleetingly.

"Yes," Bina's answer evinced her guilt. "I would like..."

"What is it then?"

Bina looked up, and her eyes moved restlessly. "Are you angry?" she asked unsure. Then she asked again, plaintively, "Are you still angry, Milada?"

Milada shook her head slowly. "Not anymore. But I am worried about you. How can you act like that?!"

Bina dodged the question. "I know what you want to say. I won't stay here. Let me go, please!"

"Do you have any money?"

"No, I don't need any. Swap me out for someone else. Send me away, far away. Here people know I'm an idiot. I am an idiot. If I stay here, I'll just think this is where I used to be, where I used to think about home, where I was happy. That makes me angry. And then I get upset with myself. But if I leave, I'll be all right. Nobody will know anything about my past. Nobody will be offended and say, 'Bitch, what a stupid bitch you are!'"

"Yes, but..."

"Here, see, I got an answer to my letter." Bina pulled out a letter and opened it. "It's in German," she added when Milada looked at her unsure.

"Jesus, Spizzari has a place for you. What a horrible idea!" Milada wore a grimace as she thought to herself Spizzari is the same old calculating, selfish person she ever was. She is unwavering and does not negotiate with anyone. She makes her own way. She does what she wants! And now she wants to force Bina into a narrow corner with no way out. It's dreadful.

In response to Milada's visible concern Bina offered, "It doesn't matter anyway."

These simple words of resignation and hopelessness grabbed Milada. She said warmly, taking Bina's smooth, fat hands in her work-worn hands, "Bina, you have done some stupid things. This time, be smart! Think before you leave us! Leaving here means going to a worse situation. Bina, do consider..."

Bina Michal stared off in the distance. "Everybody laughs about my misfortune." She extended her hand to ward off Milada's response. "I know. First..." She broke off, then completed her sentence, "I think I will choke, and then I want to scream like a wild animal."

Milada offered, "You shouldn't drink."

"I'm not usually drunk," Bina said softly. She turned beet-red in shame.

Milada had to look away to spare her. She had to remember how much beautiful humanity this young woman had had. How much, she wondered, was left to be destroyed?

Milada surveyed case after case from her memory. Each had been a tragic situation; one after another. In one single night Bina's self-respect was ruined, never to be salvaged. She heard a voice within scream for help.

Horner's contorted theories and foolhardy notions were no help at all. Milada's own wishes looked pitiful; they fluttered uselessly in the wind. From afar she heard Gustav's calm voice, "Fanny will have a bed in the clinic for tuberculosis patients. She mustn't come back to Red House. The plan is to save her."

Gustav's sparse words quashed theorizing. Horner's words were as much as colored bubbles drifting over a morass of suffering. Real help was unadorned and inconspicuous. It accorded with reality and was anchored in life. He was able to do this, Gus was. He was free. By comparison everybody else she knew was enslaved.

After a moment Milada spoke calmly, "Bina, I'd like to give you some advice. Look for work as a domestic servant. You are strong and not afraid of hard work. Put your past behind you. I'll go with you to a company that places people in service positions."

"I can't work anymore," Bina countered quickly with defiance.

"Why do you say that? You worked hard for many years growing up."

"That was with my family. I was content, and work was fun. Now I drink, laugh, scream, and put things—lots and lots of bad things—out of my head day and night. Hard work is for people who don't think. I don't know how it happened, but I can't work hard anymore. I'm always tired."

Once again Bina wore a look of indifference. She stared off into the void. She had the appearance of a dumb animal.

Milada knew what she had said was true. Bina's statements described the destruction of her life force. Her energy had been drawn out over many hours and spun into a silk cocoon; the threads bound her strength and quelled the energy of her sleeping limbs. Her fear of the world was not imaginary. She did not slink away mentally into a dark corner of life. She had used up her physical being every night in orgiastic excitement. And during the day she had lain abed, dull and half asleep. And now her body rejected refreshment and healthful activity; her body refused to heal.

You people who are privileged and free: how do you expect these depleted humans to have joy and courage? Can you honestly expect them to have strength and uplifting thoughts or wishes? Do you actually believe you can make a wounded, infected finger gently latch onto something sound? Take your entitlement and be gone!

These human beings are not responsible for their personal degeneration. It befell them and overcame them like an illness.

Your arrogance, your hatred, and your indescribably tyrannical morality have pulled them out of the soil they are rooted in. They are torn from the earth that should naturally be the source of their strength and will to live. You have sheared them of warmth, approval, and opportunity in life.

Milada knew about this entropy and said, firmly pressing Bina's hand in her own hands, raw from work, "Bina, maybe it's better for you to decide what you want by yourself. You might think this over more carefully in another setting. I'll go talk with Spizzari myself. I want to tell you one thing. If you stay or leave, don't give up on yourself! As long as you don't give up, life can't take you down. That's the absolute truth."

Spizzari's office was located in the middle of the Jewish Quarter in the tiniest of corners. A narrow door, hardly high enough to enter, opened upon a low, though rather large, chamber, blackened by smoke. It looked like both kitchen and bedroom. There amidst suitcases, baskets, and bins of clothing and laundry sat Margot, dry and mildewed. She sat with her deformed left hip in a large, brown-leather armchair. When she heard the door open, she quickly bent over her large account books. She squinted with her terribly reddened eyes at the person who had pushed her way in and sighed audibly when she recognized Milada. In response to Milada's question, she pointed silently to the back. And Milada went through the door behind the drapery out into the courtyard. There she ascended the wooden spiral staircase to the sanctum sanctorum of the company. It was the office of the older sister. Above it hung the company's sign, which read, harmlessly enough, "Sales and Distribution of Cosmetics and Parisian Specialties."

Milada knocked at the door. Once Madame Spizzari had looked through a peep hole and determined to her satisfaction what the nature of the business was, she put her large apron on a hook and opened the door.

The rather portly lady had a double chin and bright blond hair, shot through here and there with dark-white strands and combed flat. One of her eyes was sharp as a hawk's; the other, dead and unmoving under its heavy lid. This was a woman known in the most varied of circles. She was one of the most feared traffickers and sometime liaisons, a person connected in the underworld, Madame Nelly Spizzari—by marriage Mrs. Spitzer. She had been a dancer, as she was proud to say, and was the legally married wife of the wine dealer Jochele Spitzer. The burden of his other half had driven him to the mad house.

She usually sat at her large, respectable desk, strewn with newspapers and print material, surrounded by bookshelves the height of a man. The shelves ran around the periphery of the room and were draped with green fabric. Large and small packages lay about, tied-up, sealed bundles with samples, small boxes with

Oriental rarities made of wax or ebonite, secret preparations, and other specialties, as well as books and photographs with covers, picturing innocuous garden gazebos. There was all manner of materials, completely transparent; it was an indescribable arsenal of items, small items, which she sold to cognoscenti at a high price.

Spizzari had accrued a respectable fortune, "nickels and dimes," not thanks to this business of sales and distribution; nor did her wealth come from the offices of her sister Margot. She made her money from dealing in prostitution and trafficking girls in public brothels. Everything was "perfectly reliable," as she said. "Not one pound of flesh leaves here and goes over the border to Se." Her word for that disgusting place, "Se," meant to any brothel outside the Austro-Hungarian Empire.

Madame Spizzari had become a pedant in the matter of her three-pronged business. She was averse to transacting any business in this office that, according to her sensibilities, belonged elsewhere.

For that reason she gave Milada a friendly nod and pulled back one of the green draperies to reveal a brown-lacquered door, which was usually rather cleverly hidden from view. The room she conducted Milada into was entirely dark and grim. Spizzari switched on the light to reveal a small, bleak space like an antechamber with two rustic armchairs and a rather long, little table, upon which were bowls with cigars and cigarettes of various sorts together with other goods. A bottle of cognac with six glasses and a pack of cards, which probably owed its presence there to odd chance, completed the furnishings. The room apparently had no windows.

In one corner there was a thick, black valise that looked like a box. It was closed with an English lock.

Madame Spizzari gestured invitingly.

"It's nice you came and not your boss." She uttered the word "boss" with disdain. "She only talks small talk."

She was very familiar with Milada. She had watched her growth in "the business" and was always ready to praise her actions and her reliability. “Thank God you and I have no unfinished business with each other. Isn’t that right?”

“I think that’s right, Madame Spizzari. As you know Miss Michal wants a change of scene.”

“That’s really good for all of you and for her. Doesn’t it make sense?”

“Well, what kind of offers do you have for her then? I can only think, Nelly, you’re talking about Galicia.”

“Wherever did you hear that? I’m not *meshugge*. I haven’t lost my mind. Would I send someone from Goldscheider’s old business to Galicia? That would be disadvantageous. It sounds like you’ve learned Miller-tallk, my child.” Spizzari was in a good mood, put on her horn-rim glasses, and opened the mysterious, black valise with a key that dangled from her watch chain. As she was leafing through her papers and notes, holding some back with her fingers, opening letters, and lovingly smoothing out little bits of rolled-up paper, she asked in passing, “Doesn’t she owe you 530? What kind of interest do you charge, Madame Milada?”

“It’s 350, Madame Spizzari, and the interest rate is 30%, as you know. But we would rather have an exchange. We need someone new. We’re looking for fresh people for the salon in the fall, let’s say beginning in August.”

“In August the Jew Redisch in Zagreb is closed down. That’ll cost you another 25%. Prime beef isn’t cheap. Well?” she said, as she pulled out a letter. “You have to give a little in a deal! You’re such a Gypsy girl. This time of year there’s high demand.”

“Not a penny, Madame Spizzari. You know our principle. You don’t have any particular offers at the moment?”

“Do wait a minute, my child. I can’t make you a low-grade offer like Lehmann in Kosick makes in Slovakia. You can’t manage to come up with any money? Well, let’s see now. Olmuetz, Ostrau in Saxony, Znojmo or Bruenn in Slovakia, nothing there. Aussig, Aussig, where the weavers are. No, too bad, they don’t pay.” She raised her horn-rim glasses to her forehead. “Those weavers have good wares, but the girls come from home almost naked. It's an old-fashioned habit of theirs. Naturally you'll pay through the nose. It'll run you 45%.”

“Not a consideration.”

“Madame, this Michal has been in your house going on six years and she was never a beauty, *nebbish*, just my opinion.”

“Only four years, Nelly. I wasn't the one who took her on. Don't you have anything else?”

“What is not clear? I said ‘nothing.’ Aussig is not on the table. I do have...” She put her hands together above a piece of paper. “Are you interested in a good, solid deal, Madame Milada? I'll be honest with you. You're not *meshugge* and willing to spend 45% for Usti nad Labem where the wares go for 25%. I'd like to do business with you and do business with you down the line. You understand. What do you say about Budweis in Bohemia? It's with Fischer's establishment.’

“Well...”

“What do you mean ‘well’? If they want to do business with you, they'll pay double for your good Michal. You can believe me. People with money just smell different. Miller smells like an old book of psalms. But Fischer! He works with princes and counts. Do they need girls? No, they don't. They can have all the girls they want right on over to the Red Sea. They have to want to get rid of one.”

“Get rid of her, Madame Spizzari, and she's from Budweis?”

“Don't tell me my business. You know your little business, but you don't know much about what business is,” Spizzari replied in a bad mood. “I didn't select that girl for you, and she's not for trade. This girl is a unique item.” If Fischer hadn't had bad luck, this girl wouldn't see the big city. She was involved in some kind of scandal with a lieutenant. The police are done with her. Fischer's girl hasn't racked up any debts. Fischer will pay you 40%. Well? Is it a deal?”

“Have you got a photograph of this girl?”

"Yeah, I've got one." She pulled a picture out of the letter and gave it to Milada.

"Pretty good, huh? Is it a deal? Can we agree? Fischer is a gentleman. Fischer knows how to write, boy, does he! He'll be losing money with this girl. I'm telling you a scandal with an officer is a dicey situation. If Fischer gave you 30%..."

"Nelly, it's 40."

"40...30, what's the diff? If Fischer made a deal with old Miller here, he'd wretch. I'm offering you my hand to shake on it. You can charge the girl the regular fee. I'll eat the rest as my cost for making the deal."

"That would be a good deal, my dear Nelly, a good deal for you. But not for us. If the girl from Fischer owes nothing, that means she hasn't got a stitch on her back. We know how that works. Our Bina is outfitted and ready to show. Fischer needs to send this girl with a wardrobe or pay 75% cold cash. Charging the girl, Nelly, is another matter. That's money we can't count on."

"You've got a good head on your shoulders," Spizzari muttered with annoyance.

Milada went on, "Get some cash back from Fischer when he's in a hard place. I know how he is. He'll give in when it comes down to it."

"Dear soul that you are!"

"Well, Madame Spizzari, I can well understand taking on someone the police are interested in. That's not an issue for me. But working with Fischer is not easy. He's in tight with police commissioner Sucher. As I said, I'm not here to make things difficult for you. Either Fischer pays 75%, 50 to us and 25 to you, or the girl comes with a complete wardrobe. In all events, we'll keep Bina's wardrobe for the next girl that comes our way. We are within our rights, as you know. I'm sad enough to see our Bina get into the business." The old pride of Red House was alive in the young manager.

"That's really a hard bargain! We don't know if the apple has a worm in it. If you give me 12½ up front, cash, I'll deliver your wares."

"I can't do that. I'd be out of pocket. Listen, Madame Spizzari, drop the bargaining. We don't pay out cash when we don't know money's coming in." Spizzari shook her head in defeat.

"Fischer picks up the tab. He'll be the death of me, that man will. What about the money I'll be out, Madame Milada?"

"We'll cover that, of course."

"I could run my feet raw going to your place."

"We'll take care of that when you deliver her. If I have to, I'll take care of that myself. It's as secure as dealing with a bank," Milada concluded, extending her hand as she rose.

Spizzari took her hand firmly.

"I like you. You've got a good head, hard as a nut. I've always liked you. Your hands are strong. *Nebbish*, if I say so myself, your hands are used to work. Will there be anything else, Madame?"

"It's also true," Milada said casually, "you're getting your money."

"Well, not that you'll profit from this! It'll all sift out in the long run."

Spizzari stood a moment, considering, then removed her horn-rim glasses, tucked the letter from Fischer in her ample bosom, locked up the valise, and waved Milada to come over to her.

Milada could hardly believe her eyes. Immediately in response to a hidden move Spizzari made, the gray wall slid aside and revealed a white-lacquered door with a golden button. This door, too, opened, and there Milada saw the most charming, beautifully attired bathroom she had ever seen. Her work had taken her to many hotels, private residences, and spas for travelers, but the extraordinary luxury here was a unique and novel sight: a dizzying array of pink marble, sparkling crystal, and watered satin, above which hung branches and blossoms of cherries. There were a hundred lights, and each was reflected a hundred-fold. Perfume billowed in clouds. And when water flowed into the shell-shaped tub, soft music played from a hidden source.

"Jesus," said Milada.

"I see you're impressed," Spizzari replied, and even her dead eye rolled in her head with delight.

"What's this for?"

"For this, right next to it..." The satin curtain the color of water was pulled aside, and a bedroom became visible, also furnished in stylish lavishness. The guest stood awestruck.

"It's fit for the Emperor," Milada replied humbly.

"I entertain His whole *mishpocheh*, His cronies," Spizzari said in response. "So now you know what Old Spizzari does." She led the way back. "I've got twenty rooms like this, a Black man at the door, a gambling salon, and a glass conservatory," she clacked with her tongue. "My child, I looked at Nice on the French Riviera. You can make millions there. Well, Madame Milada, does pious Madame Miller have anything like this over there in Red House?"

"This is like something out of a dream," Milada said and stared at the brown shelves that hid the bright extravagance very well.

Spizzari took Milada by the hand and said seriously, "Tell me, Madame, wouldn't you be interested in selling?"

"Selling?!" Milada was a bit taken aback. She had never even taken such a possibility into consideration. Sell Miller's Red House! If other people had their hands in the business, she would be redundant, pushed out. She was not prepared for Nelly's suggestion. It came too early for the plans she had. But there it was, unsummoned and unwelcome. It felt like fate.

Milada countered this suggestion competently by saying, "Oh, if there is a decent offer. There's a lot of capital and work involved in this business."

"The capital, my child, is a small matter. And when you talk about the work involved, we'd have to say, just between us, Miller doesn't know what she's doing. In our industry, we know who runs things in Red House. Of course, we want to take certain people into account. You can think about it. It doesn't hurt to ask. The real issue is: do you want to sell?"

"Well," Milada threw out, "When it gets down to it, I have to tell you I am second in command there. But I have my own capital."

"I do know! Believe me, people in the industry are aware of you!" Spizzari called out with electricity in her voice. "Certain people have the situation around their little finger."

"Here's the situation," Milada said. "I have taken over Goldscheider's loan. And I've got a second loan, a smaller one, with Kessler, who sold Miller Red House. It is only a matter of formality that I'm not joint owner. To convince Miller of anything takes time. She doesn't trust anybody. I'd have to persuade her to sell. If you approached her today, she would name you a hugely inflated price. But if I bring it up to her when she is in distress, believing she is in some crisis and having seizures from anxiety, at a moment the future looks dark to her, and at that same time mention a standstill in the business," Milada coughed, "Then I'd be able to persuade her."

"I'm telling you, you've got a real head on your shoulders, Madame Milada!" Spizzari shouted out, enchanted. "It a pleasure working with you. Now, sure as God has given us breath!" she broke off. Milada went to the door. Both of them had had enough.

A rare honor followed that only the initiated can appreciate. Nelly accompanied her guest to the stairway, bowed, and called after Milada, "Watch you don't trip, my child!" Then Milada was left standing in the street. She knew instinctively and with a certain gratification that, for the first time in her life, she had transacted business well and entirely on her own—consciously and toward some favorable outcome. She was also aware the dangerous, heady wrangling about costs had only begun. Real things would change. This was no juggling act with phantoms. No, this was a slow move forward; it involved thinking over hard facts. Now she was looking at taking the risk. It would be victory or defeat! In the midst of her revolving thoughts, she felt a rush. She experienced a sense of free will about her future.

The thought struck her on her way that this would be the moment to visit Gustav Brenner. She had tried writing to him countless times and had destroyed letters she had begun without a real reason. She had destroyed them as the result of an unconscious fear rationality would set in the moment she actually met him again. She stopped in her tracks. She was almost shocked at the enormity of the idea. It filled her with joy.

Visit him! Why not, then? She had time to take the road over the banks of the river. "I just have to tell myself this visit is nothing unusual," she thought. He had invited her in his letter. And he had sent her his greetings with his friend David Seidner. If she put aside all romantic flights of fancy, she could see there was nothing really to worry about. She picked up the tempo of her steps on her way and quelled her feverish protests with deliberate reasoning. The embankment was ahead of her. The dirty waves of the river rushed past her. Children of workers dipped their feet in the flow. There were soldiers with their girlfriends strolling along the gravel path. The sun poured forth its gold on the roofs and windows of the houses along the embankment. Milada had arrived at her destination. The blind windows of the warehouse, black from age, were covered with screens. They looked unfriendly. A sign, worn by weather, announced, "David Brenner, Warehouse, Wholesale Iron, Steel and Wire." Heaps of iron plates, iron bars, wheels, chains and nets lay about the street in layers. Directly in front of the entry was a huge mound of trash, rusty nails, shavings, bent-up metal sheets, and sharp, shiny strips of tin. Two older boys were kneeling in front of this mound, pulling usable pieces out of the shavings and discarded metal. Milada stood there undecided for a while, just watching the boys. Then a wagon, loaded with sheets of iron, rattled through the entrance, pushing her aside. The driver yelled at the straining horse, and he lashed it to drive it forward.

Milada pushed her way inside the gate, accompanied by the children's stares of curiosity. She made her way through a square, dark courtyard, filled with crates, barrels, and carts.

"That's as far as you can go," a man working there instructed her. "The old man is in the front."

"And the young man, the doctor?"

"Him? You'll find him over in the new building."

She went back through the yard and quickly opened a door at the front by the gate. There was a chime. An older man of large, slim build and with a small, close-cropped, white moustache stepped out in front of the upholstered door of the office.

"Who are you looking for?"

"Mr. Brenner."

"Senior or Junior?"

"The doctor," she explained strategically.

He narrowed his eyes. "It's your dubious pleasure to make the acquaintance of Brenner, Senior. The doctor, my good lady, lives on the next level, the next door to your right. My pleasure."

Taken aback she climbed the winding metal stairs, which were scrubbed clean. Had that been an employee? Or could it have been...? No, it could not have been. There was no resemblance. The thought made her a bit calmer. She found Gus's calling card on a white-lacquered door, the first door that looked inviting to her. All of a sudden she was clear-headed and calm. She took stock of her situation and put together what she would say, her first words. She even planned out what to say when she left. When she rang the bell, she did not feel so much as a twinge of anxiety. Her voice resounded loudly throughout the house. She listened, then tried again. There was not a sound. Nothing. At this moment the stress of the last hour overwhelmed her, and she began to shiver in this strange house. A sob she had squelched for a long time rose up in her throat. Her wish to see him again must have been burning inside her. Her longing was uncontrollable. Every protest, each logical reason, the whole process of considering back and forth—all of it had been lies. All she wanted was to see him. She felt she had to see him. All that was real was her desire. And here she was, standing in front of a locked door.

She was rudely awakened out of all her dreaming by the simple fact this student was not home on a lovely day in spring. She looked through the glass scope in the door, as if somehow it would open the door for her. She knocked loudly, although she must have known it was in vain. "Well, no luck," she thought with resignation. "I can't expect anything more from him. It's over."

Yet she followed her impulse and wrote her name on the board by the door, then the words "was here."

Setting aside all clarity about the way she had acted, she left the building as unobtrusively as possible.

Gustav Brenner strolled homeward, taking his time, on this mild spring evening. He had bought himself supper on the way and had decided to spend his evening studying in his apartment. In fact he was upset when Joe turned down his offer to study together. Seidner just gave an all-knowing smile and shook his head.

"How ridiculous," thought Gus. "Seidner makes you think the only thing there is to do is hang out in the cafés or go visit girls. He acts like that's all there is." That was Seidner. Springtime was not good for him. He was forever wandering the streets like a cat looking for a kitty. Just disgusting. Gustav, for his part, could not get past his bourgeois upbringing, and that was not such a bad thing. He had his "patrician forebearers" to thank for this. All right, let Joe laugh at him. He was independent, yet the world of expectations of his family hung over him. And, God help him, however he wiggled and squirmed, his origins did place obligations on him.

Joe Wallner was completely unhampered, that was for sure. He had had enough with expectations. He wanted no fetters on his being. And that was fine, too. He had no ambition—of any sort. He was an "either-way" kind of guy, as he said of himself. He had no great wants.

And then there was David Seidner, his other pal! Dear God, he—Gus was certainly not prejudiced—Seidner was, after all, only a Jew. He was "temperamental due to a well-established practice of monetary exchange." Seidner always had to be right. He was an achiever and a climber, someone who plays around in the social register. He was from Hungary, had a trust fund, wrote journalism, and chummied it up with extravagant people. He already had a reputation in the big city. He was a guy who wanted to have it all. And, most likely, he was gifted at just about everything.

And then there was Gus. Without exaggeration he could say his patrician rearing truly had no room for debauchery of any kind. His breeding disposed him to calmness and to the straight and narrow. There was a touch of the Philistine in that. His Great-Uncle Benno—on his mother's side, naturally—had been an elected member of Parliament and a Philistine at that. He was proud to have the descriptor "Philistine" added to the bottom of his portrait.

It was easy for his friends to make light of these people in his family, advisors in the Emperor's court, counselors in the government, and presidents. He knew these relatives and their weaknesses and oddities; he did not shuffle over them. They were also fine, upright people who did not deviate one iota from the straight and narrow. They were decent.

And that did mean something. Of course, there would always be something to make fun of. Here was what was essential: that he remain true to the stuff he was born with. He was, after all, Gustav. And he possessed a strength that was awesome when one took the family's earnest interest into account. Yes siree, and he was going to devote the day to his studies!

As he reached the stairwell of his house he was in a good mood, and he raised his walking stick with the white handle. He hummed the university's rousing commercium song that he sang with his buddies, "Gaudeamus igitur"!

He stood gobsmacked at his door. "Milada was here"—astonishing! But she had left, Milada, the manager at Red House! Yes, but how could that be?

It had slipped his mind that in his letter to her he had almost pled with her to come. He had also forgotten that the last time Seidner had said he planned to go to Red House, he had said, half in jest and with a swagger, "Give Milada my regards." Seidner had asked him then whether he intended to see her again. These acts dissolved in his mind at the moment he was overcome with embarrassment and vexation. He took the eraser and wiped her name and her message off the board.

He found it indecent and shocking she had come by on the spur. He called it an "ambush."

In the final analysis she was not his set. He had understood that at the time and had broken off socializing with her for that reason. How inappropriate for her to come crashing into his sphere unannounced!

He had brought his supper along in a package. He opened it, poured himself a glass of fine, golden wine, lit a cigarette, opened the top portion of his window, and pushed his desk chair up to the desk to study.

"Milada was here." Splendid. Gustav's father must have stood watch as he always did. He had taken note of the strange feather hat and the imitation diamonds and immediately sniffed something wild. He knew a thing or two about such matters. At his next encounter with his father Gustav could count on the obligatory glances, manner of speaking, and the probing jabs. The patriarch would mobilize his repertoire of tactics to keep his son in line.

"Milada was here." She had taken liberties. The persistence of this woman. No, he could not say this attribute fit her. But this manager of a brothel did have something unusual about her. There was nothing sleazy about her. Joe picked up on that right away. He had said she had the eyes of a Sphinx who dreams of wondrous things. To be fair, there was something to what Joe said, quite a lot.

He leaned back, inhaled the smoke of his cigarette, and tried to recall her face. But all that emerged was an image of her large, gray eyes. This image afforded a bridge to his memories. Words she had spoken came to mind; they were like a secret script that becomes legible when heated.

"I need some good offices to live," and "We need help here, such a lot of help." Once again he was gripped by her mysteriousness. It surrounded her like a mandorla.

Was it romance, and he had misunderstood? Some crazy fantasy? What was it about her? God only knows. In his thoughts she assumed the typical longing for deliverance from her station and salvation. Then he imagined she was clinging to him. "That's what you get from these damned ideas of the Social Democrats," Gus swore. "They can make you crazy. They'll make you do crazy things." Milada did look like an anarchist, a revolutionary. Was she like the gray-eyed assassin Charlotte Corday? No, more like the militant anarchist Louise Michel. Happy to have come upon this comparison, he let himself dream off.

There was an old lithograph of this famous militant in his mother's possession. When he was a child he was drawn to Michel's deep eyes, which avoided the camera and looked very far off into the distance. Her lips had an imperious set that attracted him. They beckoned him.

"Gus, love only what is happy!" That was the advice his mother often gave him. How was it possible to affect the dark disposition of his soul? How could she guide him, when his soul always gravitated sharply—though in secret—to the dusky, deep, and recondite?

Could he be satisfied playing with his little cousins Franzi, Betty, and Loni? He had enough of eating nice tidbits, reading together in circles, and going to plays. His friend Joe was not the one who made these activities look miserable and empty. It was Gus's own disposition that caused him to rebel against the surfeit of rosiness and sweetness of his upbringing. He was interested in metal, especially in stainless steel. It had the sound of reality about it.

Then he recalled the feelings he had about his activities at Red House back then. They were unquestionably ethical and untouchable. None of his friends was as selfless, unambitious, or free of ulterior motives as he was. No one had approached his disinterest in gratification. Joe was far from it. What Joe did he did only impulsively. Joe admitted as much. He said he acted out of disdain for humanity. He, Gus, by contrast, was moved by good conscience and rationality.

He did want to help Fanny. He wanted to bring a bit of light and life into her prison.

He sat with his head resting on his arms and let his thoughts ramble well into the evening. He loosened his collar and closed his eyes. The mystery came ever closer. It leaned down over him and kissed the eyes of the young man. He opened his eyes wide. They were hot and drunk with desire.

This girl! There was something strong, free, and elemental about her. Joe had recognized it. He had said at the time a man needs to protect himself from girls like that. Gus rumpled his brow. He had heard this tune from the time he was a boy. This lullaby had permeated his whole life: Protect yourself! Protect yourself, be cautious, and never jump into anything.

He heard his mother's voice, "Don't get hurt! Don't hurt yourself! Don't let anything get too close! Be cheerful!" As long as she was alive, she guarded him like a rare jewel. He was her only child, and all the love in her lonely heart was for him. He loved her, too. Certainly. He had loved her insanely. His childhood had been wrapped up in this attachment. He had not been allowed to cross the street by himself or go to the country with friends from school.

He had often sat in front of chocolate and cakes and quietly swallowed his tears, longing to build snowmen with the kids in front of his window, to play football or go canoeing. "My sweet boy, that's dangerous. Take care of yourself!" And he clung to Mother's skirt and let himself be comforted.

Then Mother died. Then there were three people in her place. There was Grandmother with her thousand old-lady fears and her shaking, ivory hands, which she used to make the sign of the cross on his brow and chest. Then there was his Auntie, wife of the Counselor, who promised him a very high position with the State if he remained worthy. This aunt brandished the model of his dear departed Uncle Benno in front of him like a switch. Lastly there was the Old Man, his father, who tracked his every move like a spy.

Gus felt his father perpetually breathing down his neck. He could not figure out how this came to be, but he did know his father spied on him, knew everything he did, and took note of it all. He stationed himself at the back of Gus's neck and kept vigil.

"Crawl around wherever you want to. I know what you're doing, just like God."

Father probably listened at his door and opened his mail. Gus cursed the net of protection Father had cast over him.

Was he not a grown man? Could he not do as he so wished? Auntie Counselor would faint dead away if she knew a girl from that house had come to see him.

"Order is good fortune," Uncle Benno used to say. And order had described the bounds of Gus's experience—up until this moment. Now he had to break free. He had to free himself of them emotionally.

Flirtation and marriage were Grandmother's concern. It hovered over him constantly. Nonsense! He wanted to live for himself and finally have a life with other people. He wanted to live as they did. He wanted to be Gus Brenner and a man of the world. He imagined himself a cavalier! He was timid, fearful inside, and trapped. His grandmother had made him that way. It was the fruit of her child-rearing.

Had he ever had the courage to get close to a woman?

"Make sure to protect yourself from Jewesses! Keep seamstresses out of your way. A servant is the most rotten of creatures," and so on. Those messages were supposed to shield him from attachments.

If he ever fell in the clutches of a girl from one of those categories, she would certainly get her just rewards. He had never really heard that warning in exactly those words. Filled with thoughts of propriety their brains did not allow them to articulate the consequences.

How Gus envied Joe! His manner was free and confident. Just look at what all Joe had experienced! And look at how he came across! His experience gave him the playful superiority he had on his side and his certain light undertone of disdain. His attitude said, "Just let them." Gus jumped up and paced around the room, taking large steps.

He had had enough of his family's program. He wanted to live fully, doing as he pleased. And he wanted to do it without worrying about his aunt's position or Uncle Benno's good name. Let the lineage of ancestors go to hell! In all events he would never become a judge or care about what the minister of transport had to say.

Gus wanted to show them he was capable of taking something on and carrying through without their gossip or judgement.

He sat back down at his desk and pulled out a sheet of paper. How should he begin? "Dear Madame"—not good. "Dear Love"—no, not that. Those were too mannered. The best opening was simply, "Milada! Would you like to visit on Monday afternoon? I would not ask you to be here alone with me."

He shook his head. That sounded ironic. He wanted something different. He took out another sheet of paper and wrote lively and off the top:

> Milada, would you like to come again next Monday? We shouldn't let the unfortunate coincidence we missed each other this time deter our relationship. Don't you agree? I would be delighted to see you after this long time apart. Au revoir!
>
> Gus Brenner

That sounded the best. And then he was off directly to the post office! Otherwise, the maid would put it with the business letters, and it would fall into his father's web. Excited with all these thoughts and pleased with himself like never before, he put his hat on top of his rumpled blond hair and left the house.

And this letter arrived at Red House. Milada, like every girl in love, put it under her pillow, and during the day she carried it hidden in her black purse, tied tightly around her waist. When she knew nobody was looking, she pulled it out with the tips of her fingers and looked at the small, quickly executed letters of her name with rapt amazement. Life was coming her way, offering her its hand. See him again! Hear his voice! Call him by name! It seemed luck was limitless.

Mr. Teobald Sucher, Police Agent, detective and right-hand man of the Municipal Chief, sat in Division II of the Imperial Board of Directors. He was fuming.

This large man with his beard, trimmed in the going fashion and still coal black, had his reasons for being unhappy with the way things were going in his world. In his twenty years heading the "Canal," as Division II was called in the office, nothing like this had ever happened.

We should mention Sucher had a sensitive nose!

"A smuggler!" said Treulich, Commissioner First Class, an incompetent nitwit in the Division. There was a memorandum from his boss the Municipal Chief that he, Sucher, was, in future, to move in more restricted circles. If he did otherwise and disregarded this order, he would be assigned to internal affairs.

How sweet! Out of the blue! Sucher's means and interests were severed from those of his boss. Too very sweet!

The Municipal Chief—as everyone in the world knew—supported the business of brothels, the quartering of soldiers, and by-the-numbers regulations. As a friend of bourgeois order he understood regulations were on the books for a purpose. People in the right circles never turned to him in vain when they were interested in navigating the legal paragraphs on prostitution without penalty.

And he, Mr. Sucher, his so-called right-hand man, shared the Municipal Chief's understanding of the law. Sucher was the Chief's disciple. He was the one who delivered. He was, as long as he could remember, never opposed to the principles or wishes of his boss. Quite the contrary. Sucher had always practiced what the Chief preached and promoted him where possible. He was the one who, day by day, had willingly dished out orders for both Commissioners in Division II. This work never troubled him. And today he had gotten a rebuke, clearly a snub, that was in effect throughout the district. But why? Why??

It must have been because of that person of ill repute, Gerson. He had rescued her from the clutches of a midwife. He was, in effect, her benefactor. Sucher had, in fact, set her up like a princess with a man by the name of Jonasch. Sucher had paid for her to have her own room. Did a girl ever have it so good with Amschel or Klepper? It could only be because Sucher vouched for this girl Gerson that he had been sent this memorandum.

Sucher had a significant position in the Division, and he acted as privy councilor. He kept the books and was responsible for audits. Who might have been behind the memo from the Chief? Who was a player here? There was Commissioner First Class Treulich, a reprobate. And there was the other Commissioner, Baron Landskron. Were they concerned about what he did? Treulich was alcoholic and lazy and only had time for rolling cigarettes and pinching wenches.

Landskron, known as "Our Baron," wore a moustache trainer in the office and smelled of perfumes like a ballerina. You did not bring a prostitute into the office when the Baron was there. He ran those poor women out the door with curses. He told the Chief to his face he had to vomit and had spells when he was assigned to audits. So who was the man behind the memo?

Who was the head of Division II? Was it the Municipal Councilor himself? He was the man who held one hand up in the air and had the other down below. That is to say he was the middleman between orders from the top and the duties at the lowest level. Or was it Treulich who found the breakfast menu of the Blue Star more interesting than all matters of the Division put together? It had been none of these. Sucher had brought this insult on himself.

Wherever there was something going on—be that with the police, in the brothels, or in the hospital—wherever help was needed, Sucher was on call. Sucher arrived on the spot and dragged information out of the prostitutes. He never made a scene, and he never wasted time talking. If you were not compliant, in a jiffy you either got your name on the police watch list or spent time in the clink. And now this meritorious official had been dressed down. He had gotten this comeuppance on account of one idiotic dame. This meritorious official became sick and tired to death of his work. So there we are, let us see what transpires.

He tossed the newspaper extra on his desk and immersed himself in reading about the sensations in town.

He let Miladda stand there in front of his desk a good long while. She was there at the Police Bureau to take care of the registation of the new girl from Fischer. Sucher knew very well who she was, but he made her wait. He had been given a rough time, so he wanted to give someone else a rough time.

He growled while he looked askance at the papers Milada presented. "That doesn't matter to me. Those are issues for

Commissioner Dr. Treulich. It's not my job to look over the register of clients. It's all one and the same to me."

"Mr. Sucher, you know very well we have always squared things with you," Milada said insistently and pushed several documents over to him. A silver coin rolled across the table and into his hand. "It'll be taken care of soon. The new girl will arrive in a week."

He deposited the money in the pocket of his vest and shoved the papers aside. "That doesn't work anymore. If the girl doesn't show up at the station in person, she won't be registered."

"I'll bring her to you myself, Mr. Sucher."

"Does she have all her credentials in order? Where's she coming from?" asked Sucher and, once again, looked critically at the papers Milada had produced.

"From Bohemia, Budweis," Milada said with confidence.

Sucher looked up at her and made a point of winking to show he knew the score.

"Are you saying Fischer is giving you someone?" he asked derisively. "That has to be real nice wares."

"She worked for him as a waitress."

"That's not possible," Sucher snapped coarsely and shoved the papers back over to Milada. "She won't get a passbook. Not from me. You'll have to go to the Municipal Councilor for that."

"But Mr. Sucher..."

"That won't happen," he hollered once again. "Go take your case to the Councilor and see if he has time for it. Just like he said, no whore can leave his office without his stamp of approval. For my part, I don't give a damn," he spoke with venom. "The way the wind is blowing in the District now girls like that are thrown right out. I'm not allowed to issue any more of those little registration books."

"All right, Mr. Sucher. But you don't need to make things difficult for me. We will do our best for this to work out. You know how things go in our industry. I want to clear things up before she starts here."

"Yeah, that's how people think it goes. Sucher can make it all happen. He's as helpful as God. But I'm just some dumb guy who does things for them. The boss man over there in the Division will grab me by the balls! Treulich is a dope, and the Baron is a darling, and I'm the guy who takes the hit. The man who never takes the hit is the Councilor, His Grace. He gets the rewards, and I get the shaft. It doesn't help my state of mind. I tell you, this gal Gerson better not come my way ever again."

"Do you have something against her?" Milada asked agreeably.

"She's a lousy bitch and acts like she's a saint. The whole thing started when she was fourteen. Streber, who works for Thomas, took the girl to Dr. Lamberg for an examination. But Lamberg threw her out, saying the dumb little thing was a virgin. One hour later Streber brings her back to Lamberg and says her problem has been fixed. So she gets a registration book and works with Thomas who says she does abortions. Thomas makes good money. One year later the girl is in a bad way, half dead from an abortion. And what does she do? She throws away her registration book and says she doesn't want to work anymore. She says she'll never do it again.

What can anybody do with her then? They said just let her go. Is that right, I ask you? You have to have a heart. Why did I have to get involved in this? I kept Rosa Gerson at my house, treated her like a daughter. She couldn't do the work of a maid. So I asked my girlfriend Carlotta, 'What can we do with her? A masseuse maybe?' All right, so I took her to Jonasch over on Prince Street and paid for a room for her. 'I'll pick up Rosa's tab,' I told Jonasch.

"We put out an ad for her to do work, nice work. Jonasch is a good guy, but he has to make a living, too. Rosa needs decent food and clothes. I ask you now, can I send a good kid like that to a brothel if she doesn't want to go? I couldn't make her go even when the Chief told me to send her. I'm well aware of the legal statutes.

"Of course, the police wouldn't have made a profit," Milada thought to herself.

"You have to understand her upkeep costs money, and after a while Jonasch had some claim to payment. So far the story's all right.

"Then some damn busybody who wants to uphold the letter of the law comes on the scene, a Jew, wouldn't you know, a real slouch. He makes a big stink about how Jonasch is exploiting the girl. Jonasch tells him she's not a licensed prostitute, and she doesn't want to do that. The Jew said he'd go to the newspapers and bring in a lawyer. He made all kinds of threats. And stupid Jonasch gave him my name! My name!

"And when that Jew heard my name, he started raising Cain! Of course, he liked it that I was a police agent, a confidant of the Chief. He started a real smear campaign. In a flash he was upstairs in the Ministers' office making a big fuss. I don't know what all he said. He just kept complaining till everyone in town knew about the filthy mess.

"Madame, the words he used are 'filthy mess.' And our Mr. Councilor—you can say what you want about him, he does have some things to his credit—knew just what to do in such instances. He told this man—even though he's a Jew—he would clear the matter up. Know what he told this guy?

"'Yes,' says the Councilor, 'This girl will leave Jonasch when somebody pays off her debts. But then, on the double, she'll have to go to a brothel because she did dishonorable business with her body.' The Councilor told the Jew he had proof. He offered the Jew an option. Either she goes to a brothel or the Jew marries her. 'Those options would be about the same, ha-ha. That's how the law is written,' the Councilor said. Madame, you can just imagine how this Israelite let loose. 'So what does that mean?' the Jew wanted to know. The Councilor explained she has no employment and no place of residence. Since she is not a registered prostitute, the police were keeping tabs on her for illegal solicitation.

According to the law a girl has to be a legally married woman, in good employ, or a registered prostitute. Once she's officially one of these, she can do what she wants. That's the whole story," Sucher announced. "Once you get mixed up in these situations, you have to live with the consequences," he said.

"So now what?"

"Nothing. The Jew's probably off to buy a bridal wreath," Sucher sneered.

The door opened, and Commissioner Dr. Treulich, under whose jurisdiction this case fell, walked in the room, carrying a bundle of files under his arm. Milada knew him.

People called him, for short, Commissioner Fats. He personally oversaw the books with Sucher. Because of the nature of his work he was an especially careful man and quite pleasant.

Today, though, he looked irked. He had just come from making a presentation to the council members. They had wanted to have all outstanding debts from the fiscal year finished out. This damned situation with Rosa Gerson, whom he called "the masseuse," had come up. It had been written up in the paper, and now it had come down under his finicky jurisdiction.

"So what do you want?" he was short with Milada.

"A new prostitute has to be registered, Sir. I'm from Goldscheider's, Sir. All the paperwork is in order."

"Don't bring your people into my office," Treulich said curtly and slammed the door closed.

Sucher bowed and scraped, "Yes, Sir, Doctor Commissioner, Sir!" Treulich admonished him, "You should leave before the Chief arrives. Today the ministers are not kindly disposed."

Milada wanted to say something. But Sucher took hold of her shoulders and shuffled her out the door. He closed the door of the Police Bureau solidly behind her. His treatment was crude. Sucher was unpleasant.

In the fall he routinely came by Red House to see her with

offers for new girls. On those visits Sucher was cordial enough. Now he was acting like a complete ass!

But Milada was unshaken by Sucher's behavior. She was now a free agent. Gustav was somewhere waiting for her. She walked in the open air of the summer and made an effort to put the recent, ugly experience at the police department out of her mind. What had just happened hung like a dark veil over the rosy sunshine of the day. The scene kept coming back to her. The feeling of joy that had buoyed her up all week long, the feeling she wanted to hang onto, just would not return. "These thoughts are stupid!" she thought with sadness. "I could have lived without this ugly event the very day I am going to visit Gus! Why does everything have to be spoiled?" Usually, she was able to brush off crudeness and disrespect from city officials as long as things worked out for her. But this time she had been soft and vulnerable. The thousands of sweet emotions that had recently welled up in her had made her sensitive and undermined her defenses. She had wanted to be kind to people today and keep herself free of upsetting thoughts.

Why had this idiot Sucher been able to treat her so shabbily and dispose of her summarily? Did he have the right to do this only because he cared to? Had she no rights? Not even the right to protect her own happiness? Could just anybody come along and rough up her soul and trounce on her special day?

She felt rage course through her body. Her hands were balled into fists. She picked up her pace. Why did she keep getting into these situations? Again and again? Why had she not grabbed Sucher by the lapels and shaken him, this idiot? Why had she not shaken the coward till he whined for mercy?

Her furor surged through her like an electric current. It passed. She almost felt cleansed.

She had gone to the Police Bureau to transact necessary business. It was a legal formality. Yet they had treated her like a criminal or a mongrel they had, out of mercy, not sent to the pound. And she was supposed to lick their hand in gratitude. She was supposed to lick the hand of the asshole who gives every prostitute and pimp a hard time. Sucher was worse than the nastiest madam of any brothel. And then there was that other man, Commissioner Fats, who oversaw the account books. He made the girls march in front of him naked while he was liquored up with champagne and cognac. Although the summer breeze was warm, she felt chilled. At the moment she was smarting from oppression like a whipped dog, she could not be touched by love. In that condition she could not feel fortunate or dream her private dreams. One man had thrown her out the door like a bundle of trash. Another would receive her with open arms and would be happy to see her.

Poor dear Gustav! He had no idea about all this. For him a prostitute was a woman who gives. He knew prostitutes only in the context of the salon where they were laughing, young, and lovely. He had no clue about their deepest suffering and their ignominy. He knew nothing of the whole tortuous tragedy of their humanity. She dwelt on the facts Sucher felt he had every right to throw her out and Treulich showed her less dignity than a rotten cur. She remembered how Sucher had looked at her like a downtrodden serf. Once she had given him a few pieces of silver, she was an object to him. He saw her as nothing and had no qualms about taking advantage of her. At that moment she was mortified about visiting Gus.

She foresaw a string of lamentable, empty hours that dragged on. Time would become flat and mundane. She felt the fever of his expectation, and she imagined her inability to offer him anything in return. She also imagined the sobriety that, like gray, winter skies, would occlude his desire. Doubt pelted her like the sands of a desert. It battered her and buried her.

Milada struggled to escape these thoughts and to get beyond them. She wanted to understand what had closed in upon her. She listened eagerly to the conversation of two schoolgirls with their arms around each other's shoulders as they chatted away.

Finally she arrived at the entrance to the Brenners' house. There she heard the clatter of sheets of iron being thrown into the back of a wagon. The noise drowned out the sound of her own footsteps. She turned her head and saw an old man standing in the courtyard. But he was looking at something else and did not look around. She entered the new wing unnoticed. Inside the spiral staircase was dimly lit and smelled of moisture and fresh mortar. Gustav's voice fell like a bright light over the banister. She stood stock still.

"Hi, Milada! Come on up the steps! I've already made myself comfortable."

"Hi there, Doctor!" she replied. The sound of her own voice almost surprised her. It was the first time in her life she heard her own voice. She thought it sounded raw, unpleasant, and forced.

"How will it be to see him again?" she thought in fear. "I can't be doing this." He offered her his hand. She took hold of it eagerly. How warm and strong his hand was!

"Welcome!" he said excitedly and motioned her to enter ahead of himself.

"You might have lit a candle," she commented and tried to orient herself in the dark room.

He took her umbrella and put it in a corner. "Why do I need light? I know my way around here, and my friends should get to know it, too. It's pleasant. Isn't it, Madame ?"

He opened the door, and red light streamed into the room. She saw the shimmering river through the wide window hung with muslin curtains. The river was broad and flowed sleepily. In the distance she saw the green hills of summer rise up. And above it all was the sun, regal in its purple robe as it took leave of this Earth. Red streaks like tears shot through the whole of it.

"How beautiful!"

"Isn't it? If I had lit a candle, the effect would have been lost. You have to step out of the darkness to appreciate the light. Take off you wraps!"

She took off her hat and jacket and adjusted the hairpins in her thick, brown hair

He took her things and put them in the next room, came up behind her and embraced her lightly. "A mirror?"

"No thank you."

He walked across the room and whistled. They did not speak for a moment. "Everything here is very luxurious," she said as she surveyed the table, set with a white cloth, fine foods on a platter, a basket of fruit, and three bottles of wine.

"I was expecting company," was his ready reply.

She had never looked directly at his face. Ever so slowly and gingerly she took in the pleasure of his presence. She was there with him and heard his voice. His being enveloped her like a sweet, never-ending caress.

"Tell me, Madame," he started speaking, unsure, and became brusque in his insecurity, "Weren't you surprised I wrote you?"

"I thought you wanted to see me again," she answered softly, surprised by the gentle tone her voice had. She lifted her misty gray eyes to look at him tenderly. Sparks flashed in her eyes. .

"How young he is! How beautiful and how young!" Her eyes sang.

"Madame Milada!" He came close to her. "I want to tell you—I hate talking in vagaries, as you probably know—you, Madame, fascinate me. I am taken... I take you to be a true lady, regardless. But I hate where you live. And I despise the people there."

"I'm not bound to live there," Milada replied very pointedly. "I'm free to go at any moment. I don't have to run away. I can simply leave."

"So then leave! Why would you stay there? Whatever ill fate, uncertainty, or deceit—I don't know what it might be—brought you to that place, don't think you deserve to stay. Don't you see how these circumstances degrade you?"

"It's not about what I deserve, Sir. I stay because I love the people. These sick, damaged, disturbed people are family to me. They are the family I belong to."

"I thought you might say that," he spoke with bitterness. "It's some kind of mistaken notion of humanitarianism that makes you say that, some drippy sentimentality! I'm sure of this, Madame." He slammed his hand on his chest. "These prostitutes do not deserve sympathy. You don't have to sacrifice yourself for them. Their lifestyle comes from wantonness, shamelessness, and a need for theater."

"You're talking about those prostitutes you have seen on the streets, the women who put on thick makeup. They are the hungry women who approach you in the night and reach for your trousers. You mean the women who'd do anything for your money. Those creatures have waded through a river of suffering and have been washed up on the banks. That is how piteously people act at the end when they want to survive." Milada heaved a deep sigh. "They are as you describe them. But, Mr. Brenner, I see how they started out. I watch them struggle wildly, resisting. They are desperate. I see them around me as they waltz across the glittering dance floor. They float and then stumble, pick themselves up, look ahead with horror, and slide backwards hopelessly. I see them arrive one day at the terrifying moment when they are stopped short. They raise their arms, pleading, and finally sink, slowly, slowly, inexorably, watching Death grin at them. I watch them exhaust all means until they are as you, Sir, describe them." She continued undeterred, "When these girls start in this business, they are innocent and sweet. They laugh. They laugh at everything. They make the life of people like you, Sir, lighter and gay. When they're young, people don't despise them. These girls are not aware of hatred and scorn. They have no thought of the reality: they are deceived, and they are bound to suffer. They have no inkling they will be exploited, abandoned, and left to do anything to survive. And they get to this point because of you, Gustav, and all the others and your desire. When a man has had enough of her, he leaves. And after the first lover who begged for her, comes the second and the third. For men this woman is no longer the lovely muse who offers love but rather the desperate old woman who begs. As the result of having been desirable and sexual, she is now, for the rest of her existence, the whore."

His brow was furrowed. "And does all this also count for those who are born with a frivolous nature? What do men fantasize about naturally frivolous girls? What about those girls who chose to indulge themselves rather than do decent work? You can't convince me, Madame, that those girls who want out have no way of getting out. That's just ridiculous!"

"My dear Mr. Brenner, it's a gruesome injustice that those girls who are naturally frivolous," she halted a moment, "—and there are some of those—are channeled into a life of such suffering. Their ruin is unstoppable. People who are strong and secure mercilessly exploit those who are weak and confused."

"That strikes me as a convenient view of the situation," he said haughtily.

"I came to this view after long, bitter consideration and after years of experience, my own knowledge of the facts." Her worry and distress caused her to avert her eyes. She was looking for the right words. "There are people who are born with a thirst for blood and predation. They would commit murder without thinking. They would murder for enjoyment if their dark, dangerous impulses were not checked by iron-clad laws. 'Thou shalt not kill' is the hallmark of religions. The mad house or the gallows are the devices that keep people in line. Humans learn to control themselves. The mark of a good law is it will become unnecessary. But show me, Sir, the law that proscribes harm in the realm of sex. Show me one single, solitary piece of law that is upheld against the practice of sexual harm. If there is one, it is countermanded by another that makes doing harm permissible and, by people's standards of belief, acceptable. On this legally ambiguous ground people have erected the guillotine of morality. They are ready to execute the victims of sexual predation for the assurance of their propriety.

"Please, have no illusion I came up with these ideas on my own! I'm not so smart as to think this all through myself. I take a lot from my reading. Most of the books came from my teacher, Horner."

The young man was unchanged. He resisted. "Those are the poorly digested ideas of socialism," he declaimed in anger. "What you're saying is nothing new. There's nothing convincing in any of it. Horner—what can I say about him?—he always did enjoy sloshing around in pity. You certainly can't deny what we see over and over again: There are scores of young girls, living in relatively good circumstances, who follow their desires and get involved with a man to satisfy themselves. They get into prostitution because they're oversexed. They willingly throw away all social mores. They do this because prostitution is comfortable and offers them a life of luxury not possible in the context of middle-class domesticity. The interest in prostitution is inborn, I'm telling you. It doesn't come from society. A whore has no natural maternal feelings. She doesn't want a child. She hates children. A genuine woman is first and foremost a mother." He sat down and proceeded triumphantly. "We have cloisters, facilities, houses for unmarried women, the Salvation Army, and charitable organizations of all kinds for girls who want another life. Why don't you read other books than those Horner has approved for you? In England a well-born lady isn't uncomfortable doing welfare work to fight prostitution. And what is the result of her misplaced interest in doing good? Nowhere is the scourge of prostitution as rampant as in English cities with social welfare programs.

"I knew right off you, Madame, are in the wrong place. You came from the parochial girls' school and were thrown off the path by Horner's impotent philosophy. You were shunted off into some mythic land of milk and honey, the new morality. I revile the filth of the world you were born into. Milada, I have told you before, good lady, and I'll repeat it: Let's drop all this talk. Don't lecture me, and don't try to educate me or change who I am. I want you to know this: I don't need you to convince me. I respect you! I'm no longer interested in knowing how a girl with your education, your intelligence, and your femininity, Madame, landed in this milieu. It's not important to me to know who brought you there. I don't want to know." He stamped his foot. Milada shuddered. "I'm content to know some person somewhere in this world committed a crime against you. The end. I'm not going to waste another word on this."

Milada tried to speak, but he put his hand over her mouth.

"Don't talk, Milada! I'm warning you. I don't think I could bear it. I don't want to know anything more. Not. One. Thing. I just want to enjoy the day. I was so looking forward to today."

She shook her head forcefully as if to free herself of his warning. Yet the touch of his hand gave her such great happiness! At the same time she thought, "How alien this beloved person is to my inner life! Horner with all his debauchery was closer to me. The man here with me now only wants to enjoy the end of this summer's day." She shook her head again to ward off doubt. Did we cause him to think like this?

"Milada," he said, suddenly softly, and she felt his breath on her forehead. She was shocked at how his breath calmed her. She listened to his voice, and it quelled all rebellion in her.

"I'm afraid you take this world too seriously. Being so serious doesn't help. Sometimes you seem like someone who picks up all the strange, unclaimed suitcases you find on the street and feel compelled to drag them around."

She opened her eyes to see his face and smiled a smile of exhaustion.

"That's how it is, isn't it? Milada? You have to let go of some of this weight, one piece at a time. Free yourself up. At least for a while. You have such sad eyes. They're gray as the mist. I've thought I should make your eyes bright. Then they'll send out bursts of light like the sun. Then the mist will disperse. Driving the mist away intrigues me. Why do we have to worry about these things today?"

He pulled her next to himself on the sofa. "My life has been hard, too. I was thrown back and forth between a tyrannical father and poor Mama, who was ill. She loved me. She was the only person on Earth who did. I will tell you, Madame, more another time." He extended his hands to her.

"So let's be happy, both of us, all right?"

"Jettison baggage," she thought. "Who can do that! Maybe just stop and rest for a while before getting back on the path. That would be nice." She reached out her hand to his.

Enchanted he stroked her hair and turned red like a young boy.

"How will I get along in life without help, if nobody's there to help me and walk at my side?" she wondered, troubled. "Let mindlessness take over!" she heard Horner's hoarse voice from somewhere.

Gustav's hand rested on her cheek and took away the pain of her thoughts. She told herself, "I'm tired to the bone, but now I'm at home. I can relax."

"Do come with me to the next room, Milada. This was Mama's room." He opened the door to the adjoining room. It was a bright, white nest. The furniture was highly polished. There were crocheted white throws over the pieces of furniture, also over the piano. There were fine, milk-colored glasses, filled with a woman's hair, and vases and knickknacks all around. On each elegant chair there was a pillow, and the brass bed was decorated with pieces of needlework and ribbons.

"Lovely, isn't it? Mama had a taste for art. She set store by it." Milada tried to listen to Gustav. He talked on about his friends and his studies.

"I'll never be able to say anything to him he finds interesting. Nothing I have to say intrigues him. He doesn't want to know a thing about my world. I have no way of entering his world. All of it is absolutely alien to me."

He kept up the banter. "Ollie is a great girl. You'll like her. She's always on top of things and witty. She's forever up to something. She's genius at managing things and free as a bird. Joe says she's like a domestic wild animal. By the way, you'll get along well with Joe. He'll be fully attentive to you and your ideas. He's somewhat of a demagogue and quite political. Back when we were in school together Joe was quite the anarchist. Come over here, Milada, I want to show you something." He opened the window, and Milada saw about twenty small flowerpots with cacti on a board. "I take care of them by myself. They were Mama's favorite flowers. 'They don't need much, they just bloom anyway,' she always said. But they've never bloomed for me. I'm waiting for the day they do. When I was a little boy she promised me if I was good, they would put on scarlet-red blossoms. So every morning I would run to open the window, hoping to see the miracle. They're not very pretty at the moment, but the idea they might bloom... Oh, dear God, I almost forgot! I have something for you, Milada!"

He slammed the window closed and ran out of the room and came back after a while with his arms behind his back. "I should have given you this when you first came in." He handed her a bunch of flowers.

She turned red, and her eyes glowed.

"For me?"

"Yes, camelias. I thought a long time about what to get you. I thought about you. I wasn't sure what kind of flower would suit you. I finally decided on camelias. It's the flower with the most dignity. I always imagined camelias would say to me, 'Something that looks like me doesn't need an aroma.'"

"I wish I could tell you," she said between quivering lips, "how much I..."

"Don't cry," he said tenderly. "Please, no don't." He held her tight.

He looked at her, blinking back tears. "You're so pretty now."

She stood with ramrod posture, unmoving. A kind of fear, which traversed her body gently and sweetly, kept her from moving. The strangeness and specialness of the situation, together with her feelings, made her giddy, as if she had drunk wine. She thought and talked without her usual restraint. It felt as if her eyes were closed and had sunk into a deep, deep sleep. And she awoke in a dream, laughing and uttering words of drunkenness. She lifted her arms and threw them around the neck of her beloved, while he put flowers in her hair and loosened it so that it tumbled down her back and into his hands. She laughed a soft laugh fine as silver. She said over and over, "Let's not laugh!" She had no idea why she had said that. She was as delighted as a child. She had awakened. Her cheeks burned, and her limbs quivered. This child, blushing deep red, wound the veil of his dreams around his expectant body.

She was one of the oh-so-many thousands who are filled with joy as they greet the wholeness of their being in the being of another...

They sat together a long time on the divan in close embrace. He spoke at length about good fortune, sun, freedom, mountains, and being alone.

She only felt the warm breath of his mouth. She stroked the hand he used to hold her face.

She heard her own voice. It was the strangest voice she had ever heard coming from herself. It came from a hidden depth she had never known. It opened eagerly and freed up dark impulses within her.

While she spoke, tears flowed from her eyes at the nakedness of her soul. She did not hide her tears or brush them away. They fell on Gustav's hands on her lap.

"You see, my love, your tears are the most natural reaction. I understand you. Your environment has hurt you. You will be entirely refreshed when you are free of that place and come to me in my land." He was as moved as she. She shook her head.

"I beg you, please, don't speak! You don't know yourself. None of this is really new. I promise. There are all kinds of things you can do with your compassion. There's the daughter of Dr. Farkas, for example. Do you know her? No? Just listen to her story. She leaves home, tells herself she has to be a nurse in a hospital. Now she works in the ward with Dr. Pahlen. See! She's an educated girl from a nice family in the neighborhood. Your situation is just like hers. My point is she sees a lot and suffers. It will destroy her. She will be destroyed as a woman, too. It is inevitable. I ask you to consider who can take on work like this? Nobody. Not everybody is as free of prejudice as I am. There is no denying this fact: people have to stay within the bounds of their own group. This type of humanitarianism, if we can call it that, doesn't work in our times. It's possible that it will someday down the line. But then it will be the work of other people in the future. Today it is misplaced. Believe me!"

She could hear only half of what he said. His words dissolved in the joy that filled her. One thing was completely clear to her. He was good to her, he loved her.

In that moment she felt this was the highest grace she had ever known in her poor life.

He said, "I want to talk to you. I have lots of things to tell you. I've been through a lot myself nobody has any idea about."

She nodded her head in agreement and replied, "I can't talk as freely as you do. I am not like that. But we certainly should show our emotions!" She placed his hand on her pounding heart. "Believing we can be open and honest is very beautiful. We do not have to talk. There is no need to put everything into words. They are only empty. What matters is understanding the other person knows about my life and knows my thoughts. We can know each other's desires. When the other loves me, he can know me without explanation. No, rather it goes like this: when the other knows everything about me, then he loves me. How shall I say this? Gus,

I'm dumb. What's the right way to put this?

She looked at him. Under her radiant gaze the blue eyes of this young man filled with tears. Never had anyone listened to him so entirely like this. "The right way to put this," he began...

They heard footsteps on the stairs. The sound was accompanied by laughter and loud talk.

Gus got up, upset. "Be quiet. It's Joe and Ollie. Wait here, be still. Dry your eyes."

"Hey, buddy, we're here!" A large, slim girl flew through the door into the room. She narrowed her black eyes and looked around suspiciously. When she saw Milada she turned towards the door with an affected gesture. "Joe, behave yourself," she said in a formal, bookish tone. "Do enter. There's a lady here visiting."

"Joe put on a bright-red fake Jew nose to be funny. There he was walking around in public, speaking Yiddish. It was embarrassing to be out with him. It was crazy!" She took off her wide feather hat and her short jacket. She stood there in a dress of dark-blue linen that was closed to the neck. Her small, soft shoulders were covered by a wide lace collar. Her boyish bobbed hair fell over her low brow, and she had a turned-up nose and a wide, soft mouth that showed she enjoyed sensuality. She was adorable. This was her reaction to meeting Milada.

Gus began introducing his guest, "Milada, this is Ollie Polly, our friend..."

"Thanks, Gus. My real name is Olga Pollini. My father was Italian."

"And he made dolls, as you can see," said Joe. "Hello. Today the bit of aristocratic decorum she has by birth is readily apparent. She informed me from now on I may only walk proprietously on her left side."

"Oh, come on, Joe. Be quiet now. You talk big."

"Ollie, you come on. Give me back my shirt button." Joe held his shirt closed at his chest.

"I don't have it," she said in annoyance. "Heavens, drop the topic."

"I beg the indulgence of those with fine sensibilities," said Joe in resignation. He looked around, near-sighted, at the people in the room. "This lady felt the perverse need to use the small, red garnet pin I use to keep my shirt closed to replace the garter she was not wearing. I want to say one thing here. Ollie Polly arrived this afternoon without a garter, which is to say she came to visit half-clothed. We don't know what else she is or is not wearing underneath her blue gigot frock."

"You're getting unpleasant again. Now hush!"

"You can tell me I'm in the wrong, but don't tell me that's bad." Joe turned away indignant. "Gus, you need to know girls today are never more shameless than when they have deceived us. When she rocked up this afternoon at my place, boisterous and ill-tempered, slamming around, I knew right away what the drama was about. Our mothers had an air of innocence about themselves after they treated us badly. Mothers used to act all sweet and cuddly. The generation today has a more evolved behavioral style. You've told me plenty enough today, Ollie. Your outburst against me and everything about me said it all."

Olga responded, "Please stop! What do you mean I lashed out at you? What do you think I said anyway? Tell me, Joe, what did you hear me say?"

"Everything. You said you weren't at work because your aunt was ill. But you also said you had been in Prater Park with this aunt. You said she was goodly and poor, and that your dear mother had sent you last night to your aunt with a warm meal. A story right out of Grimm's fairy tales, Little Red Riding Hood. Then you told me this impoverished aunt had given you a gold necklace. It wasn't from the Big Bad Wolf. Your stories don't add up. You even told me you dance the czardas. On the one hand you said this aunt had a fever; on the other, she wanted you to button up against the cold. On top of that you told me I offend people with the way I look. More than that, no, you didn't say anything hurtful. You threw that all out in one long blast. I couldn't get a word in edgewise. No contest. I have nothing to say in my defense."

Gus said, "Ollie, your aunt must be very generous to you, and your dress is buttoned up to the neck. All that points to miracles and wonders." He was laughing.

"Let's table this discussion," Joe said philosophically. And let's get out of the alcove of Gustav's mother."

Joe poured everybody a glass of wine and offered Olga and Milada a glass. "Congrats, Gus! You're on the right path now. Keep going!"

"You all have wine like this in your own cellar? Your father must have an awful lot of money, right?" said Ollie.

Joe grumbled, "We went down there. It was locked."

Gustav was in a good mood, "Serve yourselves up some of this food! Please, take some fruit!" He spoke quietly to Milada, "Please, go serve yourself, eat."

This was the first time Milada was in a group of people from this set. Ollie was unlike anybody she had ever known. Milada knew femininity only as it was expressed in her sphere. If you were young or old, pretty or homely, smart or simple, or whether you fell somewhere in-between—even if you were bold and mouthy—you always deferred to men. You always subordinated your will to a man's.

This Ollie, however, was a different cut. Her passion for having fun and being light-hearted was written all over her face. She talked to her lover with confidence. She was both coquettish and in charge. Her tone evinced her uncontested dominance and control. This encouraged Milada.

Gisi might be prettier than another girl, and Fanny could spin a better yarn than the others. And yet none of the girls she knew would dare to speak up around men.

Ollie picked through the basket of fruit, cracked almonds and put the nuts in Joe's mouth. She told Gustav about the ongoing bickering in Bruckner's Fashion Salon where she worked as a model. She mimicked the fat women who came there to shop, pretending to raise her lorgnette, "Hopefully this will look good on a fuller figure."

In everything she said or did there was a natural and luscious femininity—from her feather hat and open-lace hose to her bubbly laughter and the way she stamped her foot when Joe was joking. Her style was fundamentally strong and powerful and seemed to triumph over any criticism or petulant remark. "I am who I am, and if you don't like it, you can leave. I'm Ollie." That's what the expression in her eyes stated when she looked at the person across from her who had nothing to say.

"So what does she think? That she's like me because she can charm Gus?" Ollie was very annoyed. She was used to roping any other woman in a small, intimate gathering into a friendship. Women readily subordinated themselves to her and looked up to her. And Ollie was free to put other women down as she cared to, and they had to accept it.

Ollie did not find this new "lady" worth her regard. Milada sat there solicitously following Gustav's every move with her eyes. She carefully peeled an apple before giving it to him. Ollie took a look under the table to see what was going on, but there was nothing to see. Where did this woman come from? She acted so precious and demure. Ollie leaned backwards.

Gus said, "Gray clouds are gathering." He leaned toward Milada and looked at her. "When we see those clouds in the distance, it's going to rain soon."

"Oh, no, I'm so happy," she whispered eagerly. "I can't express it. It's so huge."

So now they're whispering to each other?! Ollie had had enough. "I'm hungry as a bear. Could you pass me the platter, Madame?"

"Of course," said Milada, handing it to her.

"Oh, my God! You've got all your hairpins stuck every which way in your bun. How did you manage to put your hair up so carelessly?" said Ollie, harmlessly, as she went to pin Milada's hair up properly. "If you lean backwards, you'll stab yourself." Innocently she quickly pulled the hairpins out of Milada's hair. "Wow, who has hair like this! And here I am by comparison with my little rat's tail. I wish I had hair like this! If I had your hair I'd use it to my advantage. I'd go someplace wonderful! I wouldn't hang around here. I'd get myself to America. That's for sure! People notice hair like this. You look like you're really somebody with this luxurious mop. But you don't wear it right. You need to show it off. Wear it down."

And to show Milada how regal and marvelous her femininity was, Ollie swiftly loosened the heavy, chestnut-brown bun. Milada's hair, glowing copper, fell about her like a robe.

"My God!" said Joe, who stopped eating to look. "Luxurious," he said and put his glasses on to see.

Ollie said, "I'm not done yet!" She fished some narcissus buds out of her belt that the head of the Brenner house had given her when she arrived. She tucked them around Milada's head. "Well??"

"How charming you look now," said Gus and kissed her shoulder.

Very pleased with herself, Ollie took her seat again. She wanted to admire her handiwork and see what kind of girl Milada was.

"I never felt this light," Milada said. She felt giddy. "Now all my thoughts can take wing. There's nothing to hold them down. It's wonderful."

Ollie ventured, "People should go around naked. Then they'd have no worries or cares."

"Crazy damn notion," Joe observed.

"You should give it a try," said Ollie, and her voice sounded maternal. "I've always said our worries come from wearing clothes."

"If you have to pay for them, yes," said Joe.

Ollie ignored Joe. "One day we'll all be six feet under. We

won't have any memory of this Earth. I try to keep that in mind."

"We'll have to see if we can't rent you a little changing station. Ollie's philosophical as all hell today," Joe said to the group.

"That's because of the company."

"Am I making everybody somber?" Milada wanted to know. "I'm having such a good time with you. I hope I'm not making people uncomfortable. I'd like to be as happy as a child. I just don't know what a happy child feels."

"It's different for everybody. Me, my happiest moments from childhood were when I had a cold," said Joe.

Ollie rushed on to say, "And me, I...can't say." She broke off.

"Wonderful things!" Joe ventured.

"That's not true."

"But you said so yourself."

Ollie set her glass of wine down. "I said?!" She was uncertain.

"Sure. I'm truly sorry, Ollie. You can tell us about your happy memories."

"You can't say, you meanie, what's true. My childhood was not at all like you think it was. I'll tell you..."

A gruff voice in the hallway interrupted them, "Everybody, lights out! I'm turning in."

"This is earlier than he usually comes over here," Joe said, checking his watch.

"It goes without saying. This evening I have guests," Gus said. "I will tell you all something. You can't come get me out of the house after midnight. It's getting truly strange. He haunts me like a ghost. He looks in on me with a lantern. The last time he did, I jumped and yelled out in surprise."

"He jumped, too. And he yelled louder than you," said Joe.

Ollie remarked, "It's enough to make you mad. I think it's downright ruthless. It's obvious what he's doing. Joe, compared to Gus's situation you can't complain about anything."

Joe picked up on what Ollie said, "I haven't said, Gus. We two were thoughtless to surprise you like this. Your lady friend won't know what to think of our rude behavior."

"Don't mention it, Joe!" said Gus. "You have no idea how much I enjoyed your surprise," Gus smiled over at Milada.

"I swear by my personal protector the god Pan! Both of us were drunk. And we threw away all caution. We acted like Germans, charging in on you! Gus, I see Ollie and I were two idiots."

Joe apologized and looked down at his glass sullen. Ollie drummed on his back.

"Big oaf. You've said enough now," Ollie comforted him.

"Go ask the Big Bad Wolf," Joe blubbered. "He'll tell you what that means."

"He's pretty drunk," said Ollie with resignation. "He should watch it. He knows he can't tolerate that much."

Joe raised his glass in a toast to Milada, "Esteemed Lady, a poor man asks for your favor. And you, Ollie, are a snake. You're already composing a letter of apology for my behavior. Rip it up. I'm not getting drunk today. Today I'm living carefully. To prove it, as soon as I've drunk this glass of wine, I'll tell you how much money you deposited in your account today."

"You're talking gibberish."

"I'm not the type to disguise the truth with mystical mumbo-jumbo. I rummaged around in your purse when you were out. The bank receipt was in there."

Gus set down his glass.

Joe roared on, "Oh, oh, Ollie. You did this after we had talked about it? Pierrette, the sad clown looking for love, is dead," Joe's voice was gloomy. "She's gone never to return. She doesn't understand the value of her life. She's desperate. The reptile has turned into an ant. And the cricket isn't making music anymore. The cricket is saving money. The charming, poor grisette Mimi Pinson is knitting socks to sell. But she's dying of a fatty heart."

Ollie felt guilty. She gripped the basket of fruit with both arms and stuffed chocolates in her mouth, grabbed up lots of berries, and put quite a few on Joe's plate. "Now he's going to start up with the old harangue," she said with disdain. "In a while he'll be passed out and snoring."

Joe continued, "Who, I ask you, is able to delude himself into loving some wench with a sizable annual income? Furthermore, this wench then opens a bank account using his sweet name. Who spends the precious days of his youth building a golden altar and makes sacrifices at this altar that one day will be turned into a building with revenue potential? Ollie Polly, my soul has seen you dancing hectically toward the grave. In you I saw most sublime, tragic Grisette, the seamstress who made her own way but was undone. Be gone! You are becoming bloated. Every part of your body is getting fat and all the edges of your being are sharp. Olly, betake yourself from me! For a long time now you have stunk to me of onions and pomposity. You, you were the essence of sacrifice in the spring. You meant delectation. To me you were the sweet, thoughtless figure of girlhood, closing her eyes. You were sumptuous, budding like a flower, and absolutely, wildly attractive.

"You robbed me forever of spontaneity in concourse with the opposite sex. That is your greatest sin. I can no longer love. I can only speculate. Gus, my manhood perishes at the hand of another."

Ollie got very upset when anyone spoke of her bank deposits. She kept her money in two or three places. At times she bought lottery tickets and always kept her finances a fiercely guarded secret. She could bite and scratch like a cat if a friend wanted to poke around in her private affairs, asking where she got her money. No one dared ask how much she had or why she was saving her money.

Of course, Ollie's finances became a continuous point of contention for both of them because she reacted so viciously. She spoke sharply with contempt and glared at Joe, "Well, lunkhead, you can be happy. You never contributed anything to my account, so you don't have to worry."

Joe replied, "I was waiting for that. I would curl up with shame to contribute to the accretion of your fat being. You were born to throw money around, to laugh and throw away an armload of blossoms at the first gust of wind. You are so profligate that big, fat middle-class women out for a stroll cross themselves at the sight of your promiscuity and squandering. Ollie, you would be impossible in the secure, ordered world of domesticity! Your small butterfly soul would perch on its big backside and develop calluses from being obedient. How you would long to gather blossoms, rose petals, and spend nefarious days in springtime! 'Nothing's as good as rain in July,' you'd say, 'because my garden will grow huge!' Oh, Ollie, oh."

"Oh, oh," Gus echoed.

"What made you so attractive, charming, and irreplaceable was your thoughtless dalliance. Dalliance gave you all your qualities and allowed your small, predatory brain to become elegant and sly. What has given you that certain colorful cast in life? It has been playing about day by day. It's been your singsong existence and tra-la-la. Oh, there was your impassioned longing at age seventeen for a feather hat, silk ruffles, and gloves of gauze! What became of that longing? Wines dissipated it, dear Pierrette. You can't regret the loss of longing enough. In winter you were sweet and warm and agreeable, and in the summer you could parade about with your arms and neck bare. In the summer, dear grasshopper, you sang, and in the winter you danced. Scrupulousness, the mind of a child, and your fond disregard of values gave you charm and fire. You did not think. You desired. You did not care, you consumed. You didn't gorge yourself, you nibbled tidbits. You were godlike. Pierrette, what happened to your magic? The spell has been broken. Pierrette, you should not have a coin purse in your possession."

Joe's glass was empty. In a flash Gus returned from the next room with another round, which he placed on the table.

"So that's what you want to make of me," Ollie said softly to herself.

Milada sat with her elbows on the table and listened. She had her hands in her glistening hair. She listened with dreamy eyes, and her mouth was half open and hot. Gus leaned his head on her temple, and her curls surrounded his bright cheeks.

"Isn't Joe remarkable?" Gus asked softly. "Things mean more to him than he lets on. He performs."

"I can tell," said Milada in response.

Joe stared contemplatively at his glass full of wine.

"Where did your sweet magic go, I ask? What became of your youthful, physical desire for adventure? Do you have any idea? You spent passion, love, and lust richly in the evening, and early the next morning you drank hot chocolate. You had chocolate with pastries. Remember, Ollie?

"Oh, these wenches, wenches! Who put order and decency in your golden chaos? Who took advantage of you, you shop girls, chamber maids, seamstresses—all butterflies in our life? Who harmed your desire? Who taught you to tally the accounts? Ollie Polly, the sweetest of little dreams, you've ended up chopped liver. Oh, oh."

Ollie used her fingers to push her lightly fastened hair forward. "That's sure some stupid talk, isn't it?" she said in a whisper as she turned to Milada. "Guys are like that though. For them it would be just dandy not to be bothered about such basic things as money or buying food. They just want to be in love and fly off into space with their fancy thoughts. They're not interested in practicality. It ruins their interest in a nice meal. But afterwards, when their dreams are played out, it's done and over. And we're supposed to be happy with our beautiful emotions. Forget that! I won't be hanging on any of their necks asking for anything. I want my life to be better."

She got up and went over to the piano and lifted the keyboard cover. "Come over here, you oaf, and accompany me."

He got up. "Ollie, you've taken away my faith in women," he blubbered. "I used to believe in your stupidity. I counted on this one rich source of femininity. There's no help for me. Nymphs, dryads, goddesses—they're all empty illusions. Smoke and mirrors. Vain talk."

He stood up weaving and looked at Milada with his swollen eyes. "Madame, just take a look at her. She's made for man's desire. And she saves her money. She's thinking of her future. She lives and loves carefully!" He walked over to Ollie, put his arms around her and sang with a full bass, "On this settee I want to die."

Ollie added, "Keep going. You are and remain a dope."

"I'm one of those dopes who's dead serious. When they are laid in a coffin, they aren't bound for heaven. Ollie, I promise you that. It's true. I'm not drunk yet. Circe, you'll have to work very hard to get me drunk!" He lifted Ollie up high, turned her around in the air and sang, "And this settee, you will inherit it. / But first I have to die."

Gus spoke with sparkling eyes, "This guy really knows women! And they follow him around like sheep. He's a great guy! He's a true idealist. Just listen to this! He made a pledge not to touch Ollie unless she wants him to. That's the craziest!"

Gus sang along with Ollie's lovely soprano voice, "Oh, old brotherliness / Whither hast thou gone?"

"The whole thing's strange and heavenly. It's so positively beautiful," Milada thought. "These are wonderful people."

"Have more to drink, Milada! You have the eyes of a sphynx. You smile and the mists gather to tears. My love, you are so silent. Do you have a nickname? Milada is so difficult."

"It's like me," Milada said as she got up.

"Oh, no," Gus said with fire in his eyes. "You are slim and sinewy as a young boy. I like that." And he pressed his blond head against her hips.

Joe called out from behind the piano. "She looks like a gazelle that's fleeing and wants to fly over a wide, wide chasm. Jump! Jump!"

"I'd like to call you Mila. Is that all right?"

"All right, little brother Gus! *Ergo bibamus*, let us then drink to that!" Joe called out.

Ollie sat at the piano with her feet dangling from the bench. "Play something by Wagner!" she said and rolled her eyes upward. "Play the passage where Tristan drinks the love potion. Yes, play that!"

Joe sang a student commercium. His voice rang out.

In the Black Whale in Ascalon
A man drank day by day
Till stiff as any broom-handle
Upon the floor he lay.

Ollie hit him over the head with a score of music. He laughed, stood up with a full glass of wine, and went over to Gus and Milada. "Madame Milada, this man here, our Gus, is a lucky fellow. Take a good look at him. He is a person of eternal youth. All hail to the student I mentor. Long live your style!"

Joe emptied his glass and pulled Ollie down on his lap. "Now I'm going to compose a poem. Here it comes, the first verse." He tapped out the rhythm with his fingers.

Young boy green from the country, come on down,
Dum-diddy-dum...
Ride your horse to town.
More than anywhere
The city has its maidens fair.
Proud ones, honest ones, small,
Fat, sweet, fine ones, has them all.
Yes, it's got some maidens fair,
Has a lot of maidens there.

Ollie played low notes on the piano with her elbows.

"I've got to leave now," Milada announced suddenly, pinning her hair up.

"Oh, no. You can't do that, my precious! You want to take off, but you shouldn't." Gus stroked her cheek. "Mila, kiss me, please!" he begged her softly.

Joe interrupted, "Ollie, your turn. Keep up the beat." Ollie carried on,

> Young boy green from the country, come on down,
> Dum-diddy-dum...
> Ride your horse to town.

Ollie hollered out, "I'm keeping it going," and threw her feet up in the air.

"Ollie, we're not yet to the refrain. When we get there, we'll sing together in perfect harmony," Joe hollered above the music.

"Please come with me, Mila. They're making too much noise. Once Ollie's in the swing of it, it's better to leave. Come to my room. I want to tell you something."

Milada gave him an intense look. She followed him. Ollie gave her partner in song a scowling look. For a moment Ollie was overcome with jealousy and annoyance. She hoped Joe, old big lunk there, wouldn't fall asleep in the middle of the song. Resolutely she took away his glass.

"It's empty," Ollie declared to Joe who was looking solemnly at his glass.

Gus's bedroom was lit with the light of the moon. The night breeze moved the muslin curtains. Gus clapped his hands.

"Isn't it pleasant here? There's no smoke and no noise. It's lovely for us here, isn't it?"

Milada stood at the window, braiding her hair, which shone in the moonlight.

"Why don't you leave your hair down?" Gus asked. He was unhappy.

"Having my hair loose feels strange," she answered softly.

"Please be happy, my dear!" Gus said tenderly. "Just a moment, I'll get us some wine." Gus took a dark, round bottle from a shelf. "It's just for you, the very best."

"Thank you, no. I don't want to drink any more."

Milada surprised herself with her tone. It was empty and formal. How was she acting? He was entirely tender, completely warm. And she? An indescribable constriction encircled her senses like a band of iron. She thought with a shudder, "I can't help it. There is no burning ember in me. I have nothing to offer him. I'm done with all this."

She took hold of his hand, "I'd like to be like Ollie," Milada said in pain. "Happy and light and willing, just like Ollie. But I can't. You'll see how I am soon. You'll be appalled at me. I'll never be able to be like her."

Gus stomped his foot. "You don't have to be like that. I love you just as you are. You're luscious as wild fruit. Don't you know? I'm crazy for you. I was taken with you from the moment I first saw you. I hold you and your reserve in higher regard than all the Ollies in the world. I don't fall apart when someone's temperamental. Milada, what is it about you that attracts me so much? I don't know what's going on with me. And I have always tried to understand what moves me. It's not just sensuousness or desire. You're beautiful, it's true. But that's not what moves me about you. Mila, I've never seen a woman like you."

He fell to his knees before her and pressed his head to her skirt. From the next room they could hear the slow rhythm of the piano music and Ollie's high voice forging ahead.

He whispered to her ardently, "I am dying for you."

"Gus, Gus," she held his head in her cold hands. She pressed her lips to his.

"That wasn't a kiss," Gus was aroused. He pulled her down next to him on the bed. She took hold of his hands, pushed them away from herself. Her voice was halting and heavy.

"I know this is strange, I know. But you will laugh about this once I'm gone. They'll laugh about it, too. Everybody knows what I'm returning to. I'm not afraid of what people think. I don't need their forgiveness. I've got nothing to lose. I'm well aware. But I don't want to be your lover for this one hour. I don't want that."

Her voice was soft, yet every word weighed heavy in the dark room.

"Don't say that!" Gus spoke wildly and shook her by the arm. "Look what you're telling me."

"You have no idea how difficult this is for me, how I've struggled. I would lose myself, my humanity, and the whole of my being in this one moment. That's all I have. And tomorrow you wouldn't know if it had been me or someone else."

"That's not true," he gritted his teeth and pressed her arm. "Don't say such things! I'm not drunk on alcohol. Ask Ollie if I would bring her or anybody else in here. That's not what I want from you. I want to feel you, all of you, just as you are. I want to drink you in, to understand."

She did not have the strength to push him away.

He pulled her down. She felt the force of his arm around her body.

"I don't want anything from you," he whispered at her throat. "But, please, please, be quiet now!"

Ollie had stopped singing. There was still the light sound of the piano.

Gus had begun to breathe heavily. His breath moved the hair of her temples. Joe had fortunately fallen asleep,

Some time elapsed. Her head sank slowly. Suddenly Milada rose up. She was sure she had heard a voice calling. It was loud, sharp, and angry. It must have gotten quite late.

She sat up in distress. But she was thrown back down on the bed.

"Stop torturing me!" Gustav whispered. His hot breath blew across her. "Why are you doing this to me? Why??"

He groaned in her ear. How often had this happened to her!

Many horrible images and many desolate memories flooded over her and suffocated all her desire. She had experienced this hundreds of times. There had never been anything about this that had to do with her, with Milada. All he desired was her poor body, which had no will. This body made him groan and quake—him and all the others. "Let go, let go," she said, pushing away his groping hands. In this moment she saw with horrifying clarity not all these men. Rather she saw one old, haggard man, the one Goldscheider had sent to her when she was fifteen. He had placed a pink rose on her breast. He was the first. After him came a train of men, some young, some old; others friendly. or vile and base. She groaned with disgust and held up her arms in defense. A soundless battle took place in the dark. She fought off his greed, his male right of plunder. For her this was not Gus who demanded her. The greed of all the men with their demands and rights hit her with brutal force. For her this was the passion of all those men who had possessed her, bought her, and lapped at her exhausted, unwilling body.

"Let go, let go!" She grabbed hold of his arms and held on with all her might. "Gus, I'm telling you," Milada's voice was harsh and threatening. "I won't be any pleasure for you."

He released her.

"Don't scream," he said between clenched teeth. "They'll hear."

She jumped up and straightened her hair and clothes. She saw his deeply wounded, humiliated male pride in his bitterness. "Nobody will believe you did not have me," she said in nameless sorrow and looked over at him. He had buried his head in the pillow. "Let me go. I can't explain it to you."

He did not answer.

She unlocked the bedroom door and looked into the adjoining

room. Joe sat at the piano, leaned way back in his chair. That was the same posture he had had when they left. He was playing one tune after another with a light, effortless touch. Joe played soft, sweet variations of various melodies, lovely chords that flowed and dissolved into longing. Forgetting this world, Joe looked up at the mural on the ceiling of the room.

Ollie was perched in an armchair. She wore the expression of a bitter child as she watched Joe playing. She jumped up as if rescued when she saw Milada. Her rival! The woman who had won!

"How boring Joe is!" she said in exasperation. "He's tweedled away the whole evening with his idiotic plunking on the piano there. Enough!" she yelled loudly.

Joe slammed down the lid of the piano. He winked at Ollie.

"So, you see! I'm not drunk."

"You're being mean."

"I promise, my sweet love, I won't play another round."

Milada picked up her hat.

"Madame Ollie, won't you accompany me? It's gotten late, I do believe."

"Well past midnight," Joe announced.

Milada looked up in surprise. She had the feeling many hours had flown by.

"I didn't realize I'd lost track of so much time," Ollie said while yawning.

"Ollie," Joe said putting his hands around her face. "Be sure to take your things with you. And take my garnet pin. It's yours now."

"Gus, go get some candles for us to go down the stairs!"

The girls put their wraps on quickly. And Gus illuminated the stairwell. He was pale and nervous and bit his upper lip. Milada took his hand and looked at him lovingly. He shook his head in disapproval, but she did not notice.

"I'll write to you," Milada said. He nodded heavily without speaking.

"You big lunk, are you going to come get me tomorrow?" Ollie asked Joe.

"It would be my pleasure! But do bathe, Ollie. Bathe," Joe called to her over the banister.

"Keep your voice down, Joe," Gus pulled him back in the apartment.

Ollie pulled a long face as they left. The guard at the front was half asleep but opened the gate for them, letting them out onto a street filled with the light of the moon and empty of people.

Ollie began the conversation on the way, "My guy's quite sweet actually. I'll say that for him. But he doesn't give me anything."

"Miss Ollie, so what is it you do?"

"Me? I'm a model for a fashion studio," Ollie answered curtly. "It's not the greatest. Most of my time is spent at the tailor's. They pin the dress up, adjust it, and you try it on again. What do I get from this business? Not even one summer hat or a decent dress."

They walked side by side for some while, not talking.

"Which street are you taking now?" Milada wanted to know.

"I live on Grabner Lane. Let's walk through the downtown, though. I find it so lovely at night."

"Then you can accompany me a bit. I live..." Milada continued, "just around the corner from the Hotel Louvre de Lux."

"Nice part of town!" Ollie laughed. "I know it quite well. That's where Bruckner my employer used to have his shop. Now he's got a fine place in the Glass Palace."

"Do you feel safe going home on your own?" asked Milada.

"Me? Feel safe? Jesus! I'm a night creature. If someone approaches me and he's a nice guy, I take him along a-ways. If he's unpleasant, I give him what for. You can believe me." Ollie broke off. She stopped short. "All the stuff Joe was saying today, you shouldn't take it too seriously. True, I'm not a saint, but I'm not a bad person either."

Quickly Ollie unpacked her philosophy of life.

"You see, people like us have no capital and no security. We've got no advantage in this life. What we have going for us is just being young, pretty, and happy. Our men are used to having everything given to them based on their pretty faces and works of art. Men can stay in the game a long time, but for me it will be over soon. Watch me now. See how I act." Ollie stood still and put her right hand on her hip, so that Milada could admire her. "Here comes some old, used-up guy who'd like to take a look. That doesn't cost me a thing. I'd be completely *meshugge* to want to send him away so Joe can keep his illusion.

"I tell you straight up. I make some money from men. And it doesn't hurt a soul. If I didn't take advantage of these opportunities my troubles would ruin me. For a while I gave it up because of Joe. I do have a relationship with him. But without this other income I'd starve." And here she sucked in her cheeks to look emaciated.

"So you have troubles, Ollie?" Milada asked.

"Oh, a lot. My sister is sixteen. She's really foolish. It's scary! She does it with officers, just like a slut, don't you know. Of course afterwards she hasn't got a penny. She bought a Persian lamb jacket for 250 gulden. She didn't save anything. And then she takes dresses she's hardly worn to the charity store. It's enough to make me sick. And our mother's pretty critical. When Mom sees what she's doing, there's always a fight. I've got my own bad luck, too," Ollie sighed. "I've seen a lot in my life. With Joe, too. Today he laughed and sang, but six months ago you should have seen how we fought! Jesus and Mary! It makes me want to cry just thinking. He said he couldn't stand my making money. I was supposed to belong to him and only him. He fought with me just about every day. But what was I supposed to do? It costs me eighteen gulden for breakfast, supper, and a room. And Joe has no money. He tutors here and there a bit. I never wanted anything from him, and I never got anything, promise to God! Look here, Madame. Do you think he cares what'll happen to me one day?

He likes me a lot, but not as much as he used to. There's a lot of hate hidden in him. And meanness. He never once asked himself what I'll do once he's satisfied. And however much he says he loves me, one day it will come to this: he'll leave. When I pick someone up, he wants to leave me. If I'm down or really sick, he doesn't come around. What's a poor girl to do? You know as well as I do. I don't want to starve. I don't want that. I've seen enough poverty in my own family. And I've seen other ways to live. I work in nice shops and see lots of very nice things. I've learned about fashion. Am I supposed to wear a worn-out blouse or a faded straw hat by Girardi?" Ollie looked at Milada as if all happiness hinged on her answer to this one question.

"I do understand," Milada nodded in agreement. "If somebody looks as good as you do, she has to dress well."

"So then you know. I liked Joe from the beginning." Again Ollie stopped. "But I talk too much. You can't really be interested in my situation."

"Yes, I honestly am," said Milada. "Please, keep talking."

"My first impression of you, Madame, was you're far too haughty for me. But I was wrong."

"And why did you think I was haughty?"

"Well, because you've got Gus. He's such a sweet, rich man. You're really lucky. The guy who pays me is old and disgusting, but I can't complain. To tell the truth I'd be glad for somebody more appealing."

"So what do you want to do with the money?" Milada asked out of curiosity.

"Hmmm," Ollie's expression intimated there was much to tell. "I've got some ideas. But first I need to put together the funds. My mom and brother owe money. After I pay off their debts, I'd like to start my own business, do something I like. Can you imagine? I'd like to sell ball gowns and outfits of pure silk. I know a woman who can get me the best clothes. She has things from princesses, dresses they wore only once. With a business like that I'll be able to live the highlife. Naturally, I'll be with Joe if he still likes me." She was quiet for a moment.

Then Ollie continued, lively, "But you won't need anybody besides Gus. He'll make sure you live well, right?"

"I wouldn't know. I have so little time. I'm always busy."

"But then you have the whole sweet night for him, don't you?" Ollie laughed and cocked her head to the side.

"Actually that's when I'm not free."

"Actually? What kind of business are you in then?" Ollie wanted to know.

"Wait just a moment. It's around the corner here. I can show you where I work."

Ollie looked around carefully. She was familiar with the neighborhood. Then she took a good long look at Milada's tranquil face.

The two women crossed Kaerntner Street, walked along the side of the Louvre de Lux, and at the entrance to a small alley Milada stopped. One single red lantern burned at the end of the alley. It illuminated the front of the two-story house, which stood out proudly from the shabby buildings around it.

"That, Madame Ollie, is our business."

Ollie was taken aback. "Holy Mother! But, no, you're kidding me."

"It's the truth. I'm the manager there," Milada said.

"That's Red House," Ollie was able to say.

"That's right. I'm the manager of Red House."

Ollie looked at Milada with horror rising in her eyes, as if to ask, "Really?!"

Milada answered with a look that said, "Yes, really."

"Good night, then, Madame Ollie. I have to run now."

Mechanically Ollie put her hand in Milada's to say goodbye. She could only utter, "Good..." Ollie withdrew her hand and ran off.

Three days later Milada went to visit Gus in the dark of the evening.

She became his lover without holding back.

She received the following letter:

Mila, Dear!

I just returned from a café where I saw Joe again. He was completely sober. Exactly as I had expected he told me he holds you in high regard. He is not judgmental at all, not at all. There is no issue. Honestly.

When I reflect on the evening yesterday I clasp my hands together in gratitude. The time together dissolved any bitterness in my heart toward you. Never again leave me in such distress, feeling so absolutely miserable, as you had on Monday. My suffering wasn't because you left me. This torture bound me to you even more. Leave me often, my love. I crave this pain from a woman. But the words you spoke on Monday when you left were poison. In the darkness they return to me, as if whispered by evil tongues, "There will be none of this."

Dear Mila, I won't ask you any questions. I don't want to know about the others. I'm not asking to know anything about you. This I do know: Our happiness requires utmost privacy. I implore you most sincerely to stay away from people who have anything to do with me. Tell them nothing of your public life, nothing whatsoever about yourself. I will make sure you and I will be completely alone in the future. Ollie was unpleasantly surprised at your openness. She was thrown and had to promise Joe and me she would never mention what she knew about you to anyone. It's my intention to rent a room somewhere far away for us for the future. Of course the room will have a piano for Joe.

Please do come Friday! My greetings! Send me your answer!

Gus

Milada replied:

Dear Gus!

Am writing in great haste before afternoon mail. Miller's in bed ill. Cannot come. Horrible, isn't it? Be a sweetheart and come here. I can see you in between my tasks. I can take a few minutes to see you in my room. My love, we have a lot to talk about. The way you write is very strange to me. I tell myself Gus wouldn't talk to me like that in person. The words you wrote came from your pen and not from your soul. I know you better. I wish you would accept the way I see you. I want your beauty to shine forth in all you do and care to do. We have no need of secrecy.

Please do love living in your Milada.

Gus was riddled with dreadful uncertainty.

"Milada can't come," Gus spoke to Joe who was sprawled out across the settee smoking. "She wants us to go see her. What do you think, Joe?"

"So then let's go," said Joe.

"But I find it miserable, God knows. It's really awful—don't you think?—to go over there."

From behind a cloud of smoke, Joe quoted Goethe's Mephisto: "You're in bed with the devil, you are. And now you're afraid of the flame?"

Gus turned red. "You won't be able to believe that she..."

"Please, spurned lover, don't go through the roof. But mostly don't make things complicated. She can't come. You want to see her. Ergo, go see her."

"Joe, do me a favor and take my situation seriously."

Joe sat up straight and made a face of mock seriousness. He clenched his teeth and bared them. "Is this how I should look?"

"You're being a clown," Gus said, pacing around the room. He stopped pacing, fished Milada's letter out of his valise, and handed it to his friend without saying a word.

Joe turned it around in his fingers, went to the window, and read it through. He said thoughtfully, "It's just like I thought. These women are dangerous when we don't pay for the favors we enjoy. Oh, you man in love, don't get upset. I'm not talking about money. What I'm talking about is more than money." Joe put his hand in the air, then lowered it, and lit a fresh cigarette.

"Yes, do you see something behind this, Joe?" Gus asked. He was flattered at Joe's reading of Milada's letter. "The way you dissect things worries me."

"My friend, come over here a moment. Promise me this! Don't let yourself be used. Don't commit to anything with her, and don't get into any obligation unless you've spoken to me first. Apart from keeping this promise to me, you can do any damn fool thing you want." Joe put out his hand to shake on the deal.

There was such obliging earnestness in Joe's words Gus gave his hand in pledge, just as he knew to do from the long tradition of his breeding.

"Fine! I counted on you as a sound, decent person, Gus. You are, after all, the son of David Brenner."

Business at Red House had dropped off significantly in the summer months, just as it always did. Just as always, Miller complained and tried to make up for her losses through every manner of stringency. The complement of girls grew smaller. Those who could afford it went to a spa and took the waters. Putzi was one of those. One day, suddenly, she came by some money, and just as secretively as she had arrived, she sailed off into the wide world. Lefty Anna, too, had come to the end of her time at Red House. She was slated for the provinces. She had become so sharp and annoying that even the most good-natured regular guests had had enough of her. In her place there was a new girl who sniffled around the house, a fat Pole named Lola. She was the paragon of stupidity and let people push her around.

At the same low point of the summer Zimmermann had palmed off a small blonde on Red House. She was the picture of the mouthy blonde. She was trashy through and through. Her name was Mitzi Chvojka. She had been the star and darling at Zimmermann's. She was useful, pleasant-enough, and extremely talkative. Mitzi cooked up every possible kind of nastiness behind her richly curl-covered, sloping brow.

It had also come time for Bina Michal to leave Red House. She had gotten notice that she was going to Budweis in Bohemia. She took it in stride, nodded, and did not even ask about the conditions or expectations. Milada was surprised Bina answered all her questions with resignation, "It's all the same to me."

"If they don't treat you right, Bina, don't take it! Don't put up a fuss, but do defend yourself. That always works out."

Bina just shook her head. "Nobody's going to bother me," she replied dully.

One evening late in July she moved out. Nelly Spizzari came to pick her up in a small carriage. Nelly snooped around some in the house and gave Milada a knowing look. Spizzari spoke to Miller, "In a few days here you'll have the new girl from Budweis. Fischer wrote me she's very afraid of the police."

Miller replied, "Now isn't that sweet! Next thing you'll know Nelly will be sending me unregistered girls."

"My dear lady, you worry too much about your business," Spizzari said with a sneer and took her leave.

In the hallway there was a lot of kissing and embracing as Bina moved from one person to the next.

"Here, Bina, it's a little silk scarf for you," Gisi wept as she tied it around Bina's neck. "There's such a draft in carriages."

Milada sent her off with these words, "Keep your head up, Bina! Don't take any guff off of anyone!"

Then the carriage rattled off. One last time Bina thrust her head out the window, but Milada was not there at the door waving to her, as Bina had expected. Red House was shuttered and seemed to stare at her blankly.

Bina sighed and told herself, "Milada's doctor must be waiting upstairs for her." She hardened her heart to the disappointment of the last moment.

Milada's relationship to the Doctor, as people in the house generally called Gus, had taken on a legitimacy. This had happened fast as lightening, as was usual in these circles. The attentiveness of bourgeois people to the relationships of others and their burdensome gossip simply had no place here. In this world people are much less envious. They have more good humor and are more gracious about the most natural of human dealings.

"She's got it good," one or the other of the girls said with a sigh. Nobody troubled herself with speculations that were untoward or convenient. Nobody prophesied unhappiness or circulated ugly rumors. There was no speculation about the reasons for their relationship. There were no jealous concerns about how it would end. People did not talk of how this man or that man could be involved with a certain girl. And Gus, who had come from a narrow world of sexual proscriptions, found this easy way of accommodating him and accepting his attachment to Milada a comfort; it put him at ease.

People simply took Gus and Milada as a couple. Even Miller accepted their attachment without complaint. She greeted him with reverence when she ran across him in the hall. She always took the opportunity to praise him and to comment "this Brenner" had become most dignified. Gus for his part had made sure, after quite an argument with Milada, that he paid Miller for his meals. He usually paid with a large bill and left the remainder as tip.

For the girls in the house the daily visits of the Doctor provided a welcome change of pace.

Exactly as formerly, a crowd of enthusiastic girls greeted him when he arrived at Red House. It was difficult for him to break loose of their attentions. He excused himself from their company with an air of masculine arrogance, hoping Milada would chasten them. But she did not intervene. Was it a fortuitous instinct on her part or only her security as his lover? Her behavior showed she had no plans or expectations.

She had become young. She lived free of obligations. She experienced a new, vibrant childhood. She took delight in small things and spoke silly, drunken words. She often laughed aloud for no apparent reason and let her laughter fall where it might.

She blossomed. And she flung the thousand late flowers of her nature across the short, gray alley. When she was out on a walk with Gus, he tossed flowers all about, carelessly and merrily. She laughed at the girls who danced around Gus, and she laughed at his rumpled brow and exaggerated protests. She mimicked his anger at Miller and took childlike pleasure in repeating the words of praise for Gus that fell from Miller's sour lips when he was not around.

"Miller says she thinks you're a nobleman. Wait, wait! Who is this?" Milada asked imitating Miller.

"You're being silly!" Gus grumbled.

"You don't deserve her love."

Gus pulled a long face. Milada took him by the neck and begged him, "I couldn't bear one mean word about you. So, my little Gus, be on the look-out when the girls are around. Mitzi is especially mean."

"She's amusing at least."

"I don't like her."

"Me, either. I don't like any of them. They don't get any sympathy from me."

Milada was quiet.

And so Gus could tell Joe in all honesty, "I swear to you, I am taking her further and further away from her old ways. We don't talk about it anymore. I can tell that I'm freeing her up. If she ever had plans for changing me, she's given them up entirely."

Joe replied in English, since he always hoped to attain to the phlegmatic disposition of the English, "All right."

Gus had, for his part, surrendered to the atmosphere of Red House completely and without hesitation. His soft, vain nature always craved flattery. He was lulled into a pleasant state of mind; he enjoyed the uncritical admiration he received. His was passionately attracted to Milada as a woman. And he admired her. Every single second he found it grand that he loved her

He arrived late in the afternoon, laden with books and paperwork, and sat down at Milada's desk. He claimed he could study there better than at home. At home he was distracted by the noise of people loading iron and the sight of the bright river. Rather soon after starting to study at Red House, he brought along some personal effects. He put his cigarettes and pipe in a case next to her ring of keys, and he hung the well-worn, fine, traditional jacket he wore to work next to Milada's house apron.

Soon the room was filled with his loud, warm voice as well as with the elegant aroma of the Egyptian woman. Like a small, pampered boy, he demanded Milada be around him all the time. And if she could not get away from work, he gave an ear-piercing whistle that, as Milada claimed, drew her as if she were on a string.

Then he took her in his arms and instructed her, "Your darling Gus is here. Milada mustn't be elsewhere." He held her so tightly that she repeated the nonsense whole cloth. She was entirely filled with his tenderness and with his creativeness in their hours of lovemaking. She was swept away with his way of talking and even cherished their arguments over nothing. She was infatuated with his inventiveness in making up little verses and rhymes. These ditties swirled in his mind, and, to charm her, he recited them with great to-do. Milada was so dazed by his charms she walked around the spaces she had known since childhood as if in a dream. He was so playful in presenting her with a completely new and strange world that she went about her chores with abandon. His world shone out for her like a broad, green panorama before the eyes of a prisoner. Milada, who had been reserved, was now filled with this new sphere to the point of being heady and distracted. When someone from the neighborhood addressed her in passing, she could not think what to say. In the middle of her chores—whether taking care of linens, cleaning up, getting the girls ready, or lacing them up—she became aware of the presence of an intense feeling of joy. It caught her up short a few seconds, and she put her hand on her heart and stared off into the mists. She no longer paid rapt attention to the events in the house. Milada was calm.

Her great happiness at being in love did Milada much good, yet she bore a grim, bleeding wound that caused her waves of pain. This wound overshadowed what was healthy and whole. Milada was tormented by a constant, escalating horror of the past. Her memories arose in her like strange ghosts, looking for light. She could not imagine her lover with his laughing eyes would ever be able to dismiss the misery of her early childhood. She could not imagine herself stripped of romantic appearances standing before him. He could not see the neglected, repellent urchin she actually was.

Slowly a fear crept into her awareness his love and affection would have to cool and fade away if he found out about the thousands of ugly things she had been through, the constant humiliations and rejections that had harmed her, body and soul. She never forgot those. Very early in life she had known rejection. She recalled the curses and blows from her mother and her mother's lovers. And, shrouded in dusk, she saw a figure who at times saved her. A woman named Janka was etched in her memory. This had been a time that remained pure and unstained.

The most oppressed children had enjoyed childhood. But she had not. Once in a surge of passion Gus had held her in his arms and stammered, "How I wish I had known you earlier, Milada, had known you and protected you from the terrible things here!" At the time she had believed that he had thought about where she lived and had felt her pain with a shudder.

Once she was seized by an apprehension of some betrayal, of some danger—the essence of which was unclear and terrifying—and she burst in on Gus, who was sitting in her room studying. She stared at him out of her mind. The trigger for her panic had been a door slamming closed.

Gus had been pouting about her absence and said, “Mila, there you are! I’ve been so bored without you.”

She pressed his head against herself, “Gus, never ever leave this place without telling me, ‘I’ll be back tomorrow.’ Or else...”

“Or else what?”

She smiled with an effort, lifted her finger as a warning, “Or, tell me ‘I’m never coming back.’”

He looked at her in astonishment, “What’s gotten into you?”

“Cowardice!” she mumbled and, for a short, blessed moment, she shook off the fear that had gripped her for hours on end.

She was most happy and at peace when she sat near him with her head bent toward him, listening to his stories. Gus had a great need to share. He knew how to tell stories well and make them vivid, and he was quite proud of this. He liked to tell stories about the mother he had adored and about the patrician family she had come from. Other stories were about the miniatures, porcelain, and fine old Viennese furniture in the house. Grandma had lived in the midst of this décor, herself a relic of a bygone era. As an elder she had not gone out much and had stopped reading the newspaper or any new books. Her interests were arrested in her apartment. Grandpa had been a gaunt old man with blue eyes and a brown Prince Albert coat. And how he had loved beautiful objects! He had sought out and purchased items, and he placed them all around the house. He had assembled a virtual museum. By the time he died he must have had three-hundred pieces of ivory miniatures alone. “Just imagine, Mila, what a stiff-necked man he was! He would not allow a mean person or somebody who was ill to set foot in his home; he wouldn't stand for it. He broke off his friendship with his best friend when his friend had an ulcerated sore on his nose. But at the same time he could be as sweet as a child. Aunt Alma says I'm cut from the same mold, but I don't think so. I'm not a thoroughgoing aesthete. I also have a lot in me that's botched. I have that from him, from my father's side. I don't have any delusions about him. He's a brutal, self-made man, but unlike most self-made people, he is not down to earth. He's intolerably pretentious about his wealth. He's also authoritarian. My poor mama suffered under his thumb. You know, Mila, the silence between the two of them was deafening. It was a burden to me as a child."

Milada stroked his hands, kissed them, and said softly, "All that is over. It's over now."

"I often think how Mother was sacrificed. She was a lovely, sweet woman with the most extraordinary good heart ever! I have fond memories of her poems and her fairytales. All the wonderful things she introduced me to! Her world was alive. The inanimate things around her—from items on her shelves to the smallest ball of yarn—took on life in her hands. What wonderful games we devised. We went on marvelous expeditions in two rooms. They were a world for us! Papa lived downstairs, and only on the most needful occasions of her life did she go downstairs to see him. One time, after she had gone down to visit, servants brought her upstairs unconscious." Gustav leapt up. "Since that time, from that hour on, I hate this man who calls himself my father."

He was entirely swept away. He was heroic. And Milada admired him. He was fearless, a shining knight—*who, we mention as an aside, happened to get five hundred gulden every month from this man who called himself Gus's father. Moreover this father regularly put up with being presented a sizable amount in bills, which he paid with palpitations.*

"How happy your mother must have been to have you!"

"That's true. But before I was born she lived alone with him for six years, that is to say, alongside him. She stayed in this horrible, dark, deafening house, filled from top to bottom with chunks of iron, this woman who came from a paradise. I can't understand it. Why did he ever choose her? She didn't fit with him or his nature at all. She bottled up the rich treasure of her soul. Her face changed abruptly in his presence. When she was ill, she cried out when he came near her. At the end of her life I didn't let him near her. I believe, Mila, that's why he hates me so terribly much."

"Oh, Gus, nobody hates you. He doesn't either. Who could hate you?" she said, shaking her head vehemently.

"Why should I care he hates me? Believe you me, our relationship of hate is deserved. I understand his hate. I would be disgusted if he loved me. In that I'm like Mama. To his credit, when it comes to money, he is completely honorable. That's all I want from him."

"When you're finished with your studies and are a licensed physician, you won't take his money."

"Mila, that'll be a while. Just getting through university will take some time. I'm not sure I want to study medicine. Mama had great plans for me. Grandma always told me that, too. But Mama died and took everything with her, including my future."

Milada laid her hand on his mouth, "Don't talk like that, Gus. You can do anything you want. With your wonderful capabilities you'll succeed. Easily."

"Girl, let me tell you what I often think. I belong in nature. It feels right. I should have become a farmer or a woodsman, something along those lines. You can't believe how wonderful I feel in the mountains. The small and mean parts of me dissolve, as they do for every human being. I throw myself on the beautiful earth, hug it. But how can I tell my father this? There's no way of talking with him. On my soul I swear I want to change my course. God, how I would love to have an estate in the country, somewhere in Corinthia. It's easy to get land in Tyrol. And then! With that, dear God!"

He pulled Milada close to him. "I would be very happy to live there. I wouldn't have any constraints. I could get away from conventions and leave cares behind me. What do you think people would say about that? I'd like to take you along with me, my darling, and keep you there and be happy with you. Then the whole crew of people in the Imperial State with all their plans for my becoming an administrator can go stand on their head. I'll sing while they do."

"Gus, are you saying this on my account? That would be... Tell me, is this all because of me?" She moved aside and look at him earnestly. She raised her forefinger, "Are you really studying when you come here?"

"But of course I am! I've been at the books all afternoon. But what's nicer is kissing you from your forehead right on down."

She lay down in his arms and asked, "Don't you drop your schoolwork. I'm considering what I will be in your life. Do you like that?"

"It's sweet, girl. Very sweet. What do you want from me? Ambition? I don't have any. At least not now. Just let me be happy! Let me dissolve in you. That's a huge order, you're so deep." He kissed her greedily.

She pulled back. "That's not all," she declared decisively. "You can't drop your schoolwork on my account. Love won't make me proud, if..."

"If I don't do well on my exams. Don't moralize to me, sweetheart! Other people do that plenty enough. By the way, tomorrow I will be with family. We are having a celebration at Aunt Councilor's. Do you know what that means? There'll be girls with blond pigtails, pale as watered tea, turning somersaults. They'll be dry, like the cakes they serve. We'll have piles of whipped cream as sweet and gooey as my aunt's conversation. The high point of the day is Asti spumanti in liqueur glasses. Ugh. And that's why tomorrow my brown darling has to stay by herself."

She listened dreamily. "Gus," she said after a while. "There's something I want to ask of you. He opened her folded hands and answered grandiosely, "Speak, and it will be done, m'lady."

"Take me out to the country! Let me lie on the ground in the forest the whole day long, where all I see are the colors of the sky. And you. Miller. will have apoplexy if I take vacation time. But I want to go very badly."

"I'll slay Miller without further ado," he replied in earnest.

She laughed and put her face close to his. "You've certainly made me set my heart on this."

"Seeing Miller slain? Yes, I made you want that."

"I'd never thought about going out to the country before. I'd never even wanted to leave this alley. But now it appeals to me, draws me. It feels as if the earth has something to tell me."

"You can be sure of that, Milada. The earth speaks."

"When I'm close to you, like I am now, when I feel your presence, warm and alive, I have the sense I've already begun a trip to the country. It's as if I were inside you and closer to the earth. It seems I've been away from the earth this whole time."

Gus shook his head. "I can't imagine not knowing the countryside. As long as I can remember I've always been moved by the power of Nature. It gives me resilience. The business of everyday living makes me agitated. I need sensation, encouragement, and a wealth of perceptions that aren't always available in the city. In Nature I have no expectations. Everything is in harmony and good. In daily life in the city I find a lot makes no sense to me. When I'm high in the mountains I am in touch with myself, like the time I stood on the Matterhorn in icy rain while snow fell in an avalanche. I was finally able to grieve about my mother's death. One year after the catastrophe of losing her, up there, I cried." His voice was muffled.

"Oh, Gus, I don't have a connection with anything that immense or pure. It must feel good to love something that is not human. It is beyond our will and apart from our feelings. It never changes. Experiencing Nature allows people to bear great bitterness."

Gus recited this ditty:

When a girl betrays you
Find the love of another
Or better still, leave town
Take your knapsack and go a-wandering.

"Nature is good for that, too," she nodded. "But now I have to go downstairs."

"I don't know myself whether Nature helps with betrayal. For the moment I'd like to enjoy myself."

"Well, with your permission, I must go."

"But I haven't enjoyed myself," he protested. "I can't help it. I'm raw right now."

He enclosed her in his arms and kissed her eyes, which she closed under the hot breath of his mouth. He kissed her lips, and her smile faded.

"Love me. Do love me in spite of yourself," he whispered to her. She did not move.

She sighed and pulled him down on herself. She buried her head in his shoulder to hide the deathly cold expression that came over her face. She was cold as ice. She felt horror. And his young, exuberant love rushed over her silent body.

In silence she let the full measure of his caresses flow over herself. She pressed his pale face against herself to soothe him. She kissed his eyes. They were transfixed and burned with passion at the shudder of this weary woman's body.

"Love me. Love me like I love you!" he pled. Milada's wore a tense, brooding expression. She looked off into the void in response to his plea. She saw, in rapid succession, a multitude of oppressive images. She was flooded with visions and sounds that blotted out the splendor and happiness of her life. With painful clarity she recalled degrading embraces when some man's whipped-up lust triumphed. It was the tired force of habit.

Far too much had happened to her. She froze at the glow of this type of passion. His precious face now looked alien. It was distorted and conveyed nothing to her. She was captive to a monstrous fear at these moments. Milada wanted to get up, call his name, and shake him back to himself. But the sheer weight and force of his body held her down. "What's happening?" she froze in fear. "Don't I love him? This is Gustav after all. It is Gus."

And the feeling of being a prostitute—after having so much sacred joy—flew through her precisely at this moment. She could not stand the man she had chosen and desired.

Some minutes later, when, quiet and spent, he buried his head in her breasts and put his exhausted arms around her, then her tenderness returned. Then she felt passion for him. In these moments the conundrum of love hit her; it struck her in her tormented flesh.

"I could love someone more than I love him. It would be love without pain or regret. That love would be for someone small, weak, and helpless, a person who would die without my love... A child!"

With a terrible rage she looked down at herself. Her body contained her longing only for the sake of ruining her without pity.

Bina Michal had arrived at her new place of residence two weeks before a telegram arrived at Red House: "Sick Auntie arrive by train tonight 9:30. Signed Great Fellow, Budweis."

That was the way Fischer in Budweis sent telegrams to people working with his agents.

Milada took a coach to the train station.

In the meantime Gus was sitting comfortably with Joe in a wine cellar. The two of them had picked up Ollie at work and walked her home. Joe sat with legs outstretched in front of his glass of wine, taking cigarettes from Gus's cigarette case, which lay open for him. Gus was talking away eagerly, unpacking all his experiences.

"You should see what ridiculous letters Milada gets from Horner. You can't believe what kind of panegyrics he writes about her. His writing is excellent though."

"I remember one good phrase of his, 'the revulsion and avarice peculiar to the human.' The language is odd but good," Joe offered.

"There's no question he has a good mind. He was, of course, attached to Mila. But he's gone now. He couldn't take my showing up in her life."

How much satisfaction lay in Gustav's pretty young face! He stroked his English mustache and leaned forward across the table to speak in confidence.

"Come with me, Joe, and read her writing. You'll see how well she understands the philosophers she's read. It's astonishing! She has a way of expressing herself that's fresh and novel to read. It suggests the ingenious perception of a child. I'd love to see her study at university. Old pal, that's a good idea, now that I think about it. Let's all three go to Berlin. That would be a solution to getting her away from here."

"That's one costly solution," Joe said dryly.

"Not an issue!" Gus was quite worked up. "I can sell my collection of miniatures. That would bring a tidy sum. What do you think?"

Joe let out a whistle. "And what do you imagine I would be doing in all this?"

"You could tutor her for the university entrance exams. She'd sail through them. Just between us: living here is done and over. Well, old pal, what do you say to that? You could tutor her in Berlin as easily as here. You could live with us."

Joe flicked the ashes off his cigarette. "Do you honestly think she'll go along with this just that easily?" Joe said, rolling his eyes to show doubt.

Gus looked at Joe in astonishment. "Mila? Go along with me? On the instant. You don't know her. It's clear to me you have no idea what all she'd be open to. If I suggested we go to Africa, she'd be ready on the instant. Want to make a bet?" Gus was worked up. "She'd do it for me. We're only talking about going to Berlin here. Africa is too far away for me." Gus put out his broad hand to shake on the bet. "It's a deal then. I have the impression you don't do well with prophesying the future, Joe. Maybe you think my girl has plans for disappointing me massively. Let me assure you she hasn't done one single thing against me, ever."

"That just shows me she's much smarter than I'd ever given any woman credit for being. She's seen right through you."

Gus's reply was sharp, "Thanks for that, Joe. You're saying she thinks I'm too stupid to know what she's planning? Well, you might be right." He leaned back and fiddled with the chain of his watch.

Joe opened his eyes wide. Usually his eyes were swollen and sleepy, but now they looked sharp and piercing.

"Oh, so you're annoyed," Joe said. "Just think it over, you dope. Think about our friendship. You know very well that... But trying to tell you anything is a waste."

"Joe, my friend, I think you and Seidner have basically always underestimated me. And I pretty much put up with it. But most likely Mila doesn't share your opinion of me. She has her own opinion." After a while Gus drew his friend, whose face was knitted in annoyance, back into conversation, "Let's not let this point ruin the evening. You're my good friend. Just a second and I'll order a really nice Tokay, and we can drink to the triad in Berlin."

Joe, ill at ease, mumbled Virgil's line about a snake in the grass in Latin, "*Latet anguis in herba.*" And Gus went off to fetch the bottle of wine. He shook his head and sank down, looking at his empty glass.

At that moment a small carriage pulled up in front of Red House. First Milada got out. Behind her was a small, well-nourished Jewish boy. He wore jackboots and a red cap he kept pushing back and forth across his head of tight curly hair. Behind him, wrapped in a heavy blue veil and hidden under an old-fashioned Indian shawl, the new girl from Olmuetz in Moravia crawled out of the carriage.

Fischer's son Fischer Junior had come along. He spoke up about the family business, "We've got connections all the way to Turkey. The Sultan got the girls in his harem from my father!"

She said not a word. Her black eyes showed distress. Her pale face was long and narrow. Milada wondered, "This scared little girl was supposed to have been involved with an officer?! Hard to believe."

Fischer Junior offered, "She has to get used to the light first. Right, Lolo?" He poked her. "Then she'll start talking. Right, Lolo?"

The girl breathed a sigh of relief when her escort took his leave. Milada took Lolo to her room, brought her a coffee and a pastry, and helped her put her things up in the closet. She came with a very carefully selected wardrobe. After a while Lolo sat on the edge of the bed and looked at Milada vacantly.

"That should do it," said Milada. "I've got to go downstairs now. Today you can rest up. And tomorrow you'll be ready to go."

"Are you the manager?" Lolo asked with a deep, hoarse voice that sounded rusted out and destroyed.

"Yes, I am. Address me formally as Madame," Milada told her dryly.

"Are there officers downstairs?"

"We don't have officers here."

She opened her eyes wide in surprise. "No?! Officers don't come to your house? Not one single officer?" She grabbed her head and swayed, "Jesus, my God! Jesus, my God!" she sighed heavily.

"I'd say you can be glad about that. You're free of them here," Milada was short.

"I just want to die," Lolo whimpered. "I want to lie down and die." She began to cry loudly. Milada shrugged. "It's all right. You'll be fine here," she said to calm her. "Make sure the madam doesn't see you crying like this. She doesn't want a scene. She doesn't put up with crying."

In the afternoon at two o'clock the house was quiet. It stayed quiet a few hours. The girls were sound asleep. The porter collected dirty dishes, and the laundress began her work without making a sound. In the evening she lay down to sleep on the floor.

Miller took a short nap in the office. And Milada sat in her room, writing letters and leafing through the newspaper Gus brought her daily. The July sun burned hot and sparkled through the drawn curtains. Milada wore a very light, soft-blue negligee that covered her but left her lovely back bare.

"Look here," she said to Gus. He was lying on the bed and smoking. There were beads of perspiration on his forehead. He was in a bad mood, unhappy with himself.

It had been three days since he had had the conversation with Joe about the Berlin project, and he had not had the chance or been in the frame of mind to talk about it with Milada. He had become more attached to going through with it. Yet what had seemed to him at first such a simple matter and such an easy thing to do now looked complicated. There were obstacles. Milada was bound to her work, personally bound to it. She had an emotional attachment and a sense of duty. There were hundreds of other reasons she was committed to Red House. Oh, God, how he avoided bringing up the topic! He knew instinctively she was not free to go. She was always completely, actively engaged in her work. At base he knew he was secondary. Her personal pleasure was second to the importance of her job.

What if she rejected the idea out of hand? What if she tried to get him to give up the idea altogether? What if, as Joe had suspected, she had absolutely no intention of looking for another kind of work? Then he would look like a fool. Despite love and passion he would be disgraced. This prospect bothered him. She had her own head. Her sense of independence was nigh onto unpleasant. Her refusal would be a fiasco after his conversation with Joe. Getting Milada to go along with his plan had become almost a point of honor with Gus.

Milada sat down next to Gus and opened a letter. "It's from Fanny," she explained.

> Dear Milahda!
>
> Ive bin playin zither at the spa. Im doing good cuz I cann play the zither and dans. It iz fun and gives me energy but thats about it. Olympia iz still in the hospital about the same just like me with my lungs. Comm on over. Im gettin a bit scared. Can you gett my red silk dres from Zimmermann? She iz a bich. Say hello to evrybudy from me. To Bina for sure. Not to that bich. Forever and love. I cant leave. Fanny

"Charming," said Gus, with the corners of his mouth turned down.

"Want to go downstairs?"

"Don't think about it," he shook his head.

"Gus, you're getting lazy."

"You don't say," he propped his head up on his arm.

"My old man is right," he said suddenly and feigned a yawn. "I should go away."

"Is that what he wants?"

Gus nodded assent. "Yes, today after breakfast I had the dubious pleasure of seeing him. He behaved pleasantly enough and asked about my travel this summer. He was honey-sweet. And Berlin? Want to know something?" He pushed her away from himself. "He's gotten wind of you and me."

Milada bit her lip. "And what makes you say that?"

"You don't know the man. He picks up on everything. When

I was in high school he was already poking around. It was bizarre. How is it he knows about you and me? I have no idea. Who told him? I don't know. But he finds out everything. Maybe he bribed Ollie."

"So then take a trip!"

Gus shrugged. "It doesn't really matter. Whether I do or not, he'll be unpleasant."

"So what are you going to do, Gus?"

"Go off on a trip, of course." He lay back down. It was possible an uncomfortable scene might ensue. This topic might be the tip of an iceberg. All he had to say was, "Come with me, *vederemo*!"

Milada walked over to the window and peeked through the shutters to the harsh light of the street below. She was not thinking of anything in particular. She was only hypnotized by the harshness of the light. She gazed out at the street a while. Then she became somewhat light-headed, and she sat back down to her letters. She reread the following to make sure she understood what it said.

Dr. Lamberg has filed a suit against Mitzi. For the third time she has not paid him his fee. He will not conduct another examination on her.

Milada threw down the letter. "Just take a look at Lamberg! He's making thousands with these examinations, but when..."

Gus replied sharply and with a shaky voice, "I thought we might talk about other matters, Milada."

She looked at him in surprise. He had his arms crossed, and intense anger smoldered in his eyes.

"Do you honestly not care whether I go away and leave you here? Do you think you're made of marble?"

"But Gus! You would only be leaving for a few weeks. I've had to accept that ever since I've known you," she said and looked at him in amazement.

"This time if I leave, it will be for years," he replied. "And who knows if I'll ever be back."

"Gus!" she did not raise her voice. She only lifted up her arms.

He jumped up and knelt before her. There was something in her face that terrified him. It was gray as lead and stark. All power upon life failed her.

"You have to understand. I knew this would happen," he inhaled deeply with a feeling of victory.

(His first thought was, "Joe needs to see this.")

He embraced her tenderly. "You don't have to pretend you are invulnerable."

(Gus was thinking, "So look what's happened to stupid Joe's bet now.)

"I hadn't really known," Milada murmured, helpless. "I thought it would be for a short while."

"You shouldn't think, my darling, and you should not have to know. You must listen to me and trust me." He pulled her down next to him.

"Look here, my love, for three days I've been thinking about us, and I've been distressed. I wanted to spare you my turmoil. I wanted to come to some resolution on my own. My old man has found out about us. He hates me and never wishes me any joy in life. He knows how to curtail our involvement, Mila! He has that kind of power. I know what I'm saying. This wouldn't be the first time he has quashed my happiness with his fist. I need to plan my defense. I have to arm myself when he advances. He has other means to use against me. You, Mila, and your situation are in his sights. All he has to do is make a signal, and you'll be forced to leave town. These thoughts and ideas, these prospects cut me up. I have no peace. I cannot pay attention to my studies. It's my constant concern for you that makes me suffer so. This milieu! Mila, I am a man. I can't get past this place. I suffer a lot." He put his head on her shoulder and sighed.

She thought, "What does this mean? The end? Has the curtain now been pulled aside? Is my good fortune gone?" In doubt, she looked down to the bottom of her soul. She believed everything had taken flight. She found no words to comfort him; she could not come up with one good word. She did not understand one iota. He said he had known all along it would come to this. "What can I say to him?" she wondered. "He's expecting some kind of reply." But Milada did not deign, even as she was faltering, to use the crutch of a lie. She simply remained quiet.

"I know. I feel it. I will be destroyed for our love. You live here, and I live far away in another world. The horrible nights you spend here are torment enough for me. I have tried not to think about you here. But home alone I put the pillow over my head. The thought plagues me. I see… Oh, hell!" Gus stood up. "Mila, if I want to keep from going mad, this situation has to end. Don't look at me like that! I can't take it from you. I would sooner die than have you look at me like that. Mila, you have to understand. No woman will ever possess me like you do. I will never lose myself in anyone again."

"Lose?" she murmured.

He moved his hand across his forehead. "Just feel how hot I am!" He enjoyed feeling her cool fingers for a moment on his head. Then he came up with a fresh tack.

"Mila, listen! I've been talking with Joe. He knows what I'm going to say. He knows how I feel. Joe and I have come up with a plan. It's not something I just dreamed up at the moment. I've considered it from all angles. We'll leave here and go to Berlin, all three of us." Gus looked at her. She propped her head up in her hands and listened attentively. There was a deep furrow in her brow. She weighed his every word, and that made him uncomfortable.

"All three of us will go to Berlin. I know my way around there. Life there is very different. It's bigger, freer, and more stimulating. People there are living in this century. Here people are only talking about it. There you live among millions of people independently as yourself. You don't know who is breathing down my neck here. I have aunts, uncles, and cousins, and all of them are in prominent positions. They are in my private life as if they reside in my home. Here I am forever in the fold of the family."

"And because of this you're telling me I should go to Berlin?"

"Isn't that reason enough, Milada? My future is in..."

She put her hands up to cover her eyes. "I'm trying to think this through, Gus."

He tugged on his moustache.

"Joe and I have pledged neither of us would ever marry. That's an established pledge," he said nervously. "It might look like our motives are purely selfish. But that's not true. Joe holds you in high regard. He knows very well I once..."

He sat down and took her hands from her eyes. He was ill at ease.

"Look at me when I'm talking to you. When you are elsewhere in your thoughts it makes me nervous. Joe and I want you to study medicine in Berlin. You are gifted, and here all your gifts are wasted on this profession! I can imagine you practicing in a children's hospital. You would enjoy that enormously. Do you doubt you could do that? Isn't work like this possible? Couldn't it happen?

"I'm too old," she said with the expression an adult has when speaking to a dear child.

"You'd be done with your studies in six or seven years."

"Gus, you have no idea how tired and old I am," she said with the most intense expression a human can wear. "A fresh start!" she sighed. "If you'd come to me with that offer five years ago, maybe. But now it's too late."

"So you're not going with us? You're refusing?" he said and stood up.

"I'm bound to Miller by contract. As long as she runs the business, I have to be here. But that's not the reason. For that matter she could enter the cloister tomorrow. And she would probably like to do that. Once she's gone, I'm free. Free? Free?"

She shook her head a bit.

He stomped his foot. “So you don’t love me? Everything you said was a lie or a whim?” He threw himself on an armchair and buried his head in the upholstery.

Joe had been right all along. He had been taken for a fool. But why? What was keeping her in Red House? He did not really care a whit about Berlin. But now there was no going back. He had to keep going with his act.

“Are you worried about money? I...” That was brutal, but before he could speak she had surrounded him with her arms.

“Don’t talk like that,” she said softly.

“Don’t play games with me. You hide from me behind a bulwark of games. It’s wearing me out.”

She had taken up her favorite position, standing at the window. He fiddled nervously with his cigarette. He had crumpled it.

“Gus, you have more good fortune than I do,” she said finally, exhaling. “You have words to say what you think. I can’t find words to express myself. I have such nonsensical longings. I fumble around in my thoughts. Everything looks gray and shadowy. I know I can’t make myself clear to you.”

She walked over to his chair and knelt next to him. “Gus, I’m not alone. It’s not possible for me to be happy in such an ill-fated way. I can’t feel satisfied when others go hungry.”

“I do understand that,” he said magnanimously and, at the same time, he felt freed up since he had yet another way to approach this plan cleverly. “You have girls here around you who believe in you. You have more or less become a savior to them. That’s fairly much the way it is. They would see your leaving your position here—your flight, as you frame it—as a betrayal or something like that. It’s fair to expect that reaction from them. Yet all these girls, I assure you, can be rehabilitated and live in the middle class. I’m good friends with the president of the Magdalene House. Just give me addresses for these girls. Fanny would certainly be eligible. The people at Magdalene House would take her on and put her to better work than you could ever provide her. Then you'd be free of them, free!"

"Gus, how wonderfully easy and free of horror everything in the abyss is when your finger points to it. Free? Once Horner told me, 'If you only had an inkling, girl, what it means to be free! A person can be free of obligation and free of what he has the ability to do, but only God is free of desire and need. The finest attribute of godliness would be absolute freedom. You,' Horner said to me, 'can unwind the spool of string on which you hang like a kite. The length of string may get longer, but you'll eventually find the string on the spool has an end. Then you'll be pulled back, even if you had been sailing high in the clouds.' That's what Horner said. At this moment I'm aware of the end of that string."

"So you're sacrificing me to some fixed notion you have?" he asked derisively and very much in control.

She looked at him as if pleading, with a long, compelling gaze. "Can't you accept, Gus, I've seen and experienced a lot of suffering here? Don't you take seriously that from my earliest childhood everything has been anguish for me? My life was wretched until I had those sacred hours with you. Can't you just let my reality be? Do you think you can extinguish all the years of my life with one breath? As if they were little flames for you to blow out? Gus, when I laughed, it was in a way wrong. I was having fun when I kissed you. I shouldn't have fallen in love. I shouldn't have given myself over to anyone. I am not free. People like me are bound to be solitary. I didn't have the strength to go on living when you came into my life. I made a mistake. I love you."

Completely shaken Gus bent down to her. He was torn between two clutches of iron. Why talk about these painful feelings and listen to her talk about them? "I'm not actually going to leave her. Berlin or no Berlin. Only because everybody wants me to? I'm not going to leave her."

The other claw held him against his weak will. He had lost his bet with Joe! "In a minute you, the fool, will throw yourself at her and beg for forgiveness. And Joe with his supercilious self-satisfaction will have won once again."

Milada continued. "Wherever I go in life, I'll take the experiences of these days I've had with you. Living like I have has enriched my soul. A new life in Berlin would oppress me. I wouldn't have the resilience I would need with my limited strength. Milada would be no more. Don't object, just listen. I want you to hear me."

She brushed her hand across her forehead. "Once I wanted to come to understand the meaning of lives like these. I wanted to understand what we are, why we are relegated to the corners and forced to live a life robbed of will. I hoped to grasp why we had to be destroyed. And when I finally saw—because of Horner—," she stood up, born by her thoughts, "then the rebellion began. We began to invent a new world, we two. We wanted to create things completely fresh. We wanted new laws. Don't laugh! Those ideas were exhilarating. That was my youth. I will be thankful to him my whole life that I dreamed like that. Things changed for me. I started studying. There were lots of books.

"Serious ideas, hard numbers, and iron-clad laws gave me something solid to hang onto. There were ideas that threw me back; ideas that moved me forward; and there were some that swept me up and gave me solace. My rage cooled and died. For a while the rage in my heart was quelled. Then a thousand tiny seedlings began to sprout. Now I feel only love. And I have to help, Gus. I don't know life by looking on. I don't watch with envy from afar. I know how to grab life. It takes a lot of money. And more than that it takes love. I know things, Gus, all your friends at the Magdalene House don't know. For some people it takes only a little push to fall all the way down; for others, only a smile to pick themselves back up. All of us need to be endlessly forgiven. We need a hand that doesn't turn into a fist. You told me the truth. You hadn't saved one person until now. But what does it mean to save someone? Is a moment of good luck, of rest, of trust not some salvation? Oh, Gus, when we give a hungry man something, isn't it possible we have avoided some crime or kept someone from being destroyed? That person has gotten some relief, and perhaps he will not be tempted to be violent. His hunger is sated, and he's become calm. You have performed some act that is a bulwark against further crime. Any act of kindness I perform for these girls is real, and that one minute is blessed. Gus, I have to help. My compassion for people like me burns in my breast. It hurts like a wound. One thing and one thing only has ever moved me: the love I feel for these suffering creatures."

As Milada spoke, Gus's face hardened. His typical goodly, effeminate mouth had drawn into a hard line. If Milada had looked at him then, she would have seen how similar his iron face was to David Brenner's. But she was facing the window, and her gaze was directed to the sunlight. It was painful to her eyes, and she closed them against the discomfort.

"My father is a wealthy, landed man," she said softly, as if talking to herself. Each word was punctuated with a shudder.

"He presides over his estate, so people say, like a prince. My mother came from a mountain village of poor, hungry weavers. She was beautiful and sweet! She laughed and sang. All the men's hearts begged for her. But my father did not want to marry her. He pushed her away. So she left with me, before I was born, and came to this house. She never got close to anyone. She crucified her own dignity. She had me here. I took in this air. Heaven told me my first fairy tales. When it rained, I opened my mouth to drink in the drops. I played with the leaves that fell and fought with the ones that blew away. When it was cold, I heard, go find yourself a blanket!

"I went outside and found the sun. If I was hungry, I heard, go find yourself something to eat! I went outside, and the alley always yielded enough. No one had mercy on me. The street was my home. It mothered me. Don't I have thousands of sisters just like me?" Her voice broke.

Milada's words shot through Gustav's body like an electrical current.

Power was the only thing that would work. He had to resort to power. Otherwise she would slip away from him.

He pulled her over to himself with physical force and pressed kisses hard against her mouth as she sobbed.

"I love you, Mila. No one has ever excited me like you. I don't love you as just a woman. I love you as a human being, your wonderful self."

He lifted her head to himself and looked directly into her eyes. "Can you live without me? Do you think you can?"

He pressed his head tight against her shoulder in anger. He was hurting her.

"Then I will have to leave. Do you understand that? I have no other choice. Do you understand me? I wanted to spare you. Why are you forcing me to do this?" He let go of her and turned his face away. His brow was furrowed.

"I gave my word of honor."

She looked at him, puzzled, "Why? Your...?"

He stomped his foot. "Why? For what? Don't torture me for details. I am an officer in the military. Word of my relationship with you has apparently gotten around, anonymously, in certain circles. The situation has become very, very difficult among those of some standing. The commander of my regiment has called me up for breaking my word of honor. He's going to send me abroad since I refused to break off my relationship with you."

Milada covered her face with her hands.

"Milada, you have no idea how judgmental people are. You live in a pleasant bubble of delusion. Everything you think or say affects me. I see your soul in all that. But the world will chew you up with all your plans. You have no idea how much dirt people have heaped on our involvement. You manage a brothel. And I, your lover, spend my time in a brothel. You hold an opinion of this place that is benevolent. But I assure you in certain circles people see us very differently. For them I am… It's better I say nothing further.

"What are all those filthy souls to me in comparison to you if you stay with me, Mila? I have nothing on Earth but you."

Gus glowed with satisfaction at himself. He had struck the right tone. His discomfort and tension had slowly given way to a theatrical, imperious feeling of security. Her words had initiated his need to use force. He teared up at this feeling of security, and his voice swelled with disdain and longing.

"Mila, you are all I have on Earth."

Milada was pale. She listened. The light in her eyes was extinguished. She made a gesture of defense with her firm, calm hands. Her hands seemed to push something away.

"Then, of course, you must leave. I support you and will not ask you to do anything for me. It's dreadful to think you have had to go through this on my account. Please do not ask me. If you want me and if you want to take me with you, then I will go. Will you ever forgive me, dearest? My poor dear!" She laced her fingers together and pressed them to her forehead.

The pain in her flat outcry reached Gus. It punctured the shelter of his vain, satisfied masculinity. He chose a known style of behaving. He would be the happy, free-spirited boy. Yes, that would be the right tack to take. It would surely do the trick.

"Oh, Mila, please don't think I regret leaving this place. Quite the opposite. I'm thankful to you for the exchange. I might not have chosen it on my own. But now, now I am limitlessly happy about a new life with you and Joe. In Berlin you will know what it means to feel comfy. It just takes getting to know Berlin." He held her in his arms.

"And what about your father? Will he…?"

"Hold your tongue, I beg you. I don't want to hear anything

more about it. You'll learn to dance French dances, and you'll eat lovely cream cakes. We'll lead a respectable life. I wish away all the marks of trouble on your face. Be gone!" She laughed lightly. Gus continued, "Well done! As your reward you may stop worrying. For the next six hours I'm going to set the itinerary. Listen up, Mila! Go downstairs and fetch ice-cold champagne, the very best. We'll enjoy drinking up the bottle and practice celebrating like the Prussians of Berlin. Then I'll go home. And at eight o'clock you'll come over. Joe will be there. I ask you, please, make no mention of what I said about the military, heaven forbid! Some things must remain completely secret. *Allez, demoiselle*!"

Gus threw himself down on the bed and let go a sigh of relief. And as she went down the stairwell, slowly, tipsy as if drugged, trying in vain to salvage her usual, careful sobriety, at this never-ending-seeming moment, his voice rang out. He was awash in the past and a future taking form, sketchily in a blue haze. The sound of his singing filled the house, as he inverted the lyrics of the old soldier's tune, "*Muss i denn*" about leaving one's girl behind: "I've got to go, must go, and quit this town. And you, my love, will come along."

Milada stopped for a second to listen. The girls stirred in their afternoon naps. Miller heard. She became enraged and waggled her head back and forth.

Chapter 6
Solitude

The Immortals lift up lost children.
—Goethe

The new girl from Budweis, Lolo, plagued Miller nonstop. It also plagued Miller that she had had to trade out lovely, good, capable Bina Michal for this newcomer. Milada had to listen to Miller complain about how slovenly, disagreeable, and resentful Lola was. She completely lacked any style or charm, and she was entirely uninterested in the business. Lolo sat around in the salon and hardly replied when someone spoke with her. Of course, she was not earning her keep. Miller could really use someone to liven up the salon, which was mostly filled with people from abroad looking for something special. They were not taken with this girl who had no spark. Miller sulked and carped, just as she always did when she got wind of any loss of income.

After Lolo's initial howling outburst upon arrival Milada got nothing further out of her. She stayed unapproachable and obstinate, and she gave this response to all warnings and demands: "I'm working, getting it done. Don't worry." She was pretty enough to please customers. Her coal-black eyes glistened when she was not upset and were fixed straight ahead. Lolo usually sat slumped down in a large, upholstered chair, looking apathetic. She tugged at her hairdo so that it was askew. And when someone addressed her, she popped up as if she had been napping. Rather remarkably, she became popular right away with the other girls. They knew her to be soft and agreeable, and she lent others her perfumes, combs, and dresses. She did what the girls asked of her without complaint.

Men who came to be entertained took no interest in her. They dropped her after a few miserable visits. And so, very soon, and much to Miller's dismay, she sat in the salon all by herself. She sat, stared off into space, and tugged at her hair.

"So, what does she say to all of you?" Milada asked the girls.

"She says the people at Fischer's took her money. She doesn't talk much with us."

"She says she's scared and has a lot of worries. That's about it." "She's fearful but doesn't say why," another girl offered.

So Milada went directly to Lolo. "What's going on with you? Yesterday a gentleman complained to the madam about you. Listen here, my dear, you can't keep acting like this."

"I didn't say anything bad to anyone," Lolo replied.

"I didn't think you had. But you let them know you're not interested. You don't chat with them. You look put out, just like you do now. At least look at me when I speak. I don't bite. Be a little forthcoming. What's bothering you?"

Milada stroked Lolo's curly, blue-black hair lightly. With gentle, kind strokes Milada ran her hand over the girl's brow, which was furrowed with resentment.

"Madame, oh, Madame!" Lolo fell on her knees. "Please let me leave this place. For God's sake let me leave so I won't die. I'm worth nothing here as it is."

"Don't be like that, Lolo! You were at Fischer's for two years. You got to know this work there. Don't put me on."

"But at Fischer's I had only Karl. Nobody else, I swear on my mother's soul. There was nobody else. But Karl's commander, a man named Steger, wanted to have me so we had the worst bad luck. I begged Karl, 'Let him come. I promise he won't mean anything to me. Who knows what he'll do to you, Karl! Just let it happen.' But Karl was firm. He didn't want that. Then it happened. Steger gave me money and a ticket. That was my last day there. David Fischer captured me and took the ticket, too."

Lolo's soft, round face resumed its look of shock and horror.

"That is the absolute truth, Madame. I swear to God. On my soul."

"Stop crying. I wish you'd said something before. Now tell me the whole story, calmly. How did you get mixed up with Fischer in the first place? You're from Prague, aren't you?"

The girl nodded. "My name isn't really Lolo. I'm Leopoldine Schwarza. They call me Poldi, and I'm from Prague. My father..." She stopped, filled with fear.

"Keep going," Milada prompted her.

"Madame, please don't tell anybody about this. Papa would lose his position, and that would be the end for him."

"It's just between us. Tell me about it."

Lolo confessed everything. She had come from a respectable family. Her father was the porter for Duke Czernin at the palace outside the city. She was never allowed out of the house. But young Poldi accompanied the wife of Councilor Winter, at the lady's request, on her regular walk in Czernin Park. At the time Karl was a young cadet and Lady Winter's daughter Aglaia was fifteen. The two girls were like friends. One day Lady Winter told her, "Poldi, do be a good girl and do what the people at court ask." If she did, said the lady, nothing bad would happen to her. She said Poldi was like a daughter to her. Poldi was happy at the time.

When Karl was made a lieutenant and returned to the palace, Lady Winter sent Aglaia away to Switzerland. Poldi missed her friend and cried. The lady told her, "Now you have Karl here to love." Poldi was given Aglaia's clothes to wear. There were blouses and fine pinafores. She was dressed very well.

In the evening the aristocrats went to the theater. Poldi served tea, cut the cakes, and arranged the sandwiches. She was responsible for serving the lieutenant, who sat alone. Poldi was the only one who sat with him. He said otherwise the food would not taste good to him. He often told her he would be stationed somewhere else and that he would take her along as a servant.

Lolo's eyes glowed like stars as she spoke. Her pupils were large, and she was charged with happiness.

Then all of a sudden everything changed. If she had known what would happen to her, she would never have said anything to anybody. She only told Karl because she was scared and felt deathly ill. Karl went directly to his mother. Oh, God, what a horrible day that was! Everybody knew and was yelling. Lady Councilor was yelling, even the cook. But Karl yelled the most. Lolo was locked in the cellar. Later that evening Karl came to her, stroked her, and told her to be quiet. He promised her that her parents would never hear about what happened. He promised he would never leave her, never. Two days later Karl put her in a coach and took her to Mrs. Kratochvil. Mrs. Kratochvil could not walk and was in a wheelchair. That woman was very skilled. And although Lolo was left in a lot of pain, it was done. Lola stayed on with Mrs. Kratochvil for five months. Karl paid for her stay, but Lolo still had to cook and clean. Kratochvil had many aristocratic clients. They even arrived in royal carriages.

Karl was sent to Budweis. But Lolo was not allowed to live with him as his mistress. Her presence aggravated people too much for that. She was sent to Fischer's as a maid. Karl made sure her work was only serving as a housemaid. Karl spoke directly with

Fischer Senior who promised by all that is holy she would work only as a housemaid.

For a while all was well. Then came the horrible scene with Karl's commander. At Fischer's in public view the commander grabbed her and kissed her and announced loudly that all the girls there were available to any guest. He said since Lolo was not living with Karl, she was available to him. Poldi begged Karl to let the commander have his way, but Karl supposedly refused. He said he would sooner hack the man to pieces. And then the trouble began. Karl slapped his commander's face as a public insult and challenge. His superior pulled a revolver and shot. She fell to the floor unconscious and did not see what happened after that. Things went from bad to worse. The commander went to Fischer and made a scene. He threatened to close Fischer down. It was miserable.

David Fischer, the son, stuck Lolo in a room with a concealed door. It was where the officers gambled. That evening an orderly came to see her. He brought a few lines Karl had scribbled in pencil, some money, and a ticket to Prague. Karl had written she was to go away immediately. She should pay Fischer if he demanded money and go stay with Kratochvil in Prague. There Karl would be in touch. He probably had to go north to Galicia. It might be even worse. She cried the whole night through.

David Fischer told her the police had arrived and searched for her and that Karl was under arrest. Fischer claimed the police wanted her because she had started things. The police were also looking into Kratochvil's business in Prague, so he said.

She had to leave the room in the dark of the night and go down to the basement. There she sat a long, long time until she cried herself to sleep.

After some time David fetched her and said the police believed she had left a good while ago. He told her his father had had to pay very heavy fines on her account. He named the sum of one hundred fifty gulden, which, he claimed, she now owed them. Karl had to accept a transfer with the military to Galicia if he wanted to have anything further to do with her. According to David he was bound to this because he had given his word of honor.

Lolo continued telling Milada her story, "Madame, when David Fischer hauled me out of the basement, I swear by all that is holy, he stole all my money. He took Karl's note, the ticket to Prague, and the money. He took it all. I told him at the time he'd stolen it, but he swore at me for talking too loudly. For that he locked me away another two weeks. When I cried, he threw me in the basement in the dark and left me hungry until I apologized to him." Lolo sobbed, "For a while he brought me the news from the papers. He told me Karl was in prison for three months in Galicia.

"Then he took me to the train station. I spent the whole night before that in the basement. We left at 5:00 the next morning. We came here, Madame. And David told me I had to stay here. Otherwise, I would be thrown out and sent back to Prague."

Lolo wrung her hands. "My poor father! And Karl has no idea where I am. Oh, Madame, I love him so very much. If he only knew where I am! If he knew, he'd be so unhappy. For his sake I can't say anything about all this. I must keep quiet, I have to."

"Lolo, you weren't smart," said Milada after having listened to her attentively. "That Jew boy certainly did steal your money. Everything he told you about the police and about Karl's arrest was a dreadful lie. If you'd screamed at the top of your lungs at the train station, he'd have run off."

"But then Karl would have been drummed out of the military," Lolo wept. "Fischer did know about Kratochvil."

Milada was quiet. She pressed her lips together and nodded.

"Yes, of course. You had to protect Karl," she said quickly. "Lolo, listen, as it is, you're in a nasty mess. But that's all right. We'll make sure David Fischer gets what he deserves. It might be possible to scare that Jew boy so much that he coughs up some money. Then you can leave a free agent. If we can't get him to come up with some money, then, girl!" Milada stood quietly for a moment, concerned. "Hush now! Even in a bad situation, you can stay on top of things. Focus on Karl. You saved his honor with your sacrifice. You have your integrity intact. Now we have to send Kratochvil a letter to ask whether Karl has written her. Let's do that. And you keep calm. I may be able to help."

"Oh, Madame, Madame!"

Lolo took Milada's hand, and Milada used her other hand to stroke Lolo's hot brow to calm her.

The response to Milada's inquiry to Mrs. Kratochvil came from David Fischer in Budweis. He sent a crude letter, claiming to know nothing about the girl. He said he never saw any money. If, by any means, he had ever come by any money, then it had gone, by rights, to cover the rotten gambling debts of that Lieutenant Karl. Lolo, wrote David, is, after all, a slippery little liar. He wrote Milada that Lolo, as a child of ten in her parents' home, had had sex with the boys. He knew that, he wrote, from Kratochvil. He offered to replace Lolo with other young girls if she was too much trouble.

Milada threw the letter down on the floor. "I am telling you, Gus, David stole her money. But there's more to it. He usurped her father's right of consent. Lolo was underage. What he did was absolutely illegal. That will hang him."

"Mila, Mila, what all have you gotten yourself into these past few weeks!" Gus said, wringing his hands. "You've kept Miller under wraps, sold the business, saved Fanny, and now you're involved in this sweet-smelling transaction with Lolo! I'll tell you what'll come of all this. We won't be able to leave for Berlin. Joe is already making arrangements for an apartment."

Milada said, "It will all work out, Gus. The most difficult part has already been taken care of. Miller is giving her confession today. And tomorrow she is signing the final paperwork for the cloister. I still have to make sure that's in order. I can't have that hanging over my head. Right? If I only knew how to get to that guy Fischer. If I can catch him in an illegal act, then it's all over for him. He'll go to hell in a handbasket."

"Is everything Lolo said vetted?"

"Of course. I'll testify to that. Sucher will, too. But we have to proceed with caution. If Treulich at police headquarters hears of this, or, let's say. even the Baron, just as a matter of personal pride, they'll give Fischer an official citation. Sweet Jesus, here I am looking to get out of this business, and I don't have to think about good credit with the police!"

"So, how's Sucher involved in all this?" Gus asked.

"He liaises with Fischer."

"A tidy little business among buddies. Where are you in your negotiations with Spizzari about selling Red House?"

"In good shape! She's paying. She's paying me, Kessler, who sold Miller the house, and Miller."

Both were silent.

"Gus, would you like to hear Lolo speak for herself?"

He sprawled out across the chair. "Somebody should. I think you aren't disinterested enough." Milada looked at him as if making a plea.

"Gus, it would be great if you would intervene," she said timidly.

Gus smiled to himself. Again, he could call Joe out on his bet about how submissive she was to him.

He twisted the corners of his English-style moustache and spoke up clearly, "I'll do nothing of the sort. The matter looks scandalous. I have to decline getting involved in this smut."

Milada looked mildly distressed. "Do you have reasons?"

"Among other things I promised Joe to keep out of such matters," he said with hesitation.

"You promised Joe!? He doesn't seem like the type to ask that of you. He's a free spirit and has no prejudices."

Gus chuckled ironically. "You're wrong there. Joe embodies the traditional values of the Empire more than any man I know. Furthermore, I should tell you, he has some experience in these matters."

"Shouldn't we be able to get beyond his experiences? Doesn't each new insight from experience tear down the walls between people? I've always found that so. Don't you find it somewhat selfish to let things be decided by someone else's personal experience?"

Gus crumbled what was left of his cigarette and said, "Mila, you find people far too altruistic. People aren't idealistic by nature."

"Oh, Gus," she said warmly as she walked over to him, "I watched how you treated Fanny when she was ill. I saw how you dressed her wounds without hesitation."

"I am a physician," Gus chimed in.

"But you were also pleased to see her recover, weren't you? You wanted to help her, Gus. That goes beyond the limited definition of physician."

He clasped her hands and held her tight. "Mila, if I did not know we will be far away from here in six weeks, I wouldn't do it."

She looked at him earnestly, "And when we're in Berlin, can we simply forget about the less fortunate, can we? Can you and I forget?"

"Let's just wait and see where we end up," he said uncomfortably as he stood up.

Gustav was never especially given to carrying through on things. Milada backed off completely. She saw he needed to regain his feeling of superiority.

"So will you listen to Lolo tell her story?"

"It's possible." He resumed his position in the armchair and his posture of exceptional piteousness.

After a while Lolo entered. She looked around in distress, full of sorrow. Once again she told her story in broken phrases. Milada kept interrupting her with short, precise questions. Lolo's answers gave a clear picture of what had taken place. Milada encouraged her to give exact information about her parents' knowledge and consent. She asked Lolo whether she could imagine her father would ever have given permission for her to lead such a life. At that point Lolo raised her arms and cried out convincingly, genuinely, "No, no! He would have taken his revolver and killed himself first."

Milada and Gus exchanged glances. Before either Milada or Gustav could stop her, she bent down on her knees in front of him and begged him, weeping copiously, to set her free. Gus spoke impulsively, "Mila, she has to leave, regardless of the conditions. We'll send her back to Prague. And that dog Fischer must be beaten so he never forgets."

Gustav sank into silence. His face registered his concern, and he proceeded to smoke cigarette after cigarette.

Impeccably dressed, with a very light Panama hat set on his head, Gustav went, mid-morning, to the Imperial Police Headquarters and, in a rather arrogant tone, demanded to speak to Commissioner Dr. Treulich.

He was calm and, basically, in a good mood. He kept in mind Joe was wrong to construe this or a similar situation as an affair. Absurd! He was simply going to make a deposition with the appropriate authorities. That was all. He was pleased he did some things without Joe's knowledge. Gus would be able to prove to Joe, without wanting to look good, that on some particular points, dear fellow, he was not right.

Furthermore, at this moment Gus was interested in justice. "The most loyal of citizens is morally obliged to speak up against despotism and tyranny," Uncle Benno had said. Gus told himself he was upholding the traditional values of his family.

When Gustav arrived at police headquarters Sucher was having a meal. He inquired what the nature of Gustav's business might be. He was—heaven forfend!—not asking out of personal curiosity. His question was merely pro forma, as Dr. Treulich was interested in having cases sorted out into categories.

Gus looked Sucher up and down. “Mr. Sucher, Sir, may I not speak with the Commissioner myself? Yes or no?” He pulled out his calling card, “Do give him this.”

Sucher laughed impertinently and took Gustav’s calling card. Taking the small steps of a servant Sucher walked across the office and opened a side door with care. Inside Dr. Treulich was yawning behind his newspaper. He acknowledged Gus by raising his eyebrows. “He’s here for some undisclosed matter,” Sucher announced to the Commissioner, handing him the card and looking over the head of the visitor. He closed Treulich’s door summarily.

“Permit me to introduce myself, Gustav Brenner.”

“How might I assist you?”

“My apologies, Mr. Commissioner, for interrupting,” Gus said with a slight, elegant bow. He launched into his well-worded speech without pause. He laid out the somewhat complicated story of Lolo’s situation, cleverly avoiding too much detail. He got right to the core of the matter.

The Commissioner listened attentively, interrupted Gus a few times with questions, and took notes about his answers on a tablet in front of himself.

Gus spoke with the propitious awareness he would surely be taken seriously. He felt he was speaking more and more fluidly and convincingly as he went along. Finally, he came to the end.

“If you please, Mr. Brenner, how long ago was the alleged theft? I mean how much time has elapsed since the person who had possessed the money discovered it was missing?”

“About—I cannot say with certitude—four to six weeks, I’d say.”

“So, that’s very favorable. That’s all I need. Please remain a while. The further matter of the alleged false information on the document...” He scratched his head with his pencil, “That’s admittedly the domain of the Administrative Councilor himself.

We have strict orders to report events such as this immediately. My job is to take your deposition. Therefore I must ask you for your personal information."

"My information?"

"It's only a formality," said Dr. Treulich, writing down the dates Gus had given. Half muttering, Treulich shoved the transcription across his desk, "Please sign. Fine, thank you. I'll have the girl brought here in the next few days. I am familiar with Red House because of our audits. It's immensely decent, this establishment of Goldscheider's. There's never been any irregularity there. But there's always some complaint and lying in these establishments."

"I have the distinct impression this is the truth," Gus said with reserve.

"Of course, of course," the fat man was in a hurry. He was thankful to his visitor for this interruption in the off days of July. "At another time you, Sir, may also not have come forward. I find it—just between us, naturally very much in confidence—completely appropriate of you to come to me with this." He lowered his voice without meaning to, "When men such as yourself intervene without reservation in situations like this, we take it seriously since there may not be sufficient protection in the legal statutes. The system, let us not deny it, has holes."

"No longer, Dr. Commissioner," Gus said, radiating. "All complaints should come to you, Sir! You are a man of stature."

"No, but I try," Dr. Treulich played down Gus's compliment.

"Doctor, Sir, I mean it sincerely. I had been concerned my visit might have gone entirely differently. I'm glad I was mistaken. I leave today much relieved. You are a man of stature! Admittedly now we must hope there is due diligence in overcoming obstacles." Gus cast a look over in the direction of the office where the files were kept.

Dr. Treulich countered by casting a meaningful look upward to the heavens, to the sacred higher powers.

"You see, my colleague," Treulich began jovially, "Each and every profession has its good and its bad sides. One ought stay on the side of right, as you do." He ran his hand over his sparse hair.

"I'm not one to impose, Sir," Gus laughed, happily. "I'm not the ambitious sort."

And then it turned out that Dr. Treulich did in fact know Gustav Brenner! He was the son of Brenner of the Imperial Ironworks, yes, but of course. He, Treulich, was an honorary member of the university's drinking club Franconia, and at the evening meeting with members of Teutoburger Club, Gus had given an address. Oh, yes, he remembered warmly, and what a fine, warm address it had been.

The two gentlemen shook hands again. Gus presented his open cigarette case, made of gold. "Milada would certainly be surprised to see this," he thought. "She wouldn't even dream of owning such an item." At this moment he felt glad down to his soul he had come on this mission.

The two chatted this and that. They talked about how the next generation of club members just did not have the right spirit and about how the members of Club Lothringia had admitted a Jew—what a disgrace! Then Gus took his leave.

"I'm truly in your debt, Dr. Commissioner."

"But that's just doing my duty."

"My honor, Sir. The honor is mine."

Gus walked through the office with the files, not deigning to look over toward Sucher, who stood up to acknowledge Gus only grudgingly. He then went directly to his colleague the Commissioner to retrieve the written transcript of Gus's deposition, which was required for this case. Sucher had recognized the name on the calling card. This visit interested him.

In the meantime, Milada had made a visit to the Emmaus Cloister. It was a large, whitewashed building with no adornment. It belonged to the Order of the Sisters of the Venerable Cross of Jesus. The many bars on its windows and tightly closed, brown gate fit well with the physiognomy of the quiet street.

She was filled with faint, diffuse memories. She saw Janka trying to force a small, resisting child, who smelled of musk-scented soap, through the narrow door of the cloister. She could feel the cool, thin hand of the gray woman on the top of her head. With a voice full of compassion, the woman had said, "Oh, poor child!" How long ago that was! It seemed impossible she had experienced this herself. Yet this deeply hidden childhood memory of her first visit to the cloister had retained a peculiarly intense olfactory imprint. The sensory memory filled her with hundreds of unrecognized attachments as she walked down the narrow corridor to the main office.

"You'll likely want to speak to the sister who is our manager?" the young nun who had opened the door for Milada said. She eyed Milada's calling card tentatively.

"I'd like to speak with Mother Superior."

The glimmer of a smile crossed the mouth of the serious nun. "No one may speak with Mother Superior," she said and left without a sound. Small girls in blue-linen uniforms with their hair in tight braids walked in pairs past the widows and looked at Milada with curiosity. An older nun motioned with her hand for Milada to follow over to the other side of the courtyard. It was planted with chestnut trees.

"We received your petition," a low, voice behind her said with no inflection. "We are inclined, in accord with certain binding regulations, to enter into the negotiations you're interested in." Milada turned around. Before her was an elderly, haggard nun with stern, compassionless, and pale features.

"Would you mind closing the window for me?"

"Yes, Sister," said Milada shyly. She sat down stiffly on the hard, black-leather chair.

"You will address me as Sister Steward," the nun informed her as she looked out over the courtyard. Then she pulled the green curtains to. There was no light in the room.

"You have been authorized by the woman petitioning to conduct the negotiations on her behalf. Do you have the necessary papers with you?"

Milada nodded.

The nun took a form out of her valise and opened it out on her desk.

"Here is the application to the cloister we require. There are two copies. Both are signed by the two parties. Dr. Heinrich von Görz, as you see, has prepared them. You will give me the necessary information. Name?"

Milada rose to answer, supporting herself a bit on the desk. "Miss Josephine von Miller-Gerrold."

"Age?"

"Fifty-two years old."

"Employment?"

Milada faltered. "I'm not sure," she said with hesitancy.

"We must have the type of employment in the lay world for this last year."

"Owner of a house of pleasure at 2 Red House Alley," Milada said hastily.

The nun murmured, "Owner of a municipally registered guesthouse. And what is it she wishes?"

"To retire from the world," Milada continued dryly.

The nun repeated as she wrote, "The petitioner, filled with regret and tortured by the vileness of her former work, now wishes to spend the rest of her years in clerical seclusion, performing religious acts and penance." Milada nodded agreement. There was a moment of quiet. Milada looked at the curtain, which was moving slightly in the wind, and for a moment she had the distinct impression her eyes and the nun's met while looking at a dark blotch on the curtain. Milada felt there was a moment of mutual understanding. It was just a moment, then the nun looked down at her paper.

"And what does the woman petitioning offer?"

"She has money in cash and in bonds in the amount of forty-five thousand gulden. She also has four thousand gulden in property, an estate outside Vienna."

"The woman petitioning humbly offers the Cloister funds and property, possessions of both kinds. She asks only for mercy. She wishes to submit in this holy asylum to the rules of the Order with no conditions and with total resignation. Now you must sign for her."

Milada obeyed.

"We are empowered to relay your request to the appropriate authorities. We have a branch of this cloister in the town of Triestingtal, The Sacred Heart of Mary. There are two places available there for those who are weary of this world. Our Mother Superior is the one to decide who will be accepted, based on merit and urgency. In two weeks you will receive written notice of her decision. The amount you have indicated must be handed over directly to Dr. Heinrich von Görz on the day the acceptance is in effect. Three days after you receive notification the portals of asylum will be open to the penitent. I have nothing further to say."

"We beg your consideration," said Milada and bowed deeply to the stiff, indifferent nun who remained seated. Then she left via the corridor, where she was received by the small, gray porter.

"Praise be to Jesus Christ," the porter greeted her as she hurried by.

Since Milada did not reply, the porter finished the invocation herself, "Forever, amen."

There was a charged, unspeakable accusation in the voice of this woman who had renounced the world.

Two days after Gustav's visit to police headquarters Lolo was called up, much to the chagrin of Madame Miller. Miller prophesized only trouble and aggravation would come of this running-around. With all her might she declared that she had had enough of being sullied by these worldly affairs. Ever since the sale of the business her temperament and interests had changed fundamentally. Her mistrust and her greed for money, even her natural, mean-spirited behavior had disappeared.

Every third day she went to confession. She closed herself in her room and fasted, and nervously avoided any contact with the girls. They were delighted with this strange holiness; it was a continual source of merriment for them.

Lolo returned from police headquarters radiant. She told of the wonders there, how friendly and good the gentlemen at the station had been to her. When she arrived one man had told her nothing bad would happen if she told only the truth.

Then she was called to the Councilor himself. He was very sweet to her. He even gave her a section of the orange he was eating. Can you imagine!

She was open and related all the things that had happened to her. Obviously encouraged, Lolo looked around the room with laughing eyes at the girls who were assembled. She kissed Milada's hand, and her true, childlike, dear personality came out.

On 24 August, it happened to be early in the morning, Miller received a summons to appear at police headquarters. The sheet of paper shook in her fingers. She turned pale with anxiety. She emitted a flood of idiotic prophesies and repeated as a refrain she had known for a long time this was coming. She was not going to leave with propriety and grace. She would no longer arrive at her heavenly destination, etc.

Milada calmed her down as much as possible. "But, Madame, nothing that terrible is going to happen. Everything here is on the up and up. It was just some minor point in the formality of the transfer."

"No, no, there's always been one thing or another amiss," Miller was disconsolate. "Now when things seem to be going so nicely, something awful is bound to happen. Now that Lolo is finally behaving herself, all of a sudden... What is going on with the police?"

Milada made a quick movement. Miller asked, "Does this have something to do with Lolo's affair? Are the police concerned about that?"

Miller spoke to the seamstress, who was sitting at the window, embroidering. "Moosemann, you will see. Something did happen! The venerable pastor always told me, 'Josephine, you are psychic.'"

Over the course of the day Miller's anxiety ramped up. Restless and possessed by one thought, she paced back and forth in her room, mumbling prayers. She had become so distraught she rambled as if in a raging fever. Milada did fear for her sanity, so she asked Karla, a prudent person, to accompany the madam to the police. As Miller tied the ribbons of her hat with her shaky fingers, she made a pledge that if this hour of misery went badly for her, she would leave Red House on the instant and spend the time before her "investiture" in deepest seclusion in a place free of sin.

Milada thought, "It's for the best. Otherwise, she might end up somewhere else."

Toward midday Miller returned. Her eyes were on fire with ecstasy. There was a suspicious glow in her cheeks, which were usually haggard. "Nothing happened to me!" she called out to Milada triumphantly. "But all of you here will be sentenced by the court. I'm packing to leave. I'm going to have peace."

"So what happened?" Milada asked. "Please, Madame, tell me clearly!" she said with annoyance. "You can't just rush off in a mad dash."

"Who's to keep me here?" Miller snapped. "Nobody. I sacrificed my life and almost sacrificed my eternal soul. What happened, you ask? The Sodomites probably asked the same question when fire and brimstone began hailing down from heaven."

Milada gave up trying to get a rational answer. She turned to Karla who had waited in the file room with Sucher. He had joked around, as was his custom, while Miller was talking directly with the Baron, Treulich's superior. Sucher told Karla there was no concern. He assured her the visit was probably another one of his acts of official capriciousness. When Miller reemerged, she was, according to Karla, babbling like she was at the moment. She babbled the whole way back to Red House.

Madame Miller then went to see Spizzari while Karla waited outside in the carriage. Karla could not say what had transpired.

When Gus showed up at Red House at three that afternoon, the place was alive with excitement. Madame Miller was gone without a trace. Gus clapped his hands and broke out laughing.

"Mila, now for the first time I believe you and I have a future together. As God is my witness, I had actually harbored a small, hidden fear about us. But I think we'll be fine. The woman is gone. She abandoned her money, her account books, and her precious larder of food. She left the girls and the jars of jam, the customers and the mincemeat! Terrific! And you don't know where she went?"

"Not a clue. She made a huge sign of the cross in the air as her goodbye. But I imagine she will want to see me before the day is over. Don't you think so, Gus?"

Milada was somewhat heavy-hearted. Spizzari had sent a Madame Irma to Red House. She was a slim, elegant blonde who looked too goodly. It seems she had been tasked with managing the house. She was to assume all of Milada's duties. Irma reported that the worthy Nelly Spizzari had, very regrettably, failed to note the travel destination of the esteemed former madam. Nelly had to abandon Miller's lovely plan to make use of the business-savvy talents of Milada. But Nelly, so said Irma, was not remiss in sending along her greetings and a good word that the current situation was not to last forever. People would come and go. "Young people want to have their fun," she told Gustav with a wink. He gnashed his teeth in anger. Madame Irma demanded Milada give her the keys. Her tone was sweet, verging on humble. She took up residence in Miller's old room and assumed the responsibilities of the job with overbearing assuredness.

"Gus," said Milada, "I'm in a dream. I have a lot to do so I don't lose my grip in this confusion. Miller's gone. Nobody needs me anymore. Am I free? I have worried about the meaning of 'free' for such a long time. And now it's a reality for me. I'm not taking it very well. 'Free' was Horner's magic word. You can't imagine what this moment means to me."

Milada pressed her hands to her temples as she did at difficult moments. "If you weren't here, Gus, I would fall apart at this freedom."

He pulled her to himself like a guardian angel. "Oh, you silly girl! Are you going to fault yourself for not having to carry this awful burden? I'm heaving a sigh of relief for you."

"All I know is I can't grasp the news and all that comes with it. The world awaits me. Till now I accepted things as they were and tried to manage situations as they arose. Everything is new and strange."

"Does it feel strange to be part of my life?" Gus asked with tenderness.

She continued without registering his words, "You might laugh. I was used to living as I did. I was accustomed to supporting the girls, giving them encouragement, and listening to their arguments over every little thing. It has been the content of my life."

"I am the man of the hour," Gustav said ironically.

"Oh, Gus!" she rested her arms on the table and looked straight ahead. "At base there was something more. These hours full of hundreds of little tasks and worries had something bigger, something whole to them. I've always known there was a larger meaning to this work."

"Well, Mila, if you're sorry about all this change..." he started off stilted, expecting to be interrupted.

"Just wait. I'll be fine when I have something I can sink my teeth into!" Milada said as she arose. "Then I'll feel better. That woman Irma downstairs has taken over my job as manager. Miller is on her own. Fanny seems to be doing all right, Lolo is happy. What am I without worries? I have a sense I'm really good for nothing."

Gus came up behind her, took a piece of paper from his vest, and began speaking as if delivering a sermon, "'Dr. Gustav Brenner agrees to rent a furnished apartment from the widow Ludmilla Köpke at Meinecke Street 8A, Berlin. It lies on the second floor and consists of three rooms; it has an alcove, kitchen, bathroom, and pantry. Et cetera.' You silly girl! You'll have plenty enough to do. Mrs. Köpke is incredibly careful. She'll make sure you keep the place in order. That's her role, separate from my demands. I expect to be cared for like a darling. You'll be my girl for everything. Can you darn socks? Mine have holes. Can you make a decent soufflé? No, you can't? How could you say no? That's not an option. Something that fluffy and delicious? It's like..." He pressed his head to her bosom and looked at her, blinking with eyes of love.

She ran her hand over his head. "I don't know how to cook," she said pondering. Milada was impassive while he kissed her and acted flirtatious.

There was a discrete knock at the door. Madame Irma appeared at the threshold with her face powdered white and said, "Madame Milada, come downstairs. There are two gentlemen here from the police."

"An audit?" said Milada and followed her in disbelief.

"They were asking about Miller. I told them she's no longer here. There they are." Two secret agents were standing on the ground floor in the entry hall. Milada knew them.

One spoke, "I have an order to arrest Leopoldine Schwarza from Prague. She uses the name Lolo in the brothel. Is she employed here?"

"What has she done?" Milada asked.

"I don't know. It's not clear. The police station in Prague can answer that. Miss Lolo has to pack up a small suitcase of essentials."

The sound of men's voices brought the girls out of their rooms. They surrounded the two agents and asked them questions, The girls screamed out and backed off. "Where is the girl?"

"She's with Rosie." "No, she's downstairs in the kitchen." "Is this about Lolo?"

Mitzi had gone off to fetch Lolo. She showed up, pale and in shock.

"What's the matter? What's going to happen to me?" she asked softly.

"So then you're Lolo? Madame, get yourself dressed," one of the men said pleasantly, adding in Czech, "*Slecno*, quickly." His German was broken, "You can take a bundle of your things. Go put that together. Madame Manager, we have a carriage waiting."

The other agent said over his shoulder to his colleague, "She won't need much. The girl will be wearing a state-issued uniform soon enough."

No one laughed. The girls looked at Lolo, who was white as a sheet. Lolo was staring at Milada in shock.

"Jesus, where are they taking me?" Lolo took a step backwards, "Are they taking me to Fischer?"

Milada went over to her right away. "Lolo, stay calm. Be collected. Nothing's going to happen to you. I will..." Milada spoke forcefully to the girls who had gathered, "Go to your rooms, please."

"You don't have to give us orders anymore," Mitzi challenged her. The other girls also resisted Milada's authority.

Milada spoke, "Please, Mr. Jewonka, wait in my room. I'll bring everything to you right away. Come," Milada said to Lolo, as she held her. "Don't be afraid of giving a testimonial. Keep your head up!"

Gustav had watched the two men enter with astonishment.

"Imagine, Gus. Lolo is being arrested."

"Arrested? Why then? Do the gentlemen have a legitimate reason?"

"Oh, Jesus," one of the agents said, laughing.

"I know Mr. Jewonka well," Milada said motioning him away. "Are you here under Treulich's orders?"

"For one, it's top secret, so it's not your business. And two, the orders come from the Administrative Councilor himself."

Then Lolo broke out crying and screaming. She clung to Milada. "What's going to happen to me? I did nothing wrong."

"Nothing will happen to you, Lolo," Milada said emphatically. "I promise to come see you tomorrow. Calm down. Gus, you stay here and talk with her. I'm going upstairs to get her things."

Gus, completely taken aback at this turn of events, turned to the agents. His demeanor was authoritative. "Your department has overstepped its boundaries. Do you understand me? You are making a regrettable mistake. Tell the Commissioner I said so. I will get to the bottom of this tomorrow. Lolo, please, don't cry. This is most certainly an error. People will have to answer to me for this."

Milada arrived with Lolo's hat and coat. She came up behind Gus and said under her breath to him, "It's all right, stay calm."

"We're not going to take her head off," said Jewonka, helping himself to a cigarette from Gus's golden case. "After all's said and done, she'll still be here tomorrow. *Slenco*, hurry up."

"There now, see. Just go along sweetly with the gentlemen."

Lolo held on to Gus, shaking, "Please, Sir, don't leave me, don't leave me."

"You all should leave now," said Gus, waving them away. He walked over to the window. He was distraught and felt claustrophobic. He felt both compassion for the girl and a certain, angry resentment about the situation he had been thrown into. His first impulse was to run out of Red House, slip away, and never see these people again. He understood how people in this milieu could never be at peace. Look how much he had been through these last few months! This milieu fouled up every possible good moment and destroyed any sane thoughts or pleasant occurrence.

He was phlegmatic, melancholic, galled, and bitter—just like Miller.

He had to put an end to all this! He paced impatiently with his face screwed up in fear and his lips pressed tightly together. This presentation of emotion was, fundamentally, a screen for his miserable, selfish state of mind. So this is what his mission to the police had been turned into! He had aided and abetted this mess. This was what he got for putting his good name on the line. A shiver ran through him. Now he had to answer for his action. He had to raise Cain, fight for justice.

He did not have the character of Michael Kohlhaas, the legendary martyr for justice whom Kleist had immortalized as the rebel. He wanted peace, tranquility, and a pleasant life. He felt humiliated. Milada expected him to be in charge, as did everybody at Red House, right on down to the porter. Their opinion of him mattered to him, as did the judgement of others in general.

His feelings of resentment grew and eclipsed any positive thoughts he might have had. This situation was about his dignity. His whole feeling of worth hinged on this. How had it happened that he was saddled with this kind of onus? Milada knew how vulnerable he was. He asked himself whether Milada intended, ultimately, to put him in this position. Was she trying to educate him bit by bit? Was she hoping to make a savior and apostle out of him? Could it be that Joe had assessed his relation to her more clearly than he had? And now this was unraveling right before he was set to go to Berlin!

"Poor, poor Lolo!" said Milada, entering the room. "Do you have any idea, Gus, what all this means?"

"The whole situation is because of Sucher. He's perfidious. It could only be that bastard who's behind this," Gus fumed.

She shook her head, "I don't think so. I'm afraid they will put the blame on her for the story in Prague. I feel so sorry for her, the poor, poor thing." Milada sighed.

"I'm going to go see Treulich tomorrow," Gus was livid.

Milada did not respond. He looked up at her to see what she was thinking.

Naturally she accepted the whole situation as a duty that must be executed. Resolve to go forward claimed all Gus's bourgeois manhood but was nothing unusual to her. It looked as if he, too, had been implicated. He had been hitched to the same cart of manure she was.

He rumpled his brow, "I'm sorry, I have a headache. I'm going outside for some air. Want to come with me?"

She answered animatedly, "No, I've got to stay here to see if Miller sends word. They need me inside, too. You look so pale!" she said kindly, leaning her head on his shoulder. "Gus, the apartment in Berlin with Köpke is starting to look like a sanatorium."

She closed her eyes. And he stood there stock-still, looking away.

"Gus, want to know something? I'm starting to see a new life dawn through the fog. I'm going to seize my own good luck. I feel it deep in my heart." Words failed him. He kissed her on her forehead with his old tenderness.

Mr. Theobald Sucher happened to be sitting over his full breakfast when he saw Gus enter. He wiped his greasy fingers quickly and discretely on some paperwork. He was smiling, so in a good mood.

"How might I serve you, Doctor?"

"I'd like to speak with Commissioner Treulich."

Sucher raised his eyebrows. "Most sincerely I regret to inform you the Doctor is on vacation. Do you have an address for him?"

"When did he leave?"

"He left August 14th."

"So how is it I got this chit of paper yesterday, signed by him?" Gus said, throwing the document down on the table. Leisurely

Sucher put on his glasses and began reading attentively.

"Yes, that is correct. Dr. Treulich left it on his desk. He simply forgot it. It was a personal letter," said Sucher, displaying regret.

Ah-ha! Gus understood what was going on. Treulich had made himself unavailable, mum. That was how bureaucrats operated.

Gus looked up and saw Sucher's insolent smirk.

"Here you have my calling card," Gus blurted out. "Let the Administrative Councilor know I am here."

"In regard to this matter?"

"Certainly."

Sucher wagged his head, "You will have to forgive me, Sir. I advise you against this, I strongly advise you."

"You may keep your advice to yourself, Sir. I must insist."

Sucher took Gus's calling card, "Next flight up, Office 1 on your left. Follow me, please," he said officiously.

Sucher returned after a while, snickering, "This is quite the story! A rash cavalier dares to do something like this!" He took a big swig from his glass. Sucher thought people would be delighted to watch this young darling take a tumble. It is the stuff of comedic theater. Ha-ha! He rubbed his hands.

Sucher had obviously put something wily together. The day after Gustav had been here for the deposition Mr. Salomon Fischer of Budweis had come by police headquarters for a visit. Together Fischer and his old business pal Sucher, encouraged by the unavailability of Dr. Treulich, had taken care of the situation to the complete satisfaction of all parties involved.

Several seconds after Sucher had handed Gustav's card to the bureaucrat in the antechamber of the Administrative Councilor, Gus was permitted to knock at the door of the holiest of holies. After hearing a nasal "Come in!" Gus entered his office. He made a deep bow and greeted the Councilor.

"You'll have to wait," the Administrative Councilor said as he continued writing.

When he reached the end of a sentence, he called out brusquely, "So what do you want?"

"Sir, I take the liberty of speaking on behalf of Poldi Schwarza. I'm speaking to you because of a negative letter I received yesterday. It was a personal letter to me."

The Councilor picked up the topic of conversation. "But of course. What else are you here for?" he interrupted Gus rudely.

"I do not understand how this negative letter is connected to the sudden, unforeseen arrest of the girl. An interest in human decency brings me here today."

"Mr. Brenner, Sir, before you continue, I would like to put one question to you, if I may." The Councilor raised his pointy head, which looked like that of a vulture. It rested on his short, fat neck, as he looked up at Gustav. The light, refracted through his thick glasses, appeared menacing.

"How did you arrive at the decision to submit a serious deposition in support of a prostitute? How ever did you come up with this idea, I'd like to know." He pushed up his glasses, which were so thick they were dark, and his small, ugly, green eyes became visible. "You've made a defamatory claim against a respectable man with no previous convictions. And you did this for a shameful whore? Sir, that is an extreme act that will put you on a collision course with the judge on the bench."

Gus was sweating. He stammered, "Councilor, Sir, my sense of human decency compels..."

"Balderdash! Your duty as a young man is, above all else, to keep your precious nose out of shit. Do you understand? Do you perhaps have some personal relation to this individual? Is she your sister? A cousin of yours?"

Gus gathered himself, "If you permit me, Sir..."

"Some relation to this girl would be your only reason before the law for coming forward on her behalf. If you're not related to this prostitute, you have no cause to act as her guardian. Why would we consider your intervention? Sir, your folly will cost you, I promise you that. Are you aware I can throw you in the slammer for getting involved in a legal case? You have the audacity to raise some spurious rumors from disreputable sources to the level of a formal, legal accusation? Rumors like this are the order of the day in brothels. Are you willing, in your dubious role as a visitor in a brothel, to get mixed up in legal proceedings with the police? And here you are talking about errors and overstepping boundaries when we already have formal police testimony? You have a lot of nerve!" He snorted and slammed his hand on the desk.

"Sir, Councilor, I am a citizen and a university student..."

"I guarantee you that you won't be for long," the bureaucrat said dryly. "Keep your spot at the university. It's where you belong, and desist spending time in brothels. Stop consorting with sluts, and keep yourself out of legal entanglements if you value your studies."

"Councilor, Sir..."

"My God, just keep quiet. The girl in question will be taken care of by the authorities responsible for her. Do you know what it means to vouch for a person of this sort? Think what would happen to you, a young, inexperienced lad, if I charged you with complicity. End of discussion! We have no need to draw this out further."

In no time his glasses fell back on his nose, and he bent down over his desk.

Gus found his way to the door as if navigating through red fog. He gasped for air. He fumbled for words, but words stuck in his throat. He was unable to utter a single, solitary word. He stumbled into a chair in the adjoining room and caused the clerk in training to jump in surprise. As he proceeded to the door he had but one dull thought in mind. He had to look as collected as possible since Sucher would be downstairs laughing at him. That would be too much to bear. He pulled himself together enough to nod formally to Sucher who came over to him.

"With all due respect, Doctor, Sir, have you concluded your visit with the Councilor?"

When Gustav was back out on the street he fell apart. His face was dark red and glowed as if he had been slapped. However much he tried to control his lips, they quivered.

The humiliating, poisonous rebukes, accusations, and threats consumed him. They rained down upon him like lashes from a whip. Had he brought this on himself? He had simply stood there and let this man talk to him like that. He had not punched him right in the eye with the fists he made. He took the insults.

Had this villain done his dirty deed? Lord God, what had these women done to him? How far had his relationship with Milada driven him?

He ran up and down the alleys aimlessly in the heat of the August sun as if mad. He had no destination in mind. He ran into passersby and stood there with his hand to his forehead and shook his head violently. People on the street walked past him and looked back over their shoulder in astonishment.

He was gripped by this thought: The people who had pilloried him owed him an apology. He had struggled enough. No, resisting would not make things better. He had to go on with his head held high. He had to take his licks. How all of them had trammeled and abused him! These horrible women! The words of the Councilor taunted him, "Is she your sister? A cousin of yours?"

For the love of God! The most horrible of consequences from this dreadful humiliation danced in his head. Gustav imagined his illustrious Grandmother and his Aunt would find out. Dear God, what if one of them had witnessed this scene at the police station! He had not looked around himself to see whether someone had been watching. What if the newspapers got wind of this story? The thought was too painful to entertain.

Exhausted from the emotional turmoil, he took a carriage.

He went to see Joe. He wanted to relate the whole humiliating scene. He would ask his friend for help and throw himself at his feet. What remained for him after this disgrace? As things stood he was looking at suicide.

"Suicide," he uttered the word softly two times. Shivering, he pressed himself into the corner of the carriage.

Finally, he arrived at Joe's. He stumbled up the four steps, tortured by the fear he could never again meet up with his friend.

"Suicide. Suicide," hammered in his brain. "Dear Lord, how will this day end!"

Joe was in the middle of shaving. He had just raised his shaving brush to lather up when he saw Gus in the mirror. Gus tumbled through the doorway, out of breath and drenched with sweat. Joe dropped his brush in the basin and rushed over to Gus who had thrown himself down, wordless, across the bed. He began wailing in bewilderment. His very young, healthy male body thrashed about on the mattress as if he were engaged in mortal combat.

Joe wondered whether Gus's father might have beaten him with his fists. "Buddy, what is it? Talk to me! For Christ's sake, man, don't blubber like a hysterical girl! You haven't committed murder, have you?"

Joe took his hand. He held it tight.

Joe sat down on the edge of the bed and said, "Have a good cry, pal, if it helps!"

He speculated about what might have happened. "Milada? His old man? The relationship between Gustav and his father had rules, definite rules. His father would not have done something without warning. And Milada? Had she pulled the wool from his eyes? Had she decided to end things definitively? *Vederemo*! We will see!"

His chin was soaped up and itched. He used the corner of his shirt to wipe his wet face. Joe began to do what he did when he had to think, he hummed.

Gus sat up abruptly and wiped the tears from his eyes and off his blond moustache. He gripped Joe's hand and started to talk.

He was wrathful as he related the events of his day from beginning to end. He halted at points but kept on animatedly. He described Lolo's arrest, Milada's despairing request to him, and his own distress at the situation of this broken girl. He told of Sucher's insolence and how it galled him. The final part of his tale was his confrontation with the Administrative Councilor.

Without holding back or shuffling over matters, Gus described the brutal scene with the Councilor to his friend. He then started talking about his own state of mind and concluded, with a feeling of relief and with flat affect, "suicide."

"And that's the whole story?" asked Joe after a while, heaving a sigh.

"That's not enough?" Gus's reply was bitter. "It's enough to destroy my life."

"I'm asking if the bastard just tossed out some threats or if he might sue."

"Sue?"

"Well, it's customary for the person who's been accused of some illegality to counter with a suit of character defamation. You complicated matters when you claimed Fischer knew Lolo was underage. This is one hell of a rotten mess! However things go, the situation is miserable at best. Miserable! What were you thinking, my friend, to get mixed up in this?"

"I don't need you to tell me what I did wrong!" Gustav said woefully.

"I did warn you often enough. But that's irrelevant at this point. *Vanitas vanitatum*!" Joe remarked at the futility of reminding Gus of his warning.

"Joe, this time you are being unfair to me. It was..."

"It was your need to look like a big man, my friend. How often have you wanted me to praise the valor of your motives? You always want me to remark on your accomplishments. You were champing at the bit to be the big hero, and then you charged ahead. Look where you landed, pal. Didn't you realize you are weighed down? That you are being pulled under?"

"So what do I do now?" Gus lamented.

"You need to leave town—fast as you can. You need to break off your chummy relationship with the girls at Red House. You can't be seen there anymore. You'll destroy your reputation and your career. Everything you ever wanted in life is at stake. People can only shrug their shoulders over your situation as it is now."

"Who's shrugging their shoulders?"

"Who isn't? For months now you've been spending your days in that brothel. You even go around with a girl from there."

"Joe, don't bring her into this!"

"You're an idiot. The girl's been trying to tell you what she is. She grew up in that brothel. She started keeping a record of her health exams for the police when she was sixteen years old. That's a fact. You can't tell me any differently. She's taken over the job of the madam there for the last four years because the regular madam is a nitwit. She's in charge of a company of whores and does business with the most unsavory characters. And you honestly believe you were her one and only?"

"Joe, that's just not true," Gus said through his clenched teeth. "You can rake up her whole miserable past, but people cannot find one rotten deed or a single breach of confidence in my past."

Joe put his arm around Gus's shoulder. "Is that really raking up her past? Her profession is a stigma in itself. And even if she had the brains and the heroism of Aspasia—admittedly much maligned—she can't counter the facts.

Gus was both embarrassed and numb. He tried to defend himself, "I didn't know she'd kept a health record for the police at one time. Joe, I'm sure she does love me. You have nothing to say there."

"I'm happy to concede that! You are a charming, attractive guy. All right, she loves you. But does that mean she's the right partner for you? You are the son of a patrician family. You're Gustav Brenner, the aesthete. Dear friend, you can't chain yourself to her for all eternity! Don't louse up all your options. What do you need to live? Water and air. Not this woman. Keep that in mind." Gus clutched his head.

"You're saying put it all—all of it—behind me!" Gus groaned. He had a flood of things to say on behalf of his beloved, but he suppressed them. He put them out of his mind and turned to feelings of regret. His furor was muffled.

"I saw her as a martyr. I can't drop her. I can't, Joe, I just can't!" He despaired.

"So what are you going to do?"

"You're right. I have to go away, take a trip," he lamented.

"With Milada?"

"Don't ask me that! What has to happen will happen."

"Oh, Pythoness, you Oracle of Delphi, assume your place on your sacred tripod," said Joe, walking over to his shaving mirror.

Gus sat down in an armchair, "Joe, you see I'm in this miserable situation, yet you make jokes. Now you're the one who's trying to look like the big man! I have to tell you your way of joking gets to me. When you make light of my situation, I'd rather not to come to you when I need a friend. If you weren't so judgmental, I wouldn't be in this mess."

Joe inspected his fingernails. "I'm sorry. I thought you'd come to accept the oddities of my behavior. In short: I don't want to play the thankless role of the hangman in your tragedy. I'll do whatever you decide you want me to do. But you have to make a decision."

"I'm going to shoot myself."

Joe turned toward Gus with an undefinable grin. "Now there's a sweet division of tasks," he thought to himself. "Gus makes a decision, but I'm the one who is supposed to pull the trigger."

"There's one thing you have to know," Gus was agitated. "If Milada hid things from me, she did it out of love. I don't know about her life. I've never asked. It was my fault for not asking. I was too self-involved. I am certain she is smarter, better, and more noble than any of the girls from our class we're supposed to marry. If we're just talking about affection, there is no one more worthy of being my wife than she is."

Unhurried, Joe soaped up his shaving brush. He thought, "I need to prompt him to make some decision here before things fall apart. I've got to think clearly." He hummed a few bars from "The Marriage of Figaro."

As Joe shaved and hummed, Gus brooded.

"I'm not going to put foot in Red House ever again. I was aware of that before all this came up. She has to burn her bridges—all of them. I'll give her an ultimatum."

Joe sang on like a bird in the forest.

"I wish I weren't so upset! I can't put up with any more drama. I'm done with begging and their coercion. On top of it all, the heat this summer is getting to me. It's wearing me out."

Joe hummed away, this time Wagner's "Wotan's Farewell to Brunhilde."

"I'm leaving. I'm going to the mountains again. I'll be in a completely different setting. It will heal me. Should we hike through the Harz Mountains and see Blocksberg Peak? How about it? Are you interested?"

"At the moment I can't shake on it. My hand's full of soap. Great, pal, but first you've got to put your affairs in order."

Gus looked upward. "Berlin's still on the docket," he said. He looked like he was making a plea. Please keep Berlin in the plans. I'll leave for Munich today. I'll leave on the 5:55 train. I won't see Milada before I go. I'm all right making this sacrifice, but don't make me leave her forever. Write to her and tell her everything. You can tell her I had to go because of my mental state. Tell her I gave you my solemn word never again to go to Red House. Joe, I'm giving you my word right now. Let her know I'll be waiting for her in Berlin, no question about it. I'll be waiting there. Write this decision has cost me a lot, but..."

"I've got it," said Joe with his face lathered up. "Let me read it back to you: *The Robbers* by Friedrich Schiller, Act I, Scene 1. Quoth the father of his son in exile, 'But don't let my son despair!'"

Gustav had to laugh against his will at the scene of Schiller's naïve, revolutionary hero exiled in the forest. He laughed away his sorrow and pain. The decision to leave had done him much good. He took the rapid-transit train for Munich at 5:55. He had good friends there and his lovely cousin of the Niederheim Family. He looked forward to restoring his health completely in the company of these good people. He shed himself of his ugly troubles and emerged the gentleman restored. He was again the fine fellow.

"I'll wire you money for your ticket to meet me, Joe. You know my father is always generous in these matters."

"Without exception," Joe confirmed Gus's statement.

"When do you think you'll be able to join me?"

"I'm thinking in four or five days," Joe replied. Gus was full of sunshine. He was in his old best mood.

"Listen, pal, I don't want to be selfish here. Does Ollie maybe want to meet us in Berlin?" Joe waved his hand to refuse for her.

"Are you mad? Tomorrow she'll be over me. For God's sake, don't you both worry about me. Girls grow on trees, no matter where we are."¬

Gus doused his face with water from the basin. "Thank God!" he said, splashing water. "This is the first time I've felt any relief in months." He combed his moustache and his straw-like blond hair. He donned his Panama.

"I'm going to go home now. First off, I'm going to take care of business with my father. We'll talk over dinner at the university. Farewell! Want to go with me to the train?"

"Probably. But you've got to go now, or I'll nick myself with this razor." Joe was always especially worried about cutting himself.

When he was finally finished with the contortions of shaving, Joe sat down at his desk and composed the following letter, even though it was time for his breakfast.

Most esteemed Mr. Brenner:

We must substantially alter the plans we made at our last exchange. New, completely untoward circumstances have arisen. For the time being I will gloss over a chapter in this story. I shall embellish in a future conversation with you face to face. Suffice it to say Gus has gotten into quite a difficult situation and has decided to leave this afternoon for Munich. I am to meet up with him there in four or five days. The following is a description of the situation: Gus will leave without saying goodbye to W., but he leaves with the best of intentions and aspirations. At the end of September, he expects to take up residence in Berlin in a domestic arrangement with W. She remains the centerpiece of his plans.

As of this moment I believe if he carries through on his plans for Berlin, he will be at significant risk. This entirely unsophisticated personage is unpredictable. She employs the manipulative tactics of her disreputable lifestyle and should not now, or ever, be in a position to influence Gus. He has a labile, dependent, and malleable character. A situation of domesticity with W. would ensure her influence over him. A venture in cohabitation would result in an unsatisfactory marriage. There is no doubt about it. We have to act ruthlessly before the first link in this chain is forged. You and I would be powerless should this transpire.

The situation of the moment strikes me as opportune for an intervention to halt the implementation of his plan. I must emphasize again a definitive curtailment can come only from W. herself.

I therefore request the immediate transfer of funds in the amount you had formerly stipulated. W. is a woman of some means. This fact complicates making her an offer. I ask your permission to make arrangements to meet with you in our established manner at the Chess Club. I shall await the opportunity to inform you of all details of this matter.

I commend myself to you in friendship. Yours sincerely,

Joseph Wallner

Joe also composed the following letter.

Mila,

You will receive this letter from Joe, which I send you with a thousand heartfelt greetings. I write you in distress and in haste in a café, scribbling in pencil, which I have at hand. I must say farewell.

Mila, I have to leave! I had to go without seeing you, Dearest. It was not an option. I am distraught, and my state of mind is as miserable as can be. Ask Joe how I am. He can tell you everything. Please do not blame yourself. It is better for me to leave for a while. What happened recently, unbearably brutal as it was, has shown me what I had not understood before. You will have an address for me soon. For the moment I am in Munich in Hotel Residence. Joe will tell you what I would like you to do, what I expect.

I must insist, Mila, and it is my most urgent request: Leave Red House and look for a living situation befitting your new life.

Mila, I made a heavy, moral sacrifice for your sake. Never forget that! Joe will explain everything to you, my sudden departure without saying goodbye and my current condition. I have much to do to find my equilibrium. Do fare well! There is a storm brewing outside. Oh, how miserable my situation is! Both internally and externally. And you, my Love? Do not lament, my girl! We can bear anything, thinking of our future in Berlin. It will come to pass, it must. Farewell, dear Mila. I kiss your gray eyes, the eyes that have so often shown me love.

You may expect to hear from me soon from Munich.

Yours always,

Gus

Joe penned a third letter.

Dear Madame!

On behalf of our mutual friend Gustav I ask, most urgently, that you pay me a visit. Should you be unable to come in the morning, I will remain at my place all afternoon in expectation of your arrival. *Au revoir*, Joe

The day was rainy and cool. A sprinkle of cold rain soaked Milada's light clothing through and made her damp. She looked pale from lack of sleep and was obviously chilled. When she entered the room Joe was standing with his back to an open window. He closed it summarily.

Joe looked at her disapprovingly. "Madame, why didn't you bring an umbrella?"

"I forgot to. I left the house in a rush. What's happened? Where is Gus?"

"Before I answer this and similar questions, read this letter."

Milada's voice sank. "He's left?" She gave Joe a piercing look a few seconds long, then she took the letter and opened it. While she read her eyebrows knit together, throwing a dark shadow over her face. She had hardly read half the letter when she began rereading from the top. She read it through slowly and carefully.

"I don't understand this letter," she said in a stringent tone and with a stringent demeanor. She looked up at Joe.

"It was written in haste and under duress. You, Madame, should know the reason he left. There was a scandalous scene at police headquarters because of people at your house." Joe then gave a credible account of what had happened from what Gus had told him the previous day.

She listened to him while attending to her inner voice. After a few moments of silence she said, "So that's what went on. That's why he left. But why didn't he come see me first? Why didn't he tell me himself? That would have been the natural thing to do. Did he think I would disapprove?"

"Madame Milada, you have to make a serious attempt to understand his sensibilities. Gus felt truly distraught after the scene at police headquarters. Yesterday afternoon before he left, he couldn't eat his usual roast beef sandwich. I was quite shaken to see this. He had maybe two sips of his soup. A person can't go on like that."

Milada looked at him with distrust. "You can't be serious," she said in a reserved tone.

"No, unfortunately. Madame, I tell you this in earnest. May I offer you a seat? You don't look well. Can I get you a cup of tea? A cigarette? No? Well, all right. What were we saying? For me, for my family, maybe for you, too, missing a meal would not be a crucial matter. Right? But for Gus not being able to eat is a serious symptom. I was the one who suggested he take this trip. I suggested this, thinking of his constitution and knowing you would support the idea. If he'd stayed, he would've become unbearable. I came up with the idea of a vacation because of his condition. He had lost all interest in living. When we see him again he'll be his old, hale and hardy self. I have to say, you, Madame, were rather thoughtless to bring him into this whole situation with the girl. What did you imagine Gus would do? Did you think he was some kind of beast of burden for your social issues? Was that appropriate for his delicate constitution? Do you honestly think so?"

Milada looked serious. "I simply thought that as a man he would fare better with the police. I imagined he would not fall apart and cry, although that was what he did. So why did he cry? I've been thrown out of lots of offices! I'm very aware I have no access. I am not privileged. But Gus is a man. He does have access and privilege. I can't understand why Gus would be humiliated by the Administrative Councilor. Everybody in the houses knows he's a scoundrel who works with the nastiest scoundrels. I just can't comprehend why Gus didn't come see me. I would have told him right off, 'Gus, what will get this girl out of this situation is money. We've got to come up with a plan. We're talking about practical matters here, not about one man's bad mood. Someone's life is at stake.'"

Joe replied, "But, dear child, if we're going to wage war and we want to be victorious to some degree, then we have to put the appropriate people on the battlefield. We don't send hot heads off on diplomatic missions. We post people who smile and flatter for such negotiations. Milada, Madame, do you still think you chose the right man for your task? I ask you in all seriousness, this is no trifling question. Please do take a seat. We need to discuss matters thoroughly.

"Our friend Gustav, who's probably sitting down to a large, dark beer and a chunk of veal as we speak, is a charming man, a cavalier, and a person who wants to find beauty. He partakes of things with elegance. But for all that he is, he is not the man to whom we may go with ugly, oppressive business matters, those matters we might squarely situate on the dark side of the planet. I have been unhappy with you for a good while, Milada. You have brought him down. All that's happened has taken its toll on his goodness. It's made him raw and dissatisfied. His sacrifices were like a curse for him. He had been the best of all buddies. He used to get along with his fellows. Then he mistrusted even me. And this change was your doing. You got him off track.

"Gus threw around thousands of gulden for you as if they were nothing. He does not like a brouhaha. Being embattled takes a certain type of assertiveness he simply does not have. When you disrupt his pleasant demeanor, you affect his nobility. That is doing him harm. I must confess I did underestimate Gus. I firmly believed he would leave much sooner than he did. But his love for you, his overwhelming attraction to a woman, kept him hanging on. I have to say again I feel guilty toward him for not having seen what was coming."

"So what are you telling me, Sir?"

"Please call me Joe. I use titles only in public conversations."

"All right then, Joe, Sir, what did Gus do that was so detrimental? What did he experience? And what do you think I asked him to do?

Joe threw up his hands in despair. "How simple could it be!? Had you no notion, Madame, that it was an affront to his sensibilities to have the unvarnished nature of love and of these provocative girls in the house in front of him every hour of every day? Can you not appreciate that, from his perspective, being made a witness to this tragic theater of characters spurned by society is tantamount to martyrdom? Dear God, customarily a man pays and goes on his way. Men do not become involved in the stories or lives of these girls; they don't waste the capacity of their souls on devalued, lost girls. Do you not understand this? Gus is the most emotional person I know. He has most certainly suffered physically from witnessing ugly events, and you have been completely oblivious to this.

"It is doubtlessly true that unhappy people are not society's aesthetes.

"As a child of three Gus avoided playing with a girl his age because she limped. His mother was delighted at this because it showed he was as extremely sensitive as she was. Gus told his mother, 'I'd be happy to give her a coin, but she has to go away.' This incident was recited to him so often as praise, that it became the leitmotif of his development. As I have been saying, Gus is what he is supposed to believe he is. He is charming. People are delighted to welcome him on their committees, at their teas, and in their social gatherings. He was born to orchestrate ceremonies, such as engagements, christenings, and funerals. He is what the ancient Romans called an *arbiter elegantiarum*; he's a judge of taste and etiquette. For the love of God, that is not the person to put on difficult tasks. One cannot humiliate him with the misery of people beyond his ken. We cannot heap misery upon misery on this man! You can't expect a rose to have the qualities of an onion that's spicy and stings the eye." Joe pulled his chair up directly in front of Milada. "You have to understand. I've known Gus for twelve years. When he was thirteen, he was a bit asthmatic, so his family sent him to the Riviera where my family was. After he returned home I kept up with him. I tutored him for the university entrance exams; I became his coach, *maitre de plaisir*. I was supposed to introduce him to the finer pleasures of this world.

"We lived next door to each other. I was his companion and always respected him as useful. But I kept my distance from the web of his well-being, which he had carefully spun for himself. For instance, I knew not to upset his rosy mood on a summer afternoon by mentioning some inconvenient suicide. That would make him bitter—and rightfully so. Treating him incautiously could result in losing him. Do not laugh, Madame. That is his right, just as it is your right to take sustenance from the suffering around you. Each of us tries to meet the expectations of our milieu. You can't expect a straight line to follow the artistry of a curve.

"A frog jumps, and a bird sings. That's the nature of things. Don't meddle with the machinery of laws you cannot change."

He lit a cigarette.

"In a word Gus belongs to a type that is most common in our era and a type you've likely had very little chance to get to know closely. He is what we call, in common parlance, a philistine.

"Gustav Brenner expects his life to run like clockwork. He calculates each hour of his life, subtracts the amount of experience and enjoyment, and is always sure of the bottom line in the account of his activities. He's the kind of man who says, 'I'm not going there. A little Jewess will be there, and she might be dangerous to me.' Or he says, 'I believe I'll do something philanthropic.' And he takes out his address book and jots down the name of half a dozen charities, to which he donates ten gulden, the annual amount. He is capable of deciding to fall in love. People this secure can, each and every morning, find their golden shirt buttons without looking; they're right in place. They wind their watches at the appointed hour every evening after the most outrageous acts of debauchery. They never forget their walking sticks. They never pick up their belongings and move because every item has its determined, inalterable place. In sum he is a person who takes the measure of his abilities with a yardstick, meters his impulses, and calculates his every mood. A person like this is armed against any irregularity or unforeseen event. He illuminates the length of his street with the hard light of certitude. I also want to ask you, after telling you all this, to reread the letter from Gus. Maybe on second reading you'll better understand it. Please, take your time."

Obediently Milada pulled out the letter and read it through one more time.

"And so?" said Joe.

After a moment she said quietly with a voice that was veiled, "I understand. I see it was only a mistake, my mistake. I am often the one at fault. Give me a moment." Her voice trailed off. She put her hands to her eyes, and put her head down on her knees.

"Madame, I'm sure you are resilient. You'll only have to rearrange some deep-rooted concepts and principles. Real facts never fit neatly into our brain pans. I caution you. Don't cultivate a blind hatred of philistines. In your lifetime you will come to appreciate them.

"I don't know what plans you have. I don't know what your aims are. But in the future do take note of the kind of person you are engaging. You should always count on having discordant feelings. Always think with your rational mind and with your lizard brain, both. These are the two aspects of our bodily existence.

"You will come to appreciate Gus's charming conviviality in all its complexity as a fascinating theater of exceptional egoism. Just look how cleverly the year in Berlin was arranged!

"You really ought to go to Berlin. He's keeping that option open for you. He's also invited me and Ollie. We'll have an apartment with food, a piano, and university studies. A lieutenant with the guard will surely materialize for Ollie. This whole living arrangement is fundamentally only the setting for Gus's sense of well-being. We are props on the stage for his leading role as happy lover. He shuffles us around with a graceful sleight of hand. The trick is solely for his felicitous future state of mind. He's not concerned about us, he doesn't ask. I think several times before inviting someone to meet me at a café. But Gus! Anybody is acceptable, and he tosses away half of what he experiences with his conversational partner like wine that's gone bad. He just orders another bottle, a more expensive one. We are a fungible commodity.

"Gus, as you just read in his letter, loves you. He doesn't intend to give you up. What are we going to do? Are we going to Berlin?" Milada looked up at Joe, looked him in the eye. Joe wore the expression of a person who knows people.

"You, Sir, should probably go," she said. "But Berlin has nothing to offer me."

"Oh, are you sure? You will be denying my friend an important sense of security. A year in Berlin will certainly play a big role in his life. You don't stand to lose anything. I must beg you to reconsider before declining."

"Why are you plaguing me with all this, Sir, Joe?" she said with sorrow. "You're much more clever than I am. You know full well I gave you the answer you want, although I don't yet know myself how I'll cope with this."

Joe looked upset. "Actually, no. I hadn't thought you would make it so easy for me."

He paced around the room.

"You've been honest with me. I'll be honest with you. Gus is crazy about you. He doesn't consider giving you up. He dreams of being reunited with you. He and I wouldn't be happy if you don't go to Berlin. We want to make sure he's well taken care of. That's absolutely the case. You may understand what I'm about to tell you only in part. Gus's stability may depend upon your decision here. I'm speaking openly with you. Although he may be devastated as a result of your decision, you should not be swayed by his condition. That's needless to say.

"But enough of this. Gus loves you more than ever. Take all outcomes into consideration. Then give me your answer again."

She did not answer. Joe went to his desk and lit a cigarette.

"One question," she said spontaneously, and she walked over to him.

"I ask you to tell me the whole truth. Why does Gus have to go to Berlin in the first place?"

"Why? I assume, in the first place, for your sake. You are supposed to study medicine or something of the sort. I understood Gus to say the situation in Red House, your residence, has become untenable."

"Was there no other pressing reason for him to leave town? Joe, pay close attention to what I'm asking. Don't hide anything from me. I do understand very well. Doesn't Gus have to leave?"

"Have to, have to? As far as I know, no, he doesn't have to. But wait, you've jogged my memory. He and I did once make a stupid bet. He bet you would go with us to Berlin without hesitation. I bet—whether I was sure or just being obstinate—you wouldn't go. Maybe it was a *point d'honneur* with him. He is, after all, impulsive."

"Only a bet. But one he had to win," she said almost without breathing.

"Have to? Why did he have to?" Joe pursued her question.

"Because he gave his word as an officer."

"Gus? Gus, an officer!? Well..."

Milada told Joe the whole story, "Yes, Gus gave his commanding officer his word he would serve in a foreign country since he did not want to break off his relation to me."

Joe interrupted her, "Told his superior? Nonsense! Gus was never in the military. He was never an officer."

"He isn't an officer?" Milada repeated, not registering.

"But I just told you he had asthma. My God, what are you saying?"

"Never mind," she said, sitting back down. "It's already a thing of the past."

"So Gus told you?..." Joe yelled, surmising what Gus must have said. Joe's eyes were bulging out of his head.

Milada nodded.

"Oh, damned vanity!" Joe stood there, enraged, and he turned bright red. There he was on behalf of a braggart and a liar. May he rest in hell!

"Now I do understand you." Joe spoke soothingly above her. "Now you are giving me real information. I have more to tell you, things that you'll find of interest. First off, we have an offer for you."

"Are you still talking about Gus? What do you mean, 'we'?"

"I'm talking about Gus's father, of course."

"His father?! You'll have to excuse me. It's just beginning to dawn on me. I'm trying to grasp what's going on. You'll have to tell me why Gus's father came to you and you to me."

"Why are you involved? That should be relatively obvious. He wants to see his son thrive. And how am I involved? His father and I have collaborated for a good long while. I'm sure you must find me quite rotten! But your opinion of me doesn't matter now. Gus's father pays me to be the middleman. Gus does not get along with his father. But his father is very attached to him. Despite their differences the two do care about each other. You have to believe me about this. The father is a man of great strength; the son is not one tenth that man.

"In comparison to Gus's father, other men are weaklings. But that aside we have an offer to make you. Before I launch into it, would you, please, accept a cup of tea? You look, if I may, unwell. And your teeth are chattering. I won't accept no for an answer. It'll wait until we've had some tea."

Joe lit a burner, put the kettle on, set out some cups, and brought some tea cakes from the cupboard. As he worked, he hummed to himself. His humming became louder and happier.

"Please, do sit over there on the sofa. Please put the throw over your shoulders. Dear God, your clothing is soaked through and through. Here, like this. Now don't you feel better?"

Milada sat without moving at all. She was wrapped up in Joe's blanket. As she began to warm up she was filled with exhaustion. She had been awake for the last thirty-six hours. She had not had a minute of rest. She had run after Miller, had gone to the police about Lolo, and throughout all this she had been worried why Gus had not come to see her. Lolo had likely been taken away before Milada had a chance to see her. At the police station Milada had been abruptly turned away.

On top of these occurrences , she had received a dreadful message from Horner. And, after all these events, Joe's note arrived, asking her to visit. Everything had happened in such rapid succession she was thrown back and forth; she was torn apart. Then, in Joe's company, pleasant tranquility set in. All the disruption was quelled. Nothing more could bother her. Joe's humming filled the room. It rose and fell softly; it bubbled along with the simmering water.

"So, here is your tea! A little too dark, but never mind. It'll be fine, won't it?"

"You're kind," Milada said with gratitude.

"Well, not entirely. You must think I'm Pontius Pilate here. Milada, I find you impressive. Not because you are willing to give up Berlin. But in general. Between you and me things couldn't work out any more propitiously for you. I'm glad—glad for you. Do you believe me?"

Joe lit a cigarette and offered her the plate of cookies.

"You would have had to know Gus's mother and the milieu he grew up in. Dear Lord, you would then understand much more and be more sympathetic. I must have asked myself a hundred times how David Brenner could have sought out such a strangely odd union. He was an adventurous spirit; also, fanciful. He was an excellent mathematician, an educated philosopher, and someone who knew people. He told me he had kept his distance from women for years. Then he was entirely smitten. He was overcome with passion. This woman was a stupid joke in comparison to him. She was entirely unsuited to him.

"There were her flowing dresses with ne'er a wrinkle, her figure, starved to the bone with fasting, her wishes, fantasies, demands, her petulance and vanity, her bloodless tenderness, and her idiosyncratic, secretive religiosity about physical realities; and her artificiality. She was a spoiled, dissipated waste of a human being.

"She was so conceited she imagined herself to be too sublime to serve David Brenner as an 'object of pleasure'!

"God knows at the time I was in hog heaven to have my expensive cigars between my lips.

"When Gus was six years old, he had to be taken from her. She had damaged him with her holy visions, demands from God, and her rules. At the time he was thin as a rail, as malnourished as she was. She shunned all meat and fat as the prison of the soul. And so on. She ran after spiritualists, held seances, and brought home all manner of strange riffraff. She swore Gus was the most excellent spirit medium. She imagined he had been created to usher in the new order. When his father threatened to put the young boy in an academy of the Free Masons if the insanity did not stop, she reeled backwards in a swoon. She fell to the floor, and David tried to lift her, but the boy pushed his father away.

"David Brenner was able to keep his son from going mad, but he alienated him. Gustav came to hate and despise his father, so much so that, when his mother was dying, Gus, in his agony, threw his father out of the room, saying, "Don't ruin her last moments on Earth." If not these words exactly, then a similar lovely sentiment. You would have to know David Brenner as I do. You'd see what goodness his son is missing out on. Madame, are you feeling better now? You look quite refreshed. Would you like a cigarette? No? I'm afraid I'm quite morose here.

"We offer 20,000 kronen, paid to you in cash, the moment you hand me a farewell letter to Gus."

Milada flushed in surprise. "20,000 kronen to me?" she repeated, hardly able to imagine what Joe had just offered.

"You understood perfectly. You must have some plans for yourself. With this you are closer to putting them into effect. When gold rains from above you need not concern yourself whence it came."

"For me? 20,000 kronen, this huge sum of money?"

Oh, just like a woman, Joe was ashamed to think. She is swept off her feet and the boyfriend is gone from her mind. "As you see we were not trying to take advantage of you. We took you seriously in consideration of Gus. David Brenner believed his son wouldn't have wanted you to receive less. Gus is used to generous sums. He would find a less generous amount a ridiculous affront. All the more since he knows you are well off."

"I still don't understand. I told you I'm not going to Berlin. That should keep you from offering this huge sum."

Joe shook his head. "You haven't yet understood in full. You tell me in earnest, 'I'm not going to Berlin.' But what if Gus doesn't let go of you? Let's say he holds on to you, swears he'll stay with you, and tells you what you have to do. You don't know him like I do. He's stiff-necked and petulant. However absurd or outrageous his plan, there's no way of stopping him. There's another aspect to this, Milada. Gus has meant a lot to you. But your feelings are not under discussion. We want assurances. That's why we've made this offer. It commits you to separate from him. It ensures Gus is cut off from you, too."

She said forcefully, "And you trust me? What if I take the money and then..."

"Milada, I wouldn't mistrust you. But, you see, we do ask for something in writing. Gus's vanity has to be at stake, otherwise he won't let go. We ask you to send him this explanation: 'Of my own volition I have accepted 20,000 kronen from your father David Brenner. In return I agree, once and all, to break off all contact with you. I agree to this since all those concerned see that your situation in life can only be damaged by continuing our relation.' So you do see we are not making you out Dumas's Marguerite Gautier, the woman who leaves her lover for a bribe and lets him think she has betrayed him. Offering Gus this reason spares his dignity, don't you agree? You may take your time to think this over."

Joe went to his desk and laid a sheet of paper on top. He then began milling around the room.

"Joe, Sir!"

"Yes?"

"Do you promise me one thing?"

"What is it?"

"I am unpleasantly aware that you've brought me here to complete your mission as an obligation to your friend. You're not concerned about me. In a few minutes," she indicated the desk, "I will be gone. I've never had to make a plea as humbly as I do now. Strange, isn't it? At the moment I am about to be wealthy, I feel like a beggar.

"Yesterday, my entire inner riches fell away. A lot happened all at once. There were internal events, which are, of course, of no interest to you. Red House changed hands. I don't have the duties I had had. The girls in the house are against me, probably to please the new madam. I also received word from Horner. He's in a madhouse. You can't imagine what these losses mean to me. And now I'm losing Gus. But this loss is not so much Gus as it is the idea of a man, of power and freedom. It seems I can't do anything right in life. I'm angrier than a small child. I have no way of gauging anything. I am disoriented, and nothing makes sense. You've told me a lot today that is true, and I'm glad to know these things. Joe, Sir! I beg you, don't send me away immediately after I've written the letter to Gus. I want solid answers to some questions. I would like to salvage something from this for myself. Maybe you can help. Perhaps you can tell me if this is true or you can count on that or this will last. I will take you at your word and disappear from your sight forever. Will you give me that much?"

Joe looked as disgruntled as he could. Beneath the furrows on his brow his eyes were fixed on her. He was restless.

"You're welcome to stay. As long as you'd like. As far as I'm concerned you can stay all night. I'm fine with that. You can sleep." He pulled down the covers of the bed and pointed to the sofa, "I'll stay there."

She bent down and took his hand. He pulled it away, "Stupid girl," he grumbled.

"I'll sit down and write the letter now," she said and went to the desk. He nodded. Milada wrote:

> I received at my own request 20,000 kronen from your father. In return I am obliged to ignore any attempt you make to contact me. I ask you to abide by my promise. It is best for both of us.
>
> I do this for two reasons. Firstly, with this money it is possible for me to realize a part of my dreams. These dreams belong to me more than you or my love for you do. My dreams consume me and sustain me more than does your love. Secondly,

I have to think of your future. It will be happier and less endangered if I disappear forever.

Milada

Joe took the letter and nodded. "Not too sentimental. Not too short. It's exactly right."

Joe put the letter in an envelope, sealed it, and put a stamp on it, and Milada wrote Gus's address on the envelope. Then Joe handed her a check. Without looking at it, she tucked it hurriedly in her bag.

Joe took out his watch. "It's time for my supper. I'm going to the university cafeteria. You can get my meal as part of this room and board downstairs from the kitchen. Afterwards I suggest you cover up warm and get some sleep. When I come back, you should be rested."

He grabbed his hat and jacket.

"If you'd like to read, you'll find my little library under the pillow."

And with that he took his leave. The shadows of twilight lay across his small student quarters.

Milada could speak no more. With a heavy motion Joe turned on the little lamp before he went on his way. Then he pulled a book out of his pocket and held it out to her.

"Here, take it, Milada. Take it with you for a time when you have solitude. 'The starry sky above me, and the moral law within.' Those are what is eternal for Kant. It helps make sense of living."

He stood a moment in front of her.

"You want to make sense of the evil of prostitution? Hmm. Your body, Milada, is a cosmos in miniature. If you suffer terrible headaches and go to an experienced doctor for that, he won't be interested in hearing about your woes. 'How's your digestion?' he will ask. 'Are you regular?' Or you may complain of indigestion. 'Are your teeth in good order?' he will ask. This is how a man of science works.

"The massive body of this society is like the human body, always at war with bacteria and microbes. It may win out over them or succumb to them for a while. One of the afflictions of the body politic is called prostitution. The source of this disease is tied up with a host of other problems that feed on the health of the organism. Prostitution is a necessity in our lifetime and will remain so until such a time as the relation between the sexes evolves to a higher plane. In that future vulgar prostitution will serve no purpose; it will fall away. I believe this evolution is possible.

"You want to be useful. You want to do good, to save people. Dear Lady, once again I must quote a poet. 'If you want to do good, you have to wrap yourself in the tattered rags of justice on Earth to keep warm.' If you want to do something about the misery of your sphere, then don't waste your mental energy on large, high-flown projects, on overhauling systems or inciting revolutions. Such projects make the will ineffectual. Horner's will was broken by this.

"Don't take Horner as your model! Certain foods can ruin digestion; these ideas can ruin the mind. People are small. They should keep at performing small acts. Between heaven and earth there are only seeming heroes. They can't get along in the world as we know it without the institution of prostitution. You can't rescue the prostitute of today any more than you can write the laws for permits or for her decent living standards.

"You've told me on occasion about your childhood. About the dreadful loneliness and neglect you experienced as the child of a prostitute. You spoke of being buffeted back and forth between paying customers and women who were tarted up, one of whom was your mother. There are lots of children like that. Go rescue one of these children before she gets into prostitution. Snatch these children from tomorrow's greedy jaws. Take on these girls with large eyes, urchins on the street in need of nourishment for their little bodies and nurturance for their souls. The working prostitute can no longer be saved.

"Madame, you can protect children. You can wrap them in your coat. You have enough money for that. You can't create utopia. Protecting children would not wreck your strength; it would not ask the impossible of you. Establish an asylum like this! The children you take on to give them a life are a gift to the divine within. This work is like actualizing one of Horner's delusional fantasies. Don't you think so, too?"

Joe was quiet. The flame of the lamp rose, and a hazy, red glow enveloped the two of them. A thousand stars looked in through the window. It seemed you could reach out and touch the sky.

Milada's soft voice came from out the corner where she sat motionless, her hand to her forehead.

"I do now know what my life is about. I could have lived through the years of sadness by haggling, scraping, and serving—for money or for love—much more easily if I had not felt in my heart that all of it, however vivid it seemed, was only a fleeting image I might put out with a wet finger. Now for the first time I see how truly insubstantial and shadowy what I experienced was.

"But I also see that my experience was the start of a new direction I must take. Much had to happen before I was ready to move in this direction and forge a path. I needed these many events—my early years, Miller, Horner, Gus, and now these hours with you—to find my way. I now grasp its value. I'm thankful to you."

She got up and reached for her hat. She was joyous and moved. It showed on her stern face.

"But it's nighttime," he said. "You're going? I do see a little apartment like mine does not bid you to stay." He turned down the flame of the lamp. She said, "Oh, no. It was wonderful here. Everything. But I have a lot to take care of. They still need me in the house. They'll be waiting for me."

She extended both her hands to him.

He took them with his right hand and pressed them. "Farewell."

"Good evening." He walked briskly to the door.

"It's dark. Be careful," he called after her.

"I can find my way," she answered.

A Missive and Psalter in Honor of the Sacred Scarab!

To Milada, Queen of Prostitutes, *reginae prostibulorum*, my laudable pupil,

in perpetual praise by a man drawn under by vile devils

All hail to you, Sacred Scarab!
Now you sit on high,
You are swollen with vanity's glow,
Atop your head sits a small crown,
Your piss is a juice of gold,
Ha, ha, ha, we were fine together, you and I!
Do not laugh at my expense overly much
Up there on your pile of shit!
If you do, you'll explode in slop.
Cave, my Scarab, take heed!
My darling creature of filth!
In my nightlife you alone
Are a spot of gold!
What would I be without you?
A worn-out dead man,
A fool.
If I be bound and held down,
Should I be wrapped in rags and tatters,
I will only laugh ha ha ha
And think to myself I am the creator!
I know that from millions of stinking beetles
In stinking, rotting, foul shit,
I found the one that is a treasure,
One sweeter than the sweetest wine.

I found you!
All hail to you, Sacred Scarab!
Thou art full of sun,
In filthy shit.
Thou hast the sun within,
The glow of vanity!
Be, however, aware
I, your creator,
Am only a fool.
All of life is only half.
So take this advice:
Don't leave your imperial realm!
Snot-nosed boys are out there.
For snot-nosed boys there is no difference:
Asphodius or the Scarab are both the same.
Wham, his foot will squash you,
And the spot of gold in my life as a fool
Will be gone, turned to shit.
Cave, my Scarab!
Your teacher, guide, and imposter,
Arnold Egidy Horner
a.k.a. The Limp Dick

Madame von Miller had taken a room in a small rooming house for laborers who were deaf and mute on the outskirts of town. From early till late in the day she sat at the window of her room, busily reading old editions of *The Catholic Mountain Reporter*. Or she stood in the kitchen, keeping an eye out for the postman and trying to make the wife of the shoemaker, a woman who was deaf and mute, understand the wonder of God's grace that was awaiting her. Miller used gestures and vocalizations to convey this. She plied Milada, who came almost daily, with questions. She beset her with her doubts and outbursts of impatience.

"I tell you I will have no more good fortune in this life. You'll see, Milada. I won't. And on top of that I'm haunted by temptation! When I try to pray, vile faces appear to me. They're the faces of people from that place."

Even though she had tried to part with her past in her fear for her soul, she was secretly tortured by monstrous visions. She worried about the money Spizzari would make from the business now that her watchful eye was no longer there. She knew about the remodeling Spizzari planned, and she was dying to know more. Yet she hid her interest behind sobs of horror; she maintained she wanted nothing more to do with that place.

The rose-colored makeup she wore in Red House to mask the wrinkles in her cheeks had been washed away, and her skin was now visible. It was leathery and covered with yellow splotches. She parted her hair and wore it straight down. There was no rustle of silk on her sunken body. She wore only flat-black clothing, to which she had applied white stripes around the neck and sleeves to simulate the robes of a nun.

To Milada she said, "If you only knew how very happy I already am! I live in peace. I don't shudder at night. And I don't have the noise and godless traffic of those bitches. God spare me! May they never come to mind again!"

On those days Milada did not visit, Miller sent a servant to fetch her right away. Once Milada was there Miller assailed her with the most bitter accusations and threats.

"There is no reward in this world for my toil and trouble," Miller quoted an old saw. "What did I make you into? A lady, a princess! And now in the most troubled days of my life, you abandon me. Of course you're serving that Jewess Spizzari now. You kept your endearments to yourself when I was there. The new woman will make money off that place, won't she?" Miller was both curious and greedy.

"You made good money there yourself, Madame."

"I made money with you. You knew how to do business, Milada. Where did the large amount of capital you got come from?"

"You, Madame, made three times what you put into that business."

"I beg you, please, don't always talk about money. It distresses me. I have very different pleasures ahead of me. Jesus is my refuge."

Basically, she was overcome with the irrational fear Milada would abandon her before the cloister sent word to Red House she had been accepted. Miller begged her and made her promise to be open with her about her plans and options. Miller told her she could speak honestly with her, just like with a mother.

"My plans are not set, Madame. I'm not going to Berlin. I can't stay in Red House either. They are remodeling. I'd like to go somewhere in the countryside. I'd prefer to go to the mountains for some rest."

"The mountains? Milada, if you stick with me until I have word from the cloister, then you can go stay in my little house in the mountains, I promise in God's name. I got this little refuge for my last years from the blessed priest. That dear departed man thought of this out of his concern for me. I'd rent it to you for very little. I don't want to make money off of you."

"A little house in the mountains, Madame," Milada repeated right after her. "Eventually I'd like to buy such a house."

"Now there's a good idea. It has four rooms downstairs and four rooms upstairs. You could rent it out to people in the summer. Once a general even stayed there. There's a garden in front with a picket fence and flowers. And it has a plot for potatoes and vegetables. The air up there in the mountains is wonderful. You'll hear how people up there sing my praises. They call me Miss Fini."

"Well, if you wouldn't want too much for it," Milada said with hesitation since she knew showing any enthusiasm would cost her money.

"Milada, why don't you buy it! See here," said Miller caught up in sentimentality, "You've been a poor thing from childhood on, just like me. If I can help you with that and since it is already land from the Church, the Sacred Virgin will certainly pardon me. We could say it'll be in the family. I've always thought, Milada, you'd enter a cloister one day."

Milada got in touch with the lawyer in L——zer and before she realized it the idea of buying this from Miller had seduced her. She was entranced with the idea of being far away from the world she had known! She was carried away thinking of putting together a place for her plans, an asylum for children! Why not?

The thought magnetized her more and more. Miller did not have to persuade her.

"It's so beautiful there, looking out over the mountains. They call it Sunny Heights. You have only the sky and the sun all around you. The peak they call Mattern looks like an old man. It's right outside your window. The farmers call the mountains around you the Bold Red Women. The glow of the rhododendrons fills the valley. You can get to the Pastor's Forest from your garden. From there you can see the lovely surroundings."

Without scrutinizing the aims and goals of her decision Milada moved on her idea, and the little house in Sunny Heights was soon in her possession.

On 1 August Milada brought Miller news of her acceptance in the cloister. The mail came early in the morning. She was still in bed. "I am unworthy," she prayed, stammering. "May I have mercy," and she pressed the large envelope to her heart.

From this moment on till her "investiture," which as to follow in fourteen days, she withdrew from Milada. Her absence was obvious. On several occasions she excused herself because of migraines. Milada had been visiting routinely out of habit. She kept coming routinely, too, undeterred by Miller's unavailability. One day Milada got a card Miller had left for her.

I am rushing toward life in heaven. Live your life in Christ.
Farewell, Sister Josefine

Milada stared at the card for several minutes without perceiving what she had read. She opened the door to the room Miller had inhabited in the rooming house. It was cleaned out. Drawers and cupboards were hanging open, and the smell of lavender, which Miller used in her clothing in large quantities, hung in the air of the small room.

The wife of the shoemaker, who was deaf and mute, stood in the doorway and gestured to Milada. Then she returned with a neighbor woman who helped Milada understand Miller had left. She had been planning her departure for a few days, and that morning she had left in a carriage with a doctor.

Back on the street Milada tried to collect the thoughts that washed over her like a tide. She could see her shock was actually humorous. Yet the disappearance of this woman did leave a hole in her life.

Spizzari had given Milada a room in Red House for one year for her work arranging the sale. It came with board and provisions. She found it inappropriate simply to turn Milada out.

Now Spizzari entertained her own selfish plans while smiling ever so sweetly to Milada about staying on. She said it was "from here on out."

She hid her delight over Milada's break with Gustav. And she avoided talking with Milada about it.

All she said was, "You can live here as you used to when crazy Miller was here. You can stay on in my establishment. Nothing will change. My business is your business."

Milada declined the offer. She kept herself apart from the new business. Getting involved would be dicey. What she said was that she intended to take a break, rest, and spend some time to herself.

"That's smart, my child," Spizzari replied, glad about Milada's plan.

There were two matters Milada had to take care of. She wanted assurances about Lolo's fate. And she wanted to visit Horner who had been committed to a mental institution at the beginning of the summer. The report was he was happy there and cried when they threatened to send him somewhere else. She was drawn more and more closely to her small property. She wanted to see it and was looking forward to making the transition from her old home of desolation to the little house on the sunny mountain top.

In Sunny Heights

The beautiful last rays of autumn sun lit Milada's departure for the mountains of Styria. High up in the mountains snow glittered. The forests glowed in a riot of red. In the villages all was still. The still of winter was in the offing.

Dr. Stüber the lawyer was waiting for her to arrive at the L——zer train station. He had been most complimentary and had put himself, very devotedly, at her disposal. But he had to shake his head in disapproval of Milada's outfit. She wore yellow shoes made of Russian leather, a traditional, loden-green suit, and a hat with a wide brim.

"I suggest you not wear this citified costume to go up there, my esteemed, dear lady. You've got a couple of hours of steep travel to get up to the high mountains. In G——g we're having winter weather. It's cold enough to snow. I've let Katie know we're on our way. She'll make sure the place is properly heated. He asked the cab driver, "Can you take this lady from the city on up there?"

"I surely can," the young man nodded.

"You will enjoy it up there. But, my dear young lady, how do you think you're going to get around? The ground is hard stone up there, and the ice is slick. I'd like to suggest shoes with cleats, what we wear around here. You'll need a shearling coat and something..."

he cleared his throat, "Something on your legs, if I may say so."

Milada looked down at her clothing. "This is going to have to do for the first few days. After that, if you don't mind, I'll turn to you for advice about the right kind of gear for the weather. Will that be all right?"

To show his pledge he laid his hand on his heart.

"I'm going to need your advice quite often, Doctor Stüber. I intend to build up there."

"Build!? Up in the Heights?" he said in astonishment. "Oh, dear God. Do you mean a house for nuns?"

"No, a roomy, practical little house, Doctor Stüber, for lay purposes. Could we start in March?"

"A building, a building! In March the sun isn't strong enough. The ground won't be dry enough until May, my dear lady."

She exhaled deeply and looked with astonishment at the gold that twilight had laid across the scenery. "How beautiful it is!" she exclaimed.

"It is. We can't complain. Winter up here also holds its charms, as we say."

The doctor was an old bachelor who enjoyed the company of women. His fantasies were dried out, like kindling, and could easily catch fire. Talking with this woman from the city who was traveling on her own with her serious, gray eyes and warm laughter was the most romantic experience he had had in many years.

The black horse and the young cab driver were waiting to take Milada up to her house. They were becoming impatient.

"We will have to make good time," he said and cracked the whip.

Before Milada climbed into the old, heavy cab, she said, "Thank you, Doctor Stüber. And please don't tell people about our plans to build."

"It's safe with me, dear lady, safe."

"She said 'our plans,'" he whispered, charmed. "She's an attractive person."

Evening fell astonishingly quickly. The sun went out like a flame and greedily took all light with it. The rock cliffs came closer, shadowy and huge. The sky was hemmed in. Stars emerged. The horse pulled in jerks. The cab rattled behind. Dogs barked. Now and again, there was a call, and the cabby called back. The night was deep and dark.

"Do you know the way?" Milada leaned out and called once.

"Me, no. But the horse does," the young man said with a certainty that was enviable.

They stopped at an inn at the foot of the Mattern.

"That's as far as we can go with the horse," the driver said.

"The lady from the city's here?" Rosie from the inn was curious to know. "Katie's been up there twice already today," she told the cabby and picked up Milada's suitcase. "The old folks say some fool city woman is coming."

"Is it a long way to the top?" Milada wanted to know.

"It's a good fifteen minutes," was the answer.

Milada drank a glass of mulled wine and wrapped a plaid blanket around her shoulders. It was hardly any protection against the cold wind and snow. She followed Rosie as she climbed up the slope. The cab driver led the way, carrying a lantern.

"It's like drinking ice water. Just do it," Milada told herself to stay tough.

"Up here they call the place The Little Light. You've got a nice place to call home."

"Yep, where the old biddy used to live," said the young man.

"Shut your big mouth, boy," Rosie told him.

"Take your time, be careful!" was the first greeting Milada had at Sunny Height.

Katie was almost ninety years old. She greeted Milada with an old-fashioned welcome. Katie offered Milada her hand. It was hard and shriveled.

"You're frozen through and through! The woman at the inn

should have loaned you a jacket. Jesus, Jesus, you're freezing."

The smell of poppy seed cake filled the room, which had been made ready for her arrival.

An old cast-iron stove glowed and emitted a pleasant warmth for the woman from the city. There was a pot of milk, a piece of goat cheese, a loaf of black bread, and a basket of heather. Katie apologized there was not a pot of hot soup. She had not known when the new woman would arrive. But tomorrow, she promised, she would have some soup.

Milada reassured her everything was much nicer than what she was used to. She drank the milk right up. She remarked at the wonderful, thick featherbed. To whom, she asked, should she say her thanks for this? Katie was pleased to say it had come from her own trousseau. She had spun the linen cover and stuffed it with down herself. She ran her hand over it to straighten it. "It keeps forever. Madame, you don't have to worry about winter storms with this. They can be real hard. You don't have to be scared of the bats either. They like to flap against the windowpanes." Then she left her guest to her surroundings, saying, "Just take your time." To be thrifty Katie took the candle with her. Who, after all, needs light to eat or to sleep?

It was the deepest silence, solitude without a sound. Thousands of stars twinkled above. Milada tried to open a window, but it was frozen shut. Milada undressed, ate some of the bread, and pulled the featherbed over herself. It was a yard deep.

Can this be? Can this really be? She asked herself in amazement. Early this morning I was still in Red House. I said goodbye to Karla and Gisi. "What will it be like without you?" she sighed. Karla stared at her with anger in her eyes.

"It would have been better if you'd decided to stay here with us."

"Karla, if you want I will pay for you to leave here. You can come with me." Milada had often offered Karla this when Karla was unhappy.

Karla shook her head no. "I belong here. And you do, too," she answered recalcitrantly.

How could Milada ever make her grasp she had a new life? Was there a way to make her understand she was leaving this life far behind? But would this new venture work out for her? Would she have the strength to put her plan into effect?

A thousand doubts filled her mind. She was fearful and timid under this strange roof. Will I be able to pull it off?

She closed her eyes. The bit of bread in her tired hand fell to the floor. Would she pull through all the difficulties and dangers till this strange place becomes home, home to her own asylum for children? Will she do it?

"Take your time, take your time," the shaky voice of old Katie comforted her. "Take my time, take my time up here on the mountain."

The high plateau was wide and vast. The forest rose up all around. The sound of wind in the trees was constant, powerful music. The wind was all one heard.

At the back of the house was a small door that led to the Pastor's Forest, which dropped off abruptly. It was eerie and somber and without a sound. There was never a human voice in the forest.

Animals were kept in barnyards. The forest was closed to the public. It was too wet for hunting or for lumbering. When the sun rose, the snow glittered like silver on the peaks. In the caverns and hollows sunlight made a flood of colors.

Twilight fell all of a sudden. It took Milada many days to adjust to watching the sun's rays shine out like a torch one minute and the next disappear into shades of blue and black. Since she got cold once the sun was down, the old women told her to go inside. And so she did.

People up here had not forgotten their Miss Fini.

"Oh, dear Lord!" Katie sighed. She had served four different priests at the parish house. There was no convincing her that Miller had not died. Katie simply could not accept she would have given up her house.

"May she receive her eternal rewards. She had her share of sorrows and woes."

Katie's good, old face was covered in wrinkles. Yet her arthritic, knotted and deformed fingers spun yarn from early in the morning till late at night. Milada asked her whether she wanted to stop working.

"As long as a body can eat, a body has to work," was her considered answer. "If the mouth can eat, then the hands can keep going."

Milada asked Katie if she had ever been married.

Katie turned bright red. She dropped the spindle and gestured no. She was sorry, sorry, but, no, she was a virgin. Everybody knew this. She told Milada she was free to ask people if that was not so. She told Milada at the Easter festivities she carried a single white lily at the front of the procession. It was not proper for someone who served a priest ever to marry. But nowadays people have new-fangled ideas.

Often, she fell asleep while spinning. She slept through the night in her chair, always sitting in the same position, bent forward to spin. She had a large, gray chair, a gift from the current priest. She looked proud and happy as a queen in her chair.

"I'm doing real good," she was pleased to say of herself. "I eat every day, sit, and sleep, and the Good Lord protects my dear chastity."

Once a cranky old blind woman, the mother of the landholder, took Milada aside and said, "It must be a burden to take care of doddery old Katie." This woman lived with her sister Vronele up on the plateau. People called her The Rock. "Katie's not any use to anybody anymore. And then she's so uppity about her chastity," the old blind woman hissed.

A farmer woman sold Milada a sturdy fur coat and a pair of

high leather boots. Milada tromped around the woods in these. The stiff wind chapped her pampered complexion. “Go inside, go inside,” Katie warned her. “It’s blustery out there in our mountains.”

But Milada was not content to stay in the heated house. When the wind blew, it called her. The sunlight drew her outside.

When it snowed, she ran around the plateau, catching large flakes in her hands.

Her eyesight had become accustomed to the narrow tunnel of Red House Alley, but it now became sharp. Her eyes were drawn to the blue of the horizon. On sunny days it was so bright she had to avert her eyes.

She ran all over, from one elevation to the next. She looked at the wonderful land formations in this world of mountains. She slid down to the village below, where smoke plumes rose, coming ever nearer to the dark trees in the woods. It seemed the smoke looked out over the Heights with love and greeted the windows, behind which the old women were working away at this and that. Every day was filled with new sights. They enchanted her. She never tired of looking.

Yet in the midst of these precious new experiences, which opened up her recovering soul, she had visions from the past. She saw ghosts from Red House Alley. They were threatening. Sometimes they haunted her so intensely she stopped in her tracks while hiking. She murmured, “I won’t forget. I won’t forget any of it.” Fanchon, Horner, Lolo—Horner. Terrifying!

She had visited Horner. She stood next to him and listened to his idiotic, self-satisfied laughter. With horror—a horror she could not describe—she looked at his filthy, fat fingers, which fumbled with colored marbles.

The attendant at the asylum told her, “Today he’s behaving very well. But he can be uncontrolled, intractable and wild.”

The patient babbled outrageous, senseless, and vile things. The marbles were his pupils. He taught them, reprimanded them, and swore. And his former connection to people, which Milada had known so well, had deteriorated. It was a shadow of what it had been.

Her visit had made virtually no difference to him. He had spat at her secretively out of malice. He laughed at the attendant, a man who would break your heart.

Milada left after ten minutes, shaken by the horror. It was a dreadful ending!

She had no luck tracking down Lolo. All that she found out was that she had been sent back to Prague.

Snow fell for three days running. It made a defensive wall around the house. The Rock, whom Milada had supplied with food, had to shovel the snow from the door every day.

Milada's hands were chapped from the cold. She treated them by making a poultice of boiled milk and poppy seeds. "Poppy does help heal," said Katie, concerned for her young guest. Milada had also developed a bad cough. For her cough she took syrup from poppy seeds, sweetened with mallow.

Milada sat by the stove and read Goethe's *Sorrows of Young Werther*. Tears streamed down her face at Werther's restless joy in love and his soulful turbulence and despair that it was unrequited.

"Laborers carried his coffin. No priest accompanied him to the grave."

"That's what I want for myself," she thought and spoke these words aloud.

The three old women, Katie, The Rock, and Vronele moved up close to the fire in the stove. They talked about illness and death and about the meal after the burial ceremony. They listed the people who would likely be there. The Rock made cutting remarks about the priest who sent his assistant the curate to help when a "wretched thing" had died. She also spoke bitterly about the wealthy wife of the man with the lumber company. That woman, said The Rock, had never in her life given anybody anything. When someone died, she sent a small wreath of broken bits and pieces of fir and pine. Yes, The Rock had a mean word to say in any conversation. When snow fell and there was little comfort, even sitting by the stove, Milada brewed up a pot of the tea people in the region made of dried strawberry and blackberry leaves, laced with lemon and a good cognac. Then the old women grew merry, forgot about their aches and pains, and sipped at their tea, smiling together and nodding.

On one such occasion, while sitting with these women, Milada, without thinking about her listeners, began spontaneously to talk about her plans. She told them about the many small children who grow up in the city and have the most terrible needs. She spoke of how they have only filth and ugliness before their eyes. They grow up without knowing the warmth of love.

She told them at one time she, too, had suffered from this great hunger of the soul. She said she had become closely attuned to helping children who are in need. Milada let them know she had come up to these mountains to have the solitude to think through her plans. And she found this little, hidden house to be the right place for children to thrive. Here they could live among people who also knew life to be hard but who were less damaged and more compassionate than people living at a fast pace in the city.

Milada presented all this in language that was plain, like the terse language of the people in the mountains. Old Katie lit up right away. Her sparkling, black eyes darted around the group and showed her approval.

"Oh, Jesu, Jesu, the poor, little wretched things! So let's take on a child up here. It wouldn't be a bad thing if one of us was still here. A child needs to learn to laugh and play. Yes, surely. Madame, if you put a little one in my arms, I'll rock and sing that little one to sleep like a baby bird that needs a nest.

The woman they call Rock asked, "Will we have to leave this house?"

Milada assured her that would never happen. The three old women who had lived there would always have a home in the new house for young children. And it will be a nicer house. Only for the short while the house is being built will they have to live somewhere else.

The women talked among themselves back and forth. They threw out ideas. Maria from Hotwitzer should be able to make the children's clothes, and Hanna from Zirbelholz should be able to outfit the house, and Rosie from Fatting had two daughters who could work as servants.

Milada retreated to her room upstairs, supplied with lots of practical suggestions and warm well-wishes. She was aglow with anticipation. How unusual! What had happened to her that she was filled with this happiness? When she picked up her copy of Goethe's novel, her hands were shaking.

The winter's sun was cold, cold, cold. Snow had ceased falling. It lay pure white, leveling high points and low. On such a morning Milada received Dr. Stüber. He had been in Upper Reutling to see a man who was dying. And on his return trip he dropped by to see this interesting young lady of his. He found her with the three worn-out, old women, sitting around a bowl of potato gruel, swimming in butter and poppyseeds. He was happy to join them and dropped his paternalistic habit of gushing compliments. There was much serious talk there in the room at the stove where the women did their spinning. Doctor Stüber pulled out pen and paper, and the women pulled up their chairs to him and were quiet as mice, acting like the pastor had come to visit. The Rock brought out a bottle of strong rose wine. And the two non-locals talked between themselves. This was a scene of serious planning for a serious undertaking. They calculated how high the structure would have to be and how the interior would be laid out. Doctor Stüber could not conceal his astonishment at the business acumen and generative contributions of this sweet young lady.

Milada played down his compliments. "I'm used to doing practical business. Do I look that inexperienced, Doctor, Sir?"

"Not exactly that, but it is always amazing to see new blossoms in the spring, I'll have to say. May does have its blossoms, now, doesn't it?"

The Doctor tucked away his notes and sketches and promised to take the whole matter to his close friend the architect Stadlinger in Oberdorf. Stadlinger had just completed a home for workers, an orphanage, and a hospital there. "The man is trustworthy," he said. "If I can recommend anyone without reservation, it's Stadlinger, my dear Lady. We'll sit down the hill in Adinger and watch as the house goes up."

"Now what do you old ladies have to say about the fine replacement that old scarecrow Miss Fini sent us?"

Katie made the sign of the cross and admonished the Doctor not to speak ill of the dead.

"Well, well, I'm not going to spend eternity in hellfire over this," said the Doctor, winking at Milada.

"It wasn't necessary for you to talk bad about Miss Fini," The Rock finished up this informative exchange.

A small boy arrived at the house in the relentless pouring rain. He brought word from the mayor of the town. The Mayor sent his greetings to the new lady. He asked her to come down right away. An important letter had arrived for her.

Milada asked the boy if she had to go down into town to get the letter herself or whether she could give him sixpence for going down to the Mayor.

"Yes, Madame," said the boy and held out his small, brown hand to receive the coin. "But the Mayor won't give it to me," he said hurriedly, slipping the money into his pants pocket.

"It's probably one of those registered letters," said The Rock.

"You'll have to go down there to fetch it yourself."

So Milada set out on her way with the boy. He was a grandchild of Rosie in Fatting. She had twelve illegitimate children. As Miss Fini had noted with aggravation and sighs, "Each and every one of 'em was from a different father." Fini had spent many a curse on Rosie. Rosie's oldest child was a girl named Jula. Jula had made a break with this lifestyle and married. Little Dieter was Jula's legitimate son. He was a smart little boy and very proud of his father. "He's my very own daddy just for me," said the boy confidently.

Milada teased him, "Are you sure you don't want to loan him out?"

"Nope, Lady. He'd come back to me anyways, even if I loaned him out."

Milada walked along the snow-covered main street of the village. The only sound around was the ringing of cow bells and the calls of coachmen, driving their horses on.

Curiosity-seekers pressed their faces against the windowpanes to see who was on the street. Occasionally a little old woman greeted her as she passed.

"Who could have written to me?" Milada speculated.

The most likely person would be Kessler who had sold Miller Red House. Milada had given him her exact address. Fanchon or Gisi would not send off a letter into the blue. There probably was not anything of importance going on in Red House anyway.

For a brief, miserable moment she thought it might be Gus. To distract herself she shook her head and started up a conversation with little Dieter. Dieter ran into the courtyard and came back with the Mayor. He invited her into his overheated office and gave her a glass of juniper-berry wine. Then, awkwardly, he took a registered letter out of his shabby valise.

"This came three days ago, but nobody recognized the name. Then a little girl in Grüssing said she knew there was a new lady up in Miss Fini's old house. Is that right? Is that you up there?"

Milada acknowledged that she was that person, took off her

mittens and put her hand out.

"I can't give it to you just like that. First you have to sign for it."

He handed her a receipt and a large pen. "You have it directly from me." Then Milada took the letter from him. On the back of the envelope, written at an angle with red ink was: Karla Zechmeister / 3 Mohren Street / Prater Park, then "Very urgent to be delivered in person." Likely this message had prompted the Mayor to take this seriously. She did not open the letter until she had arrived home and was alone in her room. She read. It was eight pages long.

Dearest Milahda!

You will probably be surprised to hear where I am writing from. I am at 3 Mohren in Prater Park where I landed with Fanny.

Dear Milahda, there's not much worth talking about at Red House now. It's a hell I'm telling you. What that new woman has done and what goes on there all the time. It's hard to tell you. That woman only has people like herself there. There's a woman you can't trust named Irma. She locks the girls up and beats them. But this is not the worst thing that goes on there. It is a shame you're not there. All the old girls we knew got swapped out. That woman says they were old news. Werkel works upstairs, I want to spit. Gisi took off for a week with Bert the soldier guy. Only Mitzi is still there. She's got a good job like Irma. Mitzi picks up girls and brings them to the house. She plays like she's a lady with a hat and gloves. She gets girls off the street, there are hundreds of them. And our Rosie as you probably read in the papers is already dead. They found her behind the house. You should've seen her, blood everywhere. Gisi's Bert paid for me to get out. He (Bert) paid Nelly 100. She was glad about that. He came and picked me up with a coach. I snuck out while he threw my clothes out the window. Dear Milahda, enough said about what all is going on there. Mitzi has an important job there. She's sleeping with a girl who's 12 and she gets 100 gulden off her for sleeping with men. And on top of that Mitzi beats her. Milahda, they take the clothes from the girls. They only have corsets so they can't leave. It's just like what Zimmermann does. Girls and women show up in veils, and they lock them in the attic. If they have syphilis they're gone. Sucher comes and the fat Commissioner. They get drunk. Then Nelly is safe. No bills no payments. There's not an hour of peace. Everybody is fighting and bitching. There's a new girl upstairs who screams and cries but it doesn't help. She can't write. The place is falling apart and the girls can't get out. Dear Milahda, I am on my knees and thankful to be gone. Otherwise I'd be like Rosie. Dear Milahda, I have to tell you this so you know. Dear Milahda, Fanny is miserable and suffers but she won't go to the hospital. I think a lot that if you could come Fanny would dance and sing for joy. Our boss Puszta is mean but he doesn't bother me because Bert and Karl pay for me to stay. Dear Milahda, I have to go and have a lot more to tell you. I hope you're well and think about you hundreds of times. Write me: Karla Zechmeister 3 Mohren Prater. I hope this letter gets to you. Yours, Karla. Fanny sends her greetings and kisses just like me. Her pose on stage at the tavern is "Living Marble." I hope you write back soon.

Milada read the passage about Rosie two, then three times, to take in the news of her death. What had happened to her? Milada was not generally fearful or sentimental. What was going on in the house while she was sitting on the mountain top, dreaming the day away?

She was suddenly seized with distress and jumped up, holding her forehead. Had she really had any right to pick up and leave and let happen what will? Was she not one of them? Had she not known she was one of them and always said so?

Joe had, in her defense, said, "You can't save them." He had given her thousands of examples of failures. He had shown her she did have a right to leave. She knew this as a fact, yet her heart ached. Her heart would not have given up on these people.

What she did in leaving came about from her selfishness. It was evident again and again. Ultimately her will to survive won out! She had chased around after ideas, coddled ideas, allowed herself to look good because of these big ideas, and then let the small, hopeless ones die.

Just do not bend down to help! Horner's selfishness had nurtured an unholy selfishness in her. *Cave*, beware, my Scarab! That is what his admonition meant.

Why had she not taken Rosie along? She was a little girl, just a child, who laughed and cried in one breath, who played with danger and with vice as a child plays with dolls.

Milada remembered Rosie's tale of the big doll that walked in the glass cabinet. It touched her. Her story belied tragedy. It was her way of telling about her despair. She had clung to this straw from childhood, the last bit of good in her life. Rosie was throwing light on her childhood, but Milada had been judgmental about her attachment to a doll. She had been indefensibly thoughtless. She had not listened to what Rosie was telling her in her own way.

Horner would have a good laugh over this! His Scarab had kept herself at a safe remove.

Milada threw the window open, as if to get free of the ridiculing laughter of a fool. She felt this laughter was suffocating her. Everything she had done, every small step she had taken, and each big decision she had made only masked her fixation to save herself.

This view of herself had the ring of truth. In the yellow-white light that surrounded the pale snow of the high peak of the Mattern the image of her virtue as cold came into clear focus.

"There is a new girl upstairs who screams and cries, but it doesn't help," the words from Karla's letter went round and round in her head. It was a warning! It was a call that came to her over the mountains and one she had to follow. The three old women threw up their arms when Milada told them she was going to take a trip.

"Oh, my dear heart! Now, when the snow is so deep?" And, "But you have a cough!" And, "The train could get stuck in the snow."

But Milada packed her bag and sent a message via the cabby to Doctor Stüber in L.

On a dreary November day when gray fog covered Sunny Heights and its inhabitants Milada made her way between steep, hanging precipices to the train station. There the trusty face of her friend the Doctor was waiting for her. He was sad.

"That's a disturbing story," he said by way of an accusation. "We old folks have a hard time tearing ourselves away from what we love."

Milada comforted him and told him she would return. She was sure of it. Then she gave him the task of making sure construction on the house would proceed. She asked him to make sure the architect Stüber trusted knew the conditions they had agreed upon. She trusted the person he trusted.

They shook hands. The large, cotton handkerchief of the Doctor fluttered for a moment like a red bird in the breeze. It was his wave goodbye.

Milada looked out the window. Her gaze clung to the forest above and then to the sky.

She set out to meet her destiny.

Chapter 7
Spizzari's System

One dewdrop slips Into an ocean of light!
—Buddhist proverb

Nelly Spizzari was the embodiment of supreme efficiency and of directed focus beyond what any of the entrepreneurs in charge of Red House had been to date. She knew the games and strategies required in this profession, and she put them into practice with admirable equanimity. From the onset of any negotiation she never reconsidered anything. The execution of business ran, so she was wont to say, as if by itself. The most varied of temperaments within her domain bent under the pressure of her cold will.

She encouraged the girls to trust her by extending a benevolent-seeming camaraderie, but then she caught them in the jaws of her machinery. It held her victims, both those who fled to her and those she had enticed, with teeth of iron.

She always kept one or two well-trained favorites who enjoyed almost limitless power. For some reason, unbeknownst to anyone but God, she called this her "Turkish system."

Spizzari was scurrilous and brutal. She never shrank from exercising her domestic rights as the mother of the house. When someone arrived, she relieved them of their baggage and all their valuables. She locked these items away, even the most intimate of garments. In so doing she cut the new arrivals off completely from any contact with the outside world.

She promoted all kinds of gossip, arguments, and secrecies. She encouraged a regular system of internal spying and always succeeded in disrupting any harmony among the ladies. Nelly Spizzari had long been involved in trafficking girls and had learned that to make a solid profit she had first to break the will of these living wares.

Under Nelly's regime Red House had lost its esteem in the trade.

It was demolished in one sweep.

Nelly had no use for anything associated with bourgeois values. She thus attracted people who were hungry and homeless. Nelly took on anybody her procurer Mrs. Bacher drummed up. Bacher was an old, broken Jewish woman who was completely given over to Spizzari. She also took on a number of boys Bacher brought her for two gulden a head. She generally kept these creatures in the house as long as she could put them to good use. Then, when they no longer provided her any income, she turned them back out on the streets, plucked and ruined. Spizzari was friendly with the most notorious elements of the smart set and with the *Edelschweine-rasse*, the royal tribe of swine. She demanded prostitutes offer services that even the most unscrupulous rejected with disgust.

These finicky responses were foolishness the girls had to get over.

As a result of her practices the complement of ladies in the house had become a panoply of phenomena. There was a masseuse for horse riders from the circus, stars from variety shows who were homeless, stranded maid servants, apathetic prostitutes, and even nymphomaniacal daughters of the middle class. These middle-class girls called Nelly Mama, kissed her hand, and were happy to stay on.

Spizzari tethered all these types to her wagon of insatiable greed. Yet it was not greed alone that prompted her to play the most audacious games in the business.

She was attracted to outright risky adventures. They enticed this fat woman whose disposition was otherwise quite banal. She enjoyed deliberately getting into nasty contests with the law and its enforcers, the police. She was never in a state of more extreme excitement than when there was an audit in the house and she hid terror-stricken children and "decent" women in closets and in the basement. During an audit she admonished the girls to silence with threatening looks.

When the police arrived at the door, she bolted upright and slapped her thigh with delight. Her good eye had the glow of the devil.

She was particularly fond of taking very young girls from the hands of their monstrous parents. Nelly paid them a monthly sum. She performed all kinds of gruesome procedures on these children herself, stitching them up to cash in on their simulated virginity. She hid the symptoms of those who were ill and shuffled them out of the sight of the physician conducting examinations. She took all the money of the girls she had impounded, always telling them there had been some miscalculation, so that they owed her. The money she got in this way ended up in the pockets of her favorites or in the pocket of her darling nephew, an idler, to whom she had a foolish attachment. Usually she forgot about the money that went to these special individuals.

When she was in a good mood, she adorned the ladies who ran around the house half-naked with jewelry. She invited them to coffee, stuffed them with sweets and plied them with liquor. The most destructive consequence of her administration was the complete ruin of those girls she had taken over from the group Miller had had.

Although Josephine Miller had been greedy, her girls had been used to decent pay, which gave them the semblance of earning money. The real profit had, of course, gone to the madam when new girls arrived.

Spizzari mercilessly took every penny they had, down to the smallest tip. If the girls did not hand over the money willingly, they were subjected to body searches, and their rooms and bedding were thoroughly shaken down until the cash she expected was produced.

The girls who were used to Milada's humane treatment rebelled, and they riled up the girls who arrived later. Some tried to escape. But their attempts were foiled by the ever-watchful concierge and the even-more watchful Mrs. Bacher. In all events Spizzari soon realized it was necessary to clear these "undesirables" out of her despotic realm. In these cases, Mr. Stratti was brought on the scene. What his relation to Spizzari was no one knew, and people were afraid to investigate or express their surmisals aloud. In the house he was known as Trusty.

His whole external appearance suggested his personal relation to the madam. He was dark and buttoned-up, and he had a thin, black moustache with curled-up corners and piercing, small eyes. What most clearly indicated his relation to the madam was his impeccable smoking jacket for the salon, which he wore with a small rosette.

Sometimes in the afternoon, when Spizzari was having coffee with the girls, most casually she announced, "I expect Stratti will likely be here this evening."

Then some of the girls put down their coffee cups in horror and exchanged knowing glances. For whom was he coming?

Most often her esteemed partner arrived at night, amidst the hooting and hollering of the guests. Then he came up behind this or that unfortunate girl and accompanied her to her room. He did this while looking like a paying guest. But once she had dressed, Trusty, who wore an impenetrable expression, escorted the trembling girl right out the door of the house.

His usual procedure was this: he drove the terrified girl around and around the city on a long, circuitous route to confuse her and make her even more fearful. Then he deposited her at a train station with the message he really did have other business to attend to. He expressed his regret. He gave a ticket to the girl who was trying to keep herself collected, supplied her with a few coins, and whisked her off to some other city. Her departure left a feeling of terror in Red House, and Spizzari knew just how to exploit that.

A few weeks after she took over Red House, there was a nasty affair. Had Spizzari not moved on things immediately, it could easily have had ugly consequences. Little, seventeen-year-old Rosie, who had come to the house via the widow from St. Pölten, was one of the last of Miller's group to remain.

After Mitzi had become the madam's new favorite and risen in the hierarchy, Rosie gave up hope of ever again being in Mitzi's favor. The two had once been bosom friends. Rosie found Mitzi's new arrogance and cruelty so insufferable that she began having attacks of rage. This gentle country girl, now infuriated, roused the others to rebel, too. Rosie told them Spizzari had no right to lock them up or to beat them. She defended herself by slamming and crashing about and by biting the long, loveless fingers of Madame Irma. And, so, gradually, the fate of Number 311—which happened to be the address of Stratti, the man Spizzari touted as the devil himself—loomed before her.

One afternoon Mitzi informed Rosie in a derisive and mocking tone that Trusty was coming by that day. Mitzi told her to guess for whom he was coming. Rosie, who had long suffered Mitzi's abuse, imagined the terrifying visit was for her. And in a minute when no one was watching her Rosie jumped from the window in the corridor of the "barracks" to the courtyard below.

Spizzari immediately ran to the police. She gave her testimony to the event as a complaint and stated convincingly she was not at fault. She claimed she had warned Miller about this crazy girl, but she had not had the heart to throw her out herself. In her account this girl was slated to leave Red House that day. Spizzari testified she had given her money and clothing! Six blouses, six pairs of pants, three corsets, and two silk dresses. The police were free to ask the man in her service at Number 311 for confirmation. He had been at the house to pick up these items. This man could attest to the fact the girl looked gorgeous. He was surprised such a lovely girl was leaving the house. Oh, yes, Spizzari commented, the ladies in her house really had it good.

When the physician, whose job it was to examine the girls for health cards, declared Rosie suffered from extreme hysteria, the case was dropped.

Spizzari was actually quite pleased to be rid of this last recalcitrant girl from Miller's business. There were plenty of other fish in the sea.

The infamous Mrs. Bacher slunk around employment agencies and train stations, and she brought back more girls from her hunting forays than could be used in Red House.

When she was at her limit with tiredness, she called it *nebbich* tired, she sat down on a chair outside the door of the barracks on the third floor and did her knitting. She made sure none of the girls escaped to go out in public and spread rumors about the house.

Mrs. Bacher was useful.

Milada arrived from Styria in the middle of the afternoon, at the time the house was always quiet.

Bacher had conducted the girls back to their barracks after supper, and they were all asleep. There were also ten older retired women there who occupied two rooms and five beds. The windows were closed, and the locks on the windows were set up high.

It was Bacher's job to open both the doors and the windows in the corridor for some air while the girls slept.

That must have been how things were when Rosie made her leap.

Nonetheless the ever-cautious Bacher stationed the concierge in the hall while the rooms were, according to protocol, being aired out via the corridor.

Spizzari herself led Milada to the small room reserved for her. It was near the barracks and contained the furniture she had had before. “You should feel at home here,” she said in a tone that was motherly.

She then showed Milada around in the house with pride and pleasure.

On the first floor next to the salon there were two “Turkish” rooms, ostensibly named after her Turkish system. They were decorated with traditional elegance and had an adjoining booth, whose entrance was cleverly concealed by an oil painting.

Spizzari used her good eye to give Milada a hidden wink as she fiddled with the mechanism to open the room. Much to her astonishment Milada found Madame Irma sitting in this room with its chic décor. Irma was furiously filing her fingernails but arose and bowed deeply to the guest.

On an ottoman there was a thin girl Milada guessed to be about twelve. She was wearing a pink dress and was asleep.

“Who is that?” Milada asked, raising her eyebrows.

“That’s little Lisa. You can’t believe what good business she is. You’d never guess looking at her. But you ought to see what her father lays on me. When he does show up, the two of them have it out. What a low life that father is!” She turned to her darling Irma and asked, “Is she quiet now?”

“She can be a hellion,” was the dismissive reply.

“A spanking should correct that,” Spizzari mumbled and looked at the sleeping child whose rouged cheek twitched under Spizzari’s gaze.

“This room is actually for *jeux*, just for fun and games. But I’m letting Lisa stay here. One reason is something like this is always such an attraction for the gentlemen. The other reason is when her father comes, the drunken ass, then she kicks and screams. You can't imagine what a show those trashy people put on."

Spizzari continued the tour with Milada.

On the second floor, next to the dismally elegant bedroom and bath, there was a row of rooms that were called, for their uniform, color-themed décor, the Yellow, Red, and Blue Room.

Nobody lived in these rooms. They were purely for receiving guests. Spizzari lived on the ground floor. Next to her bedroom were two dressing rooms. Here in large, bolted closets she kept all the items of clothing she had taken from the "ladies." The girls had only what was on their backs, a silk top and an apron in the Empire style. In colder weather this item of apparel was cut more like a pajama top. Milada did not speak. She registered what she was seeing.

"Are the girls all right staying upstairs in those two rooms?" was all she asked. "Don't they want more?"

"Whatever are you saying! They have it good here. They play and laugh together and tell each other their silly stories. Would they be better off separated in their own room, like they were stuck in a hole? They come downstairs for meals and for coffee. They have the most beautiful life. They are such little bitches though! And if they're not happy, they let you know. You can believe me, my child. I listen to them and do as they ask."

Soon thereafter Milada was to witness just how much truth there was in Spizzari's words.

Two hours later Mrs. Bacher shook the ladies to wake them. She brought them water and a sponge as they got up and stumbled around. She encouraged them to hurry up since the wealthy Madame Manager was visiting and was waiting downstairs to have coffee with all of them.

"You can say what you want about this visitor! I know just who she is," said Mitzi. "I know her better than you do. She had a thing with some man named Brenner. He's an ass and as stuck-up as they come."

Bacher repeated herself, wagging her head back and forth, "Yes, but she's got money."

Spizzari was sitting in the salon in front of the fireplace, and there was a table set with all the paraphernalia for coffee.

The madam prepared their coffee with great care and poured it in the cups, while sucking in the fine aroma.

Milada sat at the window, looking out at the melancholy, drizzling rain.

Across from Milada, Lisa was sprawled out in an armchair, nibbling on a piece of cake. She was virtually naked, and her little legs were blue from cold.

Lisa looked Milada up and down, feeling both trust and defiance. She gave Milada the name the Tall Stick. Well, was The Stick part of the regime of Red House? What was this woman doing there? Nobody was going to do anything to Spizzari's darling. Spizzari was happy to have her little girl. If she wanted, she could play like a fresh, untouched thing! That was worth something.

The ladies arrived in the salon. They were not pulled together. They had not put on all their makeup, were half asleep, and chattering. Their hair was hanging loose or tied up sloppily with a ribbon. Johanne, an especially tall girl with flaxen hair, had thrown a Turkish shawl around herself over the baby top. She held the corner of the shawl to her cheeks because they hurt. She was in pain and tromped around the salon angrily.

"Behave yourself, my child," Spizzari said offhandedly. Milada turned her practiced eye to the girls who entered the salon.

They were to a person played-out, used-up older girls. They eyed Milada with mistrust, then sat down with a sigh, disinterested.

Red House had never accommodated inmates like these.

Perhaps, Milada thought, this one or that one might have looked better, younger, maybe even attractive, if she was dressed well and had her hair carefully coiffed. And, at that, she would have to be viewed in the soft light of evening. While the girls sat around yawning, exasperated, carping, emitting crass, mean laughter, and ridiculing little Lisa's straggly, blue legs, their appearance made a most forlorn, joyless impression.

In this setting Madame Irma in her green-silk evening attire with its matching hairnet looked good by contrast. She knew how to powder her mobile face to disguise the signs of tiredness.

A girl named Winkler, who looked a bit like a Gypsy, was smart, and had a wild crop of black curls, and Irma were the two attractions in the house, alongside thirteen-year-old Lisa.

Lisa could at times become quite unruly and had to be controlled with beatings and shoves. Irma and Winkler were best able to keep Lisa in line.

When there were guests in the salon, Lisa approached them in the most brazen manner. She was ready to bite when she felt there was competition. She wanted to serve them all—all by herself.

"She's such a little brat!" Irma told Milada with a sigh.

The madam offered coffee to two fat girls with puffy features and red hair. They accepted the coffee from her and kissed her arms in return. These two had not had a roof over their heads for a good, long time. They were well-known, old prostitutes in town who had held jobs at the Prater Park and had decided not to go the route of vegetable monger or toilette maid. They took their last bit of money and had their hair dyed flaming red. Then, when they ran across Bacher, they told her they were available to do anything.

Spizzari used them in her "Chamber of Mirrors," a repugnant show of the fashionable, mobile *poses plastiques*, depicting vices and perversions. The chamber required personnel be continuously changed out.

Anatola and Kora played in-house exotic Creoles from some far-flung, distant shore for this private human zoo. They painted their fingernails gold and sat cross-legged on the floor.

"Where is little Julie?" Spizzari wanted to know. "I get upset when someone is missing."

"She's probably asleep," said Keller, a girl with a not-altogether-perfect figure. Keller had a small, pointy face, which looked like the face of a child.

Keller had come to the salon right after having given birth. She had a light cough and varicose veins. She made every effort to stay on in the salon because Spizzari was paying for her daughter Millie's room and board. In her current state she could no longer work as a maid servant.

Johanne said with gall, "Today we couldn't get a wink of sleep."

She lashed out at the two girls playing Creoles who were perfuming their feet. "Don't those icky things ever give a body any rest? They've got that Hungarian guy Pista with them. They dance for joy around him."

One of the Creoles twisted her mouth and replied mockingly, "*Ha't*, well," she began in Hungarian, "She's pissed off István, our Pista, doesn't like her."

Johanne was livid, "That Hungarian's a thief."

Lisa yelled out, "But me, he likes me! I tell you he was one in a hundred to me. Isn't that right, Mama?" She looked at the Creoles as if mounting a challenge.

Spizzari said to be conciliatory, "Lisa, just drink your coffee and stop picking fights."

"But it's true. They'll tell my father that I do it for fifty."

"Shut up, you brat!" Madame Irma said and punched Lisa with her fist.

"Oh, God, the pain! Pull 'em out!" Johanne complained and pulled her shawl up around her mouth.

Anatola, one of the Creoles, said indignantly, "She's stinking up the whole house with her rotten teeth." She waved a fan to dispel the odor.

Spizzari addressed Irma, "Where is little Julie? I'm asking you, please. Where is she?"

"I'll go get her. Give me the key," Kora said dutifully.

"I'm going," Bacher said waving away Kora's offer. "But, Madame, Julie is asleep. She's wiped out."

"Nonsense. She's just not used to the good life," Spizzari said and looked around majestically at the assembled group. "Warm up a cup of coffee for Julie."

Bacher left and returned with a pale, haggard girl. The girl's glassy eyes darted quickly around the salon.

"Is one of those men still here?" she asked with a raspy voice.

Nobody answered her question, and she sat down, distracted, without removing her hat from her frazzled, brown hair.

The concierge arrived. Irma stood up and went over to him. She called out to these girls, "Lisa, Johanne, Winkler!"

"Gracious Lady," said the concierge, "There are customers in the Chamber of Mirrors."

Spizzari arose and signaled to the Creoles to follow her. They left the salon.

It was obvious they were open for business. The whole house was a blaze of activity.

Doors flew open and closed, china and glassware clanked, and bare feet ran down the halls.

A maid entered the salon. She looked tubercular, had flagging features and empty, blue eyes that bulged out of her head. She was loaded down with silken dresses.

The ladies undressed and dressed with Bacher's help. They rolled up their hair in curls, pinned it up with ribbons, and applied the rouge that was sitting in a pot on the window ledge. They paid no attention to Milada. Their preparations for the evening were complete.

The Creole Kora returned with a tall, pimply-faced boy, the Hungarian Cousin Pista. He greeted Spizzari like an old colleague and stretched out on the carpet.

"*Ha't*, well, I ordered Goldmucki for you. He'll be here at nine. He'll come do his work. He's a *betya'r*, a thief," Pista said in his broken German as he ran his hands over Lisa's bare legs. She squealed out in anger.

Lisa had brought an elegant, young Japanese man into the salon, and she defended her conquest against the advances of the other girls, who saw in him a bit of exoticism for everybody.

He ordered a bottle of champagne, and Lisa was charmed and threw her arms around his neck, saying, "*Aime*, you, me. *Aimer*!" He smiled a melancholy smile and stroked her round, child's face.

A girl had come in wearing street attire. She had an expensive Girardi straw hat on her head. She looked hysterically out of her mind. She pushed the ottoman she was sitting on up close to Cousin Pista and kept kissing his hand and whispering a few words to him. She laughed, revealing her yellow teeth.

Without deigning to look at her, Pista smoked the cigarettes she had generously laid out in front of him.

She was thoroughly destroyed by poor health. She was one of those deeply tragic cases of a woman driven to prostitution by some dark, insatiable need.

Since she was well-to-do the police were not concerned about her passion, all the more since people largely avoided her. Only rarely did a half-grown youth or some ill-informed stranger fall into her web.

Now she haunted Spizzari's salon even though it cost her dearly in cover charges to be there. The owner had enough concerns as it was, so she tolerated her, but barely. Eventually she was thrown out.

Every time one of the Creoles returned to the salon to call for a new customer, this unfortunate woman withdrew and waited.

"Nothing for me," she complained as Spizzari passed her by.

The man from Japan sat at a table with Lisa and drank while she incessantly combed his pockets for some coins.

"Now you see how things are here, Madame," Mitzi said with pride to Milada who had not moved for hours from her spot by the window. "But just you wait and see how it is when Rudy shows up and the whole salon is full."

"Madame Milada has seen something of the sort already," said Spizzari modestly.

Mitzi came back, "Certainly not! No one has ever seen a madam like ours!"

"Oh, look here!" Lisa shouted. "The yellow rhinoceros agrees!" she said, clapping her hands. Then she grabbed the Japanese man and tried to pull him off his chair. But his face had become a layer of stone.

With one motion of his hand the man pushed her away.

"Listen here, Nelly!" he said in good German. "Get this little pipsqueak out of your house. She's not amusing anymore. If you don't get rid of her, you won't see me or my friend Xaniroff here ever again." He threw a one-hundred krone bill down on the table and went to the door while Irma ran behind him, distraught.

He had been one of the best customers of the house.

"Didn't I tell you to keep your goddamn trap shut?" Spizzari hurled a warning at Lisa. "You just wait till your father comes, you stupid idiot!"

"It's over now with the *poses* in the Chamber of Mirrors. Our Japanese guest is not coming back," said Irma, hopeless. Kora and Anatola started crying bitterly since that would be the end of them.

"How was I supposed to know he understood German?" Lisa groaned, down on her knees on the floor.

"Get the hell out of here, you brat. You did, too, know he spoke German," Irma replied, giving her a punch.

Spizzari said furiously, "Get her out of here before I kill her."

Irma went over to Lisa and hauled her out kicking and screaming, much to the amusement of the others in the salon.

From the sound of the noise coming from the next room it was clear Lisa's punishment was not over.

Madame Irma was soft and had long, thin, gruesome fingers.

It was nine o'clock that evening. Mrs. Bacher was grumpy and slinking around in the corridor.

"Julie, Julie, Ju-lie," she called around.

"Oh, dear God, she's out like a light. She's been asleep from two till now." Bacher turned the lamp up, went over to the bed, and stared.

She said aloud, "Wouldn't you know, sprawled out every which way all over the bed with her hands wrapped up in the blanket. Impossible to pull her out." Julie's mouth hung open. A fly out of season rested on the broad, recently rouged surface of her face. The fly's feet were caked with the makeup that ran in streaks along her nose.

Mrs. Bacher clasped her hands together and began to laugh through her sealed lips. She looked malicious and designing.

"Such a stupid lump," she thought.

"Julie, Madame Julie, Ju-lie," she said as she used her small fists to hammer on the woman's chest.

"Who knows what Spizzari was thinking when she picked this one up," Bacher thought. "Must be she picked her up from some farm, a cow of a woman. A piece of ass."

Little Julie began to yawn.

Happy and unaware, just as she had been at home when the cock had begun to crow in the cool of the morning, Julie stretched her arms and buried her tousled, blond head deep in the soft pillow and kept yawning. She took a deep breath. Julie now took hold of Bacher's scrawny fist and held it tight.

Julie let her go. Her luscious face looked pained. She was still groggy.

Bacher told her, "Just wait till the madam hears about this. I told her you'd be in the Blue Room a long time ago. I never slept that dead out in my life."

Julie replied, sitting up, "Jesus, I can't go over there. That room makes me crazy."

She propped her head up in her hands, and her pink-silk top fell over her shoulders, revealing her very young, voluptuous body. Her neck was strong and tough, brown from work in the sun. The head of this farm girl was round with light, shiny eyes. Her short blond hair, which was not thick, fell in ringlets around her face. Her bobbed hair changed the look of her healthy, sensuous face. Until recently she had worn her hair in a tightly braided wreath, close to her head.

"Get up, Madame. I can tell you the madam's very angry. They just took Lisa off and beat her." Bacher's eyes glowed.

"The visiting stranger lady is downstairs. People say she's rich. Afterwards I'd like to...." Bacher trailed off. "Madame Julie, get yourself washed up and fix your hair. Your clean clothes are laid out for you. I'll be waiting for you in the Blue Room. Hurry up. The house is full of guests."

Bacher left, and Julie stared after her, still groggy from sleep.

Bacher's words buzzed around her like annoying flies. She tried to ward them off. She raised her hands and put her head against the wall. But nothing helped. They were still there and came at her from all sides; they came nearer and nearer. Get up, make the bed, put on the jewelry, put on her clothes, and go downstairs, and then...

Down there in the Blue Room, the old man was waiting.

Awful, what she had to do down there.

Irma was waiting behind the door. If Julie balked, then she was up against what she had been through before when Winkler and Irma held her down.

Oh God, oh, God, she was better off dead. It was better to lie in the ice-cold water of a mill and be clobbered with the turning wheel.

She got up and washed her hands and face. She sat with the cloth for her makeup in her hand and with her unhappy reflection in the mirror in front of her.

Oh, God, dear Holy Mother in heaven! Then the endless night began again. There was noise, disturbance, and laughter. And there was the harsh madam who called her and sent her here and there, who demanded this and that, and who dictated what she had to say to the gentlemen. The madam told her what lies she had to tell. Over and over until the next morning there were horrible things to do, things this healthy girl from the farm railed against.

Julie knew very well what she was being groomed for. She was being set up to please that filthy old man who stood there and... Her mind went blank. Disgust choked her.

She had only been there eight days. To her it seemed it had been that many years. If she defended herself with all her might, as she had at first, they came together and overpowered her. That had happened when she tried to leave. They beat her severely.

Oh, God in heaven, there was no more help on Earth for her. Everybody laughed at her. They enjoyed themselves at her expense. And her father! He had abandoned her, too. He liked money too well. She had been happy at home, especially recently when she had worked as a waitress at the Inn of God's Eye. But Father was not content with the little money she got in tips. "You've got to go to the city, a healthy girl like you. You'll make good money there." That is the way he spoke. "Then your old pa will have a better life."

One day Bacher came to see her. Bacher's daughter peddled blouses and aprons in the area. Bacher had big plans for pretty Julie.

Julie put her right elbow in front of her eyes and wept copiously. She blubbered but was able to keep down the constriction in her throat. But ultimately, the sense of being completely lost overwhelmed her, and she sat down on the edge of the bed and had a good cry.

Then she heard someone turn the knob of the door. It was Bacher, or maybe it was the madam. Julie did not look up to see.

"Dear God in heaven, please just let the Earth open up and swallow me," were the words she did not say aloud.

She was unable to move her arms for fright. They seemed to be cut off.

Jesus, Mary, and Joseph, who was this? Julie had never seen this woman. What did she want with her? Julie was in a state of such extreme agitation the unexpected appearance of this woman terrified her.

A strange woman stood there and regarded her.

"Lord Almighty, just look at the state of this operation. And right here in the middle of the girls' shared room there's a girl crying her eyes out." Milada shook her head in disbelief as she surveyed both bedrooms.

"First, please make your bed," said Milada, pointing to the blanket on the floor.

"I was just going to do that," Julie said as she got up.

Milada looked at her watch. "It's past nine o'clock, and just see how you're dressed. Do things like that go on here? Get up, girl, and keep going. Crying won't make any difference."

There was something in Milada's tone that got through to Julie. Without speaking Julie got herself up with some difficulty, even though she was still sobbing.

"Be quiet now. Hang up your clothes. Put your dresses up. Do you have any vinegar? Your face is swollen. You can't go downstairs looking like that. Just a minute."

Milada left and returned with her travel bag. She poured some drops of a solution into the basin of fresh water Julie had brought.

"So now make yourself presentable. Comb your hair. Putting your hair in order is the first thing. No, not like that. You want to make big curls. No, try braiding it and wrapping the braids around your face like you used to."

Under Milada's watchful, gray eyes Julie got herself ready. She brushed out her hair, braided it, and wound it around her head. It was the first time since she had been there that she wore her hair in the traditional way. "I don't like to look like this, so countrified," she whispered softly as she wept.

"It's fine like that," Milada was perfunctory.

"I've got to put on my makeup."

"No, don't worry about it. You're as red as a poppy. You come from the country after all, don't you?"

"I'm from a village in Styria, Groß-Söding. It's in the forest area," Julie answered, and a ray of happiness shone on her frightened face.

"And your parents?"

"There's just my father."

"So tell me. What did you do until now?"

The large girl put her head down and shifted her weight from one foot to the other.

"You can tell me. I was here in Red House for years myself. I'm familiar with everything that happens here. You're probably not very happy here, right?"

Julie's eyes were full of tears. She wanted to reply to this woman. She wanted to remain brave.

"I've been really scared here."

"So you don't like it here at all?"

Julie's eyes spoke for her, no.

"Are you homesick?"

"Not really that much."

"What's making you so unhappy?"

"I'm afraid," Julie whispered. "I'm terrified. This place is horrible."

"You won't die. You have to be patient, that's all. You'll get used to things. That madam is difficult though, right?"

"It's not so much her."

"Do the girls here bother you?"

"They're not that bad."

"So what makes you afraid? Did you do something?"

Julie was calm. It was as if she were making a confession. "I'm terrified of everything, absolutely terrified." She spoke freely. "Nothing good will come of me. What will happen to me? What will I be at the end of this life?" The pitch of her voice rose quickly. As she spoke, she was further gripped by the fear she had said too much. She started to tremble. "Please don't say anything about this to anybody, please." And Julie moved away from Milada.

Milada wore an unusual expression. The fair, taut skin under her eyes, the type of skin people who have suffered have, quivered. Her brow was furrowed. Julie was flushed and looked afraid. She had become distant. Milada was not looking at Julie but at another, familiar face. It was Bina Michal.

Do right by this inexperienced girl. She is not the person for your plans, but she is strong enough to conduct her own life. Take care of this girl. She lacks some things. You have to be aware of her limits.

"I must go downstairs, or I'll catch hell."

Milada did not hear her. She looked off in the distance.

"At ten o'clock the gentleman will be in the Blue Room," Julie spoke up for Milada to hear. "I have to go downstairs."

Milada spoke with composure, "Julie, listen to me. You don't need to be afraid for yourself anymore. Nothing bad is going to happen to you. I promise. You will get out of here."

Julie almost fell to her knees. "Oh, Madame! But my father? She pays him. If I leave, he'll send me back here."

"You'll work for me. You'll be able to send your father money from what you earn. Don't say a word of this to anybody. Keep going."

Julie radiated good luck. This could happen to her, a prostitute? She was only a child after all, laughing and weeping at the same time. For her destruction was far away.

"Go downstairs now, keep going."

Milada pushed her out the door and listened to the fall of her solid footsteps down the hall. Then she left the "barracks" quickly without anyone seeing her.

One week passed. Milada was still in the house observing. She tracked down Karla at the Prater Park and heard the details of Rosie's horrifying death. Milada also saw Fanny there.

It was late one evening, and Fanny stood in a booth at the fair, clothed with a bit of pink tricot and a glittering skirt. She was on a podium, and people came around to look at her.

She used avant-garde mobile poses like Clara Ward. She stretched out her arm, holding a small, gray dove. The dove was puny, hungry, and joyless. Fanny looked the same. She flatly refused Milada's offer to go to the mountains.

Then it was Saturday, the day of the week when people in the house were usually more light-hearted.

But on this Saturday the regular, merry atmosphere did not set in. A dismal autumn rain fell in the morning, and the girls in the barracks were chilled and huddled up to each other for warmth. Irma had a migraine and was curled up in the Chamber of *jeux*. She was immobilized. She was not available to pacify Lisa who was crying. Lisa's drunken father had been there and rained a heap of blows on her for various transgressions. Lisa thrashed about, swearing she would rather be butchered than ever go to the salon again.

Spizzari was spewing wrath and gall about a neighbor. He had yelled at her through a window in the corridor when he heard Lisa being flogged. He found the constant screaming in the house indecent, just as he found Nelly Spizzari herself. This neighbor said he would try to get this "meat market" shut down once and for all. The long and short of it was this: on this Saturday it was impossible to cheer the girls up for work; they were dispirited.

At three in the afternoon the skies cleared, and Spizzari's mood changed for the better. She had the porter call up two carriages, got the girls dressed, adorned them heavily with jewelry, and took them to a nice confectioner's shop. This was her conventional ploy when she thought the neighbors were going to spread negative rumors.

Lisa had to stay back because people would see she was a child. Nelly made sure she got a whole tray full of chocolate for not going along. She carried it around triumphantly.

Two hours later the general mood in the house had lifted. The ladies were having coffee. Milada, at the behest of Spizzari, had replaced Irma since she was ill. Milada minded the coffers. She was supposed to reaccustom herself to the business.

There were guests in the house, even the man from Japan had thought better of his rash departure and came by with his friends. They much enjoyed the *poses plastiques* of the Creoles in the chamber.

"Julie," Spizzari turned to address her as she sat stiffly, holding her coffee cup, "That little student will be coming today. Do try to take more initiative."

Then the madam gave her one of her lectures, which do not bear repeating. They were intended as motivation for the girls and for the guests. For Julie they meant never-ending torture. Julie put down her empty coffee cup with a sigh.

Ever since she had spoken with Milada she was a changed person.

Once she was assured of a future the farmer's daughter acquired a kind of cleverness and acquisitiveness. The woman visitor had made a firm promise to get her out of there. But as long as she was there, why not, so thought Julie, make some money? The madam kept a ledger of the girls' clients and did pay the girls for entertaining them. All the girls had told her that.

Winkler kept a calendar and recorded everything. It looked like she had already racked up four thousand, maybe more.

Hope of a shower of money made the country girl dizzy. Her aim was to pick up a wealthy client who returned regularly. Irma had a man like that, and so did Lisa. She stopped sleeping in the afternoon. Instead, she sat perfumed and made-up in the salon. She watched the door. She heaved a sigh when, much to the amusement of others, a certain client did not show. She took interest in others' activities. Her charming, fresh face began to look worried. Her eyes lost their luster, and her lower lip began to sag. She began to imitate the madam taking money when the girls threw it in her lap. Julie imitated her without being self-aware, almost reflexively.

When the doorbell rang, Mitzi ran out and came back in, calling, "Julie!"

Julie jumped up. Spizzari called to her in jest, "Don't let him seduce you, do you hear?" The girls, too, laughed aloud to see Julie's new behavior. But their joking did not bother her. It was a customer after all.

"It looks like we're going to have more rain," Milada said as she walked in. She had tied the purse for the money around her waist, just as she had done before. She wore a black-silk dress and over it the apron of a manager.

"Whether we're in for more rain or not, I'm glad you're back in the house, my dear. With your current situation you shouldn't be out in town too often," said Spizzari.

She arranged her skirts and slid over for Milada to sit down next to her. But Milada shook her head and went over to the window. After pulling the curtains aside for light, she took a piece of silk from her purse and started sewing pearls on it.

"What are you making?" Johanne asked with her thin voice as she went over to Milada.

"A little purse," Milada answered dryly.

"Probably for snuff," Mitzi broke in and jostled the woman next to her, a sleepy, fat woman who said only "Yes, Jesus" or "No, Jesus." This woman was in awe of Mitzi.

"You are clairvoyant," Milada said without looking up.

Mitzi looked at her sleepy companion.

"Old men like to sniff tobacco."

Milada looked up and her pupils dilated. Her face had been pale but now grew animated. She knew Mitzi was referring to Gustav's father. This was not news to her. Karla, too, had asked whether Brenner Senior was not keeping her and sending her as much money as she wanted. Milada did not tell Karla straight out no because this story would be useful for her plans. Milada thought it useful, too, for Spizzari to believe this fiction. Nelly Spizzari always liked good gossip.

"Keep your nose out of other people's business," was all Milada said by way of reply. She laid the bit of fabric across her knee and smoothed it out.

"But of course."

Spizzari laid out the tableware for coffee. "I ask you to think twice about speaking to Madame Milada like that," Nelly said in an unholy tone to Mitzi, who stood with her fists ready for a fight. "You should hope to have her good fortune someday. Listen, everybody, Julie's down in the Blue Room. She's making progress."

Mitzi broke out in a vitriolic laugh, and Spizzari took a cup of coffee over to Milada and placed it on the window ledge.

"My child, there's a draft here at the window," Spizzari said out of concern.

"I'm fine."

"Young people these days don't worry about such things."

She fiddled around in the folds over her large bosom and pulled out a needle she used to pin the curtains closed. Her cold laugh parted her thin lips.

Milada moved her chair forward, apparently to have better light. She moved the chair so far that she pulled away from Spizzari's hand.

Soon thereafter guests arrived, took up the tables in the salon, and ordered their meal. Milada took down their orders on a notepad, as she had done in the past. She oversaw the waitresses who brought their food to their table on elegant, silver platters.

Paul Menzel, Rudy, and the Hungarian Cousin Pista made a loud entrance. Menzel was dressed elegantly and fashionably. Spizzari greeted him with a kiss, but he seemed not to notice.

"He's such a charming man," she assured people in a loud voice, making big eyes as emphasis.

An older man sat with tall Johanne, drinking his wine. Every so often he turned around, brandishing his glass, and called out this command, "Lisa!"

But Lisa did not appear. Appearing in the salon would have been beneath her, and Spizzari was well aware of this.

Dolly served small pastries and sardines, English cakes, and oysters. She laid these delicacies out on the buffet. Spizzari occupied herself, flitting from table to table, talking animatedly and gesturing liberally. She kept returning to her "friends," flattering them ongoing. It was, however, completely irrelevant whether the guests were regulars or strangers. She promoted the girls to everyone and did not charge if they did not take her recommendations.

When the Creoles arrived, rather exhausted from their performances, there was a clear, while unspoken, competition between them and the hysterical girl Lisa, who sat bloodless and alert on the ottoman.

The Creoles and Lisa vied for the attention of the Hungarian Cousin Pista. He conducted himself with stoic calm. He let himself be torn back and forth and stayed with the one that drew him most forcefully.

Finally, Lisa became hysterical and ferocious and tugged at Pista wildly. The Creoles grumbled and left.

"Pista, you should be ashamed of yourself," Nelly reprimanded him.

"She should get some attention, the poor bitch," Pista said cynically while he grabbed hold of Lisa's hair with his hand. On his fingers he wore lots of rings, which made his hands look effeminate.

The older man now bellowed out, "Lisa! Dear God, I want to have her."

Spizzari passed by Milada and gave her this command, "My dear, do not serve that old geezer one more thing. He's not a reliable customer."

At midnight two men arrived in the salon. Spizzari greeted them with a deep curtsy. The older of the two offered her the rare act of cordiality from an aristocrat to an underling: He presented his fingertips for her to kiss. At his side was a tall, young man who had the long, narrow face of old aristocratic bloodlines. This young man looked around in the salon with embarrassment. He plied his way around the room from table to table, chair to chair, and girl to girl with the grace of a dance instructor. "Over there, by the window, gentlemen!" Nelly directed them. She looked the young man over, approvingly like a mother. She spoke to Milada, "Do take good care of our guests, my dear." Nelly cast an eye over to the young man, and he blushed. "I have some fine bottles in the cellar, wines, of course." And with that she disappeared.

"Look over there," the older of the two aristocrats spoke. "The woman with the Girardi straw hat is named Gellner. She has come down a notch. Her father was a councilor in the Imperial Court,"

"Would the gentlemen like a wine?" Milada asked them.

"Two bottles of Moselle. Or would you prefer a sweet wine?"

"A Tokay would be nice."

"One Moselle and one Tokay then."

"Look over there," the young man replied. "That woman is interesting," he said as he pointed to the widow from St. Pölten who entered the salon quietly. She took a seat in an armchair and folded her hands under her breasts. Her eyes were half closed.

"You'd swear that woman comes from good circles."

"She does look rather misunderstood," the older man replied with a slight laugh. "So how do you like the madam?"

"Ugly as hell!" the young man answered.

"But she was once a beauty! She was so beautiful it was a sin, Otto!" the older man said, looking at Spizzari, who had just put her colossal backside out the door.

Milada served them their drinks.

"Who is she?"

"The manager. A usual type," was the answer.

The old man Spizzari called a geezer had been chugging his drinks with Johanne. He started getting obstreperous. "Get away! I want Lisa. Madame, I want little-little Lisa." He pounded his fist on the table.

Rudy sang out in a pleasant voice:

Such a very small lady
Such a very small lady
Such a very very very
A very small lady.

"Is it a yes, or is it a no?" the elderly, drunken man asked Spizzari threateningly. She had just returned to the salon with Julie. "When I want something, I must have it, or I will close this place down. That's the law."

Spizzari hissed, "Get him out of here."

"Just look at me! A man of some standing, ladies and gentlemen. I'm a bureaucrat in the State. And when I want Lisa, then..."

Spizzari called over Winkler, a good-sized woman.

Winkler knew how to cajole. "Oh, sweet uncle, please come along with me. Of course, you'll get what you want. Such a sweet uncle you are! You don't want to put up a fuss with me, do you?" She wrapped her arms around him and pushed him toward the door.

"He's an old freeloader," Spizzari said to Milada, who rushed behind him with the tab. "I'll bet he doesn't have any money on him."

She looked over at the table with the two aristocratic gentlemen. The Creoles were hanging around them, hoping for a tip. They were showing the men their tattooed legs.

Spizzari took Julie on a tour around the tables.

"Hello, Julie! Good evening, Julie! Let's invite her to join us, all right?"

"No, it's not all right. I'm out of money."

"Oh, my! Bring us a bottle of Rüdesheimer, Mitzi!"

"Toast to Madame Julie! A toast to the virgin of Red House!"

Spizzari went over to the table with the two aristocratic gentlemen. She had Julie in tow and shoved the Creole Anatola out of the way. She held Julie's hand tightly. Julie was beet-red and was crying. "She's not used to going around on her own," she said to Otto and winked at the older man.

"She's genuinely straight from the country and a virgin."

"We weren't looking for anything, dear Nelly. For the time being," he added. He knew very well what it would cost.

She turned to Julie, "Sit down and have a drink with the gentlemen if they ask you to." She suppressed a sigh of disappointment that the gentlemen were not interested.

Rudy and Ferdie spoke loudly as they held Julie between themselves.

"So little Julie, don't you love me, my sweet love?"

"Drink up, have something to drink," Mitzi shouted, pushing a glass of wine under Julie's nose.

"I think the lovely, young man there is making her nervous," Spizzari sniffled. She persisted with her game.

Rudy announced quietly, "I'll pay a ton of money for her."

"Julie, come over here to me, my candy girl. I'll show you how to smoke. A real lady like you needs to know how to smoke." Rudy stuck a cigarette in her mouth and lit it. She inhaled and spat the cigarette out of her mouth. It flew clear across the table. She watched it fly, dully.

"So now I've tried one," she croaked out for all to hear.

She joined in the guffawing that broke out, especially since she could see Spizzari took it well and was also laughing.

Then Ferdie felt encouraged. He fiddled around with Julie's voluptuous bosom and said, "This, Julie, is what you'll have to learn from me. There's an art to smoking and looking good," He lit a cigarette, inhaled the smoke, and cast a look over to Rudy.

"See, little Julie, you have to draw in the smoke, inhale deeply, and then swallow some wine quickly. That keeps the smoke at the back of your throat, and the wine goes right to your little tummy." Ferdie rubbed his stomach. "And then you blow it out like this." He exhaled the smoke.

"Right," Rudy backed him up. "If you don't drink wine after inhaling, then the smoke explodes in your mouth. That's how it works."

"So you try it now, my little kitten. Inhale, then hold it. You're such a saucy little thing. One, two, three, now you've got it! Now take a big swig, and let the smoke out."

Everybody took a step back, laughing. Julie snorted and choked and spewed wine out of her mouth and nose in every direction. She first turned red, then blue. She grabbed her throat with both hands and pitched forward, throwing glasses and bottles every which way. Her struggle caused people to laugh harder.

"What a great way to go!" Rudy said, slapping his thigh.

Then a shrill sound shattered the laughter. In the midst of this crazy scene people all heard Mitzi's voice as she contributed crude, hair-raising yelps to egg Julie on. People were telling bawdy jokes as Julie's expense, and the men were laughing wildly. Julie was in the throes of a coughing fit and became helpless right in front of them.

Their enjoyment over her distress and the gruesomeness of their laughing ramped up.

The girls were encouraged to be unrestrained, and they pointed to Julie's nakedness, as the girl from the country lay there dazed and losing consciousness.

Julie could not grasp what was going on. In fear she looked to see Spizzari. But Spizzari had left the scene. Jesus, Mary, what did these people want with her? Mitzi was swept away and sprawled on the floor. She hollered out to Rudy who tried to help her up. But Mitzi screamed, “No, leave me alone!”

The Creoles had taken off their robes and draped them around themselves like models. They danced the czardas with bare legs. The Hungarian Cousin accompanied them with yelps and handclapping.

The lethargic widow from St. Pölten was caught up in the frenzy. She thumped Julie and said, “Why aren’t you dancing, stupid girl? Take off your clothes and dance. That’s what the men want to see. Dance!”

Julie’s eyes grew huge. What was this about? She had never seen people act like this.

The widow was carried away and clapped her hands. “Hike up your skirt, you stupid girl. We are waiting, you whore.”

Julie tried to pull away. She fought against the hands that were holding her down. At that moment she understood what they were doing. There was nothing funny about it. She was not going to stand for this. She was a creature of God and not some piece of meat for the men standing around.

Like an evil being the widow was circling around Julie. Then she sprang on her and, with her bare hands, tore off Julie’s skirt. “Dance!” she yelled, “Or we’ll make you dance.”

Julie drew her arm back and slapped the widow on the cheek. The widow screamed in response.

But no one paid any attention.

The groups of people broke up. All their fervor was spent. And sobriety caught hold. They were ashamed of themselves. Shame enveloped them. They spoke little. Rather than say anything they made small, empty sounds, like hmm and ahh.

“Look at Julie,” Ferdie mumbled belatedly as he looked at her trying to pull up her skirt with her trembling fingers.

Mitzi was, in fact, the one who helped her arrange and fasten her skirt. She shot the whimpering widow a reprimanding look. Spizzari waddled into the salon and was short with people and told them to control themselves. She went directly over to Julie.

Julie took a seat. She was debilitated. She had prevailed, but she was exhausted to the core.

Her strength and her will were gone, but so was her fear. She had no further wishes. She thought about taking Spizzari's hand off of herself, but it no longer mattered.

The madam placed her hand on Julie's shoulder. "Take your time, my child. Recover from your craziness. What a temper you have! When you are calm, then go downstairs to see the gentleman in the Blue Room. He's expecting what you just impressed others with. You impressed them! The gentleman says you have an attitude like Schiller's Joan of Arc. He'll give you what he had intended to spend for the Creoles' performance."

A piece of gold glittered in Julie's hand. What was that for? The madam had never spoken to her like this before. Julie had expected she would have to...

She sobbed and reached for Spizzari's hand.

"So go downstairs now," the madam said in her motherly tone. The madam looked up at Milada. Milada had just presented the bill to the three officers who used these names in the brothel: Rudy, Ferdie, and Karl.

When morning arrived the salon was almost empty. The overheated frenzy of the evening before had blown over. There were a few listless girls hanging around. And Dolly was turning off the lamps and the large chandelier.

Milada sat together with Spizzari at the fireplace and calculated. But the madam, who usually was very attentive to calculations, was distracted. She put the money Milada paid her in her purse without counting it through, while listening to any noise coming from the corridor. She wore an unusual expression on her fat face. It might have been eagerness or possibly anxiety. Suddenly she sat bolt upright, lifted her finger, and the look of the devil shone in her good eye. Julie stood in the doorway. She wore a pink house coat that was closed at the throat. It was decorated with ribbons and lace. Julie had her hair combed and was in a very good mood. Behind her was a gentleman, whom she kept from entering the salon. He whispered something in her ear.

Julie laughed and shook her head no.

Mitzi was at the buffet table and could see Julie and this gentleman as they approached. She gave out a yelp and clapped her hands.

"Jesus and Mary! It's the doctor. My God, it's Gustav Brenner."

Julie was dispirited and looked around the room. A smile like Spizzari's appeared on Mitzi's flat face. Milada took a moment to look at the couple. Then her eyes roamed in circles, driven, afraid to stop. They hesitated and kept searching for a place to light. They landed on the face of the man. He returned her gaze, threateningly. Yes, he saw her looking at him, and he understood what she asked, "You, what are you doing here?" His face hardened.

The glint of his teeth, as shiny and ardent as those of a predator, was his answer. Gus laughed out loud. Her gaze did not affect him. His face was a sheet of iron. She knew speaking would be useless.

Mitzi slithered over to them stealthily as a snake.

"Doctor Gustav, what a surprise to see you again. And then, to find you like this." Mitzi was flattering. "You're elegant today. Your goatee becomes you. It would be easy to fall in love with you."

He answered, "You've changed a lot yourself."

"But of course. Since the old Bible-toting madam is gone there are lots of changes. We've got a new madam who's as good as gold."

Julie poured her gentleman a cup of coffee and added too much sugar. She encouraged him, hovering, "Go on, drink. Drink it up."

She folded her arms in contentment like a child, looking at him the whole time.

The lovely doctor seemed to be in love with Julie. He came every day, for her and her alone, only for her.

And how happy she was!

She drew him away from Mitzi to herself and began speaking softly in her best German, a language she had worked to pick up in the salon. "I do love the city. I was gettin' tired of livin' out there in the country. To home we was proud of our schoolin'." She continued in this vein for a while, always whispering. Gus fiddled with the lace of her clothing and, from time to time, laughed aloud.

Suddenly he pushed away the half-empty coffee cup.

"What am I drinking here? Can't I get anything decent to drink? I'd like the nice Moselle wine you used to have."

"A bottle of Moselle!" Spizzari was delighted.

"I'll go get it," Julie said, scurrying over to the buffet.

Gus poured Julie and himself a glass and toasted to her, "Cheers, my sweet love."

Mitzi approached the couple from behind and put her hand on Gus's shoulder, "You'll be here every day, is that right?"

"Yes," he replied. "But I'm only coming to see her. I like her, nobody else."

He threw his arm around Julie. Mitzi was poised to laugh, but a disapproving look from Gus kept her quiet. Mitzi turned and left.

He poured more wine and drank eagerly, taking large gulps. He thought to himself, "What the hell am I doing? I'm a buffoon here."

He was captive to the dark figure, sitting over her notebook. He turned away from the unshaken eyes that looked through him to direct the waitress.

"Drink up," he said impatiently as he held a full glass of wine to Julie's mouth.

"I can't drink any more," she said uncomfortably. "I can't tolerate very much."

"My heart is glad, life is not sad," he repeated as if lost, staring straight ahead of himself. "A fellow has to get around to find the right fit. Then he'll be all right." Julie looked dazed and stroked his stomach. "Does it hurt?" she asked sympathetically.

Spizzari interceded. "She's a bit unpolished. She's a country girl, Doctor. She's still naïve. But she is healthy, obedient, and is not at all deceptive," she said, approaching Gustav.

He kissed Julie. "Amen," he said pretentiously. "She was promised, and then copulated. Your ceremonial words over the troth were good, Nelly. A champagne over here to celebrate! It's a big occasion. Let's toast!"

The champagne cork popped. "Come on, my love! Let's drink and get royally drunk. Long live those who are right! Bravo, that works. Sweet wine is flowing down the throat of my sweetheart. You are right. Let everything that is sour, rotten, or broken perish! *Pereat*! Even if it is wine, woman, or song, let it all die away. *Pereat*!"

He wiped his brow.

"You clown, oh you clown, you do what Joe does. You make yourself the fool. Instead of being icy you show her how you suffer!"

In the midst of the sloshing thoughts that ran through his mind there was this shred of clarity.

Milada simply sat there, either calculating the day's proceeds or pretending to. She gave the waitress commands and put his champagne on ice. Ha ha ha. And he was overloud and laughed and laughed in fits, recklessly. He drank champagne for this his wedding.

"Why do we say 'icing' champagne? How stupid!" And as he spoke he had a moment of stark sobriety. He sat upright in his chair.

"What's your name anyway, girl?"

"Julie Hintersberger," she answered.

He wiped his brow with his hand. "Little Julie is fine. Julie, listen up. I'm sleepy and tired after my trip. Tomorrow I'm going to... But that's already taken care of, right?" He was nervous and turned to Spizzari.

"Certainly. The Blue Room is reserved for her. Mrs. Bacher is already informed."

"I'll send cigarettes and books over to you tomorrow. I have to study for my classes. I can get some studying done in the..."

Milada got up and walked across the salon. She wanted to leave, but his riveting stare caused her to stop in her tracks.

"I'll be back tomorrow, as I said, little Julie. Now I'm going to pay up for the drinks."

He threw a bill on the table next to Milada. Then he extended his elbow to escort Julie. And, at his side, Julie crossed the salon. It was the first time she felt triumphant.

"You'd be better off sliding along on the floor," Mitzi called out in anger and stomped off. She looked over at Milada, "He didn't have to take up right away with just any little number."

"My goodness, naivete and innocence can be sold. Thanks be to God," Spizzari said portentously. She folded up the bills and wished one and all a good night. She went off to her apartment.

The lamps went out. The pale morning light shone through the open shutters. Dolly yawned and put her hands on her hips.

"Dear Lord, this copulation," she said softly, mournfully.

Upstairs a door creaked on its hinges as it was shut. Mrs. Bacher was closing the door of the barracks.

There was thick smoke, the smell of wine and of dead flowers hung in the air. There were cushions on the floor and on the tops of tables. Cigarette butts were strewn about, and pieces of bread and oyster shells lay all around the salon.

Milada went mechanically over to the window. The chimes of the clock at the Soldiers' Hospital reverberated through the air. Their sound, strangely, was comforting to her. Why does this ridiculous situation shake me up? What am I afraid of? What makes me shudder like this? Have I become more vulnerable because I've found my own direction? Now that I've found it can I lose it again? She shook her head to dispel this last thought.

I could indeed!

From the depth of a wound that had not closed pain arose. It threatened to overtake the security she had attained. It was pitiless.

With an ineffable feeling of well-being Julie awoke the next afternoon in her own bed.

She was lying in a lovely room, decorated with blue curtains and a blue rug. She stretched out across the generous brass bed. For the first time since she had been at Red House she felt the softness of a blanket, the smoothness of fresh linen sheets, and the suppleness of a fine mattress. Her pleasure was boundless. She submersed herself, after having regarded herself thoroughly in the mirror on the wall, in the enticing fantasy one of her friends from her village would be at the door, looking in on her. How lovely that would be!

At home she was always considered fashionable and well-groomed, and at every dance she was the best. But having this good fortune had never occurred to her, not even in her dreams. A man of the city! A doctor! Such a lovely, charming man!

She was deliriously happy and shut her eyes.

"Aah," she yawned and drew in the perfume-laden air.

Then she rang the bell for the maid who quickly brought her coffee with milk and bread filled with raisins. "It's like paradise," she thought in her headiness.

Things tasted entirely different than they did upstairs where everything was thrown together in disgusting disarray and where she had to bathe together with everybody in the same bathwater. She got up out of bed.

Draped over the armchair was a rose-red dress with lace. There were new slippers and embroidered stockings.

No, this could not be! Could not! She was treated almost as royally as Irma, and Irma had it the best here. She quickly ran to the door and tried it! Dear God, it was open! She could come and go as she pleased. She dressed quickly, forgetting makeup and powder, and ran directly to the office of Spizzari.

"Well, our Julie," she said well pleased.

"I only wanted to ask," Julie said humbly, "If I'm allowed to go to church."

Spizzari and Irma exchanged glances.

"You certainly may! Go do your duty. That's part of it. Irma will give you clothes to go and accompany you."

Julie took her white-bound prayer book, which had innumerable pictures and scraps of shiny paper in its pages and which emitted the odor of a fusty chest. With her head lowered she descended the steps with Irma. Irma was bored.

"Now she's off to show gratitude for this heavenly grace, the earthly heifer," Mitzi said viciously behind Julie's back. Spizzari raised her finger in a warning and said in a tone that discomfited her darling, "Make sure you swallow your meanness. Grant me my peace and quiet. I don't want to hear one word about your shenanigans. If I do, I'll throw you in with the others."

These were indeed the golden days for the girl. Whatever she said, went. What she wanted, the others wanted, too. She gave them chocolates and licorice candies. She let people cajole her and vie for her favor. She gave them a running tale of what he had said to her and she to him and how lovely it was to "love" him. And despite her rough High German, which her sweet rusticity shuffled over, her voice took on a tone of kindness, almost reverence.

"I done told him he shouldn't give me fancy things. But he be so good and sweet what I like do make him happy."

Behind her back the ladies found her speech highly amusing. Among themselves they mimicked her broad accent in the salon. Spizzari's admonitions and their respect for the rich doctor curtailed their usual misbehavior.

Daily Gustav visited Red House around six o'clock in the evening.

Julie stood in the hallway well before this time, listening for his arrival. When she heard his voice, she flew to greet him. Once she almost knocked Madame Milada over in her rush, so hurriedly did she fly upon recognizing his step.

Then the two of them sat together in her room, and he unpacked what he had brought her. He told her to give some of the treats to the other girls, and he promised when they were gone, he would bring more.

He asked her whether she was content and whether the madam was good to her. She assured him everything was fine. Gus also asked about this girl and that, and once he asked about Milada. Julie took her time answering him. She considered her answers and made an effort to express herself in her best formal German.

But after a few days these paltry topics of conversation were exhausted. They sat together in silence while he smoked and traced out the flower patterns on the carpeting with his walking stick.

She stared at him and found his eyes as clear as the sunny skies at their most beautiful. She found him smarter and better than any of the other men who came to Red House. In the four days she had known him she had become terribly enamored of him.

If someone were to beat her now, beat her to death... But, no, no one could beat Julie ever again.

No, no, this would not happen in the Blue Room where men were happy. Julie felt sure of this deep in her heart when she sat next to him. But she did not dare tell him this. She did not even dare take hold of his hand, that fine, white hand with the rings.

Every so often he would pick up a book, leaf around in it and read while walking back and forth around in the room.

At those times Julie ran out of the room and asked the girls in the barracks to please be quiet. And she asked the janitor not to hammer around on the doors because the Doctor was studying. If she had her way she would have silenced the doorbell to the house. She was almost afraid to breathe. She sat in an armchair with her hands folded and, in her simplicity, failed to see he was not turning the pages, only staring at the print on the page as if lost.

At ten o'clock in the evening they went to the salon. Gustav took his evening meal there. She did not move from his side. Nor did she suffer anyone speaking to him or anyone trying to get his attention. She stood beside his seat until he had been served everything he might want.

Gus had to laugh over her seriousness himself. She polished his glass until it shone and folded his napkin, and she nodded assurances at each bite he put on his fork. She brushed away each breadcrumb and cigarette ash that managed to fall on his clothing. She tended to these duties with intensity until he bade her take a seat and eat. She then followed his order and, glowing, ate with gusto.

At eleven o'clock he left the house. Julie accompanied him to the door of the house. And there, filled with tender care for her loved one, she lapsed into her dialect and whispered in his ear, "God protect you, my treasure. Stay true to me."

She was allowed to go to her own room without having to spend time in the salon. But she sat wide awake for a long, long time, thinking about everything that had happened and about what they had said to each other. She recalled each and every word he had uttered, his laughter, and his eyes as he left.

She stroked his books, she gathered up the butts of his cigarettes like treasures, took out the remaining tobacco and put it in a box.

While she was immersed in these thoughts, she became keenly aware of what she had to speak with him about. She wanted to tell him about the disgust she felt about staying in the house and about the fear she lived with. She wanted him to know what went on in the house horrified her.

And she wanted to tell him Madame Milada had as much as promised to take her away with her. But she did not want to leave with her. She wanted to be with no other person on Earth than with him. Her whole life long, only with him!

And she promised herself she would talk with him about this the next time she saw him. He would understand her even though she did not know how to express herself in educated, elegant language.

But the next day when he was there the game of silence and tenderness continued. She could only demonstrate how dear he was to her. She was incapable of holding a conversation with him.

Her throat was constricted, completely closed off by hallowed awe. Humbly, in silence, she folded her hands and smiled at him, as tears welled up in her eyes and clouded her sight.

But Gustav's tense, agitated gaze looked right past this simple soul. He spurned her attentions just as he disregarded her growing body, which quaked at his slightest touch.

In these miserable few days all Milada was only able to find out about Gustav's stay came from Joachim Kessler. The following was the limited information he gave her.

Gustav had come back to town three days after Milada had arrived in Red House. He had come circuitously from Berlin with very little luggage. He was not staying at his father's place, but rather in a small, out-of-the-way hotel on the outskirts of town. It looked as if he did not intend to stay long since he paid his hotel costs daily.

During the day he did not leave his hotel.

Late in the afternoon he regularly visited Red House where he stayed until evening fell. From there he returned to his hotel room. Milada could get no information from Gus's old companion Joe. Joe had left his old apartment to go to Berlin.

It was quite likely Joe knew Gus had taken this trip for revenge. But Joe was powerless to restrain Gus and let things play out as they would. Milada rejected the idea of turning to Joe.

If Gus did confront her as his enemy, she wanted to take up the fight with him on her own. She expected it would come to that. He had come to Red House to exact revenge. He wanted to expose her betrayal to all the world.

Fine. But why did he want to pull the simple girl Julie into the whirlwind of his impassioned vengeance? What did he want with her? Could he not be more direct? More immediate?

What did it prove to show Julie that the first girl from the country he found was as much as nothing to him after Milada?

The vanity of this petty man was oh-so lamentable! His plan was concocted of pure vanity.

To humiliate Milada he had to deal some creature a fatal wound. Then his vanity would be satisfied, and he could leave victorious.

He would have his precious male pride intact: Nobody ever insulted me and got away with it. Amen. Let him have his way, she thought. Milada could only bear up under it.

She was dissatisfied with every response she had arrived at in her brooding. She kept changing her mind, as if she had forgotten an item, had inadvertently dropped it¬ along the way, and now must stoop to retrieve it. She returned to her concern for the girl, the ingenuous girl! How could she extricate her from his grasp unharmed?

She considered the situation from the position of the girl who felt such sympathy for him. She saw Julie lived solely and passionately from the affection he feigned. Milada saw Julie's spirit would be dashed if this attachment was torn out of her life.

She had seen how Bina Michal was destroyed by the betrayal of those people she had valued most.

Milada wanted to protect this girl from that fate.

She buried her head in her hands and brooded. She despaired. "What will come of this? How will this pitiful ruse play out?"

She was unsuccessful in trying to talk with Julie. Julie avoided her anxiously and with trepidation. Surely, she must have heard the rumors that circulated in the house about Milada's affair with Gustav.

Or had Gustav warned Julie himself? Milada sat in the salon every day and listened to what the ladies said when they gathered. She listened closely to their chatter, even though the air in their midst was filled with derision, innuendoes, and gibes. People in the house mistrusted Milada and avoided her. She was ill at ease and felt oppressed. Everything she had worked to achieve vanished. The floor under her gave way ever since Gustav had set foot in the house.

Early in the morning Milada went to the salon and helped Dolly clean up. That is how she found out that Gus had given Julie a ring. While they were picking up Dolly also told Milada he had given Julie his photograph to hang in her room and that he had promised to take her to Berlin as his "housekeeper." Milada and Dolly followed all these little maneuvers of his courtship with suspicion since they surmised what his true motivation was.

He sent Julie letters via a servant, just as he had sent them before to Milada. He took her to their room and served her wine and fruits, just as he had before.

He did these things so that Milada would find out about them and suffer knowing how he repeated his attentions. He brushed away the dust that had accumulated on days gone by with a forceful hand.

Gustav sat in the Blue Room with a few books and paged around in them mindlessly while using his left hand to crush out his half-smoked, cold cigarette.

His features had become older, sharper. In the gray light of the rainy day his face looked pale and drawn with tension. On this particular day he had come earlier than was his custom. Julie was still asleep. She shook herself awake, happily surprised, and got herself ready. She was sitting next to him in her rose-red dress, not daring to move.

She watched as he let the book slide out of his hands while he edged closer. He opened and closed his hands. She placed her hand on his restless fingers. He did not read or smoke, nor did he look at her. What was going on with him? The silence lasted a long time—a very long time.

Then Julie started talking. Her discomfort came through in her voice and was moving. She spoke about Mitzi. She told him how Mitzi was forever picking on her and saying vicious things about her.

Julie spoke about little Lisa. Julie told him what a fresh mouth she had and how unschooled Lisa was. She said yesterday a man had given her a sound slap. She talked about her father back home and about the letter he had sent, saying he wanted to visit his daughter soon to meet the gentleman doctor. "Father's not just anybody. He behaves like a gentleman. He looks forward to sharing a meal with you."

Suddenly Gustav jumped to his feet. She was astonished.

Was he bothered that she spoke of what concerned her? She blushed and was slack-jawed. Gus ordered her, "Go to the madam and ask if you are allowed to go out with me. Can you go around the meadows in Prater Park? The air here is stifling, and I've got a headache." He ran his hand over his brow. She yipped with delight. She opened the window, put her arms around him tenderly, and asked what would help him feel better. "Warm salt water," she told him, was what her father always recommended. Would he perhaps like that? Or might he like a splash of cologne? It was so refreshing.

He was impatient and dismissed her suggestions, pushing her away from himself. He wanted her to go ask the madam and get ready quickly.

Spizzari nodded her approval graciously.

"Amen," Milada thought. He has to put the meadows in Prater Park on his agenda. He cannot leave out one step in this dance of deceit.

Julie reported to the madam, "'We won't be back for coffee. We'll eat out,' is what he said."

She nodded to the girls and disappeared, accompanied by Mrs. Bacher, who had given her proper clothes for the occasion.

Johanna said, "Just wait and see! She won't die a prostitute." She raised her finger to indicate the truth of her prediction.

Spizzari replied to Johanna, "You won't either, you could get to be eighty." The steps of Gustav and the girl resounded through the corridor.

Milada knew his footfall well. She heard the front door open and close with a dull thud. Mitzi ran to open the window to look out.

"Wouldn't you know! It's a carriage." She slammed the shutters closed.

"She's in his thrall," Spizzari grinned as if she were the mother.

"Eventually he'll come 'round to me if what he's lookin' for is a prostitute," Johanna threw out. She surprised herself that she had said this. Nobody spoke.

Except for the disinterested part-time women who smoked cigarettes and looked down at their feet, everyone in the room stared at Milada. *Schadenfreude* shone in their eyes. She sat in a corner by the windows, bent over her work.

She did not flinch, rather bore the meanness of their gaze like the annoyance of insects buzzing around.

"I'll come out to greet him this evening when he returns," she thought, cold and determined. "I've had enough of his stupid plan."

The pale, frosty light of December lay in the room. Cold smoke filled the room.

A feeling of essential moroseness occupied these young creatures. Nothing interested them, and a heavy, dull net, finely woven, had been cast over them. The clock's ticking was monotonous, and rain drizzled against the windowpanes. It was quiet enough to hear the pearls Milada counted on her lap clicking against each other. Spizzari was picking her teeth with a hairpin. From time to time she looked over at the photographs in the daily newspaper as she watched the pot, waiting for the coffee water to boil.

"Dear Lord, this rain is going on and on. It feels like it'll never stop," Winkler said, looking up from her book.

"That girl's out with him for a ride in the park, and here I am dying of boredom," Mitzi muttered and kicked off her slippers.

Mitzi closed her book with a clap and stuck it behind herself. "Reading these romance novels scrambles your mind."

"Then darn your stockings," Spizzari said, pointing to her sewing.

"But, Mama! I promise to God I've darned a lot, maybe seven or eight stockings. It's true, isn't it, Irma? It doesn't matter what I do I can't stop thinking. I just keep thinking! Sewing makes me sad. I don't see how Milada can keep on sewing." People looked at Milada, but she did not react. Once again silence in anger descended on this solitary human being.

Johanna brought out a pack of cards. She laid them out, "What's in the cards? The cat is on the left, and the dog's on the right, and the dog's covering up the lies."

"I'm going to confront him and ask, 'Gus, what are you doing with this girl? I'm not going to let you sacrifice this girl,'" Milada said resolutely to herself. "'Long before you and your stupid plan came into her unhappy life, I had plans for her. My plan won't destroy her.'" Milada put her needlework aside and looked up.

She was surrounded by faces, pale and ravaged, faces forged of pure hate and meanness. These people looked at her with unveiled hatred.

"All they can do is hate," Milada thought. As she exhaled, she felt the distress of these last few days fall from her. The oppressive weight her soul had borne changed into a freely taken, vital decision.

Her decision dispelled all the humiliation she had let in. It banished all doubt and all regret. Now she had to act. She looked forward to the moment she would approach him in front of everyone and ask, "What do you want from me? Leave this other girl out of your game, man."

She felt her blood coursing through her as if she were delivering this message at that very moment.

Milada's resolve came too late.

One hour after Julie had taken off on her excursion, Gustav deposited her at the door of Red House. Shaken and sobbing, she reached out her hand in parting. He did not see her gesture and called out something to the cab driver. Then in one movement he slumped back into the upholstered seat and groaned.

In the salon everyone heard the carriage had arrived. They had been listening for it.

"Ah ha! Now the lovely lady returns," Mitzi said cuttingly as she opened the door.

Milada set her needlework aside and looked at the entrance with an icy stare.

She was calm. Only the delicate skin under her eyes quivered.

Julie entered, alone. Her face was swollen and red from crying as she climbed the stairs.

"She's by herself. And she's crying and crying," Mitzi called out excitedly to the people in the salon.

Yes, Julie's eyes were blank and sunken. There were traces of tears down her cheeks, and she clutched the fur-trimmed coat, which had been thrown over the rose-red silk dress for her outing.

Spizzari looked at her. "Where is he?" she asked.

The girl only blinked in answer.

"He left," she was able to say. The fur coat fell off her shoulders, and she folded her hands over her abdomen.

"What do you mean, 'left'? Where did he go?" Spizzari asked unfeeling.

"He left," she repeated in pain. "He has to go back to Berlin," she broke out in a sob. "But he's comin' back. He won't leave me here. He'll come get me," she assured her adversaries with such emotion they were ashamed.

Spizzari stood up. "Gone," she said, and a horrible thought

arose in her mind. "So did he pay you?"

"Yes, he did," Julie sobbed. Expressionless she reached into the pocket at the waist of her dress. "I stuffed this away. It's wrapped in paper." This calmed Spizzari who was unconcerned about the girl's deep sorrow. Tears flowed over her words.

A bit of fine paper appeared. Julie unfolded it. Something bright flickered out of the paper at Spizzari. She was pleased and snapped, "It's gold."

"What's this? Just one gold coin?" Spizzari looked at it closely.

This, too, looked suspicious to Spizzari.

It rang as it fell on the marble-top table. Spizzari turned bright purple, gasped aloud, and, in a single bound, landed in front of Julie.

"You stupid cow!" she gasped. "You cow, what did you let him do to you?" Furious, she waved her hands around in the air.

"There were the food, the drinks, and living the good life. And she lets him have all these tidbits, that coward, that lowlife! All for a souvenir."

Her voice gave out. The coin clinked as it fell on the floor. She raised her hand and gave Julie, who covered her eyes with her arm, a sound slap in the face.

Lots of girls spoke up to drown out Julie's scream. They had questions and things to contribute. Their faces were lit up, eager, as they danced a gruesome dance around the crying girl.

"I'm going to make criminal charges. I'm sending her back home with a swift kick. I could have gotten a piece of garbage cheaper than this." She tore at Julie's sleeve, and Julie did not resist. She was so given over to the pain, Julie let the madam do what she wanted.

Milada got up from her seat.

The gold coin lay on the floor. Milada recognized it right away.

She might have picked it up, stuck it away somewhere, and diverted people from their viciousness, but she did not want to. Was this not what he intended? His wounded pride needed this pathetic show of vengeance. Fine, then he can have it outright.

She turned her severe, gray eyes to Julie. Seeing her, they lost their severity. They showed her compassion and understanding.

Then one of the girls bent down. “Look, it has something engraved on it. Yes, here it is, Jesus!” She looked up at Milada and understood it all. Then Mitzi, who had an idea what the inscription was, ripped it out of her hand. “This is priceless,” Mitzi laughed. “In remembrance of spring 1890.” She turned it over, “To Gustav from Milada.”

“Well it certainly was remembrance for him.” An outcry went around the circle of girls who explained to each other what the engraving meant. They pointed at Milada. She stood there calmly and weathered the storm. The madam stared at her, scarlet red. Irma, Winkler, and Mitzi pitched forward in laughter and tried to make clear to the others exactly what this coin signified.

“Well, now we do understand,” Keller said to Julie. “He has to be the biggest ass.”

“Jesus,” Mitzi said with delight. “Rudy and Ferdie will have a good laugh over this. Just look at the little thing in her red-silk dress.”

Milada recognized instantly that Gus’s vanity had destroyed this young girl.

Her soul feared worse. He had exposed her private experience of love to these people, and they had used the opportunity to tear it to shreds. So be it. Was it not some kind of cleansing?

“So, what did he say to you, the rogue?” the madam yelled over the voices of the girls, trying to get their attention. “He has to pay up, the idiot. He has to pay.”

“He done said,” Julie blurted out, “He’s to be in Berlin a while.” Julie’s arms hung at her side, and her face was twisted in pain with the effort of getting these words out of her constricted mouth. “He done said the lady there will exchange the coin for cash.” She pointed to Milada.

A storm of laughter broke out anew.

Mitzi threw herself down across the floor in gales of laughter, squealing like a pig. Winkler erupted in crude spurts and stomped her feet.

Milada opened her black purse, looked inside, and then left the salon so quickly that she left the door open. The girls heard her unlock a door upstairs.

Spizarri sat down, completely enervated. She knew very well what had transpired. But she was in no way interested in this little romance. For her this was about the money. Thank God, the scoundrel had at least paid for his drinks every day!

She thought how much costly food she had given that cow to chew for those five days. And then she had to pay for the laundry and her clothes. The whole outlay was only for this theater! What a churl!

"Well, your groom sure is lovely, I have to say! I'll bet he'll take you to Berlin on the train with a fifth-class ticket."

"I should've gotten a few bottles of wine out of the man."

Keller chimed in, "We all should've done that. But what should Julie have gotten from all this?"

Milada came back and went directly over to Mitzi who was eyeing the gold coin lovingly. She said curtly, "Give it to me."

"Go on, Mitzi, give it to her," Johanna said with embarrassment.

Mitzi took her time and let it roll to the floor, where it clattered.

"There it is," said Mitzi impertinently, shoving it aside with her foot.

Milada stooped to retrieve it, carefully brushed it off, and put down two paper bills in front of Spizzari. And said shortly, in a business-like tone, "It's correct."

Spizzari's eye was a keen as a hawk's. She recognized at a glance the amount of the notes. And then she was calm. She looked disdainfully at the girls standing around and said, "Don't make such a scene here, you useless people! Go get yourselves dressed and ready. Somebody could show up any minute now."

The girls were having a good time. They returned to the barracks. They looked forward to getting together and talking. An event like this was rare.

Standing stock still, Julie let the girls file by her. Her face was aflame, and her brow was furrowed. Each word they called out to her was like a thrust to the heart.

Her heart quaked and shriveled. She did not utter another word.

What might she have said? There was nothing more for her to hope for. She was the last to leave. She wanted to go her room and lock the door. She knew what she wanted, oh, yes.

A sigh moved her.

Spizzari salvaged some pride by pronouncing this in her motherly-seeming tone, "Well, what are we going to do with you now, Julie? You're useless here. I'm going to have to give you up. You're a laughingstock for the guests and for the girls here." She turned to Milada and continued, "Who can use her now? She's not fit for anything. She just doesn't learn."

In some measure Spizzari was actually ashamed of herself.

In the two weeks Julie had been at Red House she had indeed made herself a constant target of ridicule. She was worthless. She could not be of any value on the street. She would be picked up right away by a policeman, and then she would talk about the way Bacher had held her captive.

Sending her away—the most common means of disposing of someone—was not an option with Julie. Spizzari was beholden to her father. What would she say to the old sot when he came to the city and asked to see his daughter? Moreover, when she was first pleased at having taken Julie on, she had committed to sending her father regular payments. He would not bother Spizzari as long as the payments kept coming, but after that? At this moment all these thoughts crossed the mind of the scheming madam.

"How can we get around these commitments?" she asked Milada.

"Madame Spizzari, why not keep her on here as a maid? Dolly already has more than enough to take care of. Julie can be put to serving. I can train her to do this work. You will be able to save by having a servant in the house. Well?"

Spizzari weighed out the benefits of Milada's suggestion. Using her as a maid servant would be a way out of her obligations, at least for the time being. In fact it was a very good option. "For a few weeks, for a few months even," Spizzari granted her. "After that people will have forgotten, and we can put her back to work as a girl in the house."

"Nice, you are right here, my child."

To Julie she said, "Go pack up your things to put in the attic. You'll be fine sleeping there, and then you'll be available on call. You can thank Madame Milada and put an end to your foolishness."

Spizzari rang for the porter who accompanied Julie with a smirk.

The madam then spoke to Milada completely devoid of consideration, "So what do you think of that rogue now? He certainly had one hell of a week at our expense, didn't he?"

"Mere stupidity, Madame Spizzari," Milada replied, laughing. "The best thing to do is put the whole incident to rest." With that she went out the door.

"Maybe you had a bit of it coming," Spizzari thought vindictively after she had left.

The madam slurped up the last drop of coffee in her cup. She pulled the banknotes out of her pocket, smoothed them out lovingly, and put them in her large pocketbook with a shiny, nickel-plated opening that greedily snapped them up.

In the meantime, Julie had cleared her personal items out of the Blue Room. The porter helped her lug her heavy wooden suitcase up the steps to a small, dank corner of the attic. It was the same little corner where Milada had spent her young years, the rat chamber of old Red House. Wisps of spider webs, laden with soot, hung from the rafters down to the floor. There was an iron bed, a chest, which was upended in the corner, and a broad window seat, situated invitingly under a gable. Those paltry items constituted the furnishings. There were bits of leftover food, newspapers, and the base of a candle on the window ledge. Bacher had stayed here at times.

Dull and uncomprehending, Julie had thus far done what people had asked of her. The porter, Bacher, and even Dolly had told her what to do and pushed her around. Now she sat on her suitcase and, looking down, shot quick glances up at the porter. "That woman has gone downstair now," Julie thought. All she wanted was to be left alone. She did not want to see anybody or hear what they said. Oh, to be left completely alone!

While the porter set the chest upright and cleared it of old rolls of wallpaper, Julie looked sideways over at the door. It had no lock. But that did not matter. She could simply shove the chest in front of the door to secure it. That would work for a while. But then? A heavy veil occluded her vision. She saw blood.

"Bacher will come get the red dress," the porter said. "I'll come wake you in the morning before I go to bed. Be sure to turn out the light." The attic door slammed shut, and Julie was alone.

She sat in place on her suitcase of wood, empty and still.

"Just a little while longer, just a little. There are some footsteps on the stairs. There might be rumbling downstairs."

Cold fear crept over her. She jumped to her feet. There was nothing left to do except die. She should die over there at the window. She opened her eyes wide in terror and looked upward. Hang herself, that was what she wanted to do, just like the wife of her uncle had done when their house burned down. Yesterday Gustav sat at her side and cared for her. It was yesterday at this time—and again now! The tension left her body. Endless longing loosened her muscles. She could not resist its power. "Gus, oh, my dear Gus!" she groaned, "Please, come!" She was quaking and pressed her pleading lips together to suppress her sobs. Where in this wide world could he be? He was gone, utterly gone. In Berlin.

And he had left her there to die once he had carried through on his plan. That is what he had wanted, not her. A few hours ago, she had held his arm, caressed it. And now? She clutched her head with her hands.

No, she could not bear this.

What now? What did she have to do to stop this pain? She ripped open her suitcase, rummaged through the clothing her mother had washed, starched, ironed, folded, and packed for her. She tore aside the contents till she got to a ball of clothesline at the bottom. "When you wash your things, you'll have something to dry them on."

Julie unrolled the ball of rope. Yes, it would work.

Once again, she heard someone coming up the stairs. Who was coming to see her, who? She was fit for battle.

The door opened, and Milada entered. She surveyed the chaotic mess, Julie's distress, and the length of clothesline in her hands.

She knew she had come at the right time. "It's good you are putting things together here," she said kindly in an even tone. "It'll be more comfortable here. I know this little room very well. Over there on the window ledge I kept my flowers and my little bird. The sun shines in here at five in the morning." As she spoke, she picked up a few items of clothing made of coarse homespun linen. Each had a red label. She placed them on the bed.

Julie did not move at all. But she was overcome with hot, wild fury. She felt the blood pounding in her head. Her blood was in revolt.

"What do you want with me? Get the hell out of here, all of you, you damned idiots. Leave me alone. I hate all of you. May the devil take you all." She grabbed Milada by the hand and slung her against the bed, where her head knocked against the wall. Milada was stunned for a minute.

But soon she came to. She called out assertively, "Julie!"

"I told you! Leave me alone! You can do what you want with

me afterwards, but for now I want peace and quiet." She turned away from Milada.

Milada took her arm and forcefully turned Julie to face her.

"Julie, Julie, didn't you know how things were between me and him? Do you honestly believe what that man did was against you? Do you think what he did makes you the fool? He hardly knows you. For him you are the person he hired from the madam. You happened to be the first person who crossed his path. It could have been you or anybody else, it didn't matter to him. He had nothing against you. What he did was not directed at you. It was directed at me. He wanted to hurt me. He was aiming for the heart." She took Julie's hand. "Why are you so attached to Gus? Forget about him. You knew him for five days. He was a man visiting the house, a guest who paid the madam for you. What did you imagine a visitor is? Did you think he'd stay for a year? Be part of your life? Foolish girl! It's rare for a guest to spend the night. Men come here to rent a girl like they rent a horse. Do you understand? It's dangerous for a girl to be as dumb and emotional as you." Milada spoke softly, almost in a whisper, but each and every word was clear to Julie.

The anger that had made her arms and legs stiff gradually let up. She was relaxed. She dropped the piece of rope. She yielded. She looked up and saw Milada's face. She thought of Gustav and this woman here. What had she been in their relationship? It was true. The whole game was between them. She was outside their involvement. She had no place in this man's life. She looked down at herself. What had she wanted from him? Jesus, Mary, and Joseph! How God had abandoned her for her to think as she had. Heaven and Earth were turned upside down. As if she had been thrown down, she fell on her knees and folded her hands. "Gus is gone," she said. "I love him so dearly. Jesus, Mary, and Joseph, what's happening to me? I don't know who I am. Everything's swirling. I wanted to die." She grabbed Milada. "It's good you came. You are very good. Please don't be angry with me about what happened. I'm miserable. I don't know what got into me. Look what has happened."

Milada placed her hand lightly on Julie's head.

"Silly girl! Why would I be angry with you? Don't worry. What I promised you earlier still stands. You'll leave this house with me. We'll get out of this swamp and be in clean, fresh waters. Understand?"

"Yes, oh God," Julie whispered, deeply moved.

"You won't be a lady in the salon in Red House anymore. It's not right for you. You will work there. You'll learn a lot here about running a business. Are you prepared to follow me?"

"Yes." That word came from deep in her heart and resounded clearly, and Madame Milada nodded her approval.

"When the girls tease and taunt you, don't let it bother you. Tell yourself, 'they can't see into my soul. They are free to have a good laugh over anything on the outside.' They need their laughter. I've been letting people laugh at my expense for twenty years. And I'm still alive."

Julie nodded. "I'll do my best," she said quietly, and as she spoke the old, honest look she had had returned to her round face.

"I can leave now and be at peace. Tidy up your room now, Julie. I'll bring you some flowers tomorrow. You'll see how plants flourish here. Look at me. There you go! Things will work out for us."

Milada laughed.

Then she gave Julie a hug that admitted to no resistance. She took her hand and kissed it heartily. She calmed her. This soul would learn to love.

She stood in front of the door to Julie's room. There was noise and a disturbance down below, piano playing, crashing about, and the laughter of the girls. She also heard Lisa's high, shrill screaming above the cacophony. The rhythm of the life of prostitution rose up for Milada to hear. The people downstairs who lived under Spizzari's system would be ruined.

"Useless life," said the old woman up on the mountain when she scraped mold from the corners of the attic with a fireplace tool.

"Useless life," Milada thought. That applies to the girls in the salon. When the old woman up in the mountains found a violet growing in the grass of the garden, she dug it up carefully and warmed its roots and leaves in her worn hands. "It's a sign late in fall of the spring that is to come," she muttered, pleased.

How much Milada had learned in her time up on Sunny Heights!

People, please, stretch out your hands and save those on the margins, struggling to live. Stretch out your hands to the depth of life. You can save those who have a fragile hold on life. You can make them your own.

Those who latch onto the face of love and appreciate the warmth of a hand are good and felicitous.

We do not comprehend the secret harmony that fills all things and keeps them alive.

We do not know what it means to individuals in a moment of dread, a time of diminished will, to have someone at their side who believes there is something higher in their soul. We cannot say what it means to these individuals to know someone sincerely wants their higher being to emerge. It was in moments of despair that Jesus was at the side of humanity!

We do not know what it will mean one day to lift up someone from an oppressed class who is not free. We cannot know what it might mean to help set that person on the path to living with others. Blessed is the hand that offers help. Who knows whether there will be many, perhaps very many, others who come to us as we pass on this bridge? Who can know? The uncertainty of what is to come or how people will judge us must not deter us from offering help.

Around Christmas Milada received a long letter from L——zer with lots of inserts. Doctor Stüber sent his greetings with many expressions of devotion to his dear, young lady. He wrote of most pleasant matters that were incumbent upon her. He conveyed his most earnest and heartfelt sentiments and wishes for the coming year. In this same letter he informed her of a truly wonderful surprise. His friend the architect Stadlinger in Oberdorf had let him know he was now prepared to begin construction on the home for young children up on Sunny Heights. The architect attributed the realization of this undertaking to the foresight of the lovely, gentle benefactress.

Doctor Stüber enclosed blueprints, an estimate of the costs, and an itemization of the necessary interior furnishings that were to be made of wood. For the last items he would, owing to favorable circumstances, be able to engage the carpenter in the region. The Doctor vouched for the suitability and stability of this carpenter's work. He implored her to examine the written materials closely and to have a trusted expert examine them as well before committing to them. However, he did want to assure her the most scrupulous attention had been given to the preparation of the itemization of costs. In all these matters he was behooved to insert a small yet strong word of praise for the good architect in Oberdorf. If weather conditions should be favorable, according to the statement of this architect, he could commence work in the beginning of March. This would allow the wood to cure over the course of the summer. Stüber finished his letter with an expression of hope the dear, young lady, who had won the affection of the people in the mountains, would return to Styria before such a time as the building started in order to exchange ideas about this or that detail in person.

In closing he stated he was most humbly devoted and commended himself to her.

Milada spread the blueprints out in front of herself. On those pages she saw, with great pleasure, the realization of her plans taking shape.

Black lines connected the small buildings. The windows, which were sketched in blue, smiled happily at her. The flues in the chimneys sparkled. Even the roof timbers were tinged with gold. Every detail had been executed in miniature with loving care. If she only knew how many hours Doctor Stüber had sat with a brush, painstakingly tinting the colorless sketches he had gotten from the architect in Oberdorf! His dear, young lady ought to have a sense of her project. His paint set added bright, colorful life all around to the architect's dry representation. Surrounding every house, he had painted in a garden of roses and trees, turnips and shrubbery.

From among the sketches Milada chose a Swiss-style farmhouse with two stories. She liked the front with four windows, each with three sections. She wanted a pointed roof that overhung the house and a wooden porch with steps and a railing that attached to the side of the house. There was a plaque on the front that had been left empty. Here the Doctor had inked in with red letters:

From Our Strength as a Tribute to God

Milada pulled out her pen, struck through the inscription and wrote:

From Our Strength as Tribute to Our Life

With the stroke of her pen she had abolished any need for children who were to live in the house to feel indebted to charity.

Once again Julie slept the heavy, deep sleep a person from the country earns through physical work. There sleep comes in tandem with the uncertainty of the life of the animals and of farming.

She had finished the day's work just before midnight.

An almost endless row of pots and pans, dishes, and glassware was in spanking clean array. The damp kitchen tiles shone, as did Julie's sweaty face. She had worked up a ravenous hunger for her evening meal, which she ate alone in the kitchen.

"By the grace of God, thank you. I've eaten well," she said

aloud and wiped her mouth. She tucked up the kerchief on her head, put her kitchen mules in the corner, slipped past the noisy salon downstairs, and went on up to her small room.

Julie had used a piece of string to fasten a cheap colorized picture of Saint Johanna with a little sheep over her bed. She had set a broken jug full of branches of pussy willows and periwinkle on the window ledge. The branches were budding. It was the end of February, and the sun was gathering force. Before lying down to sleep Julie knelt down and began, haltingly, an intimate conversation with her guardian saint. Before she finished, she fell asleep. She usually did. She lay there with her shoes on and her arms outstretched in an attitude of flight.

Noise and music, laughter and squealing filled the house. The slamming of the shutters at the front door rang down the halls and caused the rusty iron bed, in which she lay, to sing along as if it wanted to join the nightly choral din.

Of course, this made Julie toss and turn. She threw aside her blanket and moaned. Her fear grew and weighed heavily on her mind and soul.

She dreamt someone climbed the stairs to her room, stopped at the door, and whispered in a low voice. She tried to jump up, hold the door closed, or run and hide, but her arms and legs were frozen stiff. She could not move but tried to struggle free. She saw evil eyes glowing out of the dark at her. "Jesus, Ma..."

She bolted up in bed, awake and covered in sweat.

"They're making noise downstairs. They don't know I'm here," she thought.

Usually when she awoke, she fell right back to sleep, and her snoring rose up from deep in her pillow.

When the clatter in the house settled down and then finally stopped Julie slept sweetly and deeply. All horror left, and her fear of invisible ghosts vanished. Her troubled soul was filled with images of joy.

Her dreams carried her home. She walked back and forth over the square in front of the church, wearing a red feather hat. There were lots of people gathered around her. They pressed in upon her and whispered. Her father was there in his uniform, bespangled with decorations. He escorted her into the church. And, yes, the venerable Father came down from the pulpit and walked over to her. Julie smiled in her sleep to think all this had happened in front of everybody back home!

A gentle, early-morning light streamed through a hole in the roof into her attic room. In a short while the entire space was filled with light, and the budding branches on the window ledge stretched upward.

There was a heavy knock at her door. “Julie, Julie!” the porter hollered.

It was six o’clock in the morning and time to get up.

She yawned loudly and rose from the bed. The house was quiet. She quickly got herself ready for the day. She pulled on a blouse and skirt for housework, tied a gray shawl over her head, picked up the bowl the porter had put by the door, and hurried out into the still of the morning in the alley. She exchanged greetings with a woman peddler, started a conversation with the milkman whose wagon was on the corner. She petted his horse, stuck her hand in the feed sack, stirred around in the grain, and made small talk with the milkman, laughing off his crude jokes. The two exchanged stories until she let out a “Jesus, I gotta get to work!” And then she ran back in the house.

The farm girl with the natural need for exchange and a feeling for neighborliness was now again awake.

She was as trustworthy as they come. She enjoyed chatting with everyone who came across her path. But she could not chat too long since once the nightlife in the house was extinguished, her hard day’s work began. Water splashed and flowed in rivulets over the tiles as Julie swept them clean, just as Madame Milada had shown her.

Once the hallway and the stairwell had been scrubbed clean, she pushed her hair out of her eyes, opened the doors to the salon, and went in. There was gray fog from the smoke, and the smell of flowers and perfume lingered. It rolled toward her like a cloud. She had stepped into the "God-forsaken" mess. She dusted, stood chairs back up, and had a good time giving tablecloths a sound shake out of open windows. She would have liked to sing, but the madam had forbidden that.

Milada was often here when Julie started her work as a maid. She had taught Julie how to sweep, wipe up, and polish. And she had praised her work, saying, "She's useful and knows how to clean." Julie was proud of that.

When she finished, she stood back and admired her work. She tiptoed out of the salon and went to the kitchen to make breakfast. Dolly and the cook slept in the adjacent room, so Julie had to be as quiet as a mouse.

The coffee for breakfast in the warm kitchen did smell delicious, and in the morning she always had a hearty hunger. She felt good to have the kitchen to herself and to work on her own. She never regretted this work after having been a lady in the salon who slept in while someone else went to work down in the kitchen. She had the resilience of a fundamentally sound soul, and she quickly snapped back to her early state of being. The moment she took off the perfumed silk gown and the lace-covered evening jacket and donned the coarse, red-wool, homespun dress her transformation was complete. The three-week-long dream of being a lady disappeared entirely, and she stepped forth as the work-a-day farm girl she actually was. She did like men. But if a man looked at her lustfully and she was not interested, she turned him away. She had been nurtured in the bosom of Nature and was not material for prostitution!

Within Red House she quickly became uninteresting and nothing special. She was beneath them. The indolent ladies of the house were happy enough to look down on her.

There was nothing more about her to laugh at. She had put aside any pretention of speaking High German with the makeup and hair curlers.

One small aspect of her former life in the house remained. Once a week Bacher, at the madam's request, took a piece of aromatic soap and a tiny bottle of perfume up to her in her room.

"So that she doesn't completely forget about taste," Spizzari told Bacher, whose reply was a knowing smile.

Julie left the ominous package of soap and scent on the window ledge untouched. Eventually Bacher shrugged and took it along. She had a little business on the side and could get some money for it.

The madam had at first seemed charmed at Milada's idea to employ Julie as a maid, and her respect for the practical knowledge of this younger person grew.

"I tell you, Madame Milada, if you wanted to go into business here, I would be out of work. You have a real flair for the profession."

But gradually Nelly came to harbor a secret resentment she was not making optimal use of this "solid," pretty thing, which Julie was, as a prostitute. Her economic potential in Red House was untapped.

To be sure the cook did praise her assistant over the moon. This level of order and cleanliness, so she claimed, had never existed in the house. It was readily apparent!

"Well, just because Julie is good at housekeeping doesn't mean that's all she is good for," Nelly thought to herself.

Perish the thought! Julie was in the house and occupied, so there was no real hurry.

At the beginning of March Milada traveled to Styria to meet with the men to make final plans for building the house. She had liquidated her assets to have all her money available and took it to Dr. Stüber who had offered to oversee the agenda of the children's home. Before she departed Milada had made Julie fully aware of her plans, and Julie's enthusiasm accompanied Milada on her trip to the mountains.

"I wish you was already back here," Julie said with a sigh and some fear.

Julie missed Milada's constant, calm presence. She felt secure around Milada. Without her Julie was filled with discomfort and angst. Once Milada had left, Julie became more reclusive. Bacher came over to her on the stairs and around the house to get her to talk about this and that.

And the madam looked at her again.

Julie wondered what they had in mind for her. She withdrew and was quiet as a mouse. She avoided contact with people when she could.

One morning she was hesitant to take the madam her coffee in her quarters.

"Don't be such a stupid girl," the cook said with venom. "The madam won't rip the crown off your head."

Julie had to serve her coffee. Spizzari was still in bed. She looked over the well-built frame of the maidservant. She could not but do otherwise. She was forever assessing people as wares. She suddenly put down her newspaper and said with substance, "Bina Michal was an even more useless thing than you. Now she's having a good time with champagne and officers in Budweis, I'm letting you know."

Julie left Nelly's apartment pale as a sheet.

"I just want Madame Milada to come," Julie cried at night when she was chilled through from cold and fear. A horror of the salon gripped her more strongly than ever before. When the entry hall was full or the stairwell creaked, she folded in terror. Fear gripped her fingers.

When she fell asleep she often dreamt of Gustav. She sat next to him in the Blue Room. She asked him something, but he was not listening.

She took hold of his hands, held him close to her, and whispered something to him urgently.

It seemed to Julie her life depended on his knowing what she said. But he was disinterested and stood to leave. The sound of her own weeping woke her from this dream. She was drenched in sweat.

The pleasure she had taken in her work began to fade. She kept out of the madam's sight as far as she was able. At the sound of the madam's voice, Julie was unable to swallow. Julie's hearty appetite had always roused a fit of laughter from the cook, but now Julie only stared at her bowl, unable to lift the spoon.

"So what's wrong? Why aren't you eating?" asked the cook.

"I et cake from Mrs. Keller," she told a bold lie and got up from the table.

That was not true. What was honestly happening with Julie? She could not bear the sight of other people eating. When Julie watched as Dolly tore a piece of meat with her teeth Julie had such violent nausea the whole kitchen seemed to swirl before her eyes.

Seized with panic she threw open the kitchen door and stepped out into the courtyard. The sound of the bell at the back door woke the madam up. Nelly went to the kitchen and saw Julie outside through the window in the door.

Julie, terrified of the madam, used her apron to cover the glass of the window.

Spizzari spoke to her in her affected motherly tone, "I don't like seeing you standing around idle, my dear." She came closer to Julie. "After supper this evening put on some nice, clean clothes and make an effort to be part of this business, girl. Idleness is the devil's playground," she said threateningly, waving her index finger in Julie's face.

Julie stood stock still, then she began to wail aloud. She pressed her hands against her belly and crept with constricted arms and legs to a spot behind the garbage cans. There she stayed, making strange guttural sounds. When she emerged from behind the garbage, she was green and pallid, and a dark shadow, which ran from her nose to her mouth, covered over her expression of utter disgust. She left the kitchen and let Spizzari know she was ill. Spizzari was disgruntled and shook her head.

Julie lay in bed. She held the pillow to her head and wailed. The room smelled of the chamomile tea Mrs. Keller had put on the window ledge for her. Toward evening Spizzari went up to see Julie. She had reserved a good client for Julie, a man who liked girls from the country. Julie, in her farmer's apron and kerchief, would be right for him, exactly what he had ordered. Spizzari believed Julie's illness was feigned. But when she peeked in the ice-cold room and smelled the acrid odor of that space, she shook her head in dismay and left without saying a word.

After a couple of hours of restful sleep Julie awoke, feeling warm, and stretched out in her bed. She was surprised she was in her own bed. She then had a dull memory of collapsing and Dolly and Keller bringing her upstairs to bed.

She felt rested and much better. She was strong enough to get up. She hastily put on her skirt and jacket. What were the people downstairs doing without her?

She made up the bed, tidied up the room, and felt a hefty pang of hunger in her stomach and throughout her abdomen. She remembered she had a piece of old, stale bread. She picked it up and bit off a chunk, washing it down with the cold, overly sweet tea. Still swallowing, she ran out the door of her room. She went to the door of Milada's room and stood there a moment. Oh, if the lady were only here! She truly missed her protector. She sighed and ran down to the kitchen.

There she found her afternoon coffee waiting for her on the shelf. She drank it down greedily and asked what was for dinner.

"A lady in the salon gets a lovely meal. A maidservant gets noodles," the cook said portentously.

"It only has to fill you up," Julie replied insolently. The cook raised her spoon in warning. "If I'd known you would run away because of guests!"

"And who knows? It could have been Gus again!" Dolly gushed as she smirked.

Julie fixed her eyes straight ahead. Why, all of a sudden, were they treating her like this? Up to this moment she had been comfortable in the kitchen.

"Your jokes are stupid," Julie's voice was shaky. And a sick feeling crept up from the pit of her stomach.

The cook had worked as a waitress in a cheap nightclub, and she appreciated Spizzari's point of view. She had also had quite an enlightening talk with the madam earlier that day. The cook started slamming and banging around with pots and pans. Julie set herself to the task of washing up the dirty dishes from the afternoon coffee.

"You're back here for now, but there's no helping you. I'd like to know what you're doing. Is it so terrible here? Is it dirty? You've got to be where the men are. They might wear fancy duds but they're all naked underneath. They stink. But you have to pull yourself together and get over this. Mind what that Jewess Spizzari wants you to do! You can crawl in a church window and hide behind the pulpit, but she'll find you and drag you out. I'm telling you, if it's not today, it'll be tomorrow. A brothel is not a crystal palace, just so you know."

Julie did not respond. She kept washing dishes with slower and slower motions. She stood close to the fire in the stove, but she was shaking with the cold that had set in her heart.

So that is how matters stood? She was to be put to work as before? There was nothing she could do. When Lisa was headstrong and resisted, Winkler and Irma held her down. That is what they would do to her. Her strength was entirely gone. She felt such constriction around her neck she imagined her collar was strangling her. She unbuttoned the collar.

No, she did not want to! She did not want men hanging on her neck. She did not want to pretend she loved each of these men. Ugh, she was disgusted. She could not let one single man near her, even if they flogged her like a horse! Her aversion at the fate she was up against triggered her courage.

"Madame Milada got me maid's work, and that's how it is. I'm a maid here. Leave me alone."

"Madame Milada?! You think she has more to say than the madam?"

"Sure, yes," Julie was firm.

"Well, she's smart. Smarter than you. She got herself some money, the Bohunk. She took up with the doctor's old man and said goodbye to the son with his pretty face. That's what she did! She did what a prostitute has to do. She didn't get all sentimental and fall in love like you."

The house had come alive with business. The doorbell rang. There was a steady stream of guests. Irma stood on the porch steps, receiving people and wishing them a good evening with an obsequious little laugh.

Mrs. Bacher brought a whole retinue of prostitutes who were on call to the kitchen. They came for supper. They ate up their meat in haste and washed it down with a large mug of beer.

The cook had a flattering word for each one of them and gave them a friendly pat on the hand.

With the exception of Mitzi, Irma, Winkler, and Keller the group that arrived was made up of "fresh," pretty young things who were new to the business. This was obvious since they were taken in by the cook's flattery.

"That's how good you could have it," the cook told Julie. "Why don't you go have a look in the salon? What's wrong with you?" Julie sat by the stove, white as a sheet. "I don't know," she muttered. "I'm cold." She sunk her head.

"Jesus, what's wrong with her?" Dolly said loudly as she stood at the kitchen door with a tray in her hands. The cook was angered and shut the door in Dolly's face. She knelt down to Julie, who was losing consciousness. She flicked water on her to bring her back.

"So what is it? Why are you like this?" The cook rubbed Julie's cheeks with her rough hands. "What's wrong? Well?"

"She's probably hungry," Dolly said. "She hasn't eaten anything today."

Julie opened her eyes, moved over to a chair and sat down. She made an effort to laugh. But instead of laughing, her face took on a grimace of loathing as the cook held a spoonful of broth to her mouth. "Take it away!"

"You think you're nauseated but it's really hunger," the cook said. "Take a sip, there you go!"

Julie started choking. She gathered her skirt together, lifted it to her mouth, and spat convulsively.

"Go to bed, Julie," Dolly said with concern. She was at base soft-hearted. "Why did you get out of bed? For the love of God, just look at you!"

Holding her skirt in a ball with one hand and her painful stomach in the other, Julie left the kitchen. She had never in her life had pain like this.

She crept up the stairs, step by step, and sat down on the bed. She held her head in her hands. Her skirt smelled of vomit.

"What is this, what is it?" she grumbled. "I was always healthy. Why am I ill? What's happening to me?" She thought of the broth and shuddered.

"Stop thinking about food," she told herself and tried to push the thought out of her mind.

She thought of Milada who had sent her a card from Styria. Milada had indicated with red ink the spot on the green meadow where the little house would stand.

Her thoughts turned to home and to her father reading from the old Bible one Sunday while her brother smoked a cigar and she waved shyly to the boy at the window. Her gesture encouraged the boy, and he came to the door and said, "Mr. Hinterberger, we need Julie at the dance." That set off quite an argument, but in the end she went off to the dance.

Then there was her sister Marianne, who married the most poverty-stricken woodsman. She must be sitting in her little hut, complaining. Oh, well...

Julie heard the voice of the innkeeper where she had worked at God's Eye as he turned out the lamps at end of the day, "Well, folks, it's time to go home to bed."

Amidst her pain and suffering, wrapped in her blanket and filled with good memories of home, Julie fell asleep. Partially awake she remembered to secure the door with the chest. But she could not bring herself to get up.

Three days later Milada showed up. She had returned to Red House. She found Julie emaciated, pale, and trembling. Her usually bright eyes were dull, swollen, and sunken. "So what's wrong, Julie? What's happened to you?"

"I'm just feeling a little off," Julie tried to put on a good face. She acted as if she had good news for Milada but held her hand a little too long. "Things are better now, all better."

"She had a bad case of influenza," Keller offered. Keller had been given permission to care for Julie. "Now Winkler's got it and Schorsch, too." Schorsch was Nelly's nephew and darling.

"It's over now. You're getting better, Julie!"

"Yes, I'm pretty healthy again. I'm having trouble eating though." She laughed self-consciously, "You can believe me."

Milada was encouraging, "You could stand to put on some weight. If the work is too much for you, the madam can find someone to help out."

Julie replied, pointing to Keller, "She's already helping." Keller nodded emphatically.

Milada had entered a special agreement with Keller right before she had left on her recent trip to Styria. One day old Keller's daughter had brought her nine-month-old baby girl to Red House. She put the child down in the hallway. Keller wrung her hands and wept. She picked up the little bundle while Spizzari protested, cursing and hollering she was not going to be responsible for anyone who cost her money. Keller's daughter wanted to leave. At that moment Milada arrived, perceived what the situation was, and took the desperate mother aside.

Milada gave Keller money for the child's care and promised her she would soon take on the baby girl. Milada pledged to raise the child, and Keller thanked Milada profusely and wept profusely. Milada's set down one condition: Spizzari must not know of the arrangement. Keller's daughter vowed to keep it secret. "Of course, I'll do that! If the old hunter her father is worried, I'll work as a maid. He never cared for me, nobody does."

The baby's name was Crystal. She was a poor, neglected child of laborers and had the serious eyes of an old soul. Crystal was the first small child Milada embraced and the first one to join the home on Sunny Heights.

The home was in the making.

Milada traveled with her dear, old friend Doctor Stüber to Oberdorf. There she consulted with the architect and the Doctor about the project. Feeling gratitude to the two men and great trust in them, she told them the story of her decision to found this home. She also told them about her own life. Both men listened attentively. Their respect for her was genuine. They were honored to work with her.

"It's all well and good. We'll make it happen," the architect said and offered her his hand.

Milada returned to Red House for the last time to retrieve her few possessions from the world she had inhabited. She was moving to her new home. It was the middle of the night.

Julie awoke in her bed. The whole house was astir. She sat bolt upright. Her head hurt, and her feet were immobile.

Last night in the evening there was noise, but what was happening now? Yes, she was rather nauseated, and Milada was going to have a physician come see her. But was this commotion about her? No, it was not.

She could not say why, but she was ashamed of herself. When she had to vomit she slipped away into a corner. She lied, too, and accepted the meals she was given, pretended to be hungry, then tossed the food in the fire. But had anything helped? She needed to get better.

What time could it be? Would she be able to get up today?

They were making quite a fuss downstairs. A door slammed shut. But she was no longer afraid of sounds at night as she had been. Who could do anything to her now that she was so ill? She pulled the sheets up over herself and moaned.

If she moved the tiniest little bit her stomach turned.

She wished either Dolly or Keller would come look in on her. There she was the long night through all by herself! Oh, Jesus!

She reached for a towel. She belched, and a bitter liquid filled her mouth.

Blood? She wondered. Her thought was: And now I die.

Holy Mother of God! How did she deserve this? She tried to pray. But she could not. The words were stirred through with the fear of death.

She surely must have contracted typhus. Keller had told her this is how typhus starts.

In a fever she tossed and turned. Something had to happen. Her pain was intolerable. Would she go to the hospital? Or go home? They certainly would gawk. "Holy Mary, pray for us sinners now and in the hour of..." She had always been very healthy. "Healthy as a horse," Father had said. "Nothing will ever happen to her!" But now?

The doorbell downstairs rang and rang. The front door opened and closed again. Would it ever stop? She thought she would like some of the wine that was on the table, a nice, sweet one. Mitzi had kept the bottle from her. Keller had hidden it behind her back. What a stupid game! Give it to me, both of you! They were such bitches. She had such a terrible thirst. Jesus, what was happening? The bottle moved across the room by itself toward her. Hah! Could that be? No, it was her sister's daughter Rosie. And there she had almost believed the bottle had moved itself. . .

Rosie is such an angel. Your auntie is here in a silk dress. How about that?

Maybe not Rosie, but a child. Mitzi's child? Take a closer look. Jesus, how this child is floating around! But it is a child. Yes, a child.

Julie awoke. She was soaked in her own sweat and shivering. Her throat was dry, and she breathed heavily. What a stupid thing to dream! The house was very quiet. The gray light of morning was breaking. She felt as if she had been beaten.

She suddenly threw off her covers, put her hands on her belly, and pressed down. Something was moving in there. She tried it again. She got control of herself and fell back against the bed. She understood. She knew what was happening to her. But it was not possible. Holy Mother Ann in heaven! She looked down at her legs and held them out stiff. It was not possible! She had simply overworked herself moving heavy furniture in the salon.

Stunned, and without thinking what she was doing, she went to the door. She wanted to tell Dolly she had strained herself moving furniture. Dolly would have a good laugh about that. She tried to laugh at herself, but her teeth chattered from fear.

The hallway was dark. Downstairs on the ground floor, the gas must be on. They would have to empty the house. Empty? What then? She sat on the stairs, and her hair fell over her pale face.

A minute ago she had had the fear of death. Death would have been good, yes, death would be fine. With horror she looked down at her body once more. She held her arms out away from her body.

Would it still be there, the thing inside? And what about tomorrow? And the next day? Eventually everyone would see what was happening with her, her father, too. Jesus! He would beat her to death. And Madame Milada would find out! She could not bear the shame. She would be better off jumping out the window as Rosie had.

She ran down the hallway to the barracks. There Bacher's chair was empty except for her knitting. She slipped on by and arrived at Milada's door. She stood there at the threshold. She called out, "Madame, Madame!" She was overcome and closed her eyes. Then the key turned from within. The door opened, and Julie flew in. Milada lifted a candle to see. "It's you, Julie! What is it? I wasn't sure if somebody was here. But here you are and barefoot, when you're not well!"

"Madame, don't be angry," Julie folded her hands and stammered out in a flood of tears how distressed she was.

Milada brought her a chair. "You're feeling miserable, aren't you? Are you in pain?"

"Yes, terrible pain."

"We'll bring the physician tomorrow to see you." She buttoned up her robe and looked at her watch. "It's 5:45 in the morning. Go back to bed. You're not getting up until we know what you have."

Julie looked at Milada, who was holding her hand. "Madame, something is happening to me."

"Go on to bed. You don't have to be humble. Tomorrow the doctor..."

Julie took firm hold of Milada's arm. "No, I don't need a doctor, Madame. I'm not ill. It's something else. I'm going to have a baby." Her voice trailed off.

Milada felt a shock run through herself. It was as if she were hearing a voice off in the distance. "What? What are you saying?"

Julie let out a deep breath.

"I'm sure. It was like this with my sister Marianne. Jesus, the shame. I am done for."

"There is no shame!" Milada was loud and clear. She was immensely moved. "Are you absolutely sure, Julie? Is there a chance you're imagining this?"

"It's moving," Julie whispered, and her face glowed.

Milada took a few steps back, without realizing what she did. "It's moving? The baby? Is that true? The baby is already alive?"

Milada had the sense this could not be the farm girl Julie she had met only months ago, the same girl she had taken on to protect. A rush of new feelings shot through her and shattered the isolation of her soul.

"Julie, it's from Gus," she said.

Julie's response was a sob. "I was only with him." She was exhausted.

"Don't cry. There's no reason to cry." Milada stroked Julie's hair. This gesture was somewhat forced and uncomfortable. Milada was surprised at the unaccustomed feelings she had. Everything Julie had said was new to her. She had never spoken with anyone about such things before.

"Madame, what will I do? I can't go on."

Milada bent over her. "Don't say that! That's silly talk!" Milada's voice was firm. She then spoke right from her heart, "It's great good fortune. Listen to me! It's such wonderful luck I can hardly believe it." Milada spoke more softly, and then she could no longer speak.

Milada cried.

After a while she collected herself, and she spoke with the open joy of a child. She was surprised at her own emotion. "I never thought of anything like this. I never thought anything like this would happen in Red House! It is a miracle."

"What will the madam say about this? And, Jesus, what if she writes Father?"

"Keep quiet about this. You and the baby will come with me. And the child will have a good life. Let's you and me make a vow to keep this quiet, all right?"

She paced around the room with ever faster steps. "When you think about it, it's as if the hard life I've had was for this moment. Just in time there will be a roof over this child's head. Just see how it falls together."

"If I live with you," Julie said softly, "I will work hard. I can do it. For the child."

Milada nodded.

"It won't be easy. It'll be just the two of us. There'll certainly be a lot of work to do. There are so very many poor mothers. Many of them will bring their children to me. They don't want them to suffer. I had not understood how huge the need was, Julie!" She stood facing Julie. "This will be family. This will be my one family on Earth. My path is right in front of me!"

She went to the window, opened it, and opened the shutters. She went back over to Julie. Milada was laughing.

"Yes, Julie. There will be many children who will come to me. You are coming with your child. If I stop to think about it, in a way this was the fate I had coming."

Julie stared at Milada.

"I'm poor. I've got nothing to pay you with. In the beginning the child won't need much. I do look forward to having this baby."

What transpired that evening was intense. Julie was overcome with emotion. She trembled violently.

"Quiet now, we've spoken enough. Go back to bed quickly. Or lie down here on my bed."

"That wouldn't be right," Julie declined, fearfully.

"You can stay here. You mustn't think only about yourself." Milada sat on the edge of the bed while Julie crawled into bed and took Milada's arm.

"Know what? The madam wants me to work in the salon. But I can't. I'm afraid."

"Nonsense! Go to sleep! You need rest. Nobody can force you to do anything anymore. We'll leave this place very soon. It's truly beautiful where we're going." Milada's words had the effect of a lullaby on Julie. They calmed her.

Julie closed her eyes and went to sleep. Only the hand that held Milada's arm moved occasionally. Milada watched as Julie slept, and she was at peace.

The line on Julie's face that had registered disgust vanished.

Was there not an invisible hand that passed over Julie's youthful features? Had it not offered her dignity and reality? The soul of a mother? Julie's breathing was even.

Milada thought back over this miraculous set of events. Her most intimate thoughts enfolded this hour like a shining castle. And held it forever safe. The love for Gustav, this time of luster and blossoms, as hopeless and lost as it had seemed to her, was going to unfold. Its very deepest meaning would ripen into life.

Milada's own depleted body was no longer capable. Then Julie arrived, strong and healthy, and she conceived and gave her this child.

She recognized, full of awe, nothing is lost, not one emotion, nor a single thought. There is a place for everything, a deep, harmonious acknowledgement. Of all the valorous deeds Milada, in her strength, had performed, the only one to endure was saving an unprotected child. Its light breath was in the belly of this farm girl who had been the object of mockery at Red House. It moved. It was alive!

And what love had wrought through her tough determination carried this child through life replete with security. As mysteriously as this love had begun, its completion was manifest in this child as the meaning of Milada's days on Earth.

Oh, mystery, not to be proved, You gather together in one drop of dew all the magnificence of light!

Milada heard the porter on the steps coming to wake Julie. Milada went out to meet her. The day began.

On this very same day the architect laid the cornerstone of the new house.

Translator's note

This translation of Else Jerusalem's *Der heilige Skarabäus* is based on the 1909 edition of the novel. It is complete, sentence by sentence; nothing has been omitted or glossed. In a few instances, when characters in polyglot Vienna speak foreign languages, I added an appositive in English. Jerusalem's text also contains many dialects of German and social registers to indicate the vertical and horizontal social mix of the setting. The narrative matrix of the novel is, however, consistently standard High German; the tone, uniformly literary. The translation emulates these varieties of speech.

In a few cases I have added vocabulary to clarify terms for the contemporary reader, such as "*poses plastiques*" for "*poses*," a performance art common in European cities at the time of composition. I have also supplied the titles of books or works of music with the authors' or composers' names.

Jerusalem made liberal use of dashes to indicate a disruption, lacuna, or syncope in a conversation or in a character's train of thought. Dashes also denote a move among voices: between the narrator's voice, characters' voices, and individual characters' interior monologues (precursors to the use of stream of consciousness in English). The dashes serve a metric function as well. They allow the reader a moment to consider what the character does not voice or take under awareness. In those passages where a break is especially pronounced, I retained the dashes. But this translation dispenses with many of the dashes for coherence.

At various points throughout the novel, the omniscient narrator breaks frame and addresses readers personally with the familiar "*Ihr*" or "you," as in, "you people." I have added italics to mark these passages. This innovative narrative voice makes impassioned pleas directly to readers (compare the italicized epigraph "To You!"). This personal, dramatic voice functions like the classical chorus and prefigures the player in Brechtian theater who steps out of the proscenium arch to deliver a lecture or analysis. The author speaks off the page to connect with readers. We hope this immediacy comes across to you.

Afterword

by Stephanie G. Ortega

The Viennese author Else Jerusalem (1876–1943) published her first novel, *Der heilige Skarabäus* (The sacred scarab), a critique of prostitution presented as naturalistic *bildungsroman*, in 1909. It was published by S. Fischer Verlag in Berlin. At the beginning of the 20th century, Fischer was a highly visible and internationally prestigious publishing house, known for the works of up-and-coming new authors, such Thomas Mann, Arthur Schnitzler, and Hermann Hesse.[1] Samuel Fischer's aim was to make great works of literature easily available to the public; he backed talented writers and promoted what he considered masterpieces in the making.[2] For an unknown woman author to have her premier novel published by Fischer was a coup.

1 Wikipedia. "S. Fischer Verlag." 11.2.24. de.wikipedia.org/wiki/S._Fischer_Verlag?wprov=sfla

2 Baur, Eva Gesine. "Samuel Fischer—das trauige Glückskind," Welt Print. 24.12.2009.de/welt_print/kultur/literatur/article5628766/Samuel-Fischer-das-traurige-Glueckskind.html.

The book was a windfall for the publishing house. Jerusalem's unprecedented work was wildly successful. In the novel's first two years on the market, the press brought out twenty-two printings of 1,000 copies each, and between 1911 and 1933 Fischer released twenty more.[3] Its popularity went beyond the German-speaking world. Translations appeared in Russian, Hungarian, Dutch, Finnish, French, and English in a heavily abridged form.[4,5]

The compelling story of a prostitute and her world of prostitution was parlayed into film in 1928 by the popular Weimar filmmaker Richard Oswald, who originated the "educational film" (*Aufklärungsfilm*) on taboo topics.[6] He produced and directed the silent film *Die Rothausgaße* (The red house alley), which was released in English as *The Green Alley*. He freely adapted Jerusalem's novel for viewers eager to see the eternally evocative fairytale-like love story of a valiant man from the bourgeoise and a captive woman of the demimonde (e.g., the blockbuster *Pretty Woman*). The film premiered in Berlin only after rounds of censorship for its treatment of a prostitute as weak-willed and of a brothel as innocuous.[7]

Three years after Samuel Fischer's death in 1933, the National Socialists forced the Fischer family to sell the press in Berlin and banned Jerusalem's novel for being *unsittlich* (indecent).[8] The ban against Jerusalem's work remained in force until the Nazis'

---

3 Kneihs, Johann. "Der heilige Skarabäus." Goodreads.com/book/show/29971143-der-heilige-skarabus.

4 Spreitzer, Brigitte. "Else Jerusalem—eine Spurensuche." *Der heilige Skarabäus*. Das vergessene Buch. DVB Verlag, 2016.

5 *The Red House*, translated by R. L. Marchant. New York: The Macaulay Company, 1932.

6 Wikipedia. "Richard Oswald." 11.2.24. de.wikipedia.org/wiki/Richard_Oswald?wprov=sfla.

7 Wikipedia. "Die Rothausgasse." 11.3.24. de.wikipedia.org/wiki/Die_Rothausgasse?wprov=sfla1. The film, also entitled *Im Haus der roten Laterne* (In the house of the red lantern), is no longer publically available.

8 Kneihls, Johann. Ibid.

defeat in 1945, but after the War this formerly best-selling novel languished in obscurity. There were no further editions, and scholars of literary history were unaware of the novel's existence.[9] Even as a document of social history it was largely unknown until 2016, when the Viennese press Das vergessene Buch (The forgotten book) reissued the novel with an extensive afterword by Professor Brigitte Spreitzer. This edition and Dr. Spreitzer's work have done much to raise awareness in the German-speaking world of Jerusalem's life and writing.

Context of composition

Else Jerusalem's novel was radical, outside classification and without antecedent. It was accepted for publication in 1908 at the end stage of the glorious Habsburg Monarchy (1282–1918) and the powerful Austro-Hungarian Empire (1867–1918). This cultural and political entity had cohered—tenuously—as a multi-ethnic polyglot society of fifty million people (Austrian German-speakers, Hungarians, Czechs, Slovaks, Slovenes, Serbs, Croats, Bosnians, Romanians, Poles of Galicia, Russians of Ukraine, and Italians of Tyrol and Triest)[10]—all of whom were citizens as of 1867. This

---

9 Two prominent studies of prostitution in late-Imperial Austria are Nancy Wingfield's sociological study, *The World of Prostitution in Late Imperial Austria* (Oxford: University of Oxford Press, 2017), and Christiane Schönfeld's collection of essays in literary history, *Commodities of Desire: the Prostitute in Modern German Literature* (Glen Oak, California, Camden, 2001). Neither scholarly treatment of the literature on prostitution mentions Jerusalem's radical tale of a prostitute with a brain and agency who comes to consciousness and into money. Schönfeld instead treats Margareta Böhme's bestseller, the notorious novel about a provocative escort who is victimized and ruined, *Tagebuch einer Verlorenen* (1905); it was compared favorably to the novels of Émile Zola. Böhme's work is known to audiences worldwide via G. W. Pabst's 1929 film *Diary of a Lost Girl*.

10 Perloff, Marjorie. "The Making of Austro-Modernism" In: *Edge of Irony: Modernism in the Shadow of the Habsburg Empire*. Chicago: University of

uneasy composite polity was at the brink of dissolution, just as Vienna, its capital in the Austrian sector Cisleithania, had become the epicenter of a cultural florescence. The time was the afterglow of turn-of-the-century stability and prosperity in Vienna, Austro-Hungary, and Europe, the grand *fin-de-siècle*.[11] Poverty and overcrowding had become endemic in the capital. The population of Vienna grew from 726,000 to around 2,000,000 between 1880 and 1910. Emperor Franz Josef (1830–1916), beloved rallying symbol for much of the 19th century, was approaching eighty and becoming weak with age. The Empire he administered had recently annexed Bosnia and Herzegovina, an act that precipitated the Bosnian Crisis, the devastation of World War I, and the dramatic dissolution of Austro-Hungary. (The resulting nation-state Austria had a population of only six million, primarily German-speakers.[12])

By 1908, the Viennese Secession, which had been established in 1897 as the vanguard of Modernism and hope, was no longer a viable movement. The Secessionists, mainly visual artists, had exhorted all artists in the name of progress to tear away artificiality, hypocritical propriety, the tradition of pleasure and diversion, distracting decoration, and commercialism in the arts.[13] Its most prominent artist, Gustav Klimt, had stepped back from his initial

---

Chicago Press, 2016. This brilliant study of the literary expression of despair/hope uses analyses of writings of the era to demonstrate how this paradox was bridged with irony.

11 Schorske, Carl E., *Fin-de-Siécle Vienna: Politics and Culture*. New York: Alfred A. Knopf, 1979. This Pulitzer-Prize-winning study is the proverbial classic on the socio-historical situation of Vienna prior to World War I. Schorske's work is a landmark of what he calls "panoptic" and "architectonic" analysis, which today we would call multi-disciplinary. He documents the overlap of crisis of cultural disintegration and explosion of creativity in this epicenter of Modernism. This book remains a topical primer and an enjoyable read.

12 Perloff, idem.

13 Daviau, Donald G. "Hermann Bahr and Gustav Klimt: A Breakthrough of Modernity in Turn-of-the-Century Vienna, *German Studies Review*. Vol. 3 No. 1 (Februrary 1980).

polemic about revealing the raw, excruciating nature of the human psyche (compare his dark mythic paintings for the University of Vienna,1900–1904, with his portraits of society women, such as his iconic *The Kiss*,1908). Klimt became a member in good standing of the establishment: the status quo and dynastic order prevailed.[14]

Many artists in the Modernist movement were squarely bourgeois. Jerusalem railed against the complacency of the members of the Modernist literary movement *Jung Wien* (Young Vienna) who presented themselves as revolutionaries. She found them just as interested in reputation and money as their predecessors, quashing their Freudian Oedipal pretense of surpassing their fathers. In her novel, Joe, the learned Bohemian, is her mouthpiece. He explains to the protagonist Milada that people with a social conscience, "unhappy" people, do not make good modern Aesthetes.

Setting of the novel

Red House Alley is set between 1865 and 1892, at the height of turn-of-the-century Viennese prosperity, the incandescent phase of the Belle Époque. One bit of information allows us to date the story definitively. Milada gives her lover Gustav a gold coin as a memento of their love affair when they were twenty-four. It bears this engraving: "Summer 1890." The action of the novel begins a year before Milada's birth as a flashback and extends two years past the year of their affair.

---

14 Sark, Kat. "Vienna Secession – Klimt, Freud, and Jung." 13.3.24 suitesculturelles.wordpress.com/2021/08/24/vienna-secession-klimt-freud-and-jung/. This essay tracks the power of the Viennese elite to erode the radicality of the Modernists by analyzing the trajectory of Klimt's production. Compare Sark's view of *The Kiss* with James Fox's comments on this painting in the episode "Vienna 1908" in the BBC series *Bright Lights, Brilliant Minds: A Tale of Three Cities* (2016). Fox argues for 1908 as the tipping point of Viennese Modernism and sees Klimt's portraits of society women as indicative of their affluence and society's approbation of Modernist style.

There are other indications of the era. The currency used in Red House is the gulden, subdivided into kreuzer. At the end of the novel Milada receives payment for ending her association with Gustav in the new currency, kronen, introduced in 1892. Milada's pay-off establishes her as wealthy in the terms of the flourishing new economy.

The glamour and titillation of prostitution is blatantly missing in Jerusalem's presentation of the sex industry of the Belle Époque. Depictions of Red House and the girls and women who work there and around the city are never alluring. Jerusalem contrasts the oppressive, denigrating conditions of the prostitutes in her novel with that of popular novels of the era, which romanticize them.

The archetypical upper-middle-class Gustav finds Milada reminiscent of Émile Zola's wildly seductive, hypersexed figure Nana (*Nana*,1890). He also tells Milada women and girls choose to be prostitutes because they are lacking moral sense, want an idle, indulgent life, and spurn their natural, valorizing instinct to motherhood. He is vocal about the disgust he feels for prostitutes at the same time he is captivated by a sexualized vision of his lover, a prostitute. Milada, by contrast, feels used and depersonalized during sex because of recurring trauma. She is never flirtatious. Gustav says he is in love with her just as he denies he ever knew she was a prostitute. He despises prostitutes and loves Milada (he says she attracts him because she is boyish, a hint of homoeroticism). Gustav's values are received from his "proper," protective family and the masculinist bourgeois community he knows through the university and its drinking clubs. Gustav's paid companion Joe says of the aesthete Gustav that "he is what he is supposed to believe he is." His conflicted reaction to prostitutes as provocative and disgusting comes with his class identity. There is no room in his mental economy for the humanity of what he calls "these creatures."

Gustav also personifies the values of the waning monarchy and its militarism. The figure Gustav is often called by the Austrian-German diminutive Gustl, meaning Little Gustav (translated here as Gus). Jerusalem's Gustl or Gus is an homage to Arthur Schnitzler's character Gustl from his 1901 novella *Leutnant Gustl*.[15] The originary Gustl is a fatuous twenty-four-year-old, obsessed with honor and reputation, who routinely visits brothels and has been challenged to a duel over an affair. The thought world of both Schnitzler's and Jerusalem's Gustl is revealed unvarnished via interior monologue so the reader sees the gap between their selfish motivation and codified postures of honor. Their hypocrisy is laid bare.

There is only one short passage in *Red House Alley* in which anyone suggests prostitution is the good life. "It's been wonderful," says Olympia, former manager of Red House. Milada reflects:

> What images might be dancing in her brain empty of blood! Perhaps Goldscheider's salon [an uptown brothel], the black-silk dress of the barmaid, the apron for money, and music! Or maybe even moments as far back as Paris, laughing and living, ravishing parties, a spin in the park on a sunny day, dances where dazzling naked flesh was in its glory, and passionate love in her heart!

Milada wonders about Olympia's fond memories as she watches her die a miserable early death in a charity hospital without a stitch, having given her last, worn piece of clothing to another

---

15 Klingenstein, Susanne. "None but the Brave (*Leutnant Gustl*) by Arthur Schnitzler, 1901." Encylopedia.com/arts/encyclopedias-almanacs-transcripts-and maps/none-brave-leutnant-gust-arthur-schnitzler-1901. Klingenstein recaps the plot of the novella to show how Schnitzler satirized society's infatuation with honor codes and militarism. She also gives the history of the high-profile scandal that resulted from his attack on officers in the Imperial Army as a Jew. He was relieved of his status as an officer in the military. The very short novella appeared in 1982 in *Plays and Stories* by Arthur Schnitzler as "Lieutenant Gustl," available at Depts.washington.edu/vienna/documents/Schnitzler/Schnitzler-lt-gustl.htm.

terminally ill prostitute. Olympia's need to construct a story of her glamorous life is self-deception, part of Jerusalem's tragic satire.

With *Red House Alley*, Jerusalem does what artists of the Viennese Secession of the 1890s claimed to do: unveil hypocrisy and expose raw, dark truth. The suffering psyches Jerusalem portrays are not those of the elite, hypersensitive artist. They are the emotions of hapless girls and women in the flourishing sex industry. Jerusalem used the principles of the revisionist movement about observation and creativity to critique the sexual fantasies of the times. Milada is neither a mysterious ancient sphinx (as Joe and Gustav see her) nor a magical, mythic glittering sacred scarab that ingests and transforms dung (as her crackpot tutor Horner sees her). She is a prostitute who inveterately embraces her background and role in society, a figure with a developed sense of compassion and personal dignity. Milada is, in fact, heroic in the face of discrimination and personal harm. Her heroism carries the story in the face of a literary tradition of girls and women who are either projections of male fantasies (e.g., *The Happy Hooker*), or the lascivious, unwitting victim.[16]

Red House Alley chronicles Milada's coming of age in the worst possible circumstances of the Belle Époque. It documents the contemporaneous practices and institutions of prostitution and sex trafficking. Here, too, the novel's presentation of the burgeoning institutionalization of prostitution and brothels is historically

---

16 Boa, Elizabeth. "Taking Sex to Market: *Tagebuch einer Verlorenen* and *Josefine Mutzenacher: Die Lebensgeschte einer wienerischen Dirne, von ihr selbst erzählt*," Eds. Woodford, Charlotte, and Benedict Schofield. *The German Bestseller in the Late Nineteenth Century*. Martelsham, UK: Boydell and Brewer, 2012. This essay in a collection on popular literature addresses Margarethe Böhme's 1905 titillating *Tagebuch einer Verlorenen* (*Diary of a Lost Girl*, which was made into Pabst's 1928 film) and Felix Salten's 1906 pornographic novel. *Josefine Mutzenbacher*. Salten, a Viennese Jew, contemporary and acquaintance of Jerusalem, published this work of graphic pornography anonymously and became wealthy. The Nazis did not ban it.

accurate. The stages of Milada's development correspond to the iterations of the brothel through its successive owners.

From Milada's birth until her appearance in a junk shop at age six (1866 to 1872), she lives with her mother Katerine, an independent prostitute, and her mother's companion Janka, in a flophouse managed by the downtrodden, vicious housekeeper Lorinser and owned by an unseen retired officer Katerine was involved with earlier. Milada continues to the age of eleven (1877) in this unstable, unstructured environment, where street prostitutes pay rent on a daily basis—or flee.

At the conclusion of Milada's brief but transformative education in a charity school, the entrepreneur Goldscheider buys the property, a transaction initiated and facilitated by the police agent Sucher. The seedy flophouse is reconstituted as an upscale, state-approved brothel with published prices that advertises in the newspapers. Its prostitutes are supplied with room and board, clothing and necessities of daily life, as well as with customers. The girls and women must keep a registration book and undergo health examinations by a state-licensed physician twice a week. Red House is now recognized and acclaimed. It also a venue of public entertainment with a restaurant, bar, and gambling room. Milada's mother is briefly retained as a regular until she falls ill, loses her situation, and dies in a charity hospital (c.1878).

As an orphan, Milada is a contractual ward of Red House for four years, indentured as a maid. When she is fifteen, the business-minded Madame Goldscheider puts Milada to work as a prostitute while training her in the business of Red House, which includes sex trafficking. Goldscheider sells the business when Milada is twenty, leaving Milada to run the house (c. 1879 to 1887). She manages the business with skill, while the inept, unthinking new owner Miller lives in Red House—"counting her money with fingers that still smelled of incense from the church"—while anxiously hoping to disentangle herself from the immorality and stress by entering a cloister (c. 1887 to 1891). The allure of Red House lapses with Miller's reluctance to engage in the parallel business of illicit trafficking.

In 1891, Milada, now part owner, negotiates the sale of Red House to a wealthy, psychopathic madam, Spizzari, who caters to courtiers of the House of Habsburg (*Edelschweinerasse*, roughly, a royal tribe of swine), a clientele more exclusive than the former lower-level aristocracy. That same year, Milada receives a substantial fortune from Gustav's father for cutting him off. In the scene where she accepts the money, she recognizes she does not love her callow lover and has been, rather, infatuated with his privilege (which she calls freedom). In that scene, she also recognizes that she no longer has to participate in the sex industry: she chooses to leave the corruption of Vienna and the destructive business of commercial sex and to save a few children from a life of prostitution by establishing a home for them in remote Styria (1892).

Milada's life spans the course of the institutionalization of prostitution in the Austro-Hungarian Empire: first, the chaotic, unregulated flophouse; then, the acclaimed, state-licensed brothel managed in accord with codes in the industry; further, the public brothel that falters because it is strictly a brothel; and finally, the officially registered, exclusive brothel with no social or governmental constraints (employing girls as young as twelve) and with the flair of fashionable, dehumanizing spectacles (presenting "Creoles" in gruesome *poses plastiques*). The trajectory of the sex trade in Jerusalem's fiction aligns with historical fact.[17]

---

17 Prokopovych, Markian. "Prostitution in Vienna in the Long Nineteenth Century." Essay in *Trafficking in Women 1924–1926: The Paul McKinsie Reports for the League of Nations*, Vol. 2. Eds. Chaumont, Jean-Michel, and Magaly Rodriguez Garcia. New York: United Nations, 2017. This essay offers detailed information about the location of brothels in Vienna. Just as Red House is set in an obscure alley off a major thoroughfare, maps in this article show density of houses of prostitution in prosperous, high-traffic areas.

Although there had been punitive legislation in Cisleithania against prostitutes in place from the 1850s to the 1870s, prostitution had flourished. By 1900, there were an estimated 50,000 registered and free-lance prostitutes in a city of over 1.7 million inhabitants.[18] In 1875 or so, the police agent Sucher facilitates the sale of Red House to be made into a proper brothel. Two years earlier, the concern over public health prompted the first regulatory legislation of the "tolerated" sex trade, and the Moral Police (*Sittenpolizei*) were tasked with oversight, which duty meant enforcement of health codes and registration of prostitutes.[19] Jerusalem's portrait of Sucher as both enforcer of the law and profiteer is a statement about the hypocritical corruption in Vienna. Sucher, the police force, the city officials, and the Imperial government all profit in a system that maintains men's rights to act on their "natural instincts."

Jerusalem understood the societal context of the period of her novel's setting. She witnessed first-hand the internationally famous trial of the infamous Viennese madam Regine Riehl in 1906. Nancy Wingfield devotes the first chapter of her study of prostitution in this era to this watershed media event that opened debate in polite society on the efficacy of regulation.[20] Else Jerusalem and the educator Coelestine Truxa—likely model for the director of Milada's school—were the only two women admitted to the court room of sixty witnesses. Here they heard the prostitutes' testimonies about their abusive treatment, such as confinement to the brothel, confiscation of clothing, beatings, threats of violence and banishment, confiscation of tips, and so on. Details of their physical and psychological abuse appear in *Red House*

18 Graziana, Edith. "Book Review: *The Red House* by Else Jerusalem" Edith's Miscellany, 2016. Lagraziana.blogspot.com/2016/05/red-house-by-else-jerusalem.html.

19 Prokopovich, idem.

20 Wingfield, idem. "The Riehl Trial," pp. 17–46.

Alley, where they become established practices during the period of regulation in the 1870s and 1880s. Beatings and emotional abuse lead Jerusalem's simple character Rosie to commit suicide. The tragedy and extreme horror of Rosie's death move Milada to revisit the late, exclusive Red House where her awareness that she is powerless reaffirms her decision to leave.

The Riehl trial brought the abuse of the sex trade to light, and this event is still the touchstone of discussion about violence and corruption in the industry. As recently as 2024, a documentary about the trial, Stefan Ludwig's *Aufstand im Bordell* (Rebellion in the brothel), was aired on Austrian national television.[21] At a time when the public was concerned about the sanctity of bourgeois morality and the protection of the family, Jerusalem was concerned with the lives of the girls and women that "proper" citizens claimed not to see.

A common belief resulting from the scandal around the trial was that Jews like the famous madam Riehl were the ones responsible for this societal ill. Jerusalem does address the role of Jews in the sex trade in her fiction. Of the four madams of Red House, both Goldscheider and Spizzari are Jews; the agents Fischer, senior and junior, who traffick women outside Vienna, and Kessler, who sold Red House to Miller, were also Jews. They are as complicit as the Gentiles. Red House does not discriminate in its exploitation or victimization: Jewish prostitutes are oppressed no more or less than those of the other ethnicities. Jerusalem's treatment of the many ethnic groups within the Empire was even-handed in the face of the anti-Semitism that was open and endemic in society. This was the same city with the same pervasive prejudice against Jews where the young Adolf Hitler arrived in 1908 to study art and where he absorbed its messages about fear and blame.

---

21 Ludwig, Stefan. *Aufstand im Bordell*. Documentary for Austrian national channel OR2, televised on 5.2.24.

Biography

Else Jerusalem was born in Vienna as Else Kotányi in 1876 on November 23 as the third of six children. Her mother, Henriette Deutsch, was Viennese, and her father, Maximillian, was a prosperous wine merchant originally from Hungary. Else attended public school and then spent eight semesters at the University of Vienna studying philosophy, though, as a woman, she was not formally enrolled and, therefore, was not awarded a degree.[22]

When she was twenty, the newspaper *Wiener Rundschau* published two of her literary sketches. Two years later, in 1899, the German press Georg Heinrich Meyer published a highly controversial collection of three short novellas about female sexuality, entitled *Venus am Kreuz* (Venus on the cross or Venus crucified), a reaction to Leopold von Sacher-Masoch's 1870 scandalous novel *Venus im Pelz* (*Venus in Furs*) about sado-masochistic relationships. Her novellas touched upon the subject she would return to a decade later in *Red House Alley*: prostitution.

By 1901, she was an influential voice in the middle-class women's movement.[23] That year she gave a speech, "Über unsere Erziehung zur Ehe" (On our education for marriage), which was published the following year with the title *Gebt uns die Wahrheit* (Tell us the truth). In it, she advocated for sex education for young women so that they were informed about the reality of married life. That same year, she married Alfred Jerusalem (1874–1945), a wealthy Jewish psychologist and factory owner. They had a traditional wedding in

22 Wunderlich, Dieter. "Else Jerusalem" *Buchtipps und mehr*. Dieterwunderlich.de/Else-Jerusalem.htm. Wunderlich's careful, succinct biography is the source for much information. Brigitte Spreitzer's "Else Jerusalem—eine Spurensuch" is the other source, which includes private letters.

23 Lorentz, Elizabeth "Review of *Shifting Voices: Feminist Thought and Women's Writing in Fin-de-Siécle Austria and Hungary*." *Modern Austrian Literature*, Vol. 42, pp. 113–15.

the *Stadttempel* or main temple of Vienna. The following year, she gave birth to a daughter, Anna Edith Jerusalem (1902–1987), and one year after that to a son, Friedrich "Fritz" Albert Jensen (1903–1955). During her first pregnancy, she published a collection of stories, *Komödie der Sinne* (Comedy of the senses).

During the first years of the 20th century, Jerusalem participated in the Modernist literary group Young Vienna. Here she associated with prominent writers, such as Hermann Bahr, Felix Salten (of *Bambi* fame), and Arthur Schnitzler. She wrote articles for local journals, such as her critique of Otto Weininger's influential 1903 *Geschlecht und Charakter* (*Sex and Character*) in *Die Zukunft*. Her invitation to attend the Riehl trial was recognition of her prominence as a feminist intellectual. She undertook research into prostitution and the lives of prostitutes toward what became *Red House Alley*.

The success of her novel gave Jerusalem the opportunity to travel for readings. At a reading in Vienna in the summer of 1909, she met the embryologist Viktor Widakowich (1880–1930). They fell in love. Alfred Jerusalem agreed to divorce Else, but Viktor's wife Antonia signed the papers only begrudgingly. In January of 1911, Else renounced the Jewish faith and was baptized in the Lutheran Church. That same month Else and Viktor married and set sail for Buenos Aires, where he had accepted a position on the faculty of the University of Buenos Aires and as director of the City's zoo. While the newly married couple was on board, Antonia committed suicide by swallowing morphine, leaving their two-year-old son behind.

In April 1912, Else, who now used the Christian surname Widakowich, gave birth to a daughter, Miriam.

She returned to Vienna in 1913 to take custody of her daughter Edith, but she and Alfred decided instead to leave Edith with her father. Viktor was in any case opposed to having Else's older child with them in Buenos Aires because he was unwilling to have people there know about their earlier marriages. Her marriage to Viktor lasted five more years and was effectively over by the time she published her first story in Argentina, which was translated from German into Spanish, "El chal de encajes" (The lace shawl) in 1917.

Else returned to Europe in 1925. On board the ship, she became acquainted with Albert Einstein, with whom she corresponded for years thereafter. She returned to Europe again in 1928 to visit Berlin and see Oswald's film of *Red House Alley*. Her name and that of her novel were featured on posters for the film while the leading players in an all-star cast were not even mentioned.[24] While she was in Berlin, the publisher Erich Caesar Reiß published her play *Steinigung in Sakya* (Stoning in Sakya) under the name Else Jerusalem-Widakowich. The play was performed in Erfurt, Germany, while she was in the country.

Else Jerusalem-Widakowich was never comfortable in Buenos Aires. She missed the cultivation of Vienna and found the society of European émigrés in the rapidly growing, "colonial" city crass. Rather than accustom herself to upper-class society there, she conducted ethnographic research on Indigenous women.[25]

Miriam Widakowich remained in Buenos Aires and married a German, Siegfried Weyland. She had a daughter, Ines, who was born in 1936. Ines's attached letter tells of her awareness of her grandmother's novel, which she read in its entirety for this publication.

Else's daughter Edith was allowed to travel with her husband Herbert Stein to Argentina since her mother was there. Edith remained from the Annexation of Austria in 1938 until the end of the War, when she returned to Vienna.

In 1939, Else Widakowich published *Die Dreieinigkeit der menschlichen Grundkräfte* (The trinity of intrinsic human strengths), a treatise on education, with Verlag die Gestaltung in Zurich. This

---

24 Filmplakat: *Im Haus zur roten Laterne* (1928), Filmposter-Archiv. Filmposter-archiv.de/filmplakat.php?id=30332

25 Bittermann-Wille, Christa. "Jerusalem, Else" *Frauen in Bewegung* 1848–1938. fraueninbewegung.onb.ac.at/node/898.

work admonishes caregivers and educators to allow children to explore their own inclinations and talents. It was a manual on hands-off parenting that also endorsed nurturing by other caregivers. The uncoupling of biological motherhood from mothering is a radical leitmotif in her novel.

Else Widakowich died in a hospital in Buenos Aires in 1943 of cerebral sclerosis. The same year, National Socialists killed her older sister Hilda Pollak, a painter in Prague, and Hilda's husband, also a well-known painter, in Dachau concentration camp. A younger brother, Paul, is also presumed to have died in the Shoah. The City of Vienna has put a *Stolperstein* or commemorative cobblestone in front of his house with the dates 1885 to 1944.[26]

Else's son Fritz grew up in Vienna with his father, used the surname Jensen, and became a medical doctor. He joined the Communist Party and formed an underground medical service for fellow travelers. He was a physician with the International Brigade in the Spanish Civil War (1936–38), then served with the Chinese Communists against the Nationalists and the Japanese. After his mother's death and the defeat of Nazism, he returned to Vienna. Fritz worked as a journalist in China in 1953 and died two years later in a terrorist bombing on board a flight to Indonesia with a Chinese delegation.[27] A monument in Beijing commemorates his work. In 2008 the University of Vienna regranted Fritz Jensen the medical degree it had revoked in 1940.[28] Although he knew his mother only the first seven years of his life, he was an idealist and activist—though in a separate key—much like his mother.

26 Kotányi, Paul. Geni.com/people/PaulKot%C3%A1nyi/6000000028046736743.

27 University of Vienna *Memorial Book*. Gedenkbuch.univie.ac.at/en/person/friedrich-albert-fritz-jerusalem-jensen. Retrieved 22.3.24.

28 University of Vienna *Memorial Book*. Gedenkbuch.univie.ac.at/en/person/friedrich-albert-fritz-jerusalem-jensen. Retrieved 22.3.24.

The happy end, reception and reality

The penultimate chapter of *Red House Alley*, "Solitude," finds Milada traveling to Styria to look into setting up a home for children. Here, two older professional men hear about her intention and about her difficult life. They support, respect, and admire her. Her seeming fate as the object of ineluctable scorn is instantaneously reversed. She has a fresh start and will offer that to others, insistent that they feel no obligation to her or anyone as charitable benefactors. Milada simply wants them to feel free.

This happy ending has troubled reviewers from the moment Jerusalem's novel was first published.[29] Reviewers who applaud the book's realistic portrayal of prostitution often are unsettled by the felicitous conclusion, which holds its own anguish.

But a home for pregnant single women and their children was not a fantasy of Jerusalem's. A woman she most likely knew through her work in the feminist movement in Vienna and through her work with Coelestine Truxa, the other woman at the Riehl trial with Jerusalem, was Bertha Pappenheim (1859–1936), a close friend of Truxa's. Pappenheim had been the patient of Josef Breuer whose case Sigmund Freud famously wrote up as Anna O. She had given him the term "talking cure" for psychoanalysis.

Pappenheim had taken charge of her own cure,[30] and at age thirty moved with her mother to Frankfurt, where her mother's supportive family lived. There Pappenheim founded social and political reform groups for Jewish women. She also set up relief organizations, such as community homes and schools for children.

---

29 Spretizer, Brigitte. Idem.

30 Kaplan, Marian. "Bertha Pappenheim." *The Shavi/Hyman Encyclopedia of Jewish Women*. 31 December 1999. Jewish Women's Archive. Encyclopedia/article/pappenheim-bertha. Kaplan quotes Ernest Jones as saying she healed herself. She was the real discoverer of the cathartic method.

She believed the most important work of her life began in 1906, when she founded the *Mädchenwohnheim* (Home for Girls) in Neu-Isenburg for illegitimate children and Jewish women endangered by prostitution. This home offered them an education to become self-supporting. Pappenheim was adamant the residents feel autonomous and not feel they were the recipients of charity.

Compare her feelings about independence with those of Jerusalem's Milada. When Milada reviews the architectural sketches for the home, she stops at the inscription over the door:

> Here Milada's friend and supporter, the Doctor, had inked in with red letters:
>
> From Our Strength as a Tribute to God.
>
> Milada pulled out her pen, struck through the inscription and wrote:
>
> From Our Strength as Tribute to Our Life.
>
> With the stroke of her pen she had abolished any need for children who were to live in the house to feel indebted to charity.

It is very likely Else Jerusalem patterned the uplifting ending of her novel on Bertha Pappenheim's work. Neu-Isenburg flourished under her hand, despite strong opposition from the conservative Jewish community. By 1928, there were 152 residents in the home. Pappenheim died there in 1936. In the wake of *Kristallnacht* (the Night of Broken Glass, November 9–10, 1938), the home was burned to the ground, and in 1942 the Gestapo sent the remaining residents to the concentration camp Theresienstadt.

Jerusalem's imaginative story was, in fact, an historical reality—but one that ended in an unimaginable nightmare.

Postscript

by Ines Weyland

This is a personal account of my relationship with my grandmother Else Jerusalem: of how I became acquainted with her long after her death and well past my youth, of how I became interested in her life and work and grew to respect, admire, empathise with her, and love her.

This account is the result of a voyage of discovery prompted by the fact that academics interested in her work contacted me. They referred me to information about her on the Internet I was not aware of. Ariel Magnus, an Argentinian novelist, got in touch with me because he was planning to write a novel in which Else and Albert Einstein, whom she befriended while they were both on a boat to Argentina, were to be protagonists. He asked me for information about her, and this led me to research her life and work further. He translated her treatise "Gebt uns die Wahrheit!" (Tell us the truth) into Spanish. Reading it, I discovered that she was a feminist writer as well as a philosopher and a sociologist.

Around that time, I found out there was an English translation of her novel with the title *The Red House* and read it. It was only later that I learned it was an abridged version. It was not until Dr. Stephanie Ortega finished translating the full original German version that was I able to read it in its entirety.

After watching the first program, "Vienna 1908," in the 2014 BBC television series *Bright Lights, Brilliant Minds: A Tale of Three Cities*, in which James Fox interviewed Dr. Brigitte Spreitzer, I began to realize the significance of the novel in its historical context. This prompted me to read *The Red House* a second time. I then made a connection between the life of its protagonist and Else's experience of emigration to Argentina. Milada, the daughter of a prostitute, who was brought up in the brothel where her mother worked, made the difficult decision to give up her relationship with the man she loved, a decision that proved to be the right one for her personal fulfilment and happiness. My thought was that Else, in deciding to leave her husband to go to Argentina with my grandfather Victor Widakowich—though fully understandable because she was in love with him and he was an exceptionally talented man—made a big sacrifice. Vienna would have continued to foster her creativity much more than the more sterile and alien culture and unfamiliar language of Argentina. She was also embarking on a relationship and life that would lead to emotional loss and turmoil. These thoughts filled me with great sorrow.

However, it comforts me to know that in spite of all her difficulties in Argentina, she carried on writing and produced short stories, two plays, essays, and a philosophical treatise. She also kept actively involved with progressive movements as well as with a circle of intellectuals and writers. My mother, Miriam, told me that she went back to Europe frequently. These trips were perhaps a way of keeping in touch with her roots and gaining inspiration from her exchanges with European writers and thinkers. More importantly, as Brigitte's research shows, in her later years she finally found peace of mind through reflecting on, analysing, and learning from her painful experiences.

In working with Brigitte, with whom a very rewarding relationship developed, and exchanging ideas with her, I was encouraged to look for more information about Else and found documents and letters I did not know I had in my possession. They were in a suitcase I brought to this country after Miriam's death, whose contents I had never examined carefully. I took them to Brigitte in Graz. She read them over a summer and kindly transcribed them all. She then brought them to me in London because she did not want to risk them being lost in the post and summarised the important passages for me. These letters helped us fit together many of the pieces of the jigsaw of Else's life, and we acquired a better understanding of what living in exile in Argentina must have been like.

In spite of knowing and understanding Else better, many gaps are left. I regret not having asked Miriam the questions I so much wish I had asked her while she was alive. Miriam, of course, spoke to me about Else, and she wrote a very brief biography in an album with family photos that she gave to my son, Miguel. The following is one of the passages:

> Of her forebears I know very little. My mother told me that her father, Maximiliano Kotanyi, was Hungarian, an adventurous man, who liked good wine, women and his violin, taking little care of his wife and six children. My mother had a very difficult character, which manifested itself in the context of family life. On the other hand, she possessed in great measure what the French call "esprit." Because of her witticisms, her *joie de vivre*, and the jokes she made up, which were sometimes sharp, although always original, she was the centre of attention within social circles both in Buenos Aires and Vienna. At our mansion in Belgrano (a district of Buenos Aires), she

> hosted some of the most illustrious personalities of the time, including the President of the republic, Hipolito Irigoyen, and wealthy ranchers, who felt honoured by her invitation. She also befriended scientists, including and Albert Einstein. It was amusing to see the great scholar accompanying her to the market and helping her with her shopping for food, whilst on other occasions attending together the many social gatherings organised by the most prestigious mathematicians that sought to honour the great scientist. All this happened in 1925... My mother's end was sad, as she died from arteriosclerosis, alone and mostly forgotten.

Notes and cards Miriam wrote to Else as a child, which Else kept among her correspondence, show how much Miriam loved her. I believe that as an adult Miriam's perception of Else was very much influenced by their difficult relationship. She also idolised her father, Victor, who separated from Else when Miriam was very young. As a result, she never conveyed to me that her mother was not only a talented writer but also a philosopher and radical feminist thinker. Nor did she tell me about her substantial literary output. Did she not know about it? I also wonder if she reflected on the possibility that Else's creativity may have been hampered by the strictures of a very conservative society.

One thing I remember that Miriam told me is that Else was only half Jewish. I now know this is not correct. Both her parents were Jews. Miriam never identified with her Jewish heritage as she was sent to a Catholic convent school since Else had converted to Christianity when she decided to marry Victor and move to Argentina. It is clear that Else was not religious either before or after her conversion. Miriam also rejected religion in her adult life, and so did I.

Recently I learned that many of Else's relatives died in concentration camps. Before then I was horrified by the accounts of what the Nazis did, but the profound distress these discoveries elicited in me was something new. I remembered another occasion when I felt great sadness at the realisation Edith, Else's daughter by her first marriage, had been alive until 1987, had been in England twice, and yet, because I did not know of her existence, we had never met. My mother had never told me that she had a half-sister, who, as I discovered through my research, had spent eight years in Argentina to escape Nazi persecution. Some years ago, I met Shoshana Duizend, who was a close friend of Edith's and kept her copious diaries. What I learned from these diaries is that Edith did not have a positive opinion of Else's novel. I imagine she must have felt resentful towards her mother, an understandable feeling, given she felt her mother had abandoned her as a child. What Edith probably did not know is that Else had wanted to take her to Argentina, as I found out through one of Victor's letters, but she did not because he was opposed to it.

My mother did, however, tell me a lot about Fritz Jensen, her half-brother, whom she may never have met. I inherited his book *China Siegt* (China victorious), published in Vienna in 1949. From the dedication at the start of the book, I learned that he was married to a Chinese woman called Wu An, and from photographs at the end of the book I could see what he looked like: an interesting and kind face.

I know that Else's wisdom and strength of character enabled her, to a great extent, to overcome the personal travails she faced in life: two daughters who were not close to her, a son who became a communist and moved to China and with whom she must have completely lost touch, two marriages that broke up, a granddaughter, me, who was six at the time of her death and with whom she was not encouraged to have a relationship. Then there was her admission to the psychiatric hospital where she died, devoid of the care and affection that she needed and which Miriam could not provide. All of this evokes a lot of sadness in me. This is why this has been not only an intellectual journey but also a very emotional one.

I wish to thank Brigitte Spreitzer for her in-depth research into my grandmother's work and life and for furthering the revival of interest in her literary career by contributing to the publication of the 2016 Austrian edition. I also wish to express my gratitude to Stephanie Ortega for all the time and effort she devoted to this English translation, which has made the book accessible to me and my son Miguel and to English-speaking readers. Her afterword contains a wealth of information about the book's historical and cultural context, and her erudite analysis of the novel will hopefully lead to a fuller understanding and appreciation of its background and purpose as well as to an awareness of Else's contribution to radical sociological and feminist thinking. Having now read the whole text, I see my grandmother's novel evinces a very good understanding of human psychology.

Else Jerusalem was born into a Jewish-Hungarian family in Vienna in 1876. She studied at the University of Vienna but as a woman was denied a diploma. Her first book, *Venus am Kreuz*, a collection of novellas, was published in 1899. She married in 1901, had two children, and remained active in intellectual and social affairs. In 1909, she published her novel *Der heilige Skarabäus* (The sacred scarab), based on her independent research on prostitution in Vienna. It became a bestseller throughout the German-speaking world. In 1910, she divorced her first husband, married the embryologist Viktor Widakowich, and emigrated with him to Argentina. There, she had a daughter and wrote for German-language journals. She died in Buenos Aires in 1943.

Stephanie Gorrell Ortega grew up in the United States and graduated from high school in West Germany. She attended Mount Holyoke College and the University of Texas, Austin, where she earned a doctorate in German literature. She has taught at the Free University of Berlin; S.U.N.Y., Buffalo; the University of the Witwatersrand, Johannesburg; and Texas State University. She has edited and translated with *Poesie*, *Slavic Review*, and *Dimension*. She lives in Austin, Texas.

Sophie Haydock is an author, editor and journalist based in Folkestone, Kent. She is also curator of Folkestone Book Festival. Her debut novel, *The Flames*, is about the women who posed for the scandalous Austrian artist Egon Schiele in Vienna a century ago. It was named by *The Times* as one of the Best Historical Fiction Books of 2022. The Italian translation, *Le Fiamme*, won the Premio Letterario Edoardo Kihlgren for debut novel in Milan. Sophie's second novel, *Madame Matisse*, is about the women who were integral to the life of the French artist Henri Matisse. Visit: sophie-haydock.com.

Red House Alley
By Else Jerusalem

First published in this edition by Boiler House Press, 2024
Part of the UEA Publishing Project

Translation based on *Der heilige Skarabäus*, Fischer
(Berlin, 1909) as reissued by Henricus BoD (Berlin, 2020)

Cover Design and Typesetting by Louise Aspinall
Typeset in Arnhem Pro

ISBN: 978-1-915812-36-0

Milton Keynes UK
Ingram Content Group UK Ltd.
UKHW020812251024
450128UK00009B/190

9 781915 812360

LITTLE DEMON *in the Details*

NORDIKA NIGHT

Little Demon in the Details

Book Cover by Rotoscope Design

Editing by Jenn Heathers

Line Editing by Sarah (sh.editsbooks)

Contact: nordikanight@gmail.com

ISBN: 978-1-7389757-0-9

Content Warnings:

- some violence/blood/murder

- a main character with childlike coping methods

- minor dominant and submissive tendencies

- panic attacks/PTSD

- abandonment issues

- a manipulative character (more in a fun way)

- neglectful/absent/cruel parents

- instances of degradation/degrading terms during sex

BRATTITUDE:
a mood or mannerism reflecting brattish or immaturely rebellious behaviour.
Comes with bitchfits.
It's a whole personality.

Little Demon in the Details

NORDIKA NIGHT

1 Blake

I'VE NEVER SEEN A guy in lingerie before. From behind, I almost think he's a chick. The way the bodysuit hugs his taut little ass and dips into the cinch of his waist almost fools me. But when the cop pulls his hands behind his back, making his hips jut forward, there's no mistaking the bulge in the front of the panties. His skin might be smooth, but it's as toned as it is tight. His legs are slender, but there's a quality to them that isn't soft and curvy. He's masculine in feminine clothing. He's boyish without being girly. The lace and the silk don't downplay his gender but enhance it instead.

"It's a sex club!" he shouts at the cops. There's no malice in his tone. He's playful, almost cocky about the trouble he's landed in. The insolent glint in his eyes suggests this is all a game to him, and the way he's sticking his ass out and biting his bottom lip, giving the gathered crowd a show, proves he likes the attention. *Craves* the attention.

"It's a strip club," the cop tells him sternly. "No sex allowed."

I watch from the sidewalk, narrowing my eyes at this guy in black satin and lace. There's a moment where he's being manhandled, not disrespectfully, and he's contemplating. Thinking. Trying to decide what kind of trouble he wants to get into. His hips *almost* thrust. His ass *almost* presses into the officer's groin. His cuffed hands *almost* cop a feel. I see it all plain as day. The deviance in him and the dislike for authority he's trying to mask in flirty nonchalance.

Then my brother ruins it.

"Goddammit, Ben." He grabs this guy by the bicep, talking to the cop like this has happened before. "He wasn't selling sex. I promise. He's just a bit touchy." The cops back off a little, knowing who my brother is.

A *bit touchy*? The guy is all devil and no angel. His size doesn't make him innocent, and his boyish looks don't detract from his danger. He's a ticking time bomb, but I don't know what his explosion entails. How does my brother know him?

My brother, Bronson, wraps a coat around this Ben kid's shoulders, and I light a cigarette to study the scene before me. Details have always been my thing, but I'm having a hard time deciding what's going on here, how this relates to Bronson, and why we're meeting outside a strip club in the first place.

The guy—somewhere in his late teens to early twenties—continues to treat this whole thing like it's a joke, even going so far as to proposition a cop. Bronson smacks him upside the head for that, and I don't miss the flare of anger in Ben's amber eyes. Deviant little fucker, isn't he?

I inhale nicotine and watch a woman I don't know step in, taking over for my brother. Once she shows up, the cops take their hands right off the boy, almost looking like they wished they'd never been called here. A bunch of apologies are shared, and then the woman is leaving with the kid. He looks over his shoulder, lace-clad ass barely peeking out from the bottom of Bronson's coat, and gives me a mischievous look.

I just take another drag and watch him go.

When the cops leave, the crowd disperses. Half go back into the club and the other half carry on down the busy sidewalk. Bronson runs his hands through his dark hair and shakes his head at me with an exhausted laugh.

"Well, welcome home," he says, pulling me in for a side hug. "Nothing like the threat of arrest as a welcoming party." He claps his hands on my cheeks. "Fuck, you've gotten older, Blake."

"It's been five years," I agree. I'm not typically a sentimental person. Attachments and me don't get along, even ones to my family. I'm loyal to my brothers, but I don't need to see them every day to keep that bond strong. We talk when we need to, and we keep our space when we don't. "Who's the boy?"

"Boy?" Bronson scoffs. "He's a fucking demon. Come on. I'll explain over a coffee."

I look at the strip club he asked me to meet him at, raising a brow in question.

"I never wanted to meet you here. It's just... fuck, it's a long story." He starts walking towards a 24/7 diner down the street, so I smoke and walk next to him in silence. Five years since I've been in this city. Five years since I've seen my brother and the rest of my family. Five years since I committed my first murder and buried the body where no one could find it, passing a test that led to five years away. Five years since I left to live out my dad's expectations for me. Five years of becoming someone new.

They were life-changing years, and I'm not the same person now as I was back then.

I toss my butt down the sewer and follow Bronson inside. The place isn't as retro as I remember it being the last time I was here. It's had a renovation, an upgrade, and it gives off the country charm appeal in the middle of the city. The sign tells us to seat ourselves, so I scan the packed place, the smell of midnight breakfasts and coffee comforting me.

He picks a booth along the window, which works well for me. I like being able to pay attention to more than one thing at a time, and if my brother is my only focal point, I'll get awkward because eye contact isn't my favourite thing. I'd rather watch than be looked at. With coffees ordered and menus in front of us, I lean back in the booth to really look at him.

Bronson is eight years older than I am, and it shows. He's rugged and worn from whatever he's been doing the past five years, but he covers it in nice clothing and a suitable haircut, appearing classically rich rather than shoddy rich. His dark hair is longer on the top, one of those styles that requires products, and his eyes, the same dark blue as mine, are tired.

"Dad call you back home?" he asks me, even though he already knows the answer.

"Something like that. Who's the kid?"

The waitress drops coffee and a bowl of individual creams at the table, so I doctor up my drink while he takes his time getting his explanation in order. I've never minded shitty coffee. The bitterness speaks to me and the sugar and creamer I put in mask that bitterness like my personality masks the distaste inside me. I'm cynical by default, and I don't know if I learned that mentality or if I was born with it.

"Dad's making me marry someone," Bronson says, looking defeated about it, like he's already gone through all the arguing and fighting with our dad.

"What about Miranda?"

The question hurts him. It's clear by the look on his face and the unabashed pain in his eyes. He schools it a second later, taking a drink of coffee. "I mean, I'm still with her. The marriage is a business arrangement and nothing more, but she's only going to go along with that for so long. She'll leave me, and Dad won't give a shit."

"So… the kid?" Is that who he has to marry?

"That's her brother." He rubs his temples, clearly more stressed than he is excited to see me. "I'm marrying Olivia Palmerston."

What the actual fuck? "*The* Palmerstons? Those ones?"

"Those ones."

Dad *has* been busy while I've been gone. The Palmerston family is old money, affluent wealth, and high society. They own over half the land plots in this city, spanning throughout the country, and whatever they don't own, they have a hand in controlling. They're shady people who make clean money through even shadier deals, but on paper, there's nothing evasive or criminal about them. They bully their way to success, and if the person can't be bullied, they buy them. It's when they can't be bullied or bought where our family steps in. While the Palmerstons are rich and clean, we're rich and dirty.

"A Palmerston and a Carter," I muse over the union of our families. "Never thought I'd see that."

Bronson sighs, waving off the waitress to give us a minute. "Apparently, Will Palmerston has been hiring Dad, and even Grandpa, for decades. The whole marriage thing came about when our family took over the natural gas refinery. We aren't just dirty hitmen for hire anymore, Blake. Dad bought a mine, and with that mine comes government control, funding, and politics. Which pipelines run where and what green bullshit we're doing to save the planet. With the Palmerstons owning everything else and us owning the mine, I guess that meant it was time to unite our families. Fucking bullshit if you ask me."

I'd conveniently been left out of all that. The Carter family earned their wealth through illegal work. We're in the security business. If someone needs to be found, relocated, protected, or killed, you call the Carter family. We are a secret only the elite and wealthy know about, but money doesn't discriminate against reputation. We've worked with mafias and cartels, industrial companies, billionaires, landowners, political figures, and even smaller governments in other countries. We're a small family, but our reputation over the past century has reached global levels.

"So, I'm guessing you don't know why you're home?" Bronson asks.

"He just told me to come home and prove myself. Said he had a job for me." My dad is the biggest asshole I know, but I don't hate him for it. He's had to be harsh in order to raise us to be killers and protectors.

"Things are changing around here, man. And Will Palmerston is losing his shit over the kid. I swear to fuck if he got arrested tonight, we would have been hired to off him. He's Olivia's younger brother. He's twenty-three, but he's a damn handful, to say the least. That's why I asked you to meet at the strip club. We got a call that he was there, and... I just knew it'd need monitoring."

"Ben?" I recall what Bronson called him outside the club.

"Yeah, that's what he's called because Will doesn't want him using his first name. It's a family name or some shit, and apparently, he hasn't earned the right to it." He laughs. "Olivia cares about him, which is why she helped him outside the club tonight. He's a full-time job, Blake. And I'm sick of watching out for him."

I wrack my brain for the complete list of the Palmerston family tree, but I'm blanking on who he could be by name. "What's his real name?" I ask again, not even sure why I'm intrigued. Maybe because I know what it's like to be the youngest and most overlooked member of the family, or maybe because that lace riding up his ass crack is still on a loop in my head.

"Mercer Bentley Palmerston," Bronson says. "Goes by Ben."

Mercer Bentley Palmerston. Pretentious as fuck name. "Why was he in cuffs tonight?"

Bronson snorts. "Because he's a fucking brat. Pissing off his family and acting out is his hobby. No, his job. You'll get to meet him this weekend. We're having an engagement dinner." He shakes his head at that, calling the waitress back. "You ready to order? Let's catch up. We've been apart for five years, and neither of us is the same."

MY DAD RIDES THAT line between military and executive. He'd never be caught dead in a suit, but he wears black tactical gear covered by a nice jacket. He's rich but likes to get his hands dirty, smart enough to run the business but craves the labour, authoritative and commanding but unhinged and a touch crazy. He's my role model.

"I got the report," he says, showing me through his new home. I don't know when he bought it, but it isn't the home I grew up in. It's bigger, fancier, and more secure. A bunker above ground. "You far exceeded your training. Master Nero said he was hard on you, but you took it and found your place."

I nod because I don't know what else to do. I haven't seen this man in five years, but he didn't even say hello. When we turn twenty-five, as long as our father deems us fit by making us pass a test, we go for training. To learn the things he can't teach us while running a business. We're trained under masters, special ops guys, weapons specialists, military leaders, medics, private investigators, and combat specialists first. After we've graduated through combat, we're trained in spy tactics, technology, and team planning.

For the past five years, I've learned every way possible to kill someone, find and keep someone alive, torture for information, deal with a hostile subject, and work as part of a team or as a solo entity. I've learned how to spy, study patterns, recognize malignancies, and be discreet. I liked the training. Kept me busy and gave me a life skill not many have. Where I draw issue is… my dad. I love him, in the only way he raised us to love, but I do not enjoy the prospect of being at his beck and call. Perhaps I just have to adjust to it. Maybe trusting him is the first step.

"You met with Bronson last night," he says, not phrasing it as a question because he already knows.

"Yes."

"And he told you about the engagement to the Palmerston girl?"

Girl? She's thirty-five. "Yes."

Dad nods curtly. "Good. This marriage will unite two very powerful families, Blake. I know you're probably thinking I'm being greedy. Speak freely."

Hate when he says that. "A little. Bronson is already in love with Miranda. Has been for what, eight years now? Why him?"

"Are you suggesting yourself?"

Fuck no. "You're greedy to unite families for money. Selfish for demanding your son sacrifice everything for you to have it."

Dad smiles, liking my honesty. "I'm not doing it for money, Blake. The Carter family is more than enough for me."

"Then why do it? Why tie us to the Palmerstons?"

"In time. Be patient." He gestures to the patio out back. "For now, I have a job proposition for you."

Without so much as a drink offer, I follow my dad to the patio and light a cigarette while he snips the end off of a cigar. I can already tell this meeting won't be casual; it's a business meeting and a welcome home wrapped into one cold encounter. I'm not surprised, and to be honest, I'm more than okay with it. I don't need warm welcomes and fake smiles. I did his training, and now I'm back, ready to be his soldier.

"What's the job?" I ask, ready to get it out of the way.

"The Palmerstons," he says. "It barely took any convincing for them to agree to this union. I want to know why."

2 Blake

An engagement party with the Palmerston family is a big affair. Guys like me don't belong in places like this. Mansions that resemble country clubs with wait-staff, high-end party favours, and decorated gardens aren't my scene, but I've learned the art of blending in.

While the Palmerston family is vast and cultured, the Carter family is smaller and more intimate. There must be over seventy-five Palmerstons here, and that's probably not even all of them, but there are only twelve Carters. My dad and his three sons, my uncle and his four kids, and my aunt and her two children. My aunt is the only one out of my father and his siblings who is married, but her husband is away on a job.

That's it. The entire Carter line. We have a few hired members of our organization, but their identities are known only to a select few of us, and in all fairness, I'm sure I don't even know them all. They don't know my guy either.

As I look around the party, I note all the acting. This is a pissing match more than an engagement party, and the top elite families in the area are here. So why didn't Will offer his daughter's hand in marriage to one of them?

Olivia seems alright, almost as reluctantly accepting of this marriage as Bronson, but the two of them put on a good front. More acting.

"You grew up."

I turn to find my middle brother, Brandt. "I thought you were on a job?" I grin, giving him a quick hug.

"Who says this isn't my job?"

I wouldn't put it past Dad to give us the same job. I'm surprised he put me on this in the first place. Most of us, all my cousins and my brothers, are put on a singular job as a test when we first get back from our five-year training. Dad wants to evaluate us, so we go on a heist, a murder, a torture, or a ransom negotiation to see how we handle it. Why did I get a long con job as my first? Looking into Olivia's family isn't going to be easy, but I've got a few ideas.

"Just be glad that's not one of us," Brandt says, tilting his drink at the head of the garden where Bronson and Olivia are receiving congratulations. "Sometimes it pays not to be the first-born."

I doubt that has anything to do with it. I have a feeling our dad is punishing Bronson for something, or at least trying to prove something to him, and testing me and Brandt to see if we can dig anything up on the Palmerstons. "No doubt."

"Still as quiet as ever." Brandt nudges me. "You've never been a big talker."

Listening is more my thing. People reveal a lot when they talk, even if they aren't blurting secrets. It's all in the tone of their voice, how much enthusiasm they pack behind their words, the hand gestures, and the rambling. The tight lips mean more, but lies are my favourite.

"Don't have much to say," I tell him.

We both turn at the sound of shouting. Something crashes inside, and the sound of hushing follows. Brandt raises a brow at me, but from across the room, my dad gives me a subtle nod. He wants me to check it out. I pat Brandt on the shoulder and head inside, seeking the commotion but being subtle about it.

A younger woman who looks a lot like Olivia has her back to someone and her arms out. She's shielding someone while her mother hisses curses at her. The kitchen staff carry on preparing appetizers and drinks, trained to ignore this.

"He's not allowed to be here, Samantha!" their mother seethes. "I'm calling a service to take him away."

"No!" Samantha shouts. "No, you can't, Mom. You don't understand what they do to him there."

"I don't care. I'm tired of this. I'm tired of him interfering with family business. If he won't follow the rules, he isn't welcome here."

As Samantha keeps arguing, I get a glimpse of the lingerie kid. From my position at the far end of the kitchen, I catch sight of his dark clothing. He's out of place here, neither dressed for the event nor dressed like he was that night outside the club. No lingerie in sight. His hoodie is black and baggy, and his sweatpants are dark grey, but his hands are busy. The little shit is adding something to a mixing bowl right behind their backs. His dark hair peeks out the front of his hood, and he's confident enough to not even check if they're watching him. He's someone who gets away with a lot.

"He's going back to the reform home. Your father will sign off on it."

"No!"

This gets Ben's attention. A look of true fear washes over his face, but he wipes it clean and remains defiant when he looks at his mother. "Fine. Not like I give a shit."

He totally gives a shit. He's terrified. I don't know what kind of reform home they sent him to in the past, but whatever it was, he's afraid of going back. If anyone is going to spill secrets about the Palmerston family...

"Mrs. Palmerston?" I step into view, letting them get a good look at who I am. They know me as Bronson's brother and my father's son, so they respect me. Recognition registers, and just as she's about to tell me she's in the middle of something, I butt in. "I'm here to take Ben."

"Oh," she sighs, her shoulders sagging. "I should have known he'd already have it planned. Very well. You're taking him to the home?"

I nod. I'm taking him to *a* home, but not whatever one she's talking about.

"Please, don't do this," Samantha begs. "I'll watch out for him. I'll make sure he stays in line. Please."

"You've tried. You've all tried. He's... maybe this time will help." Mrs. Palmerston sighs, like it actually does hurt her a little to send her son away. Not enough to stop her, though. "We must make an appearance at the party. Please, make sure he gets there safely."

I nod again, and when Samantha turns to say something to Ben, I wait.

"I hid a phone for you there last time, do you remember where?" she asks him. He rolls his eyes, but he nods. "Call me. I'll find a way to get you out of there, Ben. Just... just be patient. You don't make this easy on yourself." That's about all she has to say to him, and on her way by, I see the worry in her eyes. I stare at her, hoping she can read the silent truth in my eyes. *I'm not taking him there.* She tilts her head at me, and I nod. Done. Her shoulders sag and she gives Ben one more look before leaving.

The prick glares straight at me while he continues to dump whatever powder into the mixing bowl. No shame. No respect. No remorse. There's even a wicked glint in his eyes as he does it, never once taking them off mine. Bronson wasn't wrong when he called this guy a demon.

"Pack your shit," I tell him.

"They usually ship it there."

"Pack it anyway."

He smirks, knowing I'm up to something. "Going to follow me up to my room to make sure I pack that lacy little number you eye-fucked me in the other night?"

"Mm," I agree, nodding my head at the door.

He scoffs, tosses the little baggie into the trash can, and sways his tiny hips as he walks. All swagger. Too bad his sweats are too baggy for it to have the desired effect. Amateur. I lean against his closed bedroom door while he takes his sweet-ass time packing every item of clothing in his closet. Suits, lingerie, lounge clothes, pyjamas, you name it. He brings it all. He packs a laptop, his phone charger, and some sort of handheld gaming device, and then he stares at me like I'm wasting his time. A part of me wants to demand he carry it all down to my vehicle, but I don't have the time to get crafty with demanding respect. That can come later.

I pick up half the bags and hang them over his shoulders, forcing him to carry his share, and I take the rest. The walk down the hall and out of the estate is infuriatingly slow because he *accidentally* drops all his bags a million times just to bend over and put his ass in my face. I have the patience of a saint, so fuck you, little demon.

I catch Bronson's eye on the way out, give him a little nod, and then do the same to my dad. Without another word, the valet brings my Denali around, and I make him load all his bags in the back. When he complains, I don't give a shit and just tell him whatever he doesn't load gets left behind. No skin off my back. When he goes to open the back door, I slam it shut and nod at the passenger door.

"I'm not a driving service."

"Not rich either. This vehicle is... so common." He cringes at it.

"Good for blending in. Get in. Now."

He digs his heels in, proving once again that he has some form of a problem with authority or orders. Not sure which yet.

I bend down to get in his face, my blue eyes on his amber ones. "I'm leaving. Right now. You're either coming with me or you're going to that reform home with them. You choose." I walk around the hood, climb in, and start the vehicle. When I put it into gear, he huffs and dramatically opens the door, throwing himself onto the seat like it's the hardest thing he's ever done. I take off.

"Seatbelt."

An eye roll, but he does it.

He sulks for a bit. Well, he doesn't say anything. Instead, he fills the silence with huffing, sighing, foot tapping, and fucking with the window button. After he gets tired of that, he asks me where we're going. And he doesn't fucking stop.

"Seriously, man. Are you taking me to some dungeon to fuck the life out of me? Wouldn't put it past my parents to hire someone for that. It'd be poetic, in a way. They hate my sexuality, and so they'd love to kill me with it."

Pretty sure he loves the sound of his own voice.

"Why haven't I seen you before?"

"Are you mute?"

"Take me through a drive-thru. I'm hungry."

"Where the hell are you taking me?"

"I have to piss."

"I will jump out of this vehicle and scream bloody murder if you don't answer me. I'll do it."

I have no doubt he will. He seems like the type. Dramatic, no fucks given to how much the show ruins his life. He wants attention, but only certain kinds of attention. I don't know anything about him, but it's obviously a cry for help. Did his parents ever listen to him, or is he so ridiculous he got their attention and then squandered it? I've been in a vehicle with him for thirty-five minutes and I'm already debating opening the door and shoving him out. His family probably wouldn't mind.

I tune him out and focus on the road. I have a few options for housing. My Dad bought me an apartment for my return, just like all of us get when we complete training. I got to pick it and everything. But do I really want to take this little hoodlum there? I also own a studio apartment, which is my favourite. It's industrial, wide open, woody and modern, but it's mostly all one big room and I don't know this guy well enough yet.

I turn towards the east side of the city, deciding on the gifted apartment from my dad. At least I'll be within close driving distance to the rest of my family, and the kid can have his own bedroom until I kick him to the curb. That's mostly for my benefit.

By the time I pull into the parking garage under the building, he's gone quiet. I don't trust his quiet because it means he's up to something. I park in my spot and lock the doors as soon as he tries to get out.

"Hey!"

"What have you been doing the past ten minutes?" I ask, voice level, eyes calm but hard.

"Nothing." He gives me the puppy eyes. So I keep waiting. "I was just being a good boy. Don't you want me to be a good little boy?"

Manipulative little fuck, more like. "I'm not letting you out until you tell me. I've got time."

He holds his ground and my eye contact for way longer than I thought he would. He's a fucking brat, but he's the easiest person I've ever held eye contact with, and I don't know what that means. Ten whole minutes later, he scoffs and puts his hands into his hoodie pocket. Out comes my credit cards, the key card to the elevator, about a hundred dollars' worth of cash, and my pack of cigarettes.

I fucking hate that I'm impressed.

I hold my hand out, and he sets everything in my palm, but he makes a show of stealing a single cigarette and tucking it behind his ear, just so he gets away with something. I'll let him have it this time. My wallet, which usually stays in my back pocket, got moved to my jacket pocket for the drive. I hate sitting on it. I won't make that mistake twice.

"Enjoy your cigarette," I tell him. "You just bought yourself the stairs. And all your bags. I'm on the top floor, so you might have to make a few trips."

He crosses his arms and stares at me like he won something. He thinks he can just leave.

I point to the security guard and the cameras, and then I hold up my cell phone. "Hey, it's Blake Carter. There's a guy in my car, dressed in black, and he needs to make his way up to my apartment on his own. Don't let him leave the building."

He produces my lighter from his hoodie and lights his cigarette. "I'll be all sweaty and sore when I get there. Will you rub me down in the shower?"

I grab the lighter and take his cellphone for good measure, get out of the vehicle, and walk to the elevator. My heart is pumping, but I can't tell if it's from frustration, rage, or fatigue.

Also, not sure why my dick's a bit stiff.

3

Mercer

FUCK HIM FOR MAKING me do this. If he thinks I'm this easy to humiliate, he's in for a long fucking game. I'm a goddamn master at button-pushing, and it won't take me long to find his. I'm not dumb enough to think he's actually helping me by taking me away from the family who wants to put me into a fucking mad scientist lab. He has an agenda. I'll just have to figure out what it is.

I'm sweaty and exhausted by the time I get all my shit up fifteen flights of stairs. It took me three trips, and the only reason I did it was because I tried to escape first. He has this place on lockdown, and before I make another attempt, I'll have to do more reconnaissance.

I've raised my fist seven times to knock on his door, but I can't bring myself to do it. It feels like letting him win, and I can't stand that. Nevermind the fact that I already did all these steps three times over and practically gave him the win. There's a camera above the door, and I know he's watching me, but the asshole won't make the first move and open the door for me. He's going to wait me out, see how long it takes me to submit, and put the rest of whatever plan he's concocting into place after he learns all my weaknesses. I wish I stole a second cigarette to kill more time. But I wasn't lying when I said I needed to pee, so that, and only that, is what makes me knock.

This asshole, whose name I only learned because I peeked at his driver's licence when I stole his wallet, opens the door with a peace offering. A bottle of water. I take it, hesitant to take a drink because I wouldn't put it past him to roofie it or something. Then I remember I'm the manipulative one, unscrew the cap and chug it until it's dripping down my chin and neck. Blake watches, but his eyes won't follow the drips. He either has great restraint, is a sadist, or isn't gay. I'll find out eventually.

"Did I pass your test, master? Do I get a gold star?" I blink at him with pure innocence.

His jaw twitches, but he locks it down. Damn. "Grab your shit." He stalks past me to grab a bag and then reconsiders the position. *Smart man.* Won't allow me to be between him and his lockable apartment door. I smirk at that. He grabs the bags closest to him and forces me to carry the rest.

The apartment is furnished but doesn't feel lived in. The furniture all looks and smells new, and the countertops and cabinets barely have fingerprints. It's an open-concept layout with a giant kitchen, a dining area, and a living room with a fireplace and mantel. There's a grand piano in the corner, overlooking the city through floor-to-ceiling windows. Real *Fifty Shades* style. Oh, I hope he makes me his sub. Where's the red room?

After peeing, I sadly learn there's no red room. Just his master bedroom, a bathroom, laundry room, and finally the spare bedroom he drops my bags in. It's a nice room, and everything is tidy and clean, still containing that new furniture smell. The far wall is all windows, looking over the downtown area of the city as the sun sets.

"Did you just move in or something?" I ask, forgetting to be difficult for a second.

"Yes." He pushes the ensuite bathroom door open, showing me it's there. "This room is yours for as long as... until it isn't. Make yourself at home."

"Why?" I ask, heaving all the bags off my shoulders. I'm sweaty and disgusting, and grossed out by myself. "Why bring me here?"

"Would you rather go wherever they were going to send you?"

No. "But why? You don't know me."

"My brother is marrying your sister."

"So, you're doing it out of the goodness of your heart? You know my parents will kill you for this. Probably hire your dad to do it."

"Probably," he agrees. "What's the name of the reform home they take you to? I want to be ready if your parents ask about it. Have a story in place."

"Northern something," I tell him. "Reform for troubled boys who need to find their path to righteousness." Gag. "Gay camp." It's a lie. No point in telling him about the mad scientist lab on the property because that's where I really get sent, and fuck my parents for it.

He's already got his phone out, probably Googling it. "Not gay camp. Behavioural correction camp." He raises a brow at me and I blush for the first time. Okay, so maybe my parents don't care that I'm gay, and maybe they don't even care that I'm troubled. But they do care about my lack of respect and all the bad press I bring to the family. Or at least, that's what it looks like to my mom. My dad just straight up hates me and my brain.

I hide my guilt and sultry up my voice. "Is this going to be my new behavioural correction camp, Master Blake?"

"Call me that again and it will," he gruffs. "Shower. Get dressed. Meet me in the kitchen in an hour." He leaves without a response. And he still has my phone.

I grew up in luxury that felt like a cell, and this place is no different. It might not be as fancy and over the top as my family home, but it is just another frilly prison with a warden to keep me in line. Did my father hire him to keep me contained, or does Blake Carter have a hidden agenda? He wouldn't be helping me out of the goodness of his heart, so why did he keep me from that facility?

I still have his business card in my pocket. It came out of his wallet with the credit card and I'm not sure why I'm keeping it, but I run my fingers over it and check out my new prison cell. The bedroom is nice, new, and spacious enough for me to get up to no good. The bed is a king, settled with the headboard against the wall, so I'll definitely be changing that. I need a wall on the side to sleep against, and I might be tiny, but I'll find a way to shove it where I need it. There's a little reading nook with a chair and a lamp, and set up like a display item is a violin. Weird. Does this apartment have a music theme or something?

I crease the business card as I walk into the ensuite bathroom. A soaker tub sits in front of more floor-to-ceiling windows, one way glass, I'm assuming. The shower is big enough for three, and the stone and tile work look well done. Spinning, I catch my reflection in the vanity mirror. Still look like a fucking joke, I guess. I put zero effort into my appearance today, wanting to be moody and broody in my hoodie and sweats, but my wild hair matches the vibe, and my puffy eyes show that *zero effort* doesn't apply to my sleep schedule. As in, it takes me a fuck ton of effort to be able to sleep.

I want to defy his order to shower, but I really am gross and sweaty from the trip up here. Fuck him for making me do that. I lock the bedroom door, then the bathroom door, and then wait, listening to see if he's going to do anything about it. When I hear him in the kitchen, pots clanking around and bottles of something clacking together, I relax. Just a bit.

I make the shower hot and fast, wrapping myself in a towel to rifle through my bags. Well, shit. I forgot all my skincare products and there's nothing in the bathroom cabinets but unwrapped toothbrushes, toothpaste, and extra bottles of the same shampoo, conditioner, and body wash from the shower. I'll have to rectify that immediately, and I'm sure I can find a way to make him feel like shit about it.

The shower is a vulnerable place, but not because I'm afraid of showing some skin. Nakedness doesn't scare me; being unaware and slippery does. With that said, I throw on a new pair of sweatpants, acting like I don't give a single fuck about being here, and slip into a tank with massive armholes. Nipple slips are fun and I'm curious to see if he'll look. My radar is a bit off and I can't read him yet. He looked that night outside the club, but I couldn't tell if he was analyzing me like a job or eye-fucking me like I'd accused him of doing.

Just to give the finger to his one-hour stipulation, I wait another twenty minutes.

I leave my feet bare, my toes squishing into the cushy rug of the bedroom and then chilling against the wooden floor of the hallway. He's left his bedroom door open, so I peek inside, trying to get a read on him, but it's as bland and brand new as the rest of the apartment. No clues other than a single open duffle bag with clothing spilling onto the bed.

Blake is in the kitchen, putting together a pre-made salad, and pulling trays out of the oven. I'm sure he just ate at the engagement party, so is he doing this for my benefit? I try to spy on him, but he's impossible to sneak up on.

"Sit," he demands, and my back straightens. My feet stay rooted, refusing to cross the threshold of hardwood to tile that marks the territory line between us—the kitchen and the living area. He doesn't even look at me, focused on the salad, but a ghostly smirk hints on his lips. "You must be hungry," he amends. "Want to sit?"

Yes, I'm hungry, you dick, and fuck you for already knowing me. I choose to lie. "I already ate."

"Mm," he hums, adding nothing.

Mm? What's *Mm* mean?

When the buzzer rings and Blake goes to the door, I sit at the island while he isn't looking. Still feels like a win, so I pick cucumbers from the salad and listen to him at the door, secretly hoping it isn't anyone from my family.

"I can take them. Thanks." Blake closes the door and returns with bags of groceries. He side-eyes me at the island, munching on cucumbers, but he doesn't comment on it. He holds up three different salad dressing options, and I pick all three just to be annoying, but he still doesn't so much as curse at me.

Committed to all three options now, I make myself a little bowl and layer balsamic on top of Greek and mix it all together with sundried tomato. "What's *Mm* mean?" I ask.

"No meaning. Just a sound."

"Mm," I try it out. "A condescending sound."

"If that's how you take it." He puts groceries away like I'm not even here. He's still wearing his outfit from the party, and as good as he looks in casual partywear, it doesn't suit his energy. He looks like the kind of guy who should be wearing tactical gear or those sexy spy suits, covered in blood with a murderous high in his eyes. Or a prison suit. He could rock a prison onesie, no doubt. Or a towel, slung low on his hips to show off six abs and a V.

Speaking of blood. I know about the Carter family, and I know what they specialize in. "Am I a job?" I've already asked, but I'm waiting on an answer.

"What makes you ask that?" He turns, sliding another salad bowl across the island. "Can you make me a salad?"

"Say please." I smile at him. He pulls the bowl back and I grab it from him. "Jeez. I'll make the salad."

"Doesn't the childish act get annoying?" he asks.

"Not really."

"You like reducing yourself to nothing more than an annoying nuisance?"

"Are you trying to tell me I'm something more than that?" I slide his bowl of salad to the stool next to mine. "Am I a job?"

"What makes you ask that?" he asks again.

Ugh, he's hard to distract. "Feels like something my dad would do. Or my uncles. Really any of them. Pretend to ship me off to a reform home and then... *oh, no! Ben never came home*!" I mock my mother's voice. Hate her. Hate her most of all because she feels sorry for me but doesn't have a fucking backbone.

"Ben?" he asks, pulling one more tray from the oven and putting it on a coaster thing on the island. "That's what you like being called?"

I study the assorted finger foods. Nothing classy like my parents would have. It's all chicken fingers and meatballs, and little pastry things with spinach and feta inside. "That's the name I'm allowed to be called." Still stings. Even after all these years.

"I'm not going to call you that," he says, putting balsamic on his salad.

"What're you going to call me? Let me guess! Little boy?"

"Haven't decided yet."

"Sweetheart?"

"Mm."

"You could always go with a classic. Most guys like you just call me babe. Or baby boy."

"I'm sure they do," he says. "Probably also call you pet, brat, good boy, bad boy, and slut."

"Mm." I smirk into my salad and get brave enough for a meatball.

"Mercer," he says, making my head whip in his direction. "Think I'll just call you Mercer. That's your name, isn't it?"

A rush of something fills me up from toes to tits, and I can't place the suffocation of it. Pride? Unworthiness?

How can I mix those two up? I've never earned that name, not even when I was a kid. I've been unworthy of the family name right from the start, and I know my parents regret giving it to me and only me. Whoever originally had this name is long dead, and here I am, the little family embarrassment, bringing shame to the legacy of it. I look away from his eyes, not wanting him to catch any hint of vulnerability.

"So, for the twentieth time, am I a job?"

"No," he says. "An impulse. I improvised."

I bite the meatball off my fork, letting my teeth scrape against the tines. "Because this situation somehow benefits you?"

"Mm," he says. "Get me that bottle of tequila and I'll tell you how it benefits me." He nods across the kitchen.

I tilt my head at him, studying.

"I'm good at reading people. You don't like authority and being told what to do, so here's my shot at deciding if you work on a rewards system. Gonna go get the bottle in exchange for information, or shall we try the next method?"

"Mm, what's the next method?" I bat my lashes. Liking this *mm* business.

"I drag you the fuck over there to get the bottle like a *good little boy*, and then you whimper at my feet all night because you might hate orders and authority, but you fucking crave that shit in your sex life like the *little slut* you are," he says, a timbre to his tone but not a single increase in his volume of voice. "If you want the next method, I can find a way to add in the rest of the pet names. Your choice, *baby*."

My nips are hard and I'm grateful I wore a baggy tank and pants. With a cute as fuck smile, I slide off the stool and feel his eyes on me while I strut my shit over to the bottle of tequila. I set it on the island and push my ass out while I reach up into the cupboard for glasses, but humiliation soon wins.

"Too short?" he asks, smug as fuck. "Maybe if you stick your ass out a bit more."

I hate him. Decision made. He steps up behind me, chest to my back and upper thighs to my ass. My breath hitches so I cover it with a scoff, but there's no hiding the goosebumps on my arms.

"Five foot eight?" he guesses, voice whispering against my ear.

"Five foot nine, thank you." I spin so we're face to face, hoping it'll trip him up. It doesn't. Like, at all. "Seven? Seven and a half?" I ask him.

He presses his hips against me, letting me feel all seven and a half inches he's packing. "Eight, thank you." He comes down with two tumblers and backs away. "Come eat. I know you didn't eat any of the food at the party. You just poisoned it."

I snort. "It wasn't poison. I'm not that... dramatic."

"Mm," he says, waiting for me to sit back down. Once I'm on my stool, he goes on. "Two reasons. The first being that reform camp, or whatever the fuck it is, hasn't worked on you yet, and judging by what your sister said, bad shit happens to you there." He looks at me, but I give nothing away. "The second reason is that... I don't fully trust your family and I'm kind of wondering why they agreed to this marriage between Bronson and Olivia."

I pout my lower lip. "So, it's not a sex thing?"

He eyes me up and down, and when he's done, I can't tell if he thinks I'm pathetic or sexy. Just fucking tell me if you're gay! *Gah!* I'm usually pretty good at telling, but Blake Carter remains a mystery so far.

I pick up a chicken tender and dunk it in my salad dressing. "You think I'm privy to all the inside information with the Palmerston family? If you haven't noticed, I'm the pariah. The black sheep. The family member they shove in a closet and only parade around on occasion so no one assumes they offed me. Oh, and my leash is very tight when they parade me." *And I'm usually drugged.*

"And what, you want everyone to think it's your deviant flirting and cumslut personality that put you in that dark closet?" he asks, almost like he knows it's something else. "I don't buy it. You're acting out. The sluttiness is a direct *fuck you* because of something else."

He really is good at reading people. Luckily, he'll never find my red button because it's been buried so damn deep I can't even find it anymore. "Are you slut shaming? Because being a cumslut is so much more than a personality."

"Sure it is. But in your case, it's a cry for attention."

I toss the chicken on the counter and shove my salad away. "I want Thai food."

Blake simply smiles.

4 Blake

I WAVERED BACK AND forth about putting cameras in his room, but in the end, I decided not to. Not because I respect his privacy, but because he wants attention so badly, he'll use the cameras as a chance to put on a show.

After hanging up the phone with a contact who is looking into that reform home for me, I listen to grunting, groaning, and scraping sounds from across the hall. Soon, imaginative curses join in, and after a while, a frustrated groan containing more rage than I thought him capable of having. I climb out of bed in nothing but a pair of sweats, and cross the hall, listening outside his door for a moment. I don't even try the handle because I know it'll be locked, but when I hear him call himself useless, my chest cracks a bit.

I knock. "Mercer?"

"Don't call me that!" Bratty to his very core.

"Need help with something?"

"No. Fuck off."

"Okay." I have no plans to fuck off, but it gets his ass moving to the door. It swings open, and his flushed, sweaty face almost smashes into mine.

"Thought you were fucking off?" He composes himself. "Thought you didn't need me?"

"Well, it's not my fault your bed weighs a metric fuck ton and your floors are so new that I'm honestly a little guilty about scratching them." He glances behind him where there are actual gouges in the hardwood from the legs of the bed. "Just a smidge, though."

I don't care about floors, but I'll let him sweat it. "Need the bed moved?"

"I... yes." Vulnerability. Just a flash of it. "Against a wall."

I lean against the doorframe and cross my arms. "Okay, no problem. Carry on."

He scowls at me, and the harsh expression looks nice on his pretty face. "Blake."

"Mercer."

"I told you not to call me that."

"Mm."

Wanting to hold his ground and his independence, he gets back to pushing the bed. He leaves even more gouges in the floor, sticks his ass out real nice, and makes sure to look over his shoulder at me every few seconds to confirm I'm still watching. Oh, I'm watching. Taking a break to fan himself, he decides to pull his shirt off, using it to wipe his forehead.

"I'm usually the one on the bed, not thrusting into it," he says, all sultry-like.

"It shows. You have zero strength." When that gets a nice glare from him, I add, "You're pushing with your arms. Get your legs into it."

"They're still shaky from all the stairs," he pouts. "Aren't you going to help me?" Another pout. Puppy dog eyes. Batting lashes.

So fucking cute. "Did you ask for help?"

"No," he scoffs and gets back to pushing. After moving the massive bed less than three inches and gaining another sheen of sweat on his lower back, he mutters a very quiet, "Help."

Not willing to waste yet another opportunity to press up behind him, I lean into his back, put my hands on the bed beside his, caging him right in, and barely contain my boner when he shivers. "Say please," I throw his taunt back at him.

"Help," he mumbles again instead.

"Where are we pushing it? We're not moving in the direction of any wall, so what did you have in mind?"

He presses his ass into my groin, and I bite my lip to hide any reaction. "It's stupid, but..." He points to the wall of windows.

"That counts as a wall?" I ask. "That's safe enough for you?"

He turns his head. "How do you know it's for safety reasons?"

I grab his chin and force him to look at me, all serious now. "Is that safe enough for you? Answer me honestly."

His breathing stutters for a second, but he lets it out calmly. "I think so. I... I want to try it. It's the farthest from the door."

I study his eyes and find them genuine, even though he's trying to hide it. "Hands on the bed then." I release his jaw.

Together, but mostly me, we leave a trail of gouges across one half of the room until the side of the bed butts up to the window wall. There's a small gap where he could roll right through, but he stuffs a few pillows down there and seems satisfied with it. As he sprawls out on his back, chest heaving after all that *hard work*, I step back to... look.

I've had two bi experiences, but never with men like him. My experiences start and stop at the athletic type, and Mercer is the farthest thing from a jock. He's smaller than me by a lot; at least five inches in height and probably a sixty or more pound weight difference. He's all bite and no brawn, but I don't think that makes him a weaker opponent.

Mercer has learned how to use his body as a weapon, a distraction, and a taunt, and I have no doubt he's just as dangerous as I am. He's slender without being delicate, firm without being overly toned, and graceful while being rambunctious. He's the bull *and* the china shop. His dark hair is mussed up and messy on purpose, adding to his wild boy image, but it doesn't overly fit his lingerie energy. Maybe he likes it that way.

He gives off bottomy vibes, but I get the impression he craves more control than he lets on. He's just never found anyone to experience it with. Sure, he's submissive, but it's the fight to submission that riles him up, and I have a feeling that if he wins the fight, he expects to be the dominant one. He's exciting.

Truly a brat through and through, though. He's going to find all my buttons and push them without care. He doesn't give a shit that I'm a trained killer because there's at least a small part of him that has a death wish. He respects himself to some degree, but he also doesn't think he deserves that respect, so he neglects and degrades himself, too. He's a clusterfuck, and disarming him like he's a bomb is intriguing to all these new parts of me.

Yes, I want answers and information out of him, but I also want him to, I don't know, rise up stronger than he is right now. His strength is currently superficial, and I want to teach him how to live and breathe that power and use it as a weapon.

"Well?" Mercer asks, snapping me back to the here and now. "Did you analyze me and figure me out while you were eye-fucking me for the second time?" He makes a show of running his hands over his hips, up past his chest, and around his throat. My eyes follow, but I hide the attraction in my gaze. "Need me to put on something see-through and lacy so you can finish?"

Lace and silk act as body armour to him, but I haven't yet figured out what he's protecting himself from if he's so promiscuous. "I'll give you the full report when I'm done with it," I say instead. "Goodnight, Mercer."

"Don't call me that."

I close his door behind me and leave it up to him to lock. I leave my door open, climbing into bed with a hard dick and a filthy mind, and one ear waiting to hear if he locks his. About an hour later, after edging myself unintentionally, the lock clicks and I smile to myself. An invitation, was it?

THE NEXT MORNING, I'M up and agitated by six. Mercer has been fucking around in his room with music blaring for two hours already, and as much as I want to go in there and throttle him, I leave him be. I need him to think he has some control, and when he realizes he hasn't succeeded in drawing a reaction out of me, he'll switch gears and try the next thing.

Unlike the diner coffee, the latte I make at home isn't bitter. Whoever stocked this apartment did so with fine taste, and I resent how delicious the coffee is. On my third one, my phone rings.

"Blake," I answer, walking with my coffee to gaze out at the city fifteen stories below. "What'd you find?"

"It's legal," Aaron says, getting back to me about the reform home. "Well, the part they show to the world is legal... but I did some digging." Of course he did. That's his favourite line. "On the outside, it's a treatment centre for youth with behavioural disorders or borderline personality disorders. Highly rated and recommended, especially among the elite. It's clean on paper, has a lot of government funding, and is even part of a university study program. Caters to youth, but has an adult wing as well."

"But?"

"But it's straight out of *One Flew Over*."

"*The Cuckoo's Nest*?"

"Yeah. It has a dark side. Old school methods, sure, but even new ones. Military ones. Dangerous and completely illegal ones."

"Like?"

"Mind manipulation, brainwashing, mind mapping, and not that I can find proof yet, but I think they're even experimenting with brain chips. I've got someone on the inside now, looking for Ben's file. Nothing in the computer system, but I wouldn't expect it to be tied to the main facility. Whatever is in his file there is the standard bullshit about him being manipulative and coercive. Says he's got borderline personality disorder and frequents different personas to get his way."

I don't doubt that, but I don't think he has a disorder. His manipulations come from a place of protection, and maybe that lines up with a medical condition, but maybe not.

"But that's just what looks nice on paper. That's what is on file in case anyone ever looks into it. My girl on the inside is digging, and she never comes up empty, so I'll get back to you when I know more."

His girl on the inside is his wife. She's a therapist, so she'll have good reason to snoop around, and Aaron is a master at fabricating reasons. I trust them both as if they were family—sometimes even more than family.

When I feel Mercer listening from the hallway, I don't react. I want him to trust me, so he can eavesdrop all he wants for now.

"Send me a list of doctors and professionals who were listed in that file. Even if they're fake names or doctors that have never seen him, I want to look into them."

"I'll look, too. You got it. No record of any other Palmerston ever being there within the past few decades, but there was a Palmerston there about seventy years ago. Redacted first name, but I'll find it."

"What's the age out? He's twenty-three, so if it's a centre for youth, how do they justify sending him there?"

"Twenty-five, with an exception for up to thirty-five if the patient has a child ego, which I'm assuming is a dissociative identity disorder thing. According to his limited file, he was in the youth wing."

"Alright. Thanks, Aaron. Let me know."

Information gets me places, but I'm not a hacker. Aaron is one of the only friends I trust with this, especially because I want to keep it from my dad for now.

"It's in a building on the property over from the main facility," Mercer says, standing in the hall without making a sound. "I eavesdropped on that whole conversation, and you're old, so your phone volume is really high. I heard everything."

"Thirty is old?"

"Ancient."

"Feel like telling me everything you know about that place?" I ask, motioning to the kitchen. "If I make you coffee?"

"And breakfast?"

Crafty. "Fine."

He smirks like he won, skipping over to the island in a pair of little shorts and a hoodie, looking like a bedheaded mess. Cute, though. "Also, I need skincare products. I left all mine at home."

It's on the tip of my tongue to tell him this is his home now, but I bite it back. If his parents are the type to send him to a place like that, I'll never let them get a hold of him again. It has nothing to do with me maybe wanting to fuck him and everything to do with the vulnerability I sometimes see in his eyes.

I pull his phone from the dish towel drawer and slide it across the counter. “Order whatever you want. It’s your room. Your space.”

“Whatever I want?” It’s a dare, but I nod anyway.

“You have money?”

“Tons of it. Hush money.”

I figured.

I go searching for frying pans and utensils, having no idea where anything is in this place yet. While he shops and I make breakfast, I ask him questions.

“How many times have you been there?”

“Seven.”

“What age did it start?”

“Eleven, I think. Or maybe I turned eleven there.” He gasps at something. “So expensive! I’m buying it anyway.”

“Do you remember what they did to you? Were you always in the secondary building?” I crack a few eggs in the pan and scramble them because… fuck over easy. I’m not that good of a cook. The coffee machine finishes, so I slide him a latte.

“I remember everything, *Blake*, but I won’t share it all with you. The first time I went, I stayed with another kid in the main facility. I was there for, I don’t know, maybe like a few months or something? But when I went home, Mom and Dad weren’t happy with whatever way I’d been fixed, and the next time I was in the other building. It’s not as creepy as a dungeon, but it has padded cells and white rooms and really bright lights that make you crazy.”

I keep my back to him, stirring the eggs and dropping bread in the toaster. “Why’d they send you there?”

“For being gay.”

Evasion. “Why’d they really send you there?”

“Because I’m… smart. Or I was.”

I turn around to face him, but he keeps his face in his phone. “Smart?”

"A quick learner, good memory, analytical mind, pretty eidetic memory when it comes to numbers and sequences, patterns, things like that. 46125047560925." He glances at me, smirking.

No fucking way. "Is… is that my credit card number?"

"Yes, I'm using it to buy my new things." He grins again. "Want me to ramble off your address, social insurance number, licence number and plates, and the details on your business card?"

"You stole my business card?"

"By accident. But I'm keeping that one as a souvenir."

The toast pops, so I butter it and plate the eggs. Simple breakfast, but whatever. I remain standing on the opposite side of the counter, wanting to keep this conversation going.

"Eat."

"Make me."

Fucking hell, I will if he keeps this up. "Show some respect, and if you can't muster respect, show some appreciation for the breakfast I just cooked for you in the apartment I'm letting you live in to avoid that place."

"Fiiiiine," he complains, dramatically pressing a button on the screen of his phone. "I'm done shopping anyway. And it's not like you're doing it out of the goodness of your heart. You're using me for information."

True.

I join him on the other side of the island. We eat for a little, the silence full of tension and scraping forks. His scraping fork because he's annoying like that. To cover the sound, I ask, "So, your dad didn't like that you were smarter than him?" It's a guess.

Mercer looks at me. "You know, you're the only one to ever think that."

"Am I right?"

"Are you gay?" he asks.

"No."

"Do you wanna fuck me?" he asks with no shame.

"You make my cock hard, but I haven't decided if your personality turns me off yet. Am I right about your dad?"

"Partially right. And you get hard *because* my personality turns you off. Don't act like my attitude isn't an aphrodisiac to you. You're itching to put me in my place."

"Where's your place?"

"Don't you want to knock me down a few pegs? Kick my pedestal? Knock me off my high horse and all that?"

"No. I think you manage that pretty well on your own." His face falls, but he schools it. "I'm not your daddy, Mercer. I'm not here to put you down and keep you quiet."

"Then what?" he asks.

"I'd rather make you *scream*; help you claw your way to the top. You'll need an attitude adjustment to get there, but I don't mind using your own tools against you." I grab his stool and pull it closer to me. "I won't fuck you unless you're begging for it, and we both know your pride won't let you beg. Guess we're at an impasse."

At my limit of restraint, I leave him there to finish his breakfast. I have places to be today, and if he wants to tag along, fine. He's not a prisoner here, but he's smart enough to know his parents currently think he's at that facility. The ruse won't last long, and I'll have to hold my ground when I'm confronted about it.

5

Mercer

WITH MY CELLPHONE BACK and Blake out of the apartment, I call my sister to let her know where I am. By early afternoon, both my sisters have bullied their way into Blake's apartment, and now I can't get them out. I don't hate my sisters because they're stuck in the same life I'm stuck in. The difference is that they're both allowed in that life where I'm not.

I can't hold it against them, but I also can't help being envious. They care, but they also blame me for most of it. They see my rebellion and think it started out of nowhere, so fuck them for having blinders on. Samantha is the only one who ever actually tries to make a difference for me, even if she isn't successful.

I hate pitying myself, but I'm only human. How is it my fault that my dad hates me? Over the years, sure, I've given him plenty of reasons to despise me, but that was only after he sent me to that disgusting place when I was a kid. I hate that man as much as he hates me, and my hatred has nothing to do with him being better than me. He's my father, and he single-handedly ruined me. On purpose. And my bitch of a mother went along with it just to stand at her husband's side. Fuck them all. The whole Palmerston family, even my sisters, at times.

"I don't get it," Olivia says. "Why would he kidnap you?"

Leave it to her to think me so unworthy of saving that someone like Blake Carter wouldn't do something drastic to protect me from a terrible situation. I mean, he has ulterior motives, but even with his sketchy morals, it's more than either of my sisters have ever done for me. The difference? Blake Carter isn't afraid of my family.

"I'm not a prisoner here." But I'm smart enough to stay put for a few days. If my parents find out I'm here instead of where they want me to be, I really will be kidnapped. I need to win Blake over to my side before that happens. Too bad I've learned to be so insufferable that I've completely forgotten my people-pleasing skills.

"Yeah, but he's up to something, right?" Olivia asks Samantha. "It's a play. It has to be."

Punch to the little confidence I have left. Thanks.

"I don't know," Samantha says. "I saw the look on his face when he took Ben. It honestly seemed like he was just trying to help him. Keep him safe."

My chest wants to warm at that, but my diminished worth reminds me I'm nothing but a hindrance and an annoyance. Blake doesn't care about me.

I'd rather make you scream and help you claw your way to the top.

I swallow unease and get itchy. My skin is on fire and my thoughts won't slow down. They're all too negative and hateful to be productive, and the longer I simmer in them, the more hostile I'll become. I need a release, a way to burn off this agitation so I don't become fucking homicidal and stupid. A shaky breath leaves my lips while my sisters bicker unaware.

Nobody cares about me. Life would be easier for Samantha and Olivia if I died, and they no longer had to worry about me. My parents would be pleased with the news, and they'd probably use my funeral as a business strategy to play on sympathy. I don't have any friends, never went to a traditional school, don't have any life skills or talents, and I'm not good enough to become someone's boyfriend. Alone in birth, tortured through childhood, and scared and alone during adulthood. Life has always been bleak, but it's hitting hard right now.

My sisters talk about me. Above me. Ignoring me.

My teeth chatter with how hard I'm trembling. They don't notice. No one ever notices. My mind leaves the apartment to delve into different realities where I'm the joke of my own life, and then it comes back to the apartment, reminding me I have no right to be here. I'm sweating, shaking, fidgety as fuck and about to explode. Can I hear anything?

"Get out."

"But wait! Just let us say goodbye! Tell us what you want with him."

"Get. Out."

Time is spinning and my legs are cramping. Am I running? My escape route is so cluttered I can't even find it, but my body is fatigued like I've been sprinting through the maze of it for weeks. The double-walled glass latte mug comes into view, dried milk foam crusting on the inside. How long has it been there? When did I last drink a latte? I'm thirsty. My throat is screaming for a drink, but my mouth is flooding with saliva. Nauseous.

A door slams. I feel it but can't find it. I'm unworthy. I'm nobody. I'm unwanted. I'm scared. Nobody sees me.

"Mercer."

I'm unworthy of the name.

"Mercer, look at me."

I'm looking but I can't see.

"I'm going to touch you." Hands jar me from my state, but not enough to find reality. "Tell me what kind of help you need."

All the help. Or don't help me. Let me die. Let me go. My mind is running, running, running, unable to latch onto a command. I'm telling it to stop, but it won't listen. I have no authority over my own brain, and now I'm spinning out to space with no tether.

"Get on your knees, Mercer." Dominant. Controlling. A command.

Without knowing why, I slip off the stool to kneel. A blanket of calm settles on top of my panic, both battling for the win.

"Look at me." I look at black pants and black boots. "Look up at me, little boy. Now."

Little boy.

When I look up through blurry eyes, the calm blanket wins. My trembles lose their vibrancy, and my lungs take in a satisfying breath. Body awareness comes back to me, and the ache in my knees has nothing on the ache in my groin. I swallow the saliva in my mouth and breathe harder than should be required. My body is telling me we fought a war, but I can't remember if I won.

"Better?" Blake asks, voice firm.

I nod and swallow.

"I'm taking you to bed."

"No," I cry.

"You need rest after that. We can talk about it later."

I sink down to the floor, unwilling to walk to my room. I just got my mind back! Don't lock me away to lose it again. "No." My eyes burn, and my fight-or-flight instinct is all fucked up because they both think survival is on this floor. At this man's feet.

"I'm taking you to bed." He grabs my arm and flips me over until he can pick me up. I ragdoll to make it harder for him, but he's bigger than me. Stronger than me. "Time to sleep."

"No!" I scream this time. "No. Please, no. Not alone." I bury my face in his neck, hiding from him while clinging to him.

He pauses his steps, but I can't look to see where we are. "You're afraid to be alone?" When I don't answer, he strokes a hand through my hair and asks again. "Mercer, answer me."

"Not always. Just right now."

"I'll sit with you on the couch, okay?"

I nod against his chest.

When Blake tries to set me on the end of the couch, my fucked-up instincts keep me clutched to him so hard he can't pry me off. With a sigh, he settles with me on his lap. My fingers end up in my mouth and my cheek gets sweaty against his chest, but I can't move. I can't. Not yet. I don't even know this man, and he's probably more of a danger to me than I know, but I… I don't have anyone else. He's better than a stranger in a club for now.

Blake pulls my fingers from my mouth, but a minute later, I end up sucking on them again. I don't know why. Maybe because it's distracting. Comforting. Familiar. Something to satisfy a few of my senses. Touch, taste, the sound of my sucking. When he pulls them out again, I whimper.

"Shh." He runs a hand down my back and then he's prying my lips open with his thumb hooked on my bottom teeth. I open willingly, letting him push two fingers all the way back to my throat. He pushes them in and out, making saliva drip down my chin to soak into his t-shirt, and then he stops forcing it. He stays still, so I end up holding his hand to keep his fingers in my mouth. A new taste. A new texture.

I squeeze my thighs together and peer up at him. He's watching me, but I can't read the expression on his face. It almost looks caring, but I've never seen it on anyone before, so I can't be sure.

"You okay, Mercer?"

I suck on his fingers and nod.

"Tell me what you need. With words."

He tries to take his hand away, but I hold it there until I'm ready. I release his wet fingers and let drool drip down my chin. "Call me… a pet name." *Remind me I'm nobody but look at me while you do it. Show me what caring looks like and let me decide if it's real.* See me.

He licks his lips, his blue eyes darkening. "Tell me what you need, little demon. What's going to feel better?" When my thighs squeeze again, he notices. "You need to come, baby?"

"Yes."

"Such a little slut, aren't you?"

My legs tremble. "Yes."

"So fucking desperate for it," he growls, shoving his fingers into my mouth again. He fucks my throat with them, staring me straight in the eye. When I try to look away, he uses those fingers in my mouth to keep my head from turning. "You're such a little slut that you're going to come in your pants, aren't you?"

I choke on his fingers and love the burn of it. I nod, my hips thrusting into nothing and my thighs squeezing so tight they ache. The material of my sweatpants isn't restricting enough to rub, but my boxer-briefs do.

With Blake looking at me with heat in his eyes, his fingers in my mouth, and his boner against my ass, I whimper and whine, already losing my resolve in an unsteady state. I slide my thighs together, building that ache in my gut, so fucking desperate to embarrass myself in front of him. When I reach down to rub my cock, Blake shakes his head at me with a growled, "No."

I'm moaning like a tramp around his fingers, wiggling on his lap, eyes leaking tears, and my face covered in saliva. I don't stop staring at him, and when he slowly shoves his fingers as far as they'll go down my throat, my hips move, and the orgasm starts.

"Good boy," he purrs.

I fucking lose it. I come in my pants, slicking my thighs and my groin while my eyes roll back and my lips part even more. Blake pulls his fingers from my mouth and the most desperate, anguished moan of my life breaks free. I try to bury it in his chest, but he grips my chin and forces me to look at him while I come. It's extending the orgasm and embarrassing me at the same time, and I have no idea why I'm into this, especially since I just had a fucking breakdown, but I start to shake with the force of it. Exhausted, I slump against him, breathing against his neck, ready to pass out and never think of that again.

"Tell me why that helped," Blake demands.

I don't have an answer for him. Not one I'm willing to admit.

"Tell me."

"I don't know," I cry out. *Because it was so jarring it forced my brain to stop spinning.*

"Stand up."

He orders me to stand three more times before my shaky legs allow it. I stand right in front of him, between his spread legs, ready to run the hell away and hide in my closet until I can face this. Blake doesn't let me.

"Tell me or show me. Your choice."

I can't tell him because I don't know. I can't admit to him that having him order me around gave my brain the break it needed to think for itself. I can't tell him that the orgasm released all my panic, and that the humiliation of it eased a little of my self-loathing. It doesn't make sense. I'm ashamed, but I'm lighter. Sex usually does the trick for me. A rough, hard fuck with a nameless man and a curt goodbye is more than enough, but nothing has ever calmed me like this. I can't say that. I can't tell him because it's fucking pathetic.

So instead, I pull my sweatpants away from my body, peeling them down to show him my light blue boxer-briefs. They aren't light blue anymore. They're soaked and sticky and warm, and I kind of like the way it feels enough to have my dick twitching again.

"Show me," Blake demands.

Shaking, but getting a little of my defiance back, I lick my lips and unstick my boxers from my body, pulling them down enough to show Blake the slick mess all over my cock, balls, and groin. With him staring at me, my cock hardens fully right in front of him. I'm about to say something snippy, but Blake reaches forward. Without touching my dick, he swipes those same two fingers through the cum on my lower belly and holds them up.

"Suck them clean."

I bend down to suck them, but Blake shakes his head.

"Kneel, little slut."

God-fucking-dammit. I drop to my knees, unsure why I'm following orders now that the panic is over. Especially when it's the one thing I hate most. I'm in a trance, and when I snap out of it, I'll make him pay for this. I take his fingers into my mouth, slowly sucking them. I make a show of licking between them, and when I open my mouth as an invitation for him to jam them down my throat, I look into his eyes as he does it. He almost grins.

"Feel better?"

I nod.

"Tell me."

"I feel better."

"Good. Go clean up. We're going out to dinner." He helps me stand. "And, Mercer?" I look back at him. "You will be punished for spending seven grand on my credit card today."

My lips don't even fight the smirk, they just let it happen. "Don't call me Mercer." I strut my shit back to my room, feeling better than I have in ages.

6 Blake

FAMILY DINNER ISN'T SOMETHING I've been to in a very long time, but now that I'm home—now that we're all home and through the training—Dad wants to make it a thing. I brought Mercer for multiple reasons. One, he needs to know he isn't a prisoner in my apartment. Two, it's a power move to show my dad I'm doing something. Three, it'll show Bronson that I'm not afraid of babysitting this little brat after he complained about being sick of him. Four, it's a *fuck you* to the Palmerston family and I'm hoping my dad tells them Mercer is staying with me. It'll make Will Palmerston sweat, thinking I know something about the facility. I've got Aaron on it, so if Will tries to make some calls to ensure nothing ties back to him, I'll find out.

Olivia is here, but I can tell Bronson is itching to leave, probably meeting up with Miranda after dinner. He's in love with her, and Olivia knows it, but I can't predict how it's going to turn out. Olivia keeps looking at Mercer, subtly trying to tell him to give a signal if I'm coercing him in any way.

Mercer is a little shit, so he pretends not to notice. He's back to acting cocky and casual, his little meltdown forgotten for the time being. My fingers still tingle from being at the back of his throat.

"Yeah, everyone was really sick towards the end of the night," Olivia tells us. "So the engagement party ended a little early. Some are claiming food poisoning, but no one can narrow down why half the people got ill but others didn't when they were eating the same things."

I glance at Mercer, wondering just what he put in that mixing bowl.

"Shame," he says, faking sympathy.

"So, Ben," Bronson says from across the table. "How's it living with Blake? He's never lived with anyone before."

I put another half-serving of lasagna onto his plate, and he glares at me. Sue me. He's skinny and needs to eat more.

"He's a dick," Mercer says nonchalantly. "But I'm a bigger dick, so it's okay. The pissing contests are fun."

My dad watches this like it's funny. He thinks I'm earning Mercer's trust and weaselling my way into their family secrets, but I'm not even close. Not yet. It doesn't surprise me that Will ripped him from the family tree simply for being smarter than him. He used Mercer's lifestyle and extracurriculars as an excuse to exile him even more. Powerful men are always threatened by other powerful men, and this time, it is his own kid who overpowers him. I have no doubt Mercer rebelled just to piss them all off, which doesn't make his situation any easier, but he's living with the cards he was dealt, and to be honest, I think he's just trying to survive without losing himself.

"But you're comfortable there, right, Ben?" Olivia asks, trying to get him to admit I'm hurting him. I don't think she has the right, since she was willing to let him be shipped off to that facility again.

"So comfortable," Mercer croons. "He loves it when I walk around in my lingerie. Tonight, when we get home, I'm going to model a few new sets for him." He looks right at me, blinking beautifully. "Isn't that right, baby?"

His games are fun despite how badly they make me want to choke him. "Mm."

"Mm." He licks his lips.

"Eat."

"Yes, Daddy," he mutters, just because he knows I hate it.

Brandt snorts and Bronson tries to hide his laugh, but they both fail miserably. Olivia doesn't know what to think, and my dad still assumes this is all a part of my plan. All in all, I'm glad I brought him to dinner. Things worked out well for me. I also got a new job at the end of dinner. A name on a slip of paper that was burned immediately after I memorized it.

On the drive home, I keep my wallet in my back pocket, unwilling to make the same mistake twice.

"Can we go to a club or something?" Mercer asks after fucking with the music selection and changing every song without letting more than ten seconds of it play. "I'm so bored."

"I thought you were modelling for me?"

"Mm." He smirks and changes the song.

"Mm."

"I'm just saying, for a whack job psycho killer, you're pretty boring." He tucks his feet up on the seat. "Who has such a badass job and just sits at home drinking tea every night?"

"I don't drink tea, and I've not been home in five years. This is my first week here."

"So live a little!" he says. "Come on, Blakey."

"Don't call me that."

"Don't call me Mercer." What a little shit. "Just drop me at a club then. Actually, take me home first so I can change into a sexy little suit, and then drop me at a club. Or I can take your car, even though I hate this car. I don't even care what club I go to; I just want to dance and get my slut on."

"Do you need something in your mouth to shut up?"

His whole attitude shifts, ready for a new game. The rambling boy is gone and out comes the demon. "I need a cock in my mouth," he says with the voice of a skilled phone sex worker. "Please, Blake."

"Please, what?"

He leans over the console, batting his dark lashes at me and giving me his innocent eyes. I'm three seconds away from offering up my cock for him to warm because he seems like he needs it. Instead, he goads me. "Take me to a club so someone with more than eight inches can shove their cock down my throat."

I try not to make it obvious, but my grip on the wheel tightens. "Okay, baby. Whatever you need."

If that's how he wants to play it, I'll play right back. Mercer leans back in his seat like a victor, but by the end of the night, he'll be eating that victory and rethinking his game.

He's a little tipsy, but not dysfunctional. And definitely not off his game. There's a swarm of jocks and big burly men surrounding him, eager to take him home and make him their cumslut. I know he lied about being five foot nine, actually being closer to five foot seven, but I hadn't been lying about eight inches. Maybe even a little more, but anything past that is a waste anyway. He's tiny, and that's half his allure. Guys want to manhandle him, and he wants to take it like a greedy bitch.

Unfortunately, he's all talk. He's a tease, and I don't know if this is normal for him or if it's different because I'm here. He's purposefully leading on an entire entourage of men, pissing them off the more he plays.

I've threatened to leave five times already, and each time, he pretends he needs me for something. Does he know how transparent he's being? His game is seduction and manipulation, but he's not playing with this group of men. He's playing with me, and his victory will only come after I get possessive of him. That's not going to happen. Not externally. Internally, I'm slamming my cock down his throat to choke off all his taunts, making him weep pretty tears for me while I kill every man in this club who has looked at him.

"Blake," he purrs, leaning over my lap like he's having the time of his life. His pants are tight, and his shirt rides up, showing me his toned stomach and smooth skin. "I picked one."

"Which one?" I ask, playing along.

"That one," he says, pointing to an older guy with a ripped body. "Looks like a good daddy with a big cock."

"Mm." I settle my heart rate and lick my lips. "Better go secure him so we can get the fuck out of here. I've got my own plans tonight."

That does it. His amber eyes whip to mine and his dark hair flows with the movement. "What plans?"

"You think you're the only one who can get laid?" I finish my drink and set the empty glass down. It's just soda, but he thinks I'm drunk. "I secured my hookup two hours ago. Just been waiting for you. Didn't know you took so long to pull."

He scowls at me. "That's what happens when you have options, Blake."

"Mm," I hum again. "Hurry up then."

Mercer, predictably, turns into a petulant dick. He pulls the adult version of a hissy fit by getting all moody and saying he's not feeling it. Of course, that's my fault because I ruined his fun. What an asshole I am, eh? He practically drags me from the club, thinking he's preventing me from bringing home whoever I picked, but he's wrong. He's whiny on the drive, keeps huffing and puffing and telling me what a terrible wingman I am because I ruined his vibe.

When we get home, he strips out of his club clothes and puts on baggy sweats and a hoodie that looks a lot like one of mine. It is mine. Fucking thief. Kind of like how it looks on him, though. Big and enveloping and touching him everywhere my hands want to be.

"Will you make me a snack since you ruined my night?" Mercer asks, pouting like usual.

"I told you I have plans." I smirk at him. "I'm gonna grab a quick shower."

I leave him open-mouthed in the living room and jump in the shower. When I hear the buzzer and then the knock on the door, I almost feel sorry for what I know Mercer is about to do.

7

Mercer

THIS FUCKING BITCH. BLAKE. Not the scantily clad bimbo standing in the doorway. Rationally, I know she's probably a nice person with a big brain and a good heart, but right now, she's threatening to take what I feel entitled to.

"Hello," I pour on the silk, adding a sweet smile and batting my lashes. "Can I help you?"

"Blake," she says, and I take back all the nice things I thought about her. She's a bitch and so is he. Both of them are just bitchy bitches and I will not stand for it.

"What about him?" I block the door and make sure she notices I'm wearing Blake's hoodie. It's a flex, and I'm more than okay with it.

She notices but isn't deterred. "Look, he called me over. Can you just let me in? I didn't expect there to be a kid here."

I'm twenty-three, bitch! "I didn't expect Blake to be into haggard older women."

Okay, she's not haggard, and she's not even old, but the kid comment hurt. She's somewhere in her late twenties, and her perfectly done makeup and healthy-looking skin show *she* hasn't been missing *her* skincare products for the past few days like I have. Her clothes are label brand, her hair is done all wavy and sultry, and the dark strands fall perfectly around her high cheekbones. I hate her.

"Haggard?" She lifts a sculpted brow at me.

"Desperate? Worn? Been around the block a few times? Whatever you prefer." I rake my eyes up and down her little body, trying to show distaste even though she's infuriatingly beautiful. "Oh, you're a hooker? That makes more sense."

She steps closer to me, and there aren't a lot of times in my life where I'm bigger than someone, so I straighten to my full five feet, seven inches, and try to act intimidating. "Is this an act? Protective little brother?"

Possessive little bastard, more like. I smile at her, showing all my teeth. "Whatever act it is, it's not going to be worth your time. You should go."

"Where's Blake?"

Oh, this one doesn't give up, does she? Female version of me, which makes me like her just a little, but hate her all the more. "Tied up."

"Tied up?"

"Are you going to keep repeating everything I say? Is this a game?"

"Look, you little asshole, I'm..." she pauses, looking over my shoulder like I no longer exist. "Hey, Blake." Her bitchy smile turns seductive and my blood burns.

"Dee," Blake greets her with a calm, gravelly voice. "Come in." His fingers grasp the back of my neck, steering me from blocking the doorway. "Have a fun night?" he asks her, digging his fingers into my neck harder.

"It was alright. Work was busy."

"Prostituting is hard," I say.

Blake's fingers squeeze harder, and I don't even care that he's trying to punish me for that because he's still touching me. "Been a while," he says to her.

"What, five years? Maybe six?" Her grin is flirty, and I want to scratch it off her face. "You look good, babe."

"Babe?" I scoff. "Smart. Better to use pet names so you don't mix up the names of your clients." Dee seethes at me, but Blake's fingers squeeze so hard I wince. "What?"

"Should have brought that daddy home," Blake whispers against my ear, his nose tickling my hair. "Come on, Dee. Ignore him." He releases my neck and takes her hand.

There's a moment of complete defeat. Trauma floods my brain, reminding me how unworthy and completely forgettable I am. *Ignore him.* Story of my life. *Ben doesn't exist. Ben wasn't there. Ben isn't coming. Go hide Ben. Make sure Ben isn't in the shoot. Turn off Ben's mic. Ignore Ben. He's just acting out; ignore him.*

I get that itchy feeling. It starts in my fingers and spreads up my arms, burning and grating until it envelops my chest and makes it hard to breathe. The prickles infiltrate my lungs, but I refuse to let this bitch see me weak. I breathe in the smell of Blake's hoodie, remembering my former moment of weakness when he comforted me against his body. I hate that it happened, and I hate it even more that he saw me like that, but I've gained a Pavlovian reaction to his scent. It settles me. It coats my lungs in comfort instead of prickles, enough to keep them working, to keep my mind from spiralling. I pull the sleeves over my hands and bunch the fabric in my fists, letting it ease the itchiness.

When I turn around, Blake is steering Dee down the hall, but his eyes are looking at me. Checking on me. Checking in. His eyes ask me if I'm okay, and... just because he cares, I think I am. Unwilling to let his comment break me, I offer him a devil's smirk as a reminder that if I'm not getting laid, he's not getting laid. *Good luck*, my grin says. He has no idea how fucking annoying I can be. So annoying, his former comment to ignore me won't be possible.

Don't forget me.

Don't ignore me.

See me for who I am and notice me because I'm worthy.

Look through the bullshit and accept all my broken.

Someone. Please. See me.

THE STANDARD TRICKS DON'T work. I found the vacuum and ran it outside his door. I blasted kid cartoons on the TV. I knocked and asked a million questions, and Blake answered every single one of them without so much as a huff of annoyance. Dee glared at me every single time and even called me an attention whore. Blake looked annoyed at that. I flooded the bathtub and shouted for help, but Blake just gave me towels and a bucket. I made a show of calling an old hookup right outside his door, but Blake only slammed it in my face. I marched away at that point, but when I came back, the door was wedged open again.

Time for desperate measures.

A grilled cheese sandwich is going to save me from this nightmare. I've been cooking it for twenty minutes already, and the char on both sides is almost ready. It's nearly three in the morning, and the rest of the building is going to hate me, but I can bat my lashes and play innocent pretty well. When I get a good smoulder going, I leave it for another few minutes just to make sure the pan is really rolling with the burning smell, and then I stand on a bar stool and hold it to the smoke detector.

I wince at the first beep, feel victorious at the second, and scramble back to the floor on the third. I shove the barstool back into place and start my acting.

"Oh no!" I gasp, throwing the pan back on the stove. "Oh no. Oh no. Oh no!" Shit, I need a new line. "No good fucking burner. I just wanted a grilled cheese!"

Blake appears half naked and frustrated all to hell, switching the stove off and fanning the smoke detector. "What did you do, Mercer?" he growls at me.

"I was just trying to make a snack." Batting of the lashes. Shuffling of the feet. Twisting of the sweatshirt material in my hands. Pure innocence in the eyes. Throw in a little pout. "I'm sorry." I'm not even a little sorry.

He starts opening windows to air the place out, but it's far too late for that. I hide my victorious grin in his hoodie when the alarm system for the whole building goes off, telling us to evacuate and that fire crews are on the way.

This buys me all of Blake's attention. He grips my chin hard, snarling in my face. "You little shit."

"It was an accident."

"Bullshit." His jaw clenches and I know he wants to say more, but Dee comes out in her dress, doing an early walk of shame with her heels in her hand.

"This isn't worth it, Blake. Sorry." She looks at me with actual respect. "Well played, attention whore." She doesn't even put her shoes on before leaving the apartment and joining the other pissed off residents in the stairwells.

"Go get me a pair of pants and a shirt," he demands. "While I clean up your mess."

Shoved towards his bedroom, I enter it with a satisfying warmth in my chest. I'm going to get a real talking to about this stunt, and I'm really looking forward to it. But like the little shit he called me, I scan the room for evidence. The condom is still unopened, and the room doesn't smell like sex. But why? They were in here forever. Did Blake stall? Win for me either way. I grab a pair of sweats and a t-shirt from his hamper, drop the t-shirt back in, and walk down the hall. By this time, the building manager is at our door, ushering us out.

"Where's the shirt?" Blake asks, stepping into the pants.

"Oh. I forgot."

He growls at me again, but he doesn't have time to scold me. "It was just a burned grilled cheese. You can call off the fire department." He's talking to the building manager, and I don't think he even notices his clamped grip around my wrist. "I've got the windows open to air it out. I'm sorry. We don't need to waste the fire crews' time."

"They'll come check it out anyway. It's procedure. Just head downstairs and wait at the cluster point until they clear the building. Mind if I grab a key off you to show them the source?" He's in a robe, and I do feel a bit shitty about waking him up.

Blake hands over a key with another string of apologies, and then he's tugging me down the stairs and I'm tripping on accidental purpose into his bare back. He's not a bulky guy, but he's lean-strong. Lots of tone and definition without being the hulk, and fuck me, it's hot. Literally. Every time I touch his obliques because *whoops* I've tripped again, his skin scorches my hands. Halfway down the fifteen flights, he snaps completely, losing his cool.

Like a superhero without the cape and lacking the do-gooder mentality, he hoists me up and carries me piggyback style down the final seven flights. I smile against his neck and don't even try to keep my boner from pressing into his lower back.

"We're having a serious chat about wasting the time of emergency responders, little demon."

Guilt hits me hard, ruining my victory. I hadn't thought of that. I figured they'd clear the building, see the burned sandwich, and tell everyone they could go back home. The fire department never even crossed my mind, and now I feel bad about it. What if someone is in trouble but the fire crews are here because I'm a needy prick with attention issues? I rest my forehead against Blake's shoulder and sigh.

"I'm sorry."

"No you're not," he barks.

"I am about the fire department."

He opens the door outside, but instead of taking me to the cluster point across the street where everyone else is, he takes me down the sidewalk until we're between two other buildings. Dropping me, he wraps a hand around my throat and pushes me against the brick wall of a café.

"Fuck with me all you want. Play your games, make a fuss, be a fucking brat, I don't care. But don't involve anyone else."

"You involved someone else by inviting her over." I glare at him because, obviously, this is all his fault. "You did it to rile me. Well, I'm fucking riled, Blake! Not what you were expecting?"

"I don't mean her. I mean the residents in the building, the manager, and the fire department. No more of that. You want my attention so bad, you find more creative ways to get it without involving anyone else. Am I clear?"

"Yes, Daddy."

He tightens his fingers around my throat, cutting off air and blood flow in one calculated grip. "I am *not* your daddy. You have a daddy, and he's the majority of the reason you are the way you are, so if you want me to treat you like he treats you, by all means, keep calling me that. It won't be fun. It won't be sexy, and you'll end up more hurt than you already are. If you want my attention, find something else to call me. Understood?"

Reality hits hard. He sees me. Or at least, he sees a part of me. I've never had anyone notice that before, and it means more to me than he'll ever know. I'll never call him Daddy again. I nod in his grip.

"Tell me."

"Understood."

"Good." He releases my throat, but his eyes keep me pinned to the wall. "You're volunteering at the next fireman's breakfast. To make it up to them for this shit show."

"Blake!" I complain.

"Actions have consequences."

"Just spank me or something. Tie me up and humiliate me."

"No," Blake says with a bite. "You want sexy consequences, you learn to play the game right. If you want to pull bullshit like this again, you'll join the goddamn fire department and become a firefighter. This is the consequence of being an asshole to everyone else and wasting their time. Lesson learned?"

Ugh. Fuck Dee. She started this. "Fine." I'd make a terrible firefighter anyway.

Blake looks around the corner of the building when red and blue flashes light up our alley. And his pecs. Jeez, they reflect off his muscles like strobe lights spotlighting everywhere I want to touch. Do not even regret *forgetting* the t-shirt.

"Step one," Blake says to me, gripping my chin again. "You're going to apologize to the fire crews and the residents of the building."

I grit my teeth, holding in a complaint. I *do not* want to do that. I hate taking ownership of my fuck ups.

"If you do, and you do it sincerely, I'll forgive you for ruining my night."

"I don't need forgiveness."

His smile is almost as wicked as mine, and it scares me a little. "Either I forgive you, or I call someone else over to take care of this." He grabs his hard dick. "And I'll gag you and tie you up right where you can see me fuck her. You won't be able to move or speak, and I'll be able to fuck someone like I've wanted to all night."

"No chick is going to go for that, but good try."

"You think there aren't exhibitionists in this city? Think again, little boy. So, are you apologizing to them or am I calling someone over?"

I'm usually more of a strutter, but I stomp my sorry ass over to the cluster point to make all my *sincere* apologies.

Ugh. He didn't fuck her, so I win, but the night did not turn out like I planned. I still lost.

8 Blake

MOST OF MY PAYMENTS come in the form of cash that gets filtered through family-owned businesses and paid out to me as some sort of wage. The majority of it goes into an offshore account, but I like to keep a steady income of legitimately sourced money. Keeps me clean on paper. And I need to be clean right now.

After finding the guy whose name was on the paper my dad gave me, I make contact with the client and let them know what I found.

He's feeding information to a company in direct competition with his wife's company. That was the job, but now I wait to see if she extends the job. She'll be in touch with my dad, and it'll go from there.

Sitting in my car, building up the level of stoic calmness I'll need to deal with Mercer, Will Palmerston calls my cell. I knew it'd only be a matter of time before he figured out I have Mercer, and I'm not really doing anything to hide it, so I expect the call.

"Blake Carter," I answer.

"Mr. Carter," he greets me, starting this conversation out professionally. "I hear you have my son."

"He's staying with me, yeah." I scrunch up the bag of pastries from the café, not wanting them to cool too much before I get them upstairs.

"He was meant to be somewhere else," Will says.

"Oh? Where?"

"A facility that helps him manage his mental health. He needs to be there. I'm sure you understand."

"Sure. What's the name of the place? I can take him over."

Will doesn't answer right away because he doesn't want to reveal the name. He knows our family deals in information extraction and discreet jobs, and he doesn't want me looking into it. "May I ask why you have him living with you?"

"Just figured our families are going to be joining soon and I'd take the time to get to know him. He doesn't seem so bad."

"So bad?"

"Yeah, he's a smart guy."

"Indeed." There's an edge to Will's voice that pleases me immensely. "Ben is a lot to handle."

"I'm doing alright so far. I'll kick him out if he gets to be too much, and if he wants to leave on his own, he's welcome to."

"I'd like for you to bring him home, please."

"How come?"

"Because he's ill. He needs medication and care."

"I'm capable of getting him those things. Anything else I should know?"

There's a moment of silence where Will gathers himself and weighs his options. He doesn't want to reveal anything too telling, but he also doesn't want to let me get away with this. He hates his son, that much is clear, and now I'm standing in the way of his whipping post. If I send Mercer back there, he'll be degraded, blamed, mentally whipped, and shamed just because Will needs to do it to feel better about himself. When he's done, he'll ship Mercer to that facility in the hopes the experimental medicine will make him forget it all, or that the time there will diminish his self-worth enough that he'll be too timid to confront anything. Will wants compliance, and he wants to belittle Mercer to get it. Not going to happen.

Will clears his throat and lightens his tone. "Just that many have tried to do what you're doing. They've all failed. You'll learn soon enough that Ben is too much to handle."

"I'm looking forward to getting to know him better. Anyway, I better go. I'll let Mercer know you called to say hi."

Will audibly cringes at the name, but I hang up before he can say anything else. Fucking dick. I finish my smoke and steady myself for whatever Mercer has been up to while I've been gone.

Pastries in hand, I ride the elevator to the top, mentally ticking off things I've done and still have to accomplish today. With my phone open and my eyes reading an email, I walk out of the elevator and trip over a fuck ton of boxes. My phone goes flying and I almost crush the pastries.

"Mercer!" I shout. I'm the only apartment on this level, but my voice is loud enough to be heard seven stories down. "Get out here!"

He swings the door open in a pair of... no wait, it's a one-piece romper thing. Loose and flowy and oddly sexy. "What?" he snarks at me. "Oh! My shopping!" He bends to pick up the tiniest box in the hall. "Mind grabbing these for me?" He slams the door in my face.

I find my phone and debate taking him to that facility despite what I just told his dad. There isn't a chance in hell I'm carrying anything for him, but when I glance at the label on one of the boxes, I get even more agitated. It's from the Secret Locker, a sex shop, and I don't even want to know what's in it. Skin care products, my ass.

Stepping over the boxes, I head inside and completely ignore him at the kitchen island, sifting through a box that actually does contain skincare products. After his fire alarm stunt and his increasing brattiness, I'm going to have to find a way to get through to him. I'm also cancelling this credit card.

"Get those boxes to your room or I'm throwing them out. You have ten minutes." I walk through the apartment and close my bedroom door behind me. With my back pressed to the door, my hand rubs the ache in my pants, trying to decide what to do with it.

Sex has always been a simple transaction for me. A night of fun and then it's over. Good sex, long and drawn-out fucks, and quickies are all perfectly acceptable. I typically go for someone who puts out those vibes, seems down to fuck, and half the time, they pick me before I pick them. What they all had in common was the fact that they were easy, low-maintenance, and clear about their intentions.

Mercer is none of those things.

He's the most complicated person I've ever met, and I don't think he knows the root or reason for the things he desires. To be honest, I don't think he even knows what he desires, just that he has this itch that needs to be scratched. He's blunt and upfront while still being confusing, and his acts of rebellion and attitude are sometimes real and sometimes fake. Reading and understanding him changes minute by minute, and his needs shift on a whim.

He had a panic attack, or something like it, and the only reason I knew to give him a command was because I learned about brain manipulation tactics in my training. It's a torture method for extracting information, but it worked just as well on Mercer. It stopped the spin of his mind and jarred him into a moment of clarity. Usually, that's the moment an informant spills all their secrets, but with Mercer, he calmed down and gathered himself. But then his needs conflicted themselves again. He required comfort, more gentle than I assumed he'd want, which settled him, but when he got too settled, too calm, he needed to be shocked back to life with dirty talk and an orgasm. He's a mess of instability, and because he's so confusing, he's making my dick hard.

I rub it, listening to him grunt and groan outside my door. Boxes slam into walls and drop on the hard floor, and a second later, he starts talking to himself. Saying dumb shit about the things he bought and calling me an asshole for making him carry it all. My dick gets even harder because that's just fucking insane, and maybe I'm into insane. How dare I make him carry his own shit that he used my money to buy without my permission after he stole and memorized my credit card? *How fucking dare* I?

"I bought the best lollipops," he says, maybe to me, maybe to himself. "I'm sucking one." I hear the wrapper crinkle, and then I hear the hard candy clack off his teeth.

Ah, fuck. The memory of my fingers in his greedy mouth, his tongue slipping between them, the amount of saliva dripping down his chin. I'd rather shove my fingers back into his mouth than let him suck that lolly.

If there's anything I've learned about Mercer, it's that he needs to be held accountable. He's sexually suggestive, and usually, that gets him his way. But I meant what I said. I'm not fucking him until he begs, and if he won't beg, I'll be jerking off like a fucking teen for the foreseeable future.

WAKING UP AT THREE in the morning fucking sucks. Especially because it's exactly what Mercer wants me to do. He's not being audibly loud, but his energy is loud, and fuck me, I can't ignore it. Taking a quick piss and throwing on some sweats, I run a hand through my hair and walk past his open bedroom door.

He doesn't hear me because he has headphones on. He's leaning against the headboard of his bed, body angled towards the wall of windows, one leg bent and the other resting on top of it. His foot is bouncing to whatever he's listening to, and his hands are busy with that handheld gaming system he brought from his parents' house. This is angsty teenager Mercer, and he's pretty damn cute.

He's being quiet, so why did he wake me up?

"When I'm not acting out, no one notices me," he says, scaring the shit out of me. He doesn't look at me, and his foot keeps bouncing. "Which means I notice a lot of things because no one remembers I'm around."

The sadness he's trying to mask as nonchalance gets to me. It reminds me of the day I found him in the middle of a panic attack, and then it reminds me of the night Dee came over. His sisters talked over him, about him, without including him in the conversation. I told Dee to ignore him, and the little bit of panic I saw in his eyes when I said that hits me even harder now. He's just a boy who wants to be seen.

"Did you know my father had been trying to buy that gas plant for years?" he asks, but he still doesn't look at me. "He kept getting held up because of permits and red tape, something to do with city bylaws, and then, bam, your dad buys it."

Interesting. I step into his room, and when he still doesn't look at me, I take a chance and sit on the edge of his bed, leaning against the footboard.

"You wanted to know why my dad agreed to the engagement so easily?" he asks rhetorically. "Well, I'd wager a guess and say it has something to do with that mine."

"How's that come into an engagement, though? It's not like Bronson owns the mine."

He pretends not to hear me. "But my best guess is that the Palmerston family is finally running out of all that old money, and the Carter family is coming into new money. The engagement is the first of many proposed business arrangements. You wait a year and see. Your dad trusts my dad as a smart businessman, because on paper, he is a smart businessman. So, with that trust, Will Palmerston will pitch all these ideas to Brendan Carter, and the next thing you know, the Palmerston family will be back in the financial green."

"So, he's building a tie to my family and garnering trust to save himself?"

Again, he pretends not to hear me. "And while the Palmerston family reigns supreme, like it has for generations, he'll slowly and subtly diminish the credibility of the Carter family. If I had to make a prediction, and I'm pretty good at predictions, Will might slip the Carter name and the family business to less than stellar clients, you'll start getting calls from low-level thugs and terrorists and people with no discretion, and sooner or later, give or take two to five years, the Carter family business will be in ruins because your reputation will be next to nothing."

I don't bother responding this time, but I trust his take. He's perceptive as shit, smart, and manipulative, but those are all the reasons Will is threatened by him, so they're all the reasons I'm going to trust him.

"Without the income from your namesake business, your dad will be under a significant amount of stress. With that stress, he'll start delegating the mine to someone else so he has the time to build up and fix the hitman-for-hire business, and it'll give my dear old daddy a clear path to takeover. Brendan will be distracted and agitated, and William will slide right into 'taking on more responsibility to help out the in-laws' over at the mine. He's such a good guy like that, you know? Suddenly, things will be in the Palmerston name. Little things at first, like bills and accounts and contracts, and Will will hold his hand to his heart and say, 'oh, I had to do it because they wouldn't let me sign off unless it was in my name. I was just making it easier on you while you dealt with your family stuff,' and by this time, your dad will be suspicious as fuck."

Mercer probably knows that my dad is already suspicious, but again, I don't say anything.

"Eventually... well, you get the picture. It's a long-con takeover bred by fear of reputation and financial hardship, and we can all guess how that will go."

I don't know exactly what comes over me, but I grab his ankle and yank him down the bed. He drops his game, gasps, and stares at me with those shocked amber eyes. I pull him straight onto my lap, force his legs open, and make him straddle me. I remove the headphones and steady his hips.

"I want to make a deal with you, Mercer."

"What deal? I'm not a very reliable deal maker."

I don't doubt that. "What do you want out of life?"

He opens his mouth on a quick-witted reply and then closes it. After a major internal debate that looks like it hurts his brain, he eventually says, "I don't have a fucking clue."

"You've never been allowed to want anything, have you?"

"Don't psychoanalyze me, Blake Carter."

"I'll do whatever the fuck I want to you, Mercer Bentley Palmerston."

He grins at his full name. "What's the deal? It better be worth my time and the hard-on you just gave me by getting all handsy."

"I'll never ignore you," I tell him and he basically melts on top of me, but he doesn't want to melt, so he swallows and straightens his spine, grinding that hard-on against my lap for good measure. "I'll be honest with you if you're honest with me. I want to help you rise to the top."

"I don't need you to get me to the top. I'm capable."

"I know," I admit. "You have the skills, the smarts, and the mind to be more than... this. The neglected and hated son act must be getting old, yeah?"

"It got old fifteen years ago."

"Then I want to show you how fucking powerful you can be when you aren't hated and neglected. I know you don't need my help, but you need to fucking respect yourself. I can help with that part."

"Why?" He looks at my eyes, my mouth, checking for lies and coercion. "Why do you care?"

"Because I saw your ass in lacy lingerie, and it fucked up all my brain wires." I smirk at him.

"I knew you eye-fucked me."

"Because you don't trust anyone," I tell him the truth. "No one. Not even yourself. Aren't you sick of being beaten down over and over again, being sent to that place, and not having the power to get out from under his control? You're an adult, but you don't get to act like one. It's gotta be tiring, no?"

"Yes," he whispers. "Though it's mostly my fault."

"I know," I laugh. "You egg it on and never actually try to get away because you don't know where the fuck to go. I've been there. I might not act out the same way you do, but I know what it's like to be neglected."

He rolls his eyes at me. "Sure you do." He stays on my lap but grabs a lolly from his pile and shoves it in his mouth. "So, the deal is that we help each other?"

"No." I snatch the candy from his mouth and put it in mine. "The deal is that we learn to trust each other." Shit, this is a good lolly. Strawberries and cream or something. "Deal?"

"I'll think about it," he says, trying to grab the sucker stick.

"Open," I demand.

"I still don't trust that my dad didn't hire you to take care of me as a job. Either keep me out of his way or kill me. Haven't decided yet."

"Open."

"Say please."

Not a chance. I grip his chin and squeeze until his lips pop open. I lean in until my lips are brushing his, revelling in the feel of his small body trembling with need on top of mine. "Better start begging soon, Mercer." I lick his lips, and just as he leans in to take more, I shove the lolly back in his mouth and stand up. I set him on the bed and make a point of adjusting my dick right in front of his face. "Night, baby."

9

Mercer

I won't beg. It's not because I'm above it, but because he wants me to. Instead, I'll taunt him until he's desperate enough to give in without me having to beg. He might be strong-willed and stoic, but I'm fucking persistent. Plus, persistence and games will help my mind stay afloat through the emotions I'm drowning in after he said all that shit to me last night.

I will never ignore you.

I almost died right then and there. Everyone ignores me. *Everyone.* And now that I've had time to think about it, I know I don't deserve his attention. I've done nothing nice to get it, and eventually, he'll realize that. He'll start ignoring me because the type of attention I attract isn't sustainable long term. For now, I'm going to revel in his promise and push all his buttons to see how committed he is to keeping it.

"Will you open this for me?" I ask, setting a box on the kitchen island.

Blake pours himself a glass of water from the tap like a heathen, standing right over the sink to drink it. "A box? You can't open a box?"

"The tape is really stuck on there."

"Use a knife."

Take my fucking bait, asshole. I widen my eyes and make them a little watery. "Please."

He turns his sweaty, post-workout chest towards me, and I try really hard not to ogle his abs. All six of them sit nicely above a deep V and eight inches of pleasure. God. Fuck him for being so goddamn perfect. "Are you begging?"

"I'm asking nicely. Like a good boy."

"Mm," he hums his favourite non-word. "Sounds like begging."

So cocky. I tilt my head but keep my eyes on his, flinging open the drawer at my hip. Taking out a random knife, I start hacking at the box. I'm stabbing the damn thing with a serrated bread knife, making a mess, probably puncturing the goods inside, but I don't care because he's going to do what I want him to do without me having to beg.

"Jesus fuck," he groans, grabbing my wrist. He takes the knife from me and sets it down, pulling out a smaller one. "Try this."

Fucker. I take it, stab at the box again, and he lets me go for all of six terribly placed stabs.

"You are the worst and most obvious manipulator I've ever met." He takes the second knife from me, and I grin in victory. He stands right behind me, and as much as I love the heat of his chest on my back, it's not the position I was hoping for. I want to see his face. "Not what you were planning?" he says right beside my ear. "I know you're trying to pull a reaction out of me over whatever's in this box." He cuts it open and drops the knife, tearing open the flaps to reveal paper packaging. "Sure you don't want to do it yourself so I can sit over there and gasp and cringe and fucking gag at whatever the hell is in here?"

I slam my ass back, hitting his groin. "Sure. Go sit over there and start gagging. I can think of other ways to gag you if you prefer."

"How original. Your cock, I'm guessing?" he asks, moving to stand beside me again.

"Sure." I shrug, reaching into the box. "Or duct tape, a ball gag, a towel shoved into your mouth. Or this." I pull out an eight-and-a-half-inch dildo. "Bigger than yours, according to what you claim."

It's a big, blue, silicone dick and he doesn't even shy away from it. It's still in the packaging, but he takes his time studying it. Suction cup to stick to whatever surface I want fucking me, veins, a big head with all the right ridges. He grins.

"Seriously? That does it for you?"

"Why not?"

"It can't even come. You're a terrible cumslut if you think a non-jizzing dildo does the trick." He snorts like that's a great insult. *It is!* Fuck him! "Sort of disappointed. I had such high expectations for your slutty boy status." He shakes his head at me.

There aren't many times I'm rendered stuck for a come-back, but right now is one of them. I act like I'm not secretly scorned by his words and keep going through the box. When I find a bottle I completely forgot I ordered, I hold it up for him.

"They *can* come," I tell him, feeling justified now. "This is cum scented and flavoured lube. You put it in toys that can jizz."

"Interesting," he says, taking the bottle and smelling it. He cringes. "Not my favourite cum scent. Where's the jizzing toy then?"

I didn't order one. "You rushed me to finish shopping that morning, so I didn't pick one yet!"

"Mm," he hums again, refilling his water. "What else ya got in there, hm? What are you trying to rile me with?"

"You're taking the fun out of it," I complain.

"Oh, am I? Sorry, when you stalked out here all prancy and dancy, claiming you couldn't open a fucking box, I just assumed we were playing to win. I don't like losing, so seeing that grumpy look on your face is a nice little bonus. Did I win?"

"I'm not grumpy." I scowl into the box.

"Of course not." He finishes his water. "Want to show me the rest now, or do you need a minute to re-evaluate the game? We can wait until later when you get your swagger back."

I throw the big blue dick at him. "Fuck you, Blake."

He laughs, catching it. "Come on. Get dressed. We're going out."

"YOU CONFUSE ME," BLAKE says from behind the wheel of his Denali. "With your outfit choices."

I bullied him into taking me through a drive-thru to get a brownie fudge sundae, so I lick the spoon and look down at my outfit. I chose comfort because it resembles how I feel around Blake. Sweats, and a grey hoodie I stole straight from the dryer before he folded his laundry, my feet shoved into socks and slides, and a grey Blue Jays ball cap even though I know nothing about baseball. I just liked the blue jay.

"Why?"

"I got all these warnings about what a sexual deviant you are, and the first night I saw you, you set the standard high in that lingerie. Haven't seen you in it since." He shrugs. "You're more of a lazy hoodlum than a fancy sex symbol."

"Are you saying my hoodlum look isn't sexy?"

He grins at the windshield. "No, I'm not saying that. At all."

The timbre behind those words makes me believe them. "You said we're going out. In my life, if someone says we're going out, that means one of two things. The first being that I need to look a certain way, set a standard, comply with the Palmerston dress code because I'm being shown to the public to keep murder theories away. The second being that I'm going to be tricked into something."

"Like what?"

"Like that behavioural facility or a secluded house so I'm out of the way with a fucking warden keeping an eye on me. In either of those cases, I like to dress for… practicality. If I run, I want to be warm. If I'm attacked, I want to conceal weapons. If I'm stranded, I want my pockets jammed full of burner phones and granola bars, even though I have no one to call except the police. Or a reporter who'd probably get to me faster. So for those cases of 'we're going out', I like pants with lots of pockets and a lot of layers to hide things in."

"What's the reason behind today's choice then?" Blake asks, and I'm not sure if I can admit to him that he makes me comfortable yet.

"You don't require any effort." I take a bite of chocolate and brownies and caramel bits. "That's not the full truth, but it's the only part you're getting."

Blake lights a cigarette and nods to accept that. "Thanks. But what about the lingerie? When does that come back into play?"

"It's never out of play." I smirk, lifting my hips a bit. I lift the hoodie and roll down the waistband of the pants a little, showing him a nice peek at a bit of navy-blue lace. "Don't judge a book by its cover, Blake."

He smiles for real. "I don't know why, but that makes me feel better."

Kill me now for blushing.

I finish my ice cream and then complain about how full I am, but when we pass a McDonald's, I still ask for a Big Mac. Blake says no, telling me we're going to dinner after.

"After what?"

"I have a job to do," he says, pulling into an underground parking garage. I was too preoccupied with staring at him driving to notice what building it is. "Thought you might be interested in helping."

"Are you going to pay me?"

"Sure. What's your price, baby?"

"Your dick without having to beg," I deadpan.

"Mm," he hums, wheeling into a parking space. "Might want to wait in the car then. I can handle this one without you."

"A blowjob without having to beg for it," I compromise.

"You want to give or receive?"

I grit my teeth for a second and then decide to own it. "Give."

"Alright," he agrees. "At a time of my choosing."

We shake on it, even though I feel duped, and then we're moving around to the back of the vehicle. Blake pulls out a few devices, a few knives, and even a gun. I hold out my hand for one, but he scoffs at me.

"You couldn't even cut a box open. No."

"Yeah, I suck at kitchen knives," I agree. I steal a dagger right from his fingertips, flip it around a bunch of times to be fancy, and then hold it to his neck. "These, on the other hand, are my favourite."

He swallows, the roll of his throat pressing into the blade. "I'll take that blowjob now."

As tempted as I am to drop to my knees in this highly watched parking lot, I grin at him and shake my head. "Job hasn't been completed yet."

"Oh? Now you have boundaries?" He squeezes my wrist and takes the dagger from me. "Fuck you for being a cock tease." He hands it back and gives me three more. "We shouldn't need them, but it never hurts to be prepared. Any other weapons skills I should know about? Secret black belt or anything?"

"Damn good archer," I admit proudly. "But no. Knives and daggers are my thing."

He laughs, closing the hatch. "When I'm done with you, you'll be good with kitchen knives, too. You need to learn to cook."

I follow him as he starts into the building. "Never been good at cooking because I hate following directions."

"I couldn't tell."

I smile. A real one. Not a smirk or a grin or anything playful and condescending. It feels so nice on my face I immediately wipe it away.

Blake avoids the lobby and somehow has a key to a private elevator. I feel like a legit spy as we slink along walls and make our way down a corridor with nothing but closed doors with 'private' on the nameplates. He produces another key to unlock one of them, and all that's behind it is a set of stairs. He's sexy when he's in stealth mode, and it's getting harder and harder to walk at this clip with a stiffy.

"For being small, you're louder on your feet than I thought." He pauses to peer around a corner.

"Well, your super dangerous spy game is getting me hard and the lace is rubbing in all the right places. Sue me."

"Serves you right. Your super sexy knife skills put me in the same predicament, but you don't hear my footsteps, do you? Learn faster."

I learn on the go and by the time we get to the final door, Blake is pulling out all the spy movie moves. He has a device with a 3D image of an eyeball, holds it to the retinal scanner, puts on a finger condom to press to the print scanner, and then types in a code. The green light buzzes and we're in.

"A server room?" I ask, even though it's rhetorical. This is obviously a server room, but I still don't know what building we're in. "What is this place?"

"The competition," Blake says, pulling out a camera. "I got hired to find out if this woman's husband was leaking information to a competing company, and it turns out he was. This is the company he leaked information to, so I got rehired to wipe their servers."

"You know computers and tech that well?"

"Not even close. I have someone to do it remotely. I just need to get him some information. This isn't my main job."

"What is?"

"The husband," he says with a wicked smirk. "Whatever she decides to do with him."

"Mm, violence gets you horny, doesn't it?"

"Sometimes. Hurry up. We've got less than ten minutes in here. Use your super brain and start documenting all the main server numbers on the back."

There are way too many servers in here for him to take a picture of them all before ten minutes run out. "Just move. Put the camera away and get whatever else you need here. I'll do the server codes."

He pauses to look at me.

"If I see them, I won't forget them. I promise."

He hesitates for all of one breath and then nods. I don't know why that means so much to me. He starts plugging things into the main computer, and I start trying to memorize everything I can get my eyes on. My memory isn't photographic; I can't recall everything I've ever seen, but when it comes to numbers and sequences, even colour codes and patterns, it doesn't leave me. Ever. I'm a great card shark.

Just as Blake is packing up his equipment at our ten-minute mark, asking if I got everything memorized, the door alarm beeps. I start to panic, but Blake doesn't. As cool as a fucking cucumber, he snatches me around the waist and pulls me between two very hot control towers. His ass hits the floor and my ass hits his dick. His groan is silent, but my heartbeat isn't.

"I want 24/7 security on this door," someone says. "Frank's wife is getting suspicious, and I wouldn't put it past her to try to shut us down. Our patent is almost ready."

Blake hands me his phone, the camera already recording. He nods towards the front of the room, where we can vaguely see two shadows. We can hear fine, so hopefully the camera picks up the audio over the hum of all these machines.

"What's Frank getting out of this? Other than a divorce." The second guy laughs.

"Millions," the first one scoffs. "He's been stalling her on the patent for months. We're almost there."

"Okay, this is going to take me about twenty minutes. I just have to swap these decks out. You can call security and request a detail for this floor starting tonight."

Things go silent after that, so Blake takes his phone from me and stops the recording. I settle in, knowing we're going to be here for a while, but again, Blake doesn't allow that. Silently, he shifts back until his back is pressed to the wall and his ass is on the floor, legs spread, and he taps my hip to turn me around. It's dark, but I can see the glow of his face, and I don't trust it. I don't trust it so much my mouth waters and I keep staring at how fucking hot that look is.

Kneeling in front of him, he pulls my face to his and whispers the same command he gave me the other night. "Open."

I don't know if I comply or if it instinctually happens when he pushes my head down, but a second later, my tongue hits the tip of his cock and all my senses fine tune or turn off or something. To the soundtrack of humming tech equipment and security being ordered, I finally get my first taste of Blake Carter. And I'm not about to pass it up.

I lick the warm, salty tip of his cock just to tease him, but the insatiable slut in me needs more. With one of his hands on the base of his cock and the other on the back of my head, I dip down to take him into my mouth. My lips run the length of him, feeling all the ridges and veins until I hit his hand on the base. On the way back up, I let my teeth lightly graze him, and I lick the slit when his legs tremble. Oh, fuck yeah. I can read you, Blake Carter.

"Yes, 24/7 security starting tonight. Two stations. One outside the door and one by the elevator."

I remove his hand and suck him all the way down, craving the fill of him in my throat. I have a feeling he kept his hand there so I wouldn't gag, but lucky for him and this stealthy blowie, I'm not a gagger. I swallow around him, constricting the head in my throat. The hand he had there ends up in his mouth to stifle his groan.

The lacy restriction of my panties has my cock trapped torturously, but it only makes this hotter. I'm a sucker for punishment, but more than that, I'm a pleaser. But only when it comes to sex. I want to make *him* beg. Planting my hands on his thighs and trying to keep the sucking noises to a minimum, I bob up and down his shaft, wishing I could drag this out so it never ends. I don't worry about swallowing, just let the drool drip down his cock to soak his trimmed pubes. Love a guy who manscapes. With my nose pressed to his skin and my drool soaking my face, I realize he was being humble about those eight inches. Not by much, but goddamn. Eight and *a half*.

Both hands land on the back of my hood and he holds me there. His hips thrust so he's gently fucking my throat, and I move one hand to my dick, easing the ache just a bit. My eyes water and my throat burns, but my mind delves into such a blanket of calm that I feel entirely safe in this completely unsafe situation. I have no idea what happens if we get caught here, but I'm too comfortable to care. And I trust him. Holy shit, I trust him. Plus, I have knives.

Blake stops thrusting his hips, but he uses his hands on my head to make me fuck his cock with my mouth. I breathe through my nose and try not to make slurping sounds, but honestly, it's harder not to moan. I'm so fucking into this I'm about to come in my pants again. A tiny whimper escapes me, and Blake pulls me up.

Staring straight into my eyes with a look I've not yet seen on his face, he checks in on me. I'm crying, drooling, probably snotting, begging him with my eyes to let me go back down to suck him. "You going to come, baby?" he whispers so quietly I barely hear it.

My hand is still rubbing my cock through my sweats. I nod.

He releases my face, and when I drop down to swallow his dick, he stops me. Pushing me upright, he glances behind me before hooking his thumbs in my pants and tugging them down a bit. My hard cock presses against the panties and Blake bites his lip at the sight of it. "Can't ruin these," he says. "Fuck, Mercer. You aren't ruining these with cum." He tugs them down and puts my hand on my cock. I start stroking on instinct. He leans me forward, angling my body over his, and then he whispers in my ear, "Cover my cock in cum, baby. Then suck it all off."

Oh god. My forehead rests on his shoulder, and I bite the fabric of his jacket to shut myself up. I'm a goddamn three pump chump before I'm damn near crying into the fabric, coming all over his dick. His fingers touch my cock, pointing it right where he wants it, and it makes me tremble so hard I feel like I'm coming again.

"Mmmm." His coat eats my sounds, and his hand soothes my back.

"Good boy," he whispers, pushing me up again. His thumbs swipe the tears under my eyes, and then he looks down at the mess I made all over him. His gaze tells me what to do. His eyes are telling me to be a good little cumslut and clean up my mess. He's daring me, no... commanding me, to be his good boy.

"Two minutes," one of the men says. "All the codes will be changed in two minutes."

He tucks me into my pants and I fall forward, swallowing him into my mouth and sucking the taste of my cum off his cock. I lick all around the base, whimpering for more. When I've gathered it all in my mouth, I show him. Blake squeezes my cheeks to make it drip down my chin with all my drool, and then his tongue licks from chin to lips. I'm going to come again. Jesus fuck.

He pushes me down and I suck him until he's shaking with restraint. Pressing my lips right under his tip and shallowly bobbing my head, he firms up his hold on my hair to keep me there. His release hits my tongue with a warm spurt, the liquid filling my mouth. I swallow what I can and take him deeper until he's done, but the taste of him and the way he trembles set me off again. I've never had a hard time coming more than once in a row, but fuck me, I definitely ruined the lace, even if the load was smaller. I keep it quiet, my little secret, and then I suck in a silent breath, licking him clean. I wait on my knees for him to tell me I did good.

His cheeks are flushed, his dark hair is messier for some reason, and his eyes are calm and chaotic together. He runs his thumb over my bottom lip, and then he pulls me close. When his lips meet mine, it's so unexpected that I freeze. I've never really been kissed before. Quickies don't always like kissing, and even if they did, I don't think it'd be anything like the way Blake kisses. He's slow and calculated, not at all in a rush, conveying how good of a slut I am with gentle caresses and shared tastes. His thumb runs over my lip again, even though he's still kissing me, and when his mouth moves, I know he's mouthing the words, 'good boy.'

"Okay, let's get out of here. It's fucking hot."

"Everything is changed? Even the code to get out?"

"Yep."

The door opens at the same time those words register and ruin our kiss. We don't know the new code to get out. For the first time, Blake looks a little worried. He pushes me to my feet and we both watch the door swing closed in slow motion. He makes a run for it, but I'm faster. Not with my jelly legs, but with my throwing knife. I time it perfectly, and just as the door jars shut, my knife lands between it and the doorframe, preventing it from latching. Okay, I'm impressed with myself. When did I get this cool?

Blake pauses, waiting to see if anyone is going to come back and notice that. When no one does, he checks the door and smiles when it still opens. He puts my knife back in place, tugs up his pants, and kisses me again.

"Fuck, Mercer. You earned a second blowjob for that bit of brilliance. Let's get out of here." He tugs me towards the door. "I don't even care how sweaty we are, I fucking love server rooms all of a sudden."

I'm waiting for the other shoe to drop, but I still feel comfortable and safe.

10 Blake

After telling Mercer where we're going for dinner, he pulls the world's biggest hissy fit. So bad, in fact, that I end up taking him home to calm down for a minute. Well, at least thirty-eight minutes because my ears are already bleeding from all his complaints, and I stopped replying to them thirty-six minutes ago when I realized they were rhetorical bitch-fests.

I don't care. That blowjob was the hottest shit of my life, and even his asshole voice isn't detracting from it. Those knife skills are also up there on the spank bank list. Goddamn. Feisty little hoodlum on the streets, lingerie wearing badass in the sheets. Literal perfection. I really hope he begs for sex soon.

I don't think he's taken a breath in four minutes, but I let him continue. His cheeks are red and his eyes are glossy, and his little body is all taut and tight and turning me on.

"—send me back there. If you think I'm going to stand for that shit, you haven't seen the best of my knife skills yet, Blake Carter. How fucking dare you spring this on me like it's no big deal? I'm not welcome there! Did you miss the part where my mother tried to ship me off to a brainwashing camp that my dad sanctioned? No. I'm not going. You go. Feel free to stick the turkey knife in my dad's windpipe while you're at it. I'll take leftovers. And don't forget dessert."

He's pissed, but he still sways his hips down the hall, retreating to his bedroom for safe keeping. Makes me feel pretty good that he feels safe there. I don't bother following. He's pulled this trick three times already, and he always comes back.

I finish the dregs of my latte, really regretting not getting him to write down all those numbers in his memory before springing a formal dinner at his parents' on him. My dad issued the invite, but I knew Will asked him to. This is a test. Will wants to see how much I know and what my relationship with *Ben* is like. Well, he's about to find out. I'll drag Mercer there if I have to.

"You know what?" He's storming my way again, as predicted. This time he has a lolly in his mouth, but he whips it out to use as a prop, embellishing his hand gestures. "Fuck you, Blake!" He points the candy right at me. "You're the only person who knows the truth about that place. I confessed that to you in trust, and even knowing that, you're going to make me go there? You once asked me to respect and be grateful for the breakfast and the apartment you were nice enough to offer me. Well, now I'm asking you to respect the truth I told you and cut me a fucking break!" Lolly, right in my face. Then he sucks it hard, crunching the candy, and tugs it back out. He wants to add more, say more, but I think he's finally hit his word limit.

"You done?" I finish my latte. Shit, this non-bitter coffee is getting addictive.

"No, I'm not done," he snaps, not ready to deflate yet. "I'm far from done."

"You're done," I tell him, standing. I grab his chin and hold it, but the little shit doesn't stop crunching the candy beneath my fingers. "This is your chance to shove it in his face that you won."

"Won?" He smacks my hand away. "How'd I win? I'm in hiding."

"Then come out of hiding. Show him you aren't scared of him."

His eyes drop and his munching stops. He swallows the jagged bits, wincing a little. He doesn't say it, but his actions do. He *is* scared. Of that place, his dad, his situation, and now that I'm noticing more about him, he's also scared of being invisible.

"It doesn't have to all be real, Mercer. Fear is rational, but he's a predator. You're never going to stop being afraid of him if you don't become a bigger predator."

"I can't be bigger, Blake. I'm a twinky little nobody. I got all my mom's genes and none of his manly ones. He'll always be bigger than me."

"I don't mean in size, you little shit. And if you ever diss your body again, I'll punish you. I mean in lethality. Be more lethal. Or at least be intimidating enough to make him sweat. How'd you do it before, huh? Your dad hates you. Why?"

"Because I'm smart."

"Right. You threatened him with your brain. You don't need size to beat him. You already have everything you need to win."

He huffs. Or scoffs. Or laughs condescendingly. I can't always tell the difference. "Like what? What do I have?"

"You are the most persistent person I've ever met. You *do not* give up, and that's not an insult. Your attitude is bigger than this world. Use it. Your smarts are right here." I tap his head. "Stop being afraid of them just because he made you hate yourself for them. And while your body might be small, it's fucking deadly with some knives. You have assets and skills. Stop pretending you don't." I grip his chin again. "And this one doesn't matter at all because you're strong either way, but you have me. I know you've been alone in this forever, but you aren't anymore. For whatever that's worth."

He blinks, and his eyes gloss over even more. Then he gets mad. "Stop making me weepy! It's not a good look on me!"

"It's a perfect look on you," I correct. I smack his ass as he marches away. "Put on something that doesn't meet the Palmerston dress code!"

"I am!" he screams. His door slams a second later.

I DON'T UNDERSTAND HOW anyone can grow up in a place like this. Is it a home or a fucking museum? Will and Penny Palmerston are older parents, having started their family later in life. Because business comes first, right? Whatever. I'm pretty sure Mercer was an oopsie, yet another thing for him to feel shitty about, but that's not his fault. They're old enough to fit the old white money stereotype, and they do nothing to staunch it. They embellish it, live up to it, and literally turned their house into a museum. No wonder Mercer hates it here.

He was all stoic and calm in the car on the way over here, then he had a mini-for-him-freakout, and after that, I let him drive. It took him an additional thirty minutes to get us here, but he did it in the end. We drove around a lot of country blocks until he stopped sweating.

Now, I'm inside, sipping some expensive brandy, and Mercer is waiting outside because he wants to make a dramatic entrance. On his own. All the power to him. I've got my eyes on all his family members, so I know they aren't kidnapping him.

Both my brothers stand with me, neither of them asking where Mercer is. We shoot the shit for a bit, but I'm not the best conversationalist, so I let them talk around me. Dad is chatting with Olivia, Samantha, and Penny, and Will is staring at me. I smile at him like I don't know what the fuck he wants, and eventually he comes over.

"Blake," he greets me. "Bronson. Brandt."

We all say hi, even though it's awkward as hell. I'm not good at being social with anyone, let alone this prick.

"Where's Ben?" His tone is light and casual, but I know the question is anything but. "Couldn't convince him to come?" Ah, there it is, the condescending bullshit I expected.

"Why should I have to convince him to come to his own family's home?"

"He's always been defiant," Will says, waving off my question. "I'm not surprised he's not here."

The stage could not have been set any better for a grand entrance, but Mercer still doesn't come in. I won't be pissed at him if he dipped, but eventually, I want him to face this man, look him straight in the eyes, and tell him to go fuck himself.

"Just let me know when you've had enough of him, and I'll come take him off your hands."

"Oh? You need him for something? I thought he was supposed to be somewhere?"

Will smiles at my brothers. "He'll get there when the time is right. Gentlemen," he says as a goodbye even though we're all still in the same room.

We watch him go and I'm not surprised to find blank faces on both of my brothers. We weren't raised in this kind of wealth. We were well off, but our upbringing wasn't pretentious. We didn't play money games and network at social events. We weren't conducting business meetings over dinner or watching our dad try to schmooze with potential clients. Our business spoke for itself; our dad didn't have to go out there and drum it up, being deceptive and charming all wrapped up in one. My grandpa built the reputation, my dad expanded on that reputation, and word of mouth spread from there. Dad is a worker and salt-of-the-earth business owner, not whatever Will Palmerston is.

"Why the actual fuck are we marrying into this family?" Brandt asks under his breath, still watching Will. He's treating his daughters with the most compassionate attention, and my heart hurts a little more for Mercer, who never got that level of love. Or any love.

"I thought it was for money," Bronson says. "Now I'm not so sure."

Dad looks over at the three of us, his expression knowing. He can tell what we're all thinking, and I swear he's daring us to figure it out. If what Mercer told me is true, Will has already planned the entire takeover of our family business and the natural gas mine, so what the hell does Dad plan to get out of this? I know my dad well enough to understand he's already sorted through all the details Mercer laid out, but is he missing something? Is he playing another angle?

"You fucking the Palmerston boy?" Brandt straight up asks me.

"Nope."

"You wanna be?" Bronson asks.

I grin into my brandy glass and lock eyes with Will Palmerston. "If he breaks down and begs me for it."

WE'RE ALL SEATED AROUND the dining room table and Mercer still hasn't shown up. I don't fucking blame him because I'm itching to leave.

Just as salads are being placed on the table, the dining room doors bang open and there's my little brat. Dressed to fucking impress in a leather suit fit for an assassin, he slays his entrance. Leather pants with slits up the sides, showing a little skin, black boots with a small wedge, and a sleeveless black top with a corset cinched up the back. His eyes are lined with black, giving him a catlike look, and his dark hair remains as chaotic as it has always been, just without the hood this time.

His eyes seek mine for a fraction of a second to top off his bravery reserves, and then he's all snark and sass. "Family," he greets them all. "Carter boys."

I half wonder if this is a costume or if he'd actually wear something like this. I mean, he owns the clothing, obviously, since it came from his closet, but where would he typically wear this outfit? I'm kind of in love with it, but then again, I love his hoodies and sweatpants, too. The guy can wear no wrong. I wonder what kind of panties he's got on under there.

"Damn," Brandt whistles at him. "Strut that shit, hot stuff."

Mercer winks at him, not at all giving a fuck that his parents are wide-eyed and currrently having heart attacks. I catch Will's eye, and silently remind him of his earlier words. *He's always been defiant.*

Dad nods at Mercer and even shakes his hand, Bronson gives him a grin, and Olivia and Samantha are caught somewhere in the middle. They're happy to see him, annoyed that he is once again making things harder on himself, and worried about what their father will do. He doesn't even smile at them. I pull out the chair next to mine and push it in for him when he sits down.

"Blake," he greets me.

"Mercer," I greet him loud enough for the table to hear. There are a few sharp inhales, but nobody comments on the name just yet.

"Sorry I'm late," Mercer says, digging right into his salad. Turning to me, he adds, "These people don't even offer three dressing choices."

I laugh at that and pick up my fork. Oh, this is fun. When his bratty attitude isn't aimed at me, I'm rather fond of it. I think I'm fond of it regardless of where it's aimed, to be honest.

"Why are you late?" Will asks, finally opening his mouth. What a way to greet your son, jackass.

"Couldn't get my corset done up tight enough," Mercer says through a full mouth.

"Perhaps that's a sign you shouldn't wear... that."

"Mm," Mercer hums, making me laugh again. Shit, he's kinda funny.

"Mm," I echo. "Looks badass. I hope you have daggers hidden in there somewhere."

Mercer smirks at me, flashing a hilt at his waist. "So, family? What's up?"

I sit back, enjoy all fucking seven courses while Mercer runs this show and doesn't lose his edge even once. By dessert, Dad, Brandt, and Bronson are all laughing with him, Samantha and Olivia have loosened up, and Penny is quietly observing. If I'm not mistaken, there's a little tear in her eye for the lost family dinners they could have had fun at if they'd only accepted him. Too bad she missed out by being a shitty mom. I can't put all the blame on her because it must be scary being married to a tyrant, but still; she could have helped him in secret.

Will, on the other hand, isn't happy, and for whatever reason makes sense to him, he's looking at me as the one to blame. I'll take it. Gladly. That's right, asshole; I reminded your son he has fucking confidence.

"Ben, I'd like to speak to you in private," Will says at the end of dinner. "It'll only take a moment."

I really don't want that to happen, but I look at Mercer for direction. Whatever he's comfortable with, I'll have his back. "I won't ignore you," I mouth the words to him.

Mercer motions his dad over to the corner of the room, compromising. "Sure."

"In the hall."

"Here's fine."

Will's looking around, making sure my dad doesn't get the wrong—but totally right—impression. He's nervous, not because he cares, but because he's a prideful man who won't settle for a tainted reputation.

"Another time," Will says to Mercer. "I wouldn't want to be rude to our guests."

Mercer's smile is sad yet victorious. "Blake?" I barely catch the wobble in his voice. "I have somewhere to be. Want to go, or shall I steal a vehicle?"

"I'm ready to go," I tell him, placing a hand on his back when I get to him. He's shaking. Maybe not shaking, but agitated. Jittery. "You fucking killed it, little boy."

"I know." He hugs his sisters, says a timid goodbye to his mom, laughs when my brothers and dad say bye to us, and then he's trying way too hard to keep his back straight and his hands steady until we get to the Denali. I don't understand why I get this instinct, but I grab him a hoodie of mine from the trunk. He pulls it over his head and sucks on the sleeves like it's a safety blanket.

We're halfway down the lane when his breathing turns to hyperventilating. His fingers end up in his mouth next, and I call his name three times before he sort of responds to it.

"Seatbelt off," I demand.

On autopilot, he complies, starting to whimper.

"Come here." He leans over the console, not even looking at me. I stop the car to check on his eyes, and when they start to well with tears he's not ready to let fall, I reach inside the hoodie and loosen the corset.

"Tell me what you need."

He trembles, shaking his head.

Again, on instinct, I open my pants, pull out my semi-hard cock, and push his head down. When he releases his fingers and wraps his wet mouth around my dick, his shaking stops.

"You don't have to suck it, baby. Just stay there and relax until we get home." I stroke my hand down his back and make sure I drive safely.

Mercer relaxes.

11 Blake

I CAN TELL NO one has ever taken care of Mercer before. He has no healthy concept of what comfort is. At some point in his adolescent or adult life, he learned to bury his emotions in sex. That, paired with a self-soothing method bred from a lonely childhood, he's turned thumb-sucking into something sexual and submission into a way to shut down his brain to give himself a break.

I understand it, to an extent. I'm still going to talk to someone about it to learn how not to harm him while he's in this state, but I don't want to dismiss his needs. I promised him I wouldn't ignore him, and that includes right now.

He kept my cock in his mouth the whole drive, even relaxing enough to rest his cheek on my stomach while he did it. As soon as I pulled him off and lifted him from the car, he put his fingers back into his mouth and hid his face in my neck. I carried him up to the apartment, and now we're standing in his bathroom.

I've tried to be gentle with him, helping him to strip down to get in the shower, but he's not responding to that. He doesn't want me to do it, and I'm not sure if it's because he thinks it's a weakness, or if he just doesn't know how to accept a gentle touch.

Trying a different tactic, I lean back against the vanity and watch him stand there like a defeated little doll. Fuck, he's beautiful, even in turmoil, but I never want him to suffer alone. "Take your clothes off, Mercer. Now." I make my voice harder than I feel, but it gets him moving.

He needs a Dom. I'm not a Dom in the BDSM sense, but I can be dominant when he needs me to be. Mercer pulls the hoodie off and drops it to the floor. The bathroom fills with steam, but he waits, wanting me to command him again.

"All of it," I tell him. "One piece at a time. Look at me while you do it."

His eyes are less glossy when they meet mine. He undoes the ties on his leather pants, tugging them down and letting them settle on the tile. Standing there in the corset and a pair of red silk panties, his eyes on mine and his lips glistening with saliva, my cock reacts. I rub it through my pants, nodding at the top. When he turns around to show me all the ties, he looks over his shoulder to keep eye contact. I want to take a picture of him like this and jack off to it until it's crusty and ruined. Holy shit.

"Come here, little boy."

He backs up until his ass hits my legs. I undo the loosened ties, then push him away and spin him to face me again. Slowly, he pulls the top off and hooks his thumbs in the band of the red panties.

I stop him. "Let me see your ass in these. Hands on the counter."

His breath shakes out of him, but he does it. He grips the edge of the vanity and sticks his ass out for me to admire. I step behind him and run my hand over his tight ass, the silk fabric not much smoother than his supple skin. He's hairless and tight, so fucking smooth, his creamy skin begging for teeth marks.

"Fuck, this ass, Mercer." I don't even have to add gravel to my voice. It's just there, giving away my desire. I press my hips against him, letting my hands skate over his ass, around his hips, and over the hard bulge in the front of the panties. "You have no fucking idea how bad I want to fuck it."

His eyes meet mine in the mirror, but his voice stays hidden. No begging. Not now. I wouldn't make him beg right now, anyway. I wouldn't accept begging in a moment like this, not while he's still in a vulnerable state.

I slide the silk down his legs to pool at his ankles, letting my cock dig into the crack of his ass. His dick juts out in front of him, nudging the counter and already leaking. "Get in the shower. Right now."

"Alone?" He finds his voice.

"What do you need?" I spin him.

"Don't leave."

"I won't." I steer him into the shower and back away.

"Stay close."

I lean right against the tile, staying in the opening of the shower. When he's satisfied I'm not going to leave, he steps under the water. I try to keep my eyes on his, the liner already running from his tears worsening now under the spray of the shower, but soon, I'm following drops down his chest and flat stomach. His thighs clench together, making his dick stand out even more, and holy fuck, it's going to be hard to stay rooted to this spot.

"Blake," he whispers.

It's begging without manners. I want to give in to it. I won't. "Wash your hair."

While he washes and conditions his hair, the hot water soothes him enough to chase off the majority of his panic. I still don't know if these are panic attacks or PTSD episodes, but I plan to talk to him about them after he rests. He washes his face with his new skincare products, getting rid of all the smeared makeup, and then he soaps up a sponge.

When the suds slip over his nipples and he bites his lip, that's how I know he's back to his usual manipulative self.

In a totally unexpected slip of accidental fate, he drops the sponge, and *oh would you look at that!* It lands right by my feet. His pouty lips are fucking sinful, but his eyes are goddamn demonic. With a bit of blackness still smoked around the edges, he's harshly cute, sinisterly sexy, defiantly desirable, and I can't fucking help the groan when he bends down to pick it up and...*oh, no!* He falls forward. Face right into my dick.

"So fucking predictable, Mercer." My hands itch to latch onto his hair and hold him against my pants.

He doesn't even stand back up. He nuzzles his face against my cock, soaking my pants with his wet hair. "Let me suck your cock, Blake."

"Mercer..."

"I *need* it," he whines, mouthing my dick through my pants. "You asked me what I need. I need to suck a dick. Your dick."

"So cock hungry." My fingers snake into his hair, still silky from the conditioner. "Finish washing first."

"Don't make me wait. I can't wait anymore." He looks up at me with his chin on my bulge. "I can't wait, Blake."

"You need to learn patience and delayed gratification." I tug on his hair to pull him off my dick. "Finish showering first."

He sighs as he stands, shooting me a pissed off look. He sulks for a few minutes, making a show of washing his body, and then something happens. His sulk turns to determination, and I have no idea what's coming. I watch him skeptically, narrowing my eyes while he shimmies to the other end of the shower where he has a little shower caddy.

"Mercer... what're you doing?"

"Maybe you need to learn delayed gratification," he says, turning around with a fucking dildo in his hands. It's not the blue one. It's purple, a lot smaller, and has a suction cup on the base. The length of it is twisted like licorice, and the head of it is a little bigger than the rest, but it's not that thick and definitely not eight inches. Maybe five inches.

"Don't," I warn him.

He smirks at me. "Or what?"

"Or—" I cut myself off, realizing I don't have a fucking threat to stand on. If I deny him my dick, he'll fuck that one. If I give him my dick, he wins because he's the brattiest little shit that ever fucking lived. I'm stuck, giving in and letting him have his way, or suffering through this because I don't want him to have his way. Either way, I lose.

Mercer slaps the dildo to the wall. "Or? Were you finished?"

God, he's like a tiny dog. He's got that little dog syndrome where he's all fucking bark, and I know his bite will be deadly. If I give him an inch now, he'll take a mile later. I'm not slipping up just because he's goading me into it.

"Better make it a good show, baby." I lean against the wall again, my cock aching already. "Right here." I pat the glass wall. "So I can see you from all angles."

"You think you deserve to see me from all angles?" He runs a hand down his length.

"Okay, I'll leave while you fuck that tiny dick."

"Don't leave." A little bit of that vulnerability sneaks back into his voice, so I stay where I am and nod at the glass. I won't threaten to leave him again; scaring him isn't my goal.

The toy pops when he pulls it off the wall, but it suctions perfectly against the glass. He pours water-resistant lube over it, slicking it up and adjusting it until it's at the right height. His fingers dip between his legs, and his lips part on a breathy gasp when he pushes one inside himself. My restraint is already slipping. I want to bury my tongue in his ass and open him up for my pleasure.

"Tight?" I ask, my voice lower.

"Mm," he hums, adding a second finger. He bites his damn lip and drops his head, looking down at his cock. He works it with his other hand, and then the little shit looks at me through his lashes, and I swear to fuck I almost come in my pants.

"Fuck this toy, baby. Show me how well you can take a cock."

He pulls his fingers out and rubs more lube over the toy. As he backs up to it, I make sure I'm in the perfect position to watch it enter him. Right at the edge of the glass. He reaches back to hold it steady with one hand, and slowly, so I can see every fucking stretch and pucker of his tight little hole, he pushes back until the purple dildo is buried in his ass.

Fuck, I wish that was my cock.

Mercer moans, and my eyes jump to his face. I grip his chin, tilting his head towards mine. Drunk on pleasure and high on manipulation, he looks at me with the sexiest, lustiest expression I've seen in my life. "Tell me what to do."

Get off that dildo and fuck my cock. "Fuck it, little demon."

Mercer isn't shy. He gyrates his hips, changes angles, speeds up and slows down until he's leaking from the tip of his cock. I stand behind the glass, getting a feel for what he'll look like bent over for me. I stand at the side of the shower, watching it penetrate him. I get soaked when I move inside, wanting to see him from the front as he fucks that thing like it's the best sex of his life. His moans aren't forced, and his groans are better music than the piano in my living room. He's a masterpiece and he knows it.

"Stop," I command.

He stops, panting but looking at me. "Blake," he begs me to let him keep going.

"Put it on the floor and ride it. Now."

He whimpers, moving faster than I thought possible. He sticks it to the tile floor and kneels over it. Right in front of me. Facing me. So fucking hot. His legs shake a little, but he gets his feet under his knees instead of kneeling fully and rides it like he owns it.

"Can I come?" he asks on a hitched breath. "Please. I need to come." He grabs his cock.

"Hands off."

He removes his hands and presses them to the walls. One on the glass and one on the tile, me in between. "Mmmmm, Blake. Let me come."

I want to watch his bouncing cock come without any friction so badly that I nod. "Come, baby."

When he puts his mind to it, or maybe when he's not paying attention at all, he's quick to follow orders. Within seconds, Mercer's movements slow, his breath holds, and his cock twitches. Cum spurts from the tip in two long bursts, and when he wiggles his hips, a third pulse shoots free. He stays quiet, holding his breath until the intensity settles, and then he inhales harshly. I'm leaking in my boxers, and if I don't touch my dick soon, I'm going to come in them for real.

I watch his eyes scan the floor for his cum, but the water is already washing it away. "No," he pouts.

A wicked grin tilts my lips. "What's the matter? My little cumslut need some cum?"

He trembles, still slow fucking the dildo. "Yes."

"Bet you wish you learned some patience, eh? If you had just showered and waited, it could have been my cock in your ass, filling you with the cum that thing can't give you." I rub his cheek. "Poor cumslut."

He whimpers, groaning like he's literally in pain because he doesn't have any cum. "Blake." His eyes look up at me again. Begging. "I'm begging. Fuck, you win. I'm begging. Please fuck me."

I shake my head. I want to fuck him more than anything, but I wouldn't last a pump right now.

He sinks down on the dildo, cock still standing straight and hard. "I need it, Blake."

"Cum?"

"Yes." He trembles. "Please."

To see him on the floor, riding a fake dick, after an orgasm but still so unsettled… I lose my sense of the game. I'm unbuttoning my pants and before they're even down, Mercer's hands are pulling me forward. He frees my cock and takes it into his mouth, letting out a moan of relief.

"Fuck, Mercer." I want to grab his hair, but I force myself not to. "That's it, baby. Your mouth is so fucking perfect."

He's greedy. His mouth feels nothing like it did in the car. That was a comfort thing, this is a needy, desperate, sex-crazed craving to swallow a load. With my cock in his mouth, he starts shaking again. My abs tighten and my balls draw up, ready to fill his mouth and claim him already.

When I look down, his fingers are brushing the top of his shaft, and I almost lose it right then. "You going to come again, baby?"

He nods on my cock. He sucks me harder, and when he moans, white cum shooting from his cock again, it vibrates against me and I roll into bliss. I fill his mouth so full he chokes, and then I press my hand to his head to keep him there. I come down his throat and don't stop until I can manage to breathe.

Mercer gasps, saliva and cum stretching from his lips to my tip. He licks it all up and then licks the fingers that were touching his own cock. I yank him to his feet, not even bothering to ease him off the dildo. I lick the mess off his lips and kiss him. He whines again, but the sound comes out sounding so satisfied.

"Good shower?" I rasp against his lips, barely coherent.

He grins. "Mm," he says. "Guess I got my way anyway."

Fucking fuck! I walked right into that one.

12

Mercer

I'VE BEEN STOMPING AROUND my room and the hallway for over thirty minutes. It's the middle of the night and I'm the one who kicked Blake out of my room and bathroom, but now I'm... needy or something equally as pathetic. I hate sensitive intimacy. Or I used to. Why do I seek him for comfort that isn't all about sex and release? What the hell is he doing to me to have me pacing the halls outside his door at the witching hour, seeking the warmth of his body even though I don't *want* to want it?

"Mercer," he groans.

"Don't call me that!" I bark because I'm sensitive and pissy and fucking edgy. *Gah!*

"Are you walking around like an elephant because you want my attention?"

"No." I shake my head at myself. "Yes," I mumble.

He doesn't even say anything. He just lifts the blankets, stays right where he is, and waits. My move now, and I hate making it. With an irritated-at-myself huff, I stalk into his room and settle on the very edge of his bed, my head barely on a pillow. Blake drops the blankets, enveloping me in his warmth.

"I don't cuddle," I say, backing up towards him. Backing up so far that my ass hits his groin and my back hits his chest. "I hate cuddling."

"Okay," he says, half asleep.

I back up a little more because...

"I'll be your wall, Mercer." Goddamn him for getting it. His arm drapes over my hip, and I resent myself for grabbing his hand and forcing it against my chest. I still hate cuddling. "Now go the fuck to sleep."

I debate wiggling just to irritate him, but I'm too tired. Sleep is an evasive bitch, and I need a good romp in the sheets with her.

"Don't tell me what to do," I say to make myself feel better. But I'm drifting, comfortable against the wall of Blake's body, trying to remain impassive about it.

I'M NOT SOME TRAUMATIZED victim of a horrific event. My dad never beat me and my mom always fed me. Despite hating the attention I bring to myself and the clothing choices I make, they don't even care about my sexuality too much. My aunts and uncles don't care about me period, so it's not like any particular one of them did anything horrendous to me. My cousins ignore me as much as my aunts and uncles do, and being homeschooled most of my life left me with no real friends. My sisters like me well enough, but not so much as to make much of a difference in my life, and I barely know our older brother. I forget I have an older brother most times. Probably got brainwashed to forget.

There's no particular thing that sparks my trauma, and at this point in my life, I feel like a hypocrite even referring to it as trauma. I might remember everything they did to me at the facility, but none of it was particularly painful, torturous, or degrading. Just little medical procedures that left me with a sore head and a fuzzy mind. Some therapy that made me second guess my own instincts and not trust my own brain, but otherwise, there's nothing as a focal point to explain all my broken bits. They didn't saw my head open or restrain me in torture devices while they poked and prodded at my brain matter.

I'm just a scared, lonely, unwanted guy, and feeling that over the course of twenty-three years left me with cracks in my confidence and holes in my worth. My breakdown happened over time. I never got the chance to become someone because no one was ever watching. No one ever cared. So I learned not to care. When I was a young kid, I'd get in trouble for asking questions and showing up. I stopped doing that. By the time I was a teen, I got the attention I so desperately wanted by being troublesome. I *started* doing that. More and more until I had this reputation I never planned on having and a moral compass that told me to be a fucking brat in order to gain anyone's attention. Even if it was negative attention.

The panic attacks, or whatever they are, started when I was six. I don't think they're panic attacks, but what do I know? The only therapy I'm familiar with is the kind my dad ordered, and those sessions had nothing to do with healing me and everything to do with reprogramming my mind. Too bad my mind was already too broken to hit the reset button and none of the work they did there helped. Nothing changed me. I morphed into this version of myself solely through trial and error, neglect, rewards and punishments, and a timid personality that craved attention. Any attention. Does it make me a bad person if I secretly wish the therapy and the brain wires worked? If only I could have been the person my dad wanted me to be, then maybe I'd be loved.

But the episodes never went away. They started as itchy moments of uncertainty and grew into agitated whiteouts that left me aware but completely unable to react.

They don't hurt, but they scare me. They don't incapacitate me entirely, but they render me useless. They sometimes go away on their own after hours of trying to snap out of them, or they stay until my body gets too exhausted to handle them and I fall asleep. Sometimes sex helps. Sometimes it doesn't. Sometimes distractions jarring enough to my senses pull me out of them, but sometimes not. Until Blake Carter commanded me to look at him, I had no surefire way to bring myself out of that state.

His commands work better to reprogram my mind than all the therapy did. His orders give my brain a job, which makes my body able to do the job, and the itching eases. Something about the way he handles me makes me so comfortable I act on trust, which actually makes me really uncomfortable because I don't trust anyone. I don't trust and I certainly don't act on trust.

My mind is waking up. Or maybe my body is. One of them is coming to, and the wall behind me is moving, and something hard is pressing into my ass.

"What the fuck?!" I gasp, shooting upright, kicking out my feet, trying to register the here and now.

"Ohhhhhh."

I shoot to the edge of the bed, looking behind me. Blake's grabbing his balls, burying his face in the pillows, trying hard not to cry, and I'm just sitting here like a startled deer when it all comes back to me. The elephant stomping, the huffing and puffing, the non-cuddling.

"Kill me now," Blake groans.

"Shit, I'm sort of sorry!" I squeak at him.

"Sort of? You ruined my chances of having kids, you little demon. My nuts are in my throat."

I don't mind ruining the offspring chances. I want him to be mine and only mine anyway. "Maybe if you cough they'll come out your mouth."

He groans something that sounds like a *fuck you*, and I do a quick body assessment. My foot doesn't even hurt, so I couldn't have kicked him that hard. My knee is a little tender though, not sure what from. Despite the unfortunate wake-up call he didn't ask for, the night went alright. Well, it must have because I feel rested. Either my on-again-off-again relationship with sleep is back *on*, or... or Blake made me comfortable enough to sleep deeply.

"You drugged me!" I immediately accuse because it's the only explanation. "You gave me sleeping pills or something."

He rolls over, mostly on his front, still cupping his junk. "You should come with a warning label. Little Demon: All. The. Hazards. *All of them.* I'm sewing it in all your clothes."

I'm fond of this new pet name, but I'm not admitting that. "Did you drug me?" I settle into a yoga position, legs crossed, arms relaxed on my knees.

"Sure, Mercer. If it's easier for you to believe you slept well because I drugged you, go for it." He hiccups. "I think I'm gonna throw up."

He has a sexy back. Like, who the fuck has a back like that? There aren't even any tattoos or remarkable marks. It's just skin. Tanned, smooth, silky skin shrink-wrapped to muscles that move every time he breathes. His spine sticks out all knobby-like by his neck, and his lower back has those dimples that are like perfect little thumb holders. If I straddled his ass and wrapped my fingers around his hips, my thumbs would fit perfectly there. I shall now call them Mercer's thumb rests. His ass crack could be a nice little cock warmer, too.

Okay, do not get stiff while he's suffering ball-busting agony. Which isn't my fault.

"Walls don't move," I tell him. "You said you'd be my wall."

"I breathe, asshole," he says, but it's muffled by the pillow. "Go make me coffee. You owe me."

"Own you?"

"Owe! Hurry up!"

I climb out of bed, still dressed in all his clothes. "Not a morning cuddler then. Noted."

Despite his command, I *do not* hurry. I have a very luxurious shower with all my new products and fond memories of last night, then I do a face mask because, why not? Then I spend a considerable amount of time in front of the mirror, trying on ten thousand outfit combinations only to throw on the same sweats and hoodie from pre-shower, and *then* I go make his coffee.

Nothing feels like me anymore. I can't decide on a style. I'm still feeling all weirdly comfortable and relaxed, so the hoodlum look fits my current mood. Blake is already up and sitting on the couch, still not wearing a shirt, so I make us both a coffee. I like a cappuccino and Blake likes a latte, so I make them right and hold his out to him.

"I already made one because you took too long." He glares at me, his blue eyes accusatory. He takes it from me anyway and then points at his phone. "My buddy Aaron is on the phone. Aaron, Mercer is here."

"Hey, Mercer," this Aaron says, and I squint my eyes at Blake like he's cheating on me even though I don't do boyfriends and totally do not want him to be mine. I'm so good at lying to myself.

"Hey." I plop down and spill hot coffee on Blake's bare chest.

"Warning label," he hisses. "You still got all those server numbers and codes in your head?"

I nod and sip.

"Start spouting them off. Aaron is my tech guy." He leaves his phone on my lap, speaker still on. Blake pulls out a second phone, and here I am, thinking one phone to snoop on is going to be a handful, but this guy has two.

As I'm rambling off numbers, sequences and codes to Aaron, categorizing them all by server and location in the room, something weird happens. Neither Aaron nor Blake questions my memory. Blake is matching up my numbers with the photos he took of the room, and Aaron is jotting them all down and only chiming in to say, 'okay, next.' They believe me. Trust me. They aren't second-guessing me and calling that sort of memory recall impossible because of who I am and the trouble I bring to myself. For the first time in maybe my whole life, I'm being taken seriously.

The weight of it hits me hard. It's heavy and enlightening together, and I can't decide if I'm floating away or sinking under the responsibility. Blake, of fucking course, notices. None of my little details slip past him. He pulls my feet onto his lap, rubs them through my socks, and doesn't say a word about it. He does point to his dick and make an X with his fingers so I know not to kick there again. Don't Xs mark the spot?

"Okay, got 'em all. Thanks, man. Killer mind." Aaron is no longer on my shit list. "While I have you guys, I got a bit of new information on that facility. Now a good time or you wanna wait until later?"

I look at Blake, wondering what he's going to say. He doesn't say shit. He shrugs his shoulders to ask my opinion. The weight of this day is already more than I'm used to carrying. I need to go back to bed and test my relationship with sleep to make sure it wasn't a fluke last night.

"Okay," I tell Aaron. "Now is good. I dunno what you're gonna say, but if I detect even a hint of pity in your voice, I will find where you live and put your dick in a sausage grinder."

Aaron laughs, but Blake snorts. "Don't believe him, man. He sucks at kitchen utensils. If he ever threatens you with a dagger, run for your life, but kitchen products are generally a safe threat."

I push my foot into the X that marked the spot, and Blake groans again. And gets hard. Sucker for pain or just a responsive cock? I'll find out.

"Okay," Aaron says, cutting in like a buzzkill. "There are a lot of elite kids there. Against their will. It's not just a place that experiments illegally with psychological therapy and minor surgical procedures, but it seems to be a hub for 'training' the kids of well-to-do parents how to act, walk, and talk the way the parents want them to. You weren't the only elite son there, Mercer. Politicians' kids, government officials', CEOs', and even some children with parents in the FBI, CIA, or secret service. Some of their therapy is legit and recorded. It's when those methods don't work that they tend to go off-grid and get sent to the other facility at the back of the property. So, naturally, I want to shut it down."

Blake rolls his head in my direction. "Aaron has a big ol' heart for kids in trouble."

"Fuck you. That's because I was a kid in trouble." Blake smiles at this. "But here's the real kicker. You know that older brother of yours, Mercer? The one you never really see?"

"Yeah..."

"He sort of runs the place. He's the one who makes deals and negotiations with the parents of these kids. He's basically a recruiter. What do you want to do with that information?"

I'm shocked. Stunned. Don't even know why. Barely know the guy. Haven't seen my brother in years. Incapable of talking or responding. I'm processing, and maybe my brain is glitching, but I need a second. Then I need a jump start.

"We'll call you back. Thanks, Aaron. Be in touch soon."

Blake grabs my cheeks, making my lips squish out like a fish. "You short circuiting?"

"Maybe," I mumble through chubby cheeks.

"Do you ever have sex when you aren't in a negative mind space?"

"What the fuck kind of question is that at a time like this?" I smack his hand away.

Blake laughs, grinning at me with that cheeky look I'm learning to love. Or think fondly of. "Brought your brain back on board, didn't it?"

Sometimes I forget he is literally trained to read people. "Don't make me dick-kick you again, Carter."

13
Blake

Mercer's experiments with fashion and style have taken a turn tonight. Camped outside the main building of the facility we just found out his brother runs, he looks like... me. He wanted to scope the place out, disappeared into his room, and came back out in tactical gear.

Our jackets are the same. We have the same pair of boots on, but his are a few sizes smaller. His pants are black and full of pockets, but they're almost identical to mine. When I hold binoculars to my eyes, he mimics the motions. It's freaking me out.

"Why do you look like me?" I finally break down and ask.

From the passenger seat of the Denali, he keeps the binoculars to his face and sucks on a lolly. "Because you haven't taken my bait yet, so this is my way of testing my theory."

"What theory?"

"That you're egotistical and want to fuck yourself." He drops the binoculars to his lap. "Is it working? You wanna fuck mini-you?"

“I wanna fuck mini *you*,” I snap at him. “You just like playing games too much.”

“So, fuck me. Right here. This mission is a bust, anyway. My brother isn’t here.” He scoffs like he’s been dragged into boredom even though this was his idea.

“Was that begging?”

“It most certainly was not.” He crosses his arms and shifts the sucker from one cheek to the other. “We both know you’re going to stick your dick in me way before I resort to begging, so can we stop pretending otherwise?”

“You begged me in the shower.”

“I wasn’t in my right mind. That doesn’t count.”

Of course the rules change when they suit him. Plus, now I feel like I can’t fuck him until he changes out of those clothes, or it’ll prove some point that I want to bang myself. He’s seriously impossible. But there’s no denying I want him. I don’t know exactly what it is about him, or maybe it’s everything about him, but he’s changing my concept of sex and attraction.

The old me would have been beyond annoyed by his manipulative displays. I would have kicked him out of my apartment after the fire alarm incident. The new me wonders how much farther he can take this and if he has any morals or limits when it comes to getting what he wants. He’s making me impulsive and volatile, two things I’ve been trained not to be. I’m calculated and calm, able and skilled at reading people and situations, and patient about the way I handle things. The more time I spend near Mercer, the more my training goes down the drain. Only with him so far, and I won’t let myself slip when it comes to work and jobs.

I put the car in gear and pull out of the lot. We’ll come back another time to do some recon on his brother. Mercer hasn’t said what he feels about the whole thing yet, but he’ll come to a conclusion eventually. He claims not to know his brother and says he hasn’t seen him in over a year. When my phone rings, I try to answer it through the Denali's Bluetooth, but it doesn't work because Mercer has booted my phone out and connected his own. He smirks at that.

"Mr. Blake Carter's line, his little demon speaking. How may I help you?" Mercer takes it upon himself to answer. "I'll let him know. Anything else?" I'm not even mad he's taken this role. "Oh, that's juicy. Will we get to meet in person?"

"What's he saying?" I cut in.

Mercer shushes me. "Great. We'll be there. What should I wear?"

We're almost home by the time he stops gabbing with Aaron, and when he finally hangs up, I've smoked three cigarettes and gotten a boner. "What'd he say?"

Mercer's expression is unsettling. I don't trust it even a little, but goddamn my dick for getting harder. "Fuck me and find out."

"You know I can just call him back, right?"

Mercer shoves my phone down his pants. "They're purple tonight," he says. "Same colour as that dildo I fucked in the shower. Not lacy, but strappy and satin." He taps his dick, which almost looks like it's sitting on top of my phone, like he tucked my cell under his hard-on and covered it all with panties and pants. "And no, to answer your question from days ago. I don't typically have sex in a good mind space, but my mind is right and dandy at the moment, so are you going to take advantage of it or not?"

I want to. But I'll be the master manipulator tonight. He's going to beg before he gets my dick, so fuck him for thinking he's going to win.

"Are you submissive?" I ask him.

He scoffs. Or huffs. Or laughs condescendingly. "You seriously think I'm going to tell you that? You haven't even put in the work to find out. You're lazy at foreplay, Blake Carter."

He's submissive when he needs comfort after an episode, but I don't know if he's submissive when he's in the right frame of mind. But after weeks of build up I'm counting as foreplay, I'm done waiting. I want him, and we both know it, so whatever sex we have tonight is going to come after he begs and shows me just how fucking feisty he can be.

THE BUSIER I MAKE myself appear, the harder Mercer tries to distract me. Aaron called again when we were in the elevator—Mercer almost came when it vibrated against his dick—and apparently, the wife of Frank has another job for us. My family doesn't know about Aaron, but he has access to all my accounts and devices. But that job will take planning, and right after I hung up with Aaron, my dad called with another job.

Sean Pendleton. Dead. By Friday.

Those were the only words he said. Friday is in two days. Now I have a murder to plot on top of Mercer's attention to keep.

I'm sitting on a stool at the island, a secure laptop on the surface, and a rum and coke next to it, trying to research Sean Pendleton. Mercer, still dressed like me, is in the kitchen trying to prove to me he can cook something. I accused him of being a useless houseboy, and he loves nothing more than to prove himself to someone who might actually see his worth. The effort he puts into making a snack speaks volumes, but I keep the information to myself. He's never had to prove himself to anyone before, and now that he's been given the chance, he's going to win at it because he's learning to value himself. But he's going to be a little demon about it. Naturally.

"Blake?" he croons my name in a voice dripping with innocence. I peek up at him over the screen, eyes wide, lips pouty, hair a mess. "How many ounces are in a cup?" He's got mixing bowls and measuring cups all over the place. I don't even know what he's attempting to make.

"Asks the guy who is literally a numbers genius?" I lift a brow.

He fans himself, pretending the oven is making him hot. "Ugh, cooking is warm work. Better take this off." He unzips the jacket and folds it over the back of a chair. "That's better."

Cups and ounces forgotten. I get back to my research, ignoring my cock's needs. After pulling some ingredients from the fridge, he takes his long-sleeved tee off, and my eyes snag on a purple top. It hugs his body and comes up over his collarbones to wrap around the base of his neck like a pretty little collar. Fucking hell.

"So, who is Sean Pendleton?" he asks timidly. The shy-boy act doesn't mesh with his little demon personality, but it's just as sexy. He gets back to mixing ingredients in a bowl meant for salad.

"Some bookie who works with the Six."

"The gang?"

"Yeah. Guess he's been skimming. A lot."

"All that skimmed money and he'll be too dead to do anything with it all. Poor Sean Pendleton."

I click through some online images of this chubby accountant to familiarize myself with his appearance. As I'm scanning his socials and getting a feel for where he spends his time, something crashes.

I look up to find Mercer, lacking pants now too, kneeling on the countertop, reaching for something high up in the cupboard. His fine little ass is on full display because the purple panties he taunted me with earlier are a thong, and the way the string disappears between his cheeks is breaking all my resolve.

"No food in that cupboard, little demon. Whatcha looking for?" There's a plastic bowl still wobbling on the floor where it fell, and Mercer waits until it settles.

"I thought I saw flour up here." He looks back at me, still with the innocent act. "Help me?"

Okay, he's not verbally begging, but this is coercive begging if I've ever seen it. Getting up, I round the island and come up behind him. His ass is right at face level, and I'm not strong enough to resist the temptation of it. My hands run down the front of his thighs and I bury my face in his ass. His skin smells like expensive body lotion, and I bet he tastes like it, too. I graze his cheek with my teeth, nipping him lightly.

"Flour's in the pantry." I nip his other ass cheek. To be honest, I don't think I own flour. "What are you making?" I grab his hips, spin him around, and sit his bare ass on the cool granite. His copper eyes and dark hair go fucking perfectly with this vibrant shade of purple. Everything about him is a pleasure to admire, right down to the way he looks back at me.

"It's a surprise," he whispers, licking his fuckable lips. "I'm trying to make you happy. Aren't I a good boy?"

"Mm," I hum, running my hands up his thighs. Goosebumps rise on his skin, but I rub them away when I drag my hands back down. "Do you want to be a good boy?"

"Yes." He leans against the cupboard, making sure I can see all of him in this two-piece purple ensemble. "I want to be so good for you."

I smirk, leaning in until his legs widen on their own and his hard cock brushes against my abs. I lick his lips and make him whimper before whispering, "Bullshit. You want to be a bad boy. Don't you, little demon?" I pull back to look at him.

The wideness of his eyes narrows. The switch from good boy to bad boy happens instantly. His act goes out the window and familiar defiance joins the party. But his next move actually does surprise me.

From somewhere beneath the purple, he pulls a dagger and holds it to my throat, shifting it until it presses snuggly to my pulse point. "So bad," he agrees. "I can be the demon you need me to be. Now fuck me."

"Beg." My cock is so hard it hurts.

"Fuck. Me." He presses the tip of the dagger hard enough to sting.

His amber glare clashes with my blue one, and we're caught in a tense battle of lusty eyes. I want to win by making him beg for it with manners and he wants to win by getting what he wants without begging. We both want to fuck, but we're committed to the game. Our torture is self-inflicted. When the oven beeps to signal its rise to temperature, our heat levels snap. I grip his wrist and twist the dagger away from my neck, but the little shit has another one pressed to my other side. I glance down at it, panicking just a bit.

"Fuck no. I don't trust you with that one." It's a kitchen knife, probably for chopping vegetables, because it's much, *much* bigger than the dagger.

"Fuck me before I accidentally kill you," Mercer demands like a bossy bitch. "I really don't want to take on the Sean Pendleton job, so you better hurry up before this thing slips." To exaggerate his point, the knife slides a bit, nicking my skin. "Oops."

Game on, baby.

I push his hand away and wrap mine around his neck. The knife clatters to the counter, and I use the hold on his throat and a hand under his ass to bring him off the countertop. As soon as his feet hit the floor, I spin him to face the island and bend him the fuck over it. My palm smacks across his bare ass, and for the first time tonight, he moans like he's winning.

"Mm." His hands knock ingredients and bowls to the ground. "Spank me, D... Blake."

Just because he wants to get spanked, I stop. One red handprint on his ass is enough for me right now. I kneel behind him, my hands skimming his skin. I hook a finger in the strap of his thong and pull it from between his ass cheeks, letting it go to snap against his skin.

"Fuck," he pants.

"Bend over. Chest on the counter." He complies easily this time. I spread his ass and press my thumb to his tight hole. "Such an eager slut, eh, baby?"

"Yes."

I run my tongue over his hole and feel his whole body tremble. When I do it again, he pushes his ass against my face and tries to take charge. I love it. I devour him until he's dripping, tongue fucking him until I know his cock will be leaking just from the build up. My boy's response to stimulation is so fucking beautiful, and the fact that he can come multiple times just gives me a goal I can't wait to obtain. When he's flushed and agitated, wanting more, I stand up.

"Turn around, Mercer."

He straightens his body and turns to face me. His cheeks are rosy, and his eyes are doing all the begging his tongue won't.

"Am I still lazy at foreplay?" I ask, palming my cock.

He shakes his head but won't answer. I wait. "Took you long enough to give in to it."

"Is it so hard to say no? To admit you were wrong?"

He clenches his jaw and rubs himself.

"Show me, but leave the panties on."

Mercer grabs his dick and pulls it out, letting the purple thong wrap around it. The tip is glistening, and even the shaft is wet, precum already coating him. I bend down to lick it, and his hands latch onto the counter for balance.

"Ready to get fucked?"

"Yes."

"Beg."

"Blake…"

I grin at his defiance. I lift his hips and set his ass on the island again. "Heels on the counter. Spread your legs." I help him get into position. He's mostly sitting up, cock jutting proudly. When he puts his heels on the counter and opens his legs, I get the most perfect view of his hole with the G-string slid over. He lifts his smooth balls while I eye-fuck him.

"Why are you wearing so many clothes?" he pouts.

I won't be for long. The box of sex toys he stabbed is still on the floor beside the pantry, so I rifle through it. I find the cum flavoured lube but keep rooting around. I want my cum to be the only taste in his mouth tonight. When I find another sample size bottle they probably threw in as a freebie, I flick the lid open and stand in front of him again.

"I want you to finger yourself. Slow. Give me a show."

He snatches the bottle from me like he's going to win this show. He won't win. He'll be begging soon. Mercer is a master of seduction, though. While he fingers himself and I strip, it becomes a fifty-fifty chance on which of us will snap first. By the time I'm naked, he's flushed and leaking. His two middle fingers pump in and out of his ass, curling and stretching and driving me wild. His gaze shifts from my eyes to my cock, and when he moans, he watches the tip of my dick glisten in excitement.

I pull his fingers from his ass and step between his legs. With both hands on his hips, I angle him until my cock presses against his hole. Then I stay still.

"Blake," he whines.

"Mm?" I hum against his wet lips. He kisses me, biting my lips and sucking my tongue like it's going to tempt me into thrusting. It's close, not going to lie. "Need something, baby?"

"Fuck me."

"Hmm?" I bite his lip and nudge him a little more.

His arm wraps around my neck and his legs go around my waist, trying to physically force me to fuck him. I'm bigger and stronger. I kiss down his neck and tangle my fingers in his hair, yanking his head back.

He whimpers and groans, so close to losing. "Blake, fuck." He tries to tighten his legs again.

"What do you need, little demon?" I press against him a bit more, teasing the fuck out of him.

He groans for so long and with such emotion, I pull his hair again. "Fuck. Fine." He looks at me. "Fuck me," he begs.

"Say please."

He damn near cries. "Please. Please. Please. Please, fuck me, Blake. Fuck me!"

Unable to wait another second, I force his head forward so I can see his face, eyes connected, and slam inside him. Mercer's eyes widen before rolling back, his choked gasp turning into a moan. His tight hole constricts my cock so hard that my knees quake and my forehead falls forward. His heels dig into my ass, holding me there while he adjusts to my size. A warmth spreads through me, and I can't decide if it's a feeling of absolute pleasure, like this is exactly what I've been craving my entire life, or if it's a sense of rightness, like Mercer is mine and he was always meant to be mine. How long have I been unknowingly searching for this bossy little brat?

"Mmmmm." It's his outright refusal to mutter praise.

"I knew you'd beg." I rock a bit, drawing out more of his moans. "You're my little slut now, Mercer."

"Fuck, yes," he groans. "Fuck me like I'm your slut." His legs release my hips, giving me full permission and free rein to do whatever the hell I want to him. He's offering himself up as mine—mine to have, to use, to worship, to punish, to praise. Just mine. I've never seen a person more worthy of all my attention.

I push him until his back hits the counter, his amber eyes looking up at me with all the praise his words won't say. *Yet.* He moves my laptop out of the way and waits to see what I'm going to do with him. I hook his knees over my elbows, drag his small body right to the edge, and slow fuck him until he's nice and worked up—loosened up.

"How much can you take, Mercer?"

"Everything. Give me everything."

"No limits?"

"Blake, if you don't start fucking me real good, I'm going to get that blue dildo." He literally snaps his fingers at me. "No limits. Get on with the fucking!"

Grabbing the purple collar around his neck, I yank him up until our noses brush. "So bossy." I hold him right there and fuck him hard and fast. One hand on his hip, holding him in place, and one wrapped around the collar. Mercer's body bounces, jarring and jolting with each thrust, his mouth sometimes open against mine, and our foreheads clacking together. He's experiencing bliss and I'm experiencing damnation, and the concoction is more than my sensitive dick can handle. Every breath comes out staccato and choked until he reaches between our bodies to fist his dick.

I stop. "No."

"Blake," he begs.

I pull him off the counter and stand him upright, losing my connection with him to prove a point. He can boss me around all he wants, but it's going to delay his satisfaction. This. *This* is the lesson he needed to learn in the shower the other night. He doesn't get what he wants exactly when he wants it, and it's not all about the speedy orgasm. It's about the dynamic we create together, and fuck if he thinks he's going to rush our connection.

"Blake! I didn't play all these games for you to just—"

I shove him to his knees, hook my thumb over his bottom teeth, and yank his jaw open. My cock goes down his throat the next second, and Mercer's fingernails dig into my ass, pulling me in even closer.

"Learned to watch your mouthy attitude yet, you little demon?" I stroke his cheek and hold him in place, suffocating him until his eyes water. "Or are you just a slut for punishment?"

He whimpers around my cock, almost making me come, so I yank him off and watch strings of saliva stretch from his lips to my dick. "Blake."

"How's it taste?" I smack his cheek and hold him off from devouring me like he wants to.

"Like watermelon lube," he snips at me.

I pull him to his feet and fold him over the counter again. "Hands where I can see them," I demand. As soon as they hit the countertop, I sink into him until my thighs touch his ass. "I don't want you coming yet."

"I can come more than once," he says, voice breathy. "Please. I need it so bad."

"There's the begging I asked for." I wrap my fingers around his lean waist, watching my cock push in and out of him. "Fuck, baby. This purple thong is everything." I snap the strap, a bright red line colouring his ass. "Legs together."

Mercer steps his feet together, closing his legs. It makes him constrict my dick harder. All of this, the sight of it, the feel of it, and the fucking energy of it, is putting me in a conflicting place. I want to dominate the fuck out of him and treat him like the brat he is, but it's our first time and I want to treasure him like the good little boy he so badly wants to be. How can I combine both? Since when did I turn sentimental? How many first times have I had with others without caring about making it something special?

My fingers run up and down his spine, loving the way he reacts to a gentle touch even though he claims to hate it.

He's touch starved and doesn't even know it. The glide of my cock in his ass is pure perfection, but he's losing his edge because of the tickle of my fingertips.

"Blake, I'm gonna come like this. Let me. Please, let me."

I reach around the front of him, taking his cock in a loose fist. I lean over him and press my lips to the top of his spine. Fucking him, kissing him, and gently stroking him, Mercer loses his mind but remains a good boy.

"Blake. Can I? I can't... I can't stop... fuck."

"Come, Mercer," I whisper. "I give you permission."

Mercer rocks his hips until he finds a good rhythm, his ass fucking my cock and his dick fucking my fist. To know he's eager and confident enough to take exactly what he wants without shame is the biggest turn on I've ever come across. The glide of him along my shaft is exhilarating to my body and mind, and when his dick throbs in my hand, his fingers digging into the granite, I almost come in his ass.

"Mm, Blake." Cum coats my hand in warm pulses, and Mercer keeps his hips moving. He babbles a bunch of sexy sounds, and I clench my ass muscles to keep from coming too soon. His body jolts upright and the back of his head hits my shoulder.

"Such a good boy, Mercer."

"Call me a demon," he rasps, lust dripping from his voice.

"My demon. Mine."

"Mm, yes."

When he stops fucking himself on my cock, I thrust forward a few times, milking him just a little more. He whimpers, leaning back on me for stability. As impatient as I am to start fucking him again, chasing my orgasm and pulling another out of him, I pause to savour this moment. Mercer, satisfied, pliant, calm, and docile, looking like a wet dream and a beautiful man, touching me everywhere he can because he trusts me. It's a big moment, and the power of it swells in my chest.

He might be playing a game still, but I'm not. There will be time for rough fucks and punishment later, but right now, I want him to know he's fucking cherished. I kiss the side of his neck and lick the salt from his skin.

"All tuckered out, little boy?" I suck, leaving a purple bruise just above the hem of the collar.

"No. I won't be done until I swallow your cum and go to bed with it deep in my ass." He pushes his ass back onto my cock. "Can your age keep up with me, oh wise one?"

I shove my cum coated fingers into his mouth until he chokes. "Is your bratty attitude all for show or are you going to live up to the expectations I have for you, little demon?"

He slurps on my fingers. "Find out."

14

Mercer

B LAKE TURNED THE OVEN off, and then he carried my ass into his bedroom. I mean, a bedroom fuck wasn't really on my agenda, but I can't deny the comfort of his bed in the position he has me in. Face buried in the blankets, wrists pinned behind my back, knees damn near touching my ribs, and ass in the air so he can piledrive me like I'm not breakable. I'm a fucking slut for it. *Fuck me like I'm invincible and treat me like the mouthy brat I am.*

The purple thong drapes over the bedside lamp and this heathen ripped the top when he tore it off me. Naked and unafraid, I bury my moans in the blankets so he doesn't know how much I love this rough fuck. The kitchen sex was softer than I thought it would be, but I caught that spark of sentimentality in his eyes. He wanted the first time to be special. I won't admit it, but it made me feel wanted and appreciated like I never have before. He cares about more than my body and the back-and-forth games we play. I feel it in my chest even though I can't fully comprehend it.

Thankfully, this aggressive pounding is damn near giving me a concussion I'm grateful for because it's preventing me from thinking about anything except pleasure and the desire for more of it. Blake should be like any other guy I've fucked. But he's not. He feels different, and I don't know if that's because of how hard I worked to get his attention or because he treats me differently than anyone else, but I'm so here for it I'm already anticipating a second hookup. A part of me wondered if I'd leave once I got what I wanted from him, but screw my damn mind for wanting more than this hot-as-fuck sex!

Blake's dick hits so deep I fold like a suitcase, the power of his thrusts sending my upper body up the bed. Without my hands free to stop my slide, I end up flat on my stomach and Blake won't have that. He flips me over like I weigh nothing, folding me in half to slam back in.

"Fuck," I groan, loving this angle. Loving how easily he manipulates my body. "More."

"So fucking desperate for my cum," he growls at me. "Where do you want it?"

Everywhere. I want to bathe in it. I might have a cum kink, but I also have a Blake fetish. Not only do I want his cum inside me, all over me, filling me, but I want *him* all over me. I want his body against mine, his lips connected with mine, and his hands all over my skin. A desperation washes over me and I whimper, needing him everywhere.

"I got you, baby," he says.

He keeps the sex rough, but his mouth turns soft. He fucks my ass so hard our bodies rub together, but the way his teeth graze my lips and his tongue edges with mine adds a level of gentle passion to this filth. Jesus, I'm here for it. How am I craving rough and soft together?

"Blake," I beg, wrapping my arms around his neck to keep his mouth on mine. Never really needed a kiss during sex before, but I can't stop. If he abandons my lips, I might die.

I'm burning up from something. The sex, maybe. The feeling of the sex, probably. The way his body fits with mine and doesn't feel overwhelming even though he's bigger than me. The way he gives me power by seeing me, knowing what I need even though I don't know it, and the way he rasps noises against my lips that sound like a lot more than just moans. They're wordless words that convey a feeling I want to accept but don't want to hear, and that more than anything, is heating me up so much I'm on the brink of too many things. Coming. Falling for him. Needing him for more than his body. I'm teetering on the tip of the dagger, and one wrong move will send my heart slipping down the blade.

"Fuck, Mercer," he groans, sliding a hand under my lower back. "Come with me. Again. Right now, little boy." He pushes up on my lower back and that's it for me.

Cum slicks between our abs and my choked breaths go straight into Blake's moaning mouth. We aren't even kissing, but he doesn't pull away. He fucks his cum into my ass and slides our slippery bodies together until the tension settles into something exhausting and euphoric. A sense of bliss that comes from exertion, like a rush of endorphins and an earned sweat.

I take all of thirty seconds to enjoy the bubble of blissfulness, really sinking into it. Just when I'm ready to pull back and be a mood ruiner because this is *deep*, Blake does it for me. He sits up on his heels, pulls out, and turns full caveman at the sight of his cum leaking out of my sore ass. He stares for so long I almost get self-conscious, but when his eyes meet mine, I see the thoughts inside the blue of them.

He's telling me something better than his words can. He's saying I just turned him into an addict. He's saying that this first fuck is out of the way and stamped into our memories as a good time, and now he's going to go full beast mode because it doesn't have to be gentle and sentimental every time. With his eyes, Blake is daring me, no, warning me, to be exactly who I am so he can have me as myself.

I will never ignore you.

He bends forward, tongue salivating to lick his mess from my ass. I sit up and grab his hair, forcing his face right in front of mine. "If you take that cum from my body, you'll be fucking another load into me."

"You want to keep me in there all night, little demon?"

Preferably *all life*. Longer than the night. I want him inside me all the time, and I hate him for making me this way. If I'm always full of him, he can never abandon me. "I'd rather you put your cock back inside me to keep it all in there until you're ready to come again."

Blake smiles, running his thumb over my bottom lip. "Okay. Let me clean you up and take care of you first."

"I don't want you to take care of me. Just stay here with me, all filthy and sweaty."

"At least let me clean off your cum." He runs his fingers through it all over our stomachs. "And get you something to drink. Make sure the oven is really off."

He starts to climb off the bed, and I think I get scared. "Blake..." Don't leave me. Don't ignore me. Don't walk away from me. I'm trying to be sexy and manipulate him into another round, not this emotional mess of neglect issues. "Blake..."

"I'm right here," he says, taking my hand and hoisting me into his arms like I'm special. "I'm not going anywhere."

I try not to cling to him. But I do. I'm a weak-willed bitch.

After rinsing us off in the shower, making me pee and brush my teeth, getting me a bottle of water, and making sure the oven really is off, he leaves everything else on the counter and brings me back to his bed. I'm yawning by this point, but I don't want him to see it because another good fuck is definitely happening. Or a blowie. Something. I just need him in my body.

He tries to pull the blankets over our bodies, but he's struggling for some reason. I look back at him and realize I'm holding his hand so tight he can't even grip the blanket to pull it over us. He smirks at me but doesn't say anything, not complaining about how long it takes him.

"What were you even cooking out there?" he asks, settling in behind me.

I pull his arm around my body and scootch back until his still-hard dick presses against my ass. "I don't know. I just put a bunch of shit in a bowl to get your attention."

"You got it, Mercer. My attention. Fuck, you've got it." He nuzzles into my neck and I don't hate it. I opposite of hate it.

"Fuck me one more time."

"You're falling asleep." He kisses my neck.

"Please." My eyes close, but I'm still latched onto his hand like he's going to disappear.

"In the morning, baby. Sleep first."

"At least put it in me then. Please, Blake."

"Guess you got over your aversion to begging." He laughs, pulling my hips so he can slide inside me. I'm still recovering, so he goes slow and gentle, and when he's fully seated inside me, I finally feel comfortable enough to trust sleep. "I'm right here. I'm not going anywhere."

"I hate cuddling," I remind him, holding tighter, feeling more and more relaxed.

"I know." He's calling me a liar. "Don't kick me in the balls again."

"No promises."

I SCRUTINIZE MY FACE in front of the bathroom mirror. My eyes are still the same shape and colour, but something within them swirls differently. My skin is flushed and healthy, and the purple mark on my neck from Blake's hedonistic mouth stands out against the paleness of my complexion, but I like the look of it all. My hair is the same dark mess, jutting up just how I like it, falling in weird places, acting chaotic because my mind is so messy it affects my hair. But something about me is different.

I don't recognize myself, but at the same time, I'm peeking through my appearance because something about the person glancing back at me from within feels familiar. I've never seen him before, but I get that homey feeling, like a childhood memory still fuzzy in details, but you just *know* it's a good memory. Like a song you swear you've never heard before; you can't sing the lyrics, but you know the music. It's a vibe or a feeling, maybe a sixth sense. It's knowing and not knowing together. Someone is clawing their way to my surface, and I think I want to let him.

I wash and moisturize my face, give my teeth another brush, chug some water because I'm parched, and stare at the mess in the kitchen. I should clean it up...

I skip down the hall to find Blake still in bed. He's sprawled out on his back, chest bare, blankets only pulled up to his V, and damn near sparkling in the sun coming through the windows. He looks restful, and after I woke him up for a quickie that somehow turned into a non-quickie, I know I should let him sleep while I clean the kitchen. But the sun is spotlighting him like he's a prize, and my needy self wants to be close to him.

I crawl onto the bed and pull the blankets down. His semi-hard dick stays flopped on his thigh, and my mouth salivates at the prospect of tasting it first thing in the morning. I lean down to lick it, figuring it needs to wake up as much as he does. I pop the head into my mouth and give it a swirl around my tongue, pleased when he hardens fully.

"This is so much better than a kick to the balls," he says, sleepy but happy sounding.

"I like to keep you on edge." I suck him down without any real intent. Just to taste him, maybe even to feel close to him. "Why'd you fuck me without a condom?"

"Because I made Aaron hack your medical records and I know you get regular checks and stay on PrEP."

Nosy bastard. "What about my reassurance of your health?"

"Didn't hear you asking about it last night."

I nuzzle my face into his groin, laying down on his legs. "You make me irresponsible."

"Mm," he agrees. "I printed off my last test results. It's in the kitchen drawer if you want to look at it. I haven't hooked up with anyone in... a while."

"Not even Dee?"

"You know the answer to that," he says, eyes still closed. "Which reminds me. That fireman's breakfast is tomorrow. I signed you up. You gotta be there at five."

"In the fucking morning!?"

"Mm."

Now I want to bite his dick instead of lick it.

"Then I have to do the Sean Pendleton job. Then we're going to that gala."

Okay, full sulk mode engaged. I don't want to do the breakfast. I don't want to miss him when he goes to merc Sean Pendleton. I don't want to go to the gala. I drop his dick and sigh.

"Come here." He tugs me up his body and rests my head on his chest. His fingers tingle down my spine and my sweatpants get all bunched up, but I like the position. "Your dad specifically asked me not to bring you to that gala."

"Good. Then I won't go." Which pisses me off because I don't want Blake to be there without me. He's going to look all hot and irresistible in a suit, and I can't have anyone thinking they can get up in there.

"Oh, you're going. And he's going to be distracted all night because we defied him, and it's going to give my brother a chance to snoop on him."

"Bronson?"

"Brandt," he answers. "Bronson has to remain the good boy because he's engaged to your sister."

"Pretty sure my sister is gay but would never say it because it would upset Daddy's plans." My fingers trace the ridges of his chest. "Why do you care about me? Is it just to piss my dad off?" Yep, that was an insecurity straight from my mouth.

"Don't ask me questions you're not emotionally ready to hear answers to, Mercer."

My heart sinks. I forgot it was in my chest there for a bit, but bam, there it is. Bleeding all over the place, reminding me it was sitting on that dagger point. "Right. I'm a job."

Blake snorts a laugh, but his fingers keep tickling my spine. "Sometimes I don't think you know yourself. You're Mercer Bentley Palmerston, for fuck's sake. What kind of answer is going to make you get all squirmy and weird? Think about it."

Well, taunts and jibes and being neglected are the norm for me. Harsh barbs and passive-aggressive insults aren't anything new. Being a task or a job is a role I'm familiar with, and being a letdown is basically my status quo. What would make me uncomfortable is… depth. The heartfelt kind. Feelings deeper than sexual attraction and mutual orgasms. The spark of sentimentality in his eyes last night when we finally had sex for the first time.

Why does he care about me? Because I mean something to him. Not to his dad or my dad. Not for a job. Not because he wants to rescue me or heal me. He just cares. About me. Mercer Bentley Palmerston.

He's right. That does make me uncomfortable because my instincts tell me not to trust it or believe it. Lies are pretty when they're bred from insecurities and come from sexy lips. But I want to hear it so badly. I'm craving that discomfort.

I told him not to make me weepy!

"But you took me because you wanted information about my family, right?"

"Sure," he says. "I saw an opportunity and took it."

"But?" I ask, feeling stupid for being so desperate to know.

"No buts." He shifts his body until he's sitting up, leaning against the headboard. Tilting my chin, he adds, "I saw the opportunity, but you caught my attention before that moment in your parents' kitchen. Honestly, I might have created the opportunity just because I wanted to see you in the black lacy thing again." He smirks. "Where'd that one go?"

"It's dead. My dad probably burned it. Olivia took me there that night and all I got was a disappointed look and a demand to take off the ridiculous outfit." Which is the sad part. I don't even merit a firm scolding or an angry yell. I'm not even worth that effort anymore. "How would you punish me?"

"What do you mean?"

"If I did something you didn't like, how would you react?"

"Depends what you did," Blake says. "If you waste emergency responders' time, I'll make you volunteer." He laughs, pushing me onto my back and hovering above me. "If you accidentally on purpose poisoned an entire engagement party..." He shrugs, tugging my pants down. My cock springs free, and I start to breathe a little harder. Almost nervous. "I might reward you instead of punish you." He notices me tense up and stops immediately. "Talk to me, Mercer."

I shake my head because it's fucking dumb. "Nothing."

"Mercer." He pulls my pants back up.

"I'm just... it's new to me to be... fuck." I run my hands down my face, mortified. "I don't stutter!"

Blake laughs, pulling my hands free. "Out with it, demon."

"I'm usually where you are," I tell him, eye contact and everything. "I'm not used to being the one on the... receiving end."

His eyes soften a little. "You've never been blown?"

"I mean, not really. I've had a mouth on it, but not like a full..." Kill me now. I'm a twenty-three-year-old slut and I've never gotten a blowjob.

"You don't want it? Not interested?" He tilts my chin. "Be honest. No wrong answer."

"I'm self-conscious, I think."

"You?" Blake grins. "Mercer Bentley Palmerston? Guy who struts his shit in lingerie, sets a fire alarm off at three in the morning, and has no fucking shame about baking a batch of nothing just to get noticed?" He lifts a brow.

I smack him. "I like to perform. It gets me off to be the one *doing* the *doing*, you know? I don't have to worry about anything other than taking it, making it feel good, and enjoying it myself because the other person is so focused on their own pleasure. But a blowjob... that's all their attention on me and how I'm reacting. It's dumb because I seek attention, but... not that kind. I get stage fright or something, like I'm supposed to respond a certain way."

"You don't have to respond any certain way. Not with me. But it's okay if you don't want it. Explain this servicing kink to me." He settles in beside me and honestly expects me to talk about it. He even plays with my fingers.

Well, okay then. "It makes me so hard to see you react to me. That's what gets me off. Yeah, it's you. Everything about you. I want you like..." I shut myself up because this isn't what he asked. "I like to fight for your attention, and then I like it when you force me to do something. So, when you asked if I was submissive before? Yeah, no, I'm not. Only if I lose the fight, and to be honest, I don't mind losing. It's the fight I like, and when I lose it to someone like you who can actually take control and steer a sexy situation, that's when the servicing thing comes into play. After you've earned the right to put me where you want, then I get to shine by putting *you* where I want. I get to be the one to draw all the reactions out of you, control what you feel and how you feel it, and make you come by playing into how well I can read you. It's not a game, but it's a puzzle or something, and I love solving it. You. I… like solving you."

Blake doesn't say anything for a while, but when I look at him, he's deep in thought, actually thinking everything I'd said over with an open mind. "You become submissive to manipulate the dominance," he laughs. "Fuck, you really are a genius. And a manipulative little brat. So impressed." He turns his head to look at me. "I get it. I respect it. But I have an idea."

"What?"

"I want to be the one to suck your cock first. So, when that happens, we'll do it when I have something else to focus on, too. That way, you don't have to worry about responding a certain way, and I get to taste you. We'll sixty-nine or something. Or fuck, I don't care, you can shove a vibrating plug up my ass and draw all my attention there."

Um, what? "You'd bottom?" I gasp, not at all expecting that.

Blake shrugs. "Maybe." He pauses. "Okay, probably not, but I'd at least try a toy. Would you top? Are you vers?"

"Maybe. With a strong preference for bottoming." I pause this time. "Okay, whatever. I'm a full-time bottom."

Blake licks his lips, then mine, then his again, savouring the combined taste of us. "Maybe we try the blow job thing first?"

I roll my eyes at him. "Okay."

"Okay? That's it?" He acts shocked. "When did you become so compliant, Mercer?"

"You're tricking me into it."

"Bullshit. You're too smart to be tricked." He bends down to kiss me, and just when I think it's going to get sexy again, he pulls back, flips me over, and smacks my ass. "Now go clean your mess in the kitchen and I'll watch you houseboy while I drink my coffee." He jumps out of bed with way too much pep in his step.

I should have dick-kicked him again.

15 Blake

BRONSON PULLS UP IN front of my apartment and I climb into the passenger seat. I light a smoke and check my phone, making sure my target is still where he's supposed to be. I won't be completing the Sean Pendleton job until tonight, but I need to keep a tracker on him all day in case anything goes awry.

"Why am I picking you up? Don't you have like three vehicles?"

"Mercer took my Denali to the fireman's breakfast, and I need to grab a pickup for tonight. Dad has one ready to go." Sean is still at his pervy buddy's place, so as long as he stays there until mid-afternoon, I should be good.

"Fireman's breakfast?" Bronson laughs.

"Don't ask. It's punishment." Actually, I'm not too into punishment in the literal sense. I'm into consequences. If and when I ever do punish Mercer, it won't be hurtful or shameful. It'll all be a part of the puzzle he plays with me.

"You actually into him, Blake?"

"Yeah," I admit, because there's no point in hiding it. "He's feisty as fuck and I'm pretty into it."

Bronson laughs again. He doesn't stop laughing. He laughs so hard his eyes water and he snorts. Real cool. Would never know he's a fucking serial killer. "If I'd known that you coming home and falling in love with Ben was the key to taming that little brat, I'd have ended your training a year ago."

"His name is Mercer. And I don't want to tame him. I want to challenge him. He hasn't had it easy, man." I pocket my phone. "And I never said shit about falling in love."

"I know he hasn't had it easy," Bronson admits, letting the love thing go for now. "That family is so fucked."

"How so?"

"Well, Olivia and Samantha aren't shit people, but they're so compliant to Will's every wish that it almost makes them shit people. They want to please him."

"No they don't. They just don't want to cause waves."

Bronson steals a cigarette from my pack. "Yeah, you're probably right. But because they don't want to make waves, they let Ben, I mean Mercer, get shit on his whole life. They love him and want to protect him, but they don't know how, and you have to admit he doesn't make it easy."

No. He doesn't. But I understand why he acts out now that I know him. He's so much more than a brat. He's manipulative and resentful, but mostly, he's afraid of being alone, suffering from a life of neglect, and confused about himself because his redeeming qualities are what drove his own father to send him for medical brainwashing. I wonder if his brother worked on him or even knew he was there. I'll be finding out.

"But yeah, it's like they aren't terrible people, but they're terrible by proxy. Olivia is more of a bitch than Samantha, but I can't place her issue. Plus, Penny is the typical battered wife."

"You think he beats her?" I didn't get that vibe. Will isn't the hands-on abusive type.

"Nope. I think he cut her down, made her lose her worth, and turned her into his little minion. She does whatever he says because she's learned it's easier than not doing it. Even when it comes to Mercer."

"Yeah, she was all for sending him to that facility the day of your engagement party. She called it a reform home, though."

"Maybe she doesn't know the extent of it," Bronson says. "That's what I mean, though. She's a shell of a person, and I think after all this time, she doesn't even have the capacity to ask questions anymore. She lets Will run the show and goes along with everything he does."

Which is a survival tactic. I can't blame her for self-preservation. Where I can place blame is on her treatment of Mercer. Will must have said he was sick, concocted some bullshit behavioural diagnosis, presented it to Penny, and she never questioned it. She should have fucking questioned it, especially because it was about her son. I'll never forgive her for that one thing alone. All the rest I can look past, but not that.

"Mercer thinks the Palmerstons are going broke. That's why they agreed to the marriage."

Bronson looks at me with a confused expression, so I explain everything Mercer told me about the slow slide into taking over our family's legitimate businesses while our *family business* goes to ruins to distract Dad.

"Dad's not dumb. He probably saw this coming. He would have looked into everything about them before even suggesting it."

"Yeah, which makes me think he's playing at another angle. I've got my guy looking into everything to do with the Palmerston businesses, finances, and accounts. I just want Dad to admit outright what's going on."

"He won't." Bronson laughs. "He'll make you and Brandt figure it out while I play the perfect fiancé."

"When's the wedding?"

"I don't know. Supposed to be picking a date this week. Miranda is... fuck, Blake. She's going to leave me."

"We'll figure something out." I hope. Now that I'm learning what attachments and feelings are, I want to help Bronson keep the woman he loves.

As I'm scanning the tracking app to ensure Sean Pendleton is where he's supposed to be, a text pops up. I smirk at it even without reading the whole thing. Of course he altered his contact information.

Little Demon: *your abs are shit compared to these fire gods.*

Blake: *if you *accidentally* light yourself on fire to get their attention, I'm not visiting you in the burn unit.*

Little Demon: *I'd never risk my skin like that.*

Little Demon: *but I could *choke* on something to get mouth-to-mouth.*

Blake: *you don't even choke on an eight-inch dick, but good try.*

Little Demon: *compliment?*

Blake: *mm.*

Little Demon: *mm.*

"Not in love, my ass," Bronson scoffs.

THE REASON IT IRKS me to be a soldier for my dad is because we have a different outlook on morals. If I'm his hitman, my job is to conduct the hit so he can collect the money. That's it. He doesn't want me looking into the person more than is necessary to get the job done. But my mind doesn't work like that. I want to know whose life I'm snuffing out and what kind of destruction it will leave behind. I don't mind killing, to be honest, but there's more to a death than just ending a life. There's an aftermath.

Frank's wife wants him dead. An accidental death. There are a number of ways it could be carried out. Car accident, medical condition, gas leak, carbon monoxide poisoning, hit and run, you name it. I had no problem stopping him from ruining her life and her business because the proof of his actions were right there in front of me. But does leaking information merit death?

Dad thinks so. Frank's wife thinks so. Brandt has no issues with it. Bronson says Frank chose his path in life and this is where it led him. But me? I'm not sure. It depends on the situation. It depends on the destruction the death will leave behind.

Addicts aren't bad people even though they do shit things to get their fix. We don't turn our backs on them. Thieves steal for reasons that make sense to their situation, but they get let out of prison after serving their time. Even some murders are accidental, and those people suffer for eternity for what they've done. People are redeemable. Some people.

Is Frank?

"You made her wait the obligatory four days after the order?" I ask my dad. "To make sure she didn't change her mind?"

"Yes."

"And she realizes she's killing the father of her kids?"

"I think she gets it."

"Does she? Does she know how it's going to affect those kids?"

"Blake, what's the problem here?"

"The problem is that this is our life all over again." I stare him straight in the eyes.

Dad flinches at my words, but he can't deny them. "Your mother was a different circumstance altogether."

"How so? She did something bad, and you had her stopped. She didn't react the way you wanted her to, and you had her killed. I've watched you regret it every single day since it happened. I watched my brothers lose their mother, and if you think it hasn't turned us into cold-hearted people, you're mistaken."

"I know you don't believe me, Blake, but I did it to protect my sons. All three of you."

I nod, shoving my hands in my pockets. I've heard this a hundred times, but he never elaborates and no matter how hard I get Aaron to dig into it, he can't find anything. Mom tried to out the family business to the FBI. It backfired because the agent working the case was in Dad's pocket and had even hired us for jobs. Dad stopped her from trying to ruin us by discrediting her, shaming her, and making her look mentally ill to the public. Apparently, she was schizophrenic and the voices in her head were feeding her lies about our family. Did my mom have a mental illness? Maybe. I might believe that, but I don't think it was that one. All her medical records have been wiped, so Aaron can't confirm anything for me.

"Are you ever going to tell me what you were protecting us from?"

"From her."

"She was our mother!"

"She was a terrible person!"

"Right," I laugh. "So you keep saying. Maybe someday you'll tell us why. For now, I want to make damn sure this woman has a full understanding of what it means to kill her husband. I don't give a fuck if she's a cold-hearted bitch who wants him gone because he betrayed her. That's fine. I want to know what his relationship with his kids is like, how it's going to affect them, and if she's even a better parent to them. For all we know, we're taking away the only good parent those kids have." I pull my smokes from my pocket.

"I'll do my own research. Does she have a deadline for this thing?"

"Not yet."

I nod again. "Alright. I've got the other job to do tonight, and then I'll see you at the Gala."

"You don't question his death?" Dad asks.

"I did my research on him. He's not a parent, has a record for stalking kids, and when I followed him yesterday, he jerked it to kids on a playground. I have no questions about his death."

I leave my dad's kitchen and hop in the truck I'll be taking to the job tonight. I believe my dad when he says our mom was a terrible woman. I saw the signs, even when I was a kid. I know she was planning to do something to the three of us, her sons, but I don't know what. What I wish is for our dad to open up to us and tell us what actually happened. Right now isn't the time to think about it because I have to head home, get ready, and make sure Mercer knows to be ready for the gala when I get back. That in itself is going to be the biggest job of my night.

I NEVER WANTED TO be one of the people in Mercer's life that told him he couldn't wear something, but... he can't wear that. Not because I give a shit what anyone will think about it, but because I'll lose my mind and sport wood all night. Hard wood. Impossible to conceal wood. My mood will plummet because I'll be single-minded, and then I'll get edgy and short-tempered, and being around these assholes is enough to test my patience as is. I don't need Mercer and his badass suit adding to the fraying thread of my restraint.

"Don't," he snips at me. "Don't even try to make me change. I worked on this all fucking day, and if you force me to take it off, I won't go." He crosses his arms.

I can't even place why this outfit is beyond my ability to comprehend. It's basically just a suit. A black and charcoal grey suit with buckles and decorative buttons all over the place. It's grungy without being tattered, and classy without conforming. Maybe that's why I like it so much—it's his personality in clothing form. The matte black button-up fits so perfectly under the charcoal vest, and the way it all tapers down to his waist and hips, showing off some snaps and fasteners that draw the eye, has my fingers itching to use them as handholds and force him exactly where I want him. Or maybe it's the way the pants hug his tight little ass, the pockets overexaggerated and not at all detracting from the view.

Every piece of this outfit was made for him, right down to how it gives him a swagger he didn't have before. It's manly and fashionable while being chaotic and edgy. Paired with the subtle liner that darkens his demon eyes, making the amber pop and glisten, and the mess of hair on his head that remains true to his usual form, I'm seriously speechless. I can't even.

I've never reacted like this to a damn suit.

"I didn't expect you to be dressed already," I say because I can't find anything else to say. "I still have a job to do."

"Oh, right. Well, I figured you knew, but I'm totally coming with you on that." His arms uncross, showing me the fit of the vest again.

Fucking hell, I want to rip the buttons open and devour him, but I don't want to ruin the suit because I want him to wear it whenever the fuck I tell him to. "It's a murder, Mercer."

"Yes. I'm coming."

"To a murder?"

"What the hell is wrong with you? Did you forget your brain at your dad's?" He scoffs. Or huffs. Or laughs condescendingly. "I'm coming. I'm starting to think you're just a mediocre idiot who can't form words. I need to see you off some child molester to feel better about you. Trust me, your reputation needs it." He snaps his fingers. "Let's go!"

I grab him by the bicep. Even the fabric feels perfect under my rough hands. "I can't focus on a murder when you look like that."

"Like what?" he asks, smirking because he thinks I'm going to drop to my knees and worship his sexiness.

"Like yourself," I tell him honestly. "This. This whole fucking thing is you." I run my eyes up and down the height of him.

He trips over his attitude for a second, stumbling back because I've shocked him. "Me? You think this is me?"

So fucking much. I lick my lips and turn him around, spinning him in a slow circle to admire every last bit of him. "Mm."

"It's just a suit." Which translates to him saying, 'I'm just me.' "What about my hoodlum look?"

I love his hoodlum look just as much, but it isn't as jarring as seeing him in this because it's more familiar now. This is his confidence and his style. It's his defiance to be different, but his compliance to belong. It's begging for attention while being unsure if he's worthy of it. It's a statement that he's Mercer Bentley Palmerston, and he's no longer afraid. It's conflicting and confusing and goddamn phenomenal, just like the complicated mess he is. It's proof that he knows he's seen by someone. By me.

"What time is it?"

He looks at the clock on the stove, but before he has time to tell me I have to be at a literal murder in thirty-five minutes, I'm forcing him to his knees and unbuckling my tactical pants. I want to fuck him, but I can't risk getting cum on that suit.

Mercer looks up at me, still trying to decide if he wants to fight me on this. I don't give him the chance. I read his body language, decide he's willing and eager to be forced, and press my dick to his lips. He opens, taking a languid lick that doesn't at all match the hurried and desperate drive in me.

"Wait." He pops off my dick, even though I have a hand on his head, ready to push him where I want him. "I suck you off, you take me to the murder. Yes?" I push on his head, but we both know he's the one in charge here. "No murder, no blowjob."

Taking him on a job is irresponsible, but I can't think straight when he looks like this. It even turns me on that he has the balls to negotiate with me while my cock bobs in front of his face. "Fine. Blowjobs and murder."

"Such a pushover." He gloats.

"So fucking mouthy." I pull his head forward, hoping to surprise him, but my little demon slut has his lips parted and his tongue ready.

I don't know if it's him, the outfit, the time we've been living together, or the games he's been playing, but I'm realizing how much I need him. Need him to push my buttons and keep me on edge, to challenge me and entice me into his game, and to seek me when he needs comfort. I don't know how deep my feelings for him run, but I know that I'm addicted to him.

Not wanting to ruin his eyeliner, I make sure he can breathe tonight. I keep one hand on the back of his head, but let him dictate the pace and depth. His mouth is as greedy as he is, and Mercer doesn't shy away from making noise. He hums around my shaft like he's in heaven, and the enthusiasm and pure enjoyment that sparkles up at me from his glossy eyes is what sets this apart from any other blowjob I've received. Mercer loves to serve, and now that I know that about him, I want to pay attention to him in action. And fuck me, the boy knows how to suck a cock.

I stroke his cheek, making sure his eyes don't water and ruin his look. "You love this, don't you?"

He whimpers around my cock, palming the front of his pants.

"Such a good boy, Mercer. Look at you down there on your knees for me, giving me everything I want. So perfect, baby." I stare at him, unable to look away. He slows his pace, dragging his lips over my cock and then sucking the tip. When he tongues my slit, my thighs clench. "When I come, I need you to swallow. If you get even a drop on this suit, I'll lose my mind. Fuck, you in this suit, Mercer..." I admire the fuck out of him, and when I see his cheeks flush from the praise, my balls draw up.

Mercer knows it. He knows how to read my body. He sucks me like he's desperate for my cum, and when my fist tightens in his hair, he moans along my cock and drinks me down. I refuse to close my eyes. Watching him while suffering overwhelming pleasure caused by him is my new favourite thing to do. My cock pulses, coming down his throat, and Mercer takes it all and begs for more.

"Fuck, Mercer. So. Fucking. Perfect."

Mercer cries out, something between a whine and a moan, and the vibration of it along my cock sends tingles of aftershocks through my body. But when I notice his eyes flutter shut and his body wiggle and jitter, I know exactly what he's done.

I pull out, but Mercer licks me clean before he lets me go anywhere. When he tries to stand, I hold him still. Kneeling with him, I wipe his glistening lips before kissing them. "What'd I tell you about getting cum on this suit?"

"That you'd lose your mind. I didn't waste any," he promises.

"Are you wearing panties tonight?" I look into his amber eyes.

He blushes even more. "Yes."

"You better hope they protect your pants, demon. One drop of cum on them and I'll have to come up with a punishment for you."

Mercer swallows, almost excitedly. "What punishment?"

"Stand up."

I help him to his feet, tucking my dick away while he shuffles from foot to foot. He's trying to hide it, but he knows I know and I don't understand why he's being bashful.

"Show me."

"Blake…"

"Now." I wait. "And be fucking careful."

Slowly, he untucks his shirt, undoes the pants, and opens them wide enough to show me the black lace underneath. With shy eyes, he peels down the panties to show me his mess. Fuck, I love how easily he can orgasm. To see him covered in his own cum is the sexiest thing in the world. Especially in those panties and that suit. He's the ultimate distraction and I wish I had more time to make this creative. Instead, I'm going to delay his punishment until we get to the gala.

"What's this?" I touch a wet spot on his pants, bringing my finger to my mouth to suck it clean. "You've been bad, baby."

"I know." Still shy, but there's deviance in his voice now. "What are you going to do with me?"

I smirk at him. "Right now, you're going to run and change those panties, clean yourself up, and run back to me. If you aren't back here in four minutes, I'm going to the job without you. Later, you're going to pay for this mistake." I grab his chin and kiss his open mouth. "I can't wait to watch you squirm all night, Mercer."

"You think I'll squirm?" he scoffs. "Please."

"Mm." I smile. "Four minutes."

16

Mercer

TURNS OUT, MURDERS AREN'T for me. *Murderers*, on the other hand, have a sex appeal I had not been expecting. It wasn't the actual killing that attracted me to Blake Carter even more than I already am. It was his mentality. His brutality and his grace, all wrapped up into one sexy killer and the ease with which he completed the job. It was the look in his eyes before he went in there and the different, completely cold-blooded look he cracked for me when he got back to the truck. Blake was in some sort of murder-high, and as soon as he saw the look on my face, he softened up like butter and melted all over me, making sure I was okay.

Fuck, Mercer Bentley! Do not fall in love with a thirty-year-old assassin!

Anyway, my dick's been hard ever since and I can't decide if that's a good thing or a bad thing, but Blake kissed me in the truck, wheeled us out of there all cool and casual, and then we ditched the truck and moved on. He's been his normal, stoic, yet surprisingly kind and thoughtful self ever since. The mind fuck of his personalities—contract killer to attentive lover—has my cock all up in arms, kind of wishing to take him up on his blowjob offer here at the gala.

I'm casually leaning against the bar in the event room, sipping a mocktail because I don't think my jitters could handle a cocktail, unless it was Blake's, when someone bumps their elbow into me.

"Well, if it isn't the attention whore."

I look to my left and narrow my eyes at this bitch. "Says the actual whore."

Dee smirks as she orders a martini. "Still running with the prostitute excuse? Either way, he still called me."

"And you still left with your heels in your hand." I sip the fruity little number, loving the pineapple-*yness* of it. Mangos, maybe? Pineapple-ness? Whatever... it's tropical. "And I got breakfast with a lovely bunch of firefighters from the whole ordeal."

Dee accepts her martini and spins her back to the bar. Side by side, we eye-fuck this lame party. Blake is with his dad, and my dad is entertaining an entire horde of suck-ups. He loves that shit, so all the power to him.

"Well, you won," she says, sipping. "And that suit is... fire."

"I know," I admit to both those statements. "Your dress is infuriatingly perfect on your disgustingly flawless body." Might be due for a real cocktail now. "It'd look better with your hair up, though."

Dee scoffs. Or huffs. Or laughs at me condescendingly. Make up your mind with your sounds, woman! "You into fashion, Mercer?"

"You know who I am?" No one calls me Mercer except Blake, and some of his family now. I look at her, biting my tongue from asking how she got her eyeliner so perfect. Those lines are tight.

"I do now. Sorry for the dad hand you got dealt in life. I'm on his law team, and yeah. He's the fakest person I know."

I clink my glass to hers. "So, not actually a whore?"

"Asks the slut." She smiles.

"Touché. I don't know if I'm into fashion. Maybe. Not really. I have no idea who I am." Okay, what's in this mocktail and why is it making me confess things to my nemesis while my dick is hard about a murderer? "You're a lawyer?"

"A junior lawyer, yeah. I started law school late. Was a marketing executive first."

"How boring."

Dee laughs for real this time. "Do you ever filter yourself?"

"Should I?" I look at her.

She shakes her head. "Wouldn't be you if you did."

Just then, Blake looks at me like he does every three minutes. Noticing me standing with his attempted hookup, he excuses himself from his conversation and undoes a few of the top buttons on his walk across the room.

"Uh oh," Dee says. "You in trouble?"

I grin at Blake. "I hope so." More likely he's coming to make sure Dee and I haven't started a round of World War Gala. He subtly checks for fire alarms on his way over.

He swapped out his murder clothes for a casual set of dress pants, shirt, and blazer, and he looks damn good in them. Not a speck of blood on him. His eyes barely waver from mine as he crosses the room, not even when people try to catch him in a conversation. He smiles politely but keeps looking right at me, and I swear to all that is holy that this is a form of foreplay. Blake's own special brand, and it's working. If I don't get rid of the boner soon, it's going to get stuck as a permanent fixture on my body.

He doesn't hesitate when he gets to us. One hand slips to my lower back and he takes his place beside me. Not in front of me or angled to block me. Right at my side. "Mercer," he greets me with a deep tone. "Dee. Nice to see you. He isn't being a demon, is he?"

"Oh, he's casually insulting my job and telling me I look nice, but otherwise, he's well behaved." She smiles at Blake, but it surprises me that her smile for me is even bigger.

"Shame," Blake says. "He's fun when he doesn't behave."

"Yeah, I think we have different takes on that night," Dee laughs. "Anyway, nice to see you both. Blake, I'd say call me but your pet here bites, so don't call me. Mercer, if you're ever around..." She leaves it open-ended, and I respect her for it.

"Night, whore."

"Behave, slut."

When she's gone, Blake leans right in against my side, lips almost pressed to my ear. "I'm the only one who gets to call you a slut. My slut."

"She basically saw me in full-blown slut mode, so cut her some slack." I turn, our lips almost grazing.

"Some slack? You cut her no slack that night."

"No. But now that she's not in my way, I'm mature enough to reshuffle the deck." I meet his eyes. "Please be jealous. I've never made anyone jealous before."

Blake grins. "You made your dad jealous of your mind when you were a kid. Maybe we can make him even more jealous tonight. You up for putting on a show?"

"While I'm all for voyeurism and won't deny that exhibitionism intrigues me, I'm not really into sex shows with my dad. Hard pass." I finish my mocktail and Blake sets my glass on the bar.

"Not a sex show. I'm too possessive of your ass for that." He grins, making my stomach tighten. "I'm going to introduce you to all the high and mighty people, and while you're being whatever version of yourself you want to be, your dad will never look away."

"Yeah, because he'll be worried I'm tainting the Palmerston name."

"Exactly. Or winning them over. Either way, his attention has already been on you all night, and I'm up for making him sweat a bit more." His hand sinks down to my ass. "And if you're a good boy and keep him distracted while Brandt does his thing, maybe you'll be in for a reward rather than punishment, baby."

"You know, if I didn't know any better, I'd say you're the manipulative one in this relationship." I smirk, but it falls away pretty quickly. What the hell did I just say?

"Mm," is all Blake says. "Maybe tonight. But I'm not stupid enough to think everything about you right now, from what you're wearing, to how you're standing, and what you're saying, isn't a form of manipulation."

"And you're going to stand there and act like you aren't being all touchy-feely with me in such a public space because you don't want my dad to take notice?" I lift a brow.

"Oh, I want him to notice. I want him to know that while he neglected you, I accepted you. That he wasn't strong enough to handle someone as fucking incredible as you, but I'm strong enough to embrace you. I want him to know that his fuck ups are my rewards. You, Mercer, are mine, and I want him to know it. I caught your relationship slip-up."

"Poor word choice. You're still just my jailer." Jailer I'm falling for, even though it's a bad idea. Love might ruin the one and only good thing I've got in my life.

"Sure, baby. Whatever you gotta tell yourself." He kisses my cheek and I lock eyes with my dad, who definitely saw that. He's shocked, and it gives me a thrill. "Be honest with me, though. You doing okay here?"

Always checking in. "So far. If I have a panic attack just... just don't let my dad see it."

"I promise," he says. "And I'll give you my cock to suck on to calm you down." He smirks. "Come on, Mr. Demon. Let's meet some affluent douchebags. There are a few good ones."

Mr. Demon. I'm a mister now.

For the next few hours, my dad's face gets redder and sweatier the more times I hear Blake lie about being away at school the past five years. I meet so many people, I can't even keep their names straight. People who know about me but have never met me because my family kept me hidden. I get into a routine of following Blake's lead until I get a read on the people, and then I adjust my attitude accordingly. I'm an outright dick to some of them, a pleasure to others, and indifferent to many. Blake never takes his hand off my lower back. He never butts in while I'm talking, and he doesn't try to tone me down or encourage me to say more than I'm willing to. He is the only person in my whole life to treat me with this level of respect, and to be honest, I love it so much it's overwhelming. Verge of a panic attack overwhelming.

I never realized good feels can be just as overbearing as bad ones.

The best part about the whole process is that Dad sees it all. He sees me fit into his world, and his worry spikes. He doesn't trust me, and I can't really blame him for that, but to see him nervous gives my anxiety attack a kick in the ass, booting it away for later. The smug smile on my face doesn't go unnoticed by Blake, and by the time I swap my mocktails for actual cocktails, I'm living on the cloud above cloud nine because this night has been a revelation.

I'm fucking worth something.

But I can only handle so many self-realizations in one night. I'm at my tolerance limit for this party, and I don't even know the occasion for the event. Blake, aware as ever, notices and pulls me away to the side of the room for a break.

"Where's Aaron?" I ask before he can ask me if I'm alright. I don't have an answer to that question right now. "He told me on the phone he'd be here."

"He's here," Blake says, a cheeky smile on his face. "You've met him and his wife."

I narrow my eyes at him. "How'd I act?"

"Bratty and funny." Blake laughs. "He's my guy, not the Carter family's guy. So his identity stays a secret between me and him. I introduced them as a Mr and Mrs so you wouldn't hear their first names," he says, grinning.

"I don't get to know?" I pout, hating how it feels to be on the outside of any inside when it comes to Blake. I'm so needy it's despicable.

"I trust you," Blake says. "I wanted you to meet his wife, anyway."

"Why?"

He ignores the question. "Cock hard?"

It's been in different stages of hardness all night. Currently, it's pressing nicely against the satin panties I picked after ruining thc lacy ones. "Yes."

"I have a question. I want you to be honest when you answer. It doesn't have to be right now, okay?" He turns his back to the room, giving me all his attention. I've never felt more nervous and more special at the same time.

"Okay..."

"I know you like the fight. That the build up and the battle for control is an aphrodisiac to you. I get that. And I also get that you like losing the fight to become submissive and control the sex in that role."

"But?"

"But when you're not in that mood, you need to be dominated. I saw it that first night you had a panic attack when your sisters were over. You need orders and direction to function."

My cheeks flush and I don't know why. He's already seen me like that on more than one occasion, so it makes no sense to be embarrassed about it now. Except I am. Because living it and talking about it while in the right frame of mind are two totally different things.

Blake lightly grips my jaw, meeting my eyes. "Tell me how to dominate you while never making you feel like you're less than me. I want you to rise to the top of whatever you see for yourself in life. You've been beaten down since you were a kid, and I refuse to do that to you. Tell me the right way to give you what you need without ever making you feel worthless." He leans in to press his lips to mine. "Think about it, okay?"

"I don't need to think about it," I snap at him, falling in love with this murderer with attuned feelings. "I already know the answer."

"Tell me."

I grin at him. "Oh, Blake. I thought you knew me better than that."

"What's that mean? Tell me, Mercer."

My hand skims his chest, and my grin turns to one of pure innocence. "Make me."

17

Mercer

HE'S NOT SOFT. HE has feelings, but he's not a soft lover like I thought he might be.

Locked away in some fancy changing room, Blake has taken complete charge and put me in place. He didn't do it nicely, and now I'm panting with a hard dick, trying to decide which version of him I'm falling harder for. The thoughtful man who wants to pay attention to all my feelings, or the aggressive dominant who wants to step up to the plate to play my game. I think I love them both because they both see me. No matter which version of himself he's being, he sticks to his promise of not ignoring me.

I'm a fucking slut for it. All of it. The hard and the soft. The way he gives me all his attention.

His blue eyes meet mine, and within them, the order is clear. Don't fucking move. I stay still while he wraps his tie around my wrists, securing them in front of my body. My defiance will come in another form tonight, so I'll let him have this win because he's earned it.

He asked me how to dominate me without making me feel worthless... Well, by loving me. By doing exactly what he's doing. By respecting me. By proving to me that he cares without treating me like I'm broken. I know he hasn't said it, and it's way too soon to even feel it, but Blake Carter loves me. I can feel it. I think it's his love and attention that has this new version of me clawing to the surface, fighting tooth and nail to break free so I can become someone who accepts his love and knows how to love him back.

My mind plays tricks on me, though. It tells me it's his attention I love rather than the man himself. It's the focus he has on me because no one else has ever made me their spotlight. My mind tells me that Blake will get tired of loving me because once the fun of this game stops being new and exciting, he'll go back to people like Dee who come when he calls and always offer him a no-strings-attached night. I'm all the strings, tangled up like webs. Pull the wrong one and I'll go off the deep end, but keep tugging on them individually and he'll get so caught in my mess he won't be able to leave. Then he'll resent me for it.

"Stop," Blake growls at me, snugging up the tie. "Whatever the fuck you're thinking about, just stop." He lifts my bound wrists over his head to wrap around his neck. With me kneeling on a padded bench in the changeroom, he's still taller than me, but he bends to be at eye level. "Do I need to get you out of your head, demon?"

Yes, please. That's exactly what I need. "You can try."

His smirk makes my nipples harden. He took my clothes off before he got rough with me, claiming he didn't want to ruin them. All that remains are my satin panties and the tie around my wrists.

"Mm," he hums, reaching behind me. "Open your mouth."

When I don't, he bites my lip, making me hiss. I'm not usually one for pain with my pleasure, choosing to make the fight more mental than physical, but damn if that bite of pain doesn't feel nice coming from his teeth. My lips pop open on a gasp when he bites me again, and then he's shoving something into my mouth. Something cold.

"Suck on that and stop thinking," he demands, stepping back to admire his work.

With my wrists tied in the front and my panties pulled taut over my hard and leaking cock, I suck on the ice cube and watch him unbutton his shirt. Blake doesn't have any tattoos, yet his body is my bad boy fantasy. Movies and books taught me to see bad boys as an image, the way they dress and the ink on their skin; their dark hair and brooding eyes. Blake doesn't have any of that. He dresses in whatever suits his needs for the day, his skin is tanned but bare, and his eyes don't brood. They're wide open and attentive, swirling shades of blue at me with an intensity that makes him forceful. His bad boy vibe comes from his actions rather than his look, because what man can look at me like that and actually handle me?

Only Blake.

He's dangerous because of the slow and deliberate way he undresses like I don't warrant hurrying. He's powerful because of the confidence he has in himself, but he's even more powerful because of the confidence he has in me to handle whatever he throws at me. He's a true bad boy because he asks me what I need and then delivers what I ask for. He doesn't tiptoe around me, chicken out when I'm at my lowest, and he stands his ground when I try to manipulate him. The best part is that he doesn't get offended when I win. Like in the shower that night. Blake is the ultimate bad boy because he knows how to handle himself and he does the work to make sure I'm handled like I want to be.

"I think we got off on the wrong foot, Mercer," Blake says as the ice cube melts to drip down my chin. "Actually, I think *you* got off on the wrong foot."

"How so?" I watch his shirt slide off his shoulders to reveal toned pecs, cut abs, and a V that leads to the best prize of my life.

"You fucked up," he says, starting on his pants. "You mistake respect for softness."

I swallow a mouthful of saliva and water, my tongue cold and my cheeks tight. I did do that. I expected Blake to own me sexually the first time we had sex, but he didn't do that right away. He fucked me how he wanted to, which was respectful and sentimental, and I assumed that meant he was a gentle lover.

"All this attitude you throw around is for something, right? You act out to get attention, but you've never really cared what kind of attention it gets you." He leaves his pants open and takes a slow breath. "What kind of attention did you want from me?"

All of it. Undivided. Love. Understanding. I want him to see me and still look at me because I'm worthy of being looked at. I want him to look under my mask and understand why I wear it. I want him to notice me because every outward part of me shows the truth of all the inward parts of me, and then I want him to peel my layers back and still give me all his attention because the mess he finds underneath is still worth it.

"You wanted me to play your game. You wanted to be a brat and have me tame you, right?" he asks, stepping a little closer. He is right. That's the initial reaction I wanted from him. "I'm not going to tame you, Mercer."

Something hot burns in my gut. It's uncomfortable yet enticing. "Why not?"

He cups my ass and lifts me up. My legs wrap around his waist, and his eyes, too close to focus on, stay locked on mine. "Because you thrive on being unhinged, and I never want you snuffed out. Because, in order to respect who you are, I first had to get to know you. Guess what I found?" He sets my ass down on the bench and pushes my wet, cold mouth to the material over his cock. "A smart, bratty little boy with so much fire, but no idea how to keep it burning. I'm going to make you burn, Mercer."

A rush of something like adrenaline pulses through me. A desperation tenses my body but entices my mind, and before I know what I need, my hands are working to pull open his pants and tug down his boxers. The ice cube and my cool tongue glide over the head of his cock, soaking him until it melts completely. But before Blake lets me suck him, he tilts my chin up.

"I respect you," he tells me, making me whimper. "But I will fucking use you like you want to be used. I can do both. Understand?"

"Blake," I beg. My body trembles, unable to process the honesty of his words. It's all I've ever wanted, to be respected for who I am and seen *because* of who I am, and Blake does both. "Please."

With a nod, he lets go of my chin. I devour him, unable to suck him down deep enough. I get this need to be filled, choking, suffocating on him because he's the only thing that can fill me with enough pride to get through the day. I gag around his cock, but I can't stop. The feeling of him in my throat, cutting off the air I don't want to breathe, intensifies, making me fucking feral for cum. Proof. Cum is proof I'm enough. He lets me for all of a minute before he takes charge.

"You need to choke, little demon?" he rasps at me.

I hum some desperate sound, reaching for his dick. He doesn't let me. He pushes me until my body lays along the bench, my bound wrists on my chest, and then he tugs me until my head tips off the end. Looming over me, he admires my body for a few seconds, drawing out my agony, teaching me that delayed gratification he keeps going on about, and then he steps forward. Head tilted back, I look up at his straight and proud cock, his balls tight and pulled up.

"Open."

I open my mouth as wide as I can, tilting my head back even more so he can really fuck my throat. Blake bends his knees a little, the tip hitting my tongue. And then he pushes all the way inside my mouth and down my throat, his balls resting against my nose. I'm suffocating blissfully, blacking out from pleasure, and choking on the only man I've ever fallen for.

I choke, coughing around him. Pressure builds in my head, and my hands itch to push him off or pull him closer. When I cough a second time, my throat on fire, he pulls out. I gasp, but that's about all I manage before he slides his cock back in. This time, he fucks my mouth like he owns it, and the way my body reacts to that is overwhelming. I'm seconds from coming because he's claiming me. It makes me sick, but I'm far past being ashamed of my sickness. Blake thrusts in and out of my throat until I'm clenching my thighs and trying not to come in a second pair of panties.

"Good boy," he purrs at me, pulling out again. "Trust me?"

"Yes." My voice is hoarse. "Yes."

Reaching forward, he grabs my legs and tugs me down the bench a little. Instead of my head hanging over the end, it rests on the padded surface. Blake hovers over me, and when he bends forward, all I can focus on is getting his dick back into my mouth and sucking the cum out of him until he's ready to go again. I lift my hands to grab his shaft, angling it so I can get him deeper. Then I tense.

"Blake."

"Suck my cock, baby."

I do as I'm told and barely hold back from bucking my hips off the table when I feel his fingers slide my panties to the side and his tongue lick my cock. I suction my lips around his cockhead and whimper when he takes me into his mouth. Holy shit, that's good. My legs squirm and my body sweats. Everything feels way too fucking good and way too fast, but I'm a greedy cock whore all of a sudden. With Blake's mouth on me, I'm not overthinking anything. I don't care that he might be too focused on my reactions, because my reactions are all fucking natural. I want to be deeper inside him. I want to watch him. I want to lift my ass off this bench and fuck his throat like he fucked mine.

Blake slides his hands under my ass and pulls up, lifting my hips for me. I moan, knowing this is going to be over way sooner than I want it to be.

"Suck, Mercer."

Right. I lick the tip of him and take him back into my throat. I'm bobbing my head, loving every minute of it, but this is the first time in my life I've sucked a dick without my full attention being on it. There are too many points of pleasure, and I can't pick one to focus on.

But I'm a selfish little slut, and Blake's mouth on me wins out. "Blake," I moan. "Holy fuck."

He squeezes my ass, takes me down his throat, and swallows. I cry out around his cock, coming down his throat and writhing on the bench.

"Oh, fuck. Oh, fuck."

Blake pulls out of my mouth, and I'm still trembling when he lifts off my body and pulls me into a sitting position. He tugs me until I'm on his lap, straddling him and the bench, and then he kisses me when I pretty much cry for it. His tongue is coated in my cum, and I can't get enough of it. I'm an emotional wreck, but I think it feels good. Really good.

"Maybe I'm a slut for your cum too," he says against my lips. "Mm."

Oh my fuck. He's infuriatingly perfect. "I hate you." My forehead rests against his while I try to come back down to Earth. I don't know why this orgasm is hitting harder than most, but if I had to hazard a guess, and I'm a pretty accurate kind of guy, I'd say it's because that was my first blowjob and now I'm addicted. To Blake's mouth. To Blake.

Blake laughs, and just when I think he's going to kiss me again, he lifts me up. He carries me over to a wall, hooks my tied wrists over a coat hook on the wall, and presses my face against the wallpaper.

"Fuck, this ass is mine now, little boy." He smacks it. "I'm gonna fuck it until you come on the wallpaper." He grabs my hips and tugs, angling me so that my ass is sticking out for him. I arch my back to give him better access, basically inviting him to fuck me whatever way he wants. Shit, I want that so badly.

"Blake, hurry up," I complain, cock already hard and leaking again.

"So fucking greedy, Mercer. How many times have you come tonight?" He smacks my ass again. "Answer me."

"Twice. Two times." My wrists pull at the tie over the hook, desperate to touch something.

"You think you deserve a third?" he asks, his fingers brushing the hem of my panties. "You're nothing but a selfish, greedy little brat who always gets what he wants, right?"

"Yes," I agree. "Give it to me. Please, Blake. I can beg now." Because I am a greedy brat and I *do* always manipulate my way into getting whatever I want when it comes to my dick. If begging will get me there tonight, I'll beg on my knees.

"You got cum on your pants after I told you not to," he says with the voice of the devil. "That doesn't earn you a third orgasm, now does it?"

I stick my ass out, hoping to entice him. "No. I'm such a bad boy. Are you going to spank me?"

Crack! His palm stings even through the satin. I cry out blissfully, apparently very into pain with my pleasure now.

"You tried to make me jealous with the firefighters, didn't you?"

Oh god. "Yes." *Crack*! "Fuck, yes. I tried to make you jealous."

"Maybe I should go back out there and find Dee to make you jealous."

Anger overcomes me. Maybe fear. Maybe insecurity because he picked her over me once before. My cheeks heat in either shame or fury, and I spin so hard, twisting the tie another notch around my wrists until my back hits the wall and my pissed off gaze hits his curious one.

"Oh?" Blake mocks. "That's what did it? A little competition to really bring out the brat in you?" He grips my chin. "Are you jealous, little demon?"

Deep down, I know he doesn't want her. I know this is a way to get a rise out of me, and fuck me, it's working. Insecurities are coming to the forefront and that part of my brain that tells me I'm a worthless, forgotten, pathetic little boy, confined to his room and silenced by demand, is taking over my steely attitude. I want the brat to win, but the pitiful boy in me is taking over.

"There he is," Blake says while I start to panic. "There's Ben. The boy who can't cope with being ignored and forgotten. The timid, meek parts of you that win more than you want them to. How does it feel to have Ben back?"

My eyes blur with tears and my breathing can't decide on fast or slow. Are we having a panic attack or not? My fight-or-flight mode is stuck in anticipation, waiting to see which way this will go. We're on the verge of something, but I don't know what and I don't know what to prepare for. Why is my cock still hard?

"Answer me, Ben."

"Don't call me Ben!" I scream at him.

"Wasn't so long ago you were telling me not to call you Mercer. Who are you? Ben or Mercer?" He leans down, right in my face, scaring me and empowering me. "Ben or Mercer?"

"Mercer!" I yell, and with the declaration of my name, my real name, those tears fall down my cheeks and an anguished cry of self-love that hurts so fucking badly comes straight from my chest. "Mercer."

Blake unties my hands and the second they're free, my fingers slip into my mouth. I stand there like a pathetic fool, half panicked, half confident, unsure of what to expect next. From him or from me.

"If you're Mercer, why are you scared? Mercer doesn't get ignored. Mercer isn't hidden from the world. Mercer isn't a child." He steps back and I step forward, seeking comfort from him even though he's hurting me. "Mercer is mine. Mercer is yours. Mercer is fucking badass with all the strength in the world. He doesn't need to suck his fingers and hide from his family. My Mercer is the strongest person I know."

I want to take my fingers from my mouth but removing them feels like too much. The taste and sensation are the only things keeping me from spiralling. But maybe they aren't the only things. Maybe Blake is holding me up just by standing there, reminding me who I am and what I'm capable of. I'm crying, but I can still see. I'm scared, but I'm not useless. I'm overwhelmed, but I'm not buckling under the pressure.

"Who's winning? Ben or Mercer?" he asks.

A shaky breath breezes past my wet fingers. "I... I don't know yet." He asked how to dominate me without making me feel worthless. Well, I guess this is his lesson.

"Take the panties off, demon. Now."

My fingers leave my mouth, but the tears don't stop. I shimmy out of the satin and let it settle around my ankles. I whimper, needing him to touch me. Fill me. Take away the emotions too strong for me to handle. I step forward, reaching for him, but he steps back.

"Don't," I beg him, crying harder. "Don't ignore me."

"I'll never ignore you," he states. "Show yourself you can stand on your own two feet."

"I can't. I can't. Blake! I can't!" My fingers go back to my mouth and my knees ache when I crash onto them. I look up at him, needing him to pick me up, hold me close, fill me full of him so I can breathe again. "Don't leave me."

"I'll never leave you, baby. Get up. Stand up, Mercer. Don't let Ben win."

I'm itchy all over. I'm shaking without knowing the source. Agitated and alone, I don't know how to soothe myself, and my fingers aren't helping. I buckle forward instead of standing. On all fours, I stare at the carpeted floor wondering how the fuck this game turned into a healing journey. Blake said he'd never hurt me, but he's hurting me right now. Maybe healing hurts and he knows it, and a man like Blake isn't afraid to make it hurt if it's going to help me later. Maybe this is therapy, better than anything I've ever had before because it's working.

Yeah, I'm on on the floor at his feet, but I'm not reaching for him anymore. I'm weak and pathetic, but I'm being weak and pathetic all on my own. No aids. No sex. No loss of consciousness. I'm still on my hands and knees, which means I haven't crumpled completely yet.

There's more Mercer than there is Ben.

"Stand up, Mercer."

My chest heaves and my back hurts. Naked and at a low point, I swallow my pride—maybe I swallow Ben—and look up at this man who sees me. There's no disgust or disappointment in his eyes. The blue of them is cool and calm, admiring my effort even if it landed me on the floor.

"Get to your knees," he says, giving me a task to do halfway to standing. "Just your knees."

My arms are jelly, but I push my hands into the carpet and struggle into an upright position. It's exhausting, but it's rewarding, and I think something like my ego gives me enough strength to look at him again. He nods at me, and I don't know what it means, but my mouth seeks his cock and he lets me.

I hold him in my mouth until my eyes stop crying, and then I start to suck him off. The taste of him settles my nerves and the feel of his smooth, hard skin builds me back up, reminding me I'm a greedy little cumslut who belongs to this man. This man who named me Mercer.

Blake's hand runs through my dark hair, and then he steps back. His dick pops out of my mouth and I'm not even surprised when I try to follow it. "Stand up as Mercer and I'll fuck you, baby."

Incentive. Strength. Trust, because I know his promise has merit. Blake will wait in this room with me even if it takes me three days to stand on my own, and no matter how tired, hungry, and drained he is, he'll fuck me because he told me he would. Blake has never lied to me.

When I lift my left foot and plant it on the floor, my chest cracks open with memories of being pushed down. All the times I cowered on the floor because my parents didn't want me to be seen. All the men I let degrade me because I thought it'd build a tolerance to disrespect and, sooner or later, I'd stop letting it control me. All the pitying looks and sad eyes from my sisters, who wanted to help but never did.

It hurts.

When I press my hand on the carpet to push myself up, I whine, crying for the boy who gripped his blankets and hid in the dark, trying to figure out what everyone hated about him so much. As I push up, I'm reminded of all the times I've been pushed back down. That sudden rises have deadly falls. That words are nice even if they're lies, and sometimes, they only hurt later when you stop believing the lie.

"Blake, don't leave."

"I'm not going anywhere. I promise."

"I mean ever," I say, knowing it's psychotic. We barely know each other. "You'll break me."

"I won't break you, Mercer. Stand up and look at me."

With one more heave and a shuddering breath, I rise as Mercer Bentley and look at the man who reminded me who the fuck I am. Trembling all over, but not from panic, from pride, I meet his eyes and feel myself get stronger.

"You're going to ruin my life," Blake says with a smile on his face. "And make it fucking fun. You're going to be my brat when you want to be, my partner all the time, and my good little boy when you need to be reminded how fucking important you are. You know what I'm going to be for you?"

I shake my head, crying again. Desperate to know what he's going to be for me. Wondering if he's as psychotic as I am, falling this hard this soon.

"Everything. Yours. You fucking own me, Mercer. I'm not going anywhere."

My chest cracks wide open and my bleeding heart bleeds even more. This bleed is purifying, though. It's cleansing all the tainted blood and filling me back up with the blood Blake pumps through my veins. I can't cope with it all, so instead of crumbling to the floor again, I look him right in the eyes, not ashamed of crying in front of him, and ask for what I want.

"Fuck me." No begging.

Blake's lips are on mine in a second, and his fingers are probing my hole. "Oh, fuck, Mercer. You didn't?"

"I did."

"Such a brat." He slowly works the small plug from my ass. "You're prepped and ready for me, baby?"

"Always." I wrap my arms around his neck. "Fuck me, Blake."

Usually one to fine-tune the details, everything evades me. One second, Blake's fingers are in my ass, and then the next, I'm crying out his name as he slams his cock inside me. My back hits that wallpaper and Blake's mouth never leaves my skin. When his words of praise come, I almost cry again just because they feel so good.

"I'm so fucking proud of you, little demon," he rasps against my neck, fucking me hard against the wall. "Tell me you're proud of yourself. Say it."

"I'm proud," I admit honestly. "You make me stronger."

"No," he groans, wrapping a hand around my throat. "I remind you that you're strong. Everything else is all you."

"Blake," I moan, already about to burst. "You told me you'd fuck me until I came on the wallpaper. Spin me around."

Blake's laugh is vile. "You think I'd waste your cum on wallpaper?" Oh my god, he's perfect. "Cover me in cum, baby. I want to smell like you for the rest of the night."

I clench up, rolling into physical and emotional satisfaction. My ass clamps down on Blake's cock and his choked moan fills my mouth as he comes inside me. I slick the front of his body with cum, and the way he keeps rubbing us together spreads my mess. I love a mess, and I love our mess more than anything.

"Mercer," he moans my name. "Fuck."

I'm cooked. Done. Dead to the fucking world. Literally cannot hold myself up for one second longer. I ragdoll in his arms and the two of us fall to the floor. We stay there like that for a long time, just breathing and thinking and being close. It's one of the best feelings of my whole life.

"Blake?"

"Yeah, baby."

"Thanks for... seeing me."

He smiles at me, still sweaty and exhausted. "I'll never stop looking, Mercer."

I blush like an asshole because holy shit, he's a romantic murderer.

We take our time cleaning up, even though I don't let him dote on me, but true to his word, he doesn't really wash off that well. I'm smug as shit as we leave that changing room, knowing he's got my cum on him for the rest of the night. Take that, Dee.

"I need to pee," I tell him as we pass the bathroom. "I'll meet you out there?"

Blake kisses my lips. "I'll be at the bar. This thing is winding down. Hurry up." He smacks my ass and I watch him enter the event room again.

Smiling like a dorky kid, I take a pee and enjoy the new-found strength in my appearance in the mirror. Whoever that guy is trying to break through my eyes, he's getting closer and closer every day.

I don't hate galas so much anymore.

I wash my hands and leave the bathroom, only to run right into my dad. Something happens in my chest, but I have armour now. It slides into place, reminding me I'm not ignored. That I'm worthy.

"Ben," Dad says. "I… I wanted to offer you a drink and my apologies." He holds out two glasses, both with a serving of scotch. "It's long overdue."

Hesitantly, I take the drink. "Is it?"

"This," he motions between us, "is long overdue."

18 Blake

I don't hate much about Mercer, but I do hate that he doesn't enjoy aftercare. The little shit doesn't want me to coddle him, or make sure he isn't suffering an emotional drop from that turmoil he just lived through, and he doesn't want pampering. Maybe he'll come around the more he gets used to it, but for now, I let him go to the bathroom for a moment on his own, hoping he'll tell me if he needs anything else. Or at least, brat his way into getting whatever he needs from me. At least he's done that in the time I've known him.

He wanted to sleep in my bed? He stomped his feet in the hallway until I told him he could. He didn't want to be alone in the shower? He goaded me into staying. He's resourceful enough to get what he wants without having to outright ask for it, so I hope tonight is no different.

The event is winding down. My dad and Bronson are just getting ready to leave, but Olivia isn't with them. Brandt must already be gone because I don't see him anywhere, but the entire Palmerston family is still here. Olivia and

Samantha are with Penny, chatting to a group of socialites, and Will is... Wait, where's Will?

"You've got a little something there," Dee says, setting her empty glass on the bar top. Yeah, a little something is definitely on my shirt, but fuck it. I don't care. "Not gonna lie, Blake. I never expected you to be bi."

I shrug, scanning the room for Will Palmerston. "Dabbled a bit. Settled here."

"Crash landed, more like," she laughs. "He's such a dick, but I like him. For you. I couldn't date him. He'd be dead inside a week."

I smile at that. I don't underestimate the patience and anger management it might take to handle Mercer. "Oh, I think you might be dead inside a week, too. He makes it fun. Too bad he doesn't have any friends."

Dee scoffs, knowing exactly what I'm saying. "Please! You think he and I can be friends without hating each other in an hour?"

"He told me to take it easy on you when you called him a slut. I think that speaks volumes." I smirk at her. "He'll probably bite you if he sees me talking to you, though."

"So whipped."

Mm. Not even going to deny that. "Have you seen Will Palmerston?"

"No, not in a while. I avoid him whenever I can."

Typically, so would I, but I don't trust him when Mercer isn't at my side. That thought makes me pause for a second. I'm not giving Mercer enough credit. He's strong, proficient, and learning to believe in himself, so he's more than capable of handling his asshole of a dad. Tonight has proved that. Not only did he stand his ground at the gala, but he did it as himself, not even once faking who he is. Mercer is capable of more than anyone has ever given him credit for, and I won't be yet another person to treat him like a child.

I pause for another second.

But on the other hand, he is my *precious little baby* and I will stop at nothing to ensure he is safe.

"I gotta go," I tell Dee. "Time to be the overprotective boyfriend he secretly wants but will never admit to. Text me if you see Will."

"Wait, is he in trouble?"

"Will?"

"Mercer."

I start walking in the direction of the bathrooms. "I don't know yet." But I won't risk not finding out.

Over the past five years, I have been trained to develop many skills. How to read a situation, how to identify the exit points of a room, and how to put together clues to develop a story as close to what really happened as possible. I learned how to read people, how to interpret their intentions, and how to predict their actions before they've acted on them. I was taught how to kill, how to protect, and how to get someone to safety without anyone knowing. I'm a honed and toned assassin, a bodyguard, and a very efficient spy. But more than anything, I learned to listen to the gut instinct ingrained in me since birth. I became familiar with differentiating a gut feeling from fear. I know how to separate dread from actual instinct, and I'm capable of trusting my gut no matter my feelings on a situation.

Right now, my gut is telling me something is off. But I've also never been in a relationship before, and now I have a new protective impulse to separate from my gut instinct. I'm working through it, trying not to panic while I read the scene.

The bathroom is empty, apart from a tumbler with amber liquid in the bottom; smells like scotch. Mercer isn't inside, and he isn't in the hallway either. Poking my head back into the event room, I scan the room, looking for his dark hair and sexy suit, not seeing him after one sweep. I trust my eyes. He's not in there. If he was, my eyes would have found him immediately.

Olivia, Samantha, and Penny are still where I saw them last, but Will remains missing. Turning away from the event room, I enter the hall again. And run right into Will.

"Blake," he greets me with a smile, noticing the cum on my shirt. "We're just getting ready to head out. Are you and my son sticking around for a bit?"

His voice is steady, and his hands are damp from having just washed them. His smile is the fakest thing about him, but it's the barely there perspiration on his forehead that gives me pause. Will is an exceptional businessman, so he can hold a poker face with the best of them. His eyes won't shift, his voice won't waver, and his hands won't shake. But he's sweating, which hints at physical exertion that no one can hide.

"I was glad to see you brought him despite my protests. He's really thriving under your care," Will compliments me, and that's my first real red flag. This man, who hates the fact that I have his son living with me, wouldn't sink low enough to offer a compliment because, as much as he'd never admit it, Mercer's manipulative personality came from somewhere. Me having Mercer is a game to Will, and no matter how well he does, how much he changes, or how well behaved he seems in my company, Will won't ever admit to it because it is a direct insult to him. I'm accomplishing something he failed to even try, and businessmen are nothing but prideful and proud. Particularly Will Palmerston.

"Are you?" I push. "Never thought I'd see you glad to have your orders defied."

Will chuckles. "Well, Ben is the one area of my life I've done poorly with. I am man enough to admit that, and I'm grateful that you've taken him on as your... project."

"I haven't. He's pretty fucking perfect just how he is." My smile is feline. "Where is he?"

Will doesn't give anything away. "I thought he was with you." He pats my shoulder with another chuckle. "I'm sure he'll pop up. Have a good night, Mr. Carter."

I notice three things when Will passes me. One, he smells like whatever amber liquor is in that tumbler in the bathroom. Two, his phone has not stopped vibrating in his pocket since I ran into him. Three, he's coming from the one and only exit at the far end of the hall. The distance between the bathroom and that exit is barely twenty steps, and if Mercer was going to be ambushed and taken, this would be the perfect place to do it.

Blake: *I need you. Bathroom.*

I shove my phone in my pocket and recheck the bathroom first. I sniff the glass and get the same whiff of expensive scotch. Nothing else. No chemical smell, no sediment in the bottom, no oily residue on the top. Doesn't mean anything. The counter has drips and splashes from the tap, and the basket of towels is dwindled down to only a few. The room doesn't smell like Mercer, but I know he was in here; I watched him walk through the door.

"Blake?"

I don't turn to look at Aaron, but I see his blond head and navy-blue rimmed glasses in the mirror. He's taller than me, but build-wise, we're the same. I love my brothers with everything I have, but Aaron is the only person in the whole world I trust without question.

"I need you to track Mercer's phone." I check the powder room and the single toilet room. "Something's happened."

Aaron already has his phone out, plugging something into it from the pocket of his suit. I want to smile at how Mercer treated him when he unknowingly met him a few hours ago. It took him all of a minute to decide he liked the guy and wanted to be his true self, and after that, he was all snark and sass and full-on brat mode. Loved it, and honestly, it reinstated that feeling of rightness with Mercer.

"Says he's still here," Aaron shows me. "Heading to the front entrance."

"Will has his phone then." I push through the doors and run into Keira, Aaron's wife. "I'm checking this exit. Will you check the front?"

Aaron nods, taking Keira with him. I run out the side door, seeing nothing except an empty side lane that leads to the back parking lot. No vehicles, no signs of Mercer, and no clues. I text my brother, telling him to check the security footage.

Panic wants to claw its way up my throat, but I swallow it down to remain productive. Wherever the fuck he is, I'll find him. I don't care who I have to burn to get there. Mercer is mine, and nothing is going to take him from me unless he wants to leave on his own.

I'll find you, little demon.

Jogging around front, I'm just in time to see Will and his family climbing into the back of a vehicle. Their driver closes the door, and when I catch up to Aaron, I watch them drive away. I have no proof that Will did anything, but that gut instinct I trained to trust is telling me he is involved in this.

"Is the tracker moving away?" I ask Aaron.

"Yep."

"Who did Will have contact with in the past few minutes?" I ask him.

"Your dad," Keira tells me. "And Bronson. They talked for half a minute just before the car pulled up."

"Blake, your dad was with Trevor Palmerston." Aaron gives me a look. A look that says my world is about to be turned upside down. A look that hints at deception on the part of my own family. "It doesn't mean anything, though."

Trevor fucking Palmerston. Mercer's older brother. The one who works at that facility.

"Blake!" I turn at the sound of my name, seeing Dee run towards me with Brandt behind her. "Brandt got footage of the side exit camera before it was wiped." She hands me her phone.

I look at my brother before I watch it, trying to get a read on what the fuck is happening. Whatever is on this screen is going to either push me into a rage or break my fucking heart. He shakes his head at me, as if to say, we have no idea what the hell we're stepping into.

On the screen of Dee's phone, I watch an eight-second clip of Mercer, completely unconscious, being put into the back seat of a vehicle. Will is barely in the frame, but I catch sight of him talking to Trevor Palmerston.

A blanket of numbness calms my rage, reminding me that nothing other than a clear mind and a determined heart will help Mercer right now. It doesn't matter who took him. All that matters is tracking him, finding him, and getting him out of there alive. Everything else can come later. Mercer Bentley is my only priority.

Because I fucking love that little brat.

IT'S BACK TO MY training. Mercer is now a job. A rescue mission like all the others I've been trained for. Except this one has my heart racing and my mind dipping into gutters of hellish outcomes I can't handle. He's a job, but he's the most important job of my life. Because he's mine, and I barely got the chance to claim him.

Through the earpiece, Aaron's voice comes from his station at my apartment. "Will is still at home. Double-checked the camera feed to make sure it wasn't on a loop. It's not. He's there and so is the whole family."

"Trevor?" I ask, fastening all my gear and loading my weapons.

"He's there, too. No signs of Mercer ever being there, but I'm trying to run that partial plate number. I've got an alert out if it shows up on any traffic cams."

It won't. Whoever took him is a professional, and it's already been three hours since he went into that bathroom. When I find Mercer and bring him back home to me, I'm never letting him forgo aftercare for a moment alone again. Never.

Will might be at home right now, but if he's planning something with Mercer, he'll lead me to him eventually. For now, I focus on option one.

Brandt signals that he's ready. Dressed in the same dark tactical gear as me, he secures the earpiece and talks to Aaron even though he has no idea who Aaron is in real life. "Get anything back on that tox screen?"

"Roofies," Aaron says. They tested the glass of scotch in the bathroom.

Which means after three hours, Mercer is probably still out or groggy, depending on the dosage. I hope he's out of it so he's not scared, but I also hope he's aware and able to fight back. I hate that this is the only place I know to look for him. I'm banking on Will assuming I don't know about the second facility at the back of the property, because if he thinks I know about it, he wouldn't have brought Mercer here. And I don't know where else to look. I'm going off the fact that Trevor Palmerston was at the gala, and not much else.

"Let's go," Brandt says.

With Aaron monitoring the property, Brandt leads the way across the lawn. The second facility is a smaller building with none of the charm and fanciness of the main building. This one is a rectangular brick block with no personality, which means it's going to be hard to break into. Because it's unknown to the public, there don't seem to be any outside guards, and even the parking lot is underground. From the air, this place would look abandoned, which is exactly what it's listed as on the land registry site, according to Aaron. It used to be a military barracks until the land was purchased by Northern Horizons.

An internal moral debate isn't even on my mind tonight. When we find a back service door propped open so a man can smoke outside, I kill him without hesitation. Without knowing anything about him. Without caring. A single stab to the jugular, and a quick step back to avoid his blood spray. Brandt drags him by the feet until he's out of sight, and I kick dirt over the trail. Done. Entrance to the building: secured.

Guns raised, we enter a stairwell that doesn't go up, only straight onto this level or down to the next.

"How many sub-level floors?" I ask Aaron.

"Three," he says. "Very bottom used to contain holding cells for hostages when it was a military building. Might be easily renovated into secure patient rooms."

Sold. Brandt nods at me, and we descend the stairs to the very bottom level.

The stairwell echoes, but not near as loudly as my heartbeat in my ears. I tamp it down and steady my breathing, refusing to let emotions cloud my control. I know what I'm doing. I'm trained for this. Mercer is a job.

When we pass the second level, we pause to listen. Hearing nothing other than muffled voices, we keep descending. At the bottom floor, Brandt pauses by the door. He's three years older than me, which means he's three years out of training. He's just as capable as I am, if not more, and I trust his instinct. Once we emerge through that door, we'll be on a ticking clock. There are no cameras in the stairwell, but I'm ninety-nine percent certain there will be cameras on the patient floor. This will have to be a quick sweep, and the worst part about it is that we don't have key cards, codes, or any way to open each room if there are no windows in the doors.

"Hostage?" I ask Brandt.

"Probably our best bet," he agrees.

We wait by the doors, listening for movement, people, or sounds. Other than random banging, the hum of the electricity, and something being wheeled down the hall, we don't hear anything telling. Until a woman's voice has us alert. She's coming down the hall, pushing something like a cart, and either singing or talking to someone. If she's alone, this will be easier, but if she's not, we're ready.

Brandt puts his hand on the doorknob, and when her cart passes by, he opens the door. She's smaller than me, Mercer's size, so I clamp one hand over her mouth and wrap the other around her upper body, pulling her to my chest. She screams against my gloves, but I muffle the sounds, waiting for Brandt to clear the area. He taps my shoulder, and we pull the woman into the stairwell.

"Key card?" Brandt asks her, keeping one eye through the cracked door to the hall.

She can't speak, so I loosen my hand, ready to suffocate her if she screams. "Lanyard," she says. "It's on my lanyard."

Brandt breaks it off her neck. "It'll get us into all the doors?"

"Yes. I just deliver midnight medications. Please, don't hurt me."

I zip-tie her wrists behind her back, check all her pockets, and tape her mouth. "Do you know if Mercer Palmerston is here? Ben Palmerston?"

She shakes her head, crying now.

"Has Will Palmerston or Trevor Palmerston been here tonight?"

She shakes her head again.

I tape her ankles together so she can't run, and after making sure she isn't in possession of a panic button or a phone, we leave her in the stairwell.

"Make this quick," Brandt says.

We settle into a rhythm of checking and securing each room. Most of them have young, sleeping patients in them, and when we check their faces, they're either too drugged or too slow to react to us. The rooms are padded and white, with bright fluorescent lights just like Mercer told me. After checking all twenty rooms on this floor, we head to the second floor. Three nurses and a doctor end up tied in the stairwell, none of them knowing if Mercer is here.

"He knows," I say to Brandt. "Will knows we know about this place. Mercer isn't here."

Just to be sure, we check every floor, every room, and every closet. On the way out, my nerves are shot and my breathing is shaky. I grab the doctor from the stairwell and bring him outside.

Brandt keeps an eye out, knowing there will be security coming any minute now. "Are there other facilities like this one?"

"No! This is the only one." The doctor trembles, not so tough to be doing illegal work now that he's held at gunpoint.

"Where would Will Palmerston take his son if he isn't here?"

"Trevor? He works out of a recruiting centre downtown sometimes."

Interesting. "Mercer. Ben."

"Oh. I, uh, I don't know. Please! I don't know."

"But your main job is to brainwash young adults and kids?"

"It's for their own good!"

Bullshit. A silenced bullet goes through his right eye, and I'm walking across the lawn before his body even hits the dirt.

"Wanna check the recruiting centre?" Brandt asks.

"Aaron, can you look into it? Find out where it might be."

"On it."

I'm not one to panic. I handle high-stress situations with a clear, calm mind. A job is a job until it's complete, and nothing so far has been strong enough to sway me from my path. Fear doesn't overtake me even though I feel it, but tonight, it might win.

Where the fuck are you, Mercer?

"A building on Sycamore is owned by the Palmerston family," Aaron says. "Registered as a sub-corp to Northern Horizons. Might be it. No pings on the radar with that partial plate in that area tonight, though."

"Security cameras?" Brandt asks as we reach the vehicle.

"Looking."

He drives and I climb into the passenger seat, checking my phone for anything from Bronson or my dad. Nothing. Dad is looking into other buildings Will owns, and Bronson is supposed to be at the Palmerston house with Olivia.

On a whim, I text Mercer's phone.

Blake: *I'm on my way, baby.*

If Will has it, I hope he sees it, and I hope he fucking sweats.

19

Mercer

I HATE THAT MY fingers are in my mouth. I hate it even more that my dad sees it. No matter how hard I try, I can't pull them out, though.

My mind belongs to me, but it isn't my own. Weird questions and memories are fleeting by too fast for me to come up with answers to them. Like why Blake's apartment is music themed, but I've never seen him play an instrument, or if Dee's open invitation to hang out was a taunt or a genuine offer. But mostly, I'm just wondering if I really was a job to Blake Carter. Was this the end goal? Help me, earn my trust, break down my walls, and then send me back to my dad so his psychotherapy finally works?

I suck on my fingers and blink through the grogginess of my mind. I'm aware but not alert, and I'm scared without being able to do anything about it. My legs don't want to move and my panic attack can't fully come because my body is too lazy to let it.

Through blurred vision, I squint one eye to look around. It's a familiar room, somewhere I've spent a lot of time, but it's also different this time. My dad is here, and I don't think I've ever seen him here before.

"Baby," Dad says, looking at a phone. "He calls you baby. Suits you, since you're sucking your fucking thumb like one."

I force myself to pull my fingers from my mouth. Is that my phone? Did Blake text me?

"I admire your persistence and your ability to bounce back," Dad says. "It's just coming at the wrong time, Ben."

Mercer.

"I've had plans in place for a very long time, and you being with the youngest Carter boy isn't good for those plans. I admit, you've been dealt a terrible hand in life. This mess started long before you were born, and I *am* sorry you got caught in the crossfire, but I can't have you earning a backbone right now."

"Why?" My voice isn't powerful, reminding me how useless and weak I am. "What do I have to do with any of it?"

Dad smiles at my phone and then puts it into his jacket pocket. He looks at me for the first time, really scrutinizing my appearance. I'm still wearing the suit from the gala, but it's rumpled and damp, and ruining the couch I've been placed on. This living room sits in a cabin, one I've been kept at many times before, guarded and secure while my family does something important they don't want me fucking up. Wonder what it is this time?

Through the haze of the drugs, I'm terrified. More terrified than I've ever been before because this is the first time I've ever stood up to my dad. I put on a show tonight, blending into his world to goad him, and look how it turned out. I asked for this. I egged it on and brought my own fate just by being... myself. A brat. A hoodlum. A man learning to own his confidence. But Blake isn't here to save me from fate this time, and despite my progress lately, I don't know if I have what it takes to save myself.

I'm nobody. I'm Ben.

"You have to do with all of it," Dad says, giving me his full attention, maybe for the first time in my life. I hate how much I like it. "Because of who you actually are."

It's a struggle, but I push myself into a half-sitting, mostly slouching position, like it's going to help me hear better. Like turning the music down in the car to read the road signs better. It's useless, but it makes me feel like I'm doing something to stay alert, and I can already tell that whatever he's going to say will hurt. Whatever meagre bits of armour I have left are sliding into place, but I'm on my own for this one. No Blake. No one to call for help. No one to act out to. Just me, a lonely boy, in a room alone with my father for the first time.

There's a part of me that feels important, too. Maybe it's because my dad is going to tell me something truthful for once, or maybe it's because something I've done has caused him to actually worry. Not about me, but about whatever plan he has. I'm not just degrading the Palmerston name anymore, I'm actually worthy of being a threat. Just like Blake told me to be.

I pull the sleeve of my shirt down over my fingers, balling the fabric up as much as I can instead of sucking my fingers. "Who I am?"

"You're a smart guy, Ben. Too smart for your own good sometimes," Dad says, the chair groaning as he leans back and crosses his legs. "You saw something you shouldn't have when you were a kid. Something that put a few too many pieces of the puzzle together in your mind, and you figured it out. Do you remember?"

Remember what? Saw something I shouldn't have? Something traumatic? I comb through my mind, trying to recall anything he could be talking about, but my childhood is the same monotonous week over and over again until I got sent to the facility for the first time.

"You were ten." Dad laughs like it's funny. "A damn ten-year-old kid almost ruined everything. Do you remember the woman? The one who came to the house to talk to you about the centre Trevor worked at?"

It was so long ago, I barely remember being ten. All I remember about the night he's referring to is a lady with dark hair and red lips, telling me they were going to fix my brain. I can remember the numbers on her licence plate as we walked to the car, the pattern of her necklace, and the number of times her heels clacked against the pavement while she walked ahead of me. Her facial features evade me, and anything she might have said is gone.

"Who was she?"

"She was the woman who helped me buy that place. She took Trevor under her wing and taught him to do what she did. Which was to help young adults find their way to the centre."

"To be mind controlled."

Dad smiles again. It's his charming business smile, and I've never actually seen it directed at me before. It's... nice. Looks good on him. "Business is business, Ben."

Mercer.

"Why'd you send me there? What'd I do? I was just a kid."

"A smart kid. A kid who learned the truth somehow, and to this day, I have no idea how you did it."

"What fucking truth? I don't know anything!" My throat burns with the force of my honesty. "I have no idea what you're talking about." I cough, bringing my fingers to my mouth.

"Because we washed it from your memory." Dad stares at my fingers, so I remove them and fuck with the sleeves again. "Ben, you are the one and only thing standing in the way of everything I've ever wanted. Everything I've ever worked for. And I've put in too much effort and too much time to let you get in my way now."

"I'm not in your way! I... just let me go. I'll change my name and leave the family for good. No one wants me anyway."

"The Carter boy does," Dad says.

"Dad, please." I push myself up, not sure what I'm begging for, but getting the feeling my life isn't guaranteed for much longer. My skin itches and my throat burns, panic rearing its head. "Dad."

"*Dad*," he echoes with a huff. "Do you even realize you're nineteen years younger than Trevor? Twelve years younger than your sisters?"

An uneasy feeling churns in my stomach, and my eyes take in the pattern of the wood panelling on the walls. The hand clock ticks every second, showing 3:59. Then 4:00.

I've never been wanted. I've never been a part of the family. I've been hidden and kept a secret. My name changed to Ben and stayed Ben until Blake found me. "I'm... not yours." I chew my fingers, biting my nails until they bleed and sucking the blood away to give me something to taste. To smell. To do.

"Not my son," Dad—Will—says. "My nephew."

I look at him, ripping my eyes from my pants to search for something real in his eyes. Not his son, but still family. But he still treated me like I was nothing. Like I *am* nothing.

But I'm not nothing, because memories from that night of the lady with the red lipstick came to get me start blurring through my mind like he just unlocked them.

My name. My real name, on a birth certificate with two different parents. The numbers and dates of my birth, and the dates of my parents' deaths. A final will and testament with my name mentioned in it, and the age eighteen. I figured it out once before, and Will sent me to that place to forget.

"You needed me to turn eighteen for something."

"Your mother was my sister. Cheryl. Our father's favourite. Her and her husband, your birth father and the man whose name we refused to call you, got something I wanted in the will. When they died, they had it set up to go to you when you turned eighteen."

My mind clears and the answers spell themselves out for me. “You killed them.”

Will sighs, lost in memory. “Tried to kill you, too. You were barely born, but you were in the way, and for that, I’m sorry.”

“You’re sorry? For killing your sister and her husband, and attempting to kill a baby?” That unease in my gut worsens and toughens, preparing for where this night ends.

“I don’t take joy in what happened to them, Ben.”

Mercer!

“And I don’t have the stomach to harm a child, but...”

“But you’d hire someone to do it.” I laugh, knowing where this is going. “You hired the Carters, didn’t you?”

“Not exactly.” Will rubs his temples. “Not Brendan Carter. His wife.”

The woman with dark hair and red lipstick. Blake’s mom. She was the one who came to get me that night, taking me to the centre for the very first time. “But I was already ten by that point.”

“Yeah, things didn’t go according to plan when you were still an infant. Brendan found his wife with you. He had no idea who you were or where she got you, but he caught her trying to smother a baby. He saved you and committed his wife to that facility for having a manic episode. After that, we worked together to keep you alive but unaware until you turned eighteen. We found the stipulations in your mother’s will, but by the time you turned eighteen, someone had already taken what was rightfully yours. What should have been mine.”

I tilt my head at this man who tried to kill me as a child, tortured me through adolescence, neglected me and abandoned me, and never even cared about me because I was nothing more than a safeguard to a safety deposit box to him.

“What was it?” I ask, my interest in this dwindling by the second. My moments are numbered now. There’s no longer any reason to keep me alive. "I'm twenty-three. Why am I still alive if my eighteenth birthday didn't get you what you wanted?"

"If you'd have just stayed out of my way, none of this would have had to happen." He nods at the door to the porch, and a man in black with a gun in his hand walks inside. My grim reaper, come to claim me after far too much life has been lost and lived. I should have died twenty-three years ago. I should have died at eighteen. I'm young, but I'm past my second—maybe third—expiry date, and tonight, it has come.

Death chills me. I can't even call it fear. Just the ticking clock of fate, run down to the final minutes.

My rise to confidence ends. My games with Blake, gone. My lessons in love are over. That person crawling to my surface, battling his way into my eyes, no longer gets to fight for us. We hit our limit, and as the tears calmly slip down my cheeks, I remind myself that I am worth something. My life might have been pointless, but Blake saw me. He sees me. He understands and respects me, and the few weeks I've spent with him have been enough to settle my breathing, pull my fingers away from my mouth, and meet the barrel of that gun with readiness in my heart.

Blake helped me live, and I'll greet death grateful that I got him in any small capacity. I got to be his little demon.

"I am sorry for this, Ben." Will glances back at me before leaving the cabin like a coward.

Eyes strained but voice strong, I finally correct him. "Mercer."

20 Blake

I WATCH A HITMAN walk into the cabin, and I see Will Palmerston walk out a few seconds later. The rage inside me wants to kill him, but the heart in my chest knows Mercer is my priority. The heart in my chest *makes* Mercer my priority. Nothing is worth it if he doesn't make it through this.

I don't know the hitman, which means I don't know his execution style. If he's a *walk-in-and-take-the-shot* type, I merely have seconds.

"Go, Blake," Aaron says in my ear. "Now."

There's no one else on the property, and Will's back is to me. Ideally, I'd like him to think his hit worked and Mercer is dead, but if he sees me, none of that will be possible. I don't care.

I sprint to the front porch, not making a sound. My breathing slows, and I refuse to let my heart stutter. On soft feet, I climb the three steps and grip the knob. I pray for silent hinges, but I don't get that. The door squeaks as I open it, and I only have a second to make a decision. Closing it so Will doesn't suspect anything, I take in the scene in a single heartbeat.

Mercer, eyes pointed straight at the barrel of the gun, head held high, tears on his smooth cheeks, ready to die. Over my dead fucking body. The man looks behind him at the same time Mercer notices me. His eyes widen and cry harder, but my eyes take in the vest on the hitman. Bulletproof. I can't shoot him anywhere but the head to ensure he doesn't kill Mercer.

The man whips the gun back in Mercer's direction, and when his finger feathers the trigger, I make a split-second decision to shoot his hand.

My life, and Mercer's, flashes before my eyes. In this fragment of time, grid-locked into an instance where one or all of us dies, I know with absolute certainty that I'm in love with Mercer Bentley. The clarity of it is astounding, like the fog has lifted and revealed everything true to me. The difficult yet thrilling path life with Mercer will take me on. The comfort he'll seek from me and the strength he'll find all on his own. His lingerie and his hoodlum look, and the way he cuddles me while telling me how much he hates it. The way our lives are going to mesh together like oil and water but the determination to make them fit will be stronger than any chemical reaction. Mercer is mine and I'm his, and he is not fucking dying tonight.

A second gun appears in the hitman's hand, aimed at me.

My bullet pierces the man's palm, and the second one blows off his trigger finger. As I dodge the bullet coming my way, I rip a dagger from my belt. While the gun drops and Mercer blinks, reacting late to the gunshot, I scream his name.

"Mercer! Catch!"

He looks in my direction, but not at me. At the single dagger soaring through the air. His feet push into the floor as he stands, and the hilt of the dagger hits his palm. Tonight,

Mercer doesn't hesitate. Tonight, Mercer stands on his own two feet as himself, the guy with knife skills and worth.

I aim for the man's head, but Mercer beats me to it. No sooner than the hilt hits his palm does he flip it around and expertly fling it at the hitman. It pierces the man's eyes, and when he screams, Mercer keeps going. He yanks it free and jams it right into the guy's windpipe, cutting off his scream. Not a breath later, my third bullet, silenced, pierces his skull and he drops to the ground at Mercer's bloody feet.

My breathing fills my ears, but the tick tock of the clock drums loudly. Standing still, holding my breath, we wait. Wait to see if Will is going to check that he is dead after hearing gunshots. Wait to see if another attack is coming. I stare straight into his amber eyes, filling him with strength he doesn't even need because he already has his own. Mercer stares back, showing me how scared he is, but showing me how much he trusts and loves me, too. His chest rises and falls, but the longer we stand here listening, the harsher his breathing gets.

The sound of Will's vehicle leaving greets my ears a moment later, and the body of the hitman vibrates. Mercer, covered in blood, reaches into the man's jacket pocket and pulls his phone out.

"It's... he's asking if the job is done." His eyes water, reality and his near-death experience settling into his bones. His soul. As a contract killer, I know how to confirm a death. Will wants photo proof.

"Hey, baby." I smile at Mercer, stepping over the dead body to get to him.

At the sound of my voice and the pet name, it gives Mercer's mind permission to shut the fuck down. "Blake," he whimpers, barely holding onto himself. "Blake."

I catch him as he falls, lowering with him. "I'm right here. I got you." I cradle him, promising myself I'll never let him go again. "You did fucking good, little demon."

His fingers lift, aiming for his mouth, but I tug them to a stop.

"They're bloody, baby. I need you to do one more thing for me, okay?" I stroke my fingers through his dark hair and try to keep him as calm as possible. "And then we're getting the fuck out of here."

He grips the material of my jacket hard, not wanting to let go. He waits, staring with his big, scared eyes, listening for what I need him to do.

"I gotta put you down in all this blood, Mercer. We have to send a photo to your dad to prove you're dead. Just for now, okay? It buys us time."

"Blake."

"If we don't do it, he'll turn around and come check. We have to hurry, okay?" I wait for him to nod, even though there's none of him behind it. He's just doing what I tell him to do, and for now, I'll have to accept that.

I put him down on his back, the blood pooling all around him from the hitman. He cries, but he doesn't move. I turn his head to the side, make sure there's a pool of blood behind it, and I even put more blood in his hair. I take the phone from his grip and hate this. Everything about it. Everything about the way he looks dead is building something unhinged and lethal inside me. My breath shakes out of me, staccato and scared.

"Say something to remind me you're alive." I open the camera app.

"He's not my dad," Mercer says.

"What? Close your eyes, baby."

He closes them and I snap the photo, pulling him up faster than I set him down. I send it to Will and then delete it from the camera roll. Delete it from the trash bin, too.

"I really wanna go home now, Blake. Please." He shakes in my arms. "Please."

"Where's home, Mercer? Tell me where you feel safe."

"With you."

A text comes through the phone. *Clean it up. I want him missing, not dead.*

If this story doesn't end with me killing Will Palmerston, I will flip my shit. Actually, if this story doesn't end with Mercer taking his fucking power back and knocking his father down to the gutters where he belongs *before* I kill him, I will flip my shit even more. My mission in life just became Mercer's redemption, and I will stop at nothing to help him get it.

Hauling Mercer into my arms, letting him shake in the comfort of my safety, I glance around the cabin to make sure nothing leads Will to believe Mercer is still alive or that I was ever here. I'll call my dad to order a cleanup as soon as I get him in the vehicle. I snap a photo of the hitman first, just to get an ID on him later.

"How'd you find me?" Mercer asks, voice brittle but still there.

"I texted your phone and your dad was stupid enough to turn it on." I jostle him a bit so I can carry him with only one arm. "No matter what it took, Mercer, I would have found you." I'm just lucky I found him in time. "Ready?"

He nods, and then his arms wrap around my neck when I start walking. I turn off all the lights, close the door behind me, and head into the woods. We've got a bit of a walk, but it'll give my heart time to calm down.

I almost lost him.

I almost fucking lost him.

Rage bubbles up unexpectedly. Rage will get me nowhere, so I tamp it down and focus on walking through the forest in the dark. A job is a job, like I said before, and this job won't be over until Mercer is safely back in my home, clean of all this blood and being a brat again. I thought about taking him to my studio apartment so he isn't seen by anyone for a few days, but it'll look suspicious to Will if I'm not where he thinks I should be. On the other hand, if I go to the studio apartment and essentially go missing for a bit, it'll make

Will sweat. He'll assume I'm looking for Mercer, and he now knows I'll stop at nothing to find him.

I tap the earpiece in my ear and say, "Dad?"

"Here."

"I've got him. Will needs to think he was executed. Where should I go?"

"Did you recognize the hitman?"

"No."

"Then come here. We'll hide Mercer, and having all of us together will make it look like we're searching for him."

I look down at the boy in my arms, thankful he's breathing even though he's hurting. "Will you come to my dad's with me for a few days?" I ask him. "While we come up with a plan."

"You'll be there?"

"Yes. I won't leave you."

Mercer nods, and I convey the message to my dad. "I need a cleanup crew at the cabin. No DNA."

"I'll take care of it," Dad says.

I have too much to think about. Like how Will fooled Aaron with the live feed of their house, and who else he was working with at the gala to get Mercer out of there. And what the fuck Trevor Palmerston has to do with any of it.

The forest is mostly silent, other than insects and rustling leaves, but the loudest sound of all is probably my heart. I've never reacted to a job like this before, and even though I have him back in my arms, I can't shake the fear. Its claws are in me, reminding me how close I came to losing him forever—proving how much he's come to mean to me. How? How did that even happen? How did I fall for Mercer so quickly, and what the hell was I thinking? It's no wonder people with my lifestyle marry only for convenience. They say love gives you a weakness, and I learned that lesson tonight, but no part of me wants to pull away from him when he needs me. When I need him. How am I supposed to manage everything all at once?

Mercer intrigued me with lacy lingerie and a smoking grilled cheese sandwich, and now I'm a fucking goner.

"Aaron?" I say after clicking into his channel.

"I heard," he answers because I gave him access to the channel with my dad. "What do you want me to do?"

"I need to know what Will and Trevor are doing at all times."

"On it. Patch me into the phone you took from the hitman, and I'll monitor it, too."

"Are you still at my apartment?"

"Yeah. We're leaving, though."

Smart. Mercer's dad will be monitoring it now to keep tabs on me, so if Aaron and Keira want to keep their identity hidden, they have to go. "You're welcome at my dad's place. Both of you. They'll find out who you are, but..."

Aaron laughs. "You act like this is the first time we've been in this situation."

True, but it's different this time because... I'm in love with the client. This isn't a random job from a random client. This is my family. It's personal. It's a betrayal and the start of a war with no certain ending. This is a battle for love and life, and I'm not the only subject involved. I can't act on instinct with the Palmerston family because my instinct is to kill them all for what they've done to Mercer, morals aside. But Mercer might have a difference of opinion, and I'll—begrudgingly—have to respect it.

"Just keep in touch and watch your back. Thanks. For everything."

Aaron says goodbye right as I get to the truck I parked at the edge of the forest. We're only an hour from the city, but that's a whole hour Mercer will have to sit on his own, soaked in blood, trembling from shock after the night he's had. The whole damn day, really. A fireman's breakfast, a sexy outfit, the Sean Pendleton murder, the gala, the emotional healing and sex in the changing room, and now this? He looked that gun in the eye and greeted the whisper of death, then he stabbed someone twice, and fuck, he's gotta be exhausted.

"You okay to sit over here on your own while I drive?" I set him on the passenger seat, but he doesn't let go of my neck. "Mercer, look at me." I tilt his chin.

He's not crying. He's not trembling anymore, either. He's simply… blank. He isn't even trying to put his fingers in his mouth. His amber eyes blink at me a few times, but there's nothing in them except questions I don't have answers to and pain from everything he's been through tonight. I don't know what happened between the gala and here, but I won't ask until we're somewhere I can keep him safe.

"Do you trust me?"

He blinks.

"I won't let anything happen to you, do you hear me? I've got you. You're safe, Mercer." I cup his cheeks and bend down to be at eye level with him. "We just need to get to my dad's house."

Mercer shakes his head, his lower lip starting to tremble. "Blake." His voice is begging, but it's more scared than anything. Whatever he learned tonight, he thinks it's going to change my view of him. I don't know what it is, but that will never happen. Never.

I'VE NEVER LIVED IN this house before, but my dad has a bedroom set up for me. He takes one look at Mercer, covered in blood, clinging to me like I'm the only thing keeping him alive, and nods respectfully. Falling for the youngest Palmerston probably wasn't a part of my dad's plan, but he's smart to accept it without commenting. I love my dad, but he won't sway me away from Mercer, even if there is some diabolical plan to ruin the Palmerstons. I'll just make Mercer *not* a Palmerston.

Dad leaves soon after to make sure the cleanup goes to plan, calling Brandt and Bronson on his way out. I want to touch base with all of them, but they aren't my priority right now.

Mercer doesn't protest when I set him on the tiled floor of the bathroom, and he doesn't make a sound as I strip him of his bloody clothing and throw it all in a garbage bag. I fucking loved that suit, so I'll make sure he gets another one just like it. He does, however, protest when I try to put him in the shower.

"No," he whines, clutching my jacket.

"I'm just undressing, baby. One second."

Naked, I wrap my arms around him and step us both into the shower. The water burns on first contact, but Mercer doesn't even flinch. He stands there with his hand constantly on me, shifting with my movements as I wash him, afraid that if he lets go, I might disappear. I scrub under his nails, in every dip and crevice of his body, and triple wash his hair, more for my benefit than his. When I saw him covered in blood with closed eyes for that photo, it shook me. Dead bodies are nothing to me, but this one... it's mine. Mine to love. Mine to protect. Mine to own. And I never want to see it dead again.

Mercer trails me with a towel around his shoulders, his hands still clinging to the one around my waist as I sift through a closet of Brandt's things, looking for something to wear.

"You okay, little demon?" I ask him, sliding sweatpants up his legs.

He holds my shoulders, watching my hands work. "I don't know."

"Wanna talk about it?" I tug a hoodie over his head and help him slip his arms through.

He shakes his head, chest heaving.

"Mercer, whatever happened, whatever you learned, or whatever he said, it won't make me run. I promise. I'm here, okay? I'm not going anywhere." I grip his chin and kiss his lips. "Do you hear me?"

"How'd your mom die?" he asks timidly, looking anywhere but my eyes.

"My mom?" I tilt my head, wondering why this is what he asks, of all things. "Uh, she died because she betrayed our family. I don't really know the details of it. Why?" I stand straight to get dressed in my own hoodie and sweats.

"I think—I think it was because of me." Mercer looks at me. "I met her. I didn't know who she was at the time, but I met her when I was a kid."

What the fuck? "You're sure?"

Mercer shrugs, so I grab his wrist and drag him to the kitchen because the boy needs to drink something or eat something, despite the hour. I leave him there for all of three seconds, grabbing a family photo from the living room. It's old, I was only a teen in it, but my mom is there.

"Is this the woman you met?" I ask Mercer, handing him the photo.

He takes it, studying it while his memory works to recall her. I don't doubt him, and I trust his memory more than anyone else's, but I can't for the life of me figure out how my mom relates to him as a child.

"That's her," he says, flipping the photo over and setting it face down on the island. "I met her when I was ten, but she knew me as a baby."

I slide him a can of Pepsi and a bag of chips, sitting down with him. "You can tell me if you want."

"Do you love her?"

"I did. I mean, she was my mom, but to be honest, I never really knew her that well. She wasn't healthy, and she spent a lot of time at some hospital."

Mercer nods like he already knows this. "Yeah, at Northern Horizons, where she met my dad. Well, not my dad."

"Mercer?"

"Will Palmerston is actually my uncle, I guess."

I open the can for him and dump a few chips on the counter so he can snack slowly. "I'm listening, baby."

He crosses his legs on the stool, turns it to face me, and sips the pop. "Will Palmerston killed my parents, his sister and her husband. Cheryl Palmerston, and my dad, Mercer."

No fucking wonder Will never wanted him to have the name. It'd lead right back to his dead parents, and he couldn't have that.

He chews a chip, getting a little more life into him. "My grandfather apparently left most of the family money to Cheryl, or at least, something Will wanted, so he killed them because it was supposed to revert to him in the event of their deaths. Instead, it went to their kid. Me." He spins his stool to face away from me. "And I don't know how it happened, but your mom was already in my dad's pocket when I was a baby, and she tried to kill me."

I spin him back around. "Don't hide from me, Mercer." As shocked as I am about all of this, I want him to know I won't disregard anything he says.

"I'm trying not to taint your image of your mom," he says. "I'm sorry."

"It's not your fault." I smile at him. "If my mom tried to kill a baby, I'd rather my image of her be tainted. She failed?" I mean, obviously.

"Obviously," Mercer scoffs, taking another sip. There's my boy. "I don't know how or why she failed, though."

"I do."

We both spin on our stools, seeing my dad and brothers walk in. Their clothing is different from when they left, so I know they took care of the cabin.

"I'm sorry for the night you've had, Mercer," Dad says to him, setting some take-out bags on the counter.

"It wasn't all bad," Mercer says with a shy little grin just for me.

"You knew she tried to kill Mercer as an infant?" I ask my dad, opening the bags and shoving a bunch of food in front of my little demon.

"I knew she tried to kill a baby, yes." He stands on the opposite side of the island while Bronson stands with him, and Brandt takes a seat beside Mercer. "I didn't know it was you, though. Not then. The police took you away, and I stayed focused on my wife. Something was seriously wrong with her, and at the time, I honestly thought she was just mentally ill."

Are we finally going to get the true story about what happened to our mom? I look at my brothers, seeing their rapt attention on our dad. We've been waiting for this truth for a long, long time.

"That place made her ill," Mercer offers.

"It'd be easier to think that," Dad says, smiling at Mercer. "But the truth is that she wasn't the woman I thought she was. She had another agenda, and unfortunately, it had everything to do with Will Palmerston. They were after the Palmerston fortune together, and I didn't learn that until... later."

"She took me there when I was ten," Mercer says. "Came to my house, talked to my parents, and then talked to me about a place that would make me feel better. At the time, I was pretty down on myself because no one loved me, and she convinced me it was a problem with me instead of my family. I went with her."

If my mom was alive, I'd murder her all over again. I look at my dad, finally understanding why he did what he did.

Mom was a terrible person, and even though we're also terrible people, she fucked over family, and no one fucks over our family.

"I'm sorry," Dad says to Mercer. "My wife wasn't a good person, and I'm sorry for what she did to you."

Mercer almost puts his fingers in his mouth, but he eats a fry instead. "Thank you."

"So, you fucking knew about this?" Bronson snaps. "And you're making me marry one of them?"

Dad sighs, rubbing his temples. "I've had a plan in place since Mercer turned seventeen. My son falling for him wasn't a part of that plan, but I think it's time to fill everyone in."

Fucking finally.

21

Mercer

AFTER THE DAY I'VE had, I don't even feel guilty about stealing a second cheeseburger from the bag. Near-death experiences and shock impact my appetite, and Blake is shoving food and drinks at me like they're the only things keeping me going, so I'm indulging. Eating gives me something else to focus on, so that's a bonus.

Still, I latch onto Blake's shirt when he tries to leave me. We're moving to the living room to be more comfortable, and Blake is carrying all the food. I hate needing him so much, and I can't fully recall when he became my safety zone, but my world might literally end if he moves too far away from me.

"Take this," he says, shoving paper bags at me. I hold them, and a second later, I realize why. It's so Blake can touch me, steering me to the couch with all my snacks.

He sits us down together, letting me snuggle in close enough to probably annoy the shit out of him with my munching. Blake hands me a to-go cup of soda, but before I even take a drink of it, Brandt holds up a bottle of rum as an offering. I pop the top and let him fill it up, needing the booze to settle me down enough to process without going into an episode.

Holy shit. I haven't had a panic attack. How? How have I not? Am I too shocked to panic?

"Does rum go well with roofies?" I ask, just to be a little shit.

Brandt laughs, but Blake doesn't. He gets grumpier.

"Get on with it, Dad," Blake says. "Mercer needs to sleep."

"I'm not a fucking baby," I snip at him. He grins, and his family snickers. "I can leave if you want to have this as a family thing." Except I can't leave because I'm glued to Blake and unwilling to let him detach himself from me.

Blake starts to scold me for offering to leave, but Brendan cuts him off. "You are family, Mercer. And this has just as much to do with you as it does us."

Am I goddamn blushing? I pull my hood up to hide my face, grateful Blake put me in my hoodlum look for the night. I mumble a thanks around a mouthful of cheese, bread, and beef.

"Your real parents hired our family when you were born," Brendan says. "I knew your dad from childhood, but had lost touch with him over the years. I knew he married a Palmerston, but other than dealing with Will and your grandfather, I wasn't that close with any of them. When you were born, your mom showed up at my door. Literally. She knocked, barely out of the hospital from having you."

"Why?" I ask.

"Because your grandfather had died a few months prior, and around the time of your birth, his final will and testament were released for the family to read over. When she saw it and learned that she had been given almost everything to do with the Palmerston name, including businesses and estates, she knew her days were numbered."

What a way to be graced with gifts; in danger because of them. I settle against Blake, no longer eating. I set the burger down and focus on the drink instead. “She hired you to kill Will?”

“No,” Brendan says, shaking his head. “She used me as a scapegoat, actually. And for a connection. A lawyer. She wanted her will set up and in place before she left my house. She wanted everything in her name to go to you, but she knew that’d put you in danger, so she made a few stipulations. In the event of your death, everything would go to a charity. But if you made it to eighteen, it’d be in your name.”

But it isn’t. “I’m twenty-three,” I remind him.

“There was another stipulation,” Brendan says with a smile. “Your mother was a smart lady. On the day of your seventeenth birthday, I got a letter. Everything meant for you, came to me. That’s how we became owners of the gas mine and all the subsidiary businesses beneath it. It’s also why Will is so pissed at us. And if I had to guess, it’s why Will agreed to the marriage between Bronson and Olivia. He wants to rework the legalities of it because that’s what he wanted from your grandfather’s will.”

“What? You've owned it all this time?” Blake scoffs, his hand squeezing my thigh. “Why do you own it? And why are you trying to marry into that family?” I can tell Blake is mentally berating himself. He’s a big picture guy, and he has no idea how this all ties together.

“Because Cheryl trusted him to get it to me,” I fill in, picking up on where this is going. “Or to keep me alive long enough to take Will down first to ensure my safety.”

Brendan nods. “And the betrothal gave me an in with the family.”

Bronson stands, snatching the bottle of rum off the sofa table. “You needed an in so you could find out if this is a murder mission or a rescue mission,” he says, putting it all together.

“If Will is acting alone or if the rest of the Palmerstons are in on it, too,” Blake adds.

"I needed to determine if your sisters, uh, cousins, were aware. As well as Penny. I've always known Will and Penny weren't your parents, but it didn't benefit your safety in the grand scheme of things to make that public knowledge. It would have given away Cheryl's plan, and if Will was aware I knew anything about it before your seventeenth birthday, he would have attempted murder again. I am sorry for the things you've lived through, Mercer." Brendan smiles at me, and I honestly think he means it.

Blake looks at me, checking in. His blue eyes search the lines of my face, looking for any panic or doubt. When he looks at me like this, I know he loves me. He hasn't said it, and maybe he won't, but I feel it. I feel him being the only person to ever truly care about my wellbeing, and me as a person. The real me.

"I'm okay," I tell him. I'm overwhelmed to high hell, but I'm managing. I guess I do that now. *I manage*. New life skill.

"I became the owner of the gas mine, including the businesses beneath it, but that wasn't made public knowledge until you turned eighteen. On your eighteenth birthday, Will learned the truth. He figured out that Cheryl had made arrangements to bypass him, and he was not happy about it. So, guess what he did?" Brendan grins.

"He cozied up to you," Brandt laughs. "Which made it pretty damn easy for you to pitch a betrothal, old man."

"Hey, watch it. It was supposed to be you getting married to one of the Palmerston girls, but Will wanted it to be Bronson, and I haven't figured out why."

"Because he wasn't single and Will was testing your commitment to joining forces," Blake says. He looks at Bronson and asks, "So? What's your take? Do the sisters know? Does Penny know?"

"I think Will believes women should be seen, not heard, so they're in the dark about most things. They just believe whatever he tells them. Pretty sure they have no idea about the facility Mercer went to, either."

And I never told them. Why? Because no one fucking believes me. I lost my voice for the truth a decade ago and am only now starting to get it back. I have a question, though, and I'm not sure if it's my place to ask. I take a sip, let the rum burn my throat, and go for it.

"Why'd you have your wife killed, though?"

"I didn't, actually," Brendan admits. "Not to say I wouldn't have, but it wasn't me."

"Will," I fill in. "She failed at whatever she was supposed to be doing, and he killed her for it."

Brendan nods, and now it's my turn to check in on Blake. My dad killed his mom. His mom tried to kill me. We're woven together in such a bad way, it makes any future between us seem impossible. He leans in until his nose tickles my hair.

"I'm not going anywhere, baby. I promise." His lips brush my cheek, and he lifts my straw to my mouth before he turns his focus back to his dad. "I was a teen when she died, so what happened then? What'd she do?"

"Mercer was first sent to that facility. All the times I tried to help her mental health by sending her there, she fooled me. She actually worked there as a recruiter under Will's leadership. She trained Trevor, but Will didn't want Mercer knowing Trevor worked there. He was still pretty young at the time. So your mom brought Mercer to the facility, and she did it as a ruse." Brendan sighs. "She tried to double-cross Will. She found out about me being a part of Cheryl's plans. I'm not sure how, but she thought she could kill Mercer herself, cut Will out of the deal, and come back home to our marriage to reap the benefits coming my way."

"And Will killed her for it." Blake shakes his head. "Or hired it, anyway."

"He tried to hire me," Brendan laughs. "Told me about my wife's betrayal, spun a tale, left Mercer out of it, and tried to get me to kill her. When I told him no, he took matters into his own hands, scared she'd come back and tell me who

Mercer really was. But I did act on it. I hired someone to tail her for a few days. It was because of that tail that I know how and when she died, and where her body is."

"You didn't tell the tail to intervene if someone attempted murder?" Bronson asks.

Brendan looks his son in the eye. "No, I didn't."

The three brothers share a look, and after a few seconds, they all nod. Apparently, they're okay with that. Sheesh. The security alarm on the wall, partially hidden behind a curtain, blinks the late hour at me, and fatigue sets in despite my nerves being as fried as these french fries are.

"So, what now?" Brandt asks. "How does Mercer get everything back?"

I shake my head. "I don't really wanna know that right now. I went from sexy firemen to a sexy suit, to almost dying, to straight up murdering someone tonight. I'm just... done."

"My bullet killed him," Blake says, trying to take the weight off my shoulders so I don't have to be a murderer.

I roll my eyes at him. "I know your kill count is high, but mine is now one, thank you."

He grins. "My murderous little demon."

"I'm a one-and-done murderer, thanks. I'd rather be the voice in the earpiece from now on."

Blake smiles again and then looks at his dad. "Thanks for finally telling us, you dick," he says with a huff of laughter. "You don't think we would have understood that?"

"I know you would have, but everything comes at the right time for a reason." Brendan looks between Blake and I. "We'll talk more tomorrow. When everyone is rested and levelheaded."

Blake doesn't hesitate. He snatches me up like I'm his luggage, says a quick goodnight, and carries me and a cheeseburger back to the bedroom while I sip the rest of my drink.

"You still gonna be a brat after this?" he asks, kicking the door shut.

"It's my personality," I confirm.

His only answer is a grin.

HE'S STILL THERE. THAT other guy in my soul—the one trying to claw his way to the surface. I can see him if I lean in really close to the mirror, peering through my fears, my bloodshot eyes, the overwhelming information from yesterday, and the events that changed me for life. To be honest, I don't mind changing since I barely know who I am anyway, but becoming a murderer at twenty-three hadn't been on my list of life goals. Although, murdering my would-be-murderer feels half decent.

It's that half-decent thought that makes me think the real Mercer Bentley is still in there, fighting his way to the surface to meet me for the first time.

I tiptoe away from the mirror in this unfamiliar bathroom, for once not wanting to wake Blake. The skincare products in this place are utter shit, so I steal a toothbrush, splash some water on my face even though I never do that and don't know why some people do, and then silently slink into the bedroom. One look at Blake on his back, arm behind his head, leg cocked, has me rethinking my former plan to be quiet. He's slept long enough and I'm a needy bastard. Pretty shameless about it, too.

I'm not ready to think about everything from last night, but I'm also not ready to let it beat me, so I climb up the bed and settle right on his lap, straddling him.

"Why do you have instruments in your apartment?" I ask. When he doesn't answer, I ask three more times to annoy him because I already know by the pace of his breathing that he's awake. His hand slides up my thigh, and he shifts his body a bit, making it so I'm resting right on his hardening dick.

"Because I want to learn to play them," he says in a sleep-gravelled voice.

"You don't play any of them?" I wiggle on his lap until he blinks his eyes open, showing me that deep blue gaze that's become the lighthouse in all my storms.

"The piano, a little," he says. "But none of the other ones. I like music, but I don't really know a lot about it. Maybe that's why I like it."

He's such a mystery at times, and a completely open book at others. I debate making a joke about him playing the flesh flute last night, but decide that even my street cred can't take that level of lameness. He's watching me, and I didn't have to do anything to get his attention other than sit here. I like the way it feels when Blake looks at me, and despite being an attention whore, I don't want him to ask me if I'm okay. I just want his attention, maybe his love. I want to be seen by him because he's the only person I feel comfortable being around without fully knowing who I am. I'm not wearing a mask. I'm not faking anything. I'm just me—confused, uncertain, not-okay, bratty me.

"You learned a lot last night," he says instead, fingers kneading my legs.

"Mm." I roll my eyes, using his favourite non-word.

Blake must realize I'm not ready to talk about it because he starts talking about himself instead. "I've never been as afraid as I was last night."

"Why?" Yeah, I'm an insecure bitch and I need to hear him say it.

He bucks his hips a bit, leaning against the headboard and bringing me with him to stay on his lap. "Losing you isn't an option for me anymore."

Oh. My. Fucking. Gawd. I choke on feelings and blush from trying to hold them in so hard. But it's no use. My eyes water and my hand smacks this romantic murderer right on his taut pec. "I told you not to make me weepy!" I groan, hiding in my hoodie. I try to climb off him, but he holds me in place. "Blake."

"Where's my bratty demon? Who is this shy boy?" he laughs. "Kinda cute like this."

"Do not call me cute, Blake Carter." I fight him. "I'm sexy! Manly!"

"Adorably manly," he agrees, still laughing. "And so fucking sexy."

I swear to all that is holy, if this man does not stop complimenting me, I will combust. *This!* This is what I wanted, and now I'm cracking under the attention. I'm a terrible cumslut and a horrible attention whore. I wiggle on his dick, just to turn this sexual. I can handle sexual.

"Uh-uh," he says, squeezing my hips to keep me still. "You gotta learn to take the good without getting sex out of it."

"No," I pout.

Blake's laugh is fucking magical. I'm glad when he pulls me down so I can hide in his neck. He wraps his arms around me, rubs his stubbly jaw all over my hair, and just holds me there. Pushing my hood off completely, his fingers weave through my hair, lightly tickling. With the steady beat of his heart against my chest, the warmth of him all around me, and the feeling of absolute safety, I relax and let myself feel things.

I almost died. The man who I thought was my dad tried to have me murdered. And he left instead of watching it happen. For money? How the fuck is it my fault that he didn't get what he was after, and why should I have to die for it? Especially if he knows Brendan Carter is now in possession of it. What purpose does it all serve, and why am I so insignificant that my life is good for nothing but a well-timed death?

I killed someone. Blake likes to take credit for it, but I know the blade I shoved through his windpipe caused his death. I don't like that I did it, but I'm proud of myself for doing it. It saved my life, and now that I know I have some worth—at least in Blake's eyes—I'm proud that I defended myself. But the reality of it sits a little differently in my mind. Yeah, I killed him when the option presented itself to me, but if Blake hadn't shown up, I would have stared that bullet straight in the eye until it embedded between mine. Does that make me weak?

I'm not the Palmerston I thought I was. I'm Cheryl Palmerston's kid. A woman, a mother I never met, who tried to protect me before she died. And my name... my birth father's name. No wonder Will never wanted to call me that. How do I even begin to mourn for two lives I hadn't known were lost until a few hours ago? Am I expected to mourn for them?

I'm not Ben anymore. I'm not the useless kid who got shoved into his bedroom and forgotten about or shipped off to a facility to force my mind to think a certain way. I'm no longer Will Palmerston's youngest child, and I'm also not a brother. I'm Mercer Bentley... no last name because I don't want to be a Palmerston anymore.

I'm Mercer Bentley.

My eyes water with the realization that literally everything about me, my life, and my uncertain future has changed. I'm dead. Or, at the very least, I'm presumed dead by Will, and soon enough, he'll declare me missing. How long am I going to be in hiding? How long will I be Blake's little secret? How long can I handle being invisible again? I don't even have a home.

Hating it, I cry. Silently and without gumption. I'm sad, but unclear about why. I'm scared, but I can't decide what's terrifying me the most. I'm uncertain and overwhelmed, and everything is ebbing against me in gentle waves, filling me up with doubts and questions until I'm full to bursting with unease.

Blake rubs my back. "This is rock bottom, baby."

Weirdly, it doesn't feel like the lowest I've ever been. I'm not alone this time.

"Remember how I said I wanted to make you scream as you clawed your way to the top?" he asks, massaging my scalp. "This is our starting point. Me and you, Mercer. Wherever the fuck you wanna go in life, no matter who you are or who you want to be, it's me and you."

"B-but?" I ask.

"Look at me." He tugs on my hair and tilts my chin. His blue eyes meet mine, and with absolute conviction, he says, "There are no buts to the way I feel about you. Do you understand what I mean?"

Tears streak paths down my cheeks and his face blurs in front of mine. I told him once that everyone who claims to love me does it with a *but* attached to the end. Blake is telling me he loves me, and I can't decide if I'm worthy of it or not. But I nod, and Blake's thumb swipes my cheek. The balled material of my sleeves ends up in my mouth, but Blake pulls it free and kisses me instead.

"Fuck knows how you did it, little demon, but you did." His lips move against mine, kissing and confessing together.

"Did what?"

"Made me yours."

A sob rips free from my chest and my arms fly around his neck. I can't get close enough to him. He lifts me up until my legs wrap around his waist, and he holds me just as tightly.

"I'll find a way to get us out of here, Mercer. We're going home."

Home.

22

Mercer

After Aaron ran interference, putting up a blocker that would jam any audio or video feed around, in, or near Blake's apartment building, we went back home. Home for now, anyway. I'm trying to accept it without too many questions. Luckily, my mind is fried and my body is even more fried, and since Blake refused me sex all day, I'm crashing hard.

He puts me to bed, settles in behind me, and I'm out before his arm wraps around me.

Somewhere in the depths of my sleeping mind, I'm realizing that maybe someone thought I was worthy. A mom who was killed when I was a baby and a dad who died because she did. Maybe they noticed me. Maybe they loved me. Maybe. But in the forefront of my sleeping mind, I'm remembering that someone notices me *now*. Not maybe. For sure. I'm cherished as myself and seen as the real me. I'm encouraged and empowered because a man took notice of me and reminded me to love myself. His attention sparked my own internal attention, and for the first time in way too long, I'm seeing parts of me I forgot existed.

Like the strength to get through the other night. Like the pride I'm remembering to feel for myself for getting through every single day of my life. Like the understanding I'm showing myself for reacting to things the way I do, for becoming who I am today. The events of our lives shape us, and mine always beat me down, shaping me into a flattened version of a timid boy who just wanted to be seen. But under Blake's penetrating gaze, I remembered that I'm allowed to see myself, too.

Without thrashing, ball-busting, or dick-kicking, my eyes blink open to the most beautiful morning view. Blake's cock. "Hello, handsome," I tell it, content to just stare at the length of it.

Blake scoffs, standing at the side of his bed. "Move over, sleep demon." He climbs back in and pulls me against his chest. "You snore."

"No. I wouldn't do that."

"Well, you do."

"No."

"Denial?"

"You're just a liar." Snoring is unbecoming and I refuse to believe I do it. Snoring isn't cute. "I'm too cute."

"I thought you were sexy and manly?" he mocks me. "You kept me up all night with it," he insists, continuing to lie. "I think you should give me a massage because you wedged your bony hips into mine all night, and then you should suck my handsome cock and make me a coffee."

I snore.

Blake doesn't laugh, but I feel his lips pull into a smile and his arms tighten around me. The next time I wake up, he's the one snoring, and I take a video just to prove it to him later. On his phone, because I no longer have one. I do a bit of snooping, make sure he's not being shady, and finally drag my ass out of bed. I want to do something special for him before I go back to full brat mode, so I have a quick shower and head to the kitchen.

A while ago, after that night Blake let me have the daggers, I hid a few around his apartment. I snatch one from under the hall table, grip it between my first two fingers, and aim it at my target.

"Morning," I announce myself to this very comfortable couple in the kitchen. Mr. Sexy Blond with Glasses and Mrs. Sexy Blond without Glasses. "Who the fuck are you?"

The blond guy smiles at me, and I recognize him from the gala last night. My brain rapid-fires information at me, and I recall Blake telling me I was bratty and funny to this particular couple. I don't drop the dagger, but I match his smile.

"Well, well, well. We finally meet… properly."

"Actually, we met properly last night," Aaron says. "And you met my wife, Keira."

I lower the dagger and smile at her. "Pleasure is all yours," I say to Aaron. "Your phone voice is sexier." I take his fresh latte right out of his hand and sit down at the island with Keira. "Sorry for the dagger."

"No, you're not." She laughs, and I can't deny that.

"Did you break in, or does my housekeeper know you're here?" I tug on the sleeves of the hoodie I stole from him, covering my hands completely. The pants are his, too, and maybe the t-shirt I'm wearing also belongs to him. I might have gotten it all out of his dirty hamper because the smell of him is such a fucking comfort and I needed it. I'm whipped.

"Housekeeper?" Blake asks, walking down the hall without a shirt on. As much as I love the view, I'm fucking seething. That body is mine to look at and mine alone. The dagger flies right by his head and sticks into the ridiculous photo of a bunch of piano keys on his wall. He doesn't even flinch, but he sure as shit smirks deeper. "Morning, demon." He steals the latte I already stole and yanks his hoodie right off my body and throws it on. He sets a gentle kiss on my sneering lips that feels a lot like a taunt, so I call him a dick and grab a new hoodie from the couch. He steals my spot at the island while I do that.

Okayyyy. Who's the brat now?

I hip check Aaron out of my way because fuck everyone this morning. I pop my hip, turn my back on the crowd, and revel in the fact that they're watching me anyway. I press the start button on the coffee machine and focus on the grind of the beans.

I have a lot of things to think about today, but I'd rather be distracted. Which is why my mind is running twenty miles a minute, coming up with all sorts of ways to piss Blake off enough to avoid him asking all the questions he wants to ask. Coming up with an idea on the fly, I undo the drawstring of the sweatpants I'm wearing and stand straighter. If he wants to show off his body to the unwanted company, I can *accidentally* do the same. With my hip no longer cocked, the too-big pants slide right down to my ankles and pool there like a cozy little foot wrap.

"Mercer," Blake warns.

I watch the coffee drip into the already frothed milk for just a beat too long, making sure Blake knows I'm intentionally defying him, and then I bend forward to pick up the pants. Fortunately for my audience, I'm wearing the best underwear. They're red briefs, nice and tight against my ass, and right across the cheeks, they say, 'spank me.'

Pulling them up dramatically slowly, I gasp in actual surprise when a firm hand smacks against my ass, shocking me for real, but feeling blissfully crisp. The sting of it has me turning around, looking at Blake with stunned innocence.

"Careful what you beg for, little boy," Blake says. "You once told me you were semi-interested in exhibitionism." He tugs the pants up and ties the drawstring extra tight, double knots it and everything.

"I didn't beg."

"Just like you don't snore?"

"Exactly like that." I glare at him. "It's not my fault your pants are so big. You should cut back on the sugar in your lattes."

"Or you could stop stealing all my clothes and wear ones that actually fit you," he counters.

I scoff at him. "Please. Stop acting like your caveman parts don't want me in your clothes." I pat him on the chest and then pretend he doesn't exist. "Aaron, what's for breakfast?"

"Coffee, pancakes, and difficult conversations," Aaron says without missing a beat.

I tip my head back and groan at the ceiling. "Pancakes first."

It's a trick because as soon as Blake and Aaron start making pancakes, Keira makes herself a fresh coffee and sits with me at the island. Blake telling me he wants me to meet Aaron's wife comes back to mind, and I scrutinize this beauty like she's the prettiest devil. Well, Dee might also take that title. What's her deal and why did Blake want me to meet her in the first place?

"I feel like you're about to con me into something," I say, sipping. Loudly.

"I am. Sort of," she says. "Not con, but offer you something you probably won't want."

I turn on my stool, deciding to face her fully while she tricks me. "Advice?"

"Not really."

"Information that I'll block like I'm blocking everything from last night?" I guess again.

"Actually, more of a way to process all that information," she says, smiling at me while I scowl. "I work with people who have similar life situations to you, Mercer."

"Are we talking about a banker who helps invalids manage their newfound billions? A family crisis line that helps sons evade their murderous non-dads? A grief therapist who helps process deaths we never knew about?" Should I admit I'm a one-and-done murderer, or is that up for secrets?

"I'm a psychologist who specializes in long term PTSD."

Oh. Is that me? Do I have long term PTSD? It can't be me because I don't have any one significant thing that traumatized me. I don't even know if I am traumatized or if I'm just... beaten down a bit. A lot.

"Mercer, you have a strong fear of abandonment, and—"

"I know that." I stand up. "Trust me, I fucking know. I also know how pathetic it is." I forget my coffee and head for the hallway, needing another shower because I feel dirty now. Not dirty. Just messy and childish and fucking dumb.

"It's not pathetic," Keira says. "It's not pathetic at all, Mercer."

I look at Blake, wondering if he set this up. If he did, I will dick-kick him again. I feel little when he looks at me, but once I get over my own shit, I realize he isn't looking at me in any particular way. He's just watching me, loving on me, being all supportive and charming.

"Fuck you, Blake," I snap at him. "Keira, I have a window wall and a bed. Let's go. Pancakes can be delivered to us." I don't check to see if she follows because I kind of hope she doesn't. I hear all three of them laugh a little, and then Keira is handing me my coffee before we enter my bedroom.

Two hours and seven pancakes later, I've learned something. That trauma can be long and drawn out rather than blunt and singular. That the fear of abandonment can start in childhood and morph into something debilitating throughout the course of life. That neglect, belittling, gaslighting, and shame aren't my fault. That even though I wasn't in the war, my life was a war and caused PTSD episodes, which are my panic attacks.

I fear abandonment. I fear neglect. I fear being invisible. I fear being a nobody and then dying. I fear intimacy and honesty because I'm preconditioned to not trust anyone. I have trust issues and behavioural reactions to help me cope with my fears.

Well, goddammit! I'm a brat because it's my coping method! Gah! I really wanted that to be my actual personality, and like hell am I letting it go. The brat life is for me, and I'm not giving it up.

Keira says processing my trauma is a good first step, but learning to trust myself and those around me is another good step. I don't trust anyone, not even myself, but maybe Blake is winning me over a bit in the trust department. So, that's going to have to be my step one. She says my self-soothing methods are bred from childhood, and that seeking sensory distractions is quite common.

She asked me to practice appreciating good attention and recognizing bad attention.

Yeah, whatever. I'm in a pissy mood after the two blonds leave, and since Blake is the only one around, he's the one I'm going to take it out on.

23 Blake

Mercer won't talk to me, but it's a little bit funny. While giving me the silent treatment, he's being the loudest fucking attention whore I've ever met. I've earned it, I guess. I bombarded him with Keira after a stressful and emotionally upsetting night, and now he's going to make me pay for it. I'll pay whatever price he wants because he actually talked to her and that's more than I ever could have hoped for.

He's 'borrowing' my laptop, which means he's just snooping through it. After a bunch of huffing and some eye rolls, he switches tactics and angles the screen so I can see what he's doing on there. He's researching the next fireman's breakfast, and right there on the screen, he has the volunteer form open and mostly filled out.

He's also terrible at the silent treatment because his bratty mouth wants to run, and he's barely holding himself back from making snippy one-liners that'll punch me right in my pride. Well, time to entice him.

"Busy next Saturday?" I ask, smirking at my phone, doing research on Frank and his wife.

"With abs," he answers. "You wouldn't understand."

When did I become a person who enjoys being talked to this way? He told me I was a puzzle, or at least sex was a puzzle, so maybe it's my turn to play some games with him. I pull my shirt over my head and make sure he gets a nice view of my very hard-earned and defined six-pack.

"Wouldn't I?" I ask, walking by him.

He glowers at me, not liking when the game gets flipped on him. His next move is a pathetic one, but I fucking love it. He takes his sweet ass time finding a porn video he thinks will rile me, and when he puts on headphones he *accidentally* forgets to connect to the laptop, the man moans and '*daddies*' come straight through the speakers.

I unplug the internet modem, and the screen pauses on a furry chest that I know for a fact grosses Mercer out.

He stands, pulling the headphones off. "You think you can out-brat me, Blake Carter?"

"It's kind of fun to be an asshole." I shrug, grinning at him. "I see why you do it."

"Good fucking luck, *little boy*," he sneers the pet name, hoping it'll make me angry. It doesn't. Especially because he looks jealous. Jealous of his own mouth muttering a nickname meant for him. I kind of love how complicated and hypocritical he is. I laugh, and he smacks my chest.

Oh, this is going to be fun. I have like three thousand things I need to do today, including forcing Mercer to talk about his family, figuring out how to keep him in hiding a bit longer, and unravelling the whole Palmerston family, but this one takes the cake. Because now that Mercer knows who he is, feels safe enough in this apartment, and has an understanding of his mental health, it's time to get back to our original dynamic.

Mercer gets to be the brat.

I get to put him exactly where I want him.

Let the games begin.

MERCER COMES ON STRONG, not one to let someone intimidate him at his own game. I'm liking the competitiveness he's showing, but I'm barely holding my fists in check.

Leaning in the doorway like the little demon he is, Mercer bats his lashes and bites his sexy lip like a total flirt, drawing the eyes of the pizza delivery guy. At first, I thought the guy would laugh it off and leave with his tip, but when Mercer casually played with the strings of his hoodie, the guy paused and started to flirt back.

Now I'm holding myself back from knocking out a twenty-year-old delivery prick. If I really wanted to, I could kill him, erase the evidence, and get rid of the body like it never happened. Tempting.

"Oh, you're too kind," Mercer feigns modesty and licks his lips. "Do you have to get back right away?"

"Well, uh..." The guy looks over Mercer's shoulder, catching my murderous look. He swallows hard enough for me to hear it, matching the sound with the roll of his throat and the sweat under his uniform hat.

Mercer looks at me, rolling his eyes. "Oh, don't mind him. He's a teddy bear." Leaning into the guy, he stage-whispers, "Between you and me, he can't fuck me like I want to be fucked. Maybe you can do better?"

I'm across the room and slamming the door within two breaths, wrapping my hand around Mercer's throat and tossing the box of pizza to the floor. I press his back to the door and glare down at his victorious smirk.

"Problem, baby?" he asks, his thighs already rubbing together.

"Can't fuck you like you want to be fucked?" I squeeze his neck a bit tighter. "If I fucked you like I wanted to, you'd cry and beg me to stop. So, say that again, *baby*. Who can't handle who?"

Mercer drops the innocent act, shoving me in the chest so hard I almost lose my grip on his throat. "Fuck you, Blake! It's not my fault you treat me like I'm breakable!" He shoves me again, so I use the momentum to take his legs out and push his back to the floor. "Ow! You heavy bitch!"

"Not breakable?" I ask, straddling him. "You're already breaking, little boy."

"Yeah, because this is domestic violence. Not sex."

"Then why's your dick hard?" I sit on it, pinning it to his body. "Or are you just a cock tease, Mercer? Want me to call the pizza boy back to see if you can tease him hard enough that he actually beats you?"

He scoffs. "You're such an asshole."

"Mm," I agree. "Your move. Or is this all you wanted? Just to make me jealous and have me overpower you?"

"Well, you aren't fucking me yet, so it's clearly not all I wanted." He glares. "And you better thank whatever devil you pray to that the pizza landed upright. I would have been a two-time murderer for that alone."

Fuck, he's sexy when he's full of attitude. He was right earlier. I can't out-brat him, but I *can* dominate him. That's the game we play. That's our dynamic. And over time, I've come to crave it as much as he does. When he huffs, his cheeks turning pink, I pin his wrists to the floor and bend over him.

"You think you're winning, Mercer?"

He grins right in my face. "Who has all your attention right now?" His grin turns triumphant. "Never challenge my brattiness again, baby."

Everything clicks together and I laugh. "Oh, I get it."

"What?" He squirms, trying to break free of my hold. "What do you get?"

"You learned that your bratty attitude and attention-seeking behaviour is your way of coping." I smirk. "And now you're all bummed out because it's not just who you are, so you're upping your game to prove a point to yourself."

He scoffs. Or huffs. Or laughs condescendingly. "Get out of my head!" he shrieks at me. "Those are my thoughts! How do you know them?" He makes a great effort to slip free, but it's all for nothing.

"Good at reading people, remember?" I pull him to his feet by his wrists, dragging him away from the forgotten pizza and into the living room.

"Stop manhandling me," he snaps at me, smacking my shoulder. "Fucking barbarian."

He's such a little liar. *My* little liar. This barbarian act is exactly why he acts like a bratty little shit. He wants me to manhandle him. He told me he enjoys the fight for dominance, and he admitted to loving being submissive while manipulating me. When I win the first round and put him on his knees, that's when he really gets to shine by manipulating everything I feel. I understand him now—get him and the puzzle he pieces together.

But he's complicated, too. He acts out for attention, not punishment. Mercer has been scolded and degraded his entire life, and despite the tough front he puts on, I know he's sensitive to being mocked. Which is why I won't make fun of him, degrade him, tease him harshly, or make him question his actions. I will give him the attention he wants, and I'll do it all without punishing him for acting the way he does.

I can do puzzles, too, and my people reading skills give me an edge he doesn't have.

I grin at him, pushing on his shoulders until his tight little ass hits the coffee table. "Stay."

"Make me." He stands.

I just glare at him, and he glares back. Our stares contain different energies, though. His is challenging and defiant whereas mine is calm and authoritative. It reminds me of the night I saw him outside the strip club—that exact look crossed his face when the officer told him what to do. He *does* have a problem with authority, but it's not what I originally thought. It's not an unwillingness to comply; it's the need to fight the system that never made sense to him—that never encouraged him. Mercer wants to fight, and in return, he wants someone to fight back. A worthy opponent who rises to his challenges instead of staunching them.

So instead of making him stay, I give him a job. "Ready to show me what else you ordered in that sex shop box? Mm? I'm ready to gasp and cringe."

"About fucking time," he scoffs, strutting over to the kitchen with swagger. The box in question is still on the floor at the end of the island, so he picks it up and brings it back, sitting his ass on the coffee table where I initially commanded him to sit. So easy.

I grin, sinking down onto the couch opposite him. He knows he played right into my hands, but he's too amped up about the shock value he thinks he's going to pull out of me with whatever that box contains. I've already seen most of it in passing since I used lube from that box, but I'm a willing spectator, and I know he's going to pull out all the best tricks. As he roots around in there, keeping everything hidden, I eye-fuck the hell out of him.

His hoodlum look might be my favourite one. Especially when he wears sexy underthings beneath it. He's the epitome of a little demon, from the way his amber eyes hold all the fires of hell, to the way every move is calculated to manipulate. If Mercer chose to, he could con Earth into rotating the opposite way; he just needs to learn to trust his instincts. He'll get there.

"Just so we're clear, this is my 'does Blake bat for my team?' question box. At the time I ordered it, I didn't know if you'd dick me down or not, and these treats were ordered specifically to find out."

"Mm." I watch him with excitement, honestly curious how he thought some sex toys would bring me out of the closet. Not that I was in the closet, but my bi experiences were few and far between before I dragged him back to my apartment and made him mine. "You've set the stage, baby. Get on with the show."

He side-eyes me. "You're missing a few," he says.

"A few what?"

"You've used little boy, baby, babe, cumslut, little demon, my personal favourite, and bad boy. You're still missing baby boy, pet, brat, and sweetheart." His grin is fucking vile, and I love it. "Find a way to work those in. You know, really try them all on for size."

Oh, I will. "Are you stalling?"

He whips out a small box. "I never stall." Opening it, he removes a little bulbous-shaped thing with a silicone T-bar on the end for easy removal. Also in the box is a little remote with only three buttons. "Intensity. Vibration style. Off button." He points to them all in turn. He clicks it. "Mm, charged."

He's begging for it to go in his ass, so now it's my turn to shine. "I'm not cringing yet, baby boy." I smile, tugging on the front of his hoodie to pull him to his feet. The box topples to the floor, and Mercer topples onto my lap.

"Blake," he complains.

"Brat?" I retort, manhandling him over my lap until his ass is right there, ripe for the smacking. I spank him over his sweatpants and give him a firm squeeze.

"Jesus," he groans.

I love the way he fits on my lap. Small enough to maneuver easily, but feisty enough to put up a fight. I take the toy from his hand, knowing I should probably wash it, but I shove it into his mouth instead. "Get that nice and wet for me, pet." I tug the back of his sweats down, exposing his dark grey underwear. Fuck me, he has the sexiest ass I've ever seen. Even in boxer-briefs. "No panties tonight?"

"I can't be sexy all the time," he whines around the toy in his mouth.

I smack him for saying that. "You *are* sexy all the time, sweetheart. In anything you wear, and completely naked, you are a fucking wet dream." I tug the boxer-briefs down, running my palm over his smooth ass, already pinking up from my spanks. I shove him to the side a little, getting his ass right over my lap. "How many times can you come in a row?" I slide my hands all over him, dipping between his cheeks to spread him open. I spit right on his hole, rubbing it in. His dick hardens against my leg.

"On my own or with someone?"

My teeth clench and I don't answer.

"With someone, usually only once because I flee the scene or don't feel completely comfortable with them. Plus, tops are selfish and just like to get themselves off."

I smack him. "Don't talk about other men in this ass, Mercer. It's mine now."

"Mm," he hums at me, and I can only imagine he's still grinning. "On my own, if I edge properly, sometimes five times. My record is six, but by that point, barely any cum came out."

Dry orgasms. Still sexy. I slide my fingers through the spit and into his tight hole. Mercer squirms on my lap, a rasp leaving his lips. "Give me the toy... what name am I missing?"

"None. You used them all." His voice is breathless now, but there's still some fight left in him.

"Good. Give me the toy, little demon."

He moans, popping the toy out of his mouth and handing it to me behind his back. He turns his head to watch me, so I smack his ass again, watching the flush creep over his cheeks—ass and face. Slowly, I work the small toy inside him. It doesn't go in very deep, but it flares out to fill him and press in all the right places.

"Here's what's going to happen," I start, smoothing a hand over his ass before pulling his boxers back up. "You're going to show me everything in that box, and I'm going to control this toy. The game is willpower. Who will crack first, Mercer? Will I bend you over and fuck you because I get jealous of this toy, or are you going to reach your cum limit without ever begging for it?"

"So, getting fucked means losing?" he scoffs. "I'll lose. Fuck me now, Blake."

I laugh, sitting him up and taking his sweatpants completely off. On my lap and facing me, his cheeks are already flushed and his eyes are glowing, living for this challenge. "You can't touch your cock. I won't fuck you until you beg. And the game isn't over until you tell me it is."

"I can come, though?"

I nod at his dick straining against the material. "Sure. In those."

A new challenge lights him up, and he laughs at me. "Oh, fucking hell, Blake. I'm allowed to come? You realize that you're the one who is going to lose, right? If I can come, and you have to watch it, I will use that to my advantage until you're the one begging."

That's my boy. I lean forward, pressing a smirking kiss to his grinning lips. "I expect nothing less. Guess we'll see who has more control."

24

Mercer

It's him. He has more control. I'm damn near delusional with need, and Blake is as calm as ever. He's either too good at hiding his desires, or I'm just a weak-willed little slut. I refuse to believe I have no effect on him, so fuck that thought for daring to even graze my mind.

The pizza is cold on the floor by the door, and my underwear is slick and sticky with a combination of two orgasms and way too much precum. I'm sweating, no longer wearing my hoodlum look, and Blake might have a rosy tint to his cheeks, but otherwise, he's cool and collected.

He presses the button on the remote, making my ass clench and my cock jolt. "Next."

I groan, almost buckling forward and falling right off the table. The box is nearly empty beside me, and if I don't start begging soon, I'll be using more of these toys to get the relief he's currently denying me. Yeah, I got off twice already, but I'm greedy! My dick isn't done yet, and he knows it, so now he's denying me the third.

I hold up the next item from the box. I'm hoping it's going to rattle him at least a little. "Bought this one just for you," I tell him, sounding like a drunk floozy. "I know you liked it." I hook the straps over my fingers and unfold it so he can get a good look.

Blake licks his lips, and from beneath the material of his black boxer-briefs, his cock gives an enthusiastic throb. Finally. "Put it on," he demands.

When I don't jump to action, he fucking growls at me. "Fuck," I groan at the sound of it, and then whimper, dropping the lace to squeeze my thighs when he ups the intensity of the rolling vibrations in my ass. "Ah, fuck." I'm panting, squeezing my legs, trying with everything I have not to touch my cock and lose the game. A bead of precum seeps through the grey fabric and, fuck me, I'm totally going to lose, aren't I?

"Put. It. On."

My eyes lift to watch Blake and his asshole voice. Goddamn, the caveman act is hot. Grinning at him, I muster up the nerve to say for the second time, "Make me."

Blake doesn't hesitate. His hands latch behind my knees and he pulls me forward until I'm on his lap. Selfishly, I grind against him, rubbing my cock all over his legs just to get a little friction going. My wet boxers slide against his leg until he cups my ass to bring me forward, smashing my dick against his abs instead. Even better. I rub against him shamelessly, my eyes on his and his eyes penetrating my fucking soul.

Hooking his thumbs into the waistband of my boxers, he asks, "Ready to beg yet, little demon?"

Yes. Yes, so ready. "Not even close." I groan, clenching my ass around the toy. "Are you?" I drop down to wiggle on his dick, but before he can react, he flips me onto my back beside him. Hovering over me, he tugs my underwear down to reveal my shiny cock and the previous two messes I made. He looks, and his eyes darken right before me.

"Maybe," he answers my question. "But I think you'll break first." He grabs the lacy number off the floor and easily maneuvers me into it. Blake slides my legs through the holes, tugs it up and over my ass, and then sits me up to get the straps over my shoulders. I don't assist him at all, but he doesn't let that deter him. He leans back to admire me, and fucking finally, a glistening bit of moisture dampens his boxers.

"Mm," I hum, running my hands over the lace. "You like?" It's the same, or as close as I could find, to the black lingerie I wore the night he eye-fucked me outside the strip club. It hugs my torso, accentuates my hips, and makes my ass look phenomenal.

"Mm," he answers, twisting my legs to flip me over onto my stomach. He smacks my ass in the lingerie, and I hump the fucking couch like a nympho.

I grind my dick against the cushion, letting my hips gyrate and my ass roll. The buzz from the toy, the rock of my hips, the firmness of the cushions, and Blake's eyes on me have me ready to bust again.

"Blake," I moan. "Fuck, I'm gonna—"

He lifts me by my hips, and I'm humping the air on the way up. He situates me on his lap again, my back to his chest, and then he settles into a reclined position.

"Beg me, baby," he rasps against my neck, pulling and tugging on my hips so my ass grinds against his dick. "Beg me to fuck you."

I want to. So badly. "The toy is doing fine."

He clicks it off and pisses me off. "Don't you want my thick cock filling your tight ass, little boy?"

Yes. Yes. Yes.

"Think how easily I could slide these to the side and bury my cock inside you, Mercer." He snaps the fabric, making me gasp. "Or I could stand you up right now and tongue fuck you with that toy still inside until you come all over this pretty lace."

Oh god. "Blake."

"Yeah, baby?" he runs his hands up my legs, bypasses my dick, and continues up my hips and stomach. "Beg. Me."

It's on the tip of my tongue to beg. To ask him to fuck me until I can't think anymore. To beg him to pump me full of cum, cover me with it, force me to swallow it, anything. Instead, I rock on his lap until he inhales harshly. "Are you jealous of the toy yet?" I ask. "It's made me come twice already, and you haven't made me come once." I lean back, wrapping my arms around his neck and resting my head on his shoulder. "It feels so fucking good in my ass, Blake. Even when you turn it off, it still feels so good." I add a moan to embellish. "Mmm, I'm gonna come again so hard. My ass is gonna squeeze the toy so tight. Don't you want it to be your cock?"

He groans, sounding damn close to snapping. "That toy can't come. Don't you want my cum, demon?"

"Yes."

"My little cumslut needs cum, doesn't he?"

"Fuck yes." I grind down hard on him.

"Beg me."

I close my eyes, hyper-fixated on every place his hands touch me, his breath against my neck, and the beat of his heart against my back. My feet dig into the couch and my hands tangle in his dark hair, lost to the sensation of him, the situation, the game, and the best edging of my life. I picture him sliding the panties to the side, his jealousy making him rip the toy from my ass, and his cock replacing it a second later. One hard thrust and he'd be buried inside me, fucking me like he owns me.

"Ah, fuck," I moan, my cock leaking.

"Beg me to fuck you, Mercer."

I moan louder, thrusting my hips back and forth, so close to coming in this brand-new outfit. "Oh, god, Blake. I can't stop it." I tighten my fingers in his hair.

"Mercer," he growls.

The throatiest moan leaves my lips, and that's how I win the game.

Blake shoves me forward until I crash to my knees on the floor. My hands brace on the coffee table, and he's behind me a second later, pulling the toy out and spanking my ass. "Fuck," he groans, spitting on my hole.

My chest hits the table hard, and my forehead lands on the surface of it. Blake thrusts his hips and buries his cock inside me to the root.

"Fuck." I'm rasping out shallow breaths, trying to move back to fuck his cock, but he's not having it.

He holds me in place, a tight grip on both of my hips, fucking me hard and deep with the panties pushed to the side. "You fucking brat," he accuses, pumping in and out of me. "Such. A fucking. Brat." He slams into me hard.

"Blake!" I scream his name, crashing against the table in a tsunami of orgasmic bliss. He fucks me through it, not giving a single shit that I'm coming in my lacy lingerie. My stomach clenches and my ass clamps hard around his dick. "Fuck me full of cum, Blake. Oh. My. God."

He yanks on my hair, bringing me upright. One arm wraps around my throat and the other wraps around my waist, caging me to him so he can go wild. He picks up the pace, fucking me like the barbarian I called him, and sinking his teeth into the base of my neck.

He growls against my skin, and holy fuck, it breaks me completely. I'm not sure if one orgasm has ended and another started or if this is one massive rolling thing, but I'm trembling all over, seeping through the lace, coating myself in my cum as he fills me with his.

"Fuck, Mercer," he says against my neck, his voice deep and gravelly. "Holy fuck, you're mine."

Goddamn right I am. My legs are shaking and my cum is dripping to the floor, but I keep my hands on the table just in case he lets go and I fall forward. There isn't an ounce of strength left in me, and I'm pretty sure there isn't a drop of cum left either.

Blake pushes me forward until my chest hits the flat top of the table. "Push."

"No," I whine. "I want it."

"Show it to me, baby. I'll finger it back inside." He smooths his hand over my ass cheek and then pulls out slowly.

The loss of him inside me is jarring, but I push his cum out simply because I love how possessive it makes him. To my utter delight, it's his tongue I feel against me instead of his fingers. He licks his cum from my hole and then shoves it back inside me. My cock is still in semi-mode, but if I orgasm again, I might die. It wants to wake up for this, but I'll have to just enjoy the feeling without getting off to it.

He hums delight with his tongue still buried inside me. The warmth and gentleness of it is the perfect come down from this euphoric high. His hands spread me open, and he keeps licking, trying not to waste any of his cum.

"Sit on your ass, baby." He leans back, helping me turn around to sit with my back against the table. "Stick your tongue out."

I open my mouth and stick my tongue out. The tip of his hard cock rests against it, tasting like cum already. Up on his knees, he looks down at me, slowly stroking his length in front of my face.

"I want you full of me tonight, Mercer." He licks his lips and holds my head in place. "I want my cum in your ass, in your throat, in your stomach, and on your lips for the rest of the night."

Okay, there might be one more orgasm left in me. I whine on the floor, my hand fondling my dick. I lick his slit and make him tremble, a pulse of precum exploding against my tastebuds.

"Are you proud of yourself?" he asks. "For winning."

I nod with my tongue sticking out, proud as shit, thank you.

"It's justified, baby," he says, smirking at me. "You're a fucking brat, through and through."

I run my thumb over the tip of my dick, loving that he said that.

"My brat. All. Fucking. Mine." He groans, his release coating my tongue and sliding down my throat. His hand keeps my head still, and on instinct, I don't swallow, letting it gather on my tongue. Blake's eyes close momentarily, his abs clenching and his hand slowing on his shaft. As soon as he's empty, he surprises the fuck out of me by bending forward and kissing me with his cum still in my mouth.

I moan into the kiss, swapping it back and forth until I swallow it. He tilts his head down, forehead against mine, and spits whatever is left in his mouth onto my dick. I rub it against my shaft, over the tip, and moan into his mouth as the fifth orgasm washes through me. It's weak and drawn out, but the subtleness of it is exactly what I need to finish this incredible night.

We stay on the floor, coming back to reality slowly. "Was that everything in the box?" Blake asks.

"No. There's one more thing."

He huffs out a small laugh. "Save it for the next time we play." He grips my chin and looks me right in the eye. "I won't lose a second time, baby."

"We'll see." I smirk at him.

He winces and complains when he does it, but he picks me up and carries me down the hall, mess and all. "Where are we going?"

"I'm plugging you, bathing you, feeding you, and putting you to bed."

I scoff. "I don't need the aftercare."

He kicks his bedroom door open. "I don't care. I need it."

Oh. I go completely warm. Gooey. Holy shit, I love him. Instead of telling him that, I say, "Then you can heat up the pizza we stole."

"Stole?"

"You slammed the door in his face before I paid him."

Blake laughs, setting me on the edge of the bathtub to start the water. "Poor guy. But next time, no ordering pizza, and no answering the door. You're supposed to be dead, Mercer. Let's keep Will believing that for as long as we can. We need to plan first."

Right. Reality. Ew.

"Tomorrow." He kisses my lips.

25 Blake

Brandt and Bronson are 'searching' for Mercer, making it look like we're in hysterics over him being missing. The ruse won't last because Will is smarter than that, but for now, it gives us a little time. Mercer is taking his sweet time getting ready, and I have no doubt he will be in his hoodlum look when he decides to leave his bedroom. He's stalling because my dad is here. For the first time.

While I wait for his coffee to brew, my dad paces around my apartment. He spends a lot of time near the piano, probably wondering why I requested it when he was hiring someone to design this place. There's an instrument in each room, but the piano is my favourite.

"Do you still play?" he asks, fingers brushing the keys.

"A little. I'm not as good as I used to be." Piano wasn't really my focus over the past five years while I was away, but I played when I could.

Learning to play the piano is the only memory I have of my dad being solely fatherly. He taught me when I was a kid. I'd been having a hard time focusing, mostly because I was a busybody who didn't know how to slow down. I was tested for neurodivergence, but never registered anywhere on the scale. I was simply hyperactive and had a busy mind, so my dad taught me to play the piano one summer, and I guess it just stuck. It was the first thing I remember ever calming my mind, and through the course of my life, I've learned to channel that calmness in other ways.

"You were never one to half-ass anything," Dad laughs. "You got so mad when you weren't instantly incredible at the piano. Glad you stuck with it."

Not sure what to say to that because father-son conversations aren't our thing, I hand him the coffee and change the topic. "What's Will saying?"

"Nothing yet. It's been two days, so he'll want to wait until you approach him. The public will assume Mercer was with you after the gala, so he's gotta keep that appearance, too. He won't act until you ask him where Mercer is, and then he'll pretend you were the one to bring it to his attention."

I figured as much. He already knows I know, since he read that text message I sent, but I'll have to play this carefully.

"Are you planning to give it back to him?" I ask my dad, needing to know his intentions before this goes any further.

"It's already his, Blake. I'm just the CEO for right now, but legally, he owns it all. The mine, the subsidiary companies, the accounts, all the assets, and even a lot of the properties and businesses that Will thinks he currently owns."

"But Will thinks you own it?"

"He thinks I own the gas plant. I'm not sure what else he thinks." He sips the coffee. "I just want our family business, Blake. I'm not a businessman when it comes to these types of things. They belong to Mercer, and when he decides to do something with them, I already have a contract drawn up to remove my name from everything, if that's what he wishes."

I tilt my head, studying everything about his body language, voice, and reactions. "No greed?"

"Not about this."

"No malicious intent?"

"Not towards him or those companies."

"Why not?"

He sighs, moving to the window to peer out at the city. "For one, I've been hating this fucking mine since it got put into my name. Way more trouble than it's worth. For two, I made a deal with his mother. For three, my only goal in any of this is to ruin Will Palmerston. And fourthly, and this one is the biggest." He turns to face me. "You love that boy, Blake. You love him."

Yeah, I fucking do. "Bronson loves Miranda. You had no problem fucking them over."

"I did have a problem with it," he corrects. "I hadn't been planning on involving Bronson, but when Will put up that stipulation, I made a move. And Miranda, for how much she claims to love him, was more than willing to take a buyout to leave him. Three million if she leaves after they're wed."

Jesus fuck. My poor brother. "You're sure?"

Dad nods, not looking pleased about it. "I have the conversation on video, and her signature on the contract."

"Bronson is gonna be crushed." I glance down the hall, wondering if Mercer is eavesdropping instead of joining the conversation. Avoidance won't work forever, so I'll force him to face it if he doesn't do it on his own. "But he's not marrying Olivia, right?"

"I had never planned to let it get that far, no. I just needed a reason to be closer to Will. And now we have to decide what we're doing with that family."

"Mercer should have a say in that."

Dad nods. "He won't remain dead for long. I give it three days max. Probably sooner."

"I know."

The bedroom door bangs against the wall, and Mercer makes his dramatic entrance. His hoodlum look is nowhere to be found, and my eyes roll when I see what he's decided on. Me. He's dressed like me again. Tactical pants, a jacket with a lot of pockets, the collar popped up, and his Blue Jays ball cap.

"No. Go change." I point down the hall. "No more testing me to see how self-indulgent I am. Go find another look."

He scoffs at me. Or huffs. Or laughs condescendingly. "Relax your ego, bad boy. This isn't my Blake look."

"What is it?"

"This is my..." he pauses, glancing at my dad. "I can't say his name, but it's my 'man in the mic' look. I want to work like your buddy does."

"Aaron?" my dad says.

My head whips to my dad. "You know Aaron?"

"It's your job to read situations and the people in them, Blake. It's my job to read my sons." Dad grins. "I've known about Aaron since you were teens."

I groan, but Mercer is pleased by this news. "Okay, Papa Carter. Do you have an Aaron, or is the job open?" He gives my dad a cute as fuck smile. "I'm pretty smart with numbers, and I'm a fast learner."

Dad laughs. "Won't you be a little busy managing your billion-dollar corporations?"

Mercer grimaces. Then pouts. With blinky eyes and everything. "Don't make me do the billionaire thing."

"You don't want it?" I ask.

"Do I have to want it?" he asks back.

"No, but it's yours to do with as you please," Dad tells him. "You don't have to make that decision right now, Mercer, but no one else can make it for you."

Mercer barely thinks about it, skipping over to the coffee machine. "As long as William Douchebag Palmerston doesn't get it, I don't really give a shit." He presses the button for a latte.

I look at Dad, and he looks at me. We both shrug, deciding we won't press it for now. Mercer can think about it for real and then ask questions about it when he's ready.

"It's blood money."

"It's a gift from your birth mother," I correct.

"Who died for me to have it. I almost died because of it. We're all gonna almost die for it. So, hence, blood money." He spins to face us. "So, is the Aaron position open?" he asks my dad.

Dad laughs, in a good mood this morning. "If you honestly want training, we can arrange that."

Mercer beams a victorious smile. "Excellent. So, when do I get to rise from the dead?"

"Three days," Dad tells him.

Mercer grins. "So, you're telling me I'm basically Jesus then?"

HE HASN'T RISEN FROM the dead yet, but we are on a mission together. I call it a job; he calls it a mission. So naturally, now I also call it a mission because I'm the biggest fucking pushover for this guy. It's pathetic.

Trevor Palmerston is the mission. Mercer's former elder brother is at an office building downtown, and we're waiting for him to leave for his next appointment. Aaron was able to tap into his emails and phone, so unless it's a ploy or a decoy, we have his schedule. Now we wait.

"So, did you ever off what's her name's husband?" Mercer asks. "You know, Frank? The leaking information guy who led to me showcasing my dagger skills for you." He looks at me, blinking his big amber eyes. He's also behind the steering wheel because he conned me into letting him drive in case there was going to be a car chase, which he claims he'd be good at. I have doubts, but I'm still sitting in the passenger seat like a goon.

Pushover. *Again.*

He's all confidence and swagger today, and I'm loving it. The timid boy from that eventful night is on lockdown, and in his place, Mercer has added sass, self-worth, certainty, and a big old helping of avoidance. He doesn't want to talk about it yet, but at the very least, he's interested in Trevor's whereabouts.

"No. Pretty sure my dad is going to give that job to one of my brothers instead."

"Why? Lose your murderous edge?"

"My dad thinks I have." I huff at that. "Because I have morals."

"You killed Sean Pendleton without a second thought," Mercer reminds me, sipping from the thermos I warned him not to bring. If he has to pee, he's going to have to fucking hold it.

"Not without a second thought. I did my background checks on him and came to the conclusion that I was fine delivering his death. But Frank, he's a shady person trying to screw over his wife's business, but he's a good dad, and his kids love him. From what I'm gathering, they live with him and not their mom, so it comes down to them. Do I want to orphan them by killing their dad, or do I want to enrage a client by not following through on a job?" I look at Mercer. "What would you do?"

"Is it a responsibility thing?" he asks. "Like, you don't give a fuck if Frank dies, you just don't want to be the one responsible for it?"

Maybe. Maybe not. "I don't know. It's not really one thing or the other. It's a gut instinct, and I've learned to trust those."

Mercer nods like he understands that. On the third nod, he tilts his ball cap down and shoves his massive thermos onto my lap. "Speaking of gut instinct, this is the fourth time that red car has driven by us. It's the third time with this driver, but the first time, it was a female driver. I have the plate number if you want to run it."

Patterns and numbers. Sometimes I forget I have such a valuable brain with me. I dial Aaron and wait for him to speak through the Denali's Bluetooth.

"Hey," he says simply.

"Blondie!" Mercer beams. "It's Blake's little demon here, and I have a number for you to run. Ready?"

While Mercer rambles off the plate number and actually gossips with my supposed best friend, I scan the area for any other inconsistencies. Trevor hasn't left the building yet, unless he tricked us, and his vehicle is still parked up the street. I squint my eyes at it, wondering, not for the first time, why an executive would park on the street instead of in a parking spot with his name on it.

I don't know much about Trevor other than that my mom supposedly trained him to do this job. She used to do it, according to Mercer, but I can't figure out what he has to do with any of this. Mercer said he never ran into Trevor when he was at the facility.

"Like, do I need to wear a uniform?" Mercer asks Aaron.

"You're never seen in this job," Aaron laughs. "You can be naked."

"Oh, that's fun, but I do like being seen," he pouts. "Isn't it like the movie montages where they show *Batman* in the field, and then screen flip to *Alfred* in the *Batcave*?"

"If you want to believe this is a movie, sure."

There's the red car again. Mercer smacks me on the arm, pointing at it. It's a female driver again. Mercer smacks me again, and now I see Trevor leaving the building. As soon as he starts walking down the front steps toward his vehicle, the red car slows.

"Get down," I tell Mercer, drawing a gun even though there's nothing I can do about it. "Get down, right now." I push his head down, but he still peeks.

"What's going on?" Aaron asks.

The passenger window of the red car rolls down, the snout of a rifle poking through. The next second, bullets pierce Trevor's body, making him jerk around in a death dance while the patrons on the street scream. I keep my eyes on the red car.

"You got that plate?"

"Yes," Mercer whispers.

It's probably a stolen car, but why did the driver and the passenger switch seats so often?

Trevor is dead. The car is speeding off. Mercer is looking at me with his hand on the gearshift. "Are we pursuing?" he asks. "Blake! Are we pursuing? Aaron? Can I high-speed chase this?"

"No," we say at the same time.

"Ohh. Boring."

I guess he's completely ignoring the death that just happened. "Go, Mercer. We can't be here. Drive slow and head west." He looks at me, blinking those beautiful eyes again, so I add, "Please, baby."

He smirks, setting off onto the street before it gets completely barricaded.

"Julia Hentz," Aaron says. "That's who owns the car. Recognize the name?"

"Hentz?" Mercer asks, taking his thermos back to sip as he drives. "Olivia has a friend named Jules, last name Hentz. Could be her."

"Any issues with Jules and Trevor?"

Mercer shakes his head. "Don't know if they even know each other. I barely know Trevor. Knew."

Mercer has my seat all the way forward, and my mirrors are all fucked up and wonky, but he doesn't appear to need to swap spots anyway. For once, he's a blanket of calm. Actually, he's calm and snarky.

"Hey, Siri," he says. "Play my road chase playlist."

The *Fast and Furious* soundtrack starts playing, and Mercer slips on a pair of sunglasses. "Don't worry, boys. It's not *Tokyo Drift*."

Read the situation, Blake. Why would a wayward woman, who may or may not be friends with Olivia, murder Trevor Palmerston in full daylight? Who else was in that car with her? Did us being parked there have anything to do with it? I wouldn't put it past Will to murder his son and blame it on us.

The screen on the dash of the Denali lights up with an incoming call. "Listen in, Aaron. This is Samantha." I press the button to pick up the call, silencing Mercer's road tunes. "Hello."

"Blake Carter?" she asks. "This is Samantha Palmerston."

Mercer locks up for a second, but then he scoffs silently, dramatically displaying a gag reflex. I still don't know how he feels about his sisters not being his sisters because he won't talk about it, but I can tell there's at least a little disdain there.

"Yes?"

"I..." She pauses, which makes me sit up a little straighter. "I would like to hire you to complete a job."

Well, that isn't what I was expecting. "What job?"

"You handle sensitive information and get it into the right hands, correct?" she asks.

"Yes."

"Well, Mr. Carter, I have some sensitive information. Information that could get me killed."

Does she know her brother just died? Does she know something about Olivia's maybe-friend being involved in the murder? Does she know Mercer is missing yet? What the fuck is going on?

"What do you want me to do with it?" I ask.

"I think that you love my brother," she says, and Mercer's grip on the steering wheel tightens as he keeps driving.

"Not to assume, but I can see it. I saw it, the night of the gala."

"Okay?" I won't confirm that because I don't want Mercer to hear it this way for the first time, even though I've sort of already told him.

"I believe he's missing, and I believe you already know that. You don't have to confirm or deny it, but I have some information that might be of use to you. To help you find him."

I look at Mercer, but he won't look at me. "You think he's still alive?"

Samantha doesn't answer me, but she says, "I think my sister and my father had him taken."

"What makes you think that?" I listen to her breathing, the way the phone shuffles around, the absolute lack of background noise, and the hitch in her voice. She's nervous, but I don't know if she's nervous because she's lying to me to set me up for something or if it's because she's going behind Will's back to reach out to me.

"A... contract that I found claiming that Ben, uh, I mean Mercer, is actually the sole owner of all Palmerston companies, and that in the event of his death, they revert to my father."

Mercer's stabby finger punches the mute button. "That wrinkly old dick fudged me up a fake will? The fucking audacity!"

I unmute the call. "What are you asking me, Samantha?"

"I will pay you to find him before it is too late."

"I will do that anyway. You have my word. What else?"

"I know the name of the lawyer who created this contract. She's a woman well known to my family, and I believe my sister is actually... *with* her. I don't know for certain, but my suspicion is that Olivia and my father are working together. I've... I wouldn't be inclined to tell you this, but since Ben—Mercer's life is on the line, I have no other choice. I just want my brother home."

Mercer stabs the mute button again. "Numbers are my thing, Blakey, not this. What's this bitch getting at? Is she sincere? Do your people reading thingy."

I unmute the call again. "Before I do anything, I want to know something."

"Okay," she agrees timidly.

"You told Mercer you hid a phone for him at the facility, right?"

"Yes."

"Which means you knew what they did there?"

"It's a behavioural facility for troubled youth," she says. "Is that what you mean?"

No. But it proves she doesn't know what really happens there. Or she's a good phone actor. Aaron, who is still listening in on this call, sends a live-feed video through to my phone. It's camera footage from a Mini Mart parking lot where Samantha is sitting in her car. She's alone, no gun to her head, and her hood is up to hide her face. She's betraying her father, and seeing her this nervous makes me more comfortable.

"Tell me where the phone is. If I can find it, I'll trust that you genuinely care about Mercer's wellbeing."

When Samantha does her best to explain where the cellphone is hidden, Aaron shoots me a thumbs up. He's still got Keira on the inside there, so he'll get her to look for it.

"Okay, I'll look for it. What's the lawyer's name?"

MERCER IS A STOMPY little shit right now. I've never seen anyone huff, scoff, sigh, and groan so dramatically in all my life. He's sucking on a lollipop, complaining that it isn't as good as the ones he bought, chewing Aaron's ear off about anything and everything.

"Who the actual fuck buys peach lollies, Blondie?" Mercer points it at him. "Fucking psychopath." He shoves it back into his mouth. "Okay, so what does it mean? The phone is legitimately there, which I told you it was because I used it before, and now I'm all up in limbo wondering what the fuck we do next."

"You need to learn some chill if you want to be the next me," Aaron tells him.

"I will chill when I get the job!" he shouts. "This mission is my life, so excuse me for not being a goddamn cucumber about it." He huffs, so I grab him around the waist and plonk him down on my lap. "Don't get handsy with me while I'm trying to be stern, Blake Carter."

I tug that lolly right out of his mouth and kiss him just to shut him up. "If you're going to ramble, use that brilliant mind of yours and ramble useful things, little boy." I pop the lolly back in, grateful that it's a step up from his fingers in his mouth. Not that I mind him sucking his fingers, but it's nice to see progress in his coping mechanisms. He hasn't broken down once since the gala. He's attached to my hip and clingy as hell, but I'm more than happy to be his safety net.

"Useful things," he huffs. "Okay. I want proof of something."

"What?"

"These wills and end-of-life arrangements are all about Mercer Palmerston, right? Well, apparently, my birth daddy took my birth mommy's last name, so how do we know that old bastard isn't still kicking around, and all these monies aren't going to him?"

Aaron spins his laptop, showing Mercer a bunch of screens. "His death certificate. His body. His middle name was Franklin. These wills name Mercer Bentley Palmerston, with your date of birth. I already looked into it." Aaron grins.

"But now you're finally looking in the right places. Keep going."

Mercer preens, proud as punch. "Okay, next. Who benefits from Trevor dying?"

"Olivia," I answer. "She becomes the eldest heir."

"Yes, but whyyyyy?" he drones. "Because of the monies?"

Monies? Why can't he just say money like a normal rich kid? "Because her and Will become the sole owners of... everything."

"Yes, but we all know Will, that weathered fuckwit. And he's a greedy son of a gun. He won't allow Olivia to own anything." Mercer crunches the candy. "Which means she's doing his dirty work with this Julia bitch, and when he gets what he wants, she's off to the chopping block next."

"We've got eyes on her," Aaron says. "Not really to protect her, though. Do you want her protected?"

Mercer blanches, not having decided that yet. "I kind of want Samantha protected," he admits. "Even though I don't trust her yet. I at least want the option to maybe, potentially, in an unlikely twist of fate, trust her. Or at least not hate her."

"We can do that, baby," I tell him. Protection is a big part of the Carter business, and if I don't do it, I can contract it out to any one of my cousins, aunts, uncles, or brothers.

Mercer mumbles a quick thanks before wiggling on my lap just to rile me up. "Why isn't your apartment this cool?" he asks me, gawking around at Aaron's place.

It's industrial, open concept, full of brick walls and exposed beams, and has those old-fashioned windows that tilt up instead of sliding up. It is cool, and I'm glad he likes it, because the industrial apartment I own is right next to this. Me and Aaron always wanted to be neighbours. Aaron grins at me, but he hides it from Mercer.

"Aaron bats for both teams," I tell him. "Wanna hop on his lap instead?"

To test me, he tries to get up. Not fucking happening. I wrap my arms around his middle and pull him against my chest. “Good try, little demon. You’re mine, and I have no problem staking my claim.”

“Then get a cooler apartment,” he says, but his voice has gone breathy, and his hand conveniently sits on his lap, covering his hardening dick.

“It’s on the news,” Aaron says, turning up the volume and mirroring his screen to the TV on the wall.

We all watch the news, reporting on the gunfire downtown. The red car has been identified, but they’re asking anyone with information to come forward. Trevor Palmerston’s name is left out of it, claiming a sole victim was gunned down and pronounced dead at the scene.

What’s Will going to say next? One son is missing, and one is dead. How does this benefit him? There has to be a bigger picture. Why can’t I see it?

Mercer goes back to gawking at Aaron’s apartment and all the tech equipment he has. So, I run through everything I know in my head.

Mercer purposefully aggravated Will by wearing lingerie and getting into the wrong kind of trouble, bringing attention to himself and the Palmerston family, but Will never did anything except send him to that facility. Why? Why try to kill him now? Is it because of me? Because of the betrothal between Olivia and Bronson? I do believe Mercer when he said Will was setting up for a long con to take over the Carter owned businesses, but something must have happened recently to have him upping his schedule. Knowing that it would sever ties between our family and his. Pissing off the Carter family isn’t smart, so Will must have a fall-back plan to take us down. But what?

On top of that, Olivia now seems more involved than I initially thought. That first night I saw her taking Mercer from the police outside the club, she seemed irritated with him, but concerned about him. Does she care, or was she simply playing a part? Samantha doesn't seem to have anything to do with any of it, which is the only reason she's able to look at it from an outside perspective. She notices things between her sister and her father because she's either full of resentment that she's not on the inside, or she's genuinely concerned about Mercer.

Trevor is a wildcard. Other than knowing my mom trained him and he worked at that facility, I have no idea what he had to do with anything. I don't know what his death means, either. Yes, it bumps Olivia to the eldest Palmerston heir, but is that all?

The original will from Cheryl, Mercer's birth mom, played into my dad's hands, but I had Aaron look it over. My dad is only the acting CEO, with everything firmly placed in Mercer's name. He's not getting anything out of this other than having to keep these businesses afloat for my boyfriend while not wanting to do any of it.

I fell in love with Mercer Bentley, and I have no idea if that is why Will tweaked his plans, or if it's because of something else. Mercer has never been protected before, and now he's protected by me and my family. Did that make Will nervous?

Will's end goal is money. Owning all the Palmerston businesses, corporations, estates, and properties. If that's what he wants, Mercer is in his way. My dad is in his way. I'm in his way. Olivia might be his scapegoat, but her days are numbered, like Mercer said, because Will won't be anything less than top dog. If he's already suffering financial hardship because he doesn't own Mercer's portion, it might be enough to make him act hastily.

Simply put and broken down, Will needs to acquire the mine and everything that comes with it. To do that, he needs Mercer dead. For Mercer to be dead, he needs to silence me and my family. So, essentially, we need to die for his plan to work. Samantha has no part in this, and I'm assuming Penny, Will's wife, has no idea what's going on.

Trevor, on the other hand, seems to be a man who enjoyed his job at that facility. He wasn't close with his family and had very little to do with any family businesses other than Northern Horizons, but he was an heir to the fortune.

My fingers drum on Mercer's thigh, a theory forming.

"It's Olivia," I say, working through my theory. "She's thwarting Will's original plan."

"Will's original plan being a slow takeover?" Aaron asks.

"Yeah, like Mercer said. He planned to marry into the Carter family and slowly gain access to everything we own, hoping that it'd never actually go into Mercer's name. Or he already knew it was in Mercer's name and planned to either manipulate Mercer into giving it to him or kill Mercer to take it over."

"How's Olivia change that?" Mercer asks.

"She's her father's daughter. She just killed Trevor, she thinks you're dead, and Samantha will be next. That will make her the only heir."

"Because she has no idea I actually own all that shit, she still plans to marry Bronson," Mercer picks up my train of thought. "And take it all through him because she thinks the Carter family owns it."

"Then she has Bronson murdered, and she gains access to everything he owned through whatever prenup she dictated."

"Then her and her lawyer girlfriend run off into the sunset with everything, while the rest of us are dead or diminished to nothing." Mercer hops off my lap. "Yes. She fucked with Will's plans, and that's why he's making countermoves now."

Aaron shakes his head. "If she's smart enough to do all that, she wouldn't be dumb enough to have her lawyer girlfriend, as Mercer put it, shoot Trevor in broad daylight in her own car."

"Because the legal documents are already completed. She doesn't need the lawyer anymore, and if she goes down for murder, Olivia can cut her out of the deal." I mull that over. "Or it wasn't her who did it. Mercer said the driver kept changing, and I saw it, too."

Mercer gasps. Three times. "She made her hubby do it! She'll claim she had no idea what he was going to do, her husband goes away for murder, and lesbo girlfriend and Olivia are free and clear to put the rest of their plan in place without anyone looking over their shoulders."

"Which means Samantha isn't safe," Aaron says. "We should put her in a safehouse."

I nod to agree, pulling my phone out to call my dad. "What about Penny?"

"Fuck her," Mercer says. "She'll side with Will every fucking day because she's nothing without him."

Works for me. I climb off the couch to pace, calling my dad. As soon as he picks up, I feel Mercer tugging on the back of my shirt, trying not to get in my way, but being clingy because that's who he is. A boy with abandonment issues and a fear of being alone. I smooth a hand over his hair, showing him he isn't bothering me.

"Blake," Dad answers. "Trevor Palmerston is dead, and no one can find Samantha."

Fuck.

26

Mercer

THE ITCHINESS IS BACK, and it's not for the reason I thought it would be. My breathing is off, my legs are weak, and my fingers are tempted to end up in my mouth.

Blake is leaving me. And I fucking hate that I can't handle that.

"Look at me, Mercer," Blake says at the door to Aaron's apartment. He palms my cheeks, bends down, and swipes his thumb under my eyes. I didn't realize I'd started crying. "I'm coming back."

Don't forget me.

"I promise you, baby, I'm coming right back."

Don't leave me.

"We're going to get Samantha, and then I'll be right back here. It's safest for you to stay with Aaron."

But what about your safety? "Don't go," I beg. My entire family is after his life. "Please, Blake."

Blake smiles at me, pulling my fingers from my mouth. "Nothing, not your fucking family or the fate of the universe, will keep me from you. Do you hear me, Mercer? You're my little demon, and I will never leave you alone."

I cry harder, a mix of fear and emotion. "But?"

He licks his lips, meeting my eyes with his. "There are no buts. Not about this, and not about the way I feel for you. No buts, baby."

I cling to his jacket, gripping it between my fingers, desperate to keep him here. "But what if…" I trail off.

Blake nods at Aaron. "He has an earpiece for you. We can talk the whole time. Does that help?"

I sigh out a shaky breath. Maybe a little, but he can still die out there without me. Not that I'm some hero who can save him, but I don't want him to die without me. How pathetic is that?

"Plus, you're going to have to get used to wearing it if you wanna be the guy in the mic, right?" He smirks. "I'm coming back. I promise." The way he promises tells me that even if he does die, he will come back to tell me he tried. That even if something goes terribly wrong, Blake will find his way back to me because he will never lie to me—will never break a promise to me.

He's been doing this far longer than he's known me, and I need to learn to trust him. I do trust him and his capabilities, but I don't trust the danger out there. Now that we know what's happening, he's a target to more than one person simply because he loves me.

Like Keira said, it's time for me to start trusting myself. "If you don't talk to me the whole time and come back to me when you promised, I will turn full serial killer, and you'll be my first victim."

Blake laughs. "Deal." He grips my chin, pressing his lips to mine. "No buts, baby."

I wrap my arms around him and admit I feel the same. "No buts." *I love you, Blake.*

I stare at the closed door for five minutes after he's gone, contemplating breaking his rule and following him. Realistically, I know I'd only be a hindrance, and my whereabouts need to stay hidden to keep both of us safe, but the temptation is there. I no longer feel safe if Blake isn't around. That asshole became my safe place. He's my wall, the lock on my door, the only person who sees me and loves me because of it.

"Better get over here," Aaron calls. "Blake's already bitching that you aren't talking his ear off." He holds up a set of headphones with a mic. "Time to start training to be me, Mercer."

I'm still shaking, but I ignore the itch and join Aaron at his hacker's paradise set-up. "Do I get a cool code name?" I sit down in a swivelly computer chair. *Shit, that's comfy.* I throw on the headphones, feeling even cooler.

"Little Demon," Blake's voice comes through immediately. "That's your code name, baby. Or Blake's Little Demon. I like that better."

"Mm." My shakes settle and the itchiness mostly goes away. Gosh, it's sick how dependent I am on him. I went from being a scared and lonely boy to being his shadow, and I don't know how to differentiate the two personalities. My abandonment issues cling to him, but my newfound sense of self reminds me I've got what it takes to stand on my own two feet. I *killed a guy*! I can handle a few hours without my master, surely.

For good measure, I tuck my nose into Blake's hoodie and breathe him in. There. Shakes mostly gone, replaced only by a nervous energy that is more normally associated with worrying about him being a murder target.

"What can this little demon do?" I ask Aaron.

"The biggest thing we can do is clear their path," Aaron starts teaching me. Blake and Brandt are together tonight, and the two of them are heading to Samantha's last known location. They contacted her, telling her to stay put, but she's no longer on the camera feed of the parking lot she was in.

"Okay. Clearing their path," I parrot. "How?"

"Traffic cams, any cameras we can tap into to make sure there isn't anything unexpected waiting for them. On this screen, you'll see everything I can hack into. But on this screen, you'll see the ones we're watching for. Or watching out for, more like."

I see the screen with multiple camera feeds of the roads and areas they're heading into. On another screen, I see Will, sitting down with a detective to either play his part about my disappearance or to talk about Trevor's death. Next to that view, Olivia sits at home, but the image is grainy.

"How are you getting that? Are there cameras in the house?" I ask.

"It's from an open laptop sitting on the kitchen table. I tapped into the webcam."

So fucking cool. I don't even know how to be this cool, but I'm here for it. Kind of wish I had black-rimmed glasses for this moody look. I'd look sexy as a gamer boy.

"On top of that, we're monitoring bank account activity, including offshore accounts. Sometimes it tells us where they are or what they intend to do."

"Or if they've hired a hitman," I scoff.

"Or that, but your, uh, Will never leaves a trail like that. He's too business savvy," Aaron says.

"Are you still alive, Blakey?"

"Mm," he hums.

"And this is security access codes," Aaron goes on, showing me sequences of numbers that draw my interest. "Northern Horizons, all the businesses Will owns, Olivia's known locations, your family home, and even the door security alarms at the gas plant. We're tracking secure employee web portals as well as their lock codes to access parts of the buildings. We want to know all the moving parts. Who is going where and when and why they're there. If we know where everyone is, we know how to avoid them."

I let my eyes roam all the different screens, wondering how long it took him to focus on this many things at a time. Patterns, sequences, numbers, and puzzles are where I excel, but this is an even bigger puzzle that my brain wants to learn how to solve.

I match the personal identification codes to names, trying to memorize who has what access to where. The numbers keep shifting as workers at these buildings access different areas or restricted spaces, but my mind snags on one.

"Wait." I point to it on the screen. "That's Trevor's access code at the... what is that building?" I try to scan the list, looking for the ID number on the list of buildings.

"Fuck," Aaron hisses. "Blake, someone using Trevor's code just entered your dad's house." Aaron pulls up another screen while Blake talks in the background. "Can you tell him?" He nods at the new screen that's dialling Brendan Carter.

"Carter," he answers.

"Brendan, it's Blake's Little Demon." I snug the mic up to my mouth, feeling so badass even though Brendan might be in danger. "Someone just entered your house using an ID tag linked to Trevor." I look at Aaron. "Why would Trevor have an ID code for the Carter house?"

"He doesn't. But it shows that whoever put in security at the Carter house, also did it at Northern Horizons because the systems are linked illegally. Good catch," Aaron says.

"I'm tapping into my camera feed," Brendan says. "But after this, I want it disabled. We'll redo it tomorrow."

"Don't stay there tonight, Dad," Blake says.

"I won't." There's a pause while both Brendan and Aaron tap into the footage at the Carter home, so while they're doing that, I keep scanning the traffic cams to make sure Blake and Brandt's path remains clear.

"Might be nothing," I start, feeling unsure if this is worth mentioning. "But there is a black SUV parked at every intersection for the next seven blocks."

On the screen, I watch the vehicle Brandt is driving turn a corner to avoid the area. Brandt curses, then says, "Thanks, Little Demon. It's not nothing."

As soon as they divert their route, the SUVs all start moving. "They're moving."

"Do you recognize this woman?" Brendan says.

My eyes flick to the security camera screen to see a woman in the kitchen of Brendan's house. I wait until her face partially catches a camera, like she knows where they all are. "That's Olivia's friend, Jules," I say at the same time Aaron says, "Julia Hentz."

"Keep an eye on her," Brendan says. "We're at the police station." Brendan and Bronson are keeping up appearances, ready to confront Will at the cop shop to ask about me and my whereabouts. It's the perfect time to leak that information to see what Will does with it. "Call me if anything happens."

"Those SUVs are one block east of you guys, spanned out from a few blocks back to a few ahead. Your path to that Mini Mart is blocked," I say, pulling out a phone Blake gave me to try calling Samantha again.

She's not with Olivia. She isn't with Will. Trevor is dead. Julia is breaking and entering. So where the fuck could she be?

"Where's Keira?" I ask Aaron. "Should we be monitoring her safety?"

"Always am," Aaron says. "She's working." To Blake and Brandt, he adds, "You can cut through the parking garage of the Morrison Hotel. It spans two blocks and will shoot under the road and spit you out on the east side of them. Take a right in 400 metres."

"On it," Brandt says. "Julia?"

"Just snooping so far," I answer. "In the living room now."

"What's Dad keep at that house that she'd be looking for in the living room? Most people go for the home office or a safe," Blake says.

I think back to the night we sat in Brendan's living room after my big murder night. I remember cheeseburgers and a rum-filled drink, and a really bad case of the *clingys*. What else? As Brandt pulls into the parking garage and Brendan and Bronson enter the police station on all the cameras, my mind reels, trying to recall in perfect memory if anything stood out to me in the living room of that house. Julia is scanning the hearth, the shelves, the side tables, and picking up all the photos and picture frames. Her hands run along the wall, feeling for something in the dark.

"The security alarm box," I blurt, remembering it blinking the time at me. "It's hidden behind the curtain by the patio door. She's looking for it."

"She's how they're synching them," Blake says. "So fucking smart, baby."

So the security alarm company isn't to blame, Olivia's girlfriend is. But why? "Why, though? What is she hoping to achieve?"

"My dad's whereabouts," Blake answers.

"More than likely, she's tapping into the alarm so she knows exactly when he's home and when he isn't," Aaron makes her screen bigger. "Not sure why yet."

"Are we clear to exit the garage?" Brandt asks.

I scan the traffic cams again, seeing their marker one block east of where the SUVs are. "You betcha, Brandty. They're now one city block west of you."

He laughs, and Blake groans. Wow, my shakes are completely gone and a new sort of buzz is humming me up with energy and the wiggles. "I feel like a badass," I tell them all. "I'm so getting laid when you get back, Blake."

"Mm," he agrees, making me smile. "Watch our back. We're at the variety store." I check the screen, watching Blake get out of the vehicle while Brandt keeps it running.

He disappears inside the store for a few seconds, but comes out just as quickly. When he leaves the camera's reach around the back of the building, my shaking comes back, and my eyes fixate on the place he disappeared.

Aaron taps my knee, nodding at a monitor that shows the back of the building. *Oh, phew.* There's his sexy ass in tactical gear and bad boy mode. Blake checks in all the shadowed areas, behind the dumpsters, and inside parked staff vehicles. Nothing. No Samantha.

"I'll pull footage from the past few hours," Aaron says, getting right on it. "Will take me a bit."

The phone Blake gave me starts blaring Latino rap, showing a number I don't recognize. I pick it up, but don't say anything.

"Ben." Olivia's voice snakes down my spine and sets my skin to goosebumps. My eyes shift to the grainy footage of her at the house, sitting at the kitchen island now with a glass of wine in front of her. She looks straight at the laptop sitting across the room on the dining room table and smiles. "Caught you on camera outside Trevor's building today. Parked there with your boyfriend. Not dead, after all."

I don't know what to do. What does she want? I hate freezing up, but she hasn't given any indication about her intentions yet, so I stay silent.

"By now, I'm sure you've put the pieces together. You were always a smart kid. Smarter than the rest of us. Took me until yesterday to figure out that you aren't who I thought you were, *cousin*."

I get sweaty and freezing all at once.

"Dad doesn't know you aren't dead yet, and if you want to keep it that way, you'll meet with me tomorrow at that same cabin. Alone."

"No. I don't give a fuck what he knows."

"Okay," she laughs. "What about her? Do you give a fuck about her?" She walks over to the laptop we're spying on her through, tilting the screen down to the floor.

Samantha. Either alive and unconscious or already dead. Olivia nudges her, and she groans, slipping down the wall with no coordination.

"Noon tomorrow, Ben. At the cabin."

"Mercer," I correct.

She hangs up on me. I go still.

"Heading home," Blake says. "I'll call Dad. Mercer? Listen to me. I'll be home in twenty-five minutes. No buts, okay?"

Aaron grabs my chair and spins me to face him. "Do not shut down. If you shut down, she wins. This is where you shine, Mercer. This is where you put your mind to use, lean on the rest of us to help you, and figure something out. You are not alone in this, hear me? You are not alone."

I am not alone. For the first time in my life, I have something like a real family. That bitch slaps me back into my body and the brilliant mind I'm learning to use. I crack my knuckles, nod at him, and face the monitors again.

"I want their trip home monitored. I want to know what Julia is doing. And I want every geographic map and aerial footage of that cabin." My fingers hover over the keyboard, not knowing how to obtain all that. I look at Aaron for another lesson. "Help me, I'm poor."

Aaron laughs. Blake laughs. Brandt laughs. *My fucking family.*

27 Blake

THE WAY HE MELTS into my body, his back to my chest and his arms reaching back around my neck, does me in. The fit of him. The feel of him. The *fucking* him. There's no bratty attitude and no ulterior motive tonight because this isn't a game. This is—for the very first time—simply sex with Mercer. It's *everything.*

My arms weave around his waist, sliding up his chest to pin him to me as tightly as I can. I thrust my hips upward, fucking him slow and deep while he moans with his head leaned back against my shoulder. His body is a masterpiece; a lean, smooth, beautiful tool he loves using to manipulate. But he's not manipulating me tonight.

As soon as I walked into Aaron's apartment, honestly braced for Mercer's panic attack, he surprised the shit out of me by finishing whatever job he was doing with Aaron before so much as acknowledging me. I mean, I knew he knew I was there because he visibly relaxed, so I kissed him and let him do his thing. When he finished, he took off the headphones, stood up and stretched, and then just...

hugged me. No witty snips or mocking comebacks. No taunts or teases.

A healthy reaction to an unhealthy situation, and I'm so proud of him.

I grind into him, my hands wandering his chest and shoulders to keep him as close as possible. The way he's breathing harshly, moaning with each subtle thrust and grabbing at the back of my neck, is pure bliss. My tongue runs up the side of his neck, tasting the sweat on his skin and feeling the way we mingle together. I suck under his ear, leaving a mark to claim him by.

I've never been in love before, and if this is how intense it is, call me a fucking goner, because there's no coming back from this.

"Blake," Mercer moans, twisting his head.

I grip his jaw and turn his head even more, bringing his lips to mine. I suck his tongue into my mouth and drag my teeth over his bottom lip before releasing him. The whine of satisfaction he lets out is the best music to complement the way we're joined. I keep my forehead pressed to the side of his, my free hand sliding down his stomach to grip his cock.

"Mm." He trembles against me.

I stroke him at the same slow pace as I fuck him, making sure he feels every languid drag of my cock inside his tight ass. When he tugs on my hair and lets out a breathy moan, I capture his mouth to taste it.

"Fuck, Mercer," I breathe against his lips.

I don't even know what else to say. Words evade me and feeling consumes me. The sensation of having him like this, knowing he wants it as badly as I do, proves to me he's the one. I didn't know I was waiting for him, but now that I have him, I can't imagine ever letting go.

Dropping his dick and letting my hands wander, I grip his hips and rock him on my cock, gyrating until I find the angle that has precum leaking from his tip.

"Oh, god," he groans, sucking in a quick breath. "Fuck."

When he buckles forward, landing on his stomach, I lean over him and keep my cock buried deep inside him. He meets me with each thrust, lifting his hips and pushing his ass back while he grips the blanket in a tight fist. I love it, all of it, but I hate not being able to see him. I need to see his eyes.

Mercer groans in frustration when I pull out, but it turns into a gasp when I flip him onto his back. Grabbing him behind the knees, I tug until I'm between his legs. He blinks up at me, lip caught between his teeth.

"So swoony, Blake," he mocks with a little smirk.

Yeah, sentimental, more like. I drape his legs over my hips and push inside him to fuck him missionary. There are those amber eyes. Usually so full of either trouble or panic, tonight they relay nothing but absolute comfort and whatever he portrays as love. When he cries out in pleasure, his hands reach around my neck, and he doesn't even have to pull me down. I go on my own, kissing him like he's the only sustenance I need to survive.

One of these days, everything with his family is going to be resolved, and when it is, I'll have to go back to my job. Leaving him for days at a time seems impossible and I have no idea how I'm going to do it—survive it. I've never been attached to anything before; not a place, a person, or a home. Mercer is all those things to me. He tied me down so fucking tight, I'm going to turn into the needy one.

Against my lips in a raspy whisper, he says, "Fuck me like there are no buts, Blake."

Fuck me like you love me.

He keeps his arms around my neck, and I snake one under his lower back. The other tangles in his hair, and I roll my hips, making him tighten his legs around my waist. Every time I fuck him, it's with no buts because I've been in love with Mercer since before the gala, and there's nothing I wouldn't do for him. He fucking has me. For how possessive

I get, I know it's him who holds all the power. Mercer is mine, but he has no idea how irrevocably he owns me.

His cock rubs against my abs with every motion of my hips. My mind stays right here with him, not wandering to the trouble coming his way tomorrow. For now, he's all I'm focused on. His little moans and the way his heels dig into my ass have me bending forward to kiss him again. With my lips pressed to his and his ass hugging my cock, I'm on that razor's edge of pure bliss.

"No buts, Mercer. No fucking buts."

He cries out as he comes, his cock spurting between our bodies and his fingers tugging at the back of my neck. When he squeezes my dick with the force of his orgasm, it's over for me.

"Mm, Blake," he moans against my mouth.

I fill him with cum, my hips slowing and my breathing increasing until he completely steals it away with a life-changing kiss. Dipped in bliss and soaked in love, we morph together until the orgasms ebb and the need to stay connected overwhelms. I settle over him, chests flush, wrapping my arms around his back and burying my face in his neck.

"I lov—"

"Don't," he snaps at me, yanking on my hair to look me straight in the eyes. "You got to half-ass say it first, so I get to whole-ass say it first."

I smirk at him, holding in a laugh. "Well, get on with it then, little demon."

"Now there's pressure on it," he complains.

"Alright, then I'll say it. I lo—"

"You shut your sexy mouth!" He slaps a hand over my lips. His amber eyes meet my blue ones, and even though he's being a little demon, it just makes his declaration mean more. "I love you, okay? With no buts. Fuck knows how that happened, since you were my jailor and all," he scoffs. His hand leaves my mouth. "You saw me." He swallows audibly.

"And loved me anyway." Vulnerability and insecurity flash in his eyes, but when he blinks, it's gone. "I love you, Blake. Sorry?"

I laugh for real. It feels amazing, and I never want this moment to end. "Mm." I kiss him. "Your love is a lot to handle," I agree.

"If you don't say it back within the next five seconds, I will have a full-blown meltdown."

"You told me not to make you weepy," I tease.

His eyes water a little. "Make me weepy. I only said that because you're bound to be an ugly crier and I was trying to be modest because I'm not."

"Modesty isn't a good look on you, baby." I push my weight onto my elbows and stay right in his face. "One of the many things I love about you, Mercer."

More tears well in his eyes. "Again."

"I love you, Mercer."

"But?"

"No buts."

He struggles not to get weepy, but in the end, he lets out a dramatic whine, covers his face, and doesn't complain when I uncover it.

"I fucking love you." I kiss him.

"Love me harder," he demands.

Any-fucking-time.

AARON OFFERS ME A coffee with a grin. "Good night?"

I take the coffee and hide my own grin. Great night. We're still in his apartment, but I decided not to tell Mercer about the apartment next door until he gets through this day. He doesn't need anything else to distract him before he meets Olivia at the cabin. Strapped with daggers. Highly tracked. Full of audio and video. In a bullet-proof vest. I'm not taking any chances, and I'll be less than ten feet away from him at all times.

"He loves me," I tell Aaron with a smirk. "Said so himself."

"Kind of flattered it happened here," he laughs.

"Don't get smug," I warn. "Keira make it home?"

"She's gonna stay with Kev until this is all over," he says, waving me off.

Aaron and Keira are married, but they have an open relationship. She has another boyfriend named Kevin, and he has a boyfriend named Ian. Sometimes they all hang out together, but I've never tried to dive too deep into their dynamics. It works for them, so whatever. It always blew me away because I could barely handle a one-night stand, and here he is, loving life with a wife and a boyfriend. Aaron is nothing if not attention oriented, so maybe that's why.

But so am I. And now I have a new fixation, who is currently deciding what kind of outfit today will require. I miss his panties and lingerie, but after all this, I'll get him back in his hoodlum look with all the sexy lacy underthings. Hot damn, he's fucking perfection.

"Okay, before we dive into what's happening today," Aaron says, sitting down at the kitchen table. "Frank." He raises a brow, asking me what I plan to do with him. "We pissing his wife off or killing him?"

"I thought Brandt took that over?"

Aaron nods. "Yeah, but we both know you're a control freak and will want the final say."

I sit down with him, keeping an eye on the hall. Aaron's apartment has more bedrooms than mine, which means more privacy. Mine only has one actual bedroom, and other than it and the bathroom, everything else is out in the open. I hope Mercer loves it.

"I want to expose him instead. If we incriminate him for leaking secure information, especially to the competition, it'll benefit her more. The kids get to keep their dad, even if he gets fined or goes to jail for a bit, and her business will flourish with all the media attention. The company he leaked information to will fail, and she'll be right back at the top."

Aaron spins a laptop toward me. "Figured you'd say that." He shows me the whole plan. Evidence, reports, proof of information, and footage of everything except the time me and Mercer were in that server room. Fuck, love him and how well he reads me. "I'll put it through the fake private investigation company, getting her to sign off on it like she hired them instead of us, and send it through?"

"If she'll sign it, yeah." I nod at him. "Thanks."

"Okay, next thing," he says, closing the laptop. "Can I actually train Mercer?"

"If he wants to learn it, then yeah."

"Good. He's got a fucking brilliant mind. He'd be good at this," Aaron compliments my boy, making me smile into my coffee. "But are you sure it's smart for him to work with you? Be your man in the mic, as he calls it?"

Yeah, no. Probably not the best idea. Not at the start, anyway. He needs to learn from Aaron because Aaron is the best, but he'd be better paired with one of my brothers or my dad until we learn to separate work from our relationship. I can't be worrying about him, and he can't be worrying about me without distractions happening.

Just as I'm about to answer, Brandt, Bronson, and my dad walk in the apartment door without even knocking.

"Alright. What the actual fuck?" I stand up, confused. "I swear I kept him a secret. How do you all know about Aaron?"

"I told you it's my job to read my sons," Dad says with a smile.

"I didn't," Bronson admits. "Until yesterday."

I look at Brandt, waiting for him to answer. He shrugs. "We fucked a few times."

Well, Jesus fucking Christ. I'm not even going to touch that one right now, but I give Aaron a glare for supposedly being my best friend and most well-kept secret and keeping that big-ass lie from me. I rub my temples and drain the coffee, needing another one already.

"Blake's in love," Aaron chimes in, getting the attention off himself.

"Old news," Brandt says.

Bronson laughs. "He's been in love since he saw that devil outside the strip club in black lacy lingerie." He grins at me. "Right, man?"

Wrong. I was *intrigued* then, but I didn't know how incredible the person inside that insanely sexy body would turn out to be. "Can we focus on the cabin job?" We have less than five hours to finish planning it.

"Where's Mercer?" Dad asks.

Finally taking the intro he didn't take at that family dinner so long ago, Mercer struts his shit down the hallway. Dressed in tight-fitting black tactical gear and combat boots, he flips a few daggers between his fingers and glares at all of us with dark-lined eyes and thick lashes. With his hair properly messed up and his spine straight, he owns the look.

Lethal. Sexy. In-fucking-charge. That's his look.

"Today is my one and only shot to be the assassin, so I'm dressing the part. After this, I'm back in my hoodlum-slash-gamer boy look to be Little Demon in the mic." He twirls the daggers and sheaths them in holsters strapped to his hips. "Boys," he greets everyone with a saucy smirk. "Blakey."

My cock twitches in my tactical pants, and I debate stripping him from that outfit to fuck him full of more cum to carry into this job.

See? This is what I mean by distractions.

28

Mercer

Looking at her now, I wonder how I could have ever mistaken her expressions for compassion. All these years, Olivia made me believe I was my own worst enemy, but she still felt a little sorry for me. Today, I know that's bullshit, and for the first time, I'm not afraid to stare it in the eye.

Everything else? Yeah. Fucking terrified. But not that. Not the blatant dislike and disrespect she has for me. Luckily, I'm a petty bitch and hate her just as much.

Blake is in my ear, but he isn't speaking, and my assassin's look isn't intimidating to Olivia. I don't need her to be intimidated; I just need her to know I'm not that little boy she sometimes checked on in his bedroom.

My eyes shift to Samantha. She's drugged, probably with the same drug Will used on me, passed out on the couch. Her chest is still moving, and every now and then, she makes sleepy sounds, so keeping her on the breathing side of living is my biggest goal. According to Blake, my biggest goal is keeping *myself* alive.

"I'd say it's nice to see you, Olivia, but truthfully, you're looking even more haggard than Dee. Tired, much?" That gets Blake talking—more like reaming me out for running my mouth, but I like his voice in my ear. We've swapped roles today, and I'd much rather be the man in the mic than standing in this bullshit cabin where I almost died and actually murdered someone.

Olivia is aware of the mouth I have on me, so she doesn't take the bait. She leans against the back of Samantha's couch, looking down at her. "She always did have a soft spot for you," she says, as if it made her weak. "Too bad she didn't have a backbone. One stern warning to drop it from Mom or Dad and she did."

I painted my nails for the occasion. A blackish-purple shade called '*are you jelly*?' It seemed fitting. I made Blake buy it for me on the credit card number I stole. No regrets. I inspect my nails, giving Blake the signal that I'm alright so far.

"And you did?" I ask. "Had that backbone you're accusing her of not having?"

"Yeah, I just didn't have a heart." She laughs. "Well, not really for you, anyway. You made the bed you sleep in."

"Got me in Blake Carter's bed, so... are you jelly?"

Her smile is cat-like and confident. "Guess he won, yeah?" she mocks me, and I don't understand why. "All this time, I thought marrying the eldest Carter was the way to go, but Blake had it figured out before me."

"Don't listen to her, baby. It has nothing to do with money," Blake says in my ear.

"He gets you to fall in love with him, takes everything you own, and then you end up dead anyway. Brilliant. It's what I would have done. Too bad I had the wrong Carter boy."

I hate that my insecurities come roaring to the surface of my skin, prickling my goosebumps to make me itchy. I trust Blake. I *love* Blake. Why the hell are her words piercing my new armour?

"Why'd you want to meet?" My *'are you jelly'* fingertips tickle the hilt of a dagger. I don't know if I have what it takes to maim or kill her, but having the weapons makes me feel better. Knowing how to use them skillfully makes me feel even better. All that time I spent locked in this cabin as a teen wasn't for nothing.

"We have business to discuss. We can either do it the easy way, which means you give me everything you own in exchange for her." She hooks her thumb at the couch. "Or I get my lawyer to rework the will and company transfer documents for when you die."

"Jules?" I ask, still tickling the dagger. It keeps my fingers out of my mouth. "Isn't she already going down for the murder of Trevor? That's how you set it up, right?"

Olivia's face hardens at the same time the front door bangs open. Julia Hentz, the lawyer, has a gun to Blake's temple and his hands are bound behind his back. I jump at the intrusion, and as soon as I go to help Blake, he subtly shakes his head at me. He's fine. Maybe this is a part of his plan.

"I didn't kill Trevor," Julia says, pushing Blake inside the cabin and closing the door. "My husband did it in a jealous rage. Thought I was having an affair with him."

Didn't seem like a jealous rage. Five circles of the block and at least two swaps in the driver's seat don't add up. Plus, I'm not as stupid as she thinks I am.

I turn my attention away from Blake, even though it surprises me how angry I am to see him bound with a gun to his head. "So, it's just the businesses you're after?"

"And all the assets and accounts that go along with them." Olivia steps toward me, leaving at least ten feet between us, but it still feels too close. "I want them so Will can't have them."

"He doesn't have them now, and he never will," I say, meaning it.

Olivia laughs. “Really, Ben? You think he won’t find a way to kill you or con you into giving him everything he feels entitled to?”

“Mercer,” I correct out of habit now. “Why’d Trevor have to die?” I barely knew anything about the man I thought was my brother. He didn’t spend much time in my life; I didn’t see him at the facility, and he didn’t appear to be very close with the Palmerston family, apart from attending functions and events when required.

“Because Julia’s husband was jealous,” Olivia says, aware that we’re both carrying listening devices. She hasn’t specifically said anything to incriminate herself, and even offering Samantha’s life in exchange for this deal proves nothing. No one knows Samantha is here, and she hasn’t mentioned her name.

“Okayyyyy,” I drone. “So, to sum it all up, you want me to sign over everything I own or else you’re going to kill us both?” I motion between me and Samantha, my nails glistening in the sun through the window.

“Him, too,” she mouths, nodding at Blake. “And Brandt to the west. Brendan to the east, and my future hubby just outside.”

Good. She doesn’t know about Aaron. But I do wonder how she knows the whereabouts of everyone else. Are there others here working with her or does she have surveillance up? If she does, Aaron would have caught on and disarmed it. Unless he’s keeping it live for a reason that I haven’t figured out yet. Gah, seeing everything is harder than I thought it was.

“What about Will?” And Penny?

“Can we get on with this?” Julia barks at the two of us, shucking up her hold on my man. “We have no idea who else is coming, Liv.”

I glare at her, not liking her touching him. Blake, the fucking bastard, smirks at me. I do more than tickle the hilt this time, tugging it free to rest in my grip at my side.

Olivia waves her off like she means nothing, which only makes her angry. I don't want her angry with Blake in her grasp, so I turn to my former sister, waiting for her to answer my question.

"Will won't last much longer. He's of no concern to you." She flips her dark hair over her shoulder. "I'm only interested in our deal right now. So, what's it going to be, Ben?"

"Well, I'm not giving you anything," I tell her. A lot of hours of research spent with Aaron last night delayed the best sex of my life, and after finding something that stuck, I called my new potential bestie to strike a deal. Potential is a loose term; she's still my nemesis for the time being. "I have my own lawyer now, and I'm warning you, she's a savage little whore."

Olivia widens her eyes at me, unsure for the first time since I showed up. "What?"

"Yeah, she undid all your forged documents and had them declared null and void. Whatever plans you had in place for my death or Will's death are now undone, so you might want to start again." I shrug, acting nonchalant even though this dagger is sitting heavy between my fingertips. "On top of that, I have a new executor of my will, and when I die, my assets will go somewhere you'll never be able to obtain them." I smile at her.

"Ben," she seethes at me. "What did you do?" She closes the distance between us, her back to Samantha. I stay my hand and meet her eyes. "What the fuck did you do?"

"I thought this was a *Game of Thrones* type situation? You're after what's mine, but you'll take out the Carters and Will to get it, and in return, Will is also trying to take out the Carters and me to get it. Aren't we all fighting for the same throne? I didn't think there were any rules to this game."

When the last word leaves my lips, the plan—that got slightly muddled by Blake being in here—goes into motion. That dagger between my fingers flies to my left, embedding in Julia's right hand. Blake knocks the gun from her grasp, and then my second dagger heads straight for *his* hands. I'm not used to throwing with my nails painted, so it's just a titch too far to the right. Blake catches it... blade first. Blood drips down his fingers, but he works to cut his bindings.

"Warning label," he complains to me.

Meanwhile, as I'm ignoring him, Brandt, Bronson, and Brendan—the B team—already have Samantha secure, and a bag and zip ties are being placed over Olivia's head and wrists.

"A Team? You there?" I ask the mic in my ear.

"Here," Aaron says. "Surveillance all around the property, but no other bodies I'm picking up. She has no men."

Blake's knee is pressed to Julia's spine, and her wrists are being tethered behind her back. He's bleeding all over her, and when he glares his *warning label* bullshit at me, I just blink my big ol' eyes.

"No buts?"

"A fucking but or two today, Mercer," he scoffs at me. "Your aim is impeccable. You did that on purpose!"

I'll take the blame because there isn't a chance in hell I'm pointing fingers at my painted ones. Blake will make me stop wearing the polish, and I've grown rather fond of the colour.

"Exit path is clear," Aaron says to all of us. "Three approaching vehicles from the north. Better move."

And with that, I let them do all the heavy lifting of the ladies and follow them from the cabin. There's no time to do a sweep for bugs and cameras, but Aaron—being the A team, way cooler than this B team—is confident he can remotely destroy them.

Brandt has Olivia over his shoulder, kicking and screaming, and Brendan has Julia in his arms. She might be knocked out because Blake got a bit bloody-handsy with her when he lost his temper with me. I walk behind Blake as he clears our path, and Bronson brings up the rear with a groggy Samantha. Too many unconscious girls around for my liking, thanks.

"You okay, little demon?" Blake asks, eyes scanning the forest.

"Legs are a bit tired. Piggyback?"

"Do not pull a trip move like you did that night on the stairs."

"What night?" I play innocent.

"The fire alarm night."

Ah, look at all these fond memories we're creating.

I smile at him to cover up how badly I'm shaking, and when he turns ahead, knowing our exit is more important than my tired legs, I subtly put my fingers into my mouth.

29 Blake

MERCER FUCKS WITH THE window button. He messes with the radio. He gets sick of the radio and complains about not having his own phone to connect to the sound system. He tilts his seat back. He tilts it forward. His feet cross on the seat, then rest on the dash, then stomp on the floor mat. He huffs and fucking scoffs, and then he crosses his arms and puts on a pouty face.

Then he goes quiet. I notice it this time.

"Goddamn you, Blake," he complains even more. "You ruin all my fun."

I grin. Yeah, I no longer keep my wallet in my jacket pocket while driving. I tighten my bandaged hand around the steering wheel, looking over at Mercer in his hoodlum look. And I know for a damn fact he has a lacy blue bodysuit on under there.

"I found other fun things," he says, leaning back to sit in his chair.

In his greedy fucking paws, he has a gun he has no idea how to use, my phone, and the pack of cigarettes I haven't smoked in a while.

"Mercer, I'm fucking serious about you and warning labels. Put the gun down." I hold my hand out for it.

With an eye roll, he slaps it on my palm, and I tuck it back into the holster on the opposite side of him. "I'm smoking this. Why don't you smoke these anymore?"

Because I don't want to smell like cigarettes when I kiss you. It's not something I've ever thought about before, but it's on my mind now. Maybe also because he's a better stress reliever than those things.

He lights a cigarette and cracks the window, completing his hoodlum look. So hot. He points my phone at my face to unlock it and then helps himself. "I'm snooping."

"I figured."

"I also know your password, but thought I'd respect your privacy by making you aware I'm doing it." He clicks into my messages, sifts through them, and then checks my web browser history. He takes a drag. "Why have you been googling men's tailors? Having a suit made for something I don't know about, you secretive dick? No wonder I need to snoop."

"I'm trying to find that suit you wore to the gala," I tell him, pulling into a Starbucks because he whined when I passed the last four. "What do you want?"

"A pumpkin spice latte."

"It's spring."

"A pumpkin spice latte."

"It's *spring*. They don't have that. Pick something else."

"Well, I don't want Starbucks then," he sasses, taking another drag. "I want a milkshake now."

I pull up to the drive-thru and roll down the window. "Do you have pumpkin spice lattes?"

"No, sorry."

I step on the gas and cross the street for a milkshake. Fucking pushover. Mercer grins into my phone, knowing he won. "You won't find that suit anywhere," he says. "I sort of made it when I was bored once. It was a regular suit. I just sewed a bunch of buckles and clasps and stuff on it. Don't judge me. It was a lonely time in my life."

My heart hurts for the life he's lived. "How're your therapy exercises from Keira going?"

He scoffs. No wait. He laughs condescendingly. For sure this time. "None of your business, nosy."

"Says the guy snooping through my phone."

"Hey, I'm the one with trust and abandonment issues. I'm allowed to snoop and be overbearing because it's justified."

I let out a long breath, kind of loving the feeling of being annoyed by him. "What kind of milkshake?"

"Chocolate. A big one. I'm feeling extra salty, so I gotta even that out with some sweets." He takes another drag and taps his purple nails on my phone screen, sifting through all my emails now.

I order him a big chocolate milkshake, settle for a shitty McDonald's coffee, and pull back onto the street. "You ruined me for bitter coffee," I tell him, even though he isn't the one that put that fancy coffee machine in my apartment.

"Thank you, Blake. I love ruining you," he says with attitude and a smile. "I haven't had a panic attack like I used to in a while," he answers my question finally. "They start, but I can sometimes pull myself out of them now. She told me to take notice of good attention and bad attention."

"And?"

He groans. "Don't fish for compliments."

I laugh. "You saying I give you good attention, baby?"

"You might, but you're also draining because you require so much of mine."

"Mm." I can't stop smiling at how big of a hypocrite he is.

"Mm," he echoes. He tosses the cigarette butt and rolls up the window. "Okay, real talk." He looks at me. "What the fuck do I do, Blake?"

About Olivia and Samantha. About Will. About the money and the companies and the gas plant he now owns. About his life being in danger. About coming back from the dead.

"Also, I'm homeless," he adds, sucking on the straw.

"You're never homeless, Mercer."

"You gonna lock me in your ivory tower forever? Because I'm so much more than a sleeping beauty, and those firemen might come for me again."

"I'll fight them off." I look at him. "You're mine now, baby. I'm never letting you go. Wherever you wanna live, I'll be there."

"I wanna live with Aaron," he snarks. "Love that place and all his nerdy shit."

"We can get you nerdy shit." Damn, can't wait for his hacker look. "As for the rest of it, we'll sit down and think it all through. It's in your hands now. We're just here to act out whatever you pick."

"Is it wrong if I don't want it?" he asks. "I know my birth mumsie left it as a gift and literally lost her life for it, but it feels tainted now. It'll never be free of the Palmerstons if I own it. I don't even want to be a Palmerston anymore."

I can think of a way to change his last name, but I keep that thought to myself for now. "What would you rather do with it? If you sell it all, you still get the money."

"Think your dad will keep it?"

I honestly thought so at first. When I first got back from my five years away to notice my dad had purchased a gas mine, I figured he was trying to be as big and mighty as Will. Now that I know he's only holding onto it for Mercer, I highly doubt my dad wants the headaches that come with being that wealthy and influential. At the end of the day, Brendan Carter is a man who likes to get his hands dirty with actual blood, not political games and business negotiations.

"I don't know, Mercer. What do you want out of life?"

"What a lame question." He slurps his milkshake.

"Answer it anyway. You've never had the option to decide before."

"Hot sex. A hacker's apartment like my new idol Aaron. To be the man in the mic. Sexy outfits." He tucks his head and mumbles, "You."

As soon as I try to comment on all that, he turns the radio on loud. *Frank Thomas has been charged and is awaiting trial regarding the Thomas-Henderson breach of information. His wife, Annabelle Thomas, CEO and founder of Thomas Tech Inc, is pressing charges and filing a lawsuit against patent theft. Henderson Industries is under investigation until the trial is over, but we all know there's probably no coming back from this.*

"Went the high route, I see," Mercer says. "Do I have to do this? I don't even like her."

"She's on your side now, Mercer. You don't have to like her."

"Fine, but you aren't coming with me. I don't want you near that whore."

I roll my eyes and pull over to park on the side of the street. When I try to get out, Mercer stops me with a look. "What?"

"I'm serious. You aren't coming. Circle the block a few times or something."

I love to hate him. "You're impossible."

"I know."

Dee rips open his door. "Blake," she greets me. "Asshole," she greets Mercer. "You ready?"

He scoffs. She scoffs back. Condescending laughter follows from both of them. Godspeed to their time spent together.

I pull Mercer back by his hoodie, planting a kiss on his lips. "I'm going to meet with my dad. I'll come pick you up when you're ready." I slap a new phone to his chest. "Call me."

There's a quick flash of fear in his amber eyes. He still doesn't like it when we're apart, and the selfish, egotistical part of me likes that. The compassionate part of me knows that it hurts him. He blinks it away, unwilling to look weak in front of Dee, and then he hands me his milkshake, only a quarter of it gone. "I'm full." He smirks and hops out, slamming the door and sauntering ahead of Dee.

She gives me a head shake through the window and then follows him. "I'll drop him off," she shouts through the cracked window. "Just tell him where and I'll get him there. If I don't kill him first."

I'll kill her if she does. I nod, and get back to driving, sipping the goddamn milkshake that is ten times better than my coffee.

OH, HOW THE MIGHTY have fallen.

Will knows he's fucked. His oldest daughter is unhinged, and now that he isn't in control of everything, he's trying to earn back my dad's favour. I'm just sitting here trying not to slam a knife through his eye socket for everything he ever did to Mercer, but mostly, for attempting to murder him that night in the cabin.

"The situation has gotten out of hand," Will says to my dad. We're in a public place, the facility my mom worked at and where Mercer stayed, because Will isn't dumb enough to be alone with the Carter family right now. "And I'd just like it to end. I've already lost my son."

"You have a heart for him but not for Mercer?" I ask in a calm tone. Outside, I'm a still lake. Underneath, I'm the deepest, deadliest cave in the ocean.

Will avoids the question. "I'd just like my daughters back. Please."

Samantha is being cared for by Aaron and Keira, even though we're unsure how much to trust her yet. Olivia and her lawyer girlfriend are… being held in a secure location. The only reason I'm comfortable having Mercer out of my line of sight is because I know where all his enemies are at this very moment. Plus, I'm tracking him, sort of spying on his conversation through a bug in his phone, and Aaron is monitoring his whereabouts. I might have even discreetly told Dee to call me if Mercer even blinked wrong. He doesn't need to know how insanely protective of him I am. As long as he knows I'm protective in general.

"Really?" Dad asks him. "You'll stop your plan to obtain these businesses if we give you your daughters back? Somehow, I don't believe that. The Palmerston fortune is dwindling, and you're just as desperate now, if not more so, than you were two years ago when we struck this betrothal agreement."

"My family wasn't in danger then!" Will barks.

"Mercer was," I say, shifting my weight from foot to foot because I'm too pent up to sit down. "How many times have you tried to kill him, Will? How many times did you try to get my mom to kill him?"

And that's the kicker. My mom, the woman who birthed me, tried to kill the man I love. As. A. *Baby*. What kind of evil bitch does that? I understand that money is power in this world, but I've never craved power so strongly that I'd murder a child to gain it. I don't understand the financial games these one-percenters play, and I probably never will. I'd rather be poor in money but rich in Mercer. Does he care about money that much? Would he leave me if I had nothing to offer him but love?

"I don't trust you," Dad says to Will. "I don't trust that Samantha will be safe with you. I don't trust that you won't strike a deal with Olivia to join forces and come after us together. Where's your wife, Will?"

Will's cheeks turn red with rage, and his temple throbs.

"She's here, right?" I ask him, already knowing the answer. "You didn't want her to know about any of this, so you drugged her, which gave her hallucinations, and then you claimed they came from the loss of Trevor, and had her committed to the facility you own."

"To keep her safe!" Will shouts, drawing looks from people in the lobby. We're in an office off to the side, but it has glass panel walls so we can't murder him here. Too bad.

My dad stands, ending this meeting before it really began. That was the point of it. To show Will that we hold the power, and that he is now at our mercy. Whatever we decide to do with his daughters, he can't control. Whatever we decide to do with the businesses and money he feels entitled to, that's on us. We are at the top, and he has no power right now.

"We'll speak with Samantha and give her the option to go back to you, but don't hold your breath. As for Olivia..." Dad zips his jacket and pushes his chair in. "We'll be in touch."

"And what am I supposed to do until then? The media is breathing down my neck about Trevor, and Ben is still missing."

"He won't be for long." I grin at Will.

The paleness of his face is worth everything. Shock registers, and fear quickly follows it. *Yes, that's right, you coward. Mercer is alive and well, and now you know you didn't beat us. Fuck you for even trying.*

My baby boy is out there strutting his hot ass around downtown as we speak, and he'll be pronounced as found anytime now. "But if you ever so much as look at him again, I won't botch the hit like you did."

He glares at me, but the roll of his throat shows he's taking my threat seriously. He knows I know everything, and the way that makes me smile is diabolical.

"We'll be in touch," Dad says, holding out his hand.

Reluctantly, even though we didn't keep up our end of the bargain by bringing his daughters to him, Will slaps a USB drive against my dad's palm. The non-redacted records of my mom's time here, including her work history, the patients she recruited, and the families she personally worked with to get their kids into this facility. Dad wants to go through every single one of them to ensure no other babies were harmed or died because of her. After he's done, Aaron will use the information to shut the illegal part of this place down.

On the way out to the car, Dad asks, "How's your moral compass when it comes to killing a thirty-something-year-old Palmerston woman who hasn't had the chance to have babies yet?"

"It's pointing right at death." Olivia shouldn't spawn evil, and my compass has no problem snuffing her out.

With Mercer's permission? Maybe. Maybe even without it.

30

Mercer

OH, SHE'S OFF HER damn rocker if she thinks I'm going to take fashion advice from a raggedy old ho. Despite the combination of sleek black and a shade of purple that complements my '*are you jelly*' nails exceptionally well, I roll my eyes at the outfit she holds up.

"Ew."

"Oh, stop." She shoves the outfit against my chest and pushes me into the changing room. "You know I'm right."

I slide the curtain shut with dramatic flair. "I'm not in my uppity city boy phase right now." I hang the outfit on the wall hook and start stripping.

"No, you're just in your attention whore, twinky little brat phase," she calls me out.

Always, but I'm not telling her that. "Actually, I'm in my gamer boy phase." I slide on the pants and resent how good they feel against my skin. Expensive material and a snug fit that accentuates my toned ass and lean legs. Damn her. I stare at myself in the mirror, kind of admiring how the pants look with just the navy-blue bodysuit as a top. Then

I admire the love bite Blake left on the side of my neck, feeling pretty smug about wearing him in front of Dee.

“Well, you can pair it with grungy shoes,” Dee says through the curtain. “Hurry up and stop eye-fucking yourself in the mirror. We all know you’re hot shit. You most of all. We have places to be.”

“What’s wrong with my hoodlum look?” I take the shirt off the hanger and slip it over my head. It’s a deep shade of blackish purple that looks nice against my paler skin. It’s a sweater, but with only three-quarter sleeves, and if I’m being honest, that’s what makes me the most nervous. What if I can’t ball up the material if I get panicky?

“It doesn’t belong in a meeting where you want to be taken seriously,” she answers. “What’s your shoe size?” Dee asks.

“None of your fucking biz.”

She huffs and then slides the curtain open, crowding all my space.

“Um, hello?”

“Yeah, hi,” she says. “Put these on.” She shoves a pair of shoes at me. Matte black slip-ons that I actually love.

“I told you I’m not into fashion,” I scoff at her, but put the shoes on. And fuck her again because they complete the look and fit perfectly. I appear as a casually dressed hoodlum who should be taken seriously, and that’s exactly what she was going for.

She starts fussing with my outfit. Tucking and untucking the shirt, giving a nod of approval to my lacy bodysuit, and hiking up the pants a bit.

“Are you my fucking mom?” I huff, letting her work her magic.

“Ever had one of those?” she retorts.

Ah, she’s the devil. I go back to looking at myself in the mirror. My eyes are bright and not too tired-looking today, despite my lack of sleep last night. That person inside me, the one clawing his way to the surface, appears even closer in the light of this fluorescent dressing room. I smirk at him, willing him to keep on coming. I've never felt stronger than I do lately, even if my whole family is trying to kill me.

"How do you get your eyeliner so perfect?" I ask as she tucks just the side of the sweater into the waistband of my pants, tugging it so it artfully hangs.

"That a compliment, Mercer?"

"A question. If you're going to be a bitch about it, you can just fuck off. I have enough attitude for one dressing room."

She smiles, kneeling in front of me to roll the hem of my pants. "Practice. And the right liner. I'll show you sometime." She stands. "There. Respectable asshole with a chip on his shoulder. My work here is done." She rips off all the tags to take to the cashier and packs my hoodlum look into a bag. "We have twenty minutes to get there. Move it, sassy."

Sassy. I scoff at that. She's the sassy one.

ON THE WAY TO this café, I bought a pair of sunglasses. Now I'm hiding behind them, letting Dee do all the talking while I soak in the sun on the patio and pay attention in secret. This place has pumpkin spice lattes, thank the heavens.

"It's a possibility," Dee's lawyer friend says. He's her boss or something, and she wanted to get his opinion and approval before setting anything in stone. "It gives Mercer ownership through a shell company. His name will mostly stay out of everything, but he'll own it all. Or..."

I don't wanna own it all, but I don't know what else to do with it.

"I thought we might set it up so he has majority control, but he isn't the only target if someone tries to come for him," Dee says. "Shareholders."

The guy nods. "He'll get to pick them. Or we can open it to other clients, get a good mix of shareholders."

They both look at me, so I tilt my cup until the foam hits my nose. I don't know anything about running a business, and Dee is trying to set it up so that my businesses are run for me, but I'm still the owner of the holding companies. Or something like that. "Yes?"

"Do you want to gift a portion of your stock to others? Sell it? Pick shareholders? Keep it close in the family?" Dee asks.

"I'll think about it." I lean back in my chair. "They're running themselves right now, aren't they?"

"Yes, and we're vetting all the CEOs currently in place, but it still leaves you as the sole owner of everything. We're trying to put fail-safes in place to protect you if anyone tries to come for it. Shareholders are one option, or dividing business ownership rights with a new incorporation license," Mr. Bigshot Lawyer says. "In the event of your death, no one person would gain ownership. You can will your portion to someone, but it protects the business as a whole. We'd keep you as the majority share owner."

I just want to be the new Aaron. I frown.

"And in place of you, you can hire someone to act as your representative, so you don't have to be publicly or physically involved in meetings and business decisions," Dee adds.

"Like you?"

She leans back and widens her pretty eyes at me. Actually succeeded in shocking the bitch. Finally. "Me?"

"Why not? I'll pay you more than this guy."

He laughs. "Are you poaching my lawyers, Mr. Palmerston?"

"Ugh, don't call me that. Just Mercer. And yeah, if she has the balls to do it."

Dee stumbles over her words. It'd be cute if she wasn't so whorish. She ignores me and faces her boss. "I'll get these drawn up for approval and then we'll narrow down the specifics of the corporation's... structure." She closes her laptop and puts her iPad in her bag.

We say a long and drawn-out goodbye to her boss, so I order another pumpkin spice for the drive. When we get in her Mercedes, she scoffs at me.

"What the fuck was that?" She smacks my shoulder. "What was that!?"

I rub my arm. "Look, lady, you forced me to go to a meeting about a topic I'm unfamiliar with and didn't have time to research, so fuck you for that. Also, don't you want to be a millionaire? It sounds pretty perfect to me. You get to be my face, do all your high and mighty bullshit, and run a corporation with the legal smarts to do it well. Plus, you know business and marketing since you did that boring ass job first, right?" I shrug. "And we all know you want to be my face."

When she just stares at me, I take a sip.

"Ohhhh." I laugh. "You'd rather just be a prostitute?"

"Oh, fuck you, Mercer," she snaps at me, starting the car. "The preferred term is escort."

I grin. "Mm."

"Ugh."

"And you made me dress up for a meeting in a coffee shop, which is bullshit. It's also bullshit that you think he would have taken me less seriously in my hoodlum look. I have the money and the power, so he'll take me seriously no matter what I'm wearing."

"It's your attitude that makes people not take you seriously," she says, driving down a busy street at rush hour, hitting all the red lights. "Except Blake Carter, apparently."

"Mm," I say again.

"I think our hangouts will have to be capped at two hours tops. I'm at my limit with you."

"Ditto."

DEE DROPPED ME OFF at Blake's apartment. When I stepped into the building, he was waiting for me, which made me super suspicious. The whole way up the elevator, I glared at him until he buckled under the pressure of it.

"What?" he had asked.

"She has your number. Make her lose it or get a new one."

He threw me over his shoulder, spanked my ass, and told me to shut my mouth and pack a bag.

I packed seven bags.

Now we're standing in the twin to Aaron's apartment, and I'm swooning and scoffing and speechless. It's industrial, open concept, wide and spacious, and has a hallway bathroom and a bedroom with an ensuite off to one side. There're so many windows! That old kind like in Aaron's apartment, and a massive balcony that faces open space. It's mostly empty, though. A few pieces of furniture, but definitely not set up.

And that's not even the best part. Blake, my calm, cool cucumber, is stuttering like a sexy fool.

"It's, I mean, I bought it forever ago, but I never... and when you said you liked... I just, you know? Like it was meant... to be? Because we're both... and I want you to feel like it's yours as much as... fucking hell." He takes a deep breath, and I watch his whole show instead of the apartment. He straightens his back and composes himself.

"I bought it. Never moved in. Will you fucking live here with me, you satanic little demon?"

Oh, yay! My nickname got a descriptor!

"I dunno, Blake," I muse, pacing around the wide-open space like I'm not pissing myself in excitement. "Where will I put all my things?"

Angrily, he points a stern finger at the bedroom.

"Where will your piano that you never play go?"

Another finger point to the floor space in front of the windows.

"I mean, it's cute." I dawdle just to rile him up some more.

"But?"

He's set me up too perfectly. I look at him and let him see the real smile on my face. "No buts, Carter. But I promise you this," I step up to him, poking him in the chest, "you and me in all this open space? It'll be a sexy hell that even you get sick of."

His smile is almost shy. "Then it's a good thing my best friend lives next door."

I recoil at that. "Hell no. Aaron is mine now. Get a new best friend." I already hate the suggestion, and he knows it. "You know what? Fine. You can have Aaron, but I get Keira. No other friends. Ever. Unless they are completely horrendous people you would never be attracted to. I'm talking ugly, terrible personalities, and the works."

He wraps a hand around my throat and uses his thumb to tilt my chin up. "You'll move in here with me?"

"Yes."

"You're sure? You don't like the other apartment better? Want a different place completely? Want a house instead of an apartment?"

"Me and lawn work? Hell no." A thought occurs. "Unless it has a pool. I'd make a sexy pool boy."

"And we'd still have to hire a pool boy who'd do more than just be the aesthetic of it." He kisses my lips and pulls back. "Move in here with me?"

"What temperature do you like the thermostat at?"

"Oh my god," he groans. "Whatever you like it at! We both know I'm a fucking pushover for you."

"Exactly the answer I was looking for." I wrap my arms around his neck and let him pull me into his arms. My legs go around his waist and my dick just gets hard... because how can it not against those abs? "Okay, roomie. As long as you'll be my wall."

"Mm," he agrees. "And I'll fuck you against the rest of them." His lips press to mine, and I smile without meaning to. "What's this?" he teases. "Horny and happy? Guess you do fuck in the right frame of mind."

"It's new."

"You're welcome."

"Less talking. More wall-fucking."

SAMANTHA'S A WRECK. PUFFY eyes, snotty nose, tangled hair, and a mountain of used tissues on the table in front of her. She's been crying since she woke up.

But now she's white. As a ghost. "Oh my god!" she shrieks, partly in fear but mostly from shock. "Ben? Ben!" She rushes me.

"Mercer," I correct.

"Mercer!" She flings her arms around me and hugs me. It's weird because, while she's really the only person who has hugged me my whole life, those hugs were timid and empty, but this one is full of love and relief. "I can't believe you're here. Alive, I mean."

I hug her back, feeling both awkward and grateful. "Brandt is a moody dick and kept my life-or-death situation a bit of a secret to see how you'd react." I pat her back. "Wanted to see if you actually cared about me. I'm… kind of surprised that you do."

"Of course I do, Mercer. I always have." She lets me go, smiling at me like a right proper mess. "I've just been more afraid of Dad."

"He's not my dad," I tell her. "He killed my parents and pretended I was his so he could kill me at eighteen and take my fortune."

"Right," she says softly. "What a mess."

"You or this situation? Because damn, girl."

Brandt and Blake are chatting outside the front door of this inconspicuous little house in the suburbs. And by chatting, I mean they're probably standing there silently with the odd word thrown in. Brandt has been watching Samantha, making sure she's okay, and testing her headspace. As per his report—because I'm a guy who gets reports now—he says she's been an emotional wreck over me. Not anyone else. He even had to tell her that Trevor died. I guess she was a bit sad about that, but like me, she didn't know him very well.

"I know. I'm disgusting." She chokes out a weak laugh. "I've been so confused."

So, real lickety-split, I give her the breakdown. "Will wants everything in my name. So does Olivia. She tried to barter with me for your life, but I've got the B team on my side, and we got you out of there. Now we also have Olivia and Julia in the basement of some building, trying to decide what to do with them. Also, my new lawyer is a skank. Escort, excuse me."

"Uh, what?"

"Oh! And Blake bought me an apartment because he loves me with no buts."

Okay, guess I was a little desperate to tell someone that. Dee wouldn't appreciate it the same way.

"What lawyer?"

"I poached a lawyer from Will's legal team, and now she's mine, but I'm trying to double-poach her to become the acting whatever for all these things I own." I sit down on the couch and watch her sit across from me. "What do you want to do, Samantha? What's next for you?"

"Do I get a choice? I mean, up until you came in, I honestly thought the Carter family might kill me."

"I own their moves when it comes to you, and I don't want you dead. You're the only one who ever even tried to help me." I mean that, too. "Thanks for that."

"It wasn't enough," she sighs. "I'm sorry."

Since I'm in a good mood because of Blake's love, I wave it off. "Bygones. No point dwelling on it anymore, as long as you aren't in this thing with Olivia."

Samantha sinks against the couch. "She's been off ever since the engagement to Bronson. I don't trust her anymore." She looks at me, smiling. "I don't have any skills, Mercer. I have a business degree, but I never did anything with it because Dad wouldn't let me. I don't know what I want or what I even can do."

"Will you go back there? To that house?"

She laughs, sounding tired. "Honestly? I kind of want to walk away and disappear. Dad doesn't care about me enough to come looking. I've always wanted to go to Japan." She shrugs. "Maybe now is the time."

Go to Japan and disappear? Wow. I wasn't expecting it to be that easy.

"Okay, how about this?" I turn to face her. "I haven't looked through the whole business profile yet, but there is a hotel chain somewhere in Asia that I own. What if you take that over? I think it's a ritzy one, but there aren't a lot of locations. I can get the business file for you?"

"You just want to gift me a hotel chain?" She laughs. "What have I ever done to deserve that?"

I grab her hand and squeeze it, even though it's probably snotty. "Tried."

She starts to tear up, so I hug her.

"Just think about it," I say against her hair. "And for all I know, I could be completely wrong. It might be a restaurant chain or a strip club chain or something. I'm guessing about the hotel business."

She laughs and hugs me tighter. "Thank you, Mercer. Thank you."

Okay, so at least I got a happy ending with her. Everyone else? Yeah, not gonna happen.

31 Blake

MERCER IS A TYRANNICAL dictator.

To distract himself from the decision he has to make about Olivia and Julia, he's bossing me around, and making this new apartment his home. I know he's doing it for attention, but I've been fake ignoring him for the past two hours. For one, I have to get back to my actual job, so research is a must, and I'm not going to lie, I've been tracking Samantha to make sure she leaves the country. But mostly, it's just to get him to try harder. I love it when he begs for attention, and it's become a new sort of game to see how far he'll take it.

"Blake!" Mercer shouts.

"Mm?" I keep my eyes on my laptop.

I watch the screen of my laptop fall shut, replaced by Mercer's amber eyes, messy dark hair, and accusatory expression. "There's about to be a few buts, Blake."

"What buts?" I ask, leaning back. Mercer ordered a new dining room set with six chairs—you know, because we're only two people, but *just in case*. The thing is made from reclaimed wood and pipes, definitely fits the theme of the apartment, and probably cost more than my Denali. He says he's in his rustic home phase.

"I love you, but you're ignoring me. I love you, but you're an asshole. I love you, but if you don't treat me like the *new me* I am, I will go to the bedroom to be Ben."

"I have that kind of power, huh?" I grab the front of his shirt and slide his ass down the table until he's right in front of me. "I can turn you back into Ben? Come on. You're stronger than that, baby." I tug a little more, making him spread his legs to rest his feet on my chair.

"I've never had a home that feels safe before," he says honestly. "I'm trying to nest and you're ruining it." His bottom lip sticks out.

Work vanishes from my mind. His words hit me hard, like he knew they would, and now I want to make this the best house decorating, nesting, homecoming night he's ever going to have.

I slide my hands up his legs and look up at his face. "You have all my attention, Mercer. What do you want me to do? Hang pictures? Move the bed without gouging the floor? Make you a drink and turn on the right music? Tell me."

"Mm," he muses, grinning at me like the devil he is. "A drink sounds nice."

I smile at him and start to get up, but his socked foot lands on my chest to keep me in the chair. "A drink for you," he says, nodding at his dick.

Fucking honoured that he'd let me suck his cock without anything else to distract me from paying too close attention to his reactions like he feared, I lean forward and nip at the inside of his ankle. "Yeah? You gonna come down my throat?"

"If you keep talking like that, I'll come in my pants," he says with a breathless sigh.

Not wanting him to change his mind, I hook my fingers in the waistband of his black sweatpants, encouraging him to lift his ass as I pull them down. His cock springs free, no panties or boxers to hold it in check. Slowly, I pull the pants off his legs, tossing them to the floor and admiring the way his slit glistens with precum. I lean forward and lick it, drawing a cry from Mercer already. His fingers grip the edge of the table, and my tongue runs down his shaft, looking up to meet his eyes for permission.

He rakes his teeth over his bottom lip, shimmying to the very edge of the table and looking like all my fantasies come to life. "New house, new rules," he says right before he reaches forward and pushes my head down.

My hands spread his legs, and my mouth goes willingly. I suck the head, skimming my tongue under his crown until his hands get even more greedy. He pushes, and I slide down his shaft, swallowing as much of him as I can until he groans low and sultry. He's leaking already, and the taste of him has my dick pressing against the front of my pants, dampening the material of my boxers.

Mercer plants one hand on the table behind him, leaning back to angle his hips for better access. With his eyes on me, I thrive. I bob on his cock, tongue flicking over the tip every time I draw my lips upward. His thighs tremble and my chest tightens, hooked on this new experience. Him, for once, at my complete mercy. I won't squander it.

"Blake," he moans when I pull back, letting strings of saliva stretch between us. My fingers dig into his thighs and his eyes darken with lust. "Fuck. More."

Languidly, I flatten my tongue and run it over the tip. "You gonna give me something to drink, little demon?" I mouth his length and come back up again to suck the head.

"If you earn it. This is self-serve. You gotta tap your own keg." He frees my head and uses his hand to lift his hoodie up to his chest, giving himself a better view. "I like how you look down there."

"Mm?" I grin, licking my wet lips to take him into my mouth again. I like how I feel down here.

He groans, and when I bottom out, my nose to his skin, he coughs, choking on a gasp. "Fuck."

I don't give him time to overthink his reaction or make him feel like he has to act a certain way. I find a rhythm, deepthroating him slowly while sucking the head hard every time I pull back, that has him shaking with restraint. He's not going to last, and I already know what I'm going to do with his cum when I get it. When his thighs try to close and he starts squirming, I close off my throat, ready for him to fill my mouth.

"Ah, fucking fuck," he moans, head tipped back.

Mercer comes with a tremble. His breathing stops altogether and his cock throbs in my mouth, giving me the best taste of him. I suction my lips around him, not wanting any to drip out, sucking him through the rest of his orgasm. He's still messy when I pull my mouth away, but his eyes meet mine and he knows I'm up to something.

Standing, I push his chest to make him lie on his back, and then I hook my arms under his knees and fold him in half. With his pretty little hole on perfect display, I spit his cum all over him, watching it drip down his balls and coat his crack. I lick my lips to savour the rest.

"Oh my god," he moans. "You're fucking filthy."

I push my finger and his cum inside him, gathering as much as I can to fill him. "You love it, you little cumslut."

His cock twitches, hardening fully again already. His docile, dazed nod is as sexy as his parted lips and glazed eyes. This is my Mercer. The one who loves cum and uses sex as a coping mechanism. The sexual deviant who knows exactly what he wants, and finally, I know exactly how to give it to him. I add another finger, pushing his mess inside him.

"You want me to fuck you full of cum, little demon?" I curl my fingers and make him writhe in anticipation. "Tell me."

"Yes," he moans, legs widening all on their own, eyes on me. "Fuck me full of cum. I need it, Blake."

“Beg me, baby.”

“Blake, please.” His voice takes on a desperate tone, whining. “Please fill me up. Fuck me so hard I break.”

I tug on the front of his hoodie to bring him to a sitting position. “I’ll never break you, Mercer.” I pull his sweater and shirt over his head. “But I’ll wreck you tonight.”

He whimpers. “Yes.”

Pulling my fingers from his ass, I hook them over his bottom teeth and drag his jaw down. He looks at me with a combination of defiance and submission, still debating which way he wants to go with this. His tongue laps at my fingers, sucking his own taste from them until I pull away.

“Blake,” he whines.

I pull my shirt off and throw it on the floor with his pants. I nod at the floor in front of me. “On your knees.”

Mercer complies, getting to his knees while cum glistens on his inner thighs. His hands reach for my pants, but I step back. He whimpers again.

“You do what I say when I say it, understand?”

Commands. He wants them, even though he wants to fight for control. While a battle of want rages in his eyes, I wait for him to submit or fight back. And now that I know him, even if he does submit, he’ll still be manipulating me through the pleasure he brings me. He’s the perfect conundrum, and I can’t believe he’s mine.

He nods. “Yes, Blake.” A flash of deviancy lights up his whiskey eyes. Atta boy.

“Take my cock out,” I demand.

Mercer doesn’t hesitate because he wants to complete this command. With steady fingers and big eyes, he slides my sweatpants down but leaves my boxers in place. To be a brat, he defies orders by pressing his face to my cock, mouthing it through the material. His eyes look up at me and the challenge in them is tempting. Before I get the chance to grab his jaw and put him in place, he pulls back like nothing happened and slides my boxers down my legs, grinning at me.

"Now what?" he asks, batting his lashes.

I step out of my pants and tell him, "Open."

Before his lips are even all the way parted, I shove my cock into his mouth and press on the back of his head. "Get me nice and wet, so I can fuck your tight ass, baby."

He chokes only once, settling his jaw and loosening his throat. With my hand encouraging him, he sucks my cock and doesn't try to be sexy about it. He's sloppy and loud, drooling down his chin and all over my shaft, soaking me like I told him to. He gags silently when I slide down his throat, but he shifts his eyes up to look at me while he does it. So fucking sexy.

Mercer squirms on the floor, his knees sliding together and his fingers itching to touch his cock. He doesn't, yet. But if I know him, he won't be able to hold out for long. I tangle my fingers in his hair to fuck his face harder, and when he starts to moan, I go faster.

"So submissive," I tease him. "Love getting your face fucked by a thick cock, don't you?"

He hums his agreement around my length, the vibration of it going back to my balls and making my ass clench.

"Reach behind you and make sure that cum is still in your hole, little boy."

With my cock choking him, he reaches back to comply. Fingering himself with his cum as lube, his eyes leak as much as his dick does. I've never seen a more beautiful mess.

"Good boy."

He cries out around my cock, trembling all over. Okay, my boy loves some praise. Noted.

Grabbing the back of the chair I was just on, I drag it over to where we are and then pull out of his mouth. My cock glistens and drips with spit, and Mercer's heavy breathing makes him drool down his chin. I sit on the chair and crook my finger at him.

"Come here."

Mercer stands, his fingers wet. He steps between my legs and waits for his next order. "You think you're ready to get fucked?" I meet his eyes after admiring every inch of him.

"Yes, Blake."

"You sure?"

"Yes, Blake."

"Better show me. Turn around and bend forward. Show me that ass I own."

Mercer turns, bending at the same time. Right in front of me, he spreads his ass cheeks and shows me his puckered, glistening hole. My cock aches to be inside him, but my mouth ends up there instead. I hold him by his hips and tongue fuck his ass until he's begging me to stop.

"Blake, I'm gonna come like this," he rasps. "Fuck me. Please, fuck me."

I swirl my tongue once more, gathering his cum and smacking my lips. "You fuck me, baby. Show me you're ready." I turn him around.

Mercer straddles my lap, eyes on my lips. I grin to taunt him, and he licks them because he can't help himself. I smack his ass and squeeze it, loving the way he fits in my palms.

"Fuck my cock, baby. Open yourself up so I can ruin you."

With one arm over my shoulder for balance, he reaches back to grab my cock, lining it up. Slowly, he sinks down, and I watch every expression on his face as he fills himself full of me. His eyes blink, his lips part, his cheeks turn pink, and then he bites his lip. When his ass hits my thighs, my abs clench with restraint. I want to fuck into him so hard and so fast, but I want to draw this out even more.

"How's my cock feel, Mercer?"

"So. Fucking. Good," he whispers.

I put his other arm around my neck and then grab his legs, planting his feet on the sides of the chair. "Then fuck it."

Using his feet for leverage, he slides up until just the tip is inside him. Meeting my eyes and yanking on my hair, he slams back down.

"Ah, fuck," I groan. "So good, baby. Fuck me harder."

Mercer rides my cock with no shame. His dick bounces between our bodies, hard as lead and dripping precum. When his legs get tired, he switches from fucking me to gyrating on my lap, hitting all the right angles and making his face flush harder.

"I'll come," he warns.

"Feeling good, sweetheart?"

"So good."

I grab his dick and squeeze the tip hard, making him bite back a hiss. "No coming yet, Mercer." I kiss him and give my hips a thrust.

"Mm," he whimpers.

I grab him under his thighs and stand up with him still on my dick. Mercer wraps his arms around me, sucking his own brand against the side of my neck. The slice from his dagger burns on my palm, salty sweat coating the two of us. Taking him over to where the piano now sits, I set his ass right on the keys, making them shout a discordant tone.

Cocky, Mercer grins at me. "We gonna make music, Blake?"

I smirk back, letting his legs drop to wrap around my hips. "We're gonna break the sound barrier, baby." I slam into him, clanging the keys, making him scream, and jarring the piano. I fuck him so hard his eyes can't stay open and his legs vice around my hips. The sound of skin slapping, keys going off, Mercer moaning, and me grunting have us both sweaty and delusional.

"Blake... oh, fuck, *yes*." He's so close.

So I lift him up and spin him around, forcing him to slap his hands down on the keys. As soon as he's braced, I thrust into him hard and fast, spit and cum and pure desire making us savage.

"Harder," Mercer demands.

I slam into him and wrap my hand around the front of his neck. "You think you can boss me around, Mercer?"

"Yes. Fuck me harder, Blake. You haven't wrecked me yet." He slams his ass back, taking charge.

I hold him steady and pound into him. My hips piston and his legs weaken. His fingers tickle the ivory, creating music that should sound terrible but doesn't. When he cries out and his ass clenches around my cock, I pull his hands away from the keys and shut the lid.

"Hold on tight, Mercer," I warn against his ear. "Come all over this piano."

Thrusting upward, I fuck him until he bursts. He clamps down on me, his ass spasming all around my sensitive dick. His cum hits the wooden lid of the keys, the back of the piano, and the floor. He cries out in pleasure, and when he starts to breathe again, I reach around and massage his balls.

"Oh, god," he pants at the extended pleasure. "Fuck. Give me your cum. Please. I need it, Blake."

"Mm, fucking take it, Mercer." I bury myself deep and go still, filling him with my pleasure and rubbing his balls at the same time. "So fucking perfect, little boy."

He moans, another weak spurt of cum shooting from his cock.

I pull out fast and spin him around again, lifting his useless legs and sitting him on the piano. Bending, I lick our cum from his ass, sucking it into my mouth. He's yanking on my hair, already knowing what I'm going to do, bringing my mouth to his to swap cum like he can't get enough of it. I spit it into his mouth and he gives it back. It drips down our chins and my fingers swipe through it to shove it back into his mouth.

"There's my little cumslut," I purr against his lips. We're all teeth and tongue and sloppy uncoordinated kisses, and it's goddamn perfect.

"I want more." He kisses me. "Fuck me again. Fuck my throat. Fuck anything. Just give me more cum, Blake."

I kiss him lightly and step back. But I don't keep enough of a hold on him because his legs can't hold him up and he slides down the front of the piano. I barely catch him under his arms before he crashes to the floor.

Laughing, I yank him back up. "Wrecked." I smile at him.

"So wrecked," he agrees weakly. "Still want more, though."

I leave my laptop and all that work on the table, carrying Mercer first to the bathroom and then to the bedroom. When I try to set him on the bed, he clings to me harder.

"Finally admitting you want some aftercare, Mercer?" I smooth his dark hair back.

He nods but doesn't say anything. That's good enough for me. I tuck him into my chest, his face buried in my neck. "I hate cuddling," he whispers.

"I know." I smile at his lie. "If you wanna act like I'm forcing you to be here, you can."

"Thank you." He snuggles in. "I..."

I kiss the top of his head. "Love you, too, Mercer."

"No buts?"

"No buts." And I'm proud of him. He straight up asked for my attention instead of manipulating me into it. I don't know if that's progress or comfort, but it's something to be admired.

32

Mercer

"WHY ARE YOU WALKING like that?" Bronson asks as soon as I walk into Aaron's apartment.

Because I got dicked-down and bred by the god of thunder last night. "Exercise." I breeze past him and sit at my new station next to Aaron's. His is cooler, but I'll get there. "Coffee," I demand Bronson.

"I'm not your bitch," he barks at me.

Ugh, these Carter boys will need some training. When Aaron gives me an accusatory look, I try to ignorc it, but he wins.

"Ugh, fine," I groan, getting out of my chair. I'm not supposed to be here for *man behind the mic* duties. I steal Aaron's coffee and head out to the balcony, slamming the sliding door behind me.

"Morning," Keira says, smiling at me. Her smile falls a second later. "You okay?"

"I got fucked. Let it go." I plop onto the patio couch, wincing at my sore ass. "Can we get this over with?" Therapy. No fun. "And if you try to tell me that being a brat isn't who I am one more time, I will do everything in my power to prove you wrong. Trust me, you won't like it."

Keira laughs, setting down her iPad to give me her full attention. "How are things going?"

"That's such a vague and therapist-esque question."

"Okay, let me rephrase. Are you keeping your shit together with everything going on, or is it overwhelming you?"

I'm distracting myself by making my new apartment into a home and getting fucked in it like it's nobody's business. "I'm overwhelmed, Keira. I'm supposed to decide the fate of my sister and make decisions about a bunch of companies when I've never had decision-making power before. It's a tad overwhelming, don't you think?"

"I definitely think," she agrees. "So, how are you coping?"

"Meditation and internal thought assessment."

She tilts her head at me.

"Sex and fancy nail polish." I'm on a purple kick, so I repainted this morning because I woke up at the ass crack of dark. "This one's called '*yank my doodle*,' and I definitely got my doodle yanked last night. But I feel good about it, even if my legs are jelly and my ass aches."

"Feel good about it, why?" she asks.

I roll my eyes. "Because I didn't have to be a brat to get good attention." I sip the lukewarm coffee. "Doesn't mean I'm not one," I tack on in a mumble.

"How did you get his attention? Or was he already paying attention to you?"

"I asked for it like a mature adult. It was weird."

"But it worked." She laughs. "See? He loves you, and he doesn't need to be manipulated into paying attention to you."

"Maybe not, but he likes being manipulated."

"That's because he's a sadist and a masochist." Dee, that whore, struts a bomb outfit out onto the patio like she belongs here. "And you're his favourite devil."

"He didn't hurt me," I retort, glaring at her for being here.

"Your wince and wobbly walk say otherwise." She sits beside me, not caring that I'm two seconds away from biting her. "And let me guess, you begged him to break you."

I hate her. I hate her for knowing me. "Who invited you?"

"You wanna know how I know Blake?" Dee asks, smirking. "My brother is Keira's boyfriend."

"You have a boyfriend?" I gasp. "How did I not know this? Wait, Aaron?"

"Aaron is her husband," Dee says, like I'm dumb. "Anyway, I'm here because you and I have business to discuss. So hurry up and get *therapied* so we can get down to it. I'll wait."

"Leave." I glare at her.

"No."

I hate that I want her to stay. Keira must sense this because she moves on. "Have you given much thought to what you want to do about your family?"

"Too much thought, but never settle on anything. It might be pathetic, but I sometimes wish something would just happen without me having to give permission so that I can either feel good or bad about it after it's already done."

"It's not pathetic," Keira says. "It's displacement. Have you tried talking to Olivia?"

Not since she got locked up wherever the Carters are keeping her. "No. She was going to kill me. How do I talk to her after that?"

"I think you first need to decide if you want to," Keira says. "How are your panic attacks and PTSD episodes?"

I glance at Dee, but she's ignoring us in favour of her phone. "I'm getting better at managing them. At least, I think I am. Sometimes they start, but they don't fully develop. Other times, I surprise myself by not having one. And sometimes I still have a full-blown meltdown with my fingers in my mouth and all the itchies." I shrug. "Depends."

"And your sleep?"

"Fucked to exhaustion," Dee says for me. "Better than a sleeping pill."

She's not wrong, but I narrow my eyes at her anyway. "I feel safer when I sleep now. Because I trust the person in the house with me."

"Good. That's a huge improvement," Keira says. "You've learned to trust someone, maybe even more than one person." She doesn't let me correct that. "Are you thinking about how you're going to prepare for when Blake goes back to work? His job takes him away from home for days, sometimes weeks at a time."

My cheeks burn and my skin itches. A heaviness presses on my chest, and the cup of coffee in my hand trembles slightly. Blake leaving for work—for anything—is not something I'm ready for, but it's going to come whether I want it to or not. I know I have abandonment issues, but I thought they'd improve when I developed a level of trust with Blake. I know he's coming back to me. I know he isn't leaving me or our relationship every time he walks out the door, but I still feel like it's the end of the world whenever he walks away from me. I even sat on the counter and chatted his ear off while I painted my nails and he was in the shower this morning because being in a different room felt impossible. What the hell is wrong with me?

"We can work on some exercises for that," Keira offers. "Keeping yourself busy is one of them."

"I can do that," Dee says. "Since you're a brat and put ideas in my head about this business arrangement."

"See?" I tell Keira. "She knows I'm a brat."

"All too well, Mr. Fire Alarm."

Best grilled cheese sandwich I ever made.

I THINK IT'S THE lack of remorse on her face that wants me to just snap my fingers and have my beast murder her. Olivia isn't sorry; she's pissed off she got caught. The look in her eyes tells me she's looking for a way out of this, to get back to her plan, to take what she thinks she can from me without a single regard for my life.

Maybe she never gave a shit about me or my life. If I was dead, she'd have one less obstacle in her way to getting the Palmerston fortune. Maybe she fooled me all these years, pretending to look out for me, picking me up at clubs when I got the family into trouble, and compassionately scolding me while reminding me it was mostly my fault. I thought that was her being a sister—angry at my actions but still caring about me regardless of them.

"All new security systems at Dad's place and the gas plant," Brandt tells Bronson behind me.

Bronson doesn't answer, but he hasn't said much since a few hours ago when Brendan told him that the woman he's in love with accepted hush money to go away. Maybe I should offer him the task of killing Olivia just to ease his broken heart. Poor chap.

"What do you think?" Blake asks me as I stare at my former sister through a camera screen. "Want to talk to her?"

Not really, but I should. It might help me make a decision. I slip my hand into his and play with his fingers. "I need you to break it down for me, Blake. None of this 'whatever you want to do, we'll do' bullshit. I need options. Preferably only two options, but three if you must." Because I can't process something so open-ended. I need to narrow it down and think about what the actual outcome is going to be.

"Option one, we kill her and make it look like she died of natural causes. We have doctors on our payroll who can help with that, and it'll keep the heat off you."

I nod.

"Option two, you release her. But I'm warning you right now, Mercer, if she so much as looks at you wrong, I'll be implementing option one without your permission."

Another nod. I link my fingers with his.

"Option three, we create a set-up."

"What kind of set-up?"

Brandt comes to stand at my side. "There're a few ways we can do it, depending on which outcome you want. We can kill her and frame Will, essentially putting him behind bars for life. Kills two birds with one stone."

"Or we frame them both for white-collar crimes, ruin their reputations, strip them of everything they own, and set them back to the bottom of the totem pole. The government will seize everything in their names, though. Not sure if you're okay with that. They may or may not go to prison, depending on the case and their lawyers." Blake squeezes my hand.

"I already have more money and companies than I know what to do with, so I don't care what happens to theirs," I say. "So, murder, freedom, or prison. Those are my options?"

"Or freedom with nothing to their names," Brandt clarifies.

"Will tried to kill me multiple times." I start running through my choices. "And never with his own hands. He hired people to do it for him."

Blake's hand tightens around mine, thinking of his mom.

"I don't know if Olivia actively tried to kill me, but she would have killed me and Samantha if I didn't comply with her orders that day." Luckily, the Carter B team showed up before she could. "So, what do they deserve?"

And whatever choice I make for Olivia, the same fate will have to come to Julia or she'll nark on us.

"I vote bullet to the brain and a missing body," Bronson says, stepping up to Blake's side and adding another option to my growing list. "For her and Will."

Normally, I'd think that's his bitterness talking since his heart is hurting, but I know it's not. The Carter boys are trained to keep level heads, and nothing deters them from that during a job. Not even when I was missing; Blake kept his cool until he found me and completed the job.

"What's the blowback on that, though?" I ask. "If I'm the only remaining Palmerston, I'll look guilty. Especially because I now own so many of their assets."

"I vote reputational ruin," Brandt says. "Strip them of everything they are, ruin them, leave them with nothing and no allies, no money to pay high profile lawyers, and see how they make out. They might go to jail, but even if they don't, their lives will be over."

Blake nods, squeezing my hand. "That's my vote, too. You're more powerful than they are now, Mercer. It'll be a long and drawn-out case with a huge media following, but it gives you the chance to tell your story. We won't be able to prove Will murdered your birth parents, but we can prove his corruption and collusion."

"How though? He's always been squeaky clean."

"Because Aaron is a fucking boss," Bronson says. "When he digs, he finds what he's looking for. And I just met the guy. Been admiring his work for years without knowing it was him."

"That's why he's my idol." I smile. "What about Julia?"

"We can take her down with them. Or we prove she was an accessory to Trevor's murder. She's not getting out of this intact," Brandt says.

Olivia is pacing like a caged animal in the small room she's being kept in. If I set her free, no matter what happens, she'll come for me. But for the first time in my life, I think I'm prepared for that. I have more power. I'm stronger. And unlike her, I have a fucking family now. A murderous one.

"And now that I have Dee as my CEO and lawyer for the corporations, everything is protected from a single attack," I say, nodding. "I vote reputational ruin and possible prison time."

The door opens and closes behind us, Brendan walking in. "I think that's a great choice, Mercer." He steps up beside his sons. "It'll take us a few days to get everything in order, but it's also a great learning opportunity for you." He looks at me. "Brandt has an opening for his *man in the mic* position. You interested?"

I don't think I've ever smiled wider. "Yes, please. And you won't even have to call me Little Demon." I laugh at Brandt.

Blake bends down and laughs against my lips. "You're still my little demon, Mercer." He kisses me. "I'm so fucking proud of you. I told you I'd help you claw your way to the top, but guess what? You did it all on your fucking own, baby. I love you."

Holy, I love this man. "Thank you."

For seeing me and loving me anyway.

For not ignoring me.

For looking beneath my masks and understanding why I wear them.

"I love you with no buts, Blake Carter."

Bronson groans, not wanting to hear it while he shatters. Brendan stays silent. Brandt scoffs.

"I am not getting laid enough for this," he quips, heading for the door. "Think Aaron can handle a fuck buddy on top of his wife and boyfriend?"

Blake just gives him the finger and says, "Aaron is mine."

I pull back to glare at him. I thought it might be jealousy that eats me up, not wanting Blake to claim anyone but me, but it's not. It's jealousy because Aaron is mine. "Excuse me. I'm weaselling my way in with Aaron, so you can back off a bit, thanks."

Blake grabs my butt. "How's your ass feeling today, little boy?"

Ugh, he always wins. How the tables have turned.

33

Mercer

I ROLL MY EYES and squish my new company phone between my ear and shoulder, holding up a lavender shade of lace to my torso. It's a one-piece, but there are enough cut-outs that Blake can wedge his way in from anywhere.

"If I wanted to be on the phone with you at two in the morning talking business, I wouldn't have hired you to be me." Maybe I should try the black one. "With my complexion, should I wear lavender lace or a darker shade?"

"The media is breathing down our necks, Mercer. Marketing and media management are fielding calls, messages, emails, and even people showing up to get a statement. This is big news, and everyone wants to hear from you. A darker tone because you're pale. Lavender will wash you out. Go for navy or deep violet."

I drop the lavender and grab the black and navy sets I bought. My hands are shaking, but at this point, it might be nerves, excitement, or panic. Who knows? I've been shaking ever since Blake left six days ago.

"Can't you just handle the interviews?"

"I'm not a media rep, Mercer! They want you. It's your family scandal." Dee must be rolling her eyes at me by now, but I don't care.

I'm going with the navy. It matches the bruise I gave myself three days ago by sliding the driver's seat of the Denali too far forward and smacking my knees on the dashboard. "Okay, fine, but it isn't happening tomorrow."

"Yeah, yeah," she scoffs. "Have your day of sex and then call me the fuck back, okay?" She hangs up on me, even more of a brat than I am.

We still have to keep our hangouts to two hours or less. It's for safety reasons.

"It's more than just sex!" I shout into the phone, even though she's gone.

I drop my phone on the bed Blake hasn't slept in since he left, feeling sad without him. I might have called him 127 times since he's been gone, but he called me at least 42 times, so I call it even. With my undergarments picked, I debate what I'll wear over them.

My hoodlum look is still my preferred clothing choice when I'm around Blake. He made me comfortable right from the beginning, and he hasn't stopped since. I take one step towards the closet, ready to rake through all my hoodies even though we all know I'll wear one of his, when my phone rings again.

I sprint to it, hoping it's Blake. Diving onto the bed, my face falls when it's just Brandt.

"Hoodlum," I answer with my new code name since I joined his team.

"I need an address. Quick," he says, the sound of his vehicle filling the empty silence.

I hop off the bed and head to the living room where some of my new equipment is set up. I'm still training under Aaron, so I spend most of my time there, but I've got a little hacker's den started. I do a full spin in my chair and switch my phone to Bluetooth with my headset.

"For?"

Brandt rambles off a partial plate number, and a vehicle model and make.

Using my new skills and a bunch of programs Aaron helped me install, I jam all the information into my computer and wait for it to spit out an answer. While I'm doing that, I track Brandt to get eyes on where he is. And also while I'm doing that, I cross my legs because I have to pee like a motherfucker.

"Amy Daniels?" I ask.

"Sure. Address."

"15599, apartment 42, Westwick Ave. Security cameras at the front door, but don't seem to be anywhere else." I spot him on the map, taking a turn to switch directions. "Setting lights to green."

"Getting good, Hoodlum."

"I know." I pull up information on Amy Daniels, my eyes scanning it as fast as my brain will allow. "What're you doing going after a politician's daughter?"

"Trying to get laid," he snarks at me. "Since you're hogging Aaron."

"Not sorry." The clickety-clack sound of my keyboard settles something inside me. I swear it's better than white noise. So. Fucking. Satisfying. "She's not home," I tell Brandt. "Pinged that vehicle parked. She's at the Vixen in the West End."

"Well, she's about to be dead if we don't do something."

I pull up footage of the Vixen, a plush lounge for wealthy youngsters. Been there a time or two in my slutty days. The private rooms don't have cameras, but I'm able to tap into a few devices, running a facial recognition program for Amy. "Julia is there." I spot her on my screen.

"I know," Brandt says. "Guess who they're going after now?"

I laugh into the mic. "Blake is going to love this."

Amy Daniels is the daughter of a politician, but more important for tonight's shenanigans, she's the new CEO of Thomas Tech Inc, owned by Blake's client and Frank's wife. Guess Olivia and Julia found their next target.

"Want me to pull the fire alarm?" I ask.

"Nah, just get me in there and keep me off Julia's radar. I don't want them knowing we're onto them yet. We'll get Amy out, warn her, and then be on our way. Annabelle hired us again."

Guess she wasn't too pissed at Blake for refusing to kill her husband. Still hate that lady, though. I dug into her, and she's all sorts of bitchy.

I settle in for a bit of work, ready to get Brandt in and out of the Vixen Club without Olivia or Julia knowing any better. By the time I'm done, my eyes are straining but my body is wired. And Amy Daniels is safe with Brandt, so long as he doesn't try to get in her pants.

I hang the headset on the charging rack, rubbing my eyes and putting my monitors to sleep. It's almost four a.m., and Blake will be home in the morning. I hate sleeping in that bed without him, and my abandonment issues won't let me stop thinking about all the reasons he might not come back, so I pee and then settle on the couch with a blanket and Netflix.

I've had three panic attacks since he left, one full-blown meltdown, and an impromptu meeting with Keira where I got so desperate, I used my spare key and kind of interrupted them in bed. Aaron left with a bunch of complaints, and Keira, bless her therapist's heart, talked me through my anxiety. And then scolded me for taking advantage of our friendship. Guess I still have a lot to learn about boundaries.

My fingers have been in my mouth a lot, and I've cried more than I care to admit. The fear of him being gone hasn't gotten any easier to manage, but I've taken Keira's advice to find healthy ways to cope with it. Distraction being one of them, and an actual friend to talk to being the other. Fucking Dee became my friend, and I still don't know how I feel about it. She's also my business partner, so maybe that takes the edge off a bit.

She's been fielding reporters about the Palmerston case. Will lost pretty much everything, including his businesses and the licences to run them. He lost the house, his good standing with the Better Business Bureau, and his wife. Penny left his ass after she found out he tried to kill me. After she reached out to me to offer an apology, I almost forgave her, until she admitted to knowing a lot more than she ever let on. Obviously, she knew she wasn't my mother, but she *also* knew that Will was using me to obtain what Cheryl left to me in her final will and testament. I don't have any contact with Penny anymore, and to be honest, I don't even know what she's doing now.

But Will still had a good lawyer on his team. He managed to avoid prison time since most of his crimes were white-collar, and it was difficult to prove he acted individually. But at least he's a nobody now. Or, he is for the time being. He's currently trying to marry some old hag from Europe, preying on her because she knows nothing about him. She's a wealthy woman with no children and a dead husband. All the best to him. I'm done wasting my time worrying about him.

Samantha fucking sucks at running a hotel chain, but Dee helped her hire the right people to help manage it. She's currently learning to speak Mandarin, and we talk on the phone sometimes. We don't talk about family. Ever.

I ball up the sleeves of Blake's hoodie, barely noticing when the material ends up in my mouth. I miss him so much it's hard to focus on anything else, but I have been enjoying my training with Aaron and my partnership with Brandt. I just need my man home. I must doze in and out of sleep because I keep missing vital points in the movie I'm watching and the sky keeps getting lighter, but when my eyes shoot open at a sound, I barely feel rested at all.

Blake's keys jangle in the door, and then he's standing there and I'm sitting here, and we're staring, and I don't know if I should run to him pathetically because he already knows I'm pathetic, or if I should pretend I have some chill.

Relief floods me with such an overwhelming rush that I can't even stand up. My eyes water from happiness, and my smart-ass mouth won't even form a single word. Instead, I just stare at him and let the tears fall.

He didn't abandon me.

He closes the door and drops all his things, closing the distance between us. I reach for him at the same time he reaches for me, and then he's dragging my body over the back of the couch and I'm clinging to him like he's the only air I need.

"Fuck, I missed you, baby." He hugs me tight, kissing me everywhere he can.

I can't speak because I'm a blubbering idiot. The smell of him is so much stronger than this washed-out hoodie I've been wearing around the apartment for six days. I bury my face in his neck and breathe him in. It makes me cry more, but I don't care. He's here, and I survived it. He came back to me like he promised he would, and my fear of abandonment eases just the smallest fraction.

"Look at me, Mercer." He sits my ass on the back of the couch and grabs my cheeks, looking down at me. "Missed these eyes," he says, smiling. "Say something."

I kiss him instead, snot and tears and all. I kiss him until my eyes stop watering and the relief stops breaking me. When I'm calm, I rest my ear to his chest and listen to his heartbeat. I know he's been travelling all night, and I'm sure he's tired, but I can't let him go yet.

"Thanks for coming back," I whisper.

"I will always come back. I promise." He rubs my back. "Tell me what you need, Mercer."

I wipe my nose and look at him. Deep blue eyes and dark hair are my favourite combination. Sometimes, despite how cocky I am about it to Dee, I can't believe he's actually mine. "I need you to do that thing where you smother me with your body and touch me all over while I sleep."

"You mean cuddle?"

I scoff. "No."

Blake smiles, and I love it. Like, *love it*. No buts. We lock up and turn everything off, heading to the bedroom. When he climbs into bed and holds back the blanket for me, I tell him I have to pee first. I'm standing over the toilet taking a piss when Blake walks in.

I raise a brow at him.

"My turn to be clingy," he says, leaning against the vanity while I finish. "I'm not letting you out of my sight until I absolutely have to."

Oh, god. Here comes that fucking blush again. Am I swooning, too? Jesus. Do not get more weepy!

"I knew you were just as needy as me," I accuse, flushing the toilet and running my hands under the tap.

Blake crowds me from behind, pressing his dick to my ass. "So fucking needy, you don't even know the half of it, baby. I didn't even jerk off. Been saving it all for you."

I lick my lips and feel my cock stir to life. "Mm." I turn to face him, pretty much becoming down to fuck within six seconds flat.

Blake grips my jaw lightly, pressing his lips to mine. "But later, Mercer. After you've slept for at least four hours."

"You're such a cock tease."

"Hypocrite." He steers me back to bed, and I can't even describe how safe, comfortable, in love, and at home I feel pressed against his strong body with his arms caging me in.

"Can you at least put it in me?" I whisper into the darkness. "I prepped and everything, and I know we're too tired and weepy for sex, but I can keep your dick warm. It's really no trouble."

Blake's smile is felt against the back of my neck, and slowly, not in a rush at all, he nudges me into the right position, buries his dick in my pre-lubed ass, and then scolds me for getting hard and trying to grind on his cock.

"Thought it was no trouble?" he asks in a taunting tone. "I'm not fucking you until you sleep, you demon."

Yeah, we'll see about that. I'll never admit to him how good it feels to have him inside me. Connected. The reason I won't admit it is that he already knows without me having to say it.

"No buts, Blake," I whisper.

"Never any buts, Mercer."

Until he sees my new lingerie and the game I'm going to play with him. I grin as I fall asleep.

34 Blake

HE'S SOAKING THIS UP. For how nervous he was, especially with how much he bitched and moaned about doing it, he's enjoying the hell out of this spotlight.

A hundred cameras point at him, triple that many microphones and recording devices, and the flash of lights show off the twinkle of wanted attention in his whiskey eyes. A press conference daunted him so badly I'd had to physically dress him in that sexy suit while he rag-dolled and acted like a petulant child before dragging him here, but now that he's the centre of attention, he's rethinking his take.

"That boy was made for the spotlight," Bronson says, standing next to me.

The conference is being held on the front steps of the newly acquired headquarters for all of Mercer's owned companies. It's the central location for the business, but he barely spends any time in the building. Still can't believe he picked Dee to be his CEO. I also can't even believe she agreed to do it, but she's managed to unite all the COOs of the individual businesses and set a new standard. The sun beats down on Mercer, spotlighting him like he deserves, making all his words pop and his smile brighten.

"My spotlight," I tell Bronson. "Hate all these people looking at what's mine."

"You know, I truly never guessed you'd turn into a possessive dick. You were always so nonchalant and uninterested in people unless you were studying them for a job."

Mercer is like a job—the best job I've ever taken. To figure him out, peel back his layers, make him happy despite all the monsters in his closet, and to love him in a way he knows how to accept, and to protect him for the rest of his life. Every part of that boy is a puzzle. Even the easy-to-read, bratty, attention-seeking parts of him are hard to decipher because they change with his mood.

When I first saw him that night outside the strip club, I thought he had a problem with authority. Turns out, he had a problem with himself. He didn't want to follow orders because he didn't agree with the orders given, but he also used commands as a comfort method while he was in a panic attack. Commands that came from me—whether he trusted me then or my orders simply jarred him, I don't know, but he revels in that shit now.

"Love studying him," I tell Bronson, keeping my eyes on Mercer as he talks to the crowd.

News about Will, Mercer's birth parents, and the whole scandal with the Palmerston corporation has gone global, and everyone wanted to hear from the poor little boy who lost his parents, got kept in the dark and used for financial gain. Well, he's showing everyone that he's no longer that boy. He's no longer Ben Palmerston. He's Mercer fucking Bentley, the man who came out the other side and rose to the top because of his own strength and willpower. It's a sight to behold, and my dick is getting antsy about it.

"Well, watch out," Bronson teases. "Brandt already fucked your secret friend, and now he's working closely with Mercer."

"Brandt will die a slow and agonizing death if he even thinks about it." I fiddle with the pack of cigarettes in my jacket pocket, wanting one but not craving it badly enough to have one. "What's going on with Amy Daniels?"

"She's back home with security and surveillance," Bronson says. "She's Annabelle's new CEO of Thomas Tech Inc."

I shake my head at him. "I know."

Bronson laughs. "Well, shit. I didn't know. You've been in France for six days moving an entire underground gun business. Didn't know if you'd been briefed yet."

"Yeah, but Mercer calls me thirty-eight times a day and tells me everything from what colour his nails are to the jobs he's working on. In great detail. He told me about Amy Daniels yesterday morning."

"The nails are new," Bronson comments.

"I've learned he works in phases. They'll come and go." Not complaining, though. That sparkly purple polish wrapped around my dick was a nice sight. I've said it before, and I'll say it again: Mercer can wear no wrong. "Anyway, so Amy Daniels is covered? Brandt is on it?"

"Yeah, but Dad got a call from Annabelle Thomas last night. She thinks Frank has a hit out on her, so she wants us to kill him again. Dad's in negotiations."

"It's not Frank. It's Olivia Palmerston."

"Yeah," he agrees. "But Annabelle doesn't know that. Olivia is a dumb criminal."

"Why? She's probably got her lawyer girlfriend on the will to enable a division of company assets. Even if they don't get everything from Thomas Tech, they'll get enough money to get started just because of a falsified contract. Probably take that money and run, which would be best for us."

"Yeah, but she's already got the eyes of the law on her. So, what does she think she's going to do? Discreetly collect a lump sum of cash and assets, and then run off into the sunset to start a new life somewhere else?"

“Probably. She’s going after Amy because Amy has the power to divide assets.”

Bronson shakes his head. “Nah. Mercer looked over their company contracts. Everything, including CEO duties, requires Annabelle’s signature. Olivia is going after a false lead just because she thinks Thomas Tech is weak from Frank’s former information leak. She’s going to get burned, and *that* is the best thing for us. She’ll be blacklisted or imprisoned when she gets caught, and trust me, she will.”

We can hope. “Well, either way, we’ll keep an eye on all of it.” I pull my hand out of my pocket and away from the cigarettes. “See you tomorrow night?”

“Yeah.”

Mercer is just wrapping up his Q&A, so I head to the side of the steps to wait for him. Being Mercer, he drags it out as long as he can, soaking up all that attention and making me fucking feral to get him alone. I want him to shine, but fuck, he’s mine. For my eyes only. When he finally says goodbye to the gathered crowd of reporters, journalists, media crews, and the general public, I take his hand and lead him to the underground parking garage where I parked. By the time we get to the Denali, he’s shaking.

“What’s wrong, baby?” I grip his chin and force his eyes to mine. “Why are you shaking?”

He grabs at my jacket, afraid I’ll disappear. His hands tremble and his eyes are shifty, unsure of where to focus. His breathing picks up, and his mouth opens and closes without anything coming from it.

“Good attention is overwhelming too, right?”

He lets out a desperate sigh. “Yes.”

He’s crashing from the adrenaline of that conference, realizing that good feelings can be as triggering as negative ones. He’s not used to being in the spotlight, and the crash is already starting. I shove him into the passenger seat and feel my heart break when he begs me not to go. But I have to. I close his door and run to mine, getting in so he doesn’t have to miss me for more than a few seconds. By the time I close my door, Mercer has his fingers in his mouth, and his other hand is latched onto my sleeve, tethering himself to me. Someday we will conquer his fear of abandonment, but today isn't that day. Baby steps.

Keira told me to make him voice what he needs. I've been trying that method, and sometimes he answers, but most times he doesn't. "What do you need, Mercer? Anything. I'll give you anything." I push his dark hair off his forehead and pull his fingers from his mouth.

"I don't even know what's wrong with… I'm… why am I scared?" His eyes water.

"Because you just did something new and brave, and it's overwhelming. I'm so fucking proud of you, baby."

"I should be happy!" he shouts, frustrated with himself. "I liked it up there!"

"You are happy," I tell him. "But you're processing now. Sometimes that hurts."

"God," he scoffs. "How fucking long am I going to be like this, Blake? What would all those people think if they knew the owner of Bentley Inc. was a fucking pathetic mess?" He scratches at his sleeves. "How long am I going to have the emotional maturity of a fucking six-year-old?"

He has a wide range of emotional maturity, but I get where he's coming from. He can't cope with overwhelming feelings, good or bad, and his fears eat him alive. The only coping methods he has are ones he learned as a child—crying, thumb sucking that has turned into finger sucking, an overreaction to the situation, and the need for comfort. But he also has a task-oriented mind. Right now, he's spiralling into self-loathing and oncoming panic; he needs something to jar him from that.

"Tell me what you need, Mercer." I know what he needs, but he needs to know it, too.

His amber eyes glisten with angry tears when he looks at me. His lips are slick with spit and his cheeks are red, and I've never seen a more attractive mess. "Take my brain power away, Blake."

Jar him from his panic. That's what he's asking. Last time, I let him hold my dick in his mouth. This time, I'm going to force him to get aroused.

Aggressively, I bend him over my lap. With no politeness, I push his face against my groin, smothering him in the fabric of my pants. He gasps and his hands land on my thighs for balance, but I don't let up. My cock hardens beneath his face, and all on his own, he mouths it through the material. I relax my hold on his head, letting him pull back just enough to get his hands on my fly.

I love Mercer, and I never want to hurt him, but I fucking love that he can take rough play. He's not breakable, and he'd hate me for treating him like he is.

He's whimpering in desperation, his fingers fumbling with my buttons because he's so rushed. I push my seat back, giving him a bit more room, anticipation already coiling in my stomach. When he pulls my cock free, sliding his hand down the shaft, I don't give him time to decide what to do. I push on the back of his head and force myself down his throat.

My eyes close in bliss and Mercer gags around me. I hold him there, suffocating the panic from his mind and effectively killing it for the time being. When he strains, needing to breathe, I let him up. And then I grab both sides of his head and fuck his throat like I own it.

The squelching sounds from his throat and the slurping of his lips around my dick fill the vehicle with the best music. Mercer's neck muscles are strained, and his polished fingertips dig into my thighs, but when I look over at his body, he's rubbing his legs together. He fucking loves this.

"If I move my hands, can I trust you to be a good little boy and keep sucking my cock like this?"

He nods on my dick, whimpering.

I let go of his face, letting him work on his own. He deepthroats me, burying his nose to my pubic bone. My hips buck on their own, seeking more of the man I love. Fuck, he's got a mouth on him. My body heats and my stomach coils, desperate to fill his stomach full of cum already.

I grab the back of his suit jacket and pull it so he's on his knees on the passenger seat, leaning over the centre console. Reaching my hand to the front of him, I rub his hard cock through his pants, making him moan around me.

"You're slacking, Mercer. Suck me harder."

He pops off my dick to mouth off, but before he can, I shove him back down and give my hips a few hard thrusts.

"You need to get off, baby?" I rub his dick.

"Mm," he hums his answer.

"I fucking hate this suit compared to your last one," I say, giving his dick a smack. He cries out, but his hips jut forward, seeking more. "I want you to ruin it. Coat it in cum and sit in your mess until we get home."

I push on the back of his head, choking him at the same time as I tap his cock again. He humps the air, sliding his thighs together.

"Such a greedy little boy," I taunt him. "Earn my cum before you fill these panties full of your own." I know they're the red ones he wore before, and I'd love nothing more than to see them darkened with wetness.

His head overpowers my hand, and he pulls up. Saliva drips from his open lips to coat my groin, and holy fuck, he's sexy like this. Fucking lethal and turned on, fighting a battle with me while losing and winning simultaneously.

"Got something to say, brat?"

He narrows his angry eyes at me, not even bothering to lick the mess off his lips. "I hate your suit more," he seethes.

And then he takes charge. Mercer has always been this way. He craves the fight to submission, but today, after everything he's gone through, he isn't willing to submit. He leans back on his knees in the passenger seat, undoing his pants.

"I told you to ruin those," I warn him against taking them off.

"I will, asshole," he snaps, tugging them down to just below his ass. He leaves the front pulled up over his dick, making sure he comes inside them. "Lean back."

Fumbling because his pants are loose, he climbs onto my lap with his back to me. "Mercer," I warn. "I won't fuck you dry without prep."

He leans over the steering wheel and puts his ass right in my face. "Better get me wet then."

I spit on his hole and tongue fuck it into his ass. I lick down to his balls and taint, soaking him with saliva before shoving my tongue inside him again.

"Spit," he demands. I spit. "More." I spit again, watching it drip down his crack to coat his hole. When I try to push it inside him with my finger, he stops me. "No. Just fuck me."

The conviction in his voice has me grabbing his hips and pulling him back on my slick dick. I nudge him, breaking through his tight, clenching hole. "Cock in your pants, baby?"

"Yes," he growls. Hot damn.

"Good. You're a filthy brat who deserves to sit in his own mess." I pull him down on my cock, easing into him faster than I should.

Mercer moans and cries out, but he doesn't stop. He sinks down until I'm buried inside him and then wiggles around to adjust. "And you're a fucking savage who fucks little boys in busy parking lots."

"Mm," I agree. "Better start moving, little demon. Wouldn't want the crowd to catch their new favourite businessman getting a punishment fuck in the front seat of such a normal vehicle, as you called it."

"Disgraceful," he says.

I snap my hips up, fucking into him deep and hard. He falls against the steering wheel. “Hold on and plant your feet on the floor, Mercer.”

He hovers just above me, feet on the floor and hands on the steering wheel. I grab his hips and fuck him from the bottom. My hips snap upward, my cock sinking deep inside him at a fast pace. When my rhythm becomes predictable, he slams his ass back to meet every thrust. The Denali rocks and the windows fog as we both pant and groan.

“Harder,” he demands.

I press my back into the seat and use the leverage to fuck him harder. “So fucking needy.”

“More,” he cries out, ready to come.

I sweat with the effort, but fuck me is it worth it. My thighs hit his ass cheeks and spit and precum lube his ass with every goddamn thrust of my hips. I fuck him until his groans turn to desperate moans, and when he clamps down on me, I tilt my hips to hit his prostate.

“Fuck!” he cries out, coming in his pants.

I’m seconds behind him, trying my hardest to keep thrusting through his orgasm, but my own makes my movements stutter, burying my load deep in his ass.

“Ah, fuck, Mercer,” I groan against his back. “Fuck, your ass is so goddamn perfect.” I pull him down to sit on my dick, twitching inside him as the pleasure extends. “Show me your mess.”

I look over his shoulder as he opens his pants to show me red panties and his black dress pants slicked with cum. I reach around and run my hand down the length of him, spreading the mess around. He moans at the touch, head falling back to my shoulder.

“Got another one in ya, baby?”

“No,” he says, but his hips are thrusting a little, pushing his dick through my fist. “Maybe.”

I’ve never met a guy who can come so many times, and I swear to fuck it is my newest fetish. I jerk him off slowly, kissing his neck, and rocking my hips to add a little pleasure from the back.

“My filthy little demon,” I whisper against his skin.

“Yes,” he moans.

“Tell me you’re mine, Mercer.” I tighten my grip just a little, spreading cum up and down his length with my cock still buried in his ass.

“I’m yours,” he breathes, rocking in my lap. “I’m yours, Blake.”

“My greedy little cumslut?”

“Yes.”

“My bratty boy?”

“Mm, yes.”

My dick hardens inside him, making him whimper. I thrust into him gently, pushing up until his cock slides through my hand, and pulling down to circle my thumb over the tip.

“Blake,” he whines. “Can I come?”

“Come, Mercer.” I lightly clamp my teeth onto the side of his neck as he trembles, coming again.

“Mmmmmm.” His head presses against my shoulder, his ass milks my dick, and his cock spurts and throbs in my hand, most of it ending up in his pants again.

So sexy. Holy shit, he’s everything. When he collapses on my lap, I slide my fingers through his mess and shove them into his mouth, making him suck them clean.

“That take your brain power away?”

“Yes,” he whispers. “Still kind of bummed that I didn’t get to taste your cum.”

“You can keep my cock warm on the way home, and I’ll be ready to fill your mouth when we get there.” I kiss his neck. “Love you, Mercer.”

“No buts.” He turns to face me, planting a kiss to my lips.

I make him pull up his pants, mess and all, and when he gets back to his seat, he leans over and puts my semi-hard cock into his mouth, just like I told him to. Submissive after all. I grin.

35

Mercer

OH, HE'S PISSED, AND I love it!

Nothing beats that sinister look in his eyes. When he sears me with all the heat of the sun, eye-fucking me with rapt attention, and loving me even though I'm purposefully baiting him, it shows just how right we are for each other.

"We aren't going," he says with determination, pulling his phone from his pocket to call his dad.

"Oh, we're going," I tell him, snatching the phone from his grip.

"Mercer," he warns. "We're staying home. You can't flaunt that in front of me and not expect me to react to it."

"Oh, I was counting on your reaction." I grin, doing a full circle so he can see the navy set I picked out. It hugs my ass, showing a lot of cheek, but frames it perfectly. The lace sits firmly against my skin, trailing up my hips to disappear into cut-outs around my middle. The top rests nicely over my chest, going up around my throat like a collar, similar to the purple one he ruined. Dee was right when she suggested the darker tone. Plus, the navy makes my golden eyes stand out. Didn't even need eyeliner.

"What reaction were you hoping for?" he asks, standing in the bedroom with a hard dick and nothing to stick it in. "Blind rage? Because if you make me sit through a family dinner with a boner, that's all you'll get, little demon."

I strut up to him, pushing my hands under his shirt to fondle his abs. "I'm taking a lesson out of your textbook."

His teeth clench. "What lesson?"

"Remember all those times you tried to teach me delayed gratification?" I smirk at him. "It's your turn to learn."

"I don't need to learn that lesson. I'm pretty fucking familiar with it, Mercer."

"Oh?" I muse. "Just like you don't have to get therapy for your trauma, but I do?"

"What trauma?"

"Your mom was murdered, too, Blake Carter! How come I'm the only one who has to get therapy?" I widen my eyes at him. "So, since you snuck your way out of that one, I'm teaching you this one. Delayed gratification is the theme of the night." I tip up on my toes to kiss his lips. "Still no buts?"

"Mm." He grips my chin. "You'll pay for this later, baby."

Oh, I'm counting on it.

Just to be a dirty tease, I bend over right in front of him, pull the lace aside, and show him the diamond end of the snug little plug shoved up there.

He growls.

EVERYONE IS STARING AT Blake, and it's hilarious. His cheeks are flushed all to hell, and he hasn't said more than six words since we got here. Three of those were my name in a warning tone. We're eating dessert, and Blake has tried to leave twice already, but I just keep on chatting.

"Yeah, so Brandt calls me in the middle of the night, tells me he's a bit tied up, and I thought he needed an escape route. Turns out, he was literally tied up, and Blake got jelly when I had to go rescue him naked with a still-hard dick."

Everyone laughs, even Brandt, but Blake squeezes my thigh under the table. His blue eyes have warnings in them, and I know I'm pushing it. My middle name should be *pushing it.*

"What's your problem?" Brandt asks Blake.

"Nothing."

"Nothing?" I question. "Share with the fam, Blakey. Get it all out."

He glares at me, but he takes my bait and throws it back in my face. "Okay. My problem is that Mercer is wearing something I want to rip off under this hoodlum look. My biggest problem is that there is a plug in the ass that belongs to my dick. My problem, *fam*, is that every second that plug sits there and I don't get to pull it out and replace it with my cock, the higher the chances are Mercer won't fucking survive my wrath. Happy, baby?"

Delightfully so.

Everyone else coughs, chokes, holds back laughter, or some combination of all three, but I pretend like it didn't affect me. "So, anyway, we untied him and—Hey! Blake!"

The room tips upside down as my ass goes in the air and my head hangs down Blake's back. I listen to his family mock him, but the firm crack of his palm against my ass has my dick hard and that plug shifting. The door to a bedroom opens and closes, and Blake throws me on the bed.

Bouncing to face him, I laugh. "What happened to you? You used to be so calm and cucumbery. None of my shit ever got to you."

"I fell in love with you," he says with no fuss.

"What's wrong?"

"Mercer, this is going to be fucking quick. I suck at delayed gratification, okay? I just need to fuck you and I need to do it right now. You can draw it out and play games later. Please, baby, just let me fuck you." His eyes beg, and I pause my game.

Okay, hold up. He actually looks on edge. Something is grating on him, and I don't know if it's just edging and sex games, or if something else is going on.

"Blake?"

He tugs my sweatpants down to my ankles, lifts me up, and plants me on my feet. "Nothing is wrong. I just fucking need you, Mercer."

I nod my permission, understanding how that feels. He kisses me quickly, and then turns me around and bends me over. My hands land on the bed and his hand cracks against my ass again. The sting is fiercer now that my sweatpants are gone.

He moves the lacy material aside, his fingers gripping the end of the butt plug. "I'm going insane, Mercer. You in this outfit... with this plug... I just..." He slowly works the plug free. "Can I fuck you hard and fast, baby?"

My cock leaks at the question. "Yes. Fuck yes."

Lube from the plug drips from my ass, and I hear Blake spit on his cock. The next second, I'm being rammed forward as he buries himself to the root inside me. Oh, fuck yeah. Love him desperate.

Blake lets out a strained moan, and then he really does fuck me hard and fast. I plant my hands and let him grip my hips, panting with each hard thrust. It doesn't take long for my back to arch and my cock to drip steadily. He squeezes my hips, spreads my cheeks, smacks my ass, and breathes hard through all of it.

"Fuck, baby. I'm already there." He fucks me harder. "I'm gonna fill your ass and put the plug back in."

Oh, god. "Mmm. Yes."

With another smack, I lose my composure and prove to myself that I suck at delayed gratification, too. My cock ruts against the bed, and in seconds, I'm coming through the lace outfit, coating my dick. Blake groans out his release, burying himself deep and throbbing inside me. He moans my name, bruises my hips, and fucks into me until I fall forward and he lands on top of me.

"I'm sorry," he pants against my neck. "I fucking needed that. I've never been that desperate before."

"I kind of love you like that." I laugh. "Please get desperate and grumpy more often."

He runs his hands up my sides, pushing my hoodie up. "Do you even know how insane you make me, Mercer? Like fucking hell. This lingerie is everything, and you look hot as fuck in it, but it's more than that. It's just you. I need you." He kisses my neck, and I'm blushing again. "I fucking love you, baby."

"I love you, too." I smile widely, not even embarrassed about it.

Blake pulls me up, really does put the plug back in, and then throws a blanket over the cum stain on the bed like it never happened.

BLAKE IS ASLEEP, AND I'm staring at him like a creep. Our bedroom is mostly dark, and his breathing is very relaxing, but I've got things on my mind, and I like watching him when he doesn't know it.

"Blake?" I whisper.

He hums in his sleep, his hand seeking my waist under the blanket.

"It's not just sex for me," I tell him, knowing he probably can't hear me. "I know I use sex as a coping method, and I love our sex life, but... it's you. You're the only person who ever made me feel safe."

My maturity knows I should tell him this while he's awake, but I need a practice run, so this will have to be it.

I admire the stubble on his face. "I just wanted to thank you. For seeing me for who I am, even if I didn't always know my own identity. For naming me Mercer and making me love it." I place my hand on his cheek. "For seeing all my broken parts and still deeming me worthy."

Blake saved me. I don't even know if he realized he was doing it at the time, but when he practically kidnapped me from the engagement party, he saved me from enduring the facility, Will's hatred, and the future of being nothing more than a tool until my early death. Blake brought me into his home, made me feel safe there, and worked to understand my actions.

He didn't get mad at me for acting out. He didn't reprimand me for being juvenile. He saw me as a brat, and even then, he didn't try to tame me. Instead, he encouraged me, and I know that it's his influence that brought this new person to life. He didn't give me all the answers to take all the credit. No, he reminded me I'm worth something, proved it to me through his actions, and gave me the confidence boost I needed to get there on my own.

"Thank you for believing in me, Blake," I whisper, feeling warm. I lean forward to press my lips to his forehead. "Thank you for loving me, even when I didn't know what it meant." I kiss his hair softly.

Blake's arms wrap around my back and he holds me close. "Thanks for loving me back, little demon."

It's on the tip of my tongue to reprimand him while I'm trying to be sneaky. Instead, I hug him back, snuggle in close, and send up a bunch of gratitude to whoever listens, thanking them for this life, and for giving me Blake Carter.

36

Blake

THREE MONTHS LATER

Mercer is out of his nail polish phase and into his hat phase. He didn't even warn me about it. I got back from eleven days away on a job, walked into the apartment, and found him in a loose tank with big armholes, a small pair of shorts, and a summery, beachy-style fedora. His surfer boy look is hot as fuck, and I am absolutely hoping it hangs on for the rest of the summer.

Currently shirtless and in a pair of purple swim shorts and the fedora, he gives me a saucy look before continuing to chop vegetables for a salad.

"Stop giving me that nervous look," he scoffs at me. "My kitchen knife skills are on point these days, remember? The maturity thing?"

Oh, I remember. He gets mad at himself for reacting like a child, so on top of his beach look, he's been working on being a proper homeowner. Yeah, homeowner, because we put his name on the mortgage so we could be common law and own an asset together.

"It's not the knife I'm worried about, baby. It's whatever you're cooking. You sure you aren't making another batch of nothing to get my attention?"

He smiles, a free and easy one that looks incredible on his face. Tossing the chopped peppers into the salad bowl, he says, "I don't need to bake batches of nothing to get your attention anymore."

"No?" Maybe I need to pretend to ignore him a bit more just to make him try harder. But I promised him I never would, and I won't break that promise.

"Nope. You're addicted to me."

Fucking right I am. Those eleven days away were hell, and I talked to my dad about keeping my jobs closer to home for a bit. Mercer is busy as hell with his 'man behind the mic' business these days, plus he reluctantly agreed to bi-monthly work meetings with Dee.

"Am I, now?" I get off the stool and crowd him from behind, caging him in my arms. "You my drug, Mercer?" I kiss his neck and make him laugh.

He spins in my arms, still wielding that kitchen knife. "The only one you'll ever do," he says confidently. "And since you stopped smoking, I'm your stress reliever, your vice, your bad little habit, and your boyfriend."

"And my little cumslut. So many titles to fill," I tease, kissing his smile. "They seem to make you happy."

"Mostly." He drops the knife and runs his hands up my abs and chest.

"Just mostly?"

"Mm."

I pick him up and sit his ass on the counter, knocking his hat off to look at his eyes. "Tell me how to make you happier."

"You'll figure it out." He licks his lips.

"More cum?" I slide my hands up his thighs.

"I'll never say no to that, but you're satisfactory in that department."

"You want me to be home more?"

"Always, but I understand your job. Even if it gives me panic attacks and makes me pathetic."

"You're improving, though. So. Fucking. Proud." I kiss him between each word.

"Keep guessing," he says against my lips, still smiling.

"Are you back on the fish tank thing? Because you can get one, but I'm telling you, they're more work than just putting food in the top and watching them eat."

"I'm over that. I learned they poop and cloud up the water."

Sounds about right. I try to think back on our conversations since we moved in here. He's never mentioned anything about being unhappy unless it's to do with me leaving for work. Or bitching about therapy. Or Dee. Or Keira. Or the thermostat. We settled on his demand because mine was too cold for him to wear shorts in the house. We also don't share a bathroom anymore. He keeps all his skincare products and occasional makeup purchases in the one attached to the bedroom, and I keep my toothbrush in the other one.

The oven timer beeps. "Oh, guess you ran out of time." He kisses me before hopping off the counter.

I peek to see what he made, thinking it'll be some elaborate meal because he's been watching cooking shows. I lift a brow at it in question.

"What?" he scoffs. "I'm getting there!"

"Fries?"

"Yeah, but I cut them from *actual*, full-grown potatoes I bought at a *real* grocery store, and then blanched them in water before putting them in the oven, Blake! And I even put oil and salt on them!" he screams at me, defending his cooking. "Shit, I forgot to put in the chicken tenders."

To his credit, the fries actually look nice and crispy, despite how uneven and mismatched in size they are. He sets the tray on the stovetop and heads for the freezer to get the chicken tenders. I grab his wrist and bring him back to where he was between me and the island.

"Fries and salad are enough, baby. They look really good."

He blushes a little. Even his chest is flushed. "I know."

"Tell me what will make you hap—"

The Brandt line rings through the apartment, blocking my question. Mercer presses a button on his tablet, connecting the call to a speaker device.

"Hoodlum!"

"Turn on the news!" Brandt shouts, but he's kind of laughing. "Blake with you?"

"Here," I tell Brandt, clicking the news on the TV.

"Don't call my hoodlum line for fun calls, Brantley!" Mercer rolls his eyes.

"Don't call me Brantley when it's not even my name, Mercer Bentley."

The news finally clicks on at the same time my dad calls, joining Brandt's line, and Bronson is a second behind.

"*Annabelle Thomas, owner and founder of Thomas Tech Inc., has just been rushed to hospital with life-threatening injuries.*"

I look at Mercer as the reporter speaks. He shrugs, slipping into my arms in front of me.

"*Annabelle was attacked in her own home, according to police. Two perpetrators, Julia Hentz and Olivia Palmerston, were caught on the live footage from a tech device created and patented by Annabelle and Thomas Tech Inc. The device might just have saved her life, but it certainly did not save Mrs. Hentz and Ms. Palmerston.*"

The screen cuts to Julia and Olivia being cuffed and pushed into the back of an unmarked police SUV.

"*Charges are still being laid, but the big one will depend on Annabelle's recovery.*" If she dies in the hospital, it'll be murder. If she doesn't, it'll be attempted murder with whatever else they're being charged with.

"Fortunately, Annabelle's two daughters were staying with their father, Frank, when the incident occurred."

Mercer looks at me with a smirk. "Guess you and your moral compass saved those kids after all."

"Will Palmerston, Olivia's father and the man involved with the Palmerston-Bentley case, has not replied to police contact for questioning. He doesn't seem to be in the city anymore."

He's not. He's in Romania, and he is doing well there. Unfortunately.

"This is Sheri Jones, reporting live. We'll be back with more updates."

"Did that really just happen?" Bronson laughs through the speaker. "Did Olivia and Julia just solve our Olivia and Julia problem by being dumb as fuck?"

Things really do come full circle. Annabelle created the device that ended up incriminating Olivia. I didn't kill Frank when she asked me to, which ended up saving his daughters. Mercer didn't buckle under Olivia's threats, and instead ruined her reputation, which made her desperate enough to kill Annabelle.

"I just got word from the hospital," Dad says. "And a lawyer."

"What'd they say?" Mercer asks, turning his back on the TV to wrap his arms around me instead.

"Annabelle died on the way to the hospital. Julia and Olivia tried to enact a new will agreement, but it didn't stand. Guess what?" Dad laughs.

I see the whole fucking picture, and I can't help but laugh, too. "She never changed her will and now everything goes to Frank and the girls."

Fucking hell, things really did come full circle.

We share a few laughs about that, and then everyone hangs up, and Brandt sets a meeting with Amy Daniels to talk about her future with Thomas Tech.

"This is how you can make me happier, Blake." Mercer's chin rests on my chest, his big amber eyes looking up at me.

"How?"

He just smiles at me, waiting for me to figure it out on my own. Now that my mind is working right, I see his big picture, too.

He lost his birth name and became Ben. I renamed him Mercer.

Everything bad in his life has been because of his last name. I can rename him again.

I lick my lips and grin at my little demon. "You telling me you wanna become Mercer Bentley Carter?"

"Mm," he hums, grinning.

"Mm."

37

Mercer

epilogue

"IS THIS 'EURO-BOY CHIC' enough?" I ask Dee, holding up a man-purse while wearing white trousers and a white and beige lined button-down. Most of the buttons are undone to show off my non-buff chest like all the other boys I've seen walking around the Amalfi Coast.

"Yes, but it's a thousand degrees and you already sweat under pressure. Swap the pants for shorts." She flings shorts at me, hitting me in the face with them. "And hurry up. I didn't fly all the way here to watch you play dress-up."

I don't even watch her leave the hotel suite. *Good riddance, whore.*

She has a damn point, though. I switch out the white pants for white shorts, slip my feet into deck shoes, and debate a fedora. I mean, my hat phase ended when summer did, and I got sick of picking them up off the floor after Blake got handsy. But they are nice for hiding sweat, even though they make me sweat even more.

Gah! I love and hate Italy! So many new fashion options, and I'm buckling under the pressure.

"Mercer!" Blake shouts from the bathroom, steam billowing out of the propped open door. "Did you steal my razors?"

Sure as shit did. I threw them out with the room service trays last night. I like him with scruff, so fuck him for wanting to shave it all off. "No!"

"Mercer Bentley," he says in his stern voice.

I look over with my innocent eyes, blinking at all the water dripping down his chest and the lack of a towel around his naked hips. Mmm. Two days and he'll be legally mine, and then he can never escape me.

"Yes, darling?" He tried all my nicknames, so now I'm trying out a few to find one that fits him. Haven't found the winner yet.

"Where are my razors? I packed ten of them and all I can find is this." He holds up an electric trimmer that certainly does not shave down to the skin. I purposefully left that one as a compromise, since I'm mature now.

"You probably forgot them like you forgot your phone."

"You stole my phone, you fucking demon."

Sure as shit did. I threw it on the apartment floor right as we were walking out the door. He's been attached to that thing, researching our wedding venue, being a groomzilla, and taking odd jobs to keep himself sane, and I wanted all his attention on me and only me for this trip. Honestly, by now, he should have expected it.

I blink at him again. "You didn't even compliment my outfit." I pout. "See? My nails are '*seazy breezy*.'" I waggle my blunt ocean-blue nails at him.

His dick takes notice, at least.

And I take notice of it, licking my lips to get him off the razor hunt.

"Don't, you little demon," he warns me. "We have to be out there in ten minutes."

"It's *our* dinner. We can be late if we want to." I drop the man-purse and sway my hips on my way over to him. Blake watches me like I'm going to detonate or something equally as destructive, so I trail a blue nail from his chin to his cock. "Mm."

"Mercer."

I wrap my fingers around his dick and feel it harden fully against my palm. "Yes, fiancé?"

But I don't give him enough brain space to answer. I run my fist over the length of him, watching his eyes the whole time. Blake's chest inflates, and before he lets his breath out, he has an internal debate about time management and being late to dinners. On the exhale, he reaches forward to grab my chin.

"You threw them out, didn't you?"

I pump my fist and bat my lashes. "I would *never*."

"You manipulated your way into making me look how you want me to look." His hips buck, fucking my fist now.

"You always look sexy."

"You made me leave my phone behind." His cock drags through my loose fist. "You threw out my razors." He squeezes my chin harder, and now my dick is hard behind the fabric of these white shorts. "You lie and you manipulate; you think you can get one over on me?"

I circle my fingers around the head of his cock and jerk him off with purpose. Just to make him shut up.

He groans. Or moans. Or sighs in agony. So conflicting. "And now you're making us late for dinner."

"If you'd just admit defeat and let yourself come, we wouldn't have to be late." I smile at him. My charming one.

"You think you get to win all the time, Mercer?" he rasps at me, the tone of his voice not sounding nearly as threatening as he means it to be.

Aww. Such a fluffy unicorn.

"Yes," I state. With one more smirk, I drop to my knees, stroke just below the head of his dick, lick the slit, and suction my lips around him.

So. Fucking. Predictable.

Blake grips the doorframe, buckles forward, fills my mouth with cum, and curses me and '*seazy breezy*' nail polish.

I swallow his load and stand, gripping his chin this time. "You're so easy to beat these days, Blake Carter. Might have to start looking for a new man to marry in two days."

He swats my ass, but I'm already running and giggling and grabbing my man-purse. "Get dressed, heathen! We're late!"

DINNER IS BORING BECAUSE, even without his phone, Blake is being a wedding details monster. He's talking to Dee across the table—because like fuck will I let them sit side by side—going on and on about the location and the weather, double and triple checking that no one but our family will be there.

So, I tune that shit out and focus my attention on Aaron and the Carter boys.

"So, like I was saying, Brantley, it would benefit me immensely to get some field experience. Let me go on a quick murder here, a small gang war there, and it'll really up my *man in the mic* training. What do you think?"

"No," Blake says, finally surfacing from wedding talk.

"You don't own me."

"I will in two days."

I roll my eyes at him. "How very old-school caveman of you." I turn my back to the love of my life, just because I can and I know it'll get me spanked later, and face his bestie. "What do you say, A team? Let me get in on the action."

"You can't even shoot a gun." Aaron serves himself more wine. He never gets to be drunk because he's pretty much always on the clock or needs to be available, so he's taking advantage.

"I have daggers, Aaron!"

"In those white shorts?" he scoffs. "Or are they in your purse?"

Everyone laughs, probably at me and my purse, so I open the zipper and whip out a dagger. "Yes, actually. Now, can we go murder someone?"

"You realize this is our wedding trip, right?"

I spin around to face my soon-to-be hubby. "Oh, *what*? Like your constant wedding talk, incessant need to dictate the venue, and creepy Pinterest boards weren't indicative enough, Blake." I hit him with another eye roll. "Please."

Blake grabs my chair, spins it, and forces me to face him. I'm not even mad about it because he's paying angry attention to me instead of Dee.

"Once I marry your ass, Mercer Bentley, you'll be a Carter." His voice is all sex and dominance and possession and it's giving me chills.

"Yeah, but I'm always gonna be your little demon." I smile sweetly, and that's when Blake remembers that I'm holding a dagger. I press it to the white linen of his fancy shirt that honestly looks so hot on him, turning my smile into a wicked smirk. "Take me on a field trip."

"Are you so bored with life?"

No, *but I want to understand you!* "I'm greedy. You know this."

"Okay," Brendan cuts into our stare down and Blake takes the opportunity to disarm me. "Can we have a nice family engagement meal?"

Yeah, we only got engaged like six days ago, and my needy ass demanded a wedding right away. I seriously had no idea how realistically Blake would take that. It was a chore getting the Carter boys, Dee, Aaron and Keira, and Samantha here on such short notice, but we got it done.

As excited as I am to make myself a Carter and tether my life to the murderer of my dreams, I'm itchy for a whole new reason. It's not panic this time. It's a gnawing, irritating, increasingly demanding sense of… vengeance. No matter how hard I try to kick everything that happened to me, I can't let it go. I can't move on with my life because William fucking Palmerston got off too easily.

I've never been a vengeful person before. I killed a guy, claimed my one-time-murderer fame, got to be the man in the mic, ruined the Palmerston family and the reputation they had, and got to watch my bitchy non-sister get locked up for life in a separate prison from her bitchy girlfriend. It's a lot. It's enough.

It *should* be enough.

But I'm Blake's little demon, and this demon is turning devilish. I want to sic my hound on my former father, and give the command for him to be ripped apart. I don't think I'll maniacally laugh while Blake ups his murder count, but I might smirk a little bit. Just a tad. Like one of those satisfied, sinister little grins that nobody else notices. Yet everyone will notice because I'll do it with the intention of it being seen because that's just who I am.

"Let's toast," Bronson says. "To Blake finally finding the needy little bastard of his dreams."

I can toast to that. I lift my wine glass, smile at my new family, and let them celebrate me.

"I have an idea for a wedding present, Mercer," Blake whispers in my ear.

"Mm?" I lean into him.

"Fancy a trip to Romania?" he asks.

My skin prickles in anticipation and my eyes shift to his. A trip to Romania. Where Will lives. Oh, Blake Carter, I knew you were perfect.

"On one condition," Blake goes on before I have time to properly practice my sinister smirk. "You're an observer. Bark all the commands you want, but my hands will be the ones doing the killing."

Brandt, who is an eavesdropper extraordinaire, scoffs. "Really? You're going to give him his field experience like he's been begging for over the last few months and you've always said no to? Such a fucking pushover."

"Listen here, Brantley, I am like a mosquito. I will pester and suck you dry until I get what I'm after. You know this."

"He better not *know this*," Blake snips.

Now everyone is in on the conversation, talking about logistics and how bad of an idea it is, while also being weirdly excited about it. Maybe we made a mistake all those months ago when we decided to ruin him rather than kill him, but in my eyes, it was perfect. Because now that Will has married this rich woman, started to get his footing under him again, and revived enough to gain some confidence, it's the perfect time to pull the rug out from under him. And this time when he falls, he won't get back up.

The topic changes from weddings to plotting murders, but Blake's eyes are still on mine. Always attuned, paying attention, checking in.

"Up to you," he says casually.

"I have my own condition," I tell him. "Tomorrow."

"Mercer," he groans. "We can't plan a murder that fast from countries away."

Since I'm pretty heckin' familiar with begging these days, I throw on some pout, water up the eyes, and aim a bunch of blinks at my almost-hubby. "Don't make me marry you in a world where he exists, Blake."

His jaw tics with the force of my manipulation. Yeah, I was perfectly fine to marry him in a world with Will up until this very moment, but it's a good bargaining chip and I'm not above using it.

"Fuck, Mercer," he groans, giving in. "You manipulative prick!" He pulls me onto his lap and I smile, one of my real ones, against his neck.

"No buts?"

"A bit of a but, baby." He laughs into my hair. "And if we don't make it back in time for the wedding I planned meticulously, there'll be such a big but that my firm stance on no punishments will be rethought and reconsidered."

"Don't you dare try to tame me, Blake Carter." I pull back, meeting his blue eyes.

"Never. But I will take pleasure in making you face the consequences of your actions." He grins. "And they won't be as sexy as those firefighters."

If my punishment involves a naked Blake with a twitchy palm and power in his eyes, it'll be a million times better than those firefighters. Gosh, this murder side trip is worth it already.

"What should I wear?"

Because Will always took issue with my outfits, I decide to wear one he'll absolutely loathe. Just to send him to the underworld with a sexy me as his final thought. *Ha!*

Lace. Leather. A corset. Eyeliner. Boots with a bit of a heel on them that I made Blake buy me late last night just for the occasion. I'm in my fierce assassin phase tonight.

Outfit aside, I'm in *man on a mission* mode now. Aaron is our man in the mic, and Brendan is with him to ensure all our bases are covered. Bronson and Brandt are with us, Samantha stayed in Italy at the hotel with Keira, and Dee scoffed at me before we left. She usually calls me a slut, but on our way out the door, she called me a murder slut, and I didn't hate it. Still hate her, though. Mostly.

"I can't believe how bullshit this is." I huff with binoculars pressed to my eyes. "He traded in one mansion and got a bigger one. I feel even better about mission 'Whacking Will' now."

"No one calls it that," Bronson says.

"Uh, we all call it that. It's the mission name." I glare at him.

"We never had mission names before you." Brandt tucks some guns into his tactical gear like it's a casual Monday evening. "We never even called them missions. You're tainting the family."

"Improving," I amend.

"Mercer, if you so much as step out of line or somewhere I can't see you and reach you at all times, I will lock you in the car until this is over," Blake says. He grips my chin and forces me to remove the binoculars from my face. "I'm marrying you tomorrow. Don't fuck that up. Got it?"

"*I'm* marrying *you* tomorrow, so give me some fucking credit." I smack his hand away, but he grabs me again.

"I love you, Mercer, but I'm serious. This job is not well planned, and it's dangerous. I trust you, but things go wrong on jobs sometimes. Respect the situation."

I blow out all my witty comebacks and nod. "I'm respecting it. I promise."

Blake presses a kiss to my lips, savours the taste, and then nods. "Then let's move."

Operation 'Whacking Will' is a go.

And I've learned how to walk silently with a boner since the server room job.

Will lives in an old but impressive stone mansion with his rich elderly wife and her two dogs. After Bronson and Brandt secure the hounds by plying them with treats and snacks in the yard, we move inside. Security in a place this old isn't hard to get past, and I'm already getting a super secret spy rush from all the slinking we're doing.

It's kind of fun to hear Aaron in my ear, being me from back in Italy. According to him, the house is empty apart from three live-in staff members, the Romanian woman, who is asleep in her bed, and Will, who is asleep in his own bed.

"Knew you'd show up eventually."

Okay, so not asleep in his own bed. Something squeezes in my chest, but no itchies come. I'm not even pulling down my sleeves to ball up the fabric. No. I'm touching dagger hilts and keeping my eyes on the man who ordered my death too many times over. Blake, who has never once stepped in front of me during our entire relationship, does so now. But it doesn't feel demeaning. It's protective, and I love him for it.

"You always were an ungrateful brat, Ben," Will says.

A grateful brat, more like. "It's Mercer. Nice place you have here." I step to the side of Blake, letting him protect me but also letting myself meet eyes with the one and only man I've ever wanted to kill. "Have you started poisoning your wife yet? Plotted her murder? Hired a new hitman who won't botch the job?"

I don't even care that he calls me Ben. To him, I'll always be Ben, and luckily for me, he'll only get to think it for another few minutes until Blake shuts his brain off with a bullet. But when Will smiles at me, something inside me shrinks. Ben is still in there, and sometimes—at the worst of times—he shows up to remind me how neglected and fearful we've always been. This is why I'm the man in the mic. Behind my screens, people like Will can't taunt little timid boys out from beneath my skin. I'm stronger there because I'm in control, important, and powerful. Out here, I'm a liability, and that fact is only just settling in.

"Heard you're getting married," Will says.

From my side, Blake presses his shoulder to mine, reminding me how strong we are together. "Apologize for everything you've ever done to him and maybe I'll make this fast," Blake seethes at Will.

Will snorts. It's a gross sound and gives me the hee-bie-jeebies. "I can't believe you settled for him. You're Blake Carter. What're you doing with a scared boy?"

Blake looks at me with love in his eyes and a smile on his face. "He's not a scared boy. He's my little demon, and it's about time you met him properly."

I'm stunned into awe for a split second, and then I realize that was a lead-in. A lead-in to what? I'm not sure. But when Aaron says something about the drone above us not picking up any approaching heat sensors, and the glint in Blake's eyes darkens, and Bronson and Brandt move in closer, I act the way I *think* I'm supposed to act. Even though Blake made me promise to be a spectator.

I've got fucking knife skills, and I don't want to spectate this time.

My fingers are nimble on the hilt of the first throwing knife. It soars past Blake's head and sticks the landing right in the base of Will's throat. The second one comes with a twist and twirl that I execute perfectly before the hilt wobbles to a standstill right in the middle of Will's stomach.

"Mercer!" Blake shouts.

"Hoodlum!" Brandt scolds.

"Goddammit," Bronson mumbles.

"What?" I ask, looking at Will as he stumbles to his knees, bleeding in all the right places. "You set me up to make a move! You called me a little demon!"

Will can't really talk anymore since there's a dagger sticking out of the hollow of his throat, and when he falls to his side in a heap of agony, reality sets in.

"I told you *not* to act!" Blake scolds me. "Watch only, remember?"

"Yes, I remember. But I thought you changed your mind when you said that bit about Will meeting your little demon." I walk towards Will's body. "Excuse me for getting your signals mixed!" *God. He's such a dick sometimes.* I kick Will. "You awake?"

Oh no. He's not awake. He doesn't move and there's blood soaking into the fancy rug, and the dogs are snacking outside, and *oh my god.*

He's dead. I turn my back and stomp around, fingers in my hair, wishing for my hoodlum look. "How dare you, Blake Carter! I told you I was a one-and-done murderer!"

"You did this, demon," Blake scoffs at me.

"Because you set me up perfectly. I've never heard a more perfect intro than that! Now I'm a two-time murderer and that just doesn't have the same ring to it! Gosh!" The stress!

"He's still alive," Bronson says. "Got a bit of a pulse."

My eyes shoot to Blake. "You better off him before he dies from my knives. I don't want a two-time rep, Blake."

"Fucking warning label," Blake groans, shooting Will between his closed eyes. "There. Still a one-and-done, Mercer. Happy? Was this climactic enough for you or do you need more flair? We can string him up and bat at him like he's a piñata if you want. We can waterboard his dead body just to get you that field experience you were after. Hm? Want to cut him open and see all his vile parts just to get an anatomy lesson?"

"I'm sensing some hostility, Blake." *The piñata option sounds fun, though.*

Blake doesn't often lose his cool, so he gathers himself on his way over to me. "You manipulated me into this murder, conned me into bringing you here, and broke a promise to me."

"You offered this as a wedding gift," I remind him.

"Yes. Wedding gifts usually come after the wedding." He lifts a brow. "Are you okay?"

I glance at Will's body. "You're sure I'm not a two-time murderer?"

"Yes."

I smile at him. "Then no bats and waterboarding! Let's go. Don't make us late for our wedding, Blake!"

"Jesus fuck," he groans.

I sit on the front steps of the Romanian mansion, feeding the dogs treats and smoking Blake's cigarettes while the three Carter boys clean up my mess. Apparently, the murder wasn't supposed to be bloody. Suffocation was the plan, but no one told me, so how was I supposed to know? While they work, I think it all over.

I mean, it was pretty easy. He didn't even have guards or anything. And these pups are little sweethearts. I'm debating stealing them, but the little old lady in her bed might be heartbroken, so I'll just spoil them while I have their attention. But like... Will's dead now, and it feels good, but it wasn't as dramatic as I thought it would be. He called me a brat, Blake said some swoony shit, and bam, dead. Chapter over. No more men who look at me like I'm still Ben Palmerston.

Blake walks out with sweat on his forehead. Sitting down, he asks again, "You okay, baby?"

"It was kind of boring," I tell him, offering him one of his own cigarettes that he refuses.

He laughs. "Not all murders are like they are in the movies. What were you expecting?"

"I don't know. Like at least one explosion and maybe an evil henchman or something. A death threat right before he died, at the very least. And we can't even blow the house up or anything because his widow is sleeping so peacefully. I hope she has a touch of dementia and forgets she ever married him." I take a drag. "Can we steal the dogs?"

"No."

"Can I steal something?"

"Fine, but make it small. You already packed thirty-seven suitcases."

I grin. "Can I blow something up?"

"We don't need the attention." He squeezes my thigh. "You're honestly okay?"

I stub out the cigarette and drop it on the ground, but Blake puts it in his pocket because he thinks like a CSI actor and claims it has DNA. "I mean, it was a lame murder for sure, and I'm glad I'm not a double-murderer, but... something feels better now that he's gone. Not just for me, but for anyone else he decides isn't worth living if they're in the way of his greed. Maybe we saved the old lady."

"Maybe."

"I guess I just feel sorta lighter. That's all. I thought it was all vengeance and retribution that I wanted, but I think it was just something more subtle than that."

"Freedom," Blake says, voicing my feeling. "You are one hundred percent free to be you now, Mercer. It's not subtle. It's powerful, and it's okay to feel it."

I straddle his lap and look into his eyes. "You sure you wanna marry me? I'm a lot to handle."

"Mm." He grins.

"And I lie sometimes."

"You lie about lying."

"Not on purpose," I scoff. "I just want you to be sure you're making the right choice. I mean, I'll die if you leave me or change your mind, but at least I'm pretending to give you the option to think about it."

Blake laughs, squeezing my ass. "I don't need to think about anything, baby. I was yours the night you wore lingerie outside that club. I'm just glad I got the chance to make you mine, too. I'm marrying you tomorrow. For the rest of my life, it'll be me and my one-time-murdering little demon. No buts, Mercer."

Oh my god, I'm so pathetically in love with him. "When we get back to the hotel tonight, I'll make you a grilled cheese sandwich."

"Like fuck you will. You are banned from grilled cheeses." He tilts my head back and smiles at me. "I'm liking this corset, but I miss your hoodlum look."

"You really like my hoodlum look?" I wrap my arms around his neck.

He nods. "Yeah. You look cute as fuck in it, but also because… you told me I don't require any effort and that's why you wear it. It means I make you comfortable."

I knew he'd figure that out. "Wait until you see what I'm wearing to our wedding." I smirk. It's the off-white version of that suit he fell in love with, the one with all the buckles and clasps. Dee helped me make a new one, and I can't wait for him to see me in it. And peel me out of it.

"As long as you wear lace under it, I don't care if you wear a hoodie, baby. I just love you and can't wait to marry you. You're the neediest little boy I've ever fucking met, but I love giving you everything you want."

My eyes water with the declaration. "*Do not* make me weepy!"

"No buts, Mercer."

"No buts, hubs."

Finally, the *perfect* nickname.

THE END

From Nothing Series

GARRON PARK
LOT 62

GARRON PARK
Where hope dies and no one ever gets ahead. Until…

LOT 62
Every fairytale had a villain, and this way of life was ours…

Garron Park & Lot 62 are a completed duet in the From Nothing series.
MM, rivals-to-still-rivals-but-also-lovers
Aggressive love language
Hurt/Comfort
Trailer park setting – rags to rags, no riches – underdogs
Steamy – Lots of tension – a sexy build-up
Touch him and die vibes
Bi-awakening/GFY
Motocross

Canadian.
Coffee Obsessed.
Terrible Internet.
Lover of MM books.
Living life with my dog, Waylon!

NORDIKA NIGHT

IG: nordikanightauthor
FB readers group: Nordika's Nightmares
TikTok: nordikanight

Printed in Dunstable, United Kingdom

82744831R00214